IRB WORLD RUGBY YEARBOOK 2007

EDITED BY PAUL MORGAN AND JOHN GRIFFITHS

VSP

Vision Sports Publishing
2 Coombe Gardens,
London, SW20 0QU

www.visionsp.co.uk

This First Edition Published by
Vision Sports Publishing in 2006

1-905326-11-4

All pictures by Getty Images unless otherwise stated
Illustrations by Ann Cakebread

Typeset by Palimpsest Book Production Ltd, Grangemouth, Stirlingshire

Printed and bound in the UK by
CPD

INTRODUCTION

FROM JOINT EDITOR – PAUL MORGAN

Over the years, I always collected the Rothmans Rugby Yearbooks with relish. The first one was published in 1972 and is still fetching a good price on the rugbyrelics web site today. My collection doesn't go back that far but many are piled on an ever-creaking shelf in my office.

So it was with some dismay when I discovered, three years ago, the book was going to be removed from our shelves, possibly forever. I knew I had to do something about it, as I know our great game of rugby union deserves an official, annual, publication covering the world game.

No look at the rugby year would be complete without the Englands and New Zealands, obviously, but I believe it would also not be complete without nations like Georgia and Uruguay either. We had to draw a line somewhere, on the countries we covered, in depth, and I drew one under the 20 nations who qualified for the 2003 World Cup. Many more nations than the yearbook has covered before.

The journey from day one to publication has been a long, and often arduous one, so it would be remiss of me not hand out a few hero-grams.

John Griffiths' statistics – which have graced the book for many years – were crucial, and those of others like Hugh Copping, Geoff Miller and John Lea, who filled in some of the gaps.

Of course to Jim Drewett and Toby Trotman at Vision Sports Publishing for sharing my vision for the book and supporting me along the way.

Principal writer Iain Spragg for his tireless work. The players including John Eales, Francois Pienaar, Sean Fitzpatrick, Michael Lynagh and Will Greenwood, who joined our writing team and one of the best wicketkeepers in the rugby world, our proof-reader and fact-checker, Howard Evans.

The correspondents from around the world, almost too numerous to mention, were a great source of inspiration. They all share my passion.

Emirates were great partners and at the IRB nothing could have happened without Greg Thomas championing the project, along with Chris Thau . . . and last but not absolutely not least the many, many days and weeks spent on this book by the inexhaustible Dom Rumbles.

With any new project there is pain along the way and few suffered more pain than Julie, Ricky and Debi at our world-class typesetters, Palimpsest Book Production Limited. If patience really is a virtue Julie and the team are the most virtuous people I know!

All that is left is for me to hope you enjoy the rebirth of the IRB World Rugby Yearbook and rejoice with me in the knowledge that the IRB and Emirates have committed to it for three seasons so it will be back – at least – in 2007 and 2008.

Any comments are always gratefully received and any recommendations for future editions should come to me at Rugby World Magazine. Email me at paul_morgan@ipcmedia.com

RUGBY'S DEVELOPMENT JOURNEY CONTINUES

DR. SYD MILLAR, CHAIRMAN, INTERNATIONAL RUGBY BOARD

In 1987 the game of rugby took a huge step forward in terms of global appeal and promotion with the kick-off of the first-ever IRB Rugby World Cup in New Zealand and Australia. Little did we know that this historic tournament would change the face of the game forever. The evolution rugby has experienced since those pioneering days has been phenomenal.

The International Rugby Board is delighted at this success and the fact that Rugby World Cup is now one of the largest international sporting events in the world.

Twenty years later we are now looking forward to the sixth Rugby World Cup that will be hosted by the French Rugby Federation in 2007. Importantly, the success of Rugby World Cup is now driving the development of the game worldwide and interest in hosting the Tournament has heightened due to the profile it provides and the legacy it leaves behind. Indeed for Rugby World Cup 2011 three countries were locked in the bidding process.

It is history now that New Zealand won the right to host the 2011 Tournament but there is so much more to the successful development of rugby worldwide than the awarding of a single tournament to a host nation. The negative coverage in certain sections of the media has missed this point. Investment in infrastructure, high performance initiatives, development programmes and tournament structures on a consistent basis and over a long period are the keys to the success of global development.

Rugby World Cup, the game's premier event, takes place once every four years. While the placement of the tournament does play a role in the development of rugby, it's what happens during the rest of the four-year cycle that really grows the game.

Across this cycle the IRB invests in several other major events, all of which play a part in the development of rugby. The Under-21 World Championship in France was hugely successful in terms of development, promotion and legacy a year before Rugby World Cup 2007. The Under-19 World Championship was held in Dubai, the first time a major rugby tournament has been held in the Middle East. And the IRB Sevens Series takes place annually in eight locations around the world including Wellington, California, Hong Kong and London. We have also just completed a highly successful Women's Rugby World Cup in Edmonton, Canada.

But the health and development of the game received a significant boost in August 2005 when – based on the revenue generation provided by Rugby World Cup – the IRB launched an unprecedented, three-year US$50 million strategic investment programme aimed at increasing global playing standards and competitiveness. The IRB's commitment to such major goals is reflected by the fact that as well as re-investing in our traditional base – the Tier 1 Unions – we have committed around US$32 million to development programmes in Tier 2 and Tier 3 Unions.

This includes US$15 million of investment in high performance and infrastructure in Fiji, Samoa, Tonga, Japan, USA, Canada and Romania. Investment of US$14 million has gone into new international and provincial cross-border tournaments and US$2.5 million has been provided for selected Tier 3 Unions that have the potential to move up. The new tournaments that have been created are:

- Pacific Rugby Cup – a six-team cross-border competition between two representative teams from each of Fiji, Samoa and Tonga
- Pacific 5 Nations – featuring the national teams from Japan, Fiji, Samoa and Tonga, plus the Junior All Blacks. In 2007 it will be expanded to include an Australian representative team.
- North America 4 – a four-team cross-border competition between two representative teams from each of USA and Canada.
- Nations Cup – a competition that provides matches for the A teams of Italy and Argentina. This year they played against Portugal and Russia
- Expanded Churchill Cup – this competition comprises England A (or Saxons), USA, Canada, New Zealand Maori and this year the A teams from Scotland and Ireland thanks to the investment programme.
- Funding has also been provided to allow a Romanian representative side to play in the European Challenge Cup (the competition below the European Cup)
- The IRB is also planning a South American tournament involving provincial teams from Argentina and perhaps some Tier 3 Unions from the continent.

This US$50 million investment programme is on top of the US$22.5 million the IRB invests annually in its 115 member Unions in the form of tournaments, grants, and education and training resources. The total investment in the game over the next three years is over US$110 million.

On the field we are also confronting several key issues at present. An essential element of rugby is its physicality which has to be appropriately balanced with the safety of participating players. The IRB continues to take the issue of injury prevention very seriously and as the world's governing body we are continually reviewing all aspects of the game. The Laws are constantly reviewed by relevant experts, and experimental laws are continually trialled throughout the world.

We now have our first ever Medical Officer to assist the ongoing work of the Medical Advisory Committee (MAC). Work is already underway on a global injury definition protocol for rugby to assist in improved collation and more consistent analysis of injury research data. The IRB also invests in injury research and this year is funding RFU research on tackle injuries.

An IRB Law Project Group is investigating the tackle and post-tackle area in terms of Law and safety, and experimental laws are being trialled in South Africa. In addition the Group is also looking at the scrum. Already in place are a number of Law variations at the Under-19 level aimed at ensuring that the game is appropriate for the physical development of players in that age group.

The IRB believes that the contested scrum is an integral part of the game and that rugby is unique in that its playing charter provides the opportunity for individuals of all shapes and sizes to play the game. That said, the experts in the Project Group will work hand in hand with the IRB Medical Officer and MAC and all recommendations on any future Law changes will be presented to the IRB Council in due course.

CONTENTS

Emirates

INTRODUCTION

FROM GARY CHAPMAN – PRESIDENT, EMIRATES GROUP SERVICES

It's no exaggeration to say Rugby is in our blood!

From sponsoring the Dubai Rugby 7s back in 1988, now part of the IRB World Sevens Series, we have seen our logo, together with the IRB's, at many of the world's major tournaments.

In January 2006 Emirates signed a three-year, multi-million pound, sponsorship deal to become the first Official Sponsor of the IRB's International Referees.

This agreement means that all IRB match officials will wear Emirates branded kit at all IRB tournaments such as the RBS Six Nations, the Tri-Nations, Under-19s and Under-21s World Championships, IRB World Sevens Series as well as at many of the other rugby internationals.

More recently Emirates have become the Official Carrier for the 2007 Rugby World Cup in France.

We are very proud to become a significant partner of IRB on the world rugby scene - we place much value in our partnership with the IRB and rugby in the knowledge that people who watch and support this great game are the same people who travel regularly.

When it comes to sponsors, no other airline has such an exciting sponsorship portfolio as Emirates.

In that other game, we sponsor Arsenal Football Club, The Emirates Stadium, Hamburg Football Club, Paris St Germaine, The Asian Football Federation as well as being the official partner of the 2010 and 2014 FIFA World Cup events. Other exciting sponsorships where you see the Emirates logo include sailing, golf, cricket, horse racing and motor racing.

But, we have to admit, it's rugby which has a special place in our hearts.

RUGBY WORLD CUP 2007

A PARTY ON THE HORIZON

The next Rugby World Cup is just around the corner. So Gavin Mortimer reveals some of the plans that are afoot and predicts an unforgettable Rugby World Cup in France, in 2007

Dave Rogers/Getty Images

Bernard Lapasset is planning a Rugby World Cup to remember.

Only the French could pull it off. The centrepiece of their promotion of the 2007 Rugby World Cup is 'Le Train du Rugby', a four-carriage train that between May 9 and November 18 2006 visited 112 French towns and covered over 10,000 kilometres. Imagine if they'd tried that in Britain in the lead up to the 1999 World Cup. There'd still be people at a remote station in the north of Scotland waiting for the train to turn up. That's not a slight on the organisation of the 1999 RWC, more a dig at the less than impressive British rail system. But in France, the rail network is world class, and what better way for the organisers of next year's World Cup to convey their message than by teaming up with SNCF, the national rail company. And what is the message? That RWC 2007 is going to be one smooth ride.

For the French, you see, the tournament is personal. It's the first time in the 20-year history of the World Cup that the main organiser is not an Anglophone country; then there is also the memory of last year when London got the nod ahead of Paris to host the 2012 Olympics. Any defeat at the hands of Perfidious Albion hurts the French, and that one was particularly painful. So why not show that France has shrugged off the disappointment by staging the greatest ever Rugby World Cup. Bernard Lapasset, president of the Fédération Française de Rugby [FFR], says they 'want to show that France can do it even better'.

Such sentiments are echoed by Jean-François Lamour, the Minister for Sport. "France must hold its own when it comes to organising sports events," he says. "The image of our country depends on it. We're very proud to be organising it for the first time [and] it's going to be a great adventure."

Monsieur Lamour has put his government's money where his mouth is, financing the World Cup to the tune of 27m euros. Among other things, this has helped pay for the employment of 200 full-time staff before and during the tournament, covered the costs of training the 6000 unpaid volunteers who will be on hand at all ten French stadiums to assist spectators, and, of course, it's got the train on the track.

One might wonder if Le Train du Rugby isn't early, about a year early, but its arrival was timed not just to launch the build-up to the World Cup but also to coincide with the centenary of France's first Test match. That was against New Zealand, on January 1 1906 at Parc des Princes, a match which ended in a 38–8 thumping for the home side. Nonetheless, the correspondent for the *Daily Telegraph* thought that despite the scoreline it had been the 'greatest day ever known' in French rugby. For not only had they scored eight points but the public had been enraptured by the spectacle. "I came back from the game in a delirious crowd of young Frenchman," wrote the correspondent. "They dreamt of the day when [rugby] football shall become a national game in this country."

One hundred years on and rugby is indeed a national game in France, but it still lags some way behind football in popularity. Sure, in the south of the country rugby is a way of life, every bit as important to the people as it is in Cardiff and Christchurch. But in the north of France, rugby has had less of an impact. No one can quite explain why this is, though countless theories have been suggested over the years, from religion to weather to temperament to class structure. But Bernard

Lapasset knows that the biggest challenge facing him and his team is to ensure all his compatriots feel part of RWC 2007. "We want to share this experience with all of France, not just the rugby community," he says. "We must convince the public to join us, we must show them that it's safe to bring the family to a match and to join in the excitement."

The Rugby Train began its voyage on May 9 in the symbolic town of Le Havre on the Normandy coast. It was here in 1872 that the first ever match of rugby was played in France between two teams of British wine merchants. Before the train departed the people of Le Havre had the opportunity to hop on board and find out more about rugby. The inside of the first carriage was a replica of the dressing room in the Stade de France, the second was a mini pitch complete with crowd cheers and player grunts, the third was the inside of a clubhouse and the fourth was devoted to RWC 2007. Moving through the carriages, past walls displayed with photographs, cups and jerseys, were some of the biggest names in French rugby, including national coach Bernard Laporte and Philippe Sella, France's most capped back with 111 appearances, who happily signed autographs for fans.

The pair were on the train again a few weeks later when it chugged into Arcachon, a town 150km north of Biarritz on the Atlantic coast that is famous for its oysters. Along with several other well-known names from French rugby, Laporte and Sella played an exhibition game of beach rugby as local children swarmed over the train. Two weeks later the train stopped at Menton, burial place of William Webb Ellis, and its journey came to an end on November 18 in Paris, the same day France played New Zealand at the Stade de France.

In Sella's opinion the Train du Rugby has been a knockout success. "The object was to promote rugby throughout France and to launch the World Cup into the consciousness of the French public," he says. "From what I've seen it's been very well received and I think we've got the message across that rugby is a great game to play. Certainly the children seem to have enjoyed the chance to throw a ball around."

The north/south divide was evident during the train's tour, says Sella, although he adds that the divide is more blurred than it was during his playing days. "Of course, the heart of rugby in France is in the south-west but rugby is becoming more popular elsewhere. In the south-east there is an increasing passion for rugby, particularly in the Rhones-Alps (Bourgoin are in the French Top 14 and three clubs from the region are in Division Two) and progress is being made in and around Paris. Racing Club used to be one of the strongest clubs in France [they won the inaugural French Club Championship in 1892] but now it's Stade Francais and they're doing a great job in attracting new fans. It was magnificent to see 79,000 people at the Stade de France last season to watch them play Toulouse.

"I suppose the one area where it's more difficult to attract fans is in the north-west in Alsace-Lorraine. There are no professional teams and there's less interest in rugby, but the train was still popular when it stopped."

With the one millionth ticket sold in August 2006, the FFR are well on their way to reaching their stated ambition of selling 2.2 million by the time the World Cup opens with France playing Argentina on September 7. Sella has an emphatic message to all those overseas fans still undecided as to whether to make the trip. "The rugby is going to be great, as is the ambiance and the spirit of friendship among the supporters, but remember that there is a lot more to experience than just rugby: the food, the wine, the scenery. It will be a wonderful occasion!"

The ten host French cities have been well chosen by the RWC organisers. Naturally, they all boast stadiums worthy of hosting World Cup matches, but each one has something different to offer the rugby tourist: Bordeaux has its wine, Montpellier its sunshine, Lyon has gastronomy, Toulouse has architecture, Marseille its history and then there's the beauty of Paris.

The French capital will represent the heart of RWC 2007 with the 80,000 capacity Stade de France hosting both semi-finals and the final on October 20. As well as the action going on inside the stadium there will be a cornucopia of festivies in the immediate vicinity. "The success of a sporting event depends as much on what goes on outside the stadium as inside," says Didier Paillard, the mayor of St-Denis, the Parisien suburb which is home to the Stade de France. "It's what we learned during the 1998 football World Cup." A giant screen nearby will transmit all the matches and there will be live bands and parties to suit all tastes. But Monsieur Paillard has also arranged for a series of workshops and programmes to educate locals youngsters in the benefits of leading a sporty life.

So things are looking good for RWC 2007. Tickets are selling like hot *gateaux*, there are no last-minute worries about unfinished stadia and the organisers have all the staff in place. What's there to worry about? Just one thing, the only thing that is out of the organisers' hands – the rugby. That's down to Bernard Laporte and his boys. "If one wants the World Cup to be really huge in France then the French public must be won over by our style and by our results," says Laporte. "That's down to us." Le Train du Rugby ran perfectly in 2006. Now France must hope the wheels don't come off when the action begins in September 2007.

RUGBY WORLD CUP RECORDS 1987-2003

(FINAL STAGES ONLY)

OVERALL RECORDS

MOST MATCHES WON IN FINAL STAGES

26	New Zealand
24	Australia
22	France
20	England

MOST OVERALL PENALTIES IN FINAL STAGES

39	J P Wilkinson	England	1999-2003
36	A G Hastings	Scotland	1987-95
35	G Quesada	Argentina	1999-2003

MOST OVERALL POINTS IN FINAL STAGES

227	A G Hastings	Scotland	1987-95
195	M P Lynagh	Australia	1987-95
182	J P Wilkinson	England	1999-2003
170	G J Fox	New Zealand	1987-91

MOST OVERALL DROPPED GOALS IN FINAL STAGES

8	J P Wilkinson	England	1999-2003
6	J H de Beer	South Africa	1999
5	C R Andrew	England	1987-1995
5	G L Rees	Canada	1987-1999

MOST OVERALL TRIES IN FINAL STAGES

15	J T Lomu	New Zealand	1995-99
11	R Underwood	England	1987-95
10	D I Campese	Australia	1987-95
10	B P Lima	Samoa	1991-2003

MOST MATCH APPEARANCES IN FINAL STAGES

22	J Leonard	England	1991-2003
18	M O Johnson	England	1995-2003
17	S B T Fitzpatrick	New Zealand	1987-1995

MOST OVERALL CONVERSIONS IN FINAL STAGES

39	A G Hastings	Scotland	1987-95
37	G J Fox	New Zealand	1987-91
36	M P Lynagh	Australia	1987-95

LEADING SCORERS

MOST POINTS IN ONE COMPETITION

126	G J Fox	New Zealand	1987
113	J P Wilkinson	England	2003
112	T Lacroix	France	1995
104	A G Hastings	Scotland	1995
103	F Michalak	France	2003
102	G Quesada	Argentina	1999
101	M Burke	Australia	1999

MOST TRIES IN ONE COMPETITION

8	J T Lomu	New Zealand	1999
7	M C G Ellis	New Zealand	1995
7	J T Lomu	New Zealand	1995
7	D C Howlett	New Zealand	2003
7	J M Muliaina	New Zealand	2003

MOST CONVERSIONS IN ONE COMPETITION

30	G J Fox	New Zealand	1987
20	S D Culhane	New Zealand	1995
20	M P Lynagh	Australia	1987
20	L R MacDonald	New Zealand	2003

MOST PENALTY GOALS IN ONE COMPETITION

31	G Quesada	Argentina	1999
26	T Lacroix	France	1995
23	J P Wilkinson	England	2003
21	G J Fox	New Zealand	1987
21	E J Flatley	Australia	2003
20	C R Andrew	England	1995

MOST DROP GOALS IN ONE COMPETITION

8	J P Wilkinson	England	2003
6	J H de Beer	South Africa	1999
3	G P J Townsend	Scotland	1999
3	A P Mehrtens	New Zealand	1995
3	J T Stransky	South Africa	1995
3	C R Andrew	England	1995
3	J Davies	Wales	1987

MATCH RECORDS

MOST POINTS IN A MATCH

BY THE TEAM

145	New Zealand v Japan	1995
142	Australia v Namibia	2003
111	England v Uruguay	2003
101	New Zealand v Italy	1999
101	England v Tonga	1999

BY A PLAYER

45	S D Culhane	New Zealand v Japan	1995
44	A G Hastings	Scotland v Ivory Coast	1995
42	M S Rogers	Australia v Namibia	2003
36	T E Brown	New Zealand v Italy	1999
36	P J Grayson	England v Tonga	1999
34	J H de Beer	South Africa v England	1999
32	J P Wilkinson	England v Italy	1999

MOST TRIES IN A MATCH

BY THE TEAM

22	Australia v Namibia	2003
21	New Zealand v Japan	1995
17	England v Uruguay	2003
14	New Zealand v Italy	1999
13	England v Tonga	1999
13	Scotland v Ivory Coast	1995
13	France v Zimbabwe	1987
13	Australia v Romania	2003
13	New Zealand v Tonga	2003

BY A PLAYER

6	M C G Ellis	New Zealand v Japan	1995
5	C E Latham	Australia v Namibia	2003
5	O J Lewsey	England v Uruguay	2003
4	K G M Wood	Ireland v United States	1999
4	A G Hastings	Scotland v Ivory Coast	1995
4	C M Williams	South Africa v Western Samoa	1995
4	J T Lomu	New Zealand v England	1995
4	B F Robinson	Ireland v Zimbabwe	1991
4	I C Evans	Wales v Canada	1987
4	C I Green	New Zealand v Fiji	1987
4	J A Gallagher	New Zealand v Fiji	1987
4	J M Muliaina	New Zealand v Canada	2003

MOST CONVERSIONS IN A MATCH

BY THE TEAM

20	New Zealand v Japan	1995
16	Australia v Namibia	2003
13	New Zealand v Tonga	2003
13	England v Uruguay	2003
12	England v Tonga	1999
11	New Zealand v Italy	1999
11	Australia v Romania	2003
10	New Zealand v Fiji	1987

BY A PLAYER

20	S D Culhane	New Zealand v Japan	1995
16	M S Rogers	Australia v Namibia	2003
12	P J Grayson	England v Tonga	1999
12	L R MacDonald	New Zealand v Tonga	2003
11	T E Brown	New Zealand v Italy	1999
11	E J Flatley	Australia v Romania	2003
11	P J Grayson	England v Uruguay	2003
10	G J Fox	New Zealand v Fiji	1987

MOST PENALTY GOALS IN A MATCH

BY THE TEAM

8	Australia v South Africa	1999
8	Argentina v Samoa	1999
8	Scotland v Tonga	1995
8	France v Ireland	1995

BY A PLAYER

8	M Burke	Australia v South Africa	1999
8	G Quesada	Argentina v Samoa	1999
8	A G Hastings	Scotland v Tonga	1995
8	T Lacroix	France v Ireland	1995

MOST DROP GOALS IN A MATCH

BY THE TEAM

5	South Africa v England	1999
3	Fiji v Romania	1991
3	England v France	2003

BY A PLAYER

5	J H de Beer	South Africa v England	1999
3	J P Wilkinson	England v France	2003
2	J P Wilkinson	England v South Africa	2003
2	P C Montgomery	South Africa v New Zealand	1999
2	C Lamaison	France v New Zealand	1999
2	J T Stransky	South Africa v New Zealand	1995
2	C R Andrew	England v Argentina	1995
2	T Rabaka	Fiji v Romania	1991
2	L Arbizu	Argentina v Australia	1991
2	J Davies	Wales v Ireland	1987

RUGBY WORLD CUP TOURNAMENTS 1987-2003

FIRST TOURNAMENT : 1987

IN AUSTRALIA & NEW ZEALAND

POOL 1

Australia	19	**England**	6
USA	21	**Japan**	18
England	60	**Japan**	7
Australia	47	**USA**	12
England	34	**USA**	6
Australia	42	**Japan**	23

	P	W	D	L	F	A	Pts
Australia	3	3	0	0	108	41	6
England	3	2	0	1	100	32	4
USA	3	1	0	2	39	99	2
Japan	3	0	0	3	48	123	0

POOL 2

Canada	37	**Tonga**	4
Wales	13	**Ireland**	6
Wales	29	**Tonga**	16
Ireland	46	**Canada**	19
Wales	40	**Canada**	9
Ireland	32	**Tonga**	9

	P	W	D	L	F	A	Pts
Wales	3	3	0	0	82	31	6
Ireland	3	2	0	1	84	41	4
Canada	3	1	0	2	65	90	2
Tonga	3	0	0	3	29	98	0

POOL 3

New Zealand	70	**Italy**	6
Fiji	28	**Argentina**	9
New Zealand	74	**Fiji**	13
Argentina	25	**Italy**	16
Italy	18	**Fiji**	15
New Zealand	46	**Argentina**	15

	P	W	D	L	F	A	Pts
New Zealand	3	3	0	0	190	34	6
Fiji	3	1	0	2	56	101	2
Argentina	3	1	0	2	49	90	2
Italy	3	1	0	2	40	110	2

POOL 4

Romania	21	**Zimbabwe**	20
France	20	**Scotland**	20
France	55	**Romania**	12
Scotland	60	**Zimbabwe**	21
France	70	**Zimbabwe**	12
Scotland	55	**Romania**	28

	P	W	D	L	F	A	Pts
France	3	2	1	0	145	44	5
Scotland	3	2	1	0	135	69	5
Romania	3	1	0	2	61	130	2
Zimbabwe	3	0	0	3	53	151	0

QUARTER-FINALS

New Zealand	30	**Scotland**	3
France	31	**Fiji**	16
Australia	33	**Ireland**	15
Wales	16	**England**	3

SEMI-FINALS

France	30	**Australia**	24
New Zealand	49	**Wales**	6

THIRD PLACE MATCH

Wales	22	**Australia**	21

First World Cup Final, Eden Park, Auckland, 20 June 1987

NEW ZEALAND 29 (1G 4PG 1DG 2T)
FRANCE 9 (1G 1PG)

NEW ZEALAND: J A Gallagher; J J Kirwan, J T Stanley, W T Taylor, C I Green; G J Fox, D E Kirk (captain); S C McDowell, S B T Fitzpatrick, J A Drake, M J Pierce, G W Whetton, A J Whetton, W T Shelford, M N Jones

SCORERS TRIES : Jones, Kirk, Kirwan Conversion : Fox Penalty Goals : Fox (4) Drop Goal : Fox

FRANCE: S Blanco; D Camberabero, P Sella, D Charvet, P Lagisquet; F Mesnel, P Berbizier; P Ondarts, D Dubroca (captain), J-P Garuet, A Lorieux, J Condom, E Champ, L Rodriguez, D Erbani

SCORERS TRY : Berbizier Conversion : Camberabero Penalty Goal : Camberabero

REFEREE K V J Fitzgerald (Australia)

Getty Images

David Kirk becomes the first man to get his hands on the World Cup.

SECOND TOURNAMENT : 1991
IN BRITAIN, IRELAND & FRANCE

POOL 1

New Zealand	18	**England**	12
Italy	30	**USA**	9
New Zealand	46	**USA**	6
England	36	**Italy**	6
England	37	**USA**	9
New Zealand	31	**Italy**	21

	P	W	D	L	F	A	Pts
New Zealand	3	3	0	0	95	39	9
England	3	2	0	1	85	33	7
Italy	3	1	0	2	57	76	5
USA	3	0	0	3	24	113	3

POOL 2

Scotland	47	**Japan**	9
Ireland	55	**Zimbabwe**	11
Ireland	32	**Japan**	16
Scotland	51	**Zimbabwe**	12
Scotland	24	**Ireland**	15
Japan	52	**Zimbabwe**	8

	P	W	D	L	F	A	Pts
Scotland	3	3	0	0	122	36	9
Ireland	3	2	0	1	102	51	7
Japan	3	1	0	2	77	87	5
Zimbabwe	3	0	0	3	31	158	3

POOL 3

Australia	32	**Argentina**	19
Western Samoa	16	**Wales**	13
Australia	9	**Western Samoa**	3
Wales	16	**Argentina**	7
Australia	38	**Wales**	3
Western Samoa	35	**Argentina**	12

	P	W	D	L	F	A	Pts
Australia	3	3	0	0	79	25	9
Western Samoa	3	2	0	1	54	34	7
Wales	3	1	0	2	32	61	5
Argentina	3	0	0	3	38	83	3

POOL 4

France	30	**Romania**	3
Canada	13	**Fiji**	3
France	33	**Fiji**	9
Canada	19	**Romania**	11
Romania	17	**Fiji**	15
France	19	**Canada**	13

	P	W	D	L	F	A	Pts
France	3	3	0	0	82	25	9
Canada	3	2	0	1	45	33	7
Romania	3	1	0	2	31	64	5
Fiji	3	0	0	3	27	63	3

QUARTER-FINALS

England	19	**France**	10
Scotland	28	**Western Samoa**	6
Australia	19	**Ireland**	18
New Zealand	29	**Canada**	13

SEMI-FINALS

England	9	**Scotland**	6
Australia	16	**New Zealand**	6

THIRD PLACE MATCH

New Zealand	13	**Scotland**	6

Second World Cup Final, Twickenham, 2 November 1991

AUSTRALIA 12 (1G 2PG)
ENGLAND 6 (2PG)

AUSTRALIA: M C Roebuck; D I Campese, J S Little, T J Horan, R H Egerton; M P Lynagh, N C Farr-Jones (captain); A J Daly, P N Kearns, E J A McKenzie, R J McCall, J A Eales, S P Poidevin, T Coker, V Ofahengaue

SCORERS TRY : Daly Conversion : Lynagh Penalty Goals : Lynagh (2)

ENGLAND: J M Webb; S J Halliday, W D C Carling (captain), J C Guscott, R Underwood; C R Andrew, R J Hill; J Leonard, B C Moore, J A Probyn, P J Ackford, W A Dooley, M G Skinner, M C Teague, P J Winterbottom

SCORER PENALTY GOALS : Webb (2)

REFEREE W D Bevan (Wales)

Simon Bruty/Getty Images

It's ours! Nick Farr-Jones celebrates Australia's win at Twickenham.

THIRD TOURNAMENT : 1995
IN SOUTH AFRICA

POOL A

South Africa	27	Australia	18
Canada	34	Romania	3
South Africa	21	Romania	8
Australia	27	Canada	11
Australia	42	Romania	3
South Africa	20	Canada	0

	P	W	D	L	F	A	Pts
South Africa	3	3	0	0	68	26	9
Australia	3	2	0	1	87	41	7
Canada	3	1	0	2	45	50	5
Romania	3	0	0	3	14	97	3

POOL B

Western Samoa	42	Italy	18
England	24	Argentina	18
Western Samoa	32	Argentina	26
England	27	Italy	20
Italy	31	Argentina	25
England	44	Western Samoa	22

	P	W	D	L	F	A	Pts
England	3	3	0	0	95	60	9
Western Samoa	3	2	0	1	96	88	7
Italy	3	1	0	2	69	94	5
Argentina	3	0	0	3	69	87	3

POOL C

Wales	57	Japan	10
New Zealand	43	Ireland	19
Ireland	50	Japan	28
New Zealand	34	Wales	9
New Zealand	145	Japan	17
Ireland	24	Wales	23

	P	W	D	L	F	A	Pts
New Zealand	3	3	0	0	222	45	9
Ireland	3	2	0	1	93	94	7
Wales	3	1	0	2	89	68	5
Japan	3	0	0	3	55	252	3

POOL D

Scotland	89	Ivory Coast	0
France	38	Tonga	10
France	54	Ivory Coast	18
Scotland	41	Tonga	5
Tonga	29	Ivory Coast	11
France	22	Scotland	19

	P	W	D	L	F	A	Pts
France	3	3	0	0	114	47	9
Scotland	3	2	0	1	149	27	7
Tonga	3	1	0	2	44	90	5
Ivory Coast	3	0	0	3	29	172	3

QUARTER-FINALS

France	36	Ireland	12
South Africa	42	Western Samoa	14
England	25	Australia	22
New Zealand	48	Scotland	30

SEMI-FINALS

South Africa	19	France	15
New Zealand	45	England	29

THIRD PLACE MATCH

France	19	England	9

Third World Cup Final, Ellis Park, Johannesburg, 24 June 1995

SOUTH AFRICA 15 (3PG 2DG)
NEW ZEALAND 12 (3PG 1DG) *

SOUTH AFRICA: A J Joubert; J T Small, J C Mulder, H P Le Roux, C M Williams; J T Stransky, J H van der Westhuizen; J P du Randt, C L C Rossouw, I S Swart, J J Wiese, J J Strydom, J F Pienaar (captain), M G Andrews, R J Kruger Substitutions: G L Pagel for Swart (68 mins); R A W Straeuli for Andrews (90 mins); B Venter for Small (97 mins)

SCORER PENALTY GOALS: Stransky (3) Drop Goals: Stransky (2)

NEW ZEALAND: G M Osborne; J W Wilson, F E Bunce, W K Little, J T Lomu; A P Mehrtens, G T M Bachop; C W Dowd, S B T Fitzpatrick (captain), O M Brown, I D Jones, R M Brooke, M R Brewer, Z V Brooke, J A Kronfeld Substitutions: J W Joseph for Brewer (40 mins); M C G Ellis for Wilson (55 mins); R W Loe for Dowd (83 mins); A D Strachan for Bachop (temp 66 to 71 mins)

SCORER PENALTY GOALS: Mehrtens (3) Drop Goal: Mehrtens

REFEREE E F Morrison (England)

* after extra time : 9-9 after normal time

Dave Rogers/Getty Images

South Africa President, Nelson Mandela hands the trophy to Francois Pienaar.

FOURTH TOURNAMENT : 1999
IN BRITAIN, IRELAND & FRANCE

POOL A

Spain	15	Uruguay	27
South Africa	46	Scotland	29
Scotland	43	Uruguay	12
South Africa	47	Spain	3
South Africa	39	Uruguay	3
Scotland	48	Spain	0

	P	W	D	L	F	A	Pts
South Africa	3	3	0	0	132	35	9
Scotland	3	2	0	1	120	58	7
Uruguay	3	1	0	2	42	97	5
Spain	3	0	0	3	18	122	3

POOL B

England	67	Italy	7
New Zealand	45	Tonga	9
England	16	New Zealand	30
Italy	25	Tonga	28
New Zealand	101	Italy	3
England	101	Tonga	10

	P	W	D	L	F	A	Pts
New Zealand	3	3	0	0	176	28	9
England	3	2	0	1	184	47	7
Tonga	3	1	0	2	47	171	5
Italy	3	0	0	3	35	196	3

POOL C

Fiji	67	Namibia	18
France	33	Canada	20
France	47	Namibia	13
Fiji	38	Canada	22
Canada	72	Namibia	11
France	28	Fiji	19

	P	W	D	L	F	A	Pts
France	3	3	0	0	108	52	9
Fiji	3	2	0	1	124	68	7
Canada	3	1	0	2	114	82	5
Namibia	3	0	0	3	42	186	3

POOL D

Wales	23	Argentina	18
Samoa	43	Japan	9
Wales	64	Japan	15
Argentina	32	Samoa	16
Wales	31	Samoa	38
Argentina	33	Japan	12

	P	W	D	L	F	A	Pts
Wales	3	2	0	1	118	71	7
Samoa	3	2	0	1	97	72	7
Argentina	3	2	0	1	83	51	7
Japan	3	0	0	3	36	140	3

POOL E

Ireland	53	United States	8
Australia	57	Romania	9
United States	25	Romania	27
Ireland	3	Australia	23
Australia	55	United States	19
Ireland	44	Romania	14

	P	W	D	L	F	A	Pts
Australia	3	3	0	0	135	31	9
Ireland	3	2	0	1	100	45	7
Romania	3	1	0	2	50	126	5
United States	3	0	0	3	52	135	3

PLAY-OFFS FOR QUARTER-FINAL PLACES

England	45	Fiji	24
Scotland	35	Samoa	20
Ireland	24	Argentina	28

QUARTER-FINALS

Wales	9	Australia	24
South Africa	44	England	21
France	47	Argentina	26
Scotland	18	New Zealand	30

SEMI-FINALS

South Africa	21	Australia	27
New Zealand	31	France	43

THIRD PLACE MATCH

South Africa	22	New Zealand	18

Fourth World Cup Final, Millennium Stadium, Cardiff Arms Park, 6 November 1999

AUSTRALIA 35 (2G 7PG) FRANCE 12 (4PG)

AUSTRALIA : M Burke; B N Tune, D J Herbert, T J Horan, J W Roff; S J Larkham, G M Gregan; R L L Harry, M A Foley, A T Blades, D T Giffin, J A Eales (captain), M J Cockbain, R S T Kefu, D J Wilson Substitutions J S Little for Herbert (46 mins); O D A Finegan for Cockbain (52 mins); M R Connors for Wilson (73 mins); D J Crowley for Harry (75 mins); J A Paul for Foley (85 mins); C J Whitaker for Gregan (86 mins); N P Grey for Horan (86 mins)

SCORERS TRIES : Tune, Finegan Conversions : Burke (2) Penalty Goals : Burke (7)

FRANCE : X Garbajosa; P Bernat Salles, R Dourthe, E Ntamack, C Dominici; C Lamaison, F Galthié; C Soulette, R Ibañez (captain), F Tournaire, A Benazzi, F Pelous, M Lièvremont, C Juillet, O Magne Substitutions O Brouzet for Juillet (HT); P de Villiers for Soulette (47 mins); A Costes for Magne (temp 19 to 22 mins) and for Lièvremont (67 mins); U Mola for Garbajosa (67 mins); S Glas for Dourthe (temp 49 to 55 mins and from 74 mins); S Castaignède for Galthié (76 mins); M Dal Maso for Ibañez (79 mins)

SCORER PENALTY GOALS : Lamaison (4)

REFEREE A J Watson (South Africa)

Dave Rogers/Getty Images

France are vanquished and Australia have the trophy, in the hands of John Eales.

FIFTH TOURNAMENT : 2003 IN AUSTRALIA

POOL A

Australia	24	**Argentina**	8
Ireland	45	**Romania**	17
Argentina	67	**Namibia**	14
Australia	90	**Romania**	8
Ireland	64	**Namibia**	7
Argentina	50	**Romania**	3
Australia	142	**Namibia**	0
Ireland	16	**Argentina**	15
Romania	37	**Namibia**	7
Australia	17	**Ireland**	16

	P	W	D	L	F	A	Pts
Australia	4	4	0	0	273	32	12
Ireland	4	3	0	1	141	56	10
Argentina	4	2	0	2	140	57	8
Romania	4	1	0	3	65	192	6
Namibia	4	0	0	4	28	310	4

POOL B

France	61	**Fiji**	18
Scotland	32	**Japan**	11
Fiji	19	**United States**	18
France	51	**Japan**	29
Scotland	39	**United States**	15
Fiji	41	**Japan**	13
France	51	**Scotland**	9
United States	39	**Japan**	26
France	41	**United States**	14
Scotland	22	**Fiji**	20

	P	W	D	L	F	A	Pts
France	4	4	0	0	204	70	12
Scotland	4	3	0	1	102	97	10
Fiji	4	2	0	2	98	114	8
United States	4	1	0	3	86	125	6
Japan	4	0	0	4	79	163	4

POOL C

South Africa	72	**Uruguay**	6
England	84	**Georgia**	6
Samoa	60	**Uruguay**	13
England	25	**South Africa**	6
Samoa	46	**Georgia**	9
South Africa	46	**Georgia**	19
England	35	**Samoa**	22
Uruguay	24	**Georgia**	12
South Africa	60	**Samoa**	10
England	111	**Uruguay**	13

	P	W	D	L	F	A	Pts
England	4	4	0	0	255	47	12
South Africa	4	3	0	1	184	60	10
Samoa	4	2	0	2	138	117	8
Uruguay	4	1	0	3	56	255	6
Georgia	4	0	0	4	46	200	4

POOL D

New Zealand	70	**Italy**	7
Wales	41	**Canada**	10
Italy	36	**Tonga**	12
New Zealand	68	**Canada**	6
Wales	27	**Tonga**	20
Italy	19	**Canada**	14
New Zealand	91	**Tonga**	7
Wales	27	**Italy**	15
Canada	24	**Tonga**	7
New Zealand	53	**Wales**	37

	P	W	D	L	F	A	Pts
New Zealand	4	4	0	0	282	57	7
Wales	4	3	0	1	132	98	7
Italy	4	2	0	2	77	123	7
Canada	4	1	0	3	54	135	3
Tonga	4	0	0	4	46	178	3

Fifth World Cup Final, Telstra Stadium, Sydney, 22 November 2003

ENGLAND 20 (4PG 1DG 1T)
AUSTRALIA 17 (4PG 1T) *

ENGLAND: J Robinson; O J Lewsey, W J H Greenwood, M J Tindall, B C Cohen; J P Wilkinson, M J S Dawson; T J Woodman, S Thompson, P J Vickery, M O Johnson (captain), B J Kay, R A Hill, L B N Dallaglio, N A Back Substitutions: M J Catt for Tindall (78 mins); J Leonard for Vickery (80 mins); I R Balshaw for Lewsey (85 mins); L W Moody for Hill (93 mins)

SCORERS TRY: Robinson Penalty Goals: Wilkinson (4) Dropped Goal: Wilkinson

AUSTRALIA: M S Rogers; W J Sailor, S A Mortlock, E J Flatley, L Tuqiri; S J Larkham, G M Gregan (captain); W K Young, B J Cannon, A K E Baxter, J B Harrison, N C Sharpe, G B Smith, D J Lyons, P R Waugh Substitutions: D T Giffin for Sharpe (48 mins); J A Paul for Cannon (56 mins); M J Cockbain for Lyons (56 mins); J W Roff for Sailor (70 mins); M J Dunning for Young (92 mins); M J Giteau for Larkham (temp 18 to 30 mins; 55 to 63 mins; 85 to 93 mins)

SCORERS TRY: Tuqiri Penalty Goals: Flatley (4)

REFEREE A J Watson (South Africa)

* after extra time : 14-14 after normal time

Dave Rogers/Getty Images

Martin Johnson brings the World Cup to the northern hemisphere for the first time.

QUARTER-FINALS

New Zealand	29	**South Africa**	9
Australia	33	**Scotland**	16
France	43	**Ireland**	21
England	28	**Wales**	17

SEMI-FINALS

Australia	22	**New Zealand**	10
England	24	**France**	7

THIRD PLACE MATCH

New Zealand	40	**France**	13

Stuart Hannagan/Getty Images

The 2003 final was won, deep into extra time, by an unforgettable Jonny Wilkinson drop goal.

THE IRB PLAYERS OF THE YEAR

By Iain Spragg

Name: Daniel Carter
Date of Birth: 5 March,1982
Teams: Canterbury, Crusaders, New Zealand
Debut: 21/06/2003 v Wales (Hamilton)
Caps: 31
Points: 468
(All statistics up to 30.10.06)
Chris McGrath/Getty Images

The All Black No.10 had a lot to live up to in 2006. Named the 2005 IRB Player of the Year at the age of 23, Carter enjoyed a golden year in which he, at times, single-handedly tore the British & Irish Lions to shreds, scoring a record 33 points in the second Test massacre in Wellington, and establishing himself as the game's undisputed number one fly-half.

He amassed 20 points on his debut against Wales in 2003 and is already third on the all-time list of All Black scorers after a mere 31 caps and boasts a better strike rate than the only two men – Grant Fox and Andrew Mehrtens – who have so far outscored him.

So valuable is he now to the All Blacks that coach Graham Henry rested him for the first two Tests of 2006 against Ireland but recalled his talismanic playmaker for the one-off Test against Argentina in Buenos Aries. Carter kicked 10 points and scored a try to spare his side from defeat as New Zealand scraped home 25–19.

The 2006 Tri-Nations saw the fly-half in prolific form once again as the All Blacks dominated and successfully defended their crown. Carter amassed 99 of his side's 179 points – averaging 16.5 points a game – and the tournament was decided in favour of the New Zealanders with two games to spare.

He was in particularly devastating form with the boot in the All Blacks' 35–17 win over the Springboks in Wellington – landing seven penalties and two conversions for a haul of 25 points – while he maintained his impressive record of a try almost every other game when he crossed against South Africa in Rustenburg.

Still only 24, Carter has years of Test match rugby ahead of him and seems destined to be one of the stars of the 2007 World Cup.

Name: Chris Latham
Date of Birth: 8 September, 1975
Teams: Queensland Reds, Australia
Debut: 21/11/1998 v France (Paris)
Caps: 67
Points: 165

Chris McGrath/Getty Images

Chris Latham has packed a lot into his six-year career, as the Wallabies' full-back. First capped against France back in 1998 at the Stade de France, Latham has been ripping opposition defences apart with such regularity ever since that it's hard to remember a time when he wasn't an integral part of the Australian set-up.

His outstanding record of 33 tries in just 67 Tests for his country leaves him second only to the great David Campese on the all-time list of Wallaby try scorers and his form in 2006 suggested there are plenty more to come from the powerful Queensland number 15.

Bouncing back after an injury-plagued 2005 in which he missed five internationals with a hamstring injury, the new international season began with the two-Test series against England. Latham returned to the side and was, perhaps predictably, quick to help himself to international try number 31 in the first Test in Sydney's Telstra Stadium as the Wallabies romped home 34–3.

He added try number 32 in the one-off clash with Ireland in Perth and even before the start of the Tri-Nations, it was obvious the Reds full-back was back to his barnstorming best.

Latham started five of Australia's first six Tri-Nations' fixtures – scoring in the 49–0 rout of the Springboks in Brisbane – and although the Wallabies struggled at times through the tournament, his personal performances were recognised in September. Four days after his 31st birthday, he was named the Australian Player of the Year and awarded the John Eales Medal. He was the first back to receive the honour.

A veteran of both the 1999 and 2003 World Cup campaigns, Latham's powers show no signs of waning and he looks set to make another big impact in France in 2007.

Name: Paul O'Connell
Date of Birth: 20 October, 1979
Teams: Young Munster, Munster, Ireland
Debut: 3/02/2002 v Wales (Dublin)
Caps: 36
Points: 25

Tom Shaw/Getty Images

If Ireland fans were concerned that the hand injury that kept Paul O'Connell out of action for the 2005 autumn Tests would affect his performances in 2006, they need not have worried. It was as if the Munster lock had never been away.

In fact, the 26-year-old returned to the international fray even stronger than before and his typically abrasive, all-action displays in the Irish pack were as influential and eye-catching as ever.

He returned to the team for the opening Six Nations clash with Italy at Lansdowne Road in February and had it not been for a shoulder injury picked up against France in Paris, he would have been an ever-present in Eddie O'Sullivan's side throughout the tournament.

As it was, he missed the Wales game but came back for the victories over Scotland and England that clinched a second successive Triple Crown for the men in green.

First capped against Wales in 2002 – a match in which he also scored the first of his five international tries – O'Connell followed up on his Six Nations success by playing a key part in Munster's Heineken Cup campaign. Beaten finalists in both 2000 and 2002, the Irish province finally ended their European jinx by beating Biarritz at the Millennium Stadium and unsurprisingly O'Connell was once again conspicuous whenever it mattered in both the loose and tight.

He was an automatic choice for the summer tour of New Zealand and Australia and although it was to prove a winless trip for the Irish, the second row once again enhanced his reputation against the southern hemisphere giants, scoring a try in the second Test against the All Blacks in Auckland.

O'Connell has already captained his country twice in the absence of Brian O'Driscoll and will surely lead Ireland again, in the future.

Name: Richie McCaw
Date of Birth: 31 December, 1980
Teams: Canterbury, Crusaders, New Zealand
Debut: 17/11/2001 v Ireland (Dublin)
Caps: 46
Points: 40

Phil Walter/Getty Images

Richie McCaw had large boots to fill when he was appointed All Blacks captain in May this year. His predecessor, Tana Umaga, had lead his country with distinction and considerable success 21 times and when he finally decided to call time on his Test career, New Zealand were shorn of one of the All Blacks' most popular leaders of recent years.

McCaw, however, was the natural choice as Umaga's successor. The hard-tackling Canterbury man was established as the team's vice captain, had already lead his country against Wales back in 2004 aged just 23 (becoming only the 60th player in history to captain the All Blacks) and was arguably the first name down on Graham Henry's team sheet every week.

Unsurprisingly, the new captain was quickly into his stride and leading from the front. He took the team into the Tri-Nations unbeaten after wins in the three warm-up Tests against Ireland and Argentina and it was quickly apparent that McCaw would let his actions rather than words speak volumes for his captaincy.

A master at the breakdown, McCaw scored of one of the team's four tries in the first game of the Tri-Nations against Australia in Christchurch, and he repeated the trick in the next match – the 35–17 win over the Springboks at the Westpac Stadium.

When he wasn't helping to keep the scoreboard ticking over, he was spearheading a miserly All Blacks' defence, which provided the platform for their Tri-Nations success.

The only blemish on McCaw's otherwise faultless record as captain came in the final match of the competition when South Africa pulled off a surprise 21–20 win in Rustenburg.

It was McCaw's first taste of defeat as captain but after his first year in one of rugby's toughest jobs, the signs are it will prove be a rare setback on his watch.

Name: Fourie du Preez
Date of Birth: 24 March,1982
Teams: Blue Bulls, Bulls, South Africa
Debut: 12/06/2004 v Ireland (Bloemfontein)
Caps: 30
Points: 25

Dave Rogers/Getty Images

An exciting and often unpredictable scrum-half, Fourie du Preez enjoyed a breakthrough year in 2006 in which he established himself in the Springboks line-up and put himself in pole position for a starting place at the World Cup next year.

First capped against Ireland in Bloemfontein in 2004 (a year after his Super 12 debut for the Bulls against the Brumbies), the Pretoria-born number nine initially struggled to stay in the side despite tries against both New Zealand and Argentina that year and he soon found himself on the fringes of the squad.

He had to be content to make the bulk of his appearances in 2005 from the Springbok bench but bounced back this year with some commanding performances which saw him hailed as one of the international game's most dangerous line-breakers.

He started both games against Scotland in the summer, scoring the only try the second Test victory in Port Elizabeth, but found himself back amongst the substitutes for the Springboks' opening Tri-Nations clash with Australia in Brisbane.

It was to prove the only setback in an otherwise encouraging season. South Africa were routed 49–0 by the Wallabies, du Preez was summoned from the bench for the second half and the scrum-half was to start in four of the next five games in the tournament.

He fully justified his selection with tries against New Zealand in both Wellington's Westpac Stadium and his hometown of Pretoria and although South Africa lost both Tests heavily, du Preez demonstrated his ability to break down even the most well organised defences.

An accurate kicker from hand and with pace to burn, the 24-year-old Springbok will now be difficult to dislodge from the side as South Africa build for the World Cup in France.

THE WORLD RECORD BREAKERS

By Chris Thau

Record breakers, irrespective of their pursuit or field of activity, are exceptional people, strong-willed, obsessive and single-minded. In individual sports, they are supremely gifted athletes – runners, weightlifters or swimmers, etc – striving for perfection in their chosen field. They are the human expression of the Olympic slogan 'stronger, faster, higher'. In games and team sports though, a significant collective effort is required in addition to single-mindedness and talent which remain pre-requisites for any record-breaking exploit.

In rugby, a multifarious and intricate ball game, individual records of the likes of Australia's George Gregan and Japan's Daisuke Ohata – who have become the world's most capped player and top try scorer respectively – are the sum of many unquantified parts, of which what is commonly described as 'team effort' is probably the main ingredient.

Gregan who was born in Lusaka, in Zambia, went to Australia with his family when he was one year old, and he grew up in Canberra where he was educated at St Edmund's College. He made his apprenticeship at scrum-half for school and Australia age-groups (U19 and U21) where he got to understand and respect the value of team effort. He won the first of his 127 caps in 1994 against Italy in Brisbane, a match the the Wallabies were lucky to win by three points, 23-20.

His understated contribution, work ethic and leadership qualities made an immediate impact at top level and his try-saving tackle on Jeff Wilson that won Australia the Bledisloe Cup in 1994 entered the legend of Wallaby-All Black encounters. In the aftermath of the RWC 1995 as the game went professional, he joined the Canberra Brumbies professional team, who stunned the world as they won the Super 12 competitions several times. There, in his hometown of Canberra, under the astute management of coach Rod Macqueen, Gregan gave the phrase "playing for your home team" a new meaning, as he became a foundation rock on which the success of the franchise was built.

Similarly after Daisuke Ohata scored his third try against Georgia in the city of his birth Osaka, to break the world try-scoring record previously held by Australia's David Campese, his first words of thanks were addressed to his fellow players.

Jeff Brass/Getty Images

George Gregan, the world's most-capped player, taking on the New Zealand defence.

"I am very happy to break the record and would like to thank my team-mates, who facilitated it. It is great to break the record before the soccer World Cup starts," Ohata said after receiving a special award of one million Yen from the Japan Rugby Football Union and a special gold-striped shirt to mark the occasion.

Ohata, who is two years younger than Gregan, set his world record in the Test against the visiting Georgians at the legendary Hanazono Stadium in front of his parents, former school teachers from *Tokai Dai Gyosei High School* and friends. He scored his first try towards the end of the first half and from then on every time he touched the ball the expectant roar of the crowd moved up a few decibels. The levels of noise became deafening as he scored his second try, which equalled Campese's world record, some 20 minutes into the second half. From that moment on, the entire Japanese team worked for Ohata and his record. Late in injury time, as the crowd held their collective breath he gathered the ball from a lineout near the Georgian line and crashed over for his third – a world record try.

"I started playing rugby because of my father. He played rugby at high school, and influenced me to take up the game. It was always a sport that was close to me, and I started playing in the third year of elementary school. From there, I wanted to play in a team that would reach the national High School Tournament finals at Hanazono. But there are too many high school strong teams in Osaka, so I decided to join a new school, choosing it so we could build up a team and aim for Hanazono

Chris McGrath/Getty Images

Japan's Daisuke Ohata sped past David Campese's record for tries in Test matches, in 2006.

our way. I played for three years at high school, and was lucky to have such wonderful coaches. And I was selected for the Japanese high school representative team. I went on playing rugby at university in the Kansai, and put in four years of hard training at Kyoto Sangyo University. There, when I was in my third year at university, I was lucky enough to be chosen for the full Japanese national team for the first time."

Interestingly enough Ohata's 10-year try-scoring spree which commenced with a hat-trick against Korea in 1996, would have had a much higher yield, had his 21 tries, scored in non-cap matches, been considered. Even before his official international debut, the winger gave a sample of his awesome finishing power in a non-cap international against Thailand at the 15th Asian Championship when he scored four tries.

Ohata's strike rate of 1.01 tries per match (65 tries in 55 matches) is far superior to that of Campese of 0.63 (64 tries in 101 tests) tries/match. It is fair to say though, that Ohata's phenomenally high rate has been helped by the quality of opposition. Unlike Campese's record set against largely first class opposition, Ohata's has benefited from some soft opportunities, against Asian nations in particular, though he scored against virtually all nations he had played against. Had his other 21 tries scored in five non-cap matches been considered, this would have increased his world record tally to 86 tries in 60 matches – a bewildering strike rate of 1.43 tries per match.

Among the delighted spectators at Hanazono, there were two of his predecessors in the red and white Japanese jersey, the lethal Yoshihiro 'Demi' Sakata, now Professor at Osaka University and the explosive Yoshimitsu Yoshida.

"I have heard all about the wonderful players who have represented Japan in the past, and I think that there is great value in the legacy that they have left us. Similar to Sakata, who scored four tries against the Junior All Blacks, and Yoshida, who scored a try for the World XV in New Zealand, so too I want to achieve results, and leave a legacy for players to come. With the type of play that I do, I get a lot of pleasure from scoring tries. But rugby is a team game, a team with many players in it, and it is fun just to take part, to meet people, be part of a team," Ohata said.

"Breaking the world record is not the final goal of my career, and I would like to take it as far as I can. Naturally, I do not remember all my tries, but I can recall some of them I think. I believe that the try I scored at the 2003 RWC left a good impression with everybody. For me, in front of all those people, showing them the attractiveness of rugby was a valuable experience. That was a good try, I think. But, my favourite is the try I scored against Wales at the 1999 RWC."

Meanwhile, Gregan who had equalled Jason Leonard's record in Australia's Test number 448 against New Zealand in last year's final Tri-Nations game (September 2005), at Eden Park, had to deal with an unprecedented barrage of media criticism. Many made the Australian skipper, together with the then coach Eddie Jones, the scapegoat of the country's poor patch. Jones was fired by ARU after the 2005 European autumn tour which saw Australia lose three Tests out of four, with Gregan taking over as the favorite media target.

During this particularly difficult period, when his captaincy as well as his style came under fire Gregan kept his head down and went on giving his all in the matches he played, earning the respect and support of the new coach John Connolly, one of the finest man-managers in the world game. He was selected for the first Test of 2006 when he played part of a comprehensive team effort in the win over England and came from the bench in the second Cook Cup Test in Melbourne, to win his 120th cap for his country. "George is one of Australia's greatest-ever players. Part of this is because he never stops working hard," said Connolly, describing the attacks as 'unfair'. "He's probably one of the most professional players I've ever coached. George practices and does extra work away from the field to prepare himself and he has the complete confidence and trust of the other players. He's a player players want to play with, and there's probably no greater wrap as a player".

Gregan became the Wallabies captain after John Eales retired in 2001, as Australia embarked on a tour of Europe, which started off with a friendly against Spain in Madrid. He led the Wallabies throughout the 2003 RWC campaign, when the narrow defeat at the hands of England, made his critics forget the masterful display in the win over New Zealand in the semi-final. In June 2004 Gregan was appointed to the Order of Australia for his services to Rugby Union Football and in particular as the captain of the Wallabies. In October he announced that his four-year-old son had epilepsy and has launched an epilepsy awareness campaign in Australia with the slogan 'Get on the Team'.

Gregan missed the last few weeks of the 2005 Super 12 season after breaking his leg during a game against the New South Wales Waratahs in Canberra. He returned for the match against Italy in Melbourne, which the Wallabies won 61-29. During the 2006 match against South Africa in Sydney, Gregan took over from his predecessor John Eales the mantle of Australia's most capped capatin with 57 tests, with his views firmly set on Will Carling's world record captaincy of 59 internationals. "The Wallabies were at the top in 2001" Gregan said. "Some senior players were leaving, so the captaincy was something I took on as a challenge and the challenge is still there for me. Having played under Ealesy, he was such a great leader and to achieve the record that he once held is a fantastic honour.

"Captaining the Wallabies has been extremely rewarding and something that I have thoroughly enjoyed. I have had some good luck and good management along the way. I've been very fortunate to have a career in a game that I love, a game that I started playing as a ten-year-old."

All Blacks legend Wayne Smith paid a telling tribute to the scrum-half.

"Gregan" – observed Smith – "is probably the greatest Wallaby ever. He has been involved in some of their greatest Test victories. He is a warrior; you never get on top of him. He has got a huge spirit and you can't say much more than that. Form comes and goes, but his soul and depth of spirit have seen him return to the top before. He knows the drums have been beating for him for a decade probably, from time to time. He just keeps fronting. I would say, because of the character of the man, it probably inspires him more than anything."

New Zealand, captained by Richie McCaw (above, with the Tri Nations trophy) have risen to the world's number one team.

IRB WORLD RANKINGS

By Dominic Rumbles

New Zealand's dominance of the Test arena in 2006 was reflected in the IRB World Rankings during the same period. In losing just one match during a busy schedule of June Tests and a Tri-Nations, Graham Henry's team consolidated their top spot- a place that the All Blacks have occupied since June 2004.

While New Zealand continued to set the pace, there was much jostling for position amongst the other leading nations during a year of highs and lows on the international stage. England, who held top spot from October 2003 to June 2004, slipped to sixth after an inconsistent RBS Six Nations campaign and two heavy defeats in Australia, while Wales, 2005 Grand Slam champions, slumped to ninth after a disappointing campaign.

Of course for every slump there was a peak and 2006 Six Nations champions France moved to second, Ireland climbed to fifth and South Africa third. Australia's resurgence under John Connolly yielded third place during July, but defeat to South Africa saw the Wallabies swap places with the Springboks by the end of the Tri-Nations. Scotland, after improved results in 2006, moved to seventh.

With an unprecedented level of rugby being played by Tier 2 and Tier 3 nations during 2006 owing to full Rugby World Cup qualifying programme and the introduction of new IRB tournaments such as the Pacific 5 Nations and Nations Cup, there was predictably considerable movement.

Fiji jumped above Italy to 11th, while Tonga, who notched up some impressive results during the Pacific 5 Nations, moved up four places to 16th. Kenya (up seven to 37th) and Russia (up five to 19th) also made significant rankings progress.

Started in 2003, the IRB World Rankings are published every week on www.irb.com are calculated using a 'Points Exchange' system, in which the sides take points off each other based on the match result. Whatever one side gains, the other side loses. The exchanges are based on the match result, the relative strength of each team, and the margin of victory. There is also an allowance for home advantage.

Points exchanges are doubled during the World Cup Finals to recognise the unique importance of this event, but all other full international matches are treated the same, to be as fair as possible to countries playing a different mix of friendly and competitive matches across the world.

All member countries have a rating, typically between 0 and 100. The top side in the world will normally have a rating above 90. Any match that is not a full international between two countries does not count at all.

IRB WORLD RANKINGS 20.09.06

POSITION (PREVIOUS)	MEMBER UNION	RATING POINTS
1(1)	NEW ZEALAND	92.91
2(2)	FRANCE	87.53
3(4)	SOUTH AFRICA	87.05
4(3)	AUSTRALIA	86.13
5(5)	IRELAND	82.01
6(6)	ENGLAND	79.66
7(7)	SCOTLAND	77.72
8(8)	ARGENTINA	77.49
9(9)	WALES	76.34
10(10)	SAMOA	73.86
11(11)	FIJI	73.15
12(12)	ITALY	72.11
13(13)	CANADA	69.11
14(14)	ROMANIA	67.31
15(15)	USA	66.55
16(16)	TONGA	66.04
17(17)	GEORGIA	65.56
18(18)	URUGUAY	65.35
19(19)	RUSSIA	64.54
20(20)	JAPAN	63.05
21(21)	PORTUGAL	61.16
22(22)	MOROCCO	60.52
23(23)	KOREA	60.21
24(24)	CHILE	59.27
25(25)	SPAIN	56.99
26(26)	CZECH REPUBLIC	56.56
27(28)	GERMANY	56.06
28(29)	HONG KONG	55.21
29(27)	NAMIBIA	54.74
30(30)	PARAGUAY	53.82
31(31)	TUNISIA	52.66
32(32)	UKRAINE	52.54
33(33)	NETHERLANDS	51.72
34(34)	BELGIUM	51.51
35(35)	BRAZIL	50.72

36(36)	MOLDOVA	50.22
37(43)	KENYA	49.63
38(37)	POLAND	49.55
39(38)	CROATIA	48.93
40(39)	CHINESE TAIPEI	48.41
41(40)	ARABIAN GULF	48.32
42(41)	LATVIA	48.26
43(42)	SRI LANKA	48.16
44(44)	KAZAKHSTAN	47.95
45(45)	MADAGASCAR	47.95
46(46)	SWEDEN	47.71
47(47)	IVORY COAST	47.54
48(48)	SWITZERLAND	47.13
49(49)	ZIMBABWE	46.90
50(50)	UGANDA	46.78
51(51)	CHINA	46.58
52(52)	MALTA	46.43
53(53)	SINGAPORE	46.00
54(54)	COOK ISLANDS	45.87
55(55)	VENEZUELA	45.45
56(56)	PERU	45.44
57(57)	PAPUA NEW GUINEA	45.09
58(58)	DENMARK	45.05
59(59)	TRINIDAD & TOBAGO	43.97
60(60)	CAYMAN	43.87
61(61)	ANDORRA	43.54
62(62)	BARBADOS	43.13
63(63)	THAILAND	42.32
64(64)	SENEGAL	42.13
65(65)	BERMUDA	41.69
66(66)	LITHUANIA	41.19
67(67)	NIUE ISLANDS	40.96
68(68)	SLOVENIA	40.90
69(69)	GUYANA	40.35
70(70)	MALAYSIA	40.19
71(71)	HUNGARY	40.05
72(72)	SERBIA AND MONTENEGRO	40.04
73(73)	AUSTRIA	39.97
74(74)	ZAMBIA	39.96
75(75)	ST. VINCENT & THE GRENADINES	39.30
76(76)	SOLOMON ISLANDS	39.06
77(77)	JAMAICA	38.97
78(78)	MONACO	38.81
79(79)	NORWAY	38.70
80(80)	BOTSWANA	38.64
81(81)	CAMEROON	38.52
82(82)	GUAM	38.13
83(83)	LUXEMBOURG	37.93
84(84)	SWAZILAND	37.57
85(85)	ST. LUCIA	37.57

86(86)	COLOMBIA	37.53
87(87)	TAHITI	36.25
88(88)	INDIA	36.20
89(89)	NIGERIA	36.00
90(90)	BAHAMAS	35.61
91(91)	BULGARIA	35.20
92(92)	VANUATU	34.77
93(93)	ISRAEL	34.56
94(94)	BOSNIA & HERZEGOVINA	31.80
95(95)	FINLAND	

FRANCE WIN WITHOUT SETTING SIX NATIONS ALIGHT

By Will Greenwood

Dave Rogers/Getty Images

Aurelien Rougerie of France celebrates in the dressing room after France clinched the RBS Six Nations title with a 21–16 win over Wales.

I don't believe anyone would argue 2006 was a classic year for the Six Nations but it was still a fascinating tournament that produced more than one genuine upset, as well as some curious and at times inept performances from the perennial heavyweights, France and England.

The fact France clinched their third title in five seasons confirmed many people's pre-tournament predictions but Bernard Laporte and his men will be aware they failed to convince anyone that they are in great shape for the World Cup challenge on home soil next year. I wouldn't be surprised if the champagne stayed firmly on ice, even after the tense victory in Cardiff that confirmed them as champions.

My personal highlights of the campaign were the performances of Italy and Scotland. It was a breath of fresh air watching both teams, written off at the start of the season, scaring the life out of the 'bigger' sides and they enlivened the tournament in a way that the other four countries failed to do. It's ironic that the team that finished bottom – Italy – actually made the greatest strides and will have taken the most encouragement from their displays.

Ireland fans will doubtless have celebrated their second Triple Crown in three seasons with traditional gusto but it was a bad year to be a Wales or England supporter. Wales, the defending Grand Slam champions, simply fell apart at the seams on and off the pitch while England got worse as the season wore on and both teams could have few complaints about their disappointing finishes.

Overall, however, it was an intriguing year but I was a little alarmed at how dominant defences were throughout the competition. The fans want to see a Utopian world of free-flowing rugby with tries scored from all over the pitch but the reality is that it's getting more and more difficult to create space. Defences are sucking the life out of the opposition and the days of crowd-pleasing, length-of-the-pitch tries are going to become an increasing rarity.

But back to the champions, France. They began the tournament with an abysmal performance at Murrayfield but it would be wrong to suggest they were not eventually worthy winners because they blew away the top two other sides – England and Ireland. The nagging doubts about their consistency, however, remain.

The loss of Yannick Jauzion before the start of the competition was a big blow and the French midfield lacked the right balance as a result. The return of Damien Traille in the centre for the third match against Italy gave them a better shape and rescued Frederic Michalak from the guillotine.

TRIVIA

Wales made an unwelcome entry into an exclusive club in this Six Nations, becoming only the fourth team in the history of the illustrious tournament to immediately follow a Grand Slam season – as they completed a clean sweep in 2005 – with a fifth-place finish the following year. France were the first side to do it in 1968 and 1969, repeating the trick in 1988 and 1989, in between Scotland doing it in 1984 and 1985. Rugby World Magazine's team of the tournament was: Sylvain Marconnet, Steve Thompson, Pieter de Villiers, Malcolm O'Kelly, Fabien Pelous, Sergio Parisse, Allister Hogg, Denis Leamy, Harry Ellis, Stephen Jones, Chris Paterson, Mirco Bergamasco, Brian O'Driscoll, Mark Jones and Geordan Murphy.

Getty Images

Just three years after winning the World Cup, England were shocked, finishing fourth for the second year running.

Like many, I'm still not sure about Michalak. He's undoubtedly a precocious talent but I'm not convinced he's the right fly-half to lead France to the World Cup. He still doesn't dictate games in a way a side aspiring to be the best in the world needs and recent history suggests teams with mavericks at 10 don't win World Cups. Carlos Spencer and the All Blacks in 2003 spring to mind.

The major plus for the French was the return of the prodigal son, Thomas Castaignede. He was one of the few players who showed the ambition and desire to play some rugby and France looked a more potent attacking force once he had been recalled to face the Italians in Paris.

But despite lifting the Six Nations trophy once again, Laporte has a lot of soul searching to do. Does he really believe he has a team capable of winning the World Cup? Half of his side are in their 30s and while age was far from a disadvantage when England won in 2003, France have not looked anywhere near as assured in their build-up.

For second-placed Ireland, it was an encouraging campaign and his side's first-half performance in Paris aside, Eddie O'Sullivan will have been satisfied with a job well done. Only he and his players will know exactly what wrong in those 40 minutes in the Stade de France but to be 43–3 down at one stage was a real horror show. If Ireland have aspirations to be a world-class rather than leading European side, they simply cannot afford to switch off for long periods like that again.

In their other games, Ireland were of course far better. Admittedly, Wales just didn't turn up in Dublin but Ireland played the perfect tactical game in wet conditions against Scotland and took their chances at Twickenham for a famous triumph and their third consecutive victory over the English.

In the Ireland pack, Denis Leamy was absolutely outstanding and Paul O'Connell a mountain but it was Shane Horgan on the wing who really caught my eye. He is a gifted footballer who always does a job for Ireland and, in my opinion, he's been vastly underrated for too long.

Frank Hadden must have been delighted with Scotland's third place in his debut Six Nations as head coach and his team's memorable backs-to-the-wall displays against France and England were as absorbing as they were ultimately effective. They didn't play the prettiest rugby of the tournament but it was certainly riveting.

The Scotland team have been in the doldrums in recent seasons and their rejuvenation was great news for the Six Nations, if not France and England fans. Their narrow victory over Italy in Rome was their first away win in the championship since 2002 and while Hadden may still be a relative novice in terms of international experience, he clearly restored a much-needed sense of pride and commitment in his team. Jason White led the side from the front and the future now looks significantly brighter for the men in blue.

In contrast, Andy Robinson and his England team must be wondering what further embarrassments there could be on the horizon after a disastrous campaign. The comprehensive opening victory over Wales at Twickenham proved to be the falsest of dawns and even though a hard-fought but ultimately flattering win in Italy followed, it was all downhill from there.

Robinson came in for a lot of criticism for his conservative selections and as the season wore on his argument for consistency began to look a thin one. Personally I think he missed the opportunity to blood some new players once the campaign began to slip away after the defeat in Edinburgh. It was the ideal time to introduce two or three new faces once a potential Grand Slam had gone but it didn't happen.

On the field, I felt the back row lacked the right balance and the team still lacks enough ball carriers in the front five. I felt sorry for Charlie Hodgson, still not quite managing to bring his club form to the international frame, although he may have picked a different looking back line outside him. England still failed to convince that they're equipped to drag themselves out of their long-term slump.

The best that can be said for Wales' campaign was that they stayed faithful to their open, fluid style of play rather than retreat into their shells when the going got tough. It was, in truth, a toothless defence of their title but they were robbed of so many leading players through injury and that proved their downfall.

The bizarre, mid-tournament departure of Mike Ruddock did not help their cause either. It overshadowed everything else and there's no way the upheaval could have helped the Welsh players. The whole business was pure soap opera and could not have come at a worse time for a team that was already struggling.

But there were still positives. Dwayne Peel proved he can get even better at scrum-half and his partnership with Stephen Jones is as effective and reliable as any other in international rugby. The Welsh pack was competitive throughout and they finished the tournament strongly by pushing France close in Cardiff.

And so to Italy. Although they again finished the competition as the not-so-proud holders of the Wooden Spoon, they came close in all five of their games and Pierre Berbizier will have taken great heart from his side's displays. One solitary point was a meagre return for the way they played but there were clear signs, particularly in the back line, that Italy had moved up to another level.

The 'find of the tournament' for me was Mirco Bergamasco in the centre. He was outstanding defensively and his partnership with Gonzalo Canale in the midfield gave Italy the genuine threat out wide that they've lacked in past seasons. Ramiro Pez at fly-half was also impressive and the Italian pack as ever were abrasive and produced a respectable amount of ball.

It bodes well for the future of the competition that the bottom-placed team proved to be so competitive.

RBS SIX NATIONS 2006: FINAL TABLE

	P	W	D	L	For	Against	Pts
France	5	4	0	1	148	85	**8**
Ireland	5	4	0	1	131	97	**8**
Scotland	5	3	0	2	78	81	**6**
England	5	2	0	3	120	106	**4**
Wales	5	1	1	3	80	135	**3**
Italy	5	0	1	4	72	125	**1**

Points: Win 2; Draw 1; Defeat 0.

There were 629 points scored at an average of 41.9 a match. The Championship record (803 points at an average of 53.5 a match) was set in 2000. Ronan O'Gara was the leading individual points scorer with 76, 13 points shy of the Championship record Jonny Wilkinson set in 2001. Shane Horgan and Mirco Bergamasco were the Championship's leading try-scorers with three each.

Dave Rogers/Getty Images

There was only one candidate for most improved team: Frank Hadden's Scotland.

4 February, Lansdowne Road, Dublin

IRELAND 26 (2G 4PG) ITALY 16 (1G 3PG)

IRELAND: G E A Murphy; S P Horgan, B G O'Driscoll (*captain*), G M D'Arcy, T J Bowe; R J R O'Gara, P A Stringer; M J Horan, J Flannery, J J Hayes, M E O'Kelly, P J O'Connell, S H Easterby, D P Leamy, D P Wallace *Substitution:* D F O'Callaghan for O'Kelly (61 mins)

SCORERS *Tries:* Flannery, Bowe *Conversions:* O'Gara (2) *Penalty Goals:* O'Gara (4)

ITALY: C Stoica; P Canavosio, G-J Canale, Mirco Bergamasco, L Nitoglia; R Pez, P Griffen; S Perugini, F Ongaro, C Nieto, S Dellape, M Bortolami (*captain*), J Sole, S Parisse, Mauro Bergamasco *Substitutions:* A R Persico for Mauro Bergamasco (61 mins); C Del Fava for Bortolami (temp 25 to 32 mins and 66 mins); M-L Castrogiovanni, for Nieto (66 mins)

SCORERS *Try:* Mirco Bergamasco *Conversion:* Pez *Penalty Goals:* Pez (2), Griffen

REFEREE D Pearson (England)

YELLOW CARD R Pez (38 mins)

4 February, Twickenham

ENGLAND 47 (4G 3PG 2T) WALES 13 (1G 2PG)

ENGLAND: O J Lewsey; M J Cueto, J D Noon, M J Tindall, B C Cohen; C C Hodgson, H A Ellis; A J Sheridan, S G Thompson, M J H Stevens, S W Borthwick, D J Grewcock, J P R Worsley, M E Corry (*captain*), L W Moody *Substitutions:* T M D Voyce for Lewsey (20 mins); L B N Dallaglio for Worsley (temp 6 to 12 mins) and for Corry (62 mins); L A Mears for Thompson (62 mins); J M White for Sheridan (68 mins); S D Shaw for Grewcock (71 mins); M J S Dawson for Ellis (71 mins); A J Goode for Hodgson (73 mins)

SCORERS *Tries:* Cueto, Moody, Tindall, Dallaglio, Dawson, Voyce *Conversions:* Hodgson (2), Goode (2) *Penalty Goals:* Hodgson (3)

WALES: G.Thomas (*captain*); M A Jones, H Luscombe, M J Watkins, S M Williams; S M Jones, D J Peel; D Jones, T R Thomas, A R Jones, I M Gough, R A Sidoli, C L Charvis, M J Owen, M E Williams *Substitutions:* G D Jenkins for A R Jones (60 mins); G J Cooper for Peel (64 mins); A M Jones for Gough (temp 12 to 19 mins and 64 mins); A J Popham for Charvis (71 mins); L Byrne for Watkins (temp 6 to 16 mins) and for Cooper (79 mins)

SCORERS *Try*: M E Williams *Conversion*: S M Jones *Penalty Goals:* S M Jones (2)

REFEREE P G Honiss (New Zealand)

YELLOW CARD M E Williams (52 mins)

5 February, Murrayfield

SCOTLAND 20 (2G 2PG) FRANCE 16 (2PG 2T)

SCOTLAND: H F G Southwell; C D Paterson, M P di Rollo, A R Henderson, S F Lamont; D A Parks, M R L Blair; G Kerr, D W H Hall, B A F Douglas, A D Kellock, S Murray, J P R White (*captain*), S M Taylor, A Hogg *Substitutions:* S Webster for Di Rollo (28 mins); C J Smith for Douglas (41 mins); C P Cusiter for Blair (55 mins); G Ross for Parks (62 mins); S Lawson for Hall (62 mins); J M Petrie for White (70 mins); S J MacLeod for Kellock (71 mins)

SCORERS *Tries*: Lamont (2) *Conversions*: Paterson (2) *Penalty Goals:* Paterson (2)

FRANCE: N Brusque; C Dominici, F Fritz, L Valbon, C Heymans; F Michalak, J-B Elissalde; S Marconnet, D Szarzewski, P de Villiers, F Pelous (*captain*), J Thion, Y Nyanga, J Bonnaire, R Martin *Substitutions:* O Milloud for De Villiers (64 mins); S Bruno for Szarzewski (64 mins); T Lièvremont for Bonnaire (70 mins); G Bousses for Brusque (73 mins); D Yachvili for Elissalde (79 mins)

SCORERS *Tries:* Bonnaire, Bruno *Penalty Goals:* Elissalde (2)

REFEREE J I Kaplan (South Africa)

11 February, Stade de France, Paris

FRANCE 43 (5G 1PG 1T) IRELAND 31 (4G 1PG)

FRANCE: C Dominici; A Rougerie, F Fritz, D Marty, C Heymans; F Michalak, J-B Elissalde; O Milloud, R Ibañez, P de Villiers, F Pelous (*captain*), J Thion, Y Nyanga, J Bonnaire, O Magne *Substitutions:* S Bruno for Ibañez (46 mins); S Marconnet for Milloud (58 mins); R Martin for Magne (temp 37 to 40 mins and 58 mins); D Yachvili for Elissalde (58 mins); B Boyet for Michalak (68 mins); L Nallet for Nyanga (70 mins)

SCORERS *Tries:* Marty (2), Heymans (2), Rougerie, Magne *Conversions:* Elissalde (5) *Penalty Goal:* Elissalde

IRELAND: G E A Murphy; S P Horgan, B G O'Driscoll (*captain*), G M D'Arcy, T J Bowe; R J R O'Gara, P A Stringer; R Corrigan, J Flannery, J J Hayes, M E O'Kelly, P J O'Connell, S H Easterby, D P Leamy, D P Wallace *Substitutions:* D F O'Callaghan for O'Kelly (50 mins); S J Best for Corrigan (50 mins); A Trimble for Bowe (61 mins); E Reddan for O'Driscoll (76 mins)

SCORERS *Tries:* O'Gara, D'Arcy, O'Callaghan, Trimble *Conversions:* O'Gara (4) *Penalty Goal:* O'Gara

REFEREE P G Honiss (New Zealand)

11 February, Stadio Flaminio, Rome

ITALY 16 (1G 1PG 2DG) ENGLAND 31 (4G 1PG)

ITALY: C Stoica; P Canavosio, G-J Canale, Mirco Bergamasco, L Nitoglia; R Pez, P Griffen; S Perugini, F Ongaro, C Nieto, S Dellape, M Bortolami (*captain*), J Sole, S Parisse, Mauro Bergamasco *Substitutions:* C Del Fava for Dellape (56 mins); A R Persico for Sole (56 mins); S Picone for Canavosio (59 mins); C Festuccia for Ongaro (64 mins); M-L Castrogiovanni, for Nieto (64 mins); A Lo Cicero for Perugini (67 mins)

SCORERS *Try:* Mirco Bergamasco *Conversion:* Pez *Penalty Goal:* Pez *Dropped Goals:* Pez (2)

ENGLAND: T M D Voyce; M J Cueto, J D Noon, M J Tindall, B C Cohen; C C Hodgson, H A Ellis; A J Sheridan, S G Thompson, M J H Stevens, S W Borthwick, D J Grewcock, J P R Worsley, M E Corry (*captain*), L W Moody *Substitutions:* M J S Dawson for Ellis (54 mins); L A Mears for Thompson (61 mins); J M White for Sheridan (61 mins); L B N Dallaglio for Worsley (65 mins); S D Shaw for Grewcock (69 mins); J D Simpson-Daniel for Tindall (76 mins)

SCORERS *Tries:* Tindall, Hodgson, Cueto, Simpson-Daniel *Conversions:* Hodgson (4) *Penalty Goal:* Hodgson

REFEREE K M Deaker (New Zealand)

12 February, Millennium Stadium, Cardiff

WALES 28 (4G) SCOTLAND 18 (1G 2PG 1T)

WALES: G.Thomas (*captain*); M A Jones, H Luscombe, M J Watkins, S M Williams; S M Jones, D J Peel; D Jones, T R Thomas, A R Jones, I M Gough, R A Sidoli, C L Charvis, M J Owen, M E Williams *Substitutions:* G Delve for Charvis (66 mins); G D Jenkins for A R Jones (68 mins); L Byrne for Luscombe (temp 29 to 40 mins) and for S M Williams (69 mins); M Phillips for Peel (69 mins); N J Robinson for Watkins (74 mins); Mefin Davies for T R Thomas (76 mins); A M Jones for Sidoli (77 mins)

SCORERS *Tries*: G Thomas (2), pen try, Sidoli *Conversions*: S M Jones (4)

SCOTLAND: H F G Southwell; C D Paterson, B MacDougall, A R Henderson, S F Lamont; D A Parks, M R L Blair; G Kerr, S Lawson, B A F Douglas, A D Kellock, S Murray, J P R White (*captain*), S M Taylor, A Hogg *Substitutions:* C J Smith for Kerr (54 mins); R W Ford for Lawson (54 mins); C P Cusiter for Blair (60 mins); G Ross for Parks (60 mins); J M Petrie for Hogg (66 mins); S J MacLeod for Kellock (66 mins); S Webster for MacDougall (77 mins)

SCORERS *Tries*: Southwell, Paterson *Conversion*: Paterson *Penalty Goals:* Paterson (2)

REFEREE S R Walsh (New Zealand)

RED CARD S Murray (21 mins) Yellow Card I M Gough (21 mins)

25 February, Stade de France, Paris

FRANCE 37 (3G 2PG 2T) ITALY 12 (3PG 1DG)

FRANCE: T Castaignède; A Rougerie, F Fritz, D Traille, C Dominici; F Michalak, J-B Elissalde; O Milloud, R Ibañez, P de Villiers, F Pelous (*captain*), J Thion, Y Nyanga, T Lièvremont, O Magne *Substitutions:* D Yachvili for Elissalde (39 mins); S Marconnet for Milloud (51 mins); D Marty for Traille (52 mins); J Bonnaire for Magne (73 mins); L Nallet for Pelous (78 mins)

SCORERS *Tries:* Lièvremont, Nyanga, De Villiers, Rougerie, Michalak *Conversions:* Yachvili (3) *Penalty Goals:* Elissalde, Yachvili

ITALY: C Stoica; P Canavosio, G-J Canale, Mirco Bergamasco, L Nitoglia; R Pez, P Griffen; S Perugini, F Ongaro, C Nieto, C Del Fava, M Bortolami (*captain*), J Sole, S Parisse, Mauro Bergamasco *Substitutions:* M-L Castrogiovanni, for Nieto (66 mins); C Festuccia for Ongaro (68 mins); A Lo Cicero for Perugini (70 mins); A Zanni for Sole (74 mins); S Picone for Griffen (temp 3 to 10 mins and temp 61 to 67 mins)

SCORER *Penalty Goals:* Pez (3) *Dropped Goal:* Pez

REFEREE A J Spreadbury (England)

YELLOW CARD C Del Fava (63 mins)

25 February, Murrayfield

SCOTLAND 18 (5PG 1DG) ENGLAND 12 (4PG)

SCOTLAND: H F G Southwell; C D Paterson, M P di Rollo, A R Henderson, S F Lamont; D A Parks, M R L Blair; G Kerr, D W H Hall, B A F Douglas, S J MacLeod, A D Kellock, J P R White (*captain*), S M Taylor, A Hogg *Substitutions:* N J Hines for MacLeod (51 mins); R W Ford for Hall (58 mins); C J Smith for Douglas (60 mins); C P Cusiter for Blair (63 mins); G Ross for Parks (63 mins)

SCORERS *Penalty Goals:* Paterson (5) *Dropped Goal:* Parks

ENGLAND: O J Lewsey; M J Cueto, J D Noon, M J Tindall, B C Cohen; C C Hodgson, H A Ellis; A J Sheridan, S G Thompson, J M White, S W Borthwick, D J Grewcock, J P R Worsley, M E Corry (*captain*), L W Moody *Substitutions:* L B N Dallaglio for Corry (63 mins); S D Shaw for Grewcock (66 mins); M J S Dawson for Ellis (temp 50 to 62 mins and 72 mins); P T Freshwater for Sheridan (temp 38 to 40 mins and 72 mins)

SCORER *Penalty Goals:* Hodgson (4)

REFEREE A Lewis (Ireland)

YELLOW CARD D J Grewcock (22 mins)

26 February, Lansdowne Road, Dublin

IRELAND 31 (2G 4PG 1T) WALES 5 (1T)

IRELAND: G E A Murphy; S P Horgan, B G O'Driscoll (*captain*), G M D'Arcy, A Trimble; R J R O'Gara, P A Stringer; M J Horan, J Flannery, J J Hayes, D F O'Callaghan, M E O'Kelly, S H Easterby, D P Leamy, D P Wallace *Substitutions:* S J Best for Horan (68 mins); J H O'Connor for Wallace (74 mins); M R O'Driscoll for Easterby (76 mins); R Best for Flannery (77 mins)

SCORERS *Tries:* Wallace, Horgan, Stringer *Conversions:* O'Gara (2) *Penalty Goals:* O'Gara (4)

WALES: L Byrne; M A Jones, H Luscombe, M J Watkins, D R James; S M Jones, D J Peel; D Jones, T R Thomas, A R Jones, I M Gough, R A Sidoli, C L Charvis, M J Owen (*captain*), M E Williams *Substitutions:* G L Henson for S M Jones (18 mins); G D Jenkins for D Jones (45 mins); G Delve for Charvis (55 mins); Mefin Davies for T R Thomas (60 mins); B Davies for Byrne (72 mins)

SCORER *Try*: M A Jones

REFEREE J I Kaplan (South Africa)

YELLOW CARD D P Leamy (76 mins)

11 March, Millennium Stadium, Cardiff

WALES 18 (1G 2PG 1T) ITALY 18 (1G 2PG 1T)

WALES: L Byrne; M A Jones, H Luscombe, M J Watkins, S M Williams; S M Jones, D J Peel; D Jones, T R Thomas, A R Jones, I M Gough, R A Sidoli, C L Charvis, M J Owen (*captain*), M E Williams *Substitutions:* M Phillips for Peel (7 mins); A J Popham for Charvis (51 mins); G D Jenkins for D Jones (56 mins); Mefin Davies for T R Thomas (70 mins); J Thomas for Sidoli (74 mins)

SCORERS *Tries*: M A Jones, S M Jones *Conversion:* S M Jones *Penalty Goals:* S M Jones (2)

ITALY: E Galon; P Canavosio, G-J Canale, Mirco Bergamasco, L Nitoglia; R Pez, P Griffen; S Perugini, C Festuccia, C Nieto, S Dellape, M Bortolami (*captain*), S Parisse, J Sole, M Zaffiri *Substitutions:* M-L Castrogiovanni, for Nieto (24 mins); C Stoica for Canavosio (46 mins); C Del Fava for Dellape (49 mins); F Ongaro for Festuccia (66 mins); A Zanni for Parisse (72 mins); A Lo Cicero for Perugini (79 mins)

SCORERS *Tries:* Galon, Canavosio *Conversion:* Pez *Penalty Goals:* Pez (2)

REFEREE J Jutge (France)

11 March, Lansdowne Road, Dublin

IRELAND 15 (5PG) SCOTLAND 9 (3PG)

IRELAND: G E A Murphy; S P Horgan, B G O'Driscoll (*captain*), G M D'Arcy, A Trimble; R J R O'Gara, P A Stringer; M J Horan, J Flannery, J J Hayes, M E O'Kelly, P J O'Connell, S H Easterby, D P Leamy, D P Wallace *Substitution:* D F O'Callaghan for O'Connell (64 mins)

SCORER *Penalty Goals:* O'Gara (5)

SCOTLAND: H F G Southwell; C D Paterson, M P di Rollo, A R Henderson, S F Lamont; D A Parks, M R L Blair; G Kerr, D W H Hall, B A F Douglas, N J Hines, S Murray, J P R White (*captain*), S M Taylor, A Hogg *Substitutions:* C J Smith for Douglas (56 mins); C P Cusiter for Blair (57 mins); G Ross for Parks (57 mins); S Lawson for Hall (62 mins); S Webster for Paterson (69 mins); J M Petrie for White (71 mins); B A F Douglas for Smith (temp 62 to 69 mins)

SCORER *Penalty Goals:* Paterson (3)

REFEREE S J Dickinson (Australia)

12 March, Stade de France, Paris

FRANCE 31 (2G 4PG 1T) ENGLAND 6 (2PG)

FRANCE: T Castaignède; A Rougerie, F Fritz, D Traille, C Dominici; F Michalak, D Yachvili; S Marconnet, R Ibañez, P de Villiers, F Pelous (*captain*), J Thion, Y Nyanga, T Lièvremont, O Magne *Substitutions:* O Milloud for de Villiers (50 mins); J Bonnaire for Magne (57 mins); D Szarzewski for Ibañez (60 mins); L Nallet for Pelous (64 mins); L Valbon for Traille (71 mins)

SCORERS *Tries:* Fritz, Traille, Dominici *Conversions:* Yachvili (2) *Penalty Goals:* Yachvili (4)

ENGLAND: O J Lewsey; M J Cueto, J D Noon, M J Tindall, B C Cohen; C C Hodgson, M J S Dawson; M J H Stevens, S G Thompson, J M White, S W Borthwick, D J Grewcock, J P R Worsley, M E Corry (*captain*), L W Moody *Substitutions:* A J Goode for Hodgson (40 mins); T M D Voyce for Tindall (57 mins); H A Ellis for Dawson (57 mins); L A Mears for Thompson (60 mins); A J Sheridan for Stevens (60 mins); L B N Dallaglio for Worsley (60 mins); S D Shaw for Grewcock (68 mins)

SCORERS *Penalty Goals:* Hodgson, Goode

REFEREE A C Rolland (Ireland)

18 March, Stadio Flaminio, Rome

ITALY 10 (1G 1PG) SCOTLAND 13 (1G 1PG 1DG)

ITALY: C Stoica; P Canavosio, G-J Canale, Mirco Bergamasco, L Nitoglia; R Pez, P Griffen; S Perugini, F Ongaro, M-L Castrogiovanni, S Dellape, M Bortolami (*captain*), S Parisse, J Sole, M Zaffiri *Substitutions:* E Galon for Stoica (22 mins); A Zanni for Zaffiri (53 mins); A Lo Cicero for Castrogiovanni (54 mins); C Festuccia for Ongaro (61 mins); C Del Fava for Dellape (66 mins); S Picone for Griffen (temp 9 to 19 mins)

SCORERS *Try:* Mirco Bergamasco *Conversion:* Pez *Penalty Goal:* Pez

SCOTLAND: H F G Southwell; C D Paterson, M P di Rollo, A R Henderson, S F Lamont; G Ross, C P Cusiter; G Kerr, S Lawson, B A F Douglas, N J Hines, S Murray, J P R White (*captain*), S M Taylor, A Hogg *Substitutions:* M R L Blair for Cusiter (8 mins); C J Smith for Douglas (54 mins); D A Parks for Ross (61 mins); A D Kellock for Murray (67 mins); S Webster for Lamont (71 mins); D W H Hall for Lawson (75 mins)

SCORERS *Try:* Paterson *Conversion:* Paterson *Penalty Goal:* Paterson *Dropped Goal:* Ross

REFEREE A C Rolland (Ireland)

18 March, Millennium Stadium, Cardiff

WALES 16 (1G 3PG) FRANCE 21 (1G 3PG 1T)

WALES: L Byrne; D R James, H Luscombe, M J Watkins, S M Williams; S M Jones, M Phillips; D Jones, T R Thomas, A R Jones, I M Gough, R A Sidoli, M J Owen (*captain*), A J Popham, M E Williams *Substitutions:* G L Henson for Byrne (40 mins); Mefin Davies for T R Thomas (42 mins); G D Jenkins for D Jones (51 mins); D A R Jones for Popham (68 mins); J Thomas for Sidoli (74 mins)

SCORERS *Try*: Luscombe *Conversion:* S M Jones *Penalty Goals:* S M Jones (2), Henson

FRANCE: T Castaignède; A Rougerie, F Fritz, D Traille, C Dominici; F Michalak, D Yachvili; S Marconnet, R Ibañez, P de Villiers, F Pelous (*captain*), J Thion, Y Nyanga, T Lièvremont, J Bonnaire *Substitutions:* C Heymans for Castaignède (40 mins); D Szarzewski for Lièvremont (temp 26 to 34 mins) and for Ibañez (43 mins); J-B Elissalde for Yachvili (43 mins); O Magne for Lièvremont (49 mins); L Nallet for Bonnaire (55 mins)

SCORERS *Tries:* Fritz, Szarzewski *Conversion:* Elissalde *Penalty Goals:* Yachvili (2), Elissalde

REFEREE C White (England)

YELLOW CARD R Ibañez (24 mins)

18 March, Twickenham

ENGLAND 24 (1G 4PG 1T) IRELAND 28 (2G 3PG 1T)

ENGLAND: T M D Voyce; M J Cueto, J D Noon, S R Abbott, B C Cohen; A J Goode, H A Ellis; A J Sheridan, L A Mears, J M White, S W Borthwick, S D Shaw, J P R Worsley, M E Corry (*captain*), L W Moody *Substitutions:* M J Tindall for Noon (temp 28 to 39 mins and 40 mins); S G Thompson for Mears (62 mins); D J Grewcock for Shaw (62 mins); M J S Dawson for Ellis (66 mins); P T Freshwater for Sheridan (69 mins)

SCORERS *Tries:* Noon, Borthwick *Conversion:* Goode *Penalty Goals:* Goode (4)

IRELAND: G E A Murphy; S P Horgan, B G O'Driscoll (*captain*), G M D'Arcy, A Trimble; R J R O'Gara, P A Stringer; M J Horan, J Flannery, J J Hayes, M E O'Kelly, P J O'Connell, S H Easterby, D P Leamy, D P Wallace *Substitutions:* D F O'Callaghan for O'Kelly (53 mins); G T Dempsey for Trimble (65 mins); J H O'Connor for Wallace (temp 16 to 25 mins) and for Leamy (70 mins)

SCORERS *Tries:* Horgan (2), Leamy *Conversions:* O'Gara (2) *Penalty Goals:* O'Gara (3)

REFEREE N Whitehouse (Wales)

YELLOW CARD S H Easterby (67 mins)

Dave Canon/Getty Images

Ireland stunned England with a 28–24 win at Twickenham, which gave them a Triple Crown. Above Shane Horgan (left), Ronan O'Gara (centre) and captain Brian O'Driscoll get the party started.

INTERNATIONAL CHAMPIONSHIP RECORDS 1883–2006

PREVIOUS WINNERS

1883 England	1884 England	1885 Not completed
1886 England & Scotland	1887 Scotland	1888 Not completed
1889 Not completed	1890 England & Scotland	1891 Scotland
1892 England	1893 Wales	1894 Ireland
1895 Scotland	1896 Ireland	1897 Not completed
1898 Not completed	1899 Ireland	1900 Wales
1901 Scotland	1902 Wales	1903 Scotland
1904 Scotland	1905 Wales	1906 Ireland & Wales
1907 Scotland	1908 Wales	1909 Wales
1910 England	1911 Wales	1912 England & Ireland
1913 England	1914 England	1920 England & Scotland & Wales
1921 England	1922 Wales	1923 England
1924 England	1925 Scotland	1926 Scotland & Ireland
1927 Scotland & Ireland	1928 England	1929 Scotland
1930 England	1931 Wales	1932 England & Ireland & Wales
1933 Scotland	1934 England	1935 Ireland
1936 Wales	1937 England	1938 Scotland
1939 England & Ireland & Wales	1947 England & Wales	1948 Ireland
1949 Ireland	1950 Wales	1951 Ireland
1952 Wales	1953 England	1954 England & Wales & France
1955 Wales & France	1956 Wales	1957 England
1958 England	1959 France	1960 England & France
1961 France	1962 France	1963 England
1964 Scotland & Wales	1965 Wales	1966 Wales
1967 France	1968 France	1969 Wales
1970 Wales & France	1971 Wales	1972 Not completed
1973 Five Nations tie	1974 Ireland	1975 Wales
1976 Wales	1977 France	1978 Wales
1979 Wales	1980 England	1981 France
1982 Ireland	1983 Ireland & France	1984 Scotland
1985 Ireland	1986 Scotland & France	1987 France
1988 Wales & France	1989 France	1990 Scotland
1991 England	1992 England	1993 France
1994 Wales	1995 England	1996 England
1997 France	1998 France	1999 Scotland
2000 England	2001 England	2002 France
2003 England	2004 France	2005 Wales
2006 France		

England have won the title outright 25 times; Wales 23; France 15; Scotland 14; Ireland 10; Italy 0.

TRIPLE CROWN WINNERS

England (23 times) 1883, 1884, 1892, 1913, 1914, 1921, 1923, 1924, 1928, 1934, 1937, 1954, 1957, 1960, 1980, 1991, 1992, 1995, 1996, 1997, 1998, 2002, 2003.

Wales (18 times) 1893, 1900, 1902, 1905, 1908, 1909, 1911, 1950, 1952, 1965, 1969, 1971, 1976, 1977, 1978, 1979, 1988, 2005.

Scotland (10 times) 1891, 1895, 1901, 1903, 1907, 1925, 1933, 1938, 1984, 1990.

Ireland (Eight times) 1894, 1899, 1948, 1949, 1982, 1985, 2004, 2006.

GRAND SLAM WINNERS

England (12 times) 1913, 1914, 1921, 1923, 1924, 1928, 1957, 1980, 1991, 1992, 1995, 2003.

Wales (Nine times) 1908, 1909, 1911, 1950, 1952, 1971, 1976, 1978, 2005.

France (Eight times) 1968, 1977, 1981, 1987, 1997, 1998, 2002, 2004.

Scotland (Three times) 1925, 1984, 1990.

Ireland (Once) 1948

THE SIX NATIONS CHAMPIONSHIP 2000–2006: COMPOSITE SEVEN-SEASON TABLE

	P	W	D	L	Pts
France	35	26	0	9	**52**
Ireland	35	25	0	10	**50**
England	35	24	0	11	**48**
Wales	35	14	2	19	**30**
Scotland	35	11	1	23	**23**
Italy	35	3	1	31	**7**

MAJOR RECORDS

RECORD	DETAIL		SET
Most team points in season	229 by England	in five matches	2001
Most team tries in season	29 by England	in five matches	2001
Highest team score	80 by England	80–23 v Italy	2001
Biggest team win	57 by England	80–23 v Italy	2001
Most team tries in match	12 by Scotland	v Wales	1887
Most appearances	56 for Ireland	C M H Gibson	1964 – 1979
Most points in matches	406 for Wales	N R Jenkins	1991 – 2001
Most points in season	89 for England	J P Wilkinson	2001
Most points in match	35 for England	J P Wilkinson	v Italy, 2001
Most tries in matches	24 for Scotland	I S Smith	1924 – 1933
Most tries in season	8 for England	C N Lowe	1914
	8 for Scotland	I S Smith	1925
Most tries in match	5 for Scotland	G C Lindsay	v Wales, 1887
Most cons in matches	74 for England	J P Wilkinson	1998 – 2003
Most cons in season	24 for England	J P Wilkinson	2001
Most cons in match	9 for England	J P Wilkinson	v Italy, 2001
Most pens in matches	93 for Wales	N R Jenkins	1991 – 2001
Most pens in season	18 for England	S D Hodgkinson	1991
	18 for England	J P Wilkinson	2000
	18 for France	G Merceron	2002
Most pens in match	7 for England	S D Hodgkinson	v Wales, 1991
	7 for England	C R Andrew	v Scotland, 1995
	7 for England	J P Wilkinson	v France, 1999
	7 for Wales	N R Jenkins	v Italy, 2000
	7 for France	G Merceron	v Italy, 2002
Most drops in matches	9 for France	J-P Lescarboura	1982 – 1988
	9 for England	C R Andrew	1985 – 1997
Most drops in season	5 for France	G Camberabero	1967
	5 for Italy	D Dominguez	2000
	5 for Wales	N R Jenkins	2001
	5 for England	J P Wilkinson	2003
Most drops in match	3 for France	P Albaladejo	v Ireland, 1960
	3 for France	J-P Lescarboura	v England, 1985
	3 for Italy	D Dominguez	v Scotland 2000
	3 for Wales	N R Jenkins	v Scotland 2001

New Zealand had this year's trophy wrapped-up in double-quick time.

TRI-NATIONS

ALL BLACKS STAY ON TOP

By Francois Pienaar

I can't imagine there were many people who were surprised when New Zealand clinched the 2006 Tri-Nations crown. They went into the competition as the number one ranked team in the world, they were the defending champions and with their last defeat of any description almost a year old, everyone knew they were odds on to add another trophy to the cabinet.

The format of the competition had changed – each side playing an extra game home and away for the first time – but the All Blacks' appetite for winning was as strong as ever. The fact they wrapped up the title with two games to spare merely emphasised the dominance of Graham Henry's side. They were the standout team in the competition and they were worthy winners of their seventh Tri-Nations crown.

But even though the Blacks fulfilled their pre-tournament expectations and brushed off the Australian and South African challenge (with the exception of the Boks' 21–20 win in Rustenburg), I still thought it was a hugely entertaining tournament. There may have been an air of predictability about New Zealand's success but that definitely didn't detract from some of the thrilling rugby that was produced.

It may sound cliched to say that each successive Tri-Nations tournament has been better than the last but I genuinely believe that. I felt 2005 was the best I had seen at the time and I thought 2006 surpassed it.

I was at Loftus Versfeld for the South Africa and New Zealand game and some of the rugby on display took my breath away. I was sitting next to the former All Black captain Sean Fitzpatrick and neither of us could quite believe how good some of the play was. Of course, he had a big smile on his face because New Zealand produced the lion's share of it in their 45–26 win but I was still amazed at what they (and to a lesser extent the Springboks) were doing out there. It was rugby played with such precision and speed and it was amazing to watch, even though I wasn't happy to see South Africa on the wrong end of much of it.

As I said, New Zealand were worthy champions but I'm sure Graham Henry will have been just as pleased with the way he was able to change his starting line-up between games and bring in some fringe players as he was with the trophy itself.

Phil Walter/Getty Images

New Zealand were in irresistible form, winning the Tri-Nations with ease.

The All Blacks now have a tremendous squad and proved they can win home and away almost at will. They were quite simply a cut above the rest.

The worrying thing for the rest of the world with the World Cup looming next year is that Henry now seems to have such strength in depth. Daniel Carter is rightly regarded as the world's best fly-half at the moment, but Henry still had the luxury of being able to give Luke McAlister two starts in the midfield and he proved he's a world-class understudy who could step in if anything ever happened to Carter.

New Zealand also proved they have three hookers, three full-backs and three scrum-halves who are up to Test-match standard and that kind of depth is invaluable in modern Test-match rugby.

In contrast, Australia confirmed they are vulnerable if they suffer one or two key injuries. If John Connolly has a fully fit, first-choice XV at his disposal, the Wallabies are as competitive as ever, but you suspect they would be in big trouble if the likes of Mortlock, Latham or Larkham were sidelined for any length of time.

The Australian back line did look very dangerous but the question remains whether the pack can generate enough ball. Connolly is trying to rebuild in the forwards, bringing in bigger, heavier players like Blake, but the problem was never going to fix itself overnight. Judging by their Tri-Nations performances, the Wallabies are on the right track but they're not quite there yet.

It's easy to forget Australia had a nightmare 2005, losing seven in a row and failing to win a single Tri-Nations game. By comparison, second place in the 2006 Tri-Nations was a success story

South Africa had a torrid start to the competition with four straight defeats, but showed courage to bounce back and beat the Blacks and the Wallabies in South Africa in their final two fixtures.

Coach Jake White will probably still be scratching his head at how his side managed to lose 49–0 to the Wallabies in Brisbane in the first game but must have taken heart from the way they finished the competition. It was disappointing for the Boks to finish third after pushing New Zealand really close in 2005, but I'm sure they'll regroup.

White was quite ambitious in some of his selections during the tournament and that will hopefully reap its own rewards in the future. I've always maintained, even when we've had bad results, that South Africa has a big enough pool of talent to produce a really great side and the challenge for White is to successfully tap into that.

Overall, I thought the change of format – increasing each country's commitment from four to six games – was a success. Some people were worried that two extra matches may have undermined the intensity of the tournament but I thought the opposite was true. Even allowing for a couple one-sided scorelines, it was an incredibly competitive and physical tournament and as I said earlier, the skill levels on display were phenomenal.

For the neutral (if there is such a thing) I can understand that it was disappointing to see New Zealand crowned champions with two games still to play, but that was nothing to do with the new format. They were just too good.

Some people in South Africa were critical of the fact the new format meant the Boks had to play their first three games away from home. New Zealand and Australia both got two home fixtures in their first three, but I'd argue it all depends on your perspective, whether you believe it was a disadvantage.

With the benefit of hindsight, three matches on the road for the Boks at the start was an incredibly tough proposition, but you could as easily argue that three home fixtures to wrap-up the tournament gave them an edge at the business-end of the season. The fact they were out of title contention by the time the home games began reflected on Boks' performances and not on the vagaries of the fixture list.

We are talking about professional rugby here. Yes, it's harder to fly thousands of miles to fulfil a fixture than it is to play in your own backyard, but these guys are well prepared, well looked after and they're used to the schedule. I really don't agree the way the fixtures were arranged had any great bearing on the eventual outcome.

It's also important to remember that the format meant the Boks had two home fixtures against the All Blacks and two away in Australia (rather than the other way around) and I know which I would have chosen given the option.

Judging by the 2006 Tri-Nations, some people are already arguing the World Cup is the All Blacks' to throw away. I accept that if they reproduced that level of performance in France in 2007, they'll be unbelievably hard to beat, but I don't agree they are world champions in all but name.

It takes luck to win a World Cup and even New Zealand will need a slice if they're going to lift the Webb Ellis Cup. There are such small margins of error in a World Cup campaign and although they look the best team in the world today, it's not always the best team that takes the honours.

RESULTS

8 July, Jade Stadium, Christchurch

NEW ZEALAND 32 (3G, 2PG, 1T)
AUSTRALIA 12 (1G, 1T)

NEW ZEALAND: L MacDonald; R Gear, M Muliaina, A Mauger, J Rokocoko; D Carter, B Kelleher; T Woodcock, K Mealamu, C Hayman, C Jack, J Eaton, J Collins, R McCaw (captain), R So'oialo Substitutions: G Somerville for Woodcock (50 mins), A Williams for Eaton (59 mins), I Toeava for MacDonald (60 mins), P Weepu for Kelleher (65 mins), A Hore for Mealamu (62), C Masoe for So'oialo (62)

SCORERS *Tries*: Mealamu (2), McCaw, Toeava *Conversions*: Carter (3) *Penalty Goals*: Carter (2)

AUSTRALIA: C Latham; M Gerrard, S Mortlock, M Rogers, L Tuqiri; S Larkham, G Gregan (captain); G Holmes, T McIsaac, G Shepherdson, N Sharpe, D Vickerman, M Chisholm, G Smith, R Elsom Substitutions: J Paul for McIsaac (38 mins), S Fava for Chisholm (50 mins), M Giteau for Rogers (68 mins), A Baxter for Shepherdson (68 mins), S Cordingley for Gregan (70 mins), P Waugh for Smith (70 mins)

SCORERS *Tries*: Tuqiri, Fava *Conversion*: Mortlock

REFEREE J Kaplan (South Africa)

YELLOW CARD Elsom (27 mins)

15 July, Suncorp Stadium, Brisbane

AUSTRALIA 49 (5G, 2PG, 1DG, 1T)
SOUTH AFRICA 0

AUSTRALIA: C Latham; M Gerrard, S Mortlock, M Giteau, L Tuqiri; S Larkham, G Gregan (captain); G Holmes, J Paul, G Shepherdson, N Sharpe, D Vickerman, R Elsom, S Fava, G Smith Substitutions: S Cordingley for Gregan (40 mins), M Chisholm for Vickerman (40 mins), C Rathbone for Gerrard (62 mins), P Waugh for Smith (69 mins), M Rogers for Giteau (75 mins), S Hardman for Paul (75 mins), A Baxter for Holmes (75 mins)

SCORERS *Tries*: Giteau (2), Paul, Holmes, Latham, Chisholm *Conversions*: Mortlock (5) *Penalty Goals*: Mortlock (2) *Drop Goal*: Larkham

SOUTH AFRICA: P Montgomery; A Ndungane, J Fourie, W Olivier, B Habana; J van der Westhuyzen, R Januarie; O du Randt, J Smit (captain), CJ van der Linde, V Matfield, D Rossouw, J van Niekerk, P Spies, J Smith Substitutions: A van den Berg for Rossouw (38 mins), E Andrews for du Randt (48 mins), F du Preez for Januarie (55 mins), B Paulse for Habana (60 mins), J Cronje for van Niekerk (62 mins), D Coetzee for Smit (70 mins), M Bosman for van der Westhuyzen (75 mins)

REFEREE P Honiss (New Zealand)

YELLOW CARD Matfield (30 mins)

Getty Images

South Africa were humiliated in Brisbane, losing by a record score.

22 July, Westpac Stadium, Wellington

NEW ZEALAND 35 (2G, 7PG)
SOUTH AFRICA 17 (2G, 1PG)

NEW ZEALAND: L MacDonald; D Howlett, M Muliaina, S Tuitupou, S Hamilton; D Carter, P Weepu; N Tialata, A Oliver, C Hayman, C Jack, A Williams, R Thorne, R McCaw (captain), R So'oialo Substitutions: G Somerville for Tialata (62 mins), J Cowan for Weepu (67 mins), A Hore for Oliver (73 mins), C Masoe for McCaw (91 mins), L McAlister for Tuitupou (91 mins)

SCORERS *Tries*: Weepu, McCaw *Conversions*: Carter (2) *Penalty Goals*: Carter (7)

SOUTH AFRICA: P Montgomery; B Paulse, J Fourie, W Olivier, B Habana; B James, F du Preez; O du Randt, J Smit (captain), CJ van der Linde, A van den Berg, V Matfield, S Tyibilika, J Smith, J Cronje Substitutions: E Andrews for du Randt (temp 56 to 64 mins), J Muller for van den Berg (69 mins), J van Niekerk for Tyibilika (75 mins)

SCORERS *Tries*: Du Preez, Paulse *Conversions*: Montgomery (2) *Penalty Goal*: Montgomery

REFEREE J Jutge (France)

29 July, Suncorp Stadium, Brisbane

AUSTRALIA 9 (3PG)
NEW ZEALAND 13 (1G, 1PG, 1DG)

AUSTRALIA: C Latham; M Gerrard, S Mortlock, M Giteau, L Tuqiri; S Larkham, G Gregan (captain); G Holmes, J Paul, R Blake, N Sharpe, D Vickerman, S Fava, G Smith, R Elsom Substitutions: T McIsaac for Paul (61 mins), M Chisholm for Fava (61 mins), P Waugh for Elsom (61 mins), S Cordingley for Gregan (73 mins), C Rathbone for Tuqiri (74 mins), M Rogers for Gerrard (75 mins), G Shepherdson for Blake (77 mins)

SCORERS *Penalty Goals*: Mortlock (3)

NEW ZEALAND: L MacDonald; R Gear, M Muliaina, A Mauger, J Rokocoko; D Carter, B Kelleher; T Woodcock, K Mealamu, C Hayman, C Jack, A Williams, J Collins, R McCaw (captain), R So'oialo Substitutions: C Masoe for Collins (62 mins), G Somerville for Woodcock (68 mins), J Eaton for Williams (74 mins), J Cowan for Kelleher (75 mins), A Hore for Mealamu (75 mins)

SCORERS *Try*: Rokocoko *Conversion*: Carter *Penalty Goal*: Carter *Drop Goal*: Carter

REFEREE A Rolland (Ireland)

5 August, Telstra Stadium, Sydney

AUSTRALIA 20 (2G, 2PG)
SOUTH AFRICA 18 (1G, 2PG, 1T)

AUSTRALIA: C Latham; M Gerrard, S Mortlock, M Giteau, L Tuqiri; S Larkham, G Gregan (captain); G Holmes, T McIsaac, R Blake, N Sharpe, D Vickerman, R Elsom, G Smith, W Palu Substitutions: J Paul for McIsaac (49 mins), P Waugh for Smith (54 mins), M Rogers for Larkham (69 mins), C Rathbone for Gerrard (72 mins), M Chisholm for Elsom (72 mins), S Cordingley for Gregan (72 mins), G Shepherdson for Holmes (77 mins)

SCORERS *Tries*: Gerrard, Rogers *Conversions*: Mortlock (2) *Penalty Goals*: Mortlock (2)

SOUTH AFRICA: P Montgomery; A Ndungane, J Fourie, W Olivier, B Habana; B James, F du Preez; O du Randt, J Smit (captain), CJ van der Linde, J Muller, V Matfield, S Tyibilika, J Smith, J Cronje Substitutions: J van Niekerk for Tyibilika (69 mins), A van den Berg for Muller (74 mins)

SCORERS *Tries*: Fourie, Montgomery *Conversion*: James *Penalty Goals*: James (2)

REFEREE J Jutge (France)

19 August, Eden Park, Auckland

NEW ZEALAND 34 (2G, 5PG, 1T)
AUSTRALIA 27 (3G, 2PG)

NEW ZEALAND: M Muliaina; D Howlett, I Toeava, L McAlister, J Rokocoko; D Carter, B Kelleher; T Woodcock, K Mealamu, C Hayman, C Jack, J Eaton, J Collins, R McCaw (captain), R So'oialo Substitutions: G Somerville for Hayman (26 mins), L MacDonald for Toeava (43 mins), P Weepu for Kelleher (46 mins), A Williams for Eaton (54 mins), C Masoe for So'oialo (67 mins)

SCORERS *Tries*: Eaton, Jack, McAlister *Conversions*: Carter (2) *Penalty Goals*: Carter (5)

AUSTRALIA: C Latham; C Rathbone, S Mortlock, M Giteau, L Tuqiri; S Larkham, G Gregan (captain); G Holmes, J Paul, R Blake, N Sharpe, D Vickerman, R Elsom, P Waugh, W Palu Substitutions: G Smith for Waugh (temp 57 to 61 mins), M Gerrard for Mortlock (temp 61 to 64 mins), M Chisholm for Elsom (67 mins), A Baxter for Blake (69 mins), M Rogers for Larkham (69 mins)

SCORERS *Tries:* Tuqiri (2), Elsom *Conversions*: Mortlock (3) *Penalty Goals*: Mortlock (2)

REFEREE C White (England)

YELLOW CARD Waugh (78 mins)

26 August, Loftus Versfeld, Pretoria

SOUTH AFRICA 26 (1G, 3PG, 2T)
NEW ZEALAND 45 (4G, 4PG, 1T)

SOUTH AFRICA: P Montgomery; A Ndungane, J Fourie, J de Villiers, B Habana; B James, F du Preez; O du Randt, J Smit (captain), CJ van der Linde, J Muller, V Matfield, S Tyibilika, P Spies, J Cronje Substitutions: BJ Botha for van der Linde (23 mins), P Wannenburg for Tyibilika (47 mins), A Pretorius for James (59 mins), A van den Berg for Matfield (61 mins), R Pienaar for Montgomery (61 mins), W Oliver for de Villiers (77 mins), C Ralepelle for du Randt (78 mins)

SCORERS *Tries*: Fourie (2), De Preez *Conversion*: Pretorius *Penalty Goals*: Montgomery (2), James

NEW ZEALAND: L MacDonald; R Gear, M Muliaina, L McAlister, S Sivivatu; D Carter, P Weepu; N Tialata, A Oliver, G Somerville, G Rawlinson, A Williams, R Thorne, R McCaw (captain), C Masoe Substitutions: I Toeava for MacDonald (12 mins), T Woodcock for Somerville (16 mins), C Jack for Rawlinson (47 mins), J Collins for Masoe (51 mins), K Mealamu for Oliver (59 mins), J Cowan for Weepu (63 mins), S Tuitupou for McAlister (64 mins)

SCORERS *Tries*: Tialata, McAlister, Sivivatu, Muliaina, Gear *Conversions*: Carter (4) *Penalty Goals*: Carter (4)

REFEREE A Lewis (Ireland)

2 September, Royal Bafokeng Stadium, Rustenburg

SOUTH AFRICA 21 (1G, 3PG, 1T)
NEW ZEALAND 20 (2G, 2PG)

SOUTH AFRICA: J Fourie; A Ndungane, W Olivier, J de Villiers, B Habana; A Pretorius, F du Preez; O du Randt, J Smit (captain), BJ Botha, J Muller, V Matfield, P Wannenburg, P Spies, AJ Venter Substitutions: B Paulse for Ndungane (50 mins), R Pienaar for du Preez (52 mins), L Sephalka for du Randt (73 mins), B James for Habana (78 mins)

SCORERS *Tries*: Habana, Wannenburg *Conversion*: Pretorius *Penalty Goals*: Pretorius (3)

NEW ZEALAND: D Howlett; J Rokocoko, M Muliaina, A Mauger, S Sivivatu; D Carter, J Cowan; T Woodcock, A Hore, C Hayman, C Jack, A Williams, J Collins, R McCaw (captain), R So'oialo Substitutions: M Holah for McCaw (temp 48 to 51 mins), J Eaton for Jack (56 mins), B Kelleher for Cowan (60 mins), R Gear for Sivivatu (60 mins), N Tialata for Woodcock (64 mins), A Oliver for Hore (66 mins)

SCORERS *Tries*: Carter, Rokococo *Conversions*: Carter (2) *Penalty Goals*: Carter (2)

REFEREE C White (England)

9 September, Ellis Park, Johannesburg

SOUTH AFRICA 24 (1G, 3PG, IT, IDG) AUSTRALIA 16 (IG, 3PG)

SOUTH AFRICA: J Pietersen; A Ndungane, J Fourie, J De Villiers, W Olivier; A Pretorius, F du Preez; O Du Randt, J Smit (captain), B Botha, J Muller, V Matfield, P Spies, A Venter, P Wannenburg Substitutions: B Paulse for Ndungane (41 mins), J Cronje for Venter (66 mins), R Pienaar for du Preez (76 mins), L Sephaka for du Randt (76 mins), A van den Berg for Matfield (76 mins)

SCORERS *Tries*: Du Preez, Paulse *Conversion*: Pretorius *Penalty Goals*: Pretorius (3) Drop goal: Pretorius

AUSTRALIA: C Latham; C Rathbone, S Mortlock, M Giteau, C Shepherd; S Larkham, G Gregan (captain); B Robinson, J Paul, R Blake, N Sharpe, D Vickerman, R Elsom, P Waugh, W Palu Substitutions: M Gerrard for Shepherd (55 mins), A Baxter for Blake (60 mins), S Staniforth for Larkham (74 mins), B Sheehan for Gregan (74 mins), G Smith for Palu (74 mins), Blake for Robinson (77 mins), T McIsaac for Paul (79 mins), M Chisholm for Elsom (53 mins)

SCORERS *Try*: Larkham *Conversion*: Mortlock *Penalty Goals*: Mortlock (3)

REFEREE S Walsh (New Zealand)

Getty Images

South Africa ended the tournament on a winning note.

TRI NATIONS 2006

TRI NATIONS 2006: FINAL TABLE

	P	W	D	L	F	A	Bonus	Pts
New Zealand	6	5	0	1	179	112	3	**23**
Australia	6	2	0	4	133	121	3	**11**
South Africa	6	2	0	4	106	185	1	**9**

Points: win 4; draw 2; four or more tries, or defeat by seven or fewer points 1

TRI NATIONS RECORDS 1996–2006

Previous winners: 1996 **New Zealand**; 1997 **New Zealand**; 1998 **South Africa**; 1999 **New Zealand**; 2000 **Australia**; 2001 **Australia**; 2002 **New Zealand**; 2003 **New Zealand**; 2004 **South Africa**; 2005 **New Zealand**; 2006 **New Zealand**

Grand Slam winners: **New Zealand** (Three times) 1996, 1997, 2003; **South Africa** (Once) 1998

RECORD	DETAIL		SET
Most team points in season	179 by N Zealand	in six matches	2006
Most team tries in season	18 by S Africa	in four matches	1997
Highest team score	61 by S Africa	61-22 v Australia (h)	1997
Biggest team win	49 by Australia	49-0 v S Africa (h)	2006
Most team tries in match	8 by S Africa	v Australia	1997
INDIVIDUAL RECORD	**DETAIL**		**SET**
Most appearances	44 for Australia	G M Gregan	1996 to 2006
Most points in matches	328 for N Zealand	A P Mehrtens	1996 to 2004
Most points in season	99 for N Zealand	D W Carter	2006
Most points in match	29 for N Zealand	A P Mehrtens	v Australia (h) 1999
Most tries in matches	16 for N Zealand	C M Cullen	1996 to 2002
Most tries in season	7 for N Zealand	C M Cullen	2000
Most tries in match	3 for N Zealand	J T Rokococo	v Australia (a) 2003
	3 for S Africa	M C Joubert	v N Zealand (h) 2004
	3 for N Zealand	D C Howlett	v Australia (h) 2005
Most cons in matches	34 for N Zealand	A P Mehrtens	1996 to 2004
Most cons in season	14 for N Zealand	D W Carter	2006
Most cons in match	6 for S Africa	J H de Beer	v Australia (h),1997
Most pens in matches	82 for N Zealand	A P Mehrtens	1996 to 2004
Most pens in season	21 for N Zealand	D W Carter	2006
Most pens in match	9 for N Zealand	A P Mehrtens	v Australia (h) 1999

From 1996 to 2005 inclusive, each nation played four matches in a season. Since 2006 the nations have each played six matches a season.

EUROPEAN NATIONS CUP

ROMANIA ARE TRIUMPHANT

By Iain Spragg

Mark Dadswell/Getty Images

Romania are champions of the Second Division of the Six Nations.

Romania dramatically recaptured the European Nations Cup crown from Portugal in a tense, close-fought tournament that ebbed and flowed throughout and climaxed with a nerve-jangling final round of games in June that saw the Oaks crowned champions by the narrowest of margins.

In what was to become an unpredictable three-horse race between

Romania, defending champions Portugal and the powerful Georgians, Europe's second tier international tournament began back in November 2004. Yet after ten rounds of matches between the six competing nations over the ensuing 20 months, the Romanians were still tied with Georgia at the top of the table and secured their third Nations Cup title only by virtue of their superior points difference.

Coached by Robert Antonin, the Romanians lost their final match of the campaign – a 25–24 reverse in Krasnoyarsk against Russia – but even though Georgia were 24–3 winners in the Czech Republic on the same day, they were unable to run up the cricket score they knew they required to stand any chance of overhauling their more free-scoring rivals.

Meanwhile, Portugal's shock defeat to the same Russian side in Lisbon three days later put paid to any Iberian hopes of retaining the title.

Regularly referred to as the Six Nations B, the competition began with high hopes for all six sides but it was Portugal, coached by Tomaz Morais, who were the first out of the blocks with a morale-boosting win against Ukraine. Morais named a match day squad containing only two foreign-based players – João Uva of Santboiana in Cataluoa and Brive's Pedro Leal – and his side proved to strong for the home team as they ran out 38–6 winners.

For Morais, who was appointed coach in 2001, it was a victory borne out of his desire to instil more discipline in his side.

"To play in the national team, a player has to understand that he is essentially assuming a compromise where he has to play by the rules of the team," Morais said.

"We showed discipline, method, a more positive outlook and a spirit of sacrifice. My goal has always been to create a hard-working, dynamic and winning team which is always having fun. I want the players to embrace my convictions and my goals."

Meanwhile, Romania kicked off with a comfortable victory over the Czech Republic, lead by the coaching team of Josef Fatka and Petr Michovsk, in Prague. Biarritz's Moldovan-born prop Petru Balan led the way with a brace of tries and Antonin had an all-important opening win under his belt.

Georgia, however, were not so fortunate and had to travel to Russia to face a home team coached by South African Blikkies Groenewald, a member of the Bulls coaching set-up during the 2003 and 2004 Super-12 campaigns. "We have a tough path to walk, but we shall see," said Groenewald before the game. "They are a fine body of men, very enthusiastic, but in need of lots of specialised training."

The South African's caution proved to be well founded and tries

Jamie McDonald/Getty Images

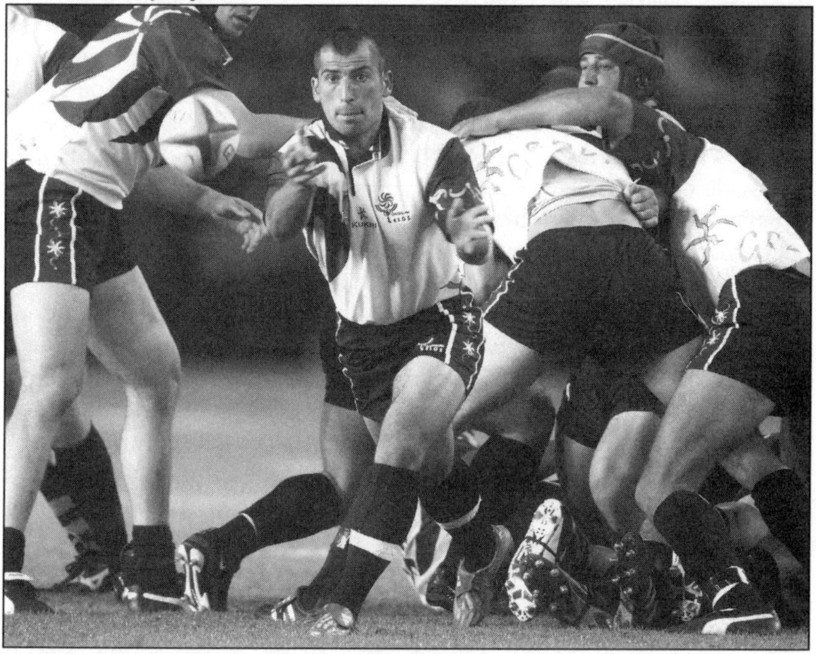

Heartbreak for Georgia as they finished second on points difference.

from Bessik Khamashuridze, Tedo Zibzibadze, Irakli Machkhaneli and Goderdzi Shvelidze eased the Georgians, coached by former Test scrum-half Malkhaz Tcheishvili and U-21 coach David Chavleishvili, to an impressive 27–15 win.

The visit of the Russians to Timisoara in February 2005 was Romania's next fixture and something of a grudge match after Romania had been beaten in Russia in early 2004 amid allegations of their food being spiked with sleeping pills before the game.

Antonin's preparations for the match were severely hampered by the loss of his leading French-based players, whose clubs refused to release them for the game and he was unable to select Balan, Beziers' captain Alin Petrache, Pau hooker Marius Tincu and Grenoble flanker Florin Corodeanu.

The absentees were not to prove disastrous, however, and Romania coasted to a comfortable 33–10 win.

Georgia's second game was a tough trip to Portugal and although the coaching team decided to hand debuts to Bidzina Samkharadze, Levan Ghvaberidze, Zviad Maissuradze, Lexo Gugava, George Kutarashvili,

Michael Sujashvili and Rezo Belkania, the new faces were unable to prevent Morais' team grinding out a 18–14 win.

The third game of Romania's campaign – an away clash with the Georgians in Tbilisi – was to prove far tougher and although Romania's powerful pack was again more than competitive, they were outscored two tries to one and Georgia emerged 20–13 winners to throw the title race wide open.

Romania, however, were back in rude health in their next game in Bucharest in March – running in 15 tries against the hapless Ukraine to register a thumping 97–0 victory, but faced Portugal four months later in a match that would mark the halfway point of the competition.

The game in Bucharest was predictably tight. The Portuguese were unbeaten at the top of the table, but tries from flanker Ovidiu Tonita and wing Ion Teodorescu and two crucial conversions from full-back Danut Dumbrava were enough to give the Oaks a 14–10 win.

Georgia demolished the Czech Republic 75–10 the next day to complete the fifth round of matches and at the halfway point, Romania, Georgia and Portugal were all locked on 13 points, each having lost one of their opening five matches. The destiny of the European Nations Cup was in the balance.

The pivotal game was to be Georgia in Romania in February 2006. Antonin and his troops had been idle in the tournament since June while the Georgians had stolen a march on them with a victory over Russia in November. A win for the visitors would put clear daylight between themselves and the Oaks.

The wintery, snow-laden clash in Bucharest was expected to be close, but once Romania had weathered Georgia's fierce opening 20 minutes, they were always in control and ran in four tries in a 35–10 victory. Scrum-half Petre Mitu scored one and landed two conversions and three penalties for a personal haul of 18 points and Romania were back in the driving seat.

The Czech Republic were the visitors to Romania in March and the omens for a shock win were not good. The Czechs had not beaten their hosts in 20 attempts since 1927 (they did manage a 6–6 draw in Prague in 1966) and their preparations were hampered by the loss of several leading players, including Robert Voves, Jiri Skall, Martin Kafka, Martin Jagr, the Czech Republic's Player of the Year in 2005, Martin Hudak, Michal Kolar and veteran hooker Lukas Rapant. It was little surprise then when they went down 50–3.

Romania turned their attention to their visit to Portugal a week later. The Portuguese had thrown away valuable points with a 19–19 draw with Russia in February and Antonin knew a first victory in Lisbon since 2001 could all but secure the title. The match itself was surprisingly one-sided considering what was at stake and Portugal were restricted to a solitary penalty as Romania ran in four tries in their 27–3 victory. Portugal's hopes were fading fast and Romania and Georgia were left to contest the honours.

Georgia won 32–12 in Ukraine in April to maintain the pressure but once Romania emulated them in early June with a comprehensive 58–0 victory in Kiev, it became obvious points difference could be decisive. Georgia could not overhaul the Oaks on points even if Antonin's side lost their final game in Russia.

Which they did. Trailing 15–13 at the break in Krasnoyarsk, the Russians mounted a spirited second-half fightback, scoring through Konstantin Rachkov and Ivan Prischepenko to establish a 25–15 lead. Substitute Danut Dumbrava landed three penalties for the Romanians to cut the advantage to a single point, but Russia held on and claimed a famous 25–24 win.

Sadly for Georgia, their triumph in the Czech Republic was to prove hollow and Romania were confirmed as champions.

There was however some consolation for the disappointed Georgians and Portuguese. The tournament had also served as a qualifying group for the 2007 World Cup and the final Nations Cup standings confirmed Romania, Georgia and Portugal as the three sides through to the final European qualifying round.

Ukraine, meanwhile, finished the campaign winless and were relegated, to be replaced next season by Spain after their victory over Germany.

RESULTS

20 November, 2004	**Ukraine** 6 **Portugal** 38	**Russia** 15 **Georgia** 27
27 November, 2004	**Czech Republic** 14 **Romania** 38	
5 February, 2005	**Portugal** 18 **Georgia** 14	
26 February, 2005	**Romania** 33 **Russia** 10	**Portugal** 19 **Czech Republic** 131
	Georgia 65 **Ukraine** 0	
12 March, 2005	**Georgia** 20 **Romania** 13	**Czech Republic** 42 **Ukraine** 5
19 March, 2005	**Romania** 97 **Ukraine** 0	**Czech Republic** 11 **Russia** 7
4 June, 2005	**Russia** 16 **Portugal** 18	
11 June, 2005	**Romania** 14 **Portugal** 10	**Russia** 72 **Ukraine** 0
12 June, 2005	**Georgia** 75 **Czech Republic** 10	
5 November, 2005	**Ukraine** 8 **Czech Republic** 47	
12 November, 2005	**Russia** 52 **Czech Republic** 12	
4 February, 2006	**Georgia** 46 **Russia** 19	
25 February, 2006	**Romania** 35 **Georgia** 10	**Portugal** 19 **Russia** 19
11 March, 2006	**Romania** 50 **Czech Republic** 3	**Georgia** 40 **Portugal** 0
18 March, 2006	**Portugal** 3 **Romania** 27	
29 April, 2006	**Ukraine** 12 **Georgia** 32	
13 May, 2006	**Portugal** 52 **Ukraine** 14	
20 May, 2006	**Czech Republic** 10 **Portugal** 18	
27 May, 2006	**Ukraine** 12 **Russia** 55	
3 June, 2006	**Ukraine** 0 **Romania** 58	
10 June, 2006	**Russia** 25 **Romania** 24	**Czech Republic** 3 **Georgia** 24
13 June, 2006	**Portugal** 17 **Russia** 37	

FINAL TABLE

	P	W	D	L	Pts Diff	Pts
Romania	10	8	0	2	294	**26**
Georgia	10	8	0	2	228	**26**
Portugal	10	6	1	3	20	**23**
Russia	10	4	1	5	88	**19**
Czech Republic	10	3	0	7	-131	**16**
Ukraine	10	0	0	10	-499	**10**

BARCLAYS CHURCHILL CUP

RUGBY CANADA USA RUGBY ENGLAND RUGBY

MAORI REIGN SUPREME

Jimmy Jeong/Getty Images

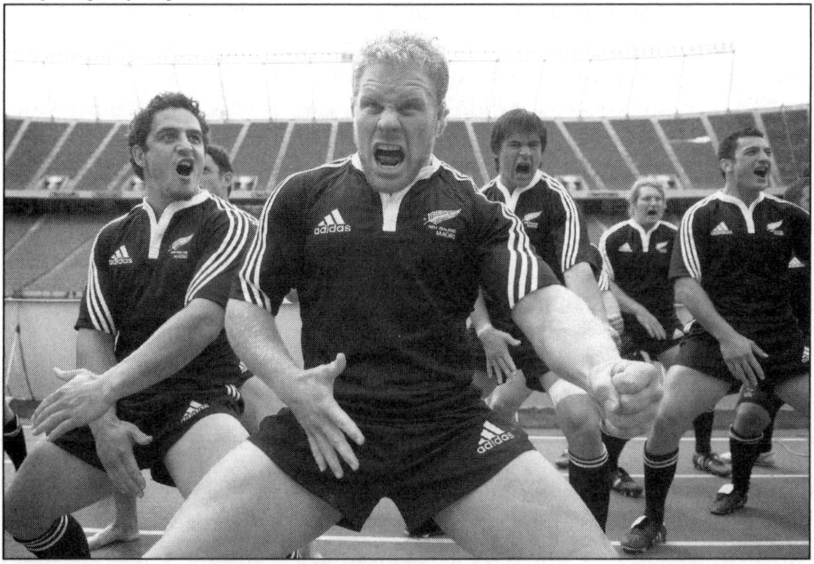

The Maori proved too strong for everyone at the Churchill Cup.

New Zealand Maori marked their return to Churchill Cup action after a year's self-imposed sabbatical by winning the expanded tournament for a second time in three years.

The Kiwis were missing from the 2005 competition because it clashed with their outstanding fixture with the Lions in New Zealand but were readmitted to the newly-expanded six team tournament in 2006 and duly swept the competition aside.

Their 52–17 win over Scotland A in Edmonton in the final was as comprehensive as it was unsurprising and confirmed the Maori as champions for the first time since 2004 when they made their bow in the competition and proved too strong for England A.

The 2006 Churchill Cup began in early June and for the first time featured Scotland A and Ireland A, who joined the rebranded England Saxons, Maori, Canada and the US Eagles in two round robin pools to determined the line-ups for the Bowl and Plate finals, as well as the Churchill Cup final itself.

The first round of games produced an immediate shock in Toronto when debutantes Scotland A, coached by Englishman Steve Bates, met the much-vaunted Saxons and pulled off a stunning win.

A titanic contest from the first whistle, the game appeared to be following the form book when England were awarded a penalty try in the second-half after persistent collapsing of the scrum by the Scots but their 7–6 lead was short lived when Simon Danielli raced over to establish a match-winning 13–7 lead. England laid siege to the Scotland line but Bates' hastily-assembled side held firm.

"That was massive, we didn't want to give points away to England, and certainly not at the end," said Bates. "For a group to come together for essentially two or three training sessions and perform on this level was huge."

Scotland A went to ensure top spot in the group with tense 15–10 win over Canada four days later and when England then beat the Canucks 41–11, the final group standings were confirmed. Scotland would play in the final proper, while England would go into the Plate final and the hosts Canada the Bowl.

The second group was topped with ease by New Zealand, who demolished America 74–6 and then overcame Ireland A 27–6 to set-up their clash with the Scots.

But first there was the business of the Bowl and Plate finals.

The Bowl game was a strictly North American affair as Canada took on their neighbours the USA at Edmonton's Commonwealth Stadium and after two group phase defeats, there was finally something to celebrate for the hosts as America were dispatched 33–18.

Wing Justin Mensah Coker helped himself to two tries while Morgan Williams and James Pritchard also crossed to give the Canucks a convincing victory in front of their own fans.

"I thought my kicking came off well, which is always a bonus when you are striking the ball well, but I have got to do more on the field," said Canada's Australian-born wing Pritchard, who had an eventful match with 18 points and a yellow card.

"When you go off for ten in the bin you just lose so much momentum and I thought that was what happened. But credit to the team they all pulled together and we got it done."

The Plate final saw the Saxons take on Ireland A and although they were vastly more experienced in terms of the Churchill Cup, it was the Irish who held their nerve to complete a 30–27 win and a highly encouraging first appearance in the competition.

The decisive moment in the match came in the 86th minute with England 27–23 ahead. Andy Beattie was yellow carded for collapsing a rolling maul and the Saxons were down to just 13 men because Dave Barnes had already received his marching orders from the referee.

Ireland took full advantage of their two extra men and bustled over replacement hooker Brian Blainey for the all-important score. Paddy Wallace slotted the conversion and Ireland were home and dry.

"Now that we have been a part of this Churchill Cup we want to come back again and win it," said Ireland captain Shane Jennings. "We kind of let ourselves down against the Maori when we lost in Santa Clara, but we won't make that mistake if we come back again."

The Maori versus Scotland A completed the tournament but any hopes the neutrals had of the Scots giving the New Zealanders a real scare were soon dashed after five minutes when the Kiwis pounced on turnover ball and No.8 Thomas Waldrom went across over for the opening try. Callum Bruce converted and the Maori proceeded to run in scores with unnerving regularity.

Scotland did hit back with scores from Alasdair Dickinson and Nikki Walker but the New Zealanders scored seven tries of their own – including two for Waldrom – to record an emphatic 52–17 win.

But despite the heavy defeat, coach Bates was determined to focus on the positives of the tournament.

"I am really proud of the guys for getting to tonight's final," he said. "It was a tough game but we knew that was going to happen I think. They get the ball going forward and once they do they are pretty difficult to stop.

"They played with a lot of pace and intensity and it's something for our guys to learn from. We'll take some great memories from this trip and hopefully it will inspire our guys to look to the future and improve our game."

Bates' New Zealand counterpart Donny Stevenson however felt the scoreline failed to do justice to Scotland's performance.

"The score might have blown out a bit in the end but we were certainly under pressure in the first half," he said. "I don't think we got out of our own 22 except on the occasions where we scored. We pride ourselves on our second half though and it was good to see it again today."

CHURCHILL CUP RESULTS

GROUP PHASE

3 June, York University, Toronto	
England Saxons 7 (1G)	**Scotland A** 13 (1G, 2PG)
3 June, Buck Shaw Stadium, Santa Clara	
USA 13 (1G, 2PG)	**Ireland A** 28 (1G, 2PG, 3T)
7 June, Twin Elm Stadium, Ottawa	
Canada 10 (1G, 1PG)	**Scotland A** 15 (1G, 1T, 1DG)
7 June, Buck Shaw Stadium, Santa Clara	
USA 6 (2PG)	**New Zealand Maori** 74 (7G, 5T)
10 June, York University, Toronto	
Canada 11 (2PG, 1T)	**England Saxons** 41 (4G, 1PG, 2T)
10 June, Buck Shaw Stadium, Santa Clara	
New Zealand Maori 27 (2G, PG, 2T)	**Ireland A** 6 (1PG, 1DG)

FINAL STANDINGS

GROUP ONE

	P	W	D	L	F	A	BP	Pts
Scotland A	2	2	0	0	28	17	0	8
England Saxons	2	1	0	1	48	24	2	6
Canada	2	0	0	2	21	56	1	1

GROUP TWO

	P	W	D	L	F	A	BP	Pts
NZ Maori	2	2	0	0	101	12	2	10
Ireland A	2	1	0	1	34	40	1	5
USA	2	0	0	2	19	102	0	0

CHURCHILL CUP BOWL FINAL

17 June, Commonwealth Stadium, Edmonton

CANADA 33 (2G, 3PG, 2T) USA 18 (1G, 2PG, IT)

CANADA: M Pyke; J Mensah-Coker, C Pack, D Spicer, J Pritchard; A Monro, M Williams (captain); D Pletch, P Riordan, R Snow, L Tait, M Burak, A Kleeberger, S McKeen, S-M Stephen

SUBSTITUTES: A Abrams, M Barbieri, M Pletch, O Atkinson, ACarpenter, E Fairhurst, D Daypuck

SCORERS *Tries:* Mensah-Coker (2), Pritchard, Williams Conversions: Pritchard (2) Penalty Goals: Pritchard (3)

USA: J Hullinger; M Palefau, P Emerick, A Tuipulotu, J Nash; J Kelly, T Meek; M MacDonald, P Bell, J Tarpoff, C Hansen, M Mangan, S Lawrence, T Clever, K Schubert (captain)

SUBSTITUTES: O Lentz, C Osentowski, B Schoener, M Aylor, M Timoteo, A Tuilevuka, B Barnard

SCORERS *Tries:* Tuilevuka, Clever Conversion: Tuilevuka Penalty Goals: Kelly (2)

REFEREE A Small (England)

CHURCHILL CUP PLATE FINAL

17 June, Commonwealth Stadium, Edmonton

ENGLAND SAXONS 27 (2G, PG, 2T)
IRELAND A 30 (2G, 2PG, 2T)

ENGLAND SAXONS: D Armitage; R Haughton, B Johnston (captain), S Vesty, A Erinle; D Walder, C Stuart-Smith; D Barnes, J Buckland, S Turner, J Hudson, N Kennedy, K Roche, D Seymour, K Horstmann

SUBSTITUTES: D Paice, M Ward, A Beattie, L Narraway, R Wigglesworth, M Horak, B Woods

SCORERS *Tries:* Vesty, Horstmann, Johnston, Erinle Conversions: Walder (2) Penalty Goal: Walder

YELLOW CARDS Barnes (75 mins), Paice (80 mins), Beattie (80 mins)

IRELAND A: B Cunningham; A Maxwell, J Hearty, M Lawlor, C McPhillips; P Wallace T O'Leary; R Hogan, J Fogarty, T Court, T Hogan, M McCullough, S Jennings (captain), N McMilan, J Heaslip

SUBSTITUTES: B Blaney, R McCormack, D Browne, J Muldoon, C Keane, E Hickey, S Keogh

SCORERS *Tries:* McCullough, McCormack, Heaslip, Fogarty Conversions: Wallace (2) Penalty Goals: Wallace (2)

REFEREE P Allan (Scotland)

CHURCHILL CUP FINAL

17 June, Commonwealth Stadium, Edmonton

NEW ZEALAND MAORI 52 (4G, 3 PG, 3T)
SCOTLAND A 17 (2G, PG)

NEW ZEALAND MAORI: S Paku; A Tahana, R Kahui, N Brew, H Gear; C Bruce, C Smylie; J McDonnell, S Linklater, D Manu, K Ormsby, P Tito (captain), L Messam, T Latimer, T Waldron

SUBSTITUTES: L Mahoney, M Noble, W Smith, J Paringatai, C Tamou, M Berquist, P Te Whare

SCORERS *Tries:* Waldron (2), Messam, McDonnell, Orsmby, Tahana, Kahui Conversions: Bruce (4) Penalty Goals: Bruce (3)

SCOTLAND A: C MacRae; S Danielli, G Morrison, M Dey, R Lamont; P Godman, R Lawson (captain); A Jacobsen, F Thomson, A Dickinson, C Hamilton, M Rennie, R Beattie, A Strokosch, D Callam

SUBSTITUTES: C Noon, T McGee, A Hall, S Gray, A Kelly, A Miller, N De Luca, N Walker, C Gregor

SCORERS *Tries:* Walker, Dickinson Conversions: MacRae (2)

PENALTY GOAL: MacRae

REFEREE N Owens (Wales)

Jimmy Jeong/Getty Images

The Maori start the celebrations after winning the Churchill Cup, hitting the half-century against Scotland.

IRB Sevens© World Series

BACK TO THE TOP

By Iain Spragg

Mark Thompson/Getty Images

Fiji celebrate winning the IRB Sevens World Series title.

Fiji finally broke New Zealand's stranglehold on the IRB Sevens title and became only the second country to be crowned champions in the history of the tournament. The Kiwis had claimed all six previous titles but 2005/06 was indisputably Fiji's season as coach Waisale Serevi and his side re-established the Pacific Islanders as the kings of the shortened game.

Confirmation of Fiji's triumph came in June at the Emirates Airline London Sevens – the last of the eight tournaments on the Sevens calendar – with a 33–14 quarter-final victory over Kenya, a result which meant nearest rivals England could not overhaul Serevi's side for the title.

Fiji, however, refused to rest on their laurels in London and faced New Zealand in the semi-final, beating their perennial rivals 21–17 in a dramatic clash that symbolised the passing of the torch from the deposed champions to the new dominant force. Samoa were dispatched in the final (54–14) and Fiji, who already held the Rugby World Cup and World Games Sevens titles, were confirmed as worthy winners.

"It's a fantastic moment for Fiji," said the veteran Serevi. "The players have made a lot of sacrifices that have paid off and I thank them and their families for that and salute them for a wonderful performance in the whole series and here today."

The 38-year-old legend, however, also hinted that his side's triumph would probably prompt him to finally bring down the curtain on his illustrious Sevens career. "I think it might be time now not only to wear the tracksuit," he admitted, "but also the big jumpers, big jackets and the pom-pom and the bags, and to be on the outside cheering for them."

The seventh IRB Sevens series began back in December in the humidity of Dubai and the tournament was to set the tone for the rest of the series as Fiji and Mike Friday's England, defending their Dubai crown, began their season-long battle for supremacy.

Both sides were made to work hard to reach the final but once there they produced an exhilarating clash which England edged 28–26 in front of a sell-out 60,000 crowd courtesy of a brace of tries from Ben Gollings and Player of the Tournament Tom Varndell. England had thrown down the gauntlet.

It was picked up by the Pacific Islanders later the same month at the George Sevens in South Africa. England were knocked out in the semi-finals and Fiji faced Argentina, conquerors of hosts South Africa, in the final.

To their credit, the South Americans pushed Serevi's side all the way but two tries from William Ryder, the coach's heir apparent, were enough to seal a 21–19 win and Fiji's first IRB title since December 2002.

The New Year saw the series move to New Zealand in February but home advantage was not enough to kick start the ailing champions defence of their title.

Comfortable victories over Kenya (28–5) and the Cook Islands (41–7) was followed by a 5–5 draw with Samoa but the Kiwis, coached by Gordon Tietjens, still made the semi-finals in Wellington where they faced Fiji.

Unfortunately for the hosts, Fiji were in no mood to reciprocate New

Zealand hospitality and booked their place in the final with a 26–14 victory. The changing of the guard was evidently quickening.

In the final, Fiji were up against the rapidly improving South Africans, semi-final victors against France, but despite a gutsy display from the Springboks they had no answer to Ryder's mercurial hat-trick and were beaten 27–22. Fiji were now the clear leaders at the top of the table.

England, however, came storming back into real contention at the USA Sevens in Los Angeles a week later, crushing the Fijians 38–5 in the final to throw the series wide open again. "It was important we did this to Fiji," said centre Mathew Tait after the final whistle. "We had to front up and we did."

Two months later, the countries decamped en masse to Hong Kong for the expanded, 24-team stage of the series. Semi-final victories over South Africa and New Zealand respectively saw England and Fiji through to the final once more and although it was again England who won the battle. The manner of victory could not have been more different from the one-sided encounter in Los Angeles.

In a tense, tight final, Fiji led 24–19 with time seemingly running out for England until Gollings scampered over in the dying seconds to level the scores. He then converted to seal a famous win and cut Fiji's lead at the top of the table to just six points.

Stung by successive final reverses, Fiji bounced back seven days later at the Singapore Sevens, thumping Friday's side 40–19 in the final to claim their third title of the season and establish a 10-point lead at the top.

The penultimate event – the Paris Sevens in May – was to prove pivotal. Although Fiji surprisingly fell to France (22–21) in the last eight, England failed to take advantage of their rival's slip-up and also went out at the quarter-final stage after their 29–17 defeat to Glen Ella's Australia.

South Africa capitalised on Fiji and England's unexpected misfortune and cruised through to the final – beating Samoa 33–12 to become only the third IRB title winner of the season.

Heading to London for the climax of the campaign, Fiji held a 14-point lead over England, who knew the Pacific Islanders would have to implode spectacularly in the capital if they were to have any chance of being crowned champions. In the end, Serevi's side more than held their nerve and their comprehensive defeat of Samoa in the final at Twickenham was a fitting end to a convincing campaign.

There was some consolation, however, for the Samoans in their 54–14 mauling as 19-year-old winger Timoteo Iosua scored one of their three tries to take his tally for the season to 40 and confirm him as the series' top try scorer, five clear of Fiji's Sireli Naqelevuki. England's Gollings was the tournament's leading points scorer with 343.

DUBAI TOURNAMENT

England (20), 2. **Fiji** (16), 3= **South Africa** (12), 3= **Samoa** (12), 5. **New Zealand** (8), 6. **France** (6), 7= **Australia** (4), 7= **Argentina** (4), 9. **Wales** (2).

GEORGE TOURNAMENT

Fiji (20), 2. **Argentina** (16), 3= **England** (12), 3= **South Africa** (12), 5. **Samoa** (8), 6. **New Zealand** (6), 7= **France** (4), 7= **Australia** (4), 9. **Wales** (2).

NEW ZEALAND TOURNAMENT

Fiji (20), 2. **South Africa** (16), 3= **New Zealand** (12), 3= **France** (12), 5. **England** (8), 6. **Argentina** (6), 7= **Samoa** (4), 7= **Australia** (4), 9. **Scotland** (2).

USA TOURNAMENT

England (20), 2. **Fiji** (16), 3= **South Africa** (12), 3= **New Zealand** (12), 5. **Argentina** (8), 6. **France** (6), 7= **Australia** (4), 7= **Canada** (4), 9. **Scotland** (2).

HONG KONG TOURNAMENT

1. **England** (30), 2. **Fiji** (24), 3= **South Africa** (18), 3= **New Zealand** (18), 5= **Samoa** (8), 5= **Argentina** (8), 5= **Australia** (8), 5= **Scotland** (8), 9. **Wales** (4), 10. **Kenya** (3), 11. **China** (1).

SINGAPORE TOURNAMENT

Fiji (20), 2. **England** (16), 3= **South Africa** (12), 3= **Argentina** (12), 5. **Samoa** (8), 6. **France** (6), 7= **New Zealand** (4), 7= **Australia** (4), 9. **Kenya** (2).

PARIS TOURNAMENT

South Africa (20), 2. **Samoa** (16), 3= **France** (12), 3= **Australia** (12), 5. **Fiji** (8), 6. **Argentina** (6), 7= **New Zealand** (4), 7= **England** (4), 9. **Kenya** (2).

LONDON TOURNAMENT

1. **Fiji** (20), 2. **Samoa** (16), 3= **England** (12), 3= **New Zealand** (12), 5. **South Africa** (8), 6. **Kenya** (6), 7= **Argentina** (4), 7= **France** (4), 9. **Portugal** (2).

FINAL RANKINGS

1 **Fiji** 144 points	8 **Australia** 40
2 **England** 122	9 **Kenya** 13
3 **South Africa** 110	10 **Scotland** 12
4 **New Zealand** 76	11 **Wales** 8
5 **Samoa** 72	12 **Canada** 4
6 **Argentina** 64	13 **Portugal** 2
7 **France** 50	14 **China** 1

PREVIOUS WINNERS

1999/2000: New Zealand
2000/2001: New Zealand
2001/2002: New Zealand
2002/2003: New Zealand
2003/2004: New Zealand
2004/2005: New Zealand
2005/2006: Fiji

IRB WORLD SEVENS SERIES 2006–07

The International Rugby Board (IRB) has announced a new international schedule for the world's leading Rugby Sevens tournament series, the IRB Sevens World Series. Following a major review of the Series by the IRB in consultation with relevant stakeholders, eight countries will once again host a tournament, but there are two new tournament locations with Adelaide (Australia) and San Diego (USA) included for the first time. Last season's IRB Sevens World Series broke all previous attendance and broadcast records and the 2006/07 series is the most eagerly anticipated to date. The series will again kick off in Dubai on December 1, visiting George (South Africa), Wellington (New Zealand), San Diego, Hong Kong, Adelaide and London before concluding with an eighth location. This location will be announced in the near future.Tournament dates are as follows:

• Dubai – Dec 1/2	• Hong Kong – March 30/31 and April 1
• George (South Africa) – Dec 8/9	• Adelaide (Australia)– April 7/8
• Wellington (New Zealand) – Feb 2/3	• London – May 26/27
• San Diego (USA) – Feb 10/11	

"The IRB is delighted to welcome Adelaide and San Diego as IRB Sevens World Series tournament hosts for the first time," said IRB Chairman, Dr Syd Millar. "The popularity of Rugby Sevens continues to grow in North America and the USA will host a tournament for the fourth successive season, while the success of Rugby Sevens at this year's Commonwealth Games in Melbourne underlines its popularity in Australia. The inclusion of these exciting new locations into the Series will serve to foster the growing global appeal of Rugby Sevens ahead of what promises to be the most competitive series to date."

Fiji may have been crowned champions of the Sevens world by winning the IRB World Sevens Series but they couldn't complete the 2006 double by landing gold at the Melbourne Commonwealth Games. The defending champions, New Zealand, won gold for the third consecutive time, beating England in the final, 29–21, in front of more than 50,000 fans at the Telstra Dome. Josh Blackie led the way for New Zealand with two tries in the final. "It's something I'll never forget," said New Zealand Sevens coach Gordon Tietjens. "I really feel for the players, they were quite magnificent." Fiji had to settle for bronze, beating Australia 24–17 in the play-off. Wales defeated South Africa 29–28 in the Plate Final, while Kenya won the Bowl Final 26–12 against Tonga.

Dave Rogers/Getty Images

The IRB Sevens World Sevens series will stop in London at the end of May, where Samoa [above, with ball] were runners-up in 2006.

UNDER 21 WORLD CHAMPIONSHIP

FRANCE 2006

BLUES-PRINT FOR THE FUTURE

Dave Rogers/Getty Images

The France side hold the Under-21 World Cup trophy aloft. Could this be a dress rehearsal for 2007?

The future of French rugby appears bright after the junior Bleus toppled defending champions South Africa in June to be crowned IRB Under-21 World Champions for the first time.

The young French side may have enjoyed home advantage in the final as tournament hosts but they were still worthy 24–13 winners over the Springboks in the Parc des Sports Marcel Michelin, a result watched by 13,000 partisan fans in Clermont-Ferrand.

What made the victory all the more impressive was the fact the French had lost to South Africa earlier in the group stages of the competition but rallied when it mattered in the final and although they were outscored one try to nil by the defending champions, the unerring accuracy of the boot of fly-half Lionel Beauxis proved France's salvation.

A compelling competition began with the three rounds of group games in early June and featured big wins in the first round for both Wales (who demolished Georgia 73–25) and New Zealand (who were 75–16 winners over Italy), while France were made to work hard by Ireland before emerging 26–8 winners. Meanwhile South Africa, who claimed the 2005 title after beating the Baby Blacks in Durban, were nearly brought down to earth with a bump by Argentina in Riom but held their nerve for a 20–16 victory.

The second round of fixtures, however, saw the young Springboks reproduce their form of a year ago with a merciless 102–17 rout of whipping boys Georgia while France remained unbeaten after a 32–3 win against Wales.

The final group games were the highlight of the tournament to date with mouth-watering matches between New Zealand and Australia, as well as the first meeting of France and South Africa.

The Anzac clash in the Stade Darragon in Vichy was a genuine nail biter but two tries from New South Wales scrum-half Josh Holmes was enough to preserve the young Wallabies unbeaten record and Australia held on to win 21–17.

"New Zealand played a very physical game and it wasn't easy," said Australian captain Julian Salvi. "But we wanted to make the semi-finals and now it's France."

The Australians were handed their French challenge after Les Bleus went down 14–10 to South Africa in the Stade au Complexe du Mas in Issoire. In another tight game, both sides scored a try apiece and it came down to a duel between the respective kickers to decide the match – the Springboks' Isma-eel Dollie landing three penalties to a penalty and conversion from Lionel Beauxis to give his side a 14–10 win.

"France are a superb team," said South Africa coach Peter de Villiers. "In the end we came out on top but the French could have won. I want to congratulate all my players – the defence was absolutely heroic today."

With the group phase over, it was time for the business end of the tournament and the games that would decide the final standings.

The first round of play-offs saw England emerge as the Home Unions top team after a 13–11 triumph over Wales while France bounced back from the disappointment of losing to South Africa by beating Australia 32–17.

South Africa continued their unbeaten run with a convincing 40–23 win over New Zealand – a repeat of the 2005 final – and the line-ups for the final set of matches were confirmed. Hosts France would contest the final against the Springboks, Australia and New Zealand would cross swords once again for third place while England and Ireland would meet in a battle of Britain for fifth.

The Anglo-Irish showdown took place in the Stade Couturier in Coumon d'Auvergne but once England had established a 15–8 half-time lead, the momentum was with the team in white and after the break, Ireland were shut out. England ran in three second-half tries in increasingly wet conditions and emerged 32–8 winners to claim fifth place.

"Against Ireland it was as ever a very physical match," said England coach Dorian West. "We controlled territory well and we can only be satisfied we finished the season with nine wins and only one loss [against New Zealand]."

The New Zealand and Australia match for third place – a rematch of the group clash which the Wallabies edged – was a titanic clash between two ambitious but evenly matched sides.

In a hugely entertaining match, the Baby Blacks outscored their oldest international rivals six tries to five and although Wallaby captain Tatafu Polota-Nau scored the last try late on to make it 39–36, New Zealand held on for a thrilling win.

"We're disappointed to finish in third place, but today we're pleased," said Kiwi coach Greg Cooper. "It's a welcome revenge after losing to the same Australian side in the group stages. We made a lot of mistakes in the match but are pleased with the way we attacked."

And so to the final and the rematch between France and the Springboks for the Under-21 crown. But while the All Blacks and Wallaby clash was an 11–try exhibition, the final was an altogether more tactical affair dominated by the kickers.

Flanker Pierre Spies scored the only try of the game in the second-half for the South Africans but six penalties and two sweetly-timed drop goals from Lionel Beauxis for a personal haul of 24 points was enough to give France the title.

"It's huge, it's like a dream," said France's captain Loic Jacquet after the final whistle. The atmosphere was electric and it's one of the biggest matches of my career. We knew we could beat South Africa after our first match against them. We made fewer errors this time."

Man-of-the-match Beauxis was quick to pay tribute to the efforts of the French forwards. "We controlled the ball really well and a lot of credit for that goes to the forwards," he said. "It's been a long road of hard work which has paid off. I would like to play in the full French international team one day."

RESULTS

ROUND ONE

9 June, Stade Darragon, Vichy	**England** 34 **Fiji** 8
9 June, Stade Emile Pons, Riom	**Italy** 16 **New Zealand** 75
9 June, Stade au Complexe du Mas, Issoire	**Wales** 73 **Georgia** 25
9 June, Stade au Complexe du Mas, Issoire	**Ireland** 8 **France** 26
9 June, Stade Darragon, Vichy	**Australia** 18 **Scotland** 14
9 June, Stade Emile Pons, Riom	**South Africa** 20 **Argentina** 16

ROUND TWO

13 June, Stade Couturier, Coumon d'Auvergne	**Ireland** 22 **Argentina** 26
13 June, Stade Antonin Chastel, Thiers	**Australia** 43 **Fiji** 20
13 June, Stade Darragon, Vichy	**England** 14 **New Zealand** 29
13 June, Stade Antonin Chastel, Thiers	**South Africa** 102 **Georgia** 17
13 June, Stade Couturier, Coumon d'Auvergne	**Wales** 3 **France** 32
13 June, Stade Darragon, Vichy	**Italy** 10 **Scotland** 26

ROUND THREE

17 June, Stade Darragon, Vichy	**Italy 17** Fiji 43
17 June, Stade Emile Pons, Riom	**Wales** 10 **Argentina** 13
17 June, Stade au Complexe du Mas, Issoire	**Ireland** 47 **Georgia** 0
17 June, Stade Darragon, Vichy	**Australia** 21 **New Zealand** 17
17 June, Stade Emile Pons, Riom	**England** 31 **Scotland** 12
17 June, Stade au Complexe du Mas, Issoire	**South Africa** 14 **France** 10

PLAY-OFFS

21 June, Stade au Complexe du Mas, Issoire	
10th v 11th Place Play-Off	**Fiji** 33 **Italy** 12
21 June, Stade au Complexe du Mas, Issoire	
9th v 12th Place Play-Off	**Scotland** 46 **Georgia** 14
21 June, Stade Darragon, Vichy	
6th v 7th Place Play-Off	**Argentina** 20 **Ireland** 42
21 June, Stade Darragon, Vichy	
5th v 8th Place Play-Off	**England** 13 **Wales** 11
21 June, Parc des Sports Marcel Michelin, Clermont-Ferrand	
2nd v 3rd Place Play-Off	**Australia** 17 **France** 32
21 June, Parc des Sports Marcel Michelin, Clermont-Ferrand	
1st v 4th Place Play-Off	South **Africa** 40 **New Zealand** 23

25 June, Stade Antonin Chastel, Thiers	
11th Place Play-Off	**Italy** 12 **Georgia** 9
25 June, Stade Antonin Chastel, Thiers	
9th Place Play-Off	**Fiji** 21 **Scotland** 19
25 June, Stade Couturier, Coumon d'Auvergne	
7th Place Play-Off	**Argentina** 28 **Wales** 12
25 June, Stade Couturier, Coumon d'Auvergne	
5th Place Play-Off	**Ireland** 8 **England** 32

3RD PLACE PLAY-OFF

25 June, Parc des Sports Marcel Michelin, Clermont-Ferrand

NEW ZEALAND 39 (3G, 1PG, 3T) AUSTRALIA 36 (4G, 1PG, 1T)

NEW ZEALAND: J Payne; L Masaga, R Kahui, S Brett, J Somerset; W Ripia, A Mathewson; J MacKintosh (captain), L Po-Ching, M Reid, R Wilson, M Patterson, S King, S Lilo, K Read Substitutions: O Tololima-Auva'a for Lilo (30 mins), M Tuu'u for Reid (50 mins), H Elliot for Po-Ching (63 mins), G Pisi for Masaga (76 mins)

SCORERS Tries: Masaga (2), MacKintosh, Brett, Mathewson, Tuu'u Conversions: Brett (3) Penalty Goal: Brett

AUSTRALIA: C Brown; L Bibo, L James, A Faingaa, D Iaone; L Johansson, J Holmes; P Cowan, G Abram, J Ulugia, T Hockings, J Horwill, M Dan, D Haydon, T Polota-Nau (captain) Substitutions: J Kennedy for Ulugia (52 mins), B Vaaulu for Brown (55 mins), S Faingaa for Abram (60 mins), P O'Connor for Horwill (68 mins), S Greally for Vaaulu (76 mins)

SCORERS *Tries:* Abram, Holmes, Faingaa, Haydon, Polota-Nau Conversions: Bibo (4) Penalty Goal: Bibo

REFEREE T Hirabayashi (Japan)

FINAL

25 June, Parc des Sports Marcel Michelin, Clermont-Ferrand

SOUTH AFRICA 13 (1G, 2PG)
FRANCE 24 (6PG, 2DG)

SOUTH AFRICA: M Delport; JP Pietersen, W Murray, B Barritt, C Mkhize; I Dollie, J Vermaak; H van der Merwe, C Ralepelle (captain), S Mxoli, N Blignaut, W Steenkamp, P Spies, H Lobberts, K Daniel Substitutions: S Spedding for Mkhize (40 mins), P Louw for Daniel (50 mins), A Strauss for Ralepelle (60 mins), J Mongalo for Speeding (74 mins), A Hargreaves for Blignaut (74 mins), B Maku for van der Merwe (74 mins), W Malgas for Vermaak (74 mins)

SCORERS *Try:* Spies Conversion: Dollie Penalty Goals: Dollie (2)

FRANCE: M Medard; F Denos, M Mermoz, G Puyo, Y Fior; L Beauxis, S Tillous-Borde; L Cabarry, L Sempere, Y Montes, D Drozdz, L Jacquet (captain), F Ouedraogo, F Alexandre, D Chouly Substitutions: T Domingo for Cabarry (40 mins), M Bourret for Fior (44 mins), G Guirado for Sempere (47 mins), N Bontinck for Alexandre (47 mins), J Le Devedec for Drozdz (53 mins), T Lacroix for Bourret (66 mins), L Cabarry for Montes (74 mins), J Tomas for Tillous (74 mins), M Bourret for Puyo (77 mins)

SCORERS PENALTY GOALS: Beauxis (6) Drop Goals: Beauxis (2)

REFEREE C Pollock (New Zealand)

FINAL STANDINGS

1 France	**7** Argentina
2 South Africa	**8** Wales
3 New Zealand	**9** Fiji
4 Australia	**10** Scotland
5 England	**11** Italy
6 Ireland	**12** Georgia

IRB UNDER 19 WORLD CHAMPIONSHIP

DUBAI 2006

NEW GROUND FOR WALLABIES

Bryn Lennon/Getty Images

There was no stopping the Junior Wallabies in Dubai as they lifted the Under-19 World Cup.

Australia claimed their first ever IRB Under-19 World Championship Division A title in 2006 with a hard-fought 17–13 victory over New Zealand. The junior Wallabies lead throughout the final at The Exiles ground in Dubai but had to weather a late Baby Blacks fight back to ensure their triumph.

"We made such a good start that the Kiwis were probably a bit shell shocked," said victorious Australian coach Phil Mooney after the final whistle. "We had the opportunities and grasped them. At 14–13, I was a bit worried but we dug deep. Hopefully we will go on to win this event lots of times in the future but this team will always be the first."

The Australians took the lead on 15 minutes when lock Daniel Linde crashed over and doubled their advantage three minutes later when wing Lachlan Turner found space. The Kiwis kept in touch courtesy of a penalty from the boot of Colin Slade, the competition's top scorer, but still trailed by 11 points at half-time.

After the break, the Baby Blacks came storming back and two tries from wing Armyn Sanders, both of which were unconverted, left the match delicately poised at 14–13 in Australia's favour. The Kiwis threw everything at their opponents in the dying minutes but it was the Wallabies who delivered the crucial coup de grace late on when centre Anthony Faingaa, the twin brother of Australian captain Saia, dropped a match-clinching goal. Australia were champions for the first time and New Zealand were beaten in the final for the second successive year after losing to South Africa in Durban in 2005.

"For Anthony to get the drop goal at the end was a great moment," said Saia Faingaa after the match. "We showed our character to come through a very difficult test. I always had faith in the boys and thought we could stick in there."

Elsewhere in Division A, it was a disappointing tournament for the junior Springboks, the defending champions. Comprehensively outplayed by both France (42–3) and England (45–18) in the group stages, the South Africans finished a lowly eighth in the final Division A standings after play-off defeats to Wales (33–21) and Argentina (26–7).

For the Home Unions, it was a mixed tournament. Ireland (who's Brian Collins was the tournament's third top points scorer with 55), Wales and Scotland finished fifth, sixth and ninth respectively in the final standings while England, coached by former international Nigel Redman, bounced back from their opening group stage defeat against Ireland (17–16) to finish third, their best ever placing in the tournament.

After their reverse against the Irish, England saw off Argentina (28–23) and South Africa to earn themselves a semi-final clash with New Zealand. The Kiwis proved too strong for England but they gained some consolation for defeat in the third place play-off against France.

France, who were beaten by Australia in their semi-final, actually lead 12–5 at one stage courtesy of four penalties from Mathieu Belie but Redman's side levelled at 12–12 with a converted try from Danny Care. Full-back David Doherty had crossed for the English in the first-half.

However, when South African referee Willie Roos blew for full-time,

Bryn Lennon/Getty Images

Tries from David Doherty and Danny Care gave England third place.

the two sides were still tied at 12 all but, according to tournament rules, England were handed third place on the number of tries scored rule.

"I cannot praise the lads enough," a relieved Redman said after the match. "It was hot, it was brutal but it's been a great tournament. We've played some sensational rugby and deserve third place."

At the other end of the Division A table, Romania finished bottom and were relegated after failing to win any of their five fixtures. They drew their final game with Japan 13–13 but were consigned to Division B rugby in 2007 as the Japanese held their nerve to win the resulting penalty shootout 4–1.

In Division B, Fiji triumphed in the tournament's second tier competition and will be playing against the elite of Under-19 rugby next year after seeing off South Pacific Island neighbours Tonga in the final – their fifth victory in 17 demanding days in the humidity of Dubai.

The Fijians began their campaign tentatively with a narrow 38–30 win over Italy in their opening match but comfortable victories over the USA (48–3) and Russia (43–3) took them into the play-off phase in confident mood. Canada were duly dispatched 20–13 to set up the Tonga clash.

The final itself was a free-flowing clash reminiscent of the rugby played by the senior Fijian team, although it was Tonga who drew first blood with a superb solo try from fly-half Richard Havili, which he converted.

Fiji hit back through with a converted score from flanker Sakenasa Aca and took control of the clash after the break, winger Seremaia Tagicakibau landing a penalty before lock James Brown crossed. Tagicakibau then crossed for Fiji's third try and although Tonga narrowed the deficit with an injury time try from replacement Semisi Fotu, it was too little too late.

"We came here not only to compete but to get promotion to Division A," said a happy Fiji coach Josua Toakula. "We achieved that and we thank God for it."

Fiji captain Andrew Durutalo added: "The plan was to not to get involved in too many rucks and to move the ball wide. Sevens rugby accounted for more than 50 per cent of our success."

In the the Division B third-place play-off, Italy ran out comprehensive 35–8 winners of Canada, outscoring the North Americans four tries to one. "I asked the guys to play with a lot of passion and I am happy with that," said young Azzurri coach Gianluca Guidi. "But I am disappointed we were not in the final against Tonga. We worked very hard over the last three days and in the second-half, we played very well."

The USA finished bottom in the Division B standings after agonisingly losing 30–28 to Korea in the 11th place play-off.

RESULTS

DIVISION A

ROUND ONE

5 April, Exiles RFC, Dubai	**South Africa** 3 **France** 42
5 April, Sharjah Wanderers, Sharjah	**Argentina** 10 **Samoa** 8
5 April, Exiles RFC 2, Dubai	**New Zealand** 38 **Wales** 14
5 April, Sharjah Wanderers 2, Sharjah	**Romania** 17 **Japan** 30
5 April, Exiles RFC, Dubai	**Ireland** 17 **England** 16
5 April, Sharjah Wanderers, Sharjah	**Scotland** 3 **Australia** 78

ROUND TWO

9 April, Sharjah Wanderers, Sharjah	**South Africa** 44 **Samoa** 0
9 April, Exiles RFC, Dubai	**Ireland** 18 **France** 26
9 April, Sharjah Wanderers 2, Sharjah	**Argentina** 23 **England** 28
9 April, Exiles RFC 2, Dubai	**Romania** 9 **Australia** 88
9 April, Sharjah Wanderers, Sharjah	**New Zealand** 90 **Japan** 10
9 April, Exiles RFC, Dubai	**Scotland** 5 **Wales** 35

ROUND THREE

13 April, Exiles RFC, Dubai	**New Zealand** 22 **Australia** 17
13 April, Sharjah Wanderers, Sharjah	**Scotland** 48 **Japan** 0
13 April, Sharjah Wanderers 2, Sharjah	**Romania** 0 **Wales** 70
13 April, Exiles RFC 2, Dubai	**Argentina** 12 **France** 19
13 April, Sharjah Wanderers, Sharjah	**Ireland** 16 **Samoa** 15
13 April, Exiles RFC, Dubai	**South Africa** 18 **England** 45

PLAY-OFFS

17 April, Sharjah Wanderers 2, Sharjah

Japan 0 **Samoa** 26

17 April, Sharjah Wanderers, Sharjah

Scotland 38 **Romania** 10

17 April, Sharjah Wanderers, Sharjah

Ireland 19 **Argentina** 13

17 April, Exiles RFC 2, Dubai

Wales 33 **South Africa** 21

17 April, Exiles RFC, Dubai

France 16 **Australia** 26

17 April, Exiles RFC, Dubai

New Zealand 24 **England** 11

21 April, Sharjah Wanderers 2, Sharjah

Japan 13 **Romania** 13

21 April, Sharjah Wanderers, Sharjah

Samoa 12 **Scotland** 18

21 April, Sharjah Wanderers, Sharjah

Argentina 26 **South Africa** 7

21 April, Exiles RFC 2, Dubai

Ireland 20 **Wales** 15

IRB UNDER-19 WORLD CUP FINAL

21 April, Exiles RFC, Dubai

NEW ZEALAND 13 (1PG, 2T)
AUSTRALIA 17 (2G, 1DG)

NEW ZEALAND: C Slade; A Sanders, T Bateman, M Sa'u, G Tweddle; T Renata, J Legg; S Cleaver, M Pomare, J Direen, C Smith, C Middleton, M Coman, S Fuglistaller, V Vito (captain) Substitutions: T Saseve for Sanders (70 mins); T Saseve for Sa'u (temp 5 to 17 mins); T Puki for Renata (41 mins); D Devereaux for Legg (temp 61 to 70 mins); A Briggs for Cleaver (49 mins); P Faasalele for Middleton (36 mins); H Matenga for Coman (36 mins)

SCORERS *Tries*: Sanders (2) Penalty Goal: Slade

AUSTRALIA: L Rosengreen; B Vaaulu, B Gillespie, Anthony Faingaa, L Turner; C Lealiifano, J Holmes; B Daley, Saia Faingaa (captain), J Kennedy, D Linde, S Wykes, A J Gilbert, D Pocock, P McCutcheon Substitutions: T Hoponoa for Daley (49 mins); P Luafutu for Gilbert (36 mins)

SCORERS *Tries:* Linde, Turner Conversions: Lealiifano (2) Drop Goal: Anthony Faingaa

REFEREE A MacPherson (Scotland)

IRB UNDER-19 WORLD CUP THIRD PLACE PLAY-OFF

21 April, Exiles RFC, Dubai

FRANCE 12 (4PG) ENGLAND 12 (1G, 1T)
ENGLAND WIN BY A VIRTUE OF TRIES SCORED

FRANCE: M Belie; M Nicolas, T Combezou, M Bastareaud, A Palisson; M Parra, T Bourahoua (captain); J Andoque, C Ponnau, S Clement, T Lassalle, A Louchard, A Burban, A Valdant, J Raynaud Substitutions: B Thuries for Palisson (42 mins); S Clement for Andoque (63 mins); J P Genevois for Ponnau (51 mins); B Sore for Clement (41 mins); D Lagrange for Louchard (67 mins); Y Maestri for Valdant (12 mins)

SCORERS *Penalty Goals:* Belie (4)

ENGLAND: D Doherty; O Dodge, T Youngs, A Powell (captain), S Kuadey; D Care, J Simpson; C Beech, J Page, D Cole, D Attwood, S McDonald, I Grieve, A Saull, D Tait Substitutions: J Turner-Hall for Youngs (temp 41 to 51 mins); Turner-Hall for Kuadey (58 mins); R Bolt for Simpson (36 mins); M Mullan for Beech (42 mins); R McMillan for Page (42 mins); T Mercey for Cole (42 mins); A Shaw for McDonald (63 mins)

SCORERS *Tries:* Doherty, Care Conversion: Doherty

REFEREE W Roos (South Africa)

FINAL DIVISION A TABLE

1 – Australia	**7** – Argentina
2 – New Zealand	**8** – South Africa
3 – England	**9** – Scotland
4 – France	**10** – Samoa
5 – Ireland	**11** – Japan
6 – Wales	**12** – Romania

DIVISION B

ROUND ONE	
4 April, Exiles RFC, Dubai	**Canada** 29 **Namibia** 10
4 April, Sharjah Wanderers, Sharjah	**Uruguay** 35 **USA** 3
4 April, Exiles RFC 2, Dubai	**Chile** 6 **Tonga** 24
4 April, Sharjah Wanderers 2, Sharjah	**Chinese Taipei** 14 **Russia** 36
4 April, Exiles RFC, Dubai	**Fiji** 38 **Italy** 30
4 April, Sharjah Wanderers, Sharjah	**Georgia** 57 **Korea** 3
ROUND TWO	
8 April, Sharjah Wanderers, Sharjah	**Georgia** 14 **Namibia** 6
8 April, Exiles RFC, Dubai	**Canada** 14 **Tonga** 29
8 April, Exiles RFC 2, Dubai	**Chile** 33 **Korea** 10
8 April, Sharjah Wanderers 2, Sharjah	**Uruguay** 21 **Russia** 3
8 April, Sharjah Wanderers, Sharjah	**Chinese Taipei** 0 **Italy** 107
8 April, Exiles RFC, Dubai	**Fiji** 48 **USA** 3
ROUND THREE	
12 April, Sharjah Wanderers, Sharjah	**Georgia** 9 **Tonga** 16
12 April, Exiles RFC, Dubai	**Canada** 86 **Korea** 0
12 April, Sharjah Wanderers 2, Sharjah	**Chile** 6 **Namibia** 14
12 April, Exiles RFC 2, Dubai	**Uruguay** 18 **Italy** 37
12 April, Sharjah Wanderers, Sharjah	**Chinese Taipei** 17 **USA** 17
12 April, Exiles RFC, Dubai	**Fiji** 43 **Russia** 3

PLAY-OFFS

16 April, Sharjah Wanderers 2, Sharjah	
Division B 10th v 11th Place Play-Off	**USA** 14 **Chinese Taipei** 15
16 April, Sharjah Wanderers, Sharjah	
Division B 9th v 12th Place Play-Off	**Namibia** 51 **Korea** 5
16 April, Sharjah Wanderers, Sharjah	
Division B 6th v 7th Place Play-Off	**Uruguay** 24 **Chile** 5
16 April, Exiles RFC 2, Dubai	
Division B 5th v 8th Place Play-Off	**Georgia** 33 **Russia** 8
16 April, Exiles RFC, Dubai	
Division B 2nd v 3rd Place Play-Off	**Tonga** 24 **Italy** 10
16 April, Exiles RFC, Dubai	
Division B 1st v 4th Place Play-Off	**Fiji** 20 **Canada** 13
20 April, Sharjah Wanderers 2, Sharjah	
Division B 11th Place Play-Off	**Korea** 30 **USA** 28
20 April, Sharjah Wanderers, Sharjah	
Division B 9th Place Play-Off	**Namibia** 57 **Chinese Taipei** 10
20 April, Sharjah Wanderers, Sharjah	
Division B 7th Place Play-Off	**Russia** 9 **Chile** 10
20 April, Exiles RFC 2, Dubai	
Division B 5th Place Play-Off	**Georgia** 38 **Uruguay** 18

20 April, Exiles RFC, Dubai

FIJI 22 (2G, 1PG, 1T) TONGA 14 (2G)

FIJI: I Keresoni; S Tagicakibau, T Mwai, L Ratulevu, M Tokalauvere; R Bativagone, T Naituna; A Durutalo (captain), P Mara, S Newa, J Vugakoto, J Brown, T Bakanivesi, S Aca, W Kotobalavu Substitutions: I Bolakoro for Ratulevu (66 mins); O Namatalevu for Tokalauvere (70 mins); M Liga for Naituna (41 mins); S Nauluvula for Mara (64 mins); F Kuruvoli for Bakanivesi (61 mins); S Vuetinavanua for Aca (70 mins)

SCORERS *Tries:* Aca, Brown, Tagicakibau Conversions: Tagicakibau (2) Penalty Goal: Tagicakibau

YELLOW CARD: Liga (64)

TONGA: S Pangata'a; V Hakalo, S Faka'osilea, S Talakai, M Uhatahi; R Havili, S Fisilau; V Pola, T Mafi, S Lea'aemanu, M Tuli, F Vea, S Kalamafoni, T Lutua, P Havea (captain) Substitutions: S Fotu for Pangata'a (47 mins); F Blake for Uhatahi (53 mins); T Ahoafi for Fisilau (temp 46 to 58 mins); L Taueli for Mafi (47 mins); D Maka for Tuli (53 mins); S Ahofono for Vea (54 mins); S Manuopangai for Havea (53 mins)

SCORERS *Tries:* Havili, Fotu Conversions: Fisilau (2)

REFEREE P Fitzgibbon (Ireland)

IRB UNDER-19 DIVISION B THIRD PLACE

20 April, Exiles RFC, Dubai

CANADA 8 (1PG, 1T) ITALY 35 (3G, 3PG, 1T)

CANADA: D Hilborn; J Durling, N Trenkel, M O'Leary, P MacKenzie; M Evans, A Paul; R Heine, Alex Lavrinenko, N Daniel, B Pettinger, W Simpson, B Johnson, Eugene Lavrinenko, B Jones (captain) Substitutions: B Grant for O'Leary (40 mins); C Brown for Paul (50 mins); G Davidson for Heine (46 mins); Heine for Alex Lavrinenko (65 mins); A Bimm for Simpson (27 mins); J Moonlight for Bimm (50 mins); S Penhall for Johnson (50 mins); A Clark for Eugene Lavrinenko (52 mins)

SCORERS *Try:* Eugene Lavrinenko Penalty Goal: Evans

ITALY: T Tebaldi; F Fronzoni, A D Corso (captain), Davide Duca, A Bacchetti; F Vezzosi, M Wilson; A Borsi, N Gatto, E Borboni, L Beccaris, N Pedrazzani, F Cristiano, S Favaro, G Turroni Substitutions: A Pauletti for Bacchetti (65 mins); L Innocenti for Borsi (40 mins); A Zampiron for Gatto (68 mins); Natale Duca for Beccaris (48 mins); M Nicolli for Pedrazzani (50 mins); D Pasqualetto for Favaro (70 mins)

SCORERS *Tries:* Favaro, Fronzoni, Innocenti, Bacchetti Conversions: Davide Duca (3) Penalty Goals: Davide Duca (3)

REFEREE A Lindsay (Australia)

FINAL DIVISION B TABLE

1 – Fiji	7 – Chile
2 – Tonga	8 – Russia
3 – Italy	9 – Namibia
4 – Canada	10 – Chinese Taipei
5 – Georgia	11 – Korea
6 – Uruguay	12 – USA

TOP 10 INDIVIDUAL POINTS SCORERS

Colin Slade	(New Zealand)	61
Seremaia Tagicakibau	(Fiji)	56
Brian Collins	(Ireland)	55
Mathieu Belie	(France)	54
Davide Duca	(Italy)	48
Alberico Passadore	(Uruguay)	43
Chris Lind	(USA)	40
Daniel Cipriani	(England)	36
Luke McLean	(Australia)	34
Samisioni Fisilau	(Tonga)	33

TOP 10 TRY SCORERS

Santiago Di Meo	(Uruguay)	5
Joshua Holmes	(Australia)	5
Giorgi Lomsadze	(Georgia)	5
Andrea Bacchetti	(Italy)	4
Timothy Bateman	(New Zealand)	4
Rokodaini Bativagone	(Fiji)	4
Jack Durling	(Canda)	4
Yu Hoon Kim	(Korea)	4
Tomasi Mawi	(Fiji)	4
Matt O'Leary	(Canada)	4

WOMEN'S WORLD CUP

BLACK FERNS IN ASCENDANCY

New Zealand maintained their virtual monopoly on the Women's World Cup with a 25–17 victory in Edmonton over old rivals England – a result which gave the Black Ferns an unprecedented third successive title and Kiwi captain Farah Palmer the perfect end to an illustrious career.

A survivor from the 2002 final in which New Zealand had narrowly beaten England, Palmer was playing her last game for her country after a decade of Test match rugby and led from the front as New Zealand repeated their successes of 1998 and 2002 to confirm their status as the women's game's number one side.

England were hoping to get their hands on the trophy they lifted for the first and only time in 1994 and although they trailed the defending champions by a mere three points in the dying minutes, full-back Amiria Marsh put the Black Ferns out of sight in injury time with a try that ensured Palmer enjoyed one last victory before hanging up her international boots.

"It's a great way to finish my career as a Black Fern," Palmer said after her final match. "I felt this final was a lot tougher than the last. We were on defence much more than in previous World Cups.

"We put a lot of pressure on ourselves because we have high standards. We know that everyone is working on how to beat us. People at home expect a win, but that's why we play an elite sport."

It was certainly clear from the group stages of the competition that the New Zealanders would once again be a force to be reckoned with. Convincing 66–7 winners over hosts Canada in their opening fixture at Ellerslie Rugby Park, the Kiwis did not concede a single point in their next two games as Samoa were brushed aside 50–0 and Scotland beaten 21–0.

England, however, also found their form early on. Coached by Geoff

Ross Land/Getty Images

Rochelle Martin [left] Jed Rowlands and Farah Palmer [right] celebrate their World Cup triumph.

Richards, they were equally frugal in defence in their victories over the USA (18–0), South Africa (74–9) and France (27–8) and were the only other side to go into the play-offs unbeaten. Les Blues did beat Ireland and Australia to finish third after the group phase, while Canada came in fourth after bouncing back from their Black Ferns mauling with comfortable wins over Spain and Kazakhstan.

The first round of play-offs saw all six fixtures won by the team that finished higher in the table than their opponents, although Ireland, who finished eighth, came within a point of upsetting the form book and beating fifth-place Scotland but a late drop goal from captain Paula Chalmers dramatically ensured a 11–10 win for Gil Stevenson's Scots.

That meant New Zealand would face England once again in the final while France would face Canada in the third-place play-off. South Africa and Kazakhstan would meet in the battle to avoid last place.

The first 23 minutes of the French clash with Canada in the Commonwealth Stadium in Edmonton was an error-ridden affair but once captain Estelle Sartini crashed over for the first try of the match, France were always in the driving seat. Wing Maria Gallo brought Canada close in the second half with a try, but the French stretched away with a second touchdown of their own and hung on for a 17–8 victory.

"Finishing third is very important for our country and for our French teams," Sartini said after the game. "The President of French rugby was in the crowd today. It was important to win in front of him. It brought recognition for us, for the women."

Disappointed Canada captain Kelly McCallum said: "This wasn't how we wanted to end the tournament. We will move on from this. The last time we played France in the World Cup we lost 41–7. I think we proved we can compete with the top teams in the world."

The final in the Commonwealth Stadium was equally hard-fought as England looked to avoid defeat in a second successive final and for the third time in the 15-year history of the competition. In contrast New Zealand, coached by Jed Rowlands, were looking to extend their impressive eight-year reign as world champions by another four years.

It was England who drew first blood with a third-minute penalty from fly-half Karen Andrew but the Black Ferns went in at half-time ahead courtesy of a try from Monalisa Codling.

Wing Stephanie Mortimer and lock Victoria Heighway added New Zealand's second and third tries, but a penalty try for England gave Jo Yapp's side hope. That hope briefly turned into expectation when flanker Helen Clayton squirmed over the Kiwi line to make it 20–17 in favour the Ferns. Amiria Marsh, however, was to have the last word of an enthralling match with her injury-time effort that confirmed England's defeat.

"When I took over after the last World Cup, I was thankful Farah and some others chose not to retire," said coach Rowlands. "I think it was important to have continuity in our squad. I'm very pleased with the performances because the other countries are getting better.

"Scoring at the last instant was a great way to finish the game and have that as the last play. We came here to score tries and we did that. For us, it's the best way to finish."

For England a second defeat in the final was difficult to stomach. "We gave everything we could," said Yapp. "New Zealand never gave up. We'll look back and say it was a good final. We always believed we could do it and that belief was there until that final try."

The other final play-off games brought victories for the USA over Scotland, a narrow 18–14 win for Australia against Ireland and a 10–5 triumph for Spain against Samoa.

The 11th place play-off saw South Africa complete a miserable tournament as they were easily beaten 36–0 by Kazakhstan, their fifth defeat in five games.

Scotland's Donna Kennedy headed a host of post-tournament retirements, after winning her 95th cap, which is a world record.

RESULTS

GROUP STAGES

31 August	
Spain 0 **Scotland** 24	**New Zealand** 66 **Canada** 7
Kazakhstan 5 **Samoa** 20	**Australia** 68 **South Africa** 12
Ireland 0 **France** 43	**England** 18 **USA** 0
4 September	
New Zealand 50 **Samoa** 0	**Ireland** 11 **USA** 24
Kazakhstan 17 **Scotland** 32	**England** 74 **South Africa** 8
Australia 10 **France** 24	**Spain** 0 **Canada** 79
8 September	
Ireland 37 **South Africa** 0	**Spain** 14 **Samoa** 12
Australia 6 **USA** 10	**Kazakhstan** 5 **Canada** 45
New Zealand 21 **Scotland** 0	**England** 27 **France** 8

PLAY-OFFS

12 September	
1st v 4th Place Play-Off	**New Zealand** 40 **France** 10
2nd v 3rd Place Play-Off	**England** 20 **Canada** 14
5th v 8th Place Play-Off	**Scotland** 11 **Ireland** 10
6th v 7th Place Play-Off	**USA** 29 **Australia** 12
9th v 12th Place Play-Off	**Samoa** 43 **South Africa** 10
10th v 11th Place Play-Off	**Spain** 17 **Kazakhstan** 12
16 September	
11th Place Play-Off	**South Africa** 0 **Kazakhstan** 36
9th Place Play-Off	**Samoa** 5 **Spain** 10
7th Place Play-Off	**Ireland** 14 **Australia** 18
17 September	
5th Place Play-Off	**Scotland** 0 **USA** 24
3rd Place Play-Off	**France** 17 **Canada** 8

FINAL

17 September, Commonwealth Stadium, Edmonton

NEW ZEALAND 25 (1G, 1PG, 3T)
ENGLAND 17 (2G, 1PG)

NEW ZEALAND: A Marsh; C Richardson, H Manuel, E Edwards, S Mortimer; A Richards, E Jensen; D Maliukaetau, F Palmer (captain), C Robertson, M Codling, V Heighway, M Ruscoe, R Martin, L Itunu Substitutions: S Willoughby for Itunu (58 mins), H Myers for Richardson (72 mins)

SCORERS TRIES: Codling, Mortimer, Heighway, Marsh Conversion: Jensen Penalty Goal: Jensen

ENGLAND: C Barras; D Waterman, S Day, K Oliver, K Shaylor; K Andrew, J Yapp (captain); R Clark, A Garnett, V Gray; J Sutton, J Lyne; G Stevens, M Alphonsi, C Spencer Substitutions: T Taylor for Lyne (61 mins), V Huxford for Gray (63 mins), S Rae for Andrew (67 mins), H Clayton for Spencer (72 mins), A Turner for Oliver (77 mins)

SCORERS TRIES: Clayton, pen try Conversions: Andrew, Rae

PENALTY GOAL: Andrew

REFEREE S McDowell (Ireland)

FINAL STANDINGS

1	New Zealand	7	Australia
2	England	8	Ireland
3	France	9	Spain
4	Canada	10	Samoa
5	USA	11	Kazakhstan
6	Scotland	12	South Africa

TOP POINT SCORERS

Heather Moyse	Canada	**35**
Emma Jensen	New Zealand	**34**
Valuese Sao Taliu	Samoa	**33**
Shelley Rae	England	**31**
Sue Day	England	**30**
Maria Gallo	Canada	**30**
Amiria Marsh	New Zealand	**30**
Tobie McGann	Australia	**30**
Kelly McCallum	Canada	**29**
Paula Chambers	Scotland	**27**

TOP TRY SCORERS

Heather Moyse	Canada	**7**
Sue Day	England	**6**
Maria Gallo	Canada	**6**
Amiria Marsh	New Zealand	**6**
Tricia Brown	Australia	**5**
Catherine Devillers	France	**5**
Valuese Sao Taliu	Samoa	**5**
Ellie Karvoski	USA	**4**
Ruan Sims	Australia	**4**
Charlotte Barras	England	**3**

STAT ATTACK

Most points by a team	202	New Zealand
Fewest points for a team	30	South Africa
Most points against a team	258	South Africa
Fewest points against a team	34	New Zealand
Most tries for a team	31	New Zealand
Fewest tries by a team	5	South Africa
Most tries against a team	41	South Africa
Fewest tries against a team	5	New Zealand
Most yellow cards by a team	3	Samoa, South Africa, Spain

Jimmy Jeong/Getty Images

Heather Moyse [right] made a huge impact at the World Cup, ending the tournament with seven tries, more than any other player.

Before England arrived in Canada they proved they were in great form winning the Six Nations Grand Slam, topping the table for the first time since 2003.

The seminal match arrived in the penultimate round when England won 28–0 in Paris, against France, with a forward-dominated game plan, that included a penalty try.

Geoff Richards' England side duly completed the Grand Slam a week later, beating Ireland 39–10.

Head coach Richards said: "Winning today and winning the title is massive. I am delighted because we have achieved our goal of winning the Six Nations Grand Slam.

"We have worked hard, we have improved and we have gathered momentum as we have gone through the tournament. We had a huge game against France last week and in some ways I thought it could be difficult to replicate but the girls did a magnificent job in difficult conditions.

"It has taken a while to win the Six Nations but with this being a World Cup year it was even more of an important goal for us. It will certainly give us confidence going to Canada because we are now in the best possible position as champions of Europe. With a lot of hard work to do between now and the World Cup we are in the right frame of minds to go out there and do the best possible job."

Donna Kennedy, the world's most-capped women's rugby player completed her 90th Test in the final weekend, against Spain.

On the domestic front Richmond overcame the disappointment of losing the Premiership title to Saracens with an impressive 35–0 victory over league rivals Worcester in the final of the Rugby World National Cup.

Richmond skipper Nicki Drinkwater led by example with tries, either side of the break, with former England international Teresa Andrews also grabbing a brace of tries. Lisa O'Keeffe also touched down for a try, while Nicky Meston added two conversions and two penalties.

Saracens won the League on the final day, having to secure just one point from their home game with Wasps, and they did just that with a 60–0 victory! It was Saracens' first title in four years. On Saracens' big day Welsh international Louise Horgan, Tash Fitt (3), Assunta De Biase, Julie Gilbert (2), Emily Ryall and Katie Hannam all touched down.

Blaydon clinched the Premiership 2 title by five points from the Leos. Blaydon won nine of their 12 league outings this season.

Waterloo won promotion into Premiership2. The Liverpool club topped the National Challenge North 1 table by an impressive 16 points before seeing off the winners of the National Challenge Midlands 1 (Camphill), National Challenge South East 1 (Blackheath) and National Challenge South West 1 (Supermarine) leagues in a round robin tournament.

WOMEN'S SIX NATIONS RESULTS

Round One
Ireland 25 **Spain** 10, **England** 38 **Wales** 15, **Scotland** 3 **France** 23.
Round Two
Wales 5 **Scotland** 0, **France** 32 **Ireland** 0, **Spain** 3 **England** 86.
Round Three
Wales 14 **Ireland** 7, **Scotland** 5, **England** 22, **France** 38 **Spain** 0.
Round Four
Wales 10 **Spain** 0, **Scotland** 9 **Ireland** 0, **France** 0 **England** 28.
Round Five
England 39 **Ireland** 10, **Spain** 12 **Scotland** 16, **Wales** 11 **France** 10.

	P	W	For	Against	Diff	Pts
England	5	5	213	33	180	**10**
Wales	5	4	55	55	0	**8**
France	5	3	103	42	61	**6**
Scotland	5	2	33	62	–29	**4**
Ireland	5	1	42	104	–62	**2**
Spain	5	0	25	175	–150	**0**

Shaun Botterill/Getty Images

England's women picked up their first Grand Slam since 2003.

A SEASON TO REMEMBER

Over the next 378 pages we will take a look at the fortunes of 20 of the world's leading countries, the 20 sides who qualified for the 2003 Rugby World Cup

INTERNATIONAL RECORDS

RESULTS OF INTERNATIONAL MATCHES

MATCH RECORDS UP TO 30TH SEPTEMBER 2006

Cap matches involving senior executive council member unions only. Years for International Championship matches are for the second half of the season: eg 1972 means season 1971–72. Years for matches against touring teams from the Southern Hemisphere refer to the actual year of the match.

Points-scoring was first introduced in 1886, when an International Board was formed by Scotland, Ireland and Wales. Points values varied among the countries until 1890, when England agreed to join the Board, and uniform values were adopted.

Northern Hemisphere seasons	Try	Conversions	Penalty Goal	Dropped goal	Goal from mark
1890–91	1	2	2	3	3
1891–92 to 1882–93	2	3	3	4	4
1893–94 to 1904–05	3	2	3	4	4
1905–06 to 1947–48	3	2	3	4	3
1948–49 to 1970–71	3	2	3	3	3
1971–72 to 1991–92	4	2	3	3	3
1992–93 onwards	5	2	3	3	–

*The goal from mark ceased to exist when the free-kick clause was introduced, 1977–78.

WC indicates a fixture played during the Rugby World Cup finals. LC indicates a fixture played in the Latin Cup. TN indicates a fixture played in the Tri Nations.

ENGLAND V SCOTLAND

Played 123 England won 65, Scotland won 41, Drawn 17
Highest scores England 43–3 in 2001 and 43–22 in 2005, Scotland 33–6 in 1986
Biggest wins England 43–3 in 2001, Scotland 33–6 in 1986

1871 Raeburn Place (Edinburgh) **Scotland** 1G 1T to 1T
1872 The Oval (London) **England** 1G 1DG 2T to 1DG
1873 Glasgow **Drawn** no score
1874 The Oval **England** 1DG to 1T
1875 Raeburn Place **Drawn** no score
1876 The Oval **England** 1G 1T to 0
1877 Raeburn Place **Scotland** 1 DG to 0
1878 The Oval **Drawn** no score
1879 Raeburn Place **Drawn** Scotland 1DG England 1G
1880 Manchester **England** 2G 3T to 1G
1881 Raeburn Place **Drawn** Scotland 1G 1T England 1DG 1T
1882 Manchester **Scotland** 2T to 0
1883 Raeburn Place **England** 2T to 1T
1884 Blackheath (London) **England** 1G to 1T
1885 No Match
1886 Raeburn Place **Drawn** no score
1887 Manchester **Drawn** 1T each
1888 No Match
1889 No Match
1890 Raeburn Place **England** 1G 1T to 0
1891 Richmond (London) **Scotland** 9–3
1892 Raeburn Place **England** 5–0
1893 Leeds **Scotland** 8–0
1894 Raeburn Place **Scotland** 6–0
1895 Richmond **Scotland** 6–3
1896 Glasgow **Scotland** 11–0
1897 Manchester **England** 12–3
1898 Powderhall (Edinburgh) **Drawn** 3–3
1899 Blackheath **Scotland** 5–0
1900 Inverleith (Edinburgh) **Drawn** 0–0
1901 Blackheath **Scotland** 18–3
1902 Inverleith **England** 6–3
1903 Richmond **Scotland** 10–6
1904 Inverleith **Scotland** 6–3
1905 Richmond **Scotland** 8–0
1906 Inverleith **England** 9–3
1907 Blackheath **Scotland** 8–3
1908 Inverleith **Scotland** 16–10
1909 Richmond **Scotland** 18–8
1910 Inverleith **England** 14–5
1911 Twickenham **England** 13–8
1912 Inverleith **Scotland** 8–3
1913 Twickenham **England** 3–0
1914 Inverleith **England** 16–15
1920 Twickenham **England** 1344
1921 Inverleith **England** 18–0
1922 Twickenham **England** 11–5
1923 Inverleith **England** 8–6
1924 Twickenham **England** 19–0
1925 Murrayfield **Scotland** 14–11
1926 Twickenham **Scotland** 17–9
1927 Murrayfield **Scotland** 21–13
1928 Twickenham **England** 6–0
1929 Murrayfield **Scotland** 12–6
1930 Twickenham **Drawn** 0–0
1931 Murrayfield **Scotland** 28–19
1932 Twickenham **England** 16–3
1933 Murrayfield **Scotland** 3–0
1934 Twickenham **England** 6–3
1935 Murrayfield **Scotland** 10–7
1936 Twickenham **England** 9–8
1937 Murrayfield **England** 6–3
1938 Twickenham **Scotland** 21–16
1939 Murrayfield **England** 9–6
1947 Twickenham **England** 24–5
1948 Murrayfield **Scotland** 6–3
1949 Twickenham **England** 19–3
1950 Murrayfield **Scotland** 13–11
1951 Twickenham **England** 5–3
1952 Murrayfield **England** 19–3
1953 Twickenham **England** 26–8
1954 Murrayfield **England** 13–3
1955 Twickenham **England** 9–6
1956 Murrayfield **England** 11–6
1957 Twickenham **England** 16–3
1958 Murrayfield **Drawn** 3–3
1959 Twickenham **Drawn** 3–3
1960 Murrayfield **England** 21–12

1961 Twickenham **England** 6–0
1962 Murrayfield **Drawn** 3–3
1963 Twickenham **England** 10–8
1964 Murrayfield **Scotland** 15–6
1965 Twickenham **Drawn** 3–3
1966 Murrayfield **Scotland** 6–3
1967 Twickenham **England** 27–14
1968 Murrayfield **England** 8–6
1969 Twickenham **England** 8–3
1970 Murrayfield **Scotland** 14–5
1971 Twickenham **Scotland** 16–15
1971 Murrayfield **Scotland** 26–6
Special centenary match – non-championship
1972 Murrayfield **Scotland** 23–9
1973 Twickenham **England** 20–13
1974 Murrayfield **Scotland** 16–14
1975 Twickenham **England** 7–6
1976 Murrayfield **Scotland** 22–12
1977 Twickenham **England** 26–6
1978 Murrayfield **England** 15–0
1979 Twickenham **Drawn** 7–7
1980 Murrayfield **England** 30–18
1981 Twickenham **England** 23–17
1982 Murrayfield **Drawn** 9–9
1983 Twickenham **Scotland** 22–12
1984 Murrayfield **Scotland** 18–6
1985 Twickenham **England** 10–7
1986 Murrayfield **Scotland** 33–6
1987 Twickenham **England** 21–12
1988 Murrayfield **England** 9–6
1989 Twickenham **Drawn** 12–12
1990 Murrayfield **Scotland** 13–7
1991 Twickenham **England** 21–12
1991 Murrayfield *WC* **England** 9–6
1992 Murrayfield **England** 25–7
1993 Twickenham **England** 26–12
1994 Murrayfield **England** 15–14
1995 Twickenham **England** 24–12
1996 Murrayfield **England** 18–9
1997 Twickenham **England** 41–13
1998 Murrayfield **England** 34–20
1999 Twickenham **England** 24–21
2000 Murrayfield **Scotland** 19–13
2001 Twickenham **England** 43–3
2002 Murrayfield **England** 29–3
2003 Twickenham **England** 40–9
2004 Murrayfield **England** 35–13
2005 Twickenham **England** 43–22
2006 Murrayfield **Scotland** 18–12

ENGLAND V IRELAND

Played 119 England won 69, Ireland won 42, Drawn 8
Highest scores England 50–18 in 2000, Ireland 28–24 in 2006
Biggest wins England 46–6 in 1997, Ireland 22–0 in 1947

1875 The Oval (London) **England** 1G 1DG 1T to 0
1876 Dublin **England** 1G 1T to 0
1877 The Oval **England** 2G 2T to 0
1878 Dublin **England** 2G 1T to 0
1879 The Oval **England** 2G 1DG 2T to 0
1880 Dublin **England** 1G 1T to 1T
1881 Manchester **England** 2G 2T to 0
1882 Dublin **Drawn** 2T each
1883 Manchester **England** 1G 3T to 1T
1884 Dublin **England** 1G to 0
1885 Manchester **England** 2T to 1T
1886 Dublin **England** 1T to 0
1887 Dublin **Ireland** 2G to 0
1888 No Match
1889 No Match
1890 Blackheath (London) **England** 3T to 0
1891 Dublin **England** 9–0
1892 Manchester **England** 7–0
1893 Dublin **England** 4–0
1894 Blackheath **Ireland** 7–5
1895 Dublin **England** 6–3
1896 Leeds **Ireland** 10–4
1897 Dublin **Ireland** 13–9
1898 Richmond (London) **Ireland** 9–6
1899 Dublin **Ireland** 6–0
1900 Richmond **England** 15–4
1901 Dublin **Ireland** 10–6
1902 Leicester **England** 6–3
1903 Dublin **Ireland** 6–0

1904 Blackheath **England** 19–0
1905 Cork **Ireland** 17–3
1906 Leicester **Ireland** 16–6
1907 Dublin **Ireland** 17–9
1908 Richmond **England** 13–3
1909 Dublin **England** 11–5
1910 Twickenham **Drawn** 0–0
1911 Dublin **Ireland** 3–0
1912 Twickenham **England** 15–0
1913 Dublin **England** 15–4
1914 Twickenham **England** 17–12
1920 Dublin **England** 14–11
1921 Twickenham **England** 15–0
1922 Dublin **England** 12–3
1923 Leicester **England** 23–5
1924 Belfast **England** 14–3
1925 Twickenham **Drawn** 6–6
1926 Dublin **Ireland** 19–15
1927 Twickenham **England** 8–6
1928 Dublin **England** 7–6
1929 Twickenham **Ireland** 6–5
1930 Dublin **Ireland** 4–3
1931 Twickenham **Ireland** 6–5
1932 Dublin **England** 11–8
1933 Twickenham **England** 17–6
1934 Dublin **England** 13–3
1935 Twickenham **England** 14–3
1936 Dublin **Ireland** 6–3
1937 Twickenham **England** 9–8
1938 Dublin **England** 36–14
1939 Twickenham **Ireland** 5–0
1947 Dublin **Ireland** 22–0
1948 Twickenham **Ireland** 11–10
1949 Dublin **Ireland** 14–5
1950 Twickenham **England** 3–0
1951 Dublin **Ireland** 3–0
1952 Twickenham **England** 3–0
1953 Dublin **Drawn** 9–9
1954 Twickenham **England** 14–3
1955 Dublin **Drawn** 6–6
1956 Twickenham **England** 20–0
1957 Dublin **England** 6–0
1958 Twickenham **England** 6–0
1959 Dublin **England** 3–0
1960 Twickenham **England** 8–5
1961 Dublin **Ireland** 11–8
1962 Twickenham **England** 16–0
1963 Dublin **Drawn** 0–0
1964 Twickenham **Ireland** 18–5
1965 Dublin **Ireland** 5–0
1966 Twickenham **Drawn** 6–6
1967 Dublin **England** 8–3
1968 Twickenham **Drawn** 9–9
1969 Dublin **Ireland** 17–15
1970 Twickenham **England** 9–3
1971 Dublin **England** 9–6
1972 Twickenham **Ireland** 16–12
1973 Dublin **Ireland** 18–9
1974 Twickenham **Ireland** 26–21
1975 Dublin **Ireland** 12–9
1976 Twickenham **Ireland** 13–12
1977 Dublin **England** 4–0
1978 Twickenham **England** 15–9
1979 Dublin **Ireland** 12–7
1980 Twickenham **England** 24–9
1981 Dublin **England** 10–6
1982 Twickenham **Ireland** 16–15
1983 Dublin **Ireland** 25–15
1984 Twickenham **England** 12–9
1985 Dublin **Ireland** 13–10
1986 Twickenham **England** 25–20
1987 Dublin **Ireland** 17–0
1988 Twickenham **England** 35–3
1988 Dublin **England** 21–10
Non-championship match
1989 Dublin **England** 16–3
1990 Twickenham **England** 23–0
1991 Dublin **England** 16–7
1992 Twickenham **England** 38–9
1993 Dublin **Ireland** 17–3
1994 Twickenham **Ireland** 13–12
1995 Dublin **England** 20–8
1996 Twickenham **England** 28–15
1997 Dublin **England** 46–6
1998 Twickenham **England** 35–17
1999 Dublin **England** 27–15
2000 Twickenham **England** 50–18
2001 Dublin **Ireland** 20–14
2002 Twickenham **England** 45–11
2003 Dublin **England** 42–6
2004 Twickenham **Ireland** 19–13
2005 Dublin **Ireland** 19–13
2006 Twickenham **Ireland** 28–24

ENGLAND V WALES

Played 114 England won 52, Wales won 50, Drawn 12
Highest scores England 60–26 in 1998, Wales 34–21 in 1967
Biggest wins England 50–10 in 2002, Wales 25–0 in 1905

1881	Blackheath (London) **England** 7G 1DG 6T to 0
1882	No Match
1883	Swansea **England** 2G 4T to 0
1884	Leeds **England** 1G 2T to 1G
1885	Swansea **England** 1G 4T to 1G 1T
1886	Blackheath **England** 1GM 2T to 1G
1887	Llanelli **Drawn** no score
1888	No Match
1889	No Match
1890	Dewsbury **Wales** 1T to 0
1891	Newport **England** 7–3
1892	Blackheath **England** 17–0
1893	Cardiff **Wales** 12–11
1894	Birkenhead **England** 24–3
1895	Swansea **England** 14–6
1896	Blackheath **England** 25–0
1897	Newport **Wales** 11–0
1898	Blackheath **England** 14–7
1899	Swansea **Wales** 26–3
1900	Gloucester **Wales** 13–3
1901	Cardiff **Wales** 13–0
1902	Blackheath **Wales** 9–8
1903	Swansea **Wales** 21–5
1904	Leicester **Drawn** 14–14
1905	Cardiff **Wales** 25–0
1906	Richmond (London) **Wales** 16–3
1907	Swansea **Wales** 22–0
1908	Bristol **Wales** 28–18
1909	Cardiff **Wales** 8–0
1910	Twickenham **England** 11–6
1911	Swansea **Wales** 15–11
1912	Twickenham **England** 8–0
1913	Cardiff **England** 12–0
1914	Twickenham **England** 10–9
1920	Swansea **Wales** 19–5
1921	Twickenham **England** 18–3
1922	Cardiff **Wales** 28–6
1923	Twickenham **England** 7–3
1924	Swansea **England** 17–9
1925	Twickenham **England** 12–6
1926	Cardiff **Drawn** 3–3
1927	Twickenham **England** 11–9
1928	Swansea **England** 10–8
1929	Twickenham **England** 8–3
1930	Cardiff **England** 11–3
1931	Twickenham **Drawn** 11–11
1932	Swansea **Wales** 12–5
1933	Twickenham **Wales** 7–3
1934	Cardiff **England** 9–0
1935	Twickenham **Drawn** 3–3
1936	Swansea **Drawn** 0–0
1937	Twickenham **England** 4–3
1938	Cardiff **Wales** 14–8
1939	Twickenham **England** 3–0
1947	Cardiff **England** 9–6
1948	Twickenham **Drawn** 3–3
1949	Cardiff **Wales** 9–3
1950	Twickenham **Wales** 11–5
1951	Swansea **Wales** 23–5
1952	Twickenham **Wales** 8–6
1953	Cardiff **England** 8–3
1954	Twickenham **England** 9–6
1955	Cardiff **Wales** 3–0
1956	Twickenham **Wales** 8–3
1957	Cardiff **England** 3–0
1958	Twickenham **Drawn** 3–3
1959	Cardiff **Wales** 5–0
1960	Twickenham **England** 14–6
1961	Cardiff **Wales** 6–3
1962	Twickenham **Drawn** 0–0
1963	Cardiff **England** 13–6
1964	Twickenham **Drawn** 6–6
1965	Cardiff **Wales** 14–3
1966	Twickenham **Wales** 11–6
1967	Cardiff **Wales** 34–21
1968	Twickenham **Drawn** 11–11
1969	Cardiff **Wales** 30–9
1970	Twickenham **Wales** 17–13
1971	Cardiff **Wales** 22–6
1972	Twickenham **Wales** 12–3
1973	Cardiff **Wales** 25–9
1974	Twickenham **England** 16–12
1975	Cardiff **Wales** 20–4
1976	Twickenham **Wales** 21–9
1977	Cardiff **Wales** 14–9

1978	Twickenham **Wales** 9–6
1979	Cardiff **Wales** 27–3
1980	Twickenham **England** 9–8
1981	Cardiff **Wales** 21–19
1982	Twickenham **England** 17–7
1983	Cardiff **Drawn** 13–13
1984	Twickenham **Wales** 24–15
1985	Cardiff **Wales** 24–15
1986	Twickenham **England** 21–18
1987	Cardiff **Wales** 19–12
1987	Brisbane *WC* **Wales** 16–3
1988	Twickenham **Wales** 11–3
1989	Cardiff **Wales** 12–9
1990	Twickenham **England** 34–6
1991	Cardiff **England** 25–6
1992	Twickenham **England** 24–0
1993	Cardiff **Wales** 10–9
1994	Twickenham **England** 15–8
1995	Cardiff **England** 23–9
1996	Twickenham **England** 21–15
1997	Cardiff **England** 34–13
1998	Twickenham **England** 60–26
1999	Wembley **Wales** 32–31
2000	Twickenham **England** 46–12
2001	Cardiff **England** 44–15
2002	Twickenham **England** 50–10
2003	Cardiff **England** 26–9
2003	Cardiff **England** 43–9
2003	Brisbane *WC* **England** 28–17
2004	Twickenham **England** 31–21
2005	Cardiff **Wales** 11–9
2006	Twickenham **England** 47–13

ENGLAND V FRANCE

Played 86 England won 46, France won 33, Drawn 7
Highest scores England 48–19 in 2001, France 37–12 in 1972
Biggest wins England 37–0 in 1911, France 37–12 in 1972 and 31–6 in 2006

1906	Paris **England** 35–8
1907	Richmond (London) **England** 41–13
1908	Paris **England** 19–0
1909	Leicester **England** 22–0
1910	Paris **England** 11–3
1911	Twickenham **England** 37–0
1912	Paris **England** 18–8
1913	Twickenham **England** 20–0
1914	Paris **England** 39–13
1920	Twickenham **England** 8–3
1921	Paris **England** 10–6
1922	Twickenham **Drawn** 11–11
1923	Paris **England** 12–3
1924	Twickenham **England** 19–7
1925	Paris **England** 13–11
1926	Twickenham **England** 11–0
1927	Paris **France** 3–0
1928	Twickenham **England** 18–8
1929	Paris **England** 16–6
1930	Twickenham **England** 11–5
1931	Paris **France** 14–13
1947	Twickenham **England** 6–3
1948	Paris **France** 15–0
1949	Twickenham **England** 8–3
1950	Paris **France** 6–3
1951	Twickenham **France** 11–3
1952	Paris **England** 6–3
1953	Twickenham **England** 11–0
1954	Paris **France** 11–3
1955	Twickenham **France** 16–9
1956	Paris **France** 14–9
1957	Twickenham **England** 9–5
1958	Paris **England** 14–0
1959	Twickenham **Drawn** 3–3
1960	Paris **Drawn** 3–3
1961	Twickenham **Drawn** 5–5
1962	Paris **France** 13–0
1963	Twickenham **England** 6–5
1964	Paris **England** 6–3
1965	Twickenham **England** 9–6
1966	Paris **France** 13–0
1967	Twickenham **France** 16–12
1968	Paris **France** 14–9
1969	Twickenham **England** 22–8
1970	Paris **France** 35–13
1971	Twickenham **Drawn** 14–14
1972	Paris **France** 37–12
1973	Twickenham **England** 14–6

1974 Paris **Drawn** 12–12
1975 Twickenham **France** 27–20
1976 Paris **France** 30–9
1977 Twickenham **France** 4–3
1978 Paris **France** 15–6
1979 Twickenham **England** 7–6
1980 Paris **England** 17–13
1981 Twickenham **France** 16–12
1982 Paris **England** 27–15
1983 Twickenham **France** 19–15
1984 Paris **France** 32–18
1985 Twickenham **Drawn** 9–9
1986 Paris **France** 29–10
1987 Twickenham **France** 19–15
1988 Paris **France** 10–9
1989 Twickenham **England** 11–0
1990 Paris **England** 26–7
1991 Twickenham **England** 21–19
1991 Paris *WC* **England** 19–10
1992 Paris **England** 31–13
1993 Twickenham **England** 16–15
1994 Paris **England** 18–14
1995 Twickenham **England** 31–10
1995 Pretoria *WC* **France** 19–9
1996 Paris **France** 15–12
1997 Twickenham **France** 23–20
1998 Paris **France** 24–17
1999 Twickenham **England** 21–10
2000 Paris **England** 15–9
2001 Twickenham **England** 48–19
2002 Paris **France** 20–15
2003 Twickenham **England** 25–17
2003 Marseilles **France** 17–16
2003 Twickenham **England** 45–14
2003 Sydney *WC* **England** 24–7
2004 Paris **France** 24–21
2005 Twickenham **France** 18–17
2006 Paris **France** 31–6

ENGLAND V NEW ZEALAND

Played 28 England won 6, New Zealand won 21, Drawn 1
Highest scores England 31–28 in 2002, New Zealand 64–22 in 1998
Biggest wins England 13–0 in 1936, New Zealand 64–22 in 1998

1905 Crystal Palace (London) **New Zealand** 15–0
1925 Twickenham **New Zealand** 17–11
1936 Twickenham **England** 13–0
1954 Twickenham **New Zealand** 5–0
1963 1 Auckland **New Zealand** 21–11
2 Christchurch **New Zealand** 9–6
New Zealand won series 2–0
1964 Twickenham **New Zealand** 14–0
1967 Twickenham **New Zealand** 23–11
1973 Twickenham **New Zealand** 9–0
1973 Auckland **England** 16–10
1978 Twickenham **New Zealand** 16–6
1979 Twickenham **New Zealand** 10–9
1983 Twickenham **England** 15–9
1985 1 Christchurch **New Zealand** 18–13
2 Wellington **New Zealand** 42–15
New Zealand won series 2–0
1991 Twickenham *WC* **New Zealand** 18–12
1993 Twickenham **England** 15–9
1995 Cape Town *WC* **New Zealand** 45–29
1997 1 Manchester **New Zealand** 25–8
2 Twickenham **Drawn** 26–26
New Zealand won series 1–0, with 1 draw
1998 1 Dunedin **New Zealand** 64–22
2 Auckland **New Zealand** 40–10
New Zealand won series 2–0
1999 Twickenham *WC* **New Zealand** 30–16
2002 Twickenham **England** 31–28
2003 Wellington **England** 15–13
2004 1 Dunedin **New Zealand** 36–3
2 Auckland **New Zealand** 36–12
New Zealand won series 2–0
2005 Twickenham **New Zealand** 23–19

ENGLAND V SOUTH AFRICA

Played 24 England won 11, South Africa won 12, Drawn 1
Highest scores England 53–3 in 2002, South Africa 44–21 in 1999
Biggest wins England 53–3 in 2002, South Africa 35–9 in 1984

1906	Crystal Palace (London) **Drawn** 3–3
1913	Twickenham **South Africa** 9–3
1932	Twickenham **South Africa** 7–0
1952	Twickenham **South Africa** 8–3
1961	Twickenham **South Africa** 5–0
1969	Twickenham **England** 11–8
1972	Johannesburg **England** 18–9
1984	1 Port Elizabeth **South Africa** 33–15
	2 Johannesburg **South Africa** 35–9
	South Africa won series 2–0
1992	Twickenham **England** 33–16
1994	1 Pretoria **England** 32–15
	2 Cape Town **South Africa** 27–9
	Series drawn 1–1
1995	Twickenham **South Africa** 24–14
1997	Twickenham **South Africa** 29–11
1998	Cape Town **South Africa** 18–0
1998	Twickenham **England** 13–7
1999	Paris *WC* **South Africa** 44–21
2000	1 Pretoria **South Africa** 18–13
	2 Bloemfontein **England** 27–22
	Series drawn 1–1
2000	Twickenham **England** 25–17
2001	Twickenham **England** 29–9
2002	Twickenham **England** 53–3
2003	Perth *WC* **England** 25–6
2004	Twickenham **England** 32–16

ENGLAND V AUSTRALIA

Played 34 England won 13, Australia won 20, Drawn 1
Highest scores England 32–31 in 2002, Australia 76–0 in 1998
Biggest wins England 20–3 in 1973 & 23–6 in 1976, Australia 76–0 in 1998

1909	Blackheath (London) **Australia** 9–3
1928	Twickenham **England** 18–11
1948	Twickenham **Australia** 11–0
1958	Twickenham **England** 9–6
1963	Sydney **Australia** 18–9
1967	Twickenham **Australia** 23–11
1973	Twickenham **England** 20–3
1975	1 Sydney **Australia** 16–9
	2 Brisbane **Australia** 30–21
	Australia won series 2–0
1976	Twickenham **England** 23–6
1982	Twickenham **England** 15–11
1984	Twickenham **Australia** 19–3
1987	Sydney *WC* **Australia** 19–6
1988	1 Brisbane **Australia** 22–16
	2 Sydney **Australia** 28–8
	Australia won series 2–0
1988	Twickenham **England** 28–19
1991	Sydney **Australia** 40–15
1991	Twickenham *WC* **Australia** 12–6
1995	Cape Town *WC* **England** 25–22
1997	Sydney **Australia** 25–6
1997	Twickenham **Drawn** 15–15
1998	Brisbane **Australia** 76–0
1998	Twickenham **Australia** 12–11
1999	Sydney **Australia** 22–15
2000	Twickenham **England** 22–19
2001	Twickenham **England** 21–15
2002	Twickenham **England** 32–31
2003	Melbourne **England** 25–14
2003	Sydney *WC* **England** 20–17 (aet)
2004	Brisbane **Australia** 51–15
2004	Twickenham **Australia** 21–19
2005	Twickenham **England** 26–16
2006	1 Sydney **Australia** 34–3
	2 Melbourne **Australia** 43–18
	Australia won series 2–0

ENGLAND V NEW ZEALAND NATIVES

Played 1 England won 1
Highest score England 7–0 in 1889, NZ Natives 0–7 in 1889
Biggest win England 7–0 in 1889, NZ Natives no win

1889	Blackheath **England** 1G 4T to 0

ENGLAND V RFU PRESIDENT'S XV

Played 1 President's XV won 1
Highest score England 11–28 in 1971, RFU President's XV 28–11 in 1971
Biggest win RFU President's XV 28–11 in 1971

1971	Twickenham **President's XV** 28–11

ENGLAND V ARGENTINA

Played 11 England won 8, Argentina won 2, Drawn 1
Highest scores England 51–0 in 1990, Argentina 33–13 in 1997
Biggest wins England 51–0 in 1990, Argentina 33–13 in 1997

11981	1 Buenos Aires **Drawn** 19–19
	2 Buenos Aires **England** 12–6
	England won series 1–0 with 1 draw
1990	1 Buenos Aires **England** 25–12
	2 Buenos Aires **Argentina** 15–13
	Series drawn 1–1
1990	Twickenham **England** 51–0
1995	Durban *WC* **England** 24–18
1996	Twickenham **England** 20–18
1997	1 Buenos Aires **England** 46–20
	2 Buenos Aires **Argentina** 33–13
	Series drawn 1–1
2000	Twickenham **England** 19–0
2002	Buenos Aires **England** 26–18

ENGLAND V ROMANIA

Played 4 England won 4
Highest scores England 134–0 in 2001, Romania 15–22 in 1985
Biggest win England 134–0 in 2001, Romania no win

1985	Twickenham **England** 22–15
1989	Bucharest **England** 58–3
1994	Twickenham **England** 54–3
2001	Twickenham **England** 134–0

ENGLAND V JAPAN

Played 1 England won 1
Highest score England 60–7 in 1987, Japan 7–60 in 1987
Biggest win England 60–7 in 1987, Japan no win

1987 Sydney *WC* **England** 60–7

ENGLAND V UNITED STATES

Played 4 England won 4
Highest scores England 106–8 in 1999, United States 19–48 in 2001
Biggest win England 106–8 in 1999, United States no win

1987 Sydney *WC* **England** 34–6
1991 Twickenham *WC* **England** 37–9
1999 Twickenham **England** 106–8
2001 San Francisco **England** 48–19

ENGLAND V FIJI

Played 4 England won 4
Highest scores England 58–23 in 1989, Fiji 24–45 in 1999
Biggest win England 58–23 in 1989, Fiji no win

1988 Suva **England** 25–12
1989 Twickenham **England** 58–23
1991 Suva **England** 28–12
1999 Twickenham *WC* **England** 45–24

ENGLAND V ITALY

Played 12 England won 12
Highest scores England 80–23 in 2001, Italy 23–80 in 2001
Biggest win England 67–7 in 1999, Italy no win

1991 Twickenham *WC* **England** 36–6
1995 Durban *WC* **England** 27–20
1996 Twickenham **England** 54–21
1998 Huddersfield **England** 23–15
1999 Twickenham *WC* **England** 67–7
2000 Rome **England** 59–12
2001 Twickenham **England** 80–23
2002 Rome **England** 45–9
2003 Twickenham **England** 40–5
2004 Rome **England** 50–9
2005 Twickenham **England** 39–7
2006 Rome **England** 31–16

ENGLAND V CANADA

Played 6 England won 6
Highest scores England 70–0 in 2004, Canada 20–59 in 2001
Biggest win England 70–0 in 2004, Canada no win

1992 Wembley **England** 26–13
1994 Twickenham **England** 60–19
1999 Twickenham **England** 36–11
2001 1 Markham **England** 22–10
2 Burnaby **England** 59–20
England won series 2–0
2004 Twickenham **England** 70–0

ENGLAND V SAMOA

Played 4 England won 4
Highest scores England 44–22 in 1995, Samoa 22–44 in 1995 and 22–35 in 2003
Biggest win England 40–3 in 2005, Samoa no win

1995 Durban *WC* **England** 44–22
1995 Twickenham **England** 27–9
2003 Melbourne *WC* **England** 35–22
2005 Twickenham **England** 40–3

ENGLAND V THE NETHERLANDS

Played 1 England won 1
Highest scores England 110–0 in 1998, The Netherlands 0–110 in 1998
Biggest win England 110–0 in 1998, The Netherlands no win

1998 Huddersfield **England** 110–0

ENGLAND V TONGA

Played 1 England won 1
Highest scores England 101–10 in 1999, Tonga 10–101 in 1999
Biggest win England 101–10 in 1999, Tonga no win

1999 Twickenham *WC* **England** 101–10

ENGLAND V GEORGIA

Played 1 England won 1
Highest scores England 84–6 in 2003, Georgia 6–84 in 2003
Biggest win England 84–6 in 2003, Georgia no win

2003 Perth *WC* **England** 84–6

ENGLAND V URUGUAY

Played 1 England won 1
Highest scores England 111–13 in 2003, Uruguay 13–111 in 2003
Biggest win England 111–13 in 2003, Uruguay no win

2003 Brisbane *WC* **England** 111–13

SCOTLAND V IRELAND

Played 119 Scotland won 61, Ireland won 52, Drawn 5, Abandoned 1
Highest scores Scotland 38–10 in 1997, Ireland 44–22 in 2000
Biggest wins Scotland 38–10 in 1997, Ireland 36–6 in 2003

1877 Belfast **Scotland** 4G 2DG 2T to 0
1878 No Match
1879 Belfast **Scotland** 1G 1DG 1T to 0
1880 Glasgow **Scotland** 1G 2DG 2T to 0
1881 Belfast **Ireland** 1DG to 1T
1882 Glasgow **Scotland** 2T to 0
1883 Belfast **Scotland** 1G 1T to 0
1884 Raeburn Place (Edinburgh) **Scotland** 2G 2T to 1T
1885 Belfast Abandoned **Ireland** 0 **Scotland** 1T
1885 Raeburn Place **Scotland** 1G 2T to 0
1886 Raeburn Place **Scotland** 3G 1DG 2T to 0
1887 Belfast **Scotland** 1G 1GM 2T to 0
1888 Raeburn Place **Scotland** 1G to 0
1889 Belfast **Scotland** 1DG to 0
1890 Raeburn Place **Scotland** 1DG 1T to 0
1891 Belfast **Scotland** 14–0
1892 Raeburn Place **Scotland** 2–0
1893 Belfast **Drawn** 0–0
1894 Dublin **Ireland** 5–0
1895 Raeburn Place **Scotland** 6–0
1896 Dublin **Drawn** 0–0
1897 Powderhall (Edinburgh) **Scotland** 8–3
1898 Belfast **Scotland** 8–0
1899 Inverleith (Edinburgh) **Ireland** 9–3
1900 Dublin **Drawn** 0–0
1901 Inverleith **Scotland** 9–5
1902 Belfast **Ireland** 5–0
1903 Inverleith **Scotland** 3–0
1904 Dublin **Scotland** 19–3
1905 Inverleith **Ireland** 11–5
1906 Dublin **Scotland** 13–6
1907 Inverleith **Scotland** 15–3
1908 Dublin **Ireland** 16–11
1909 Inverleith **Scotland** 9–3
1910 Belfast **Scotland** 14–0
1911 Inverleith **Ireland** 16–10
1912 Dublin **Ireland** 10–8
1913 Inverleith **Scotland** 29–14
1914 Dublin **Ireland** 6–0
1920 Inverleith **Scotland** 19–0
1921 Dublin **Ireland** 9–8
1922 Inverleith **Scotland** 6–3
1923 Dublin **Scotland** 13–3
1924 Inverleith **Scotland** 13–8
1925 Dublin **Scotland** 14–8
1926 Murrayfield **Ireland** 3–0
1927 Dublin **Ireland** 6–0
1928 Murrayfield **Ireland** 13–5
1929 Dublin **Scotland** 16–7
1930 Murrayfield **Ireland** 14–11
1931 Dublin **Ireland** 8–5
1932 Murrayfield **Ireland** 20–8
1933 Dublin **Scotland** 8–6
1934 Murrayfield **Scotland** 16–9
1935 Dublin **Ireland** 12–5
1936 Murrayfield **Ireland** 10–4
1937 Dublin **Ireland** 11–4
1938 Murrayfield **Scotland** 23–14
1939 Dublin **Ireland** 12–3
1947 Murrayfield **Ireland** 3–0
1948 Dublin **Ireland** 6–0
1949 Murrayfield **Ireland** 13–3
1950 Dublin **Ireland** 21–0
1951 Murrayfield **Ireland** 6–5
1952 Dublin **Ireland** 12–8

1953 Murrayfield **Ireland** 26–8
1954 Belfast **Ireland** 6–0
1955 Murrayfield **Scotland** 12–3
1956 Dublin **Ireland** 14–10
1957 Murrayfield **Ireland** 5–3
1958 Dublin **Ireland** 12–6
1959 Murrayfield **Ireland** 8–3
1960 Dublin **Scotland** 6–5
1961 Murrayfield **Scotland** 16–8
1962 Dublin **Scotland** 20–6
1963 Murrayfield **Scotland** 3–0
1964 Dublin **Scotland** 6–3
1965 Murrayfield **Ireland** 16–6
1966 Dublin **Scotland** 11–3
1967 Murrayfield **Ireland** 5–3
1968 Dublin **Ireland** 14–6
1969 Murrayfield **Ireland** 16–0
1970 Dublin **Ireland** 16–11
1971 Murrayfield **Ireland** 17–5
1972 No Match
1973 Murrayfield **Scotland** 19–14
1974 Dublin **Ireland** 9–6
1975 Murrayfield **Scotland** 20–13
1976 Dublin **Scotland** 15–6
1977 Murrayfield **Scotland** 21–18
1978 Dublin **Ireland** 12–9
1979 Murrayfield **Drawn** 11–11
1980 Dublin **Ireland** 22–15
1981 Murrayfield **Scotland** 10–9
1982 Dublin **Ireland** 21–12
1983 Murrayfield **Ireland** 15–13
1984 Dublin **Scotland** 32–9
1985 Murrayfield **Ireland** 18–15
1986 Dublin **Scotland** 10–9
1987 Murrayfield **Scotland** 16–12
1988 Dublin **Ireland** 22–18
1989 Murrayfield **Scotland** 37–21
1990 Dublin **Scotland** 13–10
1991 Murrayfield **Scotland** 28–25
1991 Murrayfield *WC* **Scotland** 24–15
1992 Dublin **Scotland** 18–10
1993 Murrayfield **Scotland** 15–3
1994 Dublin **Drawn** 6–6
1995 Murrayfield **Scotland** 26–13
1996 Dublin **Scotland** 16–10
1997 Murrayfield **Scotland** 38–10
1998 Dublin **Scotland** 17–16
1999 Murrayfield **Scotland** 30–13
2000 Dublin **Ireland** 44–22
2001 Murrayfield **Scotland** 32–10
2002 Dublin **Ireland** 43–22
2003 Murrayfield **Ireland** 36–6
2003 Murrayfield **Ireland** 29–10
2004 Dublin **Ireland** 37–16
2005 Murrayfield **Ireland** 40–13
2006 Dublin **Ireland** 15–9

SCOTLAND V WALES

Played 111 Scotland won 47, Wales won 61, Drawn 3
Highest scores Scotland 35–10 in 1924, Wales 46–22 in 2005
Biggest wins Scotland 35–10 in 1924, Wales 46–22 in 2005

1883 Raeburn Place (Edinburgh) **Scotland** 3G to 1G
1884 Newport **Scotland** 1DG 1T to 0
1885 Glasgow **Drawn** no score
1886 Cardiff **Scotland** 2G 1T to 0
1887 Raeburn Place **Scotland** 4G 8T to 0
1888 Newport **Wales** 1T to 0
1889 Raeburn Place **Scotland** 2T to 0
1890 Cardiff **Scotland** 1G 2T to 1T
1891 Raeburn Place **Scotland** 15–0
1892 Swansea **Scotland** 7–2
1893 Raeburn Place **Wales** 9–0
1894 Newport **Wales** 7–0
1895 Raeburn Place **Scotland** 5–4
1896 Cardiff **Wales** 6–0
1897 No Match
1898 No Match
1899 Inverleith (Edinburgh) **Scotland** 21–10
1900 Swansea **Wales** 12–3
1901 Inverleith **Scotland** 18–8
1902 Cardiff **Wales** 14–5
1903 Inverleith **Scotland** 6–0
1904 Swansea **Wales** 21–3
1905 Inverleith **Wales** 6–3

1906 Cardiff **Wales** 9–3
1907 Inverleith **Scotland** 6–3
1908 Swansea **Wales** 6–5
1909 Inverleith **Wales** 5–3
1910 Cardiff **Wales** 14–0
1911 Inverleith **Wales** 32–10
1912 Swansea **Wales** 21–6
1913 Inverleith **Wales** 8–0
1914 Cardiff **Wales** 24–5
1920 Inverleith **Scotland** 9–5
1921 Swansea **Scotland** 14–8
1922 Inverleith **Drawn** 9–9
1923 Cardiff **Scotland** 11–8
1924 Inverleith **Scotland** 35–10
1925 Swansea **Scotland** 24–14
1926 Murrayfield **Scotland** 8–5
1927 Cardiff **Scotland** 5–0
1928 Murrayfield **Wales** 13–0
1929 Swansea **Wales** 14–7
1930 Murrayfield **Scotland** 12–9
1931 Cardiff **Wales** 13–8
1932 Murrayfield **Wales** 6–0
1933 Swansea **Scotland** 11–3
1934 Murrayfield **Wales** 13–6
1935 Cardiff **Wales** 10–6
1936 Murrayfield **Wales** 13–3
1937 Swansea **Scotland** 13–6
1938 Murrayfield **Scotland** 8–6
1939 Cardiff **Wales** 11–3
1947 Murrayfield **Wales** 22–8
1948 Cardiff **Wales** 14–0
1949 Murrayfield **Scotland** 6–5
1950 Swansea **Wales** 12–0
1951 Murrayfield **Scotland** 19–0
1952 Cardiff **Wales** 11–0
1953 Murrayfield **Wales** 12–0
1954 Swansea **Wales** 15–3
1955 Murrayfield **Scotland** 14–8
1956 Cardiff **Wales** 9–3
1957 Murrayfield **Scotland** 9–6
1958 Cardiff **Wales** 8–3
1959 Murrayfield **Scotland** 6–5
1960 Cardiff **Wales** 8–0
1961 Murrayfield **Scotland** 3–0
1962 Cardiff **Scotland** 8–3
1963 Murrayfield **Wales** 6–0
1964 Cardiff **Wales** 11–3
1965 Murrayfield **Wales** 14–12
1966 Cardiff **Wales** 8–3
1967 Murrayfield **Scotland** 11–5
1968 Cardiff **Wales** 5–0
1969 Murrayfield **Wales** 17–3
1970 Cardiff **Wales** 18–9
1971 Murrayfield **Wales** 19–18
1972 Cardiff **Wales** 35–12
1973 Murrayfield **Scotland** 10–9
1974 Cardiff **Wales** 6–0
1975 Murrayfield **Scotland** 12–10
1976 Cardiff **Wales** 28–6
1977 Murrayfield **Wales** 18–9
1978 Cardiff **Wales** 22–14
1979 Murrayfield **Wales** 19–13
1980 Cardiff **Wales** 17–6
1981 Murrayfield **Scotland** 15–6
1982 Cardiff **Scotland** 34–18
1983 Murrayfield **Wales** 19–15
1984 Cardiff **Scotland** 15–9
1985 Murrayfield **Wales** 25–21
1986 Cardiff **Wales** 22–15
1987 Murrayfield **Scotland** 21–15
1988 Cardiff **Wales** 25–20
1989 Murrayfield **Scotland** 23–7
1990 Cardiff **Scotland** 13–9
1991 Murrayfield **Scotland** 32–12
1992 Cardiff **Wales** 15–12
1993 Murrayfield **Scotland** 20–0
1994 Cardiff **Wales** 29–6
1995 Murrayfield **Scotland** 26–13
1996 Cardiff **Scotland** 16–14
1997 Murrayfield **Wales** 34–19
1998 Wembley **Wales** 19–13
1999 Murrayfield **Scotland** 33–20
2000 Cardiff **Wales** 26–18
2001 Murrayfield **Drawn** 28–28
2002 Cardiff **Scotland** 27–22
2003 Murrayfield **Scotland** 30–22
2003 Cardiff **Wales** 23–9
2004 Cardiff **Wales** 23–10
2005 Murrayfield **Wales** 46–22
2006 Cardiff **Wales** 28–18

SCOTLAND V FRANCE

Played 79 Scotland won 34, France won 42, Drawn 3
Highest scores Scotland 36–22 in 1999, France 51–16 in 1998 and 51–9 in 2003
Biggest wins Scotland 31–3 in 1912, France 51–9 in 2003

1910 Inverleith (Edinburgh) **Scotland** 27–0	
1911 Paris **France** 16–15	
1912 Inverleith **Scotland** 31–3	
1913 Paris **Scotland** 21–3	
1914 No Match	
1920 Paris **Scotland** 5–0	
1921 Inverleith **France** 3–0	
1922 Paris **Drawn** 3–3	
1923 Inverleith **Scotland** 16–3	
1924 Paris **France** 12–10	
1925 Inverleith **Scotland** 25–4	
1926 Paris **Scotland** 20–6	
1927 Murrayfield **Scotland** 23–6	
1928 Paris **Scotland** 15–6	
1929 Murrayfield **Scotland** 6–3	
1930 Paris **France** 7–3	
1931 Murrayfield **Scotland** 6–4	
1947 Paris **France** 8–3	
1948 Murrayfield **Scotland** 9–8	
1949 Paris **Scotland** 8–0	
1950 Murrayfield **Scotland** 8–5	
1951 Paris **France** 14–12	
1952 Murrayfield **France** 13–11	
1953 Paris **France** 11–5	
1954 Murrayfield **France** 3–0	
1955 Paris **France** 15–0	
1956 Murrayfield **Scotland** 12–0	
1957 Paris **Scotland** 6–0	
1958 Murrayfield **Scotland** 11–9	
1959 Paris **France** 9–0	
1960 Murrayfield **France** 13–11	
1961 Paris **France** 11–0	
1962 Murrayfield **France** 11–3	
1963 Paris **Scotland** 11–6	
1964 Murrayfield **Scotland** 10–0	
1965 Paris **France** 16–8	
1966 Murrayfield **Drawn** 3–3	
1967 Paris **Scotland** 9–8	
1968 Murrayfield **France** 8–6	
1969 Paris **Scotland** 6–3	
1970 Murrayfield **France** 11–9	
1971 Paris **France** 13–8	
1972 Murrayfield **Scotland** 20–9	
1973 Paris **France** 16–13	
1974 Murrayfield **Scotland** 19–6	
1975 Paris **France** 10–9	
1976 Murrayfield **France** 13–6	
1977 Paris **France** 23–3	
1978 Murrayfield **France** 19–16	
1979 Paris **France** 21–17	
1980 Murrayfield **Scotland** 22–14	
1981 Paris **France** 16–9	
1982 Murrayfield **Scotland** 16–7	
1983 Paris **France** 19–15	
1984 Murrayfield **Scotland** 21–12	
1985 Paris **France** 11–3	
1986 Murrayfield **Scotland** 18–17	
1987 Paris **France** 28–22	
1987 Christchurch *WC* **Drawn** 20–20	
1988 Murrayfield **Scotland** 23–12	
1989 Paris **France** 19–3	
1990 Murrayfield **Scotland** 21–0	
1991 Paris **France** 15–9	
1992 Murrayfield **Scotland** 10–6	
1993 Paris **France** 11–3	
1994 Murrayfield **France** 20–12	
1995 Paris **Scotland** 23–21	
1995 Pretoria *WC* **France** 22–19	
1996 Murrayfield **Scotland** 19–14	
1997 Paris **France** 47–20	
1998 Murrayfield **France** 51–16	
1999 Paris **Scotland** 36–22	
2000 Murrayfield **France** 28–16	
2001 Paris **France** 16–6	
2002 Murrayfield **France** 22–10	
2003 Paris **France** 38–3	
2003 Sydney *WC* **France** 51–9	
2004 Murrayfield **France** 31–0	
2005 Paris **France** 16–9	
2006 Murrayfield **Scotland** 20–16	

SCOTLAND V NEW ZEALAND

Played 25 Scotland won 0, New Zealand won 23, Drawn 2
Highest scores Scotland 31–62 in 1996, New Zealand 69–20 in 2000
Biggest wins Scotland no win, New Zealand 69–20 in 2000

1905	Inverleith (Edinburgh) **New Zealand** 12–7
1935	Murrayfield **New Zealand** 18–8
1954	Murrayfield **New Zealand** 3–0
1964	Murrayfield **Drawn** 0–0
1967	Murrayfield **New Zealand** 14–3
1972	Murrayfield **New Zealand** 14–9
1975	Auckland **New Zealand** 24–0
1978	Murrayfield **New Zealand** 18–9
1979	Murrayfield **New Zealand** 20–6
1981	1 Dunedin **New Zealand** 11–4
	2 Auckland **New Zealand** 40–15
	New Zealand won series 2–0
1983	Murrayfield **Drawn** 25–25
1987	Christchurch *WC* **New Zealand** 30–3
1990	1 Dunedin **New Zealand** 31–16
	2 Auckland **New Zealand** 21–18
	New Zealand won series 2–0
1991	Cardiff *WC* **New Zealand** 13–6
1993	Murrayfield **New Zealand** 51–15
1995	Pretoria *WC* **New Zealand** 48–30
1996	1 Dunedin **New Zealand** 62–31
	2 Auckland **New Zealand** 36–12
	New Zealand won series 2–0
1999	Murrayfield *WC* **New Zealand** 30–18
2000	1 Dunedin **New Zealand** 69–20
	2 Auckland **New Zealand** 48–14
	New Zealand won series 2–0
2001	Murrayfield **New Zealand** 37–6
2005	Murrayfield **New Zealand** 29–10

SCOTLAND V SOUTH AFRICA

Played 18 Scotland won 4, South Africa won 14, Drawn 0
Highest scores Scotland 29–46 in 1999, South Africa 68–10 in 1997
Biggest wins Scotland 21–6 in 2002, South Africa 68–10 in 1997

1906	Glasgow **Scotland** 6–0
1912	Inverleith **South Africa** 16–0
1932	Murrayfield **South Africa** 6–3
1951	Murrayfield **South Africa** 44–0
1960	Port Elizabeth **South Africa** 18–10
1961	Murrayfield **South Africa** 12–5
1965	Murrayfield **Scotland** 8–5
1969	Murrayfield **Scotland** 6–3
1994	Murrayfield **South Africa** 34–10
1997	Murrayfield **South Africa** 68–10
1998	Murrayfield **South Africa** 35–10
1999	Murrayfield *WC* **South Africa** 46–29
2002	Murrayfield **Scotland** 21–6
2003	1 Durban **South Africa** 29–25
	2 Johannesburg **South Africa** 28–19
	South Africa won series 2–0
2004	Murrayfield **South Africa** 45–10
2006	1 Durban **South Africa** 36–16
	2 Port Elizabeth **South Africa** 29–15
	South Africa won series 2–0

SCOTLAND V AUSTRALIA

Played 24 Scotland won 7, Australia won 17, Drawn 0
Highest scores Scotland 24–15 in 1981, Australia 45–3 in 1998
Biggest wins Scotland 24–15 in 1981, Australia 45–3 in 1998

1927	Murrayfield **Scotland** 10–8
1947	Murrayfield **Australia** 16–7
1958	Murrayfield **Scotland** 12–8
1966	Murrayfield **Scotland** 11–5
1968	Murrayfield **Scotland** 9–3
1970	Sydney **Australia** 23–3
1975	Murrayfield **Scotland** 10–3
1981	Murrayfield **Scotland** 24–15
1982	1 Brisbane **Scotland** 12–7
	2 Sydney **Australia** 33–9
	Series drawn 1–1
1984	Murrayfield **Australia** 37–12
1988	Murrayfield **Australia** 32–13
1992	1 Sydney **Australia** 27–12
	2 Brisbane **Australia** 37–13
	Australia won series 2–0
1996	Murrayfield **Australia** 29–19
1997	Murrayfield **Australia** 37–8
1998	1 Sydney **Australia** 45–3
	2 Brisbane **Australia** 33–11
	Australia won series 2–0
2000	Murrayfield **Australia** 30–9
2003	Brisbane *WC* **Australia** 33–16
2004	1 Melbourne **Australia** 35–15
	2 Sydney **Australia** 34–13
	Australia won series 2–0
2004	1 Murrayfield **Australia** 31–14
	2 Glasgow **Australia** 31–17
	Australia won series 2–0

SCOTLAND V SRU PRESIDENT'S XV

Played 1 Scotland won 1
Highest scores Scotland 27–16 in 1972, SRU President's XV 16–27 in 1973
Biggest win Scotland 27–16 in 1973, SRU President's XV no win

1973	Murrayfield **Scotland** 27–16

SCOTLAND V ROMANIA

Played 10 Scotland won 8 Romania won 2, Drawn 0
Highest scores Scotland 60–19 in 1999, Romania 28–55 in 1987 & 28–22 in 1984
Biggest wins Scotland 60–19 in 1999, Romania 28–22 in 1984 & 18–12 in 1991

1981	Murrayfield **Scotland** 12–6
1984	Bucharest **Romania** 28–22
1986	Bucharest **Scotland** 33–18
1987	Dunedin *WC* **Scotland** 55–28
1989	Murrayfield **Scotland** 32–0
1991	Bucharest **Romania** 18–12
1995	Murrayfield **Scotland** 49–16
1999	Glasgow **Scotland** 60–19
2002	Murrayfield **Scotland** 37–10
2005	Bucharest **Scotland** 39–19

SCOTLAND V ZIMBABWE

Played 2 Scotland won 2
Highest scores Scotland 60–21 in 1987, Zimbabwe 21–60 in 1987
Biggest win Scotland 60–21 in 1987 & 51–12 in 1991, Zimbabwe no win

1987 Wellington *WC* **Scotland** 60–21	1991 Murrayfield *WC* **Scotland** 51–12

SCOTLAND V FIJI

Played 4 Scotland won 3, Fiji won 1
Highest scores Scotland 38–17 in 1989, Fiji 51–26 in 1998
Biggest win Scotland 38–17 in 1989, Fiji 51–26 in 1998

1989 Murrayfield **Scotland** 38–17	2002 Murrayfield **Scotland** 36–22
1998 Suva **Fiji** 51–26	2003 Sydney *WC* **Scotland** 22–20

SCOTLAND V ARGENTINA

Played 6 Scotland won 1, Argentina won 5, Drawn 0
Highest scores Scotland 49–3 in 1990, Argentina 31–22 in 1999
Biggest wins Scotland 49–3 in 1990, Argentina 31–22 in 1999 and 25–16 in 2001

1990 Murrayfield **Scotland** 49–3	1999 Murrayfield **Argentina** 31–22
1994 1 Buenos Aires **Argentina** 16–15	2001 Murrayfield **Argentina** 25–16
2 Buenos Aires **Argentina** 19–17	2005 Murrayfield **Argentina** 23–19
Argentina won series 2–0	

SCOTLAND V JAPAN

Played 3 Scotland won 3
Highest scores Scotland 100–8 in 2004, Japan 11–32 in 2003
Biggest win Scotland 100–8 in 2004, Japan no win

1991 Murrayfield *WC* **Scotland** 47–9	2004 Perth **Scotland** 100–8
2003 Townsville *WC* **Scotland** 32–11	

SCOTLAND V SAMOA

Played 6 Scotland won 5, Drawn 1
Highest scores Scotland 38–3 in 2004, Samoa 20–35 in 1999
Biggest win Scotland 38–3 in 2004, Samoa no win

1991	Murrayfield *WC* **Scotland** 28–6	2000	Murrayfield **Scotland** 31–8
1995	Murrayfield **Drawn** 15–15	2004	Wellington (NZ) **Scotland** 38–3
1999	Murrayfield *WC* **Scotland** 35–20	2005	Murrayfield **Scotland** 18–11

SCOTLAND V CANADA

Played 2 Scotland won 1, Canada won 1
Highest scores Scotland 23–26 in 2002, Canada 26–23 in 2002
Biggest win Scotland 22–6 in 1995, Canada 26–23 in 2002

1995	Murrayfield **Scotland** 22–6	2002	Vancouver **Canada** 26–23

SCOTLAND V IVORY COAST

Played 1 Scotland won 1
Highest scores Scotland 89–0 in 1995, Ivory Coast 0–89 in 1995
Biggest win Scotland 89–0 in 1995, Ivory Coast no win

1995	Rustenburg *WC* **Scotland** 89–0

SCOTLAND V TONGA

Played 2 Scotland won 2
Highest scores Scotland 43–20 in 2001, Tonga 20–43 in 2001
Biggest win Scotland 41–5 in 1995, Tonga no win

1995	Pretoria *WC* **Scotland** 41–5	2001	Murrayfield **Scotland** 43–20

SCOTLAND V ITALY

Played 11 Scotland won 8, Italy won 3
Highest scores Scotland 47–15 in 2003, Italy 34–20 in 2000
Biggest wins Scotland 47–15 in 2003, Italy 34–20 in 2000

1996	Murrayfield **Scotland** 29–22	2003	Murrayfield **Scotland** 33–25
1998	Treviso **Italy** 25–21	2003	Murrayfield **Scotland** 47–15
1999	Murrayfield **Scotland** 30–12	2004	Rome **Italy** 20–14
2000	Rome **Italy** 34–20	2005	Murrayfield **Scotland** 18–10
2001	Murrayfield **Scotland** 23–19	2006	Rome **Scotland** 13–10
2002	Rome **Scotland** 29–12		

SCOTLAND V URUGUAY

Played 1 Scotland won 1
Highest scores Scotland 43–12 in 1999, Uruguay 12–43 in 1999
Biggest win Scotland 43–12 in 1999, Uruguay no win

1999 Murrayfield *WC* **Scotland** 43–12

SCOTLAND V SPAIN

Played 1 Scotland won 1
Highest scores Scotland 48–0 in 1999, Spain 0–48 in 1999
Biggest win Scotland 48–0 in 1999, Spain no win

1999 Murrayfield *WC* **Scotland** 48–0

SCOTLAND V UNITED STATES

Played 3 Scotland won 3
Highest scores Scotland 65–23 in 2002, United States 23–65 in 2002
Biggest win Scotland 53–6 in 2000, United States no win

2000 Murrayfield **Scotland** 53–6
2002 San Francisco **Scotland** 65–23
2003 Brisbane WC **Scotland** 39–15

IRELAND V WALES

Played 111 Ireland won 44, Wales won 61, Drawn 6
Highest scores Ireland 54–10 in 2002, Wales 34–9 in 1976
Biggest wins Ireland 54–10 in 2002, Wales 29–0 in 1907

1882 Dublin **Wales** 2G 2T to 0
1883 No Match
1884 Cardiff **Wales** 1DG 2T to 0
1885 No Match
1886 No Match
1887 Birkenhead **Wales** 1DG 1T to 3T
1888 Dublin **Ireland** 1G 1DG 1T to 0
1889 Swansea **Ireland** 2T to 0
1890 Dublin **Drawn** 1G each
1891 Llanelli **Wales** 6–4
1892 Dublin **Ireland** 9–0
1893 Llanelli **Wales** 2–0
1894 Belfast **Ireland** 3–0
1895 Cardiff **Wales** 5–3
1896 Dublin **Ireland** 8–4
1897 No Match
1898 Limerick **Wales** 11–3
1899 Cardiff **Ireland** 3–0
1900 Belfast **Wales** 3–0
1901 Swansea **Wales** 10–9
1902 Dublin **Wales** 15–0
1903 Cardiff **Wales** 18–0
1904 Belfast **Ireland** 14–12
1905 Swansea **Wales** 10–3
1906 Belfast **Ireland** 11–6
1907 Cardiff **Wales** 29–0
1908 Belfast **Wales** 11–5
1909 Swansea **Wales** 18–5
1910 Dublin **Wales** 19–3
1911 Cardiff **Wales** 16–0

1912 Belfast **Ireland** 12–5
1913 Swansea **Wales** 16–13
1914 Belfast **Wales** 11–3
1920 Cardiff **Wales** 28–4
1921 Belfast **Wales** 6–0
1922 Swansea **Wales** 11–5
1923 Dublin **Ireland** 5–4
1924 Cardiff **Ireland** 13–10
1925 Belfast **Ireland** 19–3
1926 Swansea **Wales** 11–8
1927 Dublin **Ireland** 19–9
1928 Cardiff **Ireland** 13–10
1929 Belfast **Drawn** 5–5
1930 Swansea **Wales** 12–7
1931 Belfast **Wales** 15–3
1932 Cardiff **Ireland** 12–10
1933 Belfast **Ireland** 10–5
1934 Swansea **Wales** 13–0
1935 Belfast **Ireland** 9–3
1936 Cardiff **Wales** 3–0
1937 Belfast **Ireland** 5–3
1938 Swansea **Wales** 11–5
1939 Belfast **Wales** 7–0
1947 Swansea **Wales** 6–0
1948 Belfast **Ireland** 6–3
1949 Swansea **Ireland** 5–0
1950 Belfast **Wales** 6–3
1951 Cardiff **Drawn** 3–3
1952 Dublin **Wales** 14–3
1953 Swansea **Wales** 5–3
1954 Dublin **Wales** 12–9
1955 Cardiff **Wales** 21–3
1956 Dublin **Ireland** 11–3
1957 Cardiff **Wales** 6–5
1958 Dublin **Wales** 9–6
1959 Cardiff **Wales** 8–6
1960 Dublin **Wales** 10–9
1961 Cardiff **Wales** 9–0
1962 Dublin **Drawn** 3–3
1963 Cardiff **Ireland** 14–6
1964 Dublin **Wales** 15–6
1965 Cardiff **Wales** 14–8
1966 Dublin **Ireland** 9–6
1967 Cardiff **Ireland** 3–0
1968 Dublin **Ireland** 9–6
1969 Cardiff **Wales** 24–11
1970 Dublin **Ireland** 14–0
1971 Cardiff **Wales** 23–9
1972 No Match
1973 Cardiff **Wales** 16–12
1974 Dublin **Drawn** 9–9
1975 Cardiff **Wales** 32–4
1976 Dublin **Wales** 34–9
1977 Cardiff **Wales** 25–9
1978 Dublin **Wales** 20–16
1979 Cardiff **Wales** 24–21
1980 Dublin **Ireland** 21–7
1981 Cardiff **Wales** 9–8
1982 Dublin **Ireland** 20–12
1983 Cardiff **Wales** 23–9
1984 Dublin **Wales** 18–9
1985 Cardiff **Ireland** 21–9
1986 Dublin **Wales** 19–12
1987 Cardiff **Ireland** 15–11
1987 Wellington *WC* **Wales** 13–6
1988 Dublin **Wales** 12–9
1989 Cardiff **Ireland** 19–13
1990 Dublin **Ireland** 14–8
1991 Cardiff Drawn 21–21
1992 Dublin **Wales** 16–15
1993 Cardiff **Ireland** 19–14
1994 Dublin **Wales** 17–15
1995 Cardiff **Ireland** 16–12
1995 Johannesburg WC **Ireland** 24–23
1996 Dublin **Ireland** 30–17
1997 Cardiff **Ireland** 26–25
1998 Dublin **Wales** 30–21
1999 Wembley **Ireland** 29–23
2000 Dublin **Wales** 23–19
2001 Cardiff **Ireland** 36–6
2002 Dublin **Ireland** 54–10
2003 Cardiff **Ireland** 25–24
2003 Dublin **Ireland** 35–12
2004 Dublin **Ireland** 36–15
2005 Cardiff **Wales** 32–20
2006 Dublin **Ireland** 31–5

IRELAND V FRANCE

Played 81 Ireland won 28, France won 48, Drawn 5
Highest scores Ireland 31–43 in 2006, France 45–10 in 1996
Biggest wins Ireland 24–0 in 1913, France 44–5 in 2002

1909 Dublin **Ireland** 19–8
1910 Paris **Ireland** 8–3
1911 Cork **Ireland** 25–5
1912 Paris **Ireland** 11–6
1913 Cork **Ireland** 24–0
1914 Paris **Ireland** 8–6
1920 Dublin **France** 15–7
1921 Paris **France** 20–10
1922 Dublin **Ireland** 8–3
1923 Paris **France** 14–8
1924 Dublin **Ireland** 6–0
1925 Paris **Ireland** 9–3
1926 Belfast **Ireland** 11–0
1927 Paris **Ireland** 8–3
1928 Belfast **Ireland** 12–8
1929 Paris **Ireland** 6–0
1930 Belfast **France** 5–0
1931 Paris **France** 3–0
1947 Dublin **France** 12–8
1948 Paris **Ireland** 13–6
1949 Dublin **France** 16–9
1950 Paris **Drawn** 3–3
1951 Dublin **Ireland** 9–8
1952 Paris **Ireland** 11–8
1953 Belfast **Ireland** 16–3
1954 Paris **France** 8–0
1955 Dublin **France** 5–3
1956 Paris **France** 14–8
1957 Dublin **Ireland** 11–6
1958 Paris **France** 11–6
1959 Dublin **Ireland** 9–5
1960 Paris **France** 23–6
1961 Dublin **France** 15–3
1962 Paris **France** 11–0
1963 Dublin **France** 24–5
1964 Paris **France** 27–6
1965 Dublin **Drawn** 3–3
1966 Paris **France** 11–6
1967 Dublin **France** 11–6
1968 Paris **France** 16–6
1969 Dublin **Ireland** 17–9
1970 Paris **France** 8–0
1971 Dublin **Drawn** 9–9
1972 Paris **Ireland** 14–9
1972 Dublin **Ireland** 24–14
Non-championship match
1973 Dublin **Ireland** 6–4
1974 Paris **France** 9–6
1975 Dublin **Ireland** 25–6
1976 Paris **France** 26–3
1977 Dublin **France** 15–6
1978 Paris **France** 10–9
1979 Dublin **Drawn** 9–9
1980 Paris **France** 19–18
1981 Dublin **France** 19–13
1982 Paris **France** 22–9
1983 Dublin **Ireland** 22–16
1984 Paris **France** 25–12
1985 Dublin **Drawn** 15–15
1986 Paris **France** 29–9
1987 Dublin **France** 19–13
1988 Paris **France** 25–6
1989 Dublin **France** 26–21
1990 Paris **France** 31–12
1991 Dublin **France** 21–13
1992 Paris **France** 44–12
1993 Dublin **France** 21–6
1994 Paris **France** 35–15
1995 Dublin **France** 25–7
1995 Durban *WC* **France** 36–12
1996 Paris **France** 45–10
1997 Dublin **France** 32–15
1998 Paris **France** 18–16
1999 Dublin **France** 10–9
2000 Paris **Ireland** 27–25
2001 Dublin **Ireland** 22–15
2002 Paris **France** 44–5
2003 Dublin **Ireland** 15–12
2003 Melbourne WC **France** 43–21
2004 Paris **France** 35–17
2005 Dublin **France** 26–19
2006 Paris **France** 43–31

IRELAND V NEW ZEALAND

Played 20 Ireland won 0, New Zealand won 19, Drawn 1
Highest scores Ireland 29–40 in 2001, New Zealand 63–15 in 1997
Biggest win Ireland no win, New Zealand 59–6 in 1992

1905	Dublin **New Zealand** 15–0
1924	Dublin **New Zealand** 6–0
1935	Dublin **New Zealand** 17–9
1954	Dublin **New Zealand** 14–3
1963	Dublin **New Zealand** 6–5
1973	Dublin **Drawn** 10–10
1974	Dublin **New Zealand** 15–6
1976	Wellington **New Zealand** 11–3
1978	Dublin **New Zealand** 10–6
1989	Dublin **New Zealand** 23–6
1992	1 Dunedin **New Zealand** 24–21
	2 Wellington **New Zealand** 59–6
	New Zealand won series 2–0
1995	Johannesburg *WC* **New Zealand** 43–19
1997	Dublin **New Zealand** 63–15
2001	Dublin **New Zealand** 40–29
2002	1 Dunedin **New Zealand** 15–6
	2 Auckland **New Zealand** 40–8
	New Zealand won series 2–0
2005	Dublin **New Zealand** 45–7
2006	1 Hamilton **New Zealand** 34–23
	2 Auckland **New Zealand** 27–17
	New Zealand won series 2–0

IRELAND V SOUTH AFRICA

Played 17 Ireland won 2, South Africa won 14, Drawn 1
Highest scores Ireland 18–28 in 2000, South Africa 38–0 in 1912
Biggest wins Ireland 17–12 in 2004, South Africa 38–0 in 1912

1906	Belfast **South Africa** 15–12
1912	Dublin **South Africa** 38–0
1931	Dublin **South Africa** 8–3
1951	Dublin **South Africa** 17–5
1960	Dublin **South Africa** 8–3
1961	Cape Town **South Africa** 24–8
1965	Dublin **Ireland** 9–6
1970	Dublin **Drawn** 8–8
1981	1 Cape Town **South Africa** 23–15
	2 Durban **South Africa** 12–10
	South Africa won series 2–0
1998	1 Bloemfontein **South Africa** 37–13
	2 Pretoria **South Africa** 33–0
	South Africa won series 2–0
1998	Dublin **South Africa** 27–13
2000	Dublin **South Africa** 28–18
2004	1 Bloemfontein **South Africa** 31–17
	2 Cape Town **South Africa** 26–17
	South Africa won series 2–0
2004	Dublin **Ireland** 55–6

IRELAND V AUSTRALIA

Played 25 Ireland won 7, Australia won 18, Drawn 0
Highest scores Ireland 27–12 in 1979, Australia 46–10 in 1999
Biggest wins Ireland 27–12 in 1979, Australia 46–10 in 1999

1927	Dublin **Australia** 5–3
1947	Dublin **Australia** 16–3
1958	Dublin **Ireland** 9–6
1967	Dublin **Ireland** 15–8
1967	Sydney **Ireland** 11–5
1968	Dublin **Ireland** 10–3
1976	Dublin **Australia** 20–10
1979	1 Brisbane **Ireland** 27–12
	2 Sydney **Ireland** 9–3
	Ireland won series 2–0
1981	Dublin **Australia** 16–12
1984	Dublin **Australia** 16–9
1987	Sydney *WC* **Australia** 33–15
1991	Dublin *WC* **Australia** 19–18
1992	Dublin **Australia** 42–17
1994	1 Brisbane **Australia** 33–13
	2 Sydney **Australia** 32–18
	Australia won series 2–0
1996	Dublin **Australia** 22–12
1999	1 Brisbane **Australia** 46–10
	2 Perth **Australia** 32–26
	Australia won series 2–0
1999	Dublin *WC* **Australia** 23–3
2002	Dublin **Ireland** 18–9
2003	Perth **Australia** 45–16
2003	Melbourne *WC* **Australia** 17–16
2005	Dublin **Australia** 30–14
2006	Perth **Australia** 37–15

IRELAND V NEW ZEALAND NATIVES

Played 1 New Zealand Natives won 1
Highest scores Ireland 4–13 in 1888, Zew Zealand Natives 13–4 in 1888
Biggest win Ireland no win, New Zealand Natives 13–4 in 1888

1888	Dublin **New Zealand** Natives 4G 1T to 1G 1T

IRELAND V IRU PRESIDENT'S XV

Played 1 Drawn 1
Highest scores Ireland 18–18 in 1974, IRFU President's XV 18–18 in 1974

1974	Dublin **Drawn** 18–18

IRELAND V ROMANIA

Played 8 Ireland won 8
Highest scores Ireland 60–0 in 1986, Romania 35–53 in 1998
Biggest win Ireland 60–0 in 1986, Romania no win

1986	Dublin **Ireland** 60–0	2001	Bucharest **Ireland** 37–3
1993	Dublin **Ireland** 25–3	2002	Limerick **Ireland** 39–8
1998	Dublin **Ireland** 53–35	2003	Gosford *WC* **Ireland** 45–17
1999	Dublin *WC* **Ireland** 44–14	2005	Dublin **Ireland** 43–12

IRELAND V CANADA

Played 3 Ireland won 2 Drawn 1
Highest scores Ireland 46–19 in 1987, Canada 27–27 in 2000
Biggest win Ireland 46–19 in 1987, Canada no win

1987	Dunedin *WC* **Ireland** 46–19	2000	Markham **Drawn** 27–27
1997	Dublin **Ireland** 33–11		

IRELAND V TONGA

Played 2 Ireland won 2
Highest scores Ireland 40–19 in 2003, Tonga 19–40 in 2003
Biggest win Ireland 32–9 in 1987, Tonga no win

1987	Brisbane *WC* **Ireland** 32–9	2003	Nuku'alofa **Ireland** 40–19

IRELAND V SAMOA

Played 4 Ireland won 3, Samoa won 1, Drawn 0
Highest scores Ireland 49–22 in 1988, Samoa 40–25 in 1996
Biggest wins Ireland 49–22 in 1988 and 35–8 in 2001, Samoa 40–25 in 1996

1988	Dublin **Ireland** 49–22	2001	Dublin **Ireland** 35–8
1996	Dublin **Samoa** 40–25	2003	Apia **Ireland** 40–14

IRELAND V ITALY

Played 13 Ireland won 10, Italy won 3, Drawn 0
Highest scores Ireland 61–6 in 2003, Italy 37–29 in 1997 & 37–22 in 1997
Biggest wins Ireland 61–6 in 2003, Italy 37–22 in 1997

1988	Dublin **Ireland** 31–15	2002	Dublin **Ireland** 32–17
1995	Treviso **Italy** 22–12	2003	Rome **Ireland** 37–13
1997	Dublin **Italy** 37–29	2003	Limerick **Ireland** 61–6
1997	Bologna **Italy** 37–22	2004	Dublin **Ireland** 19–3
1999	Dublin **Ireland** 39–30	2005	Rome **Ireland** 28–17
2000	Dublin **Ireland** 60–13	2006	Dublin **Ireland** 26–16
2001	Rome **Ireland** 41–22		

IRELAND V ARGENTINA

Played 7 Ireland won 5 Argentina won 2
Highest scores Ireland 32–24 in 1999, Argentina 34–23 in 2000
Biggest win Ireland 32–24 in 1999, Argentina 34–23 in 2000

1990	Dublin **Ireland** 20–18	2002	Dublin **Ireland** 16–7
1999	Dublin **Ireland** 32–24	2003	Adelaide *WC* **Ireland** 16–15
1999	Lens *WC* **Argentina** 28–24	2004	Dublin **Ireland** 21–19
2000	Buenos Aires **Argentina** 34–23		

IRELAND V NAMIBIA

Played 3 Ireland won 1, Namibia won 2
Highest scores Ireland 64–7 in 2003, Namibia 26–15 in 1991
Biggest win Ireland 64–7 in 2003, Namibia 26–15 in 1991

1991	1 Windhoek **Namibia** 15–6		Namibia won series 2–0
	2 Windhoek **Namibia** 26–15	2003	Sydney *WC* **Ireland** 64–7

IRELAND V ZIMBABWE

Played 1 Ireland won 1
Highest scores Ireland 55–11 in 1991, Zimbabwe 11–55 in 1991
Biggest win Ireland 55–11 in 1991, Zimbabwe no win

1991	Dublin *WC* **Ireland** 55–11

IRELAND V JAPAN

Played 5 Ireland won 5
Highest scores Ireland 78–9 in 2000, Japan 28–50 in 1995
Biggest win Ireland 78–9 in 2000, Japan no win

1991	Dublin *WC* **Ireland** 32–16	2005	1 Osaka **Ireland** 44–12
1995	Bloemfontein *WC* **Ireland** 50–28		2 Tokyo **Ireland** 47–18
2000	Dublin **Ireland** 78–9		Ireland won series 2–0

IRELAND V UNITED STATES

Played 5 Ireland won 5
Highest scores Ireland 83–3 in 2000, United States 18–25 in 1996
Biggest win Ireland 83–3 in 2000, United States no win

1994	Dublin **Ireland** 26–15	2000	Manchester (NH) **Ireland** 83–3
1996	Atlanta **Ireland** 25–18	2004	Dublin **Ireland** 55–6
1999	Dublin *WC* **Ireland** 53–8		

IRELAND V FIJI

Played 2 Ireland won 2
Highest scores Ireland 64–17 in 2002, Fiji 17–64 in 2002
Biggest win Ireland 64–17 in 2002, Fiji no win

1995	Dublin **Ireland** 44–8	2002	Dublin **Ireland** 64–17

IRELAND V GEORGIA

Played 2 Ireland won 2
Highest scores Ireland 70–0 in 1998, Georgia 14–63 in 2002
Biggest win Ireland 70–0 in 1998, Georgia no win

1998	Dublin **Ireland** 70–0	2002	Dublin **Ireland** 63–14

IRELAND V RUSSIA

Played 1 Ireland won 1
Highest scores Ireland 35–3 in 2002, Russia 3–35 in 2002
Biggest win Ireland 35–3 in 2002, Russia no win

2002	Krasnoyarsk **Ireland** 35–3

WALES V FRANCE

Played 82 Wales won 42, France won 37, Drawn 3
Highest scores Wales 49–14 in 1910, France 51–0 in 1998
Biggest wins Wales 47–5 in 1909, France 51–0 in 1998

1908 Cardiff **Wales** 36–4
1909 Paris **Wales** 47–5
1910 Swansea **Wales** 49–14
1911 Paris **Wales** 15–0
1912 Newport **Wales** 14–8
1913 Paris **Wales** 11–8
1914 Swansea **Wales** 31–0
1920 Paris **Wales** 6–5
1921 Cardiff **Wales** 12–4
1922 Paris **Wales** 11–3
1923 Swansea **Wales** 16–8
1924 Paris **Wales** 10–6
1925 Cardiff **Wales** 11–5
1926 Paris **Wales** 7–5
1927 Swansea **Wales** 25–7
1928 Paris **France** 8–3
1929 Cardiff **Wales** 8–3
1930 Paris **Wales** 11–0
1931 Swansea **Wales** 35–3
1947 Paris **Wales** 3–0
1948 Swansea **France** 11–3
1949 Paris **France** 5–3
1950 Cardiff **Wales** 21–0
1951 Paris **France** 8–3
1952 Swansea **Wales** 9–5
1953 Paris **Wales** 6–3
1954 Cardiff **Wales** 19–13
1955 Paris **Wales** 16–11
1956 Cardiff **Wales** 5–3
1957 Paris **Wales** 19–13
1958 Cardiff **France** 16–6
1959 Paris **France** 11–3
1960 Cardiff **France** 16–8
1961 Paris **France** 8–6
1962 Cardiff **Wales** 3–0
1963 Paris **France** 5–3
1964 Cardiff Drawn 11–11
1965 Paris **France** 22–13
1966 Cardiff **Wales** 9–8
1967 Paris **France** 20–14
1968 Cardiff **France** 14–9
1969 Paris Drawn 8–8
1970 Cardiff **Wales** 11–6
1971 Paris **Wales** 9–5
1972 Cardiff **Wales** 20–6
1973 Paris **France** 12–3
1974 Cardiff **Drawn** 16–16
1975 Paris **Wales** 25–10
1976 Cardiff **Wales** 19–13
1977 Paris **France** 16–9
1978 Cardiff **Wales** 16–7
1979 Paris **France** 14–13
1980 Cardiff **Wales** 18–9
1981 Paris **France** 19–15
1982 Cardiff **Wales** 22–12
1983 Paris **France** 16–9
1984 Cardiff **France** 21–16
1985 Paris **France** 14–3
1986 Cardiff **France** 23–15
1987 Paris **France** 16–9
1988 Cardiff **France** 10–9
1989 Paris **France** 31–12
1990 Cardiff **France** 29–19
1991 Paris **France** 36–3
1991 Cardiff **France** 22–9
Non-championship match
1992 Cardiff **France** 12–9
1993 Paris **France** 26–10
1994 Cardiff **Wales** 24–15
1995 Paris **France** 21–9
1996 Cardiff **Wales** 16–15
1996 Cardiff **France** 40–33
Non-championship match
1997 Paris **France** 27–22
1998 Wembley **France** 51–0
1999 Paris **Wales** 34–33
1999 Cardiff **Wales** 34–23
Non-championship match
2000 Cardiff **France** 36–3
2001 Paris **Wales** 43–35
2002 Cardiff **France** 37–33
2003 Paris **France** 33–5
2004 Cardiff **France** 29–22
2005 Paris **Wales** 24–18
2006 Cardiff **France** 21–16

WALES V NEW ZEALAND

Played 22 Wales won 3, New Zealand won 19, Drawn 0
Highest scores Wales 37–53 in 2003, New Zealand 55–3 in 2003
Biggest wins Wales 13–8 in 1953, New Zealand 55–3 in 2003

1905	Cardiff **Wales** 3–0
1924	Swansea **New Zealand** 19–0
1935	Cardiff **Wales** 13–12
1953	Cardiff **Wales** 13–8
1963	Cardiff **New Zealand** 6–0
1967	Cardiff **New Zealand** 13–6
1969	1 Christchurch **New Zealand** 19–0
	2 Auckland **New Zealand** 33–12
	New Zealand won series 2–0
1972	Cardiff **New Zealand** 19–16
1978	Cardiff **New Zealand** 13–12
1980	Cardiff **New Zealand** 23–3
1987	Brisbane WC **New Zealand** 49–6
1988	1 Christchurch **New Zealand** 52–3
	2 Auckland **New Zealand** 54–9
	New Zealand won series 2–0
1989	Cardiff **New Zealand** 34–9
1995	Johannesburg *WC* **New Zealand** 34–9
1997	Wembley **New Zealand** 42–7
2002	Cardiff **New Zealand** 43–17
2003	Hamilton **New Zealand** 55–3
2003	Sydney *WC* **New Zealand** 53–37
2004	Cardiff **New Zealand** 26–25
2005	Cardiff **New Zealand** 41–3

WALES V SOUTH AFRICA

Played 19 Wales won 1, South Africa won 17, Drawn 1
Highest scores Wales 36–38 in 2004, South Africa 96–13 in 1998
Biggest win Wales 29–19 in 1999, South Africa 96–13 in 1998

1906	Swansea **South Africa** 11–0
1912	Cardiff **South Africa** 3–0
1931	Swansea **South Africa** 8–3
1951	Cardiff **South Africa** 6–3
1960	Cardiff **South Africa** 3–0
1964	Durban **South Africa** 24–3
1970	Cardiff **Drawn** 6–6
1994	Cardiff **South Africa** 20–12
1995	Johannesburg **South Africa** 40–11
1996	Cardiff **South Africa** 37–20
1998	Pretoria **South Africa** 96–13
1998	Wembley **South Africa** 28–20
1999	Cardiff **Wales** 29–19
2000	Cardiff **South Africa** 23–13
2002	1 Bloemfontein **South Africa** 34–19
	2 Cape Town **South Africa** 19–8
	South Africa won series 2–0
2004	Pretoria **South Africa** 53–18
2004	Cardiff **South Africa** 38–36
2005	Cardiff **South Africa** 33–16

WALES V AUSTRALIA

Played 23 Wales won 9, Australia won 14, Drawn 0
Highest scores Wales 28–3 in 1975, Australia 63–6 in 1991
Biggest wins Wales 28–3 in 1975, Australia 63–6 in 1991

1908 Cardiff **Wales** 9–6
1927 Cardiff **Australia** 18–8
1947 Cardiff **Wales** 6–0
1958 Cardiff **Wales** 9–3
1966 Cardiff **Australia** 14–11
1969 Sydney **Wales** 19–16
1973 Cardiff **Wales** 24–0
1975 Cardiff **Wales** 28–3
1978 1 Brisbane **Australia** 18–8
2 Sydney **Australia** 19–17
Australia won series 2–0
1981 Cardiff **Wales** 18–13
1984 Cardiff **Australia** 28–9
1987 Rotorua *WC* **Wales** 22–21
1991 Brisbane **Australia** 63–6
1991 Cardiff *WC* **Australia** 38–3
1992 Cardiff **Australia** 23–6
1996 1 Brisbane **Australia** 56–25
2 Sydney **Australia** 42–3
Australia won series 2–0
1996 Cardiff **Australia** 28–19
1999 Cardiff *WC* **Australia** 24–9
2001 Cardiff **Australia** 21–13
2003 Sydney **Australia** 30–10
2005 Cardiff **Wales** 24–22

WALES V NEW ZEALAND NATIVES

Played 1 Wales won 1
Highest scores Wales 5–0 in 1888, New Zealand Natives 0–5 in 1888
Biggest win Wales 5–0 in 1888, New Zealand Natives no win

1888 Swansea **Wales** 1G 2T to 0

WALES V NEW ZEALAND ARMY

Played 1 New Zealand Army won 1
Highest scores Wales 3–6 in 1919, New Zealand Army 6–3 in 1919
Biggest win Wales no win, New Zealand Army 6–3 in 1919

1919 Swansea **New Zealand** Army 6–3

WALES V ROMANIA

Played 8 Wales won 6, Romania won 2
Highest scores Wales 81–9 in 2001, Romania 24–6 in 1983
Biggest wins Wales 81–9 in 2001, Romania 24–6 in 1983

1983 Bucharest **Romania** 24–6
1988 Cardiff **Romania** 15–9
1994 Bucharest **Wales** 16–9
1997 Wrexham **Wales** 70–21
2001 Cardiff **Wales** 81–9
2002 Wrexham **Wales** 40–3
2003 Wrexham **Wales** 54–8
2004 Cardiff **Wales** 66–7

WALES V FIJI

Played 6 Wales won 6
Highest scores Wales 58–14 in 2002, Fiji 15–22 in 1986 & 15–19 in 1995
Biggest win Wales 58–14 in 2002, Fiji no win

1985	Cardiff **Wales** 40–3	1995	Cardiff **Wales** 19–15
1986	Suva **Wales** 22–15	2002	Cardiff **Wales** 58–14
1994	Suva **Wales** 23–8	2005	Cardiff **Wales** 11–10

WALES V TONGA

Played 6 Wales won 6
Highest scores Wales 51–7 in 2001, Tonga 20–27 in 2003
Biggest win Wales 51–7 in 2001, Tonga no win

1986	Nuku'Alofa **Wales** 15–7	1997	Swansea **Wales** 46–12
1987	Palmerston North *WC* **Wales** 29–16	2001	Cardiff **Wales** 51–7
1994	Nuku'Alofa **Wales** 18–9	2003	Canberra *WC* **Wales** 27–20

WALES V SAMOA

Played 6 Wales won 3, Samoa won 3, Drawn 0
Highest scores Wales 50–6 in 2000, Samoa 38–31 in 1999
Biggest wins Wales 50–6 in 2000, Samoa 34–9 in 1994

1986	Apia **Wales** 32–14	1994	Moamoa **Samoa** 34–9
1988	Cardiff **Wales** 28–6	1999	Cardiff *WC* **Samoa** 38–31
1991	Cardiff *WC* **Samoa** 16–13	2000	Cardiff **Wales** 50–6

WALES V CANADA

Played 8 Wales won 7, Canada won 1, Drawn 0
Highest scores Wales 60–3 in 2005, Canada 26–24 in 1993
Biggest wins Wales 60–3 in 2005, Canada 26–24 in 1993

1987	Invercargill *WC* **Wales** 40–9	1999	Cardiff **Wales** 33–19
1993	Cardiff **Canada** 26–24	2002	Cardiff **Wales** 32–21
1994	Toronto **Wales** 33–15	2003	Melbourne *WC* **Wales** 41–10
1997	Toronto **Wales** 28–25	2005	Toronto **Wales** 60–3

WALES V UNITED STATES

Played 6 Wales won 6
Highest scores Wales 77–3 in 2005, United States 23–28 in 1997
Biggest win Wales 77–3 in 2005, United States no win

1987	Cardiff **Wales** 46–0
1997	Cardiff **Wales** 34–14
1997	1 Wilmington **Wales** 30–20
	2 San Francisco **Wales** 28–23
	Wales won series 2–0
2000	Cardiff **Wales** 42–11
2005	Hartford **Wales** 77–3

WALES V NAMIBIA

Played 3 Wales won 3
Highest scores Wales 38–23 in 1993, Namibia 30–34 in 1990
Biggest win Wales 38–23 in 1993, Namibia no win

1990	1 Windhoek **Wales** 18–9
	2 Windhoek **Wales** 34–30
	Wales won series 2–0
1993	Windhoek **Wales** 38–23

WALES V BARBARIANS

Played 2 Wales won 1, Barbarians won 1
Highest scores Wales 31–10 in 1996, Barbarians 31–24 in 1990
Biggest wins Wales 31–10 in 1996, Barbarians 31–24 in 1990

1990	Cardiff Barbarians 31–24
1996	Cardiff **Wales** 31–10

WALES V ARGENTINA

Played 10 Wales won 6, Argentina won 4
Highest scores Wales 44–50 in 2004, Argentina 50–44 in 2004
Biggest win Wales 35–20 in 2004, Argentina 45–27 in 2006

1991	Cardiff WC **Wales** 16–7
1998	Llanelli **Wales** 43–30
1999	1 Buenos Aires **Wales** 36–26
	2 Buenos Aires **Wales** 23–16
	Wales won series 2–0
1999	Cardiff *WC* **Wales** 23–18
2001	Cardiff **Argentina** 30–16
2004	1 Tucumán **Argentina** 50–44
	2 Buenos Aires **Wales** 35–20
	Series drawn 1–1
2006	1 Puerto Madryn **Argentina** 27–25
	2 Buenos Aires **Argentina** 45–27
	Argentina won series 2–0

WALES V ZIMBABWE

Played 3 Wales won 3
Highest scores Wales 49–11 in 1998, Zimbabwe 14–35 in 1993
Biggest win Wales 49–11 in 1998, Zimbabwe no win

1993 1 Bulawayo **Wales** 35–14
2 Harare **Wales** 42–13
Wales won series 2–0
1998 Harare **Wales** 49–11

WALES V JAPAN

Played 6 Wales won 6
Highest scores Wales 98–0 in 2004, Japan 30–53 in 2001
Biggest win Wales 98–0 in 2004, Japan no win

1993 Cardiff **Wales** 55–5
1995 Bloemfontein *WC* e/**Wales** 57–10
1999 Cardiff *WC* **Wales** 64–15
2001 1 Osaka **Wales** 64–10
2 Tokyo **Wales** 53–30
Wales won series 2–0
2004 Cardiff **Wales** 98–0

WALES V PORTUGAL

Played 1 Wales won 1
Highest scores Wales 102–11 in 1994, Portugal 11–102 in 1994
Biggest win Wales 102–11 in 1994, Portugal no win

1994 Lisbon **Wales** 102–11

WALES V SPAIN

Played 1 Wales won 1
Highest scores Wales 54–0 in 1994, Spain 0–54 in 1994
Bigegst win Wales 54–0 in 1994, Spain no win

1994 Madrid **Wales** 54–0

WALES V ITALY

Played 13 Wales won 11, Italy won 1, Drawn 1
Highest scores Wales 60–21 in 1999, Italy 30–22 in 2003
Biggest win Wales 60–21 in 1999, Italy 30–22 in 2003

1994 Cardiff **Wales** 29–19
1996 Cardiff **Wales** 31–26
1996 Rome **Wales** 31–22
1998 Llanelli **Wales** 23–20
1999 Treviso **Wales** 60–21
2000 Cardiff **Wales** 47–16
2001 Rome **Wales** 33–23
2002 Cardiff **Wales** 44–20
2003 Rome **Italy** 30–22
2003 Canberra *WC* **Wales** 27–15
2004 Cardiff **Wales** 44–10
2005 Rome **Wales** 38–8
2006 Cardiff **Drawn** 18–18

BRITISH/IRISH ISLES V SOUTH AFRICA

Played 43 British/Irish won 16, South Africa won 21, Drawn 6
Highest scores: British/Irish 28–9 in 1974, South Africa 35–16 in 1997
Biggest wins: British/Irish 28–9 in 1974, South Africa 34–14 in 1962

1891 1 Port Elizabeth **British/Irish** 4–0
2 Kimberley **British/Irish** 3–0
3 Cape Town **British/Irish** 4–0
British/Irish won series 3–0

1896 1 Port Elizabeth **British/Irish** 8–0
2 Johannesburg **British/Irish** 17–8
3 Kimberley **British/Irish** 9–3
4 Cape Town **South Africa** 5–0
British/Irish won series 3–1

1903 1 Johannesburg **Drawn** 10–10
2 Kimberley **Drawn** 0–0
3 Cape Town **South Africa** 8–0
South Africa won series 1–0 with two drawn

1910 1 Johannesburg South Africa 14–10
2 Port Elizabeth **British/Irish** 8–3
3 Cape Town **South Africa** 21–5
South Africa won series 2–1

1924 1 Durban **South Africa** 7–3
2 Johannesburg **South Africa** 17–0
3 Port Elizabeth **Drawn** 3–3
4 Cape Town **South Africa** 16–9
South Africa won series 3–0, with 1 draw

1938 1 Johannesburg **South Africa** 26–12
2 Port Elizabeth **South Africa** 19–3
3 Cape Town **British/Irish** 21–16
South Africa won series 2–1

1955 1 Johannesburg **British/Irish** 23–22
2 Cape Town **South Africa** 25–9
3 Pretoria **British/Irish** 9–6
4 Port Elizabeth **South Africa** 22–8
Series drawn 2–2

1962 1 Johannesburg **Drawn** 3–3
2 Durban **South Africa** 3–0
3 Cape Town **South Africa** 8–3
4 Bloemfontein **South Africa** 34–14
South Africa won series 3–0, with 1 draw

1968 1 Pretoria **South Africa** 25–20
2 Port Elizabeth **Drawn** 6–6
3 Cape Town **South Africa** 11–6
4 Johannesburg **South Africa** 19–6
South Africa won series 3–0, with 1 draw

1974 1 Cape Town **British/Irish** 12–3
2 Pretoria **British/Irish** 28–9
3 Port Elizabeth **British/Irish** 26–9
4 Johannesburg **Drawn** 13–13
British/Irish won series 3–0, with 1 draw

1980 1 Cape Town **South Africa** 26–22
2 Bloemfontein **South Africa** 26–19
3 Port Elizabeth **South Africa** 12–10
4 Pretoria **British/Irish** 17–13
South Africa won series 3–1

1997 1 Cape Town **British/Irish** 25–16
2 Durban **British/Irish** 18–15
3 Johannesburg **South Africa** 35–16
British/Irish won series 2–1

BRITISH/IRISH ISLES V NEW ZEALAND

Played 35 British/Irish won 6, New Zealand won 27, Drawn 2
Highest scores: British/Irish 20–7 in 1993, New Zealand 48–18 in 2005
Biggest wins: British/Irish 20–7 in 1993, New Zealand 38–6 in 1983

1904 Wellington **New Zealand** 9–3
1930 1 Dunedin **British/Irish** 6–3
2 Christchurch **New Zealand** 13–10
3 Auckland **New Zealand** 15–10
4 Wellington **New Zealand** 22–8
New Zealand won series 3–1
1950 1 Dunedin **Drawn** 9–9
2 Christchurch **New Zealand** 8–0
3 Wellington **New Zealand** 6–3
4 Auckland **New Zealand** 11–8
New Zealand won series 3–0, with 1 draw
1959 1 Dunedin **New Zealand** 18–17
2 Wellington **New Zealand** 11–8
3 Christchurch **New Zealand** 22–8
4 Auckland **British/Irish** 9–6
New Zealand won series 3–1
1966 1 Dunedin **New Zealand** 20–3
2 Wellington **New Zealand** 16–12
3 Christchurch **New Zealand** 19–6
4 Auckland **New Zealand** 24–11
New Zealand won series 4–0
1971 1 Dunedin **British/Irish** 9–3
2 Christchurch **New Zealand** 22–12
3 Wellington **British/Irish** 13–3
4 Auckland **Drawn** 14–14
British/Irish won series 2–1, with 1 draw
1977 1 Wellington **New Zealand** 16–12
2 Christchurch **British/Irish** 13–9
3 Dunedin **New Zealand** 19–7
4 Auckland **New Zealand** 10–9
New Zealand won series 3–1
1983 1 Christchurch **New Zealand** 16–12
2 Wellington **New Zealand** 9–0
3 Dunedin **New Zealand** 15–8
4 Auckland **New Zealand** 38–6
New Zealand won series 4–0
1993 1 Christchurch **New Zealand** 20–18
2 Wellington **British/Irish** 20–7
3 Auckland **New Zealand** 30–13
New Zealand won series 2–1
2005 1 Christchurch **New Zealand** 21–3
2 Wellington **New Zealand** 48–18
3 Auckland **New Zealand** 38–19
New Zealand won series 3–0

ANGLO-WELSH V NEW ZEALAND

Played 3 New Zealand won 2, Drawn 1
Highest scores Anglo Welsh 5–32 in 1908, New Zealand 32–5 in 1908
Biggest win Anglo Welsh no win, New Zealand 29–0 in 1908

1908 1 Dunedin **New Zealand** 32–5
2 Wellington **Drawn** 3–3
3 Auckland **New Zealand** 29–0
New Zealand won series 2–0 with one drawn

BRITISH/IRISH ISLES V AUSTRALIA

Played 20 British/Irish won 15, Australia won 5, Drawn 0
Highest scores: British/Irish 31–0 in 1966, Australia 35–14 in 2001
Biggest wins: British/Irish 31–0 in 1966, Australia 35–14 in 2001

1899 1 Sydney **Australia** 13–3
2 Brisbane **British/Irish** 11–0
3 Sydney **British/Irish** 11–10
4 Sydney **British/Irish** 13–0
British/Irish won series 3–1
1904 1 Sydney **British/Irish** 17–0
2 Brisbane **British/Irish** 17–3
3 Sydney **British/Irish** 16–0
British/Irish won series 3–0
1930 Sydney **Australia** 6–5
1950 1 Brisbane **British/Irish** 19–6
2 Sydney **British/Irish** 24–3
British/Irish won series 2–0
1959 1 Brisbane **British/Irish** 17–6
2 Sydney **British/Irish** 24–3
British/Irish won series 2–0
1966 1 Sydney **British/Irish** 11–8
2 Brisbane **British/Irish** 31–0
British/Irish won series 2–0
1989 1 Sydney **Australia** 30–12
2 Brisbane **British/Irish** 19–12
3 Sydney **British/Irish** 19–18
British/Irish won series 2–1
2001 1 Brisbane **British/Irish** 29–13
2 Melbourne **Australia** 35–14
3 Sydney **Australia** 29–23
Australia won series 2–1

FRANCE V NEW ZEALAND

Played 41 France won 10, New Zealand won 30, Drawn 1
Highest scores France 43–31 in 1999, New Zealand 54–7 in 1999
Biggest wins France 22–8 in 1994, New Zealand 54–7 in 1999

1906 Paris **New Zealand** 38–8
1925 Toulouse **New Zealand** 30–6
1954 Paris **France** 3–0
1961 1 Auckland **New Zealand** 13–6
2 Wellington **New Zealand** 5–3
3 Christchurch **New Zealand** 32–3
New Zealand won series 3–0
1964 Paris **New Zealand** 12–3
1967 Paris **New Zealand** 21–15
1968 1 Christchurch **New Zealand** 12–9
2 Wellington **New Zealand** 9–3
3 Auckland **New Zealand** 19–12
New Zealand won series 3–0
1973 Paris **France** 13–6
1977 1 Toulouse **France** 18–13
2 Paris **New Zealand** 15–3
Series drawn 1–1
1979 1 Christchurch **New Zealand** 23–9
2 Auckland **France** 24–19
Series drawn 1–1
1981 1 Toulouse **New Zealand** 13–9
2 Paris **New Zealand** 18–6
New Zealand won series 2–0
1984 1 Christchurch **New Zealand** 10–9
2 Auckland **New Zealand** 31–18
New Zealand won series 2–0
1986 Christchurch **New Zealand** 18–9
1986 1 Toulouse **New Zealand** 19–7
2 Nantes **France** 16–3
Series drawn 1–1
1987 Auckland WC **New Zealand** 29–9
1989 1 Christchurch **New Zealand** 25–17
2 Auckland **New Zealand** 34–20
New Zealand won series 2–0
1990 1 Nantes **New Zealand** 24–3
2 Paris **New Zealand** 30–12
New Zealand won series 2–0
1994 1 Christchurch **France** 22–8
2 Auckland **France** 23–20
France won series 2–0

1995	1 Toulouse **France** 22–15
	2 Paris **New Zealand** 37–12
	Series drawn 1–1
1999	Wellington **New Zealand** 54–7
1999	Twickenham WC **France** 43–31
2000	1 Paris **New Zealand** 39–26
	2 Marseilles **France** 42–33
	Series drawn 1–1
2001	Wellington **New Zealand** 37–12
2002	Paris **Drawn** 20–20
2003	Christchurch **New Zealand** 31–23
2003	Sydney WC **New Zealand** 40–13
2004	Paris **New Zealand** 45–6

FRANCE V SOUTH AFRICA

Played 36 France won 10, South Africa won 20, Drawn 6
Highest scores France 36–26 in 2006, South Africa 52–10 in 1997
Biggest wins France 30–10 in 2002, South Africa 52–10 in 1997

1913	Bordeaux **South Africa** 38–5
1952	Paris **South Africa** 25–3
1958	1 Cape Town **Drawn** 3–3
	2 Johannesburg **France** 9–5
	France won series 1–0, with 1 draw
1961	Paris **Drawn** 0–0
1964	Springs (SA) **France** 8–6
1967	1 Durban **South Africa** 26–3
	2 Bloemfontein **South Africa** 16–3
	3 Johannesburg **France** 19–14
	4 Cape Town **Drawn** 6–6
	South Africa won series 2–1, with 1 draw
1968	1 Bordeaux **South Africa** 12–9
	2 Paris **South Africa** 16–11
	South Africa won series 2–0
1971	1 Bloemfontein **South Africa** 22–9
	2 Durban **Drawn** 8–8
	South Africa won series 1–0, with 1 draw
1974	1 Toulouse **South Africa** 13–4
	2 Paris **South Africa** 10–8
	South Africa won series 2–0
1975	1 Bloemfontein **South Africa** 38–25
	2 Pretoria **South Africa** 33–18
	South Africa won series 2–0
1980	Pretoria **South Africa** 37–15
1992	1 Lyons **South Africa** 20–15
	2 Paris **France** 29–16
	Series drawn 1–1
1993	1 Durban **Drawn** 20–20
	2 Johannesburg **France** 18–17
	France won series 1–0, with 1 draw
1995	Durban WC **South Africa** 19–15
1996	1 Bordeaux **South Africa** 22–12
	2 Paris **South Africa** 13–12
	South Africa won series 2–0
1997	1 Lyons **South Africa** 36–32
	2 Paris **South Africa** 52–10
	South Africa won series 2–0
2001	1 Johannesburg **France** 32–23
	2 Durban **South Africa** 20–15
	Series drawn 1–1
2001	Paris **France** 20–10
2002	Marseilles **France** 30–10
2005	1 Durban **Drawn** 30–30
	2 Port Elizabeth **South Africa** 27–13
	South Africa won series 1–0, with 1 draw
2005	Paris **France** 26–20
2006	Cape Town **France** 36–26

FRANCE V AUSTRALIA

Played 36 France won 16, Australia won 18, Drawn 2
Highest scores France 34–6 in 1976, Australia 48–31 in 1990
Biggest wins France 34–6 in 1976, Australia 35–12 in 1999

1928	Paris **Australia** 11–8
1948	Paris **France** 13–6
1958	Paris **France** 19–0
1961	Sydney **France** 15–8
1967	Paris **France** 20–14
1968	Sydney **Australia** 11–10
1971	1 Toulouse **Australia** 13–11
	2 Paris **France** 18–9
	Series drawn 1–1
1972	1 Sydney Drawn 14–14
	2 Brisbane **France** 16–15
	France won series 1–0, with 1 draw
1976	1 Bordeaux **France** 18–15
	2 Paris **France** 34–6
	France won series 2–0
1981	1 Brisbane **Australia** 17–15
	2 Sydney **Australia** 24–14
	Australia won series 2–0
1983	1 Clermont-Ferrand Drawn 15–15
	2 Paris **France** 15–6
	France won series 1–0, with 1 draw
1986	Sydney **Australia** 27–14
1987	Sydney WC **France** 30–24
1989	1 Strasbourg **Australia** 32–15
	2 Lille France 25–19
	Series drawn 1–1
1990	1 Sydney **Australia** 21–9
	2 Brisbane **Australia** 48–31
	3 Sydney **France** 28–19
	Australia won series 2–1
1993	1 Bordeaux **France** 16–13
	2 Paris **Australia** 24–3
	Series drawn 1–1
1997	1 Sydney **Australia** 29–15
	2 Brisbane **Australia** 26–19
	Australia won series 2–0
1998	Paris **Australia** 32–21
1999	Cardiff WC **Australia** 35–12
2000	Paris **Australia** 18–13
2001	Marseilles **France** 14–13
2002	1 Melbourne **Australia** 29–17
	2 Sydney **Australia** 31–25
	Australia won series 2–0
2004	Paris **France** 27–14
2005	Brisbane **Australia** 37–31
2005	Marseilles **France** 26–16

FRANCE V UNITED STATES

Played 7 France won 6, United States won 1, Drawn 0
Highest scores France 41–9 in 1991 and 41–14 in 2003, United States 31–39 in 2004
Biggest wins France 41–9 in 1991, United States 17–3 in 1924

1920	Paris **France** 14–5
1924	Paris **United States** 17–3
1976	Chicago **France 33**–14
1991	1 Denver **France** 41–9
	2 Colorado Springs **France** 10–3*
	*Abandoned after 43 mins
	France won series 2–0
2003	Wollongong WC **France** 41–14
2004	Hartford **France** 39–31

FRANCE V ROMANIA

Played 49 France won 39, Romania won 8, Drawn 2
Highest scores France 67–20 in 2000, Romania 21–33 in 1991
Biggest wins France 59–3 in 1924, Romania 15–0 in 1980

1924 Paris **France** 59–3	1981 Narbonne **France** 17–9
1938 Bucharest **France** 11–8	1982 Bucharest **Romania** 13–9
1957 Bucharest **France** 18–15	1983 Toulouse **France** 26–15
1957 Bordeaux **France** 39–0	1984 Bucharest **France** 18–3
1960 Bucharest **Romania** 11–5	1986 Lille **France** 25–13
1961 Bayonne **Drawn** 5–5	1986 Bucharest **France** 20–3
1962 Bucharest **Romania** 3–0	1987 Wellington WC **France** 55–12
1963 Toulouse **Drawn** 6–6	1987 Agen **France** 49–3
1964 Bucharest **France** 9–6	1988 Bucharest **France** 16–12
1965 Lyons **France** 8–3	1990 Auch **Romania** 12–6
1966 Bucharest **France** 9–3	1991 Bucharest **France** 33–21
1967 Nantes **France** 11–3	1991 Béziers WC **France** 30–3
1968 Bucharest **Romania** 15–14	1992 Le Havre **France** 25–6
1969 Tarbes **France** 14–9	1993 Bucharest **France** 37–20
1970 Bucharest **France** 14–3	1993 Brive **France** 51–0
1971 Béziers **France** 31–12	1995 Bucharest **France** 24–15
1972 Constanza **France** 15–6	1995 Tucumán LC **France** 52–8
1973 Valence **France** 7–6	1996 Aurillac **France** 64–12
1974 Bucharest **Romania** 15–10	1997 Bucharest **France** 51–20
1975 Bordeaux **France** 36–12	1997 Lourdes LC **France** 39–3
1976 Bucharest **Romania** 15–12	1999 Castres **France** 62–8
1977 Clermont-Ferrand **France** 9–6	2000 Bucharest **France** 67–20
1978 Bucharest **France** 9–6	2003 Lens **France** 56–8
1979 Montauban **France** 30–12	2006 Bucharest **France** 62–14
1980 Bucharest **Romania** 15–0	

FRANCE V NEW ZEALAND MAORI

Played 1 New Zealand Maori won 1
Highest scores France 3–12 in 1926, New Zealand Maori 12–3 in 1926
Biggest win France no win, New Zealand Maori 12–3 in 1926

1926 Paris **New Zealand** Maori 12–3

FRANCE V GERMANY

Played 15 France won 13, Germany won 2, Drawn 0
Highest scores France 38–17 in 1933, Germany 17–16 in 1927 & 17–38 in 1933
Biggest wins France 34–0 in 1931, Germany 3–0 in 1938

1927 Paris **France** 30–5
1927 Frankfurt **Germany** 17–16
1928 Hanover **France** 14–3
1929 Paris **France** 24–0
1930 Berlin **France** 31–0
1931 Paris **France** 34–0
1932 Frankfurt **France** 20–4
1933 Paris **France** 38–17
1934 Hanover **France** 13–9
1935 Paris **France** 18–3
1936 1 Berlin **France** 19–14
2 Hanover **France** 6–3
France won series 2–0
1937 Paris **France** 27–6
1938 Frankfurt **Germany** 3–0
1938 Bucharest **France** 8–5

FRANCE V ITALY

Played 27 France won 26, Italy won 1, Drawn 0
Highest scores France 60–13 in 1967, Italy 40–32 in 1997
Biggest wins France 60–13 in 1967, Italy 40–32 in 1997

1937 Paris **France** 43–5
1952 Milan **France** 17–8
1953 Lyons **France** 22–8
1954 Rome **France** 39–12
1955 Grenoble **France** 24–0
1956 Padua **France** 16–3
1957 Agen **France** 38–6
1958 Naples **France** 11–3
1959 Nantes **France** 22–0
1960 Treviso **France** 26–0
1961 Chambéry **France** 17–0
1962 Brescia **France** 6–3
1963 Grenoble **France** 14–12
1964 Parma **France** 12–3
1965 Pau **France** 21–0
1966 Naples **France** 21–0
1967 Toulon **France** 60–13
1995 Buenos Aires LC **France** 34–22
1997 Grenoble **Italy** 40–32
1997 Auch LC **France** 30–19
2000 Paris **France** 42–31
2001 Rome **France** 30–19
2002 Paris **France** 33–12
2003 Rome **France** 53–27
2004 Paris **France** 25–0
2005 Rome **France** 56–13
2006 Paris **France** 37–12

FRANCE V BRITISH XVS

Played 5 France won 2, British XVs won 3, Drawn 0
Highest scores France 27–29 in 1989, British XV 36–3 in 1940
Biggest wins France 21–9 in 1945, British XV 36–3 in 1940

1940 Paris **British** XV 36–3
1945 Paris **France** 21–9
1945 Richmond **British** XV 27–6
1946 Paris **France** 10–0
1989 Paris **British** XV 29–27

FRANCE V WALES XVS

Played 2 France won 1, Wales XV won 1
Highest scores France 12–0 in 1946, Wales XV 8–0 in 1945
Biggest win France 12–0 in 1946, Wales XV 8–0 in 1945

1945 Swansea **Wales** XV 8–0
1946 Paris **France** 12–0

FRANCE V IRELAND XVS

Played 1 France won 1
Highest scores France 4–3 in 1946, Ireland XV 3–4 in 1946
Biggest win France 4–3 in 1946, Ireland XV no win

1946 Dublin **France** 4–3

FRANCE V NEW ZEALAND ARMY

Played 1 New Zealand Army won 1
Highest scores France 9–14 in 1946, New Zealand Army 14–9 in 1946
Biggest win France no win, New Zealand Army 14–9 in 1946

1946 Paris **New Zealand** Army 14–9

FRANCE V ARGENTINA

Played 38 France won 29, Argentina won 8, Drawn 1
Highest scores France 47–12 in 1995 & 47–26 in 1999, Argentina 33–32 in 2003
Biggest wins France 47–12 in 1995, Argentina 18–6 in 1988

1949	1 Buenos Aires **France** 5–0
	2 Buenos Aires **France** 12–3
	France won series 2–0
1954	1 Buenos Aires **France** 22–8
	2 Buenos Aires **France** 30–3
	France won series 2–0
1960	1 Buenos Aires **France** 37–3
	2 Buenos Aires **France** 12–3
	3 Buenos Aires **France** 29–6
	France won series 3–0
1974	1 Buenos Aires **France** 20–15
	2 Buenos Aires **France** 31–27
	France won series 2–0
1975	1 Lyons **France** 29–6
	2 Paris **France** 36–21
	France won series 2–0
1977	1 Buenos Aires **France** 26–3
	2 Buenos Aires **Drawn** 18–18
	France won series 1–0, with 1 draw
1982	1 Toulouse **France** 25–12
	2 Paris **France** 13–6
	France won series 2–0
1985	1 Buenos Aires **Argentina** 24–16
	2 Buenos Aires **France** 23–15
	Series drawn 1–1
1986	1 Buenos Aires **Argentina** 15–13
	2 Buenos Aires **France** 22–9
	Series drawn 1–1
1988	1 Buenos Aires **France** 18–15
	2 Buenos Aires **Argentina** 18–6
	Series drawn 1–1
1988	1 Nantes **France** 29–9
	2 Lille **France** 28–18
	France won series 2–0

1992	1 Buenos Aires **France** 27–12
	2 Buenos Aires **France** 33–9
	France won series 2–0
1992	Nantes **Argentina** 24–20
1995	Buenos Aires LC **France** 47–12
1996	1 Buenos Aires **France** 34–27
	2 Buenos Aires **France** 34–15
	France won series 2–0
1997	Tarbes LC **France** 32–27
1998	1 Buenos Aires **France** 35–18
	2 Buenos Aires **France** 37–12
	France won series 2–0
1998	Nantes **France** 34–14
1999	Dublin WC **France** 47–26
2002	Buenos Aires **Argentina** 28–27
2003	1 Buenos Aires **Argentina** 10–6
	2 Buenos Aires **Argentina** 33–32
	Argentina won series 2–0
2004	Marseilles **Argentina** 24–14

FRANCE V CZECHOSLOVAKIA

Played 2 France won 2
Highest scores France 28–3 in 1956, Czechoslovakia 6–19 in 1968
Biggest win France 28–3 in 1956, Czechoslovakia no win

1956	Toulouse **France** 28–3
1968	Prague **France** 19–6

FRANCE V FIJI

Played 7 France won 7
Highest scores France 77–10 in 2001, Fiji 19–28 in 1999
Biggest win France 77–10 in 2001, Fiji no win

1964	Paris **France** 21–3
1987	Auckland WC **France** 31–16
1991	Grenoble WC **France** 33–9
1998	Suva **France** 34–9
1999	Toulouse WC **France** 28–19
2001	Saint Etienne **France** 77–10
2003	Brisbane WC **France** 61–18

FRANCE V JAPAN

Played 2 France won 2
Highest scores France 51–29 in 2003, Japan 29–51 in 2003
Biggest win France 51–29 in 2003, Japan no win

1973	Bordeaux **France** 30–18
2003	Townsville WC **France** 51–29

FRANCE V ZIMBABWE

Played 1 France won 1
Highest scores France 70–12 in 1987, Zimbabwe 12–70 in 1987
Biggest win France 70–12 in 1987, Zimbabwe no win

1987	Auckland WC **France** 70–12

FRANCE V CANADA

Played 7 France won 6, Canada won 1, Drawn 0
Highest scores France 50–6 in 2005, Canada 20–33 in 1999
Biggest wins France 50–6 in 2005, Canada 18–16 in 1994

1991 Agen WC **France** 19–13	2002 Paris **France** 35–3
1994 Nepean **Canada** 18–16	2004 Toronto **France** 47–13
1994 Besançon **France** 28–9	2005 Nantes **France** 50–6
1999 Béziers WC **France** 33–20	

FRANCE V TONGA

Played 3 France won 2, Tonga won 1
Highest scores France 43–8 in 2005, Tonga 20–16 in 1999
Biggest win France 43–8 in 2005, Tonga 20–16 in 1999

1995 Pretoria WC **France** 38–10	2005 Toulouse **France** 43–8
1999 Nuku'alofa **Tonga** 20–16	

FRANCE V IVORY COAST

Played 1 France won 1
Highest scores France 54–18 in 1995, Ivory Coast 18–54 in 1995
Biggest win France 54–18 in 1995, Ivory Coast no win

1995 Rustenburg WC **France** 54–18

FRANCE V SAMOA

Played 1 France won 1
Highest scores France 39–22 in 1999, Samoa 22–39 in 1999
Biggest win France 39–22 in 1999, Samoa no win

1999 Apia **France** 39–22

FRANCE V NAMIBIA

Played 1 France won 1
Highest scores France 47–13 in 1999, Namibia 13–47 in 1999
Biggest win France 47–13 in 1999, Namibia no win

1999 Bordeaux WC **France** 47–13

SOUTH AFRICA V NEW ZEALAND

Played 70 New Zealand won 38, South Africa won 29, Drawn 3
Highest scores New Zealand 55–35 in 1997, South Africa 46–40 in 2000
Biggest wins New Zealand 52–16 in 2003, South Africa 17–0 in 1928

1921	1 Dunedin **New Zealand** 13–5
	2 Auckland **South Africa** 9–5
	3 Wellington **Drawn** 0–0
	Series drawn 1–1, with 1 draw
1928	1 Durban **South Africa** 17–0
	2 Johannesburg **New Zealand** 7–6
	3 Port Elizabeth **South Africa** 11–6
	4 Cape Town **New Zealand** 13–5
	Series drawn 2–2
1937	1 Wellington **New Zealand** 13–7
	2 Christchurch **South Africa** 13–6
	3 Auckland **South Africa** 17–6
	South Africa won series 2–1
1949	1 Cape Town **South Africa** 15–11
	2 Johannesburg **South Africa** 12–6
	3 Durban **South Africa** 9–3
	4 Port Elizabeth **South Africa** 11–8
	South Africa won series 4–0
1956	1 Dunedin **New Zealand** 10–6
	2 Wellington **South Africa** 8–3
	3 Christchurch **New Zealand** 17–10
	4 Auckland **New Zealand** 11–5
	New Zealand won series 3–1
1960	1 Johannesburg **South Africa** 13–0
	2 Cape Town **New Zealand** 11–3
	3 Bloemfontein **Drawn** 11–11
	4 Port Elizabeth **South Africa** 8–3
	South Africa won series 2–1, with 1 draw
1965	1 Wellington **New Zealand** 6–3
	2 Dunedin **New Zealand** 13–0
	3 Christchurch **South Africa** 19–16
	4 Auckland **New Zealand** 20–3
	New Zealand won series 3–1
1970	1 Pretoria **South Africa** 17–6
	2 Cape Town **New Zealand** 9–8
	3 Port Elizabeth **South Africa** 14–3
	4 Johannesburg **South Africa** 20–17
	South Africa won series 3–1
1976	1 Durban **South Africa** 16–7
	2 Bloemfontein **New Zealand** 15–9
	3 Cape Town **South Africa** 15–10
	4 Johannesburg **South Africa** 15–14
	South Africa won series 3–1
1981	1 Christchurch **New Zealand** 14–9
	2 Wellington **South Africa** 24–12
	3 Auckland **New Zealand** 25–22
	New Zealand won series 2–1
1992	Johannesburg **New Zealand** 27–24
1994	1 Dunedin **New Zealand** 22–14
	2 Wellington **New Zealand** 13–9
	3 Auckland **Drawn** 18–18
	New Zealand won series 2–0, with 1 draw
1995	Johannesburg WC **South Africa** 15–12 (aet)
1996	Christchurch TN **New Zealand** 15–11
1996	Cape Town TN **New Zealand** 29–18
1996	1 Durban **New Zealand** 23–19
	2 Pretoria **New Zealand** 33–26
	3 Johannesburg **South Africa** 32–22
	New Zealand won series 2–1
1997	Johannesburg TN **New Zealand** 35–32
1997	Auckland TN **New Zealand** 55–35
1998	Wellington TN **South Africa** 13–3
1998	Durban TN **South Africa** 24–23
1999	Dunedin TN **New Zealand** 28–0
1999	Pretoria TN **New Zealand** 34–18
1999	Cardiff WC **South Africa** 22–18
2000	Christchurch TN **New Zealand** 25–12
2000	Johannesburg TN **South Africa** 46–40
2001	Cape Town TN **New Zealand** 12–3
2001	Auckland TN **New Zealand** 26–15
2002	Wellington TN **New Zealand** 41–20
2002	Durban TN **New Zealand** 30–23
2003	Pretoria TN **New Zealand** 52–16
2003	Dunedin TN **New Zealand** 19–11
2003	Melbourne WC **New Zealand** 29–9
2004	Christchurch TN **New Zealand** 23–21
2004	Johannesburg TN **South Africa** 40–26
2005	Cape Town TN **South Africa** 22–16
2005	Dunedin TN **New Zealand** 31–27
2006	Wellington TN **New Zealand** 35–17
2006	Pretoria TN **New Zealand** 45–26
2006	Rustenburg TN **South Africa** 21–20

SOUTH AFRICA V AUSTRALIA

Played 60 South Africa won 36, Australia won 23, Drawn 1
Highest scores South Africa 61–22 in 1997, Australia 49–0 in 2006
Biggest wins South Africa 61–22 in 1997, Australia 49–0 in 2006

1933	1 Cape Town **South Africa** 17–3
	2 Durban **Australia** 21–6
	3 Johannesburg **South Africa** 12–3
	4 Port Elizabeth **South Africa** 11–0
	5 Bloemfontein **Australia** 15–4
	South Africa won series 3–2
1937	1 Sydney **South Africa** 9–5
	2 Sydney **South Africa** 26–17
	South Africa won series 2–0
1953	1 Johannesburg **South Africa** 25–3
	2 Cape Town **Australia** 18–14
	3 Durban **South Africa** 18–8
	4 Port Elizabeth **South Africa** 22–9
	South Africa won series 3–1
1956	1 Sydney **South Africa** 9–0
	2 Brisbane **South Africa** 9–0
	South Africa won series 2–0
1961	1 Johannesburg **South Africa** 28–3
	2 Port Elizabeth **South Africa** 23–11
	South Africa won series 2–0
1963	1 Pretoria **South Africa** 14–3
	2 Cape Town **Australia** 9–5
	3 Johannesburg **Australia** 11–9
	4 Port Elizabeth **South Africa** 22–6
	Series drawn 2–2
1965	1 Sydney **Australia** 18–11
	2 Brisbane **Australia** 12–8
	Australia won series 2–0
1969	1 Johannesburg **South Africa** 30–11
	2 Durban **South Africa** 16–9
	3 Cape Town **South Africa** 11–3
	4 Bloemfontein **South Africa** 19–8
	South Africa won series 4–0
1971	1 Sydney **South Africa** 19–11
	2 Brisbane **South Africa** 14–6
	3 Sydney **South Africa** 18–6
	South Africa won series 3–0
1992	Cape Town **Australia** 26–3
1993	1 Sydney **South Africa** 19–12
	2 Brisbane **Australia** 28–20
	3 Sydney **Australia** 19–12
	Australia won series 2–1
1995	Cape Town WC **South Africa** 27–18
1996	Sydney TN **Australia** 21–16
1996	Bloemfontein TN **South Africa** 25–19
1997	Brisbane TN **Australia** 32–20
1997	Pretoria TN **South Africa** 61–22
1998	Perth TN **South Africa** 14–13
1998	Johannesburg TN **South Africa** 29–15
1999	Brisbane TN **Australia** 32–6
1999	Cape Town TN **South Africa** 10–9
1999	Twickenham WC **Australia** 27–21
2000	Melbourne **Australia** 44–23
2000	Sydney TN **Australia** 26–6
2000	Durban TN **Australia** 19–18
2001	Pretoria TN **South Africa** 20–15
2001	Perth TN **Drawn** 14–14
2002	Brisbane TN **Australia** 38–27
2002	Johannesburg TN **South Africa** 33–31
2003	Cape Town TN **South Africa** 26–22
2003	Brisbane TN **Australia** 29–9
2004	Perth TN **Australia** 30–26
2004	Durban TN **South Africa** 23–19
2005	Sydney **Australia** 30–12
2005	Johannesburg **South Africa** 33–20
2005	Pretoria TN **South Africa** 22–16
2005	Perth TN **South Africa** 22–19
2006	Brisbane TN **Australia** 49–0
2006	Sydney TN **Australia** 20–18
2006	Johannesburg TN **South Africa** 24–16

SOUTH AFRICA V WORLD XVS

Played 3 South Africa won 3
Highest scores South Africa 45–24 in 1977, World XV 24–45 in 1977
Biggest win South Africa 45–24 in 1977, World XV no win

1977 Pretoria **South Africa** 45–24	2 Johannesburg **South Africa** 22–16
1989 1 Cape Town **South Africa** 20–19	South Africa won series 2–0

SOUTH AFRICA V SOUTH AMERICA

Played 8 South Africa won 7, South America won 1, Drawn 0
Highest scores South Africa 50–18 in 1982, South America 21–12 in 1982
Biggest wins South Africa 50–18 in 1982, South America 21–12 in 1982

1980	1 Johannesburg **South Africa** 24–9	1982	1 Pretoria **South Africa** 50–18
	2 Durban **South Africa** 18–9		2 Bloemfontein **South America** 21–12
	South Africa won series 2–0		Series drawn 1–1
1980	1 Montevideo **South Africa** 22–13	1984	1 Pretoria **South Africa** 32–15
	2 Santiago **South Africa** 30–16		2 Cape Town **South Africa** 22–13
	South Africa won series 2–0		South Africa won series 2–0

SOUTH AFRICA V UNITED STATES

Played 2 South Africa won 2
Highest scores South Africa 43–20 in 2001, United States 20–43 in 2001
Biggest win South Africa 38–7 in 1981, United States no win

1981	Glenville **South Africa** 38–7	2001	Houston **South Africa** 43–20

SOUTH AFRICA V NEW ZEALAND CAVALIERS

Played 4 South Africa won 3, New Zealand Cavaliers won 1, Drawn 0
Highest scores South Africa 33–18 in 1986, New Zealand Cavaliers 19–18 in 1986
Biggest wins South Africa 33–18 in 1986, New Zealand Cavaliers 19–18 in 1986

1986	1 Cape Town **South Africa** 21–15	4 Johannesburg **South Africa** 24–10
	2 Durban **New Zealand** Cavaliers 19–18	South Africa won series 3–1
	3 Pretoria **South Africa** 33–18	

SOUTH AFRICA V ARGENTINA

Played 11 South Africa won 11
Highest scores South Africa 52–23 in 1993, Argentina 33–37 in 2000
Biggest wins South Africa 39–7 in 2004, Argentina no win

1993	1 Buenos Aires **South Africa** 29–26
	2 Buenos Aires **South Africa** 52–23
	South Africa won series 2–0
1994	1 Port Elizabeth **South Africa** 42–22
	2 Johannesburg **South Africa** 46–26
	South Africa won series 2–0
1996	1 Buenos Aires **South Africa** 46–15
	2 Buenos Aires **South Africa** 44–21
	South Africa win series 2–0
2000	Buenos Aires **South Africa** 37–33
2002	Springs **South Africa** 49–29
2003	Port Elizabeth **South Africa** 26–25
2004	Buenos Aires **South Africa** 39–7
2005	Buenos Aires **South Africa** 34–23

SOUTH AFRICA V SAMOA

Played 4 South Africa won 4
Highest scores South Africa 60–8 in 1995, 60–18 in 2002 and 60–10 in 2003, Samoa 18–60 in 2002
Biggest win South Africa 60–8 in 1995, Samoa no win

1995	Johannesburg **South Africa** 60–8
1995	Johannesburg WC **South Africa** 42–14
2002	Pretoria **South Africa** 60–18
2003	Brisbane WC **South Africa** 60–10

SOUTH AFRICA V ROMANIA

Played 1 South Africa won 1
Highest score South Africa 21–8 in 1995, Romania 8–21 in 1995
Biggest win South Africa 21–8 in 1995, Romania no win

1995	Cape Town WC **South Africa** 21–8

SOUTH AFRICA V CANADA

Played 2 South Africa won 2
Highest scores South Africa 51–18 in 2000, Canada 18–51 in 2000
Biggest win South Africa 51–18 in 2000, Canada no win

1995	Port Elizabeth WC **South Africa** 20–0
2000	East London **South Africa** 51–1

SOUTH AFRICA V ITALY

Played 6 South Africa won 6
Highest scores South Africa 101–0 in 1999, Italy 31–62 in 1997
Biggest win South Africa 101–0 in 1999, Italy no win

1995	Rome **South Africa** 40–21
1997	Bologna **South Africa** 62–31
1999	1 Port Elizabeth **South Africa** 74–3
	2 Durban **South Africa** 101–0
	South Africa won series 2–0
2001	Port Elizabeth **South Africa** 60–14
2001	Genoa **South Africa** 54–26

SOUTH AFRICA V FIJI

Played 1 South Africa won 1
Highest scores South Africa 43–18 in 1996, Fiji 18–43 in 1996
Biggest win South Africa 43–18 in 1996, Fiji no win

1996	Pretoria **South Africa** 43–18

SOUTH AFRICA V TONGA

Played 1 South Africa won 1
Higest scores South Africa 74–10 in 1997, Tonga 10–74 in 1997
Biggest win South Africa 74–10 in 1997, Tonga no win

1997	Cape Town **South Africa** 74–10

SOUTH AFRICA V SPAIN

Played 1 South Africa won 1
Highest scores South Africa 47–3 in 1999, Spain 3–47 in 1999
Biggest win South Africa 47–3 in 1999, Spain no win

1999	Murrayfield WC **South Africa** 47–3

SOUTH AFRICA V URUGUAY

Played 3 South Africa won 3
Highest scores South Africa 134–3 in 2005, Uruguay 6–72 in 2003
Biggest win South Africa 134–3 in 2005, Uruguay no win

1999	Glasgow WC **South Africa** 39–3
2003	Perth WC **South Africa** 72–6
2005	East London **South Africa** 134–3

SOUTH AFRICA V GEORGIA

Played 1 South Africa won 1
Highest scores South Africa 46–19 in 2003, Georgia 19–46 in 2003
Biggest win South Africa 46–19 in 2003, Georgia no win

2003 Sydney WC **South Africa** 46–19

SOUTH AFRICA V PACIFIC ISLANDS

Played 1 South Africa won 1
Highest scores South Africa 38–24 in 2004, Pacific Islands 24–38 in 2004
Biggest win South Africa 38–24 in 2004, Pacific Islands no win

2004 Gosford (Aus) **South Africa** 38–24

NEW ZEALAND V AUSTRALIA

Played 126 New Zealand won 84, Australia won 37, Drawn 5
Highest scores New Zealand 50–21 in 2003, Australia 35–39 in 2000
Biggest wins New Zealand 43–6 in 1996, Australia 28–7 in 1999

1903	Sydney **New Zealand** 22–3
1905	Dunedin **New Zealand** 14–3
1907	1 Sydney **New Zealand** 26–6
	2 Brisbane **New Zealand** 14–5
	3 Sydney **Drawn** 5–5
	New Zealand won series 2–0, with 1 draw
1910	1 Sydney **New Zealand** 6–0
	2 Sydney **Australia** 11–0
	3 Sydney **New Zealand** 28–13
	New Zealand won series 2–1
1913	1 Wellington **New Zealand** 30–5
	2 Dunedin **New Zealand** 25–13
	3 Christchurch **Australia** 16–5
	New Zealand won series 2–1
1914	1 Sydney **New Zealand** 5–0
	2 Brisbane **New Zealand** 17–0
	3 Sydney **New Zealand** 22–7
	New Zealand won series 3–0
1929	1 Sydney **Australia** 9–8
	2 Brisbane **Australia** 17–9
	3 Sydney **Australia** 15–13
	Australia won series 3–0
1931	Auckland **New Zealand** 20–13
1932	1 Sydney **Australia** 22–17
	2 Brisbane **New Zealand** 21–3
	3 Sydney **New Zealand** 21–13
	New Zealand won series 2–1
1934	1 Sydney **Australia** 25–11
	2 Sydney **Drawn** 3–3
	Australia won series 1–0, with 1 draw
1936	1 Wellington **New Zealand** 11–6
	2 Dunedin **New Zealand** 38–13
	New Zealand won series 2–0
1938	1 Sydney **New Zealand** 24–9
	2 Brisbane **New Zealand** 20–14
	3 Sydney **New Zealand** 14–6
	New Zealand won series 3–0
1946	1 Dunedin **New Zealand** 31–8
	2 Auckland **New Zealand** 14–10
	New Zealand won series 2–0
1947	1 Brisbane **New Zealand** 13–5
	2 Sydney **New Zealand** 27–14
	New Zealand won series 2–0
1949	1 Wellington **Australia** 11–6
	2 Auckland **Australia** 16–9
	Australia won series 2–0
1951	1 Sydney **New Zealand** 8–0

2 Sydney **New Zealand** 17–11
3 Brisbane **New Zealand** 16–6
New Zealand won series 3–0
1952 1 Christchurch **Australia** 14–9
2 Wellington **New Zealand** 15–8
Series drawn 1–1
1955 1 Wellington **New Zealand** 16–8
2 Dunedin **New Zealand** 8–0
3 Auckland **Australia** 8–3
New Zealand won series 2–1
1957 1 Sydney **New Zealand** 25–11
2 Brisbane **New Zealand** 22–9
New Zealand won series 2–0
1958 1 Wellington **New Zealand** 25–3
2 Christchurch **Australia** 6–3
3 Auckland **New Zealand** 17–8
New Zealand won series 2–1
1962 1 Brisbane **New Zealand** 20–6
2 Sydney **New Zealand** 14–5
New Zealand won series 2–0
1962 1 Wellington **Drawn** 9–9
2 Dunedin **New Zealand** 3–0
3 Auckland **New Zealand** 16–8
New Zealand won series 2–0, with1 draw
1964 1 Dunedin **New Zealand** 14–9
2 Christchurch **New Zealand** 18–3
3 Wellington **Australia** 20–5
New Zealand won series 2–1
1967 Wellington **New Zealand** 29–9
1968 1 Sydney **New Zealand** 27–11
2 Brisbane **New Zealand** 19–18
New Zealand won series 2–0
1972 1 Wellington **New Zealand** 29–6
2 Christchurch **New Zealand** 30–17
3 Auckland **New Zealand** 38–3
New Zealand won series 3–0
1974 1 Sydney **New Zealand** 11–6
2 Brisbane **Drawn** 16–16
3 Sydney **New Zealand** 16–6
New Zealand won series 2–0, with 1 draw
1978 1 Wellington **New Zealand** 13–12
2 Christchurch **New Zealand** 22–6
3 Auckland **Australia** 30–16
New Zealand won series 2–1
1979 Sydney **Australia** 12–6
1980 1 Sydney **Australia** 13–9
2 Brisbane **New Zealand** 12–9
3 Sydney **Australia** 26–10
Australia won series 2–1
1982 1 Christchurch **New Zealand** 23–16
2 Wellington **Australia** 19–16
3 Auckland **New Zealand** 33–18
New Zealand won series 2–1
1983 Sydney **New Zealand** 18–8
1984 1 Sydney **Australia** 16–9
2 Brisbane **New Zealand** 19–15
3 Sydney **New Zealand** 25–24
New Zealand won series 2–1
1985 Auckland **New Zealand** 10–9
1986 1 Wellington **Australia** 13–12
2 Dunedin **New Zealand** 13–12
3 Auckland **Australia** 22–9
Australia won series 2–1
1987 Sydney **New Zealand** 30–16
1988 1 Sydney **New Zealand** 32–7
2 Brisbane **Drawn** 19–19
3 Sydney **New Zealand** 30–9
New Zealand won series 2–0, with 1 draw
1989 Auckland **New Zealand** 24–12
1990 1 Christchurch **New Zealand** 21–6
2 Auckland **New Zealand** 27–17
3 Wellington **Australia** 21–9
New Zealand won series 2–1
1991 1 Sydney **Australia** 21–12
2 Auckland **New Zealand** 6–3
1991 Dublin WC **Australia** 16–6
1992 1 Sydney **Australia** 16–15
2 Brisbane **Australia** 19–17
3 Sydney **New Zealand** 26–23
Australia won series 2–1
1993 Dunedin **New Zealand** 25–10
1994 Sydney **Australia** 20–16
1995 Auckland **New Zealand** 28–16
1995 Sydney **New Zealand** 34–23
1996 Wellington TN **New Zealand** 43–6
1996 Brisbane TN **New Zealand** 32–25
New Zealand won series 2–0
1997 Christchurch **New Zealand** 30–13
1997 Melbourne TN **New Zealand** 33–18
1997 Dunedin TN **New Zealand** 36–24
New Zealand won series 3–0
1998 Melbourne TN **Australia** 24–16
1998 Christchurch TN **Australia** 27–23
1998 Sydney **Australia** 19–14
Australia won series 3–0

1999	Auckland TN **New Zealand** 34–15
1999	Sydney TN **Australia** 28–7
	Series drawn 1–1
2000	Sydney TN **New Zealand** 39–35
2000	Wellington TN **Australia** 24–23
	Series drawn 1–1
2001	Dunedin TN **Australia** 23–15
2001	Sydney TN **Australia** 29–26
	Australia won series 2–0
2002	Christchurch TN **New Zealand** 12–6
2002	Sydney TN **Australia** 16–14
	Series drawn 1–1
2003	Sydney TN **New Zealand** 50–21
2003	Auckland TN **New Zealand** 21–17
	New Zealand won series 2–0
2003	Sydney WC **Australia** 22–10
2004	Wellington TN **New Zealand** 16–7
2004	Sydney TN **Australia** 23–18
	Series drawn 1–1
2005	Sydney TN **New Zealand** 30–13
2005	Auckland TN **New Zealand** 34–24
	New Zealand won series 2–0
2006	Christchurch TN **New Zealand** 32–12
2006	Brisbane TN **New Zealand** 13–9
2006	Auckland TN **New Zealand** 34–27
	New Zealand won series 3–0

NEW ZEALAND V UNITED STATES

Played 2 New Zealand won 2
Highest scores New Zealand 51–3 in 1913, United States 6–46 in 1991
Biggest win New Zealand 51–3 in 1913, United States no win

1913	Berkeley **New Zealand** 51–3
1991	Gloucester WC **New Zealand** 46–6

NEW ZEALAND V ROMANIA

Played 1 New Zealand won 1
Highest score New Zealand 14–6 in 1981, Romania 6–14 in 1981
Biggest win New Zealand 14–6 in 1981, Romania no win

1981	Bucharest **New Zealand** 14–6

NEW ZEALAND V ARGENTINA

Played 13 New Zealand won 12, Drawn 1
Highest scores New Zealand 93–8 in 1997, Argentina 21–21 in 1985
Biggest win New Zealand 93–8 in 1997, Argentina no win

1985	1 Buenos Aires **New Zealand** 33–20
	2 Buenos Aires **Drawn** 21–21
	New Zealand won series 1–0, with 1 draw
1987	Wellington WC **New Zealand** 46–15
1989	1 Dunedin **New Zealand** 60–9
	2 Wellington **New Zealand** 49–12
	New Zealand won series 2–0
1991	1 Buenos Aires **New Zealand** 28–14
	2 Buenos Aires **New Zealand** 36–6
	New Zealand won series 2–0
1997	1 Wellington **New Zealand** 93–8
	2 Hamilton **New Zealand** 62–10
	New Zealand won series 2–0
2001	Christchurch **New Zealand** 67–19
2001	Buenos Aires **New Zealand** 24–20
2004	Hamilton **New Zealand** 41–7
2006	Buenos Aires **New Zealand** 25–19

NEW ZEALAND V ITALY

Played 8 New Zealand won 8
Highest scores New Zealand 101–3 in 1999, Italy 21–31 in 1991
Biggest win New Zealand 101–3 in 1999, Italy no win

1987	Auckland WC **New Zealand** 70–6	2000	Genoa **New Zealand** 56–19
1991	Leicester WC **New Zealand** 31–21	2002	Hamilton **New Zealand** 64–10
1995	Bologna **New Zealand** 70–6	2003	Melbourne WC **New Zealand** 70–7
1999	Huddersfield WC **New Zealand** 101–3	2004	Rome **New Zealand** 59–10

NEW ZEALAND V FIJI

Played 4 New Zealand won 4
Highest scores New Zealand 91–0 in 2005, Fiji 18–68 in 2002
Biggest win New Zealand 91–0 in 2005, Fiji no win

1987	Christchurch WC **New Zealand** 74–13	2002	Wellington **New Zealand** 68–18
1997	Albany **New Zealand** 71–5	2005	Albany **New Zealand** 91–0

NEW ZEALAND V CANADA

Played 3 New Zealand won 3
Highest scores New Zealand 73–7 in 1995, Canada 13–29 in 1991
Biggest win New Zealand 73–7 in 1995, Canada no win

1991	Lille WC **New Zealand** 29–13	2003	Melbourne WC **New Zealand** 68–6
1995	Auckland **New Zealand** 73–7		

NEW ZEALAND V WORLD XVS

Played 3 New Zealand won 2, World XV won 1, Drawn 0
Highest scores New Zealand 54–26 in 1992, World XV 28–14 in 1992
Biggest wins New Zealand 54–26 in 1992, World XV 28–14 in 1992

1992	1 Christchurch **World XV** 28–14	3 Auckland **New Zealand** 26–15
	2 Wellington **New Zealand** 54–26	New Zealand won series 2–1

NEW ZEALAND V SAMOA

Played 4 New Zealand won 4
Highest scores New Zealand 71–13 in 1999, Samoa 13–35 in 1993 & 13–71 in 1999
Biggest win New Zealand 71–13 in 1999, Samoa no win

1993	Auckland **New Zealand** 35–13	1999	Albany **New Zealand** 71–13
1996	Napier **New Zealand** 51–10	2001	Albany **New Zealand** 50–6

NEW ZEALAND V JAPAN

Played 1 New Zealand won 1
Highest scores New Zealand 145–17 in 1995, Japan 17–145 in 1995
Biggest win New Zealand 145–17 in 1995, Japan no win

1995	Bloemfontein WC **New Zealand** 145–17

NEW ZEALAND V TONGA

Played 3 New Zealand won 3
Highest scores New Zealand 102–0 in 2000, Tonga 9–45 in 1999
Biggest win New Zealand 102–0 in 2000, Tonga no win

1999	Bristol WC **New Zealand** 45–9	2003	Brisbane WC **New Zealand** 91–7
2000	Albany **New Zealand** 102–0		

NEW ZEALAND V PACIFIC ISLANDS

Played 1 New Zealand won 1
Highest scores New Zealand 41–26 in 2004, Pacific Islands 26–41 in 2004
Biggest win New Zealand 41–26 in 2004, Pacific Islands no win

2004	Albany **New Zealand** 41–26

AUSTRALIA V UNITED STATES

Played 6 Australia won 6
Highest scores Australia 67–9 in 1990, United States 19–55 in 1999
Biggest win Australia 67–9 in 1990, United States no win

1912	Berkeley **Australia** 12–8	1987	Brisbane WC **Australia** 47–12
1976	Los Angeles **Australia** 24–12	1990	Brisbane **Australia** 67–9
1983	Sydney **Australia** 49–3	1999	Limerick WC **Australia** 55–19

AUSTRALIA V NEW ZEALAND XVS

Played 24 Australia won 6, New Zealand XVs won 18, Drawn 0
Highest scores Australia 26–20 in 1926, New Zealand XV 38–11 in 1923 and 38–8 in 1924
Biggest win Australia 17–0 in 1921, New Zealand XV 38–8 in 1924

1920 1 Sydney **New Zealand** XV 26–15
2 Sydney **New Zealand** XV 14–6
3 Sydney **New Zealand** XV 24–13
New Zealand XV won series 3–0
1921 Christchurch **Australia** 17–0
1922 1 Sydney **New Zealand** XV 26–19
2 Sydney **Australia** 14–8
3 Sydney **Australia** 8–6
Australia won series 2–1
1923 1 Dunedin **New Zealand** XV 19–9
2 Christchurch **New Zealand** XV 34–6
3 Wellington **New Zealand** XV 38–11
New Zealand XV won series 3–0
1924 1 Sydney **Australia** 20–16
2 Sydney **New Zealand** XV 21–5
3 Sydney **New Zealand** XV 38–8
New Zealand XV won series 2–1
1925 1 Sydney **New Zealand** XV 26–3
2 Sydney **New Zealand** XV 4–0
3 Sydney **New Zealand** XV 11–3
New Zealand XV won series 3–0
1925 Auckland **New Zealand** XV 36–10
1926 1 Sydney **Australia** 26–20
2 Sydney **New Zealand** XV 11–6
3 Sydney **New Zealand** XV 14–0
4 Sydney **New Zealand** XV 28–21
New Zealand XV won series 3–1
1928 1 Wellington **New Zealand** XV 15–12
2 Dunedin **New Zealand** XV 16–14
3 Christchurch **Australia** 11–8
New Zealand XV won series 2–1

AUSTRALIA V SOUTH AFRICA XVS

Played 3 South Africa XVs won 3
Highest scores Australia 11–16 in 1921, South Africa XV 28–9 in 1921
Biggest win Australia no win, South Africa XV 28–9 in 1921

1921 1 Sydney **South Africa** XV 25–10
2 Sydney **South Africa** XV 16–11
3 Sydney **South Africa** XV 28–9
South Africa XV won series 3–0

AUSTRALIA V NEW ZEALAND MAORIS

Played 16 Australia won 8, New Zealand Maoris won 6, Drawn 2
Highest scores Australia 31–6 in 1936, New Zealand Maoris 25–22 in 1922
Biggest wins Australia 31–6 in 1936, New Zealand Maoris 20–0 in 1946

1922 1 Sydney **New Zealand** Maoris 25–22
2 Sydney **Australia** 28–13
3 Sydney **New Zealand** Maoris 23–22
New Zealand Maoris won series 2–1
1923 1 Sydney **Australia** 27–23
2 Sydney **Australia** 21–16
3 Sydney **Australia** 14–12
Australia won series 3–0
1928 Wellington **New Zealand** Maoris 9–8
1931 Palmerston **North Australia** 14–3
1936 Palmerston **North Australia** 31–6
1946 Hamilton **New Zealand** Maoris 20–0
1949 1 Sydney **New Zealand** Maoris 12–3
2 Brisbane **Drawn** 8–8
3 Sydney **Australia** 18–3
Series drawn 1–1, with 1 draw
1958 1 Brisbane **Australia** 15–14
2 Sydney **Drawn** 3–3
3 Melbourne **New Zealand** Maoris 13–6
Series drawn 1–1, with 1 draw

AUSTRALIA V FIJI

Played 16 Australia won 13, Fiji won 2, Drawn 1
Highest scores Australia 66–20 in 1998, Fiji 28–52 in 1985
Biggest wins Australia 66–20 in 1998, Fiji 17–15 in 1952 & 18–16 in 1954

1952	1 Sydney **Australia** 15–9
	2 Sydney **Fiji** 17–15
	Series drawn 1–1
1954	1 Brisbane **Australia** 22–19
	2 Sydney **Fiji** 18–16
	Series drawn 1–1
1961	1 Brisbane **Australia** 24–6
	2 Sydney **Australia** 20–14
	3 Melbourne **Drawn** 3–3
	Australia won series 2–0, with 1 draw
1972	Suva **Australia** 21–19
1976	1 Sydney **Australia** 22–6
	2 Brisbane **Australia** 21–9
	3 Sydney **Australia** 27–17
	Australia won series 3–0
1980	Suva **Australia** 22–9
1984	Suva **Australia** 16–3
1985	1 Brisbane **Australia** 52–28
	2 Sydney **Australia** 31–9
	Australia won series 2–0
1998	Sydney **Australia** 66–20

AUSTRALIA V TONGA

Played 4 Australia won 3, Tonga won 1, Drawn 0
Highest scores Australia 74–0 in 1998, Tonga 16–11 in 1973
Biggest wins Australia 74–0 in 1998, Tonga 16–11 in 1973

1973	1 Sydney **Australia** 30–12
	2 Brisbane **Tonga** 16–11
	Series drawn 1–1
1993	Brisbane **Australia** 52–14
1998	Canberra **Australia** 74–0

AUSTRALIA V JAPAN

Played 3 Australia won 3
Highest scores Australia 50–25 in 1975, Japan 25–50 in 1973
Biggest win Australia 50–25 in 1975, Japan no win

1975	1 Sydney **Australia** 37–7
	2 Brisbane **Australia** 50–25
	Australia won series 2–0
1987	Sydney WC **Australia** 42–23

AUSTRALIA V ARGENTINA

Played 17 Australia won 12, Argentina won 4, Drawn 1
Highest scores Australia 53–7 in 1995 & 53–6 in 2000, Argentina 27–19 in 1987
Biggest wins Australia 53–6 in 2000, Argentina 18–3 in 1983

1979	1 Buenos Aires **Argentina** 24–13
	2 Buenos Aires **Australia** 17–12
	Series drawn 1–1
1983	1 Brisbane **Argentina** 18–3
	2 Sydney **Australia** 29–13
	Series drawn 1–1
1986	1 Brisbane **Australia** 39–19
	2 Sydney **Australia** 26–0
	Australia won series 2–0
1987	1 Buenos Aires **Drawn** 19–19
	2 Buenos Aires **Argentina** 27–19
	Argentina won series 1–0, with 1 draw
1991	Llanelli WC **Australia** 32–19
1995	1 Brisbane **Australia** 53–7
	2 Sydney **Australia** 30–13
	Australia won series 2–0
1997	1 Buenos Aires **Australia** 23–15
	2 Buenos Aires **Argentina** 18–16
	Series drawn 1–1
2000	1 Brisbane **Australia** 53–6
	2 Canberra **Australia** 32–25
	Australia won series 2–0
2002	Buenos Aires **Australia** 17–6
2003	Sydney WC **Australia** 24–8

AUSTRALIA V SAMOA

Played 4 Australia won 4
Highest scores Australia 74–7 in 2005, Samoa 13–25 in 1998
Biggest win Australia 73–3 in 1994, Samoa no win

1991	Pontypool WC **Australia** 9–3
1994	Sydney **Australia** 73–3
1998	Brisbane **Australia** 25–13
2005	Sydney **Australia** 74–7

AUSTRALIA V ITALY

Played 8 Australia won 8
Highest scores Australia 69–21 in 2005, Italy 21–69 in 2005
Biggest win Australia 55–6 in 1988, Italy no win

1983	Rovigo **Australia** 29–7
1986	Brisbane **Australia** 39–18
1988	Rome **Australia** 55–6
1994	1 Brisbane **Australia** 23–20
	2 Melbourne **Australia** 20–7
	Australia won series 2–0
1996	Padua **Australia** 40–18
2002	Genoa **Australia** 34–3
2005	Melbourne **Australia** 69–21

AUSTRALIA V CANADA

Played 5 Australia won 5
Highest scores Australia 74–9 in 1996, Canada 16–43 in 1993
Biggest win Australia 74–9 in 1996, Canada no win

1985	1 Sydney **Australia** 59–3
	2 Brisbane **Australia** 43–15
	Australia won series 2–0
1993	Calgary **Australia** 43–16
1995	Port Elizabeth WC **Australia** 27–11
1996	Brisbane **Australia** 74–9

AUSTRALIA V KOREA

Played 1 Australia won 1
Highest scores Australia 65–18 in 1987, Korea 18–65 in 1987
Biggest win Australia 65–18 in 1987, Korea no win

1987 Brisbane **Australia** 65–18

AUSTRALIA V ROMANIA

Played 3 Australia won 3
Highest scores Australia 90–8 in 2003, Romania 9–57 in 1999
Biggest win Australia 90–8 in 2003, Romania no win

1995 Stellenbosch WC **Australia** 42–3
1999 Belfast WC **Australia** 57–9
2003 Brisbane WC **Australia** 90–8

AUSTRALIA V SPAIN

Played 1 Australia won 1
Highest scores Australia 92–10 in 2001, Spain 10–92 in 2001
Biggest win Australia 92–10 in 2001, Spain no win

2001 Madrid **Australia** 92–10

AUSTRALIA V NAMIBIA

Played 1 Australia won 1
Highest scores Australia 142–0 in 2003, Namibia 0–142 in 2003
Biggest win Australia 142–0 in 2003, Namibia no win

2003 Adelaide WC **Australia** 142–0

AUSTRALIA V PACIFIC ISLANDS

Played 1 Australia won 1
Highest scores Australia 29–14 in 2004, Pacific Islands 14–29 in 2004
Biggest win Australia 29–14 in 2004, Pacific Islands no win

2004 Adelaide **Australia** 29–14

INTERNATIONAL WORLD RECORDS

The match and career records cover *official cap matches* played by the dozen Executive Council Member Unions of the International Board (England, Scotland, Ireland, Wales, France, Italy, South Africa, New Zealand, Australia, Argentina, Canada and Japan) from 1871 up to 30 September 2006. Figures include Test performances for the (British/Irish Isles) Lions and (South American) Jaguars (shown in brackets). Where a world record has been set in a cap match played by another nation in membership of the IRB, this is shown as a footnote to the relevant table.

MATCH RECORDS

MOST CONSECUTIVE TEST WINS

17 by N Zealand	1965 SA 4, 1966 BI 1,2,3,4, 1967 A, E, W, F, S, 1968 A 1,2, F 1,2,3, 1969 W 1,2
17 by S Africa	1997 A 2, It, F 1,2, E, S, 1998 I 1,2, W 1, E 1, A 1, NZ 1,2, A 2, W 2, S, I 3

MOST CONSECUTIVE TEST WITHOUT DEFEAT

Matches	Wins	Draws	Periods
23 by N Zealand	22	1	1987 to 1990
17 by N Zealand	15	2	1961 to 1964
17 by N Zealand	17	0	1965 to 1969
17 by S Africa	17	0	1997 to 1998

MOST POINTS IN A MATCH

BY THE TEAM

Pts.	Opponent	Venue	Year
155 by Japan	Chinese Taipei	Tokyo	2002
152 by Argentina	Paraguay	Mendoza	2002
147 by Argentina	Venezuela	Santiago	2004
145 by N Zealand	Japan	Bloemfontein	1995
144 by Argentina	Paraguay	Montevideo	2003
142 by Australia	Namibia	Adelaide	2003
134 by Japan	Chinese Taipei	Singapore	1998
134 by England	Romania	Twickenham	2001
134 by S Africa	Uruguay	East London	2005
120 by Japan	Chinese Taipei	Tainan	2002

Hong Kong scored 164 points against Singapore at Kuala Lumpur in 1994

BY A PLAYER

Pts.	Player	Opponent	Venue	Year
60 for Japan	T Kurihara	Chinese Taipei	Tainan	2002
50 for Argentina	E Morgan	Paraguay	San Pablo	1973
45 for N Zealand	S D Culhane	Japan	Bloemfontein	1995
45 for Argentina	J-M Nuñez-Piossek	Paraguay	Montevideo	2003
44 for Scotland	A G Hastings	Ivory Coast	Rustenburg	1995
44 for England	C Hodgson	Romania	Twickenham	2001
42 for Australia	M S Rogers	Namibia	Adelaide	2003
40 for Argentina	G M Jorge	Brazil	Sao Paulo	1993
40 for Japan	D Ohata	Chinese Taipei	Tokyo	2002
40 for Scotland	C D Paterson	Japan	Perth	2004
39 for Australia	M C Burke	Canada	Brisbane	1996

MOST TRIES IN A MATCH

BY THE TEAM

Tries	Opponent	Venue	Year
24 by Argentina	Paraguay	Mendoza	2002
24 by Argentina	Paraguay	Montevideo	2003
23 by Japan	Chinese Taipei	Tokyo	2002
23 by Argentina	Venezuela	Santiago	2004
22 by Australia	Namibia	Adelaide	2003
21 by N Zealand	Japan	Bloemfontein	1995
21 by S Africa	Uruguay	East London	2005
20 by Japan	Ch Taipei	Singapore	1998
20 by England	Romania	Twickenham	2001
19 by Argentina	Brazil	Santiago	1979
19 by Argentina	Paraguay	Asuncion	1985

Hong Kong scored 26 tries against Singapore at Kuala Lumpur in 1994

BY A PLAYER

Tries	Player	Opponent	Venue	Year
9 for Argentina	J-M Nuñez-Piossek	Paraguay	Montevideo	2003
8 for Argentina	G M Jorge	Brazil	Sao Paulo	1993
8 for Japan	D Ohata	Chinese Taipei	Tokyo	2002
7 for Argentina	U O'Farrell	Uruguay	Buenos Aires	1951
6 for Argentina	E Morgan	Paraguay	San Pablo	1973
6 for Argentina	G M Jorge	Brazil	Montevideo	1989
6 for N Zealand	M C G Ellis	Japan	Bloemfontein	1995
6 for Japan	T Kurihara	Chinese Taipei	Tainan	2002
6 for S Africa	T Chavhanga	Uruguay	East London	2005
6 for Japan	D Ohata	Hong Kong	Tokyo	2005
5 for Scotland	G C Lindsay	Wales	Raeburn Place	1887
5 for England	D Lambert	France	Richmond	1907
5 for Argentina	H Goti	Brazil	Montevideo	1961
5 for Argentina	M R Jurado	Brazil	Montevideo	1971
5 for England	R Underwood	Fiji	Twickenham	1989
5 for N Zealand	J W Wilson	Fiji	Albany	1997
5 for Japan	T Masuho	Ch Taipei	Singapore	1998
5 for Argentina	P Grande	Paraguay	Asuncion	1998
5 for S Africa	C S Terblanche	Italy	Durban	1999
5 for England	O J Lewsey	Uruguay	Brisbane	2003
5 for Australia	C E Latham	Namibia	Adelaide	2003
5 for Argentina	F Higgs	Venezuela	Santiago	2004

10 tries were scored for Hong Kong by A Billington against Singapore at Kuala Lumpur in 1994

MOST CONVERSIONS IN A MATCH

BY THE TEAM

Cons	Opponent	Venue	Year
20 by N Zealand	Japan	Bloemfontein	1995
20 by Japan	Chinese Taipei	Tokyo	2002
17 by Japan	Chinese Taipei	Singapore	1998
16 by Argentina	Paraguay	Mendoza	2002
16 by Australia	Namibia	Adelaide	2003
16 by Argentina	Venezuela	Santiago	2004
15 by Argentina	Brazil	Santiago	1979
15 by England	Holland	Huddersfield	1998
15 by Japan	Chinese Taipei	Tainan	2002

BY A PLAYER

Cons	Player	Opponent	Venue	Year
20 for N Zealand	S D Culhane	Japan	Bloemfontein	1995
16 for Argentina	J-L Cilley	Paraguay	Mendoza	2002
16 for Australia	M S Rogers	Namibia	Adelaide	2003
15 for England	P J Grayson	Holland	Huddersfield	1998
15 for Japan	T Kurihara	Chinese Taipei	Tainan	2002

MOST PENALTIES IN A MATCH

BY THE TEAM

Pens	Opponent	Venue	Year
9 by Japan	Tonga	Tokyo	1999
9 by N Zealand	Australia	Auckland	1999
9 by Wales	France	Cardiff	1999
9 by N Zealand	France	Paris	2000

Portugal scored nine penalties against Georgia at Lisbon in 2000

BY A PLAYER

Pens	Player	Opponent	Venue	Year
9 for Japan	K Hirose	Tonga	Tokyo	1999
9 for N Zealand	A P Mehrtens	Australia	Auckland	1999
9 for Wales	N R Jenkins	France	Cardiff	1999
9 for N Zealand	A P Mehrtens	France	Paris	2000

Nine penalties were scored for Portugal by T Teixeira against Georgia at Lisbon in 2000

MOST DROPPED GOALS IN A MATCH

BY THE TEAM

Drops	Opponent	Venue	Year
5 by South Africa	England	Paris	1999
3 by several nations			

BY A PLAYER

Drops	Player	Opponent	Venue	Year
5 for S Africa	J H de Beer	England	Paris	1999
3 for several nations				

MOST CAPPED PLAYERS

Caps	Player	Career Span
127	G M Gregan (Australia)	1994 to 2006
119 (5)	J Leonard (England/Lions)	1990 to 2004
111	P Sella (France)	1982 to 1995
109	F Pelous (France)	1995 to 2006
101	D I Campese (Australia)	1982 to 1996
93	S Blanco (France)	1980 to 1991
92	S B T Fitzpatrick (N Zealand)	1986 to 1997
92 (8)	M O Johnson (England/Lions)	1993 to 2003
92	G O Llewellyn (Wales)	1989 to 2004
91 (6)	R Underwood (England/Lions)	1984 to 1996
91 (4)	N R Jenkins (Wales/Lions)	1991 to 2002
91 (3)	Gareth Thomas (Wales/Lions)	1995 to 2006
91	S J Larkham (Australia)	1996 to 2006

MOST CONSECUTIVE TESTS

Tests	Player	Career span
63	S B T Fitzpatrick (N Zealand)	1986 to 1995
62	J W C Roff (Australia)	1996 to 2001
53	G O Edwards (Wales)	1967 to 1978
52	W J McBride (Ireland)	1964 to 1975
51	C M Cullen (N Zealand)	1996 to 2000

MOST TESTS AS CAPTAIN

Tests	Player	Career span
59	W D C Carling (England)	1988 to 1996
58	G M Gregan (Australia)	2001 to 2006
55	J A Eales (Australia)	1996 to 2001
51	S B T Fitzpatrick (N Zealand)	1992 to 1997
46 (8)	H Porta (Argentina/Jaguars)	1971 to 1990
45 (6)	M O Johnson (England/Lions)	1997 to 2003
41	L Arbizu (Argentina)	1992 to 2002
41	F Pelous (France)	1997 to 2006
37	M Giovanelli (Italy)	1992 to 1999
36	N C Farr-Jones (Australia)	1988 to 1992
36	G H Teichmann (S Africa)	1996 to 1999
36	K G M Wood (Ireland)	1996 to 2003

MOST POINTS IN TESTS

Points	Player	Tests	Career Span
1090 (41)	N R Jenkins (Wales/Lions)	91 (4)	1991 to 2002
1010 (27)	D Dominguez (Italy/Argentina)	76 (2)	1989 to 2003
967	A P Mehrtens (N Zealand)	70	1995 to 2004
911	M P Lynagh (Australia)	72	1984 to 1995
878	M C Burke (Australia)	81	1993 to 2004
864 (47)	J P Wilkinson (England/Lions)	57 (5)	1998 to 2005
733 (66)	A G Hastings (Scotland/Lions)	67 (6)	1986 to 1995

MOST TRIES IN TESTS

Tries	Player	Tests	Career Span
65	D Ohata (Japan)	56	1996 to 2006
64	D I Campese (Australia)	101	1982 to 1996
50 (1)	R Underwood (England/Lions)	91 (6)	1984 to 1996
46	C M Cullen (N Zealand)	58	1996 to 2002
44	J W Wilson (N Zealand)	60	1993 to 2001
42	D C Howlett (N Zealand)	55	2000 to 2006
38	S Blanco (France)	93	1980 to 1991
38	J H van der Westhuizen (S Africa)	89	1993 to 2003
37	J T Lomu (N Zealand)	63	1994 to 2002
37*	J F Umaga (N Zealand)	74	1999 to 2005
37 (1)	Gareth Thomas (Wales/Lions)	91 (3)	1995 to 2006
35	J J Kirwan (N Zealand)	63	1984 to 1994
34 (1)	I C Evans (Wales/Lions)	79 (7)	1987 to 1998

* includes a penalty try

MOST CONVERSIONS IN TESTS

Cons	Player	Tests	Career Span
169	A P Mehrtens (N Zealand)	70	1995 to 2004
140	M P Lynagh (Australia)	72	1984 to 1995
133 (6)	D Dominguez (Italy/Argentina)	76 (2)	1989 to 2003
131 (1)	N R Jenkins (Wales/Lions)	91 (4)	1991 to 2002
129 (6)	J P Wilkinson (England/Lions)	57 (5)	1998 to 2005
118	G J Fox (N Zealand)	46	1985 to 1993

MOST PENALTY GOALS IN TESTS

Penalties	Player	Tests	Career Span
248 (13)	N R Jenkins (Wales/Lions)	91 (4)	1991 to 2002
214 (5)	D Dominguez (Italy/Argentina)	76 (2)	1989 to 2003
188	A P Mehrtens (N Zealand)	70	1995 to 2004
177	M P Lynagh (Australia)	72	1984 to 1995
174	M C Burke (Australia)	81	1993 to 2004
171 (10)	J P Wilkinson (England/Lions)	57 (5)	1998 to 2005
160 (20)	A G Hastings (Scotland/Lions)	67 (6)	1986 to 1995

MOST DROP GOALS IN TESTS

Drops	Player	Tests	Career Span
28 (2)	H Porta (Argentina/Jaguars)	65 (8)	1971 to 1990
23 (2)	C R Andrew (England/Lions)	76 (5)	1985 to 1997
21 (0)	J P Wilkinson (England/Lions)	57 (5)	1998 to 2005
19 (0)	D Dominguez (Italy/Argentina)	76 (2)	1989 to 2003
18	H E Botha (S Africa)	28	1980 to 1992
17	S Bettarello (Italy)	55	1979 to 1988
15	J-P Lescarboura (France)	28	1982 to 1990

ARGENTINA

ARGENTINA'S TEST RECORD

OPPONENTS	DATE	VENUE	RESULT
Wales	11 June	H	**Won** 27–25
Wales	17 June	H	**Won** 45–27
New Zealand	24 June	H	**Lost** 19–25
Chile	1 July	A	**Won** 26–0
Uruguay	8 July	H	**Won** 45–14

PUMAS HEAD FOR FRANCE IN TROUBLED TIMES

By Frankie Deges

It never ceases to amaze the way the Argentine Pumas continue to maintain their standing in world rugby in spite of a shortened international calendar. Of course, one can look at the glass in two ways – it can either be half empty or half full. Taking with both hands each and every one of the opportunities that come their way is a testament to this team. They try to look at the glass as half full and do all they can to ensure the top half of it is also filled.

The way Agustin Pichot's side played in the five internationals of the first half of 2006 simply confirmed how much his players love playing for the light blue and white jersey; representing their country. With most of them plying their trade overseas, the opportunities to come home are few; in spite of this, they give their 110% for a cause they are prepared to bleed for.

Yes, the international season began in controversy as 60 of Argentina's representative players decided to strike against the Argentine Rugby Union (UAR), declaring themselves unavailable for selection. If someone loves playing for their country so much, why strike? A natural question with a good answer.

These are players that give their time and put the bodies on the line for what would be considered a pittance in test rugby. They do it willingly and with pride. Those back at home, where the game remains strictly amateur, were part of a special plan, with a small financial package and regulated commitment to a fitness plan to look after them.

In December 2005, the UAR Council was partially renovated, the "new" officials found the place in a complicated financial situation and their encompassing policy included dismantling some of the structures in place for the Pumas. With the excuse of lack of available funds, many things were changed and promises broken. The players, having not received the answers they were after, then decided to withdraw their services.

"There is nothing in rugby I love more than playing for Los Pumas. I know how fulfilling it can be and even in spite of this I was prepared to risk not playing again for my country because I believe so strongly in our position," said hooker Mario Ledesma, an eleven-season Puma veteran.

Fortunately, common sense prevailed and when the team took the field against a young Wales side in the season's opener, in June 2006, they had their backs against the wall.

Having not been together as a squad for seven months, it was here that the Puma "Garra" (an untranslatable word which represents spirit, passion, strength, motivation) was fully tested in a hard-fought 27–25 win in the new test destination of Puerto Madryn, in Patagonia. This was the game that confirmed the coming of age of Juan Martin Fernandez Lobbe, younger brother of Ignacio, a Puma since 1996. In only his fifth test he scored a try and was incredible on the flank.

A week later, with more training sessions on their backs and apparent renewed communication with UAR officials, the Pumas were very good in scoring what should have been a record margin against a Top 10 side. Fly-half Federico Todeschini punished every indiscretion, kicking eight penalties and converting the three tries scored: a second touchdown in the series for Fernandez Lobbe Jr and a brace from young and exciting centre Gonzalo Tiesi. The score at one stage read 45–13, Los Pumas losing interest in the last three minutes in which Wales came back with two converted tries to narrow the gap to 45–27.

Beating Wales in two Tests enabled Argentina to return to the eighth place in the IRB Rankings, one place short of their best placing, overtaking Wales who dropped to ninth.

On the back of two solid wins, the "rotation policy" of All Black coach Graham Henry almost came unstuck in Buenos Aires as again New Zealand escaped this city with a narrow, hard earned win.

On a wet night, in which the ball became slippery and hard to control, Los Pumas played a very intelligent game, reducing the risks factor and controlling the All Black forwards. The "zero mistake" plan was impossible to maintain against a well drilled side. Of the three All Black tries, the second was a gem from Dan Carter, yet it first needed a huge Puma mistake. Flanker Martin Durand scored the Pumas' only try from a blindside 30–yard run and Federico Todeschini contributed 14 points from his well-oiled right boot. He would get 80 points in the five tests.

The final minutes saw Los Pumas camped in attacking positions yet unable to break the All Black line as their defence withstood all Argentina threw at them. Replacement prop Neemia Tialata pinched a ball in the bottom of a ruck two yards from his goal line to enable his team to kick for the safety of touch and the relief of the final whistle. That was how close it was.

The first three Tests confirmed that the old heads in the team were playing some of their best rugby. Pichot, who carried throughout a groin injury that had hampered his European season, played his best rugby of the last few years; number eight Gonzalo Longo confirmed his position as the best in his position in the country, whilst hooker Mario Ledesma's lineout throwing was his most efficient, ever matching his general play.

Coach Marcelo Loffreda, in charge of the team for a seventh consecutive season, selected a renovated squad for the two RWC qualifying games against Chile and Uruguay with a satisfying blend of experience and youth. As expected both these teams were won, yet both Condors and Teros ensured that these were not easy wins. Chile was beaten 60–13 in Santiago whilst under monsoon-like conditions, Uruguay was downed 26–0 in Buenos Aires.

In winning the qualifying round for South America, Argentina's place in Pool D was confirmed. This means Los Pumas play the opening match for a third consecutive World Cup.

It is hard to imagine a year before that kick-off what the Puma lineup could be like, but the Argentina A win at the inaugural IRB Nations Cup in Portugal meant good exposure for the second-tier players – a few of whom played later in the World Cup qualifiers.

Coached by former Puma and Wallaby prop Patricio Noriega, a team selected almost exclusively from players still in the country, at the same time as Los Pumas were playing Wales and New Zealand, they managed to beat Italy A 26–12 in the opening round, were far superior to Russia, whom they beat 64–6 and in the de-facto final, home side Portugal was downed 24–19 in what was a great team effort.

The sevens squad, which has for so long been a production line for future full internationals (73 full caps first played sevens for Argentina), was less successful than in previous years as the selection policy became more open and three different coaches were used in the eight tournaments. Even so, the team still managed to finish in sixth place at the IRB Sevens, reaching one final (in George) and playing in every quarter-final.

Again, Argentina U21 failed to break into the top four in the World Championship and in fact returned from France with a seventh place, yet there were many positives in the performance of Francisco Albarracin's team. The scrum-half, in his second World Championship has class written all over him, and his side could have beaten South Africa U21 in the opening round, beat Ireland U21 and then beat Wales U21, sending them to the 5th to 8th place where, having lost by a big margin against Ireland, again beat Wales (this time more conclusively) to retain the seventh place.

In Dubai, Los Pumitas, the U19s, finished in seventh place, beating Samoa in the final game South Africa.

All of this confirms the fact that Argentine rugby continues to produce quality players and with sufficient competition and certain structures in place they could be higher in the rankings. Having for too long chased the illusion of a place in SANZAR, it now seems that the focus turns to Europe where, anyway, most of international squad players are now based, and where the players continue to arrive in droves at a younger age. Having come from the amateur game, the passion, responsibility and commitment players show when they turn professional is very well received.

The domestic scene in Argentina was again led by Buenos Aires, the biggest of 23 provincial unions and with more than 40% of the playing strength. The Aguilas (Eagles) won the National Provincial Championship, which due to financial constraints was only played by its First Division.

With a handful of internationals and a new found passion for the jersey, Buenos Aires' won the 62nd NPC beating Tucuman 34–10 in the final. Buenos Aires has won 32 NPCs, whilst in the early days of the tournament (which started in 1945) they were divided in two teams – Country winning 11 more tournaments and City taking five.

Buenos Aires' only loss in the 2006 NPC came against Tucuman in pool play – the eventual champions missing their Hindu players who had travelled to Europe. As 2005 National Club Champions Hindu· had earned an all expense paid trip to Rome where they tackled Italian Champions Ghial Calvisano. The 28–12 loss might have been hampered by the fact that this was their first match of the season, although it spelt the difference between professional and amateur rugby.

This debate is still very much open in Argentina and the Pumas' strike and a number of Council decisions ensured that people were forced to take sides. And whilst the problems between players and officials are far from resolved, what is certain is that the wounds that have been opened in the past seven months will take very long to heal and could impact on Argentina's display at next year's Rugby World Cup.

ARGENTINA INTERNATIONAL STATISTICS

MATCH RECORDS UP TO 30TH SEPTEMBER 2006

MOST CONSECUTIVE TEST WINS

10	1992	Sp 1, 2, R, F,	1993	J 1, 2, Br, Ch, P, U
7	1972	Gz 2,	1973	P, U, Br, Ch, R, 1, 2

MOST CONSECUTIVE TEST WITHOUT DEFEAT

Matches	Wins	Draws	Periods
10	10	0	1992 to 1993
7	7	0	1972 to 1973

MOST POINTS IN A MATCH

BY THE TEAM

Pts.	Opponent	Venue	Year
152	Paraguay	Mendoza	2002
147	Venezuela	Santiago	2004
144	Paraguay	Montevideo	2003
114	Brazil	Sao Paulo	1993
109	Brazil	Santiago	1979
103	Paraguay	Asunción	1995
103	Brazil	Montevideo	1985
102	Paraguay	Asunción	1985

BY A PLAYER

Pts.	Player	Opponent	Venue	Year
50	E Morgan	Paraguay	Sao Paulo	1973
45	J M Nuñez Piossek	Paraguay	Montevideo	2003
36	M Sansot	Brazil	Tucumán	1977
32	G Jorge	Brazil	Sao Paulo	1993
32	J Cilley	Paraguay	Mendoza	2002
31	E Morgan	Uruguay	Sao Paulo	1973
31	E de Forteza	Paraguay	Asunción	1975
31	J Luna	Romania	Buenos Aires	1995
30	J Capalbo	Uruguay	Tucumán	1977
30	F Todeschini	Italy	Salta	2005
30	F Todeschini	Wales	Buenos Aires	2006

MOST TRIES IN A MATCH

BY THE TEAM

Tries	Opponent	Venue	Year
24	Paraguay	Mendoza	2002
24	Paraguay	Montevideo	2003
23	Venezuela	Santiago	2004
19	Brazil	Santiago	1979
19	Paraguay	Asunción	1985
18	Paraguay	San Pablo	1973
18	Brazil	Sao Paulo	1993
17	Brazil	Buenos Aires	1991
16	Paraguay	Asunción	1995
15	Paraguay	Asunción	1975
14	Paraguay	Montevideo	1989
14	Brazil	Montevideo	1961

BY A PLAYER

Tries	Player	Opponent	Venue	Year
9	J M Nuñez Piossek	Paraguay	Montevideo	2003
8	GM Jorge	Brazil	Sao Paulo	1993
7	U O'Farrell	Uruguay	Buenos Aires	1951
6	E Morgan	Paraguay	Sao Paulo	1973
6	GM Jorge	Brazil	Montevideo	1989
5	F Higgs	Venezuela	Santiago	2004

MOST CONVERSIONS IN A MATCH

BY THE TEAM

Cons	Opponent	Venue	Year
16	Paraguay	Mendoza	2002
16	Venezuela	Santiago	2004
15	Brazil	Santiago	1979
13	Paraguay	Sao Paulo	1973
13	Paraguay	Asunción	1985
12	Paraguay	Asunción	1975
12	Brazil	Buenos Aires	1993
12	Paraguay	Montevideo	2003
10	Paraguay	Tucumán	1977
10	Brazil	Montevideo	1989

BY A PLAYER

Cons	Player	Opponent	Venue	Year
16	JL Cilley	Paraguay	Mendoza	2002
13	E Morgan	Paraguay	Sao Paulo	1973
13	H Porta	Paraguay	Asunción	1985
11	E de Forteza	Paraguay	Asunción	1975
10	P Guarrochena	Paraguay	Tucumán	1977
10	S Mesón	Brazil	Montevideo	1989
10	S Mesón	Brazil	Sao Paulo	1993

MOST PENALTIES IN A MATCH

BY THE TEAM

Pens	Opponent	Venue	Year
8	Canada	Buenos Aires	1995
8	Samoa	Llanelli	1999
8	Wales	Buenos Aires	2006
7	France	Buenos Aires	1977
7	France	Nantes	1992
7	Canada	Buenos Aires	1998
7	Japan	Cardiff	1999
7	Ireland	Lens	1999
7	Italy	Salta	2005

BY A PLAYER

Pens	Player	Opponent	Venue	Year
8	S Meson	Canada	Buenos Aires	1995
8	G Quesada	Samoa	Llanelli	1999
8	F Todeschini	Wales	Buenos Aires	2006
7	H Porta	France	Buenos Aires	1977
7	S Mesón	France	Nantes	1992
7	G Quesada	Canada	Buenos Aires	1998
7	G Quesada	Japan	Cardiff	1999
7	G Quesada	Ireland	Lens	1999
7	F Todeschini	Italy	Salta	2005

MOST DROPPED GOALS IN A MATCH

BY THE TEAM

Pens	Opponent	Venue	Year
3	SA Gazelles	Pretoria	1971
3	Uruguay	Asunción	1975
3	Australia	Buenos Aires	1979
3	New Zealand	Buenos Aires	1985
3	Canada	Markham	2001

BY A PLAYER

Pens	Player	Opponent	Venue	Year
3	T Harris Smith	SA Gazelles	Pretoria	1971
3	H Porta	Australia	Buenos Aires	1979
3	H Porta	New Zealand	Buenos Aires	1985
3	J Fernández Miranda	Canada	Markham	2001

CAREER RECORDS

MOST CAPPED PLAYERS (45 CAPS AND MORE)

Caps	Player	Career Span
87	L Arbizu	1990 to 2005
86	R Martin	1994 to 2003
77	P Sporleder	1990 to 2003
75	F Méndez	1990 to 2005
63	D Cuesta Silva	1985 to 1995
62	A Pichot	1995 to 2006
59	O Hasan	1995 to 2006
57	H Porta	1971 to 1990
55	D Albanese	1995 to 2003
55	M Ledesma	1996 to 2006
54	I Fernández Lobbe	1996 to 2006
51	M Reggiardo	1995 to 2005
50	F Contepomi	1998 to 2006
47	R Grau	1993 to 2003
46	M Loffreda	1978 to 1994

MOST POINTS IN TESTS (150 POINTS AND MORE)

Points	Player	Tests	Career span
581	H Porta	57	1971 to 1990
486	G Quesada	38	1996 to 2003
320	F Contepomi	50	1998 to 2006
279	S Mesón	34	1987 to 1997
193	L Arbizu	87	1990 to 2005
185	F Todeschini	12	1998 to 2006
153	J Fernández Miranda	29	1998 to 2006
150	JM Núñez Piossek	25	2001 to 2006

MOST TRIES IN TESTS (13 AND MORE)

Tries	Player	Tests	Career span
30	JM Núñez Piossek	25	2001 to 2006
28	D Cuesta Silva	63	1985 to 1995
23	G Jorge	22	1989 to 1994
19	R Martin	86	1994 to 2003
18	L Arbizu	87	1990 to 2005
18	F Soler	26	1996 to 2002
15	H Senillosa	23	2002 to 2006
14	FE Méndez	75	1990 to 2005
14	G Morgan	7	1977 to 1979
14	G Alvarez	9	1975 to 1977

MOST DROPPED GOALS IN TESTS (8 AND MORE)

Drops	Player	Tests	Career span
26	H Porta	57	1971 to 1990
11	L Arbizu	87	1990 to 2005
7	G Quesada	38	1996 to 2003
5	T Harris Smith	5	1969 to 1972
5	J Fernández Miranda	29	1998 to 2006

MOST CONVERSIONS IN TESTS (30 AND MORE)

Cons	Player	Tests	Career span
80	H Porta	57	1971 to 1990
68	G Quesada	38	1996 to 2003
45	S Mesón	34	1987 to 1997
41	J Fernández Miranda	29	1998 to 2006
41	F Contepomi	50	1998 to 2006

MOST PENALTY GOALS IN TESTS (30 AND MORE)

Pens	Player	Tests	Career span
103	G Quesada	38	1996 to 2003
101	H Porta	57	1971 to 1990
65	F Contepomi	50	1998 to 2006
54	S Mesón	34	1987 to 1997
42	F Todeschini	12	1998 to 2006

CAREER RECORD OF ARGENTINA INTERNATIONAL PLAYERS USED DURING THE PERIOD 1 JANUARY – 30 SEPTEMBER 2006

BACKS PLAYER	DEBUT	CAPS	T	C	P	D	PTS
H Agulla	2005 v Samoa	2	1	0	0	0	5
M Avramovic	2005 v Jp	5	3	0	0	0	15
L Borges	2003 v Pg	18	11	0	0	0	55
R Carballo	2005 v C	3					
F Contepomi	1998 v Ch	50	8	41	65	1	320
J Fernández Miranda	1998 v U	29	4	41	12	5	153
N Fernández Miranda	1994 v US	40	6	0	0	0	30
JM Hernández	2003 v Pg	18	5	2	0	0	29
F Leonelli	2001 v U	12	7	0	0	0	35
F Martín Aramburu	2004 v Ch	11	6	0	0	0	30
JM Núñez Piossek	2001 v U	25	30	0	0	0	150
A Pichot	1995 v A	60	12	0	0	0	60
H Senillosa	2002 V U	23	15	17	1	1	115
F Serra	2004 v Pg	5	1	0	1	0	8
G Tiesi	2004 v SA	9	5	0	0	0	25
F Todeschini	1998 v R	12	1	27	42	0	185
N Vergallo	2005 v Samoa	3					
FORWARDS							
R Alvarez Kairelis	1998 v Pg	28	3	0	0	0	15
M Ayerza	2004 v SA	8	1	0	0	0	5
P Bouza	1996 v U	34	10	0	0	0	50
M Carizza	2004 v SA	9	1	0	0	0	5
A Creevy	2005 v J	3					
G de Robertis	2005 v Samoa	3					
M Durand	1997 v Ch	41	7	0	0	0	35
I Fernández Lobbe	1996 v US	54	5	0	0	0	25
JM Fernández Lobbe	2004 v U	7	3	0	0	0	15
P Gambarini	2006 v W	3	1	0	0	0	5
O Hasan	1995 v U	59	3	0	0	0	15
M Ledesma	1996 v U	56	3	0	0	0	15
JM Leguizamón	2005 v J	11	2	0	0	0	10
G Longo	1999 v W	43	3	0	0	0	15
R Roncero	1998 v J	20	3	0	0	0	15
M Scelzo	1996 v US	9	9	0	0	0	45
M Schusterman	2003 v Pg	15	1	0	0	0	5

AUSTRALIA

AUSTRALIA'S TEST RECORD

OPPONENTS	DATE	VENUE	RESULT
England	11 June	H	**Won** 34–3
England	17 June	H	**Won** 43–18
Ireland	24 June	H	**Won** 37–15
New Zealand	8 July	A	**Lot** 32–12
South Africa	15 July	H	**Won** 49–0
New Zealand	29 July	A	**Lost** 13–9
South Africa	5 Aug	H	**Won** 20–18
New Zealand	19 Aug	A	**Lost** 34–27
South Africa	9 Sept	A	**Lost** 24–16

WALLABIES LOOK FOR FORWARD POWER

By Michael Lynagh

After what was a pretty horrendous year for the Wallabies in 2005, I thought they showed character to bounce back in 2006 and produce some solid results and performances. The team is still very much a work in progress under John Connolly and his coaching team, but there were signs that they're heading in the right direction, albeit slower than most Wallaby supporters would probably want.

Connolly was appointed head coach in February after Eddie Jones' sacking in December and it's important to remember he inherited a side that had lost seven matches in succession in 2005 and finished bottom of the Tri-Nations without a single victory. It had been a long time since the Wallabies had been so obviously out of sorts and there was a lot of rebuilding to be done.

I don't think Connolly performed any miracles after taking the job but he certainly steadied the ship, which is exactly what was needed. The confidence began to ebb back into the side over the year and although they finished with a couple of disappointing Tri-Nations results against the All Blacks and South Africa, I think you could say Australia are finally back on the right track.

The season began with the two June Tests against England in Sydney and Melbourne. To be honest, they were probably the ideal fixtures for Connolly after taking the reins because England were tired and under strength and the matches represented a chance to get a couple of wins on the board and set the tone for the rest of the season. Two healthy victories were duly delivered and the Wallabies were up and running. England had beaten Australia at Twickenham the previous autumn and I'm sure the two June wins helped the side start putting the previous 12 months behind them.

Ireland in Perth was the final 'warm-up' fixture. I felt sorry for the Irish because they're a good side, but they flew in on the back of a tough two Test series against the All Blacks and they just didn't have enough gas left. Australia won 37–15 and maintained their winning record in 2006.

Of course, the Tri-Nations was always going to be a totally different proposition, especially as the Wallabies' opening game was against New Zealand in Christchurch. This was a real test of whether the team had genuinely been taking steps in the right direction.

The All Blacks won 32–12, but I saw signs in the Australian performance that gave me cause for quiet optimism. It wasn't a great display, but they didn't fold when the pressure came, which had been their Achilles heel in the last 12 months.

Even more encouraging was the next game, when the Springboks were put to the sword in Brisbane and the Wallabies won 49–0. It was the result and performance that the fans had been waiting for and I sensed a new-found confidence in the team after that game throughout the rest of the tournament. The team almost visibly grew in stature.

New Zealand came to Brisbane the following week and were very

Chris McGrath/Getty Images

John Connolly [right, with George Gregan] has halted Australia's losing run but still has a long way to go.

nearly beaten. They hung on for a 13–9 victory but I think if the Wallabies had shown just a little more conviction, they could have snatched the result. They did exactly that, however, against the Springboks in Sydney seven days later – edging South Africa 20–18 – although I'd have to say it was the result rather than the performance that will live in the memory.

Connolly took his team on the road for the final two games of the campaign – playing the All Blacks in Auckland and ending with the Springboks in Johannesburg.

A lot of the Wallabies critics expected them to get blown away in Auckland but they competed physically and if it hadn't been for the unforced errors they made in the second-half, it could have been Australia rather than New Zealand who emerged 34–27 winners. It was another encouraging performance in which the team just needed to be a little more clinical.

In contrast, the Springbok game at Ellis Park was a big disappointment. South Africa won 24–16 without really being stretched and from an Australia perspective, it was a tame way to close out the tournament. They had made big improvements compared to their dismal 2005 performances but they signed off with a whimper rather than a bang.

So what did we learn about Australia, Connolly and the side's World Cup prospects? The first thing to say is Connolly was on a steep learning

Ross Land/Getty Images

Rocky Elsom was an Australian forward who shone in 2006.

curve, along with the new set-up of Michael Foley as forwards coach and Scott Johnson looking after the attack, and they all need time to settle into their new roles.

There's no doubt Connolly made the Wallabies harder to beat. There was a more solid feel about the team and although they didn't manage to beat the All Blacks and lost once to South Africa, they played with a lot more self-belief and intensity.

The back line looked dangerous. Some people have said it's the best in world rugby, but I would reserve judgement on that for now. They were certainly potent, but injuries and selection meant the line-up changed frequently and I'm not sure Connolly knows what his best back line actually is. He's looking for the right balance, but I don't think he quite found it.

It's no secret Connolly and Foley, in particular, had their work cut out with the forwards, who got some terrible stick in 2005 from the opposition and the media. I liked their approach to the problem because it was pragmatic. They said 'these are the guys we've got to work with' and just got on with it. I don't think the pack is ever going to be world-beating, but it looked as though it was becoming far more competitive.

It was no surprise that they tired to bolster the front row and the likes of Tai McIsaac and Rodney Blake are hopefully players for the future. The challenge is to develop them as Test match players without the team's results suffering.

On an individual level, I thought Stephen Larkham was outstanding earlier in the season, although it was a bit of a worry the way his form tailed off towards the end of the Tri-Nations. Perhaps that was inevitable because of the pressure the All Blacks and Springboks exerted on him in the fly-half position, but 2006 confirmed for me what an influential player he still is for the Wallabies.

In the forwards, Rocky Elsom and Wycliff Palu were both impressive and along with George Smith and Phil Waugh, they gave the back row a nice balance. Elsom just needs to cut out the unnecessary penalties that became an unwelcome feature of his game.

Nathan Sharpe was pretty solid in the second row as well and Stirling Mortlock gave the team some go forward in the midfield.

There was a lot of debate about George Gregan's place again, which I suppose is inevitable when you've been in the team as long as he has. Everyone seemed to have an opinion on his selection and I have to say I don't think he deserves the criticism he received from some quarters.

Obviously he will have to retire one day or he'll be dropped but until someone stands up and demands the number nine shirt off his back, he would still be in my team. He's still up to the physical demands of Test match rugby in my opinion and none of the other scrum-halves has yet made a convincing enough argument to start ahead of him. Gregan has got a wealth of experience and I don't think Connolly and Australia should dispense with that lightly.

I read one particular article that summed up the Gregan debate for me. The argument went that if Gregan was 10 years younger, he'd would have been flavour of the month for his performance in 2006, but because he is older and people expect more from him, the reception was more muted. I've got to agree with that.

So what of the Wallabies' World Cup prospects? There's no doubt New Zealand are now the firm favourites but Australia, and the likes of France and maybe England, are not without hope.

The All Blacks have set the benchmark to all the other sides with aspirations of lifting the trophy next year, but I'm not sure they have much room for improvement. They've got a lot of depth in their squad and the confidence that comes from winning consistently, but can they get better?

The Wallabies can certainly get better. Without doubt they need to make some dramatic improvements, but I genuinely think it would be premature to write off their World Cup chances.

AUSTRALIA INTERNATIONAL STATISTICS

MATCH RECORDS UP TO 30TH SEPTEMBER 2006

MOST CONSECUTIVE TEST WINS

10	1991 Arg, WS, W, I, NZ, E,	1992 S 1,2, NZ 1,2
10	1998 NZ 3, Fj, Tg, Sm, F, E 2,	1999 I 1,2, E, SA 1
10	1999 NZ 2, R, I 3, US, W, SA 3, F,	2000 Arg 1,2,SA 1

MOST CONSECUTIVE TESTS WITHOUT DEFEAT

Matches	Wins	Draws	Periods
10	10	0	1991 to 1992
10	10	0	1998 to 1999
10	10	0	1999 to 2000

MOST POINTS IN A MATCH

BY THE TEAM

Pts.	Opponent	Venue	Year
142	Namibia	Adelaide	2003
92	Spain	Madrid	2001
90	Romania	Brisbane	2003
76	England	Brisbane	1998
74	Canada	Brisbane	1996
74	Tonga	Canberra	1998
74	W Samoa	Sydney	2005
73	W Samoa	Sydney	1994
69	Italy	Melbourne	2005
67	United States	Brisbane	1990

BY A PLAYER

Pts.	Player	Opponent	Venue	Year
42	M S Rogers	Namibia	Adelaide	2003
39	M C Burke	Canada	Brisbane	1996
30	E J Flatley	Romania	Brisbane	2003
29	S A Mortlock	South Africa	Melbourne	2000
28	M P Lynagh	Argentina	Brisbane	1995
25	M C Burke	Scotland	Sydney	1998
25	M C Burke	France	Cardiff	1999
25	M C Burke	British/Irish Lions	Melbourne	2001
25	E J Flatley*	Ireland	Perth	2003
25	C E Latham	Namibia	Adelaide	2003
24	M P Lynagh	United States	Brisbane	1990
24	M P Lynagh	France	Brisbane	1990
24	M C Burke	New Zealand	Melbourne	1998
24	M C Burke	South Africa	Twickenham	1999

* includes a penalty try

MOST TRIES IN A MATCH

BY THE TEAM

Tries	Opponent	Venue	Year
22	Namibia	Adelaide	2003
13	South Korea	Brisbane	1987
13	Spain	Madrid	2001
13	Romania	Brisbane	2003
12	United States	Brisbane	1990
12	Wales	Brisbane	1991
12	Tonga	Canberra	1998
12	Samoa	Sydney	2005
11	Western Samoa	Sydney	1994
11	England	Brisbane	1998
11	Italy	Melbourne	2005

BY A PLAYER

Tries	Player	Opponent	Venue	Year
5	C E Latham	Namibia	Adelaide	2003
4	G Cornelsen	New Zealand	Auckland	1978
4	D I Campese	United States	Sydney	1983
4	J S Little	Tonga	Canberra	1998
4	C E Latham	Argentina	Brisbane	2000
4	L D Tuqiri	Italy	Melbourne	2005

MOST CONVERSIONS IN A MATCH

BY THE TEAM

Cons	Opponent	Venue	Year
16	Namibia	Adelaide	2003
12	Spain	Madrid	2001
11	Romania	Brisbane	2003
9	Canada	Brisbane	1996
9	Fiji	Parramatta	1998
8	Italy	Rome	1988
8	United States	Brisbane	1990
7	Canada	Sydney	1985
7	Tonga	Canberra	1998
7	Samoa	Sydney	2005
7	Italy	Melbourne	2005

BY A PLAYER

Cons	Player	Opponent	Venue	Year
16	M S Rogers	Namibia	Adelaide	2003
11	E J Flatley	Romania	Brisbane	2003
10	M C Burke	Spain	Madrid	2001
9	M C Burke	Canada	Brisbane	1996
9	J A Eales	Fiji	Parramatta	1998
8	M P Lynagh	Italy	Rome	1988
8	M P Lynagh	United States	Brisbane	1990
7	M P Lynagh	Canada	Sydney	1985

MOST PENALTIES IN A MATCH

BY THE TEAM

Pens	Opponent	Venue	Year
8	South Africa	Twickenham	1999
7	New Zealand	Sydney	1999
7	France	Cardiff	1999
7	Wales	Cardiff	2001
6	New Zealand	Sydney	1984
6	France	Sydney	1986
6	England	Brisbane	1988
6	Argentina	Buenos Aires	1997
6	Ireland	Perth	1999
6	France	Paris	2000
6	British/Irish Lions	Melbourne	2001
6	New Zealand	Sydney	2004

BY A PLAYER

Pens	Player	Opponent	Venue	Year
8	M C Burke	South Africa	Twickenham	1999
7	M C Burke	New Zealand	Sydney	1999
7	M C Burke	France	Cardiff	1999
7	M C Burke	Wales	Cardiff	2001
6	M P Lynagh	France	Sydney	1986
6	M P Lynagh	England	Brisbane	1988
6	D J Knox	Argentina	Buenos Aires	1997
6	M C Burke	France	Paris	2000
6	M C Burke	British/Irish Lions	Melbourne	2001

MOST DROP GOALS IN A MATCH

BY THE TEAM

Drops	Opponent	Venue	Year
3	England	Twickenham	1967
3	Ireland	Dublin	1984
3	Fiji	Brisbane	1985

BY A PLAYER

Drops	Player	Opponent	Venue	Year
3	P FHawthorne	England	Twickenham	1967
2	M G Ella	Ireland	Dublin	1984
2	D J Knox	Fiji	Brisbane	1985

MOST CAPPED PLAYERS

Caps	Player	Career span
127	G M Gregan	1994 to 2006
101	D I Campese	1982 to 1996
91	S J Larkham	1996 to 2006
86	J A Eales	1991 to 2001
86	J W C Roff	1995 to 2004
81	M C Burke	1993 to 2004
80	T J Horan	1989 to 2000
79	D J Wilson	1992 to 2000
75	J S Little	1989 to 2000
72	M P Lynagh	1984 to 1995
72	J A Paul	1998 to 2006
69	G B Smith	2000 to 2006
68	C E Latham	1998 to 2006
67	P N Kearns	1989 to 1999
67	D J Herbert	1994 to 2002
63	N C Farr Jones	1984 to 1993
63	M J Cockbain	1997 to 2003
60	R S T Kefu	1997 to 2003
59	S P Poidevin	1980 to 1991

MOST CONSECUTIVE TESTS

Caps	Player	Span
62	J W C Roff	1996 to 2001
46	P N Kearns	1989 to 1995
44	G B Smith	2003 to 2006
42	D I Campese	1990 to 1995
37	P G Johnson	1959 to 1968

MOST TESTS AS CAPTAIN

Caps	Captain	Span
58	G M Gregan	2001 to 2006
55	J A Eales	1996 to 2001
36	N C Farr Jones	1988 to 1992
19	A G Slack	1984 to 1987
16	J E Thornett	1962 to 1967
16	G V Davis	1969 to 1972

MOST POINTS IN TESTS

Pts	Player	Tests	Career
911	M P Lynagh	72	1984 to 1995
878	M C Burke	81	1993 to 2004
322	S A Mortlock	50	2000 to 2006
315	D I Campese	101	1982 to 1996
260	P E McLean	30	1974 to 1982
249*	J W Roff	86	1995 to 2004
187*	E J Flatley	38	1997 to 2005
183	M J Giteau	37	2002 to 2006
173	J A Eales	86	1991 to 2001

* Roff and Flatley's totals include a penalty try

MOST TRIES IN TESTS

Tries	Player	Tests	Career
64	D I Campese	101	1982 to 1996
33	C E Latham	68	1998 to 2006
31*	J W Roff	86	1995 to 2004
30	T J Horan	80	1989 to 2000
29	M C Burke	81	1993 to 2004
25	L D Tuqiri	46	2003 to 2006
24	B N Tune	47	1996 to 2006
23	S J Larkham	91	1996 to 2006
23	S A Mortlock	50	2000 to 2006
21	J S Little	75	1989 to 2000

* Roff's total includes a penalty try

MOST CONVERSIONS IN TESTS

Cons	Player	Tests	Career
140	M P Lynagh	72	1984 to 1995
104	M C Burke	81	1993 to 2004
36	S A Mortlock	50	2000 to 2006
31	J A Eales	86	1991 to 2001
30	E J Flatley	38	1997 to 2005
27	P E McLean	30	1974 to 1982
27	M S Rogers	41	2002 to 2006
26	M J Giteau	37	2002 to 2006
20	J W Roff	86	1995 to 2004
19	D J Knox	13	1985 to 1997

MOST PENALTY GOALS IN TESTS

Pens	Player	Tests	Career
177	M P Lynagh	72	1984 to 1995
174	M C Burke	81	1993 to 2004
62	P E McLean	30	1974 to 1982
45	S A Mortlock	50	2000 to 2006
34	J A Eales	86	1991 to 2001
34	E J Flatley	38	1997 to 2005
23	M C Roebuck	23	1991 to 1993

MOST DROPPED GOALS IN TESTS

Drops	Player	Tests	Career
9	P F Hawthorne	21	1962 to 1967
9	M P Lynagh	72	1984 to 1995
8	M G Ella	25	1980 to 1984
4	P E McLean	30	1974 to 1982

TRI-NATIONS RECORDS

RECORD	DETAIL		SET
Most points in season	133	in six matches	2006
Most tries in season	14	in six matches	2006
Highest Score	49	49-0 v S Africa (h)	2006
Biggest win	49	49-0 v S Africa (h)	2006
Highest score conceded	61	22-61 v S Africa (a)	1997
Biggest defeat	39	22-61 v S Africa (a)	1997
Most points in matches	271	M C Burke	1996 to 2004
Most points in season	71	S A Mortlock	2000
Most points in match	24	M C Burke	v N Zealand (h) 1998
Most tries in matches	9	J W C Roff	1996 to 2003
Most tries in season	4	S A Mortlock	2000
Most tries in match	2	B N Tune	v S Africa (h) 1997
	2	S J Larkham	v N Zealand (a) 1997
	2	M C Burke	v N Zealand (h) 1998
	2	J W C Roff	v S Africa (h) 1999
	2	S A Mortlock	v N Zealand (h) 2000
	2	C E Latham	v S Africa (h) 2002
	2	M J Giteau	v S Africa (h) 2006
	2	L D Tuqiri	v N Zealand (a) 2006
Most cons in matches	19	M C Burke	1996 to 2004
Most cons in season	12	S A Mortlock	2006
Most cons in match	5	S A Mortlock	v S Africa (h) 2006
Most pens in matches	65	M C Burke	1996 to 2004
Most pens in season	14	M C Burke	2001
Most pens in match	7	M C Burke	v N Zealand (h) 1999

MISCELLANEOUS RECORDS

RECORD	HOLDER	DETAIL
Longest Test Career	G M Cooke	1932-1948
Youngest Test Cap	B W Ford	18 yrs 90 days in 1957
Oldest Test Cap	A R Miller	38 yrs 113 days in 1967

CAREER RECORDS OF AUSTRALIA INTERNATIONAL PLAYERS (PLAYERS CAPPED SINCE THE START OF RWC 2003 UP TO 30 SEPTEMBER 2006)

PLAYER BACKS	DEBUT	CAPS	T	C	P	D	PTS
A P Ashley-Cooper	2005 v SA	1	0	0	0	0	0
M C Burke	1993 v SA	81	29	104	174	1	878
S J Cordingley	2000 v Arg	11	0	0	0	0	0
E J Flatley	1997 v E	38	5*	30	34	0	187
M A Gerrard	2005 v It	16	6	0	0	0	30
M J Giteau	2002 v E	37	13	26	22	0	183
G M Gregan	1994 v It	127	18	0	0	3	99
N P Grey	1998 v S	35	7	0	0	0	35
M T Henjak	2004 v E	4	0	0	0	0	0
L D T Johansson	2005 v NZ	3	1	0	0	0	5
S J Larkham	1996 v W	91	23	2	0	2	125
C E Latham	1998 v F	68	33	0	0	0	165
L J MacKay	2005 v NZ	1	0	0	0	0	0
D A Mitchell	2005 v SA	10	6	0	0	0	30
S A Mortlock	2000 v Arg	50	23	36	45	0	322
C Rathbone	2004 v S	23	8	0	0	0	40
J W Roff	1995 v C	86	31*	20	18	0	249
M S Rogers	2002 v F	41	13	27	13	0	158
W J Sailor	2002 v F	37	13	0	0	0	65
B R Sheehan	2006 v SA	1	0	0	0	0	0
C B Shepherd	2006 v E	4	1	0	0	0	5
S N G Staniforth	1999 v US	4	4	0	0	0	20
B N Tune	1996 v W	47	24	0	0	0	120
L D Tuqiri	2003 v I	46	25	0	0	0	125
M P Turinui	2003 v I	20	6	0	0	0	30
J J Valentine	2006 v E	1	0	0	0	0	0
C J Whitaker	1998 v SA	31	2	0	0	0	10
FORWARDS:							
A K E Baxter	2003 v NZ	38	0	0	0	0	0
R C Blake	2006 v E	6	1	0	0	0	5
A M Campbell	2005 v F	1	0	0	0	0	0
B J Cannon	2001 v BI	40	2	0	0	0	10
M D Chisholm	2004 v S	22	5	0	0	0	25
M J Cockbain	1997 v F	63	1	0	0	0	5
D N Croft	2002 v Arg	5	0	0	0	0	0

B J Darwin	2001 v BI	28	0	0	0	0	0
M J Dunning	2003 v Nm	25	0	0	0	0	0
R D Elsom	2005 v Sm	18	2	0	0	0	10
S G Fava	2005 v E	5	1	0	0	0	5
D E Fitter	2005 v I	2	0	0	0	0	0
A L Freier	2002 v Arg	8	0	0	0	0	0
D T Giffin	1996 v W	50	0	0	0	0	0
S P Hardman	2002 v F	2	0	0	0	0	0
J B G Harrison	2001 v BI	34	1	0	0	0	5
D P Heenan	2003 v W	2	0	0	0	0	0
N J Henderson	2004 v PI	2	0	0	0	0	0
S A Hoiles	2004 v S	2	0	0	0	0	0
G S Holmes	2005 v F	11	2	0	0	0	10
A Kanaar	2005 v NZ	1	0	0	0	0	0
D J Lyons	2000 v Arg	40	4	0	0	0	20
T P McIsaac	2006 v E	6	0	0	0	0	0
H J McMeniman	2005 v Sm	6	0	0	0	0	0
S T Moore	2005 v Sm	6	0	0	0	0	0
W L Palu	2006 v E	5	0	0	0	0	0
J A Paul	1998 v S	72	14	0	0	0	70
T Polota-Nau	2005 v E	2	0	0	0	0	0
B Robinson	2006 v SA	1	0	0	0	0	0
J A Roe	2003 v Nm	19	1	0	0	0	5
R U Samo	2004 v S	6	0	0	0	0	0
N C Sharpe	2002 v F	50	4	0	0	0	20
G T Shepherdson	2006 v I	5	0	0	0	0	0
G B Smith	2000 v F	69	7	0	0	0	35
D J Vickerman	2002 v F	40	0	0	0	0	0
P R Waugh	2000 v E	52	4	0	0	0	20
W K Young	2000 v F	46	0	0	0	0	0

* Roff's figures include a penalty try awarded against New Zealand in 2001 and Flatley's one awarded against Ireland in 2003

AUSTRALIA INTERNATIONAL PLAYERS
UP TO 30TH SEPTEMBER 2006

Entries in square brackets denote matches played in RWC Finals.

Abrahams, A M F (NSW) 1967 NZ, 1968 NZ 1, 1969 W
Adams, N J (NSW) 1955 NZ 1
Adamson, R W (NSW) 1912 US
Allan, T (NSW) 1946 NZ 1, M, NZ 2, 1947 NZ 2, S, I, W, 1948 E, F, 1949 M 1,2,3, NZ 1,2
Anderson, R P (NSW) 1925 NZ 1
Anlezark, E A (NSW) 1905 NZ
Armstrong, A R (NSW) 1923 NZ 1,2
Ashley-Cooper, A P (ACT) 2005 SA4(R)
Austin, L R (NSW) 1963 E

Baker, R L (NSW) 1904 BI 1,2
Baker, W H (NSW) 1914 NZ 1,2,3
Ballesty, J P (NSW) 1968 NZ 1,2, F, I, S, 1969 W, SA 2,3,4,
Bannon, D P (NSW) 1946 M
Bardsley, E J (NSW) 1928 NZ 1,3, M (R)
Barker, H S (NSW) 1952 Fj 1,2, NZ 1,2, 1953 SA 4, 1954 Fj 1,2
Barnett, J T (NSW) 1907 NZ 1,2,3, 1908 W, 1909 E
Barry, M J (Q) 1971 SA 3
Bartholomeusz, M A (ACT) 2002 It (R)
Barton, R F D (NSW) 1899 BI 3
Batch, P G (Q) 1975 S, W, 1976 E, Fj 1,2,3, F 1,2, 1978 W 1,2, NZ 1,2,3, 1979 Arg 2
Batterham, R P (NSW) 1967 NZ, 1970 S
Battishall, B R (NSW) 1973 E
Baxter, A J (NSW) 1949 M 1,2,3, NZ 1,2, 1951 NZ 1,2, 1952 NZ 1,2
Baxter, A K E (NSW) 2003 NZ 2(R), [Arg, R, I(R), S(R), NZ(R), E], 2004 S1, 2, E1, PI, NZ1, SA1, NZ2, SA2, S3, F, S4, E2, 2005 It, F1, SA1,2,3(R), NZ1, SA4, NZ2, F2, E, I(R), W(R), 2006 E1(R), 2(R), I(R), NZ1(R), SA1(R), NZ3(R), SA3(R)
Baxter, T J (Q) 1958 NZ 3
Beith, B McN (NSW) 1914 NZ 3, 1920 NZ 1,2,3
Bell, K R (Q) 1968 S
Bell, M D (NSW) 1996 C
Bennett, W G (Q) 1931 M, 1933 SA 1,2,3,
Bermingham, J V (Q) 1934 NZ 1,2, 1937 SA 1
Berne, J E (NSW) 1975 S
Besomo, K S (NSW) 1979 I 2
Betts, T N (Q) 1951 NZ 2,3, 1954 Fj 2
Biilmann, R R (NSW) 1933 SA 1,2,3,4
Birt, R (Q) 1914 NZ 2
Black, J W (NSW) 1985 C 1,2, NZ, Fj 1
Blackwood, J G (NSW) 1922 M 1, NZ 1,2,3, 1923 M 1, NZ 1,2,3, 1924 NZ 1,2,3, 1925 NZ 1,4, 1926 NZ 1,2,3, 1927 I, W, S, 1928 E, F
Blades, A T (NSW) 1996 S, I, W 3, 1997 NZ 1(R), E 1(R), SA 1(R), NZ 3, SA 2, Arg 1,2, E 2, S, 1998 E 1, S 1,2, NZ 1, SA 1, NZ 2, SA 2, NZ 3, Fj, WS, F, E 2, 1999 I 1(R), SA 2, NZ 2, [R, I 3, W, SA 3, F]
Blades, C D (NSW) 1997 E 1
Blake, R C (Q) 2006 E1,2,NZ2,SA2,NZ3,SA3
Blair, M R (NSW) 1928 F, 1931 M, NZ
Bland, G V (NSW) 1928 NZ 3, M, 1932 NZ 1,2,3, 1933 SA 1,2,4,5
Blomley, J (NSW) 1949 M 1,2,3, NZ 1,2, 1950 BI 1,2
Boland, S B (Q) 1899 BI 3,4, 1903 NZ
Bond, G S G (ACT) 2001 SA 2(R), Sp (R), E (R), F, W
Bond, J H (NSW) 1920 NZ 1,2,3, 1921 NZ
Bondfield, C (NSW) 1925 NZ 2
Bonis, E T (Q) 1929 NZ 1,2,3, 1930 BI, 1931 M, NZ, 1932 NZ 1,2,3, 1933 SA 1,2,3,4,5, 1934 NZ 1,2, 1936 NZ 1,2, M, 1937 SA 1, 1938 NZ 1
Bonner, J E (NSW) 1922 NZ 1,2,3, 1923 M 1,2,3, 1924 NZ 1,2
Bosler, J M (NSW) 1953 SA 1
Bouffler, R G (NSW) 1899 BI 3
Bourke, T K (Q) 1947 NZ 2
Bowden, R (NSW) 1926 NZ 4
Bowen, S (NSW) 1993 SA 1,2,3, 1995 [R], NZ 1,2, 1996 C, NZ 1, SA 2
Bowers, A J A (NSW) 1923 M 2(R),3, NZ, 3, 1925 NZ 1,4, 1926 NZ 1, 1927 I
Bowman, T M (NSW) 1998 E 1, S 1,2, NZ 1, SA 1, NZ 2, SA 2, NZ 3, Fj, WS, F, E 2, 1999 I 1,2, SA 2, [US]
Boyce, E S (NSW) 1962 NZ 1,2, 1964 NZ 1,2,3, 1965 SA 1,2, 1966 W, S, 1967 E, I 1, F, I 2
Boyce, J S (NSW) 1962 NZ 3,4,5, 1963 E, SA 1,2,3,4, 1964 NZ 1,3, 1965 SA 1,2
Boyd, A (NSW) 1899 BI 3
Boyd, A F McC (Q) 1958 M 1
Brass, J E (NSW) 1966 BI 2, W, S, 1967 E, I 1, F, I 2, NZ, 1968 NZ 1, F, I, S
Breckenridge, J W (NSW) 1925 NZ 2(R),3, 1927 I, W, S, 1928 E, F, 1929 NZ 1,2,3, 1930 BI
Brial, M C (NSW) 1993 F 1(R), 2, 1996 W 1(R), 2, C, NZ 1, SA 1, NZ 2, SA 2, It, I, W 3, 1997 NZ 2
Bridle, O L (V) 1931 M, 1932 NZ 1,2,3, 1933 SA 3,4,5, 1934 NZ 1,2, 1936 NZ 1,2, M
Broad, E G (Q) 1949 M 1
Brockhoff, J D (NSW) 1949 M 2,3, NZ 1,2, 1950 BI 1,2, 1951 NZ 2,3
Brown, B R (Q) 1972 NZ 1,3
Brown, J V (NSW) 1956 SA 1,2, 1957 NZ 1,2, 1958 W, I, E, S, F
Brown, R C (NSW) 1975 E 1,2
Brown, S W (NSW) 1953 SA 2,3,4
Bryant, H (NSW) 1925 NZ 1,3,4
Buchan, A J (NSW) 1946 NZ 1,2, 1947 NZ 1,2, S, I, W, 1948 E, F, 1949 M 3
Buchanan, P N (NSW) 1923 M 2(R),3
Bull, D (NSW) 1928 M
Buntine, H (NSW) 1923 NZ 1(R), 1924 NZ 2
Burdon, A (NSW) 1903 NZ, 1904 BI 1,2, 1905 NZ
Burge, A B (NSW) 1907 NZ 3, 1908 W
Burge, P H (NSW) 1907 NZ 1,2,3
Burge, R (NSW) 1928 NZ 1,2,3(R), M (R)
Burke, B T (NSW) 1988 S (R)
Burke, C T (NSW) 1946 NZ 2, 1947 NZ 1,2, S, I, W, 1948 E, F, 1949 M 2,3, NZ 1,2, 1950 BI 1,2, 1951 NZ 1,2,3, 1953 SA 2,3,4, 1954 Fj 1, 1955 NZ 1,2,3, 1956 SA 1,2,
Burke, M C (NSW) 1993 SA 3(R), F 1, 1994 I 1,2, It 1,2, 1995 [C, R, E], NZ 1,2, 1996 W 1,2, C, NZ 1, SA 1, NZ 2, SA 2, It, S, I, W 3, 1997 E 1, NZ 2 , 1998 E 1, S 1,2, NZ 1, SA 1, NZ 2, SA 2, NZ 3, 1999 I 2(R), E (R), SA 1, NZ 1, SA 2, NZ 2, [R, I 3, US, W, SA 3, F], 2000 F, S, E, 2001 BI 1(R),2,3, SA 1, NZ 1, SA 2, NZ 2, Sp, E, F, W, 2002 F 1,2, NZ 1, SA 1, NZ 2, SA 2, Arg, I, E, It, 2003 SA 1, NZ 1, SA 2(R), NZ 2(R), [Arg,R, Nm(R),I], 2004 S1(R), PI(R), SA1(R), NZ2(t&R), SA2(R)
Burke, M P (NSW) 1984 E (R), I, 1985 C 1,2, NZ, Fj 1,2, 1986 It (R), F, Arg 1,2, NZ 1,2,3, 1987 SK, [US, J, I, F, W], NZ, Arg 1,2
Burnet, D R (NSW) 1972 F 1,2, NZ 1,2,3, Fj
Butler, O F (NSW) 1969 SA 1,2, 1970 S, 1971 SA 2,3, F 1,2

Calcraft, W J (NSW) 1985 C 1, 1986 It, Arg 2
Caldwell, B C (NSW) 1928 NZ 3
Cameron, A S (NSW) 1951 NZ 1,2,3, 1952 Fj 1,2, NZ 1,2, 1953 SA 1,2,3,4, 1954 Fj 1,2, 1955 NZ 1,2,3, 1956 SA 1,2, 1957 NZ 1, 1958 I
Campbell, A M (ACT) 2005 F1(R)
Campbell, J D (NSW) 1910 NZ 1,2,3
Campbell, W A (Q) 1984 Fj, 1986 It, F, Arg 1,2, NZ 1,2,3, 1987 SK, [E, US, J (R), I, F], NZ, 1988 E, 1989 BI 1,2,3, NZ, 1990 NZ 2,3
Campese, D I (ACT, NSW) 1982 NZ 1,2,3, 1983 US, Arg 1,2, NZ, It, F 1,2, 1984 Fj, NZ 1,2,3, E, I, W, S, 1985 Fj 1,2, 1986 It, F, Arg 1,2, NZ 1,2,3, 1987 [E, US, J, I, F, W], NZ, 1988 E 1,2, NZ 1,2,3, E, S, It, 1989 BI 1,2,3, NZ, F 1,2, 1990 F 2,3, US, NZ 1,2,3, 1991 W, E, NZ 1,2, [Arg, WS, W, I, NZ, E], 1992 S 1,2, NZ 1,2,3, SA, I, W, 1993 Tg, NZ, SA 1,2,3, C, F 1,2, 1994 I 1,2, It 1,2, WS, NZ, 1995 Arg 1,2, [SA, C, E], NZ 2(R), 1996 W 1,2, C, NZ 1, SA 1, NZ 2, SA 2, It, W3
Canniffe, W D (Q) 1907 NZ 2
Cannon, B J (NSW) 2001 BI 2(R), NZ 1(R), Sp (R), F (R), W (R), 2002 F 1(R),2, SA 1(t),2(R), I (t), It (R), 2003 I (R), W (R), E (R), SA 1, NZ 1, SA 2, NZ 2, [Arg,R,I, S,NZ,E], 2004 S1,2,E1,PI,NZ 1,2,SA2,S3(R), 4(R), 2005 NZ1(R),SA4,NZ2,F2,E,I,W
Caputo, M E (ACT) 1996 W 1,2, 1997 F 1,2, NZ 1
Carberry, C M (NSW, Q) 1973 Tg 2, E, 1976 I, US, Fj 1,2,3, 1981 F 1,2, I, W, S, 1982 E
Cardy, A M (NSW) 1966 BI 1,2, W, S, 1967 E, I 1, F, 1968 NZ 1,2
Carew, P J (Q) 1899 BI 1,2,3,4
Carmichael, P (Q) 1904 BI 2, 1907 NZ 1, 1908 W, 1909 E
Carozza, P V (Q) 1990 F 1,2,3, NZ 2,3, 1992 S 1,2, NZ 1,2,3, SA, I, W, 1993 Tg, NZ
Carpenter, M G (V) 1938 NZ 1,2,
Carr, E T A (NSW) 1913 NZ 1,2,3, 1914 NZ 1,2,3
Carr, E W (NSW) 1921 SA 1,2,3, NZ (R)
Carroll, D B (NSW) 1908 W, 1912 US
Carroll, J C (NSW) 1953 SA 1
Carroll, J H (NSW) 1958 M 2,3, NZ 1,2,3, 1959 BI 1,2
Carson, J (NSW) 1899 BI 1
Carson, P J (NSW) 1979 NZ, 1980 NZ 3
Carter, D G (NSW) 1988 E 1,2, NZ 1, 1989 F 1,2
Casey, T V (NSW) 1963 SA 2,3,4, 1964 NZ 1,2,3
Catchpole, K W (NSW) 1961 Fj 1,2,3, SA 1,2, F, 1962 NZ 1,2,4, 1963 SA 2,3,4, 1964 NZ 1,2,3, 1965 SA 1,2, 1966 BI 1,2, W, S, 1967 E, I 1, F, I 2, NZ, 1968 NZ 1
Cawsey, R M (NSW) 1949 M 1, NZ 1,2
Cerutti, W H (NSW) 1928 NZ 1,2,3, M, 1929 NZ 1,2,3, 1930 BI, 1931 M, NZ, 1932 NZ 1,2,3, 1933 SA 1,2,3,4,5, 1936 M, 1937 SA 1,2
Challoner, R L (NSW) 1899 BI 2
Chambers, R (NSW) 1920 NZ 1,3
Chapman, G A (NSW) 1962 NZ 3,4,5
Chisholm, M D (ACT) 2004 S3(R), 2005 Sm,It,F1,SA1, 2,3(R),NZ1(R),2,F2,E(t&R),I(R),W(R),2006 E1(R), 2, I, NZ1, SA1(R), NZ2(R), SA2(R), NZ3 (t&R), SA3(R)
Clark, J G (Q) 1931 M, NZ, 1932 NZ 1,2, 1933 SA 1
Clarken, J C (NSW) 1905 NZ, 1910 NZ 1,2,3
Cleary, M A (NSW) 1961 Fj 1,2,3, SA 1,2, F
Clements, P (NSW) 1982 NZ 3
Clifford, M (NSW) 1938 NZ 3
Cobb, W G (NSW) 1899 BI 3,4
Cockbain, M J (Q) 1997 F 2(R), NZ 1, SA 1,2, 1998 E 1, S 1,2, NZ 1, SA 1, NZ 2, SA 2, NZ 3, Fj, Tg (R), WS, F, E 2, 1999 I 1,2, E, SA 1, NZ 1, SA 2, NZ 2, [US (t&R), W, SA 3, F], 2000 Arg 1,2, SA 2(t&R),3(t&R), F, S, E (R), 2001 BI 1(R),2(R),3(R), SA 1(R), NZ 1(R), SA 2(R), NZ 2(R), Sp (R), E (R), F (t+R), W, 2002 F 1(R),2(R), NZ 1(R), SA 1(R), NZ 2(R), SA 2(R), Arg, I, E, It, 2003 [Arg(R),R(R),Nm(R),I(R),S(R),NZ(R),E(R)]
Cocks, M R (NSW, Q) 1972 F 1,2, NZ 2,3, Fj, 1973 Tg 1,2, W, E, 1975 J 1
Codey, D (NSW Country, Q) 1983 Arg 1, 1984 E, W, S, 1985 C 2, NZ, 1986 F, Arg 1, 1987 [US, J, F (R), W], NZ
Cody, E W (NSW) 1913 NZ 1,2,3
Coker, T (Q, ACT) 1987 [E, US, F, W], 1991 NZ 2, [Arg, WS, NZ, E], 1992 NZ 1,2,3, W (R), 1993 Tg, NZ, 1995 Arg 2, NZ 1(R), 1997 F 1(R), 2, NZ 1, E 1, NZ 2(R), SA 1(R), NZ 3, SA 2, Arg 1,2
Colbert, R (NSW) 1952 Fj 2, NZ 1,2, 1953 SA 2,3,4
Cole, J W (NSW) 1968 NZ 1,2, F, I, S, 1969 W, SA 1,2,3,4, 1970 S, 1971 SA 1,2,3, F 1,2, 1972 NZ 1,2,3, 1973 Tg 1,2, 1974 NZ 1,2,3
Collins, P K (NSW) 1937 SA 2, 1938 NZ 2,3
Colton, A J (Q) 1899 BI 1,3
Colton, T (Q) 1904 BI 1,2
Comrie-Thomson, I R (NSW) 1926 NZ 4, 1928 NZ 1,2,3 M
Connor, D M (Q) 1958 W, I, E, S, F, M 2,3, NZ 1,2,3, 1959 BI 1,2
Connors, M R (Q) 1999 SA 1(R), NZ 1(R), SA 2(R), NZ 2, [R (R), I 3, US, W (R), SA 3(R), F(R)], 2000 Arg 1(R),2(R), SA 1, NZ 1, SA 2, NZ 2(t&R), SA 3, F (R), S (R), E (R)
Constable, R (Q) 1994 I 2(t & R)
Cook, M T (Q) 1986 F, 1987 SK, [J], 1988 E 1,2, NZ 1,2,3, E, S, It
Cooke, B P (Q) 1979 I 1
Cooke, G M (Q) 1932 NZ 1,2,3, 1933 SA 1,2,3, 1946 NZ 2, 1947 NZ 2, S, I, W, 1948 E, F
Coolican, J E (NSW) 1982 NZ 1, 1983 It, F 1,2
Cooney, R C (NSW) 1922 M 2
Cordingley, S J (Q) 2000 Arg 1(R), SA 1(R), F, S, E, 2006 E2,I(R),NZ1(R),SA1(R),NZ2(R),SA2(R)
Corfe, A C (Q) 1899 BI 2
Cornelsen, G (NSW) 1974 NZ 2,3, 1975 J 2, S, W, 1976 E, F 1,2, 1978 W 1,2, NZ 1,2,3, 1979 I 1,2, NZ, Arg 1,2, 1980 NZ 1,2,3, 1981 I, W, S, 1982 E
Cornes, J R (Q) 1972 Fj
Cornforth, R G W (NSW) 1947 NZ 1, 1950 BI 2
Cornish, P (ACT) 1990 F 2,3, NZ 1
Costello, P P S (Q) 1950 BI 2
Cottrell, N V (Q) 1949 M 1,2,3, NZ 1,2, 1950 BI 1,2, 1951 NZ 1,2,3, 1952 Fj 1,2, NZ 1,2
Cowper, D L (V) 1931 NZ, 1932 NZ 1,2,3, 1933 SA 1,2,3,4,5
Cox, B P (NSW) 1952 Fj 1,2, NZ 1,2, 1954 Fj 2, 1955 NZ 1, 1956 SA 2, 1957 NZ 1,2
Cox, M H (NSW) 1981 W, S
Cox, P A (NSW) 1979 Arg 1,2, 1980 Fj, NZ 1,2, 1981 W (R), S, 1982 S 1,2, NZ 1,2,3, 1984 Fj, NZ 1,2,3
Craig, R R (NSW) 1908 W
Crakanthorp, J S (NSW) 1923 NZ 3
Cremin, J F (NSW) 1946 NZ 1,2, 1947 NZ 1
Crittle, C P (NSW) 1962 NZ 4,5, 1963 SA 2,3,4, 1964 NZ 1,2,3, 1965 SA 1,2, 1966 BI 1,2, S, 1967 E, I
Croft, B H D (NSW) 1928 M
Croft, D N (Q) 2002 Arg (t&R), I (R), E (t&R), It (R), 2003 [Nm]
Cross, J R (NSW) 1955 NZ 1,2,3
Cross, K A (NSW) 1949 M 1, NZ 1,2, 1950 BI 1,2, 1951 NZ 2,3, 1952 NZ 1, 1953 SA 1,2,3,4, 1954 Fj 1,2, 1955 NZ 3, 1956 SA 1,2, 1957 NZ 1,2
Crossman, O C (NSW) 1923 M 1(R),2,3, 1924, NZ 1,2,3, 1925 NZ 1,3,4, 1926 NZ 1,2,3,4, 1929 NZ 2, 1930 BI
Crowe, P J (NSW) 1976 F 2, 1978 W 1,2, 1979 I 2, NZ, Arg 1
Crowley, D J (Q) 1989 BI 1,2,3, 1991 [WS], 1992 I, W, 1993 C (R), 1995 Arg 1,2, [SA, E], NZ 1, 1996 W 2(R), C, NZ 1, SA 1,2, I, W 3, 1998 E 1(R), S 1(R),2(R), NZ 1(R), SA 1, NZ 2, SA 2, NZ 3, Tg, WS, 1999 I 1,2(R), E (R), SA 1, NZ 1(R), [R (R), I 3(t&R), US, F(R)]
Curley, T G P (NSW) 1957 NZ 1,2, 1958 W, I, E, S, F, M 1, NZ 1,2,3
Curran, D J (NSW) 1980 NZ 3, 1981 F 1,2, W, 1983 Arg 1
Currie, E W (Q) 1899 BI 2
Cutler, S A G (NSW) 1982 NZ 2(R), 1984 NZ 1,2,3, E, I, W, S, 1985 C 1,2, NZ, Fj 1,2, 1986 It, F, NZ 1,2,3, 1987 SK, [E, J, I, F, W], NZ, Arg 1,2, 1988 E 1,2, NZ 1,2,3, E, S, It, 1989 BI 1,2,3, NZ, 1991 [WS]

Daly, A J (NSW) 1989 NZ, F 1,2, 1990 F 1,2,3, US, NZ 1,2,3, 1991 W, E, NZ 1,2, [Arg, W, I, NZ, E], 1992 S 1,2, NZ 1,2,3, SA, 1993 Tg, NZ, SA 1,2,3, C, F 1,2, 1994 I 1,2, It 1,2, WS, NZ, 1995 [C, R]
D'Arcy, A M (Q) 1980 Fj, NZ 3, 1981 F 1,2, I, W, S, 1982 E, S 1,2
Darveniza, P (NSW) 1969 W, SA 2,3,4
Darwin, B J (ACT) 2001 BI 1(R), SA 1(R), NZ 1(R), SA 2(R), NZ 2(t&R), Sp, E, F, W, 2002 NZ 1(R), SA 1(R), NZ 2(R), SA 2,

Arg (R), I (R), E (R), It (R), 2003 I (R), W (t&R), E (R), SA 1(R), NZ 1(R), [Arg(R),R(R),Nm,I,S,NZ]
Davidson, R A L (NSW) 1952 Fj 1,2, NZ 1,2, 1953 SA 1, 1957 NZ 1,2, 1958 W, I, E, S, F, M 1
Davis, C C (NSW) 1949 NZ 1, 1951 NZ 1,2,3
Davis, E H (V) 1947 S, W, 1949 M 1,2
Davis, G V (NSW) 1963 E, SA 1,2,3,4, 1964 NZ 1,2,3, 1965 SA 1, 1966 BI 1,2, W, S, 1967 E, I 1, F, I 2, NZ, 1968 NZ 1,2, F, I, S, 1969 W, SA 1,2,3,4, 1970 S, 1971 SA 1,2,3, F 1,2, 1972 F 1,2, NZ 1,2,3
Davis, G W G (NSW) 1955 NZ 2,3
Davis, R A (NSW) 1974 NZ 1,2,3
Davis, T S R (NSW) 1920 NZ 1,2,3, 1921 SA 1,2,3, NZ, 1922 M 1,2,3, NZ 1,2,3, 1923 M 3, NZ 1,2,3, 1924 NZ 1,2, 1925 NZ 1
Davis, W (NSW) 1899 BI 1,3,4
Dawson, W L (NSW) 1946 NZ 1,2
Diett, L J (NSW) 1959 BI 1,2
Dix, W (NSW) 1907 NZ 1,2,3, 1909 E
Dixon, E J (Q) 1904 BI 3
Donald, K J (Q) 1957 NZ 1, 1958 W, I, E, S, M 2,3, 1959 BI 1,2
Dore, E (Q) 1904 BI 1
Dore, M J (Q) 1905 NZ
Dorr, R W (V) 1936 M, 1937 SA 1
Douglas, J A (V) 1962 NZ 3,4,5
Douglas, W A (NSW) 1922 NZ 3(R)
Dowse, J H (NSW) 1961 Fj 1,2, SA 1,2
Dunbar, A R (NSW) 1910 NZ 1,2,3, 1912 US
Duncan, J L (NSW) 1926 NZ 4
Dunlop, E E (V) 1932 NZ 3, 1934 NZ 1
Dunn, P K (NSW) 1958 NZ 1,2,3, 1959 BI 1,2
Dunn, V A (NSW) 1920 NZ 1,2,3, 1921 SA 1,2,3, NZ
Dunning, M J (NSW) 2003 [Nm,E(R)], 2004 S1(R), 2(R), E1(R), NZ1(R), SA1(R), NZ2(t&R), SA2(R), S3(R), F(R), S4(R), E2(R), 2005 Sm, It(R), F1(t&R), SA1(R), 2(R), 3, NZ1(t&R), SA4(t&R), NZ2(R), F2, E, W
Dunworth, D A (Q) 1971 F 1,2, 1972 F 1,2, 1976 Fj 2
Dwyer, L J (NSW) 1910 NZ 1,2,3, 1912 US, 1913 NZ 3, 1914 NZ 1,2,3
Dyson, F J (Q) 2000 Arg 1,2, SA 1, NZ 1, SA 2, NZ 2, SA 3, F, S, E

Eales, J A (Q) 1991 W, E, NZ 1,2, [Arg, WS, W, I, NZ, E], 1992 S 1,2, NZ 1,2,3, SA, I, 1994 I 1,2, It 1,2, WS, NZ, 1995 Arg 1,2, [SA, C, R, E], NZ 1,2, 1996 W 1,2, C, NZ 1, SA 1, NZ 2, SA 2, It, S, I, 1997 F 1,2, NZ 1, E 1, NZ 2, SA 1, Arg 1,2, E 2, S, 1998 E 1, S 1,2, NZ 1, SA 1, NZ 2, SA 2, NZ 3, Fj, Tg, WS, F, E 2, 1999 [R, I 3, W, SA 3, F], 2000 Arg 1,2, SA 1, NZ 1, SA 2, NZ 2, SA 3, F, S, E, 2001 BI 1,2,3, SA 1, NZ 1, SA 2, NZ 2
Eastes, C C (NSW) 1946 NZ 1,2, 1947 NZ 1,2, 1949 M 1,2
Edmonds, M H M (NSW) 1998 Tg, 2001 SA 1(R)
Egerton, R H (NSW) 1991 W, E, NZ 1,2, [Arg, W, I, NZ, E]
Ella, G A (NSW) 1982 NZ 1,2, 1983 F 1,2, 1988 E 2, NZ 1
Ella, G J (NSW) 1982 S 1, 1983 It, 1985 C 2(R), Fj 2
Ella, M G (NSW) 1980 NZ 1,2,3, 1981 F 2, S, 1982 E, S 1, NZ 1,2,3, 1983 US, Arg 1,2, NZ, It, F 1,2, 1984 Fj, NZ 1,2,3, E, I, W, S
Ellem, M A (NSW) 1976 Fj 3(R)
Elliott, F M (NSW) 1957 NZ 1
Elliott, R E (NSW) 1920 NZ 1, 1921 NZ, 1922 M 1,2, NZ 1(R),2,3, 1923 M 1,2,3, NZ 1,2,3
Ellis, C S (NSW) 1899 BI 1,2,3,4
Ellis, K J (NSW) 1958 NZ 1,2,3, 1959 BI 1,2
Ellwood, B J (NSW) 1958 NZ 1,2,3, 1961 Fj 2,3, SA 1, F, 1962 NZ 1,2,3,4,5, 1963 SA 1,2,3,4, 1964 NZ 3, 1965 SA 1,2, 1966 BI 1
Elsom, R D (NSW) 2005 Sm,It,F1,SA1,2,3(R),4,NZ2,F2, 2006 E1,2,I,NZ1,SA1,NZ2,SA2,NZ3,SA3
Emanuel, D M (NSW) 1957 NZ 2, 1958 W, I, E, S, F, M 1,2,3
Emery, N A (NSW) 1947 NZ 2, S, I, W, 1948 E, F, 1949 M 2,3, NZ 1,2
Erasmus, D J (NSW) 1923 NZ 1,2
Erby, A B (NSW) 1923 M 1,2, NZ 2,3, 1925 NZ 2
Evans, L J (Q) 1903 NZ, 1904 BI 1,3
Evans, W T (Q) 1899 BI 1,2

Fahey, E J (NSW) 1912 US, 1913 NZ 1,2, 1914 NZ 3
Fairfax, R L (NSW) 1971 F 1,2, 1972 F 1,2, NZ 1, Fj, 1973 W, E
Farmer, E H (Q) 1910 NZ 1
Farquhar, C R (NSW) 1920 NZ 2
Farr-Jones, N C (NSW) 1984 E, I, W, S, 1985 C 1,2, NZ, Fj 1,2, 1986 It, F, Arg 1,2, NZ 1,2,3, 1987 SK, [E, I, F, W (R)], NZ, Arg 2, 1988 E 1,2, NZ 1,2,3, E, S, It, 1989 BI 1,2,3, NZ, F 1,2, 1990 F 1,2,3, US, NZ 1,2,3, 1991 W, E, NZ 1,2, [Arg, WS, I, NZ, E], 1992 S 1,2, NZ 1,2,3, SA, 1993 NZ, SA 1,2,3
Fava, S G (ACT, WF) 2005 E(R),I(R), 2006 NZ1(R), SA1, NZ2
Fay, G (NSW) 1971 SA 2, 1972 NZ 1,2,3, 1973 Tg 1,2, W, E, 1974 NZ 1,2,3, 1975 E 1,2, J 1, S, W, 1976 I, US, 1978 W 1,2, NZ 1,2,3, 1979 I 1
Fenwicke, P T (NSW) 1957 NZ 1, 1958 W, I, E, 1959 BI 1,2
Ferguson, R T (NSW) 1922 M 3, NZ 1, 1923 M 3, NZ 3
Fihelly, J A (Q) 1907 NZ 2
Finau, S F (NSW) 1997 NZ 3
Finegan, O D A (ACT) 1996 W 1,2, C, NZ 1, SA 1(t), S, W 3, 1997 SA 1, NZ 3, SA 2, Arg 1,2, E 2, S, 1998 E 1(R), S 1(t + R),2(t + R), NZ 1(R), SA 1(t),2(R), NZ 3(R), Fj (R), Tg, WS (t + R), F (R), E 2(R), 1999 NZ 2(R), [R, I 3(R), US, W (R), SA 3(R), F (R)], 2001 BI 1,2,3, SA 1, NZ 1, SA 2, NZ 2, Sp, E, F, W, 2002 F 1,2, NZ 1, SA 1, NZ 2, SA 2, I, 2003 SA 1(t&R), NZ 1(R), SA 2(R), NZ 2(R)
Finlay, A N (NSW) 1926 NZ 1,2,3, 1927 I, W, S, 1928 E, F, 1929 NZ 1,2,3, 1930 BI
Finley, F G (NSW) 1904 BI 3
Finnane, S C (NSW) 1975 E 1, J 1,2, 1976 E, 1978 W 1,2
Fitter, D E (ACT) 2005 I,W
FitzSimons, P (NSW) 1989 F 1,2, 1990 F 1,2,3, US, NZ 1
Flanagan, P (Q) 1907 NZ 1,2
Flatley, E J (Q) 1997 E 2, S, 2000 S (R), 2001 BI 1(R),2(R),3, SA 1, NZ 1(R),2(R), Sp (R), F (R), W, 2002 F 1(R),2(R), NZ 1(t+R), SA 1(R), NZ 2(t), Arg (R), I (R), E, It, 2003 I, W, SA 1, NZ 1, SA 2, NZ 2, [Arg,R,I,S,NZ,E], 2004 S3(R),F(R),S4(R),E2, 2005 NZ1(R)
Flett, J A (NSW) 1990 US, NZ 2,3, 1991 [WS]
Flynn, J P (Q) 1914 NZ 1,2
Fogarty, J R (Q) 1949 M 2,3
Foley, M A (Q) 1995 [C (R), R], 1996 W 2(R), NZ 1, SA 1, NZ 2, SA 2, It, S, I, W 3, 1997 NZ 1(R), E 1, NZ 2, SA 1, NZ 3, SA 2, Arg 1,2, E 2, S, 1998 Tg (R), F (R), E 2(R), 1999 NZ 2(R), [US, W, SA 3, F], 2000 Arg 1,2, SA 1, NZ 1, SA 2, NZ 2, SA 3, F, S, E, 2001 BI 1(R),2,3, SA 1, NZ 1, SA 2, NZ 2, Sp, E, F, W
Foote, R H (NSW) 1924 NZ 2,3, 1926 NZ 2
Forbes, C F (Q) 1953 SA 2,3,4, 1954 Fj 1, 1956 SA 1,2
Ford, B (Q) 1957 NZ 2
Ford, E E (NSW) 1927 I, W, S, 1928 E, F, 1929 NZ 1,3
Ford, J A (NSW) 1925 NZ 4, 1926 NZ 1,2, 1927 I, W, S, 1928 E, 1929 NZ 1,2,3, 1930 BI
Forman, T R (NSW) 1968 I, S, 1969 W, SA 1,2,3,4
Fowles, D G (NSW) 1921 SA 1,2,3, 1922 M 2,3, 1923 M 2,3
Fox, C L (NSW) 1920 NZ 1,2,3, 1921 SA 1, NZ, 1922 M 1,2, NZ 1, 1924 NZ 1,2,3, 1925 NZ 1,2,3, 1926 NZ 1,3, 1928 F
Fox, O G (NSW) 1958 F
Francis, E (Q) 1914 NZ 1,2
Frawley, D (Q, NSW) 1986 Arg 2(R), 1987 Arg 1,2, 1988 E 1,2, NZ 1,2,3, S, It
Freedman, J E (NSW) 1962 NZ 3,4,5, 1963 SA 1
Freeman, E (NSW) 1946 NZ 1(R), M
Freier, A L (NSW) 2002 Arg (R), I, E (R), It, 2003 SA 1(R), NZ 1(t), 2005 NZ2(R), 2006 E2
Freney, M E (Q) 1972 NZ 1,2,3, 1973 Tg 1, W, E (R)
Friend, W S (NSW) 1920 NZ 3, 1921 SA 1,2,3, 1922 NZ 1,2,3, 1923 M 1,2,3
Furness, D C (NSW) 1946 M
Futter, F C (NSW) 1904 BI 3

Gardner, J M (Q) 1987 Arg 2, 1988 E 1, NZ 1, E
Gardner, W C (NSW) 1950 BI 1
Garner, R L (NSW) 1949 NZ 1,2
Gavin, K A (NSW) 1909 E
Gavin, T B (NSW) 1988 NZ 2,3, S, It (R), 1989 NZ (R), F 1,2, 1990 F 1,2,3, US, NZ 1,2,3, 1991 W, E, NZ 1, 1992 S 1,2, SA, I, W, 1993 Tg, NZ, SA 1,2,3, C, F 1,2, 1994 I 1,2, It 1,2,

WS, NZ, 1995 Arg 1,2, [SA, C, R, E], NZ 1,2, 1996 NZ 2(R), SA 2, W 3
Gelling, A M (NSW) 1972 NZ 1, Fj
George, H W (NSW) 1910 NZ 1,2,3, 1912 US, 1913 NZ 1,3, 1914 NZ 1,3
George, W G (NSW) 1923 M 1,3, NZ 1,2, 1924 NZ 3, 1925 NZ 2,3, 1926 NZ 4, 1928 NZ 1,2,3, M
Gerrard, M A (ACT) 2005 It(R),SA1(R),NZ1,2,E,I,W, 2006 E1,2,I,NZ1,SA1,NZ2,SA2,NZ3(t),SA3(R)
Gibbons, E de C (NSW) 1936 NZ 1,2, M
Gibbs, P R (V) 1966 S
Giffin, D T (ACT) 1996 W 3, 1997 F 1,2, 1999 I 1,2, E, SA 1, NZ 1, SA 2, NZ 2, [R, I 3, US (R), W, SA 3, F], 2000 Arg 1,2, SA 1, NZ 1, SA 2, NZ 2, SA 3, F, S, E, 2001 BI 1,2, SA 1, NZ 2, Sp, E, F, W, 2002 Arg (R), I, E (R), It (R), 2003 I, W, E, SA 1, NZ 1, SA 2, NZ 2, [Arg,Nm(R),I,NZ(t&R),E(R)]
Gilbert, H (NSW) 1910 NZ 1,2,3
Girvan, B (ACT) 1988 E
Giteau, M J (ACT, WF) 2002 E (R), It (R), 2003 SA 2(R), NZ 2(R), [Arg(R),R(R),Nm,I(R),S(R),E(t)], 2004 S1, E1, PI, NZ1, SA1, NZ2, SA2, S3, F, S4, E2, 2005 Sm, It, F1, SA1, 2,3, NZ1, SA4, F2, E(t&R), 2006 NZ1(R), SA1, NZ2, SA2, NZ3, SA3
Gordon, G C (NSW) 1929 NZ 1
Gordon, K M (NSW) 1950 BI 1,2
Gould, R G (Q) 1980 NZ 1,2,3, 1981 I, W, S, 1982 S 2, NZ 1,2,3, 1983 US, Arg 1, F 1,2, 1984 NZ 1,2,3, E, I, W, S, 1985 NZ, 1986 It, 1987 SK, [E]
Gourley, S R (NSW) 1988 S, It, 1989 BI 1,2,3
Graham, C S (Q) 1899 BI 2
Graham, R (NSW) 1973 Tg 1,2, W, E, 1974 NZ 2,3, 1975 E 2, J 1,2, S, W, 1976 I, US, Fj 1,2,3, F 1,2
Gralton, A S I (Q) 1899 BI 1,4, 1903 NZ
Grant, J C (NSW) 1988 E 1, NZ 2,3, E
Graves, R H (NSW) 1907 NZ 1(R)
Greatorex, E N (NSW) 1923 M 3, NZ 3, 1924 NZ 1,2,3, 1925 NZ 1, 1928 E, F
Gregan, G M (ACT) 1994 It 1,2, WS, NZ, 1995 Arg 1,2, [SA, C (R), R, E], 1996 W 1, C (t), SA 1, NZ 2, SA 2, It, I, W 3, 1997 F 1,2, NZ 1, E 1, NZ 2, SA 1, NZ 3, SA 2, Arg 1,2, E 2, S, 1998 E 1, S 1,2, NZ 1, SA 1, NZ 2, SA 2, NZ 3, Fj, WS, F, E 2, 1999 I 1,2, E, SA 1, NZ 1, SA 2, NZ 2, [R, I 3, W, SA 3, F], 2000 Arg 1,2, SA 1, NZ 1, SA 2, NZ 2, SA 3, 2001 BI 1,2,3, SA 1, NZ 1, SA 2, NZ 2, Sp, E, F, W, 2002 F 1,2, NZ 1, SA 1, NZ 2, SA 2, Arg, I, E, It, 2003 I, W, E, SA 1, NZ 1, SA 2, NZ 2, [Arg,R,I,S,NZ,E], 2004 S1, 2, E1, PI, SA1, NZ2, SA2, S3, F, S4, E2, 2005 It, F1, SA1, 2,3, NZ1, SA4, NZ2, F2, E, I, W, 2006 E1, 2(R), I, NZ1, SA1, NZ2, SA2, NZ3, SA3
Gregory, S C (Q) 1968 NZ 3, F, I, S, 1969 SA 1,3, 1971 SA 1,3, F 1,2, 1972 F 1,2, 1973 Tg 1,2, W, E
Grey, G O (NSW) 1972 F 2(R), NZ 1,2,3, Fj (R)
Grey, N P (NSW) 1998 S 2(R), SA 2(R), Fj (R), Tg (R), F, E 2, 1999 I 1(R),2(R), E, SA 1, NZ 1, SA 2, NZ 2(t&R), [R (R), I 3(R), US, SA 3(R), F (R)], 2000 S (R), E (R), 2001 BI 1,2,3, SA 1, NZ 1, SA 2, NZ 2, Sp, E, F, 2003 I (R), W (R), E, [Nm,NZ(t)]
Griffin, T S (NSW) 1907 NZ 1,3, 1908 W, 1910 NZ 1,2, 1912 US
Grigg, P C (Q) 1980 NZ 3, 1982 S 2, NZ 1,2,3, 1983 Arg 2, NZ, 1984 Fj, W, S, 1985 C 1,2, NZ, Fj 1,2, 1986 Arg 1,2, NZ 1,2, 1987 SK, [E, J, I, F, W]
Grimmond, D N (NSW) 1964 NZ 2
Gudsell, K E (NSW) 1951 NZ 1,2,3
Guerassimoff, J (Q) 1963 SA 2,3,4, 1964 NZ 1,2,3, 1965 SA 2, 1966 BI 1,2, 1967 E, I, F
Gunther, W J (NSW) 1957 NZ 2

Hall, D (Q) 1980 Fj, NZ 1,2,3, 1981 F 1,2, 1982 S 1,2, NZ 1,2, 1983 US, Arg 1,2, NZ, It
Hamalainen, H A (Q) 1929 NZ 1,2,3
Hamilton, B G (NSW) 1946 M
Hammand, C A (NSW) 1908 W, 1909 E
Hammon, J D C (V) 1937 SA 2
Handy, C B (Q) 1978 NZ 3, 1979 NZ, Arg 1,2, 1980 NZ 1,2
Hanley, R G (Q) 1983 US (R), It (R), 1985 Fj 2(R)
Hardcastle, P A (NSW) 1946 NZ 1, M, NZ 2, 1947 NZ 1, 1949 M 3
Hardcastle, W R (NSW) 1899 BI 4, 1903 NZ
Harding, M A (NSW) 1983 It
Hardman, S P (Q) 2002 F 2(R), 2006 SA1(R)
Hardy, M D (ACT) 1997 F 1(t), 2(R), NZ 1(R), 3(R), Arg 1(R), 2(R), 1998 Tg, WS
Harrison, J B (ACT, NSW) 2001 BI 3, NZ 1, SA 2, Sp, E, F, W (R), 2002 F 1,2, NZ 1, SA 1, NZ 2, SA 2, Arg, I (R), E, It, 2003 [R(R),Nm,S,NZ,E], 2004 S1, 2, E1, PI, NZ1, SA1, NZ2, SA2, S3, F, S4, E2
Harry, R L L (NSW) 1996 W 1,2, NZ 1, SA 1(t), NZ 2, It, S, 1997 F 1,2, NZ 1,2, SA 1, NZ 3, SA 2, Arg 1,2, E 2, S, 1998 E 1, S 1,2, NZ 1, Fj, 1999 SA 2, NZ 2, [R, I 3, W, SA 3, F], 2000 Arg 1,2, SA 1, NZ 1, SA 2, NZ 2, SA 3
Hartill, M N (NSW) 1986 NZ 1,2,3, 1987 SK, [J], Arg 1, 1988 NZ 1,2, E, It, 1989 BI 1(R), 2,3, F 1,2, 1995 Arg 1(R), 2(R), [C], NZ 1,2
Harvey, P B (Q) 1949 M 1,2
Harvey, R M (NSW) 1958 F, M 3
Hatherell, W I (Q) 1952 Fj 1,2
Hauser, R G (Q) 1975 J 1(R), 2, W (R), 1976 E, I, US, Fj 1,2,3, F 1,2, 1978 W 1,2, 1979 I 1,2
Hawker, M J (NSW) 1980 Fj, NZ 1,2,3, 1981 F 1,2, I, W, 1982 E, S 1,2, NZ 1,2,3, 1983 US, Arg 1,2, NZ, It, F 1,2, 1984 NZ 1,2,3, 1987 NZ
Hawthorne, P F (NSW) 1962 NZ 3,4,5, 1963 E, SA 1,2,3,4, 1964 NZ 1,2,3, 1965 SA 1,2, 1966 BI 1,2, W, 1967 E, I 1, F, I 2, NZ
Hayes, E S (Q) 1934 NZ 1,2, 1938 NZ 1,2,3
Heath, A (NSW) 1996 C, SA 1, NZ 2, SA 2, It, 1997 NZ 2, SA 1, E 2(R)
Heenan, D P (Q, ACT) 2003 W, 2006 E1
Heinrich, E L (NSW) 1961 Fj 1,2,3, SA 2, F, 1962 NZ 1,2,3, 1963 E, SA 1
Heinrich, V W (NSW) 1954 Fj 1,2
Heming, R J (NSW) 1961 Fj 2,3, SA 1,2, F, 1962 NZ 2,3,4,5, 1963 SA 2,3,4, 1964 NZ 1,2,3, 1965 SA 1,2, 1966 BI 1,2, W, 1967 F
Hemingway, W H (NSW) 1928 NZ 2,3, 1931 M, NZ, 1932 NZ 3
Henderson, N J (ACT) 2004 PI(R), 2005 Sm(R)
Henjak, M T (ACT) 2004 E1(R),NZ1(R), 2005 Sm(R),I(R)
Henry, A R (Q) 1899 BI 2
Herbert, A G (Q) 1987 SK (R), [F (R)], 1990 F 1(R), US, NZ 2,3, 1991 [WS], 1992 NZ 3(R), 1993 NZ (R), SA 2(R)
Herbert, D J (Q) 1994 I 2, It 1,2, WS (R), 1995 Arg 1,2, [SA, R], 1996 C, SA 2, It, S, I, 1997 NZ 1, 1998 E 1, S 1,2, NZ 1, SA 1, NZ 2, SA 2, Fj, Tg, WS, F, E 2, 1999 I 1,2, E, SA 1, NZ 1, SA 2, NZ 2, [R, I 3, W, SA 3, F], 2000 Arg 1,2, SA 1, NZ 1, SA 2, NZ 2, SA 3, F, S, E, 2001 BI 1,2,3, SA 1, NZ 1, SA 2, NZ 2, Sp, E, 2002 F 1,2, NZ 1, SA 1, NZ 2, SA 2, Arg, I, E, It
Herd, H V (NSW) 1931 M
Hickey, J (NSW) 1908 W, 1909 E
Hill, J (NSW) 1925 NZ 1
Hillhouse, D W (Q) 1975 S, 1976 E, Fj 1,2,3, F 1,2, 1978 W 1,2, 1983 US, Arg 1,2, NZ, It, F 1,2
Hills, E F (V) 1950 BI 1,2
Hindmarsh, J A (Q) 1904 BI 1
Hindmarsh, J C (NSW) 1975 J 2, S, W, 1976 US, Fj 1,2,3, F 1,2
Hipwell, J N B (NSW) 1968 NZ 1(R), 2, F, I, S, 1969 W, SA 1,2,3,4, 1970 S, 1971 SA 1,2, F 1,2, 1972 F 1,2, 1973 Tg 1, W, E, 1974 NZ 1,2,3, 1975 E 1,2, J 1, S, W, 1978 NZ 1,2,3, 1981 F 1,2, I, W, 1982 E
Hirschberg, W A (NSW) 1905 NZ
Hodgins, C H (NSW) 1910 NZ 1,2,3
Hodgson, A J (NSW) 1933 SA 2,3,4, 1934 NZ 1, 1936 NZ 1,2, M, 1937 SA 2, 1938 NZ 1,2,3
Hoiles, S A (NSW) 2004 S4(R),E2(R)
Holbeck, J C (ACT) 1997 NZ 1(R), E 1, NZ 2, SA 1, NZ 3, SA 2, 2001 BI 3(R)
Holdsworth, J W (NSW) 1921 SA 1,2,3, 1922 M 2,3, NZ 1(R)
Holmes, G S (Q) 2005 F2(R),E(t&R),I, 2006 E1, 2, I, NZ1, SA1, NZ2, SA2, NZ3
Holt, N C (Q) 1984 Fj
Honan, B D (Q) 1968 NZ 1(R), 2, F, I, S, 1969 SA 1,2,3,4
Honan, R E (Q) 1964 NZ 1,2
Horan, T J (Q) 1989 NZ, F 1,2, 1990 F 1, NZ 1,2,3, 1991 W, E, NZ 1,2, [Arg, WS, W, I, NZ, E], 1992 S 1,2, NZ 1,2,3, SA,

I, W, 1993 Tg, NZ, SA 1,2,3, C, F 1,2, 1995 [C, R, E], NZ 1,2, 1996 W 1,2, C, NZ 1, SA 1, It, S, I, W 3, 1997 F 1,2, NZ 1, E 1, NZ 2, Arg 1,2, E 2, S, 1998 E 1, S 1,2, NZ 1, SA 1, NZ 2, SA 2, NZ 3, Fj, Tg, WS, 1999 I 1,2, E, SA 1, NZ 1, SA 2, NZ 2, [R, I 3, W, SA 3, F], 2000 Arg 1
Horodam, D J (Q) 1913 NZ 2
Horsley, G R (Q) 1954 Fj 2
Horton, P A (NSW) 1974 NZ 1,2,3, 1975 E 1,2, J 1,2, S, W, 1976 E, F 1,2, 1978 W 1,2, NZ 1,2,3, 1979 NZ, Arg 1
Hoskins, J E (NSW) 1924 NZ 1,2,3
How, R A (NSW) 1967 I 2
Howard, J (Q) 1938 NZ 1,2
Howard, J L (NSW) 1970 S, 1971 SA 1, 1972 F 1(R), NZ 2, 1973 Tg 1,2, W
Howard, P W (Q, ACT) 1993 NZ, 1994 WS, NZ, 1995 NZ 1(R), 2(t), 1996 W 1,2, SA 1, NZ 2, SA 2, It, S, W 3, 1997 F 1,2, NZ 1, Arg 1,2, E 2, S
Howell, M L (NSW) 1946 NZ 1(R), 1947 NZ 1, S, I, W
Hughes, B D (NSW) 1913 NZ 2,3
Hughes, J C (NSW) 1907 NZ 1,3
Hughes, N McL (NSW) 1953 SA 1,2,3,4, 1955 NZ 1,2,3, 1956 SA 1,2, 1958 W, I, E, S, F
Humphreys, O W (NSW) 1920 NZ 3, 1921 NZ, 1922 M 1,2,3, 1925 NZ 1
Hutchinson, E E (NSW) 1937 SA 1,2
Hutchinson, F E (NSW) 1936 NZ 1,2, 1938 NZ 1,3

Ide, W P J (Q) 1938 NZ 2,3
Ives, W N (NSW) 1926 NZ 1,2,3,4, 1929 NZ 3

James, P M (Q) 1958 M 2,3
James, S L (NSW) 1987 SK (R), [E (R)], NZ, Arg 1,2, 1988 NZ 2(R)
Jamieson, A E (NSW) 1925 NZ 3(R)
Jaques, T (ACT) 2000 SA 1(R), NZ 1(R)
Jessep, E M (V) 1934 NZ 1,2
Johansson, L D T (Q) 2005 NZ2(R),F2(R),E(R)
Johnson, A P (NSW) 1946 NZ 1, M
Johnson, B B (NSW) 1952 Fj 1,2, NZ 1,2, 1953 SA 2,3,4, 1955 NZ 1,2
Johnson, P G (NSW) 1959 BI 1,2, 1961 Fj 1,2,3, SA 1,2, F, 1962 NZ 1,2,3,4,5, 1963 E, SA 1,2,3,4, 1964 NZ 1,2,3, 1965 SA 1,2, 1966 BI 1,2, W, S, 1967 E, I 1, F, I 2, NZ, 1968 NZ 1,2, F, I, S, 1970 S, 1971 SA 1,2, F 1,2
Johnstone, B (Q) 1993 Tg (R)
Jones, G G (Q) 1952 Fj 1,2, 1953 SA 1,2,3,4, 1954 Fj 1,2, 1955 NZ 1,2,3, 1956 SA 1
Jones, H (NSW) 1913 NZ 1,2,3
Jones, P A (NSW) 1963 E, SA 1
Jorgensen, P (NSW) 1992 S 1(R), 2(R)
Joyce, J E (NSW) 1903 NZ
Judd, H A (NSW) 1903 NZ, 1904 BI 1,2,3, 1905 NZ
Judd, P B (NSW) 1925 NZ 4, 1926 NZ 1,2,3,4, 1927 I, W, S, 1928 E, 1931 M, NZ
Junee, D K (NSW) 1989 F 1(R), 2(R), 1994 WS (R), NZ (R)

Kafer, R B (ACT) 1999 NZ 2, [R, US (R)], 2000 Arg 1(R),2, SA 1, NZ 1(t&R), SA 2(R),3(R), F, S, E
Kahl, P R (Q) 1992 W
Kanaar, A (NSW) 2005 NZ2(R)
Kassulke, N (Q) 1985 C 1,2
Kay, A R (V) 1958 NZ 2, 1959 BI 2
Kay, P (NSW) 1988 E 2
Kearney, K H (NSW) 1947 NZ 1,2, S, I, W, 1948 E, F
Kearns, P N (NSW) 1989 NZ, F 1,2, 1990 F 1,2,3, US, NZ 1,2,3, 1991 W, E, NZ 1,2, [Arg, WS, W, I, NZ, E], 1992 S 1,2, NZ 1,2,3, SA, I, W, 1993 Tg, NZ, SA 1,2,3, C, F 1,2, 1994 I 1,2, It 1,2, WS, NZ, 1995 Arg 1,2, [SA, C, E], NZ 1,2, 1998 E 1, S 1,2, NZ 1, SA 1, NZ 2, SA 2, NZ 3, Fj, WS, F, E 2, 1999 I 2(R), SA 1(R),2, NZ 2, [R, I 3]
Kefu, R S T (Q) 1997 SA 2(R), 1998 E 1, S 1,2, NZ 1, SA 1, NZ 2, SA 2, NZ 3, Fj (R), Tg, WS (R), F, E 2, 1999 I 1,2, E, SA 1, NZ 1(R), SA 2, NZ 2, [R, I 3, SA 3, F], 2000 SA 1(t&R), NZ 1(R), SA 2(R), NZ 2, SA 3(R), F, S, E, 2001 BI 1,2,3, SA 1, NZ 1, SA 2, NZ 2, Sp, E, F, W, 2002 F 1, NZ 1, SA 1, NZ 2, SA 2, Arg, I, E, It, 2003 I, W, E, SA 1, NZ 1, SA 2, NZ 2
Kefu, S (Q) 2001 W (R), 2003 I, W, E, SA 1, NZ 1(R)
Kelaher, J D (NSW) 1933 SA 1,2,3,4,5, 1934 NZ 1,2, 1936 NZ 1,2, M, 1937 SA 1,2, 1938 NZ 3
Kelaher, T P (NSW) 1992 NZ 1, I (R), 1993 NZ
Kelleher, R J (Q) 1969 SA 2,3
Keller, D H (NSW) 1947 NZ 1, S, I, W, 1948 E, F
Kelly, A J (NSW) 1899 BI 1
Kelly, R L F (NSW) 1936 NZ 1,2, M, 1937 SA 1,2, 1938 NZ 1,2
Kent, A (Q) 1912 US
Kerr, F R (V) 1938 NZ 1
King, S C (NSW) 1926 NZ 1,2,3,4(R), 1927 W, S, 1928 E, F, 1929 NZ 1,2,3, 1930 BI, 1932 NZ 1,2
Knight, M (NSW) 1978 W 1,2, NZ 1
Knight, S O (NSW) 1969 SA 2,4, 1970 S, 1971 SA 1,2,3
Knox, D J (NSW, ACT) 1985 Fj 1,2, 1990 US (R), 1994 WS, NZ, 1996 It, S, I, 1997 SA 1, NZ 3, SA 2, Arg 1,2
Kraefft, D F (NSW) 1947 NZ 2, S, I, W, 1948 E, F
Kreutzer, S D (Q) 1914 NZ 2

Lamb, J S (NSW) 1928 NZ 1,2, M
Lambie, J K (NSW) 1974 NZ 1,2,3, 1975 W
Lane, R E (NSW) 1921 SA 1
Lane, T A (Q) 1985 C 1,2, NZ
Lang, C W P (V) 1938 NZ 2,3
Langford, J F (ACT) 1997 NZ 3, SA 2, E 2, S
Larkham, S J (ACT) 1996 W 2(R), 1997 F 1,2, NZ 1,2(R), SA 1, NZ 3, SA 2, Arg 1,2, E 2, S, 1998 E 1, S 1,2, NZ 1, SA 1, NZ 2, SA 2, NZ 3, Fj, Tg (t), WS, F, E 2, 1999 [I 3, US, W, SA 3, F], 2000 Arg 1,2, SA 1, NZ 1, SA 2, NZ 2, SA 3, 2001 BI 1,2, NZ 1, SA 2, NZ 2, Sp, E, F, W, 2002 F 1,2, NZ 1, SA 1, NZ 2, SA 2, Arg, I, E, 2003 SA 1(R), NZ 1, SA 2, NZ 2, [Arg,R,I,S,NZ,E], 2004S1,2,E1,PI,NZ1, SA1,NZ2,SA2,S3,F,S4, 2005 Sm(R),It,F1,SA1,2,3, 2006 E1, 2, I, NZ1, SA1, NZ2, SA2, NZ3, SA3
Larkin, E R (NSW) 1903 NZ
Larkin, K K (Q) 1958 M 2,3
Latham, C E (Q) 1998 F, E 2, 1999 I 1,2, E, [US], 2000 Arg 1,2, SA 1, NZ 1, SA 2, NZ 2, SA 3, F, S, E, 2001 BI 1,2(R), SA 1(R), NZ 1(R), SA 2, NZ 2, Sp, E, F, W (R), 2002 F 1,2, NZ 1, SA 1, NZ 2, SA 2, 2003 I, W, E, NZ 1(R), SA 2, NZ 2,[Nm], 2004 S1(R), 2(R), E1(R), PI(t&R), NZ1, SA1, NZ2, SA2, S3, F, S4, E2, 2005 Sm, F1, SA2, 3, F2, E, I, W, 2006 E1, 2, I, NZ1, SA1, NZ2, SA2, NZ3, SA3
Latimer, N B (NSW) 1957 NZ 2
Lawton, R (Q) 1988 E 1, NZ 2(R), 3, S
Lawton, T (NSW, Q) 1920 NZ 1,2, 1925 NZ 4, 1927 I, W, S, 1928 E, F, 1929 NZ 1,2,3, 1930 BI, 1932 NZ 1,2
Lawton, T A (Q) 1983 F 1(R), 2, 1984 Fj, NZ 1,2,3, E, I, W, S, 1985 C 1,2, NZ, Fj 1, 1986 It, F, Arg 1,2, NZ 1,2,3, 1987 SK, [E, US, I, F, W], NZ, Arg 1,2, 1988 E 1,2, NZ 1,2,3, E, S, It, 1989 BI 1,2,3
Laycock, W M B (NSW) 1925 NZ 2,3,4, 1926 NZ 2
Leeds, A J (NSW) 1986 NZ 3, 1987 [US, W], NZ, Arg 1,2, 1988 E 1,2, NZ 1,2,3, E, S, It
Lenehan, J K (NSW) 1958 W, E, S, F, M 1,2,3, 1959 BI 1,2, 1961 SA 1,2, F, 1962 NZ 2,3,4,5, 1965 SA 1,2, 1966 W, S, 1967 E, I 1, F, I 2
L'Estrange, R D (Q) 1971 F 1,2, 1972 NZ 1,2,3, 1973 Tg 1,2, W, E, 1974 NZ 1,2,3, 1975 S, W, 1976 I, US
Lewis, L S (Q) 1934 NZ 1,2, 1936 NZ 2, 1938 NZ 1
Lidbury, S (NSW) 1987 Arg 1, 1988 E 2
Lillicrap, C P (Q) 1985 Fj 2, 1987 [US, I, F, W], 1989 BI 1, 1991 [WS]
Lindsay, R T G (Q) 1932 NZ 3
Lisle, R J (NSW) 1961 Fj 1,2,3, SA 1
Little, J S (Q, NSW) 1989 F 1,2, 1990 F 1,2,3, US, 1991 W, E, NZ 1,2, [Arg, W, I, NZ, E], 1992 NZ 1,2,3, SA, I, W, 1993 Tg, NZ, SA 1,2,3, C, F 1,2, 1994 WS, NZ, 1995 Arg 1,2, [SA, C, E], NZ 1,2, 1996 It (R), I, W 3, 1997 F 1,2, E 1, NZ 2, SA 1, NZ 3, SA 2, 1998 E 1(R), S 2(R), NZ 2, SA 2(R), NZ 3, Fj, Tg, WS, F, E 2, 1999 I 1(R),2, SA 2(R), NZ 2, [R, I 3(t&R), US, W (R), SA 3(t&R), F (R)], 2000 Arg 1(R),2(R), SA 1(R), NZ 1, SA 2, NZ 2, SA 3
Livermore, A E (Q) 1946 NZ 1, M
Loane, M E (Q) 1973 Tg 1,2, 1974 NZ 1, 1975 E 1,2, J 1, 1976 E, I, Fj 1,2,3, F 1,2, 1978 W 1,2, 1979 I 1,2, NZ, Arg 1,2, 1981 F 1,2, I, W, S, 1982 E, S 1,2

Logan, D L (NSW) 1958 M 1
Loudon, D B (NSW) 1921 NZ, 1922 M 1,2,3
Loudon, R B (NSW) 1923 NZ 1(R), 2,3, 1928 NZ 1,2,3, M, 1929 NZ 2, 1933 SA 2,3,4,5, 1934 NZ 2
Love, E W (NSW) 1932 NZ 1,2,3
Lowth, D R (NSW) 1958 NZ 1
Lucas, B C (Q) 1905 NZ
Lucas, P W (NSW) 1982 NZ 1,2,3
Lutge, D (NSW) 1903 NZ, 1904 BI 1,2,3
Lynagh, M P (Q) 1984 Fj, E, I, W, S, 1985 C 1,2, NZ, 1986 It, F, Arg 1,2, NZ 1,2,3, 1987 [E, US, J, I, F, W], Arg 1,2, 1988 E 1,2, NZ 1,3(R), E, S, It, 1989 BI 1,2,3, NZ, F 1,2, 1990 F 1,2,3, US, NZ 1,2,3, 1991 W, E, NZ 1,2, [Arg, WS, W, I, NZ, E], 1992 S 1,2, NZ 1,2,3, SA, I, 1993 Tg, C, F 1,2, 1994 I 1,2, It 1, 1995 Arg 1,2, [SA, C, E]
Lyons, D J (NSW) 2000 Arg 1(t&R),2(R), 2001 BI 1(R), SA 1(R), 2002 F 1(R),2, NZ 1(R), SA 1(R), NZ 2(R), SA 2(t+R), 2003 I, W, E, SA 1, [Arg,R,Nm,I,S,NZ,E], 2004 S1,2,E1,PI,NZ1,SA1, NZ2,SA2,S3(R),F(R),S4,E2, 2005 Sm,It,F1,SA1,2,NZ1,SA4

McArthur, M (NSW) 1909 E
McBain, M I (Q) 1983 It, F 1, 1985 Fj 2, 1986 It (R), 1987 [J], 1988 E 2(R), 1989 BI 1(R)
MacBride, J W T (NSW) 1946 NZ 1, M, NZ 2, 1947 NZ 1,2, S, I, W, 1948 E, F
McCabe, A J M (NSW) 1909 E
McCall, R J (Q) 1989 F 1,2, 1990 F 1,2,3, US, NZ 1,2,3, 1991 W, E, NZ 1,2, [Arg, W, I, NZ, E], 1992 S 1,2, NZ 1,2,3, SA, I, W, 1993 Tg, NZ, SA 1,2,3, C, F 1,2, 1994 It 2, 1995 Arg 1,2, [SA, R, E]
McCarthy, F J C (Q) 1950 BI 1
McCowan, R H (Q) 1899 BI 1,2,4
McCue, P A (NSW) 1907 NZ 1,3, 1908 W, 1909 E
McDermott, L C (Q) 1962 NZ 1,2
McDonald, B S (NSW) 1969 SA 4, 1970 S
McDonald, J C (Q) 1938 NZ 2,3
Macdougall, D G (NSW) 1961 Fj 1, SA 1
Macdougall, S G (NSW, ACT) 1971 SA 3, 1973 E, 1974 NZ 1,2,3, 1975 E 1,2, 1976 E
McGhie, G H (Q) 1929 NZ 2,3, 1930 BI
McGill, A N (NSW) 1968 NZ 1,2, F, 1969 W, SA 1,2,3,4, 1970 S, 1971 SA 1,2,3, F 1,2, 1972 F 1,2, NZ 1,2,3, 1973 Tg 1,2
McIntyre, A J (Q) 1982 NZ 1,2,3, 1983 F 1,2, 1984 Fj, NZ 1,2,3, E, I, W, S, 1985 C 1,2, NZ, Fj 1,2, 1986 It, F, Arg 1,2, 1987 [E, US, I, F, W], NZ, Arg 2, 1988 E 1,2, NZ 1,2,3, E, S, It, 1989 NZ
McIsaac, T P (WF) 2006 E1,I,NZ1,2(R),SA2,3(R)
McKay, G R (NSW) 1920 NZ 2, 1921 SA 2,3, 1922 M 1,2,3
MacKay, L J (NSW) 2005 NZ2(R)
McKenzie, E J A (NSW, ACT) 1990 F 1,2,3, US, NZ 1,2,3, 1991 W, E, NZ 1,2, [Arg, W, I, NZ, E], 1992 S 1,2, NZ 1,2,3, SA, I, W, 1993 Tg, NZ, SA 1,2,3, C, F 1,2, 1994 I 1,2, It 1,2, WS, NZ, 1995 Arg 1,2, [SA, C (R), R, E], NZ 2, 1996 W 1,2, 1997 F 1,2, NZ 1, E 1
McKid, W A (NSW) 1976 E, Fj 1, 1978 NZ 2,3, 1979 I 1,2
McKinnon, A (Q) 1904 BI 2
McKivat, C H (NSW) 1907 NZ 1,3, 1908 W, 1909 E
McLaren, S D (NSW) 1926 NZ 4
McLaughlin, R E M (NSW) 1936 NZ 1,2
McLean, A D (Q) 1933 SA 1,2,3,4,5, 1934 NZ 1,2, 1936 NZ 1,2, M
McLean, J D (Q) 1904 BI 2,3, 1905 NZ
McLean, J J (Q) 1971 SA 2,3, F 1,2, 1972 F 1,2, NZ 1,2,3, Fj, 1973 W, E, 1974 NZ 1
McLean, P E (Q) 1974 NZ 1,2,3, 1975 J 1,2, S, W, 1976 E, I, Fj 1,2,3, F 1,2, 1978 W 1,2, NZ 2, 1979 I 1,2, NZ, Arg 1,2, 1980 Fj, 1981 F 1,2, I, W, S, 1982 E, S 2
McLean, P W (Q) 1978 NZ 1,2,3, 1979 I 1,2, NZ, Arg 1,2, 1980 Fj (R), NZ 3, 1981 I, W, S, 1982 E, S 1,2
McLean, R A (NSW) 1971 SA 1,2,3, F 1,2
McLean, W M (Q) 1946 NZ 1, M, NZ 2, 1947 NZ 1,2
McMahon, M J (Q) 1913 NZ 1
McMaster, R E (Q) 1946 NZ 1, M, NZ 2, 1947 NZ 1,2, I, W
McMeniman, H J (Q) 2005 Sm(R),It(R),F2(R),E,I,W
MacMillan, D I (Q) 1950 BI 1,2
McMullen, K V (NSW) 1962 NZ 3,5, 1963 E, SA 1
McShane, J M S (NSW) 1937 SA 1,2
Mackay, G (NSW) 1926 NZ 4
Mackney, W A R (NSW) 1933 SA 1,5, 1934 NZ 1,2
Magrath, E (NSW) 1961 Fj 1, SA 2, F
Maguire, D J (Q) 1989 BI 1,2,3
Malcolm, S J (NSW) 1927 S, 1928 E, F, NZ 1,2, M, 1929 NZ 1,2,3, 1930 BI, 1931 NZ, 1932 NZ 1,2,3, 1933 SA 4,5, 1934 NZ 1,2
Malone, J H (NSW) 1936 NZ 1,2, M, 1937 SA 2
Malouf, B P (NSW) 1982 NZ 1
Mandible, E F (NSW) 1907 NZ 2,3, 1908 W
Manning, J (NSW) 1904 BI 2
Manning, R C S (Q) 1967 NZ
Mansfield, B W (NSW) 1975 J 2
Manu, D T (NSW) 1995 [R (t)], NZ 1,2, 1996 W 1,2(R), SA 1, NZ 2, It, S, I, 1997 F 1, NZ 1(t), E 1, NZ 2, SA 1
Marks, H (NSW) 1899 BI 1,2
Marks, R J P (Q) 1962 NZ 4,5, 1963 E, SA 2,3,4, 1964 NZ 1,2,3, 1965 SA 1,2, 1966 W, S, 1967 E, I 1, F, I 2
Marrott, R (NSW) 1920 NZ 1,3
Marrott, W J (NSW) 1922 NZ 2,3, 1923 M 1,2,3, NZ 1,2
Marshall, J S (NSW) 1949 M 1
Martin, G J (Q) 1989 BI 1,2,3, NZ, F 1,2, 1990 F 1,3(R), NZ 1
Martin, M C (NSW) 1980 Fj, NZ 1,2, 1981 F 1,2, W (R)
Massey-Westropp, M (NSW) 1914 NZ 3
Mathers, M J (NSW) 1980 Fj, NZ 2(R)
Maund, J W (NSW) 1903 NZ
Mayne, A V (NSW) 1920 NZ 1,2,3, 1922 M 1
Meadows, J E C (V, Q) 1974 NZ 1, 1975 S, W, 1976 I, US, Fj 1,3, F 1,2, 1978 NZ 1,2,3, 1979 I 1,2, 1981 I, S, 1982 E, NZ 2,3, 1983 US, Arg 2, NZ
Meadows, R W (NSW) 1958 M 1,2,3, NZ 1,2,3
Meagher, F W (NSW) 1923 NZ 3, 1924 NZ 3, 1925 NZ 4, 1926 NZ 1,2,3, 1927 I, W
Meibusch, J H (Q) 1904 BI 3
Meibusch, L S (Q) 1912 US
Melrose, T C (NSW) 1978 NZ 3, 1979 I 1,2, NZ, Arg 1,2
Merrick, S (NSW) 1995 NZ 1,2
Messenger, H H (NSW) 1907 NZ 2,3
Middleton, S A (NSW) 1909 E, 1910 NZ 1,2,3
Miller, A R (NSW) 1952 Fj 1,2, NZ 1,2, 1953 SA 1,2,3,4, 1954 Fj 1,2, 1955 NZ 1,2,3, 1956 SA 1,2, 1957 NZ 1,2, 1958 W, E, S, F, M 1,2,3, 1959 BI 1,2, 1961 Fj 1,2,3, SA 2, F, 1962 NZ 1,2, 1966 BI 1,2, W, S, 1967 I 1, F, I 2, NZ
Miller, J M (NSW) 1962 NZ 1, 1963 E, SA 1, 1966 W, S, 1967 E
Miller, J S (Q) 1986 NZ 2,3, 1987 SK, [US, I, F], NZ, Arg 1,2, 1988 E 1,2, NZ 2,3, E, S, It, 1989 BI 1,2,3, NZ, 1990 F 1,3, 1991 W, [WS, W, I]
Miller, S W J (NSW) 1899 BI 3
Mingey, N (NSW) 1920 NZ 3, 1921 SA 1,2,3, 1923 M 1, NZ 1,2
Mitchell, D A (Q) 2005 SA1(R), 2(R), 3(R), NZ1, SA4, NZ2, F2(R), E, I, W
Monaghan, L E (NSW) 1973 E, 1974 NZ 1,2,3, 1975 E 1,2, S, W, 1976 E, I, US, F 1, 1978 W 1,2, NZ 1, 1979 I 1,2
Monti, C I A (Q) 1938 NZ 2
Moon, B J (Q) 1978 NZ 2,3, 1979 I 1,2, NZ, Arg 1,2, 1980 Fj, NZ 1,2,3, 1981 F 1,2, I, W, S, 1982 E, S 1,2, 1983 US, Arg 1,2, NZ, It, F 1,2, 1984 Fj, NZ 1,2,3, E, 1986 It, F, Arg 1,2
Mooney, T P (Q) 1954 Fj 1,2
Moore, R C (ACT, NSW) 1999 [US], 2001 BI 2,3, SA 1, NZ 1, SA 2, NZ 2, Sp (R), E (R), F (R), W (R), 2002 F 1(R),2(R), SA 2(R)
Moore, S T (Q) 2005 Sm(R), It(R), F1(R), SA2(R), 3(R), F2(t&R)
Moran, H M (NSW) 1908 W
Morgan, G (Q) 1992 NZ 1(R), 3(R), W, 1993 Tg, NZ, SA 1,2,3, C, F 1,2, 1994 I 1,2, It 1, WS, NZ, 1996 W 1,2, C, NZ 1, SA 1, NZ 2, 1997 E 1, NZ 2
Morrissey, C V (NSW) 1925 NZ 2,3,4, 1926 NZ 2,3
Morrissey, W (Q) 1914 NZ 2
Mortlock, S A (ACT) 2000 Arg 1,2, SA 1, NZ 1, SA 2, NZ 2, SA 3, F, S, E, 2002 F 1,2, NZ 1, SA 1, NZ 2, SA 2, Arg, I, E, It, 2003 [R(R),Nm,S,NZ,E], 2004 S2, E1, PI, NZ1, SA1, NZ2, SA2, S3, F, S4, 2005 Sm, It, F1, SA2, 3(R), NZ1, 2006 E1, 2, I, NZ1, SA1, NZ2, SA2, NZ3,SA3
Morton, A R (NSW) 1957 NZ 1,2, 1958 F, M 1,2,3, NZ 1,2,3, 1959 BI 1,2

Mossop, R P (NSW) 1949 NZ 1,2, 1950 BI 1,2, 1951 NZ 1
Moutray, I E (NSW) 1963 SA 2
Mulligan, P J (NSW) 1925 NZ 1(R)
Munsie, A (NSW) 1928 NZ 2
Murdoch, A R (NSW) 1993 F 1, 1996 W 1
Murphy, P J (Q) 1910 NZ 1,2,3, 1913 NZ 1,2,3, 1914 NZ 1,2,3
Murphy, W (Q) 1912 US

Nasser, B P (Q) 1989 F 1,2, 1990 F 1,2,3, US, NZ 2, 1991 [WS]
Newman, E W (NSW) 1922 NZ 1
Nicholson, F C (Q) 1904 BI 3
Nicholson, F V (Q) 1903 NZ, 1904 BI 1
Niuqila, A S (NSW) 1988 S, It, 1989 BI 1
Noriega, E P (ACT, NSW) 1998 F, E 2, 1999 I 1,2, E, SA 1, NZ 1, SA 2(R), NZ 2(R), 2002 F 1,2, NZ 1, SA 1, NZ 2, Arg, I, E, It, 2003 I, W, E, SA 1, NZ 1, SA 2
Nothling, O E (NSW) 1921 SA 1,2,3, NZ, 1922 M 1,2,3, NZ 1,2,3, 1923 M 1,2,3, NZ 1,2,3, 1924 NZ 1,2,3
Nucifora, D V (Q) 1991 [Arg (R)], 1993 C (R)

O'Brien, F W H (NSW) 1937 SA 2, 1938 NZ 3
O'Connor, J A (NSW) 1928 NZ 1,2,3, M
O'Connor, M (ACT) 1994 I 1
O'Connor, M D (ACT, Q) 1979 Arg 1,2, 1980 Fj, NZ 1,2,3, 1981 F 1,2, I, 1982 E, S 1,2
O'Donnell, C (NSW) 1913 NZ 1,2
O'Donnell, I C (NSW) 1899 BI 3,4
O'Donnell, J B (NSW) 1928 NZ 1,3, M
O'Donnell, J M (NSW) 1899 BI 4
O'Gorman, J F (NSW) 1961 Fj 1, SA 1,2, F, 1962 NZ 2, 1963 E, SA 1,2,3,4, 1965 SA 1,2, 1966 W, S, 1967 E, I 1, F, I 2
O'Neill, D J (Q) 1964 NZ 1,2
O'Neill, J M (Q) 1952 NZ 1,2, 1956 SA 1,2
Ofahengaue, V (NSW) 1990 NZ 1,2,3, 1991 W, E, NZ 1,2, [Arg, W, I, NZ, E], 1992 S 1,2, SA, I, W, 1994 WS, NZ, 1995 Arg 1,2(R), [SA, C, E], NZ 1,2, 1997 Arg 1(t + R), 2(R), E 2, S, 1998 E 1(R), S 1(R),2(R), NZ 1(R), SA 1(R), NZ 2(R), SA 2(R), NZ 3(R), Fj, WS, F (R)
Ormiston, I W L (NSW) 1920 NZ 1,2,3
Osborne, D H (V) 1975 E 1,2, J 1
Outterside, R (NSW) 1959 BI 1,2
Oxenham, A McE (Q) 1904 BI 2, 1907 NZ 2
Oxlade, A M (Q) 1904 BI 2,3, 1905 NZ, 1907 NZ 2
Oxlade, B D (Q) 1938 NZ 1,2,3

Palfreyman, J R L (NSW) 1929 NZ 1, 1930 BI, 1931 NZ, 1932 NZ 3
Palu, W L (NSW) 2006 E2(t&R),I(R),SA2,NZ3,SA3
Panoho, G M (Q) 1998 SA 2(R), NZ 3(R), Fj (R), Tg, WS (R), 1999 I 2, E, SA 1(R), NZ 1, 2000 Arg 1(R),2(R), SA 1(R), NZ 1(R), SA 2(R),3(R), F (R), S (R), E (R), 2001 BI 1, 2003 SA 2(R), NZ 2
Papworth, B (NSW) 1985 Fj 1,2, 1986 It, Arg 1,2, NZ 1,2,3, 1987 [E, US, J (R), I, F], NZ, Arg 1,2
Parker, A J (Q) 1983 Arg 1(R), 2, NZ
Parkinson, C E (Q) 1907 NZ 2
Paul, J A (ACT) 1998 S 1(R), NZ 1(R), SA 1(t), Fj (R), Tg, 1999 I 1,2, E, SA 1, NZ 1, [R (R), I 3(R), W (t), F (R)], 2000 Arg 1(R), 2(R), SA 1(R), NZ 1(R), SA 2(R), NZ 2(R), SA 3(R), F (R), S (R), E (R), 2001 BI 1, 2002 F 1, NZ 1, SA 1, NZ 2, SA 2, Arg, E, 2003 I, W, E, SA 2(t&R), NZ2(R), [Arg(R), R(R), Nm, I(R), S(R), NZ(R), E(R)], 2004 S1(R), 2(R), E1(R), PI(R), NZ1(t&R), SA1, NZ2(R), SA2(R), S3, F, S4, E2, 2005 Sm, It, F1, SA1, 2,3, NZ1, 2006 E1(R), 2(R), I(R), NZ1(R), SA1, NZ2, SA2(R), NZ3, SA3
Pashley, J J (NSW) 1954 Fj 1,2, 1958 M 1,2,3
Pauling, T P (NSW) 1936 NZ 1, 1937 SA 1
Payne, S J (NSW) 1996 W 2, C, NZ 1, S, 1997 F 1(t), NZ 2(R), Arg 2(t)
Pearse, G K (NSW) 1975 W (R), 1976 I, US, Fj 1,2,3, 1978 NZ 1,2,3
Penman, A P (NSW) 1905 NZ
Perrin, P D (Q) 1962 NZ 1
Perrin, T D (NSW) 1931 M, NZ
Phelps, R (NSW) 1955 NZ 2,3, 1956 SA 1,2, 1957 NZ 1,2, 1958 W, I, E, S, F, M 1, NZ 1,2,3, 1961 Fj 1,2,3, SA 1,2, F, 1962 NZ 1,2
Phipps, J A (NSW) 1953 SA 1,2,3,4, 1954 Fj 1,2, 1955 NZ 1,2,3, 1956 SA 1,2
Phipps, W J (NSW) 1928 NZ 2
Piggott, H R (NSW) 1922 M 3(R)
Pilecki, S J (Q) 1978 W 1,2, NZ 1,2, 1979 I 1,2, NZ, Arg 1,2, 1980 Fj, NZ 1,2, 1982 S 1,2, 1983 US, Arg 1,2, NZ
Pini, M (Q) 1994 I 1, It 2, WS, NZ, 1995 Arg 1,2, [SA, R (t)]
Piper, B J C (NSW) 1946 NZ 1, M, NZ 2, 1947 NZ 1, S, I, W, 1948 E, F, 1949 M, 1,2,3
Poidevin, S P (NSW) 1980 Fj, NZ 1,2,3, 1981 F 1,2, I, W, S, 1982 E, NZ 1,2,3, 1983 US, Arg 1,2, NZ, It, F 1,2, 1984 Fj, NZ 1,2,3, E, I, W, S, 1985 C 1,2, NZ, Fj 1,2, 1986 It, F, Arg 1,2, NZ 1,2,3, 1987 SK, [E, J, I, F, W], Arg 1, 1988 NZ 1,2,3, 1989 NZ, 1991 E, NZ 1,2, [Arg, W, I, NZ, E]
Polota-Nau, T (NSW) 2005 E(R),I(R)
Pope, A M (Q) 1968 NZ 2(R)
Potter, R T (Q) 1961 Fj 2
Potts, J M (NSW) 1957 NZ 1,2, 1958 W, I, 1959 BI 1
Prentice, C W (NSW) 1914 NZ 3
Prentice, W S (NSW) 1908 W, 1909 E, 1910 NZ 1,2,3, 1912 US
Price, R A (NSW) 1974 NZ 1,2,3, 1975 E 1,2, J 1,2, 1976 US
Primmer, C J (Q) 1951 NZ 1,3
Proctor, I J (NSW)) 1967 NZ
Prosser, R B (NSW) 1967 E, I 1,2, NZ, 1968 NZ 1,2, F, I, S, 1969 W, SA 1,2,3,4, 1971 SA 1,2,3, F 1,2, 1972 F 1,2, NZ 1,2,3, Fj
Pugh, G H (NSW) 1912 US
Purcell, M P (Q) 1966 W, S, 1967 I 2
Purkis, E M (NSW) 1958 S, M 1
Pym, J E (NSW) 1923 M 1

Rainbow, A E (NSW) 1925 NZ 1
Ramalli, C (NSW) 1938 NZ 2,3
Ramsay, K M (NSW) 1936 M, 1937 SA 1, 1938 NZ 1,3
Rankin, R (NSW) 1936 NZ 1,2, M, 1937 SA 1,2, 1938 NZ 1,2
Rathbone, C (ACT) 2004 S1, 2(R), E1, PI, NZ1, SA1, NZ2, SA2, S3, F, S4, 2005 Sm, NZ1(R), SA4, NZ2, 2006E1(R), 2(R), I(R), SA1(R), NZ2(R), SA2(R), NZ3, SA3
Rathie, D S (Q) 1972 F 1,2
Raymond, R L (NSW) 1920 NZ 1,2, 1921 SA 2,3, NZ, 1922 M 1,2,3, NZ 1,2,3, 1923 M 1,2
Redwood, C (Q) 1903 NZ, 1904 BI 1,2,3
Reid, E J (NSW) 1925 NZ 2,3,4
Reid, T W (NSW) 1961 Fj 1,2,3, SA 1, 1962 NZ 1
Reilly, N P (Q) 1968 NZ 1,2, F, I, S, 1969 W, SA 1,2,3,4
Reynolds, L J (NSW) 1910 NZ 2(R), 3
Reynolds, R J (NSW) 1984 Fj, NZ 1,2,3, 1985 Fj 1,2, 1986 Arg 1,2, NZ 1, 1987 [J]
Richards, E W (Q) 1904 BI 1,3, 1905 NZ, 1907 NZ 1(R), 2
Richards, G (NSW) 1978 NZ 2(R), 3, 1981 F 1
Richards, T J (Q) 1908 W, 1909 E, 1912 US
Richards, V S (NSW) 1936 NZ 1,2(R), M, 1937 SA 1, 1938 NZ 1
Richardson, G C (Q) 1971 SA 1,2,3, 1972 NZ 2,3, Fj, 1973 Tg 1,2, W
Rigney, W A (NSW) 1925 NZ 2,4, 1926 NZ 4
Riley, S A (NSW) 1903 NZ
Ritchie, E V (NSW) 1924 NZ 1,3, 1925 NZ 2,3
Roberts, B T (NSW) 1956 SA 2
Roberts, H F (Q) 1961 Fj 1,3, SA 2, F
Robertson, I J (NSW) 1975 J 1,2
Robinson, B (NSW) 2006 SA3
Robinson, B J (ACT) 1996 It (R), S (R), I (R), 1997 F 1,2, NZ 1, E 1, NZ 2, SA 1(R), NZ 3(R), SA 2(R), Arg 1,2, E 2, S, 1998 Tg
Roche, C (Q) 1982 S 1,2, NZ 1,2,3, 1983 US, Arg 1,2, NZ, It, F 1,2, 1984 Fj, NZ 1,2,3, I
Rodriguez, E E (NSW) 1984 Fj, NZ 1,2,3, E, I, W, S, 1985 C 1,2, NZ, Fj 1, 1986 It, F, Arg 1,2, NZ 1,2,3, 1987 SK, [E, J, W (R)], NZ, Arg 1,2
Roe, J A (Q) 2003 [Nm(R)], 2004 E1(R), SA1(R), NZ2(R), SA2(t&R), S3, F, 2005 Sm(R), It(R), F1(R), SA1(R), 3, NZ1, SA4(t&R), NZ2(R), F2(R), E, I, W
Roebuck, M C (NSW) 1991 W, E, NZ 1,2, [Arg, WS, W, I, NZ, E], 1992 S 1,2, NZ 2,3, SA, I, W, 1993 Tg, SA 1,2,3, C, F 2
Roff, J W (ACT) 1995 [C, R], NZ 1,2, 1996 W 1,2, NZ 1, SA 1,

NZ 2, SA 2(R), S, I, W 3, 1997 F 1,2, NZ 1, E 1, NZ 2, SA 1, NZ 3, SA 2, Arg 1,2, E 2, S, 1998 E 1, S 1,2, NZ 1, SA 1, NZ 2, SA 2, NZ 3, Fj, Tg, WS, F, E 2, 1999 I 1,2, E, SA 1, NZ 1, SA 2, NZ 2(R), [R (R), I 3, US (R), W, SA 3, F], 2000 Arg 1,2, SA 1, NZ 1, SA 2, NZ 2, SA 3, F, S, E, 2001 BI 1,2,3, SA 1, NZ 1, SA 2, NZ 2, Sp, E, F, W, 2003 I, W, E, SA 1, [Arg, R, I, S(R), NZ(t&R), E(R)], 2004 S1,2, E1, PI

Rogers, M S (NSW) 2002 F 1(R),2(R), NZ 1(R), SA 1(R), NZ 2(R), SA 2(t&R), Arg, 2003 E (R), SA 1, NZ 1, SA 2, NZ 2, [Arg,R,Nm,I,S,NZ,E],2004S3(R),F(R),S4(R), E2(R), 2005 Sm(R), It,F1(R),SA1,4,NZ2,F2,E,I,W, 2006 E1,2,I,NZ1,SA1(R), NZ2(R), SA2(R),NZ3(R)

Rose, H A (NSW), 1967 I 2, NZ, 1968 NZ 1,2, F, I, S, 1969 W, SA 1,2,3,4, 1970 S

Rosenblum, M E (NSW) 1928 NZ 1,2,3, M

Rosenblum, R G (NSW) 1969 SA 1,3, 1970 S

Rosewell, J S H (NSW) 1907 NZ 1,3

Ross, A W (NSW) 1925 NZ 1,2,3, 1926 NZ 1,2,3, 1927 I, W, S, 1928 E, F, 1929 NZ 1, 1930 BI, 1931 M, NZ, 1932 NZ 2,3, 1933 SA 5, 1934 NZ 1,2

Ross, W S (Q) 1979 I 1,2, Arg 2, 1980 Fj, NZ 1,2,3, 1982 S 1,2, 1983 US, Arg 1,2, NZ

Rothwell, P R (NSW) 1951 NZ 1,2,3, 1952 Fj 1

Row, F L (NSW) 1899 BI 1,3,4

Row, N E (NSW) 1907 NZ 1,3, 1909 E, 1910 NZ 1,2,3

Rowles, P G (NSW) 1972 Fj, 1973 E

Roxburgh, J R (NSW) 1968 NZ 1,2, F, 1969 W, SA 1,2,3,4, 1970 S

Ruebner, G (NSW) 1966 BI 1,2

Russell, C J (NSW) 1907 NZ 1,2,3, 1908 W, 1909 E

Ryan, J R (NSW) 1975 J 2, 1976 I, US, Fj 1,2,3

Ryan, K J (Q) 1958 E, M 1, NZ 1,2,3

Ryan, P F (NSW) 1963 E, SA 1, 1966 BI 1,2

Rylance, M H (NSW) 1926 NZ 4(R)

Sailor, W J (Q) 2002 F 1,2, Arg (R), I, E, It, 2003 I, W, E, SA 1, NZ 1, SA 2, NZ 2, [Arg, R, I, S, NZ, E], 2004 S1,2,NZ1(R), 2(R),SA2(R),S3(R),F(R),S4(R),E2, 2005 Sm,It,F1, SA1,2,3,F2, I(R),W(R)

Samo, R U (ACT) 2004 S1,2,E1,PI,NZ1,S4(R)

Sampson, J H (NSW) 1899 BI 4

Sayle, J L (NSW) 1967 NZ

Schulte, B G (Q) 1946 NZ 1, M

Scott, P R I (NSW) 1962 NZ 1,2

Scott-Young, S J (Q) 1990 F 2,3(R), US, NZ 3, 1992 NZ 1,2,3

Shambrook, G G (Q) 1976 Fj 2,3

Sharpe, N C (Q, WF) 2002 F 1,2, NZ 1, SA 1, NZ 2, SA 2, 2003 I, W, E, SA 1(R), NZ 1(R), SA 2(R), NZ 2(R), [Arg, R, Nm, I, S, NZ, E], 2004 S1, 2, E1, PI, NZ1, SA1, NZ2, SA2, 2005 Sm, It, F1, SA1, 2, 3, NZ1, SA4, NZ2, F2, E, I, W, 2006 E1, 2, I, NZ1, SA1, NZ2, SA2, NZ3, SA3

Shaw, A A (Q) 1973 W, E, 1975 E 1,2, J 2, S, W, 1976 E, I, US, Fj 1,2,3, F 1,2, 1978 W 1,2, NZ 1,2,3, 1979 I 1,2, NZ, Arg 1,2, 1980 Fj, NZ 1,2,3, 1981 F 1,2, I, W, S, 1982 S 1,2

Shaw, C (NSW) 1925 NZ 2,3,4(R)

Shaw, G A (NSW) 1969 W, SA 1(R), 1970 S, 1971 SA 1,2,3, F 1,2, 1973 W, E, 1974 NZ 1,2,3, 1975 E 1,2, J 1,2, W, 1976 E, I, US, Fj 1,2,3, F 1,2, 1979 NZ

Sheehan, B R (ACT) 2006 SA3(R)

Sheehan, W B J (NSW) 1921 SA 1,2,3, 1922 NZ 1,2,3, 1923 M 1,2, NZ 1,2,3, 1924 NZ 1,2, 1926 NZ 1,2,3, 1927 W, S

Shehadie, N M (NSW) 1947 NZ 2, 1948 E, F, 1949 M 1,2,3, NZ 1,2, 1950 BI 1,2, 1951 NZ 1,2,3, 1952 Fj 1,2, NZ 2, 1953 SA 1,2,3,4, 1954 Fj 1,2, 1955 NZ 1,2,3, 1956 SA 1,2, 1957 NZ 2, 1958 W, I

Sheil, A G R (Q) 1956 SA 1

Shepherd, C B (WF) 2006 E1(R),2(R),I(R),SA3

Shepherd, D J (V) 1964 NZ 3, 1965 SA 1,2, 1966 BI 1,2

Shepherdson, G T (ACT) 2006 I,NZ1,SA1,NZ2(R),SA2(R)

Shute, J L (NSW) 1920 NZ 3, 1922 M 2,3

Simpson, R J (NSW) 1913 NZ 2

Skinner, A J (NSW) 1969 W, SA 4, 1970 S

Slack, A G (Q) 1978 W 1,2, NZ 1,2, 1979 NZ, Arg 1,2, 1980 Fj, 1981 I, W, S, 1982 E, S 1, NZ 3, 1983 US, Arg 1,2 NZ, It, 1984 Fj, NZ 1,2,3, E, I, W, S, 1986 It, F, NZ 1,2,3, 1987 SK, [E, US, J, I, F, W]

Slater, S H (NSW) 1910 NZ 3

Slattery, P J (Q) 1990 US (R), 1991 W (R), E (R), [WS (R), W, I (R)], 1992 I, W, 1993 Tg, C, F 1,2, 1994 I 1,2, It 1(R), 1995 [C, R (R)]

Smairl, A M (NSW) 1928 NZ 1,2,3

Smith, B A (Q) 1987 SK, [US, J, I (R), W], Arg 1

Smith, D P (Q) 1993 SA 1,2,3, C, F 2, 1994 I 1,2, It 1,2, WS, NZ, 1995 Arg 1,2, [SA, R, E], NZ 1,2, 1998 SA 1(R), NZ 3(R), Fj

Smith, F B (NSW) 1905 NZ, 1907 NZ 1,2,3

Smith, G B (ACT) 2000 F, S, E, 2001 BI 1,2,3, SA 1, NZ 1, SA 2, NZ 2, Sp, E, F (R), W (R), 2002 F 1,2, NZ 1, SA 1, NZ 2, SA 2, Arg, I, E, It, 2003 I, NZ 1, SA 2, NZ 2, [Arg, R, Nm, I, S, NZ, E], 2004 S1, 2(R), E1(t&R), PI(R), NZ1(R), SA1, NZ2, SA2, S3, F, S4, E2, 2005 Sm, It, F1, SA1, 2,3, NZ1, SA4(R), NZ2, F2, E, I, W, 2006 E1, 2, I, NZ1, SA1, NZ2, SA2, NZ3(t), SA3(R)

Smith, L M (NSW) 1905 NZ

Smith, N C (NSW) 1922 NZ 2,3, 1923 NZ 1, 1924 NZ 1,3(R), 1925 NZ 2,3

Smith, P V (NSW) 1967 NZ, 1968 NZ 1,2, F, I, S, 1969 W, SA 1

Smith, R A (NSW) 1971 SA 1,2, 1972 F 1,2, NZ 1,2(R), 3, Fj, 1975 E 1,2, J 1,2, S, W, 1976 E, I, US, Fj 1,2,3, F 1,2

Smith, T S (NSW) 1921 SA 1,2,3, NZ, 1922 M 2,3, NZ 1,2,3, 1925 NZ 1,3,4

Snell, H W (NSW) 1925 NZ 2,3, 1928 NZ 3

Solomon, H J (NSW) 1949 M 3, NZ 2, 1950 BI 1,2, 1951 NZ 1,2, 1952 Fj 1,2, NZ 1,2, 1953 SA 1,2,3, 1955 NZ 1

Spooner, N R (Q) 1999 I 1,2

Spragg, S A (NSW) 1899 BI 1,2,3,4

Staniforth, S N G (NSW, WF) 1999 [US], 2002 I, It, 2006 SA3(R)

Stanley, R G (NSW) 1921 NZ, 1922 M 1,2,3, NZ 1,2,3, 1923 M 2,3, NZ 1,2,3, 1924 NZ 1,3

Stapleton, E T (NSW) 1951 NZ 1,2,3, 1952 Fj 1,2, NZ 1,2, 1953 SA 1,2,3,4, 1954 Fj 1, 1955 NZ 1,2,3, 1958 NZ 1

Steggall, J C (Q) 1931 M, NZ, 1932 NZ 1,2,3, 1933 SA 1,2,3,4,5

Stegman, T R (NSW) 1973 Tg 1,2

Stephens, O G (NSW) 1973 Tg 1,2, W, 1974 NZ 2,3

Stewart, A A (NSW) 1979 NZ, Arg 1,2

Stiles, N B (Q) 2001 BI 1,2,3, SA 1, NZ 1, SA 2, NZ 2, Sp, E, F, W, 2002 I

Stone, A H (NSW) 1937 SA 2, 1938 NZ 2,3

Stone, C G (NSW) 1938 NZ 1

Stone, J M (NSW) 1946 M, NZ 2

Storey, G P (NSW) 1926 NZ 4, 1927 I, W, S, 1928 E, F, 1929 NZ 3(R), 1930 BI

Storey, K P (NSW) 1936 NZ 2

Storey, N J D (NSW) 1962 NZ 1

Strachan, D J (NSW) 1955 NZ 2,3

Strauss, C P (NSW) 1999 I 1(R),2(R), E (R), SA 1(R), NZ 1, SA 2(R), NZ 2(R), [R (R), I 3(R), US, W]

Street, N O (NSW) 1899 BI 2

Streeter, S F (NSW) 1978 NZ 1

Stuart, R (NSW) 1910 NZ 2,3

Stumbles, B D (NSW) 1972 NZ 1(R), 2,3, Fj

Sturtridge, G S (V) 1929 NZ 2, 1932 NZ 1,2,3, 1933 SA 1,2,3,4,5

Sullivan, P D (NSW) 1971 SA 1,2,3, F 1,2, 1972 F 1,2, NZ 1,2, Fj, 1973 Tg 1,2, W

Summons, A J (NSW) 1958 W, I, E, S, M 2, NZ 1,2,3, 1959 BI 1,2

Suttor, D C (NSW) 1913 NZ 1,2,3

Swannell, B I (NSW) 1905 NZ

Sweeney, T L (Q) 1953 SA 1

Taafe, B S (NSW) 1969 SA 1, 1972 F 1,2

Tabua, I (Q) 1993 SA 2,3, C, F 1, 1994 I 1,2, It 1,2, 1995 [C, R]

Tancred, A J (NSW) 1927 I, W, S

Tancred, H E (NSW) 1923 M 1,2

Tancred, J L (NSW) 1926 NZ 3,4, 1928 F

Tanner, W H (Q) 1899 BI 1,2

Tarleton, K (NSW) 1925 NZ 2,3

Tasker, W G (NSW) 1913 NZ 1,2,3, 1914 NZ 1,2,3

Tate, M J (NSW) 1951 NZ 3, 1952 Fj 1,2, NZ 1,2, 1953 SA 1, 1954 Fj 1,2

Taylor, D A (Q) 1968 NZ 1,2, F, I, S

Taylor, H C (NSW) 1923 NZ 1,2,3, 1924 NZ 4

Taylor, J I (NSW) 1971 SA 1, 1972 F 1,2, Fj
Taylor, J M (NSW) 1922 M 1,2
Teitzel, R G (Q) 1966 W, S, 1967 E, I 1, F, I 2, NZ
Telford, D G (NSW) 1926 NZ 3(R)
Thompson, C E (NSW) 1922 M 1, 1923 M 1,2, NZ 1, 1924 NZ 2,3
Thompson, E G (Q) 1929 NZ 1,2,3, 1930 BI
Thompson, F (NSW) 1913 NZ 1,2,3, 1914 NZ 1,2,3
Thompson, J (Q) 1914 NZ 1
Thompson, P D (Q) 1950 BI 1
Thompson, R J (WA) 1971 SA 3, F 2(R), 1972 Fj
Thorn, A M (NSW) 1921 SA 1,2,3, NZ, 1922 M 1,3
Thorn, E J (NSW) 1922 NZ 1,2,3, 1923 NZ 1,2,3, 1924 NZ 1,2,3, 1925 NZ 1,2, 1926 NZ 1,2,3,4
Thornett, J E (NSW) 1955 NZ 1,2,3, 1956 SA 1,2, 1958 W, I, S, F, M 2,3, NZ 2,3, 1959 BI 1,2, 1961 Fj 2,3, SA 1,2, F, 1962 NZ 2,3,4,5, 1963 E, SA 1,2,3,4, 1964 NZ 1,2,3, 1965 SA 1,2, 1966 BI 1,2, 1967 F
Thornett, R N (NSW) 1961 Fj 1,2,3, SA 1,2, F, 1962 NZ 1,2,3,4,5
Thorpe, A C (NSW) 1929 NZ 1(R)
Timbury, F R V (Q) 1910 NZ 1,2,
Tindall, E N (NSW) 1973 Tg 2
Toby, A E (NSW) 1925 NZ 1,4
Tolhurst, H A (NSW) 1931 M, NZ
Tombs, R C (NSW) 1992 S 1,2, 1994 I 2, It 1, 1996 NZ 2
Tonkin, A E J (NSW) 1947 S, I, W, 1948 E, F, 1950 BI 2
Tooth, R M (NSW) 1951 NZ 1,2,3, 1954 Fj 1,2, 1955 NZ 1,2,3, 1957 NZ 1,2
Towers, C H T (NSW) 1926 NZ 1,3(R),4, 1927 I, 1928 E, F, NZ 1,2,3, M, 1929 NZ 1,3, 1930 BI, 1931 M, NZ, 1934 NZ 1,2, 1937 SA 1,2
Trivett, R K (Q) 1966 BI 1,2
Tune, B N (Q) 1996 W 2, C, NZ 1, SA 1, NZ 2, SA 2, 1997 F 1,2, NZ 1, E 1, NZ 2, SA 1, NZ 3, SA 2, Arg, 1,2, E 2, S, 1998 E 1, S 1,2, NZ 1, SA 1,2, NZ 3, 1999 I 1, E, SA 1, NZ 1, SA 2, NZ 2, [R, I 3, W, SA 3, F], 2000 SA 2(R), NZ 2(t&R), SA 3(R), 2001 F (R), W, 2002 NZ 1, SA 1, NZ 2, SA 2, Arg, 2006 NZ1(R)
Tuqiri, L D (NSW) 2003 I (R), W (R), E (R), SA 1(R), NZ 1, SA 2, NZ 2, [Arg(R),R(R),Nm,I(R),S,NZ,E], 2004 S1,2,E1,PI,NZ1, SA1,NZ2,SA2,S3,F,S4,E2, 2005 It, F1, SA1, 2,3, NZ1,SA4, NZ2,F2,E,I,W, 2006 E1,2,I,NZ1, SA1, NZ2, SA2, NZ3
Turinui, M P (NSW) 2003 I, W, E, 2003 [Nm(R)], 2004 S1(R),2,E2, 2005 Sm,It(R),F1(R),SA1,2(t&R),3,NZ1, SA4, NZ2, F2, E, I, W
Turnbull, A (V) 1961 Fj 3
Turnbull, R V (NSW) 1968 I
Tuynman, S N (NSW) 1983 F 1,2, 1984 E, I, W, S, 1985 C 1,2, NZ, Fj 1,2, 1986 It, F, Arg 1,2, NZ 1,2,3, 1987 SK, [E, US, J, I, W], NZ, Arg 1(R), 2, 1988 E, It, 1989 BI 1,2,3, NZ, 1990 NZ 1
Tweedale, E (NSW) 1946 NZ 1,2, 1947 NZ 2, S, I, 1948 E, F, 1949 M 1,2,3

Valentine, J J (Q) 2006 E1(R)
Vaughan, D (NSW) 1983 US, Arg 1, It, F 1,2
Vaughan, G N (V) 1958 E, S, F, M 1,2,3
Verge, A (NSW) 1904 BI 1,2
Vickerman, D J (ACT, NSW) 2002 F 2(R), Arg, E, It, 2003 I (R), W (R), E (R), SA 1, NZ 1, SA 2, NZ 2, [Arg(R),R,I(R), S(R)], 2004 S1(t&R),2(R),E1(R),PI(R), NZ1(R), SA1(R), NZ2(R), SA2(R), S3, F, S4, E2, 2005 SA2(R), 3,NZ1, SA4, 2006 E1,2,I,NZ1,SA1,NZ2,SA2,NZ3,SA3

Walden, R J (NSW) 1934 NZ 2, 1936 NZ 1,2, M
Walker, A K (NSW) 1947 NZ 1, 1948 E, F, 1950 BI 1,2
Walker, A M (ACT) 2000 NZ 1(R), 2001 BI 1,2,3, SA 1, NZ 1,2(R)
Walker, A S B (NSW) 1912 US, 1920 NZ 1,2, 1921 SA 1,2,3, NZ, 1922 M 1,3, NZ 1,2,3, 1923 M 2,3, 1924 NZ 1,2
Walker, L F (NSW) 1988 NZ 2,3, S, It, 1989 BI 1,2,3, NZ
Walker, L R (NSW) 1982 NZ 2,3
Wallace, A C (NSW) 1921 NZ, 1926 NZ 3,4, 1927 I, W, S, 1928 E, F
Wallace, T M (NSW) 1994 It 1(R), 2
Wallach, C (NSW) 1913 NZ 1,3, 1914 NZ 1,2,3
Walsh, J J (NSW) 1953 SA 1,2,3,4
Walsh, P B (NSW) 1904 BI 1,2,3
Walsham, K P (NSW) 1962 NZ 3, 1963 E
Ward, P G (NSW) 1899 BI 1,2,3,4
Ward, T (Q) 1899 BI 2
Watson, G W (Q) 1907 NZ 1
Watson, W T (NSW) 1912 US, 1913 NZ 1,2,3, 1914 NZ 1, 1920 NZ 1,2,3
Waugh, P R (NSW) 2000 E (R), 2001 NZ 1(R), SA 2(R), NZ 2(R), Sp (R), E (R), F, W, 2003 I (R), W, E, SA 1, NZ 1, SA 2, NZ2, [Arg,R,I,S,NZ,E], 2004 S1(R), 2, E1, PI, NZ1, SA1, NZ2, SA2, S3, F, S4, E2, 2005 SA1(R), 2(R), 3, NZ1(R), SA4, NZ2, F2, E, I, W, 2006 E1(R), 2(R), I(R), NZ1(R), SA1(R), NZ2(R), SA2(R), NZ3, SA3
Waugh, W W (NSW, ACT) 1993 SA 1, 1995 [C], NZ 1,2, 1996 S, I, 1997 Arg 1,2
Weatherstone, L J (ACT) 1975 E 1,2, J 1,2, S (R), 1976 E, I
Webb, W (NSW) 1899 BI 3,4
Welborn J P (NSW) 1996 SA 2, It, 1998 Tg, 1999 E, SA 1, NZ 1
Wells, B G (NSW) 1958 M 1
Westfield, R E (NSW) 1928 NZ 1,2,3, M, 1929 NZ 2,3
Whitaker, C J (NSW) 1998 SA 2(R), Fj (R), Tg, 1999 NZ 2(R), [R (R), US, F (R)], 2000 S (R), 2001 Sp (R), W (R), 2002 Arg (R), It (R), 2003 I (R), W (R), SA 2(R), [Arg(R), Nm, S(R)], 2004 PI(R), NZ1, 2005 Sm, It(R), F1(R), SA1(R), 2(R), NZ1(t&R), SA4(R), NZ2(R), F2(R), E(R), W(R)
White, C J B (NSW) 1899 BI 1, 1903 NZ, 1904 BI 1
White, J M (NSW) 1904 BI 3
White, J P L (NSW) 1958 NZ 1,2,3, 1961 Fj 1,2,3, SA 1,2, F, 1962 NZ 1,2,3,4,5, 1963 E, SA 1,2,3,4, 1964 NZ 1,2,3, 1965 SA 1,2
White, M C (Q) 1931 M, NZ 1932 NZ 1,2, 1933 SA 1,2,3,4,5
White, S W (NSW) 1956 SA 1,2, 1958 I, E, S, M 2,3
White, W G S (Q) 1933 SA 1,2,3,4,5, 1934 NZ 1,2, 1936 NZ 1,2, M
White, W J (NSW) 1928 NZ 1, M, 1932 NZ 1
Wickham, S M (NSW) 1903 NZ, 1904 BI 1,2,3, 1905 NZ
Williams, D (Q) 1913 NZ 3, 1914 NZ 1,2,3
Williams, I M (NSW) 1987 Arg 1,2, 1988 E 1,2, NZ 1,2,3, 1989 BI 2,3, NZ, F 1,2, 1990 F 1,2,3, US, NZ 1
Williams, J L (NSW) 1963 SA 1,3,4
Williams, R W (ACT) 1999 I 1(t&R),2(t&R), E (R), [US], 2000 Arg 1,2, SA 1, NZ 1, SA 2, NZ 2, SA 3, F (R), S (R), E
Williams, S A (NSW) 1980 Fj, NZ 1,2, 1981 F 1,2, 1982 E, NZ 1,2,3, 1983 US, Arg 1(R), 2, NZ, It, F 1,2, 1984 NZ 1,2,3, E, I, W, S, 1985 C 1,2, NZ, Fj 1,2
Wilson, B J (NSW) 1949 NZ 1,2
Wilson, C R (Q) 1957 NZ 1, 1958 NZ 1,2,3
Wilson, D J (Q) 1992 S 1,2, NZ 1,2,3, SA, I, W, 1993 Tg, NZ, SA 1,2,3, C, F 1,2, 1994 I 1,2, It 1,2, WS, NZ, 1995 Arg 1,2, [SA, R, E], 1996 W 1,2, C, NZ 1, SA 1, NZ 2, SA 2, It, S, I, W 3, 1997 F 1,2, NZ 1, E 1(t + R), NZ 2(R), SA 1, NZ 3, SA 2, E 2(R), S (R), 1998 E 1, S 1,2, NZ 1, SA 1, NZ 2, SA 2, NZ 3, Fj, WS, F, E 2, 1999 I 1,2, E, SA 1, NZ 1, SA 2, NZ 2, [R, I 3, W, SA 3, F], 2000 Arg 1,2, SA 1, NZ 1, SA 2, NZ 2, SA 3
Wilson, V W (Q) 1937 SA 1,2, 1938 NZ 1,2,3
Windon, C J (NSW) 1946 NZ 1,2, 1947 NZ 1, S, I, W, 1948 E, F, 1949 M 1,2,3, NZ 1,2, 1951 NZ 1,2,3, 1952 Fj 1,2, NZ 1,2
Windon, K S (NSW) 1937 SA 1,2, 1946 M
Windsor, J C (Q) 1947 NZ 2
Winning, K C (Q) 1951 NZ 1
Wogan, L W (NSW) 1913 NZ 1,2,3, 1914 NZ 1,2,3, 1920 NZ 1,2,3, 1921 SA 1,2,3, NZ, 1922 M 3, NZ 1,2,3, 1923 M 1,2, 1924 NZ 1,2,3
Wood, F (NSW) 1907 NZ 1,2,3, 1910 NZ 1,2,3, 1913 NZ 1,2,3, 1914 NZ 1,2,3
Wood, R N (Q) 1972 Fj
Woods, H F (NSW) 1925 NZ 4, 1926 NZ 1,2,3, 1927 I, W, S, 1928 E
Wright, K J (NSW) 1975 E 1,2, J 1, 1976 US, F 1,2, 1978 NZ 1,2,3
Wyld, G (NSW) 1920 NZ 2

Yanz, K (NSW) 1958 F
Young, W K (ACT, NSW) 2000 F, S, E, 2002 F 1,2, NZ 1, SA 1, NZ 2, SA 2, Arg, E, It, 2003 I, W, E, SA 1, NZ 1, SA 2, NZ 2, [Arg, R, I, S, NZ, E], 2004 S1, 2, E1, PI, NZ1, SA1, NZ2, SA2, S3, F, S4, E2, 2005 Sm, It, F1, SA1,2,3, NZ1, SA4, NZ2

AUSTRALIA DOMESTIC REVIEW 2006

Australian club rugby will probably look back on 2006 as a watershed year in its history. On the pitch, it was business as usual as Sydney University beat Randwick in the Tooheys Cup final to retain their crown. Off the pitch, however, it was an altogether different, and for some, disconcerting story.

The season began as usual in June but even as the players were lacing up their boots once again, the debate about the future of grade rugby was raging. The ARU wanted to introduce a new, eight-team National Competition in 2007 to bridge the gap between club and Super 14 action, while the likes of Randwick, Sydney and Eastern Suburbs feared such a tournament would signal the death knell of the club game.

Ultimately the ARU won the day and from 2007 the premier domestic competition in Australia will be the National Competition. The New Cup will continue as before but with both tournaments running at the same time, there is no doubt which which will be the pre-eminent. Australia finally had the country-wide competition it had yearned for so long.

Back on the pitch, the final New Cup competition before the 2007 overhaul began with Sydney University making a clear statement of intent on the road, dishing out a comprehensive defeat to defending Shute Shield champions Eastwood.

The Woodies had claimed the Shute trophy in May with an unexpected 17–10 win over the Students but there was to be no repeat of the shock this time around as Bill Millard's side exacted revenge for their second successive Shute Shield grand final reverse.

Sydney ran in eight tries in the 49–3 victory at TG Millner Field and although both Manly and Randwick also got off to winning starts away from home with wins over struggling Penrith and Southern Districts respectively, it seemed Millard's side were not going to relinquish their grip on the trophy without a fight.

The following week, however, that grip was discernibly loosened when Sydney travelled to the Manly Oval to tackle the Marlins. The Students outscored Manly three tries to two but Peter Hewat landed two conversions and four penalties for the home side to wrap up a surprise 26–15 triumph.

The third round of games saw Sydney bounce back against Warringah while Rod Cutler's Manly were beaten at Eastern Suburbs. But the shock of the weekend came at the North Sydney Oval as Randwick were ambushed by the unbeaten Northern Suburbs.

The match was tight throughout but the Shoremen clinched an epic clash in injury-time when Chris Burnett landed a penalty from the touchline to secure a 15–13 win. Northern Suburbs went top of the table with Randwick in second and the race for the four final places was well and truly on.

Weeks four and five saw Northern Suburbs maintained the momentum with back-to-back wins against West Harbour and Parramata but the wheels began to come off in July when they well were beaten 33–13 by Southern Districts.

Meanwhile, Eastern Suburbs, Randwick, Sydney and Manly were all maintaining the pressure and when the Students outlclassed the Shoremen in a 29–0 victory at the University Oval in week eight, the Norths' challenge for the knockout phase was in deep trouble. Manly hammered home another nail into the coffin seven days later with a 37–22 reverse at the North Sydney Oval. Defeat at Eastwood on the final day of the league season confirmed the Shoremen had blown their chance of qualification.

But while the Norths' challenge was imploding, Sydney, Randwick, Eastern Suburbs and Manly were going from strength to strength and the only question unanswered going into the final two weeks was in which order the quartet would finish in the final table.

In the end it was the Galloping Greens who had the honour of finishing first. Their 15–13 defeat at Northern Suburbs in June proved to be their only defeat of the regular season and handsome victories over Penrith (64–12) and West Harbour (68–9) in the final fortnight confirmed Todd Louden's side as the one to beat. Sydney came home in second, with Eastern Suburbs third and Manly fourth.

The first of the August semi-finals saw Manly tackle Easts at the North Sydney Oval. It was nip and tuck throughout, but it was eventually the Suburbs who emerged victorious after Chris Aho crashed over in the 70th minute to seal the game.

"We didn't take out opportunities when they presented themselves and Easts were able to," Marlins coach Rod Cutler said after his team's narrow 16–10 reverse.

Victory for Easts Ireland-bound skipper Tim McGann, however, kept him on Australian soil for a week longer after he revealed he had signed a contract with Munster.

"I hadn't told anyone before this game," McGann admitted. "I didn't want it to affect the week, but if we had lost I'd have been straight on the plane to Ireland. The Waratahs offered me a contract as well but this was just a great opportunity at Munster."

The second semi-final 24 hours later pitted Randwick against Sydney at the Coogee Oval for a place in the grand final and the two best sides from the regular season did not disappoint in terms of drama and excitement.

Trailing 18–6 with just five minutes on the clock, the Students appeared dead and buried but they picked themselves up and stunned Randwick with tries from Dean Mumm and David Lyons. Julian Huxley landed the second conversion in the dying seconds and the game went into extra time.

The momentum was now firmly with Millard's side and a a converted try from Tim Davidson proved decisive as Sydney wrapped up a thrilling 31–25 win.

Randwick now had to beat Eastern Suburbs in the preliminary final for a chance to gain revenge but made no mistake second time around at the Concord Oval. The Greens outscored the Easts four tries to two, including a brace from Paul Hannify, and were in truth comfortable 36–15 winners. Suburbs skipper McGann could book his place ticket and Randwick were on their way to the grand final.

After their previous meetings, most expected the final to be another epic encounter at Aussie Stadium but few could have predicted an exact repeat of the 16–10 scoreline from the two side's recent semi-final.

The Students dominated the first-half and lead 13–0 courtesy of a try from the influential Daniel Halangahu but the Galloping Greens stormed back after the break and closed the gap with a Matt Carraro score. But in the end Sydney's heroic defensive effort reaped its rewards and they retained their Tooheys New Cup crown with another 16–10 triumph.

"We threw the kitchen sink at them and they just kept putting us down," said Randwick captain Chris Houston. "Every time we tried to get some go-forward they just chopped us straight down and when we did make a half break they were smart enough to slow the ball down and let the troops reorganise."

Students coach Millard added: "We ended up making 307 tackles to 103. So it was about the heart and composure of the guys the way they defended and the structure was really good. Randwick were great opponents, and they built a really good team this year, and that's just good for club rugby."

Whether Millard believed the imminent announcement of the National Competition would be equally good for the club game is not a matter of record, but just days after the Students' triumph, the ARU confirmed their new-look tournament had been green lighted for 2007.

"This is a vision for the future of Australian rugby," said ARU Managing Director Gary Flowers. "It not only supports the Super 14 provinces and the Wallabies, but it will also give talented club players the opportunity to secure higher representative honours. This in fact restores club rugby as a pathway for player identification, development and selection."

The ARU also confirmed the 11-week competition would feature three teams from New South Wales, two from Queensland and one each from the ACT, Western Australia and Victoria. It will be financed by A$7.6 million of Union money over the next four years.

TOOHEY'S NEW CUP

FINAL TABLE

	P	W	D	L	F	A	BP	Pts
Randwick	11	10	0	1	457	147	9	49
Sydney University	11	9	0	2	434	150	9	45
Eastern Suburbs	11	7	0	4	339	285	8	36
Manly	11	7	0	4	318	253	7	35
Eastwood	11	6	0	5	276	317	8	32
Warringah	11	5	1	5	329	297	10	32
Northern Suburbs	11	5	1	5	247	267	6	28
Southern Districts	11	4	1	6	250	295	7	25
Gordon	11	4	1	6	217	327	1	19
West Harbour	11	3	0	8	220	383	5	17
Parramatta	11	3	0	8	241	354	3	15
Penrith	11	1	0	10	165	418	3	7

SEMI-FINALS

Friday 18 August	**Eastern Suburbs** 16 **Manly** 10
Saturday 19 August	**Randwick** 25 **Sydney University** 31

PRELIMINARY FINAL

Saturday 26 August	**Randwick** 36 **Eastern Suburbs** 15

GRAND FINAL

Saturday 2 September	**Sydney University** 16 **Randwick** 10

CANADA

CANADA'S TEST RECORD

OPPONENTS	DATE	VENUE	RESULT
USA	17 June	H	**Won** 33–18
Barbados	24 June	A	**Won** 69–3
USA	12 August	H	**Won** 56–7

PROGRAMME BREEDS SUCCESS

By Ian Kennedy

Since becoming Canada's 15th coach in 2004, Ric Suggitt has scoured the 'Big Wheat Country', and the world, looking for players of quality to build into a competitive Canadian international squad. He has also attempted to address the ongoing problem related to the unavailability of Canada's overseas professionals by developing – with the help of the International Rugby Board Tier II initiatives – young, home-grown talent. After two years of searching, after looking at scores of players, and after suffering some depressing losses, by August 2006,

Suggitt appears to have found a solid corps of players to take to the 2007 Rugby World Cup and indeed, with many of the players in their early 20s, to the 2011 RWC.

The spring of 2006 saw Canada's team begin to feel the benefits of the IRB Tier II initiatives instigated in 2005, initiatives that provided money to upgrade all of Rugby Canada's programs. It used these funds to hire former Wales Assistant Coach, Geraint John as its High Performance Director; put its elite domestic players on high performance programs, and started, with the help of the IRB and the USA, a North America Four tournament featuring Canada East, Canada West, USA East (Hawks) and USA West (Falcons). It provided a new level of competition just below the international level.

Canada's 2006 season began in April when the New Zealand Rugby Union invited Rugby Canada to send a Canada 'A' side to New Zealand for a four-game, two-week long tour to avail itself of high level coaching and to play four games against a variety of competition. Canada 'A' won only one match, but its young players soaked up valuable lessons.

Ric Suggitt used the first leg of the NA 4 to vet prospective players and found No 8 Sean-Michael Stephen, wing Justin Mensah Coker, lock Mike Phinney, centres David Spicer and Chris Pack, and the 23 year-old propping Pletch twins, Mike and Dan, in fine form. Added to this, he discovered outside-half, Edinburgh Gunner professional Anders Monro, who had been born in Canada but had never been back to his birthplace. Suggitt also re-discovered Australian-born Bedford wing and kicker James Pritchard, who had played in the 2003 RWC, but had been in the international rugby wilderness since. He invited them all to the revamped, six-team Barclays Churchill Cup in June.

Against Scotland 'A' in Nepean, a suburb of the nation's capital, with Canada featuring the Pletch twins, the first ever to prop in an international, it fought toe-to-toe for the full 80-minutes against the team that had defeated the England Saxons, 13–7, a few days earlier. The Scots hung on to win, 15–10, with Canada's points coming from a Mike Pyke try and a conversion and penalty by Pritchard. A promising start.

Canada then played the England Saxons in Toronto three days later only to lose 41–11, with veteran Nik Witkowski scoring a try and Monro kicking two penalties. It had been a huge challenge for Canada's young side, full of domestic players, to play two games against fully professional sides within three days.

In the Barclays Churchill Cup Bowl Final in Edmonton, Canada found little difficulty in defeating the USA 33–18, with wing Justin Mensah-Coker picking up two tries, captain Morgan Williams one, and Pritchard adding a try, two penalties and two conversions. The match also saw

36 year-old prop Rod Snow, with his three World Cup campaigns and 55 caps of experience, come out of 'retirement' and add much-needed stability to the set pieces.

A week later Canada flew to Barbados where they played their first World Cup Qualifying game against the 'Bajans'. Barbados proved no match for Canada as they romped to a record-setting, 11-try, 69–3 win with Pritchard surpassing former Canadian great Gareth Rees' points-in-a-game record (27) with 29. In his debut, 20 year-old South African-born full-back DTH Van der Merwe, scored two tries as a replacement in the second half.

In Columbus, Ohio in late July, Canada West defeated the US Falcons 31–20 to win the inaugural NA 4 title with Canada East defeating the US Hawks 34–18 to take the Consolation Final. Both players and management agreed that valuable lessons had been gained from their NA 4 experience, with the Falcons claiming top spot in the Pool tables and giving Canada West a very competitive match in the final.

Following a few days rest, some of Canada's NA 4 participants flew to St. John's, Newfoundland to begin preparations for the all-important, 'one-off', IRB World Cup qualifying match against the USA on August 12. After a few days training the 28-man squad members took time out to view the Rugby Canada Super League Final between the hometown Rock and the Saskatchewan Prairie Fire teams.

Played on a rainy day the local Rock team doused the visiting Fire to win the MacTier Cup 28–14, and claim their second consecutive RCSL title, but its first in front of its own 2,000 delighted fans. That win set the stage for the 41st, and arguably most-important, meeting between Canada and the USA in the 2007 Rugby World Cup Qualifier the next weekend at the same Swiler's Rugby Complex.

With so much riding on this Test that would give the winner an automatic berth in Pool B at the RWC and would send the loser to play a home-and-away series against Uruguay, Suggitt called home all of his most experienced professional players. Stade Francais lock Mike James, Claremont-Auvernge back-rower Jamie Cudmore, Agen No 8 Colin Yukes, Glasgow Warriors prop Kevin Tkachuk, Montauban centre Ryan Smith and Albi scrum-half and captain Morgan Williams returned to aid Canada's cause. When the Canada team trotted onto the Swiler's Sports Complex it boasted ten professional players with 90 caps worth of experience playing against the USA. Lock Mike James and home-town prop Rod Snow would each be playing the Eagles for the 11th time. It was arguably the best team Canada had fielded in many a year, and for the first time since taking office, Suggitt fielded no new caps.

For Rod Snow, who had played for his country through three World Cups (1995, '99 and '03), had played ten years of professional rugby with Newport in Wales and had played 56 tests as Canada's most-capped prop, his inclusion in the team marked the first time he had ever played for his country in Newfoundland in front of family and friends. Poignant indeed, and the passionate, raucous St. John's fans responded with wild enthusiasm when he ran onto the pitch.

With 5,000 Newfoundland fans behind them and with the Webb Ellis Cup at the side of the pitch as an added incentive, Canada ran rampant over a dispirited Eagles side, in a record-setting performance that ranked among Canada's best games in the past decade.

Canada ran-in seven tries in recording its biggest win, 56–7, against the USA, with wing James Pritchard surpassing his 29-point single game scoring record set against Barbados the month before. This time he scored three tries, hit three penalties and converted six of Canada's seven tries for 36 points.

Coupled with Pritchard's inspiring performance, full-back Mike Pyke, No 8 Sean-Michael Stephen, substitute outside-half Derek Daypuck and marvelously, home-town hero, prop Rod Snow scored tries. When Snow scored Canada's second try the Newfoundland fans went ballistic and when Ric Suggitt replaced him late in the game, the crowd gave this great servant of Canadian rugby a boisterous, well-deserved, standing ovation.

With the win, Canada could now sets its sights on Pool B at the Rugby World Cup where it will play Wales in Nantes, Fiji in Cardiff, and Japan and Australia in Bordeaux. Suggitt will use November 2006 Tests against Wales and Italy in November, as well as a tour to Ireland in March against the four Provinces, to build on recent successes. He is well aware that record wins over Barbados and the USA, while satisfying, won't count for much against the likes of Wales, Australia, Fiji and Japan in the Rugby World Cup.

Nevertheless, Suggitt now has a solid corps of experienced professionals as well as a group of promising youngsters that he can continue to mold into a respectable Canadian competitor on the world rugby scene.

CANADA INTERNATIONAL STATISTICS

MATCH RECORDS UP TO 30TH SEPTEMBER 2006
COMPILED BY GEOFF MILLER

MOST CONSECUTIVE TEST WINS

6	1990 Arg 2, 1991 J,S,US,F,R
6	1998 US1,2,HK,J,U,US3

MOST CONSECUTIVE TESTS WITHOUT DEFEAT

Matches	Wins	Draws	Periods
6	6	0	1990 to 1991
6	6	0	1998 to 1998

MOST POINTS IN A MATCH

BY THE TEAM

Pts.	Opponent	Venue	Year
72	Namibia	Toulouse	1999
69	Barbados	Bridgetown	2006
62	Japan	Markham	2000
57	Hong Kong	Vancouver	1996
65	United States	St Johns	2006
53	United States	Vancouver	1997
51	Japan	Vancouver	1996
51	Uruguay	Edmonton	2002

BY A PLAYER

Pts.	Player	Opponent	Venue	Year
36	J Pritchard	United States	St Johns	2006
29	J Pritchard	Barbados	Bridgetown	2006
27	G L Rees	Namibia	Toulouse	1999
26	R P Ross	Japan	Vancouver	1996
24	M A Wyatt	Scotland	Saint John	1991
23	G L Rees	Argentina	Buenos Aires	1998
22	R P Ross	Hong Kong	Vancouver	1996
22	G L Rees	Japan	Vancouver	1997
22	G L Rees	United States	Burlington	1998
22	J Barker	Japan	Markham	2000

MOST TRIES IN A MATCH

BY THE TEAM

Tries	Opponent	Venue	Year
11	Barbados	Bridgetown	2006
9	Namibia	Toulouse	1999
8	Tonga	Napier	1987
8	Japan	Vancouver	1991
8	Japan	Markham	2000
7	Hong Kong	Vancouver	1996
7	United States	Vancouver	1997
7	United States	St Johns	2006

BY A PLAYER

Tries	Player	Opponent	Venue	Year
4	K S Nichols	Japan	Markham	2000
3	S D Gray	United States	Vancouver	1987
3	J Pritchard	Barbados	Bridgetown	2006
3	J Pritchard	United States	St Johns	2006

MOST CONVERSIONS IN A MATCH

BY THE TEAM

Cons	Opponent	Venue	Year
9	Namibia	Toulouse	1999
8	Japan	Markham	2000
7	Japan	Vancouver	1991
7	Barbados	Bridgetown	2006
6	United States	Vancouver	1997
6	United States	St Johns	2006
5	Hong Kong	Vancouver	1996

BY A PLAYER

Cons	Player	Opponent	Venue	Year
9	G L Rees	Namibia	Toulouse	1999
8	J Barker	Japan	Markham	2000
7	M A Wyatt	Japan	Vancouver	1991
7	J Pritchard	Barbados	Bridgetown	2006
6	G L Rees	United States	Vancouver	1997
6	J Pritchard	United States	St Johns	2006
5	R P Ross	Hong Kong	Vancouver	1996

MOST PENALTIES IN A MATCH

BY THE TEAM

Pens	Opponent	Venue	Year
8	Scotland	Saint John	1991
7	Argentina	Buenos Aires	1998
6	United States	Vancouver	1985
6	Ireland	Victoria	1989
6	France	Nepean	1994
6	United States	Burlington	1998
6	Wales	Cardiff	2002

BY A PLAYER

Pens	Player	Opponent	Venue	Year
8	M A Wyatt	Scotland	Saint John	1991
7	G L Rees	Argentina	Buenos Aires	1998
6	M A Wyatt	United States	Vancouver	1985
6	M A Wyatt	Ireland	Victoria	1989
6	G L Rees	France	Nepean	1994
6	G L Rees	United States	Burlington	1998
6	J Barker	Wales	Cardiff	2002

MOST DROP GOALS IN A MATCH

BY THE TEAM

Drops	Opponent	Venue	Year
2	United States	Saranac Lake (NY)	1980
2	United States	Tucson	1986
2	Hong Kong	Hong Kong	1997
2	Fiji	Tokyo	2001

BY A PLAYER

Drops	Player	Opponent	Venue	Year
2	R P Ross	Hong Kong	Hong Kong	1997
2	R P Ross	Fiji	Tokyo	2001

CAREER RECORDS

MOST CAPPED PLAYERS

Caps	Player	Career span
76	A J Charron	1990 to 2003
66	W U Stanley	1994 to 2003
64	D S Stewart	1989 to 2001
57	R P Ross	1989 to 2003
57	R G A Snow	1995 to 2006
55	G L Rees	1986 to 1999
54	J D Graf	1989 to 1999
52	M B James	1994 to 2006
50	J Hutchinson	1993 to 2000
49	E A Evans	1986 to 1998
47	S D Gray	1984 to 1997

MOST CONSECUTIVE TESTS

Tests	Player	Career span
40	J Hutchinson	1995 to 1999
25	J N Tait	1998 to 2001
21	W U Stanley	1998 to 2000
17	R P Ross	1996 to 1997
17	R Smith	2003 to 2006
16	A Abrams	2003 to 2005
15	S D Gray	1991 to 1994

MOST TESTS AS CAPTAIN

Tests	Player	Career span
25	G L Rees	1994 to 1999
25	A J Charron	1996 to 2003
16	J D Graf	1995 to 1999
9	M A Wyatt	1990 to 1991
8	M Luke	1974 to 1981
8	H de Goede	1984 to 1987

MOST TESTS IN INDIVIDUAL POSITIONS

Position	Player	Tests	Span
Full-back	D S Stewart	46	1989 to 2001
Wing	W U Stanley	45	1994 to 2003
Centre	S D Gray	31	1984 to 1997
Fly-half	G L Rees	49	1986 to 1999
Scrum-half	M Williams	45	1999 to 2006
Prop	R G A Snow	56	1995 to 2006
Hooker	P Dunkley	37	1998 to 2003
Lock	M B James	52	1994 to 2006
Flanker	J Hutchinson	46	1995 to 1999
No 8	C McKenzie	25	1992 to 1997

MOST POINTS IN TESTS

Points	Player	Tests	Career
492	G L Rees	55	1986 to 1999
418	R P Ross	57	1989 to 2003
263	M A Wyatt	29	1982 to 1991
226	J Barker	18	2000 to 2004
123	W U Stanley	66	1994 to 2003
116	J Pritchard	11	2003 to 2006
90	J D Graf	54	1989 to 1999

MOST TRIES IN TESTS

Tries	Player	Tests	Career
24	W U Stanley	66	1994 to 2003
10	K S Nichols	26	1996 to 2002
10	M Williams	45	1999 to 2006
9	P Palmer	17	1983 to 1992
9	J D Graf	54	1989 to 1999
9	G L Rees	55	1986 to 1999
9	A J Charron	72	1990 to 2002
9	R G A Snow	57	1995 to 2006

MOST CONVERSIONS IN TESTS

Drops	Player	Tests	Career
52	R P Ross	57	1989 to 2003
51	G L Rees	55	1986 to 1999
24	M A Wyatt	29	1982 to 1991
24	J Barker	18	2000 to 2004
20	J Pritchard	11	2003 to 2006
9	D S Stewart	64	1989 to 2001

MOST PENALTY GOALS IN TESTS

Penalties	Player	Tests	Career
110	G L Rees	55	1986 to 1999
83	R P Ross	57	1989 to 2003
64	M A Wyatt	29	1982 to 1991
55	J Barker	18	2000 to 2004
14	D S Stewart	64	1989 to 2001
12	J Pritchard	11	2003 to 2006
9	J D Graf	54	1989 to 1999
8	M D Schiefler	9	1980 to 1984

MOST DROPPED GOALS IN TESTS

Drops	Player	Tests	Career
10	R P Ross	57	1989 to 2003
9	G L Rees	55	1986 to 1999
5	M A Wyatt	29	1982 to 1991

CAREER RECORD OF CANADA INTERNATIONAL PLAYERS UP TO 31 AUGUST 2006

BACKS PLAYER	DEBUT	CAPS	T	C	P	D	PTS
J Cannon	2001 v US	31	0	0	0	0	0
C Culpan	2009 v EA	1	0	0	0	0	0
D Daypuck	2004 v E	14	1	5	12	0	51
E Fairhurst	2001 v US	31	1	4	6	0	31
B Henderson	2005 v J	3	2	0	0	0	10
S Hunter	2005 v Ro	1	0	0	0	0	0
R McWhinney	2005 v Ro	1	0	0	0	0	0
J Mensah-Coker	2006 v ScA	5	3	0	0	0	15
A Monro	2006 v EA	4	0	0	2	0	6
C Pack	2006 v ScA	1	0	0	0	0	0
J Pritchard	2003 v NZM	11	8	20	12	0	116
M Pyke	2004 v US	12	3	2	2	0	25
R Smith	2003 v E	27	4	0	0	0	20
D Spicer	2004 v E	7	0	0	0	0	0

R Stewart	2005 v Ro	1	0	0	0	0	0
D van Camp	2005 v J	2	1	0	0	0	5
D T van der Merwe	2006 v Ba	1	2	0	0	0	10
M Weingart	2004 v J	6	0	0	0	0	0
M Williams	1999 v Tg	45	10	0	0	1	43
K Witkowski	2005 v EA	2	0	0	0	0	0
N Witkowski	1998 v US	33	5	0	0	0	25
FORWARDS							
A Abrams	2003 v NZ	19	2	0	0	0	10
O Atkinson	2005 v J	2	0	0	0	0	0
M Barbieri	2006 v EA	2	0	0	0	0	0
D Biddle	2006 v ScA	3	0	0	0	0	0
M Burak	2004 v US	14	0	0	0	0	0
H Buydens	2006 v EA	2	0	0	0	0	0
A Carpenter	2005 v US	10	2	0	0	0	10
G G Cooke	2000 v Tg	24	0	0	0	0	0
J Cudmore	2002 v US	17	0	0	0	0	0
C Dunning	2005 v EA	5	0	0	0	0	0
F Gainer	2004 v US	14	0	0	0	0	0
J Jackson	2003 v U	15	0	0	0	0	0
M B James	1994 v US	52	3	0	0	0	15
A Kleeberger	2005 v Fr	6	1	0	0	0	5
M Lawson	2002 v US	25	1	0	0	0	5
S McKeen	2004 v US	16	0	0	0	0	0
M Phinney	2006 v ScA	2	0	0	0	0	0
D Pletch	2004 v US	14	0	0	0	0	0
M Pletch	2005 v Arg	5	0	0	0	0	0
P Riordan	2003 v E	11	0	0	0	0	0
R G A Snow	1995 v Arg	57	9	0	0	0	45
S-M Stephen	2005 v EA	7	2	0	0	0	10
L Tait	2005 v US	9	0	0	0	0	0
K Tkachuk	2000 v Tg	36	5	0	0	0	25
M Webb	2004 v US	13	0	0	0	0	0
C Yukes	2001 v U	21	0	0	0	0	0

ENGLAND

By Iain Spragg

ENGLAND'S TEST RECORD

OPPONENTS	DATE	VENUE	RESULT
Wales	4 February	H	**Won** 47–13
Italy	11 February	A	**Won** 31–16
Scotland	25 February	A	**Lost** 12–18
France	12 March	A	**Lost** 6–31
Ireland	18 March	H	**Lost** 24–28
Australia	11 June	A	**Lost** 3–34
Australia	17 June	A	**Lost** 18–43

FURTHER WOE FOR ENGLAND

England welcomed 2006 with high hopes and even higher expectations but behind the bravado and renewed swagger there remained the sense of unease and anxiety that had plagued Andy Robinson's side for the previous 12 turbulent months.

The 2005 Six Nations had been an unmitigated disaster with defeats to Wales, France and Ireland condemning the team to a distant fourth-place finish in the Championship. Pride and a degree of optimism were restored in the autumn internationals with victories over Australia and Samoa and a narrow reverse against the All Blacks at Twickenham but the feeling that England were still struggling to shake off their post World Cup malaise persisted.

Were the once dominant world champions really back on track or were the performances against the Wallabies and All Blacks merely a false dawn? Would Robinson's under-fire outfit go backwards or forwards in 2006?

The beleaguered England coach and his troops would soon have the answers.

The Six Nations began in February with Grand Slam winning Wales at Twickenham and England had the chance to avenge their morale-sapping 11–9 defeat in Cardiff a year previously – the result which had precipitated their dismal campaign.

When England romped home 47–13 in a six-try rout, it suggested the world champions were actually in fine fettle and although their 31–16 victory in Rome over the Italians a week later flattered the visitors, they appeared to have rediscovered the elusive knack of winning without firing on all cylinders that had eluded them since that famous night in Sydney in 2003.

And then the wheels came off.

Scotland at Murrayfield was never going to be a walkover but in the wet and wind of the Scottish capital, England contrived to squander the lion's share of possession and Chris Paterson won a dour battle of the respective kickers with Charlie Hodgson. Scotland won 18–12 and England were sent home 'tae think again', reeling from another abject performance away from home.

"We had enough ball to win the game," said captain Martin Corry after the defeat. "We pride ourselves on the fact that we play at our best when we have quick ball but that did not happen. We have to get over this now, we have a week with our clubs and then we have to focus on France."

But there was to be no respite in Paris and a nervous, rudderless England made a catalogue of errors to gift the French a record-equalling 31–6 win in the Stade de France. Robinson's assessment of the performance as "awful" was charitable in the extreme.

The Championship finished at Twickenham against Ireland but if Robinson, his players or England's increasingly disgruntled fans were hoping for a face-saving finale, they were to be sorely disappointed. Ireland outscored England three tries to two, enjoyed the rub off the green from the video referee and emerged 28–24 winners to claim their

Dave Rogers/Getty Images

Andy Robinson has endured a tough start to his reign as England coach.

second Triple Crown in three years. England, in contrast, were now in complete disarray.

"I'm really frustrated for the boys because I thought they put in a huge effort," Robinson said after a second straight defeat to the Irish. "On another day we would have won the match and won it well.

"There is only one disappointing performance for us and that was last weekend against France. I thought against Scotland we performed very, very well but just didn't finish them off, and today I felt we played well but again we didn't finish them off.

"Against Italy and Wales we won, France was disappointing but again we gave them three tries from our mistakes.

"People have got lots of opinions and when you're losing those opinions come out even more. Everybody will be reviewed, including myself, and we'll look at how we can move forward. I'll be meeting with Francis Baron [RFU chief executive] to discuss everything, but I'm not expecting to be going anywhere."

Robinson was absolutely right. A second successive Six Nations debacle inevitably meant heads would have to roll but the head coach himself was safe and it was defence coach Phil Larder, attack coach Joe Lydon and kicking guru Dave Alred who were offered up as the sacrificial lambs by the RFU.

In their place came in Mike Ford, who replaced Larder, forwards coach John Wells and finally Brian Ashton, the Bath director of rugby charged with reigniting England's misfiring attack. Robinson now had a new coaching team in place in time for the two Test tour of Australia in the summer.

"My aim is to turn England into the best defensive team in the world," Ford said after his appointment. "If we want to do well in the Six Nations and the World Cup next year then you can't have the opposition looking at your defence and being able to say 'England do this every time'."

England's new-look defence was put to the test at the end of May when Robinson picked a young, experimental side to face the Barbarians at Twickenham and their 46–19 win suggested at least the future would be brighter than the immediate past.

But the real challenge of beating the Wallabies at home still lay ahead and England's prospects began to look bleak as a succession of influential senior players were ruled out of contention through injury or Robinson's insistence they stay at home and rest.

Corry, Josh Lewsey, Hodgson and Mark Cueto were all told to take the summer off while the likes of Andrew Sheridan and Matt Stevens missed out with injury.

Only eight of the 22 players who featured against Ireland in March made the trip and six uncapped players – Magnus Lund, Peter Richards, Nick Walshe, Scott Bemand, Alex Brown and George Chuter – were drafted in to bolster a squad captained by Worcester's Pat Sanderson.

Robinson, however, was determined to remain upbeat despite the limited resources at his disposal.

"The squad is a mix of experience and youth," he said. "I've deliberately decided to rest some players to ensure they're in the best shape they could possibly be in ahead of the World Cup in 2007.

"The key message is that we've got 16 games now in 16 months to the next World Cup. Each player involved has a fantastic opportunity to put their hand up for that. They must show the ruthlessness we need to take the chance."

Unfortunately, the only hands up in evidence during the first Test against the Wallabies in Sydney were those in surrender as Australia taught England's fledgling tourists a brutal lesson in the realities of Test match rugby.

In truth, England had their chances in the Telstra Stadium and the new-look pack provided a decent platform but there was still no disguising the gulf in class between the two sides as the Wallabies ran in three tries in a comprehensive 34–3 win.

"I was really pleased with the ambition and our ability to open Australia up," Robinson said after the match. "I thought we rattled them in defence but you have to take your chances."

But whatever Robinson was saying in public, he must have been privately concerned by his side's inability to muster more than a single Olly Barkley penalty in the entire match. It was little surprise when he announced six changes to his starting line-up for the second Test in Melbourne.

They made no difference.

England actually took the lead when Andy Goode's scuffed drop goal limped over but when George Smith scored a try a minute later after a comical rebound off Tom Varndell's face, the writing was on the wall. The imperious Wallabies ran in five further tries and England slumped to a humiliating 43–18 defeat.

The result extended England's losing streak to five – their worst since 1984 – and left Robinson's record as head coach, since he replaced Sir Clive Woodward in October 2004, as played 18, won just eight.

A year that had begun with genuine promise after a resounding win over Six Nations champions Wales had now hit a new low. Not surprisingly Robinson was determined to focus on what he perceived as the positives of a difficult tour that had once again exposed England's continuing and seemingly incurable World Cup hangover.

"I'm still confident we can put out a team capable of winning the World Cup," he said after his side's Melbourne mauling. "It is another defeat, and headlines will be created because of that, but we have got to be able to move forward. Another couple of players have come through from this tour."

"We have to take stock of where we are, find a ruthlessness and an ability to finish sides off. The forward display was pretty impressive, and we had 63% possession."

"We have got to look forward. I was pleased with some of the ambition, but we must improve our game management."

The chances of England successfully defending their World Cup crown in 2007 were decidedly slim at the start of the year. By the end of another ill-fated journey Down Under and two heavy defeats, many prudent punters would probably now rate them as non-existent.

ENGLAND INTERNATIONAL STATISTICS

MATCH RECORDS UP TO 30TH SEPTEMBER 2006

MOST CONSECUTIVE TEST WINS

14	2002 W, It, Arg, NZ, A, SA,	2003 F1,W1,It,S,I, NZ,A,W2
11	2000 SA 2, A, Arg, SA3,	2001 W,It,S,F,C1,2, US
10	1882 W, 1883 I, S,	1884 W,I,S, 1885 W,I, 1886 W,I
10	1994 R, C,	1995 I,F,W,S, Arg, It, WS, A
10	2003 F,Gg, SA, Sm, U, W, F, A,	2004 It,S

MOST CONSECUTIVE TESTS WITHOUT DEFEAT

Matches	Wins	Draws	Periods
14	14	0	2002 to 2003
12	10	2	1882 to 1887
11	10	1	1922 to 1924
11	11	0	2000 to 2001

MOST POINTS IN A MATCH

BY THE TEAM

Pts.	Opponent	Venue	Year
134	Romania	Twickenham	2001
111	Uruguay	Brisbane	2003
110	Netherlands	Huddersfield	1998
106	U S A	Twickenham	1999
101	Tonga	Twickenham	1999
84	Georgia	Perth	2003
80	Italy	Twickenham	2001

BY A PLAYER

Pts.	Player	Opponent	Venue	Year
44	C Hodgson	Romania	Twickenham	2001
36	P J Grayson	Tonga	Twickenham	1999
35	J P Wilkinson	Italy	Twickenham	2001
32	J P Wilkinson	Italy	Twickenham	1999
30	C R Andrew	Canada	Twickenham	1994
30	P J Grayson	Netherlands	Huddersfield	1998
30	J P Wilkinson	Wales	Twickenham	2002
29	D J H Walder	Canada	Burnaby	2001
27	C R Andrew	South Africa	Pretoria	1994
27	J P Wilkinson	South Africa	Bloemfontein	2000
27	C C Hodgson	South Africa	Twickenham	2004
26	J P Wilkinson	United States	Twickenham	1999

MOST TRIES IN A MATCH

BY THE TEAM

Tries	Opponent	Venue	Year
20	Romania	Twickenham	2001
17	Uruguay	Brisbane	2003
16	United States	Twickenham	1999
16	Netherlands	Huddersfield	1998
13	Wales	Blackheath	1881
13	Tonga	Twickenham	1999
12	Canada	Twickenham	2004
12	Georgia	Perth	2003
10	Japan	Sydney	1987
10	Fiji	Twickenham	1989
10	Italy	Twickenham	2001

BY A PLAYER

Tries	Player	Opponent	Venue	Year
5	D Lambert	France	Richmond	1907
5	R Underwood	Fiji	Twickenham	1989
5	O J Lewsey	Uruguay	Brisbane	2003
4	G W Burton	Wales	Blackheath	1881
4	A Hudson	France	Paris	1906
4	R W Poulton	France	Paris	1914
4	C Oti	Romania	Bucharest	1989
4	J C Guscott	Netherlands	Huddersfield	1998
4	N A Back	Netherlands	Huddersfield	1998
4	J C Guscott	United States	Twickenham	1999
4	J Robinson	Romania	Twickenham	2001

MOST CONVERSIONS IN A MATCH

BY THE TEAM

Cons	Opponent	Venue	Year
15	Netherlands	Huddersfield	1998
14	Romania	Twickenham	2001
13	United States	Twickenham	1999
13	Uruguay	Brisbane	2003
12	Tonga	Twickenham	1999
9	Italy	Twickenham	2001
9	Georgia	Perth	2003
8	Romania	Bucharest	1989
7	Wales	Blackheath	1881
7	Japan	Sydney	1987
7	Argentina	Twickenham	1990
7	Wales	Twickenham	1998

BY A PLAYER

Cons	Player	Opponent	Venue	Year
15	P J Grayson	Netherlands	Huddersfield	1998
14	C Hodgson	Romania	Twickenham	2001
13	J P Wilkinson	United States	Twickenham	1999
12	P J Grayson	Tonga	Twickenham	1999
11	P J Grayson	Uruguay	Brisbane	2003
9	J P Wilkinson	Italy	Twickenham	2001
8	S D Hodgkinson	Romania	Bucharest	1989
7	J M Webb	Japan	Sydney	1987
7	S D Hodgkinson	Argentina	Twickenham	1990
7	P J Grayson	Wales	Twickenham	1998

MOST PENALTIES IN A MATCH

BY THE TEAM

Pens	Opponent	Venue	Year
8	South Africa	Bloemfontein	2000
7	Wales	Cardiff	1991
7	Scotland	Twickenham	1995
7	France	Twickenham	1999
7	Fiji	Twickenham	1999
7	South Africa	Paris	1999
7	South Africa	Twickenham	2001
6	Wales	Twickenham	1986
6	Canada	Twickenham	1994
6	Argentina	Durban	1995
6	Scotland	Murrayfield	1996
6	Ireland	Twickenham	1996
6	South Africa	Twickenham	2000
6	Australia	Twickenham	2002
6	Wales	Brisbane	2003

BY A PLAYER

Pens	Player	Opponent	Venue	Year
8	J P Wilkinson	South Africa	Bloemfontein	2000
7	S D Hodgkinson	Wales	Cardiff	1991
7	C R Andrew	Scotland	Twickenham	1995
7	J P Wilkinson	France	Twickenham	1999
7	J P Wilkinson	Fiji	Twickenham	1999
7	J P Wilkinson	South Africa	Twickenham	2001
6	C R Andrew	Wales	Twickenham	1986
6	C R Andrew	Canada	Twickenham	1994
6	C R Andrew	Argentina	Durban	1995
6	P J Grayson	Scotland	Murrayfield	1996
6	P J Grayson	Ireland	Twickenham	1996
6	P J Grayson	South Africa	Paris	1999
6	J P Wilkinson	South Africa	Twickenham	2000
6	J P Wilkinson	Australia	Twickenham	2002
6	J P Wilkinson	Wales	Brisbane	2003

MOST DROPPED GOALS IN A MATCH

BY THE TEAM

Drops	Opponent	Venue	Year
3	France	Sydney	2003
2	Ireland	Twickenham	1970
2	France	Paris	1978
2	France	Paris	1980
2	Romania	Twickenham	1985
2	Fiji	Suva	1991
2	Argentina	Durban	1995
2	France	Paris	1996
2	Australia	Twickenham	2001
2	Wales	Cardiff	2003
2	Ireland	Dublin	2003
2	South Africa	Perth	2003

BY A PLAYER

Drops	Player	Opponent	Venue	Year
3	J P Wilkinson	France	Sydney	2003
2	R Hiller	Ireland	Twickenham	1970
2	A G B Old	France	Paris	1978
2	J P Horton	France	Paris	1980
2	C R Andrew	Romania	Twickenham	1985
2	C R Andrew	Fiji	Suva	1991
2	C R Andrew	Argentina	Durban	1995
2	P J Grayson	France	Paris	1996
2	J P Wilkinson	Australia	Twickenham	2001
2	J P Wilkinson	Wales	Cardiff	2003
2	J P Wilkinson	Ireland	Dublin	2003
2	J P Wilkinson	South Africa	Perth	2003

MOST CAPPED PLAYERS

Caps	Player	Career Span
114	J Leonard	1990 to 2004
85	R Underwood	1984 to 1996
84	M O Johnson	1993 to 2003
77	M J S Dawson	1995 to 2006
77	L B N Dallaglio	1995 to 2006
72	W D C Carling	1988 to 1997
71	C R Andrew	1985 to 1997
71	R A Hill	1997 to 2004
67	M J Catt	1994 to 2006
66	N A Back	1994 to 2003
65	J C Guscott	1989 to 1999
64	B C Moore	1987 to 1995
64	D J Grewcock	1997 to 2006
58	P J Winterbottom	1982 to 1993
55	W A Dooley	1985 to 1993
55	W J H Greenwood	1997 to 2004
54	G C Rowntree	1995 to 2006
53	B C Cohen	2000 to 2006
52	J P Wilkinson	1998 to 2003
51	A S Healey	1997 to 2003
51	K P P Bracken	1993 to 2003
51	J P R Worsley	1999 to 2006

MOST CONSECUTIVE TESTS

Tests	Player	Career span
44	W D C Carling	1989 to 1995
40	J Leonard	1990 to 1995
36	J V Pullin	1968 to 1975
33	W B Beaumont	1975 to 1982
30	R Underwood	1992 to 1996

MOST TESTS AS CAPTAIN

Tests	Player	Career span
59	W D C Carling	1988 to 1996
39	M O Johnson	1998 to 2003
22	L B N Dallaglio	1997 to 2004
21	W B Beaumont	1978 to 1982
13	W W Wakefield	1924 to 1926
13	N M Hall	1949 to 1955
13	R E G Jeeps	1960 to 1962
13	J V Pullin	1972 to 1975

MOST POINTS IN TESTS

Points	Player	Tests	Career
817	J P Wilkinson	52	1998 to 2003
400	P J Grayson	32	1995 to 2004
396	C R Andrew	71	1985 to 1997
296	J M Webb	33	1987 to 1993
243	C C Hodgson	26	2001 to 2006
240	W H Hare	25	1974 to 1984
210	R Underwood	85	1984 to 1996

MOST TRIES IN TESTS

Tries	Player	Tests	Career
49	R Underwood	85	1984 to 1996
31	W J H Greenwood	55	1997 to 2004
30	J C Guscott	65	1989 to 1999
30	B C Cohen	53	2000 to 2006
24	D D Luger	38	1998 to 2003
22	J T Robinson	39	2001 to 2005
21	O J Lewsey	40	1998 to 2006
18	C N Lowe	25	1913 to 1923
16	N A Back	66	1994 to 2003
16	M J S Dawson	77	1995 to 2006
16	L B N Dallaglio	77	1995 to 2006
15	A S Healey	51	1997 to 2003
13	T Underwood	27	1992 to 1998

MOST DROPPED GOALS IN TESTS

Drops	Player	Tests	Career
21	C R Andrew	71	1985 to 1997
21	J P Wilkinson	52	1998 to 2003
6	P J Grayson	32	1995 to 2004
4	J P Horton	13	1978 to 1984

MOST CONVERSIONS IN TESTS

Cons	Player	Tests	Career
123	J P Wilkinson	52	1998 to 2003
78	P J Grayson	32	1995 to 2004
42	C C Hodgson	26	2001 to 2006
41	J M Webb	33	1987 to 1993
35	S D Hodgkinson	14	1989 to 1991
33	C R Andrew	71	1985 to 1997
17	L Stokes	12	1875 to 1881

MOST PENALTY GOALS IN TESTS

Pens	Player	Tests	Career
161	J P Wilkinson	52	1998 to 2003
86	C R Andrew	71	1985 to 1997
72	P J Grayson	32	1995 to 2004
67	W H Hare	25	1974 to 1984
66	J M Webb	33	1987 to 1993
43	S D Hodgkinson	14	1989 to 1991

INTERNATIONAL CHAMPIONSHIP RECORDS

RECORD	DETAIL		SET
Most points in season	229	in five matches	2001
Most tries in season	29	in five matches	2001
Highest Score	80	80–23 v Italy	2001
Biggest win	57	80–23 v Italy	2001
Highest score conceded	37	12–37 v France	1972
Biggest defeat	27	6–33 v Scotland	1986
Most appearances	54	J Leonard	1991–2004
Most points in matches	379	J P Wilkinson	1998–2003
Most points in season	89	J P Wilkinson	2001
Most points in match	35	J P Wilkinson	v Italy, 2001
Most tries in matches	18	C N Lowe	1913–1923
	18	R Underwood	1984–1996
Most tries in season	8	C N Lowe	1914
Most tries in match	4	R W Poulton	v France, 1914
Most cons in matches	74	J P Wilkinson	1998–2003
Most cons in season	24	J P Wilkinson	2001
Most cons in match	9	J P Wilkinson	v Italy, 2001
Most pens in matches	66	J P Wilkinson	1998–2003
Most pens in season	18	S D Hodgkinson	1991
	18	J P Wilkinson	2000
Most pens in match	7	S D Hodgkinson	v Wales, 1991
	7	C R Andrew	v Scotland, 1995
	7	J P Wilkinson	v France, 1999
Most drops in matches	9	C R Andrew	1985–1997
Most drops in season	5	J P Wilkinson	2003
Most drops in match	2	R Hiller	v Ireland, 1970
	2	A G B Old	v France, 1978
	2	J P Horton	v France, 1980
	2	P J Grayson	v France, 1996
	2	J P Wilkinson	v Wales, 2003
	2	J P Wilkinson	v Ireland, 2003

MISCELLANEOUS RECORDS

RECORD	HOLDER	DETAIL
Longest Test Career	J Leonard	1990 to 2004
Youngest Test Cap	H C C Laird	18 yrs 134 days in 1927
Oldest Test Cap	F Gilbert	38 yrs 362 days in 1923

CAREER RECORDS OF ENGLAND INTERNATIONAL PLAYERS (PLAYERS CAPPED SINCE THE START OF RWC 2003 UP TO 30 SEPTEMBER 2006)

PLAYER BACKS	DEBUT	CAPS	T	C	P	D	PTS
S R Abbott	2003 v W	9	2	0	0	0	10
I R Balshaw	2000 v I	26	12	0	0	0	60
O J Barkley	2001 v US	16	1	4	9	0	40
K P P Bracken	1993 v NZ	51	3	0	0	0	15
M J Catt	1994 v W	67	7	16	22	3	142
B C Cohen	2000 v I	53	30	0	0	0	150
M J Cueto	2004 v C	16	11	0	0	0	55
M J S Dawson	1995 v WS	77	16	6	3	0	101
H A Ellis	2004 v SA	13	2	0	0	0	10
A J Goode	2005 v It	7	0	5	6	1	31
A C T Gomarsall	1996 v It	23	6	2	0	0	34
P J Grayson	1995 v WS	32	2	78	72	6	400
W J H Greenwood	1997 v A	55	31	0	0	0	155
C C Hodgson	2001 v R	26	6	42	40	3	243
O J Lewsey	1998 v NZ	40	21	0	0	0	105
D D Luger	1998 v H	38	24	0	0	0	120
J D Noon	2001 v C	19	5	0	0	0	25
H R Paul	2002 v F	6	0	3	0	0	6
P C Richards	2006 v A	2	0	0	0	0	0
J T Robinson	2001 v It	39	22	0	0	0	110
J D Simpson-Daniel	2002 v NZ	9	2	0	0	0	10
O J Smith	2003 v It	5	0	0	0	0	0
M Tait	2005 v W	3	0	0	0	0	0
M J Tindall	2000 v I	49	12	2	0	0	64
M C van Gisbergen	2005 v A	1	0	0	0	0	0
T W Varndell	2005 v Sm	3	2	0	0	0	10
T M D Voyce	2001 v US	9	3	0	0	0	15
N P J Walshe	2006 v A	2	0	0	0	0	0
F H H Waters	2001 v US	3	0	0	0	0	0
J P Wilkinson	1998 v I	52	5	123	161	21	817

FORWARDS							
N A Back	1994 v S	66	16	0	0	1	83
D S C Bell	2005 v It	2	0	0	0	0	0
S W Borthwick	2001 v F	27	1	0	0	0	5
A Brown	2006 v A	1	0	0	0	0	0
G S Chuter	2006 v A	2	1	0	0	0	5
M E Corry	1997 v Arg	45	4	0	0	0	20
L B N Dallaglio	1995 v SA	77	16	0	0	0	80
L P Deacon	2005 v Sm	3	0	0	0	0	0
J Forrester	2005 v W	2	0	0	0	0	0
P T Freshwater	2005 v Sm	3	0	0	0	0	0
D J Grewcock	1997 v Arg	64	2	0	0	0	10
A R Hazell	2004 v C	6	1	0	0	0	5
R A Hill	1997 v S	71	12	0	0	0	60
M O Johnson	1993 v F	84	2	0	0	0	10
C M Jones	2004 v It	8	1	0	0	0	5
B J Kay	2001 v C	41	2	0	0	0	10
J Leonard	1990 v Arg	114	1	0	0	0	5
M R Lipman	2004 v NZ	3	0	0	0	0	0
M B Lund	2006 v A	2	0	0	0	0	0
L A Mears	2005 v Sm	7	0	0	0	0	0
L W Moody	2001 v C	40	9	0	0	0	45
T A N Payne	2004 v A	3	0	0	0	0	0
M P Regan	1995 v SA	33	3	0	0	0	15
G C Rowntree	1995 v S	54	0	0	0	0	0
P H Sanderson	1998 v NZ	11	1	0	0	0	5
S D Shaw	1996 v It	34	2	0	0	0	10
A J Sheridan	2004 v C	9	0	0	0	0	0
M J H Stevens	2004 v NZ	10	0	0	0	0	0
S G Thompson	2002 v S	47	3	0	0	0	15
A J Titterrell	2004 v NZ	4	0	0	0	0	0
P J Vickery	1998 v W	47	1	0	0	0	5
H D Vyvyan	2004 v C	1	1	0	0	0	5
D E West	1998 v F	21	3	0	0	0	15
J M White	2000 v SA	35	0	0	0	0	0
T J Woodman	1999 v US	22	0	0	0	0	0
J P R Worsley	1999 v Tg	51	9	0	0	0	45
M A Worsley	2003 v It	3	0	0	0	0	0

ENGLAND INTERNATIONAL PLAYERS

UP TO 30TH SEPTEMBER 2006

Note: Years given for International Championship matches are for second half of season; eg 1972 means season 1971–72. Years for all other matches refer to the actual year of the match. Entries in square brackets denote matches played in RWC Finals.

Aarvold, C D (Cambridge U, W Hartlepool, Headingley, Blackheath) 1928 A, W, I, F, S, 1929 W, I, F, 1931 W, S, F, 1932 SA, W, I, S, 1933 W

Abbott, S R (Wasps, Harlequins) 2003 W2, F3, [Sm, U, W(R)], 2004 NZ1(t&R), 2, 2006 I, A2(R)

Ackford, P J (Harlequins) 1988 A, 1989 S, I, F, W, R, Fj, 1990 I, F, W, S, Arg 3, 1991 W, S, I, F, A, [NZ, It, F, S, A]

Adams, A A (London Hospital) 1910 F

Adams, F R (Richmond) 1875 I, S, 1876 S, 1877 I, 1878 S, 1879 S, I

Adebayo, A A (Bath) 1996, It, 1997 Arg 1,2, A 2, NZ 1, 1998 S

Adey, G J (Leicester) 1976 I, F

Adkins, S J (Coventry) 1950 I, F, S, 1953 W, I, F, S

Agar, A E (Harlequins) 1952 SA, W, S, I, F, 1953 W, I

Alcock, A (Guy's Hospital) 1906 SA

Alderson, F H R (Hartlepool R) 1891 W, I, S, 1892 W, S, 1893 W

Alexander, H (Richmond) 1900 I, S, 1901 W, I, S, 1902 W, I

Alexander, W (Northern) 1927 F

Allison, D F (Coventry) 1956 W, I, S, F, 1957 W, 1958 W, S

Allport, A (Blackheath) 1892 W, 1893 I, 1894 W, I, S

Anderson, S (Rockcliff) 1899 I

Anderson, W F (Orrell) 1973 NZ 1

Anderton, C (Manchester FW) 1889 M

Andrew, C R (Cambridge U, Nottingham, Wasps, Toulouse, Newcastle) 1985 R, F, S, I, W, 1986 W, S, I, F, 1987 I, F, W, [J (R), US], 1988 S, I 1,2, A 1,2, Fj, A, 1989 S, I, F, W, R, Fj, 1990 I, F, W, S, Arg 3, 1991 W, S, I, F, Fj, A, [NZ, It, US, F, S, A], 1992 S, I, F, W, C, SA, 1993 F, W, NZ, 1994 S, I, F, W, SA 1,2, R, C, 1995 I, F, W, S, [Arg, It, A, NZ, F], 1997 W (R)

Appleford, G (London Irish) 2002 Arg

Archer, G S (Bristol, Army, Newcastle) 1996 S, I, 1997 A 2, NZ 1, SA, NZ 2, 1998 F, W, S, I, A 1, NZ 1, H, It, 1999 Tg, Fj, 2000 I, F, W, It, S

Archer, H (Bridgwater A) 1909 W, F, I

Armstrong, R (Northern) 1925 W

Arthur, T G (Wasps) 1966 W, I

Ashby, R C (Wasps) 1966 I, F, 1967 A

Ashcroft, A (Waterloo) 1956 W, I, S, F, 1957 W, I, F, S, 1958 W, A, I, F, S, 1959 I, F, S

Ashcroft, A H (Birkenhead Park) 1909 A

Ashford, W (Richmond) 1897 W, I, 1898 S, W

Ashworth, A (Oldham) 1892 I

Askew, J G (Cambridge U) 1930 W, I, F

Aslett, A R (Richmond) 1926 W, I, F, S, 1929 S, F

Assinder, E W (O Edwardians) 1909 A, W

Aston, R L (Blackheath) 1890 S, I

Auty, J R (Headingley) 1935 S

Back, N A (Leicester) 1994 S, I, 1995 [Arg (t), It, WS], 1997 NZ 1(R), SA, NZ 2, 1998 F, W, S, I, H, It, A 2, SA 2, 1999 S, I, F, W, A, US, C, [It, NZ, Fj, SA], 2000 I, F, W, It, S, SA 1,2, A, Arg, SA 3, 2001 W, It, S, F, I, A, R, SA, 2002 S, I, F, W, It, NZ (t + R), A, SA, 2003 F 1, W 1, S, I, NZ, A, F 3, [Gg, SA, Sm, W, F, A]

Bailey, M D (Cambridge U, Wasps) 1984 SA 1,2, 1987 [US], 1989 Fj, 1990 I, F, S (R)

Bainbridge, S (Gosforth, Fylde) 1982 F, W, 1983 F, W, S, I, NZ, 1984 S, I, F, W, 1985 NZ 1,2, 1987 F, W, S, [J, US]

Baker, D G S (OMTs) 1955 W, I, F, S

Baker, E M (Moseley) 1895 W, I, S, 1896 W, I, S, 1897 W

Baker, H C (Clifton) 1887 W

Balshaw, I R (Bath, Leeds, Gloucester) 2000 I (R), F (R), It (R), S (R), A (R), Arg, SA 3(R), 2001 W, It, S, F, I, 2002 S (R), I (R), 2003 F2,3, [Sm, U, A(R)], 2004 It, S, I, 2005 It, S, 2006 A1, 2

Bance, J F (Bedford) 1954 S

Barkley, O J (Bath) 2001 US (R), 2004 It(R), I(t), W, F, NZ2(R), A1(R), 2005 W(R), F, I, It, S, A(R), Sm(R), 2006 A1, 2(R)

Barley, B (Wakefield) 1984 I, F, W, A, 1988 A 1,2, Fj

Barnes, S (Bristol, Bath) 1984 A, 1985 R (R), NZ 1,2, 1986 S (R), F (R), 1987 I (R), 1988 Fj, 1993 S, I

Barr, R J (Leicester) 1932 SA, W, I

Barrett, E I M (Lennox) 1903 S

Barrington, T J M (Bristol) 1931 W, I

Barrington-Ward, L E (Edinburgh U) 1910 W, I, F, S

Barron, J H (Bingley) 1896 S, 1897 W, I

Bartlett, J T (Waterloo) 1951 W

Bartlett, R M (Harlequins) 1957 W, I, F, S, 1958 I, F, S

Barton, J (Coventry) 1967 I, F, W, 1972 F

Batchelor, T B (Oxford U) 1907 F

Bates, S M (Wasps) 1989 R

Bateson, A H (Otley) 1930 W, I, F, S

Bateson, H D (Liverpool) 1879 I

Batson, T (Blackheath) 1872 S, 1874 S, 1875 I

Batten, J M (Cambridge U) 1874 S

Baume, J L (Northern) 1950 S

Baxendell, J J N (Sale) 1998 NZ 2, SA 1

Baxter, J (Birkenhead Park) 1900 W, I, S

Bayfield, M C (Northampton) 1991 Fj, A, 1992 S, I, F, W, C, SA, 1993 F, W, S, I, 1994 S, I, SA 1,2, R, C, 1995 I, F, W, S, [Arg, It, A, NZ, F], SA, WS, 1996 F, W

Bazley, R C (Waterloo) 1952 I, F, 1953 W, I, F, S, 1955 W, I, F, S

Beal, N D (Northampton) 1996 Arg, 1997 A 1, 1998 NZ 1,2, SA 1, H (R), SA 2, 1999 S, F (R), A (t), C (R), [It (R), Tg (R), Fj, SA]

Beaumont, W B (Fylde) 1975 I, A 1(R),2, 1976 A, W, S, I, F, 1977 S, I, F, W, 1978 F, W, S, I, NZ, 1979 S, I, F, W, NZ, 1980 I, F, W, S, 1981 W, S, I, F, Arg 1,2, 1982 A, S

Bedford, H (Morley) 1889 M, 1890 S, I

Bedford, L L (Headingley) 1931 W, I

Beer, I D S (Harlequins) 1955 F, S

Beese, M C (Liverpool) 1972 W, I, F

Beim, T D (Sale) 1998 NZ 1(R),2

Bell, D S C (Bath) 2005 It(R), S

Bell, F J (Northern) 1900 W

Bell, H (New Brighton) 1884 I

Bell, J L (Darlington) 1878 I

Bell, P J (Blackheath) 1968 W, I, F, S

Bell, R W (Northern) 1900 W, I, S

Bendon, G J (Wasps) 1959 W, I, F, S

Bennett, N O (St Mary's Hospital, Waterloo) 1947 W, S, F, 1948 A, W, I, S

Bennett, W N (Bedford, London Welsh) 1975 S, A1, 1976 S (R), 1979 S, I, F, W

Bennetts, B B (Penzance) 1909 A, W
Bentley, J (Sale, Newcastle) 1988 I 2, A 1, 1997 A 1, SA
Bentley, J E (Gipsies) 1871 S, 1872 S
Benton, S (Gloucester) 1998 A 1
Berridge, M J (Northampton) 1949 W, I
Berry, H (Gloucester) 1910 W, I, F, S
Berry, J (Tyldesley) 1891 W, I, S
Berry, J T W (Leicester) 1939 W, I, S
Beswick, E (Swinton) 1882 I, S
Biggs, J M (UCH) 1878 S, 1879 I
Birkett, J G G (Harlequins) 1906 S, F, SA, 1907 F, W, S, 1908 F, W,I , S, 1910 W, I, S, 1911 W, F, I , S, 1912 W, I , S, F
Birkett L (Clapham R) 1875 S, 1877 I, S
Birkett, R H (Clapham R) 1871 S, 1875 S, 1876 S, 1877 I
Bishop, C C (Blackheath) 1927 F
Black, B H (Blackheath) 1930 W, I, F, S, 1931 W, I, S, F, 1932 S, 1933 W
Blacklock, J H (Aspatria) 1898 I, 1899 I
Blakeway, P J (Gloucester) 1980 I, F, W, S, 1981 W, S, I, F, 1982 I, F, W, 1984 I, F, W, SA 1, 1985 R, F, S, I
Blakiston, A F (Northampton) 1920 S, 1921 W, I, S, F, 1922 W, 1923 S, F, 1924 W, I, F, S, 1925 NZ, W, I, S, F
Blatherwick, T (Manchester) 1878 I
Body, J A (Gipsies) 1872 S, 1873 S
Bolton, C A (United Services) 1909 F
Bolton, R (Harlequins) 1933 W, 1936 S, 1937 S, 1938 W, I
Bolton, W N (Blackheath) 1882 I, S, 1883 W, I, S, 1884 W, I, S, 1885 I, 1887 I, S
Bonaventura, M S (Blackheath) 1931 W
Bond, A M (Sale) 1978 NZ, 1979 S, I, NZ, 1980 I, 1982 I
Bonham-Carter, E (Oxford U) 1891 S
Bonsor, F (Bradford) 1886 W, I, S, 1887 W, S, 1889 M
Boobbyer, B (Rosslyn Park) 1950 W, I, F, S, 1951 W, F, 1952 S, I, F
Booth, L A (Headingley) 1933 W, I, S, 1934 S, 1935 W, I, S
Borthwick, S W (Bath) 2001 F, C 1,2(R), US, R, 2003 A(t), W 2(t), F 2, 2004 I, F(R), NZ1(R), 2, A1, C, SA, A2, 2005 W(R), It(R), S(R), A, NZ, Sm, 2006 W, It, S, F, I
Botting, I J (Oxford U) 1950 W, I
Boughton, H J (Gloucester) 1935 W, I, S
Boyle, C W (Oxford U) 1873 S
Boyle, S B (Gloucester) 1983 W, S, I
Boylen, F (Hartlepool R) 1908 F, W, I, S
Bracken, K P P (Bristol, Saracens) 1993 NZ, 1994 S, I, C, 1995 I, F, W, S, [It, WS (t)], SA, 1996 It (R), 1997 Arg 1,2, A 2, NZ 1,2, 1998 F, W, 1999 S(R), I, F, A, 2000 SA 1,2, A, 2001 It (R), S (R), F (R), C 1,2, US, I (R), A, R (R), SA, 2002 S, I, F, W, It, 2003 W 1, It(R), I(t), NZ, A, F3, [SA, U(R), W(R), F(t&R)]
Bradby, M S (United Services) 1922 I, F
Bradley, R (W Hartlepool) 1903 W
Bradshaw, H (Bramley) 1892 S, 1893 W, I, S, 1894 W, I, S
Brain, S E (Coventry) 1984 SA 2, A (R), 1985 R, F, S, I, W, NZ 1,2, 1986 W, S, I, F
Braithwaite, J (Leicester) 1905 NZ
Braithwaite-Exley, B (Headingley) 1949 W
Brettargh, A T (Liverpool OB) 1900 W, 1903 I, S, 1904 W, I, S, 1905 I, S
Brewer, J (Gipsies) 1876 I
Briggs, A (Bradford) 1892 W, I, S
Brinn, A (Gloucester) 1972 W, I, S
Broadley, T (Bingley) 1893 W, S, 1894 W, I, S, 1896 S
Bromet, W E (Richmond) 1891 W, I, 1892 W, I, S, 1893 W, I, S, 1895 W, I, S, 1896 I
Brook, P W P (Harlequins) 1930 S, 1931 F, 1936 S
Brooke, T J (Richmond) 1968 F, S
Brooks, F G (Bedford) 1906 SA
Brooks, M J (Oxford U) 1874 S
Brophy, T J (Liverpool) 1964 I, F, S, 1965 W, I, 1966 W, I, F
Brough, J W (Silloth) 1925 NZ, W
Brougham, H (Harlequins) 1912 W, I, S, F
Brown A (Gloucester) 2006 A1
Brown, A A (Exeter) 1938 S
Brown, L G (Oxford U, Blackheath) 1911 W, F, I, S, 1913 SA, W, F, I, S, 1914 W, I, S, F, 1921 W, I, S, F, 1922 W
Brown S P (Richmond) 1998 A 1, SA 1
Brown, T W (Bristol) 1928 S, 1929 W, I, S, F, 1932 S, 1933 W, I, S
Brunton, J (N Durham) 1914 W, I, S
Brutton, E B (Cambridge U) 1886 S
Bryden, C C (Clapham R) 1876 I, 1877 S
Bryden, H A (Clapham R) 1874 S
Buckingham, R A (Leicester) 1927 F
Bucknall, A L (Richmond) 1969 SA, 1970 I, W, S, F, 1971 W, I, F, S (2[1C])
Buckton, J R D (Saracens) 1988 A (R), 1990 Arg 1,2
Budd, A (Blackheath) 1878 I, 1879 S, I, 1881 W, S
Budworth, R T D (Blackheath) 1890 W, 1891 W, S
Bull, A G (Northampton) 1914 W
Bullough, E (Wigan) 1892 W, I, S
Bulpitt, M P (Blackheath) 1970 S
Bulteel, A J (Manchester) 1876 I
Bunting, W L (Moseley) 1897 I, S, 1898 I, S, W, 1899 S, 1900 S, 1901 I, S
Burland, D W (Bristol) 1931 W, I, F, 1932 I, S, 1933 W, I, S
Burns, B H (Blackheath) 1871 S
Burton, G W (Blackheath) 1879 S, I, 1880 S, 1881 I, W, S
Burton, H C (Richmond) 1926 W
Burton, M A (Gloucester) 1972 W, I, F, S, SA, 1974 F, W, 1975 S, A 1,2, 1976 A, W, S, I, F, 1978 F, W
Bush, J A (Clifton) 1872 S, 1873 S, 1875 S, 1876 I, S
Butcher, C J S (Harlequins) 1984 SA 1,2, A
Butcher, W V (Streatham) 1903 S, 1904 W, I, S, 1905 W, I, S
Butler, A G (Harlequins) 1937 W, I
Butler, P E (Gloucester) 1975 A 1, 1976 F
Butterfield, J (Northampton) 1953 F, S, 1954 W, NZ, I, S, F, 1955 W, I, F, S, 1956 W, I, S, F, 1957 W, I, F, S, 1958 W, A, I, F, S, 1959 W, I, F, S
Byrne, F A (Moseley) 1897 W
Byrne, J F (Moseley) 1894 W, I, S, 1895 I, S, 1896 I, 1897 W, I, S, 1898 I, S, W, 1899 I

Cain, J J (Waterloo) 1950 W
Callard, J E B (Bath) 1993 NZ, 1994 S, I, 1995 [WS], SA
Campbell, D A (Cambridge U) 1937 W, I
Candler, P L (St Bart's Hospital) 1935 W, 1936 NZ, W, I, S, 1937 W, I, S, 1938 W, S
Cannell, L B (Oxford U, St Mary's Hospital) 1948 F, 1949 W, I, F, S, 1950 W, I, F, S, 1952 SA, W, 1953 W, I, F, 1956 I, S, F, 1957 W, I
Caplan, D W N (Headingley) 1978 S, I
Cardus, R M (Roundhay) 1979 F, W
Carey, G M (Blackheath) 1895 W, I, S, 1896 W, I
Carleton, J (Orrell) 1979 NZ, 1980 I, F, W, S, 1981 W, S, I, F, Arg 1,2, 1982 A, S, I, F, W, 1983 F, W, S, I, NZ, 1984 S, I, F, W, A
Carling, W D C (Durham U, Harlequins) 1988 F, W, S, I 1,2, A2, Fj, A, 1989 S, I, F, W, Fj, 1990 I, F, W, S, Arg 1,2,3, 1991 W, S, I, F, Fj, A, [NZ, It, US, F, S, A], 1992 S, I, F, W, C, SA, 1993 F, W, S, I, NZ, 1994 S, I, F, W, SA 1,2, R, C, 1995 I, F, W, S, [Arg, WS, A, NZ, F], SA, WS, 1996 F, W, S, I, It, Arg, 1997 S, I, F, W
Carpenter, A D (Gloucester) 1932 SA
Carr, R S L (Manchester) 1939 W, I, S
Cartwright, V H (Nottingham) 1903 W, I, S, 1904 W, S, 1905 W, I, S, NZ, 1906 W, I, S, F, SA
Catcheside, H C (Percy Park) 1924 W, I, F, S, 1926 W, I, 1927 I, S
Catt, M J (Bath, London Irish) 1994 W (R), C (R), 1995 I, F, W, S, [Arg, It, WS, A, NZ, F], SA, WS, 1996 F, W, S, I, It, Arg, 1997 W, Arg 1, A 1,2, NZ 1, SA, 1998 F, W (R), I, A 2(R), SA 2, 1999 S, F, W, A, C (R), [Tg (R), Fj, SA (R)], 2000 I, F, W, It, S, SA 1,2, A, Arg, 2001 W, It, S, F, I, A, R (R), SA, 2003 [Sm(R), U, W(R), F, A(R)], 2004 W(R), F(R), NZ1, A1, 2006 A1, 2
Cattell, R H B (Blackheath) 1895 W, I, S, 1896 W, I, S, 1900 W
Cave, J W (Richmond) 1889 M
Cave, W T C (Blackheath) 1905 W
Challis, R (Bristol) 1957 I, F, S
Chambers, E L (Bedford) 1908 F, 1910 W, I
Chantrill, B S (Bristol) 1924 W, I, F, S
Chapman, C E (Cambridge U) 1884 W

Chapman D E (Richmond) 1998 A 1(R)
Chapman, F E (Hartlepool) 1910 W, I, F, S, 1912 W, 1914 W, I
Cheesman, W I (OMTs) 1913 SA, W, F, I
Cheston, E C (Richmond) 1873 S, 1874 S, 1875 I, S, 1876 S
Chilcott, G J (Bath) 1984 A, 1986 I, F, 1987 F (R), W, [J, US, W (R)], 1988 I 2(R), Fj, 1989 I (R), F, W, R
Christophers, P (Bristol) 2002 Arg, SA, 2003 W 1 (R)
Christopherson, P (Blackheath) 1891 W, S
Chuter, G S (Leicester) 2006 A1(R), 2
Clark, C W H (Liverpool) 1876 I
Clarke, A J (Coventry) 1935 W, I, S, 1936 NZ, W, I
Clarke, B B (Bath, Richmond) 1992 SA, 1993 F, W, S, I, NZ, 1994 S, F, W, SA 1,2, R, C, 1995 I, F, W, S, [Arg, It, A, NZ, F], SA, WS, 1996 F, W, S, I, Arg (R), 1997 W, Arg 1,2, A 1(R), 1998 A 1(t),NZ 1,2, SA 1, H, It, 1999 A (R)
Clarke, S J S (Cambridge U, Blackheath) 1963 W, I, F, S, NZ 1,2, A, 1964 NZ, W, I, 1965 I, F, S
Clayton, J H (Liverpool) 1871 S
Clements, J W (O Cranleighans) 1959 I, F, S
Cleveland, C R (Blackheath) 1887 W, S
Clibborn, W G (Richmond) 1886 W, I, S, 1887 W, I, S
Clough, F J (Cambridge U, Orrell) 1986 I, F, 1987 [J (R), US]
Coates, C H (Yorkshire W) 1880 S, 1881 S, 1882 S
Coates, V H M (Bath) 1913 SA, W, F, I, S
Cobby, W (Hull) 1900 W
Cockerham, A (Bradford Olicana) 1900 W
Cockerill, R (Leicester) 1997 Arg 1(R),2, A 2(t+R), NZ 1, SA, NZ 2, 1998 W, S, I, A 1, NZ 1,2, SA 1, H, It, A 2, SA 2, 1999 S, I, F, W, A, C (R), [It, NZ, Tg (R), Fj (R)]
Codling, A (Harlequins) 2002 Arg
Cohen, B C (Northampton) 2000 I, F, W, It, S, SA 2, Arg, SA 3, 2001 W, It, S, F, R, 2002 S, I, F, W, It, NZ, A, SA, 2003 F 1, W 1, S, I, NZ, A, F2, 3, [Gg, SA, Sm, W, F, A], 2004 It, S, I, W, F, NZ1, 2, A1,C(R), A2(R), 2005 F(R), A, NZ, 2006 W, It, S, F, I
Colclough, M J (Angoulême, Wasps, Swansea) 1978 S, I, 1979 NZ, 1980 F, W, S, 1981 W, S, I, F, 1982 A, S, I, F, W, 1983 F, NZ, 1984 S, I, F, W, 1986 W, S, I, F
Coley, E (Northampton) 1929 F, 1932 W
Collins, P J (Camborne) 1952 S, I, F
Collins, W E (O Cheltonians) 1874 S, 1875 I, S, 1876 I, S
Considine, S G U (Bath) 1925 F
Conway, G S (Cambridge U, Rugby, Manchester) 1920 F, I, S, 1921 F, 1922 W, I, F, S, 1923 W, I, S, F, 1924 W, I, F, S, 1925 NZ, 1927 W
Cook, J G (Bedford) 1937 S
Cook, P W (Richmond) 1965 I, F
Cooke, D A (Harlequins) 1976 W, S, I, F
Cooke, D H (Harlequins) 1981 W, S, I, F, 1984 I, 1985 R, F, S, I, W, NZ 1,2
Cooke, P (Richmond) 1939 W, I
Coop, T (Leigh) 1892 S
Cooper, J G (Moseley) 1909 A, W
Cooper, M J (Moseley) 1973 F, S, NZ 2(R), 1975 F, W, 1976 A, W, 1977 S, I, F, W
Coopper, S F (Blackheath) 1900 W, 1902 W, I, 1905 W, I, S, 1907 W
Corbett, L J (Bristol) 1921 F, 1923 W, I, 1924 W, I, F, S, 1925 NZ, W, I, S, F, 1927 W, I, S, F
Corless, B J (Coventry, Moseley) 1976 A, I (R), 1977 S, I, F, W, 1978 F, W, S, I
Corry, M E (Bristol, Leicester) 1997 Arg 1,2, 1998 H, It, SA 2(t), 1999 F(R), A, C (t), [It (R), NZ (t+R), SA (R)], 2000 I (R), F (R), W (R), It (R), S (R), Arg (R), SA 3(t), 2001 W (R), It (R), F (t), C 1, I, 2002 F (t+R), W (t), 2003 W 2, F 2,3, [U], 2004 A1(R), C, SA, A2, 2005 F, I, It, S, A, NZ, Sm, 2006 W, It, S, F, I
Cotton, F E (Loughborough Colls, Coventry, Sale) 1971 S (2[1C]), P, 1973 W, I, F, S, NZ 2, A, 1974 S, I, 1975 I, F, W, 1976 A, W, S, I, F, 1977 S, I, F, W, 1978 S, I, 1979 NZ, 1980 I, F, W, S, 1981 W
Coulman, M J (Moseley) 1967 A, I, F, S, W, 1968 W, I, F, S
Coulson, T J (Coventry) 1927 W, 1928 A, W
Court, E D (Blackheath) 1885 W
Coverdale, H (Blackheath) 1910 F, 1912 I, F, 1920 W
Cove-Smith, R (OMTs) 1921 S, F, 1922 I, F, S, 1923 W, I, S, F, 1924 W, I, S, F, 1925 NZ, W, I, S, F, 1927 W, I, S, F, 1928 A, W, I, F, S, 1929 W, I
Cowling, R J (Leicester) 1977 S, I, F, W, 1978 F, NZ, 1979 S, I
Cowman, A R (Loughborough Colls, Coventry) 1971 S (2[1C]), P, 1973 W, I
Cox, N S (Sunderland) 1901 S
Cranmer, P (Richmond, Moseley) 1934 W, I, S, 1935 W, I, S, 1936 NZ, W, I, S, 1937 W, I, S, 1938 W, I, S
Creed, R N (Coventry) 1971 P
Cridlan, A G (Blackheath) 1935 W, I, S
Crompton, C A (Blackheath) 1871 S
Crosse, C W (Oxford U) 1874 S, 1875 I
Cueto, M J (Sale) 2004 C, SA, A2, 2005 W, F, I, It, S, A, NZ, Sm, 2006 W, It, S, F, I
Cumberlege, B S (Blackheath) 1920 W, I, S, 1921 W, I, S, F, 1922 W
Cumming, D C (Blackheath) 1925 S, F
Cunliffe, F L (RMA) 1874 S
Currey, F I (Marlborough N) 1872 S
Currie, J D (Oxford U, Harlequins, Bristol) 1956 W, I, S, F, 1957 W, I, F, S, 1958 W, A, I, F, S, 1959 W, I, F, S, 1960 W, I, F, S, 1961 SA, 1962 W, I, F
Cusani, D A (Orrell) 1987 I
Cusworth, L (Leicester) 1979 NZ, 1982 F, W, 1983 F, W, NZ, 1984 S, I, F, W, 1988 F, W

D'Aguilar, F B G (Royal Engineers) 1872 S
Dallaglio, L B N (Wasps) 1995 SA (R), WS, 1996 F, W, S, I, It, Arg, 1997 S, I, F, A 1,2, NZ 1, SA, NZ 2, 1998 F, W, S, I, A 2, SA 2, 1999 S, I, F, W, US, C, [It, NZ, Tg, Fj, SA], 2000 I, F, W, It, S, SA 1,2, A, Arg, SA 3, 2001 W, It, S, F, 2002 It (R), NZ, A (t), SA(R), 2003 F 1 (R), W 1, It, S, I, NZ, A, [Gg, SA, Sm, U, W, F, A], 2004 It, S, I, W, F, NZ1, 2, A1, 2006 W(t&R), It(R), S(R), F(R)
Dalton, T J (Coventry) 1969 S(R)
Danby, T (Harlequins) 1949 W
Daniell, J (Richmond) 1899 W, 1900 I, S, 1902 I, S, 1904 I, S
Darby, A J L (Birkenhead Park) 1899 I
Davenport, A (Ravenscourt Park) 1871 S
Davey, J (Redruth) 1908 S, 1909 W
Davey, R F (Teignmouth) 1931 W
Davidson, Jas (Aspatria) 1897 S, 1898 S, W, 1899 I, S
Davidson, Jos (Aspatria) 1899 W, S
Davies, G H (Cambridge U, Coventry, Wasps) 1981 S, I, F, Arg 1,2, 1982 A, S, I, 1983 F, W, S, 1984 S, SA 1,2, 1985 R (R), NZ 1,2, 1986 W, S, I, F
Davies, P H (Sale) 1927 I
Davies, V G (Harlequins) 1922 W, 1925 NZ
Davies, W J A (United Services, RN) 1913 SA, W, F, I, S, 1914 I, S, F, 1920 F, I, S, 1921 W, I, S, F, 1922 I, F, S, 1923 W, I, S, F
Davies, W P C (Harlequins) 1953 S, 1954 NZ, I, 1955 W, I, F, S, 1956 W, 1957 F, S, 1958 W
Davis, A M (Torquay Ath, Harlequins) 1963 W, I, S, NZ 1,2, 1964 NZ, W, I, F, S, 1966 W, 1967 A, 1969 SA, 1970 I, W, S
Dawe, R G R (Bath) 1987 I, F, W, [US], 1995 [WS]
Dawson, E F (RIEC) 1878 I
Dawson, M J S (Northampton, Wasps) 1995 WS, 1996 F, W, S, I, 1997 A 1, SA, NZ 2(R), 1998 W (R), S, I, NZ 1,2, SA 1, H, It, A 2, SA 2, 1999 S, F(R), W, A(R), US, C, [It, NZ, Tg, Fj (R), SA], 2000 I, F, W, It, S, A (R), Arg, SA 3, 2001 W, It, S, F, I, 2002 W (R), It (R), NZ, A, SA, 2003 It, S, I, A(R), F3(R), [Gg, Sm, W, F, A], 2004It(R), S(R), I, W, F, NZ1, 2(R), A1(R), 2005 W, F(R), I(R), It(R), S(R), A, NZ, 2006 W(R), It(R), S(t&R), F, I(R)
Day, H L V (Leicester) 1920 W, 1922 W, F, 1926 S
Deacon, L P (Leicester) 2005 Sm, 2006 A1, 2(R)
Dean, G J (Harlequins) 1931 I
Dee, J M (Hartlepool R) 1962 S, 1963 NZ 1
Devitt, Sir T G (Blackheath) 1926 I, F, 1928 A, W
Dewhurst, J H (Richmond) 1887 W, I, S, 1890 W
De Glanville, P R (Bath) 1992 SA (R), 1993 W (R), NZ, 1994 S, I, F, W, SA 1,2, C (R), 1995 [Arg (R), It, WS], SA (R),

1996 W (R), I (R), It, 1997 S, I, F, W, Arg 1,2, A 1,2, NZ 1,2, 1998 W (R), S (R), I (R), A 2, SA 2, 1999 A (R), US, [It, NZ, Fj (R), SA]
De Winton, R F C (Marlborough N) 1893 W
Dibble, R (Bridgwater A) 1906 S, F, SA, 1908 F, W, I, S, 1909 A, W, F, I, S, 1910 S, 1911 W, F, S, 1912 W, I, S
Dicks, J (Northampton) 1934 W, I, S, 1935 W, I, S, 1936 S, 1937 I
Dillon, E W (Blackheath) 1904 W, I, S, 1905 W
Dingle, A J (Hartlepool R) 1913 I, 1914 S, F
Diprose, A J (Saracens) 1997 Arg 1,2, A 2, NZ 1, 1998 W (R), S (R), I, A 1, NZ 2, SA 1
Dixon, P J (Harlequins, Gosforth) 1971 P, 1972 W, I, F, S, 1973 I, F, S, 1974 S, I, F, W, 1975 I, 1976 F, 1977 S, I, F, W, 1978 F, S, I, NZ
Dobbs, G E B (Devonport A) 1906 W, I
Doble, S A (Moseley) 1972 SA, 1973 NZ 1, W
Dobson, D D (Newton Abbot) 1902 W, I, S, 1903 W, I, S
Dobson, T H (Bradford) 1895 S
Dodge, P W (Leicester) 1978 W, S, I, NZ, 1979 S, I, F, W, 1980 W, S, 1981 W, S, I, F, Arg 1,2, 1982 A, S, F, W, 1983 F, W, S, I, NZ, 1985 R, F, S, I, W, NZ 1,2
Donnelly, M P (Oxford U) 1947 I
Dooley, W A (Preston Grasshoppers, Fylde) 1985 R, F, S, I, W, NZ 2(R), 1986 W, S, I, F, 1987 F, W, [A, US, W], 1988 F, W, S, I 1,2, A 1,2, Fj, A, 1989 S, I, F, W, R, Fj, 1990 I, F, W, S, Arg 1,2,3, 1991 W, S, I, F, [NZ, US, F, S, A], 1992 S, I, F, W, C, SA, 1993 W, S, I
Dovey, B A (Rosslyn Park) 1963 W, I
Down, P J (Bristol) 1909 A
Dowson, A O (Moseley) 1899 S
Drake-Lee, N J (Cambridge U, Leicester) 1963 W, I, F, S, 1964 NZ, W, I, 1965 W
Duckett, H (Bradford) 1893 I, S
Duckham, D J (Coventry) 1969 I, F, S, W, SA, 1970 I, W, S, F, 1971 W, I, F, S (2[1C]), P, 1972 W, I, F, S, 1973 NZ 1, W, I, F, S, NZ 2, A, 1974 S, I, F, W, 1975 I, F, W, 1976 A, W, S
Dudgeon, H W (Richmond) 1897 S, 1898 I, S, W, 1899 W, I, S
Dugdale, J M (Ravenscourt Park) 1871 S
Dun, A F (Wasps) 1984 W
Duncan, R F H (Guy's Hospital) 1922 I, F, S
Duncombe, N (Harlequins) 2002 S (R), I (R)
Dunkley, P E (Harlequins) 1931 I, S, 1936 NZ, W, I, S
Duthie, J (W Hartlepool) 1903 W
Dyson, J W (Huddersfield) 1890 S, 1892 S, 1893 I, S

Ebdon, P J (Wellington) 1897 W, I
Eddison, J H (Headingley) 1912 W, I, S, F
Edgar, C S (Birkenhead Park) 1901 S
Edwards, R (Newport) 1921 W, I, S, F, 1922 W, F, 1923 W, 1924 W, F, S, 1925 NZ
Egerton, D W (Bath) 1988 I 2, A 1, Fj (R), A, 1989 Fj, 1990 I, Arg 2(R)
Elliot, C H (Sunderland) 1886 W
Elliot, E W (Sunderland) 1901 W, I, S, 1904 W
Elliot, W (United Services, RN) 1932 I, S, 1933 W, I, S, 1934 W, I
Elliott, A E (St Thomas's Hospital) 1894 S
Ellis, H A (Leicester) 2004 SA(R), A2(R), 2005 W(R), F, I, It, S, Sm, 2006 W, It, S, F(R), I
Ellis, J (Wakefield) 1939 S
Ellis, S S (Queen's House) 1880 I
Emmott, C (Bradford) 1892 W
Enthoven, H J (Richmond) 1878 I
Estcourt, N S D (Blackheath) 1955 S
Evans, B J (Leicester) 1988 A 2, Fj
Evans, E (Sale) 1948 A, 1950 W, 1951 I, F, S, 1952 SA, W, S, I, F, 1953 I, F, S, 1954 W, NZ, I, F, 1956 W, I, S, F, 1957 W, I, F, S, 1958 W, A, I, F, S
Evans, G W (Coventry) 1972 S, 1973 W (R), F, S, NZ 2, 1974 S, I, F, W
Evans, N L (RNEC) 1932 W, I, S, 1933 W, I
Evanson, A M (Richmond) 1883 W, I, S, 1884 S
Evanson, W A D (Richmond) 1875 S, 1877 S, 1878 S, 1879 S, I
Evershed, F (Blackheath) 1889 M, 1890 W, S, I, 1892 W, I, S, 1893 W, I, S
Eyres, W C T (Richmond) 1927 I

Fagan, A R St L (Richmond) 1887 I
Fairbrother, K E (Coventry) 1969 I, F, S, W, SA, 1970 I, W, S, F, 1971 W, I, F
Faithfull, C K T (Harlequins) 1924 I, 1926 F, S
Fallas, H (Wakefield T) 1884 I
Fegan, J H C (Blackheath) 1895 W, I, S
Fernandes, C W L (Leeds) 1881 I, W, S
Fidler, J H (Gloucester) 1981 Arg 1,2, 1984 SA 1,2
Fidler, R J (Gloucester) 1998 NZ 2, SA 1
Field, E (Middlesex W) 1893 W, I
Fielding, K J (Moseley, Loughborough Colls) 1969 I, F, S, SA, 1970 I, F, 1972 W, I, F, S
Finch, R T (Cambridge U) 1880 S
Finlan, J F (Moseley) 1967 I, F, S, W, NZ, 1968 W, I, 1969 I, F, S, W, 1970 F, 1973 NZ 1
Finlinson, H W (Blackheath) 1895 W, I, S
Finney, S (RIE Coll) 1872 S, 1873 S
Firth, F (Halifax) 1894 W, I, S
Flatman, D L (Saracens) 2000 SA 1(t),2(t+R), A (t), Arg (t+R), 2001 F (t), C 2(t+R), US (t+R), 2002 Arg
Fletcher, N C (OMTs) 1901 W, I, S, 1903 S
Fletcher, T (Seaton) 1897 W
Fletcher, W R B (Marlborough N) 1873 S, 1875 S
Fookes, E F (Sowerby Bridge) 1896 W, I, S, 1897 W, I, S, 1898 I, W, 1899 I, S
Ford, P J (Gloucester) 1964 W, I, F, S
Forrest, J W (United Services, RN) 1930 W, I, F, S, 1931 W, I, S, F, 1934 I, S
Forrest, R (Wellington) 1899 W, 1900 S, 1902 I, S, 1903 I, S
Forrester, J (Gloucester) 2005 W(t), Sm(t&R)
Foulds, R T (Waterloo) 1929 W, I
Fowler, F D (Manchester) 1878 S, 1879 S
Fowler, H (Oxford U) 1878 S, 1881 W, S
Fowler, R H (Leeds) 1877 I
Fox, F H (Wellington) 1890 W, S
Francis, T E S (Cambridge U) 1926 W, I, F, S
Frankcom, G P (Cambridge U, Bedford) 1965 W, I, F, S
Fraser, E C (Blackheath) 1875 I
Fraser, G (Richmond) 1902 W, I, S, 1903 W, I
Freakes, H D (Oxford U) 1938 W, 1939 W, I
Freeman, H (Marlborough N) 1872 S, 1873 S, 1874 S
French, R J (St Helens) 1961 W, I, F, S
Freshwater, P T (Perpignan) 2005 v Sm(R), 2006 S(t&R), I(R)
Fry, H A (Liverpool) 1934 W, I, S
Fry, T W (Queen's House) 1880 I, S, 1881 W
Fuller, H G (Cambridge U) 1882 I, S, 1883 W, I, S, 1884 W

Gadney, B C (Leicester, Headingley) 1932 I, S, 1933 I, S, 1934 W, I, S, 1935 S, 1936 NZ, W, I, S, 1937 S, 1938 W
Gamlin, H T (Blackheath) 1899 W, S, 1900 W, I, S, 1901 S, 1902 W, I, S, 1903 W, I, S, 1904 W, I, S
Gardner, E R (Devonport Services) 1921 W, I, S, 1922 W, I, F, 1923 W, I, S, F
Gardner, H P (Richmond) 1878 I
Garforth, D J (Leicester) 1997 W (R), Arg 1,2, A 1, NZ 1, SA, NZ 2, 1998 F, W (R), S, I, H, It, A 2, SA 2, 1999 S, I, F, W, A, C (R), [It (R), NZ (R), Fj], 2000 It
Garnett, H W T (Bradford) 1877 S
Gavins, M N (Leicester) 1961 W
Gay, D J (Bath) 1968 W, I, F, S
Gent, D R (Gloucester) 1905 NZ, 1906 W, I, 1910 W, I
Genth, J S M (Manchester) 1874 S, 1875 S
George, J T (Falmouth) 1947 S, F, 1949 I
Gerrard, R A (Bath) 1932 SA, W, I, S, 1933 W, I, S, 1934 W, I, S, 1936 NZ, W, I, S
Gibbs, G A (Bristol) 1947 F, 1948 I
Gibbs, J C (Harlequins) 1925 NZ, W, 1926 F, 1927 W, I, S, F
Gibbs, N (Harlequins) 1954 S, F
Giblin, L F (Blackheath) 1896 W, I, 1897 S
Gibson, A S (Manchester) 1871 S
Gibson, C O P (Northern) 1901 W
Gibson, G R (Northern) 1899 W, 1901 S

Gibson, T A (Northern) 1905 W, S
Gilbert, F G (Devonport Services) 1923 W, I
Gilbert, R (Devonport A) 1908 W, I, S
Giles, J L (Coventry) 1935 W, I, 1937 W, I, 1938 I, S
Gittings, W J (Coventry) 1967 NZ
Glover, P B (Bath) 1967 A, 1971 F, P
Godfray, R E (Richmond) 1905 NZ
Godwin, H O (Coventry) 1959 F, S, 1963 S, NZ 1,2, A, 1964 NZ, I, F, S, 1967 NZ
Gomarsall, A C T (Wasps, Bedford, Gloucester) 1996 It, Arg, 1997 S, I, F, Arg 2(R) 2000 It (R), 2002 Arg, SA(R), 2003 F 1, W 1(R),2, F2(R), [Gg(R), U], 2004 It, S, NZ1(R), 2, A1, C, SA, A2
Goode, A J (Leicester) 2005 It(R), S(R), 2006 W(R), F(R), I, A1(R), 2
Gordon-Smith, G W (Blackheath) 1900 W, I, S
Gotley, A L H (Oxford U) 1910 F, S, 1911 W, F, I, S
Graham, D (Aspatria) 1901 W
Graham, H J (Wimbledon H) 1875 I, S, 1876 I, S
Graham, J D G (Wimbledon H) 1876 I
Gray, A (Otley) 1947 W, I, S
Grayson, P J (Northampton) 1995 WS, 1996 F, W, S, I, 1997 S, I, F, A 2(t), SA (R), NZ 2, 1998 F, W, S, I, H, It, A 2, 1999 I, [NZ (R), Tg, Fj (R), SA], 2003 S(R), I(t), F2, 3(R), [Gg(R), U], 2004 It, S, I
Green, J (Skipton) 1905 I, 1906 S, F, SA, 1907 F, W, I, S
Green, J F (West Kent) 1871 S
Green, W R (Wasps) 1997 A 2, 1998 NZ 1(t+R), 1999 US (R), 2003 W 2(R)
Greening, P B T (Gloucester, Wasps) 1996 It (R), 1997 W (R), Arg 1 1998 NZ 1(R),2(R), 1999 A (R), US, C, [It (R), NZ (R), Tg, Fj, SA], 2000 I, F, W, It, S, SA 1,2, A, SA 3, 2001 F, I
Greenstock, N J J (Wasps) 1997 Arg 1,2, A 1, SA
Greenwell, J H (Rockcliff) 1893 W, I
Greenwood, J E (Cambridge U, Leicester) 1912 F, 1913 SA, W, F, I, S, 1914 W, S, F, 1920 W, F, I, S
Greenwood, J R H (Waterloo) 1966 I, F, S, 1967 A, 1969 I
Greenwood, W J H (Leicester, Harlequins) 1997 A 2, NZ 1, SA, NZ 2, 1998 F, W, S, I, H, It, 1999 C, [It, Tg, Fj, SA], 2000 Arg (R), SA 3, 2001 W, It, S, F, I, A, R, SA, 2002 S, I, F, W, It, NZ, A, SA, 2003 F 1, W 1, It, S, I, NZ, A, F3, [Gg, SA, U(R), W, F, A], 2004 It, S, I, W, F, C(R), SA(R), A2(R)
Greg, W (Manchester) 1876 I, S
Gregory, G G (Bristol) 1931 I, S, F, 1932 SA, W, I, S, 1933 W, I, S, 1934 W, I, S
Gregory, J A (Blackheath) 1949 W
Grewcock, D J (Coventry, Saracens, Bath) 1997 Arg 2, SA, 1998 W (R), S (R), I (R), A 1, NZ 1, SA 2(R), 1999 S (R), A (R), US, C, [It, NZ, Tg (R), SA], 2000 SA 1,2, A, Arg, SA 3, 2001 W, It, S, I, A, R (R), SA, 2002 S (R), I (R), F (R), W, It, NZ, SA (R), 2003 F 1 (R), W 1 (R), It, S (R), I (t), W 2, F 2, [U], 2004 It, S, W, F, NZ1, 2(R), C, SA, A2, 2005 W, F, I, It, S, A, NZ, 2006 W, It, S, F, I(R)
Grylls, W M (Redruth) 1905 I
Guest, R H (Waterloo) 1939 W, I, S, 1947 W, I, S, F, 1948 A, W, I, S, 1949 F, S
Guillemard, A G (West Kent) 1871 S, 1872 S
Gummer, C H A (Plymouth A) 1929 F
Gunner, C R (Marlborough N) 1876 I
Gurdon, C (Richmond) 1880 I, S, 1881 I, W, S, 1882 I, S, 1883 S, 1884 W, S, 1885 I, 1886 W, I, S
Gurdon, E T (Richmond) 1878 S, 1879 I, 1880 S, 1881 I, W, S, 1882 S, 1883 W, I, S, 1884 W, I, S, 1885 W, I, 1886 S
Guscott, J C (Bath) 1989 R, Fj, 1990 I, F, W, S, Arg 3, 1991 W, S, I, F, Fj, A, [NZ, It, F, S, A], 1992 S, I, F, W, C, SA, 1993 F, W, S, I, 1994 R, C, 1995 I, F, W, S, [Arg, It, A, NZ, F], SA, WS, 1996 F, W, S, I, Arg, 1997 I (R), W (R), 1998 F, W, S, I, H, It, A 2, SA 2, 1999 S, I, F, A, US, C, [It (R), NZ, Tg]

Haag, M (Bath) 1997 Arg 1,2
Haigh, L (Manchester) 1910 W, I, S, 1911 W, F, I, S
Hale, P M (Moseley) 1969 SA, 1970 I, W
Hall, C (Gloucester) 1901 I, S
Hall, J (N Durham) 1894 W, I, S
Hall, J P (Bath) 1984 S (R), I, F, SA 1,2, A, 1985 R, F, S, I, W, NZ 1,2, 1986 W, S, 1987 I, F, W, S, 1990 Arg 3, 1994 S
Hall, N M (Richmond) 1947 W, I, S, F, 1949 W, I, 1952 SA, W, S, I, F, 1953 W, I, F, S, 1955 W, I
Halliday, S J (Bath, Harlequins) 1986 W, S, 1987 S, 1988 S, I 1,2, A 1, A, 1989 S, I, F, W, R, Fj (R), 1990 W, S, 1991 [US, S, A], 1992 S, I, F, W
Hamersley, A St G (Marlborough N) 1871 S, 1872 S, 1873 S, 1874 S
Hamilton-Hill, E A (Harlequins) 1936 NZ, W, I
Hamilton-Wickes, R H (Cambridge U) 1924 I, 1925 NZ, W, I, S, F, 1926 W, I, S, 1927 W
Hammett, E D G (Newport) 1920 W, F, S, 1921 W, I, S, F, 1922 W
Hammond, C E L (Harlequins) 1905 S, NZ, 1906 W, I, S, F, 1908 W, I
Hancock, A W (Northampton) 1965 F, S, 1966 F
Hancock, G E (Birkenhead Park) 1939 W, I, S
Hancock, J H (Newport) 1955 W, I
Hancock, P F (Blackheath) 1886 W, I, 1890 W
Hancock, P S (Richmond) 1904 W, I, S
Handford, F G (Manchester) 1909 W, F, I, S
Hands, R H M (Blackheath) 1910 F, S
Hanley, J (Plymouth A) 1927 W, S, F, 1928 W, I, F, S
Hanley, S M (Sale) 1999 W
Hannaford, R C (Bristol) 1971 W, I, F
Hanvey, R J (Aspatria) 1926 W, I, F, S
Harding, E H (Devonport Services) 1931 I
Harding, R M (Bristol) 1985 R, F, S, 1987 S, [A, J, W], 1988 I 1(R),2, A 1,2, Fj
Harding, V S J (Saracens) 1961 F, S, 1962 W, I, F, S
Hardwick, P F (Percy Park) 1902 I, S, 1903 W, I, S, 1904 W, I, S
Hardwick, R J K (Coventry) 1996 It (R)
Hardy, E M P (Blackheath) 1951 I, F, S
Hare, W H (Nottingham, Leicester) 1974 W, 1978 F, NZ, 1979 NZ, 1980 I, F, W, S, 1981 W, S, Arg 1,2, 1982 F, W, 1983 F, W, S, I, NZ, 1984 S, I, F, W, SA 1,2
Harper, C H (Exeter) 1899 W
Harriman, A T (Harlequins) 1988 A
Harris, S W (Blackheath) 1920 I, S
Harris, T W (Northampton) 1929 S, 1932 I
Harrison, A C (Hartlepool R) 1931 I, S
Harrison, A L (United Services, RN) 1914 I, F
Harrison, G (Hull) 1877 I, S, 1879 S, I, 1880 S, 1885 W, I
Harrison, H C (United Services, RN) 1909 S, 1914 I, S, F
Harrison, M E (Wakefield) 1985 NZ 1,2, 1986 S, I, F, 1987 I, F, W, S, [A, J, US, W], 1988 F, W
Hartley, B C (Blackheath) 1901 S, 1902 S
Haslett, L W (Birkenhead Park) 1926 I, F
Hastings, G W D (Gloucester) 1955 W, I, F, S, 1957 W, I, F, S, 1958 W, A, I, F, S
Havelock, H (Hartlepool R) 1908 F, W, I
Hawcridge, J J (Bradford) 1885 W, I
Hayward, L W (Cheltenham) 1910 I
Hazell, A R (Gloucester) 2004 C, SA(t&R), 2005 W, F(t), It(R), S(R)
Hazell, D St G (Leicester) 1955 W, I, F, S
Healey, A S (Leicester) 1997 I (R), W, A 1(R),2(R), NZ 1(R), SA (R), NZ 2, 1998 F, W, S, I, A 1, NZ 1,2, H, It, A 2, SA 2(R), 1999 US, C, [It, NZ, Tg, Fj, SA (R)], 2000 I, F, W, It, S, SA 1,2, A, SA 3(R), 2001 W (R), It, S, F, I (R), A, R, SA, 2002 S, I, F, W, It (R), NZ (R), A (R), SA(R), 2003 F2
Hearn, R D (Bedford) 1966 F, S, 1967 I, F, S, W
Heath, A H (Oxford U) 1876 S
Heaton, J (Waterloo) 1935 W, I, S, 1939 W, I, S, 1947 I, S, F
Henderson, A P (Edinburgh Wands) 1947 W, I, S, F, 1948 I, S, F, 1949 W, I
Henderson, R S F (Blackheath) 1883 W, S, 1884 W, S, 1885 W
Heppell, W G (Devonport A) 1903 I
Herbert, A J (Wasps) 1958 F, S, 1959 W, I, F, S
Hesford, R (Bristol) 1981 S (R), 1982 A, S, F (R), 1983 F (R), 1985 R, F, S, I, W
Heslop, N J (Orrell) 1990 Arg 1,2,3, 1991 W, S, I, F, [US, F], 1992 W (R)

Hetherington, J G G (Northampton) 1958 A, I, 1959 W, I, F, S
Hewitt, E N (Coventry) 1951 W, I, F
Hewitt, W W (Queen's House) 1881 I, W, S, 1882 I
Hickson, J L (Bradford) 1887 W, I, S, 1890 W, S, I
Higgins, R (Liverpool) 1954 W, NZ, I, S, 1955 W, I, F, S, 1957 W, I, F, S, 1959 W
Hignell, A J (Cambridge U, Bristol) 1975 A 2, 1976 A, W, S, I, 1977 S, I, F, W, 1978 W, 1979 S, I, F, W
Hill, B A (Blackheath) 1903 I, S, 1904 W, I, 1905 W, NZ, 1906 SA, 1907 F, W
Hill, R A (Saracens) 1997 S, I, F, W, A 1,2, NZ 1, SA, NZ 2, 1998 F, W, H (R), It (R), A 2, SA 2, 1999 S, I, F, W, A, US, C, [It, NZ, Tg, Fj (R), SA], 2000 I, F, W, It, S, SA 1,2, A, Arg, SA 3, 2001 W, It, S, F, I, A, SA, 2002 S, I, F, W, It, NZ, A, SA, 2003 F 1, W 1, It, S, I, NZ, A, F 3 [Gg, F, A], 2004 It, S, I, W, F, NZ1, 2, A1
Hill, R J (Bath) 1984 SA 1,2, 1985 I (R), NZ 2(R), 1986 F (R), 1987 I, F, W, [US], 1989 Fj, 1990 I, F, W, S, Arg 1,2,3, 1991 W, S, I, F, Fj, A, [NZ, It, US, F, S, A]
Hillard, R J (Oxford U) 1925 NZ
Hiller, R (Harlequins) 1968 W, I, F, S, 1969 I, F, S, W, SA, 1970 I, W, S, 1971 I, F, S (2[1C]), P, 1972 W, I
Hind, A E (Leicester) 1905 NZ, 1906 W
Hind, G R (Blackheath) 1910 S, 1911 I
Hobbs, R F A (Blackheath) 1899 S, 1903 W
Hobbs, R G S (Richmond) 1932 SA, W, I, S
Hodges, H A (Nottingham) 1906 W, I
Hodgkinson, S D (Nottingham) 1989 R, Fj, 1990 I, F, W, S, Arg 1,2,3, 1991 W, S, I, F, [US]
Hodgson, C C (Sale) 2001 R, 2002 S (R), I (R), It (R), Arg, 2003 F 1, W 1, It (R), 2004 NZ1, 2, A1, C, SA, A2, 2005 W, F, I, It, S, A, NZ, Sm, 2006 W, It, S, F
Hodgson, J McD (Northern) 1932 SA, W, I, S, 1934 W, I, 1936 I
Hodgson, S A M (Durham City) 1960 W, I, F, S, 1961 SA, W, 1962 W, I, F, S, 1964 W
Hofmeyr, M B (Oxford U) 1950 W, F, S
Hogarth, T B (Hartlepool R) 1906 F
Holford, G (Gloucester) 1920 W, F
Holland, D (Devonport A) 1912 W, I, S
Holliday, T E (Aspatria) 1923 S, F, 1925 I, S, F, 1926 F, S
Holmes, C B (Manchester) 1947 S, 1948 I, F
Holmes, E (Manningham) 1890 S, I
Holmes, W A (Nuneaton) 1950 W, I, F, S, 1951 W, I, F, S, 1952 SA, S, I, F, 1953 W, I, F, S
Holmes, W B (Cambridge U) 1949 W, I, F, S
Hook, W G (Gloucester) 1951 S, 1952 SA, W
Hooper, C A (Middlesex W) 1894 W, I, S
Hopley, D P (Wasps) 1995 [WS (R)], SA, WS
Hopley, F J V (Blackheath) 1907 F, W, 1908 I
Horak, M J (London Irish) 2002 Arg
Hordern, P C (Gloucester) 1931 I, S, F, 1934 W
Horley, C H (Swinton) 1885 I
Hornby, A N (Manchester) 1877 I, S, 1878 S, I, 1880 I, 1881 I, S, 1882 I, S
Horrocks-Taylor, J P (Cambridge U, Leicester, Middlesbrough) 1958 W, A, 1961 S, 1962 S, 1963 NZ 1,2, A, 1964 NZ, W
Horsfall, E L (Harlequins) 1949 W
Horton, A L (Blackheath) 1965 W, I, F, S, 1966 F, S, 1967 NZ
Horton, J P (Bath) 1978 W, S, I, NZ, 1980 I, F, W, S, 1981 W, 1983 S, I, 1984 SA 1,2
Horton, N E (Moseley, Toulouse) 1969 I, F, S, W, 1971 I, F, S, 1974 S, 1975 W, 1977 S, I, F, W, 1978 F, W, 1979 S, I, F, W, 1980 I
Hosen, R W (Bristol, Northampton) 1963 NZ 1,2, A, 1964 F, S, 1967 A, I, F, S, W
Hosking, G R d'A (Devonport Services) 1949 W, I, F, S, 1950 W
Houghton, S (Runcorn) 1892 I, 1896 W
Howard, P D (O Millhillians) 1930 W, I, F, S, 1931 W, I, S, F
Hubbard, G C (Blackheath) 1892 W, I
Hubbard, J C (Harlequins) 1930 S
Hudson, A (Gloucester) 1906 W, I, F, 1908 F, W, I, S, 1910 F
Hughes, G E (Barrow) 1896 S
Hull, P A (Bristol, RAF) 1994 SA 1,2, R, C
Hulme, F C (Birkenhead Park) 1903 W, I, 1905 W, I
Hunt, J T (Manchester) 1882 I, S, 1884 W
Hunt, R (Manchester) 1880 I, 1881 W, S, 1882 I
Hunt, W H (Manchester) 1876 S, 1877 I, S, 1878 I
Hunter, I (Northampton) 1992 C, 1993 F, W, 1994 F, W, 1995 [WS, F]
Huntsman, R P (Headingley) 1985 NZ 1,2
Hurst, A C B (Wasps) 1962 S
Huskisson, T F (OMTs) 1937 W, I, S, 1938 W, I, 1939 W, I, S
Hutchinson, F (Headingley) 1909 F, I, S
Hutchinson, J E (Durham City) 1906 I
Hutchinson, W C (RIE Coll) 1876 S, 1877 I
Hutchinson, W H H (Hull) 1875 I, 1876 I
Huth, H (Huddersfield) 1879 S
Hyde, J P (Northampton) 1950 F, S
Hynes, W B (United Services, RN) 1912 F

Ibbitson, E D (Headingley) 1909 W, F, I, S
Imrie, H M (Durham City) 1906 NZ, 1907 I
Inglis, R E (Blackheath) 1886 W, I, S
Irvin, S H (Devonport A) 1905 W
Isherwood, F W (Ravenscourt Park) 1872 S

Jackett, E J (Leicester, Falmouth) 1905 NZ, 1906 W, I, S, F, SA, 1907 W, I, S, 1909 W, F, I, S
Jackson, A H (Blackheath) 1878 I, 1880 I
Jackson, B S (Broughton Park) 1970 S (R), F
Jackson, P B (Coventry) 1956 W, I, F, 1957 W, I, F, S, 1958 W, A, F, S, 1959 W, I, F, S, 1961 S, 1963 W, I, F, S
Jackson, W J (Halifax) 1894 S
Jacob, F (Cambridge U) 1897 W, I, S, 1898 I, S, W, 1899 W, I
Jacob, H P (Blackheath) 1924 W, I, F, S, 1930 F
Jacob, P G (Blackheath) 1898 I
Jacobs, C R (Northampton) 1956 W, I, S, F, 1957 W, I, F, S, 1958 W, A, I, F, S, 1960 W, I, F, S, 1961 SA, W, I, F, S, 1963 NZ 1,2, A, 1964 W, I, F, S
Jago, R A (Devonport A) 1906 W, I, SA, 1907 W, I
Janion, J P A G (Bedford) 1971 W, I, F, S (2[1C]), P, 1972 W, S, SA, 1973 A, 1975 A 1,2
Jarman, J W (Bristol) 1900 W
Jeavons, N C (Moseley) 1981 S, I, F, Arg 1,2, 1982 A, S, I, F, W, 1983 F, W, S, I
Jeeps, R E G (Northampton) 1956 W, 1957 W, I, F, S, 1958 W, A, I, F, S, 1959 I, 1960 W, I, F, S, 1961 SA, W, I, F, S, 1962 W, I, F, S
Jeffery, G L (Blackheath) 1886 W, I, S, 1887 W, I, S
Jennins, C R (Waterloo) 1967 A, I, F
Jewitt, J (Hartlepool R) 1902 W
Johns, W A (Gloucester) 1909 W, F, I, S, 1910 W, I, F
Johnson, M O (Leicester) 1993 F, NZ, 1994 S, I, F, W, R, C, 1995 I, F, W, S, [Arg, It, WS, A, NZ, F], SA, WS, 1996 F, W, S, I, It, Arg, 1997 S, I, F, W, A 2, NZ 1,2, 1998 F, W, S, I, H, It, A 2, SA 2, 1999 S, I, F, W, A, US, C, [It, NZ, Tg, Fj, SA], 2000 SA 1,2, A, Arg, SA 3, 2001 W, It, S, F, SA, 2002 S, I, F, It (t+R), NZ, A, SA, 2003 F 1, W 1, S, I, NZ, A, F 3, [Gg, SA, Sm, U(R),W, F, A]
Johnston, B (Saracens) 2002 Arg, NZ (R)
Johnston, W R (Bristol) 1910 W, I, S, 1912 W, I, S, F, 1913 SA, W, F, I, S, 1914 W, I, S, F
Jones, C M (Sale) 2004 It(R), S, I(R), W, NZ1, 2005 W, 2006 A1(R), 2
Jones, F P (New Brighton) 1893 S
Jones, H A (Barnstaple) 1950 W, I, F
Jorden, A M (Cambridge U, Blackheath, Bedford) 1970 F, 1973 I, F, S, 1974 F, 1975 W, S
Jowett, D (Heckmondwike) 1889 M, 1890 S, I, 1891 W, I, S
Judd, P E (Coventry) 1962 W, I, F, S, 1963 S, NZ 1,2, A, 1964 NZ, 1965 I, F, S, 1966 W, I, F, S, 1967 A, I, F, S, W, NZ

Kay, B J (Leicester) 2001 C 1,2, A, R, SA (t+R), 2002 S, I, F, W, It, Arg, NZ (R), A, SA, 2003 F 1, W 1, It, S, I, NZ, A, F 3, [Gg, SA, Sm, W, F, A], 2004 It, S, I, W, F, C(R), SA(R), 2005 W, F, I, It, S, 2006 A2
Kayll, H E (Sunderland) 1878 S

Keeling, J H (Guy's Hospital) 1948 A, W
Keen, B W (Newcastle U) 1968 W, I, F, S
Keeton, G H (Leicester) 1904 W, I, S
Kelly, G A (Bedford) 1947 W, I, S, 1948 W
Kelly, T S (London Devonians) 1906 W, I, S, F, SA, 1907 F, W, I, S, 1908 F, I, S
Kemble, A T (Liverpool) 1885 W, I, 1887 I
Kemp, D T (Blackheath) 1935 W
Kemp, T A (Richmond) 1937 W, I, 1939 S, 1948 A, W
Kendall, P D (Birkenhead Park) 1901 S, 1902 W, 1903 S
Kendall-Carpenter, J MacG K (Oxford U, Bath) 1949 I, F, S, 1950 W, I, F, S, 1951 I, F, S, 1952 SA, W, S, I, F, 1953 W, I, F, S, 1954 W, NZ, I, F
Kendrew, D A (Leicester) 1930 W, I, 1933 I, S, 1934 S, 1935 W, I, 1936 NZ, W, I
Kennedy, R D (Camborne S of M) 1949 I, F, S
Kent, C P (Rosslyn Park) 1977 S, I, F, W, 1978 F (R)
Kent, T (Salford) 1891 W, I, S, 1892 W, I, S
Kershaw, C A (United Services, RN) 1920 W, F, I, S, 1921 W, I, S, F, 1922 W, I, F, S, 1923 W, I, S, F
Kewley, E (Liverpool) 1874 S, 1875 S, 1876 I, S, 1877 I, S, 1878 S
Kewney, A L (Leicester) 1906 W, I, S, F, 1909 A, W, F, I, S, 1911 W, F, I, S, 1912 I, S, 1913 SA
Key, A (O Cranleighans) 1930 I, 1933 W
Keyworth, M (Swansea) 1976 A, W, S, I
Kilner, B (Wakefield T) 1880 I
Kindersley, R S (Exeter) 1883 W, 1884 S, 1885 W
King, A D (Wasps) 1997 Arg 2(R), 1998 SA 2(R), 2000 It (R), 2001 C 2(R), 2003 W2
King, I (Harrogate) 1954 W, NZ, I
King, J A (Headingley) 1911 W, F, I, S, 1912 W, I, S, 1913 SA, W, F, I, S
King, Q E M A (Army) 1921 S
Kingston, P (Gloucester) 1975 A 1,2, 1979 I, F, W
Kitching, A E (Blackheath) 1913 I
Kittermaster, H J (Harlequins) 1925 NZ, W, I, 1926 W, I, F, S
Knight, F (Plymouth) 1909 A
Knight, P M (Bristol) 1972 F, S, SA
Knowles, E (Millom) 1896 S, 1897 S
Knowles, T C (Birkenhead Park) 1931 S
Krige, J A (Guy's Hospital) 1920 W

Labuschagne, N A (Harlequins, Guy's Hospital) 1953 W, 1955 W, I, F, S
Lagden, R O (Richmond) 1911 S
Laird, H C C (Harlequins) 1927 W, I, S, 1928 A, W, I, F, S, 1929 W, I
Lambert, D (Harlequins) 1907 F, 1908 F, W, S, 1911 W, F, I
Lampkowski, M S (Headingley) 1976 A, W, S, I
Lapage, W N (United Services, RN) 1908 F, W, I, S
Larter, P J (Northampton, RAF) 1967 A, NZ, 1968 W, I, F, S, 1969 I, F, S, W, SA, 1970 I, W, F, S, 1971 W, I, F, S (2[1C]), P, 1972 SA, 1973 NZ 1, W
Law, A F (Richmond) 1877 S
Law, D E (Birkenhead Park) 1927 I
Lawrence, Hon H A (Richmond) 1873 S, 1874 S, 1875 I, S
Lawrie, P W (Leicester) 1910 S, 1911 S
Lawson, R G (Workington) 1925 I
Lawson, T M (Workington) 1928 A, W
Leadbetter, M M (Broughton Park) 1970 F
Leadbetter, V H (Edinburgh Wands) 1954 S, F
Leake, W R M (Harlequins) 1891 W, I, S
Leather, G (Liverpool) 1907 I
Lee, F H (Marlborough N) 1876 S, 1877 I
Lee, H (Blackheath) 1907 F
Le Fleming, J (Blackheath) 1887 W
Leonard, J (Saracens, Harlequins) 1990 Arg 1,2,3, 1991 W, S, I, F, Fj, A, [NZ, It, US, F, S, A], 1992 S, I, F, W, C, SA, 1993 F, W, S, I, NZ, 1994 S, I, F, W, SA 1,2, R, C, 1995 I, F, W, S, [Arg, It, A, NZ, F], SA, WS, 1996 F, W, S, I, It, Arg, 1997 S, I, F, W, A 2, NZ 1, SA, NZ 2, 1998 F, W, S, I, H, It, A 2 SA 2, 1999 S, I, F, W, A, C (R), [It, NZ, Fj, SA], 2000 I, F, W, It, S, SA 1,2, A, Arg, SA 3, 2001 W, It, S, F, I, R, 2002 S (R), I (R), F (R), It (R), A, SA, 2003 F 1, S, I, NZ, W 2, F 2(t+R), 3(R), [Gg(t&R), SA(R), Sm, U, W, F(t&R), A(R)], 2004 It(R)
Leslie-Jones, F A (Richmond) 1895 W, I
Lewis, A O (Bath) 1952 SA, W, S, I, F, 1953 W, I, F, S, 1954 F
Lewsey, O J (Wasps) 1998 NZ 1,2, SA 1, 2001 C 1,2, US, 2003 It, S, I, NZ, A, F2, 3(t+R), [Gg, SA, U, F, A], 2004 It, S, I, W, F, NZ1, 2, A1, C, SA, A2, 2005 W, F, I, It, S, A, NZ, Sm, 2006 W, S, F
Leyland, R (Waterloo) 1935 W, I, S
Linnett, M S (Moseley) 1989 Fj
Lipman, M R (Bath) 2004 NZ2(R), A1(R), 2006 A2
Livesay, R O'H (Blackheath) 1898 W, 1899 W
Lloyd, L D (Leicester) 2000 SA 1(R),2(R), 2001 C 1,2, US
Lloyd, R H (Harlequins) 1967 NZ, 1968 W, I, F, S
Locke, H M (Birkenhead Park) 1923 S, F, 1924 W, F, S, 1925 W, I, S, F, 1927 W, I, S
Lockwood, R E (Heckmondwike) 1887 W, I, S, 1889 M, 1891 W, I, S, 1892 W, I, S, 1893 W, I, 1894 W, I
Login, S H M (RN Coll) 1876 I
Lohden, F C (Blackheath) 1893 W
Long, A E (Bath) 1997 A 2, 2001 US (R)
Longland, R J (Northampton) 1932 S, 1933 W, S, 1934 W, I, S, 1935 W, I, S, 1936 NZ, W, I, S, 1937 W, I, S, 1938 W, I, S
Lowe, C N (Cambridge U, Blackheath) 1913 SA, W, F, I, S, 1914 W, I, S, F, 1920 W, F, I, S, 1921 W, I, S, F, 1922 W, I, F, S, 1923 W, I, S, F
Lowrie, F (Wakefield T) 1889 M, 1890 W
Lowry, W M (Birkenhead Park) 1920 F
Lozowski, R A P (Wasps) 1984 A
Luddington, W G E (Devonport Services) 1923 W, I, S, F, 1924 W, I, F, S, 1925 W, I, S, F, 1926 W
Luger, D D (Harlequins, Saracens) 1998 H, It, SA 2, 1999 S, I, F, W, A, US, C, [It, NZ, Tg, Fj, SA], 2000 SA 1, A, Arg, SA 3, 2001 W, I, A, R, SA, 2002 F (R), W, It, 2003 F 1, W 1, It, S (R), I (R), NZ(R), W 2, [Gg(R), SA(R), U, W]
Lund, M B (Sale) 2006 A1, 2(R)
Luscombe, F (Gipsies) 1872 S, 1873 S, 1875 I, S, 1876 I, S
Luscombe, J H (Gipsies) 1871 S
Luxmoore, A F C C (Richmond) 1900 S, 1901 W
Luya, H F (Waterloo, Headingley) 1948 W, I, S, F, 1949 W
Lyon, A (Liverpool) 1871 S
Lyon, G H d'O (United Services, RN) 1908 S, 1909 A

McCanlis, M A (Gloucester) 1931 W, I
McCarthy, N (Gloucester) 1999 I (t), US (R), 2000 It (R)
McFadyean, C W (Moseley) 1966 I, F, S, 1967 A, I, F, S, W, NZ, 1968 W, I
MacIlwaine, A H (United Services, Hull & E Riding) 1912 W, I, S, F, 1920 I
Mackie, O G (Wakefield T, Cambridge U) 1897 S, 1898 I
Mackinlay, J E H (St George's Hospital) 1872 S, 1873 S, 1875 I
MacLaren, W (Manchester) 1871 S
MacLennan, R R F (OMTs) 1925 I, S, F
McLeod, N F (RIE Coll) 1879 S, I
Madge, R J P (Exeter) 1948 A, W, I, S
Malir, F W S (Otley) 1930 W, I, S
Mallett, J A (Bath) 1995 [WS (R)]
Mallinder, J (Sale) 1997 Arg 1,2
Mangles, R H (Richmond) 1897 W, I
Manley, D C (Exeter) 1963 W, I, F, S
Mann, W E (United Services, Army) 1911 W, F, I
Mantell, N D (Rosslyn Park) 1975 A 1
Mapletoft, M S (Gloucester) 1997 Arg 2
Markendale, E T (Manchester R) 1880 I
Marques, R W D (Cambridge U, Harlequins) 1956 W, I, S, F, 1957 W, I, F, S, 1958 W, A, I, F, S, 1959 W, I, F, S, 1960 W, I, F, S, 1961 SA, W
Marquis, J C (Birkenhead Park) 1900 I, S
Marriott, C J B (Blackheath) 1884 W, I, S, 1886 W, I, S, 1887 I
Marriott, E E (Manchester) 1876 I
Marriott, V R (Harlequins) 1963 NZ 1,2, A, 1964 NZ
Marsden, G H (Morley) 1900 W, I, S
Marsh, H (RIE Coll) 1873 S
Marsh, J (Swinton) 1892 I
Marshall, H (Blackheath) 1893 W

Marshall, M W (Blackheath) 1873 S, 1874 S, 1875 I, S, 1876 I, S, 1877 I, S, 1878 S, I
Marshall, R M (Oxford U) 1938 I, S, 1939 W, I, S
Martin, C R (Bath) 1985 F, S, I, W
Martin, N O (Harlequins) 1972 F (R)
Martindale, S A (Kendal) 1929 F
Massey, E J (Leicester) 1925 W, I, S
Mather, B-J (Sale) 1999 W
Mathias, J L (Bristol) 1905 W, I, S, NZ
Matters, J C (RNE Coll) 1899 S
Matthews, J R C (Harlequins) 1949 F, S, 1950 I, F, S, 1952 SA, W, S, I, F
Maud, P (Blackheath) 1893 W, I
Maxwell, A W (New Brighton, Headingley) 1975 A 1, 1976 A, W, S, I, F, 1978 F
Maxwell-Hyslop, J E (Oxford U) 1922 I, F, S
Maynard, A F (Cambridge U) 1914 W, I, S
Mears, L A (Bath) 2005 Sm(R), 2006 W(R), It(R), F(R), I, A1, 2(R)
Meikle, G W C (Waterloo) 1934 W, I, S
Meikle, S S C (Waterloo) 1929 S
Mellish, F W (Blackheath) 1920 W, F, I, S, 1921 W, I
Melville, N D (Wasps) 1984 A, 1985 I, W, NZ 1,2, 1986 W, S, I, F, 1988 F, W, S, I 1
Merriam, L P B (Blackheath) 1920 W, F
Michell, A T (Oxford U) 1875 I, S, 1876 I
Middleton, B B (Birkenhead Park) 1882 I, 1883 I
Middleton, J A (Richmond) 1922 S
Miles, J H (Leicester) 1903 W
Millett, H (Richmond) 1920 F
Mills, F W (Marlborough N) 1872 S, 1873 S
Mills, S G F (Gloucester) 1981 Arg 1,2, 1983 W, 1984 SA 1, A
Mills, W A (Devonport A) 1906 W, I, S, F, SA, 1907 F, W, I, S, 1908 F, W
Milman, D L K (Bedford) 1937 W, 1938 W, I, S
Milton, C H (Camborne S of M) 1906 I
Milton, J G (Camborne S of M) 1904 W, I, S, 1905 S, 1907 I
Milton, W H (Marlborough N) 1874 S, 1875 I
Mitchell, F (Blackheath) 1895 W, I, S, 1896 W, I, S
Mitchell, W G (Richmond) 1890 W, S, I, 1891 W, I, S, 1893 S
Mobbs, E R (Northampton) 1909 A, W, F, I, S, 1910 I, F
Moberley, W O (Ravenscourt Park) 1872 S
Moody, L W (Leicester) 2001 C 1,2, US, I (R), R, SA (R), 2002 I (R), W, It, Arg, NZ, A, SA, 2003 F 1, W 2, F 2, 3(R), [Gg(R), SA, Sm(R), U, W, F(R), A(R)], 2004 C, SA, A2, 2005 F, I, It, S, A, NZ, Sm, 2006 W, It, S, F, I, A1
Moore, B C (Nottingham, Harlequins) 1987 S, [A, J, W], 1988 F, W, S, I 1,2, A 1, 2, Fj, A, 1989 S, I, F, W, R, Fj, 1990 I, F, W, S, Arg 1,2, 1991 W, S, I, F, Fj, A, [NZ, It, F, S, A], 1992 S, I, F, W, SA, 1993 F, W, S, I, NZ, 1994 S, I, F, W, SA 1,2, R, C, 1995 I, F, W, S, [Arg, It, WS (R), A, NZ, F]
Moore, E J (Blackheath) 1883 I, S
Moore, N J N H (Bristol) 1904 W, I, S
Moore, P B C (Blackheath) 1951 W
Moore, W K T (Leicester) 1947 W, I, 1949 F, S, 1950 I, F, S
Mordell, R J (Rosslyn Park) 1978 W
Morfitt, S (W Hartlepool) 1894 W, I, S, 1896 W, I, `S
Morgan, J R (Hawick) 1920 W
Morgan, W G D (Medicals, Newcastle) 1960 W, I, F, S, 1961 SA, W, I, F, S
Morley, A J (Bristol) 1972 SA, 1973 NZ 1, W, I, 1975 S, A 1,2
Morris, A D W (United Services, RN) 1909 A, W, F
Morris, C D (Liverpool St Helens, Orrell) 1988 A, 1989 S, I, F, W, 1992 S, I, F, W, C, SA, 1993 F, W, S, I, 1994 F, W, SA 1,2, R, 1995 S (t), [Arg, WS, A, NZ, F]
Morris, R (Northampton) 2003 W 1, It
Morrison, P H (Cambridge U) 1890 W, S, I, 1891 I
Morse, S (Marlborough N) 1873 S, 1874 S, 1875 S
Mortimer, W (Marlborough N) 1899 W
Morton, H J S (Blackheath) 1909 I, S, 1910 W, I
Moss, F (Broughton) 1885 W, I, 1886 W
Mullins, A R (Harlequins) 1989 Fj
Mycock, J (Sale) 1947 W, I, S, F, 1948 A
Myers, E (Bradford) 1920 I, S, 1921 W, I, 1922 W, I, F, S, 1923 W, I, S, F, 1924 W, I, F, S, 1925 S, F
Myers, H (Keighley) 1898 I

Nanson, W M B (Carlisle) 1907 F, W
Nash, E H (Richmond) 1875 I
Neale, B A (Rosslyn Park) 1951 I, F, S
Neale, M E (Blackheath) 1912 F
Neame, S (O Cheltonians) 1879 S, I, 1880 I, S
Neary, A (Broughton Park) 1971 W, I, F, S (2[1C]), P, 1972 W, I, F, S, SA, 1973 NZ 1, W, I, F, S, NZ 2, A, 1974 S, I, F, W, 1975 I, F, W, S, A 1, 1976 A, W, S, I, F, 1977 I, 1978 F (R), 1979 S, I, F, W, NZ, 1980 I, F, W, S
Nelmes, B G (Cardiff) 1975 A 1,2, 1978 W, S, I, NZ
Newbold, C J (Blackheath) 1904 W, I, S, 1905 W, I, S
Newman, S C (Oxford U) 1947 F, 1948 A, W
Newton, A W (Blackheath) 1907 S
Newton, P A (Blackheath) 1882 S
Newton-Thompson, J O (Oxford U) 1947 S, F
Nichol, W (Brighouse R) 1892 W, S
Nicholas, P L (Exeter) 1902 W
Nicholson, B E (Harlequins) 1938 W, I
Nicholson, E S (Leicester) 1935 W, I, S, 1936 NZ, W
Nicholson, E T (Birkenhead Park) 1900 W, I
Nicholson, T (Rockcliff) 1893 I
Ninnes, B F (Coventry) 1971 W
Noon, J D (Newcastle) 2001 C 1,2, US, 2003 W 2, F 2(t+R), 2005 W, F, I, It, S, A, NZ, 2006 W, It, S, F, I, 2006 A1(R), 2
Norman, D J (Leicester) 1932 SA, W
North, E H G (Blackheath) 1891 W, I, S
Northmore, S (Millom) 1897 I
Novak, M J (Harlequins) 1970 W, S, F
Novis, A L (Blackheath) 1929 S, F, 1930 W, I, F, 1933 I, S

Oakeley, F E (United Services, RN) 1913 S, 1914 I, S, F
Oakes, R F (Hartlepool R) 1897 W, I, S, 1898 I, S, W, 1899 W, S
Oakley, L F L (Bedford) 1951 W
Obolensky, A (Oxford U) 1936 NZ, W, I, S
Ojomoh, S O (Bath, Gloucester) 1994 I, F, SA 1(R),2, R, 1995 S (R), [Arg, WS, A (t), F], 1996 F, 1998 NZ 1
Old, A G B (Middlesbrough, Leicester, Sheffield) 1972 W, I, F, S, SA, 1973 NZ 2, A, 1974 S, I, F, W, 1975 I, A 2, 1976 S, I, 1978 F
Oldham, W L (Coventry) 1908 S, 1909 A
Olver, C J (Northampton) 1990 Arg 3, 1991 [US], 1992 C
O'Neill, A (Teignmouth, Torquay A) 1901 W, I, S
Openshaw, W E (Manchester) 1879 I
Orwin, J (Gloucester, RAF, Bedford) 1985 R, F, S, I, W, NZ 1,2, 1988 F, W, S, I 1,2, A 1,2
Osborne, R R (Manchester) 1871 S
Osborne, S H (Oxford U) 1905 S
Oti, C (Cambridge U, Nottingham, Wasps) 1988 S, I 1, 1989 S, I, F, W, R, 1990 Arg 1,2, 1991 Fj, A, [NZ, It]
Oughtred, B (Hartlepool R) 1901 S, 1902 W, I, S, 1903 W, I
Owen, J E (Coventry) 1963 W, I, F, S, A, 1964 NZ, 1965 W, I, F, S, 1966 I, F, S, 1967 NZ
Owen-Smith, H G O (St Mary's Hospital) 1934 W, I, S, 1936 NZ, W, I, S, 1937 W, I, S

Page, J J (Bedford, Northampton) 1971 W, I, F, S, 1975 S
Pallant, J N (Notts) 1967 I, F, S
Palmer, A C (London Hospital) 1909 I, S
Palmer, F H (Richmond) 1905 W
Palmer, G V (Richmond) 1928 I, F, S
Palmer, J A (Bath) 1984 SA 1,2, 1986 I (R)
Palmer, T (Leeds) 2001 US (R)
Pargetter, T A (Coventry) 1962 S, 1963 F, NZ 1
Parker, G W (Gloucester) 1938 I, S
Parker, Hon S (Liverpool) 1874 S, 1875 S
Parsons, E I (RAF) 1939 S
Parsons, M J (Northampton) 1968 W, I, F, S
Patterson, W M (Sale) 1961 SA, S
Pattisson, R M (Blackheath) 1883 I, S
Paul, H R (Gloucester) 2002 F(R), 2004 It(t&R), S(R), C, SA, A2

Paul, J E (RIE Coll) 1875 S
Payne, A T (Bristol) 1935 I, S
Payne, C M (Harlequins) 1964 I, F, S, 1965 I, F, S, 1966 W, I, F, S
Payne, J H (Broughton) 1882 S, 1883 W, I, S, 1884 I, 1885 W, I
Payne, T A N (Wasps) 2004 A1, 2006 A1(R), 2(R)
Pearce, G S (Northampton) 1979 S, I, F, W, 1981 Arg 1,2, 1982 A, S, 1983 F, W, S, I, NZ, 1984 S, SA 2, A, 1985 R, F, S, I, W, NZ 1,2, 1986 W, S, I, F, 1987 I, F, W, S, [A, US, W], 1988 Fj, 1991 [US]
Pears, D (Harlequins) 1990 Arg 1,2, 1992 F (R), 1994 F
Pearson, A W (Blackheath) 1875 I, S, 1876 I, S, 1877 S, 1878 S, I
Peart, T G A H (Hartlepool R) 1964 F, S
Pease, F E (Hartlepool R) 1887 I
Penny, S H (Leicester) 1909 A
Penny, W J (United Hospitals) 1878 I, 1879 S, I
Percival, L J (Rugby) 1891 I, 1892 I, 1893 S
Periton, H G (Waterloo) 1925 W, 1926 W, I, F, S, 1927 W, I, S, F, 1928 A, I, F, S, 1929 W, I, S, F, 1930 W, I, F, S
Perrott, E S (O Cheltonians) 1875 I
Perry, D G (Bedford) 1963 F, S, NZ 1,2, A 1964 NZ, W, I, 1965 W, I, F, S, 1966 W, I, F
Perry, M B (Bath) 1997 A 2, NZ 1, SA, NZ 2, 1998 W, S, I, A 1, NZ 1,2, SA 1, H, It, A 2, 1999 I, F, W, A US, C, [It, NZ, Tg, Fj, SA], 2000 I, F, W, It, S, SA 1,2, A, SA 3, 2001 W (R), F (R)
Perry, S V (Cambridge U, Waterloo) 1947 W, I, 1948 A, W, I, S, F
Peters, J (Plymouth) 1906 S, F, 1907 I, S, 1908 W
Phillips, C (Birkenhead Park) 1880 S, 1881 I, S
Phillips, M S (Fylde) 1958 A, I, F, S, 1959 W, I, F, S, 1960 W, I, F, S, 1961 W, 1963 W, I, F, S, NZ 1,2, A, 1964 NZ, W, I, F, S
Pickering, A S (Harrogate) 1907 I
Pickering, R D A (Bradford) 1967 I, F, S, W, 1968 F, S
Pickles, R C W (Bristol) 1922 I, F
Pierce, R (Liverpool) 1898 I, 1903 S
Pilkington, W N (Cambridge U) 1898 S
Pillman, C H (Blackheath) 1910 W, I, F, S, 1911 W, F, I, S, 1912 W, F, 1913 SA, W, F, I, S, 1914 W, I, S
Pillman, R L (Blackheath) 1914 F
Pinch, J (Lancaster) 1896 W, I, 1897 S
Pinching, W W (Guy's Hospital) 1872 S
Pitman, I J (Oxford U) 1922 S
Plummer, K C (Bristol) 1969 W, 1976 S, I, F
Pool-Jones, R J (Stade Francais) 1998 A 1
Poole, F O (Oxford U) 1895 W, I, S
Poole, R W (Hartlepool R) 1896 S
Pope, E B (Blackheath) 1931 W, S, F
Portus, G V (Blackheath) 1908 F, I
Potter, S (Leicester) 1998 A 1(t)
Poulton, R W (later Poulton Palmer) (Oxford U, Harlequins, Liverpool) 1909 F, I, S, 1910 W, 1911 S, 1912 W, I, S, 1913 SA, W, F, I, S, 1914 W, I, S, F
Powell, D L (Northampton) 1966 W, I, 1969 I, F, S, W, 1971 W, I, F, S (2[1C])
Pratten, W E (Blackheath) 1927 S, F
Preece, I (Coventry) 1948 I, S, F, 1949 F, S, 1950 W, I, F, S, 1951 W, I, F
Preece, P S (Coventry) 1972 SA, 1973 NZ 1, W, I, F, S, NZ 2, 1975 I, F, W, A 2, 1976 W (R)
Preedy, M (Gloucester) 1984 SA 1
Prentice, F D (Leicester) 1928 I, F, S
Prescott, R E (Harlequins) 1937 W, I, 1938 I, 1939 W, I, S
Preston, N J (Richmond) 1979 NZ, 1980 I, F
Price, H L (Harlequins) 1922 I, S, 1923 W, I
Price, J (Coventry) 1961 I
Price, P L A (RIE Coll) 1877 I, S, 1878 S
Price, T W (Cheltenham) 1948 S, F, 1949 W, I, F, S
Probyn, J A (Wasps, Askeans) 1988 F, W, S, I 1,2, A 1, 2, A, 1989 S, I, R (R), 1990 I, F, W, S, Arg 1,2,3, 1991 W, S, I, F, Fj, A, [NZ, It, F, S, A], 1992 S, I, F, W, 1993 F, W, S, I
Prout, D H (Northampton) 1968 W, I
Pullin, J V (Bristol) 1966 W, 1968 W, I, F, S, 1969 I, F, S, W, SA, 1970 I, W, S, F, 1971 W, I, F, S (2[1C]), P, 1972 W, I, F, S, SA, 1973 NZ 1, W, I, F, S, NZ 2, A, 1974 S, I, F, W, 1975 I, W (R), S, A 1,2, 1976 F
Purdy, S J (Rugby) 1962 S
Pyke, J (St Helens Recreation) 1892 W
Pym, J A (Blackheath) 1912 W, I, S, F

Quinn, J P (New Brighton) 1954 W, NZ, I, S, F

Rafter, M (Bristol) 1977 S, F, W, 1978 F, W, S, I, NZ, 1979 S, I, F, W, NZ, 1980 W(R), 1981 W, Arg 1,2
Ralston, C W (Richmond) 1971 S (C), P, 1972 W, I, F, S, SA, 1973 NZ 1, W, I, F, S, NZ 2, A, 1974 S, I, F, W, 1975 I, F, W, S
Ramsden, H E (Bingley) 1898 S, W
Ranson, J M (Rosslyn Park) 1963 NZ 1,2, A, 1964 W, I, F, S
Raphael, J E (OMTs) 1902 W, I, S, 1905 W, S, NZ, 1906 W, S, F
Ravenscroft, J (Birkenhead Park) 1881 I
Ravenscroft, S C W (Saracens) 1998 A 1, NZ 2(R)
Rawlinson, W C W (Blackheath) 1876 S
Redfern, S (Leicester) 1984 I (R)
Redman, N C (Bath) 1984 A, 1986 S (R), 1987 I, S, [A, J, W], 1988 Fj, 1990 Arg 1,2, 1991 Fj, [It, US], 1993 NZ, 1994 F, W, SA 1,2, 1997 Arg 1, A 1
Redmond, G F (Cambridge U) 1970 F
Redwood, B W (Bristol) 1968 W, I
Rees, D L (Sale) 1997 A 2, NZ 1, SA, NZ 2, 1998 F, W, SA 2(R), 1999 S, I, F, A
Rees, G W (Nottingham) 1984 SA 2(R), A, 1986 I, F, 1987 F, W, S, [A, J, US, W], 1988 S (R), I 1,2, A 1,2, Fj, 1989 W (R), R (R), Fj (R), 1990 Arg 3(R), 1991 Fj, [US]
Reeve, J S R (Harlequins) 1929 F, 1930 W, I, F, S, 1931 W, I, S
Regan, M (Liverpool) 1953 W, I, F, S, 1954 W, NZ, I, S, F, 1956 I, S, F
Regan, M P (Bristol, Bath, Leeds) 1995 SA, WS, 1996 F, W, S, I, It, Arg, 1997 S, I, F, W, A 1, NZ 2(R), 1998 F, 2000 SA 1(t), A(R), Arg, SA 3(t), 2001 It(R), S(R), C 2(R), R, 2003 F 1(t), It(R), W 2, [Gg(R), Sm], 2004 It(R), I(R), NZ1(R), 2, A1
Rendall, P A G (Wasps, Askeans) 1984 W, SA 2, 1986 W, S, 1987 I, F, S, [A, J, W], 1988 F, W, S, I 1,2, A 1,2, A, 1989 S, I, F, W, R, 1990 I, F, W, S, 1991 [It (R)]
Rew, H (Blackheath) 1929 S, F, 1930 F, S, 1931 W, S, F, 1934 W, I, S
Reynolds, F J (O Cranleighans) 1937 S, 1938 I, S
Reynolds, S (Richmond) 1900 W, I, S, 1901 I
Rhodes, J (Castleford) 1896 W, I, S
Richards, D (Leicester) 1986 I, F, 1987 S, [A, J, US, W], 1988 F, W, S, I 1, A 1,2, Fj, A, 1989 S, I, F, W, R, 1990 Arg 3, 1991 W, S, I, F, Fj, A, [NZ, It, US], 1992 S (R), F, W, C, 1993 NZ, 1994 W, SA 1, C, 1995 I, F, W, S, [WS, A, NZ], 1996 F (t), S, I
Richards, E E (Plymouth A) 1929 S, F
Richards, J (Bradford) 1891 W, I, S
Richards, P C (Gloucester) 2006 A1, 2
Richards, S B (Richmond) 1965 W, I, F, S, 1967 A, I, F, S, W
Richardson, J V (Birkenhead Park) 1928 A, W, I, F, S
Richardson, W R (Manchester) 1881 I
Rickards, C H (Gipsies) 1873 S
Rimmer, G (Waterloo) 1949 W, I, 1950 W, 1951 W, I, F, 1952 SA, W, 1954 W, NZ, I, S
Rimmer, L I (Bath) 1961 SA, W, I, F, S
Ripley, A G (Rosslyn Park) 1972 W, I, F, S, SA, 1973 NZ 1, W, I, F, S, NZ 2, A, 1974 S, I, F, W, 1975 I, F, S, A 1,2, 1976 A, W, S
Risman, A B W (Loughborough Coll) 1959 W, I, F, S, 1961 SA, W, I, F
Ritson, J A S (Northern) 1910 F, S, 1912 F, 1913 SA, W, F, I, S
Rittson-Thomas, G C (Oxford U) 1951 W, I, F
Robbins, G L (Coventry) 1986 W, S
Robbins, P G D (Oxford U, Moseley, Coventry) 1956 W, I, S, F, 1957 W, I, F, S, 1958 W, A, I, S, 1960 W, I, F, S, 1961 SA, W, 1962 S
Roberts, A D (Northern) 1911 W, F, I, S, 1912 I, S, F, 1914 I

Roberts, E W (RNE Coll) 1901 W, I, 1905 NZ, 1906 W, I, 1907 S
Roberts, G D (Harlequins) 1907 S, 1908 F, W
Roberts, J (Sale) 1960 W, I, F, S, 1961 SA, W, I, F, S, 1962 W, I, F, S, 1963 W, I, F, S, 1964 NZ
Roberts, R S (Coventry) 1932 I
Roberts, S (Swinton) 1887 W, I
Roberts, V G (Penryn, Harlequins) 1947 F, 1949 W, I, F, S, 1950 I, F, S, 1951 W, I, F, S, 1956 W, I, S, F
Robertshaw, A R (Bradford) 1886 W, I, S, 1887 W, S
Robinson, A (Blackheath) 1889 M, 1890 W, S, I
Robinson, E T (Coventry) 1954 S, 1961 I, F, S
Robinson, G C (Percy Park) 1897 I, S, 1898 I, 1899 W, 1900 I, S, 1901 I, S
Robinson, J T (Sale) 2001 It (R), S (R), F (R), I, A, R, SA, 2002 S, I, F, It, NZ, A, SA, 2003 F 1, W 1, S, I, NZ, A, F 3, [Gg, SA, Sm, U(R), W, F, A], 2004 It, S, I, W, F, C, SA, A2, 2005 W, F, I
Robinson, J J (Headingley) 1893 S, 1902 W, I, S
Robinson, R A (Bath) 1988 A 2, Fj, A, 1989 S, I, F, W, 1995 SA
Robson, A (Northern) 1924 W, I, F, S, 1926 W
Robson, M (Oxford U) 1930 W, I, F, S
Rodber, T A K (Army, Northampton) 1992 S, I, 1993 NZ, 1994 I, F, W, SA 1,2, R, C, 1995 I, F, W, S, [Arg, It, WS (R), A, NZ, F], SA, WS, 1996 W, S (R), I (t), It, Arg, 1997 S, I, F, W, A 1, 1998 H (R), It (R), A 2, SA 2, 1999 S, I, F, W, A, US (R), [NZ (R), Fj (R)]
Rogers, D P (Bedford) 1961 I, F, S, 1962 W, I, F, 1963 W, I, F, S, NZ 1,2, A, 1964 NZ, W, I, F, S, 1965 W, I, F, S, 1966 W, I, F, S, 1967 A, S, W, NZ, 1969 I, F, S, W
Rogers, J H (Moseley) 1890 W, S, I, 1891 S
Rogers, W L Y (Blackheath) 1905 W, I
Rollitt, D M (Bristol) 1967 I, F, S, W, 1969 I, F, S, W, 1975 S, A 1,2
Roncoroni, A D S (West Herts, Richmond) 1933 W, I, S
Rose, W M H (Cambridge U, Coventry, Harlequins) 1981 I, F, 1982 A, S, I, 1987 I, F, W, S, [A]
Rossborough, P A (Coventry) 1971 W, 1973 NZ 2, A, 1974 S, I, 1975 I, F
Rosser, D W A (Wasps) 1965 W, I, F, S, 1966 W
Rotherham, Alan (Richmond) 1883 W, S, 1884 W, S, 1885 W, I, 1886 W, I, S, 1887 W, I, S
Rotherham, Arthur (Richmond) 1898 S, W, 1899 W, I, S
Roughley, D (Liverpool) 1973 A, 1974 S, I
Rowell, R E (Leicester) 1964 W, 1965 W
Rowley, A J (Coventry) 1932 SA
Rowley, H C (Manchester) 1879 S, I, 1880 I, S, 1881 I, W, S, 1882 I, S
Rowntree, G (Leicester) 1995 S (t), [It, WS], WS, 1996 F, W, S, I, It, Arg, 1997 S, I, F, W, A 1, 1998 A 1, NZ 1, 2, SA 1, H (R), It (R), 1999 US, C, [It (R), Tg, Fj (R)], 2001 C 1,2, US, I(R), A, R, SA, 2002 S, I, F, W, It, 2003 F 1(R), W 1, It, S, I, NZ, F 2, 2004 C, SA, A2, 2005 W, F, I, It, 2006 A1, 2
Royds, P M R (Blackheath) 1898 S, W, 1899 W
Royle, A V (Broughton R) 1889 M
Rudd, E L (Liverpool) 1965 W, I, S, 1966 W, I, S
Russell, R F (Leicester) 1905 NZ
Rutherford, D (Percy Park, Gloucester) 1960 W, I, F, S, 1961 SA, 1965 W, I, F, S, 1966 W, I, F, S, 1967 NZ
Ryalls, H J (New Brighton) 1885 W, I
Ryan, D (Wasps, Newcastle) 1990 Arg 1,2, 1992 C, 1998 S
Ryan, P H (Richmond) 1955 W, I

Sadler, E H (Army) 1933 I, S
Sagar, J W (Cambridge U) 1901 W, I
Salmon, J L B (Harlequins) 1985 NZ 1,2, 1986 W, S, 1987 I, F, W, S, [A, J, US, W]
Sample, C H (Cambridge U) 1884 I, 1885 I, 1886 S
Sampson, P C (Wasps) 1998 SA 1, 2001 C 1,2
Sanders, D L (Harlequins) 1954 W, NZ, I, S, F, 1956 W, I, S, F
Sanders, F W (Plymouth A) 1923 I, S, F
Sanderson, A (Sale) 2001 R (R), 2002 Arg, 2003 It(t + R), W 2(R), F 2
Sanderson, P H (Sale, Harlequins, Worcester) 1998 NZ 1,2, SA 1, 2001 C 1(R),2(R), US(t+R), 2005 A, NZ, Sm, 2006 A1, 2
Sandford, J R P (Marlborough N) 1906 I
Sangwin, R D (Hull and E Riding) 1964 NZ, W
Sargent, G A F (Gloucester) 1981 I (R)
Savage, K F (Northampton) 1966 W, I, F, S, 1967 A, I, F, S, W, NZ, 1968 W, F, S
Sawyer, C M (Broughton) 1880 S, 1881 I
Saxby, L E (Gloucester) 1932 SA, W
Scarbrough, D G R (Leeds) 2003 W 2
Schofield, J W (Manchester) 1880 I
Scholfield, J A (Preston Grasshoppers) 1911 W
Schwarz, R O (Richmond) 1899 S, 1901 W, I
Scorfield, E S (Percy Park) 1910 F
Scott, C T (Blackheath) 1900 W, I, 1901 W, I
Scott, E K (St Mary's Hospital, Redruth) 1947 W, 1948 A, W, I, S
Scott, F S (Bristol) 1907 W
Scott, H (Manchester) 1955 F
Scott, J P (Rosslyn Park, Cardiff) 1978 F, W, S, I, NZ, 1979 S (R), I, F, W, NZ, 1980 I, F, W, S, 1981 W, S, I, F, Arg 1,2, 1982 I, F, W, 1983 F, W, S, I, NZ, 1984 S, I, F, W, SA 1,2
Scott, J S M (Oxford U) 1958 F
Scott, M T (Cambridge U) 1887 I, 1890 S, I
Scott, W M (Cambridge U) 1889 M
Seddon, R L (Broughton R) 1887 W, I, S
Sellar, K A (United Services, RN) 1927 W, I, S, 1928 A, W, I, F
Sever, H S (Sale) 1936 NZ, W, I, S, 1937 W, I, S, 1938 W, I, S
Shackleton, I R (Cambridge U) 1969 SA, 1970 I, W, S
Sharp, R A W (Oxford U, Wasps, Redruth) 1960 W, I, F, S, 1961 I, F, 1962 W, I, F, 1963 W, I, F, S, 1967 A
Shaw, C H (Moseley) 1906 S, SA, 1907 F, W, I, S
Shaw, F (Cleckheaton) 1898 I
Shaw, J F (RNE Coll) 1898 S, W
Shaw, S D (Bristol, Wasps) 1996 It, Arg, 1997 S, I, F, W, A 1, SA (R), 2000 I, F, W, It, S, SA 1(R),2(R), 2001 C 1(R), 2, US, I, 2003 It (R), W 2, F 2(R), 3(R), 2004 It(t&R), S(R), NZ1, 2, A1, 2005 Sm(R), 2006 W(R), It(R), S(R), F(R), I
Sheasby, C M A (Wasps) 1996 It, Arg, 1997 W (R), Arg 1(R),2(R), SA (R), NZ 2(t)
Sheppard, A (Bristol) 1981 W (R), 1985 W
Sheridan, A J (Sale) 2004 C(R), 2005 A, NZ, Sm, 2006 W, It, S, F(R), I
Sherrard, C W (Blackheath) 1871 S, 1872 S
Sherriff, G A (Saracens) 1966 S, 1967 A, NZ
Shewring, H E (Bristol) 1905 I, NZ, 1906 W, S, F, SA, 1907 F, W, I, S
Shooter, J H (Morley) 1899 I, S, 1900 I, S
Shuttleworth, D W (Headingley) 1951 S, 1953 S
Sibree, H J H (Harlequins) 1908 F, 1909 I, S
Silk, N (Harlequins) 1965 W, I, F, S
Simms, K G (Cambridge U, Liverpool, Wasps) 1985 R, F, S, I, W, 1986 I, F, 1987 I, F, W, [A, J, W], 1988 F, W
Simpson, C P (Harlequins) 1965 W
Simpson, P D (Bath) 1983 NZ, 1984 S, 1987 I
Simpson, T (Rockcliff) 1902 S, 1903 W, I, S, 1904 I, S, 1905 I, S, 1906 S, SA, 1909 F
Simpson-Daniel, J D (Gloucester) 2002 NZ, A, 2003 W 1(t + R), It, W 2, 2004 I(R), NZ1, 2005 Sm, 2006 It(R)
Sims, D (Gloucester) 1998 NZ 1(R),2, SA 1
Skinner, M G (Harlequins) 1988 F, W, S, I 1,2, 1989 Fj, 1990 I, F, W, S, Arg 1,2, 1991 Fj (R), [US, F, S, A], 1992 S, I, F, W
Sladen, G M (United Services, RN) 1929 W, I, S
Sleightholme, J M (Bath) 1996 F, W, S, I, It, Arg, 1997 S, I, F, W, Arg 1,2
Slemen, M A C (Liverpool) 1976 I, F, 1977 S, I, F, W, 1978 F, W, S, I, NZ, 1979 S, I, F, W, NZ, 1980 I, F, W, S, 1981 W, S, I, F, 1982 A, S, I, F, W, 1983 NZ, 1984 S
Slocock, L A N (Liverpool) 1907 F, W, I, S, 1908 F, W, I, S
Slow, C F (Leicester) 1934 S
Small, H D (Oxford U) 1950 W, I, F, S
Smallwood, A M (Leicester) 1920 F, I, 1921 W, I, S, F, 1922 I, S, 1923 W, I, S, F, 1925 I, S
Smart, C E (Newport) 1979 F, W, NZ, 1981 S, I, F, Arg 1,2, 1982 A, S, I, F, W, 1983 F, W, S, I

Smart, S E J (Gloucester) 1913 SA, W, F, I, S, 1914 W, I, S, F, 1920 W, I, S
Smeddle, R W (Cambridge U) 1929 W, I, S, 1931 F
Smith, C C (Gloucester) 1901 W
Smith, D F (Richmond) 1910 W, I
Smith, J V (Cambridge U, Rosslyn Park) 1950 W, I, F, S
Smith, K (Roundhay) 1974 F, W, 1975 W, S
Smith, M J K (Oxford U) 1956 W
Smith, O J (Leicester) 2003 It (R), W 2(R), F 2, 2005 It(R), S(R)
Smith, S J (Sale) 1973 I, F, S, A, 1974 I, F, 1975 W (R), 1976 F, 1977 F (R), 1979 NZ, 1980 I, F, W, S, 1981 W, S, I, F, Arg 1,2, 1982 A, S, I, F, W, 1983 F, W, S
Smith, S R (Richmond) 1959 W, F, S, 1964 F, S
Smith, S T (Wasps) 1985 R, F, S, I, W, NZ 1,2, 1986 W, S
Smith, T H (Northampton) 1951 W
Soane, F (Bath) 1893 S, 1894 W, I, S
Sobey, W H (O Millhillians) 1930 W, F, S, 1932 SA, W
Solomon, B (Redruth) 1910 W
Sparks, R H W (Plymouth A) 1928 I, F, S, 1929 W, I, S, 1931 I, S, F
Speed, H (Castleford) 1894 W, I, S, 1896 S
Spence, F W (Birkenhead Park) 1890 I
Spencer, J (Harlequins) 1966 W
Spencer, J S (Cambridge U, Headingley) 1969 I, F, S, W, SA, 1970 I, W, S, F, 1971 W, I, S (2[1C]), P
Spong, R S (O Millhillians) 1929 F, 1930 W, I, F, S, 1931 F, 1932 SA, W
Spooner, R H (Liverpool) 1903 W
Springman, H H (Liverpool) 1879 S, 1887 S
Spurling, A (Blackheath) 1882 I
Spurling, N (Blackheath) 1886 I, S, 1887 W
Squires, P J (Harrogate) 1973 F, S, NZ 2, A, 1974 S, I, F, W, 1975 I, F, W, S, A 1,2, 1976 A, W, 1977 S, I, F, W, 1978 F, W, S, I, NZ, 1979 S, I, F, W
Stafford R C (Bedford) 1912 W, I, S, F
Stafford, W F H (RE) 1874 S
Stanbury, E (Plymouth A) 1926 W, I, S, 1927 W, I, S, F, 1928 A, W, I, F, S, 1929 W, I, S, F
Standing, G (Blackheath) 1883 W, I
Stanger-Leathes, C F (Northern) 1905 I
Stark, K J (O Alleynians) 1927 W, I, S, F, 1928 A, W, I, F, S
Starks, A (Castleford) 1896 W, I
Starmer-Smith, N C (Harlequins) 1969 SA, 1970 I, W, S, F, 1971 S (C), P
Start, S P (United Services, RN) 1907 S
Steeds, J H (Saracens) 1949 F, S, 1950 I, F, S
Steele-Bodger, M R (Cambridge U) 1947 W, I, S, F, 1948 A, W, I, S, F
Steinthal, F E (Ilkley) 1913 W, F
Stephenson, M (Newcastle) 2001 C 1,2, US
Stevens, C B (Penzance-Newlyn, Harlequins) 1969 SA, 1970 I, W, S, 1971 P, 1972 W, I, F, S, SA, 1973 NZ 1, W, I, F, S, NZ 2, A, 1974 S, I, F, W, 1975 I, F, W, S
Stevens, M J H (Bath) 2004 NZ1(R), 2(t), 2005 I, It, S, NZ(R), Sm, 2006 W, It, F
Still, E R (Oxford U, Ravenscourt P) 1873 S
Stimpson, T R G (Newcastle, Leicester) 1996 It, 1997 S, I, F, W, A 1, NZ 2(t+R), 1998 A 1, NZ 1,2(R), SA 1(R), 1999 US (R), C (R), 2000 SA 1, 2001 C 1(t),2(R), 2002 W (R), Arg, SA (R)
Stirling, R V (Leicester, RAF, Wasps) 1951 W, I, F, S, 1952 SA, W, S, I, F, 1953 W, I, F, S, 1954 W, NZ, I, S, F
Stoddart, A E (Blackheath) 1885 W, I, 1886 W, I, S, 1889 M, 1890 W, I, 1893 W, S
Stoddart, W B (Liverpool) 1897 W, I, S
Stokes, F (Blackheath) 1871 S, 1872 S, 1873 S
Stokes, L (Blackheath) 1875 I, 1876 S, 1877 I, S, 1878 S, 1879 S, I, 1880 I, S, 1881 I, W, S
Stone, F le S (Blackheath) 1914 F
Stoop, A D (Harlequins) 1905 S, 1906 S, F, SA, 1907 F, W, 1910 W, I, S, 1911 W, F, I, S, 1912 W, S
Stoop, F M (Harlequins) 1910 S, 1911 F, I, 1913 SA
Stout, F M (Richmond) 1897 W, I, 1898 I, S, W, 1899 I, S, 1903 S, 1904 W, I, S, 1905 W, I, S
Stout, P W (Richmond) 1898 S, W, 1899 W, I, S
Stringer, N C (Wasps) 1982 A (R), 1983 NZ (R), 1984 SA 1(R), A, 1985 R
Strong, E L (Oxford U) 1884 W, I, S
Sturnham B (Saracens) 1998 A 1, NZ 1(t),2(t)
Summerscales, G E (Durham City) 1905 NZ
Sutcliffe, J W (Heckmondwike) 1889 M
Swarbrick, D W (Oxford U) 1947 W, I, F, 1948 A, W, 1949 I
Swayne, D H (Oxford U) 1931 W
Swayne, J W R (Bridgwater) 1929 W
Swift, A H (Swansea) 1981 Arg 1,2, 1983 F, W, S, 1984 SA 2
Syddall, J P (Waterloo) 1982 I, 1984 A
Sykes, A R V (Blackheath) 1914 F
Sykes, F D (Northampton) 1955 F, S, 1963 NZ 2, A
Sykes, P W (Wasps) 1948 F, 1952 S, I, F, 1953 W, I, F
Syrett, R E (Wasps) 1958 W, A, I, F, 1960 W, I, F, S, 1962 W, I, F

Tait, M (Newcastle) 2005 W, 2006 A1, 2
Tallent, J A (Cambridge U, Blackheath) 1931 S, F, 1932 SA, W, 1935 I
Tanner, C C (Cambridge U, Gloucester) 1930 S, 1932 SA, W, I, S
Tarr, F N (Leicester) 1909 A, W, F, 1913 S
Tatham, W M (Oxford U) 1882 S, 1883 W, I, S, 1884 W, I, S
Taylor, A S (Blackheath) 1883 W, I, 1886 W, I
Taylor, E W (Rockcliff) 1892 I, 1893 I, 1894 W, I, S, 1895 W, I, S, 1896 W, I, 1897 W, I, S, 1899 I
Taylor, F (Leicester) 1920 F, I
Taylor, F M (Leicester) 1914 W
Taylor, H H (Blackheath) 1879 S, 1880 S, 1881 I, W, 1882 S
Taylor, J T (W Hartlepool) 1897 I, 1899 I, 1900 I, 1901 W, I, 1902 W, I, S, 1903 W, I, 1905 S
Taylor, P J (Northampton) 1955 W, I, 1962 W, I, F, S
Taylor, R B (Northampton) 1966 W, 1967 I, F, S, W, NZ, 1969 F, S, W, SA, 1970 I, W, S, F, 1971 S (2[1C])
Taylor, W J (Blackheath) 1928 A, W, I, F, S
Teague, M C (Gloucester, Moseley) 1985 F (R), NZ 1, 2, 1989 S, I, F, W, R, 1990 F, W, S, 1991 W, S, I, F, Fj, A, [NZ, It, F, S, A], 1992 SA, 1993 F, W, S, I
Teden, D E (Richmond) 1939 W, I, S
Teggin, A (Broughton R) 1884 I, 1885 W, 1886 I, S, 1887 I, S
Tetley, T S (Bradford) 1876 S
Thomas, C (Barnstaple) 1895 W, I, S, 1899 I
Thompson, P H (Headingley, Waterloo) 1956 W, I, S, F, 1957 W, I, F, S, 1958 W, A, I, F, S, 1959 W, I, F, S
Thompson, S G (Northampton) 2002 S, I, F, W, It, Arg, NZ, A, SA, 2003 F 1, W 1, It, S, I, NZ, A, F 2(R), 3, [Gg, SA, Sm(R), W, F, A], 2004 It, S, I, W, F, NZ1, A1(R), C, SA, A2, 2005 W, F, I, It, S, A, NZ, Sm, 2006 W, It, S, F, I(R)
Thomson, G T (Halifax) 1878 S, 1882 I, S, 1883 W, I, S, 1884 I, S, 1885 I
Thomson, W B (Blackheath) 1892 W, 1895 W, I, S
Thorne, J D (Bristol) 1963 W, I, F
Tindall, M J (Bath, Gloucester) 2000 I, F, W, It, S, SA 1,2, A Arg, SA 3, 2001 W (R), R, SA (R), 2002 S, I, F, W, It, NZ, A, SA, 2003 It, S, I, NZ, A, F 2, [Gg, SA, Sm, W, F(R), A], 2004 W, F, NZ1, 2, A1, C, SA, A2, 2005 A, NZ, Sm, 2006 W, It, S, F, I(t&R)
Tindall, V R (Liverpool U) 1951 W, I, F, S
Titterrell, A J (Sale) 2004 NZ2(R), C(R), 2005 It(R), S(R)
Tobin, F (Liverpool) 1871 S
Todd, A F (Blackheath) 1900 I, S
Todd, R (Manchester) 1877 S
Toft, H B (Waterloo) 1936 S, 1937 W, I, S, 1938 W, I, S, 1939 W, I, S
Toothill, J T (Bradford) 1890 S, I, 1891 W, I, 1892 W, I, S, 1893 W, I, S, 1894 W, I
Tosswill, L R (Exeter) 1902 W, I, S
Touzel, C J C (Liverpool) 1877 I, S
Towell, A C (Bedford) 1948 F, 1951 S
Travers, B H (Harlequins) 1947 W, I, 1948 A, W, 1949 F, S
Treadwell, W T (Wasps) 1966 I, F, S
Trick, D M (Bath) 1983 I, 1984 SA 1
Tristram, H B (Oxford U) 1883 S, 1884 W, S, 1885 W, 1887 S

Troop, C L (Aldershot S) 1933 I, S
Tucker, J S (Bristol) 1922 W, 1925 NZ, W, I, S, F, 1926 W, I, F, S, 1927 W, I, S, F, 1928 A, W, I, F, S, 1929 W, I, F, 1930 W, I, F, S, 1931 W
Tucker, W E (Blackheath) 1894 W, I, 1895 W, I, S
Tucker, W E (Blackheath) 1926 I, 1930 W, I
Turner, D P (Richmond) 1871 S, 1872 S, 1873 S, 1874 S, 1875 I, S
Turner, E B (St George's Hospital) 1876 I, 1877 I, 1878 I
Turner, G R (St George's Hospital) 1876 S
Turner, H J C (Manchester) 1871 S
Turner, M F (Blackheath) 1948 S, F
Turquand-Young, D (Richmond) 1928 A, W, 1929 I, S, F
Twynam, H T (Richmond) 1879 I, 1880 I, 1881 W, 1882<j> I, 1883 I, 1884 W, I, S

Ubogu, V E (Bath) 1992 C, SA, 1993 NZ, 1994 S, I, F, W, SA 1,2, R, C, 1995 I, F, W, S, [Arg, WS, A, NZ, F], SA, 1999 F (R), W (R), A (R)
Underwood, A M (Exeter) 1962 W, I, F, S, 1964 I
Underwood, R (Leicester, RAF) 1984 I, F, W, A, 1985 R, F, S, I, W, 1986 W, I, F, 1987 I, F, W, S, [A, J, W], 1988 F, W, S, I 1,2, A 1,2, Fj, A, 1989 S, I, F, W, R, Fj, 1990 I, F, W, S, Arg 3, 1991 W, S, I, F, Fj, A, [NZ, It, US, F, S, A], 1992 S, I, F, W, SA, 1993 F, W, S, I, NZ, 1994 S, I, F, W, SA 1,2, R, C, 1995 I, F, W, S, [Arg, It, WS, A, NZ, F], SA, WS, 1996 F, W, S, I
Underwood, T (Leicester, Newcastle) 1992 C, SA, 1993 S, I, NZ, 1994 S, I, W, SA 1,2, R, C, 1995 I, F, W, S, [Arg, It, A, NZ], 1996 Arg, 1997 S, I, F, W, 1998 A 2, SA 2
Unwin, E J (Rosslyn Park, Army) 1937 S, 1938 W, I, S
Unwin, G T (Blackheath) 1898 S
Uren, R (Waterloo) 1948 I, S, F, 1950 I
Uttley, R M (Gosforth) 1973 I, F, S, NZ 2, A, 1974 I, F, W, 1975 F, W, S, A 1,2, 1977 S, I, F, W, 1978 NZ 1979 S, 1980 I, F, W, S

Valentine J (Swinton) 1890 W, 1896 W, I, S
Vanderspar, C H R (Richmond) 1873 S
Van Gisbergen, M C (Wasps) 2005 A(t)
Van Ryneveld, C B (Oxford U) 1949 W, I, F, S
Varley, H (Liversedge) 1892 S
Varndell, T W (Leicester) 2005 Sm(R), 2006 A1, 2
Vassall, H (Blackheath) 1881 W, S, 1882 I, S, 1883 W
Vassall, H H (Blackheath) 1908 I
Vaughan, D B (Headingley) 1948 A, W, I, S, 1949 I, F, S, 1950 W
Vaughan-Jones, A (Army) 1932 I, S, 1933 W
Verelst, C L (Liverpool) 1876 I, 1878 I
Vernon, G F (Blackheath) 1878 S, I, 1880 I, S, 1881 I
Vickery, G (Aberavon) 1905 I
Vickery, P J (Gloucester) 1998 W, A 1, NZ 1,2, SA 1, 1999 US, C, [It, NZ, Tg, SA], 2000 I, F, W, S, A, Arg (R), SA 3(R), 2001 W, It, S, A, SA, 2002 I, F, Arg, NZ, A, SA, 2003 NZ(R), A, [Gg, SA, Sm(R), U, W, F, A], 2004 It, S, I, W, F, 2005 W(R), F, A, NZ
Vivyan, E J (Devonport A) 1901 W, 1904 W, I, S
Voyce, A T (Gloucester) 1920 I, S, 1921 W, I, S, F, 1922 W, I, F, S, 1923 W, I, S, F, 1924 W, I, F, S, 1925 NZ, W, I, S, F, 1926 W, I, F, S
Voyce, T M D (Bath, Wasps) 2001 US (R), 2004 NZ2, A1, 2005 Sm, 2006 W(R), It, F(R), I, A1
Vyvyan, H D (Saracens) 2004 C(R)

Wackett, J A S (Rosslyn Park) 1959 W, I
Wade, C G (Richmond) 1883 W, I, S, 1884 W, S, 1885 W, 1886 W, I
Wade, M R (Cambridge U) 1962 W, I, F
Wakefield, W W (Harlequins) 1920 W, F, I, S, 1921 W, I, S, F, 1922 W, I, F, S, 1923 W, I, S, F, 1924 W, I, F, S, 1925 NZ, W, I, S, F, 1926 W, I, F, S, 1927 S, F
Walder, D J H (Newcastle) 2001 C 1,2, US, 2003 W 2(R)
Walker, G A (Blackheath) 1939 W, I
Walker, H W (Coventry) 1947 W, I, S, F, 1948 A, W, I, S, F
Walker, R (Manchester) 1874 S, 1875 I, 1876 S, 1879 S, 1880 S
Wallens, J N S (Waterloo) 1927 F
Walshe, N P J (Bath) 2006 A1(R), 2(R)
Walton, E J (Castleford) 1901 W, I, 1902 I, S
Walton, W (Castleford) 1894 S
Ward, G (Leicester) 1913 W, F, S, 1914 W, I, S
Ward, H (Bradford) 1895 W
Ward, J I (Richmond) 1881 I, 1882 I
Ward, J W (Castleford) 1896 W, I, S
Wardlow, C S (Northampton) 1969 SA (R), 1971 W, I, F, S (2[1C])
Warfield, P J (Rosslyn Park, Durham U) 1973 NZ 1, W, I, 1975 I, F, S
Warr, A L (Oxford U) 1934 W, I
Waters, F H H (Wasps) 2001 US, 2004 NZ2(R), A1(R)
Watkins, J A (Gloucester) 1972 SA, 1973 NZ 1, W, NZ 2, A, 1975 F, W
Watkins, J K (United Services, RN) 1939 W, I, S
Watson, F B (United Services, RN) 1908 S, 1909 S
Watson, J H D (Blackheath) 1914 W, S, F
Watt, D E J (Bristol) 1967 I, F, S, W
Webb, C S H (Devonport Services, RN) 1932 SA, W, I, S, 1933 W, I, S, 1935 S, 1936 NZ, W, I, S
Webb, J M (Bristol, Bath) 1987 [A (R), J, US, W], 1988 F, W, S, I 1,2, A 1,2, A, 1989 S, I, F, W, 1991 Fj, A, [NZ, It, F, S, A], 1992 S, I, F, W, C, SA, 1993 F, W, S, I
Webb, J W G (Northampton) 1926 F, S, 1929 S
Webb, R E (Coventry) 1967 S, W, NZ, 1968 I, F, S, 1969 I, F, S, W, 1972 I, F
Webb, St L H (Bedford) 1959 W, I, F, S
Webster, J G (Moseley) 1972 W, I, SA, 1973 NZ 1, W, NZ 2, 1974 S, W, 1975 I, F, W
Wedge, T G (St Ives) 1907 F, 1909 W
Weighill, R H G (RAF, Harlequins) 1947 S, F, 1948 S, F
Wells, C M (Cambridge U, Harlequins) 1893 S, 1894 W, S, 1896 S, 1897 W, S
West, B R (Loughborough Colls, Northampton) 1968 W, I, F, S, 1969 SA, 1970 I, W, S
West, D E (Leicester) 1998 F (R), S (R), 2000 Arg (R), 2001 W, It, S, F (t), C 1,2, US, I (R), A, SA, 2002 F (R), W (R), It (R), 2003 W 2(R), F 2,3(t+R), [U, F(R)]
West, R (Gloucester) 1995 [WS]
Weston, H T F (Northampton) 1901 S
Weston, L E (W of Scotland) 1972 F, S
Weston, M P (Richmond, Durham City) 1960 W, I, F, S, 1961 SA, W, I, F, S, 1962 W, I, F, 1963 W, I, F, S, NZ 1,2, A, 1964 NZ, W, I, F, S, 1965 F, S, 1966 S, 1968 F, S
Weston, W H (Northampton) 1933 I, S, 1934 I, S, 1935 W, I, S, 1936 NZ, W, S, 1937 W, I, S, 1938 W, I, S
Wheatley, A A (Coventry) 1937 W, I, S, 1938 W, S
Wheatley, H F (Coventry) 1936 I, 1937 S, 1938 W, S, 1939 W, I, S
Wheeler, P J (Leicester) 1975 F, W, 1976 A, W, S, I, 1977 S, I, F, W, 1978 F, W, S, I, NZ, 1979 S, I, F, W, NZ, 1980 I, F, W, S, 1981 W, S, I, F, 1982 A, S, I, F, W, 1983 F, S, I, NZ, 1984 S, I, F, W
White, C (Gosforth) 1983 NZ, 1984 S, I, F
White, D F (Northampton) 1947 W, I, S, 1948 I, F, 1951 S, 1952 SA, W, S, I, F, 1953 W, I, S
White, J M (Saracens, Bristol, Leicester) 2000 SA 1,2, Arg, SA 3, 2001 F, C 1,2, US, I, R (R), 2002 S, W, It, 2003 F 1(R), W 2, F 2,3, [Sm, U(R)], 2004 W(R), F(R), NZ1,2, A1,C, SA, A2, 2005 W, 2006 W(R), It(R), S, F, I, A1,2
White-Cooper, S (Harlequins) 2001 C 2, US
Whiteley, E C P (O Alleynians) 1931 S, F
Whiteley, W (Bramley) 1896 W
Whitely, H (Northern) 1929 W
Wightman, B J (Moseley, Coventry) 1959 W, 1963 W, I, NZ 2, A
Wigglesworth, H J (Thornes) 1884 I
Wilkins, D T (United Services, RN, Roundhay) 1951 W, I, F, S, 1952 SA, W, S, I, F, 1953 W, I, F, S
Wilkinson, E (Bradford) 1886 W, I, S, 1887 W, S
Wilkinson, H (Halifax) 1929 W, I, S, 1930 F
Wilkinson, H J (Halifax) 1889 M
Wilkinson, J P (Newcastle) 1998 I (R), A 1, NZ 1, 1999 S, I, F, W, A, US, C, [It, NZ, Fj, SA (R)], 2000 I, F, W, It, S, SA 2, A, Arg, SA 3, 2001 W, It, S, F, I, A, SA, 2002 S, I, F, W, It, NZ, A, SA, 2003 F 1, W 1, It, S, I, NZ, A, F 3, [Gg, SA, Sm, W, F, A]

Wilkinson, P (Law Club) 1872 S
Wilkinson, R M (Bedford) 1975 A 2, 1976 A, W, S, I, F
Willcocks, T J (Plymouth) 1902 W
Willcox, J G (Oxford U, Harlequins) 1961 I, F, S, 1962 W, I, F, S, 1963 W, I, F, S, 1964 NZ, W, I, F, S
William-Powlett, P B R W (United Services, RN) 1922 S
Williams, C G (Gloucester, RAF) 1976 F
Williams, C S (Manchester) 1910 F
Williams, J E (O Millhillians, Sale) 1954 F, 1955 W, I, F, S, 1956 I, S, F, 1965 W
Williams, J M (Penzance-Newlyn) 1951 I, S
Williams, P N (Orrell) 1987 S, [A, J, W]
Williams, S G (Devonport A) 1902 W, I, S, 1903 I, S, 1907 I, S
Williams, S H (Newport) 1911 W, F, I, S
Williamson, R H (Oxford U) 1908 W, I, S, 1909 A, F
Wilson, A J (Camborne S of M) 1909 I
Wilson, C E (Blackheath) 1898 I
Wilson, C P (Cambridge U, Marlborough N) 1881 W
Wilson, D S (Met Police, Harlequins) 1953 F, 1954 W, NZ, I, S, F, 1955 F, S
Wilson, G S (Tyldesley) 1929 W, I
Wilson, K J (Gloucester) 1963 F
Wilson, R P (Liverpool OB) 1891 W, I, S
Wilson, W C (Richmond) 1907 I, S
Winn, C E (Rosslyn Park) 1952 SA, W, S, I, F, 1954 W, S, F
Winterbottom, P J (Headingley, Harlequins) 1982 A, S, I, F, W, 1983 F, W, S, I, NZ, 1984 S, F, W, SA 1,2, 1986 W, S, I, F, 1987 I, F, W, [A, J, US, W], 1988 F, W, S, 1989 R, Fj, 1990 I, F, W, S, Arg 1,2,3, 1991 W, S, I, F, A, [NZ, It, F, S, A], 1992 S, I, F, W, C, SA, 1993 F, W, S, I
Wintle, T C (Northampton) 1966 S, 1969 I, F, S, W
Wodehouse, N A (United Services, RN) 1910 F, 1911 W, F, I, S, 1912 W, I, S, F, 1913 SA, W, F, I, S
Wood, A (Halifax) 1884 I
Wood, A E (Gloucester, Cheltenham) 1908 F, W, I
Wood, G W (Leicester) 1914 W
Wood, M B, (Wasps) 2000 C 2(R), US (R)
Wood, R (Liversedge) 1894 I
Wood, R D (Liverpool OB) 1901 I, 1903 W, I
Woodgate, E E (Paignton) 1952 W
Woodhead, E (Huddersfield) 1880 I
Woodman, T J, (Gloucester) 1999 US (R), 2000 I (R), It (R), 2001 W (R), It (R), 2002 NZ, 2003 S (R), I(t + R), A, F 3, [Gg, SA, W(R), F, A], 2004 It, S, I, W, F, NZ1, 2
Woodruff, C G (Harlequins) 1951 W, I, F, S
Woods, S M J (Cambridge U, Wellington) 1890 W, S, I, 1891 W, I, S, 1892 I, S, 1893 W, I, 1895 W, I, S
Woods, T (Bridgwater) 1908 S
Woods, T (United Services, RN) 1920 S, 1921 W, I, S, F
Woodward, C R (Leicester) 1980 I (R), F, W, S, 1981 W, S, I, F, Arg 1,2, 1982 A, S, I, F, W, 1983 I, NZ, 1984 S, I, F, W
Woodward, J E (Wasps) 1952 SA, W, S, 1953 W, I, F, S, 1954 W, NZ, I, S, F, 1955 W, I, 1956 S
Wooldridge, C S (Oxford U, Blackheath) 1883 W, I, S, 1884 W, I, S, 1885 I
Wordsworth, A J (Cambridge U) 1975 A 1(R)
Worsley, J P R (Wasps) 1999 [Tg, Fj], 2000 It (R), S (R), SA 1(R),2(R), 2001 It (R), S (R), F (R), C 1,2, US, A, R, SA, 2002 S, I, F, W (t+R), Arg, 2003 W 1(R), It, S(R), I(t), NZ(R), A(R), W 2, [SA(t), Sm, U], 2004 It, I, W(R), F, NZ1(R), 2, A1, SA, A2, 2005 W, F, I, It, S, 2006 W, It, S, F, I, A1(R), 2
Worsley, M A (London Irish, Harlequins) 2003 It(R), 2004 A1(R), 2005 S(R)
Worton, J R B (Harlequins, Army) 1926 W, 1927 W
Wrench, D F B (Harlequins) 1964 F, S
Wright, C C G (Cambridge U, Blackheath) 1909 I, S
Wright, F T (Edinburgh Acady, Manchester) 1881 S
Wright, I D (Northampton) 1971 W, I, F, S (R)
Wright. J C (Met Police) 1934 W
Wright, J F (Bradford) 1890 W
Wright, T P (Blackheath) 1960 W, I, F, S, 1961 SA, W, I, F, S, 1962 W, I, F, S
Wright, W H G (Plymouth) 1920 W, F
Wyatt, D M (Bedford) 1976 S (R)

Yarranton, P G (RAF, Wasps) 1954 W, NZ, I, 1955 F, S
Yates, K P (Bath) 1997 Arg 1,2
Yiend, W (Hartlepool R, Gloucester) 1889 M, 1892 W, I, S, 1893 I, S
Young, A T (Cambridge U, Blackheath, Army) 1924 W, I, F, S, 1925 NZ, F, 1926 I, F, S, 1927 I, S, F, 1928 A, W, I, F, S, 1929 I
Young, J R C (Oxford U, Harlequins) 1958 I, 1960 W, I, F, S, 1961 SA, W, I, F
Young, M (Gosforth) 1977 S, I, F, W, 1978 F, W, S, I, NZ, 1979 S
Young, P D (Dublin Wands) 1954 W, NZ, I, S, F, 1955 W, I, F, S
Youngs, N G (Leicester) 1983 I, NZ, 1984 S, I, F, W

DOMESTIC RUGBY

TROPHY SALES TO THE NORTH

Dave Rogers/Getty Images

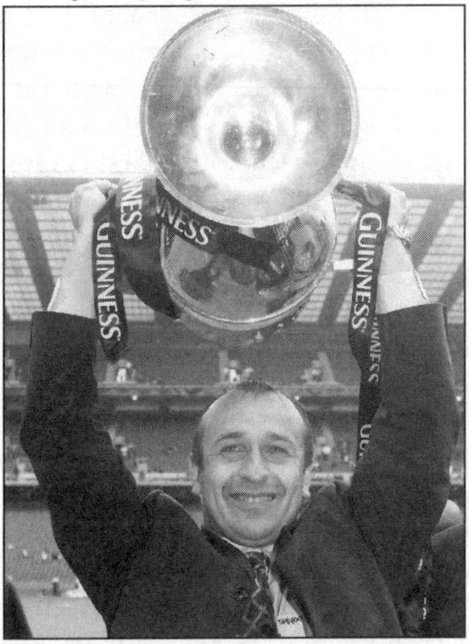

Philippe Saint-Andre celebrates Sale's first English title.

"**I think justice has** been done," said Sale Sharks Director of Rugby Philippe Saint-Andre in the aftermath of his side's comprehensive play-off final victory over Leicester. The Tigers had been clinically dispatched 45–20 at Twickenham and the Sharks were crowned Guinness Premiership champions for the first time.

Of course, Sale had 'won' the Premiership already. They had finished six points clear of Leicester in the final standings but knew they still had to successfully negotiate a play-off semi-final and then the all-important Twickenham showdown if they were to claim the club's first piece of major silverware in 145 years of asking.

After all, Wasps had 'won' the Premiership title in the three previous seasons without ever actually topping the table and Sale's season long dominance was no guarantee of success at the business end of the campaign. 'Justice', in the words of Saint-Andre, would only be done if Sale triumphed at Twickenham.

In the end, however, the result was never in doubt and Sale became the first side to top the table and be crowned champion club. The Sharks were the undisputed kings of England.

It was clear at the start of the campaign that Sale would once again be a force to be reckoned with. Finishing third behind Leicester and Wasps the previous season, they began the year with confidence and, more importantly, six victories in their opening seven games. Gloucester did manage to beat them 21–18 at Kingsholm in September courtesy of a dramatic penalty try 10 minutes into second-half injury time but the potentially morale-sapping defeat was merely a temporary setback.

Sale's first major test came in October with the visit of defending champions Wasps to Edgeley Park. The Sharks' title credentials were about to be put under the microscope and Saint-Andre knew it, describing the fixture "as the game of the season" in the build-up to the match.

In truth, it was far from a classic but a combination of Sale's abrasive pack and six penalties from the boot of fly-half Charlie Hodgson ensured an 18–10 victory. Sale went top of the table and became the team to beat.

"It was a game for men and I am pleased because tactically, we followed the game plan we worked on all week," said Saint-Andre. "We played a very rushed defence and had a lot of go-forward. We put a lot of pressure on them. We made one mistake and they scored a try but we were completely in control of the game and it is a huge victory for us because Wasps are one of the best teams in Europe."

A month later heavyweights Leicester also made the trip to Manchester and with Sale still enjoying clear water between themselves and the chasing pack, it was to be another pivotal moment in the campaign.

Both teams were depleted by international call-ups for the autumn Tests but it was Sale who held their nerve, outscored their visitors two tries to one and emerged 24–16 victors.

"We showed we are a good team even though we had 12 players missing," said Saint-Andre after the game. "It was an outstanding performance by my squad.

"To be missing all these players and still beat Leicester is great. The defence was outstanding, the spirit was there and the guys worked very, very hard."

Three Premiership wins in four followed and by the time Sale travelled to Welford Road in January to tackle Leicester in their own backyard, they were still top. The 27–27 draw with the Tigers was nothing if not dramatic and although the Sharks should really have ended Leicester's two-year unbeaten league record at home, the hard-earned points proved Sale were unlikely to fold in the second half of the campaign.

Dave Rogers/Getty Images

Martin Corry's Leicester endured heartache in the Premiership final, at Twickenham.

The Sharks outscored the home side two tries to nil thanks to Dean Schofield and Chris Jones but Tigers' fly-half Andy Goode landed eight penalties and a drop-goal – his final kick levelling the scores with five minutes left.

"A lot of people said we didn't have the hunger last week [against Bristol] and I was pleased with the commitment and character we showed," said Saint-Andre. "There was a big improvement from last year when we were beaten here."

A surprise 15–9 defeat to Saracens at Edgeley Park in March briefly suggested the pressure of topping the table for so long might begin to tell on the club but it was to prove an inexplicable blip rather than a downward spiral.

Four Premiership games remained and although a 32–21 loss at Newcastle took the club's tally of defeats to five, wins over London Irish, Gloucester and Northampton ensured Sale would finish top of the table and guarantee crucial home advantage in the play-off semi-final.

It transpired that fourth-placed Wasps would be their opponents at Edgeley Park and the home side could have been forgiven for a sense of foreboding before the game. Experts at peaking for the play-offs, the defending champions had ended the Sharks championship dream at the same stage the previous year, which made their resulting 22–12 win over the Londoners all the sweeter.

Inspired by a flawless kicking display from fly-half Charlie Hodgson, who landed six penalty attempts from six for a 16–point haul, and the only try of the match from Jason Robinson, Sale never looked in danger of falling at the final hurdle. Wasps three-year reign as champions was over and the Sharks were heading for Twickenham.

"We must savour this moment and take this mentality into the game in two weeks," Saint-Andre said after the semi-final. "We are not champions yet."

Wasps Director of Rugby Ian McGeechan was quick to pay tribute to the team that had dethroned the champions. "All credit to Sale," he said. "They held on to the ball when they had it and we didn't do as much as we should have when we had it."

The second semi-final saw Leicester take on surprise package London Irish at Welford Road but any hopes the in-form Exiles had of a debut appearance in the Premiership final were quickly extinguished by the Tigers' five-try burst for a 40–8 victory, including a late brace from substitute Leon Lloyd.

"We played well and I am very happy with that," Tigers captain Martin Corry said after the game. "We wanted to keep hold of the ball and we did. We will take that scoreline but it counts for very little if we don't reproduce it in two weeks time against Sale."

A fortnight later the two sides met on a wet, misty and unseasonally miserable May afternoon at Twickenham. Leicester were looking for a record seventh league title while Sale were hoping for the first real taste of success in the club's history.

The match exploded into life as early as the seventh minute when Hodgson launched a high, hanging kick which winger Mark Cueto plucked out of the air and Geordan Murphy's despairing grasp for the first try of the match. Sale were up and running.

Leicester responded quickly with a scrappy score from Lewis Moody but Sale hit back impressively with tries from Magnus Lund and Oriol Ripol and at half-time the Sharks enjoyed a commanding if not yet decisive 23–10 advantage.

Leicester looked to the substitutes bench for inspiration after the break – bringing on Austin Healey and Sam Vesty to inject menace into their misfiring back line – but Sale were not be overhauled. Hodgson kept the scoreboard ticking over with five penalties to add to the two he slotted in the first-half and although James Hamilton crossed for Leicester, Sale were always too far ahead and they went past the 40 point mark late on when replacement Chris Mayor raced over.

Leicester had been well and truly beaten 45–20 and Sale were the worthy champions.

"It's an amazing feeling. I can't describe how good it feels," said Hodgson, who scored 23 of his side's points. "In the end it was a comfortable win, the way we defended and turned the ball over was key.

"If you sit at the top of the league and don't win you are going to be disappointed but we are absolutely delighted with today. We will enjoy this moment. It's the first time for the club and we're going to savour every last minute."

Saint-Andre was equally happy. "We deserved this," he said. "We were in control, we were patient and we did not panic. Our kicking was also very good. They had to take a lot of risks and they made errors. Manchester is not just a football city now – it also has a rugby club."

In National One Dean Richards' Harlequins stormed back in to the Premiership with 25 wins from 26, scoring 1,001 points in the process, to top the table and ensure top-flight rugby at the Twickenham Stoop next season. Leeds were relegated from the Premiership.

In National Two, Moseley enjoyed their first season at their new Billesley Common ground, winning the title in April after a 43–12 defeat of Launceston. Fly-half Ollie Thomas top scored in the campaign with 253 points while wing Nathan Bressington contributed with 20 tries.

Meanwhile, the National Three North title was claimed by Bradford & Bingley, who earned their third promotion in four seasons to take the club to its highest ever position to date in the league structure. Led by former England Under-19 Geoff Wappett, the Bees clinched promotion with a 36–29 win against Nuneaton in April. "I always believed we were good enough to do what we've done," Wappett said. "And I think we've achieved it with a bit of style."

Stockport also had cause for celebration – claiming a North West Two title and Powergen Intermediate Cup double after beating Morley 11–6 at Twickenham.

GUINNESS PREMIERSHIP RESULTS

2 September 2005: **Sale** 26 **Newcastle** 25. September 3: **Wasps** 23 **Saracens** 11, **Leicester** 32 **Northampton** 0, **Leeds** 11 **London Irish** 27. September 4: **Worcester** 15 **Gloucester** 15, **Bristol** 19 **Bath** 16, September 10: **Wasps** 29 **Leicester** 29, **Gloucester** 21 **Sale** 18, **Bath** 9 **Northampton** 17. September 11: **Saracens** 34 **Leeds** 16, **Newcastle** 14 **Bristol** 16, **London Irish** 15 **Worcester** 20. September 16: **Sale** 29 **London Irish** 3. September 17: **Worcester** 25 **Saracens** 24, **Northampton** 9 **Newcastle** 16, **Leicester** 40 **Bath** 26. September 18: **Leeds** 23 **Wasps** 47 **Bristol** 9 **Gloucester** 41. September 24: **London Irish** 24 **Bristol** 22, **Gloucester** 28 **Northampton** 24. September 25: **Wasps** 34 **Worcester** 20, **Saracens** 32 **Sale** 40, **Newcastle** 16 **Bath** 27, **Leeds** 20 **Leicester** 28. October 14: **Worcester** 22 **Leeds** 15, **Sale** 18 **Wasps** 10, **Leicester** 16 **Newcastle** 16. October 15: **Northampton** 25 **London Irish** 23, **Bath** 18 **Gloucester** 16. October 16: **Bristol** 11 **Saracens** 23. November 4: **Worcester** 15 **Leicester** 11, **Wasps** 21 **Bristol** 16. November 5: **Saracens** 28 **Northampton** 22, **London Irish** 36 **Bath** 13, **Leeds** 11 **Sale** 17, **Gloucester** 27 **Newcastle** 20. November 11: **Sale** 24 **Worcester** 13, **Newcastle** 20 **London Irish** 23. November 12: **Northampton** 13 **Wasps** 21, **Leicester** 25 **Gloucester** 20. November 13: **Bristol** 32 **Leeds** 6, **Bath** 12 **Saracens** 12. November 18: **Worcester** 24 **Bristol** 15, **Sale** 24 **Leicester** 16. November 20: **Wasps** 28 **Bath** 20, **Saracens** 27 **Newcastle** 18, **London Irish** 25 **Gloucester** 10, **Leeds** 28 **Northampton** 25. November 25: **Leicester** 35 **London Irish** 3, **Bath** 12 **Leeds** 16. November 26: **Gloucester** 19 **Saracens** 8, **Northampton** 21 **Worcester** 22. November 27: **Newcastle** 17 **Wasps** 15, **Bristol** 22 **Sale** 14. December 26: **Worcester** 18 **Bath** 36, **Wasps** 32 **Gloucester** 25, **Sale** 34 **Northampton** 14. December 27: **Saracens** 19 **London Irish** 20, **Leeds** 10 **Newcastle** 13, **Bristol** 15 **Leicester** 3. December 31: **London Irish** 19 **Wasps** 35, **Gloucester** 31 **Leeds** 7, January 1: **Northampton** 29 **Bristol** 22, **Newcastle** 21 **Worcester** 15. January 2: **Bath** 9 **Sale** 21. January 8: **Wasps** 21 **Newcastle** 6, **Saracens** 9 **Gloucester** 19, **Sale** 31 **Bristol** 29, **London Irish** 25 **Leicester** 28, **Leeds** 25 **Bath** 14. January 27: **Bristol** 23 **Worcester** 26. January 28: **Northampton** 21 **Leeds** 18, **Newcastle** 21 **Saracens** 16, **Leicester** 27 **Sale** 27, **Gloucester** 9 **London Irish** 13, **Bath** 28 **Wasps** 16. February 10: **Leeds** 26 **Bristol** 16. February 11: **Worcester** 33 **Sale** 48. February 12: **Wasps** 19 **Northampton** 19. **Saracens** 29 **Bath** 34, **London Irish** 6 **Newcastle** 9. February 17: **Sale** 35 **Leeds** 24, **Leicester** 28 **Worcester** 22. February 18: **Northampton** 58 **Saracens** 17, **Bath** 28 **London Irish** 33. February 19: **Newcastle** 9 **Gloucester** 13, **Bristol** 9 **Wasps** 9. February 24: **Newcastle** 24 **Leicester** 16, **Leeds** 21 **Worcester** 15. February 25: **Gloucester** 15 **Bath** 18. February 26: **Wasps** 26 **Sale** 16, **Saracens** 13 **Bristol** 19, **London Irish** 30 **Northampton** 3. March 11: **Northampton** 21 **Gloucester** 20, **Bath** 20 **Newcastle** 18. March 12: **Bristol** 20 **London Irish** 21. March 25: **London Irish** 21 **Sale** 29, **Gloucester** 15 **Bristol** 20, **Bath** 12 **Leicester** 19. March 26: **Wasps** 28 **Leeds** 0, **Saracens** 29 **Worcester** 15, **Newcastle** 13 **Northampton** 32. April 7: **Leeds** 13 **Saracens** 17. April 8: **Worcester** 10 **London Irish** 12, **Sale** 18 **Gloucester** 15, **Northampton** 24 **Bath** 21. April 9: **Bristol** 23 **Newcastle** 7. April 14: **Northampton** 19 **Leicester** 24. April 15: **London Irish** 28 **Leeds** 24, **Gloucester** 27 **Worcester** 16, **Bath** 31 **Bristol** 16. April 16: **Saracens** 13 **Wasps** 12, **Newcastle** 32 **Sale** 21. April 22: **Leicester** 20 **Wasps** 19. April 28: **Saracens** 12 **Leicester** 13, **Sale** 38 **Bath** 12. April 29: **Worcester** 35 **Newcastle** 27. April 30: **Wasps** 37 **London Irish** 56, **Leeds** 7 **Gloucester** 31, **Bristol** 16 **Northampton** 19. May 6: **Northampton** 34 **Sale** 36, **Newcastle** 54 **Leeds** 19, **London Irish** 30 **Saracens** 18, **Leicester** 32 **Bristol** 3, **Gloucester** 32 **Wasps** 37 and **Bath** 25 **Worcester** 22

GUINNESS PREMIERSHIP FINAL TABLE

	P	W	D	L	F	A	BP	Pts
Sale	22	16	3	5	573	444	8	74
Leicester	22	14	3	5	518	415	6	68
London Irish	22	14	0	8	493	454	10	66
Wasps	22	12	3	7	527	447	10	64
Gloucester	22	11	1	10	483	385	13	59
Northampton	22	10	1	11	464	488	11	53
Newcastle	22	9	1	12	416	433	9	47
Worchester	22	9	1	12	451	494	9	47
Bath	22	9	1	12	441	494	8	46
Saracens	22	8	1	13	433	483	12	46
Bristol	22	8	1	13	393	445	7	41
Leeds	22	5	0	17	363	573	8	28

Dave Rogers/Getty Images

Champions at last! Sale celebrate their Premiership final win over Leicester.

PLAY-OFFS

SEMI-FINALS

14 May, Edgeley Park, Stockport

SALE 22 (1G, 5PG) WASPS 12 (4PG)

SALE: J Robinson; M Cueto, M Taylor, E Seveali'i, O Ripol; C Hodgson, S Martens; L Faure, A Titterrell, S Turner; C Jones, F Lobbe; J White (captain), M Lund, S Chabal Substitutions: S Bruno for Titterrel (50 mins); B Foden for Martens (59 mins); C Mayor (for Seveali'i, 62); B Stewart for Turner (54 mins); D Schofield for Lobbe (61 mins); Day for Lund (73 mins)

SCORERS *Try:* Robinson *Conversion:* Hodgson *Penalty Goals:* Hodgson (5)

WASPS: M van Gisbergen; P Sackey, J Lewsey, S Abbott, T Voyce; J Staunton, E Reddan; T Payne, J Ward, P Bracken; S Shaw, R Birkett; D Leo, J Worsley, L Dallaglio (captain) Substitutions: F Waters for Voyce (17 mins); J Haskell for Birkett (49 mins); R Ibanez for Ward (54 mins); M Dawson for Reddan (54 mins); A King for Staunton (59 mins); J Va'a for Payne (71 mins); M Lock for Leo (73 mins)

SCORERS *Penalty Goals:* van Gisbergen (4)

REFEREE C White (England)

14 May, Welford Road, Leicester

LEICESTER 40 (3G, 3PG, 2T)
LONDON IRISH 8 (1PG, 1T)

LEICESTER: G Murphy; A Tuilagi, O Smith, D Gibson, T Varndell; A Goode, H Ellis; G Rowntree, G Chuter, J White, Cullen, B Kay, Jennings, L Moody, M Corry (captain) Substitutions: A Healey for Ellis (temp 41 to 52 mins); W Johnson for Corry (temp 42 to 55 mins); L Lloyd for Varndell (58 mins); J Buckland for Chuter (61 mins); S Vesty for Tuilagi (70 mins); Healey for Ellis (71 mins)

SCORERS *Tries:* Lloyd (2), Tuilagi, Ellis, Murphy *Conversions:* Goode (3) *Penalty Goals:* Goode (3)

LONDON IRISH: D Armitage; T Ojo, M Catt (captain), D Feau'nati, S Tagicakibau; R Flutey, P Hodgson; N Hatley, R Russell, R Skuse, B Casey, K Roche, D Danaher, O Magne, J M Leguizamon Substitutions: D Paice for Russell (45 mins); N Kennedy for Magne (55 mins); P Murphy for Leguizamon (61 mins); G Tiesi for Feau'nati (61 mins); B Everitt for Tagicakibau (74 mins); B Willis for Hodgson (74 mins)

SCORERS *Try:* Magne *Penalty Goal:* Catt

REFEREE D Pearson (England)

FINAL

27 May, Twickenham, London

SALE 45 (2G, 7PG, 2T) LEICESTER 20 (2G, 2PG)

SALE: J Robinson; M Cueto, M Taylor, E Seveali'I, O Ripol; C Hodgson, R Wigglesworth; L Faure, A Titterrell, S Turner, C Jones, F Lobbe, J White (captain), M Lund, S Chabal (C Day 66–75).

SUBSTITUTIONS: D Schofield for Lobbe (40 mins); S Bruno for Titterrell (51 mins); B Stewart for Turner (52 mins); C Day for Chabal (temp 66 to 75 mins); C Major for Taylor (67 mins); B Foden for Wigglesworth (74 mins); Chabal for Jones (75 mins); V Courrent for Seveali'I (78 mins)

SCORERS *Tries:* Cueto, Lund, Ripol, *Major Conversions*: Hodgson, *Current Penalty Goals*: Hodgson (7)

LEICESTER: G Murphy; A Tuilagi, O Smith, D Gibson, T Varndell; A Goode, H Ellis; G Rowntree, G Chuter, J White, L Cullen, B Kay, S Jennings, L Moody, M Corry (captain) Substitutions: S Vesty for Tuilagi (46 mins); L Deacon for Jennings (50 mins); A Healey for Ellis (52 mins); J Hamilton for Cullen (54 mins); M Holford for Rowntree (59 mins); J Buckland for Chuter (62 mins); L Lloyd for Smith (64 mins)

SCORERS *Tries:* Moody, Hamilton *Conversions*: Goode (2) *Penalty Goals*: Goode (2)

REFEREE D Pearson (England)

Dave Rogers/Getty Images

Mark Cueto scores Sale's first try in their 45–20 win in the final.

OTHER MAJOR DOMESTIC WINNERS

NATIONAL ONE

NEC Harlequins

NATIONAL TWO

Moseley

NATIONAL THREE NORTH

Bradford & Bingley

NATIONAL THREE SOUTH

Cambridge

NORTH ONE

Morley

SOUTH WEST ONE

Cleve

MIDLANDS ONE

Rugby Lions

LONDON ONE

Canterbury

FIJI

FIJI'S TEST RECORD

OPPONENTS	DATE	VENUE	RESULT
Tonga	10 June	N	**Lost** 23–24
Italy	17 June	H	**Won** 29–18
Samoa	24 June	A	**Won** 23–20
Japan	1 July	A	**Won** 29–15

FIJI TARGET LONG-TERM DEVELOPMENT

By Jeremy Duxbury

All the groundwork recently carried out by the Fiji Rugby Union has paid dividends in several areas, most notably the IRB U21 and U19 World Championships, and of course the IRB World 7s. But the Fiji Test side's results in 2006 could be described as mediocre at best.

Moving away from the trend of throwing all their dollars at the

Mike Hewitt/Getty Images

Sevens genius William Ryder helped Fiji become the best in the world, again.

national team, the FRU made a conscious decision in mid-2005 to pay more attention to the youth levels of rugby and the competition structure of what is virtually a 12–month season.

The 2006 Colonial Cup, which comprises five semi-professional franchise teams, enjoyed the newly added layers of U19s and U21s – funded from the FRU's pockets – and the main provincial championship, the Sanyo Cup, was also given an U19 level for the first time.

In recent years, Fiji's age grade teams have suffered silently and gone away to tournaments ill-prepared and under-resourced. But this new initiative meant that the Fiji U19 team travelled to Dubai in April having played and camped together for some six weeks. At the FORU U21s tournament in March, the Fiji U19s got invaluable match practice against the U21 sides of Fiji, Samoa and Tonga.

Incredibly, this year was the first time Fiji had participated in the U19 World Championships, which have been held on an annual basis in one form or another since 1969.

And Josua Toakula's team didn't fail to excite, lighting up Division B with five consecutive victories and amassing a points differential of 171–63, thus earning them a berth in the top flight for 2007.

Several of these youngsters were also deemed good enough for the U21s team that competed in France in June when Fiji beat Scotland and Italy on their way to a respectable ninth place.

Skipper and Suva Grammar School hooker Andrew Durutalo was

particularly impressive, as was star centre Tomasi Mawi, who had earlier picked up a central contract with the Fiji 7s team.

A little worrying was the fact that the success of the team also caught the eyes of agents prowling the touchlines.

High-scoring wing, Seremaia Tagicakibau, later talked of wanting to become an All Black, No.8 Netava Ravouvou signed with French club Toulouse, and U21 fly-half Sisa Waqa turned down the opportunity to join the Fiji Test side in favour of club rugby in Australia.

Whilst such players will no doubt welcome the wonderful opportunities that have come their way, Fiji has no way of ensuring that their investment in these players will not turn into another nation's asset.

Another FRU initiative on the home front was revamping the 7s season so that the domestic series was run along provincial instead of club lines. Whilst 15 champions Nadroga powered their way to the BP Oil Provincial 7s title, the rise in the standard of the competition led to an immediate improvement in the Fiji 7s team on the IRB circuit, which they finally won at the seventh time of asking.

Player-coach Waisale Serevi and his posse of pals like William Ryder, Jone Daunivucu and Sireli Naqelevuki had the most consistent of seasons, winning four of the eight IRB tournaments and finishing runners-up in three others.

Of great assistance was a multi-million US dollar sponsorship with telecommunications company Digicel which allowed the FRU to contract a squad of 15 players.

But as with the age grade boys, the success of the Fiji 7s team led to a mass exodus of players to overseas clubs, meaning that for the 2006–07 IRB World 7s, Fiji will have to start all over again. Daunivucu and speedy wing Filimone Bolavucu joined French clubs Tarbes and Brive, respectively, whilst Naqelevuki went to Western Province in South Africa.

Ryder, by far the most exciting player on the 7s circuit, was momentarily linked to Perpignan, but his lack of 15s experience made it difficult for the French club to make a commitment. Ryder has yet to play the full code for a major province.

Once the BP Oil Series had finished in February, the Colonial Cup began its third year fighting to establish the franchise concept in Fiji. The Stallions (home of Nadroga, Navosa and Namosi) galloped home in style with a solid 29–15 victory in the final over the Highlanders, made up mainly of players from Suva and Naitasiri.

And one week later, the inaugural IRB Pacific Rugby Cup kicked off with the Fiji Warriors taking on the Fiji Barbarians at Ratu Cakobau Park in Nausori.

This cross-border competition that includes two teams from both Samoa and Tonga is designed to give local players some international experience as they strive to make the full Test side.

Picking what was meant to be the best 52 domestic-based players, the selectors raised some eyebrows in dropping Test centre Julian Vulakoro (the top points scorer in the last two Colonial Cups) and rampaging loose forward Sisa Koyamaibole, who at age 25 and with 33 Test caps to his name was suddenly deemed not good enough for the B and C sides.

On the coaching front, this new competition saw former Wallaby Ilivasi Tabua and former Super 12 stalwart Iliesa Tanivula return to their roots, the duo coaching the Fiji Barbarians to third-place with two excellent victories over the two Samoan sides, Upolu and eventual champions Savaii.

Akapusi Qera, top try scorer in the Colonial Cup, ended the Pacific Rugby Cup in the same fashion with four tries in five games. The Nadroga No.8 later joined English club Pertemps Bees, while his Warriors team-mates Kameli Ratuvou and Mosese Luveitasau went to Saracens and Cardiff Blues, respectively.

All this preparation and development work should have resulted in a cohesive unit for Wayne Pivac's Test side; yet the FMF Flying Fijians struggled to get out of first gear in their seven matches of June and July.

Coming off Fiji's poor tour to Europe in November 2005, the public were demanding better rugby. Though Fiji scraped victories over Italy,

Bradley Kanaris/Getty Images

Victories over Japan and Italy give Fiji hope for the World Cup.

Samoa and Japan, the losses to Tonga and the Junior All Blacks left a dissatisfied taste in the supporters' mouths which was soured further by two thumping defeats at the hands of Australia A.

It was a difficult pill to swallow – the age grade, provincial and franchise teams had all stepped up a level, but the main team continued to disappoint.

After the embarrassing 80–9 loss to Australia A in Melbourne (a record non-Test defeat for Fiji), strong calls for Pivac's head came from the provinces and public at large. Only a year out from the World Cup, the FRU decided to persevere with the New Zealander, but monitor his work more closely in the build-up to France 2007.

Now, without any Test matches until May 2007 because of the Pacific Islanders' UK tour, Fiji are left with plenty of time to think about things but no-one to play with.

Whatever happens at next year's World Cup, Fiji's efforts to improve the standard of local rugby ought really to bear fruit for the 2011 tournament.

FIJI INTERNATIONAL STATISTICS

MATCH RECORDS UP TO 30TH SEPTEMBER 2006

OVERALL MATCH RECORD

Played	Won	Lost	Drawn	PF	PA
253	123	122	8	5,190	4,825

MOST CONSECUTIVE TESTS WITHOUT DEFEAT

Matches	Wins	Draws	Periods
6	6	0	1955 to 1958

MOST POINTS IN A MATCH

BY THE TEAM

Pts.	Opponent	Venue	Year
120	Niue	Apia	1983
113	Solomons	Pt Moresby	1969
88	PNG	Pt Moresby	1969
86	Solomons	Apia	1983
86	PNG	Suva	1979
79	PNG	Pt Moresby	1969
76	Belgium	Liege	1989

BY A PLAYER

Pts.	Player	Opponent	Venue	Year
36	S Koroduadua	Niue	Apia	1983
25	N Little	Italy	L'Aquila	1999
24	S Sikivou	Solomons	Moresby	1969
24	T Makutu	PNG	Suva	1979
24	S Laulau	Solomons	Apia	1983
24	N Little	Hong Kong	Aberdeen	1996
23	N Little	Italy	Lautoka	2000
23	N Little	Samoa	Tokyo	2001

MOST TRIES IN A MATCH

BY THE TEAM

Tries	Opponent	Venue	Year
25	Solomons Is	Pt Moresby	1969
21	Niue	Apia	1983
20	PNG	Pt Moresby	1969
19	PNG	Pt Moresby	1969
18	PNG	Suva	1979
16	Solomons	Apia	1983
14	Belgium	Liege	1989

BY A PLAYER

Tries	Player	Opponent	Venue	Year
6	T Makutu	PNG	Suva	1979
6	S Laulau	Solomons	Apia	1983
5	G Sailosi	PNG	Pt Moresby	1969
4	S Yalayala	Niue	Apia	1983
4	K Salusalu	Niue	Apia	1983
4	S Yalayala	Solomons	Apia	1983
4	S Laulau	Solomons	Apia	1983
4	J Kuinikoro	PNG	Suva	1979
4	E Teleni	Belgium	Liege	1989
4	N Korovata	Hong Kong	HK	1990
4	R Caucau	Chile	Santiago	2003

MOST CONVERSIONS IN A MATCH

BY THE TEAM

Cons	Opponent	Venue	Year
19	PNG	Port Moresby	1969
18	Niue	Apia	1983
14	PNG	Port Moresby	1969
11	PNG	Port Moresby	1969
11	Solomons	Apia	1983
10	Belgium	Liege	1989
8	Namibia	Beziers	1999

BY A PLAYER

Cons	Player	Opponent	Venue	Year
18	S Koroduadua	Niue	Apia	1983
12	S Sikivou	Solomons	Moresby	1969
11	I Musunamasi	Solomons	Apia	1983
10	S Koroduadua	Belgium	Liege	1989
8	W Serevi	Namibia	Beziers	1999

MOST PENALTIES IN A MATCH

BY THE TEAM

Pens	Opponent	Venue	Year
7	Samoa	Tokyo	2001
6	Tonga	Nuku'alofa	2001
6	Tonga	Nuku'alofa	2000
6	Hong Kong	Aberdeen	1996
6	Tonga	Nuku'alofa	1967

BY A PLAYER

Pens	Player	Opponent	Venue	Year
7	N Little	Samoa	Tokyo	2001
6	I Tabualevu	Tonga	Nuku'alofa	1967
6	N Little	HK	Aberdeen	1996
6	N Little	Tonga	Nuku'alofa	2000
6	N Little	Tonga	Nuku'alofa	2001

MOST DROPPED GOALS IN A MATCH

BY THE TEAM

Drops	Opponent	Venue	Year
3	Romania	Brive	1991
3	W Samoa	Nadi	1994

BY A PLAYER

Drops	Player	Opponent	Venue	Year
3	O Turuva	W Samoa	Nadi	1994
2	T Rabaka	Romania	Brive	1991

MOST CAPPED PLAYERS

Caps	Player	Career span
60	N Little	1996 to 2005
50	E Katalau	1995 to 2003
50	J Rauluni	1995 to 2006
49	J Veitayaki	1994 to 2003
46	I Tawake	1985 to 1999
44	G Smith	1995 to 2003
43	S Raiwalui	1997 to 2006
39	W Serevi	1989 to 2003
38	I Savai	1984 to 1995
37	I Rasila	1992 to 2003
37	N Ligairi	2000 to 2006

MOST POINTS IN TESTS

Pts	Player	Tests	Career
599	N Little	60	1996 to 2005
250	S Koroduadua	27	1982 to 1991
219	W Serevi	39	1989 to 2003
105	S Baikeinuku	24	2000 to 2006
80	S Laulau	32	1985 to 1991
80	V Satala	27	1999 to 2002
80	F Lasagavibau	23	1997 to 2002
80	N Ligairi	37	2000 to 2006
65	A Tuilevu	19	1996 to 2004
60	I Batibasaga	13	1970 to 1979
60	M Bari	18	1995 to 1999

MOST TRIES IN TESTS

Tries	Player	Tests	Career
20	S Laulau	32	1980 to 1985
16	V Satala	27	1999 to 2002
16	F Lasagavibau	23	1997 to 2002
16	N Ligairi	37	2000 to 2006
13	A Tuilevu	19	1996 to 2004
12	M Bari	18	1995 to 1999
11	W Serevi	39	1989 to 2003
11	K Salusalu	15	1982 to 1990
10	S Yalayala	11	1983 to 1986
9	V Varo	7	1970 to 1973
9	J Kuinikoro	11	1977 to 1980
9	I Tiko	11	1999 to 2000
9	R Caucau	6	2003 to 2006
8	J Levula	17	1951 to 1961
8	E Lovodua	11	1958 to 1964
8	E Teleni	23	1982 to 1989
8	T Vonolagi	16	1988 to 1993
8	V Delasau	21	2000 to 2005

MOST PENALTY GOALS IN TESTS

Pens	Player	Tests	Career
125	N Little	60	1996 to 2005
41	S Koroduadua	27	1982 to 1991
27	W Serevi	39	1989 to 2003
16	S Baikeinuku	24	2000 to 2006
10	I Batibasaga	13	1970 to 1979
9	E Rokowailoa	17	1982 to 1993

MOST DROPPED GOALS IN TESTS

DGs	Player	Tests	Career
6	O Turuva	11	1990 to 1999
5	S Koroduadua	27	1982 to 1991
3	W Serevi	39	1989 to 2003
2	P Tikoisuva	20	1968 to 1979
2	T Vonolagi	16	1988 to 1993
2	T Rabaka	4	1991
2	N Little	60	1996 to 2005

MOST CONVERSIONS IN TESTS

Cons	Player	Tests	Career
104	N Little	60	1996 to 2005
56	S Koroduadua	27	1982 to 1991
39	W Serevi	39	1989 to 2003
17	S Baikeinuku	24	2000 to 2006
16	S Sikivou	6	1969 to 1973
13	A Batibasaga	6	1967 to 1969
13	I Batibasaga	13	1970 to 1979

Chris McGarth/Getty Images

Nicky Little reigns supreme when it comes to goal-kicking Fijians.

CAREER RECORDS FOR FIJI INTERNATIONAL PLAYERS (UP TO 30 SEPTEMBER 2006)

PLAYER	DEBUT	CAPS	T	C	P	D	PTS
BACKS							
S Baikeinuku	2000 v J	25	4	17	16	1	105
A Buto	Uncapped	0	0	0	0	0	0
R Caucaunibuca	2003 v Arg	6	9	0	0	0	45
J Daunivucu	Uncapped	0	0	0	0	0	0
M Kunavore	2005 v Sm	5	2	0	0	0	10
S Leawere	2003 v Tg	5	2	0	0	0	10
N Ligairi	2000 v Tg	37	16	0	0	0	80
M Luveitasau	2005 v Sm	8	4	0	0	0	20
I Nalawaniavi	Uncapped	0	0	0	0	0	0
S Rabeni	2000 v J	21	1	0	0	0	5
N Nanuku	2005 v Pt	1	0	0	0	0	0
J Ratu	Uncapped	0	0	0	0	0	0
K Ratuvou	2005 v Sm	8	3	0	0	0	15
J Rauluni	1995 v C	50	6	0	0	0	30
E Ruivadra	2002 v Tg	17	1	0	0	0	5
S Takamaiwai	2006 v Tg	1	0	0	0	0	0
J Tora	2005 v Tg	7	0	1	0	0	2
J Tuilevu	Uncapped	0	0	0	0	0	0
E Vucago	2006 v Tg	1	0	0	0	0	0
FORWARDS							
J Bale	2004 v Tg	14	0	0	0	0	0
I Domolailai	2001 v I	12	0	0	0	0	0
A Doviverata	1999 v Sp	35	5	0	0	0	25
S Koto	2005 v M	10	0	0	0	0	0
W Lewaravu	Uncapped	0	0	0	0	0	0
J Lotawa	2004 v Tg	5	0	0	0	0	0
A Naevo	1996 v HK	35	6	0	0	0	30
S Naevo	2006 v Sm	2	0	0	0	0	0
A Nagi	2001 v I	11	0	0	0	0	0
A Qera	2005 v Sm	6	1	0	0	0	5
J Qovu	2005 v M	8	0	0	0	0	0
T Rabukawaqa	Uncapped	0	0	0	0	0	0
S Raiwalui	1997 v NZ	43	3	0	0	0	15
A Ratuva	2005 v M	10	0	0	0	0	0
I Rawaqa	2002 v Sm	24	2	0	0	0	10
K Salabogi	2005 v W	4	1	0	0	0	5
R Samo	2005 v Tg	5	0	0	0	0	0
S Matadigo	2006 v Tg	1	0	0	0	0	0
N Talei	2006 v Tg	4	0	0	0	0	0
M Vasuitoga	Uncapped	0	0	0	0	0	0

FRANCE

FRANCE'S TEST RECORD

OPPONENTS	DATE	VENUE	RESULT
Scotland	5 February	A	**Lost** 16–20
Ireland	11 February	H	**Won** 43–31
Italy	25 February	H	**Won** 37–12
England	12 March	H	**Won** 31–6
Wales	18 March	A	**Won** 21–16
Romania	17 June	A	**Won** 62–14
South Africa	24 June	A	**Lost** 26–36

GLORY FOR FRANCE

To suggest France began their preparations for the 2006 Six Nations with more than one eye on 2007, the World Cup and their hopes as hosts to finally lift the Webb Ellis Cup would not be to detract from the importance of the Championship.

While it was certainly true the French would have happily sacrificed immediate Six Nations success in return for future World Cup glory on

Dave Rogers/Getty Images

It's ours! France celebrate after being confirmed 2006 RBS Six Nations champions.

home soil, coach Bernard Laporte was still acutely aware his developing line-up needed to start getting results under their belt sooner rather than later.

Laporte's team had shown plenty of promise but little killer instinct in 2005, surrendering their Championship crown to Wales and failing to beat the Springboks (twice) or the Wallabies on their summer travels. Australia and South Africa were downed in revenge in Paris in the autumn (as were Tonga and Canada) but France's progress seemed frustratingly slow. Time was running out for Laporte to shape his side for the World Cup and expectations of it all falling into place in 2006 were not high.

The French kicked off the year against Scotland at Murrayfield, where they hadn't lost for a decade. The visitors were the hot favourites to start the campaign with a win but the Scots had clearly forgotten to read the approved script. Wing Sean Lamont scored either side of the break and although France crossed late on through Julien Bonnaire and Sebastien Bruno, Chris Paterson's two successful conversions compared to two miscued two-pointers from Jean-Baptiste Elissalde was the difference and Scotland claimed an unexpected 20–16 victory.

"We didn't have the rhythm we had in November," said Laporte. "Scotland dominated us in the rolling maul. We were shaky early on and we dragged that feeling with us throughout the match."

"Paradoxically, we had one of our best second-halves, but it was too late. If we hadn't given away those 10 points at the start we'd have won.

"They stopped us playing and this is a very difficult place to come. They never let us to get into a rhythm and now I think we have a 50/50 chance of winning this championship."

Victory over Ireland at the Stade de France a week later became an absolute necessity. The French public waited in anticipation for a performance worthy of genuine World Cup contenders and for the first 47 minutes in Paris they got their wish as their side ran in six tries for a scarcely believable 43–3 lead.

But then the old frailties they showed in Edinburgh resurfaced as Ireland scored four unanswered tries of their own to set French nerves jangling and the crowd whistling their disapproval. The home side clung on for a far-from-convincing 43–31 win.

"This team is not at its best," admitted veteran flanker Olivier Magne. "Our first half was very good, the second half was not what we expected.

"It was an incredible start. We were very motivated when the match began and we did well but we have to play like that for 80 minutes. We were very determined to finish this game well and we are very motivated for the next game."

The next game was Italy at the Stade de France but once again Laporte's side flattered to deceive despite scoring five tries in what might have seemed a convincing 37–12 victory. In reality, the Azzurri pushed the home side all the way and it was only late scores from Pieter de Villiers, Aurelien Rougerie and Frederic Michalak in the closing 15 minutes that gave Les Bleus their final cushion.

Laporte declared himself satisfied with the team's display after the match but full-back Thomas Castaignede admitted Les Bleus were still far from firing on all cylinders. "In the next game against England we will have to do much better if we want to win," he said.

"At this level, whoever you play, you must do everything right and we didn't. We didn't play well in the first half when we made mistakes."

The England game was France's third in succession in Paris and this time it was the visitors and not Laporte's men who made all the mistake at crucial times.

First England spilled a speculative up-and-under in the first minute to gift Florian Fritz a try and then proceeded to give away a series of needless penalties which Dimitri Yachvili gleefully slotted over. By the time Andy Goode's late second-half pass was intercepted by Christophe Dominici for France's third try, the game was well and truly over and England were beaten by a record-equalling 31–6 scoreline. Despite not being at their fluid best, France had seen off their old rivals and were still in contention for the Six Nations crown.

Richard Heathcote/Getty Images

France coach Bernard Laporte masterminded a campaign to make his side Europe's best, again!

"The players handled the pressure very well and with a lot of determination," Laporte said. "That is what made the difference. The England team came into the match with a certain number of doubts after what happened against Scotland.

"For both teams this was a must-win match and the fact we scored early was very important. After the first try we put the pressure on for the first 15 minutes of the match.

"Our objective now is to go to Wales and win the title. This was an important match because the result was a determining factor in who wins the tournament. We haven't won the title yet, but we are on the right track."

The final round of matches in March were intriguing. France played Wales in Cardiff but knew that even if they managed to win in the Millennium Stadium their hopes of becoming champions would still depend on what happened to Ireland at Twickenham later the same day. Les Bleus could win yet still lose.

The Cardiff clash was suitably tense from the start. Wales went ahead with a Stephen Jones penalty, France levelled through Yachvili, Jones struck again and then Hal Luscombe crashed over to give the home side a 13–6 interval lead.

After the break France clawed their way back with a Dimitri Szarzewski try and after Gavin Henson and Elissalde penalties, it seemed Wales were heading for a 16–14 win. That is until Fritz stormed over with just five minutes left on the clock and Les Bleus were 21–16 victors.

Ireland now needed to beat England by 34 clear points to deny Laporte's side but could only muster a 28–24 triumph and France were confirmed as champions for the third time in five years.

Perhaps predictably, however, the French camp could only see their achievement in terms of the impending World Cup.

"We have now won 13 of the last 15 matches over three years in the Six Nations," said team manager Jo Maso. "We are undefeated in France in seven matches since November. We have also got the record number of points since 2000 in the Six Nations. This team is going to go a long way."

By comparison to their Six Nations rivals, France had a relatively quiet summer schedule. A trip to Bucharest to face newly-crowned European Nations Cup champions Romania in mid June yielded nine tries in a straightforward 62–14 win but it was the following week's fixture – South Africa in Cape Town – that would provide real evidence of France's progress.

Les Bleus had drawn 30–30 in Durban and then were beaten 27–13 in Port Elizabeth the previous summer and the one-off Newlands match now provided France will a timely test of their development. The Springboks were unbeaten in their last 13 home games stretching back two-and-a-half years while France had not won in South Africa since 2001. The stage was set for a Gallic statement of intent.

And the message from the French forwards was clear as they took the game to the Springboks, established a rock solid platform against their much-vaunted rivals and then sat back and watched their backs accept the invitation and run in four tries – two from wing Vincent Clerc – in a 36–26 win.

A year which had begun in stuttering defeat to Scotland had finished with the northern hemisphere's only summer win over southern hemisphere opposition, a first ever French win at Newlands and signs the host nation will be a genuine force to be reckoned with at the next World Cup.

"This was a good day for French rugby," said veteran captain Fabien Pelous. "We know South Africa are a physical team and we knew we had to be at the same level if we were going to exist alongside them. I think we managed that today.

"It's always a pleasure playing here in South Africa because we know it will be very tough. I like these sort of forwards games and the win will give us good confidence ahead of the World Cup.

"We still have work to do, but we showed today that if you are really committed you can go further and keep running."

FRANCE INTERNATIONAL STATISTICS

MATCH RECORDS UP TO 30TH SEPTEMBER 2006

MOST CONSECUTIVE TEST WINS

10 1931 E,G, 1932 G, 1933 G, 1934 G, 1935 G, 1936 G1,2, 1937 G,It
8 1998 E, S, I, W, Arg 1, 2, Fj, Arg 3
8 2001 SA 3 A, Fj 2002 It, W, E, S,I
8 2004 I, It, W, S, E, US, C, A

MOST CONSECUTIVE TESTS WITHOUT DEFEAT

Matches	Wins	Draws	Periods
10	10	0	1931 to 1938
10	8	2	1958 to 1959
10	9	1	1986 to 1987

MOST POINTS IN A MATCH

BY THE TEAM

Pts.	Opponent	Venue	Year
77	Fiji	Saint Etienne	2001
70	Zimbabwe	Auckland	1987
67	Romania	Bucharest	2000
64	Romania	Aurillac	1996
62	Romania	Castres	1999
62	Romania	Bucharest	2006
61	Fiji	Brisbane	2003
60	Italy	Toulon	1967
59	Romania	Paris	1924
56	Romania	Lens	2003
56	Italy	Rome	2005

BY A PLAYER

Pts.	Player	Opponent	Venue	Year
30	D Camberabero	Zimbabwe	Auckland	1987
28	C Lamaison	New Zealand	Twickenham	1999
28	F Michalak	Scotland	Sydney	2003
27	G Camberabero	Italy	Toulon	1967
27	C Lamaison	New Zealand	Marseilles	2000
27	G Merceron	South Africa	Johannesburg	2001
26	T Lacroix	Ireland	Durban	1995
26	F Michalak	Fiji	Brisbane	2003
25	J-P Romeu	United States	Chicago	1976
25	P Berot	Romania	Agen	1987
25	T Lacroix	Tonga	Pretoria	1995

MOST TRIES IN A MATCH

BY THE TEAM

Tries	Opponent	Venue	Year
13	Romania	Paris	1924
13	Zimbabwe	Auckland	1987
12	Fiji	Saint Etienne	2001
11	Italy	Toulon	1967
10	Romania	Aurillac	1996
10	Romania	Bucharest	2000

BY A PLAYER

Tries	Player	Opponent	Venue	Year
4	A Jauréguy	Romania	Paris	1924
4	M Celhay	Italy	Paris	1937

MOST CONVERSIONS IN A MATCH

BY THE TEAM

Cons	Opponent	Venue	Year
9	Italy	Toulon	1967
9	Zimbabwe	Auckland	1987
8	Romania	Wellington	1987
8	Romania	Lens	2003

BY A PLAYER

Cons	Player	Opponent	Venue	Year
9	G Camberabero	Italy	Toulon	1967
9	D Camberabero	Zimbabwe	Auckland	1987
8	G Laporte	Romania	Wellington	1987

MOST PENALTIES IN A MATCH

BY THE TEAM

Pens	Opponent	Venue	Year
8	Ireland	Durban	1995
7	Wales	Paris	2001
7	Italy	Paris	2002
6	Argentina	Buenos Aires	1977
6	Scotland	Paris	1997
6	Italy	Auch	1997
6	Ireland	Paris	2000
6	South Africa	Johannesburg	2001
6	Argentina	Buenos Aires	2003
6	Fiji	Brisbane	2003
6	England	Twickenham	2005

BY A PLAYER

Pens	Player	Opponent	Venue	Year
8	T Lacroix	Ireland	Durban	1995
7	G Merceron	Italy	Paris	2002
6	J-M Aguirre	Argentina	Buenos Aires	1977
6	C Lamaison	Scotland	Paris	1997
6	C Lamaison	Italy	Auch	1997
6	G Merceron	Ireland	Paris	2000
6	G Merceron	South Africa	Johannesburg	2001
6	D Yachvili	England	Twickenham	2005
6	F Michalak	Fiji	Brisbane	2003

MOST DROPPED GOALS IN A MATCH

BY THE TEAM

Drops	Opponent	Venue	Year
3	Ireland	Paris	1960
3	England	Twickenham	1985
3	New Zealand	Christchurch	1986
3	Australia	Sydney	1990
3	Scotland	Paris	1991
3	New Zealand	Christchurch	1994

BY A PLAYER

Drops	Player	Opponent	Venue	Year
3	P Albaladejo	Ireland	Paris	1960
3	J-P Lescarboura	England	Twickenham	1985
3	J-P Lescarboura	New Zealand	Christchurch	1986
3	D Camberabero	Australia	Sydney	1990

CAREER RECORDS

MOST CAPPED PLAYERS

Caps	Player	Career span
111	P Sella	1982 to 1995
109	F Pelous	1995 to 2006
93	S Blanco	1980 to 1991
87	O Magne	1997 to 2006
80	R Ibañez	1996 to 2006
78	A Benazzi	1990 to 2001
71	J-L Sadourny	1991 to 2001
71	O Brouzet	1994 to 2003
69	R Bertranne	1971 to 1981
69	P Saint-André	1990 to 1997
69	C Califano	1994 to 2003
65	S Marconnet	1998 to 2006
64	F Galthie	1991 to 2003
63	M Crauste	1957 to 1966
63	B Dauga	1964 to 1972

MOST CONSECUTIVE TESTS

Caps	Player	Career span
46	R Bertranne	1973 to 1979
45	P Sella	1982 to 1987
44	M Crauste	1960 to 1966
35	B Dauga	1964 to 1968

MOST TESTS AS CAPTAIN

Caps	Captain	Career span
41	F Pelous	1997 to 2006
34	J-P Rives	1978 to 1984
34	P Saint-André	1994 to 1997
27	R Ibanez	1998 to 2003
25	D Dubroca	1986 to 1988
25	F Galthié	1999 to 2003
24	G Basquet	1948 to 1952
22	M Crauste	1961 to 1966

MOST POINTS IN TESTS

Pts	Player	Tests	Career
380	C Lamaison	37	1996 to 2001
367	T Lacroix	43	1989 to 1997
354	D Camberabero	36	1982 to 1993
267	G Merceron	32	1999 to 2003
265	J-P Romeu	34	1972 to 1977
247	T Castaignède	52	1995 to 2006
243	F Michalak	42	2001 to 2006
233	S Blanco	93	1980 to 1991
207	D Yachvili	29	2002 to 2006
200	J-P Lescarboura	28	1982 to 1990

MOST TRIES IN TESTS

Tries	Player	Tests	Career
38	S Blanco	93	1980 to 1991
33	P Saint-André	69	1990 to 1997
30	P Sella	111	1982 to 1995
26	E Ntamack	46	1994 to 2000
26	P Bernat Salles	41	1992 to 2001
23	C Darrouy	40	1957 to 1967

MOST CONVERSIONS IN TESTS

Cons	Player	Tests	Career
59	C Lamaison	37	1996 to 2001
48	D Camberabero	36	1982 to 1993
45	M Vannier	43	1953 to 1961
42	T Castaignède	52	1995 to 2006
36	R Dourthe	31	1995 to 2001
36	G Merceron	32	1999 to 2003
36	F Michalak	42	2001 to 2006
32	T Lacroix	43	1989 to 1997
31	D Yachvili	29	2002 to 2006
29	P Villepreux	34	1967 to 1972

MOST PENALTY GOALS IN TESTS

Pens	Player	Tests	Career
89	T Lacroix	43	1989 to 1997
78	C Lamaison	37	1996 to 2001
59	D Camberabero	36	1982 to 1993
57	G Merceron	32	1999 to 2003
56	J-P Romeu	34	1972 to 1977
43	D Yachvili	29	2002 to 2006
37	F Michalak	42	2001 to 2006
33	P Villepreux	34	1967 to 1972
33	P Bérot	19	1986 to 1989

MOST DROPPED GOALS IN TESTS

Drops	Player	Tests	Career
15	J-P Lescarboura	28	1982 to 1990
12	P Albaladejo	30	1954 to 1964
11	G Camberabero	14	1961 to 1968
11	D Camberabero	36	1982 to 1993
9	J-P Romeu	34	1972 to 1977

Getty Images

No Frenchman has got close to Serge Blanco's try-scoring record, established 15 years ago.

INTERNATIONAL CHAMPIONSHIP RECORDS

RECORD	DETAIL		SET
Most points in season	156	in five matches	2002
Most tries in season	18	in four matches	1998
	18	in five matches	2006
Highest Score	56	56–13 v Italy	2005
Biggest win	51	51–0 v Wales	1998
Highest score conceded	49	14–49 v Wales	1910
Biggest defeat	37	0–37 v England	1911
Most appearances	50	P Sella	1983–1995
Most points in matches	155	D Yachvili	2003–2006
Most points in season	80	G Merceron	2002
Most points in match	24	S Viars	v Ireland, 1992
	24	C Lamaison	v Scotland, 1997
	24	J-B Elissalde	v Wales, 2004
Most tries in matches	14	S Blanco	1981–1991
	14	P Sella	1983 – 1995
Most tries in season	5	P Estève	1983
	5	E Bonneval	1987
	5	E Ntamack	1999
	5	P Bernat Salles	2001
Most tries in match	3	M Crauste	v England, 1962
	3	C Darrouy	v Ireland, 1963
	3	E Bonneval	v Scotland, 1987
	3	D Venditti	v Ireland, 1997
	3	E Ntamack	v Wales, 1999
Most cons in matches	23	C Lamaison	1997–2001
	23	D Yachvili	2003–2006
Most cons in season	9	C Lamaison	1998
	9	G Merceron	2002
	9	D Yachvili	2003
Most cons in match	6	D Yachvili	v Italy, 2003
Most pens in matches	34	G Merceron	2000 – 2003
Most pens in season	18	G Merceron	2002
Most pens in match	7	G Merceron	v Italy, 2002
Most drops in matches	9	J-P Lescarboura	1982–1988
Most drops in season	5	G Camberabero	1967
Most drops in match	3	P Albaladejo	v Ireland, 1960
	3	J-P Lescarboura	v England, 1985

MISCELLANEOUS RECORDS

RECORD	HOLDER	DETAIL
Longest Test Career	F Haget	1974 to 1987
Youngest Test Cap	C Dourthe	18 yrs 7 days in 1966
Oldest Test Cap	A Roques	37 yrs 329 days in 1963

CAREER RECORDS OF FRANCE INTERNATIONAL PLAYERS (PLAYERS CAPPED SINCE THE START OF RWC 2003 UP TO 30 SEPTEMBER 2006)

PLAYER BACKS	DEBUT	CAPS	T	C	P	D	PTS
B Baby	2005 v I	3	1	0	0	0	5
M Barrau	2004 v US	3	1	0	0	0	5
P Bidabé	2004 v C	2	0	0	0	0	0
D Bory	2000 v I	18	2	0	0	0	10
G Bousses	2006 v S	1	0	0	0	0	0
B Boyet	2006 v I	1	0	0	0	0	0
N Brusque	1997 v R	27	7	0	0	1	38
J Candelon	2005 v SA	2	2	0	0	0	10
T Castaignède	1995 v R	52	17	42	21	5	247
V Clerc	2002 SA	16	9	0	0	0	45
Y Delaigue	1994 v S	20	2	0	5	4	37
C Dominici	1998 v E	52	19	0	0	0	95
P Elhorga	2001 v NZ	16	3	0	0	0	15
J-B Elissalde	2000 v S	18	3	20	24	0	127
F Fritz	2005 v SA	9	2	0	0	1	13
F Galthié	1991 v R	64	10	0	0	0	49
J-P Grandclaude	2005 v E	2	0	0	0	0	0
C Heymans	2000 v It	24	6	0	0	0	30
Y Jauzion	2001 v SA	34	12	0	0	1	63
J Laharrague	2005 v W	10	3	0	0	0	15
B Liebenberg	2003 v R	12	5	0	0	0	25
L Loustau	2004 v C	1	0	0	0	0	0
J Marlu	1998 v Fj	4	0	0	0	0	0
T Marsh	2001 v SA	21	7	0	0	0	35
D Marty	2005 v It	6	6	0	0	0	30
G Merceron	1999 v R	32	3	36	57	3	267
F Michalak	2001 v SA	42	9	36	37	5	243
P Mignoni	1997 v R	17	5	0	0	0	25
A Péclier	2004 v US	2	0	9	5	0	33
J Peyrelongue	2004 v It	6	0	0	1	0	3
C Poitrenaud	2001 v SA	21	4	0	0	0	20
A Rougerie	2001 v SA	42	19	0	0	0	95
D Traille	2001 v SA	46	12	7	10	1	107
L Valbon	2004 v US	4	1	0	0	0	5
D Yachvili	2002 v C	29	2	31	43	2	207

FORWARDS							
D Attoub	2006 v R	1	0	0	0	0	0
D Auradou	1999 v E	41	0	0	0	0	0
D Avril	2005 v A	1	0	0	0	0	0
S Betsen	1997 v It	49	9	0	0	0	45
J Bonnaire	2004 v S	21	4	0	0	0	20
O Brouzet	1994 v S	71	2	0	0	0	10
Y Bru	2001 v A	18	1	0	0	0	5
S Bruno	2002 v W	16	2	0	0	0	10
S Chabal	2000 v S	24	0	0	0	0	0
D Couzinet	2004 v US	2	0	0	0	0	0
J-J Crenca	1996 v SA	39	4	0	0	0	20
V Debaty	2006 v R	1	0	0	0	0	0
P de Villiers	1999 v W	56	2	0	0	0	10
T Dusautoir	2006 v R	2	1	0	0	0	5
R Froment	2004 v US	1	0	0	0	0	0
B Goutta	2004 v C	1	1	0	0	0	5
I Harinordoquy	2002 v W	34	9	0	0	0	45
R Ibañez	1996 v W	80	6	0	0	0	30
C Labit	1999 v S	17	0	0	0	0	0
G Lamboley	2005 v S	12	1	0	0	0	5
T Lièvremont	1996 v W	35	6	0	0	0	30
O Magne	1997 v W	87	14	0	0	0	70
S Marconnet	1998 v Arg	65	3	0	0	0	15
R Martin	2002 v E	13	2	0	0	0	10
A Martinez	2002 v A	2	0	0	0	0	0
N Mas	2003 v NZ	5	0	0	0	0	0
R Millo-Chluski	2005 v SA	1	0	0	0	0	0
O Milloud	2000 v R	34	0	0	0	0	0
L Nallet	2000 v R	19	1	0	0	0	5
Y Nyanga	2004 v US	19	3	0	0	0	15
P Papé	2004 v I	12	2	0	0	0	10
F Pelous	1995 v R	109	7	0	0	0	35
J-B Poux	2001 v Fj	11	3	0	0	0	15
T Privat	2001 v SA	10	0	0	0	0	0
P Rabadan	2004 v US	2	0	0	0	0	0
W Servat	2004 v I	16	0	0	0	0	0
D Szarzewski	2004 v C	10	3	0	0	0	15
P Tabacco	2001 v SA	18	1	0	0	0	5
J Thion	2003 v Arg	28	0	0	0	0	0

FRENCH INTERNATIONAL PLAYERS

UP TO 30TH SEPTEMBER 2006

Note: Years given for International Championship matches are for second half of season; eg 1972 means season 1971–72. Years for all other matches refer to the actual year of the match. Entries in square brackets denote matches played in RWC Finals.

Abadie, A (Pau) 1964 I
Abadie, A (Graulhet) 1965 R, 1967 SA 1,3,4, NZ, 1968 S, I
Abadie, L (Tarbes) 1963 R
Accoceberry, G (Bègles) 1994 NZ 1,2, C 2, 1995 W, E, S, I, R 1, [Iv, S], It, 1996 I, W 1, R, Arg 1, W 2(R), SA 2, 1997 S, It 1
Aguerre, R (Biarritz O) 1979 S
Aguilar, D (Pau) 1937 G
Aguirre, J-M (Bagnères) 1971 A 2, 1972 S, 1973 W, I, J, R, 1974 I, W, Arg 2, R, SA 1, 1976 W (R), E, US, A 2, R, 1977 W, E, S, I, Arg 1,2, NZ 1,2, R, 1978 E, S, I, W, R, 1979 I, W, E, S, NZ 1,2, R, 1980 W, I
Ainciart, E (Bayonne) 1933 G, 1934 G, 1935 G, 1937 G, It, 1938 G 1
Albaladejo, P (Dax) 1954 E, It, 1960 W, I, It, R, 1961 S, SA, E, W, I, NZ 1,2, A, 1962 S, E, W, I, 1963 S, I, E, W, It, 1964 S, NZ, W, It, I, SA, Fj
Albouy, A (Castres) 2002 It (R)
Alvarez, A-J (Tyrosse) 1945 B2, 1946 B, I, K, W, 1947 S, I, W, E, 1948 I, A, S, W, E, 1949 I, E, W, 1951 S, E, W
Amand, H (SF) 1906 NZ
Ambert, A (Toulouse) 1930 S, I, E, G, W
Amestoy, J-B (Mont-de-Marsan) 1964 NZ, E
André, G (RCF) 1913 SA, E, W, I, 1914 I, W, E
Andrieu, M (Nîmes) 1986 Arg 2, NZ 1, R 2, NZ 2, 1987 [R, Z], R, 1988 E, S, I, W, Arg 1,2,3,4, R, 1989 I, W, E, S, NZ 2, B, A 2, 1990 W, E, I (R)
Anduran, J (SCUF) 1910 W
Aqua, J-L (Toulon) 1999 R, Tg, NZ 1(R)
Araou, R (Narbonne) 1924 R
Arcalis, R (Brive) 1950 S, I, 1951 I, E, W
Arino, M (Agen) 1962 R
Aristouy, P (Pau) 1948 S, 1949 Arg 2, 1950 S, I, E, W
Arlettaz, P (Perpignan) 1995 R 2
Armary, L (Lourdes) 1987 [R], R, 1988 S, I, W, Arg 3,4, R, 1989 W, S, A 1,2, 1990 W, E, S, I, A 1,2,3, NZ 1, 1991 W 2, 1992 S, I, R, Arg 1,2, SA 1,2, Arg, 1993 E, S, I, W, SA 1,2, R 2, A 1,2, 1994 I, W, NZ 1(t),2(t), 1995 I, R 1 [Tg, I, SA]
Arnal, J-M (RCF) 1914 I, W
Arnaudet, M (Lourdes) 1964 I, 1967 It, W
Arotca, R (Bayonne) 1938 R
Arrieta, J (SF) 1953 E, W
Arthapignet, P (see Harislur-Arthapignet)
Artiguste, E (Castres) 1999 WS
Astre, R (Béziers) 1971 R, 1972 I 1, 1973 E (R), 1975 E, S, I, SA 1,2, Arg 2, 1976 A 2, R
Attoub, D (Castres) 2006 R
Aucagne, D (Pau) 1997 W (R), S, It 1, R 1(R), A 1, R 2(R), SA 2(R), 1998 S (R), W (R), Arg 2(R), Fj (R), Arg 3, A, 1999 W 1(R), S (R)
Audebert, A (Montferrand) 2000 R, 2002 W (R)
Aué, J-M (Castres) 1998 W (R)
Augé, J (Dax) 1929 S, W
Augras-Fabre, L (Agen) 1931 I, S, W
Auradou, D (SF) 1999 E (R), S (R), WS (R), Tg, NZ 1, W 2(R), [Arg (R)], 2000 A (R), NZ 1,2, 2001 S, I, It, W, E (R), SA 1,2, NZ (R), SA 3, A, Fj, 2002 It, E, I (R), C (R), 2003 S (R), It (R), W (R), Arg, 1,2, NZ (R), R (R), E 2(R),3, [J(R),US,NZ] , 2004 I(R), It(R),S(R),E(R)
Averous, J-L (La Voulte) 1975 S, I, SA 1,2, 1976 I, W, E, US, A 1,2, R, 1977 W, E, S, I, Arg 1, R, 1978 E, S, I, 1979 NZ 1,2, 1980 E, S, 1981 A 2
Avril, D (Biarritz) 2005 A1
Azam, O (Montferrand, Gloucester) 1995 R 2, Arg (R), 2000 A (R), NZ 2(R), 2001 SA 2(R), NZ, 2002 E (R), I (R), Arg (R), A 1
Azarete, J-L (Dax, St Jean-de-Luz) 1969 W, R, 1970 S, I, W, R, 1971 S, I, E, SA 1,2, A 1, 1972 E, W, I 2, A 1, R, 1973 NZ, W, I, R, 1974 I, R, SA 1,2, 1975 W

Baby, B (Toulouse) 2005 I,SA2(R),A1
Bacqué, N (Pau) 1997 R 2
Bader, E (Primevères) 1926 M, 1927 I, S
Badin, C (Chalon) 1973 W, I, 1975 Arg 1
Baillette, M (Perpignan) 1925 I, NZ, S, 1926 W, M, 1927 I, W, G 2, 1929 G, 1930 S, I, E, G, 1931 I, S, E, 1932 G
Baladie, G (Agen) 1945 B 1,2, W, 1946 B, I, K
Ballarin, J (Tarbes) 1924 E, 1925 NZ, S
Baquey, J (Toulouse) 1921 I
Barbazanges, A (Roanne) 1932 G, 1933 G
Barrau, M (Beaumont, Toulouse) 1971 S, E, W, 1972 E, W, A 1,2, 1973 S, NZ, E, I, J, R, 1974 I, S
Barrau, M (Agen) 2004 US,C(R),NZ(R)
Barrère, P (Toulon) 1929 G, 1931 W
Barrière, R (Béziers) 1960 R
Barthe, E (SBUC) 1925 W, E
Barthe, J (Lourdes) 1954 Arg 1,2, 1955 S, 1956 I, W, It, E, Cz, 1957 S, I, E, W, R 1,2, 1958 S, E, A, W, It, I, SA 1,2, 1959 S, E, It, W
Basauri, R (Albi) 1954 Arg 1
Bascou, P (Bayonne) 1914 E
Basquet, G (Agen) 1945 W, 1946 B, I, K, W, 1947 S, I, W, E, 1948 I, A, S, W, E, 1949 S, I, E, W, Arg 1, 1950 S, I, E, W, 1951 S, I, E, W, 1952 S, I, SA, W, E, It
Bastiat, J-P (Dax) 1969 R, 1970 S, I, W, 1971 S, I, SA 2, 1972 S, A 1, 1973 E, 1974 Arg 1,2, SA 2, 1975 W, Arg 1,2, R, 1976 S, I, W, E, A 1,2, R, 1977 W, E, S, I, 1978 E, S, I, W
Baudry, N (Montferrand) 1949 S, I, W, Arg 1,2
Baulon, R (Vienne, Bayonne) 1954 S, NZ, W, E, It, 1955 I, E, W, It, 1956 S, I, W, It, E, Cz, 1957 S, I, It
Baux, J-P (Lannemezan) 1968 NZ 1,2, SA 1,2
Bavozet, J (Lyon) 1911 S, E, W
Bayard, J (Toulouse) 1923 S, W, E, 1924 W, R, US
Bayardon, J (Chalon) 1964 S, NZ, E
Beaurin-Gressier, C (SF) 1907 E, 1908 E
Bégu, J (Dax) 1982 Arg 2(R), 1984 E, S
Béguerie, C (Agen) 1979 NZ 1
Beguet, L (RCF) 1922 I, 1923 S, W, E, I, 1924 S, I, E, R, US
Behoteguy, A (Bayonne, Cognac) 1923 E, 1924 S, I, E, W, R, US, 1926 E, 1927 E, G 1,2, 1928 A, I, E, G, W, 1929 S, W, E
Behoteguy, H (RCF, Cognac) 1923 W, 1928 A, I, E, G, W
Belascain, C (Bayonne) 1977 R, 1978 E, S, I, W, R, 1979 I, W, E, S, 1982 W, E, S, I, 1983 E, S, I, W
Belletante, G (Nantes) 1951 I, E, W
Belot, F (Toulouse) 2000 I (R)
Benazzi, A (Agen) 1990 A 1,2,3, NZ 1,2, 1991 E, US 1(R),2, [R, Fj, C], 1992 SA 1(R),2, Arg, 1993 E, S, I, W, A 1,2, 1994

I, W, E, S, C 1, NZ 1,2, C 2, 1995 W, E, S, I, [Tg, Iv, S, I, SA, E], NZ 1,2, 1996 E, S, I, W 1, Arg 1,2, W 2, SA 1,2, 1997 I, W, E, S, R 1, A 1,2, It 2, R 2(R), Arg, SA 1,2, 1999 R, WS, W 2, [C, Nm (R), Fj, Arg, NZ 2, A], 2000 W, E, I, It (R), R, 2001 S (R), I (t&R), E

Bénésis, R (Narbonne) 1969 W, R, 1970 S, I, W, E, R, 1971 S, I, E, W, A 2, R, 1972 S, I 1, E, W, I 2, A 1, R, 1973 NZ, E, W, I, J, R, 1974 I, W, E, S

Benetière, J (Roanne) 1954 It, Arg 1

Benetton, P (Agen) 1989 B, 1990 NZ 2, 1991 US 2, 1992 Arg 1,2(R), SA 1(R),2, Arg, 1993 E, S, I, W, SA 1,2, R 2, A 1,2, 1994 I, W, E, S, C 1, NZ 1,2, C 2, 1995 W, E, S, I, [Tg, Iv (R), S], It, R 2(R), Arg, NZ 1,2, 1996 Arg 1,2, W 2, SA 1,2, 1997 I, It 1,2(R), R 2, Arg, SA 1,2 1998 E, S (R), I (R), W (R), Arg 1(R),2(R), Fj (R), 1999 I, W 1, S (R)

Benezech, L (RCF) 1994 E, S, C 1, NZ 1,2, C 2, 1995 W, E, [Iv, S, E], R 2, Arg, NZ 1,2

Berbizier, P (Lourdes, Agen) 1981 S, I, W, E, NZ 1,2, 1982 I, R, 1983 S, I, 1984 S (R), NZ 1,2, 1985 Arg 1,2, 1986 S, I, W, E, R 1, Arg 1, A, NZ 1, R 2, NZ 2,3, 1987 W, E, S, I, [S, R, Fj, A, NZ], R, 1988 E, S, I, W, Arg 1,2, 1989 I, W, E, S, NZ 1,2, B, A 1, 1990 W, E, 1991 S, I, W 1, E

Berejnoi, J-C (Tulle) 1963 R, 1964 S, W, It, I, SA, Fj, R, 1965 S, I, E, W, It, R, 1966 S, I, E, W, It, R, 1967 S, A, E, It, W, I, R

Berges, B (Toulouse) 1926 I

Berges-Cau, R (Lourdes) 1976 E (R)

Bergese, F (Bayonne) 1936 G 2, 1937 G, It, 1938 G 1, R, G 2

Bergougnan, Y (Toulouse) 1945 B 1, W, 1946 B, I, K, W, 1947 S, I, W, E, 1948 S, W, E, 1949 S, E, Arg 1,2

Bernard, R (Bergerac) 1951 S, I, E, W

Bernat-Salles, P (Pau, Bègles-Bordeaux, Biarritz) 1992 Arg, 1993 R 1, SA 1,2, R 2, A 1,2, 1994 I, 1995 E, S, 1996 E (R), 1997 R 1, A 1,2, 1998 E, S, I, W, Arg 1,2, Fj, Arg 3(R), A 1999 I, W 1, R, Tg, [Nm, Fj, Arg, NZ 2, A], 2000 I, It, NZ 1(R),2, 2001 S, I, It, W, E

Bernon, J (Lourdes) 1922 I, 1923 S

Bérot, J-L (Toulouse) 1968 NZ 3, A, 1969 S, I, 1970 E, R, 1971 S, I, E, W, SA 1,2, A 1,2, R, 1972 S, I 1, E, W, A 1, 1974 I

Bérot, P (Agen) 1986 R 2, NZ 2,3, 1987 W, E, S, I, R, 1988 E, S, I, Arg 1,2,3,4, R, 1989 S, NZ 1,2

Bertrand, P (Bourg) 1951 I, E, W, 1953 S, I, E, W, It

Bertranne, R (Bagnères) 1971 E, W, SA 2, A 1,2, 1972 S, I 1, 1973 NZ, E, J, R, 1974 I, W, E, S, Arg 1,2, R, SA 1,2, 1975 W, E, S, I, SA 1,2, Arg 1,2, R, 1976 S, I, W, E, US, A 1,2, R, 1977 W, E, S, I, Arg 1,2, NZ 1,2, R, 1978 E, S, I, W, R, 1979 I, W, E, S, R, 1980 W, E, S, I, SA, R, 1981 S, I, W, E, R, NZ 1,2

Berty, D (Toulouse) 1990 NZ 2, 1992 R (R), 1993 R 2, 1995 NZ 1(R), 1996 W 2(R), SA 1

Besset, E (Grenoble) 1924 S

Besset, L (SCUF) 1914 W, E

Besson, M (CASG) 1924 I, 1925 I, E, 1926 S, W, 1927 I

Besson, P (Brive) 1963 S, I, E, 1965 R, 1968 SA 1

Betsen, S (Biarritz) 1997 It 1(R), 2000 W (R), E (R), A (R), NZ 1(R),2(R), 2001 S (R), I (R), It (R), W (R), SA 3(R), A, Fj, 2002 It, W, E, S, I, Arg, A 1,2, SA, NZ, C, 2003 E 1, S, I, It, W, R, E 2, [Fj,J,S,I,E], 2004 I,It,W,S,E,A,Arg,NZ, 2005 E,W,I,It, 2006 SA

Bianchi, J (Toulon) 1986 Arg 1

Bichindaritz, J (Biarritz O) 1954 It, Arg 1,2

Bidabé, P (Biarritz) 2004 C, 2006 R

Bidart, L (La Rochelle) 1953 W

Biemouret, P (Agen) 1969 E, W, 1970 I, W, E, 1971 W, SA 1,2, A 1, 1972 E, W, I 2, A 2, R, 1973 S, NZ, E, W, I

Biénès, R (Cognac) 1950 S, I, E, W, 1951 S, I, E, W, 1952 S, I, SA, W, E, It, 1953 S, I, E, 1954 S, I, NZ, W, E, Arg 1,2, 1956 S, I, W, It, E

Bigot, C (Quillan) 1930 S, E, 1931 I, S

Bilbao, L (St Jean-de-Luz) 1978 I, 1979 I

Billac, E (Bayonne) 1920 S, E, W, I, US, 1921 S, W, 1922 W, 1923 E

Billière, M (Toulouse) 1968 NZ 3

Bioussa, A (Toulouse) 1924 W, US, 1925 I, NZ, S, E, 1926 S, I, E, 1928 E, G, W, 1929 I, S, W, E, 1930 S, I, E, G, W

Bioussa, C (Toulouse) 1913 W, I, 1914 I

Biraben, M (Dax) 1920 W, I, US, 1921 S, W, E, I, 1922 S, E, I

Blain, A (Carcassonne) 1934 G

Blanco, S (Biarritz O) 1980 SA, R, 1981 S, W, E, A 1,2, R, NZ 1,2, 1982 W, E, S, I, R, Arg 1,2, 1983 E, S, I, W, 1984 I, W, E, S, NZ 1,2, R, 1985 E, S, I, W, Arg 1,2, 1986 S, I, W, E, R 1, Arg 2, A, NZ 1, R 2, NZ 2,3, 1987 W, E, S, I, [S, R, Fj, A, NZ], R, 1988 E, S, I, W, Arg 1,2,3,4, R, 1989 I, W, E, S, NZ 1,2, B, A 1, 1990 E, S, I, R, A 1,2,3, NZ 1,2, 1991 S, I, W 1, E, R, US 1,2, W 2, [R, Fj, C, E]

Blond, J (SF) 1935 G, 1936 G 2, 1937 G, 1938 G 1, R, G 2

Blond, X (RCF) 1990 A 3, 1991 S, I, W 1, E, 1994 NZ 2(R)

Boffelli, V (Aurillac) 1971 A 2, R, 1972 S, I 1, 1973 J, R, 1974 I, W, E, S, Arg 1,2, R, SA 1,2, 1975 W, S, I

Bonal, J-M (Toulouse) 1968 E, W, Cz, NZ 2,3, SA 1,2, R, 1969 S, I, E, R, 1970 W, E

Bonamy, R (SB) 1928 A, I

Bondouy, P (Narbonne, Toulouse) 1997 S (R), It 1, A 2(R), R 2, 2000 R (R)

Bonetti, S (Biarritz) 2001 It, W, NZ (R)

Boniface, A (Mont-de-Marsan) 1954 I, NZ, W, E, It, Arg 1,2, 1955 S, I, 1956 S, I, W, It, Cz, 1957 S, I, W, R 2, 1958 S, E, 1959 E, 1961 NZ 1,3, A, R, 1962 E, W, I, It, R, 1963 S, I, E, W, It, R, 1964 S, NZ, E, W, It, 1965 W, It, R, 1966 S, I, E, W

Boniface, G (Mont-de-Marsan) 1960 W, I, It, R, Arg 1,2,3, 1961 S, SA, E, W, It, I, NZ 1,2,3, R, 1962 R, 1963 S, I, E, W, It, R, 1964 S, 1965 S, I, E, W, It, R, 1966 S, I, E, W

Bonnaire, J (Bourgoin) 2004 S(t&R),A(R),NZ(R), 2005 S,E,W,I,It,SA1,2,A1,C,Tg,SA3, 2006 S,I,It(R),E(R), W,R,SA(R)

Bonnes, E (Narbonne) 1924 W, R, US

Bonneval, E (Toulouse) 1984 NZ 2(R), 1985 W, Arg 1, 1986 W, E, R 1, Arg 1,2, A, R 2, NZ 2,3, 1987 W, E, S, I, [Z], 1988 E

Bonnus, F (Toulon) 1950 S, I, E, W

Bonnus, M (Toulon) 1937 It, 1938 G 1, R, G 2, 1940 B

Bontemps, D (La Rochelle) 1968 SA 2

Borchard, G (RCF) 1908 E, 1909 E, W, I, 1911 I

Borde, F (RCF) 1920 I, US, 1921 S, W, E, 1922 S, W, 1923 S, I, 1924 E, 1925 I, 1926 E

Bordenave, L (Toulon) 1948 A, S, W, E, 1949 S

Bory, D (Montferrand) 2000 I, It, A, NZ 1, 2001 S, I, SA 1,2,3, A, Fj, 2002 It, E, S, I, C, 2003 [US,NZ]

Boubée, J (Tarbes) 1921 S, E, I, 1922 E, W, 1923 E, I, 1925 NZ, S

Boudreaux, R (SCUF) 1910 W, S

Bouet, D (Dax) 1989 NZ 1,2, B, A 2, 1990 A 3

Bouguyon, G (Grenoble) 1961 SA, E, W, It, I, NZ 1,2,3, A

Bouic, G (Agen) 1996 SA 1

Bouilhou, J (Toulouse) 2001 NZ, 2003 Arg 1

Boujet, C (Grenoble) 1968 NZ 2, A (R), SA 1

Bouquet, J (Bourgoin, Vienne) 1954 S, 1955 E, 1956 S, I, W, It, E, Cz, 1957 S, E, W, R 2, 1958 S, E, 1959 S, It, W, I, 1960 S, E, W, I, R, 1961 S, SA, E, W, It, I, R, 1962 S, E, W, I

Bourdeu, J R (Lourdes) 1952 S, I, SA, W, E, It, 1953 S, I, E

Bourgarel, R (Toulouse) 1969 R, 1970 S, I, E, R, 1971 W, SA 1,2, 1973 S

Bourguignon, G (Narbonne) 1988 Arg 3, 1989 I, E, B, A 1, 1990 R

Bousquet, A (Béziers) 1921 E, I, 1924 R

Bousquet, R (Albi) 1926 M, 1927 I, S, W, E, G 1, 1929 W, E, 1930 W

Bousses, G (Bourgoin) 2006 S(R)

Boyau, M (SBUC) 1912 I, S, W, E, 1913 W, I

Boyer, P (Toulon) 1935 G

Boyet, B (Bourgoin) 2006 I(R)

Branca, G (SF) 1928 S, 1929 I, S

Branlat, A (RCF) 1906 NZ, E, 1908 W

Brejassou, R (Tarbes) 1952 S, I, SA, W, E, 1953 W, E, 1954 S, I, NZ, 1955 S, I, E, W, It

Brethes, R (St Sever) 1960 Arg 2

Bringeon, A (Biarritz O) 1925 W

Brouzet, O (Grenoble, Bègles, Northampton, Montferrand) 1994 S, NZ 2(R), 1995 E, S, I, R 1, [Tg, Iv, E (t)], It, Arg (R), 1996 W 1(R), 1997 R 1, A 1,2, It 2, Arg, SA 1,2, 1998

E, S, I, W, Arg 1,2, Fj, Arg 3, A, 1999 I, W 1, E, S, R, [C (R), Nm, Fj (R), Arg, NZ 2(R), A (R)], 2000 W, E, S, I, It, A, NZ 1(R),2(R), 2001 SA 1,2, NZ, 2002 W, E, S, I, Arg, A 1(R),2, SA, NZ, C, 2003 E 1, S, I, It, W, E 3, [Fj(R),J,S(R),US,I(R)]

Bru, Y (Toulouse) 2001 A (R), Fj (R), 2002 It, 2003 Arg 2, NZ, R, E 2,3(R), [J,S(R),US, I(t&R),NZ], 2004 I(R),It(R),W(R),S(R),E(R)

Brun, G (Vienne) 1950 E, W, 1951 S, E, W, 1952 S, I, SA, W, E, It, 1953 E, W, It

Bruneau, M (SBUC) 1910 W, E, 1913 SA, E

Brunet, Y (Perpignan) 1975 SA 1, 1977 Arg 1

Bruno, S (Béziers, Sale) 2002 W (R), 2004 A(R),NZ(t&R), 2005 S(R),E,W,I,It,SA1,2(R),A1(R),2(R),C,SA3(R), 2006 S(R),I(R)

Brusque, N (Pau, Biarritz) 1997 R 2(R), 2002 W, E, S, I, Arg, A 2, SA, NZ, C, 2003 E 2, [Fj,S,I,E,NZ(R)], 2004 I,It,W,S,E,A,Arg, 2005 SA1(R),2,A1, 2006 S

Buchet, E (Nice) 1980 R, 1982 E, R (R), Arg 1,2

Buisson, H (see Empereur-Buisson)

Buonomo, Y (Béziers) 1971 A 2, R, 1972 I 1

Burgun, M (RCF) 1909 I, 1910 W, S, I, 1911 S, E, 1912 I, S, 1913 S, E, 1914 E

Bustaffa, D (Carcassonne) 1977 Arg 1,2, NZ 1,2, 1978 W, R, 1980 W, E, S, SA, R

Buzy, C-E (Lourdes) 1946 K, W, 1947 S, I, W, E, 1948 I, A, S, W, E, 1949 S, I, E, W, Arg 1,2

Cabanier, J-M (Montauban) 1963 R, 1964 S, Fj, 1965 S, I, W, It, R, 1966 S, I, E, W, It, R, 1967 S, A, E, It, W, I, SA 1,3, NZ, R, 1968 S, I

Cabannes, L (RCF, Harlequins) 1990 NZ 2(R), 1991 S, I, W 1, E, US 2, W 2, [R, Fj, C, E], 1992 W, E, S, I, R, Arg 2, SA 1,2, 1993 E, S, I, W, R 1, SA 1,2, 1994 E, S, C 1, NZ 1,2, 1995 W, E, S, R 1, [Tg (R), Iv, S, I, SA, E], 1996 E, S, I, W 1, 1997 It 2, Arg, SA 1,2

Cabrol, H (Béziers) 1972 A 1(R),2, 1973 J, 1974 SA 2

Cadenat, J (SCUF) 1910 S, E, 1911 W, I, 1912 W, E, 1913 I

Cadieu, J-M (Toulouse) 1991 R, US 1, [R, Fj, C, E], 1992 W, I, R, Arg 1,2, SA 1

Cahuc, F (St Girons) 1922 S

Califano, C (Toulouse, Saracens) 1994 NZ 1,2, C 2, 1995 W, E, S, I, [Iv, S, I, SA, E], It, Arg, NZ 1,2, 1996 E, S, I, W 1, R, Arg 1,2, SA 1,2, 1997 I, W, E, A 1,2, It 2, R 2(R), Arg, SA 1,2, 1998 E, S, I, W, 1999 I, W 1, E (R), S, WS, Tg (R), NZ 1, W 2, [C, Nm, Fj], 2000 W, E, S, I, It, R, A, NZ 1,2(R), 2001 S (R), I (R), It, W, SA 1(R),2(R), NZ, 2003 E 1, S (R), I (R)

Cals, R (RCF) 1938 G 1

Calvo, G (Lourdes) 1961 NZ 1,3

Camberabero, D (La Voulte, Béziers) 1982 R, Arg 1,2, 1983 E, W, 1987 [R (R), Z, Fj (R), A, NZ], 1988 I, 1989 B, A 1, 1990 W, S, I, R, A 1,2,3, NZ 1,2, 1991 S, I, W 1, E, R, US 1,2, W 2, [R, Fj, C], 1993 E, S, I

Camberabero, G (La Voulte) 1961 NZ 3, 1962 R, 1964 R, 1967 A, E, It, W, I, SA 1,3,4, 1968 S, E, W

Camberabero, L (La Voulte) 1964 R, 1965 S, I, 1966 E, W, 1967 A, E, It, W, I, 1968 S, E, W

Cambré, T (Oloron) 1920 E, W, I, US

Camel, A (Toulouse) 1928 S, A, I, E, G, W, 1929 W, E, G, 1930 S, I, E, G, W, 1935 G

Camel, M (Toulouse) 1929 S, W, E

Camicas, F (Tarbes) 1927 G 2, 1928 S, I, E, G, W, 1929 I, S, W, E

Camo, E (Villeneuve) 1931 I, S, W, E, G, 1932 G

Campaes, A (Lourdes) 1965 W, 1967 NZ, 1968 S, I, E, W, Cz, NZ 1,2, A, 1969 S, W, 1972 R, 1973 NZ

Campan, O (Agen) 1993 SA 1(R),2(R), R 2(R), 1996 I, W 1, R

Candelon, J (Narbonne) 2005 SA1,A1(R)

Cantoni, J (Béziers) 1970 W, R, 1971 S, I, E, W, SA 1,2, R, 1972 S, I 1, 1973 S, NZ, W, I, 1975 W (R)

Capdouze, J (Pau) 1964 SA, Fj, R, 1965 S, I, E

Capendeguy, J-M (Bègles) 1967 NZ, R

Capitani, P (Toulon) 1954 Arg 1,2

Capmau, J-L (Toulouse) 1914 E

Carabignac, G (Agen) 1951 S, I, 1952 SA, W, E, 1953 S, I

Carbonne, J (Perpignan) 1927 W

Carbonneau, P (Toulouse, Brive, Pau) 1995 R 2, Arg, NZ 1,2, 1996 E, S, R (R), Arg 2, W 2, SA 1, 1997 I (R), W, E, S (R), R 1(R), A 1,2, 1998 E, S, I, W, Arg 1,2, Fj, Arg 3, A, 1999 I, W 1, E, S, 2000 NZ 2(R), 2001 I

Carminati, A (Béziers, Brive) 1986 R 2, NZ 2, 1987 [R, Z], 1988 I, W, Arg 1,2, 1989 I, W, S, NZ 1(R),2, A 2, 1990 S, 1995 It, R 2, Arg, NZ 1,2

Caron, L (Lyon O, Castres) 1947 E, 1948 I, A, W, E, 1949 S, I, E, W, Arg 1

Carpentier, M (Lourdes) 1980 E, SA, R, 1981 S, I, A 1, 1982 E, S

Carrère, C (Toulon) 1966 R, 1967 S, A, E, W, I, SA 1,3,4, NZ, R, 1968 S, I, E, W, Cz, NZ 3, A, R, 1969 S, I, 1970 S, I, W, E, 1971 E, W

Carrère, J (Vichy, Toulon) 1956 S, 1957 E, W, R 2, 1958 S, SA 1,2, 1959 I

Carrère, R (Mont-de-Marsan) 1953 E, It

Casadei, D (Brive) 1997 S, R 1, SA 2(R)

Casaux, L (Tarbes) 1959 I, It, 1962 S

Cassagne, P (Pau) 1957 It

Cassayet-Armagnac, A (Tarbes, Narbonne) 1920 S, E, W, US, 1921 W, E, I, 1922 S, E, W, 1923 S, W, E, I, 1924 S, E, W, R, US, 1925 I, NZ, S, W, 1926 S, I, E, W, M, 1927 I, S, W

Cassiède, M (Dax) 1961 NZ 3, A, R

Castaignède, S (Mont-de-Marsan) 1999 W 2, [C (R), Nm (R), Fj, Arg (R), NZ 2(R), A (R)]

Castaignède, T (Toulouse, Castres, Saracens) 1995 R 2, Arg, NZ 1,2, 1996 E, S, I, W 1, Arg 1,2, 1997 I, A 1,2, It 2, 1998 E, S, I, W, Arg 1,2, Fj, 1999 I, W 1, E, S, R, WS, Tg (R), NZ 1, W 2, [C], 2000 W, E, S, It, 2002 SA, NZ, C, 2003 E 1(R), S (R), It, W, Arg 1, 2005 A2(R),C,Tg,SA3, 2006 It,E,W,R,SA(R)

Castel, R (Toulouse, Béziers) 1996 I, W 1, W 2, SA 1(R),2, 1997 I (R), W, E (R), S (R), A 1(R), 1998 Arg 3(R), A (R), 1999 W 1(R), E, S

Castets, J (Toulon) 1923 W, E, I

Caujolle, J (Tarbes) 1909 E, 1913 SA, E, 1914 W, E

Caunègre, R (SB) 1938 R, G 2

Caussade, A (Lourdes) 1978 R, 1979 I, W, E, NZ 1,2, R, 1980 W, E, S, 1981 S (R), I

Caussarieu, G (Pau) 1929 I

Cayrefourcq, E (Tarbes) 1921 E

Cazalbou, J (Toulouse) 1997 It 2(R), R 2, Arg, SA 2(R)

Cazals, P (Mont-de-Marsan) 1961 NZ 1, A, R

Cazenave, A (Pau) 1927 E, G 1, 1928 S, A, G

Cazenave, F (RCF) 1950 E, 1952 S, 1954 I, NZ, W, E

Cecillon, M (Bourgoin) 1988 I, W, Arg 2,3,4, R, 1989 I, E, NZ 1,2, A 1, 1991 S, I, E (R), R, US 1, W 2, [E], 1992 W, E, S, I, R, Arg 1,2, SA 1,2, 1993 E, S, I, W, R 1, SA 1,2, R 2, A 1,2, 1994 I, W, NZ 1(R), 1995 I, R 1, [Tg, S (R), I, SA]

Celaya, M (Biarritz O, SBUC) 1953 E, W, It, 1954 I, E, It, Arg 1,2, 1955 S, I, E, W, It, 1956 S, I, W, It, E, Cz 1957 S, I, E, W, R 2, 1958 S, E, A, W, It, 1959 S, E, 1960 S, E, W, I, R, Arg 1,2,3, 1961 S, SA, E, W, It, I, NZ 1,2,3, A, R

Celhay, M (Bayonne) 1935 G, 1936 G 1, 1937 G, It, 1938 G 1, 1940 B

Cermeno, F (Perpignan) 2000 R

Cessieux, N (Lyon) 1906 NZ

Cester, E (TOEC, Valence) 1966 S, I, E, 1967 W, 1968 S, I, E, W, Cz, NZ 1,3, A, SA 1,2, R, 1969 S, I, E, W, 1970 S, I, W, E, 1971 A 1, 1972 R, 1973 S, NZ, W, I, J, R, 1974 I, W, E, S

Chabal, S (Bourgoin) 2000 S, 2001 SA 1,2, NZ (R), Fj (R), 2002 Arg (R), A 2, SA (R), NZ (t), C (R), 2003 E 1(R), S (R), I (R), Arg 2, NZ (R), E 2(R),3, [J(R),US,NZ], 2005 S, E,A2(R),Tg

Chaban-Delmas, J (CASG) 1945 B 2

Chabowski, H (Nice, Bourgoin) 1985 Arg 2, 1986 R 2, NZ 2, 1989 B (R)

Chadebech, P (Brive) 1982 R, Arg 1,2, 1986 S, I

Champ, E (Toulon) 1985 Arg 1,2, 1986 I, W, E, R 1, Arg 1,2, A, NZ 1, R 2, NZ 2,3, 1987 W, E, S, I, [S, R, Fj, A, NZ], R, 1988 E, S, Arg 1,3,4, R, 1989 W, S, A 1,2, 1990 W, E, NZ 1, 1991 R, US 1, [R, Fj, C, E]

Chapuy, L (SF) 1926 S

Charpentier, G (SF) 1911 E, 1912 W, E

Charton, P (Montferrand) 1940 B

Charvet, D (Toulouse) 1986 W, E, R 1, Arg 1, A, NZ 1,3, 1987

W, E, S, I, [S, R, Z, Fj, A, NZ], R, 1989 E (R), 1990 W, E, 1991 S, I
Chassagne, J (Montferrand) 1938 G 1
Chatau, A (Bayonne) 1913 SA
Chaud, E (Toulon) 1932 G, 1934 G, 1935 G
Chazalet, A (Bourgoin) 1999 Tg
Chenevay, C (Grenoble) 1968 SA 1
Chevallier, B (Montferrand) 1952 S, I, SA, W, E, It, 1953 E, W, It, 1954 S, I, NZ, W, Arg 1, 1955 S, I, E, W, It, 1956 S, I, W, It, E, Cz, 1957 S
Chiberry, J (Chambéry) 1955 It
Chilo, A (RCF) 1920 S, W, 1925 I, NZ
Cholley, G (Castres) 1975 E, S, I, SA 1,2, Arg 1,2, R, 1976 S, I, W, E, A 1,2, R, 1977 W, E, S, I, Arg 1,2, NZ 1,2, R, 1978 E, S, I, W, R, 1979 I, S
Choy J (Narbonne) 1930 S, I, E, G, W, 1931 I, 1933 G, 1934 G, 1935 G, 1936 G 2
Cigagna, A (Toulouse) 1995 [E]
Cimarosti, J (Castres) 1976 US (R)
Cistacq, J-C (Agen) 2000 R (R)
Clady, A (Lezignan) 1929 G, 1931 I, S, E, G
Clarac, H (St Girons) 1938 G 1
Claudel, R (Lyon) 1932 G, 1934 G
Clauzel, F (Béziers) 1924 E, W, 1925 W
Clavé, J (Agen) 1936 G 2, 1938 R, G 2
Claverie, H (Lourdes) 1954 NZ, W
Cléda, T (Pau) 1998 E (R), S (R), I (R), W (R), Arg 1(R), Fj (R), Arg 3(R), 1999 I (R), S
Clément, G (RCF) 1931 W
Clément, J (RCF) 1921 S, W, E, 1922 S, E, W, I, 1923 S, W, I
Clemente, M (Oloron) 1978 R, 1980 S, I
Clerc, V (Toulouse) 2002 SA, NZ, C, 2003 E 1, S, I, It (R), W (R), Arg 2, NZ, 2004 I,It, W, 2005 SA2,Tg, 2006 SA
Cluchague, L (Biarritz O) 1924 S, 1925 E
Coderc, J (Chalon) 1932 G, 1933 G, 1934 G, 1935 G, 1936 G 1
Codorniou, D (Narbonne) 1979 NZ 1,2, R, 1980 W, E, S, I, 1981 S, W, E, A 2, 1983 E, S, I, W, A 1,2, R, 1984 I, W, E, S, NZ 1,2, R, 1985 E, S, I, W, Arg 1,2
Coeurveille, C (Agen) 1992 Arg 1(R),2
Cognet, L (Montferrand) 1932 G, 1936 G 1,2, 1937 G, It
Collazo, P (Bègles) 2000 R
Colombier, J (St Junien) 1952 SA, W, E
Colomine, G (Narbonne) 1979 NZ 1
Comba, F (SF) 1998 Arg 1,2, Fj, Arg 3, 1999 I, W 1, E, S, 2000 A, NZ 1,2, 2001 S, I
Combe, J (SF) 1910 S, E, I, 1911 S
Combes, G (Fumel) 1945 B 2
Communeau, M (SF) 1906 NZ, E, 1907 E, 1908 E, W, 1909 E, W, I, 1910 S, E, I, 1911 S, E, I, 1912 I, S, W, E, 1913 SA, E, W
Condom, J (Boucau, Biarritz O) 1982 R, 1983 E, S, I, W, A 1,2, R, 1984 I, W, E, S, NZ 1,2, R, 1985 E, S, I, W, Arg 1,2, 1986 S, I, W, E, R 1, Arg 1,2, NZ 1, R 2, NZ 2,3, 1987 W, E, S, I, [S, R, Z, A, NZ], R, 1988 E, S, W, Arg 1,2,3,4, R, 1989 I, W, E, S, NZ 1,2, A 1, 1990 I, R, A 2,3(R)
Conilh de Beyssac, J-J (SBUC) 1912 I, S, 1914 I, W, E
Constant, G (Perpignan) 1920 W
Coscolla, G (Béziers) 1921 S, W
Costantino, J (Montferrand) 1973 R
Costes, A (Montferrand) 1994 C 2, 1995 R 1, [Iv], 1997 It 1, 1999 WS, Tg (R), NZ 1, [Nm (R), Fj (R), Arg (R), NZ 2(R), A (t&R)], 2000 S (R), I
Costes, F (Montferrand) 1979 E, S, NZ 1,2, R, 1980 W, I
Couffignal, H (Colomiers) 1993 R 1
Coulon, E (Grenoble) 1928 S
Courtiols, M (Bègles) 1991 R, US 1, W 2
Couzinet, D (Biarritz) 2004 US,C(R)
Crabos, R (RCF) 1920 S, E, W, I, US, 1921 S, W, E, I, 1922 S, E, W, I, 1923 S, I, 1924 S, I
Crampagne, J (Bègles) 1967 SA 4
Crancee, R (Lourdes) 1960 Arg 3, 1961 S
Crauste, M (RCF, Lourdes) 1957 R 1,2, 1958 S, E, A, W, It, I, 1959 E, It, W, I, 1960 S, E, W, I, It, R, Arg 1,3, 1961 S, SA, E, W, It, I, NZ 1,2,3, A, R, 1962 S, E, W, I, It, R, 1963 S, I, E, W, It, R, 1964 S, NZ, E, W, It, I, SA, Fj, R, 1965 S, I, E, W, It, R, 1966 S, I, E, W, It
Cremaschi, M (Lourdes) 1980 R, 1981 R, NZ 1,2, 1982 W, S, 1983 A 1,2, R, 1984 I, W
Crenca, J-J (Agen) 1996 SA 2(R), 1999 R, Tg, WS (R), NZ 1(R), 2001 SA 1,2, NZ (R), SA 3, A, Fj, 2002 It, W, E, S, I, Arg, A 2, SA, NZ, C, 2003 E 1, S, I, It, W, R, E 2, [Fj, J(t&R),S,I,E,NZ(R)], 2004 I(R),It(R),W(R),S(R),E(R)
Crichton, W H (Le Havre) 1906 NZ, E
Cristina, J (Montferrand) 1979 R
Cussac, P (Biarritz O) 1934 G
Cutzach, A (Quillan) 1929 G

Daguerre, F (Biarritz O) 1936 G 1
Daguerre, J (CASG) 1933 G
Dal Maso, M (Mont-de-Marsan, Agen, Colomiers) 1988 R (R), 1990 NZ 2, 1996 SA 1(R),2, 1997 I, W, E, S, It 1, R 1(R), A 1,2, It 2, Arg, SA 1,2, 1998 W (R), Arg 1(t), Fj (R), 1999 R (R), WS (R), Tg, NZ 1(R), W 2(R), [Nm (R), Fj (R), Arg (R), A (R)], 2000 W, E, S, I, It
Danion, J (Toulon) 1924 I
Danos, P (Toulon, Béziers) 1954 Arg 1,2, 1957 R 2, 1958 S, E, W, It, I, SA 1,2, 1959 S, E, It, W, I, 1960 S, E
Dantiacq, D (Pau) 1997 R 1
Darbos, P (Dax) 1969 R
Darracq, R (Dax) 1957 It
Darrieussecq, A (Biarritz O) 1973 E
Darrieussecq, J (Mont-de-Marsan) 1953 It
Darrouy, C (Mont-de-Marsan) 1957 I, E, W, It, R 1, 1959 E, 1961 R, 1963 S, I, E, W, It, 1964 NZ, E, W, It, I, SA, Fj, R, 1965 S, I, E, It, R, 1966 S, I, E, W, It, R, 1967 S, A, E, It, W, I, SA 1,2,4
Daudé, J (Bourgoin) 2000 S
Daudignon, G (SF) 1928 S
Dauga, B (Mont-de-Marsan) 1964 S, NZ, E, W, It, I, SA, Fj, R, 1965 S, I, E, W, It, R, 1966 S, I, E, W, It, R, 1967 S, A, E, It, W, I, SA 1,2,3,4, NZ, R, 1968 S, I, NZ 1,2,3, A, SA 1,2, R, 1969 S, I, E, R, 1970 S, I, W, E, R, 1971 S, I, E, W, SA 1,2, A 1,2, R, 1972 S, I 1, W
Dauger, J (Bayonne) 1945 B 1,2, 1953 S
Daulouede, P (Tyrosse) 1937 G, It, 1938 G 1, 1940 B
Debaty, V (Perpignan) 2006 R(R)
De Besombes, S (Perpignan) 1998 Arg 1(R), Fj (R)
Decamps, P (RCF) 1911 S
Dedet, J (SF) 1910 S, E, I, 1911 W, I, 1912 S, 1913 E, I
Dedeyn, P (RCF) 1906 NZ
Dedieu, P (Béziers) 1963 E, It, 1964 W, It, I, SA, Fj, R, 1965 S, I, E, W
De Gregorio, J (Grenoble) 1960 S, E, W, I, It, R, Arg 1,2, 1961 S, SA, E, W, It, I, 1962 S, E, W, 1963 S, W, It, 1964 NZ, E
Dehez, J-L (Agen) 1967 SA 2, 1969 R
De Jouvencel, E (SF) 1909 W, I
De Laborderie, M (RCF) 1921 I, 1922 I, 1925 W, E
Delage, C (Agen) 1983 S, I
De Malherbe, H (CASG) 1932 G, 1933 G
De Malmann, R (RCF) 1908 E, W, 1909 E, W, I, 1910 E, I
De Muizon, J J (SF) 1910 I
Delaigue, G (Toulon) 1973 J, R
Delaigue, Y (Toulon, Toulouse, Castres) 1994 S, NZ 2(R), C 2, 1995 I, R 1, [Tg, Iv], It, R 2(R), 1997 It 1, 2003 Arg 1,2, 2005 S,E,W,I,It,A2(R),Tg,SA3(R)
Delmotte, G (Toulon) 1999 R, Tg
Delque, A (Toulouse) 1937 It, 1938 G 1, R, G 2
De Rougemont, M (Toulon) 1995 E (t), R 1(t), [Iv], NZ 1,2, 1996 I (R), Arg 1,2, W 2, SA 1, 1997 E (R), S (R), It 1
Desbrosse, C (Toulouse) 1999 [Nm (R)], 2000 I
Descamps, P (SB) 1927 G 2
Desclaux, F (RCF) 1949 Arg 1,2, 1953 It
Desclaux, J (Perpignan) 1934 G, 1935 G, 1936 G 1,2, 1937 G, It, 1938 G 1, R, G 2, 1945 B 1
Deslandes, C (RCF) 1990 A 1, NZ 2, 1991 W 1, 1992 R, Arg 1,2
Desnoyer, L (Brive) 1974 R
Destarac, L (Tarbes) 1926 S, I, E, W, M, 1927 W, E, G 1,2
Desvouges, R (SF) 1914 W
Detrez, P-E (Nîmes) 1983 A 2(R), 1986 Arg 1(R),2, A (R), NZ1
Devergie, T (Nîmes) 1988 R, 1989 NZ 1,2, B, A 2, 1990 W, E, S, I, R, A 1,2,3, 1991 US 2, W 2, 1992 R (R), Arg 2(R)
De Villiers, P (SF) 1999 W 2, [Arg (R), NZ 2(R), A (R)], 2000

W (R), E (R), S (R), I (R), It (R), NZ 1(R),2, 2001 S, I, It, W, E, SA 1,2, NZ (R), SA 3, A, Fj, 2002 It, W, E, I, SA, NZ, C, 2003 Arg 1,2, NZ (R), 2004 I,It,W,S,E,US,C,NZ, 2005 S,I(R),It(R),SA1(R),2, A1(R),2,C,Tg(R),SA3, 2006 S,I,It,E,W,SA
Deygas, M (Vienne) 1937 It
Deylaud, C (Toulouse) 1992 R, Arg 1,2, SA 1, 1994 C 1, NZ 1,2, 1995 W, E, S, [Iv (R), S, I, SA], It, Arg
Dintrans, P (Tarbes) 1979 NZ 1,2, R, 1980 E, S, I, SA, R, 1981 S, I, W, E, A 1,2, R, NZ 1,2, 1982 W, E, S, I, R, Arg 1,2, 1983 E, W, A 1,2, R, 1984 I, W, E, S, NZ 1,2, R, 1985 E, S, I, W, Arg 1,2, 1987 [R], 1988 Arg 1,2,3, 1989 W, E, S, 1990 R
Dispagne, S (Toulouse) 1996 I (R), W 1
Dizabo, P (Tyrosse) 1948 A, S, E, 1949 S, I, E, W, Arg 2, 1950 S, I, 1960 Arg 1,2,3
Domec, A (Carcassonne) 1929 W
Domec, H (Lourdes) 1953 W, It, 1954 S, I, NZ, W, E, It, 1955 S, I, E, W, 1956 I, W, It, 1958 E, A, W, It, I
Domenech, A (Vichy, Brive) 1954 W, E, It, 1955 S, I, E, W, 1956 S, I, W, It, E, Cz, 1957 S, I, E, W, It, R 1,2, 1958 S, E, It, 1959 It, 1960 S, E, W, I, It, R, Arg 1,2,3, 1961 S, SA, E, W, It, I, NZ 1,2,3, A, R, 1962 S, E, W, I, It, R, 1963 W, It
Domercq, J (Bayonne) 1912 I, S
Dominici, C (SF) 1998 E, S, Arg 1,2, 1999 E, S, WS, NZ 1, W 2, [C, Fj, Arg, NZ 2, A], 2000 W, E, S, R, 2001 I (R), It, W, E, SA 1,2, NZ, Fj, 2003 Arg 1, R, E 2,3, [Fj,J,S,I,E], 2004 I,It,W,S,E,A(R),NZ(R), 2005 S,E,W,I,It,2006 S,I,It,E,W
Dorot, J (RCF) 1935 G
Dospital, P (Bayonne) 1977 R, 1980 I, 1981 S, I, W, E, 1982 I, R, Arg 1,2, 1983 E, S, I, W, 1984 E, S, NZ 1,2, R, 1985 E, S, I, W, Arg 1
Dourthe, C (Dax) 1966 R, 1967 S, A, E, W, I, SA 1,2,3, NZ, 1968 W, NZ 3, SA 1,2, 1969 W, 1971 SA 2(R), R, 1972 I 1,2, A 1,2, R, 1973 S, NZ, E, 1974 I, Arg 1,2, SA 1,2, 1975 W, E, S
Dourthe, M (Dax) 2000 NZ 2(t)
Dourthe, R (Dax, SF, Béziers) 1995 R 2, Arg, NZ 1,2, 1996 E, R, 1996 Arg 1,2, W 2, SA 1,2, 1997 W, A 1, 1999 I, W 1,2, [C, Nm, Fj, Arg, NZ 2, A], 2000 W, E, It, R, A, NZ 1,2, 2001 S, I
Doussau, E (Angoulême) 1938 R
Droitecourt, M (Montferrand) 1972 R, 1973 NZ (R), E, 1974 E, S, Arg 1, SA 2, 1975 SA 1,2, Arg 1,2, R, 1976 S, I, W, A 1, 1977 Arg 2
Dubertrand, A (Montferrand) 1971 A 1,2, R, 1972 I 2, 1974 I, W, E, SA 2, 1975 Arg 1,2, R, 1976 S, US
Dubois, D (Bègles) 1971 S
Dubroca, D (Agen) 1979 NZ 2, 1981 NZ 2(R), 1982 E, S, 1984 W, E, S, 1985 Arg 2, 1986 S, I, W, E, R 1, Arg 2, A, NZ 1, R 2, NZ 2,3, 1987 W, E, S, I, [S, Z, Fj, A, NZ], R, 1988 E, S, I, W
Duché, A (Limoges) 1929 G
Duclos, A (Lourdes) 1931 S
Ducousso, J (Tarbes) 1925 S, W, E
Dufau, G (RCF) 1948 I, A, 1949 I, W, 1950 S, E, W, 1951 S, I, E, W, 1952 SA, W, 1953 S, I, E, W, 1954 S, I, NZ, W, E, It, 1955 S, I, E, W, It, 1956 S, I, W, It, 1957 S, I, E, W, It, R 1
Dufau, J (Biarritz) 1912 I, S, W, E
Duffaut, Y (Agen) 1954 Arg 1,2
Duffour, R (Tarbes) 1911 W
Dufourcq, J (SBUC) 1906 NZ, E, 1907 E, 1908 W
Duhard, Y (Bagnères) 1980 E
Duhau, J (SF) 1928 I,1930 I, G, 1931 I, S, W, 1933 G
Dulaurens, C (Toulouse) 1926 I, 1928 S, 1929 W
Duluc, A (Béziers) 1934 G
Du Manoir, Y le P (RCF) 1925 I, NZ, S, W, E, 1926 S, 1927 I, S
Dupont, C (Lourdes) 1923 S, W, I, 1924 S, I, W, R, US, 1925 S, 1927 E, G 1,2, 1928 A, G, W, 1929 I
Dupont, J-L (Agen) 1983 S
Dupont, L (RCF) 1934 G, 1935 G, 1936 G 1,2, 1938 R, G 2
Dupouy, A (SB) 1924 W, R
Duprat, B (Bayonne) 1966 E, W, It, R, 1967 S, A, E, SA 2,3, 1968 S, I, 1972 E, W, I 2, A 1
Dupré, P (RCF) 1909 W
Dupuy, J (Tarbes) 1956 S, I, W, It, E, Cz, 1957 S, I, E, W, It, R 2, 1958 S, E, SA 1,2, 1959 S, E, It, W, I, 1960 W, I, It, Arg 1,3, 1961 S, SA, E, NZ 2, R, 1962 S, E, W, I, It, 1963 W, It, R, 1964 S
Dusautoir, T (Biarritz) 2006 R,SA
Du Souich, C J (see Judas du Souich)
Dutin, B (Mont-de-Marsan) 1968 NZ 2, A, SA 2, R
Dutour, F X (Toulouse) 1911 E, I, 1912 S, W, E, 1913 S
Dutrain, H (Toulouse) 1945 W, 1946 B, I, 1947 E, 1949 I, E, W, Arg 1
Dutrey, J (Lourdes) 1940 B
Duval, R (SF) 1908 E, W, 1909 E, 1911 E, W, I

Echavé, L (Agen) 1961 S
Elhorga, P (Agen) 2001 NZ, 2002 A 1,2, 2003 Arg 2, NZ (R), R, [Fj(R),US,I(R),NZ], 2004 I(R),It(R),S,E, 2005 S,E
Elissalde, E (Bayonne) 1936 G 2, 1940 B
Elissalde, J-B (La Rochelle, Toulouse) 2000 S (R), R (R), 2003 It (R), W (R), 2004 I,It,W,A,Arg, 2005 SA1,2(R),A1,2,SA3, 2006 S,I,It,W(R)
Elissalde, J-P (La Rochelle) 1980 SA, R, 1981 A 1,2, R
Empereur-Buisson, H (Béziers) 1931 E, G
Erbani, D (Agen) 1981 A 1,2, NZ 1,2, 1982 Arg 1,2, 1983 S (R), I, W, A 1,2, R, 1984 W, E, R, 1985 E, W (R), Arg 2, 1986 S, I, W, E, R 1, Arg 2, NZ 1,2(R),3, 1987 W, E, S, I, [S, R, Fj, A, NZ], 1988 E, S, 1989 I (R), W, E, S, NZ 1, A 2, 1990 W, E
Escaffre, P (Narbonne) 1933 G, 1934 G
Escommier, M (Montelimar) 1955 It
Esponda, J-M (RCF) 1967 SA 1,2, R, 1968 NZ 1,2, SA 2, R, 1969 S, I (R), E
Estève, A (Béziers) 1971 SA 1, 1972 I 1, E, W, I 2, A 2, R, 1973 S, NZ, E, I, 1974 I, W, E, S, R, SA 1,2, 1975 W, E
Estève, P (Narbonne, Lavelanet) 1982 R, Arg 1,2, 1983 E, S, I, W, A 1,2, R, 1984 I, W, E, S, NZ 1,2, R, 1985 E, S, I, W, 1986 S, I, 1987 [S, Z]
Etcheberry, J (Rochefort, Cognac) 1923 W, I, 1924 S, I, E, W, R, US, 1926 S, I, E, M, 1927 I, S, W, G 2
Etchenique, J-M (Biarritz O) 1974 R, SA 1, 1975 E, Arg 2
Etchepare, A (Bayonne) 1922 I
Etcheverry, M (Pau) 1971 S, I
Eutrope, A (SCUF) 1913 I

Fabre, E (Toulouse) 1937 It, 1938 G 1,2
Fabre, J (Toulouse) 1963 S, I, E, W, It, 1964 S, NZ, E
Fabre, L (Lezignan) 1930 G
Fabre, M (Béziers) 1981 A 1, R, NZ 1,2, 1982 I, R
Failliot, P (RCF) 1911 S, W, I, 1912 I, S, E, 1913 E, W
Fargues, G (Dax) 1923 I
Fauré, F (Tarbes) 1914 I, W, E
Fauvel, J-P (Tulle) 1980 R
Favre, M (Lyon) 1913 E, W
Ferrand, L (Chalon) 1940 B
Ferrien, R (Tarbes) 1950 S, I, E, W
Finat, R (CASG) 1932 G, 1933 G
Fite, R (Brive) 1963 W, It
Forestier, J (SCUF) 1912 W
Forgues, F (Bayonne) 1911 S, E, W, 1912 I, W, E, 1913 S, SA, W, 1914 I, E
Fort, J (Agen) 1967 It, W, I, SA 1,2,3,4
Fourcade, G (BEC) 1909 E, W
Foures, H (Toulouse) 1951 S, I, E, W
Fournet, F (Montferrand) 1950 W
Fouroux, J (La Voulte) 1972 I 2, R, 1974 W, E, Arg 1,2, R, SA 1,2, 1975 W, Arg 1, R, 1976 S, I, W, E, US, A 1, 1977 W, E, S, I, Arg 1,2, NZ 1,2, R
Francquenelle, A (Vaugirard) 1911 S, 1913 W, I
Fritz, F (Toulouse) 2005 SA1,A2,SA3, 2006 S,I,It,E,W,SA
Froment, R (Castres) 2004 US(R)
Furcade, R (Perpignan) 1952 S

Gabernet, S (Toulouse) 1980 E, S, 1981 S, I, W, E, A 1,2, R, NZ 1,2, 1982 I, 1983 A 2, R
Gachassin, J (Lourdes) 1961 S, I, 1963 R, 1964 S, NZ, E, W, It, I, SA, Fj, R, 1965 S, I, E, W, It, R, 1966 S, I, E, W, 1967 S, A, It, W, I, NZ, 1968 I, E, 1969 S, I

Galasso, A (Toulon, Montferrand) 2000 R (R), 2001 E (R)
Galau, H (Toulouse) 1924 S, I, E, W, US
Galia, J (Quillan) 1927 E, G 1,2, 1928 S, A, I, E, W, 1929 I, E, G, 1930 S, I, E, G, W, 1931 S, W, E, G
Gallart, P (Béziers) 1990 R, A 1,2(R),3, 1992 S, I, R, Arg 1,2, SA 1,2, Arg, 1994 I, W, E, 1995 I (t), R 1, [Tg]
Gallion, J (Toulon) 1978 E, S, I, W, 1979 I, W, E, S, NZ 2, R, 1980 W, E, S, I, 1983 A 1,2, R, 1984 I, W, E, S, R, 1985 E, S, I, W, 1986 Arg 2
Galthié, F (Colomiers, SF) 1991 R, US 1, [R, Fj, C, E], 1992 W, E, S, R, Arg, 1994 I, W, E, 1995 [SA, E], 1996 W 1(R), 1997 I, It 2, SA 1,2, 1998 W (R), Fj (R), 1999 R, WS (R), Tg, NZ 1(R), [Fj (R), Arg, NZ 2, A], 2000 W, E, A, NZ 1,2, 2001 S, It, W, E, SA 1,2, NZ, SA 3, A, Fj, 2002 E, S, I, SA, NZ, C, 2003 E 1, S, Arg 1,2, NZ, R, E 2, [Fj,J,S,I,E]
Galy, J (Perpignan) 1953 W
Garbajosa, X (Toulouse) 1998 I, W, Arg 2(R), Fj, 1999 W 1(R), E, S, WS, NZ 1, W 2, [C, Nm (R), Fj (R), Arg, NZ 2, A], 2000 A, NZ 1,2, 2001 S, I, E, 2002 It (R), W, SA (R), C (R), 2003 E 1, S, I, It, W, E 3
Garuet-Lempirou, J-P (Lourdes) 1983 A 1,2, R, 1984 I, NZ 1,2, R, 1985 E, S, I, W, Arg 1, 1986 S, I, W, E, R 1, Arg 1, NZ 1, R 2, NZ 2,3, 1987 W, E, S, I, [S, R, Fj, A, NZ], 1988 E, S, Arg 1,2, R, 1989 E (R), S, NZ 1,2, 1990 W, E
Gasc, J (Graulhet) 1977 NZ 2
Gasparotto, G (Montferrand) 1976 A 2, R
Gauby, G (Perpignan) 1956 Cz
Gaudermen, P (RCF) 1906 E
Gayraud, W (Toulouse) 1920 I
Gelez, F (Agen) 2001 SA 3, 2002 I (R), A 1, SA, NZ, C (R), 2003 S, I
Geneste, R (BEC) 1945 B 1, 1949 Arg 2
Genet, J-P (RCF) 1992 S, I, R
Gensane, R (Béziers) 1962 S, E, W, I, It, R, 1963 S
Gerald, G (RCF) 1927 E, G 2, 1928 S, 1929 I, S, W, E, G, 1930 S, I, E, G, W, 1931 I, S, E, G
Gérard, D (Bègles) 1999 Tg
Gerintes, G (CASG) 1924 R, 1925 I, 1926 W
Geschwind, P (RCF) 1936 G 1,2
Giacardy, M (SBUC) 1907 E
Gimbert, P (Bègles) 1991 R, US 1, 1992 W, E
Giordani, P (Dax) 1999 E, S
Glas, S (Bourgoin) 1996 S (t), I (R), W 1, R, Arg 2(R), W 2, SA 1,2, 1997 I, W, E, S, It 2(R), R 2, Arg, SA 1,2, 1998 E, S, I, W, Arg 1,2, Fj, Arg 3, A, 1999 W 2, [C,Nm, Arg (R), NZ 2(R), A (t&R)], 2000 I, 2001 E, SA 1,2, NZ
Gomès, A (SF) 1998 Arg 1,2, Fj, Arg 3, A, 1999 I (R)
Gommes, J (RCF) 1909 I
Gonnet, C-A (Albi) 1921 E, I, 1922 E, W, 1924 S, E, 1926 S, I, E, W, M, 1927 I, S, W, E, G 1
Gonzalez, J-M (Bayonne) 1992 Arg 1,2, SA 1,2, Arg, 1993 R 1, SA 1,2, R 2, A 1,2, 1994 I, W, E, S, C 1, NZ 1,2, C 2, 1995 W, E, S, I, R 1, [Tg, S, I, SA, E], It, Arg, 1996 E, S, I, W 1
Got, R (Perpignan) 1920 I, US, 1921 S, W, 1922 S, E, W, I, 1924 I, E, W, R, US
Gourdon, J-F (RCF, Bagnères) 1974 S, Arg 1,2, R, SA 1,2, 1975 W, E, S, I, R, 1976 S, I, W, E, 1978 E, S, 1979 W, E, S, R, 1980 I
Gourragne, J-F (Béziers) 1990 NZ 2, 1991 W 1
Goutta, B (Perpignan) 2004 C
Goyard, A (Lyon U) 1936 G 1,2, 1937 G, It, 1938 G 1, R, G 2
Graciet, R (SBUC) 1926 I, W, 1927 S, G 1, 1929 E, 1930 W
Grandclaude, J-P (Perpignan) 2005 E(R),W(R)
Graou, S (Auch, Colomiers) 1992 Arg (R), 1993 SA 1,2, R 2, A 2(R), 1995 R 2, Arg (t), NZ 2(R)
Gratton, J (Agen) 1984 NZ 2, R, 1985 E, S, I, W, Arg 1,2, 1986 S, NZ 1
Graule, V (Arl Perpignan) 1926 I, E, W, 1927 S, W, 1931 G
Greffe, M (Grenoble) 1968 W, Cz, NZ 1,2, SA 1
Griffard, J (Lyon U) 1932 G, 1933 G, 1934 G
Gruarin, A (Toulon) 1964 W, It, I, SA, Fj, R, 1965 S, I, E, W, It, 1966 S, I, E, W, It, R, 1967 S, A, E, It, W, I, NZ, 1968 S, I
Guelorget, P (RCF) 1931 E, G
Guichemerre, A (Dax) 1920 E, 1921 E, I, 1923 S
Guilbert, A (Toulon) 1975 E, S, I, SA 1,2, 1976 A 1, 1977 Arg 1,2, NZ 1,2, R, 1979 I, W, E
Guillemin, P (RCF) 1908 E, W, 1909 E, I, 1910 W, S, E, I, 1911 S, E, W
Guilleux, P (Agen) 1952 SA, It
Guiral, M (Agen) 1931 G, 1932 G, 1933 G
Guiraud, H (Nîmes) 1996 R

Haget, A (PUC) 1953 E, 1954 I, NZ, E, Arg 2, 1955 E, W, It, 1957 I, E, It, R 1, 1958 It, SA 2
Haget, F (Agen, Biarritz O) 1974 Arg 1,2, 1975 SA 2, Arg 1,2, R, 1976 S, 1978 S, I, W, R, 1979 I, W, E, S, NZ 1,2, R, 1980 W, S, I, 1984 S, NZ 1,2, R, 1985 E, S, I, 1986 S, I, W, E, R 1, Arg 1, A, NZ 1, 1987 S, I, [R, Fj]
Haget, H (CASG) 1928 S, 1930 G
Halet, R (Strasbourg) 1925 NZ, S, W
Hall, S (Béziers) 2002 It, W
Harinordoquy, I (Pau, Biarritz)) 2002 W, E, S, I, A 1,2, SA, NZ, C, 2003 E 1, S, I, It, W, Arg 1(R),2, NZ, R, E 2,3(R), [Fj,S,I,E], 2004 I,It,W,E,A,Arg,NZ, 2005 W(R),2006 R(R),SA
Harislur-Arthapignet, P (Tarbes) 1988 Arg 4(R)
Harize, D (Cahors, Toulouse) 1975 SA 1,2, 1976 A 1,2, R, 1977 W, E, S, I
Hauc, J (Toulon) 1928 E, G, 1929 I, S, G
Hauser, M (Lourdes) 1969 E
Hedembaigt, M (Bayonne) 1913 S, SA, 1914 W
Hericé, D (Bègles) 1950 I
Herrero, A (Toulon) 1963 R, 1964 NZ, E, W, It, I, SA, Fj, R, 1965 S, I, E, W, 1966 W, It, R, 1967 S, A, E, It, I, R
Herrero, B (Nice) 1983 I, 1986 Arg 1
Heyer, F (Montferrand) 1990 A 2
Heymans, C (Agen, Toulouse) 2000 It (R) R, 2002 A 2(R), SA, NZ, 2004 W(R),US, C(R),A,Arg, NZ, 2005 I,It,SA1,2,A1,2,C,SA3, 2006 S,I,W(R), R,SA
Hiquet, J-C (Agen) 1964 E
Hoche, M (PUC) 1957 I, E, W, It, R 1
Hondagné-Monge, M (Tarbes) 1988 Arg 2(R)
Hontas, P (Biarritz) 1990 S, I, R, 1991 R, 1992 Arg, 1993 E, S, I, W
Hortoland, J-P (Béziers) 1971 A 2
Houblain, H (SCUF) 1909 E, 1910 W
Houdet, R (SF) 1927 S, W, G 1, 1928 G, W, 1929 I, S, E, 1930 S, E
Hourdebaigt, A (SBUC) 1909 I, 1910 W, S, E, I
Hubert, A (ASF) 1906 E, 1907 E, 1908 E, W, 1909 E, W, I
Hueber, A (Lourdes, Toulon) 1990 A 3, NZ 1, 1991 US 2, 1992 I, Arg 1,2, SA 1,2, 1993 E, S, I, W, R 1, SA 1,2, R 2, A 1,2, 1995 [Tg, S (R), I], 2000 It, R
Hutin, R (CASG) 1927 I, S, W
Hyardet, A (Castres) 1995 It, Arg (R)

Ibañez, R (Dax, Perpignan, Castres, Saracens, Wasps) 1996 W 1(R), 1997 It 1(R), R 1, It 2(R), R 2, SA 2(R), 1998 E, S, I, W, Arg 1,2, Fj, Arg 3, A, 1999 I, W 1, E, S, R, WS, Tg (R), NZ 1, W 2, [C, Nm, Fj, Arg, NZ 2, A], 2000 W (R), E (R), S (R), I (R), It (R), R, 2001 S, I, It, W, E, SA 1,2, NZ (R), SA 3, A, Fj, 2002 It (R), W, E, S, I, Arg, A 1(R),2, SA, NZ, C, 2003 E 1, S, I, It, W, R (R), E 2(R),3, [Fj,J(R),S,I,E,NZ(R)], 2005 C(R),Tg, 2006 I,It,E,W,R,SA(R)
Icard, J (SF) 1909 E, W
Iguiniz, E (Bayonne) 1914 E
Ihingoué, D (BEC) 1912 I, S
Imbernon, J-F (Perpignan) 1976 I, W, E, US, A 1, 1977 W, E, S, I, Arg 1,2, NZ 1,2, 1978 E, R, 1979 I, 1981 S, I, W, E, 1982 I, 1983 I, W
Iraçabal, J (Bayonne) 1968 NZ 1,2, SA 1, 1969 S, I, W, R, 1970 S, I, W, E, R, 1971 W, SA 1,2, A 1, 1972 E, W, I 2, A 2, R, 1973 S, NZ, E, W, I, J, 1974 I, W, E, S, Arg 1,2, SA 2(R)
Isaac, H (RCF) 1907 E, 1908 E
Ithurra, E (Biarritz O) 1936 G 1,2, 1937 G

Janeczek, T (Tarbes) 1982 Arg 1,2, 1990 R
Janik, K (Toulouse) 1987 R
Jarasse, A (Brive) 1945 B 1
Jardel, J (SB) 1928 I, E

Jaureguy, A (RCF, Toulouse, SF) 1920 S, E, W, I, US, 1922 S, W, 1923 S, W, E, I, 1924 S, W, R, US, 1925 I, NZ, 1926 S, E, W, M, 1927 I, E, 1928 S, A, E, G, W, 1929 I, S, E
Jaureguy, P (Toulouse) 1913 S, SA, W, I
Jauzion, Y (Colomiers, Toulouse) 2001 SA 1,2, NZ, 2002 A 1(R),2(R), 2003 Arg 2, NZ, R, E 2,3, [Fj,S,I,E], 2004 I,It,W,S,E,A,Arg,NZ(t), 2005 W,I,It,SA1,2,A1, 2,C,Tg(R),SA3, 2006 R,SA
Jeangrand, M-H (Tarbes) 1921 I
Jeanjean, N (Toulouse) 2001 SA 1,2, NZ, SA 3(R), A (R), Fj (R), 2002 It, Arg, A 1
Jeanjean, P (Toulon) 1948 I
Jérôme, G (SF) 1906 NZ, E
Joinel, J-L (Brive) 1977 NZ 1, 1978 R, 1979 I, W, E, S, NZ 1,2, R, 1980 W, E, S, I, SA, 1981 S, I, W, E, R, NZ 1,2, 1982 E, S, I, R, 1983 E, S, I, W, A 1,2, R, 1984 I, W, E, S, NZ 1,2, 1985 S, I, W, Arg 1, 1986 S, I, W, E, R 1, Arg 1,2, A, 1987 [Z]
Jol, M (Biarritz O) 1947 S, I, W, E, 1949 S, I, E, W, Arg 1,2
Jordana, J-L (Pau, Toulouse) 1996 R (R), Arg 1(t),2, W 2, 1997 I (t), W, S (R)
Judas du Souich, C (SCUF) 1911 W, I
Juillet, C (Montferrand, SF) 1995 R 2, Arg, 1999 E, S, WS, NZ 1, [C, Fj, Arg, NZ 2, A], 2000 A, NZ 1,2, 2001 S, I, It, W
Junquas, L (Tyrosse) 1945 B 1,2, W, 1946 B, I, K, W, 1947 S, I, W, E, 1948 S, W

Kaczorowski, D (Le Creusot) 1974 I (R)
Kaempf, A (St Jean-de-Luz) 1946 B

Labadie, P (Bayonne) 1952 S, I, SA, W, E, It, 1953 S, I, It, 1954 S, I, NZ, W, E, Arg 2, 1955 S, I, E, W, 1956 I, 1957 I
Labarthete, R (Pau) 1952 S
Labazuy, A (Lourdes) 1952 I, 1954 S, W, 1956 E, 1958 A, W, I, 1959 S, E, It, W
Labit, C (Toulouse) 1999 S, R (R), WS (R), Tg, 2000 R (R), 2002 Arg, A 1(R), 2003 Arg 1,2, NZ (R), R (R), E 3, [Fj(R),J,US,E(R),NZ]
Laborde, C (RCF) 1962 It, R, 1963 R, 1964 SA, 1965 E
Labrousse, T (Brive) 1996 R, SA 1
Lacans, P (Béziers) 1980 SA, 1981 W, E, A 2, R, 1982 W
Lacassagne, H (SBUC) 1906 NZ, 1907 E
Lacaussade, R (Bègles) 1948 A, S
Lacaze, C (Lourdes, Angoulême) 1961 NZ 2,3, A, R, 1962 E, W, I, It, 1963 W, R, 1964 S, NZ, E, 1965 It, R, 1966 S, I, E, W, It, R, 1967 S, E, SA 1,3,4, R, 1968 S, E, W, Cz, NZ 1, 1969 E
Lacaze, H (Périgueux) 1928 I, G, W, 1929 I, W
Lacaze, P (Lourdes) 1958 SA 1,2, 1959 S, E, It, W, I
Lacazedieu, C (Dax) 1923 W, I, 1928 A, I, 1929 S
Lacombe, B (Agen) 1989 B, 1990 A 2
Lacome, M (Pau) 1960 Arg 2
Lacoste, R (Tarbes) 1914 I, W, E
Lacrampe, F (Béziers) 1949 Arg 2
Lacroix, P (Mont-de-Marsan, Agen) 1958 A, 1960 W, I, It, R, Arg 1,2,3, 1961 S, SA, E, W, I, NZ 1,2,3, A, R, 1962 S, E, W, I, R, 1963 S, I, E, W
Lacroix, T (Dax, Harlequins) 1989 A 1(R),2, 1991 W 1(R),2(R), [R, C (R), E], 1992 SA 2, 1993 E, S, I, W, SA 1,2, R 2, A 1,2, 1994 I, W, E, S, C 1, NZ 1,2, C 2, 1995 W, E, S, R 1, [Tg, Iv, S, I, SA, E], 1996 E, S, I, 1997 It 2, R 2, Arg, SA 1,2
Lafarge, Y (Montferrand) 1978 R, 1979 NZ 1, 1981 I (R)
Laffitte, R (SCUF) 1910 W, S
Laffont, H (Narbonne) 1926 W
Lafond, A (Bayonne) 1922 E
Lafond, J-B (RCF) 1983 A 1, 1985 Arg 1,2 1986 S, I, W, E, R 1, 1987 I (R), 1988 W, 1989 I, W, E, 1990 W, A 3(R), NZ 2, 1991 S, I, W 1, E, R, US 1, W 2, [R (R), Fj, C, E], 1992 W, E, S, I (R), SA 2, 1993 E, S, I, W
Lagisquet, P (Bayonne) 1983 A 1,2, R, 1984 I, W, NZ 1,2, 1986 R 1(R), Arg 1,2, A, NZ 1, 1987 [S, R, Fj, A, NZ], R, 1988 S, I, W, Arg 1,2,3,4, R, 1989 I, W, E, S, NZ 1,2, B, A 1,2, 1990 W, E, S, I, A 1,2,3, 1991 S, I, US 2, [R]
Lagrange, J-C (RCF) 1966 It
Laharrague, J (Brive, Perpignan) 2005 W,I,It,SA1, A1,2,C(R),Tg, 2006 R(R),SA
Lalande, M (RCF) 1923 S, W, I
Lalanne, F (Mont-de-Marsan) 2000 R
Lamaison, C (Brive, Agen) 1996 SA 1(R),2, 1997 W, E, S, R 1, A 2, It 2, R 2, Arg, SA 1,2, 1998 E, S, I, W, Arg 3(R), A, 1999 R, WS (R), Tg, NZ 1(R), W 2(R), [C (R), Nm, Fj, Arg, NZ 2, A], 2000 W, A, NZ 1,2, 2001 S, I, It, W (R)
Lamboley, G (Toulouse) 2005 S(R), E(R), W(R), I(R), It(R), SA1(R), 2(R), A1, 2(R), C(R), Tg, SA3(R)
Landreau, F (SF) 2000 A, NZ 1,2, 2001 E (R)
Lane, G (RCF) 1906 NZ, E, 1907 E, 1908 E, W, 1909 E, W, I, 1910 W, E, 1911 S, W, 1912 I, W, E, 1913 S
Langlade, J-C (Hyères) 1990 R, A 1, NZ 1
Laperne, D (Dax) 1997 R 1(R)
Laporte, G (Graulhet) 1981 I, W, E, R, NZ 1,2, 1986 S, I, W, E, R 1, Arg 1, A (R), 1987 [R, Z (R), Fj]
Larreguy, P (Bayonne) 1954 It
Larribau, J (Périgueux) 1912 I, S, W, E, 1913 S, 1914 I, E
Larrieu, J (Tarbes) 1920 I, US, 1921 W, 1923 S, W, E, I
Larrieux, M (SBUC) 1927 G 2
Larrue, H (Carmaux) 1960 W, I, It, R, Arg 1,2,3
Lasaosa, P (Dax) 1950 I, 1952 S, I, E, It, 1955 It
Lascubé, G (Agen) 1991 S, I, W 1, E, US 2, W 2, [R, Fj, C, E], 1992 W, E
Lassegue, J-B (Toulouse) 1946 W, 1947 S, I, W, 1948 W, 1949 I, E, W, Arg 1
Lasserre, F (René) (Bayonne, Cognac, Grenoble) 1914 I, 1920 S, 1921 S, W, I, 1922 S, E, W, I, 1923 W, E, 1924 S, I, R, US
Lasserre, J-C (Dax) 1963 It, 1964 S, NZ, E, W, It, I, Fj, 1965 W, It, R, 1966 R, 1967 S
Lasserre, M (Agen) 1967 SA 2,3, 1968 E, W, Cz, NZ 3, A, SA 1,2, 1969 S, I, E, 1970 E, 1971 E, W
Laterrade, G (Tarbes) 1910 E, I, 1911 S, E, I
Laudouar, J (Soustons, SBUC) 1961 NZ 1,2, R, 1962 I, R
Lauga, P (Vichy) 1950 S, I, E, W
Laurent, A (Biarritz O) 1925 NZ, S, W, E, 1926 W
Laurent, J (Bayonne) 1920 S, E, W
Laurent, M (Auch) 1932 G, 1933 G, 1934 G, 1935 G, 1936 G 1
Laussucq, C (SF) 1999 S (R), 2000 W (R), S, I
Lavail, G (Perpignan) 1937 G, 1940 B
Lavaud, R (Carcassonne) 1914 I, W
Lavergne, P (Limoges) 1950 S
Lavigne, B (Agen) 1984 R, 1985 E
Lavigne, J (Dax) 1920 E, W
Lazies, H (Auch) 1954 Arg 2, 1955 It, 1956 E, 1957 S
Le Bourhis, R (La Rochelle) 1961 R
Lecointre, M (Nantes) 1952 It
Le Droff, J (Auch) 1963 It, R, 1964 S, NZ, E, 1970 E, R, 1971 S, I
Lefevre, R (Brive) 1961 NZ 2
Leflamand, L (Bourgoin) 1996 SA 2, 1997 W, E, S, It 2, Arg, SA 1,2(R)
Lefort, J-B (Biarritz O) 1938 G 1
Le Goff, R (Métro) 1938 R, G 2
Legrain, M (SF) 1909 I, 1910 I, 1911 S, E, W, I, 1913 S, SA, E, I, 1914 I, W
Lemeur, Y (RCF) 1993 R 1
Lenient, J-J (Vichy) 1967 R
Lepatey, J (Mazamet) 1954 It, 1955 S, I, E, W
Lepatey, L (Mazamet) 1924 S, I, E
Lescarboura, J-P (Dax) 1982 W, E, S, I, 1983 A 1,2, R, 1984 I, W, E, S, NZ 1,2, R, 1985 E, S, I, W, Arg 1,2, 1986 Arg 2, A, NZ 1, R 2, NZ 2, 1988 S, W, 1990 R
Lesieur, E (SF) 1906 E, 1908 E, W, 1909 E, W, I, 1910 S, E, I, 1911 E, I, 1912 W
Leuvielle, M (SBUC) 1908 W, 1913 S, SA, E, W, 1914 W, E
Levasseur, R (SF) 1925 W, E
Levée, H (RCF) 1906 NZ
Lewis, E W (Le Havre) 1906 E
Lhermet, J-M (Montferrand) 1990 S, I, 1993 R 1
Libaros, G (Tarbes) 1936 G 1, 1940 B
Liebenberg, B (SF) 2003 R (R), E 2(R),3, [US,I(R),NZ(R)], 2004 I(R),US,C,NZ, 2005 S,E
Lièvremont, M (Perpignan, SF) 1995 It, R 2, Arg (R), NZ 2(R),

1996 R, Arg 1(R), SA 2(R), 1997 R 1, A 2(R), 1998 E (R), S, I, W, Arg 1,2, Fj, Arg 3, A, 1999 W 2, [C, Nm, Fj, Arg, NZ 2, A]
Lièvremont, T (Perpignan, SF, Biarritz) 1996 W 2(R), 1998 E, S, I, W, Arg 1,2, Fj, Arg 3, A, 1999 I, W 1, E, W 2, [Nm], 2000 W (R), E (R), S (R), I, It, 2001 E (R), 2004 I(R),It(R),W,S,US,C, 2005 A2,C,Tg(t&R), SA3(R), 2006 S(R),It,E,W
Lira, M (La Voulte) 1962 R, 1963 I, E, W, It, R, 1964 W, It, I, SA, 1965 S, I, R
Llari, R (Carcassonne) 1926 S
Lobies, J (RCF) 1921 S, W, E
Lombard, F (Narbonne) 1934 G, 1937 It
Lombard, T (SF) 1998 Arg 3, A, 1999 I, W 1, S (R), 2000 W, E, S, A, NZ 1, 2001 It, W
Lombarteix, R (Montferrand) 1938 R, G 2
Londios, J (Montauban) 1967 SA 3
Loppy, L (Toulon) 1993 R 2
Lorieux, A (Grenoble, Aix) 1981 A 1, R, NZ 1,2, 1982 W, 1983 A 2, R, 1984 I, W, E, 1985 Arg 1,2(R), 1986 R 2, NZ 2,3, 1987 W, E, [S, Z, Fj, A, NZ], 1988 S, I, W, Arg 1,2,4, 1989 W, A 2
Loury, A (RCF) 1927 E, G 1,2, 1928 S, A, I
Loustau, L (Perpignan) 2004 C
Loustau, M (Dax) 1923 E
Lubin-Lebrère, M-F (Toulouse) 1914 I, W, E, 1920 S, E, W, I, US, 1921 S, 1922 S, E, W, 1924 W, US, 1925 I
Lubrano, A (Béziers) 1972 A 2, 1973 S
Lux, J-P (Tyrosse, Dax) 1967 E, It, W, I, SA 1,2,4, R, 1968 I, E, Cz, NZ 3, A, SA 1,2, 1969 S, I, E, 1970 S, I, W, E, R, 1971 S, I, E, W, A 1,2, 1972 S, I 1, E, W, I 2, A 1,2, R, 1973 S, NZ, E, 1974 I, W, E, S, Arg 1,2, 1975 W

Macabiau, A (Perpignan) 1994 S, C 1
Maclos, P (SF) 1906 E, 1907 E
Magne, O (Dax, Brive, Montferrand, Clermont-Auvergne, London Irish) 1997 W (R), E, S, R 1(R), A 1,2, It 2(R), R 2, Arg (R), 1998 E, S, I, W, Arg 1,2, Fj, Arg 3, A, 1999 I, R, WS, NZ 1, W 2, [C, Nm, Fj, Arg, NZ 2, A], 2000 W, E, S, It, R, A, NZ 1,2, 2001 S, I, It, W, E, SA 1,2, NZ, SA 3, A, Fj, 2002 It, E, S, I, Arg, A 1,2(R), SA, NZ, C, 2003 E 1, S, I, It, W, R, E 2,3(R), [Fj,J,S,I,E,NZ(R)], 2004 I,It,W(R),S,E,A,Arg,NZ, 2005 SA1,2(R),A1, 2006 I,It,E,W(R)
Magnanou, C (RCF) 1923 E, 1925 W, E, 1926 S, 1929 S, W, 1930 S, I, E, W
Magnol, L (Toulouse) 1928 S, 1929 S, W, E
Magois, H (La Rochelle) 1968 SA 1,2, R
Majerus, R (SF) 1928 W, 1929 I, S, 1930 S, I, E, G, W
Malbet, J-C (Agen) 1967 SA 2,4
Maleig, A (Oloron) 1979 W, E, NZ 2, 1980 W, E, SA, R
Mallier, L (Brive) 1999 R, W 2(R), [C (R)], 2000 I (R), It
Malquier, Y (Narbonne) 1979 S
Manterola, T (Lourdes) 1955 It, 1957 R 1
Mantoulan, C (Pau) 1959 I
Marcet, J (Albi) 1925 I, NZ, S, W, E, 1926 I, E
Marchal, J-F (Lourdes) 1979 S, R, 1980 W, S, I
Marconnet, S (SF) 1998 Arg 3, A, 1999 I (R), W 1(R), E, S (R), R, Tg, 2000 A, NZ 1,2, 2001 S, I, It (R), W (R), E, 2002 S (R), Arg (R), A 1,2, SA (R), C (R), 2003 E 1(R), S, I, It, W, Arg 1(t+R),2, NZ, R, E 2,3(t+R), [S,US(R),I,E,NZ], 2004 i , i t , W , S , E , A , Arg,NZ, 2005 S,E,W,I,It,SA1,2,A1(R),2(R),C,Tg, SA3(R), 2006 S,I(R),It(R),E,W,R,SA
Marchand, R (Poitiers) 1920 S, W
Marfaing, M (Toulouse) 1992 R, Arg 1
Marlu, J (Montferrand, Biarritz)) 1998 Fj (R), 2002 S (R), I (R), 2005 E
Marocco, P (Montferrand) 1968 S, I, W, E, R 1, Arg 1,2, A, 1988 Arg 4, 1989 I, 1990 E (R), NZ 1(R), 1991 S, I, W 1, E, US 2, [R, Fj, C, E]
Marot, A (Brive) 1969 R, 1970 S, I, W, 1971 SA 1, 1972 I 2, 1976 A 1
Marquesuzaa, A (RCF) 1958 It, SA 1,2, 1959 S, E, It, W, 1960 S, E, Arg 1
Marracq, H (Pau) 1961 R
Marsh, T (Montferrand) 2001 SA 3, A, Fj, 2002 It, W, E, S, I, Arg, A 1,2, 2003 [Fj,J,S,I,E,NZ], 2004 C,A,Arg,NZ
Martin, C (Lyon) 1909 I, 1910 W, S
Martin, H (SBUC) 1907 E, 1908 W
Martin, J-L (Béziers) 1971 A 2, R, 1972 S, I 1
Martin, L (Pau) 1948 I, A, S, W, E, 1950 S
Martin, R (SF) 2002 E (t+R), S (R), I (R), 2005 SA1(t&R),2,A1,2,C,SA3, 2006 S,I(t&R),R,SA(R)
Martine, R (Lourdes) 1952 S, I, It, 1953 It, 1954 S, I, NZ, W, E, It, Arg 2, 1955 S, I, W, 1958 A, W, It, I, SA 1,2, 1960 S, E, Arg 3, 1961 S, It
Martinez, A (Narbonne) 2002 A 1, 2004 C
Martinez, G (Toulouse) 1982 W, E, S, Arg 1,2, 1983 E, W
Marty, D (Perpignan) 2005 It,C,Tg, 2006 I,It(R),R (R)
Mas, F (Béziers) 1962 R, 1963 S, I, E, W
Mas, N (Perpignan) 2003 NZ, 2005 E,W,I,It
Maso, J (Perpignan, Narbonne) 1966 It, R, 1967 S, R, 1968 S, W, Cz, NZ 1,2,3, A, R, 1969 S, I, W, 1971 SA 1,2, R, 1972 E, W, A 2, 1973 W, I, J, R
Massare, J (PUC) 1945 B 1,2, W, 1946 B, I, W
Massé, A (SBUC) 1908 W, 1909 E, W, 1910 W, S, E, I
Masse, H (Grenoble) 1937 G
Matheu-Cambas, J (Agen) 1945 W, 1946 B, I, K, W, 1947 S, I, W, E, 1948 I, A, S, W, E, 1949 S, I, E, W, Arg 1,2, 1950 E, W, 1951 S, I
Matiu, L (Biarritz) 2000 W, E
Mauduy, G (Périgueux) 1957 It, R 1,2, 1958 S, E, 1961 W, It
Mauran, J (Castres) 1952 SA, W, E, It, 1953 I, E
Mauriat, P (Lyon) 1907 E, 1908 E, W, 1909 W, I, 1910 W, S, E, I, 1911 S, E, W, I, 1912 I, S, 1913 S, SA, W, I
Maurin, G (ASF) 1906 E
Maury, A (Toulouse) 1925 I, NZ, S, W, E, 1926 S, I, E
Mayssonnié, A (Toulouse) 1908 E, W, 1910 W
Mazas, L (Colomiers, Biarritz) 1992 Arg, 1996 SA 1
Melville, E (Toulon) 1990 I (R), A 1,2,3, NZ 1, 1991 US 2
Menrath, R (SCUF) 1910 W
Menthiller, Y (Romans) 1964 W, It, SA, R, 1965 E
Merceron, G (Montferrand) 1999 R (R), Tg, 2000 S, I, R, 2001 S (R), W, E, SA 1,2, NZ (R), Fj, 2002 It, W, E, S, I, Arg, A 2, C, 2003 E 1, It (R), W (R), NZ (t+R), R (R), E 3, [Fj(R),J(R),S(R),US,E(R),NZ]
Meret, F (Tarbes) 1940 B
Mericq, S (Agen) 1959 I, 1960 S, E, W, 1961 I
Merle, O (Grenoble, Montferrand) 1993 SA 1,2, R 2, A 1,2, 1994 I, W, E, S, C 1, NZ 1,2, C 2, 1995 W, I, R 1, [Tg, S, I, SA, E], It, R 2, Arg, NZ 1,2, 1996 E, S, R, Arg 1,2, W 2, SA 2, 1997 I, W, E, S, It 1, R 1, A 1,2, It 2, R 2, SA 1(R),2
Merquey, J (Toulon)1950 S, I, E, W
Mesnel, F (RCF) 1986 NZ 2(R),3, 1987 W, E, S, I, [S, Z, Fj, A, NZ], R, 1988 E, Arg 1,2,3,4, R, 1989 I, W, E, S, NZ 1, A 1,2, 1990 E, S, I, A 2,3, NZ 1,2, 1991 S, I, W 1, E, R, US 1,2, W 2, [R, Fj, C, E], 1992 W, E, S, I, SA 1,2, 1993 E (R), W, 1995 I, R 1, [Iv, E]
Mesny, P (RCF, Grenoble) 1979 NZ 1,2, 1980 SA, R, 1981 I, W (R), A 1,2, R, NZ 1,2, 1982 I, Arg 1,2
Meyer, G-S (Périgueux) 1960 S, E, It, R, Arg 2
Meynard, J (Cognac) 1954 Arg 1, 1956 Cz
Mias, L (Mazamet) 1951 S, I, E, W, 1952 I, SA, W, E, It, 1953 S, I, W, It, 1954 S, I, NZ, W, 1957 R 2, 1958 S, E, A, W, I, SA 1,2, 1959 S, It, W, I
Michalak, F (Toulouse) 2001 SA 3(R), A, Fj (R), 2002 It, A 1,2, 2003 It, W, Arg 2(R), NZ, R, E 2, [Fj,J,S,I,E,NZ(R)], 2004 I , W , S , E , A , A r g , N Z , 2 0 0 5 S(R),E(R),W(R),I(R),It(R),SA1,2,A1,2,C,Tg(R),SA3, 2006 S,I,It,E,W
Mignoni, P (Béziers, Clermont-Auvergne)) 1997 R 2(R), Arg (t), 1999 R (R), WS, NZ 1, W 2(R), [C, Nm], 2002 W, E (R), I (R), Arg, A 2(R), 2005 S,It(R),C(R), 2006 R
Milhères, C (Biarritz) 2001 E
Milliand, P (Grenoble) 1936 G 2, 1937 G, It
Millo-Chlusky, R (Toulouse) 2005 SA1
Milloud, O (Bourgoin) 2000 R (R), 2001 NZ, 2002 W (R), E (R), 2003 It (R), W (R), Arg 1, R (R), E 2(t+R),3, [J,S(R),US,I(R),E(R)], 2004 US,C(R),A,Arg,NZ(R), 2005 S(R),E(R),W(R),SA1,2(R),A1,2,C(R),Tg,SA3, 2006 S(R),I,It,E(R)
Minjat, R (Lyon) 1945 B 1

FRANCE

Miorin, H (Toulouse) 1996 R, SA 1, 1997 I, W, E, S, It 1, 2000 It (R), R (R)
Mir, J-H (Lourdes) 1967 R, 1968 I
Mir, J-P (Lourdes) 1967 A
Modin, R (Brive) 1987 [Z]
Moga, A-M-A (Bègles) 1945 B 1,2, W, 1946 B, I, K, W, 1947 S, I, W, E, 1948 I, A, S, W, E, 1949 S, I, E, W, Arg 1,2
Mola, U (Dax, Castres) 1997 S (R), 1999 R (R), WS, Tg (R), NZ 1, W 2, [C, Nm, Fj, Arg (R), NZ 2(R), A (R)]
Mommejat, B (Cahors, Albi) 1958 It, I, SA 1,2, 1959 S, E, It, W, I, 1960 S, E, I, R, 1962 S, E, W, I, It, R, 1963 S, I, W
Moncla, F (RCF, Pau) 1956 Cz, 1957 I, E, W, It, R 1, 1958 SA 1,2, 1959 S, E, It, W, I, 1960 S, E, W, I, It, R, Arg 1,2,3, 1961 S, SA, E, W, It, I, NZ 1,2,3
Moni, C (Nice, SF) 1996 R, 2000 A, NZ 1,2, 2001 S, I, It, W
Monié, R (Perpignan) 1956 Cz, 1957 E
Monier, R (SBUC) 1911 I, 1912 S
Monniot, M (RCF) 1912 W, E
Montade, A (Perpignan) 1925 I, NZ, S, W, 1926 W
Montlaur, P (Agen) 1992 E (R), 1994 S (R)
Moraitis, B (Toulon) 1969 E, W
Morel, A (Grenoble) 1954 Arg 2
Morere, J (Toulouse) 1927 E, G 1, 1928 S, A
Moscato, V (Bègles) 1991 R, US 1, 1992 W, E
Mougeot, C (Bègles) 1992 W, E, Arg
Mouniq, P (Toulouse) 1911 S, E, W, I,1912 I, E, 1913 S, SA, E
Moure, H (SCUF) 1908 E
Moureu, P (Béziers) 1920 I, US, 1921 W, E, I, 1922 S, W, I, 1923 S, W, E, I, 1924 S, I, E, W, 1925 E
Mournet, A (Bagnères) 1981 A 1(R)
Mouronval, F (SF) 1909 I
Muhr, A H (RCF) 1906 NZ, E, 1907 E
Murillo, G (Dijon) 1954 It, Arg 1

Nallet, L (Bourgoin, Castres) 2000 R, 2001 E, SA 1(R),2(R), NZ, SA 3(R), A (R), Fj (R), 2003 NZ, 2005 A2(R),C,Tg(R),SA3, 2006 I(R),It(R),E(R),W(R),R,SA (R)
Namur, R (Toulon) 1931 E, G
Noble, J-C (La Voulte) 1968 E, W, Cz, NZ 3, A, R
Normand, A (Toulouse) 1957 R 1
Novès, G (Toulouse) 1977 NZ 1,2, R, 1978 W, R, 1979 I, W
Ntamack, E (Toulouse) 1994 W, C 1, NZ 1,2, C 2, 1995 W, I, R 1, [Tg, S, I, SA, E], It, R 2, Arg, NZ 1,2, 1996 E, S, I, W 1, R (R), Arg 1,2, W 2, 1997 I, 1998 Arg 3, 1999 I, W 1, E, S, WS, NZ 1, W 2(R), [C (R), Nm, Fj, Arg, NZ 2, A], 2000 W, E, S, I, It
Ntamack F (Colomiers) 2001 SA 3
Nyanga, Y (Béziers, Toulouse) 2004 US,C, 2005 S(R),E(R),W,I,It,SA1,2,A1(R),2,C(t&R),Tg,SA3, 2006 S,I,It,E,W

Olive, D (Montferrand) 1951 I, 1952 I
Ondarts, P (Biarritz O) 1986 NZ 3, 1987 W, E, S, I, [S, Z, Fj, A, NZ], R, 1988 E, I, W, Arg 1,2,3,4, R, 1989 I, W, E, NZ 1,2, A 2, 1990 W, E, S, I, R (R), NZ 1,2, 1991 S, I, W 1, E, US 2, W 2, [R, Fj, C, E]
Orso, J-C (Nice, Toulon) 1982 Arg 1,2, 1983 E, S, A 1, 1984 E (R), S, NZ 1, 1985 I (R), W, 1988 I
Othats, J (Dax) 1960 Arg 2,3
Ougier, S (Toulouse) 1992 R, Arg 1, 1993 E (R), 1997 It 1

Paco, A (Béziers) 1974 Arg 1,2, R, SA 1,2, 1975 W, E, Arg 1,2, R, 1976 S, I, W, E, US, A 1,2, R, 1977 W, E, S, I, NZ 1,2, R, 1978 E, S, I, W, R, 1979 I, W, E, S, 1980 W
Palat, J (Perpignan) 1938 G 2
Palmié, M (Béziers) 1975 SA 1,2, Arg 1,2, R, 1976 S, I, W, E, US, 1977 W, E, S, I, Arg 1,2, NZ 1,2, R, 1978 E, S, I, W
Paoli, R (see Simonpaoli)
Paparemborde, R (Pau) 1975 SA 1,2, Arg 1,2, R, 1976 S, I, W, E, US, A 1,2, R, 1977 W, E, S, I, Arg 1, NZ 1,2, 1978 E, S, I, W, R, 1979 I, W, E, S, NZ 1,2, R, 1980 W, E, S, SA, R, 1981 S, I, W, E, A 1,2, R, NZ 1,2, 1982 W, I, R, Arg 1,2 1983 E, S, I, W
Papé, P (Bourgoin) 2004 I,It,W,S,E,C,NZ(R), 2005 I(R),It(R),SA1,2,A1
Pardo, L (Hendaye) 1924 I, E
Pardo, L (Bayonne) 1980 SA, R, 1981 S, I, W, E, A 1, 1982 W, E, S, 1983 A 1(R), 1985 S, I, Arg 2
Pargade, J-H (Lyon U) 1953 It
Paries, L (Biarritz O) 1968 SA 2, R, 1970 S, I, W, 1975 E, S, I
Pascalin, P (Mont-de-Marsan) 1950 I, E, W, 1951 S, I, E, W
Pascarel, J-R (TOEC) 1912 W, E, 1913 S, SA, E, I
Pascot, J (Perpignan) 1922 S, E, I, 1923 S, 1926 I, 1927 G 2
Paul, R (Montferrand) 1940 B
Pauthe, G (Graulhet) 1956 E
Pebeyre, E-J (Fumel, Brive) 1945 W, 1946 I, K, W, 1947 S, I, W, E
Pebeyre, M (Vichy, Montferrand) 1970 E, R, 1971 I, SA 1,2, A 1, 1973 W
Péclier, A (Bourgoin) 2004 US,C
Pecune, J (Tarbes) 1974 W, E, S, 1975 Arg 1,2, R, 1976 I, W, E, US
Pedeutour, P (Begles) 1980 I
Pellissier, L (RCF) 1928 A, I, E, G, W
Pelous, F (Dax, Toulouse) 1995 R 2, Arg, NZ 1,2, 1996 E, S, I, R (R), Arg 1,2, W 2, SA 1,2, 1997 I, W, E, S, It 1, R 1, A 1,2, It 2, R 2, Arg, SA 1,2(R), 1998 E, S, I, W, Arg 1,2, Fj, Arg 3, A, 1999 I, W 1, E, R (R), WS, Tg (R), NZ 1, W 2, [C, Nm, Fj, NZ 2, A], 2000 W, E, S, I, It, A, NZ 1,2, 2001 S, I, It, W, E, 2002 It (R), W (R), E (R), S, I, Arg, A 1,2, SA, NZ, C, 2003 E 1, S, I, It, W, R, E 2,3(R), [Fj,J,S,I,E,NZ(R)], 2004 I,It,W,S,E,US,C,A,Arg,NZ, 2005 S,E,W,I,It,A2, 2006 S,I,It,E,W,R,SA
Penaud, A (Brive, Toulouse) 1992 W, E, S, I, R, Arg 1,2, SA 1,2, Arg, 1993 R 1, SA 1,2, R 2, A 1,2, 1994 I, W, E, 1995 NZ 1,2, 1996 S, R, Arg 1,2, W 2, 1997 I, E, R 1, A 2, 2000 W (R), It
Périé, M (Toulon) 1996 E, S, I (R)
Peron, P (RCF) 1975 SA 1,2
Perrier, P (Bayonne) 1982 W, E, S, I (R)
Pesteil, J-P (Béziers) 1975 SA 1, 1976 A 2, R
Petit, C (Lorrain) 1931 W
Peyrelade, H (Tarbes) 1940 B
Peyrelongue, J (Biarritz) 2004 It,S(R),C(R),A(R), Arg(R),NZ
Peyroutou, G (Périgueux) 1911 S, E
Phliponeau, J-F (Montferrand) 1973 W, I
Piazza, A (Montauban) 1968 NZ 1, A
Picard, T (Montferrand) 1985 Arg 2, 1986 R 1(R), Arg 2
Pierrot, G (Pau) 1914 I, W, E
Pilon, J (Périgueux) 1949 E, 1950 E
Piqué, J (Pau) 1961 NZ 2,3, A, 1962 S, It, 1964 NZ, E, W, It, I, SA, Fj, R, 1965 S, I, E, W, It
Piquemal, M (Tarbes) 1927 I, S, 1929 I, G, 1930 S, I, E, G, W
Piquiral, E (RCF) 1924 S, I, E, W, R, US, 1925 E, 1926 S, I, E, W, M, 1927 I, S, W, E, G 1,2, 1928 E
Piteu, R (Pau) 1921 S, W, E, I, 1922 S, E, W, I, 1923 E, 1924 E, 1925 I, NZ, W, E, 1926 E
Plantefol, A (RCF) 1967 SA 2,3,4, NZ, R, 1968 E, W, Cz, NZ 2, 1969 E, W
Plantey, S (RCF) 1961 A, 1962 It
Podevin, G (SF) 1913 W, I
Poeydebasque, F (Bayonne) 1914 I, W
Poirier, A (SCUF) 1907 E
Poitrenaud, C (Toulouse) 2001 SA 3, A, Fj, 2003 E 1, S, I, It, W, Arg 1, NZ, E 3, [J,US,E(R),NZ], 2004 E(R),US,C,Arg(R),NZ, 2006 R
Pomathios, M (Agen, Lyon U, Bourg) 1948 I, A, S, W, E, 1949 S, I, E, W, Arg 1,2, 1950 S, I, W, 1951 S, I, E, W, 1952 W, E, 1953 S, I, W, 1954 S
Pons, P (Toulouse) 1920 S, E, W, 1921 S, W, 1922 S
Porcu, C (Agen) 2002 Arg (R), A 1,2(R)
Porra, M (Lyon) 1931 I
Porthault, A (RCF) 1951 S, E, W, 1952 I, 1953 S, I, It
Portolan, C (Toulouse) 1986 A, 1989 I, E
Potel, A (Begles) 1932 G
Poux, J-B (Narbonne, Toulouse) 2001 Fj (R), 2002 S, I (R), Arg, A 1(R),2(R), 2003 E 3, [Fj,J,US,NZ]
Prat, J (Lourdes) 1945 B 1,2, W, 1946 B, I, K, W, 1947 S, I, W, E, 1948 I, A, S, W, E, 1949 S, I, E, W, Arg 1,2, 1950 S,

I, E, W, 1951 S, E, W, 1952 S, I, SA, W, E, It, 1953 S, I, E, W, It, 1954 S, I, NZ, W, E, It, 1955 S, I, E, W, It
Prat, M (Lourdes) 1951 I, 1952 S, I, SA, W, E, 1953 S, I, E, 1954 I, NZ, W, E, It, 1955 S, I, E, W, It, 1956 I, W, It, Cz, 1957 S, I, W, It, R 1, 1958 A, W, I
Prevost, A (Albi) 1926 M, 1927 I, S, W
Prin-Clary, J (Cavaillon, Brive) 1945 B 1,2, W, 1946 B, I, K, W, 1947 S, I, W
Privat, T (Béziers, Clermont-Auvergne) 2001 SA 3, A, Fj, 2002 It, W, S (R), SA (R), 2003 [NZ], 2005 SA2,A1(R)
Puech, L (Toulouse) 1920 S, E, I, 1921 E, I
Puget, M (Toulouse) 1961 It, 1966 S, I, It, 1967 SA 1,3,4, NZ, 1968 Cz, NZ 1,2, SA 1,2, R, 1969 E, R, 1970 W
Puig, A (Perpignan) 1926 S, E
Pujol, A (SOE Toulouse) 1906 NZ
Pujolle, M (Nice) 1989 B, A 1, 1990 S, I, R, A 1,2, NZ 2

Quaglio, A (Mazamet) 1957 R 2, 1958 S, E, A, W, I, SA 1,2, 1959 S, E, It, W, I
Quilis, A (Narbonne) 1967 SA 1,4, NZ, 1970 R, 1971 I

Rabadan, P (SF) 2004 US(R),C(R)
Ramis, R (Perpignan) 1922 E, I, 1923 W
Rancoule, H (Lourdes, Toulon, Tarbes) 1955 E, W, It, 1958 A, W, It, I, SA 1, 1959 S, It, W, 1960 I, It, R, Arg 1,2, 1961 SA, E, W, It, NZ 1,2, 1962 S, E, W, I, It
Rapin, A (SBUC) 1938 R
Raymond, F (Toulouse) 1925 S, 1927 W, 1928 I
Raynal, F (Perpignan) 1935 G, 1936 G 1,2, 1937 G, It
Raynaud, F (Carcassonne) 1933 G
Raynaud, M (Narbonne) 1999 W 1, E (R)
Razat, J-P (Agen) 1962 R, 1963 S, I, R
Rebujent, R (RCF) 1963 E
Revailler, D (Graulhet) 1981 S, I, W, E, A 1,2, R, NZ 1,2, 1982 W, S, I, R, Arg 1
Revillon, J (RCF) 1926 I, E, 1927 S
Ribère, E (Perpignan, Quillan) 1924 I, 1925, I, NZ, S, 1926 S, I, W, M, 1927 I, S, W, E, G 1,2, 1928 S, A, I, E, G, W, 1929 I, E, G, 1930 S, I, E, W, 1931 I, S, W, E, G, 1932 G, 1933 G
Rives, J-P (Toulouse, RCF) 1975 E, S, I, Arg 1,2, R, 1976 S, I, W, E, US, A 1,2, R, 1977 W, E, S, I, Arg 1,2, R, 1978 E, S, I, W, R, 1979 I, W, E, S, NZ 1,2, R, 1980 W, E, S, I, SA, 1981 S, I, W, E, A 2, 1982 W, E, S, I, R, 1983 E, S, I, W, A 1,2, R, 1984 I, W, E, S
Rochon, A (Montferrand) 1936 G 1
Rodrigo, M (Mauléon) 1931 I, W
Rodriguez, L (Mont-de-Marsan, Montferrand, Dax) 1981 A 1,2, R, NZ 1,2, 1982 W, E, S, I, R, 1983 E, S, 1984 I, NZ 1,2, R, 1985 E, S, I, W, 1986 Arg 1, A, R 2, NZ 2,3, 1987 W, E, S, I, [S, Z, Fj, A, NZ], R, 1988 E, S, I, W, Arg 1,2,3,4, R, 1989 I, E, S, NZ 1,2, B, A 1, 1990 W, E, S, I, NZ 1
Rogé, L (Béziers) 1952 It, 1953 E, W, It, 1954 S, Arg 1,2, 1955 S, I, 1956 W, It, E, 1957 S, 1960 S, E
Rollet, J (Bayonne) 1960 Arg 3, 1961 NZ 3, A, 1962 It, 1963 I
Romero, H (Montauban) 1962 S, E, W, I, It, R, 1963 E
Romeu, J-P (Montferrand) 1972 R, 1973 S, NZ, E, W, I, R, 1974 W, E, S, Arg 1,2, R, SA 1,2(R), 1975 W, SA 2, Arg 1,2, R, 1976 S, I, W, E, US, 1977 W, E, S, I, Arg 1,2, NZ 1,2, R
Roques, A (Cahors) 1958 A, W, It, I, SA 1,2, 1959 S, E, W, I, 1960 S, E, W, I, It, Arg 1,2,3, 1961 S, SA, E, W, It, I, 1962 S, E, W, I, It, 1963 S
Roques, J-C (Brive) 1966 S, I, It, R
Rossignol, J-C (Brive) 1972 A 2
Rouan, J (Narbonne) 1953 S, I
Roucaries, G (Perpignan) 1956 S
Rouffia, L (Narbonne) 1945 B 2, W, 1946 W, 1948 I
Rougerie, A (Montferrand, Clermont-Auvergne) 2001 SA 3, A, Fj (R), 2002 It, W, E, S, I, Arg, A 1,2, 2003 E 1, S, I, It, W, Arg 1,2, NZ, R, E 2,3(R), [Fj,J,S,I,E], 2004 US,C,A,Arg,NZ, 2005 S,W,A2,C,Tg,SA3, 2006 I,It,E,W
Rougerie, J (Montferrand) 1973 J
Rougé-Thomas, P (Toulouse) 1989 NZ 1,2
Roujas, F (Tarbes) 1910 I
Roumat, O (Dax) 1989 NZ 2(R), B, 1990 W, E, S, I, R, A 1,2,3, NZ 1,2, 1991 S, I, W 1, E, R, US 1, W 2, [R, Fj, C, E], 1992 W (R), E (R), S, I, SA 1,2, Arg, 1993 E, S, I, W, R 1, SA 1,2, R 2, A 1,2, 1994 I, W, E, C 1, NZ 1,2, C 2, 1995 W, E, S, [Iv, S, I, SA, E], 1996 E, S, I, W 1, Arg 1,2
Rousie, M (Villeneuve) 1931 S, G, 1932 G, 1933 G
Rousset, G (Béziers) 1975 SA 1, 1976 US
Rué, J-B (Agen) 2002 SA (R), C (R), 2003 E 1(R), S (R), It (R), W (R), Arg 1,2(R)
Ruiz, A (Tarbes) 1968 SA 2, R
Rupert, J-J (Tyrosse) 1963 R, 1964 S, Fj, 1965 E, W, It, 1966 S, I, E, W, It, 1967 It, R, 1968 S

Sadourny, J-L (Colomiers) 1991 W 2(R), [C (R)], 1992 E (R), S, I, Arg 1(R),2, SA 1,2, 1993 R 1, SA 1,2, R 2, A 1,2, 1994 I, W, E, S, C 1, NZ 1,2, C 2, 1995 W, E, S, I, R 1, [Tg, S, I, SA, E], It, R 2, Arg, NZ 1,2, 1996 E, S, I, W 1, Arg 1,2, W 2, SA 1,2, 1997 I, W, E, S, It 1, R 1, A 1,2, It 2, R 2, Arg, SA 1,2, 1998 E, S, I, W, 1999 R, Tg, NZ 1(R), 2000 NZ 2, 2001 It, W, E
Sagot, P (SF) 1906 NZ, 1908 E, 1909 W
Sahuc, A (Métro) 1945 B 1,2
Sahuc, F (Toulouse) 1936 G 2
Saint-André, P (Montferrand, Gloucester) 1990 R, A 3, NZ 1,2, 1991 I (R), W 1, E, US 1,2, W 2, [R, Fj, C, E], 1992 W, E, S, I, R, Arg 1,2, SA 1,2, 1993 E, S, I, W, SA 1,2, A 1,2, 1994 I, W, E, S, C 1, NZ 1,2, C 2, 1995 W, E, S, I, R 1, [Tg, Iv, S, I, SA, E], It, R 2, Arg, NZ 1,2, 1996 E, S, I, W 1, R, Arg 1,2, W 2, 1997 It 1,2, R 2, Arg, SA 1,2
Saisset, O (Béziers) 1971 R, 1972 S, I 1, A 1,2, 1973 S, NZ, E, W, I, J, R, 1974 I, Arg 2, SA 1,2, 1975 W
Salas, P (Narbonne) 1979 NZ 1,2, R, 1980 W, E, 1981 A 1, 1982 Arg 2
Salinié, R (Perpignan) 1923 E
Sallefranque, M (Dax) 1981 A 2, 1982 W, E, S
Salut, J (TOEC) 1966 R, 1967 S, 1968 I, E, Cz, NZ 1, 1969 I
Samatan, R (Agen) 1930 S, I, E, G, W, 1931 I, S, W, E, G
Sanac, A (Perpignan) 1952 It, 1953 S, I, 1954 E, 1956 Cz, 1957 S, I, E, W, It
Sangalli, F (Narbonne) 1975 I, SA 1,2, 1976 S, A 1,2, R, 1977 W, E, S, I, Arg 1,2, NZ 1,2
Sanz, H (Narbonne) 1988 Arg 3,4, R, 1989 A 2, 1990 S, I, R, A 1,2, NZ 2, 1991 W 2
Sappa, M (Nice) 1973 J, R, 1977 R
Sarrade, R (Pau) 1929 I
Sarraméa, O (Castres) 1999 R, WS (R), Tg, NZ 1
Saux, J-P (Pau) 1960 W, It, Arg 1,2, 1961 SA, E, W, It, I, NZ 1,2,3, A, 1962 S, E, W, I, It, 1963 S, I, E, It
Savitsky, M (La Voulte) 1969 R
Savy, M (Montferrand) 1931 I, S, W, E, 1936 G 1
Sayrou, J (Perpignan) 1926 W, M, 1928 E, G, W, 1929 S, W, E, G
Scohy, R (BEC) 1931 S, W, E, G
Sébedio, J (Tarbes) 1913 S, E, 1914 I, 1920 S, I, US, 1922 S, E, 1923 S
Seguier, N (Béziers) 1973 J, R
Seigne, L (Agen, Merignac) 1989 B, A 1, 1990 NZ 1, 1993 E, S, I, W, R 1, A 1,2, 1994 S, C 1, 1995 E (R), S
Sella, P (Agen) 1982 R, Arg 1,2, 1983 E, S, I, W, A 1,2, R, 1984 I, W, E, S, NZ 1,2, R, 1985 E, S, I, W, Arg 1,2, 1986 S, I, W, E, R 1, Arg 1,2, A, NZ 1, R 2, NZ 2,3, 1987 W, E, S, I, [S, R, Z (R), Fj, A, NZ], 1988 E, S, I, W, Arg 1,2,3,4, R, 1989 I, W, E, S, NZ 1,2, B, A 1,2, 1990 W, E, S, I, A 1,2,3, 1991 W 1, E, R, US 1,2, W 2, [Fj, C, E], 1992 W, E, S, I, Arg, 1993 E, S, I, W, R 1, SA 1,2, R 2, A 1,2, 1994 I, W, E, S, C 1, NZ 1,2, C 2, 1995 W, E, S, I, [Tg, S, I, SA, E]
Semmartin, J (SCUF) 1913 W, I
Senal, G (Béziers) 1974 Arg 1,2, R, SA 1,2, 1975 W
Sentilles, J (Tarbes) 1912 W, E, 1913 S, SA
Serin, L (Béziers) 1928 E, 1929 W, E, G, 1930 S, I, E, G, W, 1931 I, W, E
Serre, P (Perpignan) 1920 S, E
Serrière, P (RCF) 1986 A, 1987 R, 1988 E
Servat, W (Toulouse) 2004 I,It,W,S,E,US,C,A,Arg,NZ 2005 S,E(R),W(R),It(R),SA1(R), 2
Servole, L (Toulon) 1931 I, S, W, E, G, 1934 G, 1935 G
Sicart, N (Perpignan) 1922 I
Sillières, J (Tarbes) 1968 R, 1970 S, I, 1971 S, I, E, 1972 E, W

Siman, M (Montferrand) 1948 E, 1949 S, 1950 S, I, E, W
Simon, S (Bègles) 1991 R, US 1
Simonpaoli, R (SF) 1911 I, 1912 I, S
Sitjar, M (Agen) 1964 W, It, I, R, 1965 It, R, 1967 A, E, It, W, I, SA 1,2
Skrela, D (Colomiers) 2001 NZ
Skrela, J-C (Toulouse) 1971 SA 2, A 1,2, 1972 I 1(R), E, W, I 2, A 1, 1973 W, J, R, 1974 W, E, S, Arg 1, R, 1975 W (R), E, S, I, SA 1,2, Arg 1,2, R, 1976 S, I, W, E, US, A 1,2, R, 1977 W, E, S, I, Arg 1,2, NZ 1,2, R, 1978 E, S, I, W
Soler, M (Quillan) 1929 G
Soro, R (Lourdes, Romans) 1945 B 1,2, W, 1946 B, I, K, 1947 S, I, W, E, 1948 I, A, S, W, E, 1949 S, I, E, W, Arg 1,2
Sorondo, L-M (Montauban) 1946 K, 1947 S, I, W, E, 1948 I
Soulette, C (Béziers, Toulouse) 1997 R 2, 1998 S (R), I (R), W (R), Arg 1,2, Fj, 1999 W 2(R), [C (R), Nm (R), Arg, NZ 2, A]
Soulié, E (CASG) 1920 E, I, US, 1921 S, E, I, 1922 E, W, I
Sourgens, J (Bègles) 1926 M
Souverbie, J-M (Bègles) 2000 R
Spanghero, C (Narbonne) 1971 E, W, SA 1,2, A 1,2, R, 1972 S, E, W, I 2, A 1,2, 1974 I, W, E, S, R, SA 1, 1975 E, S, I
Spanghero, W (Narbonne) 1964 SA, Fj, R, 1965 S, I, E, W, It, R, 1966 S, I, E, W, It, R, 1967 S, A, E, SA 1,2,3,4, NZ, 1968 S, I, E, W, NZ 1,2,3, A, SA 1,2, R, 1969 S, I, W, 1970 R, 1971 E, W, SA 1, 1972 E, I 2, A 1,2, R, 1973 S, NZ, E, W, I
Stener, G (PUC) 1956 S, I, E, 1958 SA 1,2
Struxiano, P (Toulouse) 1913 W, I, 1920 S, E, W, I, US
Sutra, G (Narbonne) 1967 SA 2, 1969 W, 1970 S, I
Swierczinski, C (Bègles) 1969 E, 1977 Arg 2
Szarzewski, D (Béziers, SF) 2004 C(R), 2005 I(R),A1,2, SA3, 2006 S,E(R),W(t&R),R(R),SA

Tabacco, P (SF) 2001 SA 1,2, NZ, SA 3, A, Fj, 2003 It (R), W (R), Arg 1, NZ, E 2(R),3, [S(R),US,I(R),NZ], 2004 US, 2005 S
Tachdjian, M (RCF) 1991 S, I, E
Taffary, M (RCF) 1975 W, E, S, I
Taillantou, J (Pau) 1930 I, G, W
Tarricq, P (Lourdes) 1958 A, W, It, I
Tavernier, H (Toulouse) 1913 I
Techoueyres, W (SBUC) 1994 E, S, 1995 [Iv]
Terreau, M-M (Bourg) 1945 W, 1946 B, I, K, W, 1947 S, I, W, E, 1948 I, A, W, E, 1949 S, Arg 1,2, 1951 S
Theuriet, A (SCUF) 1909 E, W, 1910 S, 1911 W, 1913 E
Thevenot, M (SCUF) 1910 W, E, I
Thierry, R (RCF) 1920 S, E, W, US
Thiers, P (Montferrand) 1936 G 1,2, 1937 G, It, 1938 G 1,2, 1940 B, 1945 B, 1,2
Thion, J (Perpignan, Biarritz) 2003 Arg 1,2, NZ, R, E 2, [Fj,S,I,E], 2004 A,Arg,NZ 2005 S,E,W,I,It, A2,C,Tg,SA3, 2006 S,I,It,E,W,R(R),SA
Tignol, P (Toulouse) 1953 S, I
Tilh, H (Nantes) 1912 W, E, 1913 S, SA, E, W
Tolot, J-L (Agen) 1987 [Z]
Tordo, J-F (Nice) 1991 US 1(R), 1992 W, E, S, I, R, Arg 1,2, SA 1, Arg, 1993 E, S, I, W, R 1
Torossian, F (Pau) 1997 R 1
Torreilles, S (Perpignan) 1956 S
Tournaire, F (Narbonne, Toulouse) 1995 It, 1996 I, W 1, R, Arg 1,2(R), W 2, SA 1,2, 1997 I, E, S, It 1, R 1, A 1,2, It 2, R 2, Arg, SA 1,2, 1998 E, S, I, W, Arg 1,2, Fj, Arg 3, A, 1999 I, W 1, E, S, R (R), WS, NZ 1, [C, Nm, Fj, Arg, NZ 2, A], 2000 W, E, S, I, It, A (R)
Tourte, R (St Girons) 1940 B
Traille, D (Pau, Biarritz) 2001 SA 3, A, Fj, 2002 It, W, E, S, I, Arg, A 1,2, SA, NZ, C, 2003 E 1, S, I, It, W, Arg, 1,2, NZ, R, E 2, [Fj(R),J,S(R),US,NZ], 2004 I,It,W,S,E, 2005 S,E,W,It(R),SA1(R),2,A1(R), 2006 It,E,W,R,SA
Trillo, J (Bègles) 1967 SA 3,4, NZ, R, 1968 S, I, NZ 1,2,3, A, 1969 I, E, W, R, 1970 E, R, 1971 S, I, SA 1,2, A 1,2, 1972 S, A 1,2, R, 1973 S, E
Triviaux, R (Cognac) 1931 E, G
Tucco-Chala, M (PUC) 1940 B

Ugartemendia, J-L (St Jean-de-Luz) 1975 S, I

Vaills, G (Perpignan) 1928 A, 1929 G
Valbon, L (Brive) 2004 US, 2005 S(R), 2006 S,E(R)
Vallot, C (SCUF) 1912 S
Van Heerden, A (Tarbes) 1992 E, S
Vannier, M (RCF, Chalon) 1953 W, 1954 S, I, Arg 1,2, 1955 S, I, E, W, It, 1956 S, I, W, It, E, 1957 S, I, E, W, It, R 1,2, 1958 S, E, A, W, It, I, 1960 S, E, W, I, It, R, Arg 1,3, 1961 SA, E, W, It, I, NZ 1, A
Vaquer, F (Perpignan) 1921 S, W, 1922 W
Vaquerin, A (Béziers) 1971 R, 1972 S, I 1, A 1, 1973 S, 1974 W, E, S, Arg 1,2, R, SA 1,2, 1975 W, E, S, I, 1976 US, A 1(R),2, R, 1977 Arg 2, 1979 W, E, 1980 S, I
Vareilles, C (SF) 1907 E, 1908 E, W, 1910 S, E
Varenne, F (RCF) 1952 S
Varvier, T (RCF) 1906 E, 1909 E, W, 1911 E, W, 1912 I
Vassal, G (Carcassonne) 1938 R, G 2
Vaysse, J (Albi) 1924 US, 1926 M
Vellat, E (Grenoble) 1927 I, E, G 1,2, 1928 A
Venditti, D (Bourgoin, Brive) 1996 R, SA 1(R),2, 1997 I, W, E, S, R 1, A 1, SA 2, 2000 W (R), E, S, It (R)
Vergé, L (Bègles) 1993 R 1(R)
Verger, A (SF) 1927 W, E, G 1, 1928 I, E, G, W
Verges, S-A (SF) 1906 NZ, E, 1907 E
Vermeulen, E (Brive, Montferrand) 2001 SA 1(R),2(R), 2003 NZ
Viard, G (Narbonne) 1969 W, 1970 S, R, 1971 S, I
Viars, S (Brive) 1992 W, E, I, R, Arg 1,2, SA 1,2(R), Arg, 1993 R 1, 1994 C 1(R), NZ 1(t), 1995 E (R), [Iv], 1997 R 1(R), A 1(R),2
Vigerie, M (Agen) 1931 W
Vigier, R (Montferrand) 1956 S, W, It, E, Cz, 1957 S, E, W, It, R 1,2, 1958 S, E, A, W, It, I, SA 1,2, 1959 S, E, It, W, I
Vigneau, A (Bayonne) 1935 G
Vignes, C (RCF) 1957 R 1,2, 1958 S, E
Vila, E (Tarbes) 1926 M
Vilagra, J (Vienne) 1945 B 2
Villepreux, P (Toulouse) 1967 It, I, SA 2, NZ, 1968 I, Cz, NZ 1,2,3, A, 1969 S, I, E, W, R, 1970 S, I, W, E, R, 1971 S, I, E, W, A 1,2, R, 1972 S, I 1, E, W, I 2, A 1,2
Viviès, B (Agen) 1978 E, S, I, W, 1980 SA, R, 1981 S, A 1, 1983 A 1(R)
Volot, M (SF) 1945 W, 1946 B, I, K, W

Weller, S (Grenoble) 1989 A 1,2, 1990 A 1, NZ 1
Wolf, J-P (Béziers) 1980 SA, R, 1981 A 2, 1982 E

Yachvili, D (Biarritz) 2002 C (R), 2003 S (R), I, It, W, R (R), E 3, [US,NZ], 2004 I(R),It(R),W(R),S,E, 2005 S(R),E,W,I,It,SA1(R),2,C,Tg, 2006 S(R),I(R),It(R),E, W,SA
Yachvili, M (Tulle, Brive) 1968 E, W, Cz, NZ 3, A, R, 1969 S, I, R, 1971 E, SA 1,2 A 1, 1972 R, 1975 SA 2

Zago, F (Montauban) 1963 I, E

GEORGIA

GEORGIA'S TEST RECORD

OPPONENTS	DATE	VENUE	RESULT
Russia	4 February	H	**Won** 46–19
Romania	25 February	A	**Lost** 10–35
Portugal	11 March	H	**Won** 40–0
Ukraine	29 April	A	**Won** 32–12
Japan	14 May	A	**Lost** 7–32
Barbarians	4 June	H	**Lost** 19–28
Czech Republic	10 June	A	**Won** 24–3

GEORGIA RE-BUILDING ALMOST COMPLETE

By Zaal Guiguineshvili

The 2005/06 season was a successful one for the Lelos, Georgia's senior national side. They won five from eight Tests, played some decent rugby, finished a respectable second in European Nations Cup (ENC), comfortably reached a point where they are two wins away from Rugby World Cup 2007 Finals and now possess a core of strong players around whom a sound team can be built.

Jamie McDonald/Getty Images

Paliko Jimsheladze is a Georgia legend with more points than any player in their history.

A considerable amount of work has been achieved since the conclusion of the 2003 Rugby World Cup to rebuild the national side in the post-Claude Saurel era. The French coach had departed on a high having led Georgia to its first Rugby World World Cup finals in 2003 and achieving a new high point in the relatively short history of Georgian Rugby. With him a number of the key senior players had also retired, having given their all in the quest of booking a place to Australia.

The door opened for a period of rebuilding in an era of uncertainty and the door also opened for a new coaching set up who were charged with the brief of achieving a second Rugby World Cup qualification and taking Georgia up to a new level. Importantly the men charged with the responsibility of achieving those goals were Georgian. They were also coaches who knew the ins and outs of the game in the country. Malkhaz Tcheishvili (head coach and scrum specialist), David Chavleishvili (backs coach) and Paata Narimanashvili (defence coach), all in their 40s, were all experienced coaches and were also tremendously respected figures within Georgian rugby circles.

Tcheishvili had previously worked with the Georgia Sevens squad; Narimanashvili with the Under 19 squad that finished tenth at the IRB Under 19 World Championship on three consecutive occasions and Chavleishvili had spent a spell as Poland's coach before returning to Georgia to coach the Under 21 team. All three introduced a fresh approach to the Georgia squad that included a number of talented overseas-based players.

Back at the turn of the millennium then head coach Saurel had initiated the trend of introducing the top Georgian players to French club Rugby. Several core national team players made the switch to the French leagues and the move proved to be a successful one as the players flourished in a competitive environment, establishing themselves as key players in some of France's top teams. Such an initiative was to have a long term reward for Saurel and his squad as the experience gained playing in France paid off as Georgia made the Rugby World Cup finals in just its fourteenth season, by defeating arch-rivals Russia in its fifty-first test.

The Georgian public hoped that in Australia the Lelos would beat Uruguay and avoid finishing last in their pool but despite a strong showing this did not materialize as the national team returned home disappointed with the finish. With Saurel gone, the locals were entrusted with rebuilding the side post Rugby World Cup 2003. For one season they chopped and changed, while a new generation of players came through the ranks. More players departed for France and those who were already there gained more experience. So when the two-year-long European Nations Cup kicked off (which also served as a Rugby World Cup 2007 pre-qualifier), the Lelos were a settled side.

The competition was to prove both encouraging and successful for a youthful Georgia side. The performances were impressive and in winning all of its home matches Georgia produced record victories over both Russia and Portugal and were just pipped to the title by Romania. A new competitive era of Georgian rugby had been ushered in. Under the new coaching team a balanced squad has been nurtured and developed and there has also been a return to the natural style of Georgian rugby based upon a strong set piece and hard running, direct backs.

While in seasons past strength in depth had been an issue for Saurel and his coaching staff, the class of 2006 provide the new coaching staff with selection headaches of an altogether better variety. An effective blend of experienced campaigners and talented youngsters has been achieved, while the French connection, initiated by Saurel, continues with several players showcasing Georgian talent in the competitive and physical world of the French Top 14 competition.

It is therefore no surprise that with so many players gaining experience abroad that this new crop of players continue to make steady progress on the world stage. Indeed, it is an abundance of quality forwards that underlines Georgia's resurgence in recent years. Blessed with a core of players with Heineken Cup experience it is therefore no surprise that it is in the pack where competition for places is most intense and none more so than in the front row where an incredible 13 players were tried over the eight tests.

While the likes of impressive hooker Akvsenti Guiorgadze (44 caps) and prop Goderdzi Shvelidze (33 caps) are almost automatic choices when they are fit, there are a number of talented young players coming through to keep the pressure on the seasoned campaigners. The emergence of the immensely gifted David Zirakashvili, 23, has been a real highlight. Compared by some to iconic prop Levan Tsabadze, Zirakashvili typifies the new breed of Georgian players as a powerful scummager and dynamic ball carrier.

However, the ferocity of competition is not exclusive to the front row. The position of lock is also an area of great depth and talent. International Law student Ilia Zedguinidze, 29, who fluently speaks six languages, has already captained the Lelos in 25 of his 41 tests, scoring an incredible 13 tries. He is usually partnered by ex-basketball player Mamuka Gorgodze, 22, a latecomer to rugby, who despite that, has impressed, thus limiting another emerging star, Levan Datunashvili, to scraps of playing time.

The back row is well-established and indeed settled. Toulon-based warhorse Guia Labadze (41 caps) is back in the fold after initially taking time away from the international Game following the last Rugby World Cup. A natural leader and tremendously experienced, Labadze has formed a highly effective back row combination with Rati Urushadze, the highest-paid man in the Russian league and chief provider of line-out ball. Burly youngsters, Besso Udessiani and Zviad Maissuradze complete the jigsaw in what is also a competitive area.

At scrum half the experienced Irakli Abtssreidze, a veteran of 34 caps, is being pushed hard by talented youngster Bidzina Samkharadze. Both are key players whose service is good but the latter is a player of great promise. At fly half Georgia's most capped player Paliko Jimsheladze, with 51 caps, continues to pull the strings and is still the stand out player in the pivotal position. However, the performance of the 21–year-old Temur Sokhadze in carving the Portugal defence wide open gives the coaches a viable alternative moving forward.

The backline remains to be built around 44–times capped Makho Urjukashvili who, despite his vast experience, is still only 26 and the 42-times capped 'Antelope' Bessik Khamashuridze, with the prolific Irakli Machkhaneli of Beziers the main strike force and Bourgoin regular Irakli Guiorgadze master at breaking the line. And of course, there is rising star Otar Barkalaia at full-back who, alongside Sokhadze and Jimsheladze, can be rotated between both full-back and fly half.

As the vast majority of Lelos ply their trade in France, the issue of obtaining releases for international duty can sometimes by a tricky one. Therefore, rather frustratingly for the Georgia team management, it is rare that Georgia is able to field its best side two matches in a row. For the big matches against both Russia and Portugal the Lelos fielded a full complement of star players, while against other nations the coaches kept on plugging holes, giving youth its head and trying out a number of combinations.

This situation has already led to emergence of great prospect Rezo Guigauri, who alongside Guiorgadze stood his ground admirably in the end of season match against the Barbarians facing two incredibly experienced international players in Tony Marsh (France) and Kevin Maggs (Ireland). The visit of the famous invitational club truly was the highlight of the season. The star-studded guests visited Kakheti, the main wine-producing region of Georgia, attending a youth festival and the famous sulphur baths, donating £10,000 for the development of the Game, and provided a great rugby show in the stifling heat. The invitation of Jimsheladze and Machkhaneli to the Barbarians squad next season highlighted the growing stature of Georgian rugby on the world map.

Both players were involved in scoring Georgia's best try of 2006 during the Barbarians game. Jimsheladze, who became the first Georgian to amass 50 caps and was presented with commemorative headgear before the game, ran back a failed clearance kick, chipped and gathered, before Guigauri carried on, dummied and broke right. The ball was then moved left before Barkalaia astutely grubbered through for Machkhaneli to pick up and ground for a sensational try.

While Georgian rugby's standing on the international stage is undoubtedly improving, progress on the domestic front is yet to mirror that growth. Yet there is real reason for optimism. The visit of the Barbarians put Georgian rugby back on the map, while the IRB through its Strategic Plan, has helped to establish a multi-pupose National Rugby Academy, which will undoubtedly bear fruit for years to come.

Otherwise, as many as eight Tbilissi clubs (each running five age-grade teams) still share a meagre field in Varketili and the once-famous Kutaissi club, Aia, have been prevented from playing in their town by soccer-mad authorities. Nevertheless, ten clubs participate in the senior, U18 and U16 Championships.

At the senior grade Locomotivi went undefeated throughout the season. They claimed the league title by beating Lelo 24–9 in the final, and achieved the treble by defeating Academy 30–6 in the Grand Final of the Palm Cup and then successfully defended the Sini (Georgian version of New Zealand's Ranfurly Shield).

GEORGIA INTERNATIONAL PLAYERS

UP TO 30TH SEPTEMBER 2006

Compiled By Hugh Copping

Abashidze, V 1998 *It* (R), *Ukr*, *I* 1999 *Tg* (R), *Tg* 2000 *It* (R), *Mor*, *Sp* 2001 *H*, *Pt* (R), *Rus*, *Sp*, *R* 2006 *J* (R)
Abdaladze, N 1997 *Cro*, *De*
Abuseridze, I 2000 *It*, *Pt*, *Mor*, *Sp*, *H*, *R* 2001 *H*, *Pt*, *Rus*, *Sp*, *R* 2002 *Pt*, *Rus*, *Sp* (R), *R* (R), *I*, *Rus* 2003 *Pt*, *Rus*, *CZR*, *R*, *It*, *E*, *Sa*, *SA* (R) 2004 *Rus* 2005 *Pt*, *Ukr*, *R* 2006 *Rus*, *R*, *Pt*, *Ukr*, *J*
Alania, K 1993 *Lux* 1994 *Swi* 1996 *CZR*, *CZR*, *Rus* 1997 *Pt* (R), *Pol*, *Cro*, *De* 1998 *It* 2001 *H*, *Pt*, *Sp* (R), *F*, *SA* 2002 *H*, *Pt* (R), *Rus* (R), *Sp*, *R*, *I*, *Rus* 2003 *Rus* (R) 2004 *Pt*, *Sp*
Andghuladze, N 1997 *Pol* (R) 2000 *It*, *Pt* (R), *Mor*, *Sp*, *H*, *R* 2004 *Rus*, *CZR* (R), *R*
Ashvetia, D 1998 *Ukr* (R)

Babunashvili, G 1992 *Ukr*, *Ukr*, *Lat* 1993 *Rus*, *Pol*, *Lux* 1996 *CZR*
Bakuradze, Z 1989 *Z* 1990 *Z* 1991 *Ukr*, *Ukr* 1993 *Rus* (R), *Pol* (R)
Baramidze, D 2000 *H* (R)
Barkalaia, O 2002 *I* (R) 2004 *Rus*, *CZR*, *R*, *Ur*, *Ch*, *Rus* (R) 2005 *Ukr*, *R*, *CZR*, *Ch* 2006 *Rus*, *R*, *Pt* (R), *Ukr*, *J* (R)
Belkania, R 2005 *Ch*
Beriashvili, G 1993 *Rus*, *Pol* 1995 *Ger* (R)
Besselia, M 1991 *Ukr* 1993 *Rus*, *Pol* 1996 *Rus* 1997 *Pt*
Bolghashvili, D 2000 *It*, *Pt* (R), *H* (R), *R* (R) 2001 *H*, *Pt*, *Rus*, *Sp*, *R*, *F*, *SA* 2002 *H*, *Pt*, *Rus*, *I* 2003 *Pt* (R), *Sp*, *Rus* (R), *CZR* (R), *R* (R), *E* (R), *Sa* (R), *SA* 2004 *Rus*, *Ur*, *Ch*, *Rus* (R) 2005 *CZR* (R)
Buguianishvili, G 1996 *CZR*, *Rus* (R) 1997 *Pol* 1998 *It*, *Rus* (R), *I*, *R* 2000 *Sp* (R), *H* (R), *R* (R) 2001 *H* (R), *F* (R), *SA* 2002 *Rus*

Chavchavadze, N 2004 *Ur*, *Ch*
Chavleishvili, D 1990 *Z* (R), *Z* 1992 *Ukr*, *Ukr*, *Lat* 1993 *Pol*, *Lux*
Chikava, I 1993 *Pol*, *Lux* 1994 *Swi* 1995 *Bul*, *Mol*, *H* 1996 *CZR*, *CZR* 1997 *Pol* (R) 1998 *I*
Chikvaidze, R 2004 *Ur*, *Ch* (R)
Chikvinidze, L 1994 *Swi* 1995 *Bul*, *Mol*, *Ger*, *H* 1996 *CZR*, *Rus* (R) 1997 *Pt*
Chkhaidze, G 2002 *H*, *R* (R), *I*, *Rus* (R) 2003 *Pt*, *CZR* (R), *It*, *E*, *SA*, *Ur* 2004 *CZR*, *R* 2006 *Pt* (R), *Ukr*
Chkhenkeli, S 1997 *Pol* (R)
Chkhikvadze, I 2005 *Ch* (R)

Dadunashvili, D 2003 *It* (R), *E* (R), *SA*, *Ur* 2004 *Rus*, *CZR*, *R* 2005 *Ch*
Datunashvili, L 2005 *Ukr* (R), *R* (R), *CZR* (R) 2006 *Rus* (R), *R*, *Pt* (R), *Ukr*, *J*, *CZR* (R)
Didebulidze, V 1991 *Ukr* 1994 *Kaz* 1995 *Bul*, *Mol* 1996 *CZR* 1997 *De* (R) 1999 *Tg* (R) 2000 *H* (R) 2001 *H*, *Pt*, *Rus*, *Sp*, *R*, *F*, *SA* 2002 *H*, *Pt*, *Rus* (R), *Sp*, *R*, *I*, *Rus* 2003 *Pt*, *Sp*, *Rus*, *CZR* (R), *R* (R), *It*, *E*, *Sa* (R), *SA* 2004 *Rus* 2005 *Pt* 2006 *R* (R)
Dzagnidze, E 1992 *Ukr*, *Ukr*, *Lat* 1993 *Rus*, *Pol* 1995 *Bul*, *Mol*, *Ger*, *H* 1998 *I*
Dzagnidze, N 1989 *Z* 1990 *Z*, *Z* 1991 *Ukr* 1992 *Ukr*, *Ukr*, *Lat* 1993 *Rus*, *Pol* 1994 *Swi* 1995 *Ger*, *H*
Dzneladze, D 1992 *Ukr* (R), *Lat* (R) 1993 *Lux* 1994 *Kaz*
Dzotsenidze, P 1995 *Ger*, *H* 1997 *Pt*, *Pol*

Elizbarashvili, G 2002 *Rus* (R) 2003 *Sp* (R) 2004 *Ch* 2005 *CZR* 2006 *Pt* (R), *Ukr*, *J*, *CZR*
Eloshvili, O 2002 *H* (R) 2003 *SA* 2006 *CZR* (R)
Essakia, S 1999 *Tg* (R), *Tg* (R) 2000 *It*, *Mor*, *Sp*, *H* 2004 *CZR* (R), *R*

Gagnidze, M 1991 *Ukr*, *Ukr*
Gasviani, D 2004 *Rus* (R) 2005 *CZR* (R), *Ch* (R) 2006 *Ukr* (R), *J* (R)
Ghibradze, A 1992 *Ukr*, *Ukr*, *Lat* 1994 *Swi* 1995 *Bul*, *Mol*, *Ger* 1996 *CZR*
Ghudushauri, D 1989 *Z* 1991 *Ukr*, *Ukr*
Ghvaberidze, L 2004 *Pt*, *Sp*
Giorgadze, A 1996 *CZR* (R) 1998 *It*, *Ukr*, *Rus*, *R* 1999 *Tg*, *Tg* 2000 *It*, *Pt*, *Mor*, *H*, *R* 2001 *H* (R), *Pt* (R), *Rus*, *Sp*, *R*, *F*, *SA* 2002 *H* (R), *Pt*, *Rus*, *Sp*, *R*, *I*, *Rus* 2003 *Pt*, *Sp*, *Rus*, *R*, *It*, *E*, *Sa*, *SA* (R), *Ur* (R) 2005 *Pt*, *Ukr*, *R*, *CZR* 2006 *Rus*, *R*, *Pt*, *CZR*
Giorgadze, I 2001 *F* (R), *SA* (R) 2003 *Pt*, *Sp*, *Rus*, *R*, *It*, *E*, *Sa*, *Ur* 2004 *Rus* 2005 *Pt*, *R*, *CZR* 2006 *Rus*, *R*, *Pt*, *CZR*
Gorgodze, M 2003 *Sp* (R), *Rus* (R) 2004 *Pt*, *Sp*, *Rus* (R), *CZR*, *R*, *Ur*, *Ch*, *Rus* (R) 2005 *Ukr*, *R*, *CZR*, *Ch* 2006 *Rus*, *Pt*, *CZR*
Gueguchadze, E 1990 *Z*, *Z*
Gugava, L 2004 *Rus* (R), *CZR*, *Ur*, *Ch*, *Rus* (R) 2005 *Ukr* 2006 *CZR*
Guigauri, R 2006 *Ukr* (R), *J* (R), *CZR*
Guiorkhelidze, I 1998 *R* 1999 *Tg* (R), *Tg* (R)
Guiunashvili, G 1989 *Z* 1990 *Z* 1991 *Ukr*, *Ukr* 1992 *Ukr*, *Ukr*, *Lat* 1993 *Rus*, *Pol* (R), *Lux* 1994 *Swi* 1996 *Rus* 1997 *Pt* (R)
Guiunashvili, K 1990 *Z*, *Z* (R) 1991 *Ukr*, *Ukr* 1992 *Ukr*, *Ukr*, *Lat*
Gujaraidze, S 2003 *SA*, *Ur*
Gundishvili, I 2002 *I* (R) 2003 *Pt* (R), *Sp* (R), *Rus*, *CZR*
Gusharashvili, A 1998 *Ukr*

Iobidze, D 1993 *Rus* (R), *Pol*
Iovadze, E 1993 *Lux* 1994 *Kaz* 1995 *Bul*, *Mol*, *Ger* (R), *H* (R) 2001 *Sp* (R), *F*, *SA* 2002 *H* (R), *Rus* (R), *Sp* (R), *R*, *I* (R)
Issakadze, A 1989 *Z*
Iurini, N 1991 *Ukr* (R) 1994 *Swi* (R) 1995 *Ger*, *H* 1996 *CZR*, *CZR*, *Rus* 1997 *Pt*, *Pol*, *Cro*, *De* 1998 *Ukr*, *Rus* 2000 *It* (R), *Sp* (R), *H*, *R* (R)

Janelidze, S 1991 *Ukr* (R), *Ukr* 1993 *Rus* 1994 *Kaz* 1995 *Ger* 1997 *Pt* (R) 1998 *Ukr* (R), *I*, *R* (R) 1999 *Tg* 2000 *R* (R)
Japarashvili, R 1992 *Ukr*, *Ukr*, *Lat* 1993 *Pol*, *Lux* (R) 1996 *CZR* 1997 *Pt* (R)
Javelidze, L 1997 *Cro* (R) 1998 *I* 2001 *H* (R), *R* (R), *F* (R), *SA* (R) 2002 *H* (R), *R* (R) 2004 *R* (R) 2005 *Ukr* (R)
Jghenti, D 2004 *CZR* (R), *R* (R)
Jhamutashvili, D 2005 *Ch*
Jhghenti, G 2005 *Ch*
Jimsheladze, P 1995 *Bul*, *Mol*, *H* (R) 1996 *CZR*, *CZR*, *Rus* 1997 *De* 1998 *It*, *Ukr*, *Rus*, *I* (R), *R* 1999 *Tg*, *Tg* 2000 *Pt*, *Mor*, *Sp*, *H*, *R* 2001 *H*, *Pt*, *Rus*, *Sp*, *R*, *F*, *SA* 2002 *H*, *Pt*, *Rus*, *Sp*, *I*, *Rus* 2003 *Pt*, *Sp*, *Rus*, *CZR*, *R*, *It*, *E*, *Sa*, *SA*, *Ur* 2004 *Rus* 2005 *R* 2006 *Rus*, *R*, *Pt*, *Ukr*, *J*, *CZR*
Jintcharadze, K 1993 *Rus*, *Pol* (R) 2000 *It* (R), *Mor* (R)

Kakhiani, G 1995 *Bul*, *Mol*
Katcharava, D 2006 *Ukr* (R), *J*
Katcharava, G 2005 *Ukr* (R) 2006 *J* (R), *CZR* (R)
Katsadze, V 1997 *Pol* 1998 *It*, *Ukr*, *Rus* (R), *I*, *R* (R) 1999 *Tg*,

Tg 2000 *Pt, Mor, Sp, H, R* 2001 *H, Pt, Rus, Sp, R* 2002 *Pt, Rus, Sp, R, I* (R), *Rus* 2003 *Pt, Sp, CZR, R, E, Sa, SA, Ur* (R) 2005 *Ukr*
Kavtarashvili, A 1994 *Swi* 1995 *Bul, Mol, Ger* (R) 1996 *CZR, Rus* 1997 *Pt, Cro, De* 1998 *It, Rus, I, R* 1999 *Tg, Tg* (R) 2000 *It, H, R* 2001 *H* (R) 2003 *SA, Ur*
Kerauli, I 1991 *Ukr, Ukr* 1992 *Ukr* (R), *Ukr*
Khachirashvili, L 2005 *Ukr* (R)
Khakhaleishili, T 1994 *Kaz*
Khamashuridze, B 1998 *It, Ukr, Rus, I* (R), *R* 1999 *Tg, Tg* 2000 *It, Pt, Sp, H, R* 2001 *Pt, Rus, Sp, R, F, SA* 2002 *H, Pt, Rus, Sp, R, I, Rus* 2003 *Pt, CZR, R* (R), *It, E, Sa* (R), *SA* (R), *Ur* (R) 2004 *Pt, Sp, Rus, Rus* 2005 *Pt, Ukr, Ch* 2006 *Rus, R, Pt*
Khamashuridze, B 1989 *Z*
Kharshiladze, M 1991 *Ukr*
Khekhelashvili, B 1999 *Tg, Tg* 2000 *It, Pt, Mor, Sp* (R), *H* (R), *R* 2001 *H* (R), *Pt* (R), *R* (R), *F, SA* (R) 2002 *H* (R), *Pt, Rus, Sp, R, I* 2003 *Sp, Rus, CZR, R, E* (R), *Sa*
Khinchaguishvili, D 2003 *Sp* (R), *CZR* (R) 2004 *Pt, Sp, Rus* (R) 2006 *CZR* (R)
Khonelidze, G 2003 *SA*
Khuade, N 1989 *Z* 1990 *Z, Z* 1991 *Ukr* (R), *Ukr* 1993 *Rus, Pol, Lux* 1994 *Swi* (R) 1995 *Ger*
Khutsishvili, Z 1993 *Lux* 1994 *Kaz, Swi* 1995 *Bul* (R) 1996 *CZR* (R) 1997 *Pol* 1998 *Rus* (R)
Khvedelidze, A 1989 *Z* 1990 *Z, Z* 1991 *Ukr, Ukr* 1992 *Ukr, Ukr, Lat* 1993 *Rus, Pol*
Kiknadze, D 2004 *Rus* 2005 *Pt, Ukr* (R)
Kobakhidze, A 1997 *Cro* (R) 1998 *I*
Kobakhidze, K 1995 *Ger* (R), *H* 1996 *Rus* (R) 1997 *Pt* 1998 *It* (R), *Ukr, Rus, I, R* 1999 *Tg* (R) 2000 *It*
Koberidze, Z 2004 *Ur*
Kopaliani, A 2003 *It, SA, Ur* 2004 *Pt, Sp* 2005 *Ukr* (R), *R* (R) 2006 *Rus* (R), *R* (R), *Ukr, J, CZR* (R)
Kutarashvili, G 2004 *Pt* (R), *CZR* (R), *R* 2005 *Ch* 2006 *Rus* (R), *R* (R), *Pt* (R), *Ukr, J*
Kvinikhidze, B 2002 *R* (R) 2004 *Pt, Sp, CZR, R* 2005 *Ch*
Kvirikashvili, M 2003 *Pt* (R), *Sp, CZR* (R), *E* (R), *Sa* (R), *SA* (R), *Ur* (R) 2004 *Rus* (R), *CZR, R, Ch* 2005 *CZR* (R), *Ch* (R)

Labadze, G 1996 *CZR, Rus* 1997 *Pt, Pol, Cro, De* 1998 *It* (R), *Ukr, Rus, I, R* 1999 *Tg, Tg* 2000 *It, Pt, Sp, H, R* 2001 *H, Pt, Rus, Sp, F, SA* 2002 *Pt, Rus, Sp, R, Rus* 2003 *Rus, CZR, R, It* (R), *E, Sa* 2004 *Rus* 2005 *R* 2006 *Rus, R, Pt, J*
Lezhava, I 1991 *Ukr* (R), *Ukr* 1992 *Ukr* (R) 1995 *Bul* (R)
Lezhava, Z 1991 *Ukr* (R) 1995 *Ger* 1996 *CZR* (R), *CZR, Rus* 1997 *Pt, Cro, De* (R) 1998 *It, Rus, R* 1999 *Tg* (R)
Liluashvili, B 1989 *Z* 1990 *Z, Z*
Liparteliani, O 1989 *Z* 1990 *Z, Z*
Liparteliani, S 1991 *Ukr* 1994 *Kaz, Swi* 1996 *CZR*
Liparteliani, Z 1994 *Kaz* (R), *Swi* 1995 *Bul, Mol, Ger, H*
Lossaberidze, M 1989 *Z*

Machitidze, K 1989 *Z* (R) 1993 *Rus* 1995 *Bul, Mol, Ger, H* 1996 *CZR, CZR* (R), *Rus* 1997 *Pt, Pol, Cro, De* 1998 *It, Ukr, Rus, R* 1999 *Tg* (R)
Machkhaneli, I 2002 *H, R* (R) 2003 *It, E* (R), *Sa* (R), *SA, Ur* 2004 *Pt, Sp, Ur, Ch* (R), *Rus* 2005 *Pt, Ukr, R, CZR, Ch* 2006 *Rus, R, Pt, CZR*
Magrakvelidze, M 1998 *Ukr* (R) 2000 *Mor* (R) 2001 *F* (R) 2002 *Pt* (R), *Sp* (R), *R* 2004 *Rus* 2005 *Pt, R* 2006 *CZR*
Maissuradze, I 1997 *Cro* (R) 1998 *It* (R), *Ukr* (R) 1999 *Tg, Tg* 2004 *Rus, R* 2005 *CZR* 2006 *CZR*
Maissuradze, Z 2004 *Pt, Sp, CZR, Ur, Ch* (R), *Rus* 2005 *Ukr* (R), *R* 2006 *Rus* (R), *R* (R), *Pt, Ukr, J, CZR* (R)
Margvelashvili, K 2003 *It, E, Sa* (R), *SA*
Marjanishvili, M 1990 *Z, Z* 1992 *Ukr, Ukr, Lat* 1993 *Rus, Pol, Lux*
Matchutadze, A 1993 *Lux* 1994 *Kaz* 1995 *Bul* (R), *Mol* 1997 *Pt* (R), *Pol, Cro, De*
Matiashvili, Z 2003 *Sp* 2005 *Ch* (R)
Mchedlishvili, Z 1995 *Mol* (R) 1996 *CZR* 1997 *Cro, De* 1998 *It, Ukr, Rus, I* (R), *R* 1999 *Tg, Tg* 2000 *Pt, Mor, Sp, H, R* 2001 *Rus* (R), *Sp* (R), *R* (R), *F, SA* 2002 *H* (R), *Pt, Rus* (R), *I* (R), *Rus* 2003 *Pt, Sp* (R), *Rus* (R), *CZR, R, It, E, Sa, Ur* 2004 *Pt* (R), *Rus* 2005 *Pt* 2006 *J*
Mgueladze, L 1992 *Ukr* (R), *Ukr* (R)
Mgueladze, N 1995 *Bul, Mol, H* 1997 *Pol* (R)
Modebadze, I 2003 *SA, Ur* 2004 *Sp* (R)
Modebadze, S 1994 *Kaz* 1995 *Mol* (R) 1996 *CZR, CZR, Rus* 1997 *Pt, Pol, Cro, De* 1998 *It, Ukr, Rus* 1999 *Tg* 2000 *It, Pt* (R) 2001 *Sp* (R), *F* (R), *SA* (R) 2002 *H, Pt* (R), *Rus* (R), *Sp, R*
Mtchedlishvili, A 2004 *Ur, Ch*
Mtchedlishvili, S 2000 *It* (R)
Mtiulishvili, M 1991 *Ukr* (R) 1994 *Kaz* (R) 1996 *CZR, CZR, Rus* 1997 *Pt, Pol, Cro, De* 1998 *It, Ukr, Rus, R* 2001 *H, Pt, Rus, Sp, R* 2002 *H, Pt, Rus* (R), *Sp, R, I* (R) 2003 *Rus* (R), *CZR, R* (R) 2004 *Rus, CZR, R* (R)

Nadiradze, V 1994 *Kaz, Swi* 1995 *H* 1996 *Rus* 1997 *Pt, De* 1998 *I, R* (R) 1999 *Tg* 2000 *It, Mor, Sp, H, R* 2001 *H, Pt, Rus, Sp, R, F, SA* 2002 *H, Pt, Rus, Sp, R, I, Rus* 2003 *Rus, CZR, R, It* (R), *E* (R), *Sa*
Natchqebia, A 1990 *Z, Z*
Natriashvili, I 2006 *Ukr* (R), *J* (R)
Natroshvili, N 1992 *Ukr, Ukr* (R), *Lat*
Nemsadze, G 2005 *Ch* 2006 *Ukr* (R)
Nikolaenko, I 1999 *Tg* (R), *Tg* (R) 2000 *It* (R), *Mor* (R), *Sp* (R), *H* (R), *R* (R) 2001 *R* (R), *F* (R) 2003 *Pt* (R), *Sp, E* (R), *Sa, SA* (R), *Ur* (R)
Ninidze, I 2004 *Ur, Ch* (R)

Oboladze, D 1993 *Rus, Pol, Lux* 1994 *Swi* 1995 *Bul, Mol, Ger, H* 1996 *CZR, CZR, Rus* 1997 *Pt, Pol* 1998 *It, Ukr* (R)
Odisharia, T 1989 *Z* (R) 1994 *Kaz* (R)

Papashvili, S 2001 *SA* (R) 2004 *CZR* (R), *R* (R) 2006 *CZR* (R)
Partsikanashvili, S 1994 *Kaz* 1996 *CZR, Rus* (R) 1997 *Pol* 1999 *Tg, Tg* 2000 *It, Pt, Mor*
Peradze, G 1991 *Ukr*
Pinchukovi, D 2004 *CZR* (R), *R* (R)
Pirpilashvili, L 2004 *Rus* (R), *CZR, R, Ur, Ch* 2005 *Ukr, R* (R), *CZR* (R)
Pirtskhalava, G 1989 *Z* (R) 1995 *Ger* 1996 *CZR, Rus* (R) 1997 *Pt* (R), *Pol*
Pkhakadze, T 1989 *Z* 1990 *Z, Z* 1993 *Rus, Pol, Lux* 1994 *Kaz* 1996 *CZR*

Rapava-Ruskini, G 1990 *Z* 1992 *Ukr, Lat* 1994 *Kaz* (R) 1996 *Rus* 1997 *Pt, Cro, De* 1998 *It, Ukr, Rus, R* 1999 *Tg*
Ratianidze, T 2000 *It* (R) 2001 *H* (R), *Pt* (R), *Sp* (R), *R* (R), *SA* (R) 2002 *Pt* (R), *Rus, Sp* (R), *R* (R), *I* (R), *Rus* (R) 2003 *Pt, Sp* (R), *Rus, CZR, R*
Rekhviashvili, Z 1995 *H* (R) 1997 *Pt, Pol* (R)

Sakandelidze, S 1996 *CZR* (R) 1998 *Ukr* (R)
Samkharadze, B 2004 *Pt, Sp, Rus, CZR* (R), *R* (R), *Ur, Ch* (R) 2005 *CZR, Ch* 2006 *Rus* (R), *R* (R), *Pt* (R), *Ukr* (R), *CZR*
Sanadze, A 2004 *Ch*
Saneblidze, P 1994 *Kaz*
Sanikidze, G 2004 *Ch*
Sardanashvili, B 2004 *Ch*
Satseradze, V 1989 *Z* 1990 *Z* 1991 *Ukr* 1992 *Ukr* (R), *Ukr, Lat* (R)
Shanidze, E 1994 *Swi*
Shkinini, G 2004 *CZR, R, Ch* 2005 *Ch* 2006 *Rus* (R), *R* (R), *Ukr, J*
Shvanguiradze, B 1990 *Z, Z* 1992 *Ukr, Ukr, Lat* 1993 *Rus, Pol, Lux*
Shvelidze, G 1998 *I, R* (R) 1999 *Tg, Tg* 2000 *It, Pt, Sp, H, R* 2001 *H, Pt, Sp* (R), *F, SA* 2002 *H, Rus, I, Rus* 2003 *Pt, Sp, Rus, CZR, R, It* (R), *E, Sa, Ur* 2004 *Rus* 2005 *Pt, CZR* 2006 *Rus, R, Pt*
Sikharulidze , I 1994 *Kaz*
Sokhadze, T 2005 *CZR* (R) 2006 *Rus* (R), *R* (R), *Pt, Ukr, J*
Sujashvili, M 2004 *Pt* (R), *Rus* 2005 *Ukr, R* (R), *CZR* (R) 2006 *Pt* (R), *Ukr, J, CZR*
Sultanishvili, S 1998 *Ukr* (R)
Sutiashvili, S 2005 *Ch* (R) 2006 *Ukr* (R)
Svanidze, P 1992 *Ukr*

Tavadze, T 1991 *Ukr, Ukr*
Tchavtchavadze, N 1998 *It* (R), *Ukr* (R) 2004 *CZR, R* (R)

Tcheishvili, M 1989 *Z* 1990 *Z*, *Z* 1995 *H*
Tepnadze, B 1995 *H* (R) 1996 *CZR* 1997 *Cro* 1998 *I*, *R* (R) 1999 *Tg* (R)
Tqabladze, P 1993 *Lux* 1995 *Bul* (R)
Tsabadze, L 1994 *Kaz*, *Swi* 1995 *Bul*, *Ger*, *H* 1996 *CZR* (R), *Rus* 1997 *Cro*, *De* 1998 *It*, *Rus*, *I* (R), *R* 1999 *Tg*, *Tg* 2000 *Pt*, *Mor*, *Sp*, *R* 2001 *H*, *Pt*, *Rus*, *Sp*, *R*, *F*, *SA* 2002 *H*, *Pt*, *Rus*, *Sp*, *R*, *I*, *Rus*
Tsiklauri, G 2003 *SA*, *Ur* (R)
Tskhvediani, D 1998 *Ukr* (R)
Tskitishvili, V 1994 *Swi* 1995 *Bul*, *Mol*
Turdzeladze, T 1989 *Z* 1990 *Z*, *Z* 1991 *Ukr* 1995 *Ger*, *H*

Uchava, K 2002 *Sp* (R)
Udessiani, B 2001 *Sp* (R), *F* (R) 2002 *H* (R) 2004 *Pt*, *Sp*, *CZR*, *R*, *Rus* 2005 *Pt*, *Ukr*, *R*, *CZR*, *Ch* 2006 *Rus*, *R*, *Ukr*, *J*, *CZR*
Urjukashvili, M 1997 *Cro*, *De* 1998 *Ukr*, *Rus*, *R* 1999 *Tg*, *Tg* 2000 *It*, *Pt*, *Mor*, *Sp* 2001 *Pt* (R), *Rus*, *Sp*, *R*, *F*, *SA* 2002 *H*, *Pt*, *Sp*, *R*, *I*, *Rus* 2003 *Pt*, *Sp*, *Rus*, *R*, *It*, *E*, *Sa*, *Ur* 2004 *Pt*, *Sp*, *Rus*, *Ur*, *Ch*, *Rus* 2005 *Pt*, *R*, *CZR* 2006 *Rus*, *R*, *Pt*, *Ukr*, *J*
Urushadze, R 1997 *Pol* 2002 *R* (R) 2004 *Pt*, *Sp*, *Rus* (R), *Rus* 2005 *Pt*, *Ukr*, *R* (R), *CZR*, *Ch* 2006 *Rus*, *R*, *Pt*, *CZR*

Valishvili, Z 2004 *Ur* (R), *Ch*
Vartaniani, D 1991 *Ukr*, *Ukr* 1992 *Ukr*, *Ukr*, *Lat* 1997 *Pol* (R) 2000 *Sp* (R), *H*, *R*

Vashadze, L 1991 *Ukr* 1992 *Ukr*, *Ukr* (R), *Lat*
Yachvili, G 2001 *H*, *Pt*, *R* 2003 *Pt*, *Sp*, *Rus*, *CZR*, *R*, *It*, *E*, *Sa*, *Ur*

Zedginidze, I 1998 *I* 2000 *It*, *Pt*, *Mor*, *Sp*, *H*, *R* 2001 *H*, *Pt*, *Rus*, *Sp*, *R* 2002 *H*, *Rus*, *Sp*, *I*, *Rus* 2003 *Pt*, *Sp*, *Rus*, *CZR*, *R*, *It*, *Sa*, *SA* (R), *Ur* 2004 *Pt*, *Sp*, *Rus*, *CZR*, *R*, *Rus* 2005 *Pt*, *Ukr*, *R*, *CZR* 2006 *Rus*, *R*, *Pt*, *Ukr*, *CZR*
Zhgenti, G 2004 *Ur* (R)
Zibzibadze, T 2000 *It* (R), *Pt*, *Mor*, *Sp* 2001 *H*, *Pt*, *Rus*, *Sp*, *R*, *F*, *SA* 2002 *H*, *Pt*, *Rus*, *Sp*, *R*, *I*, *Rus* 2003 *Pt*, *Sp*, *Rus*, *CZR*, *R*, *It*, *E*, *Sa*, *Ur* 2004 *Pt*, *Sp*, *Rus*, *CZR*, *R*, *Rus* 2005 *Pt*, *Ukr*, *R*, *CZR*
Zirakashvili, D 2004 *Ur*, *Ch* (R), *Rus* 2005 *Ukr*, *R*, *CZR* 2006 *Rus*, *R*, *Pt*

THE IRB/EMIRATES AIRLINE RUGBY PHOTOGRAPH OF THE YEAR 2006

Introducing a brand new annual Rugby photography competition – open to amateur and professional photographers alike – the *IRB/Emirates Airline Rugby Photograph of the Year*.

On the following pages you will discover the five runners-up, and winner of the inaugural competition (2006), as selected by a panel of judges headed by Greg Thomas, Head of Communications at the IRB, John Jackson of the Sports Journalists' Association and Kevin Eason, art editor of *Rugby World* magazine.

The prize for the winner is a trophy and £1,500, plus a trip for two to the Emirates Airline Dubai Sevens (courtesy of Emirates Airline).

For details on how to enter the 2007 competition, see back page of this picture section.

THE RUNNERS-UP: IN NO PARTICULAR ORDER

DAVID KAPERNICK/COURIER MAIL & SUNDAY MAIL & NEWS LTD

◄ DAVID KAPERNICK
(*Courier Mail* & *Sunday Mail*, Australia)

Matt Giteau dives gleefully over the line in Brisbane to score for Australia against South Africa in the Tri-Nations.

LEE WARREN ►
(*Touchline,* South Africa)

'What do you mean penalty?!' Mike Blair accidentally tackles referee Donal Courtney as Breyton Paulse gets away in the first Test between South Africa and Scotland.

EQUIPMENT:
Canon EOS-1D Mark II

"I like this photo because of the uniqueness of the situation. I had only ever seen the referee tackled by a spectator, but never a player. I also enjoy the expression on Breyton Paulse's face, its almost as if he knows that something has happened to make his progress to the try line easier, but even he could never have guessed what exactly!"
Lee Warren

LEE WARREN/TOUCHLINE PHOTO

STU FORSTER ►
(*Getty Images*, UK)

Peter Stringer appears to be defying the forces of gravity as he scores for Munster in their epic Heineken Cup win against Biarritz Olympique.

EQUIPMENT:
Canon EOS Digital Camera with 70-200mm F2.8 Lens, 400th second at F2.8 Rated at 1250 asa.

"I like this shot primarily because I was lucky enough to get it right in front of me and for it to be vaguely sharp! The lighting at the ends of the pitch at the Millennium Stadium is poor and it's a lottery to get anything that's sharp and useable from that area. I was also pleased to get an important try in the context of the game, and being a final made it even more so."
Stu Forster

STU FORSTER/GETTY IMAGES

HENRY BROWNE
(*Action Images*, UK)

Sebastian Chabal of Sale Sharks does the blood and sweat thing during the Guinness Premiership Final at Twickenham. The glory came later.

EQUIPMENT:
Canon 1D mk2 N with a 400mm lens.

"It was pouring with rain at the Premiership final at Twickenham and Sebastian Chabal had just been taken off for a blood injury to his nose. Play had continued, but was on the other side of the pitch and slightly out of range, so I looked to see if there were any pictures to be had around the technical area. Chabal had received attention from the doctor, and was sitting on the bench. He was drenched and looking sorry for himself. I shot it first on a 200mm lens, but it was too loose, so changed to a 400mm and got my picture. I like the picture because Sebastian Chabal looks completely spent. I think this is down to his long, wet hair, the gauze stuffed up his nose and the expression on his face. For me, it shows the toughness of Rugby Union in one picture."
Henry Browne

MARK PAIN
(*The Mail on Sunday*, UK)

Cheeky! Elvis Seveali'i of Sale Sharks pulls down the shorts of LeicesterTigers' Tom Varndell during the Guinness Premiership Final.

EQUIPMENT:
Canon EOS 1D digital camera with a 400mm 2.8 lens.

"It had been a pretty quiet game for pictures up to that point, nothing amazing happening at all. I seem to remember that it was pretty drizzly as well and very gloomy light-wise. The nice thing about the shot is that, apart from which team won the trophy, it's the one thing the crowd will remember from the game as it got the biggest cheer of the day. To capture something which can remind the fans of a great moment is rewarding in itself."
Mark Pain

IRB/EMIRATES AIRLINE RUGBY PHOTOGRAPH OF THE YEAR 2006

MORGAN TREACEY/INPHO

MORGAN TREACEY
(*INPHO*, Ireland)

Mud, glorious mud. Clontarf's James Purdue dreams of the post-match shower during an All Ireland League match at Shannon.

EQUIPMENT:
Canon EOS 1D digital camera with a 400mm 2.8 lens.

"The photo was taken at Clontarf Rugby Club in Dublin. Clontarf were playing Shannon RFC in a Division 1 game in the AIB All Ireland League. It was a wet day and the pitch was very cut up. Towards the end of the game I was having great difficulty picking out players' numbers due to the amount of mud on their jerseys, and also realised that a couple of players were literally covered from head to toe in muck. I thought this would make quite an interesting image, particularly a close in of one of the players. I moved up along the line and spent a bit of time attempting to catch an interesting expression on one of their faces. This picture was taken after a lineout had been lost, and I like the look of almost despair on the mud covered player. I'm also glad that the shot came from a relatively minor league and not from say, a Six Nations or Heineken cup game. It shows that passion and drama are not confined to the professional ranks, but can be found in the amateur game where every weekend players like the one in the picture are prepared to endure terrible conditions for little or no reward other than the love of the game. Other than that I just like the look of timelessness of it. It could have been taken 30 years ago. No matter how sanitised they try to make the modern game, rugby players will always look like this after a wet wintry day."
Morgan Treacey

THE IRB/EMIRATES AIRLINE RUGBY PHOTGRAPH OF THE YEAR 2007

The IRB/Emirates Airline Rugby Photograph of the Year competition is open to all photographers, professional or amateur, and the subject matter can be from any level of the game – from mini-rugby to the Rugby World Cup Final.

To request an entry form for next year's competition, send an e-mail to:

dominic.rumbles@irb.com

Or write to:

IRB/Emirates Airline Rugby Photo of the Year Competition
c/o Dominic Rumbles
IRB
Huguenot House
35-38 St Stephen's Green
Dublin 2, Ireland

www.irb.com

GEORGIAN INTERNATIONAL STATISTICS

MOST POINTS IN A MATCH

BY THE TEAM

Pts.	Opponent	Venue	Year
88	Netherlands	Tbilisi	2002
75	Czech Republic	Kutaisi	2005
70	Bulgaria	Sofia	1995
65	Ukraine	Tbilisi	2005
47	Moldova	Sofia	1995
46	Russia	Tbilisi	2006
43	Spain	Rustavi	2001
41	Netherlands	Tbilisi	2000
40	Portugal	Tbilisi	2006

BY A PLAYER

Pts.	Player	Opponent	Venue	Year
23	Paliko Jimsheladze	Russia	Krasnodar	2003
18	Malkhaz Urjukashvili	Romania	Tbilisi	2002
18	Paliko Jimsheladze	Netherlands	Tbilisi	2002
18	Malkhaz Urjukashvili	Czech Republic	Kutaisi	2005
16	Nugzar Dzagnidze	Zimbabwe	Kutaisi	1989
15	Paliko Jimsheladze	Bulgaria	Sofia	1995
15	Archil Kavtarashvili	Bulgaria	Sofia	1995
15	Kakha Machitidze	Bulgaria	Sofia	1995
15	Mamuka Gorgodze	Czech Republic	Kutaisi	2005
15	Malkhaz Urjukashvili	Portugal	Tbilisi	2006

MOST TRIES IN A MATCH

BY THE TEAM

Tries	Opponent	Venue	Year
14	Netherlands	Tbilisi	2002
11	Bulgaria	Sofia	1995
11	Ukraine	Tbilisi	2005
11	Czech Republic	Kutaisi	2005
7	Netherlands	Tbilisi	2000
7	Moldova	Sofia	1995

BY A PLAYER

Tries	Player	Opponent	Venue	Year
3	Paliko Jimsheladze	Bulgaria	Sofia	1995
3	Archil Kavtarashvili	Bulgaria	Sofia	1995
3	Mamuka Gorgodze	Czech Republic	Kutaisi	2005

MOST CONVERSIONS IN A MATCH

BY THE TEAM

Cons	Opponent	Venue	Year
9	Netherlands	Tbilisi	2002
7	Czech Republic	Kutaisi	2005
6	Bulgaria	Sofia	1995
5	Spain	Rustavi	2001
5	Ukraine	Tbilisi	2005
5	Russia	Tbilisi	2006

BY A PLAYER

Cons	Player	Opponent	Venue	Year
9	Paliko Jimsheladze	Netherlands	Tbilisi	2002
6	Kakha Machitidze	Bulgaria	Sofia	1995
6	Malkhaz Urjukashvili	Czech Republic	Kutaisi	2005
5	Paliko Jimsheladze	Spain	Rustavi	2001
4	Malkhaz Urjukashvili	Russia	Tbilisi	2006

MOST PENALTIES IN A MATCH

BY THE TEAM

Pens	Opponent	Venue	Year
6	Russia	Krasnodar	2003
4	Zimbabwe	Kutaisi	1989
4	Russia	Tbilisi	2002
4	Croatia	Tbilisi	1997
4	Russia	Tbilisi	1998
4	Romania	Bucharest	2001
4	Russia	Tbilisi	2002
4	South Africa	Sydney	2003
4	Uruguay	Sydney	2003
4	Italy	Asti	2003

BY A PLAYER

Pens	Player	Opponents	Venue	Year
6	P Jimsheladze	Russia	Krasnodar	2003
4	P Jimsheladze	Russia	Tbilisi	2002
4	P Jimsheladze	Italy	Asti	2003
4	S Modebadze	Croatia	Tbilisi	1997
4	M Urjukashvili	Russia	Tbilisi	1998
4	M Urjukashvili	Russia	Tbilisi	2002
4	N Dzagnidze	Zimbabwe	Kutaisi	1989

MOST DROPPED GOALS IN A MATCH

BY THE TEAM

Pens	Opponent	Venue	Year
2	Russia	Tbilisi	1996
2	Ukraine	Tbilisi	1991
2	Ukraine	Kiev	1992
2	Switzerland	Chaux de Fonds	1994

BY A PLAYER

Drops	Player	Opponents	Venue	Year
2	David Chavleishvili	Ukraine	Kiev	1992

MOST CAPPED PLAYERS

Pts	Player
50	Paliko Jimsheladze
45	Malkhaz Urjukashvili
43	Akvsenti Giorgadze
43	Besik Khamashuridze
41	Guia Labadze
41	Ilia Zedginidze

LEADING TRY SCORERS

Tries	Player
12	Ilia Zedginidze
11	Tedo Zibzibadze
10	Levan Tsabadze
10	Akvsenti Giorgadze
10	Archil Kavtarashvili
9	Besik Khamashuridze
9	Malkhaz Urjukashvili

LEADING CONVERSIONS

Cons	Player
55	Paliko Jimsheladze
34	Malkhaz Urjukashvili
9	Nugzar Dzagnidze
8	Kakha Machitidze
7	Boba Kvinikhidze

LEADING PENALTY SCORERS

Pens	Player
44	Paliko Jimsheladze
32	Malkhaz Urjukashvili
22	Nugzar Dzagnidze
13	Shota Modebadze
8	Boba Kvinikhidze

LEADING DROP GOAL SCORERS

Drops	Player
4	Kakha Machitidze
3	Nugzar Dzagnidze
3	Paliko Jimsheladze
2	Niko Iurini
2	David Chavleishvili

LEADING POINT SCORERS

Pts	Player
291	Paliko Jimsheladze
212	Malkhaz Urjukashvili
105	Nugzar Dzagnidze
62	Shota Modebadze
60	Ilia Zedginidze

IRELAND

IRELAND'S TEST RECORD

OPPONENTS	DATE	VENUE	RESULT
Italy	4 February	H	**Won** 26–16
France	11 February	A	**Lost** 31–43
Wales	26 February	H	**Won** 31–5
Scotland	11 March	H	**Won** 15–9
England	18 March	A	**Won** 28–24
New Zealand	10 June	A	**Lost** 23–34
New Zealand	17 June	A	**Lost** 17–27
Australia	24 June	A	**Lost** 15–37

TRIPLE CROWN GLORY FOR IRELAND

Ireland will have shed few tears when they said goodbye to 2005 and turned their thoughts to the challenges of a new year. The men in green had not enjoyed a vintage year by their own increasingly high standards and the fear was Ireland's continued improvement under Eddie O'Sullivan's reign could be in danger of stalling.

David Cannon/Getty Images

Brian O'Driscoll helped deliver a Triple Crown for Ireland in 2006.

Not that 2005 had been an unmitigated disaster. Third place in the Six Nations – courtesy of wins over Scotland, Italy and England – was respectable enough but after two successive second place finishes, there was a sense of regression. Irish fans had come to expect more from their team.

Two hefty wins in Japan over the summer proved little but it was the autumn defeats to New Zealand (45–7) and Australia (30–14) at Lansdowne Road that caused real concern. With home advantage against the southern hemisphere powers, Ireland looked like they had gone backwards. The question was, could O'Sullivan and his coaching set-up get the team back on track in 2006?

The initial answer seemed to be no as the Six Nations began with Italy in Dublin. The game marked the return of Brian O'Driscoll seven months after controversially dislocating his shoulder in the first Lions Test in New Zealand. The talismanic skipper had been sorely missed after his painful and much-debated encounter with Tana Umaga and Keven Mealamu in Christchurch and Ireland prayed O'Driscoll would be the man to reinvigorate the team.

Against Italy, however, it didn't happen and Ireland limped to a lacklustre 26–16 victory. Crucially they had won when far from their best but they had to rely on a controversial Tommy Bowe try in the second half to put clear water between themselves and the Azzurri. Had the referee ruled Bowe had not grounded the ball, as television replays suggested, the result could have easily gone the other way.

"It was a very tough game," said the influential Paul O'Connell, who like O'Driscoll had missed the autumn internationals with injury.

"We probably didn't play that well but they played very well. They put us under a lot of pressure. We are going to have to make a big step up and improve next week in France.

"We were miles off where our ambitions are but next week hopefully we can turn things around and put in a big performance."

In fact, it was the French who produced the 'big performance' in the Stade de France as they ran in six unanswered tries and raced into an unbelievable 43–3 lead against O'Sullivan's side. To their credit, Ireland hit back with four scores of their own during a late rally but it was too little too late and they crashed to a 43–31 defeat. The wheels seemed to be coming off Ireland's challenge.

Grand Slam champions Wales were the next visitors to Lansdowne Road but they were in disarray after the shock resignation of coach Mike Ruddock. Ireland had the chance to kickstart their campaign and took full advantage of Wales' misfortune to run out 31–5 winners. The men in green were beginning to look more like their old selves.

"It's great to be in a situation where we are the authors of our own destiny in the championship," said a relieved O'Sullivan. "They scored an early try which threw the gauntlet down at us but we responded very well."

A dour 15–9 win over Scotland in Dublin followed courtesy of five Ronan O'Gara penalties to three from Chris Paterson and although it was a tepid performance, the Triple Crown remained within their grasp. All they had to do was beat England at Twickenham.

The match was a classic. The lead changed hands regularly but England led 24–21 in the dying minutes only to have the game snatched at the death when Shane Horgan scored a controversial try to clinch a famous 28–24 win, Ireland's third successive victory over England and, of course, the Triple Crown. A season that had begun with a wobble had climaxed with a bang.

"It's a fantastic day for us," said O'Driscoll. "That was the 80 minutes of rugby that we had been waiting for this team to produce. This is a big stepping-stone for us on to bigger things hopefully."

'Bigger things' meant a two Test tour of New Zealand and a one-off international with Australia in Perth. European rivalries would have to be forgotten as O'Sullivan prepared his troops for the daunting prospect of tackling the All Blacks in their own back yard. Ireland had never won hone or away against the Kiwis in 18 meetings over the past 101 years and O'Sullivan knew he would have to produce a miracle if he was going to end the sequence.

Warren Little/Getty Images

Ulster wing Andrew Trimble was an Ireland star to emerge in 2006.

In the end, he very nearly did it. The first Test in Hamilton began badly when his team conceded a first minute try to Doug Howlett but any fears of an All Black rout were quickly dispelled. O'Driscoll's converted try and three O'Gara penalties gave the visitors a 16–8 half-time lead and when Andrew Trimble scored in the second-half, Ireland led 23–15 in the Waikato Stadium. They were ultimately denied a famous victory by three Luke McAlister penalties and a late Troy Flavell score but they had pushed the All Blacks perilously close in a 34–23 defeat.

"It's very disappointing that we fought so hard for so long and then gave away some silly points in the last 10 minutes," O'Driscoll said. "We missed some first-up tackles and coughed up some ball. You can't expect to beat New Zealand if you do that."

The big question now was had Ireland missed a golden opportunity to down New Zealand or could they regroup, find another gear in the second Test in Auckland and finally beat the All Blacks?

The Eden Park clash was another close-fought clash played in terrible conditions. Again the home side made the early running with scores from Byron Kelleher and Clarke Dermody but Ireland dragged themselves back into contention with tries from Paul O'Connell and Jerry Flannery only to be denied late in the second-half when Luke McAlister, who finished the match with 14 points, crashed over to seal a 27–17 victory for the All Blacks. Ireland had come close once again but couldn't get over the final hurdle.

"When we got within three points of them we felt we had them on the rack," said O'Driscoll. "I'm sure it wasn't vintage rugby and the stats will show there were a lot of scrums for knock ons.

"We know if we put phases together we are capable of beating any team. We showed good spirit but it would've been easier if we weren't 17 points down."

O'Sullivan added: "Games like this give you a lot of confidence that you can stay with good teams. I wouldn't panic about having to play New Zealand any more.

"It turned into a boxing match and when you play New Zealand you are boxing a weight below their category so it was really a slugging match in heavy conditions that didn't quite suit us.

"We lost the ping-pong game in our half at times and we struggled to get out of it."

Ireland had little time to lick their wounds and were soon on the plane to Australia for their clash with the Wallabies, who were riding high after two comprehensive wins over England. Ireland had beaten the Australians seven times in 24 clashes – most recently at Lansdowne Road in 2002 – but after a bruising trip to New Zealand, a tired Ireland knew an eighth triumph was against the odds.

The match at the Subiaco Oval proved to be a bridge too far and although Ireland were in contention for the first hour, the Wallabies cut loose in the second half and four late tries were enough to wrap up a 37–15 win.

Although Australia led 11–3 at the break, tries from O'Gara and Neil Best in the second half gave Ireland a 15–11 advantage. But Ireland's legs began to visibly tire and five minutes later Mark Gerrard cut through the defence and the floodgates opened. Further scores from Greg Holmes, George Gregan and Cameron Shepherd followed and Australia were home and dry.

"All three Tests this summer were particularly hard as we knew they would be and they took their toll," said O'Driscoll. "I think the legs started to get heavy after three weeks of Test rugby.

"We felt we had an opportunity to come down and claim a scalp but it shows we have some way to go yet."

A disappointed O'Sullivan was left to rue his team's missed chances but was also quick to pay tribute to the Wallabies.

"I thought the scoreline was harsh," he said. "It was there for us 10 minutes into the second half and the next score was crucial. Two sucker punches in four minutes did us in at the end of the day."

"This is our 11th Test of the season, and that Wallaby side is the best we've played."

IRELAND INTERNATIONAL STATISTICS

MATCH RECORDS UP TO 30TH SEPTEMBER 2006

MOST CONSECUTIVE TEST WINS

10	2002	R,Ru,Gg,A,Fj,Arg,	2003	S1,It1,F,W1
8	2003	Tg, Sm,W2 ,It2, S2, R ,Nm, Arg		
6	1968	S,W,A,	1969	F,E,S
6	2004	SA,US,Arg,	2005	It,S,E

MOST CONSECUTIVE TEST WITHOUT DEFEAT

Matches	Wins	Draws	Periods
10	10	0	2002 to 2003
8	8	0	2003
7	6	1	1968 to 1969
6	6	0	2004 to 2005
5	4	1	1972 to 1973

MOST POINTS IN A MATCH

BY THE TEAM

Pts.	Opponent	Venue	Year
83	United States	Manchester (NH)	2000
78	Japan	Dublin	2000
70	Georgia	Dublin	1998
64	Fiji	Dublin	2002
64	Namibia	Sydney	2003
63	Georgia	Dublin	2002
61	Italy	Limerick	2003
60	Romania	Dublin	1986
60	Italy	Dublin	2000
55	Zimbabwe	Dublin	1991
55	United States	Dublin	2004
54	Wales	Dublin	2002
53	Romania	Dublin	1998
53	United States	Dublin	1999
50	Japan	Bloemfontein	1995

BY A PLAYER

Pts	Player	Opponents	Venue	Year
32	R J R O'Gara	Samoa	Apia	2003
30	R J R O'Gara	Italy	Dublin	2000
26	D G Humphreys	Scotland	Murrayfield	2003
26	D G Humphreys	Italy	Limerick	2003
24	P A Burke	Italy	Dublin	1997
24	D G Humphreys	Argentina	Lens	1999
23	R P Keyes	Zimbabwe	Dublin	1991
23	R J R O'Gara	Japan	Dublin	2000
22	D G Humphreys	Wales	Dublin	2002
21	S O Campbell	Scotland	Dublin	1982
21	S O Campbell	England	Dublin	1983
21	R J R O'Gara	Italy	Rome	2001
21	R J R O'Gara	Argentina	Dublin	2004
20	M J Kiernan	Romania	Dublin	1986
20	E P Elwood	Romania	Dublin	1993
20	S J P Mason	Samoa	Dublin	1996
20	E P Elwood	Georgia	Dublin	1998
20	K G M Wood	United States	Dublin	1999
20	D A Hickie	Italy	Limerick	2003
20	D G Humphreys	United States	Dublin	2004

MOST TRIES IN A MATCH

BY THE TEAM

Tries	Opponent	Venue	Year
13	United States	Manchester (NH)	2000
11	Japan	Dublin	2000
10	Romania	Dublin	1986
10	Georgia	Dublin	1998
10	Namibia	Sydney	2003
9	Fiji	Dublin	2003
8	Western Samoa	Dublin	1988
8	Zimbabwe	Dublin	1991
8	Georgia	Dublin	2002
8	Italy	Limerick	2003
7	Japan	Bloemfontein	1995
7	Romania	Dublin	1998
7	United States	Dublin	1999
7	United States	Dublin	2004
7	Japan	Tokyo	2005

BY A PLAYER

Tries	Player	Opponents	Venue	Year
4	B F Robinson	Zimbabwe	Dublin	1991
4	K G M Wood	United States	Dublin	1999
4	D A Hickie	Italy	Limerick	2003
3	R Montgomery	Wales	Birkenhead	1887
3	J P Quinn	France	Cork	1913
3	E O'D Davy	Scotland	Murrayfield	1930
3	S J Byrne	Scotland	Murrayfield	1953
3	K D Crossan	Romania	Dublin	1986
3	B J Mullin	Tonga	Brisbane	1987
3	M R Mostyn	Argentina	Dublin	1999
3	B G O'Driscoll	France	Paris	2000
3	M J Mullins	United States	Manchester (NH)	2000
3	D A Hickie	Japan	Dublin	2000
3	R A J Henderson	Italy	Rome	2001
3	B G O'Driscoll	Scotland	Dublin	2002
3	K M Maggs	Fiji	Dublin	2002

MOST CONVERSIONS IN A MATCH

BY THE TEAM

Cons	Opponent	Venue	Year
10	Georgia	Dublin	1998
10	Japan	Dublin	2000
9	United States	Manchester (NH)	2000
7	Romania	Dublin	1986
7	Georgia	Dublin	2002
7	Namibia	Sydney	2003
7	United States	Dublin	2004
6	Japan	Bloemfontein	1995
6	Romania	Dublin	1998
6	United States	Dublin	1999
6	Italy	Dublin	2000
6	Italy	Limerick	2003
6	Japan	Tokyo	2005

BY A PLAYER

Cons	Player	Opponents	Venue	Year
10	E P Elwood	Georgia	Dublin	1998
10	R J R O'Gara	Japan	Dublin	2000
8	R J R O'Gara	United States	Manchester (NH)	2000
7	M J Kiernan	Romania	Dublin	1986
7	R J R O'Gara	Namibia	Sydney	2003
7	D G Humphreys	United States	Dublin	2004
6	P A Burke	Japan	Bloemfontein	1995
6	R J R O'Gara	Italy	Dublin	2000
6	D G Humphreys	Italy	Limerick	2003
6	D G Humphreys	Japan	Tokyo	2005
5	M J Kiernan	Canada	Dunedin	1987
5	E P Elwood	Romania	Dublin	1999
5	R J R O'Gara	Georgia	Dublin	2002
5	D G Humphreys	Fiji	Dublin	2002
5	D G Humphreys	Romania	Dublin	2005

MOST PENALTIES IN A MATCH

BY THE TEAM

Pens	Opponent	Venue	Year
8	Italy	Dublin	1997
7	Argentina	Lens	1999
6	Scotland	Dublin	1982
6	Romania	Dublin	1993
6	United States	Atlanta	1996
6	Western Samoa	Dublin	1996
6	Italy	Dublin	2000
6	Wales	Dublin	2002
6	Australia	Dublin	2002
6	Samoa	Apia	2003
6	Japan	Osaka	2005

BY A PLAYER

Pens	Player	Opponents	Venue	Year
8	P A Burke	Italy	Dublin	1997
7	D G Humphreys	Argentina	Lens	1999
6	S O Campbell	Scotland	Dublin	1982
6	E P Elwood	Romania	Dublin	1993
6	S J P Mason	Western Samoa	Dublin	1996
6	R J R O'Gara	Italy	Dublin	2000
6	D G Humphreys	Wales	Dublin	2002
6	R J R O'Gara	Australia	Dublin	2002

MOST DROPPED GOALS IN A MATCH

BY THE TEAM

DGs	Opponent	Venue	Year
2	Australia	Dublin	1967
2	France	Dublin	1975
2	Australia	Sydney	1979
2	England	Dublin	1981
2	Canada	Dunedin	1987
2	England	Dublin	1993
2	Wales	Wembley	1999
2	New Zealand	Dublin	2001
2	Argentina	Dublin	2004
2	England	Dublin	2005

BY A PLAYER

Drops	Player	Opponents	Venue	Year
2	C M H Gibson	Australia	Dublin	1967
2	W M McCombe	France	Dublin	1975
2	S O Campbell	Australia	Sydney	1979
2	E P Elwood	England	Dublin	1993
2	D G Humphreys	Wales	Wembley	1999
2	D G Humphreys	New Zealand	Dublin	2001
2	R J R O'Gara	Argentina	Dublin	2004
2	R J R O'Gara	England	Dublin	2005

MOST CAPPED PLAYERS

Caps	Player	Career Span
80	M E O'Kelly	1997 to 2006
72	D G Humphreys	1996 to 2005
70	K M Maggs	1997 to 2005
69	C M H Gibson	1964 to 1979
69	P A Stringer	2000 to 2006
67	B G O'Driscoll	1999 to 2006
66	G T Dempsey	1998 to 2006
65	J J Hayes	2000 to 2006
63	W J McBride	1962 to 1975
63	R J R O'Gara	2000 to 2006
62	A G Foley	1995 to 2005
61	J F Slattery	1970 to 1984
59	P S Johns	1990 to 2000
58	P A Orr	1976 to 1987
58	K G M Wood	1994 to 2003
55	B J Mullin	1984 to 1995
54	T J Kiernan	1960 to 1973
54	P M Clohessy	1993 to 2002
52	D G Lenihan	1981 to 1992
51	M I Keane	1974 to 1984
51	D A Hickie	1997 to 2005

MOST CONSECUTIVE TESTS

Tests	Player	Span
52	W J McBride	1964 to 1975
49	P A Orr	1976 to 1986
43	D G Lenihan	1981 to 1989
39	M I Keane	1974 to 1981
37	G V Stephenson	1920 to 1929

MOST TESTS AS CAPTAIN

Tests	Captain	Span
36	K G M Wood	1996 to 2003
30	B G O'Driscoll	2002 to 2006
24	T J Kiernan	1963 to 1973
19	C F Fitzgerald	1982 to 1986
17	J F Slattery	1979 to 1981
17	D G Lenihan	1986 to 1990

MOST POINTS IN TESTS

Pts	Player	Tests	Career
637	R J R O'Gara	63	2000 to 2006
565*	D G Humphreys	72	1996 to 2005
308	M J Kiernan	43	1982 to 1991
296	E P Elwood	35	1993 to 1999
217	S O Campbell	22	1976 to 1984
158	T J Kiernan	54	1960 to 1973
152	B G O'Driscoll	67	1999 to 2006
125	D A Hickie	51	1997 to 2005
113	A J P Ward	19	1978 to 1987

* Humphreys's total includes a penalty try against Scotland in 1999

MOST TRIES IN TESTS

Tries	Player	Tests	Career
28	B G O'Driscoll	67	1999 to 2006
25	D A Hickie	51	1997 to 2005
17	B J Mullin	55	1984 to 1995
16	S P Horgan	48	2000 to 2006
16	G E A Murphy	42	2000 to 2006
15	K G M Wood	58	1994 to 2003
15	K M Maggs	70	1997 to 2005
14	G V Stephenson	42	1920 to 1930
14	G T Dempsey	66	1998 to 2006
12	K D Crossan	41	1982 to 1992
11	A T A Duggan	25	1963 to 1972
11	S P Geoghegan	37	1991 to 1996

MOST CONVERSIONS IN TESTS

Cons	Player	Tests	Career
101	R J R O'Gara	63	2000 to 2006
88	D G Humphreys	72	1996 to 2005
43	E P Elwood	35	1993 to 1999
40	M J Kiernan	43	1982 to 1991
26	T J Kiernan	54	1960 to 1973
16	R A Lloyd	19	1910 to 1920
15	S O Campbell	22	1976 to 1984

MOST PENALTY GOALS IN TESTS

Pens	Player	Tests	Career
121	R J R O'Gara	63	2000 to 2006
110	D G Humphreys	72	1996 to 2005
68	E P Elwood	35	1993 to 1999
62	M J Kiernan	43	1982 to 1991
54	S O Campbell	22	1976 to 1984
31	T J Kiernan	54	1960 to 1973
29	A J P Ward	19	1978 to 1987

MOST DROPPED GOALS IN TESTS

Drops	Player	Tests	Career
9	R J R O'Gara	63	2000 to 2006
8	D G Humphreys	72	1996 to 2005
7	R A Lloyd	19	1910 to 1920
7	S O Campbell	22	1976 to 1984
6	C M H Gibson	69	1964 to 1979
6	B J McGann	25	1969 to 1976
6	M J Kiernan	43	1982 to 1991

Chris McGrath/Getty Images

A hero with Munster and Ireland no Irishman has scored more points in Test matches than Ronan O'Gara.

INTERNATIONAL CHAMPIONSHIP RECORDS

RECORD	DETAIL		SET
Most points in season	168	in five matches	2000
Most tries in season	17	in five matches	2000
Highest Score	60	60–13 v Italy	2000
Biggest win	47	60–13 v Italy	2000
Highest score conceded	50	18–50 v England	2000
Biggest defeat	40	6–46 v England	1997
Most appearances	56	C M H Gibson	1964–1979
Most points in matches	313	R J R O'Gara	2000–2006
Most points in season	76	R J R O'Gara	2006
Most points in match	30	R J R O'Gara	v Italy, 2000
Most tries in matches	16	B G O'Driscoll	2000–2006
Most tries in season	5	J E Arigho	1928
	5	B G O'Driscoll	2000
Most tries in match	3	R Montgomery	v Wales, 1887
	3	J P Quinn	v France, 1913
	3	E O'D Davy	v Scotland, 1930
	3	S J Byrne	v Scotland, 1953
	3	B G O'Driscoll	v France, 2000
	3	R A J Henderson	v Italy, 2001
	3	B G O'Driscoll	v Scotland, 2002
Most cons in matches	45	R J R O'Gara	2000–2006
Most cons in season	11	R J R O'Gara	2000
	11	R J R O'Gara	2004
Most cons in match	6	R J R O'Gara	v Italy, 2000
Most pens in matches	63	R J R O'Gara	2000–2006
Most pens in season	17	R J R O'Gara	2006
Most pens in match	6	S O Campbell	v Scotland, 1982
	6	R J R O'Gara	v Italy, 2000
	6	D G Humphreys	v Wales, 2002
Most drops in matches	7	R A Lloyd	1910 – 1920
Most drops in season	2	on several	Occasions
Most drops in match	2	W M McCombe	v France, 1975
	2	E P Elwood	v England, 1993
	2	D G Humphreys	v Wales, 1999
	2	R J R O'Gara	v England, 2005

RECORD	HOLDER	DETAIL
Longest Test Career	A J F O'Reilly	1955 to 1970
	C M H Gibson	1964 to 1979
Youngest Test Cap	F S Hewitt	17 yrs 157 days in 1924
Oldest Test Cap	C M H Gibson	36 yrs 195 days in 1979

CAREER RECORDS OF IRELAND INTERNATIONAL PLAYERS (PLAYERS CAPPED SINCE THE START OF RWC 2003 UP TO 30 SEPTEMBER 2006)

PLAYER BACKS	DEBUT	CAPS	T	C	P	D	PTS
I J Boss	2006 v NZ	2	0	0	0	0	0
T J Bowe	2004 v US	8	3	0	0	0	15
K P Campbell	2005 v J	3	0	0	0	0	0
G M D'Arcy	1999 v R	23	3	0	0	0	15
G T Dempsey	1998 v Gg	66	14	0	0	0	70
G W Duffy	2004 v SA	4	3	0	0	0	15
W G Easterby	2000 v US	28	6	0	0	0	30
D A Hickie	1997 v W	51	25	0	0	0	125
A P Horgan	2003 v Sm	7	1	0	0	0	5
S P Horgan	2000 v S	48	16	0	0	0	80
T G Howe	2000 v US	14	6	0	0	0	30
D G Humphreys	1996 v F	72	7*	88	110	8	565
J P Kelly	2002 v It	17	8	0	0	0	40
K Lewis	2005 v J	1	0	0	0	0	0
K M Maggs	1997 v NZ	70	15	0	0	0	75
G E A Murphy	2000 v US	42	16	1	0	1	85
B G O'Driscoll	1999 v A	67	28	0	0	4	152
R J R O'Gara	2000 v S	63	9	101	121	9	637
D P Quinlan	2005 v J	2	0	0	0	0	0
E Reddan	2006 F	1	0	0	0	0	0
J W Staunton	2001 v Sm	4	1	2	4	0	21
P A Stringer	2000 v S	69	6	0	0	0	30
A Trimble	2005 v A	9	4	0	0	0	20

FORWARDS

N Best	2005 v NZ	5	2	0	0	0	10
R Best	2005 v NZ	4	0	0	0	0	0
S J Best	2003 v Tg	12	1	0	0	0	5
J S Byrne	2001 v R	41	3	0	0	0	15
R Corrigan	1997 v C	47	0	0	0	0	0
V C P Costello	1996 v US	39	4	0	0	0	20
L F M Cullen	2002 v NZ	18	0	0	0	0	0
S H Easterby	2000 v S	49	4	0	0	0	20
J Flannery	2005 v R	9	2	0	0	0	10
A G Foley	1995 v E	62	5	0	0	0	25
K D Gleeson	2002 v W	25	4	0	0	0	20
J J Hayes	2000 v S	65	2	0	0	0	10
T Hogan	2005 v J	2	0	0	0	0	0
M J Horan	2000 v US	40	4	0	0	0	20
B J Jackman	2005 v J	2	0	0	0	0	0
D P Leamy	2004 v US	14	1	0	0	0	5
G W Longwell	2000 v J	26	1	0	0	0	5
M T McCullough	2005 v J	4	0	0	0	0	0
E R P Miller	1997 v It	48	6	0	0	0	30
D F O'Callaghan	2003 v W	27	1	0	0	0	5
P J O'Connell	2002 v W	36	5	0	0	0	25
J H O'Connor	2004 v SA	12	1	0	0	0	5
M R O'Driscoll	2001 v R	7	0	0	0	0	0
M E O'Kelly	1997 v NZ	80	7	0	0	0	35
A Quinlan	1999 v R	23	5	0	0	0	25
F J Sheahan	2000 v US	24	5	0	0	0	25
D P Wallace	2000 v Arg	30	5	0	0	0	25
R G Wilson	2005 v J	1	0	0	0	0	0
K G M Wood	1994 v A	58	15	0	0	0	75
B Young	2006 v NZ	2	0	0	0	0	0

* Humphreys's figures include a penalty try awarded against Scotland in 1999

IRELAND INTERNATIONAL PLAYERS

(UP TO 30TH SEPTEMBER 2006)

Note: Years given for International Championship matches are for second half of season; eg 1972 means season 1971–72. Years for all other matches refer to the actual year of the match. Entries in square brackets denote matches played in RWC Finals.

Abraham, M (Bective Rangers) 1912 E, S, W, SA, 1914 W
Adams, C (Old Wesley), 1908 E, 1909 E, F, 1910 F, 1911 E, S, W, F, 1912 S, W, SA, 1913 W, F, 1914 F, E, S
Agar, R D (Malone) 1947 F, E, S, W, 1948 F, 1949 S, W, 1950 F, E, W
Agnew, P J (CIYMS) 1974 F (R), 1976 A
Ahearne, T (Queen's Coll, Cork) 1899 E
Aherne, L F P (Dolphin, Lansdowne) 1988 E 2, WS, It, 1989 F, W, E, S, NZ, 1990 E, S, F, W (R), 1992 E, S, F, A
Alexander, R (NIFC, Police Union) 1936 E, S, W, 1937 E, S, W, 1938 E, S, 1939 E, S, W
Allen, C E (Derry, Liverpool) 1900 E, S, W, 1901 E, S, W, 1903 S, W, 1904 E, S, W, 1905 E, S, W, NZ, 1906 E, S, W, SA, 1907 S, W
Allen, G G (Derry, Liverpool) 1896 E, S, W, 1897 E, S, 1898 E, S, 1899 E, W
Allen, T C (NIFC) 1885 E, S 1
Allen, W S (Wanderers) 1875 E
Allison, J B (Edinburgh U) 1899 E, S, 1900 E, S, W, 1901 E, S, W, 1902 E, S, W, 1903 S
Anderson, F E (Queen's U, Belfast, NIFC) 1953 F, E, S, W, 1954 NZ, F, E, S, W, 1955 F, E, S, W
Anderson, H J (Old Wesley) 1903 E, S, 1906 E, S
Anderson, W A (Dungannon) 1984 A, 1985 S, F, W, E, 1986 F, S, R, 1987 E, S, F, W, [W, C, Tg, A], 1988 S, F, W, E 1,2, 1989 F, W, E, NZ, 1990 E, S
Andrews, G (NIFC) 1875 E, 1876 E
Andrews, H W (NIFC) 1888 M, 1889 S, W
Archer, A M (Dublin U, NIFC) 1879 S
Arigho, J E (Lansdowne) 1928 F, E, W, 1929 F, E, S, W, 1930 F, E, S, W, 1931 F, E, S, W, SA
Armstrong, W K (NIFC) 1960 SA, 1961 E
Arnott, D T (Lansdowne) 1876 E
Ash, W H (NIFC) 1875 E, 1876 E, 1877 S
Aston, H R (Dublin U) 1908 E, W
Atkins, A P (Bective Rangers) 1924 F
Atkinson, J M (NIFC) 1927 F, A
Atkinson, J R (Dublin U) 1882 W, S

Bagot, J C (Dublin U, Lansdowne) 1879 S, E, 1880 E, S, 1881 S
Bailey, A H (UC Dublin, Lansdowne) 1934 W, 1935 E, S, W, NZ, 1936 E, S, W, 1937 E, S, W, 1938 E, S
Bailey, N (Northampton) 1952 E
Bardon, M E (Bohemians) 1934 E
Barlow, M (Wanderers) 1875 E
Barnes, R J (Dublin U, Armagh) 1933 W
Barr, A (Methodist Coll, Belfast) 1898 W, 1899 S, 1901 E, S
Barry, N J (Garryowen) 1991 Nm 2(R)
Beamish, C E St J (RAF, Leicester) 1933 W, S, 1934 S, W, 1935 E, S, W, NZ, 1936 E, S, W, 1938 W
Beamish, G R (RAF, Leicester) 1925 E, S, W, 1928 F, E, S, W, 1929 F, E, S, W, 1930 F, S, W, 1931 F, E, S, W, SA, 1932 E, S, W, 1933 E, W, S
Beatty, W J (NIFC, Richmond) 1910 F, 1912 F, W
Becker, V A (Lansdowne) 1974 F, W
Beckett, G G P (Dublin U) 1908 E, S, W
Bell, J C (Ballymena, Northampton, Dungannon) 1994 A 1,2, US, 1995 S, It, [NZ, W, F], Fj, 1996 US, S, F, W, E, WS, A, 1997 It 1, F, W, E, S, 1998 Gg, R, SA 3, 1999 F, W, S It (R), A 2, [US (R), A 3(R), R], 2001 R (R), 2003 Tg, Sm, It 2(R)
Bell, R J (NIFC) 1875 E, 1876 E
Bell, W E (Belfast Collegians) 1953 F, E, S, W
Bennett, F (Belfast Collegians) 1913 S
Bent, G C (Dublin U) 1882 W, E
Berkery, P J (Lansdowne) 1954 W, 1955 W, 1956 S, W, 1957 F, E, S, W, 1958 A, E, S
Bermingham, J J C (Blackrock Coll) 1921 E, S, W, F
Best, N (Ulster) 2005 NZ(R),R, 2006 NZ1,2,A
Best, R (Ulster) 2005 NZ(R),A(t), 2006 W(R),A(R)
Best, S J (Belfast Harlequins, Ulster) 2003 Tg (R), W 2, S 2(R), 2003 [Nm(R)], 2004 W(R),US(R), 2005 J1,2,NZ(R),R, 2006 F(R), W(R)
Bishop, J P (London Irish) 1998 SA, 1,2, Gg, R, SA 3, 1999 F, W, E, S, It, A 1,2, Arg 1, [US, A 3, Arg 2], 2000 E, Arg, C, 2002 NZ 1,2, Fj, Arg, 2003 W 1, E
Blackham, J C (Queen's Coll, Cork) 1909 S, W, F, 1910 E, S, W
Blake-Knox, S E F (NIFC) 1976 E, S, 1977 F (R)
Blayney, J J (Wanderers) 1950 S
Bond, A T W (Derry) 1894 S, W
Bornemann, W W (Wanderers) 1960 E, S, W, SA
Boss, I J (Ulster) 2006 NZ2(R),A(R)
Bowe, T J (Ulster) 2004 US, 2005 J1,2,NZ,A,R, 2006 It,F
Bowen, D St J (Cork Const) 1977 W, E, S
Boyd, C A (Dublin U) 1900 S, 1901 S, W
Boyle, C V (Dublin U) 1935 NZ, 1936 E, S, W, 1937 E, S, W, 1938 W, 1939 W
Brabazon, H M (Dublin U) 1884 E, 1885 S 1, 1886 E
Bradley, M J (Dolphin) 1920 W, F, 1922 E, S, W, F, 1923 E, S, W, F, 1925 F, S, W, 1926 F, E, S, W, 1927 F, W
Bradley, M T (Cork Constitution) 1984 A, 1985 S, F, W, E, 1986 F, W, E, S, R, 1987 E, S, F, W, [W, C, Tg, A], 1988 S, F, W, E 1, 1990 W, 1992 NZ 1,2, 1993 S, F, W, E, R, 1994 F, W, E, S, A 1,2, US, 1995 S, F, [NZ]
Bradshaw, G (Belfast Collegians) 1903 W
Bradshaw, R M (Wanderers) 1885 E, S 1,2
Brady, A M (UC Dublin, Malone) 1966 S, 1968 E, S, W
Brady, J A (Wanderers) 1976 E, S
Brady, J R (CIYMS) 1951 S, W, 1953 F, E, S, W, 1954 W, 1956 W, 1957 F, E, S, W
Bramwell, T (NIFC) 1928 F
Brand, T N (NIFC) 1924 NZ
Brennan, J I (CIYMS) 1957 S, W
Brennan, T (St Mary's Coll, Barnhall) 1998 SA 1(R),2(R), 1999 F (R), S (R), It, A 2, Arg 1, [US, A 3], 2000 E (R), 2001 W (R), E (R), Sm (R)
Bresnihan, F P K (UC Dublin, Lansdowne, London Irish) 1966 E, W, 1967 A 1, E, S, W, F, 1968 F, E, S, W, A, 1969 F, E, S, W, 1970 SA, F, E, S, W, 1971 F, E, S, W
Brett, J T (Monkstown) 1914 W
Bristow, J R (NIFC) 1879 E
Brophy, N H (Blackrock Coll, UC Dublin, London Irish) 1957 F, E, 1959 E, S, W, F, 1960 F, SA, 1961 S, W, 1962 E, S, W, 1963 E, W, 1967 E, S, W, F, A 2
Brown, E L (Instonians) 1958 F

Brown, G S (Monkstown, United Services) 1912 S, W, SA
Brown, H (Windsor) 1877 E
Brown, T (Windsor) 1877 E, S
Brown, W H (Dublin U) 1899 E
Brown, W J (Malone) 1970 SA, F, S, W
Brown, W S (Dublin U) 1893 S, W, 1894 E, S, W
Browne, A W (Dublin U) 1951 SA
Browne, D (Blackrock Coll) 1920 F
Browne, H C (United Services and RN) 1929 E, S, W
Browne, W F (United Services and Army) 1925 E, S, W, 1926 S, W, 1927 F, E, S, W, A, 1928 E, S
Browning, D R (Wanderers) 1881 E, S
Bruce, S A M (NIFC) 1883 E, S, 1884 E
Brunker, A A (Lansdowne) 1895 E, W
Bryant, C H (Cardiff) 1920 E, S
Buchanan, A McM (Dublin U) 1926 E, S, W, 1927 S, W, A
Buchanan, J W B (Dublin U) 1882 S, 1884 E, S
Buckley, J H (Sunday's Well) 1973 E, S
Bulger, L Q (Lansdowne) 1896 E, S, W, 1897 E, S, 1898 E, S, W
Bulger, M J (Dublin U) 1888 M
Burges, J H (Rosslyn Park) 1950 F, E
Burgess, R B (Dublin U) 1912 SA
Burke, P A (Cork Constitution, Bristol, Harlequins) 1995 E, S, W (R), It, [J], Fj, 1996 US (R), A, 1997 It 1, S (R), 2001 R (R), 2003 S 1(R), Sm (R)
Burkitt, J C S (Queen's Coll, Cork) 1881 E
Burns, I J (Wanderers) 1980 E (R)
Butler, L G (Blackrock Coll) 1960 W
Butler, N (Bective Rangers) 1920 E
Byers, R M (NIFC) 1928 S, W, 1929 E, S, W
Byrne, E (St Mary's Coll) 2001 It (R), F (R), S (R), W (R), E (R), Sm, NZ (R), 2003 A (R), Sm (R)
Byrne, E M J (Blackrock Coll) 1977 S, F, 1978 F, W, E, NZ
Byrne, J S (Blackrock Coll, Leinster, Saracens) 2001 R (R), 2002 W (R), E (R), S (R), It, NZ 2(R), R, Ru (R), Gg, A, Arg, 2003 S 1, It 1, F, W 1, E, A, Tg, Sm, W 2(R), It 2, S2(R), [R(R),Nm(R)], 2004 F,W,E,It,S,SA1,2,3,Arg, 2005 It,S,E,F,W,NZ,A,R
Byrne, N F (UC Dublin) 1962 F
Byrne, S J (UC Dublin, Lansdowne) 1953 S, W, 1955 F
Byron, W G (NIFC) 1896 E, S, W, 1897 E, S, 1898 E, S, W, 1899 E, S, W

Caddell, E D (Dublin U, Wanderers) 1904 S, 1905 E, S, W, NZ, 1906 E, S, W, SA, 1907 E, S, 1908 S, W
Cagney, S J (London Irish) 1925 W, 1926 F, E, S, W, 1927 F, 1928 E, S, W, 1929 F, E, S, W
Callan, C P (Lansdowne) 1947 F, E, S, W, 1948 F, E, S, W, 1949 F, E
Cameron, E D (Bective Rangers) 1891 S, W
Campbell, C E (Old Wesley) 1970 SA
Campbell, E F (Monkstown) 1899 S, W, 1900 E, W
Campbell, K P (Ulster) 2005 J1(R),2(R),R
Campbell, S B B (Derry) 1911 E, S, W, F, 1912 F, E, S, W, SA, 1913 E, S, F
Campbell, S O (Old Belvedere) 1976 A, 1979 A 1,2, 1980 E, S, F, W, 1981 F, W, E, S, SA 1, 1982 W, E, S, F, 1983 S, F, W, E, 1984 F, W
Canniffe, D M (Lansdowne) 1976 W, E
Cantrell, J L (UC Dublin, Blackrock Coll) 1976 A, F, W, E, S, 1981 S, SA 1,2, A
Carey, R W (Dungannon) 1992 NZ 1,2
Carpendale, M J (Monkstown) 1886 S, 1887 W, 1888 W, S
Carr, N J (Ards) 1985 S, F, W, E, 1986 W, E, S, R, 1987 E, S, W
Carroll, C (Bective Rangers) 1930 F
Carroll, R (Lansdowne) 1947 F, 1950 S, W
Casement, B N (Dublin U) 1875 E, 1876 E, 1879 E
Casement, F (Dublin U) 1906 E, S, W
Casey, J C (Young Munster) 1930 S, 1932 E
Casey, P J (UC Dublin, Lansdowne) 1963 F, E, S, W, NZ, 1964 E, S, W, F, 1965 F, E, S
Casey, R E (Blackrock Coll) 1999 [A 3(t), Arg 2(R)], 2000 E, US (R), C (R)
Chambers, J (Dublin U) 1886 E, S, 1887 E, S, W
Chambers, R R (Instonians) 1951 F, E, S, W, 1952 F, W
Clancy, T P J (Lansdowne) 1988 W, E 1,2, WS, It, 1989 F, W, E, S
Clarke, A T H (Northampton, Dungannon) 1995 Fj (R), 1996 W, E, WS, 1997 F (R), It 2(R), 1998 Gg (R), R
Clarke, C P (Terenure Coll) 1993 F, W, E, 1998 W, E
Clarke, D J (Dolphin) 1991 W, Nm 1,2, [J, A], 1992 NZ 2(R)
Clarke, J A B (Bective Rangers) 1922 S, W, F, 1923 F, 1924 E, S, W
Clegg, R J (Bangor) 1973 F, 1975 E, S, F, W
Clifford, J T (Young Munster) 1949 F, E, S, W, 1950 F, E, S, W, 1951 F, E, SA, 1952 F, S, W
Clinch, A D (Dublin U, Wanderers) 1892 S, 1893 W, 1895 E, S, W, 1896 E, S, W, 1897 E, S
Clinch, J D (Wanderers, Dublin U) 1923 W, 1924 F, E, S, W, NZ, 1925 F, E, S, 1926 E, S, W, 1927 F, 1928 F, E, S, W, 1929 F, E, S, W, 1930 F, E, S, W, 1931 F, E, S, W, SA
Clohessy, P M (Young Munster) 1993 F, W, E, 1994 F, W, E, S, A 1,2, US, 1995 E, S, F, W, 1996 S, F, 1997 It 2, 1998 F (R), W (R), SA 2(R), Gg, R, SA 3, 1999 F, W, E, S, It, A 1,2 Arg 1, [US, A 3(R)], 2000 E, S, It, F, W, Arg, J, SA, 2001 It, F, R, S, W, E, Sm (R), NZ, 2002 W, E, S, It, F
Clune, J J (Blackrock Coll) 1912 SA, 1913 W, F, 1914 F, E, W
Coffey, J J (Lansdowne) 1900 E, 1901 W, 1902 E, S, W, 1903 E, S, W, 1905 E, S, W, NZ, 1906 E, S, W, SA, 1907 E, 1908 W, 1910 F
Cogan, W St J (Queen's Coll, Cork) 1907 E, S
Collier, S R (Queen's Coll, Belfast) 1883 S
Collins, P C (Lansdowne, London Irish) 1987 [C], 1990 S (R)
Collis, W R F (KCH, Harlequins) 1924 F, W, NZ, 1925 F, E, S, 1926 F
Collis, W S (Wanderers) 1884 W
Collopy, G (Bective Rangers) 1891 S, 1892 S
Collopy, R (Bective Rangers) 1923 E, S, W, F, 1924 F, E, S, W, NZ, 1925 F, E, S, W
Collopy, W P (Bective Rangers) 1914 F, E, S, W, 1921 E, S, W, F, 1922 E, S, W, F, 1923 S, W, F, 1924 F, E, S, W
Combe, A (NIFC) 1875 E
Condon, H C (London Irish) 1984 S (R)
Cook, H G (Lansdowne) 1884 W
Coote, P B (RAF, Leicester) 1933 S
Corcoran, J C (London Irish) 1947 A, 1948 F
Corken, T S (Belfast Collegians) 1937 E, S, W
Corkery, D S (Cork Constitution, Bristol) 1994 A 1,2, US, 1995 E, [NZ, J, W, F], Fj, 1996 US, S, F, W, E, WS, A, 1997 It 1, F, W, E, S, 1998 S, F, W, E, 1999 A 1(R),2(R)
Corley, H H (Dublin U, Wanderers) 1902 E, S, W, 1903 E, S, W, 1904 E, S
Cormac, H S T (Clontarf) 1921 E, S, W
Corrigan, R (Greystones, Lansdowne, Leinster) 1997 C (R), It 2, 1998 S, F, W, E, SA 3(R), 1999 A 1(R),2(R), [Arg 2], 2002 NZ 1,2, R, Ru, Gg, A, Fj (R), Arg, 2003 S 1, It 1, A, Tg, Sm, W 2, It 2, S 2, [R,Arg,A,F], 2004 F,W,E,It,S, SA1,2,3,Arg, 2005 It,S,E,F,W, J1(R),2(R), 2006 F
Costello, P (Bective Rangers) 1960 F
Costello, R A (Garryowen) 1993 S
Costello, V C P (St Mary's Coll, London Irish) 1996 US, F, W, E. WS (R), 1997 C, It 2(R), 1998 S (R), F, W, E, SA 1,2, Gg, R, SA 3, 1999 F, W (R), E, S (R), It, A 1, 2002 R (R), A, Arg, 2003 S 1, It 1, F, E, A, It 2, S 2, [R,Arg,F], 2004 F(R),W(R),It(R), S(R)
Cotton, J (Wanderers) 1889 W
Coulter, H H (Queen's U, Belfast) 1920 E, S, W
Courtney, A W (UC Dublin) 1920 S, W, F, 1921 E, S, W, F
Cox, H L (Dublin U) 1875 E, 1876 E, 1877 E, S
Craig, R G (Queen's U, Belfast) 1938 S, W
Crawford, E C (Dublin U) 1885 E, S 1
Crawford, W E (Lansdowne) 1920 E, S, W, F, 1921 E, S, W, F, 1922 E, S, 1923 E, S, W, F, 1924 F, E, W, NZ, 1925 F, E, S, W, 1926 F, E, S, W, 1927 F, E, S, W
Crean, T J (Wanderers) 1894 E, S, W, 1895 E, S, W, 1896 E, S, W
Crichton, R Y (Dublin U) 1920 E, S, W, F, 1921 F, 1922 E, 1923 W, F, 1924 F, E, S, W, NZ, 1925 E, S
Croker, E W D (Limerick) 1878 E
Cromey, G E (Queen's U, Belfast) 1937 E, S, W, 1938 E, S, W, 1939 E, S, W

Cronin, B M (Garryowen) 1995 S, 1997 S
Cronyn, A P (Dublin U, Lansdowne) 1875 E, 1876 E, 1880 S
Crossan, K D (Instonians) 1982 S, 1984 F, W, E, S, 1985 S, F, W, E, 1986 E, S, R, 1987 E, S, F, W, [W, C, Tg, A], 1988 S, F, W, E 1, WS, It, 1989 W, S, NZ, 1990 E, S, F, W, Arg, 1991 E, S, Nm 2 [Z, J, S], 1992 W
Crotty, D J (Garryowen) 1996 A, 1997 It 1, F, W, 2000 C
Crowe, J F (UC Dublin) 1974 NZ
Crowe, L (Old Belvedere) 1950 E, S, W
Crowe, M P (Lansdowne) 1929 W, 1930 E, S, W, 1931 F, S, W, SA, 1932 S, W, 1933 W, S, 1934 E
Crowe, P M (Blackrock Coll) 1935 E, 1938 E
Cullen, L F M (Blackrock Coll, Leinster) 2002 NZ 2(R), R (R), Ru (R), Gg (R), A (R), Fj, Arg (R), 2003 S 1(R), It 1(R), F (R), W 1, Tg, Sm, It 2, 2004 US(R), 2005 J1,2,R
Cullen, T J (UC Dublin) 1949 F
Cullen, W J (Monkstown and Manchester) 1920 E
Culliton, M G (Wanderers) 1959 E, S, W, F, 1960 E, S, W, F, SA, 1961 E, S, W, F, 1962 S, F, 1964 E, S, W, F
Cummins, W E A (Queen's Coll, Cork) 1879 S, 1881 E, 1882 E
Cunningham, D McC (NIFC) 1923 E, S, W, 1925 F, E, W
Cunningham, M J (UC Cork) 1955 F, E, S, W, 1956 F, S, W
Cunningham, V J G (St Mary's Coll) 1988 E 2, It, 1990 Arg (R), 1991 Nm 1,2, [Z, J(R)], 1992 NZ 1,2, A, 1993 S, F, W, E, R, 1994 F
Cunningham, W A (Lansdowne) 1920 W, 1921 E, S, W, F, 1922 E, 1923 S, W
Cuppaidge, J L (Dublin U) 1879 E, 1880 E, S
Currell, J (NIFC) 1877 S
Curtis, A B (Oxford U) 1950 F, E, S
Curtis, D M (London Irish) 1991 W, E, S, Nm 1,2, [Z, J, S, A], 1992 W, E, S (R), F
Cuscaden, W A (Dublin U, Bray) 1876 E
Cussen, D J (Dublin U) 1921 E, S, W, F, 1922 E, 1923 E, S, W, F, 1926 F, E, S, W, 1927 F, E

Daly, J C (London Irish) 1947 F, E, S, W, 1948 E, S, W
Daly, M J (Harlequins) 1938 E
Danaher, P P A (Lansdowne, Garryowen) 1988 S, F, W, WS, It, 1989 F, NZ (R), 1990 F, 1992 S, F, NZ 1, A, 1993 S, F, W, E, R, 1994 F, W, E, S, A 1,2, US, 1995 E, S, F, W
D'Arcy, G M (Lansdowne, Leinster) 1999 [R (R)], 2002 Fj (R), 2003 Tg (R), Sm (R), W 2(R), 2004 F,W,E,It,S,SA1, 2005 It,NZ,A,R, 2006 It,F,W,S,E,NZ1,2,A
Dargan, M J (Old Belvedere) 1952 S, W
Davidson, C T (NIFC) 1921 F
Davidson, I G (NIFC) 1899 E, 1900 S, W, 1901 E, S, W, 1902 E, S, W
Davidson, J C (Dungannon) 1969 F, E, S, W, 1973 NZ, 1976 NZ
Davidson, J W (Dungannon, London Irish, Castres) 1995 Fj, 1996 S, F, W, E, WS, A, 1997 It 1, F, W, E, S, 1998 Gg (R), R (R), SA 3(R), 1999 F, W, E, S, It, A 1,2(R), Arg 1, [US,R (R), Arg 2], 2000 S (R), W (R), US, C, 2001 It (R), S
Davies, F E (Lansdowne) 1892 S, W, 1893 E, S, W
Davis, J L (Monkstown) 1898 E, S
Davis, W J N (Edinburgh U, Bessbrook) 1890 S, W, E, 1891 E, S, W, 1892 E, S, 1895 S
Davison, W (Belfast Academy) 1887 W
Davy, E O'D (UC Dublin, Lansdowne) 1925 W, 1926 F, E, S, W, 1927 F, E, S, W, A, 1928 F, E, S, W, 1929 F, E, S, W, 1930 F, E, S, W, 1931 F, E, S, W, SA, 1932 E, S, W, 1933 E, W, S, 1934 E
Dawson, A R (Wanderers) 1958 A, E, S, W, F, 1959 E, S, W, F, 1960 F, SA, 1961 E, S, W, F, SA, 1962 S, F, W, 1963 F, E, S, W, NZ, 1964 E, S, F
Dawson, K (London Irish) 1997 NZ, C, 1998 S, 1999 [R, Arg 2], 2000 E, S, It, F, W, J, SA, 2001 R, S, W (R), E (R), Sm, 2002 Fj, 2003 Tg, It 2(R), S 2(R)
Dean, P M (St Mary's Coll) 1981 SA 1,2, A, 1982 W, E, S, F, 1984 A, 1985 S, F, W, E, 1986 F, W, R, 1987 E, S, F, W, [W, A], 1988 S, F, W, E 1,2, WS, It, 1989 F, W, E, S
Deane, E C (Monkstown) 1909 E
Deering, M J (Bective Rangers) 1929 W
Deering, S J (Bective Rangers) 1935 E, S, W, NZ, 1936 E, S, W, 1937 E, S
Deering, S M (Garryowen, St Mary's Coll) 1974 W, 1976 F, W, E, S, 1977 W, E, 1978 NZ
de Lacy, H (Harlequins) 1948 E, S
Delany, M G (Bective Rangers) 1895 W
Dempsey, G T (Terenure Coll, Leinster) 1998 Gg (R). SA 3, 1999 F, E, S, It, A 2, 2000 E (R), S, It, F, W, SA, 2001 It, F, S, W, E, NZ, 2002 W, E, S, It, F, NZ 1,2, R, Ru, Gg, A, Arg, 2003 S 1, E (R), A, Sm, W 2(R), It 2, S 2(R),[R,Nm,Arg,A,F], 2004 F,W, E,It,S, SA1,2,3,US(R),Arg, 2005 It(R), S, E, F, W, J1, 2, NZ(R), R(R), 2006 E(R), NZ1(R),2(t&R),A
Dennison, S P (Garryowen) 1973 F, 1975 E, S
Dick, C J (Ballymena) 1961 W, F, SA, 1962 W, 1963 F, E, S, W
Dick, J S (Queen's U, Belfast) 1962 E
Dick, J S (Queen's U, Cork) 1887 E, S, W
Dickson, J A N (Dublin U) 1920 E, W, F
Doherty, A E (Old Wesley) 1974 P (R)
Doherty, W D (Guy's Hospital) 1920 E, S, W, 1921 E, S, W, F
Donaldson, J A (Belfast Collegians) 1958 A, E, S, W
Donovan, T M (Queen's Coll, Cork) 1889 S
Dooley, J F (Galwegians) 1959 E, S, W
Doran, B R W (Lansdowne) 1900 S, W, 1901 E, S, W, 1902 E, S, W
Doran, E F (Lansdowne) 1890 S, W
Doran, G P (Lansdowne) 1899 S, W, 1900 E, S, 1902 S, W, 1903 W, 1904 E
Douglas, A C (Instonians) 1923 F, 1924 E, S, 1927 A, 1928 S
Downing, A J (Dublin U) 1882 W
Dowse, J C A (Monkstown) 1914 F, S, W
Doyle, J A P (Greystones) 1984 E, S
Doyle, J T (Bective Rangers) 1935 W
Doyle, M G (Blackrock Coll, UC Dublin, Cambridge U, Edinburgh Wands) 1965 F, E, S, W, SA, 1966 F, E, S, W, 1967 A 1, E, S, W, F, A 2, 1968 F, E, S, W, A
Doyle, T J (Wanderers) 1968 E, S, W
Duffy, G W (Harlequins) 2004 SA 2(R), 2005 S(R),J1,2
Duggan, A T A (Lansdowne) 1963 NZ, 1964 F, 1966 W, 1967 A 1, S, W, A 2, 1968 F, E, S, W, 1969 F, E, S, W, 1970 SA, F, E, S, W, 1971 F, E, S, W, 1972 F 2
Duggan, W (UC Cork) 1920 S, W
Duggan, W P (Blackrock Coll) 1975 E, S, F, W, 1976 A, F, W, S, NZ, 1977 W, E, S, F, 1978 S, F, W, E, NZ, 1979 E, S, A 1,2, 1980 E, 1981 F, W, E, S, SA 1,2, A, 1982 W, E, S, 1983 S, F, W, E, 1984 F, W, E, S
Duignan, P (Galwegians) 1998 Gg, R
Duncan, W R (Malone) 1984 W, E
Dunlea, F J (Lansdowne) 1989 W, E, S
Dunlop, R (Dublin U) 1889 W, 1890 S, W, E, 1891 E, S, W, 1892 E, S, 1893 W, 1894 W
Dunn, P E F (Bective Rangers) 1923 S
Dunn, T B (NIFC) 1935 NZ
Dunne, M J (Lansdowne) 1929 F, E, S, 1930 F, E, S, W, 1932 E, S, W, 1933 E, W, S, 1934 E, S, W
Dwyer, P J (UC Dublin) 1962 W, 1963 F, NZ, 1964 S, W

Easterby, S H (Llanelli Scarlets) 2000 S, It, F, W, Arg, US, C, 2001 S, Sm (R), 2002 W, E (R), S (R), It, F, NZ 1,2, R, Ru, Gg, 2003 Tg, Sm, It 2, S 2(t+R), [Nm,Arg,A,F], 2004 F,W,E,It,S,SA1,2,3,US,Arg, 2005 It,S,E,F,W,NZ,A, 2006 It,F,W,S,E
Easterby, W G (Ebbw Vale, Ballynahinch, Llanelli, Leinster) 2000 US, C (R), 2001 R (R), S, W (R), Sm (R), 2002 W (R), S (R), R (R), Ru (R), Gg (R), Fj, 2003 S 1(R), It 1(R), Tg, Sm, W 2(R), It 2, S 2(R), [R(R),Nm(R),F(R)], 2004 W(R),It(R), S(R),SA2(R),US, 2005 S(R)
Edwards, H G (Dublin U) 1877 E, 1878 E
Edwards, R W (Malone) 1904 W
Edwards, T (Lansdowne) 1888 M, 1890 S, W, E, 1892 W, 1893 E
Edwards, W V (Malone) 1912 F, E
Egan, J D (Bective Rangers) 1922 S
Egan, J T (Cork Constitution) 1931 F, E, SA

Egan, M S (Garryowen) 1893 E, 1895 S
Ekin, W (Queen's Coll, Belfast) 1888 W, S
Elliott, W R J (Bangor) 1979 S
Elwood, E P (Lansdowne, Galwegians) 1993 W, E, R, 1994 F, W, E, S, A 1,2, 1995 F, W, [NZ, W, F], 1996 US, S, 1997 F, W, E, NZ, C, It 2(R), 1998 F, W, E, SA 1,2, Gg, R, SA 3, 1999 It, Arg 1(R), [US (R), A 3(R), R]
English, M A F (Lansdowne, Limerick Bohemians) 1958 W, F, 1959 E, S, F, 1960 E, S, 1961 S, W, F, 1962 F, W, 1963 E, S, W, NZ
Ennis, F N G (Wanderers) 1979 A 1(R)
Ensor, A H (Wanderers) 1973 W, F, 1974 F, W, E, S, P, NZ, 1975 E, S, F, W, 1976 A, F, W, E, NZ, 1977 E, 1978 S, F, W, E
Entrican, J C (Queen's U, Belfast) 1931 S
Erskine, D J (Sale) 1997 NZ (R), C, It 2

Fagan, G L (Kingstown School) 1878 E
Fagan, W B C (Wanderers) 1956 F, E, S
Farrell, J L (Bective Rangers) 1926 F, E, S, W, 1927 F, E, S, W, A, 1928 F, E, S, W, 1929 F, E, S, W, 1930 F, E, S, W, 1931 F, E, S, W, SA, 1932 E, S, W
Feddis, N (Lansdowne) 1956 E
Feighery, C F P (Lansdowne) 1972 F 1, E, F 2
Feighery, T A O (St Mary's Coll) 1977 W, E
Ferris, H H (Queen's Coll, Belfast) 1901 W
Ferris, J H (Queen's Coll, Belfast) 1900 E, S, W
Field, M J (Malone) 1994 E, S, A 1(R), 1995 F (R), W (t), It (R), [NZ(t + R), J], Fj, 1996 F (R), W, E, A (R), 1997 F, W, E, S
Finlay, J E (Queen's Coll, Belfast) 1913 E, S, W, 1920 E, S, W
Finlay, W (NIFC) 1876 E, 1877 E, S, 1878 E, 1879 S, E, 1880 S, 1882 S
Finn, M C (UC Cork, Cork Constitution) 1979 E, 1982 W, E, S, F, 1983 S, F, W, E, 1984 E, S, A, 1986 F, W
Finn, R G A (UC Dublin) 1977 F
Fitzgerald, C C (Glasgow U, Dungannon) 1902 E, 1903 E, S
Fitzgerald, C F (St Mary's Coll) 1979 A 1,2, 1980 E, S, F, W, 1982 W, E, S, F, 1983 S, F, W, E, 1984 F, W, A, 1985 S, F, W, E, 1986 F, W, E, S
Fitzgerald, D C (Lansdowne, De La Salle Palmerston) 1984 E, S, 1986 W, E, S, R, 1987 E, S, F, W, [W, C, A], 1988 S, F, W, E 1, 1989 NZ (R), 1990 E, S, F, W, Arg, 1991 F, W, E, S, Nm 1,2, [Z, S, A], 1992 W, S (R)
Fitzgerald, J (Wanderers) 1884 W
Fitzgerald, J J (Young Munster) 1988 S, F, 1990 S, F, W, 1991 F, W, E, S, [J], 1994 A 1,2
Fitzgibbon, M J J (Shannon) 1992 W, E, S, F, NZ 1,2
Fitzpatrick, J M (Dungannon) 1998 SA 1,2 Gg (R), R (R), SA 3, 1999 F (R), W (R), E (R), It, Arg 1(R), [US (R), A 3, R, Arg 2(t&R)], 2000 S (R), It (R), Arg (R), US, C, SA (t&R), 2001 R (R), 2003 W 1(R), E (R), Tg, W 2(R), It 2(R)
Fitzpatrick, M P (Wanderers) 1978 S, 1980 S, F, W, 1981 F, W, E, S, A, 1985 F (R)
Flannery, J (Munster) 2005 R(R), 2006 It,F,W,S,E,NZ1,2,A
Flavin, P (Blackrock Coll) 1997 F (R), S
Fletcher, W W (Kingstown) 1882 W, S, 1883 E
Flood, R S (Dublin U) 1925 W
Flynn, M K (Wanderers) 1959 F, 1960 F, 1962 E, S, F, W, 1964 E, S, W, F, 1965 F, E, S, W, SA, 1966 F, E, S, 1972 F 1, E, F 2, 1973 NZ
Fogarty, T (Garryowen) 1891 W
Foley, A G (Shannon, Munster) 1995 E, S, F, W, It, [J(t + R)], 1996 A, 1997 It 1, E (R), 2000 E, S, It, F, W, Arg, C, J, SA, 2001 It, F, R, S, W, E, Sm, NZ, 2002 W, E, S, It, F, NZ 1,2, R, Ru, Gg, A, Fj, Arg, 2003 S 1, It 1, F, W 1, E, W 2, [R,A], 2004 F,W,E,It,S, SA1,2,3,US(R),Arg, 2005 It,S,E,F,W
Foley, B O (Shannon) 1976 F, E, 1977 W (R), 1980 F, W, 1981 F, E, S, SA 1,2, A
Forbes, R E (Malone) 1907 E
Forrest, A J (Wanderers) 1880 E, S, 1881 E, S, 1882 W, E, 1883 E, 1885 S 2
Forrest, E G (Wanderers) 1888 M, 1889 S, W, 1890 S, E, 1891 E, 1893 S, W, 1894 E, S, W, 1895 W, 1897 E, S
Forrest, H (Wanderers) 1893 S, W
Fortune, J J (Clontarf) 1963 NZ, 1964 E
Foster, A R (Derry) 1910 E, S, F, 1911 E, S, W, F, 1912 F, E, S, W, 1914 E, S, W, 1921 E, S, W
Francis, N P J (Blackrock Coll, London Irish, Old Belvedere) 1987 [Tg, A], 1988 WS, It, 1989 S, 1990 E, F, W, 1991 E, S, Nm 1,2, [Z, J, S, A], 1992 W, E, S, 1993 F, R, 1994 F, W, E, S, A 1,2, US, 1995 E, [NZ, J, W, F], Fj, 1996 US, S
Franks, J G (Dublin U) 1898 E, S, W
Frazer, E F (Bective Rangers) 1891 S, 1892 S
Freer, A E (Lansdowne) 1901 E, S, W
Fulcher, G M (Cork Constitution, London Irish) 1994 A 2, US, 1995 E (R), S, F, W, It, [NZ, W, F], Fj, 1996 US, S, F, W, E, A, 1997 It 1, W (R), 1998 SA 1(R)
Fulton, J (NIFC) 1895 S, W, 1896 E, 1897 E, 1898 W, 1899 E, 1900 W, 1901 E, 1902 E, S, W, 1903 E, S, W, 1904 E, S
Furlong, J N (UC Galway) 1992 NZ 1,2

Gaffikin, W (Windsor) 1875 E
Gage, J H (Queen's U, Belfast) 1926 S, W, 1927 S, W
Galbraith, E (Dublin U) 1875 E
Galbraith, H T (Belfast Acad) 1890 W
Galbraith, R (Dublin U) 1875 E, 1876 E, 1877 E
Galwey, M J (Shannon) 1991 F, W, Nm 2(R), [J], 1992 E, S, F, NZ 1,2, A, 1993 F, W, E, R, 1994 F, W, E, S, A 1, US (R), 1995 E, 1996 WS, 1998 F (R), 1999 W (R), 2000 E (R), S, It, F, W, Arg, C, 2001 It, F, R, W, E, Sm, NZ, 2002 W, E, S
Ganly, J B (Monkstown) 1927 F, E, S, W, A, 1928 F, E, S, W, 1929 F, S, 1930 F
Gardiner, F (NIFC) 1900 E, S, 1901 E, W, 1902 E, S, W, 1903 E, W, 1904 E, S, W, 1906 E, S, W, 1907 S, W, 1908 S, W, 1909 E, S, F
Gardiner, J B (NIFC) 1923 E, S, W, F, 1924 F, E, S, W, NZ, 1925 F, E, S, W
Gardiner, S (Belfast Albion) 1893 E, S
Gardiner, W (NIFC) 1892 E, S, 1893 E, S, W, 1894 E, S, W, 1895 E, S, W, 1896 E, S, W, 1897 E, S, 1898 W
Garry, M G (Bective Rangers) 1909 E, S, W, F, 1911 E, S, W
Gaston, J T (Dublin U) 1954 NZ, F, E, S, W, 1955 W 1956 F, E
Gavin, T J (Moseley, London Irish) 1949 F, E
Geoghegan, S P (London Irish, Bath) 1991 F, W, E, S, Nm 1, [Z, S, A], 1992 E, S, F, A, 1993 S, F, W, E, R, 1994 F, W, E, S, A 1,2, US, 1995 E, S, F, W, [NZ, J, W, F], Fj, 1996 US, S, W, E
Gibson, C M H (Cambridge U, NIFC) 1964 E, S, W, F, 1965 F, E, S, W, SA, 1966 F, E, S, W, 1967 A 1, E, S, W, F, A 2, 1968 E, S, W, A, 1969 E, S, W, 1970 SA, F, E, S, W, 1971 F, E, S, W, 1972 F 1, E, F 2, 1973 NZ, E, S, W, F, 1974 F, W, E, S, P, 1975 E, S, F, W, 1976 A, F, W, E, S, NZ, 1977 W, E, S, F, 1978 F, W, E, NZ, 1979 S, A 1,2
Gibson, M E (Lansdowne, London Irish) 1979 F, W, E, S, 1981 W (R), 1986 R, 1988 S, F, W, E 2
Gifford, H P (Wanderers) 1890 S
Gillespie, J C (Dublin U) 1922 W, F
Gilpin, F G (Queen's U, Belfast) 1962 E, S, F
Glass, D C (Belfast Collegians) 1958 F, 1960 W, 1961 W, SA
Gleeson, K D (St Mary's Coll, Leinster) 2002 W (R), F (R), NZ 1,2, R, Ru, Gg, A, Arg, 2003 S 1, It 1, F, W 1, E, A, W 2, [R,A,F], 2004 F,W,E,It, 2006 NZ1(R),A(R)
Glennon, B T (Lansdowne) 1993 F (R)
Glennon, J J (Skerries) 1980 E, S, 1987 E, S, F, [W (R)]
Godfrey, R P (UC Dublin) 1954 S, W
Goodall, K G (City of Derry, Newcastle U) 1967 A 1, E, S, W, F, A 2, 1968 F, E, S, W, A, 1969 F, E, S, 1970 SA, F, E, S, W
Gordon, A (Dublin U) 1884 S
Gordon, T G (NIFC) 1877 E, S, 1878 E
Gotto, R P C (NIFC) 1906 SA
Goulding, W J (Cork) 1879 S
Grace, T O (UC Dublin, St Mary's Coll) 1972 F 1, E, 1973 NZ, E, S, W, 1974 E, S, P, NZ, 1975 E, S, F, W, 1976 A, F, W, E, S, NZ, 1977 W, E, S, F, 1978 S
Graham, R I (Dublin U) 1911 F
Grant, E L (CIYMS) 1971 F, E, S, W
Grant, P J (Bective Rangers) 1894 S, W
Graves, C R A (Wanderers) 1934 E, S, W, 1935 E, S, W, NZ, 1936 E, S, W, 1937 E, S, 1938 E, S, W

Gray, R D (Old Wesley) 1923 E, S, 1925 F, 1926 F
Greene, E H (Dublin U, Kingstown) 1882 W, 1884 W, 1885 E, S 2, 1886 E
Greer, R (Kingstown) 1876 E
Greeves, T J (NIFC) 1907 E, S, W, 1909 W, F
Gregg, R J (Queen's U, Belfast) 1953 F, E, S, W, 1954 F, E, S
Griffin, C S (London Irish) 1951 F, E
Griffin, J L (Wanderers) 1949 S, W
Griffiths, W (Limerick) 1878 E
Grimshaw, C (Queen's U, Belfast) 1969 E (R)
Guerin, B N (Galwegians) 1956 S
Gwynn, A P (Dublin U) 1895 W
Gwynn, L H (Dublin U) 1893 S, 1894 E, S, W, 1897 S, 1898 E, S

Hakin, R F (CIYMS) 1976 W, S, NZ, 1977 W, E, F
Hall, R O N (Dublin U) 1884 W
Hall, W H (Instonians) 1923 E, S, W, F, 1924 F, S
Hallaran, C F G T (Royal Navy) 1921 E, S, W, 1922 E, S, W, 1923 E, F, 1924 F, E, S, W, 1925 F, 1926 F, E
Halpin, G F (Wanderers, London Irish) 1990 E, 1991 [J], 1992 E, S, F, 1993 R, 1994 F (R), 1995 It, [NZ, W, F]
Halpin, T (Garryowen) 1909 S, W, F, 1910 E, S, W, 1911 E, S, W, F, 1912 F, E, S
Halvey, E O (Shannon) 1995 F, W, It, [J, W (t), F (R)], 1997 NZ, C (R)
Hamilton, A J (Lansdowne) 1884 W
Hamilton, G F (NIFC) 1991 F, W, E, S, Nm 2, [Z, J, S, A], 1992 A
Hamilton, R L (NIFC) 1926 F
Hamilton, R W (Wanderers) 1893 W
Hamilton, W J (Dublin U) 1877 E
Hamlet, G T (Old Wesley) 1902 E, S, W, 1903 E, S, W, 1904 S, W, 1905 E, S, W, NZ, 1906 SA, 1907 E, S, W, 1908 E, S, W, 1909 E, S, W, F, 1910 E, S, F, 1911 E, S, W, F
Hanrahan, C J (Dolphin) 1926 S, W, 1927 E, S, W, A, 1928 F, E, S, 1929 F, E, S, W, 1930 F, E, S, W, 1931 F, 1932 S, W
Harbison, H T (Bective Rangers) 1984 W (R), E, S, 1986 R, 1987 E, S, F, W
Hardy, G G (Bective Rangers) 1962 S
Harman, G R A (Dublin U) 1899 E, W
Harper, J (Instonians) 1947 F, E, S
Harpur, T G (Dublin U) 1908 E, S, W
Harrison, T (Cork) 1879 S, 1880 S, 1881 E
Harvey, F M W (Wanderers) 1907 W, 1911 F
Harvey, G A D (Wanderers) 1903 E, S, 1904 W, 1905 E, S
Harvey, T A (Dublin U) 1900 W, 1901 S, W, 1902 E, S, W, 1903 E, W
Haycock, P P (Terenure Coll) 1989 E
Hayes, J J (Shannon, Munster) 2000 S, It, F, W, Arg, C, J, SA, 2001 It, F, R, S, W, E, Sm, NZ, 2002 W, E, S, It, F, NZ 1,2, R, Ru, Gg, A, Fj, Arg, 2003 S 1, It 1, F, W 1, E, [R(R),Nm,Arg,A,F], 2004 F,W,E,It,S,SA1,2,3,US,Arg, 2005 It,S,E,F,W,NZ,A,R(R), 2006 It,F,W,S,E,NZ1,2,A
Headon, T A (UC Dublin) 1939 S, W
Healey, P (Limerick) 1901 E, S, W, 1902 E, S, W, 1903 E, S, W, 1904 S
Heffernan, M R (Cork Constitution) 1911 E, S, W, F
Hemphill, R (Dublin U) 1912 F, E, S, W
Henderson, N J (Queen's U, Belfast, NIFC) 1949 S, W, 1950 F, 1951 F, E, S, W, SA, 1952 F, S, W, E, 1953 F, E, S, W, 1954 NZ, F, E, S, W, 1955 F, E, S, W, 1956 S, W, 1957 F, E, S, W, 1958 A, E, S, W, F, 1959 E, S, W, F
Henderson R A J (London Irish, Wasps, Young Munster) 1996 WS, 1997 NZ, C, 1998 F, W, SA 1(R),2(R), 1999 F (R), E, S (R), It, 2000 S (R), It (R), F, W, Arg, US, J (R), SA, 2001 It, F, 2002 W (R), E (R), F, R (R), Ru (t), Gg (R), 2003 It 1(R),2
Henebrey, G J (Garryowen) 1906 E, S, W, SA, 1909 W, F
Heron, A G (Queen's Coll, Belfast) 1901 E
Heron, J (NIFC) 1877 S, 1879 E
Heron, W T (NIFC) 1880 E, S
Herrick, R W (Dublin U) 1886 S
Heuston, F S (Kingstown) 1882 W, 1883 E, S
Hewitt, D (Queen's U, Belfast, Instonians) 1958 A, E, S, F, 1959 S, W, F, 1960 E, S, W, F, 1961 E, S, W, F, 1962 S, F, 1965 W
Hewitt, F S (Instonians) 1924 W, NZ, 1925 F, E, S, 1926 E, 1927 E, S, W
Hewitt, J A (NIFC) 1981 SA 1(R),2(R)
Hewitt, T R (Queen's U, Belfast) 1924 W, NZ, 1925 F, E, S, 1926 F, E, S, W
Hewitt, V A (Instonians) 1935 S, W, NZ, 1936 E, S, W
Hewitt, W J (Instonians) 1954 E, 1956 S, 1959 W, 1961 SA
Hewson, F T (Wanderers) 1875 E
Hickie, D A (St Mary's Coll, Leinster) 1997 W, E, S, NZ, C, It 2, 1998 S, F, W, E, SA 1,2, 2000 S, It, F, W, J, SA, 2001 F, R, S, W, E, NZ, 2002 W, E, S, It, F, R, Ru, Gg, A, 2003 S 1, It 1, F, W 1, E, It 2, S 2, [R,Nm,Arg,A], 2004 SA3,Arg, 2005 It,S,E,F,W
Hickie, D J (St Mary's Coll) 1971 F, E, S, W, 1972 F 1, E
Higgins, J A D (Civil Service) 1947 S, W, A, 1948 F, S, W
Higgins, W W (NIFC) 1884 E, S
Hillary, M F (UC Dublin) 1952 E
Hingerty, D J (UC Dublin) 1947 F, E, S, W
Hinton, W P (Old Wesley) 1907 W, 1908 E, S, W, 1909 E, S, 1910 E, S, W, F, 1911 E, S, W, 1912 F, E, W
Hipwell, M L (Terenure Coll) 1962 E, S, 1968 F, A, 1969 F (R), S (R), W, 1971 F, E, S, W, 1972 F 2
Hobbs, T H M (Dublin U) 1884 S, 1885 E
Hobson, E W (Dublin U) 1876 E
Hogan, N A (Terenure Coll, London Irish) 1995 E, W, [J, W, F], 1996 F, W, E, WS, 1997 F, W, E, It 2
Hogan, P (Garryowen) 1992 F
Hogan, T (Munster) 2005 J1(R),2(R)
Hogg, W (Dublin U) 1885 S 2
Holland, J J (Wanderers) 1981 SA 1,2, 1986 W
Holmes, G W (Dublin U) 1912 SA, 1913 E, S
Holmes, L J (Lisburn) 1889 S, W
Hooks, K J (Queen's U, Belfast, Ards, Bangor) 1981 S, 1989 NZ, 1990 F, W, Arg, 1991 F
Horan, A K (Blackheath) 1920 E, W
Horan, M J (Shannon, Munster) 2000 US (R), 2002 Fj, Arg (R), 2003 S 1(R), It 1(R), F, W 1, E, A, Sm, It 2, S 2, [R,Nm,Arg(t&R),A(R),F(R)], 2004 It(R),S(R),SA1(R), 2(t&R), 3(R),US, 2005 It(R),S(R),E(R),F(R),W(R),J1,2,NZ,A,R, 2006 It,W,S,E,NZ1,2,A
Horgan, A P (Cork Const, Munster) 2003 Sm, W 2, S 2, 2004 F(R), 2005 J1,2,NZ
Horgan, S P (Lansdowne, Leinster) 2000 S, It, W, Arg, C, J, SA (R), 2001 It, S, W, E, NZ, 2002 S, It, F, A, Fj, Arg, 2003 S 1, [R,Nm,Arg,A,F], 2004 F,W,E,It,S,SA1,2,3,US,Arg, 2005 It,S,E,NZ,A,R, 2006 It,F,W,S,E,NZ1,2,A
Houston, K J (Oxford U, London Irish) 1961 SA, 1964 S, W, 1965 F, E, SA
Howe, T G (Dungannon, Ballymena, Ulster) 2000 US, J, SA, 2001 It, F, R, Sm, 2002 It (R), 2003 Tg, W 2, 2004 F,W,E,SA2
Hughes, R W (NIFC) 1878 E, 1880 E, S, 1881 S, 1882 E, S, 1883 E, S, 1884 E, S, 1885 E, 1886 E
Humphreys, D G (London Irish, Dungannon, Ulster) 1996 F, W, E, WS, 1997 E (R), S, It 2, 1998 S, E (R), SA 2(t + R), R (R), 1999 F, W, E, S, A 1,2, Arg 1, [US, A 3, Arg 2], 2000 E, S (R), F (t&R), W (R), Arg, US (R), C, J (R), SA (R), 2001 It (R), R, S (R), W, E, NZ, 2002 W, E, S, It, F, NZ 1(R),2(R), R (t+R), Ru (R), Gg (R), Fj, 2003 S 1, It 1, F, W 1, E, A, W 2, It 2, S 2(R), [R,Arg,A(R),F(R)], 2004W(R),It(R),S(R), SA2(R),US, 2005 S(R),W(R),J1,2,NZ(R),A(R),R
Hunt, E W F de Vere (Army, Rosslyn Park) 1930 F, 1932 E, S, W, 1933 E
Hunter, D V (Dublin U) 1885 S 2
Hunter, L (Civil Service) 1968 W, A
Hunter, W R (CIYMS) 1962 E, S, W, F, 1963 F, E, S, 1966 F, E, S
Hurley, H D (Old Wesley, Moseley) 1995 Fj (t), 1996 WS
Hutton, S A (Malone) 1967 S, W, F, A 2

Ireland J (Windsor) 1876 E, 1877 E
Irvine, H A S (Collegians) 1901 S
Irwin, D G (Queen's U, Belfast, Instonians) 1980 F, W, 1981 F, W, E, S, SA 1,2, A, 1982 W, 1983 S, F, W, E, 1984 F, W, 1987 [Tg, A (R)], 1989 F, W, E, S, NZ, 1990 E, S
Irwin, J W S (NIFC) 1938 E, S, 1939 E, S, W

Irwin, S T (Queen's Coll, Belfast) 1900 E, S, W, 1901 E, W, 1902 E, S, W, 1903 S

Jack, H W (UC Cork) 1914 S, W, 1921 W
Jackman, B J (Leinster) 2005 J1(R),2(R)
Jackson, A R V (Wanderers) 1911 E, S, W, F, 1913 W, F, 1914 F, E, S, W
Jackson, F (NIFC) 1923 E
Jackson, H W (Dublin U) 1877 E
Jameson, J S (Lansdowne) 1888 M, 1889 S, W, 1891 W, 1892 E, W, 1893 S
Jeffares, E W (Wanderers) 1913 E, S
Johns, P S (Dublin U, Dungannon, Saracens) 1990 Arg, 1992 NZ 1,2, A, 1993 S, F, W, E, R, 1994 F, W, E, S, A 1,2, US, 1995 E, S, W, It, [NZ, J, W, F], Fj, 1996 US, S, F, WS, 1997 It 1(R), F, W, E, S, NZ, C, It 2, 1998 S, F, W, E, SA 1,2, Gg, R, SA 3, 1999 F, W, E, S, It, A 1,2, Arg 1, [US, A 3, R], 2000 F (R), J
Johnston, J (Belfast Acad) 1881 S, 1882 S, 1884 S, 1885 S 1,2, 1886 E, 1887 E, S, W
Johnston, M (Dublin U) 1880 E, S, 1881 E, S, 1882 E, 1884 E, S, 1886 E
Johnston, R (Wanderers) 1893 E, W
Johnston, R W (Dublin U) 1890 S, W, E
Johnston, T J (Queen's Coll, Belfast) 1892 E, S, W, 1893 E, S, 1895 E
Johnstone, W E (Dublin U) 1884 W
Johnstone-Smyth, T R (Lansdowne) 1882 E

Kavanagh, J R (UC Dublin, Wanderers) 1953 F, E, S, W, 1954 NZ, S, W, 1955 F, E, 1956 E, S, W, 1957 F, E, S, W, 1958 A, E, S, W, 1959 E, S, W, F, 1960 E, S, W, F, SA, 1961 E, S, W, F, SA, 1962 F
Kavanagh, P J (UC Dublin, Wanderers) 1952 E, 1955 W
Keane, K P (Garryowen) 1998 E (R)
Keane, M I (Lansdowne) 1974 F, W, E, S, P, NZ, 1975 E, S, F, W, 1976 A, F, W, E, S, NZ, 1977 W, E, S, F, 1978 S, F, W, E, NZ, 1979 F, W, E, S, A 1,2, 1980 E, S, F, W, 1981 F, W, E, S, 1982 W, E, S, F, 1983 S, F, W, E, 1984 F, W, E, S
Kearney, R K (Wanderers) 1982 F, 1984 A, 1986 F, W
Keeffe, E (Sunday's Well) 1947 F, E, S, W, A, 1948 F
Kelly, H C (NIFC) 1877 E, S, 1878 E, 1879 S, 1880 E, S
Kelly, J C (UC Dublin) 1962 F, W, 1963 F, E, S, W, NZ, 1964 E, S, W, F
Kelly, J P (Cork Constitution) 2002 It, NZ 1,2, R, Ru, Gg, A (R), 2003 It 1, F, A, Tg, Sm, It 2, [R(R),Nm(R),A(R),F]
Kelly, S (Lansdowne) 1954 S, W, 1955 S, 1960 W, F
Kelly, W (Wanderers) 1884 S
Kennedy, A G (Belfast Collegians) 1956 F
Kennedy, A P (London Irish) 1986 W, E
Kennedy, F (Wanderers) 1880 E, 1881 E, 1882 W
Kennedy, F A (Wanderers) 1904 E, W
Kennedy, H (Bradford) 1938 S, W
Kennedy, J M (Wanderers) 1882 W, 1884 W
Kennedy, K W (Queen's U, Belfast, London Irish) 1965 F, E, S, W, SA, 1966 F, E, W, 1967 A 1, E, S, W, F, A 2, 1968 F, A, 1969 F, E, S, W, 1970 SA, F, E, S, W, 1971 F, E, S, W, 1972 F 1, E, F 2, 1973 NZ, E, S, W, F, 1974 F, W, E, S, P, NZ, 1975 F, W
Kennedy, T J (St Mary's Coll) 1978 NZ, 1979 F, W, E (R), A 1,2, 1980 E, S, F, W, 1981 SA 1,2, A
Kenny, P (Wanderers) 1992 NZ 2(R)
Keogh, F S (Bective Rangers) 1964 W, F
Keon, J J (Limerick) 1879 E
Keyes, R P (Cork Constitution) 1986 E, 1991 [Z, J, S, A], 1992 W, E, S
Kidd, F W (Dublin U, Lansdowne) 1877 E, S, 1878 E
Kiely, M D (Lansdowne) 1962 W, 1963 F, E, S, W
Kiernan, M J (Dolphin, Lansdowne) 1982 W (R), E, S, F, 1983 S, F, W, E, 1984 E, S, A, 1985 S, F, W, E, 1986 F, W, E, S, R, 1987 E, S, F, W, [W, C, A], 1988 S, F, W, E 1,2, WS, 1989 F, W, E, S, 1990 E, S, F, W, Arg, 1991 F
Kiernan, T J (UC Cork, Cork Const) 1960 E, S, W, F, SA, 1961 E, S, W, F, SA, 1962 E, W, 1963 F, S, W, NZ, 1964 E, S, 1965 F, E, S, W, SA, 1966 F, E, S, W, 1967 A 1, E, S, W, F, A 2, 1968 F, E, S, W, A, 1969 F, E, S, W, 1970 SA, F, E, S, W, 1971 F, 1972 F 1, E, F 2, 1973 NZ, E, S
Killeen, G V (Garryowen) 1912 E, S, W, 1913 E, S, W, F, 1914 E, S, W
King, H (Dublin U) 1883 E, S
Kingston, T J (Dolphin) 1987 [W, Tg, A], 1988 S, F, W, E 1, 1990 F, W, 1991 [J], 1993 F, W, E, R, 1994 F, W, E, S, 1995 F, W, It, [NZ, J (R), W, F], Fj, 1996 US, S, F
Knox, J H (Dublin U, Lansdowne) 1904 W, 1905 E, S, W, NZ, 1906 E, S, W, 1907 W, 1908 S
Kyle, J W (Queen's U, Belfast, NIFC) 1947 F, E, S, W, A, 1948 F, E, S, W, 1949 F, E, S, W, 1950 F, E, S, W, 1951 F, E, S, W, SA, 1952 F, S, W, E, 1953 F, E, S, W, 1954 NZ, F, 1955 F, E, W, 1956 F, E, S, W, 1957 F, E, S, W, 1958 A, E, S

Lambert, N H (Lansdowne) 1934 S, W
Lamont, R A (Instonians) 1965 F, E, SA, 1966 F, E, S, W, 1970 SA, F, E, S, W
Landers, M F (Cork Const) 1904 W, 1905 E, S, W, NZ
Lane, D (UC Cork) 1934 S, W, 1935 E, S
Lane, M F (UC Cork) 1947 W, 1949 F, E, S, W, 1950 F, E, S, W, 1951 F, S, W, SA, 1952 F, S, 1953 F, E
Lane, P (Old Crescent) 1964 W
Langan, D J (Clontarf) 1934 W
Langbroek, J A (Blackrock Coll) 1987 [Tg]
Lavery, P (London Irish) 1974 W, 1976 W
Lawlor, P J (Clontarf) 1951 S, SA, 1952 F, S, W, E, 1953 F, 1954 NZ, E, S, 1956 F, E
Lawlor, P J (Bective Rangers) 1935 E, S, W, 1937 E, S, W
Lawlor, P J (Bective Rangers) 1990 Arg, 1992 A, 1993 S
Leahy, K T (Wanderers) 1992 NZ 1
Leahy, M W (UC Cork) 1964 W
Leamy, D P (Munster) 2004 US, 2005 It,J2,NZ,A,R, 2006 It,F,W,S,E,NZ1,2,A
Lee, S (NIFC) 1891 E, S, W, 1892 E, S, W, 1893 E, S, W, 1894 E, S, W, 1895 E, W, 1896 E, S, W, 1897 E, 1898 E
Le Fanu, V C (Cambridge U, Lansdowne) 1886 E, S, 1887 E, W, 1888 S, 1889 W, 1890 E, 1891 E, 1892 E, S, W
Lenihan, D G (UC Cork, Cork Const) 1981 A, 1982 W, E, S, F, 1983 S, F, W, E, 1984 F, W, E, S, A, 1985 S, F, W, E, 1986 F, W, E, S, R, 1987 E, S, F, W, [W, C, Tg, A], 1988 S, F, W, E 1,2, WS, It, 1989 F, W, E, S, NZ, 1990 S, F, W, Arg, 1991 Nm 2, [Z, S, A], 1992 W
L'Estrange, L P F (Dublin U) 1962 E
Levis, F H (Wanderers) 1884 E
Lewis, K (Leinster) 2005 J2(R)
Lightfoot, E J (Lansdowne) 1931 F, E, S, W, SA, 1932 E, S, W, 1933 E, W, S
Lindsay, H (Dublin U, Armagh) 1893 E, S, W, 1894 E, S, W, 1895 E, 1896 E, S, W, 1898 E, S, W
Little, T J (Bective Rangers) 1898 W, 1899 S, W, 1900 S, W, 1901 E, S
Lloyd, R A (Dublin U, Liverpool) 1910 E, S, 1911 E, S, W, F, 1912 F, E, S, W, SA, 1913 E, S, W, F, 1914 F, E, 1920 E, F
Longwell, G W (Ballymena) 2000 J (R), SA, 2001 F (R), R, S (R), Sm, NZ (R), 2002 W (R), E (R), S (R), It, F, NZ 1,2, R, Ru, Gg, A, Arg, 2003 S 1, It 1, F, E, A, It 2, 2004 It(R)
Lydon, C T J (Galwegians) 1956 S
Lyle, R K (Dublin U) 1910 W, F
Lyle, T R (Dublin U) 1885 E, S 1,2, 1886 E, 1887 E, S
Lynch, J F (St Mary's Coll) 1971 F, E, S, W, 1972 F 1, E, F 2, 1973 NZ, E, S, W, 1974 F, W, E, S, P, NZ
Lynch, L (Lansdowne) 1956 S
Lytle, J H (NIFC) 1894 E, S, W, 1895 W, 1896 E, S, W, 1897 E, S, 1898 E, S, 1899 S
Lytle, J N (NIFC) 1888 M, 1889 W, 1890 E, 1891 E, S, 1894 E, S, W
Lyttle, V J (Collegians, Bedford) 1938 E, 1939 E, S

McAleese, D R (Ballymena) 1992 F
McAllan, G H (Dungannon) 1896 S, W
Macauley, J (Limerick) 1887 E, S
McBride, W D (Malone) 1988 W, E 1, WS, It, 1989 S, 1990 F, W, Arg, 1993 S, F, W, E, R, 1994 W, E, S, A 1(R), 1995 S, F, [NZ, W, F], Fj (R), 1996 W, E, WS, A, 1997 It 1(R), F, W, E, S
McBride, W J (Ballymena) 1962 E, S, F, W, 1963 F, E, S, W, NZ, 1964 E, S, F, 1965 F, E, S, W, SA, 1966 F, E, S, W,

1967 A 1, E, S, W, F, A 2, 1968 F, E, S, W, A, 1969 F, E, S, W, 1970 SA, F, E, S, W, 1971 F, E, S, W, 1972 F 1, E, F 2, 1973 NZ, E, S, W, F, 1974 F, W, E, S, P, NZ, 1975 E, S, F, W

McCahill, S A (Sunday's Well) 1995 Fj (t)

McCall, B W (London Irish) 1985 F (R), 1986 E, S

McCall, M C (Bangor, Dungannon, London Irish) 1992 NZ 1(R),2, 1994 W, 1996 E (R), A, 1997 It 1, NZ, C, It 2, 1998 S, E, SA 1,2

McCallan, B (Ballymena) 1960 E, S

McCarten, R J (London Irish) 1961 E, W, F

McCarthy, E A (Kingstown) 1882 W

McCarthy, J S (Dolphin) 1948 F, E, S, W, 1949 F, E, S, W, 1950 W, 1951 F, E, S, W, SA, 1952 F, S, W, E, 1953 F, E, S, 1954 NZ, F, E, S, W, 1955 F, E

McCarthy, P D (Cork Const) 1992 NZ 1,2, A, 1993 S, R (R)

MacCarthy, St G (Dublin U) 1882 W

McCarthy, T (Cork) 1898 W

McClelland, T A (Queen's U, Belfast) 1921 E, S, W, F, 1922 E, W, F, 1923 E, S, W, F, 1924 F, E, S, W, NZ

McClenahan, R O (Instonians) 1923 E, S, W

McClinton, A N (NIFC) 1910 W, F

McCombe, W McM (Dublin U, Bangor) 1968 F, 1975 E, S, F, W

McConnell, A A (Collegians) 1947 A, 1948 F, E, S, W, 1949 F, E

McConnell, G (Derry, Edinburgh U) 1912 F, E, 1913 W, F

McConnell, J W (Lansdowne) 1913 S

McCormac, F M (Wanderers) 1909 W, 1910 W, F

McCormick, W J (Wanderers) 1930 E

McCoull, H C (Belfast Albion) 1895 E, S, W, 1899 E

McCourt, D (Queen's U, Belfast) 1947 A

McCoy, J J (Dungannon, Bangor, Ballymena) 1984 W, A, 1985 S, F, W, E, 1986 F, 1987 [Tg], 1988 E 2, WS, It, 1989 F, W, E, S, NZ

McCracken, H (NIFC) 1954 W

McCullen, A (Lansdowne) 2003 Sm

McCullough, M T (Ulster) 2005 J1,2,NZ(R),A(R)

McDermott, S J (London Irish) 1955 S, W

Macdonald, J A (Methodist Coll, Belfast) 1875 E, 1876 E, 1877 S, 1878 E, 1879 S, 1880 E, 1881 S, 1882 E, S, 1883 E, S, 1884 E, S

McDonald, J P (Malone) 1987 [C], 1990 E (R), S, Arg

McDonnell, A C (Dublin U) 1889 W, 1890 S, W, 1891 E

McDowell, J C (Instonians) 1924 F, NZ

McFarland, B A T (Derry) 1920 S, W, F, 1922 W

McGann, B J (Lansdowne) 1969 F, E, S, W, 1970 SA, F, E, S, W, 1971 F, E, S, W, 1972 F 1, E, F 2, 1973 NZ, E, S, W, 1976 F, W, E, S, NZ

McGowan, A N (Blackrock Coll) 1994 US

McGown, T M W (NIFC) 1899 E, S, 1901 S

McGrath, D G (UC Dublin, Cork Const) 1984 S, 1987 [W, C, Tg, A]

McGrath, N F (Oxford U, London Irish) 1934 W

McGrath, P J (UC Cork) 1965 E, S, W, SA, 1966 F, E, S, W, 1967 A 1, A 2

McGrath, R J M (Wanderers) 1977 W, E, F (R), 1981 SA 1,2, A, 1982 W, E, S, F, 1983 S, F, W, E, 1984 F, W

McGrath, T (Garryowen) 1956 W, 1958 F, 1960 E, S, W, F, 1961 SA

McGuinness, C D (St Mary's Coll) 1997 NZ, C, 1998 F, W, E, SA 1,2, Gg, R (R), SA 3, 1999 F, W, E, S

McGuire, E P (UC Galway) 1963 E, S, W, NZ, 1964 E, S, W, F

MacHale, S (Lansdowne) 1965 F, E, S, W, SA, 1966 F, E, S, W, 1967 S, W, F

McHugh, M (St Mary's Coll) 2003 Tg

McIldowie, G (Malone) 1906 SA, 1910 E, S, W

McIlrath, J A (Ballymena) 1976 A, F, NZ, 1977 W, E

McIlwaine, E H (NIFC) 1895 S, W

McIlwaine, E N (NIFC) 1875 E, 1876 E

McIlwaine, J E (NIFC) 1897 E, S, 1898 E, S, W, 1899 E, W

McIntosh, L M (Dublin U) 1884 S

MacIvor, C V (Dublin U) 1912 F, E, S, W, 1913 E, S, F

McIvor, S C (Garryowen) 1996 A, 1997 It 1, S (R)

McKay, J W (Queen's U, Belfast) 1947 F, E, S, W, A, 1948 F, E, S, W, 1949 F, E, S, W, 1950 F, E, S, W, 1951 F, E, S, W, SA, 1952 F

McKee, W D (NIFC) 1947 A, 1948 F, E, S, W, 1949 F, E, S, W, 1950 F, E, 1951 SA

McKeen, A J W (Lansdowne) 1999 [R (R)]

McKelvey, J M (Queen's U, Belfast) 1956 F, E

McKenna, P (St Mary's Coll) 2000 Arg

McKibbin, A R (Instonians, London Irish) 1977 W, E, S, 1978 S, F, W, E, NZ, 1979 F, W, E, S, 1980 E, S

McKibbin, C H (Instonians) 1976 S (R)

McKibbin, D (Instonians) 1950 F, E, S, W, 1951 F, E, S, W

McKibbin, H R (Queen's U, Belfast) 1938 W, 1939 E, S, W

McKinney, S A (Dungannon) 1972 F 1, E, F 2, 1973 W, F, 1974 F, E, S, P, NZ, 1975 E, S, 1976 A, F, W, E, S, NZ, 1977 W, E, S, 1978 S (R), F, W, E

McLaughlin, J H (Derry) 1887 E, S, 1888 W, S

McLean, R E (Dublin U) 1881 S, 1882 W, E, S, 1883 E, S, 1884 E, S, 1885 E, S 1

Maclear, B (Cork County, Monkstown) 1905 E, S, W, NZ, 1906 E, S, W, SA, 1907 E, S, W

McLennan, A C (Wanderers) 1977 F, 1978 S, F, W, E, NZ, 1979 F, W, E, S, 1980 E, F, 1981 F, W, E, S, SA 1,2

McLoughlin, F M (Northern) 1976 A

McLoughlin, G A J (Shannon) 1979 F, W, E, S, A 1,2, 1980 E, 1981 SA 1,2, 1982 W, E, S, F, 1983 S, F, W, E, 1984 F

McLoughlin, R J (UC Dublin, Blackrock Coll, Gosforth) 1962 E, S, F, 1963 E, S, W, NZ, 1964 E, S, 1965 F, E, S, W, SA, 1966 F, E, S, W, 1971 F, E, S, W, 1972 F 1, E, F 2, 1973 NZ, E, S, W, F, 1974 F, W, E, S, P, NZ, 1975 E, S, F, W

McMahon, L B (Blackrock Coll, UC Dublin) 1931 E, SA, 1933 E, 1934 E, 1936 E, S, W, 1937 E, S, W, 1938 E, S

McMaster, A W (Ballymena) 1972 F 1, E, F 2, 1973 NZ, E, S, W, F, 1974 F, E, S, P, 1975 F, W, 1976 A, F, W, NZ

McMordie, J (Queen's Coll, Belfast) 1886 S

McMorrow, A (Garryowen) 1951 W

McMullen, A R (Cork) 1881 E, S

McNamara, V (UC Cork) 1914 E, S, W

McNaughton, P P (Greystones) 1978 S, F, W, E, 1979 F, W, E, S, A 1,2, 1980 E, S, F, W, 1981 F

MacNeill, H P (Dublin U, Oxford U, Blackrock Coll, London Irish) 1981 F, W, E, S, A, 1982 W, E, S, F, 1983 S, F, W, E, 1984 F, W, E, A, 1985 S, F, W, E, 1986 F, W, E, S, R, 1987 E, S, F, W, [W, C, Tg, A], 1988 S (R), E 1,2

McQuilkin, K P (Bective Rangers, Lansdowne) 1996 US, S, F, 1997 F (t & R), S

MacSweeney, D A (Blackrock Coll) 1955 S

McVicker, H (Army, Richmond) 1927 E, S, W, A, 1928 F

McVicker, J (Collegians) 1924 F, E, S, W, NZ, 1925 F, E, S, W, 1926 F, E, S, W, 1927 F, E, S, W, A, 1928 W, 1930 F

McVicker, S (Queen's U, Belfast) 1922 E, S, W, F

McWeeney, J P J (St Mary's Coll) 1997 NZ

Madden, M N (Sunday's Well) 1955 E, S, W

Magee, J T (Bective Rangers) 1895 E, S

Magee, A M (Louis) (Bective Rangers, London Irish) 1895 E, S, W, 1896 E, S, W, 1897 E, S, 1898 E, S, W, 1899 E, S, W, 1900 E, S, W, 1901 E, S, W, 1902 E, S, W, 1903 E, S, W, 1904 W

Maggs, K M (Bristol, Bath, Ulster) 1997 NZ (R), C, It 2, 1998 S, F, W, E, SA 1,2, Gg, R (R), SA 3, 1999 F, W, E, S, It, A 1,2, Arg 1, [US, A 3, Arg 2], 2000 E, F, Arg, US (R), C, 2001 It (R), F (R), R, S (R), W, E, Sm, NZ, 2002 W, E, S, R, Ru, Gg, A, Fj, Arg, 2003 S 1, It 1, F, W 1, E, A, W 2, S 2, [R,Nm,Arg,A,F], 2004 F, W(R), E(R), It(R), S(R), SA1(R), 2, US, 2005 S,F,W,J1

Maginiss, R M (Dublin U) 1875 E, 1876 E

Magrath, R M (Cork Constitution) 1909 S

Maguire, J F (Cork) 1884 S

Mahoney, J (Dolphin) 1923 E

Malcolmson, G L (RAF, NIFC) 1935 NZ, 1936 E, S, W, 1937 E, S, W

Malone, N G (Oxford U, Leicester) 1993 S, F, 1994 US (R)

Mannion, N P (Corinthians, Lansdowne, Wanderers) 1988 WS, It, 1989 F, W, E, S, NZ, 1990 E, S, F, W, Arg, 1991 Nm 1(R),2, [J], 1993 S

Marshall, B D E (Queen's U, Belfast) 1963 E

Mason, S J P (Orrell, Richmond) 1996 W, E, WS

Massey-Westropp, R H (Limerick, Monkstown) 1886 E

Matier, R N (NIFC) 1878 E, 1879 S

Matthews, P M (Ards, Wanderers) 1984 A, 1985 S, F, W, E,

1986 R, 1987 E, S, F, W, [W, Tg, A], 1988 S, F, W, E 1,2, WS, It, 1989 F, W, E, S, NZ, 1990 E, S, 1991 F, W, E, S, Nm 1 [Z, S, A], 1992 W, E, S
Mattsson, J (Wanderers) 1948 E
Mayne, R B (Queen's U, Belfast) 1937 W, 1938 E, W, 1939 E, S, W
Mayne, R H (Belfast Academy) 1888 W, S
Mayne, T (NIFC) 1921 E, S, F
Mays, K M A (UC Dublin) 1973 NZ, E, S, W
Meares, A W D (Dublin U) 1899 S, W, 1900 E, W
Megaw, J (Richmond, Instonians) 1934 W, 1938 E
Millar, A (Kingstown) 1880 E, S, 1883 E
Millar, H J (Monkstown) 1904 W, 1905 E, S, W
Millar, S (Ballymena) 1958 F, 1959 E, S, W, F, 1960 E, S, W, F, SA, 1961 E, S, W, F, SA, 1962 E, S, F, 1963 F, E, S, W, 1964 F, 1968 F, E, S, W, A, 1969 F, E, S, W, 1970 SA, F, E, S, W
Millar, W H J (Queen's U, Belfast) 1951 E, S, W, 1952 S, W
Miller, E R P (Leicester, Terenure Coll, Leinster) 1997 It 1, F, W, E, NZ, It 2, 1998 S, W (R), Gg, R, 1999 F, W, E (R), S, Arg 1(R), [US (R), A 3(t&R), Arg 2(R)], 2000 US, C (R), SA, 2001 R, W, E, Sm, NZ, 2002 E, S, It (R), Fj (R), 2003 W 1(t+R), Tg, Sm, It 2, S 2, [Nm,Arg(R),A(t&R),F(R)], 2004 SA3(R),US,Arg(R), 2005 It(R),S(R),F(R),W(R),J1(R),2
Miller, F H (Wanderers) 1886 S
Milliken, R A (Bangor) 1973 E, S, W, F, 1974 F, W, E, S, P, NZ, 1975 E, S, F, W
Millin, T J (Dublin U) 1925 W
Minch, J B (Bective Rangers) 1912 SA, 1913 E, S, 1914 E, S
Moffat, J (Belfast Academy) 1888 W, S, M, 1889 S, 1890 S, W, 1891 S
Moffatt, J E (Old Wesley) 1904 S, 1905 E, S, W
Moffett, J W (Ballymena) 1961 E, S
Molloy, M G (UC Galway, London Irish) 1966 F, E, 1967 A 1, E, S, W, F, A 2, 1968 F, E, S, W, A, 1969 F, E, S, W, 1970 F, E, S, W, 1971 F, E, S, W, 1973 F, 1976 A
Moloney, J J (St Mary's Coll) 1972 F 1, E, F 2, 1973 NZ, E, S, W, F, 1974 F, W, E, S, P, NZ, 1975 E, S, F, W, 1976 S, 1978 S, F, W, E, 1979 A 1,2, 1980 S, W
Moloney, L A (Garryowen) 1976 W (R), S, 1978 S (R), NZ
Molony, J U (UC Dublin) 1950 S
Monteith, J D E (Queen's U, Belfast) 1947 E, S, W
Montgomery, A (NIFC) 1895 S
Montgomery, F P (Queen's U, Belfast) 1914 E, S, W
Montgomery, R (Cambridge U) 1887 E, S, W, 1891 E, 1892 W
Moore, C M (Dublin U) 1887 S, 1888 W, S
Moore, D F (Wanderers) 1883 E, S, 1884 E, W
Moore, F W (Wanderers) 1884 W, 1885 E, S 2, 1886 S
Moore, H (Windsor) 1876 E, 1877 S
Moore, H (Queen's U, Belfast) 1910 S, 1911 W, F, 1912 F, E, S, W, SA
Moore, T A P (Highfield) 1967 A 2, 1973 NZ, E, S, W, F, 1974 F, W, E, S, P, NZ
Moore, W D (Queen's Coll, Belfast) 1878 E
Moran, F G (Clontarf) 1936 E, 1937 E, S, W, 1938 S, W, 1939 E, S, W
Morell, H B (Dublin U) 1881 E, S, 1882 W, E
Morgan, G J (Clontarf) 1934 E, S, W, 1935 E, S, W, NZ, 1936 E, S, W, 1937 E, S, W, 1938 E, S, W, 1939 E, S, W
Moriarty, C C H (Monkstown) 1899 W
Moroney, J C M (Garryowen) 1968 W, A, 1969 F, E, S, W
Moroney, R J M (Lansdowne) 1984 F, W, 1985 F
Moroney, T A (UC Dublin) 1964 W, 1967 A 1, E
Morphy, E McG (Dublin U) 1908 E
Morris, D P (Bective Rangers) 1931 W, 1932 E, 1935 E, S, W, NZ
Morrow, J W R (Queen's Coll, Belfast) 1882 S, 1883 E, S, 1884 E, W, 1885 S 1,2, 1886 E, S, 1888 S
Morrow, R D (Bangor) 1986 F, E, S
Mortell, M (Bective Rangers, Dolphin) 1953 F, E, S, W, 1954 NZ, F, E, S, W
Morton, W A (Dublin U) 1888 S
Mostyn, M R (Galwegians) 1999 A 1, Arg 1, [US, A 3, R, Arg 2]
Moyers, L W (Dublin U) 1884 W
Moylett, M M F (Shannon) 1988 E 1
Mulcahy, W A (UC Dublin, Bective Rangers, Bohemians) 1958 A, E, S, W, F, 1959 E, S, W, F, 1960 E, S, W, SA, 1961 E, S, W, SA, 1962 E, S, F, W, 1963 F, E, S, W, NZ, 1964 E, S, W, F, 1965 F, E, S, W, SA
Mullan, B (Clontarf) 1947 F, E, S, W, 1948 F, E, S, W
Mullane, J P (Limerick Bohemians) 1928 W, 1929 F
Mullen, K D (Old Belvedere) 1947 F, E, S, W, A, 1948 F, E, S, W, 1949 F, E, S, W, 1950 F, E, S, W, 1951 F, E, S, W, SA, 1952 F, S, W
Mulligan, A A (Wanderers) 1956 F, E, 1957 F, E, S, W, 1958 A, E, S, F, 1959 E, S, W, F, 1960 E, S, W, F, SA, 1961 W, F, SA
Mullin, B J (Dublin U, Oxford U, Blackrock Coll, London Irish) 1984 A, 1985 S, W, E, 1986 F, W, E, S, R, 1987 E, S, F, W, [W, C, Tg, A], 1988 S, F, W, E 1,2, WS, It, 1989 F, W, E, S, NZ, 1990 E, S, W, Arg, 1991 F, W, E, S, Nm 1,2, [J, S, A], 1992 W, E, S, 1994 US, 1995 E, S, F, W, It, [NZ, J, W, F]
Mullins, M J (Young Munster, Old Crescent) 1999 Arg 1(R), [R], 2000 E, S, It, Arg (t&R), US, C, 2001 It, R, W (R), E (R), Sm (R), NZ (R), 2003 Tg, Sm
Murphy, C J (Lansdowne) 1939 E, S, W, 1947 F, E
Murphy, G E A (Leicester) 2000 US, C (R), J, 2001 R, S, Sm, 2002 W, E, NZ 1,2, Fj, 2003 S 1(R), It 1, F, W 1, E, A, W 2, It 2(R), S 2, 2004 It,S,SA1,3,US,Arg, 2005 It,S,E,F,W,NZ, A,R, 2006 It,F,W,S,E,NZ1,2,A(R)
Murphy, J G M W (London Irish) 1951 SA, 1952 S, W, E, 1954 NZ, 1958 W
Murphy, J J (Greystones) 1981 SA 1, 1982 W (R), 1984 S
Murphy, J N (Greystones) 1992 A
Murphy, K J (Cork Constitution) 1990 E, S, F, W, Arg, 1991 F, W (R), S (R), 1992 S, F, NZ 2(R)
Murphy, N A A (Cork Constitution) 1958 A, E, S, W, F, 1959 E, S, W, F, 1960 E, S, W, F, SA, 1961 E, S, W, 1962 E, 1963 NZ, 1964 E, S, W, F, 1965 F, E, S, W, SA, 1966 F, E, S, W, 1967 A 1, E, S, W, F, 1969 F, E, S, W
Murphy, N F (Cork Constitution) 1930 E, W, 1931 F, E, S, W, SA, 1932 E, S, W, 1933 E
Murphy-O'Connor, J (Bective Rangers) 1954 E
Murray, H W (Dublin U) 1877 S, 1878 E, 1879 E
Murray, J B (UC Dublin) 1963 F
Murray, P F (Wanderers) 1927 F, 1929 F, E, S, 1930 F, E, S, W, 1931 F, E, S, W, SA, 1932 E, S, W, 1933 E, W, S
Murtagh, C W (Portadown) 1977 S
Myles, J (Dublin U) 1875 E

Nash, L C (Queen's Coll, Cork) 1889 S, 1890 W, E, 1891 E, S, W
Neely, M R (Collegians) 1947 F, E, S, W
Neill, H J (NIFC) 1885 E, S 1,2, 1886 S, 1887 E, S, W, 1888 W, S
Neill, J McF (Instonians) 1926 F
Nelson, J E (Malone) 1947 A, 1948 E, S, W, 1949 F, E, S, W, 1950 F, E, S, W, 1951 F, E, W, 1954 F
Nelson, R (Queen's Coll, Belfast) 1882 E, S, 1883 S, 1886 S
Nesdale, R P (Newcastle) 1997 W, E, S, NZ (R), C, 1998 F (R), W (R), Gg, SA 3(R), 1999 It, A 2(R), [US (R), R]
Nesdale, T J (Garryowen) 1961 F
Neville, W C (Dublin U) 1879 S, E
Nicholson, P C (Dublin U) 1900 E, S, W
Norton, G W (Bective Rangers) 1949 F, E, S, W, 1950 F, E, S, W, 1951 F, E, S
Notley, J R (Wanderers) 1952 F, S
Nowlan, K W (St Mary's Coll) 1997 NZ, C, It 2

O'Brien, B (Derry) 1893 S, W
O'Brien, B A P (Shannon) 1968 F, E, S
O'Brien, D J (London Irish, Cardiff, Old Belvedere) 1948 E, S, W, 1949 F, E, S, W, 1950 F, E, S, W, 1951 F, E, S, W, SA, 1952 F, S, W, E
O'Brien, K A (Broughton Park) 1980 E, 1981 SA 1(R),2
O'Brien-Butler, P E (Monkstown) 1897 S, 1898 E, S, 1899 S, W, 1900 E
O'Callaghan, C T (Carlow) 1910 W, F, 1911 E, S, W, F, 1912 F
O'Callaghan, D F (Cork Const, Munster) 2003 W 1(R), Tg (R), Sm (R), W 2(R), It 2(R), [R(R),A(t&R)], 2004 F(t&R),W,It,S(t&R),SA2(R),US, 2005 It(R),S(R),W(R),NZ,A,R, 2006 It(R),F(R),W,S(R),E(R),NZ1,2,A

O'Callaghan, M P (Sunday's Well) 1962 W, 1964 E, F
O'Callaghan, P (Dolphin) 1967 A 1, E, A 2, 1968 F, E, S, W, 1969 F, E, S, W, 1970 SA, F, E, S, W, 1976 F, W, E, S, NZ
O'Connell, K D (Sunday's Well) 1994 F, E (t)
O'Connell, P (Bective Rangers) 1913 W, F, 1914 F, E, S, W
O'Connell, P J (Young Munster, Munster) 2002 W, It (R), F (R), NZ 1, 2003 E (R), A (R), Tg, Sm, W 2, S 2, [R(R),A(t&R)], 2004 F(t&R),W,It,S(t&R),SA1(R),US, 2005 It(R),S(R),W(R),NZ,A,R, 2006 It(R),F(R),W,S(R),E(R),NZ1,2,A
O'Connell, W J (Lansdowne) 1955 F
O'Connor, H S (Dublin U) 1957 F, E, S, W
O'Connor, J (Garryowen) 1895 S
O'Connor, J H (Bective Rangers) 1888 M, 1890 S, W, E, 1891 E, S, 1892 E, W, 1893 E, S, 1894 E, S, W, 1895 E, 1896 E, S, W
O'Connor, J H (Wasps) 2004 SA3,Arg, 2005 S,E,F,W,J1,NZ,A,R, 2006 W(R),E(t&R)
O'Connor, J J (Garryowen) 1909 F
O'Connor, J J (UC Cork) 1933 S, 1934 E, S, W, 1935 E, S, W, NZ, 1936 S, W, 1938 S
O'Connor, P J (Lansdowne) 1887 W
O'Cuinneagain, D (Sale, Ballymena) 1998 SA 1,2, Gg (R), R (R), SA 3, 1999 F, W, E, S, It, A 1,2, Arg 1, [US, A 3, R, Arg 2], 2000 E, It (R)
Odbert, R V M (RAF) 1928 F
O'Donnell, R C (St Mary's Coll) 1979 A 1,2, 1980 S, F, W
O'Donoghue, P J (Bective Rangers) 1955 F, E, S, W, 1956 W, 1957 F, E, 1958 A, E, S, W
O'Driscoll, B G (Blackrock Coll, Leinster) 1999 A 1,2, Arg 1, [US, A 3, R (R), Arg 2], 2000 E, S, It, F, W, J, SA, 2001 F, S, W, E, Sm, NZ, 2002 W, E, S, It, F, NZ 1,2, R, Ru, Gg, A, Fj, Arg, 2003 S 1, It 1, F, W 1, E, W 2, It 2, S 2, [R,Nm,Arg,A,F], 2004 W,E,It,S, SA1,2,3,US,Arg, 2005 It,E,F,W, 2006 It,F,W,S,E,NZ1,2,A
O'Driscoll, B J (Manchester) 1971 F (R), E, S, W
O'Driscoll, J B (London Irish, Manchester) 1978 S, 1979 A 1,2, 1980 E, S, F, W, 1981 F, W, E, S, SA 1,2, A, 1982 W, E, S, F, 1983 S, F, W, E, 1984 F, W, E, S
O'Driscoll, M R (Cork Const, Munster) 2001 R (R), 2002 Fj (R), 2005 R(R), 2006 W(R), NZ1(R),2(R),A(R)
O'Flanagan, K P (London Irish) 1947 A
O'Flanagan, M (Lansdowne) 1948 S
O'Gara, R J R (Cork Const, Munster) 2000 S, It, F, W, Arg (R), US, C (R), J, SA, 2001 It, F, S, W (R), E (R), Sm, 2002 W (R), E (R), S (R), It (t), F (R), NZ 1,2, R, Ru, Gg, A, Arg, 2003 W 1(R), E (R), A (t+R), Tg, Sm, S 2, [R(R),Nm,Arg(R),A,F], 2004 F,W,E,It, S,SA1,2,3,Arg, 2005 It,S,E,F,W,NZ,A,R(R), 2006 It,F,W,S,E,NZ1,2,A
O'Grady, D (Sale) 1997 It 2
O'Hanlon, B (Dolphin) 1947 E, S, W, 1948 F, E, S, W, 1949 F, E, S, W, 1950 F
O'Hara, P T J (Sunday's Well, Cork Const) 1988 WS (R), 1989 F, W, E, NZ, 1990 E, S, F, W, 1991 Nm 1, [J], 1993 F, W, E, 1994 US
O'Kelly, M E (London Irish, St Mary's Coll, Leinster) 1997 NZ, C, It 2, 1998 S, F, W, E, SA 1,2, Gg, R, SA 3, 1999 A 1(R),2, Arg 1(R), [US (R), A 3, R, Arg 2], 2000 E, S, It, F, W, Arg, US, J, SA, 2001 It, F, S, W, E, NZ, 2002 E, S, It, F, NZ 1(R),2, R, Ru, Gg, A, Fj, Arg, 2003 S 1, It 1, F, W 1, E, A, W 2, S 2, [R,Nm,Arg,A,F], 2004 F,W(R),E,It,S,SA1,2, 3,Arg, 2005 It,S,E,F,W,NZ,A, 2006 It,F,W,S,E
O'Leary, A (Cork Constitution) 1952 S, W, E
O'Loughlin, D B (UC Cork) 1938 E, S, W, 1939 E, S, W
O'Mahony, D W (UC Dublin, Moseley, Bedford) 1995 It, [F], 1997 It 2, 1998 R
O'Mahony, David (Cork Constitution) 1995 It
O'Meara, B T (Cork Constitution) 1997 E (R), S, NZ (R), 1998 S, 1999 [US (R), R (R)], 2001 It (R), 2003 Sm (R), It 2(R)
O'Meara, J A (UC Cork, Dolphin) 1951 F, E, S, W, SA, 1952 F, S, W, E, 1953 F, E, S, W, 1954 NZ, F, E, S, 1955 F, E, 1956 S, W, 1958 W
O'Neill, H O'H (Queen's U, Belfast, UC Cork) 1930 E, S, W, 1933 E, S, W
O'Neill, J B (Queen's U, Belfast) 1920 S
O'Neill, W A (UC Dublin, Wanderers) 1952 E, 1953 F, E, S, W, 1954 NZ
O'Reilly, A J F (Old Belvedere, Leicester) 1955 F, E, S, W, 1956 F, E, S, W, 1957 F, E, S, W, 1958 A, E, S, W, F, 1959 E, S, W, F, 1960 E, 1961 E, F, SA, 1963 F, S, W, 1970 E
Orr, P A (Old Wesley) 1976 F, W, E, S, NZ, 1977 W, E, S, F, 1978 S, F, W, E, NZ, 1979 F, W, E, S, A 1,2, 1980 E, S, F, W, 1981 F, W, E, S, SA 1,2, A, 1982 W, E, S, F, 1983 S, F, W, E, 1984 F, W, E, S, A, 1985 S, F, W, E, 1986 F, S, R, 1987 E, S, F, W, [W, C, A]
O'Shea, C M P (Lansdowne, London Irish) 1993 R, 1994 F, W, E, S, A 1,2, US, 1995 E, S, [J, W, F], 1997 It 1, F, S (R), 1998 S, F, SA 1,2, Gg, R, SA 3, 1999 F, W, E, S, It, A 1, Arg 1, [US, A 3, R, Arg 2], 2000 E
O'Sullivan, A C (Dublin U) 1882 S
O'Sullivan, J M (Limerick) 1884 S, 1887 S
O'Sullivan, P J A (Galwegians) 1957 F, E, S, W, 1959 E, S, W, F, 1960 SA, 1961 E, S, 1962 F, W, 1963 F, NZ
O'Sullivan, W (Queen's Coll, Cork) 1895 S
Owens, R H (Dublin U) 1922 E, S

Parfrey, P (UC Cork) 1974 NZ
Parke, J C (Monkstown) 1903 W, 1904 E, S, W, 1905 W, NZ, 1906 E, S, W, SA, 1907 E, S, W, 1908 E, S, W, 1909 E, S, W, F
Parr, J S (Wanderers) 1914 F, E, S, W
Patterson, C S (Instonians) 1978 NZ, 1979 F, W, E, S, A 1,2, 1980 E, S, F, W
Patterson, R d'A (Wanderers) 1912 F, S, W, SA, 1913 E, S, W, F
Payne, C T (NIFC) 1926 E, 1927 F, E, S, A, 1928 F, E, S, W, 1929 F, E, W, 1930 F, E, S, W
Pedlow, A C (CIYMS) 1953 W, 1954 NZ, F, E, 1955 F, E, S, W, 1956 F, E, S, W, 1957 F, E, S, W, 1958 A, E, S, W, F, 1959 E, 1960 E, S, W, F, SA, 1961 S, 1962 W, 1963 F
Pedlow, J (Bessbrook) 1882 S, 1884 W
Pedlow, R (Bessbrook) 1891 W
Pedlow, T B (Queen's Coll, Belfast) 1889 S, W
Peel, T (Limerick) 1892 E, S, W
Peirce, W (Cork) 1881 E
Phipps, G C (Army) 1950 E, W, 1952 F, W, E
Pike, T O (Lansdowne) 1927 E, S, W, A, 1928 F, E, S, W
Pike, V J (Lansdowne) 1931 E, S, W, SA, 1932 E, S, W, 1933 E, W, S, 1934 E, S, W
Pike, W W (Kingstown) 1879 E, 1881 E, S, 1882 E, 1883 S
Pinion, G (Belfast Collegians) 1909 E, S, W, F
Piper, O J S (Cork Constitution) 1909 E, S, W, F, 1910 E, S, W, F
Polden, S E (Clontarf) 1913 W, F, 1914 F, 1920 F
Popham, I (Cork Constitution) 1922 S, W, F, 1923 F
Popplewell, N J (Greystones, Wasps, Newcastle) 1989 NZ, 1990 Arg, 1991 Nm 1,2, [Z, S, A], 1992 W, E, S, F, NZ 1,2, A, 1993 S, F, W, E, R, 1994 F, W, E, S, US, 1995 E, S, F, W, It, [NZ, J, W, F], Fj, 1996 US, S, F, W, E, A, 1997 It 1, F, W, E, NZ, C, 1998 S (t), F (R)
Potterton, H N (Wanderers) 1920 W
Pratt, R H (Dublin U) 1933 E, W, S, 1934 E, S
Price, A H (Dublin U) 1920 S, F
Pringle, J C (NIFC) 1902 S, W
Purcell, N M (Lansdowne) 1921 E, S, W, F
Purdon, H (NIFC) 1879 S, E, 1880 E, 1881 E, S
Purdon, W B (Queen's Coll, Belfast) 1906 E, S, W
Purser, F C (Dublin U) 1898 E, S, W

Quinlan, A (Shannon, Munster) 1999 [R (R)], 2001 It, F, 2002 NZ 2(R), Ru (R), Gg (R), A (R), Fj, Arg (R), 2003 S 1(R), It 1(R), F (R), W 1, E (R), A, W 2, [R(R),Nm,Arg], 2004 SA1(R),2(R), 2005 J1,2(t&R)
Quinlan, D P (Northampton) 2005 J1(R),2
Quinlan, S V J (Blackrock Coll) 1956 F, E, W, 1958 W
Quinn, B T (Old Belvedere) 1947 F
Quinn, F P (Old Belvedere) 1981 F, W, E
Quinn, J P (Dublin U) 1910 E, S, 1911 E, S, W, F, 1912 E, S, W, 1913 E, W, F, 1914 F, E, S
Quinn, K (Old Belvedere) 1947 F, A, 1953 F, E, S
Quinn, M A M (Lansdowne) 1973 F, 1974 F, W, E, S, P, NZ, 1977 S, F, 1981 SA 2
Quirke, J M T (Blackrock Coll) 1962 E, S, 1968 S

Rainey, P I (Ballymena) 1989 NZ
Rambaut, D F (Dublin U) 1887 E, S, W, 1888 W
Rea, H H (Edinburgh U) 1967 A 1, 1969 F
Read, H M (Dublin U) 1910 E, S, 1911 E, S, W, F, 1912 F, E, S, W, SA, 1913 E, S
Reardon, J V (Cork Constitution) 1934 E, S
Reddan, E (Wasps) 2006 F(R)
Reid, C (NIFC) 1899 S, W, 1900 E, 1903 W
Reid, J L (Richmond) 1934 S, W
Reid, P J (Garryowen) 1947 A, 1948 F, E, W
Reid, T E (Garryowen) 1953 E, S, W, 1954 NZ, F, 1955 E, S, 1956 F, E, 1957 F, E, S, W
Reidy, C J (London Irish) 1937 W
Reidy, G F (Dolphin, Lansdowne) 1953 W, 1954 F, E, S, W
Richey, H A (Dublin U) 1889 W, 1890 S
Ridgeway, E C (Wanderers) 1932 S, W, 1935 E, S, W
Rigney, B J (Greystones) 1991 F, W, E, S, Nm 1, 1992 F, NZ 1(R),2
Ringland, T M (Queen's U, Belfast, Ballymena) 1981 A, 1982 W, E, F, 1983 S, F, W, E, 1984 F, W, E, S, A, 1985 S, F, W, E, 1986 F, W, E, S, R, 1987 E, S, F, W, [W, C, Tg, A], 1988 S, F, W, E 1
Riordan, W F (Cork Constitution) 1910 E
Ritchie, J S (London Irish) 1956 F, E
Robb, C G (Queen's Coll, Belfast) 1904 E, S, W, 1905 NZ, 1906 S
Robbie, J C (Dublin U, Greystones) 1976 A, F, NZ, 1977 S, F, 1981 F, W, E, S
Robinson, B F (Ballymena, London Irish) 1991 F, W, E, S, Nm 1,2, [Z, S, A], 1992 W, E, S, F, NZ 1,2, A, 1993 W, E, R, 1994 F, W, E, S, A 1,2
Robinson, T T H (Wanderers) 1904 E, S, 1905 E, S, W, NZ, 1906 SA, 1907 E, S, W
Roche, J (Wanderers) 1890 S, W, E, 1891 E, S, W, 1892 W
Roche, R E (UC Galway) 1955 E, S, 1957 S, W
Roche, W J (UC Cork) 1920 E, S, F
Roddy, P J (Bective Rangers) 1920 S, F
Roe, R (Lansdowne) 1952 E, 1953 F, E, S, W, 1954 F, E, S, W, 1955 F, E, S, W, 1956 F, E, S, W, 1957 F, E, S, W
Rolland, A C (Blackrock Coll) 1990 Arg, 1994 US (R), 1995 It (R)
Rooke, C V (Dublin U) 1891 E, W, 1892 E, S, W, 1893 E, S, W, 1894 E, S, W, 1895 E, S, W, 1896 E, S, W, 1897 E, S
Ross, D J (Belfast Academy) 1884 E, 1885 S 1,2, 1886 E, S
Ross, G R P (CIYMS) 1955 W
Ross, J F (NIFC) 1886 S
Ross, J P (Lansdowne) 1885 E, S 1,2, 1886 E, S
Ross, N G (Malone) 1927 F, E
Ross, W McC (Queen's U, Belfast) 1932 E, S, W, 1933 E, W, S, 1934 E, S, 1935 NZ
Russell, J (UC Cork) 1931 F, E, S, W, SA, 1933 E, W, S, 1934 E, S, W, 1935 E, S, W, 1936 E, S, W, 1937 E, S
Russell, P (Instonians) 1990 E, 1992 NZ 1,2, A
Rutherford, W G (Tipperary) 1884 E, S, 1885 E, S 1, 1886 E, 1888 W
Ryan, E (Dolphin) 1937 W, 1938 E, S
Ryan, J (Rockwell Coll) 1897 E, 1898 E, S, W, 1899 E, S, W, 1900 S, W, 1901 E, S, W, 1902 E, 1904 E
Ryan, J G (UC Dublin) 1939 E, S, W
Ryan, M (Rockwell Coll) 1897 E, S, 1898 E, S, W, 1899 E, S, W, 1900 E, S, W, 1901 E, S, W, 1903 E, 1904 E, S

Saunders, R (London Irish) 1991 F, W, E, S, Nm 1,2, [Z, J, S, A], 1992 W, 1994 F (t)
Saverimutto, C (Sale) 1995 Fj, 1996 US, S
Sayers, H J M (Lansdowne) 1935 E, S, W, 1936 E, S, W, 1938 W, 1939 E, S, W
Scally, C J (U C Dublin) 1998 Gg (R), R, 1999 S (R), It
Schute, F (Wanderers) 1878 E, 1879 E
Schute, F G (Dublin U) 1912 SA, 1913 E, S
Scott, D (Malone) 1961 F, SA, 1962 S
Scott, R D (Queen's U, Belfast) 1967 E, F, 1968 F, E, S
Scovell, R H (Kingstown) 1883 E, 1884 E
Scriven, G (Dublin U) 1879 S, E, 1880 E, S, 1881 E, 1882 S, 1883 E, S
Sealy, J (Dublin U) 1896 E, S, W, 1897 S, 1899 E, S, W, 1900 E, S
Sexton, J F (Dublin U, Lansdowne) 1988 E 2, WS, It, 1989 F
Sexton, W J (Garryowen) 1984 A, 1988 S, E 2
Shanahan, T (Lansdowne) 1885 E, S 1,2, 1886 E, 1888 S, W
Shaw, G M (Windsor) 1877 S
Sheahan, F J (Cork Const, Munster) 2000 US (R), 2001 It (R), R, W (R), Sm, 2002 W, E, S, Gg (R), A (t+R), Fj, 2003 S 1(R), It 1(R), 2004 F(R), W(R), It(R), S(R),SA1(R),US, 2005 It(R), S(R), W(R), J1, 2
Sheehan, M D (London Irish) 1932 E
Sherry, B F (Terenure Coll) 1967 A 1, E, S, A 2, 1968 F, E
Sherry, M J A (Lansdowne) 1975 F, W
Shields, P M (Ballymena) 2003 Sm (R), It 2(R)
Siggins, J A E (Belfast Collegians) 1931 F, E, S, W, SA, 1932 E, S, W, 1933 E, W, S, 1934 E, S, W, 1935 E, S, W, NZ, 1936 E, S, W, 1937 E, S, W
Slattery, J F (UC Dublin, Blackrock Coll) 1970 SA, F, E, S, W, 1971 F, E, S, W, 1972 F 1, E, F 2, 1973 NZ, E, S, W, F, 1974 F, W, E, S, P, NZ, 1975 E, S, F, W, 1976 A, 1977 S, F, 1978 S, F, W, E, NZ, 1979 F, W, E, S, A 1,2, 1980 E, S, F, W, 1981 F, W, E, S, SA 1,2, A, 1982 W, E, S, F, 1983 S, F, W, E, 1984 F
Smartt, F N B (Dublin U) 1908 E, S, 1909 E
Smith, B A (Oxford U, Leicester) 1989 NZ, 1990 S, F, W, Arg, 1991 F, W, E, S
Smith, J H (London Irish) 1951 F, E, S, W, SA, 1952 F, S, W, E, 1954 NZ, W, F
Smith, R E (Lansdowne) 1892 E
Smith, S J (Ballymena) 1988 E 2, WS, It, 1989 F, W, E, S, NZ, 1990 E, 1991 F, W, E, S, Nm 1,2, [Z, S, A], 1992 W, E, S, F, NZ 1,2, 1993 S
Smithwick, F F S (Monkstown) 1898 S, W
Smyth, J T (Queen's U, Belfast) 1920 F
Smyth, P J (Belfast Collegians) 1911 E, S, F
Smyth, R S (Dublin U) 1903 E, S, 1904 E
Smyth, T (Malone, Newport) 1908 E, S, W, 1909 E, S, W, 1910 E, S, W, F, 1911 E, S, W, 1912 E
Smyth, W S (Belfast Collegians) 1910 W, F, 1920 E
Solomons, B A H (Dublin U) 1908 E, S, W, 1909 E, S, W, F, 1910 E, S, W
Spain, A W (UC Dublin) 1924 NZ
Sparrow, W (Dublin U) 1893 W, 1894 E
Spillane, B J (Bohemians) 1985 S, F, W, E, 1986 F, W, E, 1987 F, W, [W, C, A (R)], 1989 E (R)
Spring, D E (Dublin U) 1978 S, NZ, 1979 S, 1980 S, F, W, 1981 W
Spring, R M (Lansdowne) 1979 F, W, E
Spunner, H F (Wanderers) 1881 E, S, 1884 W
Stack, C R R (Dublin U) 1889 S
Stack, G H (Dublin U) 1875 E
Staples, J E (London Irish, Harlequins) 1991 W, E, S, Nm 1,2, [Z, J, S, A], 1992 W, E, NZ 1,2, A, 1995 F, W, It, [NZ], Fj, 1996 US, S, F, A, 1997 W, E, S
Staunton, J W (Garryowen, Wasps) 2001 Sm, 2005 J1(R),2(R), 2006 A(R)
Steele, H W (Ballymena) 1976 E, 1977 F, 1978 F, W, E, 1979 F, W, E, A 1,2
Stephenson, G V (Queen's U, Belfast, London Hosp) 1920 F, 1921 E, S, W, F, 1922 E, S, W, F, 1923 E, S, W, F, 1924 F, E, S, W, NZ, 1925 F, E, S, W, 1926 F, E, S, W, 1927 F, E, S, W, A, 1928 F, E, S, W, 1929 F, E, W, 1930 F, E, S, W
Stephenson, H W V (United Services) 1922 S, W, F, 1924 F, E, S, W, NZ, 1925 F, E, S, W, 1927 A, 1928 E
Stevenson, J (Dungannon) 1888 M, 1889 S
Stevenson, J B (Instonians) 1958 A, E, S, W, F
Stevenson, R (Dungannon) 1887 E, S, W, 1888 M, 1889 S, W, 1890 S, W, E, 1891 W, 1892 W, 1893 E, S, W
Stevenson, T H (Belfast Acad) 1895 E, W, 1896 E, S, W, 1897 E, S
Stewart, A L (NIFC) 1913 W, F, 1914 F
Stewart, W J (Queen's U, Belfast, NIFC) 1922 F, 1924 S, 1928 F, E, S, W, 1929 F, E, S, W
Stoker, E W (Wanderers) 1888 W, S
Stoker, F O (Wanderers) 1886 S, 1888 W, M, 1889 S, 1891 W
Stokes, O S (Cork Bankers) 1882 E, 1884 E
Stokes, P (Garryowen) 1913 E, S, 1914 F, 1920 E, S, W, F, 1921 E, S, F, 1922 W, F

Stokes, R D (Queen's Coll, Cork) 1891 S, W
Strathdee, E (Queen's U, Belfast) 1947 E, S, W, A, 1948 W, F, 1949 E, S, W
Stringer, P A (Shannon, Munster) 2000 S, It, F, W, Arg, C, J, SA, 2001 It, F, R, S (R), W, E, Sm, NZ, 2002 W, E, S, It, F, NZ 1,2, R, Ru, Gg, A, Arg, 2003 S 1, It 1, F, W 1, E, A, W 2, S 2, [R,Nm,Arg,A,F], 2004 F, W, E, It, S, SA1,2,3, US(R), Arg, 2005 It,S,E,F,W,J1,2,NZ,A,R(R), 2006 It,F,W,S,E, NZ1,2,A
Stuart, C P (Clontarf) 1912 SA
Stuart, I M B (Dublin U) 1924 E, S
Sugars, H S (Dublin U) 1905 NZ, 1906 SA, 1907 S
Sugden, M (Wanderers) 1925 F, E, S, W, 1926 F, E, S, W, 1927 E, S, W, A, 1928 F, E, S, W, 1929 F, E, S, W, 1930 F, E, S, W, 1931 F, E, S, W
Sullivan, D B (UC Dublin) 1922 E, S, W, F
Sweeney, J A (Blackrock Coll) 1907 E, S, W
Symes, G R (Monkstown) 1895 E
Synge, J S (Lansdowne) 1929 S

Taggart, T (Dublin U) 1887 W
Taylor, A S (Queen's Coll, Belfast) 1910 E, S, W, 1912 F
Taylor, D R (Queen's Coll, Belfast) 1903 E
Taylor, J (Belfast Collegians) 1914 E, S, W
Taylor, J W (NIFC) 1879 S, 1880 E, S, 1881 S, 1882 E, S, 1883 E, S
Tector, W R (Wanderers) 1955 F, E, S
Tedford, A (Malone) 1902 E, S, W, 1903 E, S, W, 1904 E, S, W, 1905 E, S, W, NZ, 1906 E, S, W, SA, 1907 E, S, W, 1908 E, S, W
Teehan, C (UC Cork) 1939 E, S, W
Thompson, C (Belfast Collegians) 1907 E, S, 1908 E, S, W, 1909 E, S, W, F, 1910 E, S, W, F
Thompson, J A (Queen's Coll, Belfast) 1885 S 1,2
Thompson, J K S (Dublin U) 1921 W, 1922 E, S, F, 1923 E, S, W, F
Thompson, R G (Lansdowne) 1882 W
Thompson, R H (Instonians) 1951 SA, 1952 F, 1954 NZ, F, E, S, W, 1955 F, S, W, 1956 W
Thornhill, T (Wanderers) 1892 E, S, W, 1893 E
Thrift, H (Dublin U) 1904 W, 1905 E, S, W, NZ, 1906 E, W, SA, 1907 E, S, W, 1908 E, S, W, 1909 E, S, W, F
Tierney, D (UC Cork) 1938 S, W, 1939 E
Tierney, T A (Garryowen) 1999 A 1,2, Arg 1, [US, A 3, R, Arg 2], 2000 E
Tillie, C R (Dublin U) 1887 E, S, 1888 W, S
Todd, A W P (Dublin U) 1913 W, F, 1914 F
Topping, J A (Ballymena) 1996 WS, A, 1997 It 1, F, E, 1999 [R], 2000 US, 2003 A
Torrens, J D (Bohemians) 1938 W, 1939 E, S, W
Trimble, A (Ulster) 2005 A,R, 2006 F(R),W,S,E,NZ1,2,A
Tucker, C C (Shannon) 1979 F, W, 1980 F (R)
Tuke, B B (Bective Rangers) 1890 E, 1891 E, S, 1892 E, 1894 E, S, W, 1895 E, S
Turley, N (Blackrock Coll) 1962 E
Tweed, D A (Ballymena) 1995 F, W, It, [J]
Tydings, J J (Young Munster) 1968 A
Tyrrell, W (Queen's U, Belfast) 1910 F, 1913 E, S, W, F, 1914 F, E, S, W

Uprichard, R J H (Harlequins, RAF) 1950 S, W

Waide, S L (Oxford U, NIFC) 1932 E, S, W, 1933 E, W
Waites, J (Bective Rangers) 1886 S, 1888 M, 1889 W, 1890 S, W, E, 1891 E
Waldron, O C (Oxford U, London Irish) 1966 S, W, 1968 A
Walker, S (Instonians) 1934 E, S, 1935 E, S, W, NZ, 1936 E, S, W, 1937 E, S, W, 1938 E, S, W
Walkington, D B (NIFC) 1887 E, W, 1888 W, 1890 W, E, 1891 E, S, W
Walkington, R B (NIFC) 1875 E, 1876 E, 1877 E, S, 1878 E, 1879 S, 1880 E, S, 1882 E, S
Wall, H (Dolphin) 1965 S, W
Wallace, D P (Garryowen, Munster) 2000 Arg, US, 2001 It, F, R (R), S (R), W, E, NZ, 2002 W, E, S, It, F, 2003 Tg (R), Sm (R), W 2(t+R), S 2, 2004 S,SA1,2, 2005 J2, 2006 It,F,W,S,E,NZ1,2,A
Wallace, Jas (Wanderers) 1904 E, S
Wallace, Jos (Wanderers) 1903 S, W, 1904 E, S, W, 1905 E, S, W, NZ, 1906 W
Wallace, P S (Blackrock Coll, Saracens) 1995 [J], Fj, 1996 US, W, E, WS, A, 1997 It 1, F, W, E, S, NZ, C, 1998 S, F, W, E, SA 1,2, Gg, R, 1999 F, W, E, S, It (R), 1999 A 1,2, Arg 1, [US, A 3, R, Arg 2], 2000 E, US, C (R), 2002 W (R), E (R), S (R), It (R), F (R), NZ 2(R), Ru (R), Gg (R)
Wallace, R M (Garryowen, Saracens) 1991 Nm 1(R), 1992 W, E, S, F, A, 1993 S, F, W, E, R, 1994 F, W, E, S, 1995 W, It, [NZ, J, W], Fj, 1996 US, S, F, WS, 1998 S, F, W, E
Wallace, T H (Cardiff) 1920 E, S, W
Wallis, A K (Wanderers) 1892 E, S, W, 1893 E, W
Wallis, C O'N (Old Cranleighans, Wanderers) 1935 NZ
Wallis, T G (Wanderers) 1921 F, 1922 E, S, W, F
Wallis, W A (Wanderers) 1880 S, 1881 E, S, 1882 W, 1883 S
Walmsley, G (Bective Rangers) 1894 E
Walpole, A (Dublin U) 1888 S, M
Walsh, E J (Lansdowne) 1887 E, S, W, 1892 E, S, W, 1893 E
Walsh, H D (Dublin U) 1875 E, 1876 E
Walsh, J C (UC Cork, Sunday's Well) 1960 S, SA, 1961 E, S, F, SA, 1963 E, S, W, NZ, 1964 E, S, W, F, 1965 F, S, W, SA, 1966 F, S, W, 1967 E, S, W, F, A 2
Ward, A J (Ballynahinch) 1998 F, W, E, SA 1,2, Gg, R, SA 3, 1999 W, E, S, It (R), A 1,2, Arg 1, [US, A 3, R, Arg 2], 2000 F (R), W (t&R), Arg (R), US (R), C, J, SA (R), 2001 It (R), F (R)
Ward, A J P (Garryowen, St Mary's Coll, Greystones) 1978 S, F, W, E, NZ, 1979 F, W, E, S, 1981 W, E, S, A, 1983 E (R), 1984 E, S, 1986 S, 1987 [C, Tg]
Warren, J P (Kingstown) 1883 E
Warren, R G (Lansdowne) 1884 W, 1885 E, S 1,2, 1886 E, 1887 E, S, W, 1888 W, S, M, 1889 S, W, 1890 S, W, E
Watson, R (Wanderers) 1912 SA
Wells, H G (Bective Rangers) 1891 S, W, 1894 E, S
Westby, A J (Dublin U) 1876 E
Wheeler, G H (Queen's Coll, Belfast) 1884 S, 1885 E
Wheeler, J R (Queen's U, Belfast) 1922 E, S, W, F, 1924 E
Whelan, P C (Garryowen) 1975 E, S, 1976 NZ, 1977 W, E, S, F, 1978 S, F, W, E, NZ, 1979 F, W, E, S, 1981 F, W, E
White, M (Queen's Coll, Cork) 1906 E, S, W, SA, 1907 E, W
Whitestone, A M (Dublin U) 1877 E, 1879 S, E, 1880 E, 1883 S
Whittle, D (Bangor) 1988 F
Wilkinson, C R (Malone) 1993 S
Wilkinson, R W (Wanderers) 1947 A
Williamson, F W (Dolphin) 1930 E, S, W
Willis, W J (Lansdowne) 1879 E
Wilson, F (CIYMS) 1977 W, E, S
Wilson, H G (Glasgow U, Malone) 1905 E, S, W, NZ, 1906 E, S, W, SA, 1907 E, S, W, 1908 E, S, W, 1909 E, S, W, 1910 W
Wilson, R G (Ulster) 2005 J1
Wilson, W H (Bray) 1877 E, S
Withers, H H C (Army, Blackheath) 1931 F, E, S, W, SA
Wolfe, E J (Armagh) 1882 E
Wood, G H (Dublin U) 1913 W, 1914 F
Wood, B G M (Garryowen) 1954 E, S, 1956 F, E, S, W, 1957 F, E, S, W, 1958 A, E, S, W, F, 1959 E, S, W, F, 1960 E, S, W, F, SA, 1961 E, S, W, F, SA
Wood, K G M (Garryowen, Harlequins) 1994 A 1,2, US, 1995 E, S, [J], 1996 A, 1997 It 1, F, 1997 NZ, It 2, 1998 S, F, W, E, SA 1,2, R (R), SA 3, 1999 F, W, E, S, It (R), A 1,2, Arg 1, [US, A 3, R (R), Arg 2], 2000 E, S, It, F, W, Arg, US, C, J, SA, 2001 It, F, S, W, E, NZ, 2002 F, NZ 1,2, Ru, 2003 W 2, S 2, [R,Nm,Arg,A,F]
Woods, D C (Bessbrook) 1888 M, 1889 S
Woods, N K P J (Blackrock Coll, London Irish) 1994 A 1,2, 1995 E, F, 1996 F, W, E, 1999 W
Wright, R A (Monkstown) 1912 S

Yeates, R A (Dublin U) 1889 S, W
Young, B (Ulster) 2006 NZ2(R),A(R)
Young, G (UC Cork) 1913 E
Young, R M (Collegians) 1965 F, E, S, W, SA, 1966 F, E, S, W, 1967 W, F, 1968 W, A, 1969 F, E, S, W, 1970 SA, F, E, S, W, 1971 F, E, S, W

IRELAND: DOMESTIC RUGBY

SHANNON KEEP STRANGELHOLD

Shannon maintained their virtual monopoly on the AIB Division One as they took their third successive title with a comprehensive victory over Clontarf in the play-off final at Lansdowne Road.

It was the Limerick club's eighth league title in the space of 11 years and although Mick Galwey's side were overshadowed by both Garryowen and Clontarf in the regular season, they came alive for the end-of-season play-offs to beat both their main rivals and retain their Division One crown in considerable style.

The campaign began in October and it was soon clear that the champions, Garryowen, Clontarf and Cork Constitution would be the four sides vying for the play-off places.

Clontarf contrived to lose to both Bohemian and Dungannon in the space of seven days in October to briefly jeopardise their involvement in the knockout stages but the north Dubliners were to lose only once again during the season – a narrow reverse against the Buccaneers in December – and coasted into the play-offs.

Garryowen, however, were the form team and a 18–10 defeat to Clontarf at Dooradoyle in January was the only blemish on an otherwise perfect league record that saw Paul Cunningham's side top the table and earn home advantage in May's semi-finals.

The visitors to Dooradoyle for the semi-final were Shannon and the first half went according to plan when full-back Conor Kilroy scored a try to give the home side a slender 11–5 lead.

Shannon replied after the break with a second Eoin Cahill touchdown of the match but Kilroy, who scored all 20 of his side's points, seemed to have won it for Garryowen when he landed a spectacular 40-metre penalty into a strong wind in the final minute of the match. Shannon trailed 20–18 but pulled off a dramatic escape when fly-half David Delaney converted a penalty in the fourth minute of injury time to send Galwey's team into the final.

"It's impossible to describe that game," said Galwey. "Conor Kilroy kicked a brilliant penalty and that kick probably deserved to win it for Garryowen. But I have great faith in these players and their true spirit really came through in the end – they never gave up and fair dues to them."

Defeat was a bitter pill to swallow for Garryowen boss Paul Cunningham, who announced he was leaving the club after the final whistle.

"Things didn't go our way at the end, but these players will be back," he said. "We won 14 out of 15 games in the League this year, and given the size of the competition, that's some record. Garryowen will be back challenging for titles but unfortunately, I won't be around to help them."

The second semi-final could not reproduce the drama of the first as Cork travelled to Castle Avenue to play Clontarf. The home side were on a 10–match winning run and they were never in danger of surrendering that record as wing Niall O'Brien helped himself to a hat-trick of tries in a 26–6 win. Clontarf were through to their first Division One final in three years.

"Niall [O'Brien] had a very good day," said 'Tarf's Kiwi coach Phil Werahiko. "He was with Connacht last season, is doing a degree this year and we're very lucky to have him. He's a quality finisher.

"Playing at Lansdowne Road is what every player dreams of – it's the home of rugby – and hopefully we can continue our good run of form there in the final."

They couldn't and little went Clontarf's way at Lansdowne Road on the bog day. Shannon and Ireland Under-21 hooker Sean Cronin opened up the scoring early on. Full-back Daragh O'Shea landed a 16th-minute penalty in reply for Clontarf but it was to be his side's only points of the match as Shannon completely dominated proceedings and three more tries followed.

First Eoin Cahill crossed before wing Andrew Thompson outpaced his brother-in-law Fiach O'Loughlin, the Clontarf scrum half, to add the third. The try took Thompson's personal points haul in the competition to 999, a Division One record. Substitute David O'Donovan added a fourth in injury time to add gloss to a 30–3 win and Shannon were champions again.

After the match Galwey was quick to pay tribute to his young hooker Cronin. "At the start of the season we were in trouble with the hooking position but Sean has come through the Under-20s and has had a magnificent season in both age grade and senior levels," he said. "He started the move for our first try and finished it off as well. He saved a certain try when he made up ground to stop their winger, and apart from those incidents he never flinched against big, experienced opponents. That's the kind of thing you need, he was an inspiration."

In the inaugural AIB Senior Cup final, Cork put aside the disappointment of their play-off defeat to beat St. Mary's College at Lansdowne Road. The undisputed star of the show was Cork wing Cronan Healy, who scored four tries in a 37–12 victory, but it was an emotional day for everyone connected with Cork as they dedicated victory to the memory of Cork player Conrad O'Sullivan, who died in March at the age of 25, the month before the final.

"No matter what we tried to do, Conrad was always on our minds in the build-up to the game," said Cork captain Frank Cogan. "We had to focus on the rugby, but we knew he was somewhere with us for the 80 minutes. We felt his presence, and it was great that we got the win, for us and for him."

Constitution coach Brian Walsh added: "It was a remarkable display given the last couple of weeks of heartache suffered by every member of the squad, every member of the club.

"It was very important for the players that we win this, very important to the club, very important that we should do this for Conrad and his family."

AIB DIVISION ONE

	P	W	D	L	F	A	BP	Pts
Garryowen	15	14	0	1	379	180	5	61
Clontarf	15	12	0	3	403	222	13	61
Cork Constitution	15	12	0	3	384	216	8	56
Shannon	15	13	0	2	357	200	4	56
U.L. Bohemian	15	10	1	4	345	309	7	49
Belfast Harlequins	15	8	0	7	328	330	7	39
Buccaneers	15	7	1	7	305	261	7	37
Lansdowne	15	7	0	8	337	311	4	32
UCD	15	6	0	9	295	286	8	32
Ballymena	15	7	0	8	307	313	4	32
St. Mary's College	15	6	1	8	250	305	3	29
Dungannon	15	6	0	9	264	357	5	29
Blackrock College	15	4	1	10	213	376	5	23
Galwegians	15	3	0	12	208	343	7	19
Dublin University	15	3	0	12	265	399	5	17
Co. Carlow	15	0	0	15	191	423	5	5

PLAY-OFFS

6 May, 2006	
Garryowen 20 **Shannon** 21	**Clontarf** 26 **Cork Constitution** 6

FINAL

13 May, 2006
Clontarf 3 **Shannon** 30

AIB DIVISION TWO WINNERS

Terenure College

AIB DIVISION THREE WINNERS

Clonakilty

ROUND ROBIN WINNERS

Rainey Old Boys

AIB CUP 2005–06

ROUND ONE

26 November, 2005
Buccaneers 28 **Ballymena** 16

ROUND TWO

17 December, 2005	
Terenure College 19 **Malone** 12	**Dolphin** 7 **Garryowen** 33
D.L.S.P 13 **Buccaneers** 50	**Clontarf** 30 **Dungannon** 20
Belfast Harlequins 50 **Suttonians** 12	
18 December, 2005	
Shannon 17 **Cork Constitution** 20	**Galwegians** 13 **Cashel** 9
29 December, 2005	
Greystones 14 **St.Mary's College** 39	

QUARTER-FINALS

11 February, 2006	
Galwegians 6 **Buccaneers** 23	**Clontarf** 14 **Garryowen** 15
Cork Constitution 41 **Belfast Harlequins** 13	
12 February, 2006	
Terenure College 21 **St. Mary's College** 35	

SEMI-FINALS

25 February, 2006	
Garryowen 14 **St. Mary's College** 23	**Buccaneers** 13 **Cork Constitution** 20

FINAL

8 April, Lansdowne Road, Dublin

CORK CONSTITUTION 37 (3G, 1PG, 1DG, 2T) ST. MARY'S COLLEGE 12 (1G, 1T)

CORK CONSTITUTION: R Lane; A Horgan, T Gleeson, C Quaid, C Healy; D Lyons, F Murphy; M Ross, D Murray, T Ryan, S Cottrell, J Maloney, B Cutriss, M O'Connell, F Cogan (captain)

SUBSTITUTIONS: A Ryan for Gleeson (76 mins); L Hill for Horgan (77 mins); B O'Connor for Cottrell (77 mins); J Murray for Cutriss (77 mins); J Cahill for M O'Connell (79 mins)

SCORERS *Tries:* Healy (4), Horgan *Conversions*: Lyons (3) *Penalty*: Lyon *Drop Goal*: Lyon

ST. MARY'S COLLEGE: F Lynch; J Norton, K Douglas, B Lynn, J McWeeney (captain); J Sexton, J Kilbride; C O'Byrne, P Smyth, P Collins, E Keane, G Logan, W Duggan, P Nash, A Copeland Substitutions: C Potts for Copeland (12 mins); H Gervais for Nash (40 mins); S Gibney for Kilbride (57 mins); R Gannon for Lynch (64 mins); M Duggan for Gibney (77 mins)

SCORERS *Tries:* Potts, Douglas *Conversion*: Lynn

YELLOW CARD O'Byrne (36 mins)

REFEREE G Clancy (Munster)

ITALY

ITALY'S TEST RECORD

OPPONENTS	DATE	VENUE	RESULT
Ireland	4 Feb	A	**Lost** 16–26
England	11 Feb	H	**Lost** 16–31
France	25 Feb	A	**Lost** 12–37
Wales	11 March	A	**Drew** 18–18
Scotland	18 March	H	**Lost** 10–13
Japan	11 June	A	**Won** 52–6
Fiji	17 June	A	**Lost** 18–29

PIERRE STARTS TO WORK HIS MAGIC

By Paolo Pacitti and Gianluca Barca

Sometimes the statistics do not tell the whole story. If you look at the bare facts then Italy again finished bottom of the RBS Six Nations without a win and are still looking for that crucial breakthrough in the Northern Hemisphere's showpiece International tournament. Yet,

Dave Rogers/Getty Images

Pierre Berbizier has made a big impression since taking over as Italy coach, making them believe the good times are coming.

the season was arguably the Azzurri's most successful to date as Pierre Berbizier's side not only demonstrated that they are genuinely competitive at this level, but that they possess the talent, the firepower and desire to ruffle the feathers of Europe's elite.

Indeed the 2006 RBS 6 Nations Championship table could have looked very different had results gone Italy's way. In an incredible match in the Millennium Stadium the Italians out-muscled the Grand Slam champions and needed only to convert one of four kicks at goal to secure a first Championship win on foreign soil. The performance – one of pride and passion built on formidable forward power – was not a one off. Full of confidence, Italy pushed a resurgent Scotland side all the way, denied at the death by a Chris Paterson penalty.

For the first time since 1997 when George Coste's side hammered Ireland at Lansdowne Road and France in Grenoble there was a genuine feel of optimism within the Italian camp. Also for the first time since 1997 Italy had a concrete coach in Berbizier, a man with a proven track record, clear ideas and enthusiasm in abundance. Appointed by Italy President Giancarlo Dondi following the departure of John Kirwan, Berbizier had the opportunity to work with a blend of talented young players and experienced campaigners.

Berbizier's rein started with Italy's tour to Argentina and Australia in June 2005 and he had to address a question which had been baffling his predecessors; who was the right player to fill the experienced boots of the retired maestro Diego Dominguez? The answer was to come from an unlikely source. Ramiro Pez, who had been released by Bath, and had been in the international wilderness under Kirwan, was on holiday in Cordoba when the call came from the former French scrum half to pack his bags and join the touring party.

The little fly half was to become firmly established as a member of the Italy squad and a key player in the post-Dominguez era. The confident performance that Pez displayed in the second test victory against Argentina raised a few eyebrows. The manner in which the Italians were able to control the match in Cordoba, defending strongly and playing with great authority, ushered in a new optimism ahead of what was looking like a rather interesting trip to Australia. Therefore it was a pity that one week later in Melbourne a high tackle by Sterling Mortlock ended Pez's influence on the game.

Italy lost, but the tour cemented Berbizier's job and became an important starting block in preparation for the three autumn tests which the Azzurri played against Tonga, Argentina and Fiji. In the event the three matches gave the new coach a rather varied view of the progress that his side had made and certainly showed little of what was to come later in the Six Nations. Comfortable successes against Tonga and Fiji came with a degree of success built on a solid set piece and some enterprising back play.

Without the services of tries of the tried and tested Andre Masi, absent for the whole season with a knee injury, Berbizier found in Gonzalo Canale and Mirco Bergamasco an exciting alternative for the midfield. But any progress made during the early throws of the autumn tests were undone with a dire performance against Argentina-the Pumas taking revenge in a match which the Italians would rather forget.

With six matches under his belt as head coach, the big question mark for Berbizier was how Italy would perform in a rather less forgiving Six Nations competition? The answer was encouraging. At Lansdowne Road Italy went back to their roots, playing with the usual passion and pride but also displaying new power in the pack and putting the Irish under severe pressure. Indeed the match and the championship could have taken on a completely different complexion had referee David Pearson called for the Television Match Official (video referee) when deliberating the two Ireland tries. Despite the defeat, it was clear that the 2006 Six Nations Championship, the seventh championship for Italy, would be a definitive turning point.

Under inspirational captain Marco Bortolami and the auspices of Berbizier, Italy played without the usual characteristic drops in concentration that had conditioned recent performances. Berbizier had asked

Warren Little/Getty Images

The television match official could have the made difference between Italy winning and losing in Dublin.

his team to give 100 per cent every game in order to pressurize the opposition and he was not to be disappointed.

Optimism was high within the Italy camp ahead of the England game at the Flaminio Stadium. A star was born in centre Mirco Bergamasco, who scored a try and caused significant problems for the England defence. The Italians though suffered too much in the midfield area where Mauro Bergamasco was forced to play alongside Pez to cover the number ten channel. It was another courageous performance, with England reverting to powerful forward play and making hard work of a 31–16 victory.

The concrete ideas Pierre Berbizier added to the rugby Italian style gave a new dimension, but the real acid test of the Italian resurgence would be the trip to the Stade de France against an undefeated France side. The Italians had another good start. Three penalties and a drop goal by Pez put pressure on Bernard Laporte's team before Dimitri Yachvili's introduction changed the direction of the game. It was another defeat, but Berbizier's side were making forward strides,

Right from the outset of the Six Nations the Italian management squad had targeted the final two matches of the tournament against Wales and a resurgent Scotland side. The matches were to come in quick succession, just eight days apart, but a challenge to relish for an Italian side playing with confidence owing to the emergence of Mirco Bergamasco and an extremely competitive lineout.

The showdown against Wales at the Millennium Stadium was to produce the first realistic chance of a tournament-first away win for the Italians. Indeed Berbizier's charges were the better of the two outfits on the day with the Welsh still reeling after the shock departure of coach Mike Ruddock. It could have been a comfortable victory had Pez not experienced an 'off day' with the boot, missing with four kicks at goal. However, the 18–18 draw against the Grand Slam champions was a significant result and the first draw against the Welsh in the history of Italian rugby.

Against Scotland in Rome, only a penalty scored by Chris Paterson in the final throws of injury time prevented Berbizier's team of recording a sensational victory over one of the competition's form sides. It was yet another stride forward without actually achieving a result.

In reflection the 2006 Six Nations was one of contrasting records for Italy. While Mirco Bergamasco's incredible total of 53 tackles from five games highlighted a new and aggressive approach, Ramiro Pez's 11 missed tackles highlighted that despite the attacking flair, the fly half position still threw up a few defencive concerns. The Italian Championship also started to offer some alternatives to Berbizier in that crucial position. One, Andre Marcato, who was central to Benetton Treviso's end of season push for the title, was a real prospect. The young man from Padua toured Japan and Fiji during the summer but played just 31 minutes in the rather one sided affair against Japan.

Marcato's emergence during the summer alongside the likes of Bourgoin fullback David Bortolussi, Catania winger Benjamin De Jager and Parma prop Fabio Staibano, gives Berbizier plenty of options ahead of the Rugby World Cup 2007 qualifiers in the autumn. De Jager and Staibano in particular impressed against Japan, scoring tries in the 52–6 victory.

While Berbizier underlined that tours against varied opposition are the best way of developing a squad, the Italy coach will also be boosted by the raised profile of his players owing to some outstanding performances during the Six Nations Championship. Many players now ply their trade with the big European teams competing in highly competitive tournaments like the Top 14, Guinness Premiership and the Heineken Cup. The Bergamasco brothers and Parisse continue to impress with Stade Francais, while Andrea Masi has moved to Biarritz, Salvatore Perugini to Toulouse, Fabio Ongaro to Saracens and Bortolami to Gloucester, highlighting Italy's emergence on the world stage.

For the fourth consecutive year the Italian Super 10 ended with the classic Benetton Treviso vs Calvisano final. It was defending champions Calvisano's sixth in a row, with only one win, the previous year.

The match, played at the Stadio Brianteo in Monza, was no advert for Italian rugby as the game was marred by tension and bitter rivalry which exploded into a massive brawl when the referee blew for the end of the game. Treviso won 17–12, thanks to an early try by Stuart Legg and four penalties by young number ten Andrea Marcato. South African Herkie Kruger's off day with the boot (3 out of 7) cost Calvisano dearly.

Treviso had won the regular season hands down, sixteen points ahead of Parma and Calvisano. In the semis, Benetton faced Gran, Parma's other club, which Super 10 top point scorer and Italy international Rima Wakarua had kicked into fourth place. Against Treviso, Wakarua was not enough to keep Gran's hopes alive. In the other clash, Parma was unlucky not to go through on aggregate, having beaten Calvisano three times out of four during the season.

Parma did however manage to beat the Dragons, in the Heineken Cup play off, and see off Rovigo, 28–13, in the Coppa Italia final, played early in March. They turned out to be Italy's surprise club of the year.

With rugby strongholds Rovigo and L'Aquila still struggling for money, Viadana, hard hit by injuries, finished a disappointing fifth.

At the bottom of the table, newly promoted Venice failed to stay the pace going straight back down after only twelve months in the Premiership.

Jamie McDonald/Getty Images

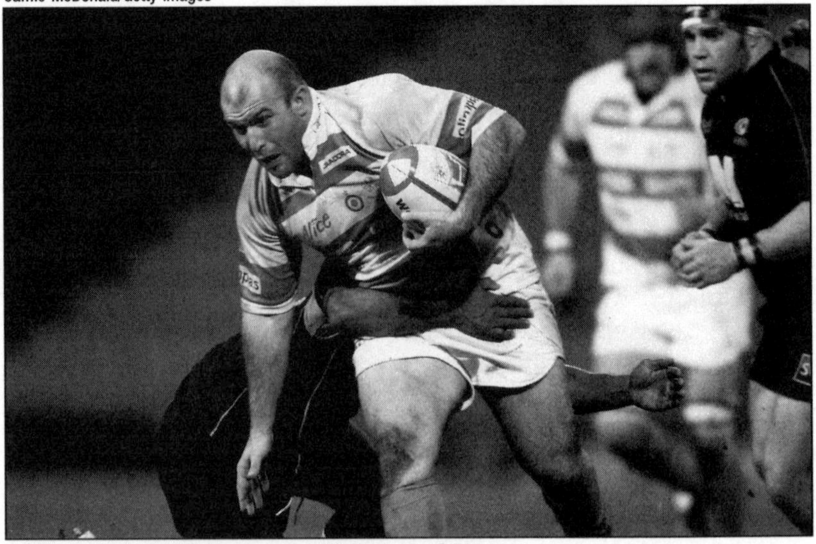

Benetton won their sixth title in a row, with a 17–12 win over Calvisano.

ITALY INTERNATIONAL PLAYERS

UP TO 30TH SEPTEMBER 2006

Compiled by Hugh Copping

Abbiati, E 1968 *WGe* 1970 *R* 1971 *Mor, F* 1972 *Pt, Sp, Sp, Yug* 1973 *Pt, ETv* 1974 *Leo*
Agosti, A 1933 *Cze* (R)
Aguero, M 2005 *Tg* (R), *Ar* (R), *Fj* 2006 *Fj* (R)
Agujari, A 1967 *Pt*
Aio, E 1974 *WGe*
Aiolfi, G 1952 *Sp, Ger, F* 1953 *F* 1955 *Ger, F*
Alacevich, A 1939 *R* (R)
Albonico, A 1934 *R* 1935 *F* 1936 *Ger, R* 1937 *Ger, R, Bel, Ger, F* 1938 *Ger*
Aldorvandi, N 1994 *Sp, CZR, H*
Alfonsetti, M 1994 *F*
Allevi, E 1929 *Sp* 1933 *Cze* (R)
Aloisio, I 1933 *Cze, Cze* 1934 *Cat, R* 1935 *Cat* 1936 *Ger, R*
Altigeri, A 1973 *Rho, WTv, Bor, NEC, Nat, Leo, FS, Tva, Cze, Yug, A* 1974 *Pt, WGe* 1975 *F, E, Pol, H, Sp* 1976 *F, R, J* 1978 *Ar, USS, Sp* 1979 *F, Pol, R*
Altissimi, T 1929 *Sp*
Ambron, V 1962 *Ger, R* 1963 *F* 1964 *Ger, F* 1965 *F, Cze* 1966 *F, Ger, R* 1967 *Pt, R* 1968 *Pt, WGe, Yug* 1969 *Bul, Sp, Bel* 1970 *Mad, Mad, R* 1971 *Mor* 1972 *Sp, Sp*
Ambrosio, R 1987 *NZ, USS, Sp* 1988 *F, R, A, I* 1989 *R, Sp, Ar, Z* (R), *USS*
Ancillotti, B 1978 *Sp* 1979 *F, Pol, R*
Andina, E 1952 *F* 1955 *F*
Angelozzi, C 1979 *E, Mor* 1980 *Coo*
Angioli, A 1960 *Ger, F* 1961 *Ger, F* 1962 *F, Ger, R* 1963 *F*
Angrisiani, A 1979 *Mor, F, Pol, USS, Mor* 1980 *Coo* 1984 *Tun*
Annibal, S 1980 *Fj, Coo, Pol, Sp* 1981 *F, WGe* 1982 *R, E, WGe* 1983 *F, USS, Sp, Mor, F, A* 1984 *F* 1985 *F, Z, Z* (R) 1986 *Tun, F, Pt* 1990 *F*
Antoni, JM 2001 *Nm* (R), *SA*
Appiani, C 1976 *Sp* (R) 1977 *Mor, Pol, Sp* 1978 *USS*
Appiani, S 1985 *R* 1986 *Pt* (R) 1988 *A* (R) 1989 *F*
Arancio, O 1993 *Rus* (R) 1994 *CZR, H, A, A, R, W, F* 1995 *S, I, Sa, E, Ar, F, R* (R), *NZ* (R), *SA* 1996 *W, Pt, W, A, E, S* 1997 *I, I* (R) 1998 *S* (R), *Ar, E* (R) 1999 *F, W* (R), *I, SA* (R), *E, NZ* (R)
Armellin, D 1965 *Cze* 1966 *Ger* 1968 *Pt, WGe, Yug* 1969 *Bul, Sp, Bel, F*
Arrigoni, A 1949 *Cze*
Artuso, G 1977 *Pol, R* 1978 *Sp* 1979 *F, E, NZ, Mor* 1980 *F, R, JAB* 1981 *F* 1982 *F, E, Mor* 1983 *F, R, USS, C* (R), *C* 1984 *USS* 1985 *R, E, USS, R* 1986 *Tun, F, Tun* 1987 *Pt, F, R, NZ*
Augeri, E 1962 *F, Ger, R* 1963 *F*
Autore, A 1961 *Ger, F* 1962 *F* 1964 *Ger* 1966 *Ger* 1968 *Pt, WGe, Yug* 1969 *Bul, Sp, Bel, F*
Avigo, L 1959 *F* 1962 *F, Ger, R* 1963 *F* 1964 *Ger, F* 1965 *F, Cze* 1966 *Ger, R*
Aymonod, R 1933 *Cze* 1934 *Cat, R* 1935 *F* (R)
Azzali, A 1981 *WGe* 1982 *F, R, WGe* 1983 *F, R, USS, Sp, Mor, F* (R) 1984 *F, Mor, R* 1985 *R, E, Sp*
Babbo, S 1996 *Pt*
Balducci, A 1929 *Sp* (R)
Baraldi, F 1973 *Cze, Yug* 1974 *Mid, Sus, Oxo* (R) 1975 *E, Pol, H, Sp* 1976 *F, R, A* 1977 *F, Mor, Cze*
Baraldi, R 1971 *R*
Barattin, A 1996 *A* (R), *E* (R)
Barba, S 1985 *R* (R), *E* 1986 *E, A* 1987 *Pt, F, R, Ar, Fj* 1988 *R, USS, A* 1990 *F, Pol, Sp, H, R, USS* 1991 *F, R, Nm, Nm, US, E, USS* 1992 *Sp, F, R, R, S* 1993 *Sp, F, Cro, Mor, Sp*
Barbieri, R 2006 *J* (R), *Fj* (R)
Barbini, G 1978 *USS* (R)
Barbini, M 2002 *NZ* (R), *Sp, Ar, A* 2003 *I, NZ* 2004 *F, I, R* (R), *J, NZ, US* (R) 2005 *W* (R), *E*
Barbini, N 1953 *Ger, R* 1954 *Sp, F* 1955 *Ger, F, Sp, Cze* 1956 *Ger* 1957 *Ger* 1958 *R* 1960 *Ger, F*
Bargelli, F 1979 *E, Sp, Mor, F, Pol, USS, NZ, Mor* 1980 *F, R, Fj, Sp* 1981 *F, R*
Barilari, S 1948 *Cze* 1953 *Ger, R*
Baroni, M 1999 *F, W* (R), *I, SA* (R), *SA* (R) 2000 *C*
Barzaghi, V 1929 *Sp* 1930 *Sp* 1933 *Cze*
Basei, JL 1979 *E, Sp, Mor* (R), *F, Pol, USS, NZ, Mor* 1980 *F, R, Fj, JAB, Coo, USS* 1981 *R*
Battagion, A 1948 *F, Cze*
Battaglini, F 1948 *F*
Battaglini, M 1940 *R, Ger* 1951 *Sp* 1953 *F, R*
Becca, A 1937 *R* 1938 *Ger* 1939 *R* 1940 *Ger*
Bellinazzo, E 1958 *R* 1959 *F* 1960 *Ger, F* 1961 *Ger, F* 1962 *F, Ger* 1964 *Ger, F* 1966 *F, Ger, R* 1967 *F*
Benatti, A 2001 *Fj* (R), *SA* (R), *Sa* 2002 *W* (R) 2003 *NZ* (R)
Bentivoglio, C 1977 *Pol*
Beretta, D 1993 *S*
Bergamasco, A 1973 *Bor, Tva* 1977 *Pol* 1978 *USS*
Bergamasco, M 1998 *H, E* 1999 *SA, E* 2000 *S, W, I, E, F, C* 2001 *I, E, F, S, W, Fj, SA, Sa* 2002 *F, S, W, I, E, NZ* (R), *Sp* (R), *R* (R), *A* 2003 *W, I, S* (R), *I, Geo* (R), *NZ, W* (R) 2004 *J, C, NZ* 2005 *I, W, Ar, A, Ar* (R), *Fj* 2006 *I, E, F, J, Fj*
Bergamasco, M 2002 *F* (R), *S, W, Ar, A* 2003 *W* (R), *I* (R), *E, F, S, S, Geo, NZ, C* 2004 *E* (R), *F, S* (R), *I* (R), *W* (R) 2005 *I, W, S, Tg, Ar, Fj* 2006 *I, E, F, W, S, J, Fj*
Bernabo, L 1970 *Mad, Mad, R* 1972 *Sp, Sp*
Bernabo, V 2004 *US* 2005 *Tg* (R), *Fj* (R)
Berni, F 1985 *R, Sp, Z, Z* 1986 *E, A* 1987 *R, NZ* 1988 *A* 1989 *F*
Bertoli 1967 *R*
Bertolotto, V 1936 *Ger, R* 1937 *Ger, R* 1942 *R* 1948 *F*
Bettarello, O 1958 *F* 1959 *F* 1961 *Ger*
Bettarello, R 1953 *Ger, R*
Bettarello, S 1979 *Pol, E, Sp, F, NZ, Mor* 1980 *F, R, Fj, JAB, Coo, Pol, USS, Sp* 1981 *F, R, USS, WGe* 1982 *F, R, E, WGe, Mor* 1983 *F, R, USS, C, Sp, Mor, F, A* 1984 *F, Mor, R, Tun, USS* 1985 *F, R, E, Sp, Z, USS, R* 1986 *Tun, F, Pt, E, A* (R), *Tun, USS* 1987 *R, USS, Sp* 1988 *USS, A*
Bettella, L 1969 *Sp, Bel, F*
Bevilacqua, R 1937 *Bel, Ger, F* 1938 *Ger* 1939 *Ger, R* 1940 *R, Ger* 1942 *R*
Bezzi, C 2003 *W, I, E, F, S, I, NZ, W* (R) 2004 *US* 2005 *Ar, A*
Biadene, G 1958 *R* 1959 *F*
Bigi, G 1930 *Sp* 1933 *Cze*
Bimbati, M 1989 *Z*
Birtig, M 1998 *H* (R) 1999 *F*
Blessano, F 1975 *F, R, Pol, H, Sp* 1976 *F, R, J* 1977 *F, Mor, Pol, R, Cze, R, Sp* 1978 *F, Ar, Sp* 1979 *F, Pol, R*
Boccaletto, L 1969 *Bul, Bel, F* 1970 *Cze, Mad, Mad, R* (R) 1971 *F, R* 1972 *Pt, Sp, Sp* 1975 *E* (R)
Boccazzi, S 1985 *Z* (R) 1988 *USS*
Bocconelli, M 1967 *R*
Bollesan, M 1963 *F* 1964 *F* 1965 *F* 1966 *F, Ger* 1967 *F, Pt* 1968 *Pt, WGe, Yug* 1969 *Bul, Sp, Bel, F* 1970 *Cze, Mad, Mad, R* 1971 *Mor, F, R* 1972 *Pt, Pt, Sp, Sp, Yug* 1973 *Pt, Rho, WTv, Bor, NEC, Nat, ETv, Leo, FS, Tva, Yug, A* 1974 *Pt, Mid, Sus, Oxo, WGe, Leo* 1975 *F, Sp, Cze*

Bona, A 1972 *Sp, Yug* 1973 *Rho, WTv, Bor, NEC, Nat, ETv, Leo, FS, Tva, Cze, Yug, A* 1974 *Pt, WGe, Leo* 1975 *F, Sp, R, Cze, E, Pol, H, Sp* 1976 *F, R, J, A, Sp* 1977 *F, Mor* 1978 *Ar, USS, Sp* 1979 *F, Sp, Mor, F, Pol, USS, NZ, Mor* 1980 *F, R, Fj, JAB, Pol, Sp* 1981 *F*
Bonaiti, L 1979 *R* 1980 *Pol*
Bonati, G 1939 *Ger, R* (R)
Bonetti, S 1972 *Yug* 1973 *Rho, WTv, Bor, NEC, Nat, ETv, Leo, FS, Tva* 1974 *Pt, Mid, Sus, Oxo, Leo* 1975 *F, Sp, R, Cze, E, Pol, H, Sp* 1976 *R, J, A, Sp* 1977 *F, Mor, R, Sp* 1978 *F* 1979 *F* 1980 *USS*
Bonfante, S 1936 *Ger, R*
Bonino, G 1949 *F*
Bonomi, M 1988 *F, R* 1990 *Sp, H, R, USS* 1991 *F, R, Nm, Nm, E* (R), *NZ, USS* 1992 *R* (R), *R* 1993 *Cro, Mor, Sp, F, S* 1994 *Sp* (R), *R, H, A, A, W* 1995 *S, I, Sa, F, Ar, R, NZ* 1996 *W* (R)
Bordon, S 1990 *R, USS* 1991 *Nm, USS* (R) 1992 *F, R* 1993 *Sp, F, Pt, Rus, F* 1994 *R, A* (R), *A, R, W, F* 1995 *I* (R), *E, Ar, F, Ar, NZ, SA* 1996 *W, A, E* 1997 *I, F*
Borsetto, L 1977 *Pol*
Borsetto, V 1948 *F, Cze*
Bortolami, M 2001 *Nm, SA* (R), *Fj, SA* (R), *Sa* 2002 *F, S, W, I, E, NZ, Sp, R, Ar, A* 2003 *W, I, E* (R), *S, Geo, Tg, C* 2004 *E, F, S, I, W, R, J, C, NZ* 2005 *I, W, S, E, F, Ar, Ar, A, Tg, Ar, Fj* 2006 *I, E, F, W, S, J, Fj* (R)
Bortolini, G 1933 *Cze* 1934 *Cat*
Bortolussi, D 2006 *J, Fj*
Boscaino, L 1967 *Pt*
Bossi, L 1940 *R, Ger*
Bottacchiara, A 1991 *NZ, USS* 1992 *Sp, F, R, R*
Bottacin, G 1956 *Cze*
Bottonelli, O 1929 *Sp* 1934 *R* 1935 *Cat, F* 1937 *Ger* 1939 *Ger*
Bove, L 1948 *Cze* 1949 *F, Cze*
Bracaglia, O 1939 *R*
Braga, M 1958 *R*
Bricchi, L 1929 *Sp* 1930 *Sp* 1933 *Cze* (R)
Brighetti, L 1934 *Cat*
Brunelli, A 1969 *Bel* 1970 *Mad* 1971 *F* (R)
Brunello, M 1988 *I* 1989 *F* 1990 *F, Sp, H, R, USS* 1993 *Pt*
Brusin, S 1957 *Ger*
Busson, G 1957 *Ger* 1958 *R* 1959 *F* 1960 *Ger, F* 1961 *Ger, F* 1962 *F, Ger* 1963 *F*
Caccia-Dominioni, F 1935 *F* (R) 1937 *Ger*
Caione, C 1995 *R* (R) 1996 *Pt* 1997 *F* (R), *R* (R) 1998 *Rus, Ar, H, E* 1999 *F, S* (R), *SA* (R), *Ur, Sp, Fj, Tg, NZ* 2000 *Sa, Fj, C, R, NZ* 2001 *I, E, S* (R), *Fj*
Caligiuri, R 1969 *F* (R) 1973 *Pt, Rho, WTv, NEC, Nat, ETv, Leo* (R), *FS, Tva* 1975 *E, Pol, H, Sp* 1976 *F, R, J, A, Sp* 1978 *F, Ar, USS, Sp* 1979 *F, Pol, R*
Caluzzi, A 1970 *R* 1971 *Mor, F* 1972 *Pt, Pt, Sp, Sp* 1973 *Pt* 1974 *Oxo, WGe, Leo*
Camiscioni, P 1975 *E* 1976 *R* (R), *J, A, Sp* 1977 *F* 1978 *F*
Campagna, M 1933 *Cze* 1934 *Cat* 1936 *Ger, R* 1937 *Ger, R, Bel* 1938 *Ger*
Canale, G-J 2003 *S* (R), *Geo, NZ* (R), *Tg, C, W* 2004 *S, I, W, R, J, C* 2005 *I, Ar, Ar, A, Tg, Ar, Fj* 2006 *I, E, F, W, S*
Canavosio, P 2005 *A* (R), *Tg* (R), *Fj* (R) 2006 *I, E, F, W, S, Fj*
Cantoni, C 1956 *Ger, F, Cze* 1957 *Ger*
Capitani, L 1989 *F, R, Sp, Ar, Z, USS*
Capuzzoni, M 1993 *Cro* 1995 *I* (R)
Caranci, A 1989 *R* (R)
Carli, M 1955 *Sp, Cze*
Carloni, C 1935 *F*
Carpente, D 2004 *R* (R), *J* (R)
Carraro, T 1937 *R* (R)
Casagrande, T 1977 *R* (R)
Cassellato, U 1990 *Sp* 1992 *R* (R), *S* 1993 *Sp, F, Pt, Cro, Mor, F* (R), *S*
Cassina, R 1992 *R* (R), *S* (R)
Castellani, A 1994 *CZR* 1995 *Ar* (R), *R* 1996 *W* (R), *S* 1997 *Ar* (R), *R, I* 1998 *S, W, Rus, H, E* (R) 1999 *F* (R), *W* (R), *Ur* (R), *Sp, Fj, Tg, NZ*
Castrogiovanni, LM 2002 *NZ* (R), *Sp, R, Ar* (R), *A* 2003 *I* (R), *E* (R), *F* (R), *S* (R), *I, Geo, NZ* (R), *Tg, C, W* 2004 *E, F, S, I, W, J* 2005 *I, W, S, E* (R), *F* (R), *Ar* (R), *A, Ar* (R), *Fj* 2006 *I* (R), *E* (R), *F* (R), *W* (R), *S*
Catotti, L 1979 *Pol, E*
Cazzini, A 1933 *Cze, Cze* 1934 *Cat, R* 1935 *Cat, F* 1936 *Ger, R* 1937 *Ger, R, Bel, Ger, F* 1939 *R* 1942 *R*
Cecchetto, G 1955 *F*
Cecchetto-Milani, A 1952 *Sp, Ger, F*
Cecchin, G 1970 *Cze, R* 1971 *F, R* 1972 *Pt*
Ceccotti, G 1972 *Pt, Sp*
Centinari, A 1930 *Sp* (R)
Centinari, R 1935 *F* 1936 *Ger, R* 1937 *Bel, F* 1939 *Ger*
Cepolino, A 1999 *Ur* (R), *Sp, Fj, Tg, NZ*
Cesani, L 1929 *Sp* 1930 *Sp* 1935 *Cat, F*
Ceselin, F 1989 *F* (R), *R*
Checchinato, C 1990 *Sp* 1991 *Nm, Nm, US, NZ, USS* 1992 *Sp, F, R, S* 1993 *Pt, Cro* (R), *Sp, F, Rus, F, S* 1994 *Sp, R, CZR, A, A, R, W, F* 1995 *Sa, F, Ar, R, NZ* 1996 *W, E* 1997 *I* (R), *F, Ar, R, SA, I* 1998 *Rus, Ar, H, E* 1999 *F, S, SA, SA, Ur, Fj, E* (R), *Tg, NZ* 2000 *S, W, I, E, F, Sa, Fj* 2001 *I, E, F, S, W, Nm, SA, Ur, Ar, Fj, SA, Sa* 2002 *F, S, W, Sp* (R), *R* (R) 2003 *Geo* (R), *NZ, Tg* (R), *C* (R), *W* 2004 *E* (R), *F* (R), *I*
Chechinato, G 1973 *Cze, Yug, A* 1974 *WGe, Leo*
Cherubini, G 1949 *Cze* 1951 *Sp*
Ciccio, T 1992 *R* 1993 *Sp, F, Mor, F*
Cicognani, E 1940 *Ger*
Cinelli, R 1968 *Pt* 1969 *Sp*
Cinti, G 1973 *Rho, WTv, ETv*
Cioni, F 1967 *Pt, R* 1968 *Pt* 1969 *Bul, Sp, Bel* 1970 *Cze, Mad, Mad, R*
Clerici, L 1939 *Ger*
Colella, A 1983 *R, USS, C, C, Sp, Mor, F, A, USS* 1984 *R, Tun, USS* 1985 *F, R, E, Sp, Z, Z, USS, R* 1986 *Tun, F, Pt, E, A, Tun, USS* 1987 *Pt, F, Ar, Fj, USS, Sp* 1988 *F, R, USS* 1989 *R, Sp, Ar* 1990 *Pol, R*
Collodo, O 1977 *Pol, Cze, R, Sp* 1978 *F* 1986 *Pt, E, A, USS* 1987 *Pt, F, R, NZ, Ar, Fj*
Colombini, S 1971 *R*
Colombo, F 1933 *Cze*
Colussi, G 1957 *F* 1958 *F* 1964 *Ger, F* 1965 *F, Cze* 1968 *Pt*
Colusso, C 1982 *F*
Comin, A 1955 *Ger, F, Sp, F, Cze* 1956 *F, Cze* 1958 *F*
Conforto, U 1965 *Cze* 1966 *Ger, R* 1967 *F, R* 1968 *Pt, WGe, Yug* 1969 *Bul, Sp, Bel, F* 1970 *Cze* 1971 *Mor, F* 1972 *Yug* 1973 *Pt*
Coppio, F 1993 *F* (R), *Pt, Cro, Mor, Sp*
Cornella, L 1999 *Sp*
Corvo, R 1985 *F* (R), *Sp, Z*
Cossara, U 1971 *Mor, F, R* 1972 *Pt, Sp* 1973 *Pt, Rho, NEC, Nat, Leo, FS, Tva, Cze* 1975 *F, Sp, R, Cze, E, Pol, H* 1976 *F, J, A* (R) 1977 *Pol*
Costa, A 1940 *R, Ger* 1942 *R*
Costanzo, S 2004 *R, C* (R), *NZ* (R), *US* (R)
Cottafava, E 1973 *Pt*
Cova, R 1937 *Bel, Ger, F* 1938 *Ger* 1939 *Ger, R* 1942 *R*
Covi, C 1988 *F, R, USS, A, I* 1989 *F, R, Sp, Ar, Z, USS* 1990 *F, Pol* (R), *R* 1991 *F, R, Nm, Nm* 1996 *E*
Crepaz, F 1972 *Pt*
Crescenzo, M 1984 *R* (R)
Crespi, U 1933 *Cze, Cze* 1934 *Cat, R* 1935 *Cat* 1937 *Ger*
Cristofoletto, W 1992 *R* 1993 *Mor, Sp, F* (R) 1996 *Pt* (R), *A, E, S* 1997 *I, F, F, Ar, SA* (R), *I* (R) 1998 *S, W, Rus, Ar, E* 1999 *F, S, W, I, SA, SA, Sp, Fj* (R), *E, NZ* (R) 2000 *E, F*
Croci, G 1990 *Sp, H, R, USS* 1991 *F, R, Nm, US, E, NZ, USS* 1992 *Sp, F* 1993 *S* 1996 *S* 1997 *I, F, F, Ar, R, SA, I* 1998 *S, W*
Crotti, R 1993 *S* 1995 *SA* (R)
Cucchiarelli, L 1966 *R* 1967 *R*
Cucchiella, G 1973 *A* (R) 1974 *Sus* 1979 *Sp, F, Pol, USS, NZ, Mor* 1980 *F, R, Fj, JAB, Coo* 1985 *USS, R* 1986 *Tun, F, Pt, E* 1987 *Pt, F, Fj*
Cuttitta, M 1990 *Pol, R, Sp, H, R, USS* 1991 *F, Nm, Nm, US, E, NZ, USS* 1992 *Sp, F, R, R, S* 1993 *Sp, F, Pt, Cro, Mor, Sp, F, Rus, F, S* 1994 *Sp, R, CZR* (R), *H, A, A, W, F* 1995 *S, I, Sa, E, Ar, F, Ar, R, NZ, SA* 1996 *W, Pt, W, E, S* 1997 *I, F, F, Ar, SA, I* 1998 *W, Rus, Ar* (R), *H, E* 1999 *F, S, W* 2000 *S, W, I, E* (R)

Cuttitta, M 1987 *Pt, F, R, NZ, Ar, Fj, USS, Sp* 1988 *F, R* 1989 *Z, USS* 1990 *Pol, R* 1991 *F, R, Nm, US, E, NZ, USS* 1992 *Sp, F, R, R, S* 1993 *Sp, F, Mor, Sp, F, F* 1994 *Sp, R, H, A, A, F* 1995 *S, I, Sa* 1996 *S* 1997 *I, F, F, Ar, R, SA, I* 1998 *S, W, Rus, Ar* 1999 *F*
Dagnini, G 1949 *F*
Dal Maso, D 2000 *Sa* (R), *Fj* 2001 *I, E* (R) 2004 *J, C, NZ, US* 2005 *I* (R), *W* (R), *S, E, F, A*
Dal Sie, M 1993 *Pt* 1994 *R, W* (R), *F* 1995 *F, Ar* 1996 *A*
D'Alberton, A 1966 *F, Ger, R* 1967 *F, R*
Daldoss, D 1979 *Pol, R, E, Sp, Mor*
D'Alessio, C 1937 *R, Bel, F* 1938 *Ger* 1939 *Ger*
Dallan, D 1999 *F, S, W* 2000 *S, W, I, E, F* (R), *C, R, NZ* 2001 *I, E, F, W, Fj, SA, Sa* 2002 *F, S, I, E, NZ, Sp, R* 2003 *W, I, E, F, S, Tg, C, W* 2004 *E, F, S, I, W, C* 2006 *J*
Dallan, M 1997 *Ar, R, I* 1998 *Ar* (R), *H, E* 1999 *SA, SA* (R) 2000 *S, Sa, C* 2001 *F, S* 2003 *Tg, C* 2004 *E, F* (R), *S*
Danieli, A 1955 *Ger, F, Sp, F, Cze*
D'Anna, V 1993 *Rus*
Dari, P 1951 *Sp* (R) 1952 *Sp, Ger, F* 1953 *Ger, R* 1954 *Sp, F*
De Angelis, G 1934 *Cat, R* 1935 *Cat, F* 1937 *R*
De Anna, E 1972 *Yug* 1973 *Cze, A* 1975 *F, Sp, R, Cze, E, Pol, H, Sp* 1976 *F, R* 1978 *Ar, USS, Sp* 1979 *F, R, Sp, Mor, F, USS, NZ* 1980 *F, R, Fj, JAB*
De Bernardo, R 1980 *USS, Sp* 1981 *F, R, USS, WGe* 1982 *R, E* 1983 *R, USS, C, C, Sp, Mor, F, A, USS* 1984 *F, USS* 1985 *R, E* 1988 *I* 1989 *Ar, Z*
De Biase, CF 1987 *Sp* 1988 *F, A*
De Carli, G 1996 *W* (R) 1997 *R* 1998 *S, Rus* (R), *Ar, H* (R), *E* 1999 *F, I, SA, SA, Ur, Fj* (R) 2000 *S* (R), *Sa* (R), *Fj* 2001 *I* (R), *E* (R), *W* (R), *SA* (R), *Ur, Fj* (R), *SA* (R), *Sa* 2002 *F* (R), *S, W, I, E* 2003 *W, I, E*
de Jager, B 2006 *J*
De Joanni, L 1983 *C* (R), *Mor, F, A* (R), *USS* 1984 *R, Tun, USS* 1985 *F, R, E, Sp* (R), *Z* 1986 *A, Tun* 1989 *F, R, Sp, Ar, Z* 1990 *R*
De Marchis, R 1935 *F*
De Marco, H 1993 *Pt*
de Marigny, R 2004 *E* (R), *F, S, I, W, US* 2005 *I, W, S*
De Rossi, A 1999 *Ur* (R), *Sp* (R), *E* (R) 2000 *I, E, F, Sa, C* (R), *R* (R), *NZ* (R) 2001 *SA, Ur* (R), *Ar* (R) 2002 *I* (R), *E* (R), *NZ, Sp, R* 2003 *W, I, E, F, S, I, Geo, Tg, C, W* 2004 *E, F, S, I, W, R*
De Rossi, C 1994 *Sp, H* (R), *R* (R)
De Santis, L 1952 *Sp*
De Stefani, M 1989 *Z*
De Vecchi, C 1948 *F*
Degli Antoni, G 1963 *F* 1965 *F* 1966 *F, Ger, R* 1967 *F*
Del Bono, G 1951 *Sp*
Del Bono, M 1960 *Ger, F* 1961 *Ger, F* 1962 *F, Ger, R* 1963 *F* 1964 *Ger, F*
Del Fava, CA 2004 *W, R, J* 2005 *I* (R), *W* (R), *S* (R), *E, F* (R), *Tg, Ar, Fj* 2006 *I* (R), *E* (R), *F, W* (R), *S* (R), *J* (R), *Fj*
Della Valle, C 1968 *WGe, Yug* 1969 *F* 1970 *Mad, Mad* 1971 *F*
Dellapè, S 2002 *F, S, I* (R), *E* (R), *NZ* (R), *Sp, Ar* 2003 *F* (R), *S* (R), *S, Geo, Tg, C, W* 2004 *E, F, S, I* (R), *W, C, NZ* 2005 *I, W, S, E* (R), *F, Ar* 2006 *I, E, W, S, J, Fj*
Delli Ficorilli, G 1969 *F*
Di Bello, A 1930 *Sp* 1933 *Cze, Cze* 1934 *Cat*
Di Carlo, F 1975 *Sp, R, Cze, Sp* (R) 1976 *F* (R), *Sp* 1977 *Pol, R, Pol* 1978 *Ar, USS* 1980 *JAB, Pol*
Di Cola, B 1973 *A*
Di Cola, G 1972 *Sp* (R), *Sp* 1973 *A*
Di Maura, F 1971 *Mor*
Di Zitti, A 1958 *R* 1960 *Ger* 1961 *Ger, F* 1962 *F, Ger, R* 1964 *Ger, F* 1965 *F, Cze* 1966 *F, Ger, R* 1967 *F, Pt, R* 1969 *Bul, Sp, Bel* 1972 *Pt, Sp*
Dolfato, R 1985 *F* 1986 *A* 1987 *Pt, Fj, USS, Sp* 1988 *F, R, USS*
Dominguez, D 1991 *F, R, Nm, Nm* (R), *US, E, NZ, USS* 1992 *Sp, F, R, S* 1993 *Sp, F, Rus, F, S* 1994 *R, H, R, W* 1995 *S, I, Sa, E, Ar, SA* 1996 *W, Pt, W, A, E, S* 1997 *I, F, F, Ar, R, SA, I* 1998 *S, W, Rus, Ar, H, E* 1999 *F, S, W, I, Ur, Sp, Fj, E, Tg, NZ* 2000 *S, W, I, E, F* 2001 *F, S, W, Fj, SA, Sa* 2002 *F, S, I, E, Ar* 2003 *W, I*
Donadona, D 1929 *Sp* 1930 *Sp*
Dora, G 1929 *Sp*
D'Orazio, R 1969 *Bul*
Dotti IV, M 1939 *R* 1940 *R, Ger*
Dotto, F 1971 *Mor, F* (R) 1972 *Pt, Pt, Sp*
Dotto, P 1993 *Sp* (R), *Cro* 1994 *Sp, R*
Faccioli, U 1948 *F*
Falancia, A 1975 *E, Pol*
Faliva, G 1999 *SA* (R) 2002 *NZ, Ar, A* (R)
Faltiba, G 1993 *Pt* (R)
Fanton, G 1979 *Pol* (R)
Farina, P 1987 *F, NZ, Fj*
Farinelli, P 1940 *R* 1949 *F, Cze* 1951 *Sp* 1952 *Sp*
Fattori, T 1936 *Ger, R* 1937 *R, Ger, F* 1938 *Ger* 1939 *Ger, R* 1940 *R, Ger*
Fava, E 1948 *F, Cze*
Favaretto, P 1951 *Sp*
Favaro, R 1988 *F, USS, A, I* 1989 *F, R, Sp, Ar, Z, USS* 1990 *F, Pol, R, H, R, USS* 1991 *F, R, Nm, Nm, US, E, NZ, USS* 1992 *Sp, F, R* 1993 *Sp, F, Cro, Sp, F* 1994 *CZR* (R), *A, A, R, W, F* 1995 *S, I, Sa* 1996 *Pt*
Favretto, G 1948 *Cze* 1949 *Cze*
Fedrigo, A 1972 *Yug* 1973 *Pt, Rho, WTv, Bor, NEC, Nat, ETv, Leo, FS, Cze, Yug, A* 1974 *Pt, Mid, Sus, Oxo, WGe, Leo* 1975 *F, Sp, R, Cze, E, Pol, H, Sp* 1976 *F, J, A, Sp* 1977 *F, Pol, R, Cze, R, Sp* 1978 *F, Ar* 1979 *Pol, R*
Fedrigo, P 1973 *Pt*
Ferracin, P 1975 *R, Cze, E, Pol, H, Sp* 1976 *F* 1977 *Mor, Pol* 1978 *USS*
Festuccia, C 2003 *W, I, E, F, S, S, I* (R), *Geo* (R), *NZ, Tg* (R), *C* (R), *W* (R) 2004 *E* (R), *F* (R), *S* (R), *I* (R) 2005 *F* (R), *Ar* (R), *Ar, A, Tg, Ar* 2006 *E* (R), *F* (R), *W, S* (R)
Figari, G 1940 *R, Ger* 1942 *R* (R)
Filizzola, EG 1993 *Pt, Mor, Sp, F, Rus, F, S* 1994 *Sp, CZR, A* 1995 *R* (R), *NZ* (R)
Finocchi, M 1968 *Yug* (R) 1969 *F* (R) 1970 *Cze, Mad, Mad, R* 1971 *Mor, R*
Fornari, G 1952 *Sp, Ger, F* 1953 *F, Ger, R* 1954 *Sp, F* 1955 *Ger, F, Sp, F, Cze* 1956 *Ger, F, Cze*
Francescato, B 1977 *Cze, R, Sp* 1978 *F, Sp* (R) 1979 *F* 1981 *R*
Francescato, I 1990 *R, USS* 1991 *F, R, US, E, NZ, USS* 1992 *R, S* 1993 *Mor, F* 1994 *Sp, H, R, W, F* 1995 *S, I, Sa, E, Ar, F, Ar, R, NZ, SA* 1996 *W, Pt, W, A, E, S* 1997 *F, F, Ar, R, SA*
Francescato, N 1972 *Yug* 1973 *Rho, WTv, Bor, NEC, Nat, ETv, Leo* 1974 *Pt* 1976 *J, A, Sp* 1977 *F, Mor, Pol, R, R, Sp* 1978 *F, Ar, USS, Sp* 1979 *F, R, E, Sp, Mor, F, Pol, USS, NZ* 1980 *F, R, Fj, JAB, Coo, Pol, USS, Sp* 1981 *F, R* 1982 *Mor*
Francescato, R 1976 *Sp* 1978 *Ar, USS* 1979 *Sp, F, Pol, USS, NZ, Mor* 1980 *F, R, Fj, JAB, Coo, Pol, USS, Sp* 1981 *F, R* 1982 *WGe* 1983 *F, R, USS, C, C, Sp, Mor, F, A* 1984 *Mor, R, Tun* 1985 *F, Sp, Z, USS* 1986 *Tun, F*
Franceschini, G 1975 *H, Sp* 1976 *F, J* 1977 *F, Pol, Pol, Cze, R, Sp* 1978 *F, USS*
Francese, A 1939 *R* 1940 *R*
Francesio, J 2000 *W* (R), *I, Sa* (R) 2001 *Ur*
Frati, F 2000 *C, NZ* (R) 2001 *I* (R), *S*
Frelich, F 1955 *Cze* 1957 *F, Ger* 1958 *F, R*
Fumei, M 1984 *F*
Fusco, A 1982 *E* (R) 1985 *R* 1986 *Tun, F, Tun* (R)
Fusco, E 1960 *Ger, F* 1961 *F* 1962 *F, Ger, R* 1963 *F* 1964 *Ger, F* 1965 *F* 1966 *F*
Gabanella, R 1951 *Sp* 1952 *Sp*
Gabrielli, P 1948 *Cze* 1949 *F, Cze* 1951 *Sp* 1954 *F*
Gaetaniello, F 1975 *H* (R) 1976 *R, A, Sp* (R) 1977 *F, Pol, R, Pol, R, Sp* 1978 *Sp* 1979 *Pol, R, E, Sp, Mor, F, Pol, USS, NZ, Mor* 1980 *Fj, JAB, Sp* 1981 *F, R, USS, WGe* 1982 *F, R, E, WGe, Mor* 1983 *F, R, USS, C, C, Sp*
Gaetaniello, F 1980 *Sp* (R) 1982 *E* 1984 *USS* 1985 *R, Sp, Z* (R), *Z, USS, R* 1986 *Pt, E, A, Tun, USS* 1987 *Pt, F, NZ, Ar, Fj, USS, Sp* 1988 *F* 1990 *F, R, Sp, H* 1991 *Nm, US, E, NZ*
Galeazzo, A 1985 *Sp* 1987 *Pt, R, Ar, USS*
Galletto, M 1972 *Pt, Sp, Yug*
Galon, E 2001 *I* (R) 2005 *Tg, Ar, Fj* 2006 *W, S* (R)

Ganzerla, R 1973 *Bor, NEC*
Gardin, M 1981 *USS, WGe* 1982 *Mor* 1983 *F, R* 1984 *Mor, R, USS* 1985 *E, USS, R* 1986 *Tun, F, Pt, Tun, USS* 1987 *Pt, F, R, NZ, Ar, Fj, USS, Sp* 1988 *R*
Gardner, JM 1992 *R, S* 1993 *Rus, F* 1994 *Sp, R, H, F* 1995 *S* (R), *I, Sa, E, Ar* 1996 *W* 1997 *I, F, SA, I* 1998 *S, W*
Gargiullo, P 1973 *FS* (R) 1974 *Mid, Sus, Oxo*
Garguillo, F 1972 *Yug*
Garguilo, F 1967 *F, Pt* 1968 *Yug* 1974 *Sus*
Garozzo, S 2001 *Ur, Ar* 2002 *Ar*
Gatto, M 1967 *Pt, R*
Gattoni, G 1933 *Cze, Cze*
Gerardo, A 1968 *Yug* 1969 *Sp* 1970 *Cze, Mad* 1971 *R* 1972 *Sp*
Geremia, G 1956 *Cze*
Gerosa, E 1952 *Sp, Ger, F* 1953 *F, Ger, R* 1954 *Sp*
Gerosa, M 1994 *CZR, A, A, R, W* 1995 *E, Ar*
Ghezzi, C 1938 *Ger* 1939 *Ger, R* 1940 *R, Ger*
Ghini, A 1981 *USS* (R), *WGe* 1982 *F, R, E, Mor* 1983 *F, R, C, Mor, F, A, USS* 1984 *F, Mor, R, USS* 1985 *F, R, E, Z, Z, USS* 1987 *Fj* 1988 *R, USS* (R)
Ghiraldini, L 2006 *J* (R), *Fj* (R)
Ghizzoni, S 1977 *F, Mor* (R), *Pol, R, Pol, Cze, R, Sp* 1978 *F, Ar, USS* 1979 *F, Pol, Sp, Mor, F, Pol* 1980 *R, Fj, JAB, Coo, Pol, USS, Sp* 1981 *F* 1982 *F, R, E, WGe, Mor* 1983 *F, USS, C, C, Sp, Mor, F, A, USS* 1984 *F, Mor, R, Tun, USS* 1985 *F, R, E, Z, Z, USS, R* 1986 *F, E, A, Tun, USS* 1987 *Pt, F, R, NZ*
Giacheri, M 1992 *R* 1993 *Sp, F, Pt, Rus, F, S* 1994 *Sp, R, CZR* (R), *H, A, A, F* 1995 *S, I, E, Ar, F, Ar, R, NZ, SA* 1996 *W* 1999 *S, W, I, Ur, Fj, E, Tg, NZ* 2001 *Nm* (R), *SA, Ur, Ar, SA* 2002 *F* (R), *S* (R), *W, I, E, NZ, A* (R) 2003 *E, F, S, I*
Giani, G 1966 *Ger, R* 1967 *F, Pt, R*
Gini, G 1968 *Pt, WGe, Yug* 1969 *Bul, Sp, Bel, F* 1970 *Cze, Mad, Mad, R* 1971 *Mor, F* 1972 *Pt, Pt* 1974 *Mid, Oxo*
Giorgio, G 1968 *Pt, WGe*
Giovanelli, M 1989 *Z* (R), *USS* 1990 *Pol, Sp, H, R, USS* 1991 *F, R, Nm, E, NZ, USS* 1992 *Sp, F, S* 1993 *Sp, F, Pt, Cro, Mor* (R), *Sp, F* 1994 *R, CZR, H, A, A* 1995 *F* (R), *Ar, R, NZ, SA* 1996 *A, E, S* 1997 *F, F, Ar, R, SA, I* 1998 *S, W, Rus, Ar, H, E* 1999 *S, W, I, SA, SA, Ur, Sp* (R), *Fj, E, Tg, NZ* 2000 *S*
Giugovaz, E 1965 *Cze* 1966 *F*
Giuliani, R 1951 *Sp*
Gorni, M 1939 *R* 1940 *R, Ger*
Goti, M 1990 *H*
Grasselli, G 1952 *Ger*
Grespan, G 1989 *F, Sp, USS* 1990 *F, R* (R) 1991 *R, NZ* (R), *USS* 1992 *R, S* 1993 *Sp, F, Cro, Sp, F* (R), *Rus* (R) 1994 *Sp, CZR, R, W*
Griffen, P 2004 *E, F, S, I, W, R* (R), *J, C, NZ, US* 2005 *W* (R), *S* (R), *F* (R), *Ar, Ar, A, Tg, Ar, Fj* 2006 *I, E, F, W, S, J, Fj*
Gritti, A 1996 *Pt* 2000 *S, W, I, E, F, Sa, Fj, C, R, NZ* 2001 *E, F, S, W*
Guidi, G 1996 *Pt, E* (R) 1997 *F* (R), *Ar* (R), *R*
Innocenti, M 1981 *WGe* 1982 *F, R, E, WGe, Mor* 1983 *F, USS* (R), *C, C, Mor, F, A, USS* 1984 *F, Mor, Tun, USS* 1985 *F, R, E, Sp, USS, R* 1986 *Tun, F, Pt, E, A, Tun, USS* 1987 *Pt, F, R, NZ, Ar, Fj, USS, Sp* 1988 *F, R, A*
Intoppa, G 2004 *R* (R), *J* (R), *C* (R), *NZ* (R) 2005 *I* (R), *W* (R), *E* (R)
Jannone, C 1981 *USS* 1982 *F, R*
Lanfranchi, S 1949 *F, Cze* 1953 *F, Ger, R* 1954 *Sp, F* 1955 *F* 1956 *Ger, Cze* 1957 *F* 1958 *F* 1959 *F* 1960 *F* 1961 *F* 1962 *F, Ger, R* 1963 *F* 1964 *Ger, F*
Lanzi, G 1998 *Ar* (R), *H* (R), *E* (R) 1999 *Sp* 2000 *S* (R), *W, I* (R) 2001 *I* (R)
Lari, G 1972 *Yug* (R) 1973 *Yug, A* 1974 *Pt, Mid, Sus, Oxo, Leo*
Lazzarini, E 1970 *Cze* 1971 *Mor, F, R* 1972 *Pt, Pt, Sp, Sp* 1973 *Pt, Rho, WTv, Bor, NEC, Leo, FS, Tva, Cze, Yug, A* 1974 *Pt, Mid, Sus, Oxo, WGe*
Levorato, U 1956 *Ger, F* 1957 *F* 1958 *F, R* 1959 *F* 1961 *Ger, F* 1962 *F, Ger, R* 1963 *F* 1964 *Ger, F* 1965 *F*
Lijoi, A 1977 *Pol, R* (R) 1978 *Sp* 1979 *R* (R), *Mor*
Limone, G 1979 *E, Mor, USS* (R), *Mor* 1980 *JAB, Sp* 1981 *USS, WGe* 1982 *E* (R) 1983 *USS*
Lo Cicero, A 2000 *E, F, Sa, Fj, C, R, NZ* 2001 *I, E, F, S, W, Fj, SA, Sa* (R) 2002 *F, S* (R), *W* (R), *Sp, R, A* 2003 *F, S, S, I, Geo, Tg, C, W* 2004 *E, F, S, I, W, R, J, C, NZ, US* 2005 *I, W, S, E, F, Ar, Ar, A, Tg, Ar* 2006 *E* (R), *F* (R), *W* (R), *S* (R), *J, Fj*
Loranzi, C 1973 *Nat* (R), *ETv, Leo* (R), *FS* (R), *Tva* (R)
Lorigiola, F 1979 *Sp, F, Pol, USS, NZ, Mor* 1980 *F, R, Fj, JAB, Pol, USS, Sp* 1981 *F, R, USS* 1982 *WGe* 1983 *R* (R), *USS, C, Sp* 1984 *Tun* 1985 *Sp* 1986 *Pt, E, A, Tun, USS* 1987 *Pt, F, R, NZ, Ar* 1988 *F*
Luchini, G 1973 *Rho, Nat*
Luise, L 1955 *Ger, F, Sp, F, Cze* 1956 *Ger, F, Cze* 1957 *Ger* 1958 *F*
Luise III, R 1959 *F* 1960 *Ger, F* 1961 *Ger, F* 1962 *F, Ger, R* 1965 *F, Cze* 1966 *F* 1971 *R* 1972 *Pt, Sp, Sp* (R)
Lupini, T 1987 *R, NZ, Ar, Fj, USS, Sp* 1988 *F, R, USS, A* 1989 *R*
Maestri, O 1935 *Cat, F* 1937 *Ger* (R)
Maffioli, R 1933 *Cze, Cze* 1934 *Cat, R* 1935 *Cat* 1936 *Ger, R* 1937 *Ger, R, Bel, Ger*
Maini, R 1948 *F, Cze*
Malosti, G 1953 *F* 1954 *Sp* 1955 *F* 1956 *Ger, F* 1957 *F* 1958 *F*
Mancini, G 1952 *Ger, F* 1953 *F, Ger, R* 1954 *Sp, F* 1955 *Cze* 1956 *Ger, F, Cze* 1957 *F*
Mandelli, R 2004 *I* (R), *W* (R), *R* (R), *J* (R), *US* (R)
Mannato, A 2004 *US* (R) 2005 *Ar, A*
Manni, E 1976 *J* (R), *A, Sp* 1977 *Mor*
Manteri, L 1996 *W, A, E, S* (R)
Marcato, A 2006 *J* (R)
Marchetto, M 1972 *Yug* 1973 *Pt, Cze, Yug* 1974 *Pt, Mid, Sus, WGe, Leo* 1975 *F, Sp, R, Cze, E, Pol, H, Sp* 1976 *F, R, J, A, Sp* 1977 *F, Mor, Pol, R, Cze* (R), *R, Sp* 1978 *F, USS* (R), *Sp* 1979 *F, Pol* (R), *R, E, Pol* (R), *USS, NZ, Mor* 1980 *F, Coo* 1981 *USS*
Marescalchi, A 1933 *Cze* 1935 *F* (R) 1937 *R*
Mariani, P 1976 *R, A, Sp* 1977 *F, Pol* 1978 *F* (R), *Ar, USS, Sp* 1979 *F, Pol, R, Sp, F, Pol, USS, NZ, Mor* 1980 *F, R, Fj, JAB*
Marini, P 1949 *F, Cze* 1951 *Sp* 1953 *F, Ger, R* 1955 *Ger*
Martin, L 1997 *F* (R), *R* (R) 1998 *S, W, Rus, H, E* 1999 *F, S, W, I, SA, SA, Ur, Sp* (R), *Fj, E* 2000 *S, W, I, E, F, Sa, Fj, C, R, NZ* 2001 *I, E, S, W* (R), *SA, Ar, Fj* (R), *SA, Sa* 2002 *F, S* (R)
Martinenghi, F 1952 *Sp, Ger*
Martinez-Frugoni, R 2002 *NZ, Sp* (R), *R* (R) 2003 *W, I, E, F, S, S* (R), *NZ*
Martini, G 1965 *F* 1967 *F* 1968 *Pt*
Martini, R 1959 *F* 1960 *Ger, F* 1961 *Ger, F* 1964 *Ger, F* 1965 *F* 1968 *WGe, Yug*
Masci, P 1948 *Cze* 1949 *F, Cze* 1952 *Sp, Ger, F* 1953 *F* 1954 *Sp* 1955 *F*
Mascioletti, M 1977 *Mor, Pol* 1978 *Ar, USS, Sp* 1979 *Pol, E, Sp, Mor, F, Pol, USS, NZ, Mor* 1980 *F, R, Fj* 1981 *WGe* 1982 *F, R, WGe* 1983 *F, R, USS, C, C, Sp, Mor, F, A, USS* 1984 *F, Mor, Tun* 1985 *F, R, Z, Z, USS, R* 1986 *Tun, F, Pt, E, Tun, USS* 1987 *NZ, Ar, Fj* 1989 *Sp, Ar, Z, USS* 1990 *Pol*
Masi, A 1999 *Sp* 2003 *E* (R), *F* (R), *S, S, I* (R), *NZ, Tg* (R), *C* (R), *W* 2004 *E, I* (R), *W, R, J, C* 2005 *I, W, S, E, F, Ar, Ar, A* 2006 *J, Fj*
Mastrodomenico, L 2000 *Sa* (R), *C* (R), *NZ* (R) 2001 *Nm, Ar* (R)
Matacchini, I 1948 *F, Cze* 1949 *F, Cze* 1954 *Sp* 1955 *Ger, F, Sp, F*
Mattarolo, L 1973 *Bor, Nat, ETv, Leo, FS, Tva, Cze*
Mattei, M 1967 *R*
Mazzantini, F 1965 *Cze* 1966 *F* 1967 *F*
Mazzantini, M 2000 *S* (R) 2001 *S* (R), *W* 2002 *E* (R), *NZ* 2003 *E* (R), *F* (R), *Geo, NZ, C* (R)
Mazzariol, F 1995 *F, Ar* (R), *R, NZ* 1996 *Pt* (R) 1997 *F* (R), *R* (R), *SA* (R) 1998 *Ar, H* (R) 1999 *F* (R), *SA, SA, Sp* (R), *E* (R), *NZ* (R) 2000 *Fj* (R), *C* 2001 *Nm, SA, Ur, Ar, Fj* (R), *SA* (R) 2002 *W* (R), *NZ, Sp* 2003 *S* (R), *I, NZ, C* (R), *W* (R) 2004 *R*
Mazzi, G 1998 *H* (R) 1999 *SA, SA, Ur* (R), *Sp* (R)
Mazzucato, N 1995 *SA* 1996 *Pt, S* 1997 *I* (R) 1999 *Sp, E*

(R), *Tg* (R), *NZ* (R) 2000 *F*, *Sa*, *Fj*, *R* 2001 *Nm*, *SA*, *Ur*, *Ar* 2002 *W*, *I*, *E*, *NZ*, *Sp*, *R*, *Ar*, *A* 2003 *E*, *F*, *S*, *I*, *NZ*, *Tg*, *W* 2004 *E*, *F* (R), *S*, *I*, *W*, *R*, *J* (R)
Mazzucchelli, I 1965 *F*, *Cze* 1966 *F*, *Ger*, *R* 1967 *F* 1968 *Pt*, *WGe* 1969 *Bul*, *F* 1971 *F* 1972 *Pt*, *Sp* 1974 *WGe* 1975 *F*, *R*, *Cze*, *Pol* 1976 *F*, *R*
Menapace, P 1996 *Pt* (R)
Michelon, E 1969 *Bel*, *F* 1970 *Cze*, *Mad*, *Mad*, *R* (R) 1971 *R*
Miele, A 1968 *Yug* 1970 *Mad* (R) 1971 *R* 1972 *Pt*, *Sp*
Milano, GE 1990 *USS* (R)
Mioni, A 1955 *Ger*, *F*, *F* 1957 *F*
Modonesi, A 1929 *Sp*
Modonesi, L 1966 *Ger*, *R* 1967 *F*, *Pt*, *R* 1968 *Pt*, *WGe* 1970 *Cze*, *Mad*, *Mad*, *R* 1971 *F* 1974 *Leo* 1975 *F*, *Sp*, *R*, *Cze*
Molari, N 1957 *F* 1958 *R*
Molinari, F 1973 *NEC*
Molinari, G 1948 *F*
Monfeli, P 1970 *R* 1971 *Mor*, *F* 1972 *Pt* 1976 *J*, *A*, *Sp* 1977 *F*, *R*, *Cze*, *R*, *Sp* 1978 *F*
Morelli, G 1988 *I* 1989 *F*, *R*
Morelli, G 1976 *F* (R) 1982 *F*, *R*, *Mor* 1983 *R*, *C*, *Sp*, *A*, *USS* 1984 *Mor*, *R*, *USS* 1985 *R*, *E*, *Z*, *Z*, *USS*, *R* 1986 *Tun*, *F*, *E*, *A*, *Tun*, *USS* 1987 *F*, *NZ*
Morelli, G 1981 *WGe* 1982 *R*, *E*, *Mor* 1983 *USS* (R) 1984 *F*
Moreno, A 1999 *Tg*, *NZ* 2002 *F* (R), *S* (R)
Moretti, A 1997 *R* (R) 1998 *Rus* (R) 1999 *Ur* (R), *Sp*, *Tg* (R), *NZ* 2002 *E* (R), *NZ*, *Sp*, *R*, *Ar*, *A* (R) 2005 *Ar*
Moretti, U 1933 *Cze* (R) 1934 *R* 1935 *Cat* 1937 *R*, *Ger*, *F* 1942 *R*
Morimondi, A 1930 *Sp* 1933 *Cze* 1934 *Cat* 1935 *Cat*
Moscardi, A 1993 *Pt* 1995 *R* (R) 1996 *S* (R) 1998 *Ar*, *H*, *E* 1999 *F*, *S*, *W*, *I*, *SA*, *SA*, *Ur*, *Fj*, *E*, *Tg*, *NZ* (R) 2000 *S*, *W*, *I*, *E*, *F*, *Sa*, *Fj*, *C*, *R*, *NZ* 2001 *I*, *E*, *F*, *S*, *W*, *Nm*, *SA*, *Ur*, *Ar*, *Fj*, *SA*, *Sa* 2002 *F*, *S*, *W*, *I*, *E*
Muraro, A 2000 *C*, *R*, *NZ* 2001 *I*, *E*, *Nm*, *SA*, *Ur* (R), *Ar*, *Fj*, *SA*, *Sa* 2002 *F*
Nathan, E 1930 *Sp*
Navarini, G 1957 *Ger* 1958 *R*
Nicolosi, M 1982 *R*
Nieto, C 2002 *E* 2005 *Ar*, *Ar*, *A* (R), *Tg*, *Ar*, *Fj* (R) 2006 *I*, *E*, *F*, *W*, *J*, *Fj*
Nisti, A 1929 *Sp* (R) 1930 *Sp*
Nitoglia, L 2004 *C*, *NZ*, *US* 2005 *I*, *W*, *S*, *E*, *F*, *Ar*, *Tg*, *Ar*, *Fj* 2006 *I*, *E*, *F*, *W*, *S*
Ongaro, F 2000 *C* 2001 *Nm* (R), *SA*, *Ur* (R), *Ar* (R) 2002 *Ar* (R), *A* 2003 *E* (R), *F* (R), *S* (R), *I*, *Geo*, *NZ* (R), *Tg*, *C*, *W* 2004 *E*, *F*, *S*, *I*, *W*, *R*, *J*, *C*, *NZ*, *US* 2005 *I*, *W*, *S*, *E*, *F*, *Tg* (R), *Ar* (R), *Fj* 2006 *I*, *E*, *F*, *W* (R), *S*, *J*, *Fj*
Orlandi, C 1992 *S* 1993 *Sp*, *F*, *Mor*, *F*, *Rus*, *F*, *S* 1994 *Sp*, *CZR*, *H*, *A*, *A*, *R*, *W* 1995 *S*, *I*, *Sa*, *E*, *Ar*, *F*, *Ar*, *R*, *NZ*, *SA* 1996 *W*, *Pt*, *W*, *A*, *E*, *S* 1997 *I*, *F*, *F*, *Ar*, *R*, *SA*, *I* 1998 *S*, *W* 2000 *W* (R), *F* (R)
Orlando, S 2004 *E* (R), *S* (R), *W* (R), *C* (R), *NZ* (R), *US* 2005 *E* (R), *F* (R), *Ar* (R), *A* (R) 2006 *J*
Orquera, L 2004 *C* (R), *NZ* (R), *US* 2005 *I*, *W*, *S*, *E*, *F*, *Ar*, *Tg* (R)
Osti, A 1981 *F*, *R*, *USS* 1982 *E*, *Mor* 1983 *R*, *C*, *A*, *USS* 1984 *R*, *USS* 1985 *F* 1986 *Tun* 1988 *R*
Pace, S 2001 *SA* (R), *Sa* 2005 *Fj*
Pace, S 1977 *Mor* 1984 *R*, *Tun*
Pacifici, P 1969 *Bul*, *Sp*, *F* 1970 *Cze*, *Mad*, *Mad*, *R* 1971 *Mor*, *F*
Paciucci, R 1937 *R*, *Ger*, *F*
Paganelli, F 1972 *Sp* (R)
Palmer, S 2002 *Ar*, *A* (R) 2003 *I* (R), *E* (R), *F* (R), *S* (R), *S*, *NZ*, *C* (R), *W* (R) 2004 *I*, *R* (R)
Paoletti, P 1972 *Pt*, *Sp*, *Yug* 1973 *Pt*, *Rho*, *WTv*, *Bor*, *NEC*, *Nat*, *ETv*, *Leo*, *FS*, *Tva* 1974 *Mid*, *Oxo*, *WGe*, *Leo* 1975 *F*, *Sp* 1976 *R*
Paoletti, T 2000 *S*, *W*, *I*, *E*, *F*, *Sa*, *C* (R), *R* (R), *NZ* (R) 2001 *F*, *Nm* (R), *Ur* (R), *Ar* (R), *Fj* (R), *SA* (R)
Paolin, G 1929 *Sp*
Parisse, S 2002 *NZ*, *Sp*, *R*, *Ar* (R), *A* 2003 *S* (R), *I*, *Geo*, *NZ* (R), *Tg*, *C*, *W* 2004 *E*, *F*, *S* 2005 *I*, *W*, *S*, *E*, *F*, *Ar*, *Ar*, *A*, *Tg*, *Ar*, *Fj* 2006 *I*, *E*, *F*, *W*, *S*, *Fj*
Parmiggiani, E 1942 *R* 1948 *Cze*
Paseli, P 1929 *Sp* 1930 *Sp* 1933 *Cze*
Passarotto, E 1975 *Sp* (R)
Pavanello, E 2002 *R*, *Ar* (R), *A* 2004 *R*, *J*, *C* (R), *NZ* (R), *US* 2005 *Ar* (R), *A* (R)
Pavesi, P 1977 *Pol* 1979 *Mor* 1980 *USS*
Pavin, M 1980 *USS* 1986 *F* (R), *Pt*, *E*, *A*, *Tun*, *USS* 1987 *Ar*
Pedrazzi, R 2001 *Nm*, *Ar* (R) 2002 *F*, *S*, *W* 2005 *S* (R), *E*, *F* (R)
Pedroni, P 1989 *Z*, *USS* 1990 *F*, *Pol*, *R* 1991 *F*, *R* (R), *Nm* 1993 *Rus*, *F* 1994 *Sp*, *R*, *CZR*, *H* 1995 *I*, *Sa*, *E*, *Ar*, *F*, *Ar*, *R*, *NZ*, *SA* 1996 *W*, *W*
Peens, G 2002 *W*, *I*, *E*, *NZ*, *Sp*, *R*, *Ar* (R), *A* (R) 2003 *E* (R), *F* (R), *S* (R), *S*, *I*, *Geo* (R), *NZ* 2004 *NZ* (R) 2005 *E*, *F*, *Ar*, *Ar*, *A*
Pelliccione, L 1983 *Sp*, *Mor*, *F*
Pelliccione, L 1977 *Pol*
Percudani, M 1952 *F* 1954 *F* 1955 *Ger*, *Sp*, *F*, *Cze* 1956 *Cze* 1957 *F* 1958 *R*
Perrini, F 1955 *Sp*, *F*, *Cze* 1956 *Ger*, *F*, *Cze* 1957 *F* 1958 *F* 1959 *F* 1962 *R* 1963 *F*
Perrone, F 1951 *Sp*
Persico, AR 2000 *S* (R), *W* (R), *E* (R), *F* (R), *Sa*, *Fj* 2001 *F*, *S*, *W*, *Nm*, *SA* (R), *Ur*, *Ar*, *Fj*, *SA*, *Sa* (R) 2002 *F* (R), *S* (R), *W*, *I*, *E*, *NZ*, *Sp*, *R*, *Ar*, *A* 2003 *W*, *I*, *E*, *F*, *S*, *I* (R), *Geo*, *Tg*, *C*, *W* 2004 *E*, *F*, *S*, *I*, *W*, *R*, *J* (R), *C*, *NZ* 2005 *I*, *W*, *S*, *E*, *F*, *Ar*, *Ar*, *Tg*, *Ar* 2006 *I* (R), *E* (R)
Pertile, J 1994 *R* 1995 *Ar* 1996 *W* (R), *A*, *E*, *S* 1997 *I*, *F*, *SA* 1998 *Rus* 1999 *S*, *W*, *I*, *SA*, *SA*
Perugini, S 2000 *I* (R), *F* (R), *Sa* (R), *Fj* (R) 2001 *S* (R), *W* (R), *Nm*, *SA*, *Ur*, *Ar* 2002 *W*, *I* (R) 2003 *W* (R), *S*, *Geo* (R), *NZ*, *Tg* (R), *W* (R) 2004 *E* (R), *F* (R), *I* (R), *W* (R), *C*, *NZ*, *US* 2005 *I* (R), *W* (R), *S* (R), *E*, *F* 2006 *I*, *E*, *F*, *W*, *S*
Perziano, L 1993 *Pt*
Perziano, M 2000 *NZ* 2001 *F*, *S*, *W*, *Nm*, *SA*, *Ur*, *Ar*, *Fj*, *SA*
Pesce, V 1988 *I* 1989 *R* (R)
Pescetto, P 1956 *Ger*, *Cze* 1957 *F*
Petralia, G 1984 *F*
Pez, R 2000 *Sa*, *Fj*, *C* (R), *R*, *NZ* 2001 *I* 2002 *S* (R), *W*, *E* (R), *A* 2003 *I* (R), *E*, *F*, *S*, *S*, *Geo* 2005 *Ar*, *A*, *Tg*, *Ar*, *Fj* 2006 *I*, *E*, *F*, *W*, *S*, *J*, *Fj*
Phillips, M 2002 *F*, *S*, *W* (R), *I*, *E* 2003 *W*, *I*, *E*, *F*, *S*, *S*, *I* (R), *NZ*, *W* (R)
Pianna, G 1934 *R* 1935 *Cat*, *F* 1936 *Ger*, *R* 1938 *Ger*
Piazza, A 1990 *USS*
Piccini, F 1963 *F* 1964 *Ger* 1966 *F*
Picone, S 2004 *I* (R), *W* (R) 2005 *F* 2006 *E* (R), *F* (R), *S* (R), *J* (R)
Pietroscanti, F 1987 *USS*, *Sp* 1988 *A*, *I* 1989 *F*, *R*, *Sp*, *Ar*, *Z*, *USS* 1990 *F*, *Pol*, *R*, *H* 1991 *Nm*, *Nm* 1992 *Sp*, *F*, *R* 1993 *Sp* (R), *Mor* (R), *Sp*, *F*, *Rus*, *F*
Pignotti, F 1968 *WGe*, *Yug* 1969 *Bul*, *Sp*, *Bel*
Pilat, C 1997 *I* 1998 *S*, *W* 2000 *E*, *Sa* 2001 *I*, *W* (R)
Pini, MJ 1998 *H*, *E* 1999 *F*, *Ur*, *Fj*, *E*, *Tg*, *NZ* 2000 *S*, *W*, *I*, *F*
Piovan, M 1973 *Pt* 1974 *Pt*, *Mid*, *Sus* (R), *Oxo* 1976 *A* 1977 *F*, *Mor*, *R* 1979 *F* (R)
Piovan, R 1996 *Pt* (R) 1997 *R* 2000 *R*, *NZ*
Piovene, M 1995 *NZ* (R)
Piras, E 1971 *R* (R)
Pisaneschi, M 1948 *Cze* (R) 1949 *Cze* 1953 *F*, *Ger*, *R* 1954 *Sp*, *F* 1955 *Ger*, *F*, *Sp*, *F*, *Cze*
Pitorri, F 1948 *Cze* 1949 *F*
Pitorri, M 1973 *NEC* (R)
Pivetta, G 1979 *R* (R), *E*, *Mor* 1980 *Coo*, *USS* 1981 *R*, *USS*, *WGe* 1982 *F*, *R*, *WGe*, *Mor* 1983 *F*, *USS* (R), *C*, *Sp*, *Mor* (R), *F* (R), *USS* 1984 *F*, *Mor*, *R*, *Tun* 1985 *F*, *R* (R), *Sp*, *Z*, *Z* 1986 *Pt* 1987 *Sp* 1989 *R*, *Sp* 1990 *F*, *Pol* (R), *R*, *Sp*, *R*, *USS* 1991 *F*, *R*, *Nm*, *Nm*, *US*, *E*, *NZ*, *USS* 1992 *Sp*, *F*, *R*, *R* 1993 *Cro*, *Mor* (R), *Sp*
Platania, M 1994 *F* 1995 *F* (R), *R* 1996 *Pt*
Ponchia, I 1955 *F*, *Sp*, *F*, *Cze* 1956 *F* 1957 *Ger* 1958 *F*
Ponzi, E 1973 *Cze*, *A* 1974 *WGe* 1975 *F*, *Sp*, *R*, *Cze*, *E*, *Pol*, *H*, *Sp* 1976 *F*, *R*, *J*, *A*, *Sp* 1977 *F*, *Mor*, *Pol*, *R*
Porcellato, G 1989 *R*
Porzio, G 1970 *Cze*, *Mad*, *Mad*
Possamai, C 1970 *Cze*, *Mad*, *Mad*
Pozzebon, W 2001 *I* (R), *E*, *F*, *S*, *W*, *Nm*, *SA*, *Ur*, *Ar*, *Fj*, *SA*,

Sa 2002 *NZ* (R), *Sp* (R) 2004 *R*, *J*, *C* (R), *NZ*, *US* 2005 *W*, *E* (R)
Pratichetti, C 1988 *R* 1990 *Pol*
Pratichetti, M 2004 *NZ*
Preo, G 1999 *I* 2000 *I* (R), *E* (R), *Sa* (R), *Fj*, *R* (R), *NZ* (R)
Presutti, P 1974 *Mid*, *Sus*, *Oxo* 1977 *Pol*, *Cze*, *R*, *Sp* 1978 *F*
Properzi-Curti, FP 1990 *Pol*, *Sp*, *H*, *R* 1991 *F*, *Nm*, *Nm*, *US*, *E*, *NZ* 1992 *Sp*, *F*, *R* 1993 *Cro* (R), *Mor*, *F*, *Rus*, *F*, *S* 1994 *Sp* (R), *R*, *H*, *A*, *A* 1995 *S*, *I*, *Sa*, *E*, *Ar*, *NZ*, *SA* 1996 *W*, *Pt*, *W*, *A*, *E* 1997 *I*, *F*, *F*, *Ar*, *SA* 1998 *Ar* 1999 *S*, *W*, *I*, *SA*, *SA*, *Ur*, *E*, *Tg* (R), *NZ* (R) 2001 *F* (R), *S*, *W*
Prosperini, C 1966 *R* 1967 *F*, *Pt*, *R*
Pucciarello, F 1999 *Sp*, *Fj*, *E* 2002 *S*, *W* (R), *I* (R), *E* (R), *Ar*
Puglisi, G 1971 *F* 1972 *Yug* 1973 *Cze*
Pulli, M 1968 *Pt* 1972 *Pt*, *Pt*
Puppo, A 1972 *Pt* (R), *Pt*, *Sp*, *Sp* 1973 *Pt*, *Rho*, *WTv*, *Bor*, *NEC*, *Nat*, *ETv*, *Leo*, *FS*, *Tva* 1974 *Mid*, *Sus*, *Oxo*, *WGe*, *Leo* 1977 *R*
Quaglio, I 1970 *R* 1971 *R* 1972 *Pt*, *Sp* 1973 *WTv*, *Bor*, *NEC*, *Nat*, *Leo*, *FS*, *Tva* 1975 *H*, *Sp* 1976 *F*, *R*
Quaglio, M 1984 *Tun* (R) 1988 *F*, *R*
Queirolo, JM 2000 *Sa*, *Fj* 2001 *E*, *F* (R), *Fj* (R) 2002 *NZ* (R), *Sp* (R), *A* 2003 *Geo* (R)
Quintavala, P 1958 *R*
Raffo, C 1929 *Sp* 1930 *Sp* 1933 *Cze*, *Cze* 1937 *R*, *Bel*
Raineri, G 1998 *H* (R) 2000 *Fj*, *R*, *NZ* 2001 *I*, *E*, *S* (R), *W*, *Nm*, *SA* (R), *Ur*, *Ar* 2002 *W* (R), *I*, *E*, *NZ* 2003 *W*, *I*, *E*, *F*, *S*, *Geo*
Raisi, G 1956 *Ger*, *F* 1957 *F*, *Ger* 1960 *Ger* 1964 *Ger*, *F*
Rampazzo, R 1996 *W* (R) 1999 *I* (R)
Ravazzolo, M 1993 *Cro*, *Sp*, *F*, *F* (R), *S* 1994 *Sp* (R), *R* (R), *CZR*, *H* 1995 *S*, *I*, *Sa*, *F* (R), *Ar*, *NZ* 1996 *W*, *Pt*, *W*, *A* 1997 *F*, *Ar*, *R*, *SA* (R)
Re Garbagnati, A 1936 *Ger*, *R* 1937 *Ger*, *Bel*, *Ger*, *F* 1938 *Ger* 1939 *Ger*, *R* 1940 *R*, *Ger* 1942 *R*
Reale, P 1987 *USS*, *Sp* 1988 *USS*, *A*, *I* 1989 *Z* 1992 *S*
Riccardi, G 1955 *Ger*, *F*, *Sp*, *F*, *Cze* 1956 *F*, *Cze*
Ricci, G 1967 *Pt* 1969 *Bul*, *Sp*, *Bel*, *F*
Ricciarelli, G 1962 *Ger*
Riccioni, L 1951 *Sp* 1952 *Sp*, *Ger*, *F* 1953 *F*, *Ger* 1954 *F*
Rigo, S 1992 *S* 1993 *Sp*, *F*, *Pt*
Rinaldo, A 1977 *Mor*, *Pol*, *R*, *Cze*
Rista, W 1968 *Yug* (R) 1969 *Bul*, *Sp*, *Bel*, *F*
Rivaro, M 2000 *S* (R), *W*, *I* (R) 2001 *E* (R)
Rizzo, M 2005 *A* (R)
Rizzoli, G 1935 *F* (R) 1936 *Ger*, *R*
Robazza, C 1978 *Ar*, *Sp* 1979 *F*, *Pol*, *R*, *E*, *Sp*, *F*, *Pol*, *USS*, *NZ*, *Mor* 1980 *F*, *R*, *Fj*, *JAB*, *Coo*, *Pol*, *Sp* 1981 *F*, *R*, *USS*, *WGe* 1982 *E*, *WGe* 1983 *F*, *USS*, *C*, *Mor*, *F* 1984 *F*, *Tun* 1985 *F*
Robertson, K 2004 *R*, *J*, *C*, *NZ*, *US* 2005 *I* (R), *W* (R), *S* (R), *F*, *Ar*, *Ar*, *A*
Rocca, A 1973 *WTv* (R), *Bor*, *NEC* (R) 1977 *R*
Romagnoli, G 1965 *F*, *Cze* 1967 *Pt*, *R*
Romagnoli, S 1982 *Mor* 1984 *R*, *Tun*, *USS* 1985 *F*, *Z*, *Z* 1986 *Tun* (R), *Pt*, *A*, *Tun*, *USS* 1987 *Pt*, *F*, *Fj*
Romano, G 1942 *R*
Romano, P 1942 *R*
Roselli, F 1995 *F*, *R* 1996 *W* 1998 *Rus*, *Ar*, *H*, *E* 1999 *F* (R), *S*, *W*, *I*, *SA*, *SA*, *Ur*, *Fj*, *Tg*
Rosi, P 1948 *F*, *Cze* 1949 *F*, *Cze* 1951 *Sp* 1952 *Ger*, *F* 1953 *F*, *Ger*, *R* 1954 *Sp*, *F*
Rossi, G 1981 *USS*, *WGe* (R) 1982 *E*, *WGe*, *Mor* 1983 *F*, *R*, *USS*, *C*, *C*, *Mor*, *F*, *A*, *USS* 1984 *Mor* 1985 *F* (R), *R*, *E*, *Sp*, *Z*, *USS*, *R* 1986 *Tun*, *F*, *E*, *A*, *Tun*, *USS* 1987 *R*, *NZ*, *Ar*, *USS*, *Sp* 1988 *USS*, *A*, *I* 1989 *F*, *R*, *Sp*, *Ar*, *Z*, *USS* 1990 *F*, *R* 1991 *R*
Rossi, N 1973 *Yug* 1974 *Pt*, *Mid*, *Sus*, *Oxo*, *WGe*, *Leo* 1975 *Sp*, *Cze*, *E*, *H* (R) 1976 *J*, *A*, *Sp* 1977 *Cze* 1980 *USS*
Rossi, Z 1959 *F* 1961 *Ger*, *F* 1962 *F*, *Ger*, *R*
Rossini, E 1948 *F*, *Cze* 1949 *F*, *Cze* 1951 *Sp* 1952 *Ger*
Rovelli, B 1960 *Ger*, *F* 1961 *Ger*, *F*
Russo, A 1986 *E*
Sacca, D 2003 *I*
Saetti, R 1988 *USS* (R), *I* 1989 *F*, *R*, *Sp*, *Ar*, *Z*, *USS* 1990 *F* (R), *Sp*, *H*, *R*, *USS* 1991 *R*, *Nm*, *Nm* (R), *US*, *E* 1992 *R*
Saetti, R 1957 *Ger* 1958 *F*, *R* 1959 *F* 1960 *F* 1961 *Ger*, *F* 1964 *Ger*, *F*
Sagramora, A 1970 *Mad*, *Mad* 1971 *R*
Saibene, E 1957 *F*, *Ger*
Salmasco, C 1965 *F* 1967 *F*
Salsi, L 1971 *Mor* 1972 *Pt*, *Sp*, *Yug* 1973 *Pt*, *Rho*, *WTv*, *Nat*, *ETv*, *Leo*, *FS*, *Tva*, *Cze*, *Yug*, *A* 1974 *Pt*, *Oxo*, *WGe*, *Leo* 1975 *Sp*, *R*, *Sp* 1977 *R*, *Pol*, *Cze*, *R*, *Sp* 1978 *F*
Salvadego, F 1985 *Z*
Salvan, R 1973 *Yug* 1974 *Pt*
Salvati, L 1987 *USS* 1988 *USS*, *I*
Santofadre, R 1952 *Sp*, *Ger*, *F* 1954 *Sp*, *F*
Sartorato, F 1956 *Ger*, *F* 1957 *F*
Savi, M 2004 *R* (R), *J* (R) 2005 *E* (R)
Saviozzi, S 1998 *Rus*, *H* (R) 1999 *W* (R), *I*, *SA*, *SA*, *Ur*, *Fj* (R), *Tg*, *NZ* 2000 *C* (R), *NZ* (R) 2002 *NZ* (R), *Sp* (R)
Scaglia, D 1994 *R*, *W* 1995 *S* 1996 *W*, *A* 1999 *W*
Scalzotto, E 1974 *Mid*, *Sus*, *Oxo*
Scanavacca, A 1999 *Ur* (R) 2001 *E* 2002 *Sp* (R), *R* 2004 *US* (R)
Sciacol, R 1965 *Cze*
Scodavolpe, I 1954 *Sp*
Screnci, F 1977 *Cze*, *R*, *Sp* 1978 *F* 1979 *Pol*, *R*, *E* 1982 *F* 1984 *Mor*
Selvaggio, A 1973 *Rho*, *WTv*, *ETv*, *Leo*, *FS*, *Tva*
Sepe, M 2006 *J* (R), *Fj*
Sesenna, D 1992 *R* 1993 *Cro*, *Mor*, *F* (R) 1994 *R* (R)
Sessa, G 1930 *Sp*
Sessi, G 1942 *R* (R)
Sgorbati, E 1968 *WGe*, *Yug*
Sgorbati, E 1933 *Cze* 1934 *Cat*, *R* 1935 *Cat*, *F* 1936 *Ger* 1937 *Ger* 1938 *Ger* 1939 *Ger* 1940 *R*, *Ger* 1942 *R*
Sgorlon, A 1993 *Pt* (R), *Mor*, *Sp* (R), *F*, *Rus*, *F*, *S* 1994 *CZR*, *R*, *W* 1995 *S*, *E*, *Ar*, *F*, *Ar*, *R*, *NZ*, *SA* 1996 *W*, *Pt*, *W*, *A*, *E* (R), *S* 1997 *I*, *F*, *F*, *Ar*, *R*, *SA*, *I* 1998 *S*, *W*, *Rus* 1999 *F* (R), *S*, *W*
Sguario, P 1958 *R* 1959 *F* 1960 *Ger*, *F* 1961 *Ger* 1962 *R*
Silini, M 1955 *Ger*, *Sp*, *F*, *Cze* 1956 *Cze* 1957 *Ger* 1958 *F* 1959 *F*
Silvestri, S 1954 *F*
Silvestri, U 1967 *Pt*, *R* 1968 *Pt*, *WGe*
Silvestri, U 1949 *F*, *Cze*
Simonelli, L 1956 *Ger*, *F*, *Cze* 1958 *F* 1960 *Ger*, *F*
Sinitich, F 1980 *Fj* (R), *Coo*, *Pol*, *Sp* 1981 *R* 1983 *USS* (R)
Sole, J 2005 *Ar*, *Tg*, *Ar* 2006 *I*, *E*, *F*, *W*, *S*, *J*, *Fj*
Soro, F 1965 *Cze* 1966 *F*, *Ger*, *R*
Spagnoli, A 1973 *Rho* (R)
Speziali, E 1965 *Cze*
Staibano, F 2006 *J* (R), *Fj* (R)
Stenta, U 1937 *Bel*, *Ger*, *F* 1938 *Ger* 1939 *Ger*, *R* 1940 *R*, *Ger* 1942 *R*
Stievano, P 1948 *F* 1952 *F* 1953 *F*, *Ger*, *R* 1954 *Sp*, *F* 1955 *Ger*
Stocco, S 1998 *H* 1999 *S* (R), *I* (R) 2000 *Fj* (R)
Stoica, CA 1997 *I*, *F*, *SA*, *I* 1998 *S*, *W*, *Rus*, *Ar*, *H*, *E* 1999 *S*, *W*, *SA*, *SA*, *Ur*, *Sp*, *Fj*, *E*, *Tg*, *NZ* 2000 *S*, *W*, *I*, *E*, *F*, *Sa*, *Fj*, *C*, *R*, *NZ* 2001 *I*, *E*, *F*, *S*, *W*, *Fj*, *SA*, *Sa* 2002 *F*, *S*, *W*, *I*, *E*, *Sp*, *R*, *Ar*, *A* 2003 *W*, *I*, *S*, *I*, *Geo*, *Tg*, *C*, *W* 2004 *E*, *F*, *S*, *I*, *W*, *US* 2005 *S*, *Tg*, *Ar* 2006 *I*, *E*, *F*, *W* (R), *S*
Tagliabue, L 1930 *Sp* (R) 1933 *Cze*, *Cze* 1934 *Cat*, *R* 1935 *F* 1937 *Ger*
Tartaglini, S 1948 *Cze* 1949 *F*, *Cze* 1951 *Sp* 1952 *Sp*, *Ger*, *F* 1953 *F*
Tassin, A 1973 *A*
Taveggia, A 1954 *F* 1955 *Ger*, *F*, *Sp*, *F* 1956 *Ger*, *F*, *Cze* 1957 *F*, *Ger* 1958 *F*, *R* 1959 *F* 1960 *Ger*, *F* 1967 *Pt*
Tebaldi, D 1985 *Z*, *Z* 1987 *R*, *Ar*, *Fj*, *USS*, *Sp* 1988 *F*, *A* (R), *I* 1989 *F* 1990 *F*, *Pol*, *R* 1991 *Nm* (R)
Tedeschi 1948 *F*
Testoni, G 1937 *Bel* 1938 *Ger* 1942 *R*
Tinari, C 1980 *JAB* (R), *Coo*, *Pol*, *USS*, *Sp* 1981 *USS*, *WGe* 1982 *F*, *WGe* 1983 *R*, *USS*, *C*, *C*, *Sp*, *Mor* (R), *A*, *USS* 1984 *Mor*, *R*
Tommasi, M 1990 *Pol* (R) 1992 *R* (R), *S* (R) 1993 *Pt*, *Cro*, *Sp*, *F* (R)
Torresan, C 1980 *F*, *R*, *Fj* (R), *Coo*, *Pol*, *USS* 1981 *R* (R),

USS 1982 *R* (R), *Mor* (R) 1983 *C*, *F*, *A*, *USS* 1984 *F*, *Mor*, *Tun*, *USS* 1985 *Z*, *Z*, *USS*
Tozzi, F 1933 *Cze* (R)
Travagli, P 2004 *C* (R), *NZ* (R)
Travini, L 1999 *SA* (R), *Ur* (R), *Sp*, *Fj* 2000 *I* (R)
Trebbi, F 1933 *Cze* (R), *Cze*
Trentin, F 1979 *Mor*, *F* (R), *Pol*, *USS* 1981 *R* (R)
Trevisiol, M 1988 *F*, *USS*, *A*, *I* 1989 *F*, *Ar*, *USS* 1994 *R*
Trippiteli, M 1979 *Pol* 1980 *Pol*, *Sp* 1981 *F*, *R* 1982 *F*, *E*, *WGe* 1984 *Tun*
Troiani, L 1985 *R* 1986 *Tun*, *F*, *Pt*, *A*, *USS* 1987 *Pt*, *F* 1988 *R*, *USS*, *A*, *I* 1989 *Sp*, *Ar*, *Z*, *USS* 1990 *F*, *Pol*, *R*, *Sp*, *H*, *R*, *USS* 1991 *F*, *R*, *Nm*, *Nm*, *US*, *E* 1992 *Sp*, *F*, *R*, *R*, *S* 1993 *Sp*, *F*, *Cro*, *Rus*, *F* 1994 *Sp*, *CZR*, *A*, *A*, *F* 1995 *S*, *E*, *Ar*
Troncon, A 1994 *Sp* (R), *R*, *CZR*, *H* (R), *A*, *A*, *R*, *W*, *F* 1995 *S*, *I*, *Sa*, *E*, *Ar*, *F*, *Ar*, *R*, *NZ*, *SA* 1996 *W*, *W*, *A*, *E*, *S* 1997 *I*, *F*, *F*, *Ar*, *SA*, *I* 1998 *S*, *W*, *Rus*, *Ar*, *H*, *E* 1999 *F*, *S*, *W*, *I*, *Ur*, *Sp*, *Fj*, *E*, *Tg*, *NZ* 2000 *S*, *W*, *I*, *E*, *F*, *R*, *NZ* 2001 *I*, *F*, *Nm*, *SA*, *Ur*, *Ar*, *Fj*, *SA*, *Sa* 2002 *F*, *S*, *W*, *I*, *E*, *Sp*, *R*, *Ar*, *A* (R) 2003 *W*, *I*, *E*, *F*, *S*, *S*, *I*, *Geo*, *NZ* (R), *Tg*, *C*, *W* 2004 *R*, *J* (R) 2005 *I*, *W*, *S*, *E*, *F*
Troncon, G 1962 *F*, *Ger*, *R* 1963 *F* 1964 *Ger*, *F* 1965 *Cze* 1966 *F*, *R* 1967 *F* 1968 *Yug* 1972 *Pt* (R)
Turcato, L 1952 *Sp*, *Ger*, *F* 1953 *Ger*, *R*
Turcato, M 1949 *F* 1951 *Sp*
Vaccari, P 1991 *Nm*, *Nm*, *US*, *E*, *NZ*, *USS* 1992 *Sp*, *F*, *R*, *R*, *S* 1993 *Mor*, *Sp* (R), *F*, *Rus*, *F*, *S* 1994 *Sp*, *R*, *CZR*, *H*, *A*, *A*, *R*, *W*, *F* 1995 *I*, *Sa*, *E*, *Ar*, *F*, *Ar*, *R*, *NZ*, *SA* 1996 *W*, *W*, *E*, *S* 1997 *I*, *F*, *F*, *Ar*, *R*, *SA*, *I* 1998 *S*, *W*, *Ar* 1999 *Ur*, *Sp*, *E*, *Tg*, *NZ* 2001 *Fj* 2002 *F*, *S*, *Ar*, *A* 2003 *W*, *I*, *E*, *F*, *S*
Vagnetti, V 1939 *R* (R) 1940 *R*
Valier, F 1968 *Yug* 1969 *F* 1970 *Cze*, *R* 1971 *Mor*, *R* 1972 *Pt*
Valtorta, L 1957 *Ger* 1958 *F*
Vene, O 1966 *F*
Venturi, E 1983 *C* 1985 *E*, *Sp* 1986 *Tun*, *Pt* 1988 *USS*, *A* 1989 *F*, *R*, *Sp*, *Ar*, *USS* 1990 *F*, *Pol*, *R*, *Sp*, *H*, *R*, *USS* 1991 *F*, *R*, *NZ*, *USS* 1992 *Sp*, *F* (R), *R* (R) 1993 *Sp*, *F*
Vezzani, P 1973 *Yug* 1975 *F*, *Sp*, *R*, *Cze*, *E*, *Pol*, *H*, *Sp* 1976 *F*
Vialetto, F 1972 *Yug*
Viccariotto, V 1948 *F*
Vigliano, S 1937 *R* (R), *Bel*, *Ger*, *F* 1939 *R* 1942 *R*
Villagra, L 2000 *Sa* (R), *Fj* (R)
Vinci I, E 1929 *Sp* (R)
Vinci II, P 1929 *Sp* 1930 *Sp* 1933 *Cze*
Vinci III, F 1929 *Sp* 1930 *Sp* 1934 *Cat*, *R* 1935 *Cat*, *F* 1936 *Ger*, *R* 1937 *Ger*, *R*, *Ger*, *F* 1939 *Ger*, *R* 1940 *Ger*
Vinci IV, P 1929 *Sp* 1930 *Sp* 1933 *Cze*, *Cze* 1934 *Cat*, *R* 1935 *Cat*, *F* 1937 *Ger*, *Bel*, *Ger*, *F* 1939 *Ger*
Visentin, A 1970 *R* 1972 *Pt*, *Sp* (R) 1973 *Rho* (R), *WTv*, *Bor*, *NEC*, *Nat*, *ETv*, *Leo*, *FS*, *Tva*, *Cze*, *Yug*, *A* 1974 *Pt*, *Leo* 1975 *F*, *Sp*, *R*, *Cze* 1976 *R* 1978 *Ar*
Visentin, G 1935 *Cat*, *F* 1936 *R* 1937 *Ger*, *Bel*, *Ger*, *F* 1938 *Ger* 1939 *Ger*
Visentin, T 1996 *W*
Visser, W 1999 *I* (R), *SA*, *SA* 2000 *S*, *W*, *I*, *F* (R), *C*, *R*, *NZ* 2001 *I*, *E*, *F*, *S*, *W*, *Nm*, *SA*, *Ur*, *Ar*, *Fj* (R), *SA*, *Sa*
Vitadello, F 1985 *Sp* 1987 *Pt* (R)
Vitelli, C 1973 *Cze*, *Yug* 1974 *Pt*, *Sus*
Vittorini, I 1969 *Sp* (R)
Wakarua, RS 2003 *Tg*, *C*, *W* 2004 *E*, *F*, *S* (R), *W* (R), *J*, *C*, *NZ* 2005 *Fj* (R)
Williams, F 1995 *SA*
Zaffiri, M 2000 *Fj* (R), *R*, *NZ* 2001 *W* (R) 2003 *S* 2005 *Tg* (R), *Fj* (R) 2006 *W*, *S*
Zanatta, R 1954 *Sp*, *F*
Zanchi, G 1953 *Ger*, *R* 1955 *Sp*, *Cze* 1957 *Ger*
Zanella, A 1977 *Mor*
Zanella, M 1976 *J*, *Sp* 1977 *R*, *Pol*, *Cze* 1978 *Ar* (R) 1980 *Pol*, *USS*
Zanetti, E 1942 *R*
Zani, F 1960 *Ger*, *F* 1961 *Ger*, *F* 1962 *F*, *R* 1963 *F* 1964 *F* 1965 *F* 1966 *Ger*, *R*
Zani, G 1934 *R*
Zanni, A 2005 *Tg* (R), *Ar* (R), *Fj* 2006 *F* (R), *W* (R), *S* (R)
Zanoletti, C 2001 *Sa* (R) 2002 *E* (R), *NZ*, *R*, *Ar* (R), *A* (R) 2005 *A* (R)
Zanon, G 1981 *F*, *R*, *USS*, *WGe* 1982 *R*, *E*, *WGe*, *Mor* 1983 *F*, *R*, *USS*, *C*, *C*, *Sp*, *Mor*, *F*, *A*, *USS* 1984 *F*, *Mor*, *R*, *USS* 1985 *F*, *R*, *E*, *Sp*, *Z*, *Z*, *USS* 1986 *USS* 1987 *R*, *Ar*, *USS* (R) 1989 *Sp*, *Ar* 1990 *F*, *Pol*, *R*, *Sp*, *H*, *R*, *USS* 1991 *Nm* (R), *US*, *E*
Zingarelli, M 1973 *A*
Zisti, N 1999 *E*, *NZ* 2000 *E*, *F*
Zoffoli, G 1936 *Ger*, *R* 1937 *Ger*, *R*, *Ger* 1938 *Ger* 1939 *R*
Zorzi, S 1985 *R* 1986 *Tun*, *F* 1988 *F* (R), *R* (R), *USS* 1992 *R*
Zucchelo, A 1956 *Ger*, *F*
Zucchi, C 1952 *Sp* 1953 *F*
Zuin, L 1977 *Cze* 1978 *Ar*, *USS*, *Sp* 1979 *F*, *Pol*, *R*

ITALIAN INTERNATIONAL STATISTICS

UP TO 30TH SEPTEMBER 2006

MOST POINTS IN A MATCH

BY THE TEAM

Pts.	Opponent	Venue	Year
104	Czech Republic	Viadana	1994
76	Croatia	Perpignan	1993
70	Morocco	Carcassonne	1993
67	Netherlands	Huddersfield	1998
66	Fiji	Treviso	2001

BY A PLAYER

Pts.	Player	Opponent	Venue	Year
29	Diego Dominguez	Fiji	Treviso	2001
29	Diego Dominguez	Scotland	Rome	2000
29	Stefano Bettarello	Canada	Toronto, Ontario	1983
28	Diego Dominguez	Netherlands	Calvisano	1994
27	Diego Dominguez	Ireland	Bologna	1997
25	Diego Dominguez	Romania	Tarbes	1997

MOST TRIES IN A MATCH

BY THE TEAM

Tries	Opponent	Venue	Year
16	Czech Republic	Viadana	1994
11	Netherlands	Huddersfield	1998
11	Croatia	Perpignan	1993
10	Portugal	Lisbon	1996
10	Morocco	Carcassonne	1993
10	Belgium	Brussels	1969
10	Belgium	Paris	1937

BY A PLAYER

Tries	Player	Opponent	Venue	Year
4	Ivan Francescato	Morocco	Carcassonne	1993
4	Renzo Cova	Belgium	Paris	1937
3	Paolo Dari	Germany	Hanover	1953
3	Martin Castrogiovanni	Japan	Tokyo	2004
3	Paolo Mariani	Poland	Catania	1977
3	Manrico Marchetto	Poland	Treviso	1975
3	Elio Michelon	Belgium	Brussels	1969
3	Elio De Anna	Czecho-slovakia	Reggio Calabria	1975
3	Vittorio Ambron	Portugal	Lisbon	1968
3	Paolo Pescetto	Czecho-slovakia	Prague	1956
3	Marcello Cuttitta	Morocco	Carcassonne	1993
3	Mario Gerosa	Czech Republic	Viadana	1994
3	Nicola Aldorvandi	Czech Republic	Viadana	1994

MOST CONVERSIONS IN A MATCH

BY THE TEAM

Cons	Opponent	Venue	Year
12	Czech Republic	Viadana	1994
10	Morocco	Carcassonne	1993
9	Croatia	Perpignan	1993
8	Spain	Parma	1994
7	Czechoslovakia	Reggio Calabria	1975
7	Netherlands	Calvisano	1994
7	Namibia	Windhoek	2001
7	Portugal	Lisbon	1996
7	Japan	Tokyo	2006

BY A PLAYER

Cons	Player	Opponent	Venue	Year
12	Luigi Troiani	Czech Republic	Viadana	1994
10	Gabriel Filizzola	Morocco	Carcassonne	1993
9	Luigi Troiani	Croatia	Perpignan	1993
8	Luigi Troiani	Spain	Parma	1994
7	Diego Dominguez	Portugal	Lisbon	1996
7	Ennio Ponzi	Czecho-slovakia	Reggio Calabria	1975
7	Diego Dominguez	Netherlands	Calvisano	1994
7	Francesco Mazzariol	Namibia	Windhoek	2001

MOST PENALTIES IN A MATCH

BY THE TEAM

Pens	Opponent	Venue	Year
8	Romania	Catania	1994
7	Fiji	Treviso	2001
6	Argentina	Lourdes	1997
6	Scotland	Rome	2000
6	Scotland	Treviso	1998
6	Ireland	Bologna	1997
6	Scotland A	Rovigo	1993
6	Tonga	Leicester	1999
6	Romania	Parma	2002
6	Argentina	Salta	2005

BY A PLAYER

Pens	Player	Opponent	Venue	Year
8	Diego Dominguez	Romania	Catania	1994
7	Diego Dominguez	Fiji	Treviso	2001
6	Diego Dominguez	Argentina	Lourdes	1997
6	Diego Dominguez	Scotland	Rome	2000
6	Diego Dominguez	Scotland	Treviso	1998
6	Diego Dominguez	Ireland	Bologna	1997
6	Diego Dominguez	Scotland A	Rovigo	1993
6	Diego Dominguez	Tonga	Leicester	1999
6	Gert Peens	Romania	Parma	2002
6	Gert Peens	Argentina	Salta	2005

MOST DROP GOALS IN A MATCH

BY THE TEAM

Drops	Opponent	Venue	Year
3	Romania	Padova	1990
3	Scotland	Rome	2000
3	Transvaal	Johannesburg	1973
2	Spain	Casablanca	1983
2	Canada	Toronto, Ontario	1983
2	Wales	Rome	2003
2	England	Rome	2006
2	England U23	Padova	1982
2	Yugoslavia	Zagreb	1973
2	Spain	L'Aquila	1969
2	Ireland	Dublin	1999

BY A PLAYER

Drops	Player	Opponent	Venue	Year
3	Diego Dominguez	Scotland	Rome	2000
3	Rocco Caligiuri	Transvaal	Johannesburg	1973
2	Stefano Bettarello	Canada	Toronto, Ontario	1983
2	Diego Dominguez	Wales	Rome	2003
2	Ramiro Pez	England	Rome	2006
2	Stefano Bettarello	England U23	Padova	1982
2	Diego Dominguez	Ireland	Dublin	1999
2	Massimo Bonomi	Romania	Padova	1990

MOST CAPPED PLAYERS

Caps	Player
90	Alessandro Troncon
83	Carlo Checchinato
74	Diego Dominguez
69	Cristian Stoica
69	Massimo Cuttitta
64	Paolo Vaccari
60	Serafino Ghizzoni
60	Massimo Giovanelli

LEADING TRY SCORERS

Tries	Player
25	Marcello Cuttitta
22	Paolo Vaccari
21	Manrico Marchetto
21	Carlo Checchinato
17	Massimo Mascioletti
17	Serafino Ghizzoni
16	Ivan Francescato
16	Alessandro Troncon

LEADING CONVERSIONS SCORERS

Cons	Player
127	Diego Dominguez
57	Luigi Troiani
46	Stefano Bettarello
30	Ramiro Pez
17	Gert Peens
17	Ennio Ponzi
16	Gabriel Filizzola
15	Rima Wakarua

LEADING PENALTY SCORERS

Pens	Player
209	Diego Dominguez
106	Stefano Bettarello
57	Luigi Troiani
37	Ramiro Pez
31	Ennio Ponzi
22	Rima Wakarua
22	Gert Peens
14	Francesco Mazzariol

LEADING DROP GOAL SCORERS

Drops	Player
19	Diego Dominguez
15	Stefano Bettarello
5	Massimo Bonomi
5	Oscar Collodo
4	Ramiro Pez
3	Pierluigi Pacifici
3	Rocco Caligiuri
3	Serafino Ghizzoni

LEADING POINT SCORERS

Pts	Player
983	Diego Dominguez
483	Stefano Bettarello
294	Luigi Troiani
203	Ramiro Pez
133	Ennio Ponzi
110	Marcello Cuttitta
107	Paolo Vaccari
105	Carlo Checchinato

JAPAN

JAPAN'S TEST RECORD

OPPONENTS	DATE	VENUE	RESULT
Arabian Gulf	16 April	H	**Won** 82–9
South Korea	23 April	H	**Won** 50–14
Georgia	14 May	H	**Won** 32–7
Tonga	4 June	H	**Lost** 16–57
Italy	11 June	H	**Lost** 6–52
Samoa	17 June	A	**Lost** 9–53
Junior All Blacks	24 June	A	**Lost** 8–38
Fiji	1 July	H	**Lost** 15–29

TROUBLES IN RECORD-BREAKING YEAR

By Rich Freeman

It is safe to say 2006 was not a vintage year for rugby in Japan with confusion reigning in both domestic and international competition. Daisuke Ohata may have become the top try scorer in test match history when he scored a hat trick against Georgia in front in his hometown of Osaka in May but that was all Japanese fans really had to cheer about on the international front until two battling performances closed out the busiest international season the national side has ever had. Head coach Jean-Pierre Elissalde bore the brunt of the criticism and finished the season having to endure some fairly difficult questioning from the local press. Elissalde had not endeared himself to many by saying that he thought the one-sided nature of many of the Top League games was holding back the Japan national team, as the players were simply not skilled enough in the basics to compete at the highest level. And the way the team succumbed to the likes of Tonga and Italy, and played so badly in defeating South Korea, the Arabian Gulf and Georgia, showed the Frenchman had a point. Elissalde, who seemed to have trouble getting his message across to players and media alike, was also not helped by a horrendous injury list that saw over a third of his first-choice team miss out on the entire international season and the antiquated way in which the game is organized and structured in Japan. It was no coincidence that the biggest story of the season was the success of Waseda University, culminating in its win over Toyota Verblitz in the quarterfinals of the All-Japan Championship, while the biggest crowd of the season was the one that watched Waseda beat Kanto Gakuin to claim the University Championship. To many in Japan student rugby is still the be-all and end-all, despite the introduction of the Top League, which has been expanded to 14 teams from the 2006–07 season.

Japan had entered the calendar year on the back of a win over Spain in November. However, that victory was offset a week later by the news that the Japan Rugby Football Union had failed in its bid to host the 2011 Rugby World Cup. The JRFU later admitted that their whole policy for the development of the game in Japan had been geared towards hosting the tournament and the lack of a back-up plan was sadly also in evidence on the field. The opening Test matches of the year saw Japan win its two RWC qualifiers in Tokyo against the Arabian Gulf (82–9) and South Korea (50–14), but the performances left Elissalde – a former assistant under Mitsutake Hagimoto – saying there were the worst performances he had seen from Japan. Things improved against Georgia (32–7) with Ohata ending the game one million yen richer and wearing a commemorative gold jersey after he passed David Campese's record of 64 tries. But the Georgians were missing a number of first-choice players and the majority of the players were playing their third game in a week in two different continents. The build-up to the game had also been shrouded in controversy when back-up scrumhalf Yuki Yatomi walked out on the national squad in order to play a pre-season friendly for Waseda University. Not for the first time, a player had put club/university before country. And not for the first time, the powers that be simply brushed the issue aside. Such is the power certain universities seem to have. Following a two-week break, the Brave Blossoms entered a five-week stretch during which they played a test every weekend. They were anything but brave in the opening game of the Pacific Five Nations, going down 57–16 to Tonga in the rugby heartland of Kita-Kyushu. A week they were on the end of another hiding when they lost 52–6 to Italy in Tokyo. With away games against Samoa and the Junior All Blacks to follow, the talk was of damage limitation and of keeping the scores under 100. The Brave Blossoms may have shipped another 50 against Samoa (53–9) but it was a much improved performance, and one week later – with the Japanese backrow of Takeshi Kikutani, Hajime Kiso and the recalled Phil O'Reilly playing out of their skins–Japan led the JABs for the opening quarter before eventually going down 38–8. Could they repeat the performance back on home soil? Led by Ono – the fourth captain of the year – and with Kosuke Endo proving himself once again to be Japan's most dangerous back in the absence of Ohata – the hosts pulled level with Fiji at 15–15 with 10 minutes left on the clock. But two late tries saw the Brave Blossoms walk away from the new tournament pointless – but not without some pride restored and hope for the future. While Elissalde was getting a hard time, the local press was raving about two homegrown coaches. Masahiro Kunda's Toshiba Brave Lupus once again proved they are the best company team in Japan, winning the Top League, Microsoft Cup and sharing the All-Japan Championship with NEC Green Rockets. Meanwhile, Katsuyuki Kiyomiya's Waseda were untouchable in the university competition before causing the biggest shock in domestic rugby when they beat a Toyota side including former All Blacks Filo Tiatia and Troy Flavell. Heading into the final three rounds of the Top League, the silverware appeared to be Sanyo Wild Knights' to lose. Having beaten Toshiba in convincing style, all Sanyo had to do was keep winning, though the Brave Lupus were keeping up the pressure by earning bonus points in every game they played. In the end it proved too much for Sanyo, who lost two of their last three games and Toshiba romped home to win back-to-back trophies. Sanyo's reversal of fortune continued in the Microsoft Cup (played for by the Top 8 teams in the Top League) and it was left to Suntory Sungoliath – who will be coached by Kiyomiya next season- to try and stop the Toshiba juggernaut. Suntory had improved considerably in the latter half of the season as a result of the input of advisor Eddie Jones, but not even the Australian could help them from derailing Toshiba. But in a strange end to a strange season, Toshiba missed out on an outright treble when they drew 6–6 with NEC and were forced to share the All Japan title – the conservatives in charge of rugby determining that no side meant no side and no extra time should be played. It was one of those years.

In September 2006 the JRFU replaced French-born national coach Jean-Pierre Elissalde with former international Osamu Ota.

JAPAN INTERNATIONAL STATISTICS

MATCH RECORDS UP TO 30 SEPTEMBER 2006

MOST CONSECUTIVE TEST WINS

5 1980 SK 1981 AU 1982 HK, C 1,2

MOST CONSECUTIVE TESTS WITHOUT DEFEAT

Matches	Wins	Draws	Periods
5	5	0	1980 to 1982

MOST POINTS IN A MATCH

BY THE TEAM

Pts.	Opponent	Venue	Year
155	Chinese Taipei	Tokyo	2002
134	Chinese Taipei	Singapore	1998
120	Chinese Taipei	Tainan	2002
91	Hong Kong	Tokyo	2005
90	South Korea	Tokyo	2002

BY A PLAYER

Pts.	Player	Opponent	Venue	Year
60	T Kurihara	Chinese Taipei	Tainan	2002
40	D Ohata	Chinese Taipei	Tokyo	2002
35	T Kurihara	South Korea	Tokyo	2002
34	K Hirose	Tonga	Tokyo	1999
31	K Hirose	Hong Kong	Tokyo	2005

MOST TRIES IN A MATCH

BY THE TEAM

Tries	Opponent	Venue	Year
23	Chinese Taipei	Tokyo	2002
20	Chinese Taipei	Singapore	1998
18	Chinese Taipei	Tainan	2002
13	South Korea	Tokyo	2002
13	Arabian Gulf	Tokyo	2006
12	South Korea	Tokyo	2003
12	Hong Kong	Tokyo	2005

BY A PLAYER

Tries	Player	Opponent	Venue	Year
8	D Ohata	Chinese Taipei	Tokyo	2002
6	T Kurihara	Chinese Taipei	Tainan	2002
6	D Ohata	Hong Kong	Tokyo	2005
5	T Masuho	Chinese Taipei	Singapore	1998
4	Y Sakata	NZ Juniors	Wellington	1968
4	T Hirao	Chinese Taipei	Taiwan	2001
4	D Ohata	South Korea	Tokyo	2002
4	R Miki	Chinese Taipei	Tainan	2002

MOST CONVERSIONS IN A MATCH

BY THE TEAM

Cons	Opponent	Venue	Year
20	Chinese Taipei	Tokyo	2002
17	Chinese Taipei	Singapore	1998
15	Chinese Taipei	Tainan	2002
11	South Korea	Tokyo	2002
11	Hong Kong	Tokyo	2005

BY A PLAYER

Cons	Player	Opponent	Venue	Year
15	T Kurihara	Chinese Taipei	Tainan	2002
12	A Miller	Chinese Taipei	Tokyo	2002
11	T Kurihara	South Korea	Tokyo	2002
11	K Hirose	Hong Kong	Tokyo	2005
10	K Hirose	Chinese Taipei	Singapore	1998

MOST PENALTIES IN A MATCH

BY THE TEAM

Pens	Opponent	Venue	Year
9	Tonga	Tokyo	1999
6	Tonga	Tokyo	1990
5	Argentina (1st Test)	Buenos Aires	1993
5	Argentina (2nd Test)	Buenos Aires	1993
5	South Korea	Tokyo	2001
5	France	Townsville	2003
5	Russia	Tokyo	2004

BY A PLAYER

Pens	Player	Opponent	Venue	Year
9	K Hirose	Tonga	Tokyo	1999
6	T Hosokawa	Tonga	Tokyo	1990
5	T Hosokawa	Argentina (1st Test)	Buenos Aires	1993
5	T Hosokawa	Argentina (2nd Test)	Buenos Aires	1993
5	T Kurihara	South Korea	Tokyo	2001
5	T Kurihara	France	Townsville	2003
5	W Ikeda	Russia	Tokyo	2004

MOST DROPPED GOALS IN A MATCH

BY THE TEAM

Drops	Opponent	Venue	Year
2	Argentina	Tokyo	1998

BY A PLAYER

Drops	Player	Opponent	Venue	Year
2	K Iwabuchi	Argentina	Tokyo	1998

CAREER RECORDS

MOST CAPPED PLAYERS

Caps	Player	Career span
80	Y Motoki	1991 to 2005
61	T Ito	1996 to 2005
56	D Ohata	1996 to 2006
46	T Masuho	1991 to 2001
44	Y Sakuraba	1986 to 1999
44	T Matsuda	1992 to 2003
43	M Kunda	1991 to 1999
41	H Tanuma	1996 to 2003
41	W Murata	1991 to 2005
40	K Hirose	1994 to 2005
40	S Hasagawa	1997 to 2003
38	T Hayashi	1980 to 1992
37	S Hirao	1983 to 1999

MOST CONSECUTIVE TESTS

Caps	Player	Career span
28	Y Motoki	1994 to 1998
26	Y Yoshida	1988 to 1995
18	S Mori	1974 to 1978
18	T Ishizuka	1978 to 1982
17	Y Konishi	1982 to 1986
17	B Ferguson	1993 to 1996

MOST TESTS AS CAPTAIN

Caps	Captain	Span
29	T Miuchi	2002 to 2005
16	M Kunda	1993 to 1998
16	A McCormick	1998 to 1999
13	T Hayashi	1984 to 1987
13	S Hirao	1989 to 1991
13	Y Motoki	1996 to 1997

MOST POINTS IN INDIVIDUAL POSITIONS

Pts	Player	Tests	Career
Full-back	T Matsuda	38	1992 to 2003
Wing	T Masuho	45	1991 to 2001
Centre	Y Motoki	72	1991 to 2005
Fly-half	K Hirose	34	1994 to 2005
Scrum-half	W Murata	33	1991 to 2005
Prop	S Hasagawa	30	1997 to 2003
Hooker	M Kunda	41	1991 to 1999
Lock	Y Sakuraba	37	1986 to 1999
Flanker	H Kajihara	31	1989 to 1997
No 8	T Ito	28	1996 to 2004

MOST POINTS IN TESTS

Tries	Player	Tests	Career
422	K Hirose	40	1994 to 2005
345	T Kurihara	26	2000 to 2003
325	D Ohata	56	1996 to 2006
137	T Masuho	46	1991 to 2001
115	T Hosokawa	11	1990 to 1993

MOST TRIES IN TESTS

Tries	Player	Tests	Career
65	D Ohata	56	1996 to 2006
27	T Masuho	46	1991 to 2001
20	T Itoh	18	1963 to 1974
20	T Kurihara	26	2000 to 2003
19	Y Yoshida	26	1988 to 1995
17	H Onozawa	29	2001 to 2005

MOST CONVERSIONS IN TESTS

Cons	Player	Tests	Career
77	K Hirose	40	1994 to 2005
70	T Kurihara	26	2000 to 2003
18	Y Yamaguchi	13	1967 to 1973
17	A Miller	10	2002 to 2003
14	N Ueyama	21	1973 to 1980
14	T Hosokawa	11	1990 to 1993
14	S Onishi	17	2000 to 2006

MOST PENALTY GOALS IN TESTS

Pens	Player	Tests	Career
79	K Hirose	40	1994 to 2005
35	T Kurihara	26	2000 to 2003
24	T Hosokawa	11	1990 to 1993
18	Y Yamaguchi	13	1967 to 1973
18	N Ueyama	21	1973 to 1980

MOST DROPPED GOALS IN TESTS

Drops	Player	Tests	Career
5	K Morita	8	2004 to 2005
3	Y Matsuo	24	1974 to 1984
2	K Hirose	40	1994 to 2005
2	K Iwabuchi	20	1997 to 2002

CAREER RECORDS OF JAPAN INTERNATIONAL PLAYERS (UP TO 30 SEPTEMBER 2006)

PLAYER	DEBUT	CAPS	T	C	P	D	PTS
BACKS							
K Ando	2006 v AG	7	0	5	5	1	28
K Endo	2004 v It	8	0	0	0	0	0
W Ikeda	2004 v SK	14	1	7	11	0	52
Y Imamura	2006 v AG	5	1	0	0	0	5
M Ito	2000 v Tg	14	1	0	0	0	5
T Miyake	2005 v Sp	4	1	0	0	0	5
H Mizuno	2004 v R	11	2	0	0	0	10
A Moriya	2006 v Tg	5	0	0	0	0	0
D Ohata	1996 v SK	56	65	0	0	0	325
S Onishi	2000 v Fj	17	1	14	5	0	48
N Oto	2001 v SK	11	4	0	0	0	20
K Takei	2004 v It	6	5	0	0	0	25
Y Yatomi	2006 v SK	1	0	0	0	0	0
H Yoshida	2001 v Sam	14	1	0	0	0	5
FORWARDS							
R Asano	2003 v Aust.A	16	0	0	0	0	0
Y Hisadomi	2002 v Ru	19	1	0	0	0	5
K Kasai	1999 v C	11	1	0	0	0	5
T Kikutani	2005 v Sp	9	2	0	0	0	5
H Kiso	2001 v CT	23	0	0	0	0	0
T Kitagawa	2005 v Sp	6	1	0	0	0	5
T Kumagae	2004 v SK	21	0	0	0	0	0
H Makiri	2005 v Ur	11	3	0	0	0	15
Y Matsubara	2004 v SK	13	1	0	0	0	5
T Nakai	2005 v Ur	11	0	0	0	0	0
H Oono	2004 v SK	13	0	0	0	0	0
P O'Reilly	2005 v SK	3	3	0	0	0	15
T Sato	2005 v Sp	8	1	0	0	0	5
T Soma	2005 v Sp	6	0	0	0	0	0
T Taniguchi	2006 v Tg	2	0	0	0	0	0
M Yamamoto	2002 v Ru	21	0	0	0	0	0
R Yamamura	2001 v W	28	1	0	0	0	5
T Yamaoka	2004 v It	13	0	0	0	0	0

NAMIBIA

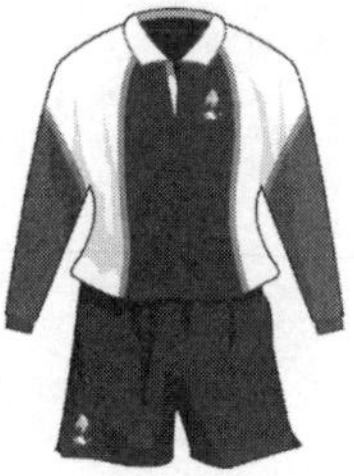

NAMIBIA'S TEST RECORD

OPPONENTS	DATE	VENUE	RESULT
Kenya	27 May	H	**Won** 84-12
Tunisia	1 July	A	**Lost** 7-24
Kenya	9 Sept	A	**Lost** 26-30

FIGHTING AGAINST THE ODDS

By Andrew Poolman

ONE of the big buzz words in the northern hemisphere at the moment is burnout. Player burnout as the Martin Corrys and Gavin Hensons of the rugby world are asked to play more and more Test matches.

In England the RFU have reached an agreement that no player will play more than eight Test matches in a season already packed with club rugby of high intensity.

Since the last Rugby World Cup in 2003, when England were victorious, and before their four Tests in the autumn of 2006, the national side has racked up an incredible 26 Tests.

Hamish Blair/Getty Images

Namibia – here represented by Erenstine Haragaes of the Rugby World Cup Choir – made their second World Cup finals appearance in 1999.

Compare that to the side that had the worst record in the 2003 World Cup, Namibia, and you'll have an idea about the almost opposite realities between the nations. Until its qualifying campaign for the 2007 World Cup started in May 2006, Namibia had played just eight Tests since losing 37–7 to Romania in its final game of the 2003 tournament.

The IRB is of course addressing the lack of matches but apart from this dearth of games the availability of the country's foreign-based professional players, mostly from South Africa, could once again be a deciding factor in the build-up to Rugby World Cup.

Although the situation has improved considerably over the last few years, the national team still finds itself without some key players for important matches due to players' commitments to provincial unions and clubs. Too often the team list put on paper by the selectors looks very different at kick-off time.

The possibility of playing in a World Cup remains undeniably the strongest motivation for any Namibian player. Even if the Namibian Rugby Union doesn't have the resources to offer players much besides that, the 1999 and 2003 World Cups remain among the proudest memories of every player involved.

As a result, the number of Namibians taking opportunities to play abroad has not slowed down in recent years. At the same time, the attitude towards accepting players back to play Test rugby for Namibia, which at certain times was met with some resistance by fans of the local clubs, has also moved towards embracing a more open approach to modern realities. In fact, more often now opportunities abroad are welcomed as a way of exposing players to higher levels of coaching and competition than they might expect locally and ultimately benefiting the national team.

A case in point is centre Hendrik Meyer, formerly with the Mpumalanga Pumas, who recently joined the Cheetahs, so shrewdly coached by former Springbok Rassie Erasmus, and became an instant hit when he scored a hat-trick in his Currie Cup debut against the Falcons.

While Namibia continues to produce individual players of some quality, the challenges of building a successful team at Test level has often fallen short of expectations. This is partially due to its inactivity at international level. If Namibia harbour dreams of competing with much better sides, then an expanded Test programme needs to be introduced that goes way beyond Rugby World Cup qualifiers and Africa Cup matches.

Unfortunately, costs make matches against South African teams too much of a rarity, but this is something that looks set to change as the IRB continues its commitment to increasing the competitiveness of the international game through providing additional funding for Tier 2 and 3 Nations.

Another issue is the domestic league structure which is not conducive to preparing the national side to the highest level. Club champions Wanderers, who beat Reho Falcon 31–16 in last year's premier league final, remain the pacesetters. United, coached by former Namibian and Cats prop Danie Vermeulen, are known as a well-organised unit capable of playing at a fast pace, while Western Suburbs have also shown significant improvement over the last two years.

Rehoboth and the University of Namibia complete the six-team premier league, while the first and second divisions consist of ten teams each. The commitment of clubs from the smaller rural towns against all odds continues to command respect.

The drawn-out league program over seven months remains an oddity, as clubs insist on a more concentrated structure at every annual general meeting.

Despite the challenges, Namibia remains confident, whether under the captaincy of Natal Sharks prop Kees Lensing or Corné Powell, who plays for local champions Wanderers. Tunisia and Morocco always provide tough obstacles, but coach Johan Venter, who took the reigns at the start of the season after a short but successful stint in the 1998 RWC qualifying campaign, has assembled a strong squad.

Venter was re-instated in February when his predecessor, Christo Alexander, was appointed as chief executive officer of the Namibia Rugby Union. Alexander took a seriously weakened team to Morocco at the end of 2005 as the withdrawal of top players and the NRU's suspension of United Rugby Club players limited his options. Three players made their Test debut while ten had only played one test, against Madagascar one month previously. The result, a 49–0 loss in Casablanca, had a predictability to it.

At the end of June 2006, the Namibians suffered a 24–7 away loss in the World Cup qualifier against Tunisia. In the build-up to the match, the headlines were dominated by coach Venter's decision to drop fly-half Morné Schreuder for the crucial encounter after the 26-year-old failed to attend team practices in Windhoek. There was initially a lot of sympathy for Schreuder, a Test regular since his debut against Madagascar in 2002 and who played in the 2003 World Cup in Australia. He had started the season by moving to Tsumeb, a town about 500 km from the capital, and taking a job there.

At a time when work commitments robbed the team of a full compliment of players for training, some claimed that the coach had robbed the team of an in-form player. However, as Venter points out, Schreuder's absence had left him no choice.

It had been just a few short weeks after Schreuder had kicked 12 out of 12 conversions in the 84–12 win against Kenya in Windhoek. It was also remembered that it was Schreuder's accurate goal kicking under pressure four years ago in Tunis which had secured the team's spot as the African qualifier for the 2003 World Cup in Australia.

Against Tunisia, the number 10 jersey was taken by Melrick Africa, a skilled player who had played most of his rugby for the national team on the right wing. The defeat in Tunis – Namibia has yet to win a Test in the northern African country after three visits – was largely blamed on a lethargic performance by the forwards. With Kees Lensing and Heino Senekal not available for the match, the team struggled in the set piece, while the backline's defence also came in for criticism.

The only players to emerge with credit from the defeat were loose forwards Jacques Burger and Pieter-Jan van Lill, both of whom play in South Africa. Burger is contracted to Griquas, while van Lill is a student at Stellenbosch. Both previously played in the Under-19 World Cup.

Withdrawal of experienced players was a key factor again as Namibia suffered its first-ever defeat to Kenya in Nairobi in early September. The 26–30 loss was especially embarrassing following the earlier big win in Windhoek. The Kenyan pace out wide exposed the visitors' defence and delivered six tries as the depleted Namibians failed to impose their traditional forward dominance.

As the qualifying campaign reaches its climax, Namibia can put together an excellent team on paper. Despite the lack of money to prepare a unit which is ready for battle, at least for the moment the team is spared of the political infighting which has hamstrung the side in the past.

At age grade Namibia continued to be represented in international competition. The IRB Under-19 World Championship provided the opportunity for young Namibians to test themselves against sides that they would not usually face.

Victories over Chinese Taipei (57–10), Chile (14–6) and Korea (51–5) followed losses against the two tougher sides, Canada (10–29) and Georgia (6–14), which secured a ninth place finish from 12 division B teams for P.J. Erasmus's team. While ultimately disappointing, the experience will hold the next generation of young international players in good stead.

However, the encouraging performances in Dubai were not backed up in qualification for the IRB Under-19 World Championship 2007 to be held in Ireland. The Namibians started the Under-19 Africa Cup in Casablanca well enough, beating Tunisia 29–14 barely one day after completing the long trip from Windhoek and via Dubai. The Namibians also beat Kenya 56–5 to set up a semi-final clash against the host team, but were defeated 22–5 by the much heavier Morocco pack. Zimbabwe subsequently beat a tired Morocco 10–3 in the final to book the African qualifier spot at the 2007 Under-19 World Cup in Ireland.

Being eliminated comes as quite a disappointment following respectable 16th and 15th places overall at the 2004 and 2003 junior World Championships respectively. Namibia even competed in Division A in 2003 before a revamp of the tournament format saw them back in the B Division again.

The Namibian youngsters were led by prop Casper Viviers, one of seven players who played in last year's Under-19 World Cup. Viviers' performance in Dubai won him a contract to play for Agen in France, marking him as one of the country's potential upcoming stars.

NAMIBIA INTERNATIONAL STATISTICS

COMPILED BY HUGH COPPING

MATCH RECORDS UP TO 20 SEPTEMBER 2006

MOST POINTS IN A MATCH

BY THE TEAM

Pts.	Opponent	Venue	Year
112	Madagascar	Windhoek	2002
86	Portugal	Windhoek	1990
84	Kenya	Windhoek	2006
82	Uganda	Windhoek	2003
79	Germany	Gera	1999
69	Zimbabwe	Windhoek	1992

BY A PLAYER

Pts.	Player	Opponent	Venue	Year
35	Jaco Coetzee	Kenya	Nairobi	1993
26	Moolman Olivier	Portugal	Windhoek	1990
25	Riaan van Wyk	Madagascar	Windhoek	2002
24	Gerhard Mans	Portugal	Windhoek	1990
22	Morne Schreuder	Kenya	Windhoek	2006

MOST TRIES IN A MATCH

BY THE TEAM

Tries	Opponent	Venue	Year
18	Madagascar	Windhoek	2002
16	Portugal	Windhoek	1990
13	Germany	Gera	1999
12	Uganda	Windhoek	2003
12	Kenya	Windhoek	2006
11	Zimbabwe	Windhoek	1992

BY A PLAYER

Tries	Player	Opponent	Venue	Year
6	Gerhard Mans	Portugal	Windhoek	1990
5	Riaan van Wyk	Madagascar	Windhoek	2002
4	Eden Meyer	Zimbabwe	Windhoek	1992
4	Melrick Africa	Kenya	Nairobi	2003

MOST CONVERSIONS IN A MATCH

BY THE TEAM

Cons	Opponent	Venue	Year
12	Kenya	Windhoek	2006
11	Uganda	Windhoek	2003
11	Portugal	Windhoek	1990
11	Madagascar	Windhoek	2002
8	Arabian Gulf	Nairobi	1993

BY A PLAYER

Cons	Player	Opponent	Venue	Year
11	Moolman Olivier	Portugal	Windhoek	1990
11	Morne Schreuder	Kenya	Windhoek	2006
8	Rudi van Vuuren	Uganda	Windhoek	2003
8	Jaco Coetzee	Arabian Gulf	Nairobi	1993

MOST PENALTIES IN A MATCH

BY THE TEAM

Pens	Opponent	Venue	Year
5	Italy	Windhoek	1991
5	Portugal	Lisbon	1998
5	France A	Windhoek	1990

BY A PLAYER

Pens	Player	Opponent	Venue	Year
5	Jaco Coetzee	Italy	Windhoek	1991
5	Rudi van Vuuren	Portugal	Lisbon	1998
5	Shaun McCulley	France A	Windhoek	1990

NEW ZEALAND

NEW ZEALAND'S TEST RECORD

OPPONENTS	DATE	VENUE	RESULT
Ireland	10 June	H	**Won** 34-23
Ireland	17 June	H	**Won** 27-17
Argentina	24 June	A	**Won** 25-19
Australia	8 July	H	**Won** 32-12
South Africa	22 July	H	**Won** 35-17
Australia	29 July	A	**Won** 13-9
Australia	19 August	H	**Won** 34-27
South Africa	26 August	A	**Won** 45-26
South Africa	2 Sept	A	**Lost** 21-20

AN ALMOST PERFECT YEAR

By Sean Fitzpatrick

There's no such thing as an All Blacks side with nothing to prove. Complacency isn't in the New Zealand rugby vocabulary but I'd have to say Graham Henry's side began 2006 with little to prove. They were ranked the number one side in the world and no-one could argue their performances in 2005 hadn't justified that status.

The way they had beaten the Lions in the summer of 2005 was crushing and they followed that up by regaining the Tri-Nations title from South Africa and then a Grand Slam in Britain and Ireland. Even though they lost to the Springboks in Cape Town, in August 2005, to ruin what would otherwise have been a 100 per cent record, it had been a good year for the All Blacks.

There were high standards to maintain in 2006, which began in June with the first of the two Tests against the Irish. There was an air of anticipation before the game because although no-one really expected Ireland to win in Hamilton, they were still Triple Crown winners and people wanted to see how many problems they could cause the Blacks.

It turned out quite a few. Henry chopped and changed in his selection, no doubt with one eye on preparations for the Tri-Nations, and Ireland took full advantage of New Zealand's uncharacteristic hesitancy. It was tight throughout and it took a late try from Troy Flavell to close the match out 34–23. The Blacks were obviously ring rusty and Ireland had nearly caught them cold.

The second Test in Auckland was the same story. New Zealand were far from their best in terrible conditions, the Ireland boys played well again and it finished 27–17 to Henry's team. It wasn't a classic match or performance but they'd done a job.

What worried me slightly about the two Tests was how we missed Dan Carter's influence. Henry had decided to rest him for the bigger challenges ahead and although I thought Luke McAlister had two decent games in his spot, particularly with the boot, he didn't really run either game like Carter can. McAlister is a good deputy but New Zealand need to keep Carter fit and healthy before next year's World Cup.

The Blacks' final game before the Tri-Nations was Argentina in Buenos Aries a week later. In my opinion, it's a fixture we don't play often enough because facing the Pumas in Argentina can tell you a lot about your players. It's a hostile situation where they will be exposed and you really learn about character in places like that. Going to Argentina toughens a team up.

The game finished 25–19 to the Blacks. Henry started with a completely different XV – including a recalled Carter – to the one that started the second Test against Ireland and they came away with what I thought was a good result. Again, it wasn't a great performance but Test match rugby isn't always about throwing the ball about and running up cricket scores. In terms of intensity, it was right up there. The experience the boys who played in Buenos Aries will have gained won't go to waste in the future.

It was now time for the Tri-Nations with Australia in Christchurch and what turned out to be a comfortable 32–12 win. South Africa were sent home from Christchurch the week after with a 35–17 reverse and it was only in the third match of the series – Australia in Brisbane for the Blesidoe Cup – that the Blacks were really stretched. It wasn't a game full of chances but New Zealand took theirs and although the Wallabies kept plugging away in the second-half, the Blacks just probably deserved to edge it 13–9.

The return match two weeks later at Eden Park was also tight. Some people thought the Brisbane game was a one-off, that Australia had produced their one heroic performance for the tournament but they again ran the Blacks very close in Auckland. Maybe they had the rub off the green with one or two of the refereeing decisions but in the end New Zealand came out 34–27 thanks mainly to the power of the pack, who out muscled the Wallabies. If Australia can find the forwards, they'll still be a threat at the World Cup next year.

The win gave Henry and his team the Tri-Nations title with two games to spare under the tournament's new, six-match format. Winning the trophy itself is always a benchmark achievement, but I suspect Henry would have been particularly pleased to see the quality of the performances improve with each game. True, the Australians came close enough twice, but the Blacks showed plenty of appetite for the fight. There was plenty of attacking rugby to enjoy, but I also thought the pack stepped up to the mark when it really mattered.

With the silverware safely in the bag, the Blacks cut loose in the next game – the clash with the Springboks in Pretoria. I was in the crowd at the Loftus Versfeld and I was amazed at some of the rugby New Zealand produced. I've rarely seen such ambitious but precise rugby played at such consistently high speed and I genuinely don't believe any side could have lived with them that day. It was the performance of the season and the final 45-26 scoreline didn't flatter them.

A week later they wrapped up their Tri-Nations with another game against the Springboks in Rustenburg. It was no surprise the South Africans were nursing a case of wounded pride after what happened in Pretoria and although I expected them to come out swinging, I didn't expect them to win.

It was tight all the way through, but when South Africa, trailing 20–18, were awarded a late penalty, I knew they were going to land it and probably hang on. There was a sense of inevitability about it all.

I thought it was a missed opportunity for New Zealand. The title may have already been safely secured but I felt it was a chance for the Blacks to hammer a stake in the ground, to show everyone that they really were unbeatable, that they could through six intense Tri-Nations matches and emerge unscathed. To have achieved that would have been a big psychological blow to everyone else ahead of the World Cup next year. Losing to the Springboks gives the rest hope.

Six Tri-Nations games isn't a million miles away from a World Cup campaign. But the difference is you can win the Tri-Nations and still lose one or two games. As the All Blacks know only two well, playing brilliantly at the World Cup but losing the one all-important match isn't quite good enough. To have won all six Tri-Nations games would have sent out a powerful message.

The other two main talking points from the season were Richie McCaw's captaincy and Henry's at times extravagant rotation policy. Both generated their fair share of column inches, although only one divided opinion.

McCaw came in as captain to replace Tana Umaga, which was a tough act to follow. There have never been any doubts about McCaw as a player, but any new captain has to make his mark quickly while maintaining his individual standards on the pitch.

He did both with what looked like ease. It was obvious from the start that he had the respect from the other players and if anything, his performances surpassed his own high standards. I don't think he really put a foot wrong and New Zealand have the man to lead them into the World Cup.

The more controversial talking point was Henry's selection policy, changing his starting line-up after each game, sometimes bringing 10 new players in even after a good victory.

I can see Henry's logic to a point. He obviously wanted to have a good look at all of his squad, to give some fringe players a chance to stake a claim and experiment with the combinations he thinks he may be forced to use if certain first-choice players pick up injuries.

Personally, though, I'm not a big fan of all this chopping and changing. However good a competition the Super 14 is, there's no substitute for the intensity of Test match rugby and I'd like to see Henry's first-choice XV, whatever that is, getting more internationals under their collective belts. I'd like to see the Test team playing together regularly as the World Cup approaches, winning games together and gaining experience as a unit.

Henry's rotation policy also failed to answer one or two selection dilemmas. He's still got a question mark over who should play scrum-half and I don't think he really found an answer to who is his best number eight.

But saying that, New Zealand looked in very good shape. They justified their world ranking and at times they were untouchable. When the Blacks committed numbers to the breakdown, cleared out the ball and produced good quality ball out wide for the backs, no-one could live with them. Henry now has to ensure they keep doing that up to and, most importantly, during the World Cup.

NEW ZEALAND INTERNATIONAL STATISTICS

(UP TO 30 SEPTEMBER 2006)

MATCH RECORDS

MOST CONSECUTIVE TEST WINS

17 1965 SA 4, 1966 BI 1,2,3,4, 1967 A,E,W,F,S, 1968 A 1,2, F 1,2,3, 1969 W 1,2
15 2005 A 1, SA 2, A 2, W,I E,S, 2006 I 1,2, Arg A 1, SA 1, A 2, 3, SA 2
12 1988 A 3, 1989 F 1,2, Arg 1,2, A,W,I, 1990 S 1,2, A 1,2

MOST CONSECUTIVE TESTS WITHOUT DEFEAT

Matches	Wins	Draws	Periods
23	22	1	1987 to 1990
17	15	2	1961 to 1964
17	17	0	1965 to 1969
15	15	0	2005 to 2006

MOST POINTS IN A MATCH

BY THE TEAM

Pts.	Opponent	Venue	Year
145	Japan	Bloemfontein	1995
102	Tonga	Albany	2000
101	Italy	Huddersfield	1999
93	Argentina	Wellington	1997
91	Tonga	Brisbane	2003
91	Fiji	Albany	2005
74	Fiji	Christchurch	1987
73	Canada	Auckland	1995
71	Fiji	Albany	1997
71	Samoa	Albany	1999

BY A PLAYER

Pts.	Player	Opponent	Venue	Year
45	S D Culhane	Japan	Bloemfontein	1995
36	T E Brown	Italy	Huddersfield	1999
33	C J Spencer	Argentina	Wellington	1997
33	A P Mehrtens	Ireland	Dublin	1997
33	D W Carter	British/Irish	Wellington	2005
32	T E Brown	Tonga	Albany	2000
30	M C G Ellis	Japan	Bloemfontein	1995
30	T E Brown	Samoa	Albany	2001
29	A P Mehrtens	Australia	Auckland	1999
29	A P Mehrtens	France	Paris	2000
29	L R MacDonald	Tonga	Brisbane	2003

MOST TRIES IN A MATCH

BY THE TEAM

Tries	Opponent	Venue	Year
21	Japan	Bloemfontein	1995
15	Tonga	Albany	2000
15	Fiji	Albany	2005
14	Argentina	Wellington	1997
14	Italy	Huddersfield	1999
13	U S A	Berkeley	1913
13	Tonga	Brisbane	2003
12	Italy	Auckland	1987
12	Fiji	Christchurch	1987

BY A PLAYER

Tries	Player	Opponent	Venue	Year
6	M C G Ellis	Japan	Bloemfontein	1995
5	J W Wilson	Fiji	Albany	1997
4	D McGregor	England	Crystal Palace	1905
4	C I Green	Fiji	Christchurch	1987
4	J A Gallagher	Fiji	Christchurch	1987
4	J J Kirwan	Wales	Christchurch	1988
4	J T Lomu	England	Cape Town	1995
4	C M Cullen	Scotland	Dunedin	1996
4	J W Wilson	Samoa	Albany	1999
4	J M Muliaina	Canada	Melbourne	2003
4	S W Sivivatu	Fiji	Albany	2005

MOST CONVERSIONS IN A MATCH

BY THE TEAM

Cons	Opponent	Venue	Year
20	Japan	Bloemfontein	1995
13	Tonga	Brisbane	2003
12	Tonga	Albany	2000
11	Italy	Huddersfield	1999
10	Fiji	Christchurch	1987
10	Argentina	Wellington	1997
9	Canada	Melbourne	2003
8	Italy	Auckland	1987
8	Wales	Auckland	1988
8	Fiji	Albany	1997
8	Italy	Hamilton	2003
8	Fiji	Albany	2005

BY A PLAYER

Cons	Player	Opponent	Venue	Year
20	S D Culhane	Japan	Bloemfontein	1995
12	T E Brown	Tonga	Albany	2000
12	L R MacDonald	Tonga	Brisbane	2003
11	T E Brown	Italy	Huddersfield	1999
10	G J Fox	Fiji	Christchurch	1987
10	C J Spencer	Argentina	Wellington	1997
9	D W Carter	Canada	Melbourne	2003
8	G J Fox	Italy	Auckland	1987
8	G J Fox	Wales	Auckland	1988
8	A P Mehrtens	Italy	Hamilton	2002

MOST DROP GOALS IN A MATCH

BY THE TEAM

Drops	Opponent	Venue	Year
3	France	Christchurch	1986

BY A PLAYER

Drops	Player	Opponent	Venue	Year
2	O D Bruce	Ireland	Dublin	1978
2	F M Botica	France	Christchurch	1986
2	A P Mehrtens	Australia	Auckland	1995

MOST PENALTIES IN A MATCH

BY THE TEAM

Pens	Opponent	Venue	Year
9	Australia	Auckland	1999
9	France	Paris	2000
7	Western Samoa	Auckland	1993
7	South Africa	Pretoria	1999
7	South Africa	Wellington	2006
6	British/Irish Lions	Dunedin	1959
6	England	Christchurch	1985
6	Argentina	Wellington	1987
6	Scotland	Christchurch	1987
6	France	Paris	1990
6	South Africa	Auckland	1994
6	Australia	Brisbane	1996
6	Ireland	Dublin	1997
6	South Africa	Cardiff	1999
6	Scotland	Murrayfield	2001
6	South Africa	Christchurch	2004
6	Australia	Sydney	2004

BY A PLAYER

Pens	Player	Opponent	Venue	Year
9	A P Mehrtens	Australia	Auckland	1999
9	A P Mehrtens	France	Paris	2000
7	G J Fox	Western Samoa	Auckland	1993
7	A P Mehrtens	South Africa	Pretoria	1999
7	D W Carter	South Africa	Wellington	2006
6	D B Clarke	British/Irish Lions	Dunedin	1959
6	K J Crowley	England	Christchurch	1985
6	G J Fox	Argentina	Wellington	1987
6	G J Fox	Scotland	Christchurch	1987
6	G J Fox	France	Paris	1990
6	S P Howarth	South Africa	Auckland	1994
6	A P Mehrtens	Australia	Brisbane	1996
6	A P Mehrtens	Ireland	Dublin	1997
6	A P Mehrtens	South Africa	Cardiff	1999
6	A P Mehrtens	Scotland	Murrayfield	2001

MOST CAPPED PLAYERS

Caps	Player	Career Span
92	S B T Fitzpatrick	1986 to 1997
81	J W Marshall	1995 to 2005
79	I D Jones	1990 to 1999
74	J F Umaga	1997 to 2005
70	A P Mehrtens	1995 to 2004
63	J J Kirwan	1984 to 1994
63	J T Lomu	1994 to 2002
62	R M Brooke	1992 to 1999
60	C W Dowd	1993 to 2001
60	J W Wilson	1993 to 2001
58	G W Whetton	1981 to 1991
58	Z V Brooke	1987 to 1997
58	C M Cullen	1996 to 2002
56	O M Brown	1992 to 1998
55	C E Meads	1957 to 1971
55	F E Bunce	1992 to 1997
55	M N Jones	1987 to 1998
55	G M Somerville	2000 to 2006
55	C R Jack	2001 to 2006
55	D C Howlett	2000 to 2006
54	J A Kronfeld	1995 to 2000

MOST CONSECUTIVE TESTS

Tests	Player	Career span
63	S B T Fitzpatrick	1986 to 1995
51	C M Cullen	1996 to 2000
49	R M Brooke	1995 to 1999
41	J W Wilson	1996 to 1999
40	G W Whetton	1986 to 1991

MOST TESTS AS CAPTAIN

Tests	Player	Career span
51	S B T Fitzpatrick	1992 to 1997
30	W J Whineray	1958 to 1965
22	T C Randell	1998 to 2002
22	R D Thorne	2002 to 2003
21	J F Umaga	2004 to 2005
19	G N K Mourie	1977 to 1982
18	B J Lochore	1966 to 1970
17	A G Dalton	1981 to 1985

MOST POINTS IN TESTS

Points	Player	Tests	Career
967	A P Mehrtens	70	1995 to 2004
645	G J Fox	46	1985 to 1993
468	D W Carter	31	2003 to 2006
291	C J Spencer	35	1997 to 2004
236	C M Cullen	58	1996 to 2002
234	J W Wilson	60	1993 to 2001
210	D C Howlett	55	2000 to 2006
207	D B Clarke	31	1956 to 1964
201	A R Hewson	19	1981 to 1984
185	J T Lomu	63	1994 to 2002
185	J F Umaga	74	1997 to 2005

MOST TRIES IN TESTS

Tries	Player	Tests	Career
46	C M Cullen	58	1996 to 2002
44	J W Wilson	60	1993 to 2001
42	D C Howlett	55	2000 to 2006
37	J T Lomu	63	1994 to 2002
37*	J F Umaga	74	1999 to 2005
35	J J Kirwan	63	1984 to 1994
32	J T Rokocoko	36	2003 to 2006
24	J W Marshall	81	1995 to 2005
20	F E Bunce	55	1992 to 1997
19	S S Wilson	34	1977 to 1983
19*	T J Wright	30	1986 to 1991

* Umaga and Wright's hauls include penalty tries

MOST CONVERSIONS IN TESTS

Cons	Player	Tests	Career
169	A P Mehrtens	70	1995 to 2004
118	G J Fox	46	1985 to 1993
88	D W Carter	31	2003 to 2006
49	C J Spencer	35	1997 to 2004
43	T E Brown	18	1999 to 2001
33	D B Clarke	31	1956 to 1964
32	S D Culhane	6	1995 to 1996

MOST PENALTY GOALS IN TESTS

Penalties	Player	Tests	Career
188	A P Mehrtens	70	1995 to 2004
128	G J Fox	46	1985 to 1993
73	D W Carter	31	2003 to 2006
43	A R Hewson	19	1981 to 1984
41	C J Spencer	35	1997 to 2004
38	D B Clarke	31	1956 to 1964
24	W F McCormick	16	1965 to 1971

MOST DROPPED GOALS IN TESTS

Drops	Player	Tests	Career
10	A P Mehrtens	70	1995 to 2004
7	G J Fox	46	1985 to 1993
5	D B Clarke	31	1956 to 1964
5	M A Herewini	10	1962 to 1967
5	O D Bruce	14	1976 to 1978

TRI NATIONS RECORDS

RECORD	DETAIL	HODDER	SET
Most points in season	179	in six matches	2006
Most tries in season	17	in four matches	1997
	17	in four matches	2003
	17	in six matches	2006
Highest Score	55	55-35 v S Africa (h)	1997
Biggest win	37	43-6 v Australia (h)	1996
Highest score conceded	46	40–46 v S Africa (a)	2000
Biggest defeat	21	7–28 v Australia (a)	1999
Most points in matches	328	A P Mehrtens	1996 to 2004
Most points in season	99	D W Carter	2006
Most points in match	29	A P Mehrtens	v Australia (h) 1999
Most tries in matches	16	C M Cullen	1996 to 2002
Most tries in season	7	C M Cullen	2000
Most tries in match	3	J T Rokocoko	v Australia (a) 2003
	3	D C Howlett	V Australia (h) 2005
Most cons in matches	34	A P Mehrtens	1996 to 2004
Most cons in season	14	D W Carter	2006
Most cons in match	4	C J Spencer	v S Africa (h) 1997
	4	A P Mehrtens	v Australia (a) 2000
	4	A P Mehrtens	v S Africa (a) 2000
	4	C J Spencer	v S Africa (a) 2003
	4	D W Carter	v S Africa (a) 2006
Most pens in matches	82	A P Mehrtens	1996 to 2004
Most pens in season	21	D W Carter	2006
Most pens in match	9	A P Mehrtens	v Australia (h) 1999

MISCELLANEOUS RECORDS

RECORD	HOLDER	DETAIL
Longest Test Career	E Hughes/C E Meads	1907-21/1957-71
Youngest Test Cap	J T Lomu	19 yrs 45 days in 1994
Oldest Test Cap	E Hughes	40 yrs 123 days in 1921

CAREER RECORDS OF NEW ZEALAND INTERNATIONAL PLAYERS (PLAYERS CAPPED SINCE THE START OF RWC 2003 UP TO 30 SEPTEMBER 2006)

PLAYER BACKS	DEBUT	CAPS	T	C	P	D	PTS
S R Anesi	2005 v Fj	1	0	0	0	0	0
B A C Atiga	2003 v Tg	1	0	0	0	0	0
D W Carter	2003 v W	31	14	88	73	1	468
Q J Cowan	2004 v It	9	0	0	0	0	0
S J Devine	2002 v E	10	0	0	0	0	0
N J Evans	2004 v E	6	1	6	5	0	32
R L Gear	2004 v PI	15	9	0	0	0	45
S E Hamilton	2006 v Arg	2	1	0	0	0	5
D W Hill	2006 v I	1	0	0	0	0	0
D C Howlett	2000 v Tg	55	42	0	0	0	210
B T Kelleher	1999 v WS	45	6	0	0	0	30
C D E Laulala	2004 v W	2	0	0	0	0	0
C L McAlister	2005 v BI	10	3	12	11	0	72
L R MacDonald	2000 v S	41	13*	25	7	0	136
J W Marshall	1995 v F	81	24	0	0	0	120
A J D Mauger	2001 v I	37	7	8	1	1	57
A P Mehrtens	1995 v C	70	7	169	188	10	967
J M Muliaina	2003 v E	43	15	0	0	0	75
M A Nonu	2003 v E	12	2	0	0	0	10
C S Ralph	1998 v E	14	8	0	0	0	40
J T Rokococo	2003 v E	36	32	0	0	0	160
K Senio	2005 v A	1	0	0	0	0	0
S W Sivivatu	2005 v Fj	8	9	0	0	0	45
C G Smith	2004 v It	6	2	0	0	0	10
C J Spencer	1997 v Arg	35	14	49	41	0	291
I Toeava	2005 v S	5	1	0	0	0	5
S Tuitupou	2004 v E	9	1	0	0	0	5
J F Umaga	1997 v Fj	74	37*	0	0	0	185
P A T Weepu	2004 v W	13	3	0	0	0	15

FORWARDS

I F Afoa	2005 v I	2	0	0	0	0	0
S P Bates	2004 v It	1	0	0	0	0	0
D J Braid	2002 v W	3	1	0	0	0	5
J Collins	2001 v Arg	35	1	0	0	0	5
C Dermody	2006 v I	2	1	0	0	0	5
J J Eaton	2005 v I	8	1	0	0	0	5
T V Flavell	2000 v Tg	17	6	0	0	0	30
C R Flynn	2003 v C	3	1	0	0	0	5
J B Gibbes	2004 v E	8	0	0	0	0	0
M G Hammett	1999 v F	29	3	0	0	0	15
C J Hayman	2001 v Sm	31	0	0	0	0	0
D N Hewett	2001 v I	22	2	0	0	0	10
C H Hoeft	1998 v E	30	0	0	0	0	0
M R Holah	2001 v Sm	36	3	0	0	0	15
A K Hore	2002 v E	15	0	0	0	0	0
C R Jack	2001 v Arg	55	4	0	0	0	20
C R Johnstone	2005 v Fj	3	0	0	0	0	0
J Kaino	2006 v I	2	0	0	0	0	0
S T Lauaki	2005 v Fj	7	1	0	0	0	5
R H McCaw	2001 v I	44	8	0	0	0	40
A J Macdonald	2005 v W	2	0	0	0	0	0
T S Maling	2002 v It	11	0	0	0	0	0
M C Masoe	2005 v W	8	0	0	0	0	0
N M C Maxwell	1999 v WS	36	5	0	0	0	25
K F Mealamu	2002 v W	38	7	0	0	0	35
K J Meeuws	1998 v A	42	10	0	0	0	50
C A Newby	2004 v E	3	0	0	0	0	0
A D Oliver	1997 v Fj	49	2	0	0	0	10
G P Rawlinson	2006 v I	3	0	0	0	0	0
K J Robinson	2002 v E	6	0	0	0	0	0
X J Rush	1998 v A	8	0	0	0	0	0
J A C Ryan	2005 v Fj	7	0	0	0	0	0
G M Somerville	2000 v Tg	55	1	0	0	0	5
R So'oialo	2002 v W	27	4	0	0	0	20
S Taumoepeau	2004 v It	3	1	0	0	0	5
B C Thorn	2003 v W	12	2	0	0	0	10
R D Thorne	1999 v SA	43	5	0	0	0	25
N S Tialata	2005 v W	9	1	0	0	0	5
M M Tuiali'i	2004 v Arg	9	1	0	0	0	5
A J Williams	2002 v E	37	4	0	0	0	20
D J C Witcombe	2005 v Fj	5	0	0	0	0	0
T D Woodcock	2002 v W	23	0	0	0	0	0

NB MacDonald's figures include a penalty try awarded against South Africa in 2001, and Umaga's a penalty try awarded against South Africa in 2002.

NEW ZEALAND INTERNATIONAL PLAYERS
UP TO 30TH SEPTEMBER 2006

Entries in square brackets denote matches played in RWC Finals.

Abbott, H L (Taranaki) 1906 F
Afoa, I F (Auckland) 2005 I,S
Aitken, G G (Wellington) 1921 SA 1,2
Alatini, P F (Otago) 1999 F 1(R), [It, SA 3(R)], 2000 Tg, S 1, A 1, SA 1, A 2, SA 2, It, 2001 Sm, Arg 1, F, SA 1, A 1, SA 2, A 2
Allen, F R (Auckland) 1946 A 1,2, 1947 A 1,2, 1949 SA 1,2
Allen, M R (Taranaki, Manawatu) 1993 WS (t), 1996 S 2 (t), 1997 Arg 1(R),2(R), SA 2(R), A 3(R), E 2, W (R)
Allen, N H (Counties) 1980 A 3, W
Alley, G T (Canterbury) 1928 SA 1,2,3
Anderson, A (Canterbury) 1983 S, E, 1984 A 1,2,3, 1987 [Fj]
Anderson, B L (Wairarapa-Bush) 1986 A 1
Anesi, S R (Waikato) 2005 Fj(R)
Archer, W R (Otago, Southland) 1955 A 1,2, 1956 SA 1,3
Argus, W G (Canterbury) 1946 A 1,2, 1947 A 1,2
Arnold, D A (Canterbury) 1963 I, W, 1964 E, F
Arnold, K D (Waikato) 1947 A 1,2
Ashby, D L (Southland) 1958 A 2
Asher, A A (Auckland) 1903 A
Ashworth, B G (Auckland) 1978 A 1,2
Ashworth, J C (Canterbury, Hawke's Bay) 1978 A 1,2,3, 1980 A 1,2,3, 1981 SA 1,2,3, 1982 A 1,2, 1983 BI 1,2,3,4, A, 1984 F 1,2, A 1,2,3, 1985 E 1,2, A
Atiga, B A C (Auckland) 2003 [Tg(R)]
Atkinson, H (West Coast) 1913 A 1
Avery, H E (Wellington) 1910 A 1,2,3

Bachop, G T M (Canterbury) 1989 W, I, 1990 S 1,2, A 1,2,3, F 1,2, 1991 Arg 1,2, A 1,2, [E, US, C, A, S], 1992 Wld 1, 1994 SA 1,2,3, A, 1995 C, [I, W, S, E, SA], A 1,2
Bachop, S J (Otago) 1994 F 2, SA 1,2,3, A
Badeley, C E O (Auckland) 1921 SA 1,2
Baird, J A S (Otago) 1913 A 2
Ball, N (Wellington) 1931 A, 1932 A 2,3, 1935 W, 1936 E
Barrett, J (Auckland) 1913 A 2,3
Barry, E F (Wellington) 1934 A 2
Barry, L J (North Harbour) 1995 F 2
Bates, S P (Waikato) 2004 It(R)
Batty, G B (Wellington, Bay of Plenty) 1972 W, S, 1973 E 1, I, F, E 2, 1974 A 1,3, I, 1975 S, 1976 SA 1,2,3,4, 1977 BI 1
Batty, W (Auckland) 1930 BI 1,3,4, 1931 A
Beatty, G E (Taranaki) 1950 BI 1
Bell, R H (Otago) 1951 A 3, 1952 A 1,2
Bellis, E A (Wanganui) 1921 SA 1,2,3
Bennet, R (Otago) 1905 A
Berghan, T (Otago) 1938 A 1,2,3
Berry, M J (Wairarapa-Bush) 1986 A 3(R)
Berryman, N R (Northland) 1998 SA 2(R)
Bevan, V D (Wellington) 1949 A 1,2, 1950 BI 1,2,3,4
Birtwistle, W M (Canterbury) 1965 SA 1,2,3,4, 1967 E, W, S
Black, J E (Canterbury) 1977 F 1, 1979 A, 1980 A 3
Black, N W (Auckland) 1949 SA 3
Black, R S (Otago) 1914 A 1
Blackadder, T J (Canterbury) 1998 E 1(R),2, 2000 Tg, S 1,2, A 1, SA 1, A 2, SA 2, F 1,2, It
Blair, B A (Canterbury) 2001 S (R), Arg 2, 2002 E, W
Blake, A W (Wairarapa) 1949 A 1
Blowers, A F (Auckland) 1996 SA 2(R),4(R), 1997 I, E 1(R), W (R), 1999 F 1(R), SA 1, A 1(R), SA 2, A 2(R), [It]
Boggs, E G (Auckland) 1946 A 2, 1949 SA 1
Bond, J G (Canterbury) 1949 A 2
Booth, E E (Otago) 1906 F, 1907 A 1,3
Boroevich, K G (Wellington) 1986 F 1, A 1, F 3(R)
Botica, F M (North Harbour) 1986 F 1, A 1,2,3, F 2,3, 1989 Arg 1(R)
Bowden, N J G (Taranaki) 1952 A 2
Bowers, R G (Wellington) 1954 I, F
Bowman, A W (Hawke's Bay) 1938 A 1,2,3
Braid, D J (Auckland) 2002 W, 2003 [C(R),Tg]
Braid, G J (Bay of Plenty) 1983 S, E
Bremner, S G (Auckland, Canterbury) 1952 A 2, 1956 SA 2
Brewer, M R (Otago, Canterbury) 1986 F 1, A 1,2,3, F 2,3, 1988 A 1, 1989 A, W, I, 1990 S 1,2, A 1,2,3, F 1,2, 1992 I 2, A 1, 1994 F 1,2, SA 1,2,3, A, 1995 C, [I, W, E, SA], A 1,2
Briscoe, K C (Taranaki) 1959 BI 2, 1960 SA 1,2,3,4, 1963 I, W, 1964 E, S
Brooke, R M (Auckland) 1992 I 2, A 1,2,3, SA, 1993 BI 1,2,3, A, WS, 1994 SA 2,3, 1995 C, [J, S, E, SA], A 1,2, It, F 1,2, 1996 WS, S 1,2, A 1, SA 1, A 2, SA 2,3,4,5, 1997 Fj, Arg 1,2, A 1, SA 1, A 2, SA 2, A 3, I, E 1, W, E 2, 1998 E 1,2, A 1, SA 1, A 2, SA 2, A 3, 1999 WS, F 1, SA 1, A 1, SA 2, A 2, [Tg, E, It (R), S, F 2]
Brooke, Z V (Auckland) 1987 [Arg], 1989 Arg 2(R), 1990 A 1,2,3, F 1(R), 1991 Arg 2, A 1,2, [E, It, C, A, S], 1992 A 2,3, SA, 1993 BI 1,2,3(R), WS (R), S, E, 1994 F 2, SA 1,2,3, A, 1995 [J, S, E, SA], A 1,2, It, F 1,2, 1996 WS, S 1,2, A 1, SA 1, A 2, SA 2,3,4,5, 1997 Arg 1,2, A 1, SA 1, A 2, SA 2, A 3, I, E 1, W, E 2
Brooke-Cowden, M (Auckland) 1986 F 1, A 1, 1987 [W]
Broomhall, S R (Canterbury) 2002 SA 1(R),2(R), E, F
Brown, C (Taranaki) 1913 A 2,3
Brown, O M (Auckland) 1992 I 2, A 1,2,3, SA, 1993 BI 1,2,3, A, S, E, 1994 F 1,2, SA 1,2,3, A, 1995 C, [I, W, S, E, SA], A 1,2, It, F 1,2, 1996 WS, S 1,2, A 1, SA 1, A 2, SA 2,3,4,5, 1997 Fj, Arg 1,2, A 1, SA 1, A 2, SA 2, A 3, I, E 1, W, E 2, 1998 E 1,2, A 1, SA 1, A 2, SA 2
Brown, R H (Taranaki) 1955 A 3, 1956 SA 1,2,3,4, 1957 A 1,2, 1958 A 1,2,3, 1959 BI 1,3, 1961 F 1,2,3, 1962 A 1
Brown, T E (Otago) 1999 WS, F 1(R), SA 1(R), A 1(R),2(R), [E (R), It, S (R)], 2000 Tg, S 2(R), A 1(R), SA 1(R), A 2(R), 2001 Sm, Arg 1(R), F, SA 1, A 1
Brownlie, C J (Hawke's Bay) 1924 W, 1925 E, F
Brownlie, M J (Hawke's Bay) 1924 I, W, 1925 E, F, 1928 SA 1,2,3,4
Bruce, J A (Auckland) 1914 A 1,2
Bruce, O D (Canterbury) 1976 SA 1,2,4, 1977 BI 2,3,4, F 1,2, 1978 A 1,2, I, W, E, S
Bryers, R F (King Country) 1949 A 1
Budd, T A (Southland) 1946 A 2, 1949 A 2
Bullock-Douglas, G A H (Wanganui) 1932 A 1,2,3, 1934 A 1,2
Bunce, F E (North Harbour) 1992 Wld 1,2,3, I 1,2, A 1,2,3, SA, 1993 BI 1,2,3, A, WS, S, E, 1994 F 1,2, SA 1,2,3, A, 1995 C, [I, W, S, E, SA], A 1,2, It, F 1,2, 1996 WS, S 1,2, A1, SA 1, A 2, SA 2,3,4,5, 1997 Fj, Arg 1,2, A 1, SA 1, A 2, SA 2, A 3, I, E 1, W, E 2
Burgess, G A J (Auckland) 1981 SA 2
Burgess, G F (Southland) 1905 A
Burgess, R E (Manawatu) 1971 BI 1,2,3, 1972 A 3, W, 1973 I, F
Burke, P S (Taranaki) 1955 A 1, 1957 A 1,2
Burns, P J (Canterbury) 1908 AW 2, 1910 A 1,2,3, 1913 A 3
Bush, R G (Otago) 1931 A

Bush, W K (Canterbury) 1974 A 1,2, 1975 S, 1976 I, SA, 2,4, 1977 BI 2,3,4(R), 1978 I, W, 1979 A
Buxton, J B (Canterbury) 1955 A 3, 1956 SA 1

Cain, M J (Taranaki) 1913 US, 1914 A 1,2,3
Callesen, J A (Manawatu) 1974 A 1,2,3, 1975 S
Cameron, D (Taranaki) 1908 AW 1,2,3
Cameron, L M (Manawatu) 1980 A 3, 1981 SA 1(R),2,3, R
Carleton, S R (Canterbury) 1928 SA 1,2,3, 1929 A 1,2,3
Carrington, K R (Auckland) 1971 BI 1,3,4
Carter, D W (Canterbury) 2003 W, F, A 1(R), [It, C, Tg, SA(R), F(R)], 2004 E1, 2, PI, A1, SA1, A2, It, W, F, 2005 Fj, BI1, 2, SA1, A1, W, E, 2006 Arg, A1, SA1, A2, 3, SA2, 3
Carter, M P (Auckland) 1991 A 2, [It, A], 1997 Fj (R), A 1(R), 1998 E 2(R), A 2
Casey, S T (Otago) 1905 S, I, E, W, 1907 A 1,2,3, 1908 AW 1
Cashmore, A R (Auckland) 1996 S 2(R), 1997 A 2(R)
Catley, E H (Waikato) 1946 A 1, 1947 A 1,2, 1949 SA 1, 2, 3, 4
Caughey, T H C (Auckland) 1932 A 1,3, 1934 A 1, 2, 1935 S, I, 1936 E, A 1, 1937 SA 3
Caulton, R W (Wellington) 1959 BI 2,3,4, 1960 SA 1,4, 1961 F 2, 1963 E 1,2, I, W, 1964 E, S, F, A 1,2,3
Cherrington, N P (North Auckland) 1950 BI 1
Christian, D L (Auckland) 1949 SA 4
Clamp, M (Wellington) 1984 A 2,3
Clark, D W (Otago) 1964 A 1,2
Clark, W H (Wellington) 1953 W, 1954 I, E, S, 1955 A 1,2, 1956 SA 2,3,4
Clarke, A H (Auckland) 1958 A 3, 1959 BI 4, 1960 SA 1
Clarke, D B (Waikato) 1956 SA 3,4, 1957 A 1,2, 1958 A 1,3, 1959 BI 1,2,3,4, 1960 SA 1,2,3,4, 1961 F 1,2,3, 1962 A 1,2,3,4,5, 1963 E 1,2, I, W, 1964 E, S, F, A 2,3
Clarke, E (Auckland) 1992 Wld 2,3, I 1,2, 1993 BI 1,2, S (R), E, 1998 SA 2, A 3
Clarke, I J (Waikato) 1953 W, 1955 A 1,2,3, 1956 SA 1,2,3,4, 1957 A 1,2, 1958 A 1,3, 1959 BI 1,2, 1960 SA 2,4, 1961 F 1,2,3, 1962 A 1,2,3, 1963 E 1,2
Clarke, R L (Taranaki) 1932 A 2,3
Cobden, D G (Canterbury) 1937 SA 1
Cockerill, M S (Taranaki) 1951 A 1,2,3
Cockroft, E A P (South Canterbury) 1913 A 3, 1914 A 2,3
Codlin, B W (Counties) 1980 A 1,2,3
Collins, A H (Taranaki) 1932 A 2,3, 1934 A 1
Collins, J (Wellington) 2001 Arg 1, 2003 E (R), W, F, SA 1, A 1, SA 2, A 2, [It, W, SA, A, F], 2004 E2(R), Arg, PI(R), A1(R), SA1, It, F, 2005 Fj, BI1, 2, 3, SA1, A1, SA2, W, E, 2006 Arg, A1, 2, 3, SA2(R), 3
Collins, J L (Poverty Bay) 1964 A 1, 1965 SA 1,4
Colman, J T H (Taranaki) 1907 A 1,2, 1908 AW 1,3
Connor, D M (Auckland) 1961 F 1,2,3, 1962 A 1,2,3,4,5, 1963 E 1,2, 1964 A 2,3
Conway, R J (Otago, Bay of Plenty) 1959 BI 2,3,4, 1960 SA 1,3,4, 1965 SA 1,2,3,4
Cooke, A E (Auckland, Wellington) 1924 I, W, 1925 E, F, 1930 BI 1,2,3,4
Cooke, R J (Canterbury) 1903 A
Cooksley, M S B (Counties, Waikato) 1992 Wld 1, 1993 BI 2, 3(R), A, 1994 F 1, 2, SA 1,2, A, 2001 A 1(R), SA 2(t&R)
Cooper, G J L (Auckland, Otago) 1986 F 1, A 1,2, 1992 Wld 1,2,3, I 1
Cooper, M J A (Waikato) 1992 I 2, SA (R), 1993 BI 1(R),3(t), WS (t), S, 1994 F 1,2
Corner, M M N (Auckland) 1930 BI 2,3,4, 1931 A, 1934 A 1, 1936 E
Cossey, R R (Counties) 1958 A 1
Cottrell, A I (Canterbury) 1929 A 1,2,3, 1930 BI 1,2,3,4, 1931 A, 1932 A 1,2,3
Cottrell, W D (Canterbury) 1968 A 1,2, F 2,3, 1970 SA 1, 1971 BI 1,2,3,4
Couch, M B R (Wairarapa) 1947 A 1, 1949 A 1,2
Coughlan, T D (South Canterbury) 1958 A 1
Cowan, Q J (Southland) 2004 It(R), 2005 W(R),I(R),S(R), 2006 I1(R),SA1(R),A2(R),SA2(R),3
Creighton, J N (Canterbury) 1962 A 4
Cribb, R T (North Harbour) 2000 S 1,2, A 1, SA 1, A 2, SA 2, F 1,2, It, 2001 Sm, F, SA 1, A 1, SA 2, A 2
Crichton, S (Wellington) 1983 S, E
Cross, T (Canterbury) 1904 BI, 1905 A
Crowley, K J (Taranaki) 1985 E 1,2, A, Arg 1,2, 1986 A 3, F 2,3, 1987 [Arg], 1990 S 1,2, A 1,2,3, F 1,2, 1991 Arg 1,2, [A]
Crowley, P J B (Auckland) 1949 SA 3,4, 1950 BI 1,2,3,4
Culhane, S D (Southland) 1995 [J], It, F 1,2, 1996 SA 3,4
Cullen C M (Manawatu, Central Vikings, Wellington) 1996 WS, S 1,2, A 1, SA 1, A 2, SA 2,3,4,5, 1997 Fj, Arg 1,2, A 1, SA 1, A 2, SA 2, A 3, I, E 1, W, E 2, 1998 E 1,2, A 1, SA 1, A 2, SA 2, A 3, 1999 WS, F 1, SA 1, A 1, SA 2, A 2, [Tg, E, It (R), S, F 2, SA 3], 2000 Tg, S 1,2, A 1, SA 1, A 2, SA 2, F 1,2, It, 2001 A 2(R), 2002 It, Fj, A 1, SA 1, A 2, F
Cummings, W (Canterbury) 1913 A 2,3
Cundy, R T (Wairarapa) 1929 A 2(R)
Cunningham, G R (Auckland) 1979 A, S, E, 1980 A 1,2
Cunningham, W (Auckland) 1905 S, I, 1906 F, 1907 A 1,2,3, 1908 AW 1,2,3
Cupples, L F (Bay of Plenty) 1924 I, W
Currie, C J (Canterbury) 1978 I, W
Cuthill, J E (Otago) 1913 A 1, US

Dalley, W C (Canterbury) 1924 I, 1928 SA 1,2,3,4
Dalton, A G (Counties) 1977 F 2, 1978 A 1,2,3, I, W, E, S, 1979 F 1,2, S, 1981 S 1,2, SA 1,2,3, R, F 1,2, 1982 A 1,2,3, 1983 BI 1,2,3,4, A, 1984 F 1,2, A 1,2,3, 1985 E 1,2, A
Dalton, D (Hawke's Bay) 1935 I, W, 1936 A 1,2, 1937 SA 1,2,3, 1938 A 1,2
Dalton, R A (Wellington) 1947 A 1,2
Dalzell, G N (Canterbury) 1953 W, 1954 I, E, S, F
Davie, M G (Canterbury) 1983 E (R)
Davies, W A (Auckland, Otago) 1960 SA 4, 1962 A 4,5
Davis, K (Auckland) 1952 A 2, 1953 W, 1954 I, E, S, F, 1955 A 2, 1958 A 1,2,3
Davis, L J (Canterbury) 1976 I, 1977 BI 3,4
Davis, W L (Hawke's Bay) 1967 A, E, W, F, S, 1968 A 1,2, F 1, 1969 W 1,2, 1970 SA 2
Deans, I B (Canterbury) 1988 W 1,2, A 1,2,3, 1989 F 1,2, Arg 1,2, A
Deans, R G (Canterbury) 1905 S, I, E, W, 1908 AW 3
Deans, R M (Canterbury) 1983 S, E, 1984 A 1(R),2,3
Delamore, G W (Wellington) 1949 SA 4
Dermody, C (Southland) 2006 I1,2
Devine, S J (Auckland) 2002 E, W 2003 E (R), W, F, SA 1, A 1(R), [C,SA(R),F]
Dewar, H (Taranaki) 1913 A 1, US
Diack, E S (Otago) 1959 BI 2
Dick, J (Auckland) 1937 SA 1,2, 1938 A 3
Dick, M J (Auckland) 1963 I, W, 1964 E, S, F, 1965 SA 3, 1966 BI 4, 1967 A, E, W, F, 1969 W 1,2, 1970 SA 1,4
Dixon, M J (Canterbury) 1954 I, E, S, F, 1956 SA 1,2,3,4, 1957 A 1,2
Dobson, R L (Auckland) 1949 A 1
Dodd, E H (Wellington) 1905 A
Donald, A J (Wanganui) 1983 S, E, 1984 F 1,2, A 1,2,3
Donald, J G (Wairarapa) 1921 SA 1,2
Donald, Q (Wairarapa) 1924 I, W, 1925 E, F
Donaldson, M W (Manawatu) 1977 F 1,2, 1978 A 1,2,3, I, E, S, 1979 F 1,2, A, S (R), 1981 SA 3(R)
Dougan, J P (Wellington) 1972 A 1, 1973 E 2
Dowd, C W (Auckland) 1993 BI 1,2,3, A, WS, S, E, 1994 SA 1(R), 1995 C, [I, W, J, E, SA], A 1,2, It, F 1,2, 1996 WS, S 1,2, A 1, SA 1, A 2, SA 2,3,4,5, 1997 Fj, Arg 1,2, A 1, SA 1, A 2, SA 2, A 3, I, E 1, W, 1998 E 1,2, A 1, SA 1, A 2,3(R), 1999 SA 2(R), A 2(R), [Tg (R), E, It, S, F 2, SA 3], 2000 Tg, S 1(R),2(R), A 1(R), SA 1(R), A 2(R)
Dowd, G W (North Harbour) 1992 I 1(R)
Downing, A J (Auckland) 1913 A 1, US, 1914 A 1,2,3
Drake, J A (Auckland) 1986 F 2,3, 1987 [Fj, Arg, S, W, F], A
Duff, R H (Canterbury) 1951 A 1,2,3, 1952 A 1,2, 1955 A 2,3, 1956 SA 1,2,3,4
Duggan, R J L (Waikato) 1999 [It (R)]
Duncan, J (Otago) 1903 A
Duncan, M G (Hawke's Bay) 1971 BI 3(R),4
Duncan, W D (Otago) 1921 SA 1,2,3
Dunn, E J (North Auckland) 1979 S, 1981 S 1

Dunn, I T W (North Auckland) 1983 BI 1,4, A
Dunn, J M (Auckland) 1946 A 1

Earl, A T (Canterbury) 1986 F 1, A 1, F 3(R), 1987 [Arg], 1989 W, I, 1991 Arg 1(R), 2, A 1, [E (R), US, S], 1992 A 2, 3(R)
Eastgate, B P (Canterbury) 1952 A 1,2, 1954 S
Eaton, J J (Taranaki) 2005 I, E(t), S(R), 2006 Arg, A1, 2(R), 3, SA3(R)
Elliott, K G (Wellington) 1946 A 1,2
Ellis, M C G (Otago) 1993 S, E, 1995 C, [I (R), W, J, S, SA (R)]
Elsom, A E G (Canterbury) 1952 A 1,2, 1953 W, 1955 A 1,2,3
Elvidge, R R (Otago) 1946 A 1,2, 1949 SA 1,2,3,4, 1950 BI 1,2,3
Erceg, C P (Auckland) 1951 A 1,2,3, 1952 A 1
Evans, D A (Hawke's Bay) 1910 A 2
Evans, N J (North Harbour, Otago) 2004 E1(R), 2, Arg, PI(R), 2005 I, S
Eveleigh, K A (Manawatu) 1976 SA 2,4, 1977 BI 1,2

Fanning, A H N (Canterbury) 1913 A 3
Fanning, B J (Canterbury) 1903 A, 1904 BI
Farrell, C P (Auckland) 1977 BI 1,2
Fawcett, C L (Auckland) 1976 SA 2,3
Fea, W R (Otago) 1921 SA 3
Feek, G E (Canterbury) 1999 WS (R), A 1(R), SA 2, [E (t), It], 2000 F 1,2, It, 2001 I, S
Finlay, B E L (Manawatu) 1959 BI 1
Finlay, J (Manawatu) 1946 A 1
Finlayson, I (North Auckland) 1928 SA 1, 2, 3, 4, 1930 BI 1,2
Fitzgerald, J T (Wellington) 1952 A 1
Fitzpatrick, B B J (Wellington) 1953 W, 1954 I, F
Fitzpatrick, S B T (Auckland) 1986 F 1, A 1, F 2,3, 1987 [It, Fj, Arg, S, W, F], A, 1988 W 1,2, A 1,2,3, 1989 F 1,2, Arg 1,2, A, W, I, 1990 S 1,2, A 1,2,3, F 1,2, 1991 Arg 1,2, A 1,2, [E, US, It, C, A, S], 1992 Wld 1,2,3, I 1,2, A 1,2,3, SA, 1993 BI 1,2,3, A, WS, S, E, 1994 F 1,2, SA 1,2,3, A, 1995 C, [I, W, S, E, SA], A 1,2, It, F 1,2, 1996 WS, S 1,2, A 1, SA 1, A 2, SA 2,3,4,5, 1997 Fj, Arg 1,2, A 1, SA 1, A 2, SA 2, A 3, W (R)
Flavell, T V (North Harbour) 2000 Tg, S 1(R), A 1(R), SA 1, 2(t), F 1(R), 2(R), It, 2001 Sm, Arg 1, F, SA 1, A 1, SA 2, A 2, 2006 I1(R), 2
Fleming, J K (Wellington) 1979 S, E, 1980 A 1,2,3
Fletcher, C J C (North Auckland) 1921 SA 3
Flynn, C R (Canterbury) 2003 [C(R),Tg], 2004 It(R)
Fogarty, R (Taranaki) 1921 SA 1,3
Ford, B R (Marlborough) 1977 BI 3,4, 1978 I, 1979 E
Forster, S T (Otago) 1993 S, E, 1994 F 1,2, 1995 It, F 1
Fox, G J (Auckland) 1985 Arg 1, 1987 [It, Fj, Arg, S, W, F], A, 1988 W 1,2, A 1,2,3, 1989 F 1,2, Arg 1,2, A, W, I, 1990 S 1,2, A 1,2,3, F 1,2, 1991 Arg 1,2, A 1,2, [E, It, C, A], 1992 Wld 1,2(R), A 1,2,3, SA, 1993 BI 1,2,3, A, WS
Francis, A R H (Auckland) 1905 A, 1907 A 1,2,3, 1908 AW 1,2,3, 1910 A 1,2,3
Francis, W C (Wellington) 1913 A 2,3, 1914 A 1,2,3
Fraser, B G (Wellington) 1979 S, E, 1980 A 3, W, 1981 S 1,2, SA 1,2,3, R, F 1,2, 1982 A 1,2,3, 1983 BI 1,2,3,4, A, S, E, 1984 A 1
Frazer, H F (Hawke's Bay) 1946 A 1,2, 1947 A 1,2, 1949 SA 2
Fryer, F C (Canterbury) 1907 A 1,2,3, 1908 AW 2
Fuller, W B (Canterbury) 1910 A 1,2
Furlong, B D M (Hawke's Bay) 1970 SA 4

Gallagher, J A (Wellington) 1987 [It, Fj, S, W, F], A, 1988 W 1,2, A 1,2,3, 1989 F 1,2, Arg 1,2, A, W, I
Gallaher, D (Auckland) 1903 A, 1904 BI, 1905 S, E, W, 1906 F
Gard, P C (North Otago) 1971 BI 4
Gardiner, A J (Taranaki) 1974 A 3
Gear, R L (North Harbour, Nelson Bays, Tasman) 2004 PI, It, 2005 BI1(R), 2, 3, SA1, A1, SA2,W,S, 2006 Arg,A1,2,SA2,3(R)
Geddes, J H (Southland) 1929 A 1
Geddes, W McK (Auckland) 1913 A 2
Gemmell, B McL (Auckland) 1974 A 1,2
George, V L (Southland) 1938 A 1,2,3
Gibbes, J B (Waikato) 2004 E1, 2, Arg(R), PI, A1, 2, SA2, 2005 BI2(R)
Gibson, D P E (Canterbury) 1999 WS, F 1, SA 1, A 1, SA 2, A 2, [Tg (R), E (R), It, S (R), F 2(R)], 2000 F 1,2, 2002 It, I 1(R),2(R), Fj, A 2(R), SA 2(R)
Gilbert, G D M (West Coast) 1935 S, I, W, 1936 E
Gillespie, C T (Wellington) 1913 A 2
Gillespie, W D (Otago) 1958 A 3
Gillett, G A (Canterbury, Auckland) 1905 S, I, E, W, 1907 A 2,3, 1908 AW 1,3
Gillies, C C (Otago) 1936 A 2
Gilray, C M (Otago) 1905 A
Glasgow, F T (Taranaki, Southland) 1905 S, I, E, W, 1906 F, 1908 AW 3
Glenn, W S (Taranaki) 1904 BI, 1906 F
Goddard, M P (South Canterbury) 1946 A 2, 1947 A 1,2, 1949 SA 3,4
Going, S M (North Auckland) 1967 A, F, 1968 F 3, 1969 W 1,2, 1970 SA 1(R),4, 1971 BI 1,2,3,4, 1972 A 1,2,3, W, S, 1973 E 1, I, F, E 2, 1974 I, 1975 S, 1976 I (R), SA 1,2,3,4, 1977 BI 1,2
Gordon, S B (Waikato) 1993 S, E
Graham, D J (Canterbury) 1958 A 1,2, 1960 SA 2,3, 1961 F 1,2,3, 1962 A 1,2,3,4,5, 1963 E 1,2, I, W, 1964 E, S, F, A 1,2,3
Graham, J B (Otago) 1913 US, 1914 A 1,3
Graham, W G (Otago) 1979 F 1(R)
Grant, L A (South Canterbury) 1947 A 1,2, 1949 SA 1,2
Gray, G D (Canterbury) 1908 AW 2, 1913 A 1, US
Gray, K F (Wellington) 1963 I, W, 1964 E, S, F, A 1,2,3, 1965 SA 1,2,3,4, 1966 BI 1,2,3,4, 1967 W, F, S, 1968 A 1, F 2,3, 1969 W 1,2
Gray, W N (Bay of Plenty) 1955 A 2,3, 1956 SA 1,2,3,4
Green, C I (Canterbury) 1983 S (R), E, 1984 A 1,2,3, 1985 E 1, 2, A, Arg 1, 2, 1986 A 2, 3, F 2, 3, 1987 [It, Fj, S, W, F], A
Grenside, B A (Hawke's Bay) 1928 SA 1,2,3,4, 1929 A 2,3
Griffiths, J L (Wellington) 1934 A 2, 1935 S, I, W, 1936 A 1,2, 1938 A 3
Guy, R A (North Auckland) 1971 BI 1,2,3,4

Haden, A M (Auckland) 1977 BI 1,2,3,4, F 1,2, 1978 A 1,2,3, I, W, E, S, 1979 F 1,2, A, S, E, 1980 A 1,2,3, W, 1981 S 2, SA 1, 2, 3, R, F 1, 2, 1982 A 1, 2, 3, 1983 BI 1, 2, 3, 4, A, 1984 F 1,2, 1985 Arg 1,2
Hadley, S (Auckland) 1928 SA 1,2,3,4
Hadley, W E (Auckland) 1934 A 1,2, 1935 S, I, W, 1936 E, A 1,2
Haig, J S (Otago) 1946 A 1,2
Haig, L S (Otago) 1950 BI 2,3,4, 1951 A 1,2,3, 1953 W, 1954 E, S
Hales, D A (Canterbury) 1972 A 1,2,3, W
Hamilton, D C (Southland) 1908 AW 2
Hamilton, S E (Canterbury) 2006 Arg,SA1
Hammett, M G (Canterbury) 1999 F 1(R), SA 2(R), [It, S (R), SA 3], 2000 Tg, S 1(R), 2(t&R), A 1(R), SA 1(R), A 2(R), SA 2(R), F 2(R), It (R), 2001 Arg 1(t), 2002 It (R), I 1, 2, A 1, SA 1, 2(R), 2003 SA 1(R), A 1(R), SA 2, [It(R),C,W(R),SA(R),F(R)]
Hammond, I A (Marlborough) 1952 A 2
Harper, E T (Canterbury) 1904 BI, 1906 F
Harding, S (Otago) 2002 Fj
Harris, P C (Manawatu) 1976 SA 3
Hart, A H (Taranaki) 1924 I
Hart, G F (Canterbury) 1930 BI 1,2,3,4, 1931 A, 1934 A 1, 1935 S, I, W, 1936 A 1,2
Harvey, B A (Wairarapa-Bush) 1986 F 1
Harvey, I H (Wairarapa) 1928 SA 4
Harvey, L R (Otago) 1949 SA 1,2,3,4, 1950 BI 1,2,3,4
Harvey, P (Canterbury) 1904 BI
Hasell, E W (Canterbury) 1913 A 2,3
Hayman, C J (Otago) 2001 Sm (R), Arg 1, F (R), A 1(R), SA 2(R), A 2(R), 2002 F (t), W, 2004 E1, 2, PI, A1, 2, SA2, It, W(R), F, 2005 BI1, SA1, A1, SA2, A2, W, E, 2006 I1, 2, A1, SA1, A2, 3, SA3

Hayward, H O (Auckland) 1908 AW 3
Hazlett, E J (Southland) 1966 BI 1,2,3,4, 1967 A, E
Hazlett, W E (Southland) 1928 SA 1,2,3,4, 1930 BI 1,2,3,4
Heeps, T R (Wellington) 1962 A 1,2,3,4,5
Heke, W R (North Auckland) 1929 A 1,2,3
Hemi, R C (Waikato) 1953 W, 1954 I, E, S, F, 1955 A 1,2,3, 1956 SA 1,3,4, 1957 A 1,2, 1959 BI 1,3,4
Henderson, P (Wanganui) 1949 SA 1,2,3,4, 1950 BI 2,3,4
Henderson, P W (Otago) 1991 Arg 1, [C], 1992 Wld 1,2,3, I 1, 1995 [J]
Herewini, M A (Auckland) 1962 A 5, 1963 I, 1964 S, F, 1965 SA 4, 1966 BI 1,2,3,4, 1967 A
Hewett, D N (Canterbury) 2001 I (R), S (R), Arg 2, 2002 It (R), I 1,2, A 1, SA 1, A 2, SA 2, 2003 E, F, SA 1, A 1, SA 2, A 2, [It, Tg(R), W, SA, A, F]
Hewett, J A (Auckland) 1991 [It]
Hewitt, N J (Southland) 1995 [I (t), J], 1996 A 1(R), 1997 SA 1(R), I, E 1, W, E 2, 1998 E 2(t + R)
Hewson, A R (Wellington) 1981 S 1, 2, SA 1, 2, 3, R, F 1, 2, 1982 A 1, 2, 3, 1983 BI 1, 2, 3, 4, A, 1984 F 1, 2, A 1
Higginson, G (Canterbury, Hawke's Bay) 1980 W, 1981 S 1, SA 1, 1982 A 1,2, 1983 A
Hill, D W (Waikato) 2006 I2(R)
Hill, S F (Canterbury) 1955 A 3, 1956 SA 1,3,4, 1957 A 1,2, 1958 A 3, 1959 BI 1,2,3,4
Hines, G R (Waikato) 1980 A 3
Hobbs, M J B (Canterbury) 1983 BI 1,2,3,4, A, S, E, 1984 F 1,2, A 1,2,3, 1985 E 1,2, A, Arg 1,2, 1986 A 2,3, F 2,3
Hoeft, C H (Otago) 1998 E 2(t + R), A 2(R), SA 2, A 3, 1999 WS, F 1, SA 1, A 1,2, [Tg,E, S, F 2, SA 3(R)], 2000 S 1,2, A 1, SA 1, A 2, SA 2, 2001 Sm, Arg 1, F, SA 1, A 1, SA 2, A 2, 2003 W, [C,F(R)]
Holah, M R (Waikato) 2001 Sm, Arg 1(t&R), F (R), SA 1(R), A 1(R), SA 2(R), A 2(R), 2002 It, I 2(R), A 2(t), E, F, W (R), 2003 W, F (R), A 1(R), SA 2, [It(R), C, Tg(R), W(R), SA(t&R), A(R), F(t&R)], 2004 E1(R), 2, Arg(R), PI, A1, SA1, A2, SA2, 2005 BI3(R), A1(R), 2006 I1, SA3(t)
Holder, E C (Buller) 1934 A 2
Hook, L S (Auckland) 1929 A 1,2,3
Hooper, J A (Canterbury) 1937 SA 1,2,3
Hopkinson, A E (Canterbury) 1967 S, 1968 A 2, F 1,2,3, 1969 W 2, 1970 SA 1,2,3
Hore, A K (Taranaki) 2002 E, F, 2004 E1(t),2(R),Arg,A1(t), 2005 W(R), I(R), S(R), 2006 I2(R), Arg(R), A1(R), SA1(R), A2(R), SA3
Hore, J (Otago) 1930 BI 2,3,4, 1932 A 1,2,3, 1934 A 1,2, 1935 S, 1936 E
Horsley, R H (Wellington) 1960 SA 2,3,4
Hotop, J (Canterbury) 1952 A 1,2, 1955 A 3
Howarth, S P (Auckland) 1994 SA 1,2,3, A
Howlett, D C (Auckland) 2000 Tg (R), F 1,2, It, 2001 Sm, Arg 1(R), F (R), SA 1, A 1,2, I, S, Arg 2, 2002 It, I 1,2(R), Fj, A 1, SA 1, A 2, SA 2, E, F, W, 2003 E, W, F, SA 1, A 1, SA 2, A 2, [It,C(R),Tg,W,SA,A,F], 2004 E1,A1,SA1,A2,SA2,W,F, 2005 Fj,BI1,A2,I,E, 2006 I1,2,SA1,A3,SA3
Hughes, A M (Auckland) 1949 A 1,2, 1950 BI 1,2,3,4
Hughes, E (Southland, Wellington) 1907 A 1,2,3, 1908 AW 1, 1921 SA 1,2
Hunter, B A (Otago) 1971 BI 1,2,3
Hunter, J (Taranaki) 1905 S, I, E, W, 1906 F, 1907 A 1,2,3, 1908 AW 1,2,3
Hurst, I A (Canterbury) 1973 I, F, E 2, 1974 A 1,2

Ieremia, A (Wellington) 1994 SA 1,2,3, 1995 [J], 1996 SA 2(R),5(R), 1997 A 1(R), SA 1(R), A 2, SA 2, A 3, I, E 1, 1999 WS, F 1, SA 1, A 1, SA 2, A 2, [Tg, E, S, F 2, SA 3], 2000 Tg, S 1,2, A 1,2, SA 2
Ifwersen, K D (Auckland) 1921 SA 3
Innes, C R (Auckland) 1989 W, I, 1990 A 1,2,3, F 1,2, 1991 Arg 1,2, A 1,2, [E, US, It, C, A, S]
Innes, G D (Canterbury) 1932 A 2
Irvine, I B (North Auckland) 1952 A 1
Irvine, J G (Otago) 1914 A 1,2,3
Irvine, W R (Hawke's Bay, Wairarapa) 1924 I, W, 1925 E, F, 1930 BI 1
Irwin, M W (Otago) 1955 A 1,2, 1956 SA 1, 1958 A 2, 1959 BI 3,4, 1960 SA 1

Jack, C R (Canterbury) 2001 Arg 1(R), SA 1(R),2, A 2, I, S, Arg 2, 2002 I 1,2, A 1, SA 1, A 2, SA 2, 2003 E, W, F, SA 1, A 1, SA 2(R), A 2, [It, C, SA, A, F], 2004 E1, 2, Arg, PI, A1, SA1, A2, SA2, It, W, F, 2005 Fj(R), BI1, 2, 3, SA1, A1, SA2, A2, W, E, S, 2006 I1, 2, A1, SA1, A2, 3, SA2(R),3
Jackson, E S (Hawke's Bay) 1936 A 1,2, 1937 SA 1,2,3, 1938 A 3
Jaffray, J L (Otago, South Canterbury) 1972 A 2, 1975 S, 1976 I, SA 1, 1977 BI 2, 1979 F 1,2
Jarden, R A (Wellington) 1951 A 1,2, 1952 A 1,2, 1953 W, 1954 I, E, S, F, 1955 A 1,2,3, 1956 SA 1,2,3,4
Jefferd, A C R (East Coast) 1981 S 1,2, SA 1
Jessep, E M (Wellington) 1931 A, 1932 A 1
Johnson, L M (Wellington) 1928 SA 1,2,3,4
Johnston, W (Otago) 1907 A 1,2,3
Johnstone, B R (Auckland) 1976 SA 2, 1977 BI 1,2, F 1,2, 1978 I, W, E, S, 1979 F 1,2, S, E
Johnstone, C R (Canterbury) 2005 Fj(R),BI2(R),3(R)
Johnstone, P (Otago) 1949 SA 2,4, 1950 BI 1,2,3,4, 1951 A 1,2,3
Jones, I D (North Auckland, North Harbour) 1990 S 1,2, A 1,2,3, F 1,2, 1991 Arg 1,2, A 1,2, [E, US, It, C, A, S], 1992 Wld 1,2,3, I 1,2, A 1,2,3, SA, 1993 BI 1,2(R),3, WS, S, E, 1994 F 1,2, SA 1,3, A, 1995 C, [I, W, S, E, SA], A 1,2, It, F 1,2, 1996 WS, S 1,2, A 1, SA 1, A 2, SA 2,3,4,5, 1997 Fj, Arg 1,2, A 1, SA 1, A 2, SA 2, A 3, I, E 1, W, E 2, 1998 E 1,2, A 1, SA 1, A 2,3(R), 1999 F 1(R), [It, S (R)]
Jones, M G (North Auckland) 1973 E 2
Jones, M N (Auckland) 1987 [It, Fj, S, F], A, 1988 W 1,2, A 2,3, 1989 F 1,2, Arg 1,2, 1990 F 1,2, 1991 Arg 1,2, A 1,2, [E, US, S], 1992 Wld 1,3, I 2, A 1,3, SA, 1993 BI 1,2,3, A, WS, 1994 SA 3(R), A, 1995 A 1(R),2, It, F 1,2, 1996 WS, S 1,2, A 1, SA 1, A 2, SA 2,3,4,5, 1997 Fj, 1998 E 1, A 1, SA 1, A 2
Jones, P F H (North Auckland) 1954 E, S, 1955 A 1,2, 1956 SA 3,4, 1958 A 1,2,3, 1959 BI 1, 1960 SA 1
Joseph, H T (Canterbury) 1971 BI 2,3
Joseph, J W (Otago) 1992 Wld 2,3(R), I 1, A 1(R),3, SA, 1993 BI 1,2,3, A, WS, S, E, 1994 SA 2(t), 1995 C, [I, W, J (R), S, SA (R)]

Kaino, J (Auckland) 2006 I1(R),2
Karam, J F (Wellington, Horowhenua) 1972 W, S, 1973 E 1, I, F, 1974 A 1,2,3, I, 1975 S
Katene, T (Wellington) 1955 A 2
Kearney, J C (Otago) 1947 A 2, 1949 SA 1,2,3
Kelleher, B T (Otago, Waikato) 1999 WS (R), SA 1(R), A 2(R), [Tg (R), E (R), It, F 2], 2000 S 1, A 1(R), 2(R), It (R), 2001 Sm, F (R), A 1(R), SA 2, A 2, I, S, 2002 It, I 2(R), Fj, SA 1(R), 2(R), 2003 F (R), [A(R)], 2004 Arg,PI(R),SA1(R),2(R),It,W(R),F, 2005 Fj, BI1(R), 2, 3, SA1, W, E, 2006 I1, 2, A1, 2, 3, SA3(R)
Kelly, J W (Auckland) 1949 A 1,2
Kember, G F (Wellington) 1970 SA 4
Ketels, R C (Counties) 1980 W, 1981 S 1,2, R, F 1
Kiernan, H A D (Auckland) 1903 A
Kilby, F D (Wellington) 1932 A 1,2,3, 1934 A 2
Killeen, B A (Auckland) 1936 A 1
King, R M (Waikato) 2002 W
King, R R (West Coast) 1934 A 2, 1935 S, I, W, 1936 E, A 1,2, 1937 SA 1,2,3, 1938 A 1,2,3
Kingstone, C N (Taranaki) 1921 SA 1,2,3
Kirk, D E (Auckland) 1985 E 1,2, A, Arg 1, 1986 F 1, A 1,2,3, F 2,3, 1987 [It, Fj, Arg, S, W, F], A
Kirkpatrick, I A (Canterbury, Poverty Bay) 1967 F, 1968 A 1(R),2, F 1,2,3, 1969 W 1,2, 1970 SA 1,2,3,4, 1971 BI 1,2,3,4, 1972 A 1,2,3, W, S, 1973 E 1, I, F, E 2, 1974 A 1,2,3, I 1975 S, 1976 I, SA 1,2,3,4, 1977 BI 1,2,3,4
Kirton, E W (Otago) 1967 E, W, F, S, 1968 A 1,2, F 1,2,3, 1969 W 1,2, 1970 SA 2,3
Kirwan, J J (Auckland) 1984 F 1,2, 1985 E 1,2, A, Arg 1,2, 1986 F 1, A 1,2,3, F 2,3, 1987 [It, Fj, Arg, S, W, F], A, 1988 W 1,2, A 1,2,3, 1989 F 1,2, Arg 1,2, A, 1990 S 1,2, A 1,2,3, F 1,2, 1991 Arg 2, A 1,2, [E, It, C, A, S], 1992 Wld 1,2(R),3, I 1,2, A 1,2,3, SA, 1993 BI 2,3, A, WS, 1994 F 1,2, SA 1,2,3
Kivell, A L (Taranaki) 1929 A 2,3
Knight, A (Auckland) 1934 A 1

Knight, G A (Manawatu) 1977 F 1,2, 1978 A 1,2,3, E, S, 1979 F 1,2, A, 1980 A 1,2,3, W, 1981 S 1,2, SA 1,3, 1982 A 1,2,3, 1983 BI 1,2,3,4, A, 1984 F 1,2, A 1,2,3, 1985 E 1,2, A, 1986 A 2,3
Knight, L G (Poverty Bay) 1977 BI 1,2,3,4, F 1,2
Koteka, T T (Waikato) 1981 F 2, 1982 A 3
Kreft, A J (Otago) 1968 A 2
Kronfeld, J A (Otago) 1995 C, [I, W, S, E, SA], A 1,2(R) 1996 WS, S 1,2, A 1, SA 1, A 2, SA 2,3,4,5, 1997 Fj, Arg 1,2, A 1, SA 1, A 2, SA 2, A 3, I (R), E 1, W, E 2, 1998 E 1,2, A 1, SA 1,2 A 3, 1999 WS, F 1, SA 1, A 1, SA 2, A 2, [Tg, E, S, F 2, SA 3], 2000 Tg, S 1(R),2, A 1(R), SA 1, A 2, SA 2

Laidlaw, C R (Otago, Canterbury) 1964 F, A 1, 1965 SA 1,2,3,4, 1966 BI 1,2,3,4, 1967 E, W, S, 1968 A 1,2, F 1,2, 1970 SA 1,2,3
Laidlaw, K F (Southland) 1960 SA 2,3,4
Lambert, K K (Manawatu) 1972 S (R), 1973 E 1, I, F, E 2, 1974 I, 1976 SA 1,3,4, 1977 BI 1,4
Lambourn, A (Wellington) 1934 A 1,2, 1935 S, I, W, 1936 E, 1937 SA 1,2,3, 1938 A 3
Larsen, B P (North Harbour) 1992 Wld 2,3, I 1, 1994 F 1,2, SA 1,2,3, A (t), 1995 [I, W, J, E(R)], It, F 1, 1996 S 2(t), SA 4(R)
Lauaki, S T (Waikato) 2005 Fj(R),BI1(R),2(R),3,A2,I,S
Laulala, C D E (Canterbury) 2004 W, 2006 I2
Le Lievre, J M (Canterbury) 1962 A 4
Lee, D D (Otago) 2002 E (R), F
Lendrum, R N (Counties) 1973 E 2
Leslie, A R (Wellington) 1974 A 1,2,3, I, 1975 S, 1976 I, SA 1,2,3,4
Leys, E T (Wellington) 1929 A 3
Lilburne, H T (Canterbury, Wellington) 1928 SA 3,4, 1929 A 1,2,3, 1930 BI 1,4, 1931 A, 1932 A 1, 1934 A 2
Lindsay, D F (Otago) 1928 SA 1,2,3
Lineen, T R (Auckland) 1957 A 1,2, 1958 A 1,2,3, 1959 BI 1,2,3,4, 1960 SA 1,2,3
Lister, T N (South Canterbury) 1968 A 1,2, F 1, 1969 W 1,2, 1970 SA 1,4, 1971 BI 4
Little, P F (Auckland) 1961 F 2,3, 1962 A 2,3,5, 1963 I, W, 1964 E, S, F
Little, W K (North Harbour) 1990 S 1,2, A 1,2,3, F 1,2, 1991 Arg 1,2, A 1, [It, S], 1992 Wld 1,2,3, I 1,2, A 1,2,3, SA, 1993 BI 1, WS (R), 1994 SA 2(R), A, 1995 C, [I, W, S, E, SA], A 1,2, It, F 1,2, 1996 S 2, A 1, SA 1, A 2, SA 2,3,4,5, 1997 W, E 2, 1998 E 1, A 1, SA 1, A 2
Loader, C J (Wellington) 1954 I, E, S, F
Lochore, B J (Wairarapa) 1964 E, S, 1965 SA 1,2,3,4, 1966 BI 1,2,3,4, 1967 A, E, W, F, S, 1968 A 1, F 2,3, 1969 W 1,2, 1970 SA 1,2,3,4, 1971 BI 3
Loe, R W (Waikato, Canterbury) 1987 [It, Arg], 1988 W 1,2, A 1,2,3, 1989 F 1,2, Arg 1,2, A, W, I, 1990 S 1,2, A 1,2,3, F 1,2, 1991 Arg 1,2, A 1,2, [E, It, C, A, S], 1992 Wld 1,2,3, I 1, A 1,2,3, SA, 1994 F 1,2, SA 1,2,3, A, 1995 [J, S, SA (R)], A 2(t), F 2(R)
Lomu, J T (Counties Manukau, Wellington) 1994 F 1,2, 1995 [I, W, S, E, SA], A 1,2, It, F 1,2, 1996 WS, S 1, A 1, SA 1, A 2, 1997 E 1, W, E 2, 1998 E 1,2, A 1(R), SA 1, A 2, SA 2, A 3, 1999 WS (R), SA 1(R), A 1(R), SA 2(R), A 2(R), [Tg, E, It, S, F 2, SA 3], 2000 Tg, S 1,2, A 1, SA 1, A 2, SA 2, F 1, 2001 Arg 1, F, SA 1, A 1, SA 2, A 2, I, S, Arg 2, 2002 It (R), I 1(R),2, Fj, SA 1(R), E, F, W
Long, A J (Auckland) 1903 A
Loveridge, D S (Taranaki) 1978 W, 1979 S, E, 1980 A 1,2,3, W, 1981 S 1,2, SA 1,2,3, R, F 1,2, 1982 A 1,2,3, 1983 BI 1,2,3,4, A, 1985 Arg 2
Lowen, K R (Waikato) 2002 E
Lucas, F W (Auckland) 1924 I, 1925 F, 1928 SA 4, 1930 BI 1,2,3,4
Lunn, W A (Otago) 1949 A 1,2
Lynch, T W (South Canterbury) 1913 A 1, 1914 A 1,2,3
Lynch, T W (Canterbury) 1951 A 1,2,3

McAlister, C L (North Harbour) 2005 BI3, SA1(R), A1(R), SA2(R), A2(R), 2006 I1, 2, SA1(R), A3, SA2
McAtamney, F S (Otago) 1956 SA 2
McCahill, B J (Auckland) 1987 [Arg, S (R), W (R)], 1989 Arg 1(R),2(R), 1991 A 2, [E, US, C, A]
McCaw, R H (Canterbury) 2001 I, S, Arg 2, 2002 I 1,2, A 1, SA 1, A 2, SA 2, 2003 E, F, SA 1, A 1, 2, [It, C(R), Tg(R), W, SA, A, F], 2004 E1, Arg, It, W, F, 2005 Fj, BI1, 2, SA1, A1, SA2, A2,W(R),I,S, 2006 I1, 2, A1, SA1, A2, 3, SA2, 3
McCaw, W A (Southland) 1951 A 1,2,3, 1953 W, 1954 F
McCool, M J (Wairarapa-Bush) 1979 A
McCormick, W F (Canterbury) 1965 SA 4, 1967 E, W, F, S, 1968 A 1,2, F 1,2,3, 1969 W 1,2, 1970 SA 1,2,3, 1971 BI 1
McCullough, J F (Taranaki) 1959 BI 2,3,4
McDonald, A (Otago) 1905 S, I, E, W, 1907 A 1, 1908 AW 1, 1913 A 1, US
Macdonald, A J (Auckland) 2005 W(R),S
Macdonald, H H (Canterbury, North Auckland) 1972 W, S, 1973 E 1, I, F, E 2, 1974 I, 1975 S, 1976 I, SA 1,2,3
MacDonald, L R (Canterbury) 2000 S 1(R),2(R), SA 1(t),2(R), 2001 Sm, Arg 1, F, SA 1(R), A 1(R), SA 2, A 2, I, S, 2002 I 1,2, Fj (R), A 2(R), SA 2, 2003 A 2(R),[It(R),C,Tg, W, SA, A, F], 2005 BI1, 2(R), SA1, 2, A2, W(R), I, E(R), S(R), 2006 Arg, A1, SA1, A2, 3(R), SA2
McDonnell, J M (Otago) 2002 It, I 1(R),2(R), Fj, SA 1(R), A 2(R), E, F
McDowell, S C (Auckland, Bay of Plenty) 1985 Arg 1,2, 1986 A 2,3, F 2,3, 1987 [It, Fj, S, W, F], A, 1988 W 1,2, A 1,2,3, 1989 F 1,2, Arg 1,2, A, W, I, 1990 S 1,2, A 1,2,3, F 1,2, 1991 Arg 1,2, A 1,2, [E, US, It, C, A, S], 1992 Wld 1,2,3, I 1,2
McEldowney, J T (Taranaki) 1977 BI 3,4
MacEwan, I N (Wellington) 1956 SA 2, 1957 A 1,2, 1958 A 1,2,3, 1959 BI 1,2,3, 1960 SA 1,2,3,4, 1961 F 1,2,3, 1962 A 1,2,3,4
McGrattan, B (Wellington) 1983 S, E, 1985 Arg 1,2, 1986 F 1, A 1
McGregor, A J (Auckland) 1913 A 1, US
McGregor, D (Canterbury, Southland) 1903 A, 1904 BI, 1905 E, W
McGregor, N P (Canterbury) 1924 W, 1925 E
McGregor, R W (Auckland) 1903 A, 1904 BI
McHugh, M J (Auckland) 1946 A 1,2, 1949 SA 3
McIntosh, D N (Wellington) 1956 SA 1,2, 1957 A 1,2
McKay, D W (Auckland) 1961 F 1,2,3, 1963 E 1,2
McKechnie, B J (Southland) 1977 F 1,2, 1978 A 2(R),3, W (R), E, S, 1979 A, 1981 SA 1(R), F 1
McKellar, G F (Wellington) 1910 A 1,2,3
McKenzie, R J (Wellington) 1913 A 1, US, 1914 A 2,3
McKenzie, R McC (Manawatu) 1934 A 1, 1935 S, 1936 A 1, 1937 SA 1,2,3, 1938 A 1,2,3
McLachlan, J S (Auckland) 1974 A 2
McLaren, H C (Waikato) 1952 A 1
McLean, A L (Bay of Plenty) 1921 SA 2,3
McLean, H F (Wellington, Auckland) 1930 BI 3,4, 1932 A 1,2,3, 1934 A 1, 1935 I, W, 1936 E
McLean, J K (King Country, Auckland) 1947 A 1, 1949 A 2
McLeod, B E (Counties) 1964 A 1,2,3, 1965 SA 1,2,3,4, 1966 BI 1,2,3,4, 1967 E, W, F, S, 1968 A 1,2, F 1,2,3, 1969 W 1,2, 1970 SA 1,2
McLeod, S J (Waikato) 1996 WS, S 1, 1997 Fj (R), Arg 2(t + R), I (R), E 1(R), W (t), E 2(R), 1998 A 1, SA 1(R)
McMinn, A F (Wairarapa, Manawatu) 1903 A, 1905 A
McMinn, F A (Manawatu) 1904 BI
McMullen, R F (Auckland) 1957 A 1,2, 1958 A 1,2,3, 1959 BI 1,2,3, 1960 SA 2,3,4
McNab, J R (Otago) 1949 SA 1,2,3, 1950 BI 1,2,3
McNaughton, A M (Bay of Plenty) 1971 BI 1,2,3
McNeece, J (Southland) 1913 A 2,3, 1914 A 1,2,3
McPhail, B E (Canterbury) 1959 BI 1,4
Macpherson, D G (Otago) 1905 A
MacPherson, G L (Otago) 1986 F 1
MacRae, I R (Hawke's Bay) 1966 BI 1,2,3,4, 1967 A, E, W, F, S, 1968 F 1,2, 1969 W 1,2, 1970 SA 1,2,3,4
McRae, J A (Southland) 1946 A 1(R),2
McWilliams, R G (Auckland) 1928 SA 2,3,4, 1929 A 1,2,3, 1930 BI 1,2,3,4
Mackrell, W H C (Auckland) 1906 F
Macky, J V (Auckland) 1913 A 2

Maguire, J R (Auckland) 1910 A 1,2,3
Mahoney, A (Bush) 1935 S, I, W, 1936 E
Mains, L W (Otago) 1971 BI 2,3,4, 1976 I
Major, J (Taranaki) 1967 A
Maka, I (Otago) 1998 E 2(R), A 1(R), SA 1(R),2
Maling, T S (Otago) 2002 It, I 2(R), Fj, A 1, SA 1, A 2, SA 2, 2004 Arg,A1,SA1,2
Manchester, J E (Canterbury) 1932 A 1,2,3, 1934 A 1,2, 1935 S, I, W, 1936 E
Mannix, S J (Wellington) 1994 F 1
Marshall, J W (Southland, Canterbury) 1995 F 2, 1996 WS, S 1,2, A 1, SA 1, A 2, SA 2,3,4,5, 1997 Fj, Arg 1,2, A 1, SA 1, A 2, SA 2, A 3, I, E 1, W, E 2, 1998 A 1, SA 1, A 2, SA 2, A 3, 1999 WS, F 1, SA 1, A 1, SA 2, A 2, [Tg, E, S, F 2(R), SA 3], 2000 Tg, S 2, A 1, SA 1, A 2, SA 2, F 1,2, It, 2001 Arg 1, F, SA 1, A 1, 2(R), 2002 I 1, 2, Fj (R), A 1, SA 1, A 2, SA 2, 2003 E, SA 1(R), A 1, SA 2, A 2, [It,Tg,W,SA,A], 2004 E1,2,PI,A1, SA1, A2, SA2, 2005 Fj(R), BI1, 2(R), 3(R)
Masoe, M C (Taranaki) 2005 W, E, 2006 Arg, A1(R), SA1(R), A2(R), 3(R), SA2
Mason, D F (Wellington) 1947 A 2(R)
Masters, R R (Canterbury) 1924 I, W, 1925 E, F
Mataira, H K (Hawke's Bay) 1934 A 2
Matheson, J D (Otago) 1972 A 1,2,3, W, S
Mauger, A J D (Canterbury) 2001 I, S, Arg 2, 2002 It (R), I 1,2, Fj, A 1, SA 1, A 2, SA 2, 2003 SA 1, A 1, SA 2, A 2, [W, SA, A, F], 2004 SA2(R), It(R), W, F(R), 2005 Fj, BI1, 2, SA1, A1, SA2, A2, I, E, 2006 I1, 2, A1, 2, SA3
Max, D S (Nelson) 1931 A, 1934 A 1,2
Maxwell, N M C (Canterbury) 1999 WS, F 1, SA 1, A 1, SA 2, A 2, [Tg, E, S, F 2, SA 3], 2000 S 1,2, A 1, SA 1(R), A 2, SA 2, F 1,2, It (R), 2001 Sm, Arg 1, F, SA 1, A 1, SA 2, A2, I, S, Arg 2, 2002 It, I 1,2, Fj, 2004 It,F
Mayerhofler, M A (Canterbury) 1998 E 1,2, SA 1, A 2, SA 2, A 3
Meads, C E (King Country) 1957 A 1, 2, 1958 A 1, 2, 3, 1959 BI 2, 3, 4, 1960 SA 1, 2, 3, 4, 1961 F 1, 2, 3, 1962 A 1, 2, 3, 5, 1963 E 1, 2, I, W, 1964 E, S, F, A 1,2,3, 1965 SA 1, 2, 3, 4, 1966 BI 1, 2, 3, 4, 1967 A, E, W, F, S, 1968 A 1, 2, F 1, 2, 3, 1969 W 1, 2, 1970 SA 3, 4, 1971 BI 1, 2, 3, 4
Meads, S T (King Country) 1961 F 1, 1962 A 4,5, 1963 I, 1964 A 1, 2, 3, 1965 SA 1, 2, 3, 4, 1966 BI 1, 2, 3, 4
Mealamu, K F (Auckland) 2002 W, 2003 E (R), W, F (R), SA 1, A 1, SA 2(R), A 2,[It, W,SA,A,F], 2004 E1, 2, PI, A1, SA1, A2, SA2, W, F(R), 2005 Fj(R), BI1, 2, 3, SA1, A1, SA2, A2, I, E, 2006 I1,2,A1,2,3,SA2(R)
Meates, K F (Canterbury) 1952 A 1,2
Meates, W A (Otago) 1949 SA 2,3,4, 1950 BI 1,2,3,4
Meeuws, K J (Otago, Auckland) 1998 A 3, 1999 WS, F 1, SA 1, A 1, SA 2, A 2, [Tg, It (R), S (R), F 2(R), SA 3], 2000 Tg (R), S 2, A 1, SA 1, A 2, SA 2, 2001 Arg 2, 2002 It, Fj, E, F, W (R), 2003 W, F (R), SA 1(R), A 1(R), SA 2, [It(R),C,Tg,W(R),SA(R),A(R)],2004 E1,2,PI,A1,SA1,A2,SA2
Mehrtens, A P (Canterbury) 1995 C, [I, W, S, E, SA], A 1,2, 1996 WS, S 1,2, A 1, SA 1, A 2, SA 2,5, 1997 Fj, SA 2(R), I, E 1, W, E 2, 1998 E 1,2, A 1, SA 1(R), A 2, SA 2, A 3, 1999 F 1, SA 1, A 1, SA 2, A 2, [Tg, E, S, F 2, SA 3], 2000 S 1,2, A 1, SA 1, A 2, SA 2, F 1,2, It (R), 2001 Arg 1, A 1(R), SA 2, A 2, I, S, Arg 2, 2002 It, I 1,2, Fj (R), A 1, SA 1, A 2, SA 2, E (R), F, W, 2004 E2(R),Arg,A2(R),SA2
Metcalfe, T C (Southland) 1931 A, 1932 A 1
Mexted, G G (Wellington) 1950 BI 4
Mexted, M G (Wellington) 1979 S, E, 1980 A 1,2,3, W, 1981 S 1,2, SA 1,2,3, R, F 1,2, 1982 A 1,2,3, 1983 BI 1,2,3,4, A, S, E, 1984 F 1,2, A 1,2,3, 1985 E 1,2, A, Arg 1,2
Mika, B M (Auckland) 2002 E (R), F, W (R)
Mika, D G (Auckland) 1999 WS, F 1, SA 1(R), A 1,2, [It, SA 3(R)]
Mill, J J (Hawke's Bay, Wairarapa) 1924 W, 1925 E, F, 1930 BI 1
Milliken, H M (Canterbury) 1938 A 1,2,3
Milner, H P (Wanganui) 1970 SA 3
Mitchell, N A (Southland, Otago) 1935 S, I, W, 1936 E, A 2, 1937 SA 3, 1938 A 1,2
Mitchell, T W (Canterbury) 1976 SA 4(R)
Mitchell, W J (Canterbury) 1910 A 2,3
Mitchinson, F E (Wellington) 1907 A 1,2,3, 1908 AW 1,2,3, 1910 A 1,2,3, 1913 A 1(R), US
Moffitt, J E (Wellington) 1921 SA 1,2,3
Moore, G J T (Otago) 1949 A 1
Moreton, R C (Canterbury) 1962 A 3,4, 1964 A 1,2,3, 1965 SA 2,3
Morgan, J E (North Auckland) 1974 A 3, I, 1976 SA 2,3,4
Morris, T J (Nelson Bays) 1972 A 1,2,3
Morrison, T C (South Canterbury) 1938 A 1,2,3
Morrison, T G (Otago) 1973 E 2(R)
Morrissey, P J (Canterbury) 1962 A 3,4,5
Mourie, G N K (Taranaki) 1977 BI 3,4, F 1,2, 1978 I, W, E, S, 1979 F 1,2, A, S, E, 1980 W, 1981 S 1,2, F 1,2, 1982 A 1,2,3
Muliaina, J M (Auckland) 2003 E (R), W, F, SA 1, A 1, SA 2, A 2, [It, C, Tg, W, SA, A, F], 2004 E1, 2, Arg, PI, A1, SA1, A2, SA2, It, W, F, 2005 Fj, BI1(R), 2, 3, SA1, A1, SA2, A2, W, E, 2006 I1, 2, A1, SA1, A2, 3, SA2, 3
Muller, B L (Taranaki) 1967 A, E, W, F, 1968 A 1, F 1, 1969 W 1, 1970 SA 1,2,4, 1971 BI 1,2,3,4
Mumm, W J (Buller) 1949 A 1
Murdoch, K (Otago) 1970 SA 4, 1972 A 3, W
Murdoch, P H (Auckland) 1964 A 2,3, 1965 SA 1,2,3
Murray, H V (Canterbury) 1913 A 1, US, 1914 A 2,3
Murray, P C (Wanganui) 1908 AW 2
Myers, R G (Waikato) 1978 A 3
Mynott, H J (Taranaki) 1905 I, W, 1906 F, 1907 A 1,2,3, 1910 A 1,3

Nathan, W J (Auckland) 1962 A 1,2,3,4,5, 1963 E 1,2, W, 1964 F, 1966 BI 1,2,3,4, 1967 A
Nelson, K A (Otago) 1962 A 4,5
Nepia, G (Hawke's Bay, East Coast) 1924 I, W, 1925 E, F, 1929 A 1, 1930 BI 1,2,3,4
Nesbit, S R (Auckland) 1960 SA 2,3
Newby, C A (North Harbour) 2004 E2(t),SA2(R), 2006 I2(R)
Newton, F (Canterbury) 1905 E, W, 1906 F
Nicholls, H E (Wellington) 1921 SA 1
Nicholls, M F (Wellington) 1921 SA 1,2,3, 1924 I, W, 1925 E, F, 1928 SA 4, 1930 BI 2,3
Nicholson, G W (Auckland) 1903 A, 1904 BI, 1907 A 2,3
Nonu, M A (Wellington) 2003 E, [It(R),C,Tg(R)], 2004 It(R),W(R),F(R), 2005 BI2(R),W(R),I,S(R), 2006 I1
Norton, R W (Canterbury) 1971 BI 1,2,3,4, 1972 A 1,2,3, W, S, 1973 E 1, I, F, E 2, 1974 A 1,2,3, I, 1975 S, 1976 I, SA 1,2,3,4, 1977 BI 1,2,3,4

O'Brien, J G (Auckland) 1914 A 1
O'Callaghan, M W (Manawatu) 1968 F 1,2,3
O'Callaghan, T R (Wellington) 1949 A 2
O'Donnell, D H (Wellington) 1949 A 2
O'Halloran, J D (Wellington) 2000 It (R)
Old, G H (Manawatu) 1981 SA 3, R (R), 1982 A 1(R)
O'Leary, M J (Auckland) 1910 A 1,3, 1913 A 2,3
Oliver, A D (Otago) 1997 Fj (t), 1998 E 1,2, A 1, SA 1, A 2, SA 2, A 3, 1999 WS, F 1, SA 1, A 1, SA 2, A 2, [Tg, E, S, F 2, SA 3(R)], 2000 Tg (R), S 1,2, A 1, SA 1, A 2, SA 2, F 1,2, It, 2001 Sm, Arg 1, F, SA 1, A 1, SA 2, A 2, I, S, Arg 2, 2003 E, F, 2004 It,F, 2005 W,S, 2006 Arg,SA1,2,3(R)
Oliver, C J (Canterbury) 1929 A 1,2, 1934 A 1, 1935 S, I, W, 1936 E
Oliver, D J (Wellington) 1930 BI 1,2
Oliver, D O (Otago) 1954 I, F
Oliver, F J (Southland, Otago, Manawatu) 1976 SA 4, 1977 BI 1,2,3,4, F 1,2, 1978 A 1,2,3, I, W, E, S, 1979 F 1,2, 1981 SA 2
Orr, R W (Otago) 1949 A 1
Osborne, G M (North Harbour) 1995 C, [I, W, J, E, SA], A 1,2, F 1(R),2, 1996 SA 2,3,4,5, 1997 Arg 1(R), A 2,3, I, 1999 [It]
Osborne, W M (Wanganui) 1975 S, 1976 SA 2(R),4(R), 1977 BI 1,2,3,4, F 1(R),2, 1978 I, W, E, S, 1980 W, 1982 A 1,3
O'Sullivan, J M (Taranaki) 1905 S, I, E, W, 1907 A 3
O'Sullivan, T P A (Taranaki) 1960 SA 1, 1961 F 1, 1962 A 1,2

Page, J R (Wellington) 1931 A, 1932 A 1,2,3, 1934 A 1,2

Palmer, B P (Auckland) 1929 A 2, 1932 A 2,3
Parker, J H (Canterbury) 1924 I, W, 1925 E
Parkhill, A A (Otago) 1937 SA 1,2,3, 1938 A 1,2,3
Parkinson, R M (Poverty Bay) 1972 A 1,2,3, W, S, 1973 E 1,2
Paterson, A M (Otago) 1908 AW 2,3, 1910 A 1,2,3
Paton, H (Otago) 1910 A 1,3
Pene, A R B (Otago) 1992 Wld 1(R),2,3, I 1,2, A 1,2(R), 1993 BI 3, A, WS, S, E, 1994 F 1,2(R), SA 1(R)
Phillips, W J (King Country) 1937 SA 2, 1938 A 1,2
Philpott, S (Canterbury) 1991 [It (R), S (R)]
Pickering, E A R (Waikato) 1958 A 2, 1959 BI 1,4
Pierce, M J (Wellington) 1985 E 1,2, A, Arg 1, 1986 A 2,3, F 2,3, 1987 [It, Arg, S, W, F], A, 1988 W 1,2, A 1,2,3, 1989 F 1,2, Arg 1,2, A, W, I
Pokere, S T (Southland, Auckland) 1981 SA 3, 1982 A 1,2,3, 1983 BI 1,2,3,4, A, S, E, 1984 F 1,2, A 2,3, 1985 E 1,2, A
Pollock, H R (Wellington) 1932 A 1,2,3, 1936 A 1,2
Porter, C G (Wellington) 1925 F, 1929 A 2,3, 1930 BI 1,2,3,4
Preston, J P (Canterbury, Wellington) 1991 [US, S], 1992 SA (R), 1993 BI 2,3, A, WS, 1996 SA 4(R), 1997 I (R), E 1(R)
Procter, A C (Otago) 1932 A 1
Purdue, C A (Southland) 1905 A
Purdue, E (Southland) 1905 A
Purdue, G B (Southland) 1931 A, 1932 A 1,2,3
Purvis, G H (Waikato) 1991 [US], 1993 WS
Purvis, N A (Otago) 1976 I

Quaid, C E (Otago) 1938 A 1,2

Ralph, C S (Auckland, Canterbury) 1998 E 2, 2002 It, I 1,2, A 1, SA 1, A 2, SA 2, 2003 E, A 1(R), [C,Tg,SA(R),F(t&R)]
Ranby, R M (Waikato) 2001 Sm (R)
Randell, T C (Otago) 1997 Fj, Arg 1,2, A 1, SA 1, A 2, SA 2, A 3, I, E 1, W, E 2, 1998 E 1,2, A 1, SA 1, A 2, SA 2, A 3, 1999 WS, F 1, SA 1, A 1, SA 2, A 2, [Tg, E, It, S, F 2, SA 3], 2000 Tg, S 1,2(R), A 1, SA 1, A 2, SA 2, F 2(R), It (R), 2001 Arg 1, F, SA 1, A 1, SA 2, A 2, 2002 It, Fj, E, F, W
Rangi, R E (Auckland) 1964 A 2,3, 1965 SA 1,2,3,4, 1966 BI 1,2,3,4
Rankin, J G (Canterbury) 1936 A 1,2, 1937 SA 2
Rawlinson, G P (North Harbour) 2006 I1,2(R),SA2
Reedy, W J (Wellington) 1908 AW 2,3
Reid, A R (Waikato) 1952 A 1, 1956 SA 3,4, 1957 A 1,2
Reid, H R (Bay of Plenty) 1980 A 1,2, W, 1983 S, E, 1985 Arg 1,2, 1986 A 2,3
Reid, K H (Wairarapa) 1929 A 1,3
Reid, S T (Hawke's Bay) 1935 S, I, W, 1936 E, A 1,2, 1937 SA 1,2,3
Reihana, B T (Waikato) 2000 F 2, It
Reside, W B (Wairarapa) 1929 A 1
Rhind, P K (Canterbury) 1946 A 1,2
Richardson, J (Otago, Southland) 1921 SA 1,2,3, 1924 I, W, 1925 E, F
Rickit, H (Waikato) 1981 S 1,2
Riechelmann, C C (Auckland) 1997 Fj (R), Arg 1(R), A 1(R), SA 2(t), I (R), E 2(t)
Ridland, A J (Southland) 1910 A 1,2,3
Roberts, E J (Wellington) 1914 A 1,2,3, 1921 SA 2,3
Roberts, F (Wellington) 1905 S, I, E, W, 1907 A 1,2,3, 1908 AW 1,3, 1910 A 1,2,3
Roberts, R W (Taranaki) 1913 A 1, US, 1914 A 1,2,3
Robertson, B J (Counties) 1972 A 1,3, S, 1973 E 1, I, F, 1974 A 1,2,3, I, 1976 I, SA 1,2,3,4, 1977 BI 1,3,4, F 1,2, 1978 A 1,2,3, W, E, S, 1979 F 1,2, A, 1980 A 2,3, W, 1981 S 1,2
Robertson, D J (Otago) 1974 A 1,2,3, I, 1975 S, 1976 I, SA 1,3,4, 1977 BI 1
Robertson, S M (Canterbury) 1998 A 2(R), SA 2(R), A 3(R), 1999 [It (R)], 2000 Tg (R), S 1,2(R), A 1, SA 1(R),2(R), F 1,2, It, 2001 I, S, Arg 2, 2002 I 1,2, Fj (R), A 1, SA 1, A 2, SA 2
Robilliard, A C C (Canterbury) 1928 SA 1,2,3,4
Robinson, C E (Southland) 1951 A 1,2,3, 1952 A 1,2
Robinson, K J (Waikato) 2002 E, F (R), W, 2004 E1,2,PI
Robinson, M D (North Harbour) 1998 E 1(R), 2001 S (R), Arg 2
Robinson, M P (Canterbury) 2000 S 2, SA 1, 2002 It, I 2, A 1, SA 1, E (t&R), F, W (R)
Rokocoko, J T (Auckland) 2003 E, W, F, SA 1, A 1, SA 2, A 2, [It,W,SA,A,F], 2004 E1, 2, Arg, PI, A1, SA1, A2, SA2, It, W, F, 2005 SA1(R),A1,SA2,A2,W,E(R),S, 2006 I1, 2, A1, 2, 3, SA3
Rollerson, D L (Manawatu) 1980 W, 1981 S 2, SA 1,2,3, R, F 1(R),2
Roper, R A (Taranaki) 1949 A 2, 1950 BI 1,2,3,4
Rowley, H C B (Wanganui) 1949 A 2
Rush, E J (North Harbour) 1995 [W (R), J], It, F 1,2, 1996 S 1(R),2, A 1(t), SA 1(R)
Rush, X J (Auckland) 1998 A 3, 2004 E1, 2, PI, A1, SA1, A2, SA2
Rutledge, L M (Southland) 1978 A 1,2,3, I, W, E, S, 1979 F 1,2, A, 1980 A 1,2,3
Ryan, J (Wellington) 1910 A 2, 1914 A 1,2,3
Ryan, J A C (Otago) 2005 Fj,BI3(R), A1(R), SA2(R), A2(R),W,S

Sadler, B S (Wellington) 1935 S, I, W, 1936 A 1,2
Salmon, J L B (Wellington) 1981 R, F 1,2(R)
Savage, L T (Canterbury) 1949 SA 1,2,4
Saxton, C K (South Canterbury) 1938 A 1,2,3
Schuler, K J (Manawatu, North Harbour) 1990 A 2(R), 1992 A 2, 1995 [I (R), J]
Schuster, N J (Wellington) 1988 A 1,2,3, 1989 F 1,2, Arg 1,2, A, W, I
Scott, R W H (Auckland) 1946 A 1,2, 1947 A 1,2, 1949 SA 1,2,3,4, 1950 BI 1,2,3,4, 1953 W, 1954 I, E, S, F
Scown, A I (Taranaki) 1972 A 1,2,3, W (R), S
Scrimshaw, G (Canterbury) 1928 SA 1
Seear, G A (Otago) 1977 F 1,2, 1978 A 1,2,3, I, W, E, S, 1979 F 1,2, A
Seeling, C E (Auckland) 1904 BI, 1905 S, I, E, W, 1906 F, 1907 A 1,2, 1908 AW 1,2,3
Sellars, G M V (Auckland) 1913 A 1, US
Senio, K (Bay of Plenty) 2005 A2(R)
Shaw, M W (Manawatu, Hawke's Bay) 1980 A 1,2,3(R), W, 1981 S 1,2, SA 1,2, R, F 1,2, 1982 A 1,2,3, 1983 BI 1,2,3,4, A, S, E, 1984 F 1,2, A 1, 1985 E 1,2, A, Arg 1,2, 1986 A 3
Shelford, F N K (Bay of Plenty) 1981 SA 3, R, 1984 A 2,3
Shelford, W T (North Harbour) 1986 F 2,3, 1987 [It, Fj, S, W, F], A, 1988 W 1,2, A 1,2,3, 1989 F 1,2, Arg 1,2, A, W, I, 1990 S 1,2
Siddells, S K (Wellington) 1921 SA 3
Simon, H J (Otago) 1937 SA 1,2,3
Simpson, J G (Auckland) 1947 A 1,2, 1949 SA 1,2,3,4, 1950 BI 1,2,3
Simpson, V L J (Canterbury) 1985 Arg 1,2
Sims, G S (Otago) 1972 A 2
Sivivatu, S W (Waikato) 2005 Fj,BI1,2,3,I,E, 2006 SA2,3
Skeen, J R (Auckland) 1952 A 2
Skinner, K L (Otago, Counties) 1949 SA 1,2,3,4, 1950 BI 1,2,3,4, 1951 A 1,2,3, 1952 A 1,2, 1953 W, 1954 I, E, S, F, 1956 SA 3,4
Skudder, G R (Waikato) 1969 W 2
Slater, G L (Taranaki) 2000 F 1(R),2(R), It (R)
Sloane, P H (North Auckland) 1979 E
Smith, A E (Taranaki) 1969 W 1,2, 1970 SA 1
Smith, B W (Waikato) 1984 F 1,2, A 1
Smith, C G (Wellington) 2004 It,F, 2005 Fj(R),BI3,W,S
Smith, G W (Auckland) 1905 S, I
Smith, I S T (Otago, North Otago) 1964 A 1,2,3, 1965 SA 1,2,4, 1966 BI 1,2,3
Smith, J B (North Auckland) 1946 A 1, 1947 A 2, 1949 A 1,2
Smith, R M (Canterbury) 1955 A 1
Smith, W E (Nelson) 1905 A
Smith, W R (Canterbury) 1980 A 1, 1982 A 1,2,3, 1983 BI 2,3, S, E, 1984 F 1,2, A 1,2,3, 1985 E 1,2, A, Arg 2
Snow, E M (Nelson) 1929 A 1,2,3
Solomon, F (Auckland) 1931 A, 1932 A 2,3
Somerville, G M (Canterbury) 2000 Tg, S 1, SA 2(R), F 1,2, It, 2001 Sm, Arg 1(R), F, SA 1, A 1, SA 2, A 2, I, S, Arg 2(t+R), 2002 I 1,2, A 1, SA 1, A 2, SA 2, 2003 E, F, SA 1, A 1, SA 2(R), A 2, [It,Tg,W,SA,A,F], 2004 Arg, SA1, A2(R), SA2(R), It(R), W, F(R), 2005 Fj, BI1(R)2, 3, SA1(R), A1(R), SA2(R), A2(R), 2006 Arg, A1(R), SA1(R), A2(R), 3(R), SA2
Sonntag, W T C (Otago) 1929 A 1,2,3

So'oialo, R (Wellington) 2002 W, 2003 E, SA 1(R), [It(R),C, Tg, W(t)], 2004 W, F, 2005 Fj, BI1, 2, 3, SA1, A1, SA2, A2, W, I(R), E, 2006 I1, 2, A1, SA1, A2, 3, SA3
Speight, M W (Waikato) 1986 A 1
Spencer, C J (Auckland) 1997 Arg 1,2, A 1, SA 1, A 2, SA 2, A 3, E 2(R), 1998 E 2(R), A 1(R), SA 1, A 3(R), 2000 F 1(t&R), It, 2002 E, 2003 E, W, F, SA 1, A 1, SA 2, A 2, [It,C,Tg,W,SA,A,F], 2004 E1, 2, PI, A1, SA1, A2
Spencer, J C (Wellington) 1905 A, 1907 A 1(R)
Spiers, J E (Counties) 1979 S, E, 1981 R, F 1,2
Spillane, A P (South Canterbury) 1913 A 2,3
Stanley, J T (Auckland) 1986 F 1, A 1,2,3, F 2,3, 1987 [It, Fj, Arg, S, W, F], A, 1988 W 1,2, A 1,2,3, 1989 F 1,2, Arg 1,2, A, W, I, 1990 S 1,2
Stead, J W (Southland) 1904 BI, 1905 S, I, E, 1906 F, 1908 AW 1,3
Steel, A G (Canterbury) 1966 BI 1,2,3,4, 1967 A, F, S, 1968 A 1,2
Steel, J (West Coast) 1921 SA 1,2,3, 1924 W, 1925 E, F
Steele, L B (Wellington) 1951 A 1,2,3
Steere, E R G (Hawke's Bay) 1930 BI 1,2,3,4, 1931 A, 1932 A 1
Steinmetz, P C (Wellington) 2002 W (R)
Stensness, L (Auckland) 1993 BI 3, A, WS, 1997 Fj, Arg 1,2, A 1, SA 1
Stephens, O G (Wellington) 1968 F 3
Stevens, I N (Wellington) 1972 S, 1973 E 1, 1974 A 3
Stewart, A J (Canterbury, South Canterbury) 1963 E 1,2, I, W, 1964 E, S, F, A 3
Stewart, J D (Auckland) 1913 A 2,3
Stewart, K W (Southland) 1973 E 2, 1974 A 1,2,3, I, 1975 S, 1976 I, SA 1,3, 1979 S, E, 1981 SA 1,2
Stewart, R T (South Canterbury, Canterbury) 1928 SA 1,2,3,4, 1930 BI 2
Stohr, L B (Taranaki) 1910 A 1,2,3
Stone, A M (Waikato, Bay of Plenty) 1981 F 1,2, 1983 BI 3(R), 1984 A 3, 1986 F 1, A 1,3, F 2,3
Storey, P W (South Canterbury) 1921 SA 1,2
Strachan, A D (Auckland, North Harbour) 1992 Wld 2,3, I 1,2, A 1,2,3, SA, 1993 BI 1, 1995 [J, SA (t)]
Strahan, S C (Manawatu) 1967 A, E, W, F, S, 1968 A 1,2, F 1,2,3, 1970 SA 1,2,3, 1972 A 1,2,3, 1973 E 2
Strang, W A (South Canterbury) 1928 SA 1,2, 1930 BI 3,4, 1931 A
Stringfellow, J C (Wairarapa) 1929 A 1(R),3
Stuart, K C (Canterbury) 1955 A 1
Stuart, R C (Canterbury) 1949 A 1,2, 1953 W, 1954 I, E, S, F
Stuart, R L (Hawke's Bay) 1977 F 1(R)
Sullivan, J L (Taranaki) 1937 SA 1,2,3, 1938 A 1,2,3
Sutherland, A R (Marlborough) 1970 SA 2,4, 1971 BI 1, 1972 A 1,2,3, W, 1973 E 1, I, F
Svenson, K S (Wellington) 1924 I, W, 1925 E, F
Swain, J P (Hawke's Bay) 1928 SA 1,2,3,4

Tanner, J M (Auckland) 1950 BI 4, 1951 A 1,2,3, 1953 W
Tanner, K J (Canterbury) 1974 A 1,2,3, I, 1975 S, 1976 I, SA 1
Taumoepeau, S (Auckland) 2004 It, 2005 I(R),S
Taylor, G L (Northland) 1996 SA 5(R)
Taylor, H M (Canterbury) 1913 A 1, US, 1914 A 1,2,3
Taylor, J M (Otago) 1937 SA 1,2,3, 1938 A 1,2,3
Taylor, M B (Waikato) 1979 F 1,2, A, S, E, 1980 A 1,2
Taylor, N M (Bay of Plenty, Hawke's Bay) 1977 BI 2,4(R), F 1,2, 1978 A 1,2,3, I, 1982 A 2
Taylor, R (Taranaki) 1913 A 2,3
Taylor, W T (Canterbury) 1983 BI 1,2,3,4, A, S, 1984 F 1,2, A 1,2, 1985 E 1,2, A, Arg 1,2, 1986 A 2, 1987 [It, Fj, S, W, F], A, 1988 W 1,2
Tetzlaff, P L (Auckland) 1947 A 1,2
Thimbleby, N W (Hawke's Bay) 1970 SA 3
Thomas, B T (Auckland, Wellington) 1962 A 5, 1964 A 1,2,3
Thomson, H D (Wellington) 1908 AW 1
Thorn, B C (Conterbury) 2003 W (R), F (R), SA 1(R), A 1(R), SA 2,[It,C,Tg,W,SA(R),A(R),F(R)]
Thorne, G S (Auckland) 1968 A 1,2, F 1,2,3, 1969 W 1, 1970 SA 1,2,3,4
Thorne, R D (Canterbury) 1999 SA 2(R), [Tg, E, S, F 2, SA 3], 2000 Tg, S 2, A 2(R), F 1,2, 2001 Sm, Arg 1, F, SA 1, A 1, I, S, Arg 2, 2002 It, I 1,2, Fj, A 1, SA 1, A2, SA 2, 2003 E, W, F, SA 1, A 1, SA 2, A 2, [It,C,Tg,W,SA,A,F], 2006 SA1,2
Thornton, N H (Auckland) 1947 A 1,2, 1949 SA 1
Tialata, N S (Wellington) 2005 W,E(t),S(R), 2006 I1(R), 2(R), Arg(R), SA1, 2,3(R)
Tiatia, F I (Wellington) 2000 Tg (R), It
Tilyard, J T (Wellington) 1913 A 3
Timu, J K R (Otago) 1991 Arg 1, A 1,2, [E, US, C, A], 1992 Wld 2, I 2, A 1,2,3, SA, 1993 BI 1,2,3, A, WS, S, E, 1994 F 1,2, SA 1,2,3, A
Tindill, E W T (Wellington) 1936 E
Toeava, I (Auckland) 2005 S, 2006 Arg, A1(t&R), A3, SA2(R)
Tonu'u, O F J (Auckland) 1997 Fj (R), A 3(R), 1998 E 1,2, SA 1(R)
Townsend, L J (Otago) 1955 A 1,3
Tremain, K R (Canterbury, Hawke's Bay) 1959 BI 2,3,4, 1960 SA 1,2,3,4, 1961 F 2,3 1962 A 1,2,3, 1963 E 1,2, I, W, 1964 E, S, F, A 1,2,3, 1965 SA 1,2,3,4, 1966 BI 1,2,3,4, 1967 A, E, W, S, 1968 A 1, F 1,2,3
Trevathan, D (Otago) 1937 SA 1,2,3
Tuck, J M (Waikato) 1929 A 1,2,3
Tuiali'i, M M (Auckland) 2004 Arg,A2(R),SA2(R),It,W, 2005 I,E(R),S(R), 2006 Arg
Tuigamala, V L (Auckland) 1991 [US, It, C, S], 1992 Wld 1,2,3, I 1, A 1,2,3, SA, 1993 BI 1,2,3, A, WS, S, E
Tuitupou, S (Auckland) 2004 E1(R), 2(R), Arg, SA1(R), A2(R), SA2, 2006 Arg,SA1,2(R)
Turner, R S (North Harbour) 1992 Wld 1,2(R)
Turtill, H S (Canterbury) 1905 A
Twigden, T M (Auckland) 1980 A 2,3
Tyler, G A (Auckland) 1903 A, 1904 BI, 1905 S, I, E, W, 1906 F

Udy, D K (Wairarapa) 1903 A
Umaga, J F (Wellington) 1997 Fj, Arg 1,2, A 1, SA 1,2, 1999 WS, F 1, SA 1, A 1, SA 2, A 2, [Tg, E, S, F 2, SA 3], 2000 Tg, S 1,2, A 1, SA 1, A 2, SA 2, F 1,2, It, 2001 Sm, Arg 1, F, SA 1, A 1, SA 2, A 2, I, S, Arg 2, 2002 I 1, Fj, SA 1(R), A 2, SA 2, E, F, W, 2003 E, W, F, SA 1, A 1, SA 2, A 2, [It], 2004 E1, 2, Arg, PI, A1, SA1, A2, SA2, It, F, 2005 Fj, BI1, 2, 3, SA1, A1, SA2, A2, W, E, S
Urbahn, R J (Taranaki) 1959 BI 1,3,4
Urlich, R A (Auckland) 1970 SA 3,4
Uttley, I N (Wellington) 1963 E 1,2

Vidiri, J (Counties Manukau) 1998 E 2(R), A 1
Vincent, P B (Canterbury) 1956 SA 1,2
Vodanovich, I M H (Wellington) 1955 A 1,2,3

Wallace, W J (Wellington) 1903 A, 1904 BI, 1905 S, I, E, W, 1906 F, 1907 A 1,2,3, 1908 AW 2
Waller, D A G (Wellington) 2001 Arg 2(t)
Walsh, P T (Counties) 1955 A 1,2,3, 1956 SA 1,2,4, 1957 A 1,2, 1958 A 1,2,3, 1959 BI 1, 1963 E 2
Ward, R H (Southland) 1936 A 2, 1937 SA 1,3
Waterman, A C (North Auckland) 1929 A 1,2
Watkins, E L (Wellington) 1905 A
Watt, B A (Canterbury) 1962 A 1,4, 1963 E 1,2, W, 1964 E, S, A 1
Watt, J M (Otago) 1936 A 1,2
Watt, J R (Wellington) 1958 A 2, 1960 SA 1,2,3,4, 1961 F 1,3, 1962 A 1,2
Watts, M G (Taranaki) 1979 F 1,2, 1980 A 1,2,3(R)
Webb, D S (North Auckland) 1959 BI 2
Weepu, P A T (Wellington) 2004 W, 2005 SA1(R), A1, SA2, A2, I, E(R), S, 2006 Arg, A1(R), SA1, A3(R), SA2
Wells, J (Wellington) 1936 A 1,2
West, A H (Taranaki) 1921 SA 2,3
Whetton, A J (Auckland) 1984 A 1(R),3(R), 1985 A (R), Arg 1(R), 1986 A 2, 1987 [It, Fj, Arg, S, W, F], A, 1988 W 1,2, A 1,2,3, 1989 F 1,2, Arg 1,2, A, 1990 S 1,2, A 1,2,3, F 1,2, 1991 Arg 1, [E, US, It, C, A]
Whetton, G W (Auckland) 1981 SA 3, R, F 1,2, 1982 A 3, 1983 BI 1,2,3,4, 1984 F 1,2, A 1,2,3, 1985 E 1,2, A, Arg 2,

1986 A 2,3, F 2,3, 1987 [It, Fj, Arg, S, W, F], A, 1988 W 1,2, A 1,2,3, 1989 F 1,2, Arg 1,2, A, W, I, 1990 S 1,2, A 1,2,3, F 1,2, 1991 Arg 1,2, A 1,2, [E, US, It, C, A, S]

Whineray, W J (Canterbury, Waikato, Auckland) 1957 A 1,2, 1958 A 1,2,3, 1959 BI 1,2,3,4, 1960 SA 1,2,3,4, 1961 F 1,2,3, 1962 A 1,2,3,4,5, 1963 E 1,2, I, W, 1964 E, S, F, 1965 SA 1,2,3,4

White, A (Southland) 1921 SA 1, 1924 I, 1925 E, F

White, H L (Auckland) 1954 I, E, F, 1955 A 3

White, R A (Poverty Bay) 1949 A 1,2, 1950 BI 1,2,3,4, 1951 A 1,2,3, 1952 A 1,2, 1953 W, 1954 I, E, S, F, 1955 A 1,2,3, 1956 SA 1,2,3,4

White, R M (Wellington) 1946 A 1,2, 1947 A 1,2

Whiting, G J (King Country) 1972 A 1,2, S, 1973 E 1, I, F

Whiting, P J (Auckland) 1971 BI 1,2,4, 1972 A 1,2,3, W, S, 1973 E 1, I, F, 1974 A 1,2,3, I, 1976 I, SA 1,2,3,4

Williams, A J (Auckland) 2002 E, F, W, 2003 E, W, F, SA 1, A 1, SA 2, A 2, [Tg, W, SA, A, F], 2004 SA1(R), A2, It(R), W, F(R), 2005 Fj, BI1, 2, 3, SA1, A1, SA2, A2, I, E, 2006 Arg, A1(R), SA1, A2, 3(R), SA2, 3

Williams, B G (Auckland) 1970 SA 1,2,3,4, 1971 BI 1,2,4, 1972 A 1,2,3, W, S, 1973 E 1, I, F, E 2, 1974 A 1,2,3, I, 1975 S, 1976 I, SA 1,2,3,4, 1977 BI 1,2,3,4, F 1, 1978 A 1,2,3, I (R), W, E, S

Williams, G C (Wellington) 1967 E, W, F, S, 1968 A 2

Williams, P (Otago) 1913 A 1

Williment, M (Wellington) 1964 A 1, 1965 SA 1,2,3, 1966 BI 1,2,3,4, 1967 A

Willis, R K (Waikato) 1998 SA 2, A 3, 1999 SA 1(R), A 1(R), SA 2(R), A 2(R), [Tg (R), E (R), It, F 2(R), SA 3], 2002 SA 1(R)

Willis, T E (Otago) 2002 It, Fj, SA 2(R), A 2, SA 2

Willocks, C (Otago) 1946 A 1,2, 1949 SA 1,3,4

Wilson, B W (Otago) 1977 BI 3,4, 1978 A 1,2,3, 1979 F 1,2, A

Wilson, D D (Canterbury) 1954 E, S

Wilson, H W (Otago) 1949 A 1, 1950 BI 4, 1951 A 1,2,3

Wilson, J W (Otago) 1993 S, E, 1994 A, 1995 C, [I, J, S, E, SA], A 1,2, It, F 1, 1996 WS, S 1,2, A 1, SA 1, A 2, SA 2,3,4,5, 1997 Fj, Arg 1,2, A 1, SA 1, A 2, SA 2, A 3, I, E 1, W, E 2, 1998 E 1,2, A 1, SA 1, A 2, SA 2, A 3, 1999 WS, F 1, SA 1, A 1, SA 2, A 2, [Tg, E, It, S, F 2, SA 3], 2001 Sm, Arg 1, F, SA 1, A 1, SA 2

Wilson, N A (Wellington) 1908 AW 1,2, 1910 A 1,2,3, 1913 A 2,3, 1914 A 1,2,3

Wilson, N L (Otago) 1951 A 1,2,3

Wilson, R G (Canterbury) 1979 S, E

Wilson, S S (Wellington) 1977 F 1,2, 1978 A 1,2,3, I, W, E, S, 1979 F 1,2, A, S, E, 1980 A 1, W, 1981 S 1,2, SA 1,2,3, R, F 1,2, 1982 A 1,2,3, 1983 BI 1,2,3,4, A, S, E

Witcombe, D J C (Auckland) 2005 Fj, BI1(R), 2(R), SA1(R), A1(R)

Wolfe, T N (Wellington, Taranaki) 1961 F 1,2,3, 1962 A 2,3, 1963 E 1

Wood, M E (Canterbury, Auckland) 1903 A, 1904 BI

Woodcock, T D (North Harbour) 2002 W, 2004 E1(t&R), 2(t&R), Arg, W, F, 2005 Fj, BI1, 2, 3, SA1, A1, SA2, A2, W(R), I, E, 2006, Arg, A1, 2, 3, SA2(R), 3

Woodman, F A (North Auckland) 1981 SA 1,2, F 2

Wrigley, E (Wairarapa) 1905 A

Wright, T J (Auckland) 1986 F 1, A 1, 1987 [Arg], 1988 W 1,2, A 1,2,3, 1989 F 1,2, Arg 1,2, A, W, I, 1990 S 1,2, A 1,2,3, F 1,2, 1991 Arg 1,2, A 1,2, [E, US, It, S]

Wylie, J T (Auckland) 1913 A 1, US

Wyllie, A J (Canterbury) 1970 SA 2,3, 1971 BI 2,3,4, 1972 W, S, 1973 E 1, I, F, E 2

Yates, V M (North Auckland) 1961 F 1,2,3

Young, D (Canterbury) 1956 SA 2, 1958 A 1,2,3, 1960 SA 1,2,3,4, 1961 F 1,2,3, 1962 A 1,2,3,5, 1963 E 1,2, I, W, 1964 E, S, F

NEW ZEALAND: DOMESTIC RUGBY

ALL SIGNS POINT TO AUCKLAND

Auckland's love affair with the Air New Zealand National Provincial Cup showed no sign of waning in 2005 as Pat Lam's side swept aside Otago in the final with a devastating surge in the last 15 minutes to land their third title in four years.

Their 39–11 victory at Eden Park in October made it 15 NPC crowns in the 30th – and in its present format, last – year of New Zealand's top domestic competition and left Auckland's tally of triumphs 10 clear of Canterbury's five final successes.

Although the eventual scoreline suggested a one-sided final, Otago were very much in the match until the final quarter when Lam's adventurous team pressed the accelerator, added four unanswered tries to the two they had already scored and finally extinguished the challenge of Wayne Graham's resolute but outgunned side.

"I felt like things were reasonably under control for most of the first half," said Auckland captain Justin Collins. "We had to keep battling away really. Otago were superb in the first half, especially in the forwards.

"But we were running them around and by the time the second half came around I think they were blowing a bit and we really pushed them and things opened up after that."

The 2005 NPC season had begun back in August. Auckland travelled to North Harbour and were relatively untroubled in a 27–10 win to start their campaign while Otago hardly broke sweat in their 29–6 victory over Bay of Plenty at Carisbrook. There were also opening day wins for defending champions Canterbury, Waikato and Wellington.

It was not until the third round of matches at the end of the month that there was a hint of a genuine upset as Canterbury travelled to Albany to face North Harbour. The 2004 champions were unbeaten in the NPC for a year but when Anthony Tuitavake scored twice for North Harbour early in the second half, it seemed their record was on the verge of being broken. Canterbury, however, refused to be beaten and two penalties from the boot of Ben Blair ensured a 23–23 draw, a near repeat of the two side's 43–43 stalemate at Jade Stadium in 2004.

Meanwhile, Auckland endured a nerve-jangling clash with Southland at Eden Park but despite Watisoni Lotawa's second try late on for the

Stags, Lam's team held on for a 38–37 win and a bonus point that sent them top of the table.

It was not until mid-September that either of the leading two sides – Auckland and Canterbury – were to lose their unbeaten records and it was the side from the City of Sails who had their colours downed by Taranaki in New Plymouth.

Auckland seemed on course for their sixth straight NPC win when they took a 13–0 lead but inspired by skipper Paul Tito, The Naki came storming back into contention, scored six tries and sent a dejected Auckland home to consider their 40–19 hammering. Defeat sent Canterbury, 23–15 victors over Waikato, to the top of the table.

"We got stuck in," said Tito after his side's surprise win. "We put our foot on their throats for 80 minutes. The boys asked for extra effort at half-time, the coach also asked for it and it was great to see the boys put it in and finish them off."

But Canterbury were themselves to suffer an unexpected reverse a fortnight later when they travelled to Carisbrook to tackle Otago. Still unbeaten, the Cantabs appeared to be on a different planet as they went a remarkable 24–0 down to their hosts inside the first 26 minutes of the clash.

Second-half tries from All Black Richie McCaw and substitute half-back Andrew Ellis made the game a contest but Otago held on for a famous 24–19 win that ended what had been threatening to be a second successive 'perfect' Canterbury campaign.

"It was a bit frustrating overall," said Canterbury captain Reuben Thorne. "We looked at the individual things – like the lineout worked well, and the scrum was pretty evenly matched, we did a lot of other good stuff in the game but you've got to do it for 80 minutes not just 60 or 70.

"A couple of little lapses, just a couple of defensive errors and maybe a little lack of urgency in that short spell of rugby cost us dearly. We'll look at it, put it behind us and hopefully rectify it for the Auckland match next week."

With their places in the semi-finals assured, the Canterbury vs Auckland game in Christchurch became a matter of pride, not to mention a battle for the Ranfurly Shield.

The game was a fascinating encounter but although Auckland displayed all of their trademark flair and adventure, they failed to cross the line and it was Canterbury who emerged the 27–12 winners thanks to tries from Blair, Corey Flynn, Thorne and Scott Hamilton.

The result saw Canterbury retain the Ranfurly Shield for another season and confirmed them as top qualifiers for the knockout stages.

The full last four line-up would see second-place Auckland entertain North Harbour, while the Cantabs would seek revenge against Otago in the first semi-final.

The blue and golds started the game as the underdogs but after weathering a fiery opening 20 minutes from the home side, they gained the ascendancy to score five tries, including two from scrum-half Chris Smylie, in a 37–22 win that ended Canterbury's reign and champions.

"I don't know whether I'm real tired or just amazed by our performance out there," said Otago captain Craig Newby. "Though we beat them two weeks ago we knew they'd be even tougher tonight. But it was an unbelievable performance from our guys. I mean five tries – you wouldn't dream it would happen at Jade Stadium."

Auckland, however, were not to be similarly ambushed the following day at Eden Park. Boasting a host of All Blacks, Auckland blitzed North Harbour in the opening 40 minutes with five tries to lead 33–7 at the break and although the visitors edged the second-half 17–5, they were finally beaten 38–24.

"It was a disappointing way to end our season but we showed great character to hang in there," said beaten skipper captain Rua Tipoki.

"The boys never gave up but it was just those errors, we can't afford those. We've been able to get away with them in the games leading up to the semis, but tonight we got punished for them."

The final was to prove even more one-sided than Auckland's passage through to it. Otago were brimming with confidence after dispatching Canterbury but Auckland were in no mood to give them a sniff of only their third NPC title.

Despite drawing first blood with a Josh Blackie try, Otago trailed 10–8 at the break and any second-half hopes they had an assault on the Auckland line were comprehensively extinguished Lam's side as the tries flowed.

Doug Howlett, Brad Mika, Ben Atiga, Mils Muliaina and Taniela Moa all crossed as Auckland ran riot and the final whistle, if not their 39–11 defeat, was a blessing for Otago when it finally came.

"We came here with nothing to lose and we were going to give it our best shot no matter what," said Otago coach Wayne Graham. "We couldn't get our game going. We couldn't get enough possession.

"I think we ran out of steam. We defended for 75% of the game and we just started to fall off a couple of tackles and a few gaps started to open up."

Lam was understandably delighted with his side's victory and was quick to pay tribute to skipper Justin Collins, who lasted 60 minutes of the game despite nursing a calf injury he picked up in the semi-finals.

"I was so proud of the guys they deserved that, Lam said. "They worked hard for it. A lot of people don't realise the amount of work that Justin has done in the last week. He led with an example that others followed."

Auckland will defend a new-look NPC competition in 2006 as the top division expands from 10 to 14 sides, split into two initial groups of seven. The new-look competition will also feature a quarter-final stage for the first time.

"The competition signals a new era for New Zealand rugby and we are delighted to be part of it," Lam said after details of the revamped tournament were unveiled. "We are privileged to have won the last Division One in the Air New Zealand NPC and look forward to the challenges that the expanded competition will bring."

The 2005 Division Two champions Hawke's Bay, who defeated Nelson Bays for the title, were promoted to the rebranded top-flight along with Counties Manukau and Manawatu, while Nelson Bays merged with Marlborough to become the new Tasman outfit, who will also play in the new Premier Division.

Meanwhile, all eight Division Three sides plus East Coast, North Otago, Poverty Bay and Wanganui from Division Two joined to form the second tier Heartland Championship for 2006.

THE NPC 2005 CHAMPIONSHIP RESULTS

12 August: **Waikato** 30 **Taranaki** 6

13 August: **Southland** 16 **Canterbury** 42, **Northland** 27 **Wellington** 43, **North Harbour** 10 **Auckland** 27

14 August: **Otago** 29 **Bay of Plenty**

19 August: **Wellington** 16 **North Harbour** 29

20 August: **Canterbury** 40 **Bay of Plenty** 13, **Taranaki** 32 **Northland** 8, **Otago** 16 **Auckland** 31

21 August: **Southland** 12 **Waikato** 14

26 August: **Wellington** 10 **Otago** 26

27 August: **Northland** 7 **Waikato** 38, **North Harbour** 23 **Canterbury** 23

28 August: **Bay of Plenty** 18 **Taranaki** 17, **Auckland** 38 **Southland** 37

2 September: **Waikato** 17 **Wellington** 41

3 September: **Canterbury** 13 **Taranaki** 11, **Southland** 28 **Otago** 22

4 September: **North Harbour** 55 **Northland** 17, **Bay of Plenty** 30 **Auckland** 41

9 September: **Otago** 21 **North Harbour** 13

10 September: **Wellington** 38 **Bay of Plenty** 32, **Northland** 10 **Canterbury** 32, **Auckland** 40 **Waikato** 30

11 September: **Taranaki** 28 **Southland** 33

16 September: **Bay of Plenty** 8 **North Harbour** 41

17 September: **Taranaki** 40 **Auckland** 19, **Wellington** 53 **Southland** 12, **Canterbury** 23 **Waikato** 15

18 September: **Northland** 3 **Otago** 41

23 September: **Canterbury** 15 **Wellington** 14

24 September: **Auckland** 53 **Northland** 7, **Otago** 26 **Taranaki** 10, **Southland** 19 **Bay of Plenty** 13

25 September: **North Harbour** 40 **Waikato** 21

30 September: **Auckland** 29 **Wellington** 22

1 October: **Otago** 24 **Canterbury** 19, **Waikato** 13 **Bay of Plenty** 17, **North Harbour** 37 **Taranaki** 3

2 October: **Northland** 15 **Southland** 21

7 October: **Taranaki** 17 **Wellington** 31

8 October: **Waikato** 25 **Otago** 13, **Bay of Plenty** 51 **Northland** 3, **Canterbury** 27 **Auckland** 12

9 October: **Southland** 22 **North Harbour** 31

FINAL TABLE

Canterbury	9	7	1	1	234	138	5	35
Auckland	9	7	0	2	290	219	5	33
North Harbour	9	6	1	2	280	158	6	32
Otago	9	6	0	3	218	145	4	28
Wellington	9	5	0	4	268	204	6	26
Southland	9	4	0	5	200	256	3	19
Waikato	9	4	0	5	203	199	2	18
Bay of Plenty	9	3	0	6	188	241	5	17
Taranaki	9	2	0	7	164	215	5	13
Northland	9	0	0	9	97	367	1	1

SEMI-FINALS

14 October, Jade Stadium, Christchurch

CANTERBURY 22 (2G, 1PG, 1T)
OTAGO 37 (3G, 2PG, 2T)

CANTERBURY: B Blair; S Hamilton, C Laulala, A Mauger, C Ralph; D Carter, A Ellis; W Crockett, C Flynn, C Johnstone, C Jack, K O'Neill, R Thorne (captain), M Tuiali'I, R McCaw

SUBSTITUTES: T Kopelani, B Franks, H Hopgood, J Leo'o, J Nutbrown, V Delesau, S Yates

SCORERS TRIES: Blair, McCaw, Hamilton Conversions: Carter(2) Penalty Goal: Carter

OTAGO: C Clare; G Horton, N Brew, S Mapusua, M Saunders; N Evans, C Smylie; C King, A Oliver, C Hayman, T Donnelly, J Ryan, C Newby (captain), J Blackie, G Webb

SUBSTITUTES: J Macdonald, G Polson, F Levi, A Soakai, T Morland, R Bambry, J Shoemark

SCORERS TRIES: Smylie (2), Newby, Clare, Blackie Conversions: Evans (3) Penalty Goals: Evans (2)

REFEREE S Walsh

15 October, Eden Park, Auckland

AUCKLAND 38 (4G, 2T) NORTH HARBOUR 24 (2G, 2T)

AUCKLAND: B Ward; D Howlett, M Muliaina, I Nacewa, T Koonwaiyou; T Lavea, S Devine; S Taumoepeau, K Mealamu, J Afoa, A Macdonald, A Williams, J Collins (captain), D Braid, J Kaino

SUBSTITUTES: J Fonokalafi, N White, K Haiu, B Mika, T Moa, J Rokocoko, B Atiga

SCORERS TRIES: MacDonald (2), Mealamu, Howlett, Rokocoko, Muliaina Conversions: Ward (4)

NORTH HARBOUR: G Pisi; V Waqaseduadua, A Tuitavake, R Tipoki (captain), Z Lawrence; L McAlister, J Poluleuligaga; T Woodcock, J Ward, M Noble, M Veale, G Rawlinson, A Boric, T Harding, N Williams

SUBSTITUTES: R Dustow, A Donald, B Wilson, R Tamihere, C McGrath, J Nasmith, A Mailei

SCORERS TRIES: Waqaseduadua (2), Pisi, Tuitavake Conversions: McAlister (2)

REFEREE B Lawrence

FINAL

22 October, Eden Park, Auckland

AUCKLAND 39 (3G, PG, 3T) OTAGO 11 (2PG, 1T)

AUCKLAND: B Ward; D Howlett, M Muliaina, I Nacewa, J Rokocoko; T Lavea, S Devine; S Taumoepeau, K Mealamu, J Afoa, A Macdonald, A Williams, J Collins (captain), D Braid, J Kaino

SUBSTITUTES: J Fonokolafi, N White, K Haiu, B Mika, T Moa, S Tuitupou, B Atiga, T Koonwaiyou

SCORERS TRIES: Mealamu, Howlett, Mika, Atiga, Muliaina, Moa Conversions: Ward (2), Atiga Penalty Goals: Ward

OTAGO: C Clare; G Horton, N Brew, S Mapusua, M Saunders; N Evans, C Smylie; C King, A Oliver, C Hayman, T Donnelly, J Ryan, C Newby (captain), J Blackie, G Webb

SUBSTITUTES: J Macdonald, G Polson, F Levi, A Soakai, T Morland, R Bambry, J Shoemark

SCORERS TRY: Blackie Penalty Goals: Evans (2)

REFEREE S Walsh

ROMANIA

ROMANIA'S TEST RECORD

OPPONENTS	DATE	VENUE	RESULT
Georgia	25 February	H	**Won** 35–10
Czech Republic	11 March	H	**Won** 50–3
Portugal	18 March	A	**Won** 27–3
Ukraine	3 June	A	**Won** 58–0
Russia	10 June	A	**Lost** 24–25
France	17 June	H	**Lost** 14–62

ON THE LONG ROAD TO RECOVERY

By Chris Thau

It was a long, long season, even by Continental standards. For reasons they describe as fairness and even-handedness, the European rugby body FIRA-AER run its senior competition, the European Nations Cup (ENC), on a home and away basis. This is why Romania's season, which ended with a 62–14 drubbing at the hands of France in Bucharest in June 2006, had commenced nearly two years earlier, on November 2004 in Prague. According to FIRA-AER this was a particularly significant season, because the position of the team in the final ENC table had particular significance for the draw for the RWC07 final round of the European zone. In other words, winning, or finishing second in the ENC was rewarded with a qualifying path that avoided clashing with the budding Six Nations power Italy – also involved the race for a place in the RWC07 starting line-up.

This is also why the new Romanian coaching team headed by former IRB Development manager for Europe Robert Antonin and former Toulouse hooker and coach Daniel Santamans made winning the ENC a priority. The match in Prague, won 38–14 by the Romanians was both the opening shot of their two-year, 16–match programme and the first of their nine wins for seven defeats of the mammoth 20–month long season, which in addition to the ENC matches also included encounters against Scotland, Ireland, Japan and Canada. The match set the Oaks on course towards their coveted objective, achieved despite a narrow and nauseating 24–25 defeat at the hands of Russia in the final round of the 10–match marathon.

While three of the players used in Prague, Tarbes lock-forward Cristian Petre, Paris Racing-Metro scrum-half Lucian Sirbu and Cluj University wing three-quarter Ioan Teodorescu played throughout the season – Petre played in all 16 matches and Teodorescu and Sirbu missed a match each – for two players centre Flavius Dobre and No8 and skipper Alin Petrache – this was the one and only appearance in this unusually long campaign.

Biarritz prop forward Petru Balan made in Prague one of his seven star appearances for his country, an average which seems fairly common for the Romanian Top 14 players based in France: Perpignan's Ovidiu Tonita played six times, Pau's duo, hooker Marius Tincu and wing forward Alex Manta, had seven and five appearances respectively – statistics which underline the difficulties the Romanian Federation is facing when trying to gather its best players for the country's international programme.

Overall, Antonin and Santamans, helped by Romanian assistant coaches, initially Virgil Nastase, then George Sava as well as, during the 2006 part of the season, former France wing three-quarter Philippe Berot as a consultant, used 46 players, half of whom play their trade in France and Italy. Interesting enough, while Romanian players are routinely employed in France and Italy as if they come from an European Union country, they do not benefit from similar employment privileges

Adam Pretty/Getty Images

Ovidiu Tonita is one of a host of Romanian stars playing overseas.

in the UK and Ireland, which perhaps explains why there is no Romanian professional player in either England, Wales or Scotland.

This 50–50 split between locally-based and overseas players has forced Antonin and Santamans to mix and match their talent, when trying to select the best combination for Romania's crunch matches. So, what is generally regarded as Romania's best back-row of Tonita, Manta and Florin Corodeanu of Grenoble only played together four times, in matches Romania badly wanted to win – against the touring Canadians, Ireland and significantly Georgia and Portugal in the crucial second round of the ENC. Similarly and not coincidently the best front row of Balan, Tincu and Petru Todirasc of Brive or Rovigo's Marcel Soccaciu, or Agen's Cezar Popescu appeared together in the same matches.

Although the same front row of Balan, Tincu and Soccaciu, appeared against Georgia in Tbilisi, in the third match of the 2005 Round of the ENC, emphasizing Romania's intentions, the Oaks, who thoroughly dominated the forwarded exchanges, failed to capitalise on their supremacy and lost a match they could and should have won. A trip to Japan for the now defunct IRB Super Cup offered Antonin and Santamans the possibility to experiment, as most of their French-based players failed to turn up due to their club commitments. Two narrow defeats at the hands of Japan and the US Eagles dampened the enthusiasm of the newcomers and resulted in some dark mutterings within ranks about the futility of the exercise.

That, however, was not the opinion of the two coaches, who saw at work some of the aspiring Romanian-based talent, of whom No 8 Cosmin Ratiu, fly-half Darie Curea and wing three-quarter Stefan Dumitru showed genuine promise. The 39–19 defeat at the hands of Scotland at the beginning of June 2005 gave the Romanians a few hints about their state of preparedness and at the same time acted as a wake-up call before the crucial match against up and coming Portuguese, arrived in Bucharest ready to upset the established order. A try by Ovidiu Tonita in the first half, before he got off injured, made the difference in a tight and unspectacular game, dominated by the never-say-die Portuguese, who made the Romanians suffer with their sizzling pace and merciless tackling.

For Romanian planners, the return match against Portugal at the beginning of March and naturally, the clash with Georgia at the beginning of February, were the main objectives of the 2006 season. The appearance in Bucharest for the Georgia match of the entire Romanian "exiles" brigade of Balan, Tincu, Toderasc, skipper Sorin Socol, Cristian Petre as well as Tonita, Manta, Corodeanu and even scrum-half Petre Mitu – who appeared to have changed his mind having declared that he was no longer interested in playing for his country – showed a degree of urgency not much in evidence before. The Romanians scored four tries to one to win 35–10 and move to the top of the ENC table, with four matches to play.

The next match against the Czech Republic was held in the unlikely venue of La Teste, a picturesque French town on the Atlantic coast, not far from Bordeaux in November 2005. With most of the Romanians, and a large number of Czechs, plying their trade in France, the two Unions agreed to use the good offices of the FFR to stage the match, which as far as the Romanians were concerned, was very much a warm-up game for the decider against Portugal a week later in Lisbon. Indeed, very much as expected and with several of their professionals missing, the Romanians won easily 50–3, to put them in the right frame of mind for the match in Lisbon the following weekend.

This time, none of the complacency displayed some eight months earlier against Portugal was in evidence and the Romanians, using their superior experience and fire power simply squeezed gallant Portugal out of the game 27–3 – scoring four tries to none in the process. The 58–0 romp against Ukraine in Kiev at the beginning of June, confirmed Romania's champion status, and although defeated by a resurgent Russia in Krasnoyarsk 25–24, they finished the campaign at the top of the ENC table – very much a case of mission accomplished.

In addition to their progress into the final round of the RWC qualifying process in Europe, probably the most significant accomplishment

Michael Cooper/Getty Images

Scrum-half Petre Mitu returned to the international scene to boost Romanian hopes.

of the Romanians was the launch onto the international scene of a new generation of players, led by the talented Contor Zenner Arad RC wing-cum-fullback Catalin Fercu. The return to international duty of former captain Romeo Gontineac, has not only added punch to the Romanian back line, but also is helping the youngsters of the likes of Ionut Dimofte, Fercu and his former Und-19 team mates, Csaba Gal, Mihai Macovei, Robert Dascalu, Florin Voicu, Stelian Burcea to settle in the increasingly competitive Romanian set-up. Giant Pau fullback Iulian Dumitras, the son of former skipper Hary, is making an impact as well, and for once, the fervent desire of coach Santamans of developing a back division to match the formidable power of the Romanian pack, is about to be fulfilled.

Meanwhile, the Army club "Steaua Bucharest" coached by former internationals Marin Mot and Leodor Costea has finished at the top of the domestic league, closely challenged by the new power in the land, the Contor Zenner club from Arad, with former champions Dinamo in the third place. "This season, for the first time in many years the National League is expanded to include two additional clubs Timisoara and Olimpia Bucharet," observed President George Straton.

The Romanian Rugby Academy, in its third year, has produced a new generation of graduates, as 17 new coaches passed the exams at the beginning of the spring. At the same time, reported National Technical Director Daniel Mitrea, 40 young players (U17–U19), including Fercu and his friends have finalised their courses at the same time, making the transition to the various international squads.

ROMANIA INTERNATIONAL PLAYERS
UP TO 30TH SEPTEMBER 2006

Compiled by Hugh Copping

Achim, A 1974 *Pol* 1976 *Pol, Mor* (R)
Aldea, M 1979 *USS, W, Pol, F* 1980 *It* (R), *USS, I, F* 1981 *It, Sp, USS, S, NZ, F* 1982 *WGe, It, USS, Z, Z, F* 1983 *Mor, WGe, It, USS, Pol, W, USS, F* 1984 *It, S, F* 1985 *E, USS*
Alexandrescu, C 1934 *It*
Alexandru, D 1974 *Pol* 1975 *JAB* 1976 *USS, Pol, F, Mor* 1977 *Sp, It, Pol, F* 1978 *Cze, Sp* 1979 *Sp, USS* 1980 *It, Pol, F* 1981 *Sp, USS, S, NZ, F* 1982 *Z* (R) 1983 *USS, Pol, W* 1984 *It, S, F, Sp* 1985 *E* 1987 *It, USS, Z, S, USS, F* 1988 *USS*
Anastasiade, N 1927 *Cze* 1934 *It* (R)
Anastasiade, V 1939 *It*
Andrei, I 2003 *W* (R), *I* (R), *Ar* (R), *Nm* (R) 2004 *CZR, Pt, Sp* (R), *Geo, It* (R), *W* (R), *J* (R) 2005 *Rus* (R), *S, Pt* (R)
Andriesi, I 1937 *It, H, Ger* 1938 *F, Ger* 1939 *It* 1940 *It*
Apjoc, E 1996 *Bel* 2000 *It* (R) 2001 *Pt* (R)
Armasel, D 1924 *F, US*
Atanasiu, A 1970 *It, F* 1971 *It, Mor, F* 1972 *Mor, Cze, WGe* 1973 *Sp, Mor, Ar, Ar, WGe* (R) 1974 *Pol*
Bacioiu, I 1976 *USS, Bul, Pol, F, Mor* 1977 *It, F, It*
Baciu, N 1964 *Cze, EGe* 1967 *It, F* 1968 *Cze, Cze, F* (R) 1969 *Pol* (R), *WGe, F* 1970 *It* 1971 *It, Mor, F* 1972 *Mor, Cze* (R), *WGe* (R) 1973 *Ar* (R), *Ar* (R) 1974 *Cze, EGe*
Balan, B 2003 *Pt* (R), *Sp, Geo* (R) 2004 *W* (R) 2005 *Ukr* (R), *S* (R), *Pt* (R) 2006 *Geo* (R), *Pt* (R), *Ukr, F*
Balan, D 1983 *F* (R)
Balan, P 1998 *H* (R), *Pol* (R), *Ukr* (R), *Ar, Geo* (R), *I* (R) 1999 *F* (R), *S, A, US, I* 2000 *Mor, H, Pt, Sp, Geo, F* (R), *It* 2001 *Pt, Sp, H* (R), *Rus, Geo* (R), *I, E* 2002 *Pt* (R), *Sp, H, Rus, Geo, Sp, S* 2003 *CZR, F, W, I, Nm* 2004 *It, W, J, CZR* 2005 *Geo, C, I* 2006 *Geo, Pt, F*
Balcan, L 1963 *Bul, EGe, Cze* (R)
Balmus, F 2000 *Mor* (R), *H, Pt* (R)
Bals, S 1927 *F, Ger, Cze*
Baltaretu, G 1965 *WGe, F*
Barascu, C 1957 *F*
Baraulea, M 2004 *CZR, Pt, Geo* (R)
Barbu, A 1958 *WGe, It* 1959 *EGe, Pol, Cze, EGe* 1960 *F*
Bargaunas, S 1971 *It, Mor* (R) 1972 *F* (R) 1974 *Cze* 1975 *It*
Barsan, S 1934 *It* 1936 *F, It* 1937 *It, H, F, Ger* 1938 *F, Ger* 1939 *It* 1940 *It* 1942 *It*
Beches, E 1979 *It, Sp, USS* 1982 *WGe, It* 1983 *Pol* (R)
Bejan, M 2001 *I, W* 2002 *Pt* 2003 *Geo* (R), *CZR* 2004 *It* (R)
Beju, C 1936 *F, It, Ger*
Bentia, G 1919 *US, F* 1924 *F, US*
Bezarau, C 1995 *Ar, F, It*
Bezuscu, R 1985 *It* 1987 *F*
Blagescu, M 1952 *EGe, EGe* 1953 *It* 1955 *Cze* 1957 *F, Cze, Bel, F*
Blasek, G 1937 *It, H, F, Ger* 1940 *It* 1942 *It*
Bogdan, V 2003 *CZR* (R)
Bogheanu, A 1980 *Mor*
Boldor, D 1988 *It, Sp, US, USS, USS, W* 1989 *It, E, Sp, Z*
Boroi, A 1975 *Sp*
Bors, P 1975 *JAB* 1976 *Sp* 1977 *It* 1980 *It, USS, I, Pol, F* 1981 *It, Sp, USS, S, NZ, F* 1982 *WGe* 1983 *Mor, WGe, It* (R), *USS* 1984 *It*
Bozian, D 1997 *Bel* 1998 *H, Pol, Ukr* (R)
Brabateanu, V 1919 *US, F*
Braga, M 1970 *It, F*
Branescu, C 1994 *It, E* 1997 *F*
Bratulescu, I 1927 *Ger, Cze*
Brezoianu, G 1996 *Bel* 1997 *F* 1998 *H, Pol, Ukr, Ar, Geo, I* 1999 *F, S, A, US, I* 2000 *H, Pt, Sp, Geo, F, It* 2001 *Sp, Rus, Geo, I, W, E* 2002 *Pt, Sp, H, Rus, Geo, I, It, Sp, W, S* 2003 *Pt, Sp, Rus, Geo, CZR, F, W, I, A, Ar, Nm* 2005 *Rus, Ukr, J, US, S, Pt, C, I* 2006 *CZR, Pt* (R), *Rus, F* (R)
Brici, V 1991 *NZ* (R) 1992 *USS, F, It* 1993 *Tun, F, Sp, I* 1994 *Sp, Ger, Rus, It, W, It, E* 1995 *F, S, J, J* (R), *SA, A* 1996 *Pt, F* 1997 *F*
Brinza, TE 1990 *It, USS* (R) 1991 *C* (R) 1992 *It, Ar* 1993 *Pt, Tun, F, F, I* 1994 *Sp, Ger, It* (R), *W, It* (R), *E* 1995 *F, S, J, J, SA, A* 1996 *Pt, F, Pol* 1997 *F, W, Ar, F, It* 1998 *Ukr* 1999 *A, US, I* 2000 *H, Geo* 2002 *H* (R)
Bucan, I 1976 *Bul* (R) 1977 *Sp* 1978 *Cze* 1979 *F* 1980 *It, USS, I, Pol, F* 1981 *It, Sp, USS, S, NZ, F* 1982 *WGe, It, USS, Z, Z, F* 1983 *Mor, WGe, It, USS, Pol, W, USS, F* 1984 *It, S, F, Sp* 1985 *E, Tun, USS, USS, It* 1986 *Pt, S, F* (R), *Pt* 1987 *It, USS, Z, S, USS, F*
Bucos, M 1972 *Mor, Cze, WGe* (R) 1973 *Sp* 1975 *JAB, Pol, F* 1976 *H, It, Sp, USS, Bul, Pol, F, Mor* 1977 *Sp, It, F, Pol, It, F* 1978 *Pol, F* 1979 *W* 1980 *It, Mor*
Buda, P 1953 *It* 1955 *Cze* 1957 *F, Cze*
Budica, C 1974 *Cze* (R), *EGe* (R), *Cze* (R)
Burcea, S 2006 *F*
Burghelea, M 1974 *Cze* (R), *EGe, F* 1975 *It*
Burlescu, S 1936 *F, It, Ger* 1938 *F, Ger* 1939 *It*
Butugan, M 2003 *Pt* (R)
Calafeteanu, VN 2004 *J* 2005 *Ukr* (R) 2006 *CZR, Pt* (R), *F* (R)
Caligari, A 1951 *EGe* 1953 *It*
Caliman, S 1958 *EGe* 1960 *Pol, EGe, Cze*
Calistrat, P 1940 *It* 1942 *It*
Camenita, Ion 1939 *It*
Capmare, C 1983 *Pol* 1984 *It*
Capusan, N 1960 *F* 1961 *Pol, Cze, EGe, F* 1962 *Cze, EGe, Pol, It* 1963 *Bul, EGe, Cze*
Caracostea, G 1919 *US, F*
Caragea, G 1980 *I, Pol, F* 1981 *It, Sp, USS, S, NZ* (R), *F* 1982 *WGe, It, USS, Z, Z, F* 1983 *Mor, WGe, It, USS, Pol, W, F* 1984 *F, Sp* 1985 *E, Tun* 1986 *S, F, Tun, Tun, Pt, F, I* 1988 *It, Sp, US, USS* 1989 *E*
Carp, C 1989 *Z, Sa, USS*
Catalin, N 2003 *Pt, Rus*
Celea, G 1963 *EGe*
Chiriac, D 1999 *S, A* (R), *I* (R) 2001 *H*
Chiriac, G 1996 *Bel* (R) 2001 *Pt, Rus* 2002 *Sp, H, Rus* (R), *Geo, I, Sp* (R), *W* (R), *S* 2003 *Sp, Rus* (R), *Geo, F, W, I, A, Ar, Nm*
Chiriac, R 1952 *EGe* 1955 *Cze* 1957 *F, Bel, F* 1958 *Sp, WGe* 1960 *F* 1961 *Pol, EGe, Cze, EGe, F* 1962 *Cze, EGe, Pol, It, F* 1963 *Bul, EGe, Cze, F* 1964 *Cze, EGe* (R), *WGe, F*
Chiricencu, M 1980 *It, Pol*
Chirila, S 1989 *Sp, S* 1990 *F, H, Sp, It, USS* 1991 *It*
Chirita, V 1999 *S* (R)
Cilinca, G 1993 *Pt*
Cioarec, N 1974 *Pol* (R) 1976 *It* 1979 *Pol* (R)
Ciobanel, P 1961 *Pol, EGe, Cze, EGe, F* 1962 *Cze, EGe, Pol, It, F* 1963 *F* 1964 *Cze, EGe, WGe, F* 1965 *WGe, F* 1966 *Cze, It, F* 1967 *F* 1968 *Cze, Cze, F* 1969 *Pol, WGe, Cze, F* 1970 *F* 1971 *F*
Ciobanu, I 1952 *EGe* (R)
Ciobanu, M 1949 *Cze* 1951 *EGe*
Cioca, R 1994 *Sp, Ger, Rus, It, It, E* 1995 *S, J* 1996 *Bel* (R)
Ciofu, I 2000 *It* 2003 *Pt*

Ciolacu, ML 1998 *Ukr* (R), *Ar* (R), *Geo* (R), *I* (R) 1999 *F* 2001 *Sp*, *H*, *Rus*, *Geo*, *W* (R), *E* (R)
Ciorascu, S 1988 *US*, *USS*, *USS*, *F*, *W* 1989 *It*, *E*, *Sp*, *Z*, *Sa*, *USS*, *S* 1990 *It*, *F*, *H*, *Sp*, *USS* 1991 *It*, *NZ*, *S*, *F*, *C*, *Fj* 1992 *Sp*, *It*, *It*, *Ar* 1994 *Ger*, *Rus*, *It*, *W* 1995 *F*, *S*, *J*, *C*, *SA*, *A* 1996 *F* 1997 *F*, *It* 1999 *F*
Ciornei, M 1972 *WGe*, *F* 1973 *Ar*, *Ar*, *WGe*, *F* 1974 *Mor*, *Pol*, *EGe*, *F*, *Cze* 1975 *It*, *Sp*
Cocor, C 1940 *It* (R) 1949 *Cze*
Codea, M 1998 *Ukr* (R) 2001 *E* (R)
Codoi, L 1980 *I*, *Pol* 1984 *F* 1985 *Tun* (R), *USS*
Cojocariu, C 1990 *It*, *F*, *H*, *Sp*, *It*, *USS* 1991 *It*, *NZ*, *F*, *S*, *F*, *C*, *Fj* 1992 *Sp*, *It*, *USS*, *F*, *Ar* 1993 *Pt*, *F*, *F*, *I* (R) 1994 *Sp*, *Ger* (R), *Rus*, *It*, *W*, *It*, *E* 1995 *F*, *S*, *J*, *J*, *C*, *SA*, *A*, *Ar*, *F*, *It* 1996 *F*
Colceriu, L 1991 *S*, *Fj* 1992 *Sp*, *It*, *It* 1993 *I* 1994 *Sp*, *Ger*, *Rus*, *It*, *W*, *It* 1995 *F*, *J* (R), *J*, *C*, *SA*, *A* 1997 *F*, *W*, *Bel*, *Ar*, *F*, *It* 1998 *Pol*, *Ukr*
Coliba, D 1987 *USS*, *F*
Coltuneac, M 2002 *Sp* (R), *W* (R), *S* (R)
Coman, T 1984 *Sp* 1986 *F*, *Tun*, *Tun*, *I* (R) 1988 *Sp* (R), *US*, *USS*, *USS* (R) 1989 *It* (R) 1992 *F*
Constantin, C 2001 *Pt* (R) 2002 *Geo* (R), *W* (R)
Constantin, F 1972 *Mor*, *Cze*, *WGe* 1973 *Ar* (R), *Ar*, *WGe* (R) 1980 *Mor* (R) 1982 *It* (R)
Constantin, I 1971 *Mor* 1972 *WGe* 1973 *Ar*, *Ar*, *WGe*, *F* 1974 *Mor*, *Pol*, *Sp* (R), *F*, *Cze* 1975 *It*, *Sp*, *JAB*, *Pol*, *F* 1976 *H*, *It*, *Sp*, *USS*, *Bul*, *Pol* 1977 *It*, *F* 1978 *Pol*, *F* 1979 *It*, *Sp*, *USS*, *W*, *Pol*, *F* 1980 *It*, *USS*, *I*, *Pol*, *F* 1981 *It*, *Sp*, *USS*, *S*, *NZ*, *F* 1982 *WGe* (R), *It*, *USS*, *Z*, *Z* 1983 *WGe*, *USS* 1985 *It*
Constantin, L 1983 *USS*, *F* (R) 1984 *It*, *S*, *F*, *Sp* 1985 *E*, *It*, *Tun* (R), *USS*, *USS*, *It* 1986 *Pt*, *S*, *F*, *Tun*, *Tun*, *Pt*, *F*, *I* 1987 *It*, *USS*, *Z*, *F*, *S*, *USS*, *F* 1991 *It* (R), *NZ* (R), *F*
Constantin, LT 1985 *USS*
Constantin, S 1980 *Mor* 1982 *Z*, *Z* 1983 *Pol*, *W*, *USS*, *F* 1984 *S*, *F* (R) 1985 *USS* 1986 *Pt*, *S*, *F*, *Tun* 1987 *It*, *Z*, *S*
Constantin, T 1992 *USS*, *F*, *It* 1993 *Pt* (R), *F*, *Sp* 1996 *Pt* 1997 *It* 1999 *F*, *US*, *I* 2000 *Pt*, *Sp*, *Geo*, *F* 2002 *Rus*, *Geo*
Constantin, T 1985 *USS*
Copil, N 1985 *USS*, *It* 1986 *S* (R)
Coravu, D 1968 *F*
Cordos, N 1958 *EGe* 1961 *EGe* 1963 *Bul*, *Cze* 1964 *Cze* (R), *EGe* (R)
Cornel, V 1977 *F* 1978 *Cze*, *Sp*
Corneliu, G 1980 *Mor*, *USS* (R) 1982 *WGe*, *It*, *Z*, *Z* 1986 *Tun*, *Pt*, *F* 1993 *I* 1994 *W* (R)
Corneliu, G 1976 *Bul* 1977 *F* (R) 1979 *It* 1981 *S* 1982 *Z*
Corneliu, M 1979 *USS*
Corodeanu, F 1997 *F*, *W* 1998 *H* (R), *Pol*, *Ar*, *Geo* 1999 *F*, *S*, *A* (R), *US* (R), *I* (R) 2000 *H*, *Sp*, *Geo*, *F*, *It* 2001 *Pt*, *Sp*, *H*, *Rus*, *Geo*, *I*, *E* 2002 *Pt*, *Sp*, *Rus*, *Geo*, *It*, *Sp*, *W*, *S* 2003 *Sp* 2005 *Geo*, *J*, *US*, *S*, *Pt*, *C*, *I* 2006 *Geo*, *CZR*, *Pt*
Costea, L 1994 *E* 1995 *S*, *J*, *J*, *Ar*, *F* 1997 *F*
Costica, M 2002 *S* (R)
Coter, L 1957 *F*, *Cze* 1959 *EGe*, *Pol*, *Cze* 1960 *F*
Covaci, F 1936 *Ger* 1937 *H*, *F*, *Ger* 1940 *It* 1942 *It*
Cratunescu, C 1919 *US*, *F*
Crissoveloni, N 1936 *F*, *It* 1937 *H*, *F*, *Ger* 1938 *F*, *Ger*
Cristea, S 1973 *Mor*
Cristian, P 2002 *W* 2003 *Pt*, *Rus*, *Geo*, *CZR* 2004 *CZR* 2005 *Ukr*, *I*
Cristoloveanu, C 1952 *EGe*
Crivat, G 1938 *F*, *Ger*
Csoma, V 1983 *WGe* (R)
Curea, D 2005 *Rus* (R), *Ukr*, *J*, *US*, *S*, *Pt*
Daiciulescu, V 1966 *Cze*, *F* 1967 *It*, *Pol* 1968 *F* 1969 *Pol*
Damian, A 1934 *It* 1936 *F*, *It*, *Ger* 1937 *It* 1938 *F*, *Ger* 1939 *It* 1949 *Cze*
Daraban, G 1969 *Cze* 1972 *Mor*, *Cze*, *WGe*, *F* 1973 *Sp*, *Mor*, *Ar*, *Ar* 1974 *Cze*, *EGe*, *F*, *Cze* 1975 *It*, *Sp*, *JAB*, *Pol*, *F* 1976 *H*, *It*, *Sp*, *USS*, *Bul*, *Pol*, *F*, *Mor* 1977 *Sp*, *It*, *F* 1978 *Cze*, *Sp*, *Pol*, *F* 1982 *F* 1983 *Mor* (R), *WGe* (R), *It*, *USS*, *W*
Dascalu, R 2006 *Ukr*, *F*
David, V 1984 *Sp* (R) 1986 *Pt*, *S*, *F*, *Tun* 1987 *USS* (R), *Z*, *F* 1992 *USS* (R)
Demci, S 1998 *Ar* (R) 2001 *H*, *Rus* (R), *Geo*, *I* (R), *W*
Demian, R 1959 *EGe* 1960 *F* 1961 *Pol*, *EGe*, *Cze*, *EGe*, *F* 1962 *Cze*, *Pol*, *It*, *F* 1963 *Bul*, *EGe*, *Cze*, *F* 1964 *WGe*, *F* 1965 *WGe*, *F* 1966 *Cze*, *It*, *F* 1967 *It*, *Pt*, *Pol*, *WGe*, *F* 1968 *Cze*, *F* 1969 *Pol*, *WGe*, *F* 1971 *It*, *Mor*
Denischi, E 1949 *Cze* 1952 *EGe*, *EGe*
Diaconu, I 1942 *It*
Diamandi-Telu, C 1938 *Ger* 1939 *It*
Dima, D 1999 *A* (R), *US* (R), *I* (R) 2000 *H*, *Pt*, *Geo*, *F*, *It* 2001 *Sp*, *H* (R), *Rus*, *Geo*, *W*, *E* 2002 *Pt*, *Sp*, *Rus*, *W* (R), *S* 2004 *CZR* (R), *Pt*, *Sp*, *Rus*, *Geo* (R)
Dimofte, I 2004 *It* (R), *W* (R), *J* (R), *CZR* 2005 *C*, *I* 2006 *Geo*, *CZR*, *Pt*, *Ukr*, *Rus*, *F*
Dinescu, C 1934 *It* 1936 *F*, *It*, *Ger* 1937 *It*, *H*, *F*, *Ger* 1938 *F*, *Ger* 1940 *It* 1942 *It*
Dinu, A 1983 *Pol*, *USS*
Dinu, C 1965 *WGe*, *F* 1966 *Cze*, *It*, *F* 1967 *It*, *Pt*, *Pol*, *WGe* 1968 *F* 1969 *Pol*, *WGe*, *Cze*, *F* 1970 *It*, *F* 1971 *Mor*, *F* 1972 *Mor*, *Cze*, *WGe*, *F* 1973 *Sp*, *Mor*, *Ar*, *Ar*, *WGe*, *F* 1974 *Mor*, *Pol*, *Sp*, *Cze*, *F*, *Cze* 1975 *It*, *Sp* 1976 *H*, *It*, *Sp*, *Pol*, *F*, *Mor* 1977 *Sp*, *It*, *F*, *Pol*, *It*, *F* 1978 *Sp*, *Pol*, *F* 1979 *Sp*, *USS*, *W*, *Pol* 1980 *I*, *Pol*, *F* 1981 *It*, *Sp*, *USS*, *NZ*, *F* 1982 *F* 1983 *Mor*, *WGe*, *It*, *USS*
Dinu, F 2000 *Mor* (R), *H* (R)
Dinu, G 1990 *It*, *F*, *H*, *Sp*, *It*, *USS* 1991 *It*, *S*, *F*, *C*, *Fj* 1992 *Sp*, *It*, *USS*, *F*, *It* 1993 *F*
Dinu, G 1975 *Pol* 1979 *It*, *Sp*
Dobre, F 2004 *W* (R), *CZR*
Dobre, G 2001 *E*
Dobre, I 1951 *EGe* 1952 *EGe* 1953 *It* 1955 *Cze* 1957 *Cze*, *Bel*, *F* 1958 *Sp*
Doja, I 1986 *Tun*, *Pt*, *F*, *I* 1988 *F*, *W* 1989 *Sp*, *Z*, *Sa*, *S* 1990 *It* 1991 *It*, *NZ*, *F*, *C* 1992 *Sp*
Doja, V 1997 *Bel* 1998 *Pol* (R), *Geo* (R), *I*
Domocos, A 1989 *Z*, *Sa*, *USS*
Dorutiu, I 1957 *Cze*, *Bel*, *F* 1958 *Sp*, *WGe*
Draghici, A 1919 *US*
Dragnea, C 1995 *F* 1996 *Pol* (R) 1997 *F* (R), *Bel*, *Ar*, *F*, *It* 1998 *H*, *Pol* (R) 1999 *F* (R) 2000 *F* (R)
Dragnea, I 1985 *Tun*
Dragnea, S 2002 *S* (R)
Dragomir, M 1996 *Bel* 1997 *Bel* 1998 *H*, *Pol*, *Ukr*, *Geo*, *I* 2001 *I* (R), *W*, *E* (R)
Dragomir, M 2001 *H* (R), *Geo* (R) 2002 *I*
Dragomir, V 1964 *Cze*, *EGe* 1966 *It* 1967 *Pol*, *WGe*
Dragomirescu, G 1919 *F*
Dragomirescu-Rahtopol, G 1963 *Bul* (R), *EGe*, *Cze*, *F* 1964 *Cze*, *EGe*, *WGe*, *F* 1965 *WGe*, *F* 1966 *Cze* 1967 *It*, *Pt*, *Pol*, *WGe*, *F* 1968 *Cze*, *Cze*, *F* 1969 *Pol*, *Cze*, *F* 1970 *It*, *F* 1971 *It*, *Mor* 1972 *Mor*, *Cze*, *WGe*, *F* 1973 *WGe*, *F*
Dragos, N 1995 *Ar* (R), *It* (R) 1997 *It* 1998 *H*, *Ar*
Dragos, N 1997 *F*, *Ar*, *F* 1998 *Pol*, *Ukr*, *Geo*, *I* 1999 *F*, *S* 2000 *Sp*, *Geo* (R), *F*
Draguceanu, CS 1994 *Sp*, *Ger*, *Rus*, *It*, *W* (R), *It*, *E* (R) 1995 *S* (R), *J*, *Ar*, *F*, *It* (R) 1996 *Bel* 1997 *W*, *Bel*, *Ar*, *F*, *It* 1998 *H*, *Pol*, *Ukr*, *Ar*, *Geo*, *I* 1999 *S*, *A*, *US*, *I* 2000 *Mor*, *H*, *Pt*, *Sp*, *Geo*, *F*, *It*
Dragulescu, C 1969 *Cze* 1970 *F* 1971 *It* 1972 *Cze*
Drobota, G 1960 *Pol*, *Cze* 1961 *EGe*, *EGe*, *F* 1962 *Cze*, *EGe*, *Pol*, *F* 1964 *Cze*, *EGe*, *F*
Dumbrava, D 2002 *W* 2003 *Sp* (R), *Rus* (R), *Geo*, *CZR*, *F*, *W*, *I*, *A*, *Nm* 2004 *CZR*, *Pt*, *Sp*, *Rus*, *Geo*, *It*, *J* (R) 2005 *Rus*, *Geo*, *Ukr*, *J*, *US*, *S*, *Pt*, *C* (R) 2006 *Geo* (R), *Pt*, *Rus* (R)
Dumitras, H 1984 *It* (R) 1985 *E* (R), *It*, *USS* (R) 1986 *Pt*, *F*, *I* 1987 *It*, *USS*, *Z*, *S*, *USS*, *F* 1988 *It*, *Sp*, *US*, *USS*, *USS*, *F*, *W* 1989 *It*, *E*, *Z*, *Sa*, *USS*, *S* 1990 *It*, *F*, *H*, *Sp*, *USS* 1991 *It*, *NZ*, *F*, *S*, *F*, *C*, *Fj* 1992 *Sp*, *USS*, *F*, *Ar* 1993 *Pt*, *Tun*, *F*, *Sp*, *F*, *I*
Dumitras, I 2002 *H* (R) 2006 *Geo*, *CZR*, *Ukr*, *Rus*, *F* (R)
Dumitrescu, E 1953 *It* 1958 *Sp*, *WGe*
Dumitrescu, G 1988 *It*, *Sp*, *F*, *W* 1989 *It*, *E*, *Sp*, *Z*, *Sa*, *USS*, *S* 1990 *It*, *F*, *H*, *Sp*, *It*, *USS* 1991 *It*, *NZ*, *F* 1997 *It* (R)
Dumitrescu, L 1997 *Bel* (R) 2001 *W* (R)
Dumitrescu, L 1997 *Ar* (R)
Dumitriu, G 1937 *H*, *F*, *Ger*
Dumitru, A 1975 *Sp* 1976 *Sp*, *Bul* 1977 *F* 1979 *It*, *W*, *F* (R) 1980 *I* 1983 *It*

Dumitru, G 1973 *Sp, Mor, Ar, Ar, WGe, F* 1974 *Mor, Sp, Cze, EGe, F* 1975 *JAB, Pol, F* 1976 *H, It, Sp* 1977 *Sp, Pol, F* 1978 *Cze, Sp, Pol, F* 1979 *It, Sp, USS, W, Pol, F* 1980 *It, Mor, USS, I, Pol, F* 1981 *It, Sp, USS, S, NZ, F* 1982 *WGe, It, USS, Z, Z, F* 1983 *Mor, WGe, It, USS, Pol, USS, F* 1984 *It, S, F* 1985 *E, It, Tun, USS* 1986 *F, I* 1987 *USS, F, S* (R), *USS, F*
Dumitru, M 1990 *F, H, Sp, It, USS* 1991 *NZ, F, F, C* 1992 *F* 1993 *F, Sp* (R), *F*
Dumitru, M 1998 *Ar* (R) 1999 *F* 2000 *Mor, H, Pt, Sp, Geo, F* 2002 *H* (R) 2003 *Sp*
Dumitru, M 2002 *Pt, Sp* (R), *H, I* 2004 *It* (R)
Dumitru, S 2005 *Rus* (R), *Ukr* (R), *US, S* (R), *Pt*
Durbac, R 1968 *Cze* 1969 *WGe, Cze* 1970 *It, F* 1971 *It, Mor, F* 1972 *WGe, F* 1973 *Ar* (R), *Ar, WGe, F* 1974 *Mor, Pol, Sp, Cze, EGe, F, Cze* 1975 *It, Sp, JAB, Pol, F*
Duta, A 1973 *Ar*
Eckert, R 1927 *F, Ger, Cze*
Enache, I 1977 *It*
Ezaru, M 2000 *Pt, Geo* (R), *F* (R)
Falcusanu, V 1974 *Sp, Cze*
Fantaneanu, G 1934 *It* 1936 *F, It, Ger* 1937 *It, H, F, Ger*
Fercu, C 2005 *C, I* 2006 *Geo, CZR, Pt, Ukr, Rus, F*
Florea, C 1937 *It, F, Ger*
Florea, G 1981 *S, NZ, F* 1982 *WGe, It, USS, Z, Z* 1984 *Sp* 1985 *USS* 1986 *Pt, F*
Florea, S 2000 *It* 2001 *Sp* (R), *Geo* (R), *I, E* (R) 2002 *It, Sp, W* 2003 *Sp* (R), *Rus* (R), *Geo, CZR, A, Ar, Nm* (R)
Florescu, I 1957 *F, Cze*
Florescu, M 1995 *F*
Florescu, P 1967 *It, Pt, Pol, WGe, F* 1968 *Cze, Cze, F* 1969 *Pol, WGe, Cze, F* 1971 *Mor* 1973 *Sp, Mor, Ar, Ar* (R) 1974 *Cze, EGe, F*
Florian, P 1927 *F* 1934 *It*
Florian, T 1927 *F, Ger*
Flutur, V 1995 *J* (R), *J, SA, A, Ar, F* (R), *It* 1996 *Bel, Pol* 1997 *F*
Flutur, V 1994 *Ger* (R)
Foca, M 1992 *It, USS, It, Ar* (R) 1993 *Pt, Tun* (R), *F*
Fugigi, C 1964 *Cze* (R) 1969 *Cze* (R) 1972 *Mor, Cze, WGe, F* 1973 *Sp, Ar, Ar* (R), *WGe, F* 1974 *Mor, Sp, Cze, EGe* 1975 *It, Sp, JAB*
Fugigi, R 1992 *Ar* 1995 *It* 1996 *Pt, F, Pol* 1998 *Ukr, Ar, I* 1999 *S, I* (R)
Fuicu, S 1976 *H* 1980 *USS, I, Pol, F* 1981 *It, Sp, USS, S, NZ, F* 1982 *Z, Z, F* 1983 *Mor, WGe, It, USS, W* 1984 *It*
Fulina, N 1988 *F, W* 1989 *It, E, Sp, Sa* (R), *USS* 1990 *It, F, H, Sp, USS* 1991 *NZ, C, Fj* 1992 *It, It* 1993 *Pt, F, Sp, F, I* 1994 *Sp, Ger, Rus, It, W, It*
Gal, C 2005 *I* (R) 2006 *Geo, CZR, Pt*
Galan, S 1985 *It* (R), *It*
Garbu, A 1992 *Ar* (R) 1993 *Tun* (R), *Sp* 1996 *Pt, Pol*
Garlesteanu, I 1924 *F, US* 1927 *F, Cze*
Gealapu, A 1994 *It, E* 1995 *F, S, J, J, C, SA, A, Ar, F, It* 1996 *Pt, F, Pol*
Gheara, C 2004 *CZR, Sp, Geo*
Gheorghe, C 1992 *It* 1993 *Tun, F* (R), *Sp* (R) 1994 *Sp* (R), *Ger, Rus, E* (R)
Gherasim, D 1959 *Cze*
Ghiata, V 1951 *EGe*
Ghica, S 1937 *H, F* 1942 *It*
Ghioc, V 2000 *It* 2001 *Pt, Sp, Rus, Geo, I, W, E* 2002 *Pt, Sp* (R), *H, W, S* 2003 *CZR, Ar* (R) 2004 *It, W* 2005 *Ukr, S* (R)
Ghiondea, N 1949 *Cze* 1951 *EGe*
Ghiuzelea, D 1951 *EGe* 1952 *EGe, EGe* 1953 *It* 1955 *Cze* 1957 *Cze*
Girbu, A 1993 *F* (R), *I* 1994 *Sp* 1995 *Ar, F* (R), *It* 1996 *F* (R) 1997 *F, Ar, F, It* 1998 *H, Pol, Geo, I*
Giucal, M 1985 *It, Tun, USS* 1986 *F, Tun*
Giugiuc, A 1963 *Bul* (R), *EGe* (R), *Cze* (R) 1964 *Cze* (R), *EGe* 1966 *Cze*
Giuglea, M 1985 *It* 1986 *Pt*
Giuglea, V 1986 *S, Tun* (R)
Glavan, I 1942 *It*
Gontineac, RS 1995 *F, S, J, J, C, SA, A* 1996 *Pt, F, Pol* 1997 *F, W, Ar, F, It* 1998 *H, Pol, Ukr, Ar, Geo, I* 1999 *F, S, A, US, I* 2000 *H, Sp, Geo, F* 2001 *Rus, Geo* 2002 *Pt, Sp, Rus, Geo, I, It, Sp, W, S* 2003 *Pt, Sp, Geo, CZR, F, W, I, A, Ar, Nm* 2004 *CZR, Pt, Rus, Geo, It, W, J, CZR* 2005 *Geo, C* 2006 *Geo, Pt, Ukr, Rus, F*
Graur, G 1958 *It* 1959 *EGe, Pol, Cze, EGe* 1960 *Pol, EGe, Cze* 1961 *EGe* 1962 *EGe, It*
Grigore, E 1982 *WGe* 1984 *Sp* 1985 *E, Tun* 1987 *It, USS, Z, F* (R), *S*
Grigorescu, V 1936 *F, It, Ger* 1939 *It*
Guramare, M 1982 *WGe* (R), *It* 1983 *Mor, WGe* 1988 *Sp* (R)
Guranescu, A 1991 *S, F* 1992 *USS* (R), *It* (R) 1993 *Pt, Tun, I* 1994 *Ger, Rus, It, W, E* (R) 1995 *SA, A, Ar* (R), *F, It*
Guranescu, S 1997 *W, Bel, Ar* (R) 2001 *Sp, H* (R), *Rus* (R), *I* (R)
Hariton, A 1973 *Mor* (R), *Ar, Ar* 1978 *Cze, Sp* (R)
Hell, T 1958 *EGe*
Hildan, CN 1998 *H, Pol, Geo* 1999 *S* (R)
Hodorca, L 1984 *It* 1985 *Tun* 1986 *Pt, S, F, Tun, Tun, I* 1987 *It, Z* (R) 1988 *F*
Holban, M 1980 *Mor* 1982 *F* 1985 *It, USS* 1986 *Pt* (R), *I* (R)
Hussar, J 1919 *US*
Iacob, D 1996 *Bel* 2001 *Pt* (R), *Sp, H, Geo, W*
Iacob, ML 1997 *W, Bel* (R), *Ar* (R), *F* (R), *It* (R) 1999 *S* (R)
Ianusevici, P 1974 *Pol, Cze, EGe, Cze* 1975 *It* (R) 1976 *USS, Bul, Pol, F, Mor* 1977 *Sp, Pol, It, F* 1978 *F*
Iconomu, I 1919 *US, F*
Iconomu, M 1919 *US, F*
Ifrim, N 1937 *F, Ger*
Ignat, G 1986 *Pt, S, F, Tun* 1988 *It, Sp, US, USS, USS, F, W* 1989 *It, E, Sp, S* 1990 *It, F, H, Sp* 1991 *It, NZ* 1992 *Sp* (R), *It, USS, F*
Ilca, V 1987 *F*
Ilie, I 1952 *EGe, EGe* 1953 *It* 1955 *Cze* (R) 1957 *F, Cze, Bel, F* 1958 *It* 1959 *EGe*
Iliescu, M 1961 *EGe* 1963 *Bul, EGe, Cze, F* 1965 *WGe, F* 1967 *WGe* (R)
Ioan, T 1937 *H, F* (R), *Ger*
Ioan, V 1927 *Cze* 1937 *It*
Ion, F 1991 *S* 1992 *Sp* 1993 *F*
Ion, G 1984 *Sp* 1986 *F* (R), *I* 1988 *USS, F, W* 1989 *It, E, Sp* (R), *Sa* (R), *USS, S* 1990 *It, F, H, Sp, It, USS* 1991 *It, NZ, F, S, F, C, Fj* 1992 *Sp, It, USS, F, Ar* 1993 *Pt, F, Sp, F* 1994 *Sp, It, W, It*
Ion, P 2003 *Ar* (R) 2005 *Rus* (R)
Ion, V 1980 *Mor, USS* 1982 *Z, Z, F* 1983 *Mor, It, USS, W, USS, F* 1984 *S* 1985 *It* (R) 1987 *It, USS, Z* (R), *F, S*
Ionescu, A 1958 *EGe, It* 1959 *EGe, Pol, Cze* 1960 *Pol, EGe, Cze* 1961 *Pol, Cze, EGe, F* 1962 *EGe, It, F* 1963 *F* 1964 *Cze, EGe, F* 1965 *WGe* (R) 1966 *Cze, It, F*
Ionescu, D 1949 *Cze* 1951 *EGe* 1952 *EGe, EGe* 1953 *It* 1955 *Cze* 1957 *F, Cze, F* 1958 *Sp, It*
Ionescu, G 1934 *It* 1936 *F, It, Ger* 1937 *It, F* 1938 *F, Ger* 1940 *It* 1942 *It*
Ionescu, G 1949 *Cze*
Ionescu, M 1972 *Mor* 1976 *USS, Bul, Pol, F* 1977 *It, F, Pol, It, F* 1978 *Cze, Sp, Pol, F* 1979 *It, Sp, USS, W, Pol, F* 1980 *I* (R) 1981 *NZ* 1983 *USS* (R)
Ionescu, S 1936 *It, Ger* 1937 *It*
Ionescu, V 1993 *Tun* (R), *F* (R) 1994 *Rus* (R) 1998 *Ukr*
Ionescu, V 1992 *It*
Ionescue, R 1968 *Cze, Cze* 1971 *F*
Ionita, F 1974 *Sp* 1978 *Pol, F*
Iordachescu, P 1957 *F, Cze, Bel, F* 1958 *Sp, WGe, EGe, It* 1959 *EGe, Pol, Cze, EGe* 1960 *Pol, EGe, Cze* 1961 *EGe* 1963 *F* 1964 *Cze, EGe, WGe* 1965 *WGe, F* 1966 *Cze*
Iordan, M 1980 *Mor*
Iordanescu, P 1949 *Cze*
Iorgulescu, V 1967 *WGe* (R) 1968 *Cze, F* 1969 *Pol, WGe, Cze* 1970 *It, F* 1971 *F* 1973 *Ar, Ar*
Irimescu, V 1960 *F* 1961 *Pol, Cze, EGe, F* 1962 *Cze, EGe, Pol, It, F* 1963 *F* 1964 *F* 1965 *WGe, F* 1966 *Cze, It, F* 1967 *It, Pt, Pol, WGe, F* 1968 *Cze, Cze, F* 1969 *Pol, WGe, Cze, F* 1970 *It, F* 1971 *F*
Irimia, I 1936 *F, It, Ger* 1937 *It, H, Ger* 1938 *F, Ger* 1939 *It* 1940 *It*
Irisescu, G 1993 *Sp* (R)
Iulian, A 2003 *CZR* (R)
Ivanciuc, I 1991 *Fj* (R) 1994 *E* 1995 *J, SA, A*

Jipescu, I 1927 *F*
Kramer, C 1955 *Cze* 1958 *Sp*, *WGe*, *It* 1960 *Pol* (R), *EGe*, *Cze*
Krantz, T 1940 *It* 1942 *It*
Kurtzbauer, C 1939 *It*
Lapusneanu, C 1934 *It*
Leonte, G 1984 *S*, *F* 1985 *E*, *It*, *USS* 1987 *It*, *USS*, *Z*, *S*, *USS*, *F* 1988 *It*, *Sp*, *US*, *USS*, *USS*, *F*, *W* 1989 *It*, *E*, *Sp*, *Z*, *Sa*, *USS*, *S* 1990 *It*, *F*, *H*, *Sp*, *It* 1991 *It*, *NZ*, *F*, *S*, *F*, *C* 1992 *USS*, *F*, *It*, *Ar* 1993 *Tun*, *F*, *Sp*, *F*, *I* 1994 *Sp*, *Ger*, *Rus*, *It*, *W*, *It* 1995 *F*, *S*, *J*, *J*, *C*, *SA*, *A*
Leuciuc, M 1987 *F* (R)
Luca, T 1995 *Ar*, *F*, *It* 1996 *F*
Lucaci, V 1996 *Bel*
Lungu, A 1980 *It*, *USS* 1981 *It*, *Sp*, *USS*, *S*, *NZ*, *F* 1982 *WGe*, *It*, *USS*, *Z*, *Z*, *F* 1983 *Mor*, *WGe*, *It*, *USS*, *Pol*, *W*, *USS*, *F* 1984 *It*, *S*, *F*, *Sp* 1985 *E*, *It*, *Tun*, *USS*, *USS*, *It* 1986 *Pt*, *S*, *F*, *Tun*, *Tun*, *Pt*, *F*, *I* 1987 *It*, *USS*, *Z*, *F*, *S*, *USS*, *F* 1988 *It*, *Sp*, *US*, *USS*, *USS*, *F*, *W* 1989 *It*, *E*, *Sp*, *Z*, *Sa*, *USS*, *S* 1990 *It*, *F*, *It* 1991 *It*, *NZ*, *F*, *S*, *F*, *C*, *Fj* 1992 *Sp*, *It*, *USS*, *F*, *Ar* 1995 *A* (R)
Lungu, R 2002 *Pt*, *H* (R), *It* (R), *Sp* (R), *W* (R) 2003 *Pt* (R)
Lupu, C 1998 *Pol* (R), *I* (R) 1999 *F* (R) 2000 *Mor*, *It* 2001 *Pt*, *H* (R), *Rus* (R), *W* 2002 *H*, *Rus* (R)
Luric, S 1951 *EGe* 1952 *EGe*, *EGe* 1953 *It* 1955 *Cze*
Luscal, V 1958 *Sp*, *WGe*, *EGe*
Macaneata, F 1983 *USS*
Maftei, V 1995 *Ar*, *F*, *It* 1996 *Bel* 1997 *W*, *F* 1998 *Ar* (R) 2001 *Pt*, *Sp*, *H*, *Geo*, *I* 2002 *Pt*, *Sp*, *Rus*, *Geo*, *I*, *It*, *Sp*, *S* 2003 *Pt*, *Geo*, *CZR*, *F*, *W*, *I*, *A*, *Ar*, *Nm* 2004 *Pt*, *Sp*, *Rus*, *Geo*, *W*, *J*, *CZR* 2005 *Rus*, *Geo*, *Ukr*, *C*, *I*
Malancu, G 1976 *H*, *It*, *USS*, *Bul*
Man, A 1988 *US*, *USS*, *USS*
Manoileanu, D 1949 *Cze*
Manole, G 1959 *Pol* 1960 *Pol*, *EGe*, *Cze*
Manta, A 1996 *Bel* 1997 *F* (R) 1998 *Ar*, *Geo*, *I* 2000 *F* 2001 *Pt*, *Sp*, *Rus*, *Geo* 2002 *Sp* (R), *H*, *Rus*, *I*, *It*, *Sp* 2003 *Pt*, *Rus* 2005 *C*, *I* 2006 *Geo*, *CZR*, *Pt*
Manu, H 1919 *US*, *F* 1927 *F*, *Ger*
Marascu, N 1919 *F* 1924 *F*, *US* 1927 *F*, *Cze*
Marasescu, A 1936 *It*, *Ger*
Marculescu, E 1936 *F*, *It*, *Ger* 1937 *It* 1939 *It* (R) 1940 *It*
Marghescu, A 1980 *Pol* (R) 1981 *It* 1983 *W*, *USS*, *F* 1984 *S*, *F*, *Sp* 1985 *E*
Marica, I 1972 *WGe*, *F* 1973 *Sp*, *Mor*, *WGe*, *F* 1974 *Mor*, *Sp*, *Cze*, *EGe*, *F*, *Cze* 1975 *It*, *Sp*
Marin, A 1979 *F* 1982 *USS* 1983 *Pol* 1984 *Sp* 1985 *USS*, *It* 1986 *Pt* 1987 *USS*, *Z*
Marin, A 1978 *Cze*, *Sp*, *Pol* 1980 *Pol*
Marin, N 1991 *Fj* 1992 *Sp* (R), *It* 1993 *F* (R), *I* (R) 1995 *Ar*, *F*, *It*
Marinache, A 1949 *Cze* 1951 *EGe* 1952 *EGe*, *EGe* 1955 *Cze* 1957 *F*, *Bel*, *F* 1960 *F* 1961 *Pol*, *EGe*, *Cze*, *EGe*, *F* 1962 *Cze*, *Pol*
Marinescu, V 1967 *Pt*, *WGe* 1968 *Cze* 1969 *Cze* (R), *F*
Marioara, F 1994 *E* (R) 1996 *Pol* (R) 1998 *Geo* (R), *I*
Mateescu, A 1959 *EGe*, *Pol*, *Cze*, *EGe* 1960 *Pol*, *EGe*, *Cze* 1962 *EGe*, *Pol* 1963 *Bul* (R), *EGe*, *Cze* (R) 1964 *Cze*, *EGe* 1965 *WGe*, *F* 1966 *F* 1970 *It*, *F* 1973 *Sp* (R), *WGe*, *F* 1974 *Mor*, *Pol*, *Sp*
Mateescu, A 1934 *It* 1936 *F*, *Ger*
Mauesescu, A 1927 *F*, *Ger*
Mavrodin, R 1998 *Geo*, *I* 1999 *F*, *A* (R), *US*, *I* 2000 *H*, *Pt*, *Sp*, *Geo*, *F*, *It* 2002 *Pt*, *Sp*, *H*, *I*, *It* (R), *Sp* (R), *W* 2003 *I*, *A*, *Ar*, *Nm* 2004 *Pt*, *Sp* (R), *Rus*, *Geo*, *W* (R), *J*, *CZR* 2005 *Rus*, *J*, *US*, *S*, *Pt* 2006 *Ukr*, *Rus*, *F* (R)
Mazilu, G 1958 *Sp*, *WGe* 1959 *EGe*, *Pol*, *Cze*
Mehedinti, S 1951 *EGe* 1953 *It*
Melinte, G 1958 *EGe*, *It*
Mergisescu, P 1960 *Pol*, *EGe*, *Cze*
Mersoiu, C 2001 *I* 2003 *Pt* (R), *Sp* (R), *Geo*, *CZR*, *F*, *W* 2004 *CZR*, *Pt*, *Sp*, *It*, *W*, *J*, *CZR* 2005 *Rus*, *Geo*, *Ukr*, *I* (R) 2006 *Pt* (R)
Mersoiu, D 2000 *Mor*, *Pt*
Miclescu 1971 *Mor* (R)
Mihailescu, S 1919 *F* 1924 *F*, *US* 1927 *F*
Mihalache, D 1973 *Mor*
Mihalascu, V 1967 *Pol*, *WGe*
Mitocaru, A 1992 *Ar* 1993 *Pt*, *Sp*, *F*
Mitu, P 1996 *Bel* (R), *Pol* 1997 *W* (R), *Bel*, *Ar*, *It* 1998 *H* (R), *Pol*, *Ukr*, *Ar*, *Geo*, *I* 1999 *F*, *S*, *A*, *US*, *I* 2000 *H*, *Pt*, *Sp*, *Geo*, *It* 2001 *Pt*, *Sp*, *H*, *Rus* 2002 *Pt*, *Sp*, *H* (R), *Rus*, *Geo*, *Sp* (R), *W*, *S* 2003 *Geo* 2005 *I* 2006 *Geo*
Miu, M 2003 *Pt*, *Sp* (R)
Mladin, V 1955 *Cze* (R) 1957 *Bel*, *F* 1958 *Sp*, *WGe*, *It* 1959 *EGe* (R) 1960 *F*
Mocanu, S 1996 *Bel* 1998 *H* (R), *Pol* (R), *Ukr* (R) 2000 *Mor*, *Pt* (R)
Moldoveanu, T 1937 *F*, *Ger* 1938 *F*, *Ger* 1939 *It* 1940 *It*
Morariu, F 1976 *H*, *USS*, *Bul*, *Pol*, *F*, *Mor* 1977 *Sp*, *It*, *F*, *Pol*, *It*, *F* 1978 *Cze*, *Sp*, *Pol*, *F* 1979 *It*, *Sp*, *USS*, *W*, *Pol*, *F* 1980 *It*, *I*, *Pol*, *F* 1981 *USS* (R), *NZ* 1982 *USS*, *Z*, *Z*, *F* 1983 *Mor*, *WGe*, *It*, *USS*, *Pol*, *W*, *F* 1984 *It*, *S*, *F*, *Sp* 1985 *E*, *It*, *Tun*, *USS*, *USS*, *It* 1986 *Pt*, *S*, *F*, *Tun* 1987 *It*, *USS*, *Z*, *S*, *USS*, *F* 1988 *It*, *Sp*, *US*, *USS*, *USS*, *F*, *W* 1989 *It*, *E*, *Sp*, *Z*
Morariu, O 1984 *Sp* 1985 *Tun*
Morariu, V 1952 *EGe*, *EGe* 1953 *It* 1955 *Cze* 1957 *F*, *Cze*, *Bel*, *F* 1959 *EGe* 1960 *F* 1961 *Pol*, *Cze*, *EGe*, *F* 1962 *Cze*, *EGe*, *Pol*, *It*, *F* 1963 *F* 1964 *WGe*, *F*
Moscu, C 1934 *It* 1937 *It*
Mot, M 1980 *Mor* 1982 *It*, *USS*, *Z* 1985 *It*, *It* 1986 *F*, *Tun* 1988 *US*, *USS*
Motoc, M 1988 *US* (R) 1989 *S*
Motrescu, P 1973 *Mor*, *Ar*, *Ar* 1974 *Mor*, *Pol*, *Sp*, *Cze* 1975 *JAB*, *Pol*, *F* 1976 *H*, *It*, *Sp*, *Bul* (R), *Pol* (R), *F*, *Mor* 1977 *Sp*, *It*, *F*, *Pol*, *It*, *F* 1978 *Cze*, *Sp*, *Pol*, *F* 1979 *It*, *Sp*, *USS*, *W*, *Pol* 1980 *It*, *Mor*
Munteanu, B 2000 *It*
Munteanu, C 1942 *It*
Munteanu, I 1940 *It* (R)
Munteanu, M 1973 *WGe*, *F* 1974 *Mor*, *Sp*, *Cze*, *EGe*, *F*, *Cze* 1975 *It*, *Sp*, *JAB*, *Pol*, *F* 1976 *H*, *It*, *Sp*, *Pol*, *Mor* 1978 *Pol*, *F* 1979 *It*, *Sp*, *W*, *Pol* 1980 *It*, *I*, *Pol*, *F* 1981 *It*, *Sp*, *USS*, *S*, *NZ*, *F* 1982 *F* 1983 *Mor*, *WGe*, *It*, *USS*, *Pol*, *W*, *USS*, *F* 1984 *It*, *S*, *F* 1985 *USS* 1986 *S*, *Tun*, *Pt*, *F* 1988 *It*, *Sp*
Munteanu, T 2004 *CZR* (R)
Musat, D 1974 *Sp*, *Cze*, *EGe*, *Cze* 1975 *It*, *JAB*, *Pol*, *F* 1976 *Mor* 1980 *Mor*
Nache, M 1980 *Mor*
Nagel, M 1958 *EGe* 1960 *Pol*, *EGe*, *Cze*
Nanu, R 1952 *EGe*, *EGe* 1953 *It* 1955 *Cze* (R) 1957 *F*, *Bel*, *F*
Nastase, V 1985 *Tun*, *USS* 1986 *Tun*, *Pt*, *F*, *I*
Neaga, D 1988 *It*, *Sp*, *USS*, *F*, *W* 1989 *It*, *E*, *Sp*, *Z*, *Sa*, *USS*, *S* 1990 *It*, *F*, *H*, *Sp*, *USS* 1991 *It*, *F*, *S*, *F*, *C*, *Fj* 1993 *Tun*, *F*, *Sp*, *I* 1994 *Sp*, *Ger*, *Rus*, *It*, *W*, *It*, *E* 1995 *F*, *S*, *J*, *J* (R), *C* 1996 *Pt*, *F*
Neagu, I 1972 *Mor*, *Cze*
Necula, E 1987 *It*, *F*
Nedelcovici, P 1924 *F*
Nedelcu, C 1964 *Cze*, *EGe*
Nedelcu, M 1993 *Pt*, *Tun*, *F* 1994 *Sp* (R), *It* (R) 1995 *Ar*, *F*, *It*
Nedelcu, V 1996 *Pol* (R) 1997 *F*, *W*, *Ar*, *F* (R) 1998 *H*, *Pol*, *Ukr*, *Ar* 2000 *H* (R) 2001 *I*, *W*, *E* 2002 *Rus* (R), *Geo* (R)
Negreci, I 1994 *E* 1995 *F*, *J*, *C*, *SA*, *A*, *Ar*, *F* (R), *It*
Nemes, I 1924 *F*, *US* 1927 *Ger*, *Cze*
Nica, G 1964 *Cze*, *EGe*, *WGe* 1966 *It*, *F* 1967 *Pol*, *F* 1969 *Pol*, *WGe*, *Cze*, *F* 1970 *It*, *F* 1971 *It*, *Mor*, *F* 1972 *Mor*, *Cze*, *WGe*, *F* 1973 *Sp*, *Mor*, *Ar*, *Ar*, *WGe*, *F* 1974 *Mor*, *Pol*, *Sp*, *Cze*, *EGe*, *F*, *Cze* 1975 *It*, *Sp*, *JAB*, *Pol*, *F* 1976 *H*, *It*, *Sp*, *USS*, *Bul*, *Pol*, *F*, *Mor* 1977 *Sp*, *It*, *F*, *Pol*, *It*, *F* 1978 *Pol*, *F*
Nichitean, N 1990 *It*, *Sp* (R), *It*, *USS* 1991 *It*, *F*, *F*, *C*, *Fj* 1992 *USS*, *It*, *Ar* 1993 *Pt* (R), *Tun*, *F*, *Sp* 1994 *Sp*, *Ger*, *Rus*, *It*, *W*, *It* 1995 *F*, *S*, *J* (R), *J*, *C* 1997 *F*
Nicola, G 1927 *F*, *Ger*, *Cze*
Nicolae, M 2003 *I* (R), *A*
Nicolau, N 1940 *It*
Nicolescu, M 1969 *Pol* (R), *WGe*, *Cze*, *F* 1971 *It*, *Mor*, *F* 1972 *Mor*, *Cze*, *WGe*, *F* 1973 *Sp*, *Mor*, *Ar*, *Ar*, *WGe*, *F* 1974 *Mor*, *Cze* (R), *EGe*, *F*, *Cze* 1975 *It*, *Sp*, *Pol* (R), *F*
Niculescu, P 1958 *It* 1959 *EGe*, *Cze*
Niculescu, V 1938 *F*, *Ger*

Nistor, F 1986 *Tun*
Nistor, V 1959 *EGe, Pol, EGe*
Oblomenco, M 1967 *It, Pt, WGe, F*
Octavian, C 1976 *USS*
Olarasu, G 2000 *Mor, H* (R)
Olarasu, M 2000 *Mor*
Onutiu, V 1967 *It, Pt, Pol, WGe, F* 1968 *Cze* 1969 *F* 1971 *It, Mor*
Oprea, N 2000 *It* 2001 *Pt, Sp* (R), *H, Rus, Geo, I, W, E*
Opris, F 1986 *F, Tun, Tun, Pt* (R), *F, I* 1987 *F*
Oprisor, G 2004 *W* (R), *J* 2005 *Rus* (R), *Ukr* (R), *US, S* (R), *Pt*
Oroian, T 1988 *F* (R), *W* (R) 1989 *It, E* (R), *Sp, Z, USS* 1990 *Sp, It* 1993 *Pt* (R), *Tun, F* (R), *Sp, I* 1994 *Sp, Ger, Rus, It, W, It, E* 1995 *F, S, J, J, C*
Ortelecan, M 1972 *Mor, Cze, WGe, F* 1974 *Pol* 1976 *It, Sp, USS, Bul, F* 1977 *Sp, It, F, Pol, It, F* 1978 *Cze, Sp* 1979 *F* 1980 *USS*
Palosanu, A 1952 *EGe, EGe* 1955 *Cze* 1957 *F, Cze*
Pana, E 1937 *F* (R), *Ger*
Paraschiv, M 1975 *Sp, JAB, Pol, F* 1976 *H, It, Sp, USS, Bul, F, Mor* 1977 *Sp, It, Pol, F* 1978 *Cze, Sp, Pol, F* 1979 *It, Sp, W* 1980 *It, I, F* 1981 *It, USS, S, NZ, F* 1982 *WGe, It, USS, Z, Z, F* 1983 *Mor, WGe, It, USS, Pol, W, USS* (R), *F* 1984 *It, S, F* 1985 *E, It, Tun, USS, USS, It* 1986 *Pt, S, Tun* (R) 1987 *It, USS, Z, F, S, USS, F*
Parcalabescu, G 1940 *It* 1942 *It* 1949 *Cze* 1951 *EGe* 1952 *EGe, EGe* 1953 *It* 1955 *Cze* 1957 *Cze, Bel, F* 1958 *It* 1959 *EGe, Pol, Cze* 1960 *Pol, EGe, Cze*
Pasache, G 2001 *E* (R)
Pascu, V 1983 *It* (R), *Pol, W, USS, F* 1984 *It* 1985 *USS* 1986 *Pt, S, F, Tun, I* 1987 *F* 1988 *It* (R)
Patrichi, C 1993 *Pt* (R), *Tun*
Paulica, I 2005 *Ukr, S* (R) 2006 *Geo* (R), *Pt, Rus, F* (R)
Pavlovici, A 1972 *Mor* (R), *Cze*
Penciu, A 1955 *Cze* 1957 *F, Cze, Bel, F* 1958 *Sp, WGe, EGe, It* 1959 *EGe, Pol, Cze, EGe* 1960 *F* 1961 *Pol, EGe, Cze, EGe, F* 1962 *Cze, EGe, Pol, It, F* 1963 *Bul, Cze, F* 1964 *WGe, F* 1965 *WGe, F* 1966 *It, F* 1967 *F*
Peter, I 1973 *Sp, Mor*
Petrache, AA 1998 *H* (R), *Pol* (R) 1999 *F, S, A, US, I* 2000 *Mor, H, Pt, Sp, Geo, F* 2001 *W, E* 2002 *Pt, Sp, H, Rus, I, It, Sp, W, S* 2003 *Pt, Sp, Rus, F* (R), *Ar* (R), *Nm* 2004 *It, W, J, CZR*
Petre, C 2001 *E* 2002 *Pt, Sp, H, Rus, Geo, I, It, Sp, S* 2003 *F, W, I, A, Ar, Nm* 2004 *CZR, Pt, Sp, Rus, Geo* (R), *It, W, J* 2005 *Rus, Geo, J, US, S, Pt, C* 2006 *Geo, CZR, Pt, Ukr, Rus, F*
Petrichei, A 2002 *S* 2003 *Sp, Rus* (R), *Geo* (R), *CZR, W* (R), *I* 2004 *Pt* (R), *Sp, Rus, Geo*
Petrisor, P 1985 *It* 1987 *USS* (R)
Peuciulescu 1927 *F*
Picoiu, M 2001 *Pt, H* 2002 *Pt* (R), *Sp, H, Rus, I* (R), *It* (R), *Sp* (R), *W*
Pinghert, C 1996 *Bel* (R)
Pintea, I 1974 *Pol* 1976 *Pol, F, Mor* 1977 *Sp, It, F, Pol, It, F* 1979 *It, Sp, USS, W, Pol, F* 1980 *It, USS*
Piti, D 1987 *USS, F* 1988 *It, Sp, US* 1991 *S*
Pllotschi, A 1985 *It, Tun* 1987 *S*
Plumiee 1927 *Ger*
Podarescu, S 1979 *Pol, F* 1980 *USS* 1982 *WGe, It, USS, F* 1983 *Mor, WGe, USS, F* 1984 *It* (R) 1985 *E, It*
Podea, C 2001 *Geo* (R), *I* (R) 2002 *I* (R), *It* (R), *Sp, W* (R) 2003 *Pt* (R), *Sp, Rus, F* (R), *A* (R)
Polizu, R 1919 *US*
Pop, A 1970 *It* 1971 *It, Mor* 1972 *Mor* (R), *Cze, F* (R) 1973 *WGe, F* 1974 *Mor, Pol, Sp, EGe, F, Cze* 1975 *It, Sp, JAB, Pol, F*
Popa, D 1993 *Tun, F, Sp*
Popa, D 1994 *Ger* (R)
Popa, I 1934 *It* 1936 *F, It, Ger* 1937 *H, F* 1938 *F, Ger* 1939 *It* 1940 *It* 1942 *It*
Popa, M 1962 *EGe*
Popa, N 1952 *EGe* (R)
Popean, A 1999 *S* (R) 2001 *Pt, H*
Popescu, C 1997 *Bel* (R) 2003 *CZR* (R), *F* (R), *W* (R), *I* (R), *A* (R), *Ar* (R), *Nm* (R) 2004 *CZR* (R), *Pt, Sp* (R), *Geo* (R), *J* (R) 2005 *Rus, S, Pt* (R), *C* (R) 2006 *CZR, Ukr* (R), *Rus, F* (R)
Popescu, C 1986 *Tun, Pt, F*
Popescu, I 1958 *EGe*
Popescu, I 2001 *Pt, Sp, H, Rus, Geo*
Popescu-Colibasi, C 1934 *It*
Popisteanu, V 1996 *Pt, F, Pol*
Popovici, F 1973 *Sp, Mor*
Postolache, N 1972 *WGe* (R), *F* 1973 *Sp, Mor, WGe, F* 1974 *Mor, Pol, Sp, EGe* (R), *F, Cze* 1975 *It, Sp, Pol, F* 1976 *H, It*
Preda, C 1961 *Pol, Cze* 1962 *EGe, F* 1963 *Bul, EGe, Cze, F* 1964 *Cze, EGe, WGe, F*
Racean, NF 1988 *USS, USS, F, W* 1989 *It, E, Z, Sa, USS* (R) 1990 *H, Sp, It, USS* 1991 *NZ, F, F, C, Fj* 1992 *Sp, It, USS, F, It, Ar* 1993 *Pt, Tun, F, Sp* 1994 *Ger* (R), *Rus, It, W* 1995 *F, S, J, J, C, SA, A*
Radoi, M 1995 *F* 1996 *Pt, Pol* (R) 1997 *F, W, Bel, Ar, F, It* 1998 *H, Pol, Ukr*
Radoi, P 1980 *Mor*
Radu, T 1991 *NZ*
Raducanu, C 1985 *It* 1987 *It* (R), *USS, Z, F, S* 1989 *It* (R), *E* (R), *Sp, Z* (R)
Radulescu, A 1980 *USS, Pol* (R) 1981 *It, Sp, USS, S, F* 1982 *WGe, It, USS, Z* (R), *Z* (R) 1983 *Pol, W, USS, F* 1984 *It, S, F, Sp* 1985 *E, USS* 1988 *It, Sp, US, USS, USS, F, W* 1989 *It, E, Sa, USS* 1990 *It, F, H, Sp* (R), *It* (R), *USS*
Radulescu, T 1958 *Sp, WGe* 1959 *EGe, Pol, Cze, EGe* 1963 *Bul, EGe, Cze* 1964 *F* 1965 *WGe, F* 1966 *Cze*
Rascanu, D 1972 *WGe, F*
Rascanu, G 1966 *It, F* 1967 *It, Pt, Pol, WGe, F* 1968 *Cze, Cze, F* 1969 *Pol, WGe, Cze, F* 1970 *It, F* 1971 *It, Mor, F* 1972 *Mor, Cze, WGe, F* 1974 *Sp*
Ratiu, C 2003 *CZR* (R) 2005 *J, US, S, Pt, C* (R), *I* (R) 2006 *Pt* (R), *Ukr, Rus, F*
Ratiu, I 1992 *It* (R)
Rentea, S 2000 *Mor*
Roman, I 1976 *Bul* (R)
Rosu, C 1993 *I*
Rotaru, I 1995 *J, C, Ar, It* (R) 1996 *Pt, F* (R), *Pol* 1997 *W, Bel, Ar, F*
Rotaru, L 1999 *F* (R), *A, I* (R)
Rusu, M 1959 *EGe* 1960 *F* 1961 *Pol, Cze* 1962 *Cze, EGe, Pol, It, F* 1963 *Bul, EGe, Cze, F* 1964 *WGe, F* 1965 *WGe, F* 1966 *Cze, It, F* 1967 *It, Pt, Pol*
Rusu, V 1960 *Pol, EGe, Cze* 1961 *EGe, F* 1962 *Cze, EGe, Pol, It, F* 1964 *Cze* (R), *EGe* (R), *WGe* (R), *F* 1965 *WGe* (R) 1966 *It, F* 1967 *WGe* 1968 *Cze*
Sadoveanu, I 1939 *It* 1942 *It*
Salageanu, AA 1995 *Ar* (R), *F, It* 1996 *Pt, F, Pol* 1997 *W, Bel, F* (R)
Samuil, V 2000 *It* (R) 2001 *Pt, E* 2002 *Pt* (R), *Sp* (R), *Geo*
Sasu, C 1989 *Z* 1991 *It, NZ, F, S, F, C, Fj* 1993 *I*
Sauan, C 1999 *S, A, US, I* 2000 *It* (R) 2002 *Geo, I, It, Sp* 2003 *Pt, Rus, Geo, CZR, F, W, I, A, Ar* (R), *Nm* (R) 2004 *CZR, Pt, Sp, Rus, Geo, It, W, J, CZR* 2005 *Rus, Geo, Ukr* (R), *J, US, S, Pt* 2006 *Rus*
Sava, G 1989 *Z* (R) 1990 *H, USS* 1991 *It, F, S, F*
Sava, I 1959 *EGe, Pol, Cze, EGe* 1960 *F* 1961 *Pol, EGe, Cze, EGe, F* 1962 *Cze, Pol, It, F*
Sava, I 1989 *S* 1990 *Sp, It* 1991 *C* (R) 1992 *Sp*
Scarlat, C 1976 *H, Sp* 1977 *F* 1978 *Cze, Sp* 1979 *It* (R), *Sp, USS, W, Pol, F* 1980 *It, USS* 1982 *USS*
Schmettau, R 1919 *US, F*
Sebe, V 1960 *Pol, EGe, Cze*
Seceleanu, I 1986 *Pt, F, I* 1990 *It* 1992 *It, USS, F, It, Ar* 1993 *Pt, Tun, F, Sp, F*
Septar, E 1996 *Bel, Pol* 1997 *W* 1998 *Pol* (R), *Ukr, I* (R) 1999 *F, S, A, US, I* 2000 *It*
Serban, B 1989 *Sa, USS, S* 1990 *It* 1992 *It, USS*
Serban, C 1964 *Cze, EGe, WGe* 1967 *Pol* (R) 1968 *Cze* (R), *F* 1969 *Pol, WGe, Cze, F* 1970 *It, F* 1971 *It, Mor, F* 1972 *F* 1973 *WGe, F* 1974 *Mor*
Serbu, M 1967 *It*
Sfetescu, E 1924 *F, US* 1927 *Cze*
Sfetescu, E 1934 *It* 1936 *F, Ger* 1937 *It*
Sfetescu, G 1927 *F, Ger*

Sfetescu, M 1924 *F, US* 1927 *Ger, Cze*
Sfetescu, N 1927 *F, Ger, Cze*
Simion, G 1998 *H*
Simion, G 1919 *US*
Simion, I 1976 *H, It, Sp* 1979 *Pol, F* 1980 *F*
Sirbu, L 1996 *Pt* (R) 2000 *Mor, H, Pt, Geo, F* 2001 *H* (R), *Rus* (R), *Geo, I, W, E* 2002 *Pt* (R), *Sp* (R), *H, Rus* (R), *I, It, S* (R) 2003 *Pt, Sp* (R), *CZR, F, W, I, A, Ar, Nm* 2004 *Pt* (R), *Sp, Rus, Geo, It, W, CZR* 2005 *Rus, Geo, Ukr, J, US, S* (R), *Pt, C* 2006 *Geo* (R), *Pt, Ukr, Rus, F*
Slobozeanu, M 1936 *F* 1937 *H, F, Ger* 1938 *F, Ger*
Slusariuc, OS 1993 *Tun* (R) 1995 *J* (R), *J* (R), *C* 1996 *Pt* (R), *F* 1997 *Bel, Ar, F* 1998 *H* (R), *Ar, Geo* (R), *I* (R) 1999 *F* (R), *S* (R), *A*
Soare, S 2001 *I* (R), *W* (R) 2002 *Geo*
Soare, S 1924 *F, US*
Socaciu, M 2000 *It* (R) 2001 *I, W, E* 2002 *It* (R), *W* (R), *S* (R) 2003 *Pt, Sp, Rus, Geo* (R), *CZR* (R), *F, W, I, A* (R), *Nm* 2004 *CZR, Pt* (R), *Sp, Rus, Geo, It, W, J, CZR* 2005 *Rus, Geo, Ukr, J, US, Pt, C* (R), *I* (R) 2006 *CZR*
Socol, S 2001 *Sp, H, Rus, Geo* 2002 *Pt, It* (R), *Sp* (R), *W* 2003 *Sp, Rus, Geo, F, W, I, A, Ar, Nm* 2004 *CZR, Pt, Sp, Rus, Geo* 2005 *Rus, Geo, Ukr, C, I* 2006 *Geo, CZR, Pt, Ukr, Rus, F*
Soculescu, N 1949 *Cze* 1951 *EGe* 1952 *EGe, EGe* 1953 *It* 1955 *Cze*
Soculescu, N 1927 *Ger*
Soculescu, V 1927 *Cze*
Solomie, GL 1992 *Sp, F, It, Ar* 1993 *Pt, Tun, F, Sp, F, I* 1994 *Sp, Ger, W, It, E* 1995 *F, S, J, J, C, SA, A, Ar, F, It* 1996 *Pt, F, Pol* 1997 *F, W, Bel, Ar, F, It* 1998 *H, Pol, Ukr, Ar, Geo, I* 1999 *S* (R), *A, US, I* 2000 *Sp, F, It* 2001 *Sp, H, Rus*
Stan, C 1990 *H* (R), *USS* 1991 *It* (R), *F* (R), *S, F, C, Fj* 1992 *Sp, It, It* (R), *Ar* (R) 1996 *Pt* (R), *Bel, F* (R), *Pol* 1997 *F* (R), *W* (R), *Bel* 1998 *Ar, Geo* 1999 *F, S, A, US, I*
Stanca, A 1996 *Pt, Pol*
Stanca, R 1997 *F* (R) 2003 *Sp* (R), *Rus* (R)
Stanciu, A 1958 *EGe, It*
Stanciu, G 1958 *EGe, It* (R)
Stanescu, C 1957 *Bel* 1958 *WGe* 1959 *EGe* 1960 *F* 1961 *Pol, EGe, Cze* 1962 *Cze, It, F* 1963 *Bul, EGe, Cze, F* 1964 *WGe, F* 1966 *Cze, It*
Stefan, C 1951 *EGe* 1952 *EGe*
Stoian, E 1927 *Cze*
Stoica, E 1973 *Ar, Ar* 1974 *Cze* 1975 *Sp* (R), *Pol, F* 1976 *Sp, USS, Bul, F, Mor* 1977 *Sp, It, F, Pol, It, F* 1978 *Cze, Sp, Pol, F* 1979 *It, Sp, USS, W, Pol, F* 1980 *It, USS, I, Pol, F* 1981 *It, Sp, USS, S, NZ, F* 1982 *WGe, It, USS, Z, Z, F*
Stoica, G 1963 *Bul, Cze* (R) 1964 *WGe* 1966 *It, F* 1967 *Pt, F* 1968 *Cze, Cze, F* 1969 *Pol*
Stroe, I 1986 *Pt*
Suciu, E 1976 *Bul* (R), *Pol* 1977 *It* (R), *F, It* 1979 *USS, Pol, F* 1981 *Sp*
Suciu, M 1968 *F* 1969 *Pol, WGe, Cze* 1970 *It, F* 1971 *It, Mor, F* 1972 *Mor, F*
Sugar, O 1983 *It* 1989 *Z* (R), *Sa, USS, S* 1991 *NZ, F*
Suiogan, K 1996 *Bel*
Talaba, D 1996 *Bel* 1997 *F* (R), *It*
Tanase, C 1938 *F, Ger* 1939 *It* 1940 *It*
Tanasescu, A 1919 *F* 1924 *F, US*
Tanoviceanu, N 1937 *It, H, F* 1939 *It*
Tarabega, I 1934 *It* 1936 *It*
Tata, V 1971 *F* 1973 *Ar* (R), *Ar*
Tatu, C 2005 *J*
Tatu, F 2003 *Ar* (R) 2004 *CZR, Pt, Sp* (R), *Geo, It, W* 2005 *Ukr*
Tatucu, I 1973 *Sp, Mor* 1974 *Cze, F*
Teleasa, D 1971 *It* 1973 *Sp, Ar* (R), *Ar* (R)
Tenescu, D 1951 *EGe*
Teodeorescu, I 2001 *I, W, E* 2002 *Pt, Sp, S* 2003 *Pt* (R), *Sp, Rus, W* (R), *I* (R), *A* (R), *Ar, Nm* 2004 *CZR, Pt, Sp, Rus, Geo* (R), *W, J, CZR* 2005 *Rus, Geo, Ukr, J, US, S, Pt, C, I* 2006 *Geo, CZR, Pt, Ukr, F*
Teodor, M 2003 *CZR* (R)
Teodorescu, I 1958 *Sp, WGe, EGe, It* 1960 *Pol, EGe, Cze* 1963 *Bul, EGe, Cze* 1965 *WGe, F*
Teofilovici, A 1957 *F, Cze, Bel, F* 1958 *Sp, WGe* 1959 *EGe* 1960 *F* 1961 *Pol, EGe, Cze, EGe, F* 1962 *Cze, Pol, It, F* 1963 *Bul, EGe, Cze, F* 1964 *WGe*
Tepurica, O 1985 *USS* (R)
Tibuleac, M 1957 *Bel, F* 1959 *Pol, Cze* 1966 *Cze* 1967 *It, Pt, Pol* (R), *WGe* (R) 1968 *Cze, Cze*
Ticlean, G 1919 *F*
Tigora, M 2004 *CZR* (R)
Tinca, A 1987 *USS, F*
Tincu, VM 2002 *Pt* (R), *Sp, H, Rus, Geo, I, It, Sp, S* 2003 *Pt, Sp, Rus, Geo, F, W* 2004 *Sp* 2005 *Geo, Ukr, C, I* 2006 *Geo, CZR, F*
Toader, M 1982 *WGe* 1984 *Sp* 1985 *E, It, Tun, USS* 1986 *S, F, Tun, Tun, Pt, F, I* 1987 *It, USS, Z, F, S, USS, F* 1988 *F, W* 1989 *It, E, Sp, Sa, USS, S* 1990 *It, F, It* (R)
Toderasc, P 2000 *It* (R) 2001 *Pt* (R), *Rus* (R), *Geo* (R), *W* (R), *E* (R) 2002 *H* (R), *Rus* (R), *Geo* (R), *I* (R), *It, Sp* (R), *W, S* (R) 2003 *Sp* (R), *Rus, Geo, CZR, F* (R), *W* (R), *I* (R), *A, Ar, Nm* (R) 2004 *CZR, Pt* (R), *Sp* (R), *Geo, It* (R), *J* (R) 2005 *J, US, S, Pt, C, I* 2006 *Geo, Pt, Ukr*
Tofan, IR 1997 *Bel, Ar, F, It* 1998 *H, Ar* 1999 *I* (R) 2000 *Mor* (R), *Sp* (R), *Geo* 2001 *Pt, Sp* (R), *H, Geo* (R), *I, W, E* 2002 *Pt* (R), *Sp, H, Rus, Geo, I, It, Sp, W, S* 2003 *Pt, Sp, Rus, Geo, CZR* (R), *F, W, I, A, Ar, Nm* 2004 *Sp* (R), *Geo* (R), *It, W, J* 2005 *Rus, Geo, Ukr* (R), *I* 2006 *Geo* (R), *CZR* (R), *Pt* (R)
Tofan, S 1985 *USS, It* 1986 *Tun, Pt, F, I* 1987 *It, USS, Z, F, S, USS, F* 1988 *It, Sp, US, USS* 1991 *NZ* (R) 1992 *Ar* 1993 *Pt* 1994 *It* (R), *E*
Tonita, O 2000 *Mor, H, Pt, Sp, F* (R) 2001 *Pt, Sp, H, Rus, Geo, I* 2002 *Sp* (R), *It, Sp, W* 2003 *Rus, Geo, F, W, I, A, Ar, Nm* 2004 *Sp, Rus, Geo, It* 2005 *Rus, Pt, C, I* 2006 *Geo, Pt*
Traian 1942 *It*
Tranca, N 1992 *Sp*
Tudor, B 2003 *CZR, A* (R)
Tudor, F 1924 *F, US*
Tudor, M 1924 *F, US*
Tudori, A 2004 *CZR* 2005 *Rus, J, Pt* (R) 2006 *Geo* (R), *CZR, Ukr*
Tudori, M 2003 *F* (R), *W* (R), *I* (R), *A* (R), *Ar, Nm* (R) 2004 *Sp* (R), *Rus, Geo, W, J* 2005 *Geo, Ukr, US, S* 2006 *Rus, F*
Tudosa, D 1999 *S* (R) 2002 *Geo* (R), *I* (R), *It* (R) 2003 *Pt, W* (R)
Tudose, T 1977 *It* 1978 *Cze, Sp, Pol, F* 1979 *It, Sp, USS* 1980 *USS*
Tufa, V 1985 *USS* 1986 *Pt, S* (R) 1990 *It* (R) 1991 *F* (R) 1995 *F* (R), *S, J, J* (R), *A* (R) 1996 *Pt* (R), *F, Pol*
Tunaru, D 1985 *It*
Turlea, V 1974 *Sp* (R) 1975 *JAB, Pol, F* 1977 *Pol*
Turut, C 1937 *H* 1938 *F*
Tutuianu, I 1960 *Pol, EGe* 1963 *Bul* (R), *EGe* (R), *Cze* 1964 *Cze, EGe, WGe* (R) 1965 *WGe, F* 1966 *Cze, It, F* 1967 *Pt, Pol, WGe, F* 1968 *Cze, Cze, F* 1969 *Pol, WGe, Cze, F* 1970 *It, F* 1971 *F*
Tutunea, G 1992 *Sp* (R)
Ungur, M 1996 *Bel*
Ungureanu, V 1979 *It*
Urdea, V 1979 *F* (R)
Ursache, V 2004 *It* (R), *W* (R), *J* (R), *CZR* 2005 *S, C* (R) 2006 *Geo* (R), *Ukr, Rus, F* (R)
Valeriu, E 1949 *Cze* (R) 1952 *EGe* (R)
Vardala, M 1924 *F, US*
Varga, G 1976 *It, USS, Bul, Pol, F, Mor* 1977 *Sp, It, F, Pol* 1978 *Sp*
Varta, N 1958 *EGe*
Varzaru, G 1980 *Mor, I, Pol, F* 1981 *It, Sp, USS, F* (R) 1983 *Mor, WGe, It, USS, F* 1984 *S, F* 1985 *Tun, USS* 1986 *F* 1988 *It, Sp, US, USS, USS*
Vasluianu, V 1989 *Z*
Vasluianu, Z 1989 *Sp, Sa*
Vaudele, N 1927 *F, Ger*
Veluda, P 1967 *It, Pt, Pol, WGe, F* 1968 *Cze, Cze*
Veluda, R 1949 *Cze* 1952 *EGe* 1967 *Pol* (R)
Veres, N 1986 *Tun, Pt* 1987 *F, USS, F* 1988 *It, Sp, USS*
Vidrascu, M 1919 *US, F*
Vidrascu, P 1919 *US* 1924 *F, US* 1927 *Cze*
Vioreanu, M 1994 *E* 1998 *H, Pol, Ukr, Ar, Geo, I* 1999 *F, S,*

A, *US*, *I* 2000 *Mor*, *Pt*, *Sp*, *Geo*, *F* 2001 *Geo* (R) 2002 *Rus*, *Geo*, *I*, *It*, *Sp* 2003 *Sp*, *Rus*, *F* (R), *I* (R), *A* (R), *Ar*, *Nm* (R)
Virgil, I 1927 *Ger*
Visan, A 1949 *Cze*
Vlad, D 2005 *S*, *C* (R), *I* (R)
Vlad, G 1991 *C* (R), *Fj* 1992 *Sp*, *It* (R), *USS*, *F*, *It*, *Ar* 1993 *Pt*, *F*, *I* 1994 *Sp*, *Ger*, *Rus*, *It*, *W*, *It*, *E* 1995 *F*, *C*, *SA*, *A*, *Ar*, *It* 1996 *Pt*, *F* 1997 *W*, *Ar*, *F*, *It* 1998 *Ar* (R)
Vlad, V 1980 *Mor* (R)
Vlaicu, FA 2006 *Ukr* (R), *F*
Vlasceanu, C 2000 *Mor*, *Pt* (R), *Sp* (R), *Geo* (R), *F* (R)
Voicu, B 2004 *CZR*, *Pt*, *Sp*, *Rus*, *It*, *J* 2005 *J*, *Pt* (R)
Voicu, M 1979 *Pol* (R)
Voicu, M 2002 *Pt* (R)
Voicu, V 1951 *EGe* 1952 *EGe* (R), *EGe* 1953 *It* 1955 *Cze*
Voinov, R 1985 *It* 1986 *Pt*, *S*, *F* (R), *Tun*
Volvoreanu, P 1924 *US*
Vraca, G 1919 *US*, *F*
Vusec, M 1959 *EGe*, *Pol*, *Cze*, *EGe* 1960 *F* 1961 *Pol*, *EGe*, *Cze*, *EGe*, *F* 1962 *Cze*, *EGe*, *Pol*, *It*, *F* 1963 *Bul*, *EGe*, *Cze*, *F* 1964 *WGe*, *F* 1965 *WGe*, *F* 1966 *It*, *F* 1967 *It*, *Pt*, *Pol*, *WGe*, *F* 1968 *Cze*, *Cze*, *F* 1969 *Pol*, *WGe*, *F*
Vusec, RL 1998 *Geo*, *I* 1999 *F*, *S*, *A*, *US*, *I* 2000 *Mor*, *H*, *Pt*, *Sp*, *F* 2002 *H*, *Rus* (R), *I* (R)
Wirth, F 1934 *It*
Zafiescu, I 1979 *W*, *Pol*, *F*
Zafiescu, M 1986 *I*
Zafiescu, M 1980 *Mor*
Zamfir, D 1949 *Cze*
Zebega, B 2004 *CZR*, *Pt* (R), *Geo* (R), *It*, *W* 2005 *Rus* (R), *Ukr* (R), *S* (R)
Zlatoianu, D 1958 *Sp*, *WGe*, *EGe*, *It* 1959 *EGe* 1960 *Pol*, *EGe*, *Cze* 1961 *EGe*, *EGe*, *F* 1964 *Cze*, *EGe* 1966 *Cze*

ROMANIAN INTERNATIONAL STATISTICS

MOST POINTS IN A MATCH

BY THE TEAM

Pts.	Opponent	Venue	Year
100	Bulgaria	Burgas	1976
97	Ukraine	Bucharest	2005
92	Portugal	Bucharest	1996
89	Morocco	Bucharest	1976
83	Belgium	Brussels	1996
83	Belgium	Brussels	1997
74	Poland	Bucharest	1998
74	Spain	Bucharest	1978

BY A PLAYER

Pts.	Player	Opponent	Venue	Year
30	Ionut Tofan	Spain	Iasi	2002
27	Virgil Popisteanu	Portugal	Bucharest	1996
27	Petre Mitu	Portugal	Lisbon	2001
25	Ionel Rotaru	Portugal	Bucharest	1996
24	Ion Constantin	Spain	Madrid	1981
23	Serban Guranescu	Belgium	Brussels	1997
22	Gelu Ignat	Netherlands	Treviso	1990
22	Ionut Tofan	Russia	Krasnodar	2002
22	Petre Mitu	Russia	Barlad	2001

MOST CONVERSIONS IN A MATCH

BY THE TEAM

Cons	Opponent	Venue	Year
12	Portugal	Bucharest	1996
11	Ukraine	Bucharest	2005
10	Belgium	Brussels	1997
9	Morocco	Bucharest	1976
9	Italy	Bucharest	1977
9	Belgium	Brussels	1996

BY A PLAYER

Cons	Player	Opponent	Venue	Year
12	Virgil Popisteanu	Portugal	Bucharest	1996
10	Serban Guranescu	Belgium	Brussels	1997
8	Danut Dumbrava	Ukraine	Bucharest	2005
7	Ionut Tofan	Spain	Iasi	2002
7	Gheorghe Nica	Morocco	Bucharest	1976
7	Ion Constantin	Spain	Madrid	1981
7	Stelian Podarescu	West Germany	Bucharest	1982
7	Neculai Nichitean	Germany	Bucharest	1994

MOST TRIES IN A MATCH

BY THE TEAM

Tries	Opponent	Venue	Year
17	Morocco	Bucharest	1976
16	East Germany	Bucharest	1951
15	Ukraine	Bucharest	2005
14	Spain	Bucharest	1978
13	Morocco	Bucharest	1973
13	Portugal	Bucharest	1996
13	Belgium	Brussels	1996

BY A PLAYER

Tries	Player	Opponent	Venue	Year
5	Gheorghe Rascanu	Morocco	Bucharest	1972
5	Cornel Popescu	Portugal	Birlad	1986
5	Ionel Rotaru	Portugal	Bucharest	1996
4	Vasile Brici	Tunisia	Bucharest	1993
4	Petre Motrescu	Spain	Bucharest	1978
4	Alexandru Marin	Spain	Bucharest	1978
4	Petre Motrescu	Italy	Bucharest	1977
4	Ion Sava	Czechoslovakia	Prague	1961
4	Gheorghe Solomie	Belgium	Brussels	1997
4	Virgil Ioan	Czechoslovakia	Bratislava	1927
4	Lucian Colceriu	Poland	Bucharest	1998
4	Dumitru Ghiuzelea	East Germany	Bucharest	1951
4	Dumitru Ghiuzelea	East Germany	Berlin	1952

MOST PENALTIES IN A MATCH

BY THE TEAM

Pens	Opponent	Venue	Year
6	Italy	Bucharest	1994
6	Portugal	Lisbon	2001
5	Russia	Krasnodar	2002
5	France	Bucharest	1991
5	Japan	Tokyo	1995
5	Georgia	Iasi	2004
5	England	London	1985
5	Scotland	Bucharest	1986

BY A PLAYER

Pens	Player	Opponents	Venue	Year
6	Neculai Nichitean	Italy	Bucharest	1994
6	Petre Mitu	Portugal	Lisbon	2001
5	Ionut Tofan	Russia	Krasnodar	2002
5	Neculai Nichitean	France	Bucharest	1991
5	Neculai Nichitean	Japan	Tokyo	1995
5	Dumitru Alexandru	England	London	1985
5	Gelu Ignat	Scotland	Bucharest	1986

MOST DROP GOALS IN A MATCH

BY THE TEAM

Pens	Opponent	Venue	Year
4	West Germany	Bucharest	1967
3	West Germany	Hanover	1965
3	Poland	Nowy Dwor	1976
3	Spain	Padova	1990

BY A PLAYER

Drops	Player	Opponents	Venue	Year
3	Valeriu Irimescu	West Germany	Bucharest	1967
3	Dumitru Alexandru	Poland	Nowy Dwor	1976
2	Alexandru Penciu	West Germany	Hanover	1965
2	Gelu Ignat	Italy	Milan	1988
2	Neculai Nichitean	Italy	Bucharest	1991
2	Neculai Nichitean	Spain	Padova	1990
2	Neculai Nichitean	Japan	Tokyo	1995
2	Ionut Tofan	Georgia	Tbilisi	2002

MOST CAPPED PLAYERS

Caps	Player
77	Adrian Lungu
70	Florica Morariu
69	Gheorghe Dumitru
68	Constantin Dinu
66	Romeo Gontineac
63	Mircea Paraschiv
58	Gabriel Brezoianu
58	Gheorghe Leonte

LEADING TRY SCORERS

Tries	Player
33	Petre Motrescu
26	Florica Morariu
26	Gabriel Brezoianu
22	Mihai Vusec
16	Gheorghe Nica
16	Gheorghe Solomie
16	Alexandru Penciu
15	Gheorghe Rascanu
15	Romeo Gontineac

LEADING CONVERSIONS SCORERS

Cons	Player
49	Petre Mitu
48	Ionut Tofan
34	Ion Constantin
33	Danut Dumbrava
27	Mihai Bucos
27	Neculai Nichitean
25	Alexandru Penciu
24	Gelu Ignat

LEADING PENALTY SCORERS

Pens	Player
54	Neculai Nichitean
46	Ionut Tofan
46	Petre Mitu
39	Gelu Ignat
37	Dumitru Alexandru
31	Ion Constantin
27	Danut Dumbrava
21	Mihai Bucos

LEADING DROP GOAL SCORERS

Drops	Player
13	Dumitru Alexandru
10	Neculai Nichitean
10	Valeriu Irimescu
7	Gelu Ignat
6	Alexandru Penciu
5	Gheorghe Dragomirescu-Rahtopol
5	Raducu Durbac

LEADING POINT SCORERS

Points	Player
306	Ionut Tofan
296	Petre Mitu
246	Neculai Nichitean
228	Dumitru Alexandru
222	Ion Constantin
194	Gelu Ignat
161	Alexandru Penciu

SAMOA

SAMOA'S TEST RECORD

OPPONENTS	DATE	VENUE	RESULT
Japan	17 June	H	**Won** 53–9
Fiji	24 June	A	**Lost** 20–23
Tonga	1 July	H	**Won** 36–0

WAYS TO SURPRISE

By Jeremy Duxbury

The ultimate loose forward in his playing days, Michael Jones now seems to be maturing nicely as a rugby coach and taking Manu Samoa steadily upward and onward. But lumped once more in a pool with England and South Africa at the Rugby World Cup 2007, the Iceman will need to summon all his strength and rugby acumen to achieve Samoa's ambitious short-term goals.

It is hard not to sympathise with this set of proud warriors. In the 2003 Rugby World Cup qualifiers, Samoa had a better head-to-head record than Fiji but the Fijians finished top virtue of a better points differential against Tonga. That meant Semo Sititi's men had to face the

Jon Buckle/Getty Images

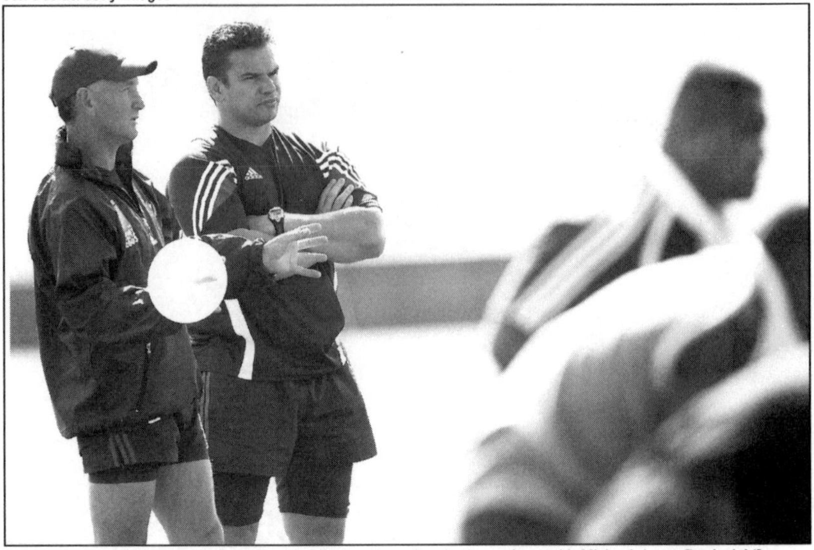

Samoa are lucky to have one of the most inspirational coaches in the rugby world, Michael Jones [back right].

Poms and the Boks on consecutive weekends in Australia whilst Fiji landed in the softest group with Scotland there for the taking.

Four years on, and Samoa finish above Fiji on points difference in the RWC 2007 qualifiers only to be given the same stone-faced opponents in pool play as the Fijians eye up their chances with an indifferent Wales side in Pool B.

If there's any lesson to be learnt from this little exercise, it may be that the World Cup pools ought to be drawn after all the teams have qualified rather than halfway through the qualifying rounds.

As for Jones, he now relishes the coaching challenges ahead after a difficult start. Taking over the reins from John Boe in early 2004, Jones suffered the ignominy of going through his first Test season without his team scoring a try. The Manu had done so superbly well six months earlier at the World Cup with that stupendous game against eventual champions England; and then 'Bang! Start again.'

Since that awkward opening period when Samoa beat Tonga by virtue of eight Roger Warren penalty goals before losing heavily to Scotland and Fiji, Jones has formed a solid unit that has achieved some impressive results.

They piled up a 36–10 victory against Fiji in July 2005, the biggest win over their island neighbours in 80 years of Test rugby. Samoa then threatened to upset Scotland's party at Murrayfield before falling 18–11,

Jon/Buckle/Getty Images

Could Samoa's Brian Lima become the first man to play in five Rugby World Cups?

and then they defeated Argentina 28–12 in Buenos Aires, albeit against a second-string Pumas side.

In 2006, Jones again found the measure of his Pacific rivals, outscoring Japan eight tries to nil in racking up a half century of points, then Tonga five tries to nil in a convincing 36–0 victory to grab second place in the inaugural IRB Pacific 5 Nations.

Joining the omnipresent skipper Sititi is the 'Chiropractor' Brian Lima, who looks set to become the first player to feature in five Rugby World Cups.

Lima is part of a powerful backline that includes the Tuilagi brothers of Leicester, Tanner Vili and Wellington's Lome Fa'atau, as well as new recruits Seilala Mapusua and Waikato's Loki Crichton, who has finally been released to play for his country.

This set of players oozes experience, yet there are also some exciting prospects among the younger ranks. Just 19, Timoteo Iosua has already made his mark. Two years ago at the FORU U18s tournament in Suva, he scored all 16 points in Samoa's 20–16 loss to Fiji, in doing so scoring points through all four methods.

In June this year, Iosua finished as top try-scorer on the IRB World 7s with a tally of 40, well ahead of other prolific players like William Ryder and Dave Strettle.

The Leififi College student is proof that Samoa's development programme is working well. A whole group of reps have emerged from the Samoa A team of 2005, including prop Donald Kerslake, lock Simaika Mika, and backs Notise Tauafao, Anitele'a Tuilagi, Douglas Sanft, Lolo Lui and David Lemi.

The Samoa U19s, having won Division B in 2005, finished 10th this year in Division A after narrow losses to Ireland (15–16) and Argentina (8–10).

Providing another level for aspiring youngsters has been the IRB's Pacific Rugby Cup, won by Savai'i Samoa 10–5 over the Fiji Warriors in a pulsating final in Apia.

The Samoans had warmed up for the competition with their own National Provincial Championship, which comprises of 16 teams in two divisions. Apia won this year's NPC and all the players in the Pacific Rugby Cup were selected from the NPC.

In the PRC final, Savai'i came back from 5–3 down at half-time in slippery conditions at the Marist Grounds in Apia. The Savai'i defence was made to work overtime to keep the Warriors at bay in the last 10 minutes. Giant No.8 Egelani Fale was a revelation for the Samoans, showing great power. Five minutes before the break, the Warriors breathed some life into their game as the forwards worked the ball downfield, before flanker Kini Salabogi jinked through to dot down in the corner. The Warriors began the second half well, but an early turnover enabled Savai'i to scramble the ball downfield and from the ensuing play centre Henry Bryce scored. Rambo Tavana converted and finished as the tournament's top scorer with 60 points. Legendary Samoan figure Peter Fatialofa coached the other Samoan team, Upolu Gold who finished fourth. A number of Samoa reps also graduated to the Pacific 5 Nations such as flanker Ulia Ulia and hooker Muliufi Salanoa.

Former Auckland team-mate Michael Jones subsequently guided Samoa to the runners-up spot in the Pacific 5 Nations behind a star-studded Junior All Blacks.

With IRB funding for Samoa's High Performance Unit amounting to £1.5million over three years, Samoa should now be able to cement their reputation as one of the toughest underdogs in World Cup history.

In recent tournaments, only a smattering of Test players have come from Samoa's domestic scene. That ratio should now even out each year as potential stars like Timoteo Iosua, David Lemi and Anitele'a Tuilagi come forward and excel.

SAMOA INTERNATIONAL STATISTICS

(TO 30TH SEPTEMBER 2006)

COMPILED BY GEOFF MILLER

MATCH RECORDS

MOST CONSECUTIVE TEST WINS

8	1990	SK,Tg 1,J,Tg 2,Fj	1991	Tg,Fj,W

MOST CONSECUTIVE TESTS WITHOUT DEFEAT

Matches	Wins	Draws	Periods
8	8	0	1990 to 1991

MOST POINTS IN A MATCH

BY THE TEAM

Pts.	Opponent	Venue	Year
74	South Korea	Tokyo	1990
68	Japan	Apia	2000
62	Tonga	Apia	1997
60	Uruguay	Perth	2003
55	West Germany	Bonn	1989
53	Japan	New Plymouth	2006
50	Tonga	Apia	2005
47	Japan	Tokyo	2001
46	Georgia	Perth	2005
43	Japan	Apia	1999
43	Italy	Apia	2000

BY A PLAYER

Pts.	Player	Opponent	Venue	Year
24	R Warren	Tonga	Apia	2004
23	A Aiolupo	South Korea	Tokyo	1990
23	S Leaega	Japan	Apia	1999
23	T Samania	Italy	Apia	2000
22	D J Kellett	Tonga	Moamoa	1994
21	M Vaea	Fiji	Apia	1991
21	E Va'a	Georgia	Perth	2003
21	R Warren	Fiji	Apia	2005
20	E Seveali'i	Japan	Apia	2000

MOST TRIES IN A MATCH

BY THE TEAM

Tries	Opponent	Venue	Year
13	South Korea	Tokyo	1990
10	West Germany	Bonn	1989
10	Tonga	Apia	1997
10	Japan	Apia	2000
10	Uruguay	Perth	2003
8	Tonga	Apia	1991
8	Japan	New Plymouth	2006
7	Japan	Tokyo	2001
7	Canada	Apia	2000

BY A PLAYER

Tries	Player	Opponent	Venue	Year
4	T Fa'amasino	Tonga	Apia	1991
4	E Seveali'i	Japan	Apia	2000
4	AI Tuilagi	Tonga	Apia	2005
3	T Fa'amasino	South Korea	Tokyo	1990
3	B P Lima	Fiji	Apia	1991
3	A So'oalo	Tonga	Apia	1997
3	D Feaunati	Namibia	Windhoek	2003

MOST CONVERSIONS IN A MATCH

BY THE TEAM

Cons	Opponent	Venue	Year
8	South Korea	Tokyo	1990
6	West Germany	Bonn	1989
6	Tonga	Apia	1997
6	Japan	Apia	2000
6	Japan	Tokyo	2001
5	Belgium	Brussels	1989
5	Japan	Apia	1990
5	Wales	Cardiff	1999
5	Uruguay	Perth	2003
5	Georgia	Perth	2003

BY A PLAYER

Cons	Player	Opponent	Venue	Year
8	A Aiolupo	South Korea	Tokyo	1990
6	T Vili	Japan	Apia	2000
6	E Va'a	Japan	Tokyo	2001
5	A Aiolupo	Belgium	Brussels	1989
5	A Aiolupo	Japan	Apia	1990
5	S Leaega	Tonga	Apia	1997
5	S Leaega	Wales	Cardiff	1999
5	E Va'a	Georgia	Perth	2003

MOST DROP GOALS IN A MATCH

BY THE TEAM

Drops	Opponent	Venue	Year
1	Fiji	Nadi	1981
1	South Korea	Tokyo	1990
1	Fiji	Apia	1991
1	Scotland	Murrayfield	1991
1	Tonga	Moamoa	1994
1	Fiji	Apia	2005
1	Argentina	Buenos Aires	2005

BY A PLAYER

Drops	Player	Opponent	Venue	Year
1	A Palamo	Fiji	Nadi	1981
1	J Ah Kuoi	South Korea	Tokyo	1990
1	S J Bachop	Fiji	Apia	1991
1	S J Bachop	Scotland	Murrayfield	1991
1	D J Kellett	Tonga	Moamoa	1994
1	R Warren	Fiji	Apia	2005
1	R Warren	Argentina	Buenos Aires	2005

MOST PENALTIES IN A MATCH

BY THE TEAM

Pens	Opponent	Venue	Year
8	Tonga	Apia	2004
5	Tonga	Moamoa	1994
5	Wales	Moamoa	1994
5	Argentina	East London	1995
5	Japan	Osaka	1999
5	England	Melbourne	2003
5	Fiji	Suva	2005
4	Tonga	Suva	1988
4	Fiji	Apia	1997
4	Japan	Apia	1999
4	Italy	Apia	2000
4	Tonga	Nuku'alofa	2002

BY A PLAYER

Pens	Player	Opponent	Venue	Year
8	R Warren	Tonga	Apia	2004
5	D J Kellett	Tonga	Moamoa	1994
5	D J Kellett	Wales	Moamoa	1994
5	D J Kellett	Argentina	East London	1995
5	S Leaega	Japan	Osaka	1999
5	E Va'a	England	Melbourne	2004
5	R Warren	Fiji	Suva	2005
4	A Aiolupo	Tonga	Suva	1988
4	E Va'a	Fiji	Apia	1997
4	S Leaega	Japan	Apia	1999
4	S Leaega	Italy	Apia	2000
4	E Va'a	Tonga	Nuku'alofa	2002

MOST CAPPED PLAYERS

Caps	Player	Career
61	B P Lima	1991 to 2006
60	T Vaega	1986 to 2001
42	O Palepoi	1998 to 2005
42	S Sititi	1999 to 2006
37	A Aiolupo	1983 to 1994
35	P R Lam	1991 to 1999
34	P P Fatialofa	1988 to 1996
32	S So'oialo	1998 to 2005
30	T Leota	1997 to 2004
29	S To'omalatai	1985 to 1995
29	T Vili	1999 to 2006
28	S Vaifale	1989 to 1997
28	E Va'a	1996 to 2003
27	T Salesa	1979 to 1989

MOST POINTS IN TESTS

Pts	Player	Tests	Career
184	E Va'a	28	1996 to 2003
180	A Aiolupo	37	1983 to 1994
160	S Leaega	17	1997 to 2002
157	D J Kellett	13	1993 to 1995
149	B P Lima	61	1991 to 2006
117	R Warren	8	2004 to 2005
114	T Salesa	27	1979 to 1989
91	T Vili	29	1999 to 2006
75	A So'oalo	19	1996 to 2001
66	T Vaega	60	1986 to 2001
64	S J Bachop	18	1991 to 1999

MOST TRIES IN TESTS

Pts	Player	Tests	Career
31	B P Lima	61	1991 to 2006
15	T Vaega	60	1986 to 2001
15	A So'oalo	19	1996 to 2001
13	R Koko	22	1983 to 1994
11	T Fa'amasino	20	1988 to 1996
11	S Sititi	42	1999 to 2006
10	G E Leaupepe	26	1995 to 2005

MOST CONVERSIONS IN TESTS

Cons	Player	Tests	Career
35	A Aiolupo	37	1983 to 1994
33	E Va'a	28	1996 to 2003
26	S Leaega	17	1997 to 2002
19	T Vili	29	1999 to 2006
18	D J Kellett	13	1993 to 1995
14	T Salesa	27	1979 to 1989

MOST PENALTY GOALS IN TESTS

Pens	Player	Tests	Career
35	D J Kellett	13	1993 to 1995
31	S Leaega	17	1997 to 2002
31	E Va'a	28	1996 to 2003
29	R Warren	8	2004 to 2005
27	A Aiolupo	37	1983 to 1994
22	T Salesa	27	1979 to 1989

MOST DROP GOALS IN TESTS

Drops	Player	Tests	Career
2	S J Bachop	18	1991 to 1999
2	R Warren	8	2004 to 2005

CAREER RECORDS OF SAMOA INTERNATIONAL PLAYERS (UP TO 31ST AUGUST 2006)

PLAYER	DEBUT	CAPS	T	C	P	D	PTS
BACKS							
A Collins	2005 v Sc	2	0	0	0	0	0
G Cowley	2005 v Sc	4	0	0	0	0	0
L Crichton	2006 v Fj	2	0	5	2	0	16
L M Fa'atau	2000 v Fj	26	8	0	0	0	40
D S Feaunati	2003 v Nb	5	5	0	0	0	25
E Fuimaono-Sapolu	2005 v Sc	5	1	0	0	0	5
T Iosua	2006 v J	1	2	0	0	0	10
B P Lima	1991 v Tg	61	31	0	0	0	149
L Lui	2004 v Fj	6	0	0	0	0	0
S Mapusua	2006 v J	3	0	0	0	0	0
K Marriner	2005 v Ar	1	0	0	0	0	0
D Sanft	2006 v J	1	0	1	0	0	2
J Senio	2005 v Tg	6	2	0	0	0	10
E Seveali'i	2000 v Fj	15	9	0	0	0	45
S So'oialo	1998 v Tg	32	4	0	0	0	20
S Tagicakibau	2003 v Nb	11	4	0	0	0	20
N Tauafoa	2005 v Au	6	0	0	0	0	0
Al. Tuilagi	2002 v Fj	8	6	0	0	0	30
An. Tuilagi	2005 v Tg	8	4	0	0	0	20
T Vili	1999 v C	29	4	19	11	0	91
R Warren	2004 v Tg	8	0	12	29	2	117
FORWARDS							
J Fa'amatuainu	2005 v Sc	2	0	0	0	0	0
A Faosiliva	2006 v J	2	0	0	0	0	0
D Farani	2005 v Tg	8	3	0	0	0	15
I Feaunati	1996 v Ir	14	2	0	0	0	10
C Johnson	2005 v Au	8	2	0	0	0	10
D Kerslake	2005 v Fj	3	0	0	0	0	0
S F Lafaiali'i	2001 v Tg	20	0	0	0	0	0
K Lealamanua	2000 v Fj	24	1	0	0	0	5
D Leo	2005 v Au	11	0	0	0	0	0
T Leupolu	2001 v Ir	14	0	0	0	0	0
M Salanoa	2005 v Tg	5	0	0	0	0	0
M M Schwalger	2000 v W	8	1	0	0	0	5
S Sititi	1999 v J	42	11	0	0	0	55
C Slade	2006 v J	3	0	0	0	0	0
P Taele-Pavihi	2005 v E	5	0	0	0	0	0
L Tafunai	2004 v Tg	8	1	0	0	0	5
P Toleafoa	2006 v J	2	0	0	0	0	0
J Tomuli	2001 v Ir	14	0	0	0	0	0
P Tupai	2005 v Au	4	0	0	0	0	0
U Ulia	2005 v Ar	7	0	0	0	0	0
J Va'a	2005 v Au	10	0	0	0	0	0

SCOTLAND

SCOTLAND'S TEST RECORD

OPPONENTS	DATE	VENUE	RESULT
France	5 February	H	**Won** 20–16
Wales	12 February	A	**Lost** 18–28
England	25 February	H	**Won** 18–12
Ireland	11 March	A	**Lost** 9–15
Italy	18 March	A	**Won** 13–10
South Africa	10 June	A	**Lost** 16–36
South Africa	17 June	A	**Lost** 15–29

HAPPY HADDEN'S GREAT START

To suggest beleaguered Scotland fans believed 2006 was going to be their year would probably be an exaggeration. After all, Scotland had mustered a mere four wins from 10 international outings in 2005 and only the most wildly optimistic supporter would have argued the side was now miraculously on the verge of great things.

It was however not all doom and gloom. Frank Hadden had finally been handed a full-time contract as coach and the memories of Matt

Williams' disastrous reign – Scotland won just three times in 17 Tests under the unpopular Australian – were already fading. The sense the side had already hit rock bottom and was finally on the way back up was palpable.

Hadden had replaced Williams after another demoralising Six Nations campaign in which they were only spared the embarrassment of the Wooden Spoon after a scrappy win over Italy.

The new coach then guided his team to much-needed victories over Romania and the Barbarians in the summer and although New Zealand and Argentina both triumphed at Murrayfield in the autumn internationals, Scotland finally looked to be enjoying life again.

The 2006 Six Nations was the next serious test of Hadden's new, more relaxed regime and it began with a performance and result that many Scotland fans must have feared were now beyond their side.

France were the visitors to Murrayfield but any Grand Slam aspirations the Tricolores harboured were quickly extinguished as Scotland exploded into life. Sean Lamont breached the French defence either side of the break and although Julien Bonnaire and Sebastien Bruno both scored in the second-half, Scotland held on 20–16 to give Hadden victory in his first Six Nations match as coach and the Scots first win over the French for seven years.

Dave Rogers/Getty Images

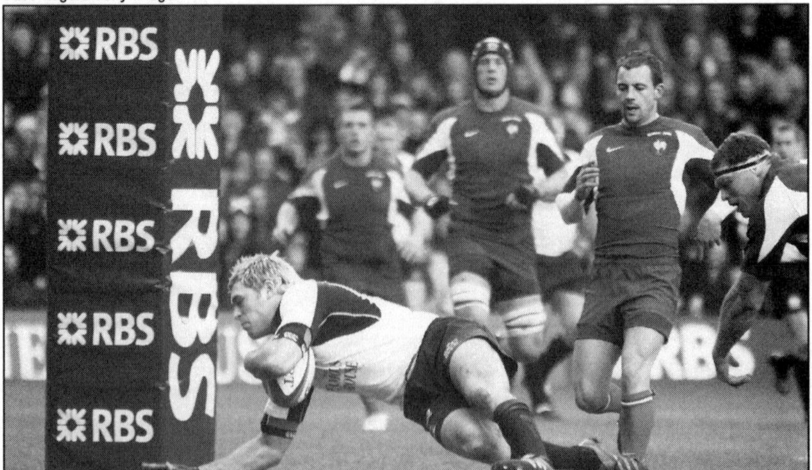

Sean Lamont was the toast of Scotland after two tries against France.

Dave Rogers/Getty Images

It was Chris Paterson's turn to take centre stage when England came calling.

"It was fantastic," Hadden said after the game. "I said we would be proud when we had done something special and I think we've done that today.

"We needed to get a result to confirm that we are on the road to something. We shouldn't forget the quality of the opposition. It was an energy-sapping contest and the guys did a great job."

The euphoria of the French match was short-lived however and a week later they crashed to a 28–18 reverse against Wales in Cardiff. Their cause was not helped by playing an hour of the match with 14 men following Scott Murray's red card for kicking and Scotland had been brought back down to earth with a bump.

A fortnight later unbeaten England came to Murrayfield with high hopes of a Grand Slam. They were sent home with their Championship dreams in tatters.

A wet and windy afternoon in Edinburgh may not have been to the visitors' liking but Scotland adapted the quicker to the conditions and Chris Paterson's five penalties outweighed the four from Charlie Hodgson and Hadden's side were 18–12 winners. Scotland had pulled off their second act of giant killing in the space of three games.

"It was an awesome defensive effort because England are such a hard team to play against," Hadden said. "Make no mistake, England played pretty well. They hold on to the ball for long spells but our defence was magnificent.

"The boys are all fit and as the game went on we gained in momentum, while England began to tire a little. Sometimes you see the bigger, heavier, stronger side wear the other team down but that didn't happen."

"I really am lost for words. It was an absolutely unbelievable effort and it's a reminder that there's more than one way to win a rugby match."

Scotland failed to string together back-to-back wins when they were edged out 15–9 by Ireland and, more specifically Ronan O'Gara's boot at Lansdowne Road but they finished the competition on a fitting high with a 13–10 win over the Italians in Rome courtesy of a late Paterson penalty.

The match in the Stadio Flaminio was far from a classic but the significance of Scotland's first Championship win on the road for four years was not lost on the coach.

"It was great to get the wins over France and England but this was the most important match for us," Hadden said. It shows how much we've come on. "It wasn't pretty at times but I thought we were always in control and deserved the result."

Scotland also deserved their third-place finish but Hadden had little time to rest on his or his side's laurels. A two Test series in South Africa loomed large and a mere four victories in 16 meetings with the Springboks did not exactly bode well. It was obvious Scotland were improving but South Africa, victorious in their previous three home clashes with the Scots, would be only too happy to send Hadden's tourists back home with two defeats and, more worryingly, back to the drawing board.

After a 66–19 warm-up victory over the Barbarians in late May, Hadden named a full-strength side for the first Test in Durban in June but worries that his rejuvenated side would be overrun by the abrasive Springbok pack persisted. By the end of the match those fears had been realised.

The Springboks raced into a 18–6 half-time lead with tries from Schalk Burger and Breyton Paulse and things got even worse in the second-half as Andre Snyman and Percy Montgomery both crossed to put the outcome beyond doubt. Simon Webster scored a consolation try three minutes from time to give the final 36–16 scoreline a degree of respectability but in truth Scotland had been well beaten.

"It was massively physical out there," Chris Paterson said after the bruising encounter. "It was so difficult for us to compete in the first half because we defended for 40 minutes.

"We defended reasonably well, but they just wore us down. Everyone is lying flat out on the dressing-room floor and we need to regroup for next week's game."

Hadden, meanwhile, was determined to focus on the positives and put the result in context. "Let's be clear, South Africa are an outstanding side, but they know they have been in a tough match," he said.

"Anybody, even the All Blacks, find it difficult to win here. It's a very, very hard place to win. They are the second ranked side in the world and we're a young side that's getting better all the time and it's another fantastic learning opportunity for us.

"The physical side of it is a completely different league, there's no question of that. Obviously, when you're more than a stone a man lighter than the opposition, it's a lot easier at home than away from home.

"But, once we came to terms with that, I thought we acquitted ourselves very well. It was another brave defensive effort, but we were just not close enough on the scoreboard. Hopefully, next week we will not be the rabbits in the headlights in the first 20 minutes."

The coach celebrated his 54th birthday in the build-up to the second Test in Port Elizabeth the following weekend but the festivities were distinctly low key as Hadden searched for a way to break down the Springbok defences.

The match itself was far closer than the Durban encounter. Scotland seemed less intimidated and although Montgomery kicked four penalties in the first half, a well-taken try from Webster kept the visitors in range and they went in at the break just 12–5 down. It could have been all-square had Webster not had a second try controversially chalked off for a knock-on but at least Scotland were in contention

Another debatable knock-on call denied Paterson Scotland's second try after the break and to add insult to injury Fourie du Preez crossed seconds after to put the Springboks firmly in the driving seat. Donnie Macfadyen's try cut the South African advantage but Montgomery's boot kept Hadden's side at arm's length and the Springboks held on for a 29–15 win that left the expectant crowd in the Boet Erasmus distinctly unimpressed.

In contrast, Scotland's coach was delighted with his side's much-improved performance even if he wasn't enamoured by the referee's performance.

"I thought we played well enough to win the game," Hadden said. "Who would have thought that the number two side in the world would have needed a couple of dodgy decisions to win?

"They bullied us last weekend so it was all about taking the game to them this time. We may have failed to become the first side to come down here and win but that doesn't take away from a hugely courageous and brave effort.

"But at the end of the day, the Springboks had every bounce of the ball and every debatable decision went against us."

SCOTLAND INTERNATIONAL STATISTICS

MATCH RECORDS UP TO 30TH SEPTEMBER 2006

MOST CONSECUTIVE TEST WINS

6 1925 F,W,I,E, 1926 F,W
6 1989 Fj ,R, 1990 I,F,W,E

MOST CONSECUTIVE TESTS WITHOUT DEFEAT

Matches	Wins	Draws	Periods
9	6*	3	1885 to 1887
6	6	0	1925 to 1926
6	6	0	1989 to 1990
6	4	2	1877 to 1880
6	5	1	1983 to 1984

* includes an abandoned match

MOST POINTS IN A MATCH

BY THE TEAM

Pts.	Opponent	Venue	Year
100	Japan	Perth	2004
89	Ivory Coast	Rustenburg	1995
65	United States	San Francisco	2002
60	Zimbabwe	Wellington	1987
60	Romania	Hampden Park	1999
55	Romania	Dunedin	1987
53	United States	Murrayfield	2000
51	Zimbabwe	Murrayfield	1991
49	Argentina	Murrayfield	1990
49	Romania	Murrayfield	1995

BY A PLAYER

Pts.	Player	Opponent	Venue	Year
44	A G Hastings	Ivory Coast	Rustenburg	1995
40	C D Paterson	Japan	Perth	2004
33	G P J Townsend	United States	Murrayfield	2000
31	A G Hastings	Tonga	Pretoria	1995
27	A G Hastings	Romania	Dunedin	1987
26	K M Logan	Romania	Hampden Park	1999
24	B J Laney	Italy	Rome	2002
23	G Ross	Tonga	Murrayfield	2001
21	A G Hastings	England	Murrayfield	1986
21	A G Hastings	Romania	Bucharest	1986

MOST TRIES IN A MATCH

BY THE TEAM

Tries	Opponent	Venue	Year
15	Japan	Perth	2004
13	Ivory Coast	Rustenburg	1995
12	Wales	Raeburn Place	1887
11	Zimbabwe	Wellington	1987
10	United States	San Francisco	2002
9	Romania	Dunedin	1987
9	Argentina	Murrayfield	1990

BY A PLAYER

Tries	Player	Opponent	Venue	Year
5	G C Lindsay	Wales	Raeburn Place	1887
4	W A Stewart	Ireland	Inverleith	1913
4	I S Smith	France	Inverleith	1925
4	I S Smith	Wales	Swansea	1925
4	A G Hastings	Ivory Coast	Rustenburg	1995

MOST CONVERSIONS IN A MATCH

BY THE TEAM

Cons	Opponent	Venue	Year
11	Japan	Perth	2004
9	Ivory Coast	Rustenburg	1995
8	Zimbabwe	Wellington	1987
8	Romania	Dunedin	1987

BY A PLAYER

Cons	Player	Opponent	Venue	Year
11	C D Paterson	Japan	Perth	2004
9	A G Hastings	Ivory Coast	Rustenburg	1995
8	A G Hastings	Zimbabwe	Wellington	1987
8	A G Hastings	Romania	Dunedin	1987

MOST PENALTIES IN A MATCH

BY THE TEAM

Pens	Opponent	Venue	Year
8	Tonga	Pretoria	1995
6	France	Murrayfield	1986
6	Italy	Murrayfield	2005

BY A PLAYER

Pens	Player	Opponent	Venue	Year
8	A G Hastings	Tonga	Pretoria	1995
6	A G Hastings	France	Murrayfield	1986
6	C D Paterson	Italy	Murrayfield	2005

MOST DROP GOALS IN A MATCH

BY THE TEAM

Drops	Opponent	Venue	Year
3	Ireland	Murrayfield	1973
2	on several	occasions	

BY A PLAYER

Drops	Player	Opponent	Venue	Year
2	R C MacKenzie	Ireland	Belfast	1877
2	N J Finlay	Ireland	Glasgow	1880
2	B M Simmers	Wales	Murrayfield	1965
2	D W Morgan	Ireland	Murrayfield	1973
2	B M Gossman	France	Parc des Princes	1983
2	J Y Rutherford	New Zealand	Murrayfield	1983
2	J Y Rutherford	Wales	Murrayfield	1985
2	J Y Rutherford	Ireland	Murrayfield	1987
2	C M Chalmers	England	Twickenham	1995

CAREER RECORDS

MOST CAPPED PLAYERS

Caps	Player	Career Span
82	G P J Townsend	1993 to 2003
76	S Murray	1997 to 2006
75	G C Bulloch	1997 to 2005
71	S B Grimes	1997 to 2005
70	K M Logan	1992 to 2003
66	C D Paterson	1999 to 2006
65	S Hastings	1986 to 1997
61	A G Hastings	1986 to 1995
61	G W Weir	1990 to 2000
61	T J Smith	1997 to 2005
60	C M Chalmers	1989 to 1999
60	B W Redpath	1993 to 2003
56	J P R White	2000 to 2006
52	J M Renwick	1972 to 1984
52	C T Deans	1978 to 1987
52	A G Stanger	1989 to 1998
52	A P Burnell	1989 to 1999
51	A R Irvine	1972 to 1982
51	G Armstrong	1988 to 1999

MOST TESTS AS CAPTAIN

Tests	Captain	Span
25	D M B Sole	1989 to 1992
21	B W Redpath	1998 to 2003
20	A G Hastings	1993 to 1995
19	J McLauchlan	1973 to 1979
16	R I Wainwright	1995 to 1998
15	M C Morrison	1899 to 1904
15	A R Smith	1957 to 1962
15	A R Irvine	1980 to 1982

MOST CONSECUTIVE TESTS

Tests	Player	Span
49	A B Carmichael	1967 to 1978
40	H F McLeod	1954 to 1962
37	J M Bannerman	1921 to 1929
35	A G Stanger	1989 to 1994

MOST POINTS IN TESTS

Points	Player	Tests	Career
667	A G Hastings	61	1986 to 1995
480	C D Paterson	66	1999 to 2006
273	A R Irvine	51	1972 to 1982
220	K M Logan	70	1992 to 2003
210	P W Dods	23	1983 to 1991
166	C M Chalmers	60	1989 to 1999
164	G P J Townsend	82	1993 to 2003
141	B J Laney	20	2001 to 2004
123	D W Hodge	26	1997 to 2002
106	A G Stanger	52	1989 to 1998

MOST TRIES IN TESTS

Tries	Player	Tests	Career
24	I S Smith	32	1924 to 1933
24	A G Stanger	52	1989 to 1998
20	C D Paterson	66	1999 to 2006
17	A G Hastings	61	1986 to 1995
17	A V Tait	27	1987 to 1999
17	G P J Townsend	82	1993 to 2003
15	I Tukalo	37	1985 to 1992
13	K M Logan	70	1992 to 2003
12	A R Smith	33	1955 to 1962

MOST CONVERSIONS IN TESTS

Cons	Player	Tests	Career
86	A G Hastings	61	1986 to 1995
55	C D Paterson	66	1999 to 2006
34	K M Logan	70	1992 to 2003
26	P W Dods	23	1983 to 1991
25	A R Irvine	51	1972 to 1982
19	D Drysdale	26	1923 to 1929
17	B J Laney	20	2001 to 2004
15	D W Hodge	26	1997 to 2002
14	F H Turner	15	1911 to 1914
14	R J S Shepherd	20	1995 to 1998

MOST PENALTY GOALS IN TESTS

Penalties	Player	Tests	Career
140	A G Hastings	61	1986 to 1995
88	C D Paterson	66	1999 to 2006
61	A R Irvine	51	1972 to 1982
50	P W Dods	23	1983 to 1991
32	C M Chalmers	60	1989 to 1999
29	K M Logan	70	1992 to 2003
29	B J Laney	20	2001 to 2004
21	M Dods	8	1994 to 1996
21	R J S Shepherd	20	1995 to 1998

MOST DROP GOALS IN TESTS

Drops	Player	Tests	Career
12	J Y Rutherford	42	1979 to 1987
9	C M Chalmers	60	1989 to 1999
7	I R McGeechan	32	1972 to 1979
7	G P J Townsend	82	1993 to 2003
6	D W Morgan	21	1973 to 1978
5	H Waddell	15	1924 to 1930

INTERNATIONAL CHAMPIONSHIP RECORDS

RECORD	DETAIL	HOLDER	SET
Most points in season	120	in four matches	1999
Most tries in season	17	in four matches	1925
Highest Score	38	38–10 v Ireland	1997
Biggest win	28	31–3 v France	1912
	28	38–10 v Ireland	1997
Highest score conceded	51	16–51 v France	1998
Biggest defeat	40	3–43 v England	2001
Most appearances	43	G P J Townsend	1993–2003
Most points in matches	288	A G Hastings	1986–1995
Most points in season	60	B J Laney	2002
Most points in match	24	B J Laney	v Italy, 2002
Most tries in matches	24	I S Smith	1924–1933
Most tries in season	8	I S Smith	1925
Most tries in match	5	G C Lindsay	v Wales, 1887
Most cons in matches	20	A G Hastings	1986–1995
Most cons in season	11	K M Logan	1999
Most cons in match	5	F H Turner	v France, 1912
	5	J W Allan	v England, 1931
	5	R J S Shepherd	v Ireland, 1997
Most pens in matches	77	A G Hastings	1986–1995
Most pens in season	15	B J Laney	2002
Most pens in match	6	A G Hastings	v France, 1986
	6	C D Paterson	v Italy, 2005
Most drops in matches	8	J Y Rutherford	1979–1987
	8	C M Chalmers	1989–1998
Most drops in season	3	J Y Rutherford	1987
Most drops in match	2	on several	occasions

MISCELLANEOUS RECORDS

RECORD	HOLDER	DETAIL
Longest Test Career	W C W Murdoch	14 seasons, 1934–35 to 1947–48
Youngest Test Cap	N J Finlay	17 yrs 36 days in 1875*
Oldest Test Cap	J McLauchlan	37 yrs 210 days in 1979

* C Reid, also 17 yrs 36 days on debut in 1881, was a day older than Finlay, having lived through an extra leap-year day.

CAREER RECORDS OF SCOTLAND INTERNATIONAL PLAYERS (PLAYERS CAPPED SINCE THE START OF RWC 2003 UP TO 30 SEPTEMBER 2006)

PLAYER	DEBUT	CAPS	T	C	P	D	PTS
BACKS							
G Beveridge	2000 v NZ	6	0	0	0	0	0
M R L Blair	2002 v C	34	4	0	0	0	20
A Craig	2002 v C	23	8	0	0	0	40
C P Cusiter	2004 v W	24	1	0	0	0	5
S C J Danielli	2003 v It	13	5	0	0	0	25
M P di Rollo	2002 v US	11	1	0	0	0	5
P J Godman	2005 v R	3	0	0	0	0	0
A R Henderson	2001 v I	38	4	0	0	0	20
B G Hinshelwood	2002 v C	19	1	0	0	0	5
R P Lamont	2005 v W	5	1	0	0	0	5
S F Lamont	2004 v Sm	22	5	0	0	0	25
B J Laney	2001 v NZ	20	4	17	29	0	141
D J Lee	1998 v I	12	1	4	7	0	34
K M Logan	1992 v A	70	13	34	29	0	220
B MacDougall	2006 v W	2	0	0	0	0	0
J G McLaren	1999 v Arg	30	6	0	0	0	30
G H Metcalfe	1998 v A	40	4	0	0	0	20
J S D Moffat	2002 v R	4	1	0	0	0	5
G A Morrison	2004 v A	6	1	0	0	0	5
D A Parks	2004 v W	25	3	2	7	3	49
C D Paterson	1999 v Sp	66	20	55	88	2	480
T K Philip	2004 v W	5	0	0	0	0	0
S J Pinder	2006 v SA	2	0	0	0	0	0
B W Redpath	1993 v NZ	60	1	0	0	0	5
G Ross	2001 v Tg	25	2	6	10	1	55
H F G Southwell	2004 v Sm	23	5	0	0	0	25
G P J Townsend	1993 v E	82	17	8	14	7	164
S Webster	2003 v I	17	6	0	0	0	30
FORWARDS							
R S Beattie	2000 v NZ	9	0	0	0	0	0
K D R Brown	2005 v R	5	1	0	0	0	5
G C Bulloch	1997 v SA	75	4	0	0	0	20
B A F Douglas	2002 v R	43	1	0	0	0	5

J P A Dunbar	2005 v F	2	0	0	0	0	0
R W Ford	2004 v A	3	0	0	0	0	0
I A Fullarton	2000 v NZ	8	0	0	0	0	0
S D Gray	2004 v A	1	0	0	0	0	0
S B Grimes	1997 v A	71	5	0	0	0	25
D W H Hall	2003 v W	11	0	0	0	0	0
C P Hamilton	2004 v A	5	0	0	0	0	0
N J Hines	2000 v NZ	36	1	0	0	0	5
A Hogg	2004 v W	28	5	0	0	0	25
A F Jacobsen	2002 v C	13	0	0	0	0	0
A D Kellock	2004 v A	11	0	0	0	0	0
G Kerr	2003 v I	33	1	0	0	0	5
S Lawson	2005 v R	10	1	0	0	0	5
M D Leslie	1998 v SA	37	10	0	0	0	50
D J H Macfadyen	2002 v C	11	2	0	0	0	10
G R McIlwham	1998 v Fj	16	0	0	0	0	0
S J MacLeod	2004 v A	8	0	0	0	0	0
C G Mather	1999 v R	10	2	0	0	0	10
E Murray	2005 v R	1	0	0	0	0	0
S Murray	1997 v A	76	3	0	0	0	15
J M Petrie	2000 v NZ	45	3	0	0	0	15
R R Russell	1999 v R	27	4	0	0	0	20
S Scott	2000 v NZ	11	0	0	0	0	0
C J Smith	2002 v C	17	0	0	0	0	0
T J Smith	1997 v E	61	6	0	0	0	30
S M Taylor	2000 v US	46	5	0	0	0	25
J P R White	2000 v E	56	4	0	0	0	20
A W Wilson	2005 v R	1	0	0	0	0	0

SCOTLAND INTERNATIONAL PLAYERS

UP TO 30TH SEPTEMBER 2006

Note: Years given for International Championship matches are for second half of season; eg 1972 means season 1971–72. Years for all other matches refer to the actual year of the match. Entries in square brackets denote matches played in RWC Finals.

Abercrombie, C H (United Services) 1910 I, E, 1911 F, W, 1913 F, W
Abercrombie, J G (Edinburgh U) 1949 F, W, I, 1950 F, W, I, E
Agnew, W C C (Stewart's Coll FP) 1930 W, I
Ainslie, R (Edinburgh Inst FP) 1879 I, E, 1880 I, E, 1881 E, 1882 I, E
Ainslie, T (Edinburgh Inst FP) 1881 E, 1882 I, E, 1883 W, I, E, 1884 W, I, E, 1885 W, I 1,2
Aitchison, G R (Edinburgh Wands) 1883 I
Aitchison, T G (Gala) 1929 W, I, E
Aitken, A I (Edinburgh Inst FP) 1889 I
Aitken, G G (Oxford U) 1924 W, I, E, 1925 F, W, I, E, 1929 F
Aitken, J (Gala) 1977 E, I, F, 1981 F, W, E, I, NZ 1,2, R, A, 1982 E, I, F, W, 1983 F, W, E, NZ, 1984 W, E, I, F, R
Aitken, R (London Scottish) 1947 W
Allan, B (Glasgow Acads) 1881 I
Allan, J (Edinburgh Acads) 1990 NZ 1, 1991, W, I, R, [J, I, WS, E, NZ]
Allan, J L (Melrose) 1952 F, W, I, 1953 W
Allan, J L F (Cambridge U) 1957 I, E
Allan, J W (Melrose) 1927 F, 1928 I, 1929 F, W, I, E, 1930 F, E, 1931 F, W, I, E, 1932 SA, W, I, 1934 I, E
Allan, R C (Hutchesons' GSFP) 1969 I
Allardice, W D (Aberdeen GSFP) 1947 A, 1948 F, W, I, 1949 F, W, I, E
Allen, H W (Glasgow Acads) 1873 E
Anderson, A H (Glasgow Acads) 1894 I
Anderson, D G (London Scottish) 1889 I, 1890 W, I, E, 1891 W, E, 1892 W, E
Anderson, E (Stewart's Coll FP) 1947 I, E
Anderson, J W (W of Scotland) 1872 E
Anderson, T (Merchiston) 1882 I
Angus, A W (Watsonians) 1909 W, 1910 F, W, E, 1911 W, I, 1912 F, W, I, E, SA, 1913 F, W, 1914 E, 1920 F, W, I, E
Anton, P A (St Andrew's U) 1873 E
Armstrong, G (Jedforest, Newcastle) 1988 A, 1989 W, E, I, F, Fj, R, 1990 I, F, W, E, NZ 1,2, Arg, 1991 F, W, E, I, R, [J, I, WS, E, NZ], 1993 I, F, W, E, 1994 E, I, 1996 NZ, 1,2, A, 1997 W, SA (R), 1998 It, I, F, W, E, SA (R), 1999 W, E, I, F, Arg, R, [SA, U, Sm, NZ]
Arneil, R J (Edinburgh Acads, Leicester and Northampton) 1968 I, E, A, 1969 F, W, I, E, SA, 1970 F, W, I, E, A, 1971 F, W, I, E (2[1C]), 1972 F, W, E, NZ
Arthur, A (Glasgow Acads) 1875 E, 1876 E
Arthur, J W (Glasgow Acads) 1871 E, 1872 E
Asher, A G G (Oxford U) 1882 I, 1884 W, I, E, 1885 W, 1886 I, E
Auld, W (W of Scotland) 1889 W, 1890 W
Auldjo, L J (Abertay) 1878 E

Bain, D McL (Oxford U) 1911 E, 1912 F, W, E, SA, 1913 F, W, I, E, 1914 W, I
Baird, G R T (Kelso) 1981 A, 1982 E, I, F, W, A 1,2, 1983 I, F, W, E, NZ, 1984 W, E, I, F, A, 1985 I, W, E, 1986 F, W, E, I, R, 1987 E, 1988 I
Balfour, A (Watsonians) 1896 W, I, E, 1897 E
Balfour, L M (Edinburgh Acads) 1872 E
Bannerman, E M (Edinburgh Acads) 1872 E, 1873 E
Bannerman, J M (Glasgow HSFP) 1921 F, W, I, E, 1922 F, W, I, E, 1923 F, W, I, E, 1924 F, W, I, E, 1925 F, W, I, E, 1926 F, W, I, E, 1927 F, W, I, E, A, 1928 F, W, I, E, 1929 F, W, I, E
Barnes, I A (Hawick) 1972 W, 1974 F (R), 1975 E (R), NZ, 1977 I, F, W
Barrie, R W (Hawick) 1936 E
Bearne, K R F (Cambridge U, London Scottish) 1960 F, W
Beattie, J A (Hawick) 1929 F, W, 1930 W, 1931 F, W, I, E, 1932 SA, W, I, E, 1933 W, E, I, 1934 I, E, 1935 W, I, E, NZ, 1936 W, I, E
Beattie, J R (Glasgow Acads) 1980 I, F, W, E, 1981 F, W, E, I, 1983 F, W, E, NZ, 1984 E (R), R, A, 1985 I, 1986 F, W, E, I, R, 1987 I, F, W, E
Beattie, R S (Newcastle, Bristol) 2000 NZ 1,2(R), Sm (R), 2003 E(R), It(R), I 2, [J(R), US,Fj]
Bedell-Sivright, D R (Cambridge U, Edinburgh U) 1900 W, 1901 W, I, E, 1902 W, I, E, 1903 W, I, 1904 W, I, E, 1905 NZ, 1906 W, I, E, SA, 1907 W, I, E, 1908 W, I
Bedell-Sivright, J V (Cambridge U) 1902 W
Begbie, T A (Edinburgh Wands) 1881 I, E
Bell, D L (Watsonians) 1975 I, F, W, E
Bell, J A (Clydesdale) 1901 W, I, E, 1902 W, I, E
Bell, L H I (Edinburgh Acads) 1900 E, 1904 W, I
Berkeley, W V (Oxford U) 1926 F, 1929 F, W, I
Berry, C W (Fettesian-Lorettonians) 1884 I, E, 1885 W, I 1, 1887 I, W, E, 1888 W, I
Bertram, D M (Watsonians) 1922 F, W, I, E, 1923 F, W, I, E, 1924 W, I, E
Beveridge, G (Glasgow) 2000 NZ 2(R), US (R), Sm (R), 2002 Fj(R), 2003 W 2, 2005 R(R)
Biggar, A G (London Scottish) 1969 SA, 1970 F, I, E, A, 1971 F, W, I, E (2[1C]), 1972 F, W
Biggar, M A (London Scottish) 1975 I, F, W, E, 1976 W, E, I, 1977 I, F, W, 1978 I, F, W, E, NZ, 1979 W, E, I, F, NZ, 1980 I, F, W, E
Birkett, G A (Harlequins, London Scottish) 1975 NZ
Bishop, J M (Glasgow Acads) 1893 I
Bisset, A A (RIE Coll) 1904 W
Black, A W (Edinburgh U) 1947 F, W, 1948 E, 1950 W, I, E
Black, W P (Glasgow HSFP) 1948 F, W, I, E, 1951 E
Blackadder, W F (W of Scotland) 1938 E
Blaikie, C F (Heriot's FP) 1963 I, E, 1966 E, 1968 A, 1969 F, W, I, E
Blair, M R L (Edinburgh) 2002 C, US, 2003 F(t+R), W 1(R), SA 2(R), It 2, I 2, [US], 2004 W(R),E(R),It(R),F(R),I(R),Sm(R),A1(R), 3(R),J(R),A4(R),SA(R),2005 I(t&R),It(R),W(R),E,R,Arg, Sm(R),NZ(R), 2006 F,W,E,I,It(R),SA 1,2
Blair, P C B (Cambridge U) 1912 SA, 1913 F, W, I, E
Bolton, W H (W of Scotland) 1876 E
Borthwick, J B (Stewart's Coll FP) 1938 W, I
Bos, F H ten (Oxford U, London Scottish) 1959 E, 1960 F, W, SA, 1961 F, SA, W, I, E, 1962 F, W, I, E, 1963 F, W, I, E
Boswell, J D (W of Scotland) 1889 W, I, 1890 W, I, E, 1891 W, I, E, 1892 W, I, E, 1893 I, E, 1894 I, E
Bowie, T C (Watsonians) 1913 I, E, 1914 I, E
Boyd, G M (Glasgow HSFP) 1926 E
Boyd, J L (United Services) 1912 E, SA
Boyle, A C W (London Scottish) 1963 F, W, I
Boyle, A H W (St Thomas's Hospital, London Scottish) 1966 A, 1967 F, NZ, 1968 F, W, I

Brash, J C (Cambridge U) 1961 E
Breakey, R W (Gosforth) 1978 E
Brewis, N T (Edinburgh Inst FP) 1876 E, 1878 E, 1879 I, E, 1880 I, E
Brewster, A K (Stewart's-Melville FP) 1977 E, 1980 I, F, 1986 E, I, R
Brotherstone, S J (Melrose, Brive, Newcastle) 1999 I (R), 2000 F, W, E, US, A, Sm, 2002 C (R)
Brown, A H (Heriot's FP) 1928 E, 1929 F, W
Brown, A R (Gala) 1971 E (2[1C]), 1972 F, W, E
Brown, C H C (Dunfermline) 1929 E
Brown, D I (Cambridge U) 1933 W, E, I
Brown, G L (W of Scotland) 1969 SA, 1970 F, W (R), I, E, A, 1971 F, W, I, E (2[1C]), 1972 F, W, E, NZ, 1973 E (R), P, 1974 W, E, I, F, 1975 I, F, W, E, A, 1976 F, W, E, I
Brown, J A (Glasgow Acads) 1908 W, I
Brown, J B (Glasgow Acads) 1879 I, E, 1880 I, E, 1881 I, E, 1882 I, E, 1883 W, I, E, 1884 W, I, E, 1885 I 1,2, 1886 W, I, E
Brown, K D R (Borders) 2005 R,Sm(R),NZ(R), 2006 SA 1(R),2(R)
Brown, P C (W of Scotland, Gala) 1964 F, NZ, W, I, E, 1965 I, E, SA, 1966 A, 1969 I, E, 1970 W, E, 1971 F, W, I, E (2[1C]), 1972 F, W, E, NZ, 1973 F, W, I, E, P
Brown, T G (Heriot's FP) 1929 W
Brown, W D (Glasgow Acads) 1871 E, 1872 E, 1873 E, 1874 E, 1875 E
Brown, W S (Edinburgh Inst FP) 1880 I, E, 1882 I, E, 1883 W, E
Browning, A (Glasgow HSFP) 1920 I, 1922 F, W, I, 1923 W, I, E
Bruce, C R (Glasgow Acads) 1947 F, W, I, E, 1949 F, W, I, E
Bruce, N S (Blackheath, Army and London Scottish) 1958 F, A, I, E, 1959 F, W, I, E, 1960 F, W, I, E, SA, 1961 F, SA, W, I, E, 1962 F, W, I, E, 1963 F, W, I, E, 1964 F, NZ, W, I, E
Bruce, R M (Gordonians) 1947 A, 1948 F, W, I
Bruce-Lockhart, J H (London Scottish) 1913 W, 1920 E
Bruce-Lockhart, L (London Scottish) 1948 E, 1950 F, W, 1953 I, E
Bruce-Lockhart, R B (Cambridge U and London Scottish) 1937 I, 1939 I, E
Bryce, C C (Glasgow Acads) 1873 E, 1874 E
Bryce, R D H (W of Scotland) 1973 I (R)
Bryce, W E (Selkirk) 1922 W, I, E, 1923 F, W, I, E, 1924 F, W, I, E
Brydon, W R C (Heriot's FP) 1939 W
Buchanan, A (Royal HSFP) 1871 E
Buchanan, F G (Kelvinside Acads and Oxford U) 1910 F, 1911 F, W
Buchanan, J C R (Stewart's Coll FP) 1921 W, I, E, 1922 W, I, E, 1923 F, W, I, E, 1924 F, W, I, E, 1925 F, I
Buchanan-Smith, G A E (London Scottish, Heriot's FP) 1989 Fj (R), 1990 Arg
Bucher, A M (Edinburgh Acads) 1897 E
Budge, G M (Edinburgh Wands) 1950 F, W, I, E
Bullmore, H H (Edinburgh U) 1902 I
Bulloch, A J (Glasgow) 2000 US, A, Sm, 2001 F (t+R), E
Bulloch, G C (West of Scotland, Glasgow) 1997 SA, 1998 It, I, F, W, E, Fj, A 1, SA, 1999 W, E, It, I, F, Arg, [SA, U, Sm, NZ], 2000 It, I, W (R), NZ 1,2, A (R), Sm (R), 2001 F, W, E, It, I, Tg, Arg, NZ, 2002 E, It, I, F, W, C, US, R, SA, Fj, 2003 I 1, F, W 1, E, It 1, SA 1,2, It 2(R), W2, I 2, [US,F,Fj,A], 2004 W,E,It,F,I,Sm,A1,2,3,J,A4,SA, 2005 F,I,It,W,E
Burnell, A P (London Scottish, Montferrand) 1989 E, I, F, Fj, R, 1990 I, F, W, E, Arg, 1991 F, W, E, I, R, [J, Z, I, WS, E, NZ], 1992 E, I, F, W, 1993 I, F, W, E, NZ, 1994 W, E, I, F, Arg 1,2, SA, 1995 [Iv, Tg (R), F (R)], WS, 1998 E, SA, 1999 W, E, It, I, F, Arg, [Sp, Sm (R), NZ]
Burnet, P J (London Scottish and Edinburgh Acads) 1960 SA
Burnet, W (Hawick) 1912 E
Burnet, W A (W of Scotland) 1934 W, 1935 W, I, E, NZ, 1936 W, I, E
Burnett, J N (Heriot's FP) 1980 I, F, W, E
Burns, G G (Watsonians, Edinburgh) 1999 It (R), 2001 Tg (R), NZ (R), 2002 US (R)
Burrell, G (Gala) 1950 F, W, I, 1951 SA
Cairns, A G (Watsonians) 1903 W, I, E, 1904 W, I, E, 1905 W, I, E, 1906 W, I, E
Calder, F (Stewart's-Melville FP) 1986 F, W, E, I, R, 1987 I, F, W, E, [F, Z, R, NZ], 1988 I, F, W, E, 1989 W, E, I, F, R, 1990 I, F, W, E, NZ 1,2, 1991 R, [J, I, WS, E, NZ]
Calder, J H (Stewart's-Melville FP) 1981 F, W, E, I, NZ 1,2, R, A, 1982 E, I, F, W, A 1,2, 1983 I, F, W, E, NZ, 1984 W, E, I, F, A, 1985 I, F, W
Callander, G J (Kelso) 1984 R, 1988 I, F, W, E, A
Cameron, A (Glasgow HSFP) 1948 W, 1950 I, E, 1951 F, W, I, E, SA, 1953 I, E, 1955 F, W, I, E, 1956 F, W, I
Cameron, A D (Hillhead HSFP) 1951 F, 1954 F, W
Cameron, A W (Watsonians) 1887 W, 1893 W, 1894 I
Cameron, D (Glasgow HSFP) 1953 I, E, 1954 F, NZ, I, E
Cameron, N W (Glasgow U) 1952 E, 1953 F, W
Campbell, A J (Hawick) 1984 I, F, R, 1985 I, F, W, E, 1986 F, W, E, I, R, 1988 F, W, A
Campbell, G T (London Scottish) 1892 W, I, E, 1893 I, E, 1894 W, I, E, 1895 W, I, E, 1896 W, I, E, 1897 I, 1899 I, 1900 E
Campbell, H H (Cambridge U, London Scottish) 1947 I, E, 1948 I, E
Campbell, J A (W of Scotland) 1878 E, 1879 I, E, 1881 I, E
Campbell, J A (Cambridge U) 1900 I
Campbell, N M (London Scottish) 1956 F, W
Campbell, S J (Dundee HSFP) 1995 C, I, F, W, E, R, [Iv, NZ (R)], WS (t), 1996 I, F, W, E, 1997 A, SA, 1998 Fj (R), A 2(R)
Campbell-Lamerton, J R E (London Scottish) 1986 F, 1987 [Z, R(R)]
Campbell-Lamerton, M J (Halifax, Army, London Scottish) 1961 F, SA, W, I, 1962 F, W, I, E, 1963 F, W, I, E, 1964 I, E, 1965 F, W, I, E, SA, 1966 F, W, I, E
Carmichael, A B (W of Scotland) 1967 I, NZ, 1968 F, W, I, E, A, 1969 F, W, I, E, SA, 1970 F, W, I, E, A, 1971 F, W, I, E (2[1C]), 1972 F, W, E, NZ, 1973 F, W, I, E, P, 1974 W, E, I, F, 1975 I, F, W, E, NZ, A, 1976 F, W, E, I, 1977 E, I (R), F, W, 1978 I
Carmichael, J H (Watsonians) 1921 F, W, I
Carrick, J S (Glasgow Acads) 1876 E, 1877 E
Cassels, D Y (W of Scotland) 1880 E, 1881 I, 1882 I, E, 1883 W, I, E
Cathcart, C W (Edinburgh U) 1872 E, 1873 E, 1876 E
Cawkwell, G L (Oxford U) 1947 F
Chalmers, C M (Melrose) 1989 W, E, I, F, Fj, 1990 I, F, W, E, NZ 1,2, Arg, 1991 F, W, E, I, R, [J, Z (R), I, WS, E, NZ], 1992 E, I, F, W, A 1,2, 1993 I, F, W, E, NZ, 1994 W, SA, 1995 C, I, F, W, E, R, [Iv, Tg, F, NZ], WS, 1996 A, It, 1997 W, I, F, A (R), SA, 1998 It, I, F, W, E, 1999 Arg (R)
Chalmers, T (Glasgow Acads) 1871 E, 1872 E, 1873 E, 1874 E, 1875 E, 1876 E
Chambers, H F T (Edinburgh U) 1888 W, I, 1889 W, I
Charters, R G (Hawick) 1955 W, I, E
Chisholm, D H (Melrose) 1964 I, E, 1965 E, SA, 1966 F, I, E, A, 1967 F, W, NZ, 1968 F, W, I
Chisholm, R W T (Melrose) 1955 I, E, 1956 F, W, I, E, 1958 F, W, A, I, 1960 SA
Church, W C (Glasgow Acads) 1906 W
Clark, R L (Edinburgh Wands, Royal Navy) 1972 F, W, E, NZ, 1973 F, W, I, E, P
Clauss, P R A (Oxford U) 1891 W, I, E, 1892 W, E, 1895 I
Clay, A T (Edinburgh Acads) 1886 W, I, E, 1887 I, W, E, 1888 W
Clunies-Ross, A (St Andrew's U) 1871 E
Coltman, S (Hawick) 1948 I, 1949 F, W, I, E
Colville, A G (Merchistonians, Blackheath) 1871 E, 1872 E
Connell, G C (Trinity Acads and London Scottish) 1968 E, A, 1969 F, E, 1970 F
Cooper, M McG (Oxford U) 1936 W, I
Corcoran, I (Gala) 1992 A 1(R)
Cordial, I F (Edinburgh Wands) 1952 F, W, I, E
Cotter, J L (Hillhead HSFP) 1934 I, E
Cottington, G S (Kelso) 1934 I, E, 1935 W, I, 1936 E
Coughtrie, S (Edinburgh Acads) 1959 F, W, I, E, 1962 W, I, E, 1963 F, W, I, E
Couper, J H (W of Scotland) 1896 W, I, 1899 I
Coutts, F H (Melrose, Army) 1947 W, I, E
Coutts, I D F (Old Alleynians) 1951 F, 1952 E
Cowan, R C (Selkirk) 1961 F, 1962 F, W, I, E

Cowie, W L K (Edinburgh Wands) 1953 E
Cownie, W B (Watsonians) 1893 W, I, E, 1894 W, I, E, 1895 W, I, E
Crabbie, G E (Edinburgh Acads) 1904 W
Crabbie, J E (Edinburgh Acads, Oxford U) 1900 W, 1902 I, 1903 W, I, 1904 E, 1905 W
Craig, A (Orrell, Glasgow) 2002 C, US, R, SA, Fj, 2003 I 1, F(R), W 1(R), E, It 1, SA 1,2, W 2, I 2, [J,US,F], 2004 A3(R), 2005 F,I,It,W,E
Craig, J B (Heriot's FP) 1939 W
Craig, J M (West of Scotland, Glasgow) 1997 A, 2001 W (R), E (R), It
Cramb, R I (Harlequins) 1987 [R(R)], 1988 I, F, A
Cranston, A G (Hawick) 1976 W, E, I, 1977 E, W, 1978 F (R), W, E, NZ, 1981 NZ 1,2
Crawford, J A (Army, London Scottish) 1934 I
Crawford, W H (United Services, RN) 1938 W, I, E, 1939 W, E
Crichton-Miller, D (Gloucester) 1931 W, I, E
Crole, G B (Oxford U) 1920 F, W, I, E
Cronin, D F (Bath, London Scottish, Bourges, Wasps) 1988 I, F, W, E, A, 1989 W, E, I, F, Fj, R, 1990 I, F, W, E, NZ 1,2, 1991 F, W, E, I, R, [Z], 1992 A 2, 1993 I, F, W, E, NZ, 1995 C, I, F, [Tg, F, NZ], WS, 1996 NZ 1,2, A, It, 1997 F (R), 1998 I, F, W, E
Cross, M (Merchistonians) 1875 E, 1876 E, 1877 I, E, 1878 E, 1879 I, E, 1880 I, E
Cross, W (Merchistonians) 1871 E, 1872 E
Cumming, R S (Aberdeen U) 1921 F, W
Cunningham, G (Oxford U) 1908 W, I, 1909 W, E, 1910 F, I, E, 1911 E
Cunningham, R F (Gala) 1978 NZ, 1979 W, E
Currie, L R (Dunfermline) 1947 A, 1948 F, W, I, 1949 F, W, I, E
Cusiter, C P (Borders) 2004 W,E,It,F,I,Sm,A1,2,3,J,A4,SA,2005 F,I,It,W,Arg(R),Sm,NZ, 2006 F(R),W(R),E(R),I(R),It
Cuthbertson, W (Kilmarnock, Harlequins) 1980 I, 1981 W, E, I, NZ 1,2, R, A, 1982 E, I, F, W, A 1,2, 1983 I, F, W, NZ, 1984 W, E, A

Dalgleish, A (Gala) 1890 W, E, 1891 W, I, 1892 W, 1893 W, 1894 W, I
Dalgleish, K J (Edinburgh Wands, Cambridge U) 1951 I, E, 1953 F, W
Dall, A K (Edinburgh) 2003 W 2(R)
Dallas, J D (Watsonians) 1903 E
Danielli, S C J (Bath, Borders)) 2003 It 2, W 2, [J(R),US,Fj,A], 2004 W, E,It,F,I,2005 F,I
Davidson, J A (London Scottish, Edinburgh Wands) 1959 E, 1960 I, E
Davidson, J N G (Edinburgh U) 1952 F, W, I, E, 1953 F, W, 1954 F
Davidson, J P (RIE Coll) 1873 E, 1874 E
Davidson, R S (Royal HSFP) 1893 E
Davies, D S (Hawick) 1922 F, W, I, E, 1923 F, W, I, E, 1924 F, E, 1925 W, I, E, 1926 F, W, I, E, 1927 F, W, I
Dawson, J C (Glasgow Acads) 1947 A, 1948 F, W, 1949 F, W, I, 1950 F, W, I, E, 1951 F, W, I, E, SA, 1952 F, W, I, E, 1953 E
Deans, C T (Hawick) 1978 F, W, E, NZ, 1979 W, E, I, F, NZ, 1980 I, F, 1981 F, W, E, I, NZ 1,2, R, A, 1982 E, I, F, W, A 1,2, 1983 I, F, W, E, NZ, 1984 W, E, I, F, A, 1985 I, F, W, E, 1986 F, W, E, I, R, 1987 I, F, W, E, [F, Z, R, NZ]
Deans, D T (Hawick) 1968 E
Deas, D W (Heriot's FP) 1947 F, W
Dick, L G (Loughborough Colls, Jordanhill, Swansea) 1972 W (R), E, 1974 W, E, I, F, 1975 I, F, W, E, NZ, A, 1976 F, 1977 E
Dick, R C S (Cambridge U, Guy's Hospital) 1934 W, I, E, 1935 W, I, E, NZ, 1936 W, I, E, 1937 W, 1938 W, I, E
Dickson, G (Gala) 1978 NZ, 1979 W, E, I, F, NZ, 1980 W, 1981 F, 1982 W (R)
Dickson, M R (Edinburgh U) 1905 I
Dickson, W M (Blackheath, Oxford U) 1912 F, W, E, SA, 1913 F, W, I
Di Rollo, M P (Edinburgh) 2002 US (R), 2005 R,Arg,Sm,NZ, 2006 F,E,I,It,SA 1,2
Dobson, J (Glasgow Acads) 1911 E, 1912 F, W, I, E, SA
Dobson, J D (Glasgow Acads) 1910 I
Dobson, W G (Heriot's FP) 1922 W, I, E
Docherty, J T (Glasgow HSFP) 1955 F, W, 1956 E, 1958 F, W, A, I, E
Dods, F P (Edinburgh Acads) 1901 I
Dods, J H (Edinburgh Acads) 1895 W, I, E, 1896 W, I, E, 1897 I, E
Dods, M (Gala, Northampton) 1994 I (t), Arg 1,2, 1995 WS, 1996 I, F, W, E
Dods, P W (Gala) 1983 I, F, W, E, NZ, 1984 W, E, I, F, R, A, 1985 I, F, W, E, 1989 W, E, I, F, 1991 I (R), R, [Z, NZ (R)]
Donald, D G (Oxford U) 1914 W, I
Donald, R L H (Glasgow HSFP) 1921 W, I, E
Donaldson, W P (Oxford U, W of Scotland) 1893 I, 1894 I, 1895 E, 1896 I, E, 1899 I
Don-Wauchope, A R (Fettesian-Lorettonians) 1881 E, 1882 E, 1883 W, 1884 W, I, E, 1885 W, I 1,2, 1886 W, I, E, 1888 I
Don-Wauchope, P H (Fettesian-Lorettonians) 1885 I 1,2, 1886 W, 1887 I, W, E
Dorward, A F (Cambridge U, Gala) 1950 F, 1951 SA, 1952 W, I, E, 1953 F, W, E, 1955 F, 1956 I, E, 1957 F, W, I, E
Dorward, T F (Gala) 1938 W, I, E, 1939 I, E
Douglas, B A F (Borders) 2002 R, SA, Fj, 2003 I 1, F, W 1, E, It 1, SA 1, 2, It 2, W 2, [J, US(t&R), F(R),Fj,A], 2004 W, E, It, F, I, Sm, A1, 2, 3, A4(R), SA(R), 2005 F(R), I(R), It(R),W(R), E(R), R, Arg, NZ, 2006 F, W, E, I, It, SA 1, 2(R)
Douglas, G (Jedforest) 1921 W
Douglas, J (Stewart's Coll FP) 1961 F, SA, W, I, E, 1962 F, W, I, E, 1963 F, W, I
Douty, P S (London Scottish) 1927 A, 1928 F, W
Drew, D (Glasgow Acads) 1871 E, 1876 E
Druitt, W A H (London Scottish) 1936 W, I, E
Drummond, A H (Kelvinside Acads) 1938 W, I
Drummond, C W (Melrose) 1947 F, W, I, E, 1948 F, I, E, 1950 F, W, I, E
Drybrough, A S (Edinburgh Wands, Merchistonians) 1902 I, 1903 I
Dryden, R H (Watsonians) 1937 E
Drysdale, D (Heriot's FP) 1923 F, W, I, E, 1924 F, W, I, E, 1925 F, W, I, E, 1926 F, W, I, E, 1927 F, W, I, E, A, 1928 F, W, I, E, 1929 F
Duff, P L (Glasgow Acads) 1936 W, I, 1938 W, I, E, 1939 W
Duffy, H (Jedforest) 1955 F
Duke, A (Royal HSFP) 1888 W, I, 1889 W, I, 1890 W, I
Dunbar, J P A (Leeds) 2005 F(R), It(R)
Duncan, A W (Edinburgh U) 1901 W, I, E, 1902 W, I, E
Duncan, D D (Oxford U) 1920 F, W, I, E
Duncan, M D F (W of Scotland) 1986 F, W, E, R, 1987 I, F, W, E, [F, Z, R, NZ], 1988 I, F, W, E, A, 1989 W
Duncan, M M (Fettesian-Lorettonians) 1888 W
Dunlop, J W (W of Scotland) 1875 E
Dunlop, Q (W of Scotland) 1971 E (2[1C])
Dykes, A S (Glasgow Acads) 1932 E
Dykes, J C (Glasgow Acads) 1922 F, E, 1924 I, 1925 F, W, I, 1926 F, W, I, E, 1927 F, W, I, E, A, 1928 F, I, 1929 F, W, I
Dykes, J M (Clydesdale, Glasgow HSFP) 1898 I, E, 1899 W, E, 1900 W, I, 1901 W, I, E, 1902 E

Edwards, D B (Heriot's FP) 1960 I, E, SA
Edwards, N G B (Harlequins, Northampton) 1992 E, I, F, W, A 1, 1994 W
Elgie, M K (London Scottish) 1954 NZ, I, E, W, 1955 F, W, I, E
Elliot, C (Langholm) 1958 E, 1959 F, 1960 F, 1963 E, 1964 F, NZ, W, I, E, 1965 F, W, I
Elliot, M (Hawick) 1895 W, 1896 E, 1897 I, E, 1898 I, E
Elliot, T (Gala) 1905 E
Elliot, T (Gala) 1955 W, I, E, 1956 F, W, I, E, 1957 F, W, I, E, 1958 W, A, I
Elliot, T G (Langholm) 1968 W, A, 1969 F, W, 1970 E
Elliot, W I D (Edinburgh Acads) 1947 F, W, E, A, 1948 F, W, I, E, 1949 F, W, I, E, 1950 F, W, I, E, 1951 F, W, I, E, SA, 1952 F, W, I, E, 1954 NZ, I, E, W
Ellis, D G (Currie) 1997 W, E, I, F
Emslie, W D (Royal HSFP) 1930 F, 1932 I
Eriksson, B R S (London Scottish) 1996 NZ 1, A, 1997 E
Evans, H L (Edinburgh U) 1885 I 1,2
Ewart, E N (Glasgow Acads) 1879 E, 1880 I, E

Fahmy, Dr E C (Abertillery) 1920 F, W, I, E
Fairley, I T (Kelso, Edinburgh) 1999 It, I (R), [Sp (R)]
Fasson, F H (London Scottish, Edinburgh Wands) 1900 W, 1901 W, I, 1902 W, E
Fell, A N (Edinburgh U) 1901 W, I, E, 1902 W, E, 1903 W, E
Ferguson, J H (Gala) 1928 W
Ferguson, W G (Royal HSFP) 1927 A, 1928 F, W, I, E
Fergusson, E A J (Oxford U) 1954 F, NZ, I, E, W
Finlay, A B (Edinburgh Acads) 1875 E
Finlay, J F (Edinburgh Acads) 1871 E, 1872 E, 1874 E, 1875 E
Finlay, N J (Edinburgh Acads) 1875 E, 1876 E, 1878 E, 1879 I, E, 1880 I, E, 1881 I, E
Finlay, R (Watsonians) 1948 E
Fisher, A T (Waterloo, Watsonians) 1947 I, E
Fisher, C D (Waterloo) 1975 NZ, A, 1976 W, E, I
Fisher, D (W of Scotland) 1893 I
Fisher, J P (Royal HSFP, London Scottish) 1963 E, 1964 F, NZ, W, I, E, 1965 F, W, I, E, SA, 1966 F, W, I, E, A, 1967 F, W, I, E, NZ, 1968 F, W, I, E
Fleming, C J N (Edinburgh Wands) 1896 I, E, 1897 I
Fleming, G R (Glasgow Acads) 1875 E, 1876 E
Fletcher, H N (Edinburgh U) 1904 E, 1905 W
Flett, A B (Edinburgh U) 1901 W, I, E, 1902 W, I
Forbes, J L (Watsonians) 1905 W, 1906 I, E
Ford, D St C (United Services, RN) 1930 I, E, 1931 E, 1932 W, I
Ford, J R (Gala) 1893 I
Ford, R W (Borders) 2004 A3(R), 2006 W(R),E(R)
Forrest, J E (Glasgow Acads) 1932 SA, 1935 E, NZ
Forrest, J G S (Cambridge U) 1938 W, I, E
Forrest, W T (Hawick) 1903 W, I, E, 1904 W, I, E, 1905 W, I
Forsayth, H H (Oxford U) 1921 F, W, I, E, 1922 W, I, E
Forsyth, I W (Stewart's Coll FP) 1972 NZ, 1973 F, W, I, E, P
Forsyth, J (Edinburgh U) 1871 E
Foster, R A (Hawick) 1930 W, 1932 SA, I, E
Fox, J (Gala) 1952 F, W, I, E
Frame, J N M (Edinburgh U, Gala) 1967 NZ, 1968 F, W, I, E, 1969 W, I, E, SA, 1970 F, W, I, E, A, 1971 F, W, I, E (2[1C]), 1972 F, W, E, 1973 P (R)
France, C (Kelvinside Acads) 1903 I
Fraser, C F P (Glasgow U) 1888 W, 1889 W
Fraser, J W (Edinburgh Inst FP) 1881 E
Fraser, R (Cambridge U) 1911 F, W, I, E
French, J (Glasgow Acads) 1886 W, 1887 I, W, E
Frew, A (Edinburgh U) 1901 W, I, E
Frew, G M (Glasgow HSFP) 1906 SA, 1907 W, I, E, 1908 W, I, E, 1909 W, I, E, 1910 F, W, I, 1911 I, E
Friebe, J P (Glasgow HSFP) 1952 E
Fullarton, I A (Edinburgh) 2000 NZ 1(R),2, 2001 NZ (R), 2003 It 2(R), I 2(t), 2004 Sm(R), A1(R),2
Fulton, A K (Edinburgh U, Dollar Acads) 1952 F, 1954 F
Fyfe, K C (Cambridge U, Sale, London Scottish) 1933 W, E, 1934 E, 1935 W, I, E, NZ, 1936 W, E, 1939 I

Gallie, G H (Edinburgh Acads) 1939 W
Gallie, R A (Glasgow Acads) 1920 F, W, I, E, 1921 F, W, I, E
Gammell, W B B (Edinburgh Wands) 1977 I, F, W, 1978 W, E
Geddes, I C (London Scottish) 1906 SA, 1907 W, I, E, 1908 W, E
Geddes, K I (London Scottish) 1947 F, W, I, E
Gedge, H T S (Oxford U, London Scottish, Edinburgh Wands) 1894 W, I, E, 1896 E, 1899 W, E
Gedge, P M S (Edinburgh Wands) 1933 I
Gemmill, R (Glasgow HSFP) 1950 F, W, I, E, 1951 F, W, I
Gibson, W R (Royal HSFP) 1891 I, E, 1892 W, I, E, 1893 W, I, E, 1894 W, I, E, 1895 W, I, E
Gilbert-Smith, D S (London Scottish) 1952 E
Gilchrist, J (Glasgow Acads) 1925 F
Gill, A D (Gala) 1973 P, 1974 W, E, I, F
Gillespie, J I (Edinburgh Acads) 1899 E, 1900 W, E, 1901 W, I, E, 1902 W, I, 1904 I, E
Gillies, A C (Watsonians) 1924 W, I, E, 1925 F, W, E, 1926 F, W, 1927 F, W, I, E
Gilmour, H R (Heriot's FP) 1998 Fj
Gilray, C M (Oxford U, London Scottish) 1908 E, 1909 W, E, 1912 I
Glasgow, I C (Heriot's FP) 1997 F (R)
Glasgow, R J C (Dunfermline) 1962 F, W, I, E, 1963 I, E, 1964 I, E, 1965 W, I
Glen, W S (Edinburgh Wands) 1955 W
Gloag, L G (Cambridge U) 1949 F, W, I, E
Godman, P J (Edinburgh) 2005 R(R),Sm(R),NZ(R)
Goodfellow, J (Langholm) 1928 W, I, E
Goodhue, F W J (London Scottish) 1890 W, I, E, 1891 W, I, E, 1892 W, I, E
Gordon, R (Edinburgh Wands) 1951 W, 1952 F, W, I, E, 1953 W
Gordon, R E (Royal Artillery) 1913 F, W, I
Gordon, R J (London Scottish) 1982 A 1,2
Gore, A C (London Scottish) 1882 I
Gossman, B M (W of Scotland) 1980 W, 1983 F, W
Gossman, J S (W of Scotland) 1980 E (R)
Gowans, J J (Cambridge U, London Scottish) 1893 W, 1894 W, E, 1895 W, I, E, 1896 I, E
Gowland, G C (London Scottish) 1908 W, 1909 W, E, 1910 F, W, I, E
Gracie, A L (Harlequins) 1921 F, W, I, E, 1922 F, W, I, E, 1923 F, W, I, E, 1924 F
Graham, G (Newcastle) 1997 A (R), SA (R), 1998 I, F (R), W (R), 1999 F (R), Arg (R), R, [SA, U, Sm, NZ (R)], 2000 I (R), US, A, Sm, 2001 I (R), Tg (R), Arg (R), NZ (R), 2002 E (R), It (R), I (R), F (R), W (R)
Graham, I N (Edinburgh Acads) 1939 I, E
Graham, J (Kelso) 1926 I, E, 1927 F, W, I, E, A, 1928 F, W, I, E, 1930 I, E, 1932 SA, W
Graham, J H S (Edinburgh Acads) 1876 E, 1877 I, E, 1878 E, 1879 I, E, 1880 I, E, 1881 I, E
Grant, D (Hawick) 1965 F, E, SA, 1966 F, W, I, E, A, 1967 F, W, I, E, NZ, 1968 F
Grant, D M (East Midlands) 1911 W, I
Grant, M L (Harlequins) 1955 F, 1956 F, W, 1957 F
Grant, T O (Hawick) 1960 I, E, SA, 1964 F, NZ, W
Grant, W St C (Craigmount) 1873 E, 1874 E
Gray, C A (Nottingham) 1989 W, E, I, F, Fj, R, 1990 I, F, W, E, NZ 1,2, Arg, 1991 F, W, E, I, [J, I, WS, E, NZ]
Gray, D (W of Scotland) 1978 E, 1979 I, F, NZ, 1980 I, F, W, E, 1981 F
Gray, G L (Gala) 1935 NZ, 1937 W, I, E
Gray, S D (Borders) 2004 A3
Gray, T (Northampton, Heriot's FP) 1950 E, 1951 F, E
Greenlees, H D (Leicester) 1927 A, 1928 F, W, 1929 I, E, 1930 E
Greenlees, J R C (Cambridge U, Kelvinside Acads) 1900 I, 1902 W, I, E, 1903 W, I, E
Greenwood, J T (Dunfermline and Perthshire Acads) 1952 F, 1955 F, W, I, E, 1956 F, W, I, E, 1957 F, W, E, 1958 F, W, A, I, E, 1959 F, W, I
Greig, A (Glasgow HSFP) 1911 I
Greig, L L (Glasgow Acads, United Services) 1905 NZ, 1906 SA, 1907 W, 1908 W, I
Greig, R C (Glasgow Acads) 1893 W, 1897 I
Grieve, C F (Oxford U) 1935 W, 1936 E
Grieve, R M (Kelso) 1935 W, I, E, NZ, 1936 W, I, E
Grimes, S B (Watsonians, Newcastle) 1997 A (t+R), 1998 I (R), F (R), W (R), E (R), Fj, A 1, 2, 1999 W (R), E, It, I, F, Arg, R, [SA, U, Sm (R), NZ (R)], 2000 It, I, F (R), W, US, A, Sm (R), 2001 F (R), W (R), E (R), It, I (R), Tg, Arg, NZ, 2002 E, It, I, F (R), W (R), C, US, R, SA, Fj, 2003 I 1, F, W 1, E(R), It 1(R), W 2, I 2, [J, US, F, Fj, A], 2004 W, E, It, F, I, Sm, A1, J, A4, SA, 2005 F, I, It, W, E(R)
Gunn, A W (Royal HSFP) 1912 F, W, I, SA, 1913 F

Hall, A J A (Glasgow) 2002 US (R)
Hall, D W H (Edinburgh) 2003 W 2(R), 2005 R(R), Arg, Sm(R), NZ(R), 2006 F, E, I, It(R), SA 1(R),2
Hamilton, A S (Headingley) 1914 W, 1920 F
Hamilton, C P (Newcastle) 2004 A2(R), 2005 R,Arg,Sm,NZ
Hamilton, H M (W of Scotland) 1874 E, 1875 E
Hannah, R S M (W of Scotland) 1971 I
Harrower, P R (London Scottish) 1885 W
Hart, J G M (London Scottish) 1951 SA
Hart, T M (Glasgow U) 1930 W, I
Hart, W (Melrose) 1960 SA
Harvey, L (Greenock Wands) 1899 I

Hastie, A J (Melrose) 1961 W, I, E, 1964 I, E, 1965 E, SA, 1966 F, W, I, E, A, 1967 F, W, I, NZ, 1968 F, W
Hastie, I R (Kelso) 1955 F, 1958 F, E, 1959 F, W, I
Hastie, J D H (Melrose) 1938 W, I, E
Hastings, A G (Cambridge U, Watsonians, London Scottish) 1986 F, W, E, I, R, 1987 I, F, W, E, [F, Z, R, NZ], 1988 I, F, W, E, A, 1989 Fj, R, 1990 I, F, W, E, NZ 1,2, Arg, 1991 F, W, E, I, [J, I, WS, E, NZ], 1992 E, I, F, W, A 1, 1993 I, F, W, E, NZ, 1994 W, E, I, F, SA, 1995 C, I, F, W, E, R, [Iv, Tg, F, NZ]
Hastings, S (Watsonians) 1986 F, W, E, I, R, 1987 I, F, W, [R], 1988 I, F, W, A, 1989 W, E, I, F, Fj, R, 1990 I, F, W, E, NZ 1,2, Arg, 1991 F, W, E, I, [J, Z, I, WS, E, NZ], 1992 E, I, F, W, A 1,2, 1993 I, F, W, E, NZ, 1994 E, I, F, SA, 1995 W, E, R (R), [Tg, F, NZ], 1996 I, F, W, E, NZ 2, It, 1997 W, E (R)
Hay, B H (Boroughmuir) 1975 NZ, A, 1976 F, 1978 I, F, W, E, NZ, 1979 W, E, I, F, NZ, 1980 I, F, W, E, 1981 F, W, E, I, NZ 1,2
Hay, J A (Hawick) 1995 WS
Hay-Gordon, J R (Edinburgh Acads) 1875 E, 1877 I, E
Hegarty, C B (Hawick) 1978 I, F, W, E
Hegarty, J J (Hawick) 1951 F, 1953 F, W, I, E, 1955 F
Henderson, A R (Glasgow) 2001 I (R), Tg (R), NZ (R), 2002 It, I, US (R), 2003 SA 1,2, It 2, I 2, [US, F, Fj, A], 2004 W, E(t&R), It(R), F, I, Sm, A1, 2, 3, J, A4, SA, 2005 W(R), R, Arg, Sm, NZ, 2006 F, W, E, I, It, SA 1,2
Henderson, B C (Edinburgh Wands) 1963 E, 1964 F, I, E, 1965 F, W, I, E, 1966 F, W, I, E
Henderson, F W (London Scottish) 1900 W, I
Henderson, I C (Edinburgh Acads) 1939 I, E, 1947 F, W, E, A, 1948 I, E
Henderson, J H (Oxford U, Richmond) 1953 F, W, I, E, 1954 F, NZ, I, E, W
Henderson, J M (Edinburgh Acads) 1933 W, E, I
Henderson, J Y M (Watsonians) 1911 E
Henderson, M M (Dunfermline) 1937 W, I, E
Henderson, N F (London Scottish) 1892 I
Henderson, R G (Newcastle Northern) 1924 I, E
Hendrie, K G P (Heriot's FP) 1924 F, W, I
Hendry, T L (Clydesdale) 1893 W, I, E, 1895 I
Henriksen, E H (Royal HSFP) 1953 I
Hepburn, D P (Woodford) 1947 A, 1948 F, W, I, E, 1949 F, W, I, E
Heron, G (Glasgow Acads) 1874 E, 1875 E
Hill, C C P (St Andrew's U) 1912 F, I
Hilton, D I W (Bath, Glasgow) 1995 C, I, F, W, E, R, [Tg, F, NZ], WS, 1996 I, F, W, E, NZ 1,2, A, It, 1997 W, A, SA, 1998 It, I (R), F, W, E, A 1,2, SA (R), 1999 W (R), E (R), It (R), I (R), F, R (R), [SA (R), U (R), Sp], 2000 It (R), F (R), W (R), 2002 SA(R)
Hines, N J (Edinburgh, Glasgow, Perpignan) 2000 NZ 2(R), 2002 C, US, R(R), SA(R), Fj(R), 2003 W 1(R), E, It 1, SA 1,2, It 2, W 2(R), I 2, [US,F(R),Fj,A], 2004 E(R), It(R), F(R), I(R), A3, J, A4, SA, 2005 F(R), I(R), It(R), W(R), E, 2006 E(R), I, It, SA 1,2
Hinshelwood, A J W (London Scottish) 1966 F, W, I, E, A, 1967 F, W, I, E, NZ, 1968 F, W, I, E, A, 1969 F, W, I, SA, 1970 F, W
Hinshelwood, B G (Worcester) 2002 C (R), R(R), SA(R), Fj, 2003 It 2, [J, US(R), Fj(R), A(R)], 2004 W, E, It, Sm, A1, 2, J, A4, SA, 2005 It(R)
Hodge D W (Watsonians, Edinburgh) 1997 F (R), A, SA (t+R), 1998 A 2(R), SA, 1999 W, Arg, R, [Sp, Sm (R)], 2000 F (R), W, E, NZ 1,2, US (R), Sm (R), 2001 F (R), W, E, It, I (R), 2002 E, W (R), C, US
Hodgson, C G (London Scottish) 1968 I, E
Hogg, A (Edinburgh) 2004 W, E(R), It, F(R), I, Sm, A1, 2, 3, J, A4, SA, 2005 F, I, It, W, E, R, Arg, Sm, NZ, 2006 F, W, E, I, It, SA 1,2
Hogg, C D (Melrose) 1992 A 1,2, 1993 NZ (R), 1994 Arg 1,2
Hogg, C G (Boroughmuir) 1978 F (R), W (R)
Holmes, S D (London Scottish) 1998 It, I, F
Holms, W F (RIE Coll) 1886 W, E, 1887 I, E, 1889 W, I
Horsburgh, G B (London Scottish) 1937 W, I, E, 1938 W, I, E, 1939 W, I, E
Howie, D D (Kirkcaldy) 1912 F, W, I, E, SA, 1913 F, W
Howie, R A (Kirkcaldy) 1924 F, W, I, E, 1925 W, I, E
Hoyer-Millar, G C (Oxford U) 1953 I
Huggan, J L (London Scottish) 1914 E
Hume, J (Royal HSFP) 1912 F, 1920 F, 1921 F, W, I, E, 1922 F
Hume, J W G (Oxford U, Edinburgh Wands) 1928 I, 1930 F
Hunter, F (Edinburgh U) 1882 I
Hunter, I G (Selkirk) 1984 I (R), 1985 F (R), W, E
Hunter, J M (Cambridge U) 1947 F
Hunter, M D (Glasgow High) 1974 F
Hunter, W J (Hawick) 1964 F, NZ, W, 1967 F, W, I, E
Hutchison, W R (Glasgow HSFP) 1911 E
Hutton, A H M (Dunfermline) 1932 I
Hutton, J E (Harlequins) 1930 E, 1931 F

Inglis, H M (Edinburgh Acads) 1951 F, W, I, E, SA, 1952 W, I
Inglis, J M (Selkirk) 1952 E
Inglis, W M (Cambridge U, Royal Engineers) 1937 W, I, E, 1938 W, I, E
Innes, J R S (Aberdeen GSFP) 1939 W, I, E, 1947 A, 1948 F, W, I, E
Ireland, J C H (Glasgow HSFP) 1925 W, I, E, 1926 F, W, I, E, 1927 F, W, I, E
Irvine, A R (Heriot's FP) 1972 NZ, 1973 F, W, I, E, P, 1974 W, E, I, F, 1975 I, F, W, E, NZ, A, 1976 F, W, E, I, 1977 E, I, F, W, 1978 I, F, E, NZ, 1979 W, E, I, F, NZ, 1980 I, F, W, E, 1981 F, W, E, I, NZ 1,2, R, A, 1982 E, I, F, W, A 1,2
Irvine, D R (Edinburgh Acads) 1878 E, 1879 I, E
Irvine, R W (Edinburgh Acads) 1871 E, 1872 E, 1873 E, 1874 E, 1875 E, 1876 E, 1877 I, E, 1878 E, 1879 I, E, 1880 I, E
Irvine T W (Edinburgh Acads) 1885 I 1,2, 1886 W, I, E, 1887 I, W, E, 1888 W, I, 1889 I

Jackson, K L T (Oxford U) 1933 W, E, I, 1934 W
Jackson, T G H (Army) 1947 F, W, E, A, 1948 F, W, I, E, 1949 F, W, I, E
Jackson, W D (Hawick) 1964 I, 1965 E, SA, 1968 A, 1969 F, W, I, E
Jacobsen, A F (Edinburgh) 2002 C (R), US, 2003 I 2, 2004 It,F,I,A3,J,A4,SA, 2005 R, Arg(R), Sm
Jamieson, J (W of Scotland) 1883 W, I, E, 1884 W, I, E, 1885 W, I 1,2
Jardine, I C (Stirling County) 1993 NZ, 1994 W, E (R), Arg 1,2, 1995 C, I, F, [Tg, F (t & R), NZ (R)], 1996 I, F, W, E, NZ 1,2, 1998 Fj
Jeffrey, J (Kelso) 1984 A, 1985 I, E, 1986 F, W, E, I, R, 1987 I, F, W, E, [F, Z, R], 1988 I, W, A, 1989 W, E, I, F, Fj, R, 1990 I, F, W, E, NZ 1,2, Arg, 1991 F, W, E, I, [J, I, WS, E, NZ]
Johnston, D I (Watsonians) 1979 NZ, 1980 I, F, W, E, 1981 R, A, 1982 E, I, F, W, A 1,2, 1983 I, F, W, NZ, 1984 W, E, I, F, R, 1986 F, W, E, I, R
Johnston, H H (Edinburgh Collegian FP) 1877 I, E
Johnston, J (Melrose) 1951 SA, 1952 F, W, I, E
Johnston, W C (Glasgow HSFP) 1922 F
Johnston, W G S (Cambridge U) 1935 W, I, 1937 W, I, E
Joiner, C A (Melrose, Leicester) 1994 Arg 1,2, 1995 C, I, F, W, E, R, [Iv, Tg, F, NZ], 1996 I, F, W, E, NZ 1, 1997 SA, 1998 It, I, A 2(R), 2000 NZ 1(R),2, US (R)
Jones, P M (Gloucester) 1992 W (R)
Junor, J E (Glasgow Acads) 1876 E, 1877 I, E, 1878 E, 1879 E, 1881 I

Keddie, R R (Watsonians) 1967 NZ
Keith, G J (Wasps) 1968 F, W
Keller, D H (London Scottish) 1949 F, W, I, E, 1950 F, W, I
Kellock, A D (Edinburgh) 2004 A3(t&R), 2005 R(R),Arg(R),Sm(R),NZ(R), 2006 F,W, E, It(R), SA 1(R), 2
Kelly, R F (Watsonians) 1927 A, 1928 F, W, E
Kemp, J W Y (Glasgow HSFP) 1954 W, 1955 F, W, I, E, 1956 F, W, I, E, 1957 F, W, I, E, 1958 F, W, A, I, E, 1959 F, W, I, E, 1960 F, W, I, E, SA
Kennedy, A E (Watsonians) 1983 NZ, 1984 W, E, A
Kennedy, F (Stewart's Coll FP) 1920 F, W, I, E, 1921 E
Kennedy, N (W of Scotland) 1903 W, I, E
Ker, A B M (Kelso) 1988 W, E
Ker, H T (Glasgow Acads) 1887 I, W, E, 1888 I, 1889 W, 1890 I, E
Kerr, D S (Heriot's FP) 1923 F, W, 1924 F, 1926 I, E, 1927 W, I, E, 1928 I, E
Kerr, G (Leeds) 2003 I 1(R), F(R), W 1(R), E(R), SA 1,2, W 2, [J(R),US,F], 2004 W(R), E(R), It(R), F(R), I(R), J, A4, SA, 2005 F, I, It, W, E, Arg, Sm(R), NZ, 2006 F, W, E, I, It, SA 1,2

Kerr, G C (Old Dunelmians, Edinburgh Wands) 1898 I, E, 1899 I, W, E, 1900 W, I, E
Kerr, J M (Heriot's FP) 1935 NZ, 1936 I, E, 1937 W, I
Kerr, R C (Glasgow) 2002 C, US, 2003 W 2
Kerr, W (London Scottish) 1953 E
Kidston, D W (Glasgow Acads) 1883 W, E
Kidston, W H (W of Scotland) 1874 E
Kilgour, I J (RMC Sandhurst) 1921 F
King, J H F (Selkirk) 1953 F, W, E, 1954 E
Kininmonth, P W (Oxford U, Richmond) 1949 F, W, I, E, 1950 F, W, I, E, 1951 F, W, I, E, SA, 1952 F, W, I, 1954 F, NZ, I, E, W
Kinnear, R M (Heriot's FP) 1926 F, W, I
Knox, J (Kelvinside Acads) 1903 W, I, E
Kyle, W E (Hawick) 1902 W, I, E, 1903 W, I, E, 1904 W, I, E, 1905 W, I, E, NZ, 1906 W, I, E, 1908 E, 1909 W, I, E, 1910 W

Laidlaw, A S (Hawick) 1897 I
Laidlaw, F A L (Melrose) 1965 F, W, I, E, SA, 1966 F, W, I, E, A, 1967 F, W, I, E, NZ, 1968 F, W, I, A, 1969 F, W, I, E, SA, 1970 F, W, I, E, A, 1971 F, W, I
Laidlaw, R J (Jedforest) 1980 I, F, W, E, 1981 F, W, E, I, NZ 1,2, R, A, 1982 E, I, F, W, A 1,2, 1983 I, F, W, E, NZ, 1984 W, E, I, F, R, A, 1985 I, F, 1986 F, W, E, I, R, 1987 I, F, W, E, [F, R, NZ], 1988 I, F, W, E
Laing, A D (Royal HSFP) 1914 W, I, E, 1920 F, W, I, 1921 F
Lambie, I K (Watsonians) 1978 NZ (R), 1979 W, E, NZ
Lambie, L B (Glasgow HSFP) 1934 W, I, E, 1935 W, I, E, NZ
Lamond, G A W (Kelvinside Acads) 1899 W, E, 1905 E
Lamont, R P (Glasgow) 2005 W,E,R,Arg,Sm
Lamont, S F (Glasgow, Northampton) 2004 Sm, A1, 2, 3, J, A4, SA, 2005 F, I, It, W, E, R, Arg, Sm, NZ, 2006 F, W, E, I, It, SA 1
Laney, B J (Edinburgh) 2001 NZ, 2002 E, It, I, F, W, C, US, R, SA, Fj, 2003 I 1, F, SA 2(R), It 2(R), W 2, 2004 W,E,It,I(R)
Lang, D (Paisley) 1876 E, 1877 I
Langrish, R W (London Scottish) 1930 F, 1931 F, W, I
Lauder, W (Neath) 1969 I, E, SA, 1970 F, W, I, A, 1973 F, 1974 W, E, I, F, 1975 I, F, NZ, A, 1976 F, 1977 E
Laughland, I H P (London Scottish) 1959 F, 1960 F, W, I, E, 1961 SA, W, I, E, 1962 F, W, I, E, 1963 F, W, I, 1964 F, NZ, W, I, E, 1965 F, W, I, E, SA, 1966 F, W, I, E, 1967 E
Lawrie, J R (Melrose) 1922 F, W, I, E, 1923 F, W, I, E, 1924 W, I, E
Lawrie, K G (Gala) 1980 F (R), W, E
Lawson, A J M (Edinburgh Wands, London Scottish) 1972 F (R), E, 1973 F, 1974 W, E, 1976 E, I, 1977 E, 1978 NZ, 1979 W, E, I, F, NZ, 1980 W (R)
Lawson, S (Glasgow) 2005 R,Arg(R),Sm,NZ, 2006 F(R),W,I(R),It,SA 1,2(R)
Lawther, T H B (Old Millhillians) 1932 SA, W
Ledingham, G A (Aberdeen GSFP) 1913 F
Lee, D J (London Scottish, Edinburgh) 1998 I (R), F, W, E, Fj, A 1,2, SA, 2001 Arg, 2004 It(R),F,I(R)
Lees, J B (Gala) 1947 I, A, 1948 F, W, E
Leggatt, H T O (Watsonians) 1891 W, I, E, 1892 W, I, 1893 W, E, 1894 I, E
Lely, W G (Cambridge U, London Scottish) 1909 I
Leslie, D G (Dundee HSFP, W of Scotland, Gala) 1975 I, F, W, E, NZ, A, 1976 F, W, E, I, 1978 NZ, 1980 E, 1981 W, E, I, NZ 1,2, R, A, 1982 E, 1983 I, F, W, E, 1984 W, E, I, F, R, 1985 F, W, E
Leslie, J A (Glasgow, Northampton) 1998 SA, 1999 W, E, It, I, F, [SA], 2000 It, F, W, US, A, Sm, 2001 F, W, E, It, I, Tg, Arg, NZ, 2002 F, W
Leslie, M D (Glasgow, Edinburgh) 1998 SA (R), 1999 W, E, It, I, F, R, [SA, U, Sm, NZ], 2000 It, I, F, W, E, NZ 1,2, 2001 F, W, E, It, 2002 It (R), I (R), F, W, R, SA, Fj(R), 2003 I 1, F, SA 1(R), 2 (R), It 2(R), W 2, [J(R),US(R)]
Liddell, E H (Edinburgh U) 1922 F, W, I, 1923 F, W, I, E
Lind, H (Dunfermline) 1928 I, 1931 F, W, I, E, 1932 SA, W, E, 1933 W, E, I, 1934 W, I, E, 1935 I, 1936 E
Lindsay, A B (London Hospital) 1910 I, 1911 I
Lindsay, G C (London Scottish) 1884 W, 1885 I 1, 1887 W, E
Lindsay-Watson, R H (Hawick) 1909 I
Lineen, S R P (Boroughmuir) 1989 W, E, I, F, Fj, R, 1990 I, F, W, E, NZ 1,2, Arg, 1991 F, W, E, I, R, [J, Z, I, E, NZ], 1992 E, I, F, W, A 1,2
Little, A W (Hawick) 1905 W
Logan, K M (Stirling County, Wasps) 1992 A 2, 1993 E (R), NZ (t), 1994 W, E, I, F, Arg 1,2, SA, 1995 C, I, F, W, E, R, [Iv, Tg, F, NZ], WS, 1996 W (R), NZ 1,2, A, It, 1997 W, E, I, F, A, 1998 I, F, SA (R), 1999 W, E, It, I, F, Arg, R, [SA, U, Sm, NZ], 2000 It, I, F, Sm, 2001 F, W, E, It, 2002 I (R), F (R), W, 2003 I 1, F, W 1, E, It 1, SA 1,2, It 2, I 2, [J, US(R), F, Fj, A]
Logan, W R (Edinburgh U, Edinburgh Wands) 1931 E, 1932 SA, W, I, 1933 W, E, I, 1934 W, I, E, 1935 W, I, E, NZ, 1936 W, I, E, 1937 W, I, E
Longstaff, S L (Dundee HSFP, Glasgow) 1998 F (R), W, E, Fj, A 1,2 1999 It (R), I (R), Arg (R), R, [U (R), Sp], 2000 It, I, NZ 1
Lorraine, H D B (Oxford U) 1933 W, E, I
Loudoun-Shand, E G (Oxford U) 1913 E
Lowe, J D (Heriot's FP) 1934 W
Lumsden, I J M (Bath, Watsonians) 1947 F, W, A, 1949 F, W, I, E
Lyall, G G (Gala) 1947 A, 1948 F, W, I, E
Lyall, W J C (Edinburgh Acads) 1871 E

Mabon, J T (Jedforest) 1898 I, E, 1899 I, 1900 I
Macarthur, J P (Waterloo) 1932 E
MacCallum, J C (Watsonians) 1905 E, NZ, 1906 W, I, E, SA, 1907 W, I, E, 1908 W, I, E, 1909 W, I, E, 1910 F, W, I, E, 1911 F, I, E, 1912 F, W, I, E
McClung, T (Edinburgh Acads) 1956 I, E, 1957 W, I, E, 1959 F, W, I, 1960 W
McClure, G B (W of Scotland) 1873 E
McClure, J H (W of Scotland) 1872 E
McCowan, D (W of Scotland) 1880 I, E, 1881 I, E, 1882 I, E, 1883 I, E, 1884 I, E
McCowat, R H (Glasgow Acads) 1905 I
McCrae, I G (Gordonians) 1967 E, 1968 I, 1969 F (R), W, 1972 F, NZ
McCrow, J W S (Edinburgh Acads) 1921 I
Macdonald, A E D (Heriot's FP) 1993 NZ
McDonald, C (Jedforest) 1947 A
Macdonald, D C (Edinburgh U) 1953 F, W, 1958 I, E
Macdonald, D S M (Oxford U, London Scottish, W of Scotland) 1977 E, I, F, W, 1978 I, W, E
Macdonald, J D (London Scottish, Army) 1966 F, W, I, E, 1967 F, W, I, E
Macdonald, J M (Edinburgh Wands) 1911 W
Macdonald, J S (Edinburgh U) 1903 E, 1904 W, I, E, 1905 W
Macdonald, K R (Stewart's Coll FP) 1956 F, W, I, 1957 W, I, E
Macdonald, R (Edinburgh U) 1950 F, W, I, E
McDonald, W A (Glasgow U) 1889 W, 1892 I, E
Macdonald, W G (London Scottish) 1969 I (R)
MacDougall, B (Borders) 2006 W, SA2(R)
Macdougall, J B (Greenock Wands, Wakefield) 1913 F, 1914 I, 1921 F, I, E
McEwan, M C (Edinburgh Acads) 1886 E, 1887 I, W, E, 1888 W, I, 1889 W, I, 1890 W, I, E, 1891 W, I, E, 1892 E
MacEwan, N A (Gala, Highland) 1971 F, W, I, E (2[1C]), 1972 F, W, E, NZ, 1973 F, W, I, E, P, 1974 W, E, I, F, 1975 W, E
McEwan, W M C (Edinburgh Acads) 1894 W, E, 1895 W, E, 1896 W, I, E, 1897 I, E, 1898 I, E, 1899 I, W, E, 1900 W, E
MacEwen, R K G (Cambridge U, London Scottish) 1954 F, NZ, I, W, 1956 F, W, I, E, 1957 F, W, I, E, 1958 W
Macfadyen, D J H (Glasgow) 2002 C (R), US, 2004 Sm,A1,2,3,J,A4,SA, 2006 SA 1,2(R)
Macfarlan, D J (London Scottish) 1883 W, 1884 W, I, E, 1886 W, I, 1887 I, 1888 I
McFarlane, J L H (Edinburgh U) 1871 E, 1872 E, 1873 E
McGaughey, S K (Hawick) 1984 R
McGeechan, I R (Headingley) 1972 NZ, 1973 F, W, I, E, P, 1974 W, E, I, F, 1975 I, F, W, E, NZ, A, 1976 F, W, E, I, 1977 E, I, F, W, 1978 I, F, W, NZ, 1979 W, E, I, F
McGlashan, T P L (Royal HSFP) 1947 F, I, E, 1954 F, NZ, I, E, W
MacGregor, D G (Watsonians, Pontypridd) 1907 W, I, E
MacGregor, G (Cambridge U) 1890 W, I, E, 1891 W, I, E, 1893 W, I, E, 1894 W, I, E, 1896 E

MacGregor, I A A (Hillhead HSFP, Llanelli) 1955 I, E, 1956 F, W, I, E, 1957 F, W, I
MacGregor, J R (Edinburgh U) 1909 I
McGuinness, G M (W of Scotland) 1982 A 1,2, 1983 I, 1985 I, F, W, E
McHarg, A F (W of Scotland, London Scottish) 1968 I, E, A, 1969 F, W, I, E, 1971 F, W, I, E (2[1C]), 1972 F, E, NZ, 1973 F, W, I, E, P, 1974 W, E, I, F, 1975 I, F, W, E, NZ, A, 1976 F, W, E, I, 1977 E, I, F, W, 1978 I, F, W, NZ, 1979 W, E
McIlwham, G R (Glasgow Hawks, Glasgow, Bordeaux-Bègles) 1998 Fj, A 2(R), 2000 E (R), NZ 2(R), US (R), A (R), Sm (R), 2001 F (R), W (R), E (R), It (R), 2003 SA 2(R), It 2(R), W 2(R), I 2, [A(R)]
McIndoe, F (Glasgow Acads) 1886 W, I
MacIntyre, I (Edinburgh Wands) 1890 W, I, E, 1891 W, I, E
McIvor, D J (Edinburgh Acads) 1992 E, I, F, W, 1993 NZ, 1994 SA
Mackay, E B (Glasgow Acads) 1920 W, 1922 E
McKeating, E (Heriot's FP) 1957 F, W, 1961 SA, W, I, E
McKelvey, G (Watsonians) 1997 A
McKendrick, J G (W of Scotland) 1889 I
Mackenzie, A D G (Selkirk) 1984 A
Mackenzie, C J G (United Services) 1921 E
Mackenzie, D D (Edinburgh U) 1947 W, I, E, 1948 F, W, I
Mackenzie, D K A (Edinburgh Wands) 1939 I, E
Mackenzie, J M (Edinburgh U) 1905 NZ, 1909 W, I, E, 1910 W, I, E, 1911 W, I
McKenzie, K D (Stirling County) 1994 Arg 1,2, 1995 R, [Iv], 1996 I, F, W, E, NZ 1,2, A, It, 1998 A 1(R), 2
Mackenzie, R C (Glasgow Acads) 1877 I, E, 1881 I, E
Mackie, G Y (Highland) 1975 A, 1976 F, W, 1978 F
MacKinnon, A (London Scottish) 1898 I, E, 1899 I, W, E, 1900 E
Mackintosh, C E W C (London Scottish) 1924 F
Mackintosh, H S (Glasgow U, W of Scotland) 1929 F, W, I, E, 1930 F, W, I, E, 1931 F, W, I, E, 1932 SA, W, I, E
MacLachlan, L P (Oxford U, London Scottish) 1954 NZ, I, E, W
Maclagan, W E (Edinburgh Acads) 1878 E, 1879 I, E, 1880 I, E, 1881 I, E, 1882 I, E, 1883 W, I, E, 1884 W, I, E, 1885 W, I 1,2, 1887 I, W, E, 1888 W, I, 1890 W, I, E
McLaren, A (Durham County) 1931 F
McLaren, E (London Scottish, Royal HSFP) 1923 F, W, I, E, 1924 F
McLaren, J G (Bourgoin, Glasgow, Bordeaux-Bègles, Castres) 1999 Arg, R, [Sp, Sm], 2000 It (R), F, E, NZ 1, 2001 F, W, E (R), I, Tg, Arg, NZ, 2002 E, It, I, F, W, 2003 W 1, E, It 1, SA 1(R), It 2, I 2(R), [J,F(R),Fj(t&R),A(R)]
McLauchlan, J (Jordanhill) 1969 E, SA, 1970 F, W, 1971 F, W, I, E (2[1C]), 1972 F, W, E, NZ, 1973 F, W, I, E, P, 1974 W, E, I, F, 1975 I, F, W, E, NZ, A, 1976 F, W, E, I, 1977 W, 1978 I, F, W, E, NZ, 1979 W, E, I, F, NZ
McLean, D I (Royal HSFP) 1947 I, E
Maclennan, W D (Watsonians) 1947 F, I
MacLeod, D A (Glasgow U) 1886 I, E
MacLeod, G (Edinburgh Acads) 1878 E, 1882 I
McLeod, H F (Hawick) 1954 F, NZ, I, E, W, 1955 F, W, I, E, 1956 F, W, I, E, 1957 F, W, I, E, 1958 F, W, A, I, E, 1959 F, W, I, E, 1960 F, W, I, E, SA, 1961 F, SA, W, I, E, 1962 F, W, I, E
MacLeod, K G (Cambridge U) 1905 NZ, 1906 W, I, E, SA,1907 W, I, E, 1908 I, E
MacLeod, L M (Cambridge U) 1904 W, I, E, 1905 W, I, NZ
MacLeod, S J (Borders) 2004 A3,J(t&R),A4(R),SA(R), 2006 F(R),W(R),E,SA2(R)
Macleod, W M (Fettesian-Lorettonians, Edinburgh Wands) 1886 W, I
McMillan, K H D (Sale) 1953 F, W, I, E
MacMillan, R G (London Scottish) 1887 W, I, E, 1890 W, I, E, 1891 W, E, 1892 W, I, E, 1893 W, E, 1894 W, I, E, 1895 W, I, E, 1897 I, E
MacMyn, D J (Cambridge U, London Scottish) 1925 F, W, I, E, 1926 F, W, I, E, 1927 E, A, 1928 F
McNeil, A S B (Watsonians) 1935 I
McPartlin, J J (Harlequins, Oxford U) 1960 F, W, 1962 F, W, I, E
Macphail, J A R (Edinburgh Acads) 1949 E, 1951 SA
Macpherson, D G (London Hospital) 1910 I, E
Macpherson, G P S (Oxford U, Edinburgh Acads) 1922 F, W, I, E, 1924 W, E, 1925 F, W, E, 1927 F, W, I, E, 1928 F, W, E, 1929 I, E, 1930 F, W, I, E, 1931 W, E, 1932 SA, E
Macpherson, N C (Newport) 1920 W, I, E, 1921 F, E, 1923 I, E
McQueen, S B (Waterloo) 1923 F, W, I, E
Macrae, D J (St Andrew's U) 1937 W, I, E, 1938 W, I, E, 1939 W, I, E
Madsen, D F (Gosforth) 1974 W, E, I, F, 1975 I, F, W, E, 1976 F, 1977 E, I, F, W, 1978 I
Mair, N G R (Edinburgh U) 1951 F, W, I, E
Maitland, G (Edinburgh Inst FP) 1885 W, I 2
Maitland, R (Edinburgh Inst FP) 1881 E, 1882 I, E, 1884 W, 1885 W
Maitland, R P (Royal Artillery) 1872 E
Malcolm, A G (Glasgow U) 1888 I
Manson, J J (Dundee HSFP) 1995 E (R)
Marsh, J (Edinburgh Inst FP) 1889 W, I
Marshall, A (Edinburgh Acads) 1875 E
Marshall, G R (Selkirk) 1988 A (R), 1989 Fj, 1990 Arg, 1991 [Z]
Marshall, J C (London Scottish) 1954 F, NZ, I, E, W
Marshall, K W (Edinburgh Acads) 1934 W, I, E, 1935 W, I, E, 1936 W, 1937 E
Marshall, T R (Edinburgh Acads) 1871 E, 1872 E, 1873 E, 1874 E
Marshall, W (Edinburgh Acads) 1872 E
Martin, H (Edinburgh Acads, Oxford U) 1908 W, I, E, 1909 W, E
Masters, W H (Edinburgh Inst FP) 1879 I, 1880 I, E
Mather, C G (Edinburgh, Glasgow) 1999 R (R), [Sp, Sm (R)], 2000 F (t), 2003 [F,Fj,A], 2004 W,E,F
Maxwell, F T (Royal Engineers) 1872 E
Maxwell, G H H P (Edinburgh Acads, RAF, London Scottish) 1913 I, E, 1914 W, I, E, 1920 W, E, 1921 F, W, I, E, 1922 F, E
Maxwell, J M (Langholm) 1957 I
Mayer, M J M (Watsonians, Edinburgh) 1998 SA, 1999 [SA (R), U, Sp, Sm, NZ], 2000 It, I
Mein, J (Edinburgh Acads) 1871 E, 1872 E, 1873 E, 1874 E, 1875 E
Melville, C L (Army) 1937 W, I, E
Menzies, H F (W of Scotland) 1893 W, I, 1894 W, E
Metcalfe, G H (Glasgow Hawks, Glasgow) 1998 A 1,2, 1999 W, E, It, I, F, Arg, R, [SA, U, Sm, NZ], 2000 It, I, F, W, E, 2001 I, Tg, 2002 E, It, I, F, W (R), C, US, 2003 I 1, F, W 1, E, It 1, SA 1,2, W 2, I 2, [US,F,Fj,A]
Metcalfe, R (Northampton, Edinburgh) 2000 E, NZ 1,2, US (R), A (R), Sm, 2001 F, W, E
Methuen, A (London Scottish) 1889 W, I
Michie, E J S (Aberdeen U, Aberdeen GSFP) 1954 F, NZ, I, E, 1955 W, I, E, 1956 F, W, I, E, 1957 F, W, I, E
Millar, J N (W of Scotland) 1892 W, I, E, 1893 W, 1895 I, E
Millar, R K (London Scottish) 1924 I
Millican, J G (Edinburgh U) 1973 W, I, E
Milne, C J B (Fettesian-Lorettonians, W of Scotland) 1886 W, I, E
Milne, D F (Heriot's FP) 1991 [J(R)]
Milne, I G (Heriot's FP, Harlequins) 1979 I, F, NZ, 1980 I, F, 1981 NZ 1,2, R, A, 1982 E, I, F, W, A 1,2, 1983 I, F, W, E, NZ, 1984 W, E, I, F, A, 1985 F, W, E, 1986 F, W, E, I, R, 1987 I, F, W, E, [F, Z, NZ], 1988 A, 1989 W, 1990 NZ 1,2
Milne, K S (Heriot's FP) 1989 W, E, I, F, Fj, R, 1990 I, F, W, E, NZ 2, Arg, 1991 F, W (R), E, [Z], 1992 E, I, F, W, A 1, 1993 I, F, W, E, NZ, 1994 W, E, I, F, SA, 1995 C, I, F, W, E, [Tg, F, NZ]
Milne, W M (Glasgow Acads) 1904 I, E, 1905 W, I
Milroy, E (Watsonians) 1910 W, 1911 E, 1912 W, I, E, SA, 1913 F, W, I, E, 1914 I, E
Mitchell, G W E (Edinburgh Wands) 1967 NZ, 1968 F, W
Mitchell, J G (W of Scotland) 1885 W, I 1,2
Moffat, J S D (Edinburgh, Borders) 2002 R, SA, Fj(R), 2004 A3
Moir, C C (Northampton) 2000 W, E, NZ 1
Moncreiff, F J (Edinburgh Acads) 1871 E, 1872 E, 1873 E
Monteith, H G (Cambridge U, London Scottish) 1905 E, 1906 W, I, E, SA, 1907 W, I, 1908 E
Monypenny, D B (London Scottish) 1899 I, W, E

Moodie, A R (St Andrew's U) 1909 E, 1910 F, 1911 F
Moore, A (Edinburgh Acads) 1990 NZ 2, Arg, 1991 F, W, E
Morgan, D W (Stewart's-Melville FP) 1973 W, I, E, P, 1974 I, F, 1975 I, F, W, E, NZ, A, 1976 F, W, 1977 I, F, W, 1978 I, F, W, E
Morrison, G A (Glasgow) 2004 A1(R), 2(R), 3, J(R), A4(R), SA(R)
Morrison, I R (London Scottish) 1993 I, F, W, E, 1994 W, SA, 1995 C, I, F, W, E, R, [Tg, F, NZ]
Morrison, M C (Royal HSFP) 1896 W, I, E, 1897 I, E, 1898 I, E, 1899 I, W, E, 1900 W, E, 1901 W, I, E, 1902 W, I, E, 1903 W, I, 1904 W, I, E
Morrison, R H (Edinburgh U) 1886 W, I, E
Morrison, W H (Edinburgh Acads) 1900 W
Morton, D S (W of Scotland) 1887 I, W, E, 1888 W, I, 1889 W, I, 1890 I, E
Mowat, J G (Glasgow Acads) 1883 W, E
Mower, A L (Newcastle) 2001 Tg, Arg, NZ, 2002 It, 2003 I 1, F, W 1, E, It 1, SA 1,2, W 2, I 2
Muir, D E (Heriot's FP) 1950 F, W, I, E, 1952 W, I, E
Munnoch, N M (Watsonians) 1952 F, W, I
Munro, D S (Glasgow High Kelvinside) 1994 W, E, I, F, Arg 1,2, 1997 W (R)
Munro, P (Oxford U, London Scottish) 1905 W, I, E, NZ, 1906 W, I, E, SA, 1907 I, E, 1911 F, W, I
Munro, R (St Andrew's U) 1871 E
Munro, S (Ayr, W of Scotland) 1980 I, F, 1981 F, W, E, I, NZ 1,2, R, 1984 W
Munro, W H (Glasgow HSFP) 1947 I, E
Murdoch, W C W (Hillhead HSFP) 1935 E, NZ, 1936 W, I, 1939 E, 1948 F, W, I, E
Murray, C A (Hawick, Edinburgh) 1998 E (R), Fj, A 1,2, SA, 1999 W, E, It, I, F, Arg, [SA, U, Sp, Sm, NZ], 2000 NZ 2, US, A, Sm, 2001 F, W, E, It (R), Tg, Arg
Murray, E (Glasgow) 2005 R(R)
Murray, G M (Glasgow Acads) 1921 I, 1926 W
Murray, H M (Glasgow U) 1936 W, I
Murray, K T (Hawick) 1985 I, F, W
Murray, R O (Cambridge U) 1935 W, E
Murray, S (Bedford, Saracens, Edinburgh) 1997 A, SA, 1998 It, Fj, A 1,2, SA, 1999 W, E, It, I, F, Arg, R, [SA, U, Sm, NZ], 2000 It, I, F, W, E, NZ 1, US, A, Sm, 2001 F, W, E, It, I, Tg, Arg, NZ, 2002 E, It, I, F, W, R, SA, 2003 I 1, F, W 1, E, It 1, SA 1,2, It 2, W 2, [J,F,A(R)], 2004 W,E,It,F,I,Sm,A1,2, 2005 F,I,It,W,E,R,Arg,Sm,NZ, 2006 F,W,I,It,SA1
Murray, W A K (London Scottish) 1920 F, I, 1921 F

Napier, H M (W of Scotland) 1877 I, E, 1878 E, 1879 I, E
Neill, J B (Edinburgh Acads) 1963 E, 1964 F, NZ, W, I, E, 1965 F
Neill, R M (Edinburgh Acads) 1901 E, 1902 I
Neilson, G T (W of Scotland) 1891 W, I, E, 1892 W, E, 1893 W, 1894 W, I, 1895 W, I, E, 1896 W, I, E
Neilson, J A (Glasgow Acads) 1878 E, 1879 E
Neilson, R T (W of Scotland) 1898 I, E, 1899 I, W, 1900 I, E
Neilson, T (W of Scotland) 1874 E
Neilson, W (Merchiston, Cambridge U, London Scottish) 1891 W, E, 1892 W, I, E, 1893 I, E, 1894 E, 1895 W, I, E, 1896 I, 1897 I, E
Neilson, W G (Merchistonians) 1894 E
Nelson, J B (Glasgow Acads) 1925 F, W, I, E, 1926 F, W, I, E, 1927 F, W, I, E, 1928 I, E, 1929 F, W, I, E, 1930 F, W, I, E, 1931 F, W, I
Nelson, T A (Oxford U) 1898 E
Nichol, J A (Royal HSFP) 1955 W, I, E
Nichol, S A (Selkirk) 1994 Arg 2(R)
Nicol, A D (Dundee HSFP, Bath, Glasgow) 1992 E, I, F, W, A 1,2, 1993 NZ, 1994 W, 1997 A, SA, 2000 I (R), F, W, E, NZ 1,2, 2001 F, W, E, I (R), Tg, Arg, NZ
Nimmo, C S (Watsonians) 1920 E

Ogilvy, C (Hawick) 1911 I, E, 1912 I
Oliver, G H (Hawick) 1987 [Z], 1990 NZ 2(R), 1991 [Z]
Oliver, G K (Gala) 1970 A
Orr, C E (W of Scotland) 1887 I, E, W, 1888 W, I, 1889 W, I, 1890 W, I, E, 1891 W, I, E, 1892 W, I, E
Orr, H J (London Scottish) 1903 W, I, E, 1904 W, I
Orr, J E (W of Scotland) 1889 I, 1890 W, I, E, 1891 W, I, E, 1892 W, I, E, 1893 I, E
Orr, J H (Edinburgh City Police) 1947 F, W
Osler, F L (Edinburgh U) 1911 F, W

Park, J (Royal HSFP) 1934 W
Parks, D A (Glasgow) 2004 W(R),E(R),F(R),I, Sm (t&R),A1,2,3,J,A4,SA, 2005 F,I,It, W,R,Arg,Sm,NZ, 2006 F,W,E,I,It(R),SA 1
Paterson, C D (Edinburgh) 1999 [Sp], 2000 F, W, E, NZ 1,2, US, A, Sm, 2001 F, W, E, It, I, NZ, 2002 E, It, I, F, W, C, US, R, SA, Fj, 2003 I 1, F, W 1, E, It 1, SA 1,2, It 2(R), W 2(R), I 2, [J,US,F,Fj,A], 2004 W, E, It, F, I, Sm, A3, J, A4, SA, 2005 F, I, It, W, E, R, Arg, Sm, NZ, 2006 F, W, E, I, It, SA 1, 2
Paterson, D S (Gala) 1969 SA, 1970 I, E, A, 1971 F, W, I, E (2[1C]), 1972 W
Paterson, G Q (Edinburgh Acads) 1876 E
Paterson, J R (Birkenhead Park) 1925 F, W, I, E, 1926 F, W, I, E, 1927 F, W, I, E, A, 1928 F, W, I, E, 1929 F, W, I, E
Patterson, D (Hawick) 1896 W
Patterson, D W (West Hartlepool) 1994 SA, 1995 [Tg]
Pattullo, G L (Panmure) 1920 F, W, I, E
Paxton, I A M (Selkirk) 1981 NZ 1,2, R, A, 1982 E, I, F, W, A 1,2, 1983 I, E, NZ, 1984 W, E, I, F, 1985 I (R), F, W, E, 1986 W, E, I, R, 1987 I, F, W, E, [F, Z, R, NZ], 1988 I, E, A
Paxton, R E (Kelso) 1982 I, A 2(R)
Pearson, J (Watsonians) 1909 I, E, 1910 F, W, I, E, 1911 F, 1912 F, W, SA, 1913 I, E
Pender, I M (London Scottish) 1914 E
Pender, N E K (Hawick) 1977 I, 1978 F, W, E
Penman, W M (RAF) 1939 I
Peterkin, W A (Edinburgh U) 1881 E, 1883 I, 1884 W, I, E, 1885 W, I 1,2
Peters, E W (Bath) 1995 C, I, F, W, E, R, [Tg, F, NZ], 1996 I, F, W, E, NZ 1,2, A, It, 1997 A, SA, 1998 W, E, Fj, A 1,2, SA, 1999 W, E, It, I
Petrie, A G (Royal HSFP) 1873 E, 1874 E, 1875 E, 1876 E, 1877 I, E, 1878 E, 1879 I, E, 1880 I, E
Petrie, J M (Glasgow) 2000 NZ 2, US, A, Sm, 2001 F, W, It (R), I (R), Tg, Arg, 2002 F (t), W (R), C, R(R), Fj, 2003 F(t+R), W 1(R), SA 1(R), 2 (R), It 2, W 2, I 2(R), [J, US, F(t&R), A(R)], 2004 It(R), I(R), Sm(R), A1(R), 2(t&R), 3(R), J, A4, SA(R), 2005 F, I, It, W, E(R), R, 2006 F(R), W(R), I(R), SA 2
Philip, T K (Edinburgh) 2004 W,E,It,F,I
Philp, A (Edinburgh Inst FP) 1882 E
Pinder, S J (Glasgow) 2006 SA 1(R),2(R)
Pocock, E I (Edinburgh Wands) 1877 I, E
Pollock, J A (Gosforth) 1982 W, 1983 E, NZ, 1984 E (R), I, F, R, 1985 F
Polson, A H (Gala) 1930 E
Pountney, A C (Northhampton) 1998 SA, 1999 W (t+R), E (R), It (t+R), I (R), F, Arg, [SA, U, Sm, NZ], 2000 It, I, F, W, E, US,A, Sm, 2001 F, W, E, It, I, 2002 E, I, F, W, R, SA, Fj
Proudfoot, M C (Melrose, Glasgow) 1998 Fj, A 1,2, 2003 I 2(R)
Purdie, W (Jedforest) 1939 W, I, E
Purves, A B H L (London Scottish) 1906 W, I, E, SA, 1907 W, I, E, 1908 W, I, E
Purves, W D C L (London Scottish) 1912 F, W, I, SA, 1913 I, E

Rea, C W W (W of Scotland, Headingley) 1968 A, 1969 F, W, I, SA, 1970 F, W, I, A, 1971 F, W, E (2[1C])
Redpath, B W (Melrose, Narbonne, Sale) 1993 NZ (t), 1994 E (t), F, Arg 1,2, 1995 C, I, F, W, E, R, [Iv, F, NZ], WS, 1996 I, F, W, E. A (R), It, 1997 E, I, F, 1998 Fj, A 1,2, SA, 1999 R (R), [U (R), Sp], 2000 It, I, US, A, Sm, 2001 F (R), E (R), It, I, 2002 E, It, I, F, W, R, SA, Fj, 2003 I 1, F, W 1, E, It 1, SA 1,2, [J,US(R),F,Fj,A]
Reed, A I (Bath, Wasps) 1993 I, F, W, E, 1994 E, I, F, Arg 1,2, SA, 1996 It, 1997 W, E, I, F, 1999 It (R), F (R), [Sp]
Reid, C (Edinburgh Acads) 1881 I, E, 1882 I, E, 1883 W, I, E, 1884 W, I, E, 1885 W, I 1,2, 1886 W, I, E, 1887 I, W, E, 1888 W, I
Reid, J (Edinburgh Wands) 1874 E, 1875 E, 1876 E, 1877 I, E
Reid, J M (Edinburgh Acads) 1898 I, E, 1899 I
Reid, M F (Loretto) 1883 I, E
Reid, R E (Glasgow) 2001 Tg (R), Arg

Reid, S J (Boroughmuir, Leeds, Narbonne) 1995 WS, 1999 F, Arg, [Sp], 2000 It (t), F, W, E (t)
Reid-Kerr, J (Greenock Wand) 1909 E
Relph, W K L (Stewart's Coll FP) 1955 F, W, I, E
Renny-Tailyour, H W (Royal Engineers) 1872 E
Renwick, J M (Hawick) 1972 F, W, E, NZ, 1973 F, 1974 W, E, I, F, 1975 I, F, W, E, NZ, A, 1976 F, W, E (R), 1977 I, F, W, 1978 I, F, W, E, NZ, 1979 W, E, I, F, NZ, 1980 I, F, W, E, 1981 F, W, E, I, NZ 1,2, R, A, 1982 E, I, F, W, 1983 I, F, W, E, 1984 R
Renwick, W L (London Scottish) 1989 R
Renwick, W N (London Scottish, Edinburgh Wands) 1938 E, 1939 W
Richardson, J F (Edinburgh Acads) 1994 SA
Ritchie, G (Merchistonians) 1871 E
Ritchie, G F (Dundee HSFP) 1932 E
Ritchie, J M (Watsonians) 1933 W, E, I, 1934 W, I, E
Ritchie, W T (Cambridge U) 1905 I, E
Robb, G H (Glasgow U) 1881 I, 1885 W
Roberts, G (Watsonians) 1938 W, I, E, 1939 W, E
Robertson, A H (W of Scotland) 1871 E
Robertson, A W (Edinburgh Acads) 1897 E
Robertson, D (Edinburgh Acads) 1875 E
Robertson, D D (Cambridge U) 1893 W
Robertson, I (London Scottish, Watsonians) 1968 E, 1969 E, SA, 1970 F, W, I, E, A
Robertson, I P M (Watsonians) 1910 F
Robertson, J (Clydesdale) 1908 E
Robertson, K W (Melrose) 1978 NZ, 1979 W, E, I, F, NZ, 1980 W, E, 1981 F, W, E, I, R, A, 1982 E, I, F, A 1,2, 1983 I, F, W, E, 1984 E, I, F, R, A, 1985 I, F, W, E, 1986 I, 1987 F (R), W, E, [F, Z, NZ], 1988 E, A, 1989 E, I, F
Robertson, L (London Scottish United Services) 1908 E, 1911 W, 1912 W, I, E, SA, 1913 W, I, E
Robertson, M A (Gala) 1958 F
Robertson, R D (London Scottish) 1912 F
Robson, A (Hawick) 1954 F, 1955 F, W, I, E, 1956 F, W, I, E, 1957 F, W, I, E, 1958 W, A, I, E, 1959 F, W, I, E, 1960 F
Rodd, J A T (United Services, RN, London Scottish) 1958 F, W, A, I, E, 1960 F, W, 1962 F, 1964 F, NZ, W, 1965 F, W, I
Rogerson, J (Kelvinside Acads) 1894 W
Roland, E T (Edinburgh Acads) 1884 I, E
Rollo, D M D (Howe of Fife) 1959 E, 1960 F, W, I, E, SA, 1961 F, SA, W, I, E, 1962 F, W, E, 1963 F, W, I, E, 1964 F, NZ, W, I, E, 1965 F, W, I, E, SA, 1966 F, W, I, E, A, 1967 F, W, E, NZ, 1968 F, W, I
Rose, D M (Jedforest) 1951 F, W, I, E, SA, 1953 F, W
Ross, A (Kilmarnock) 1924 F, W
Ross, A (Royal HSFP) 1905 W, I, E, 1909 W, I
Ross, A R (Edinburgh U) 1911 W, 1914 W, I, E
Ross, E J (London Scottish) 1904 W
Ross, G (Edinburgh, Leeds) 2001 Tg, 2002 R, SA, Fj(R), 2003 I 1, W 1(R), SA 2(R), It 2, I 2, [J], 2004 Sm, A1(R), 2(R), J(R), SA(R), 2005 It(R), W(R), E, 2006 F(R), W(R), E(R), I(R), It, SA 1(R), 2
Ross, G T (Watsonians) 1954 NZ, I, E, W
Ross, I A (Hillhead HSFP) 1951 F, W, I, E
Ross, J (London Scottish) 1901 W, I, E, 1902 W, 1903 E
Ross, K I (Boroughmuir FP) 1961 SA, W, I, E, 1962 F, W, I, E, 1963 F, W, E
Ross, W A (Hillhead HSFP) 1937 W, E
Rottenburg, H (Cambridge U, London Scottish) 1899 W, E, 1900 W, I, E
Roughead, W N (Edinburgh Acads, London Scottish) 1927 A, 1928 F, W, I, E, 1930 I, E, 1931 F, W, I, E, 1932 W
Rowan, N A (Boroughmuir) 1980 W, E, 1981 F, W, E, I, 1984 R, 1985 I, 1987 [R], 1988 I, F, W, E
Rowand, R (Glasgow HSFP) 1930 F, W, 1932 E, 1933 W, E, I, 1934 W
Roxburgh, A J (Kelso) 1997 A, 1998 It, F (R), W, E, Fj, A 1(R),2(R)
Roy, A (Waterloo) 1938 W, I, E, 1939 W, I, E
Russell, R R (Saracens, London Irish) 1999 R, [U (R), Sp, Sm (R), NZ (R)], 2000 I (R), 2001 F (R), 2002 F (R), W (R), 2003 W 1(R), It 1(R), SA 1 (R), 2 (R), It 2, I 2(R), [J, F(R), Fj(t), A(R)], 2004 W(R), E(R), F(R), I(R), J(R), A4(R), SA(R), 2005 It(R)
Russell, W L (Glasgow Acads) 1905 NZ, 1906 W, I, E
Rutherford, J Y (Selkirk) 1979 W, E, I, F, NZ, 1980 I, F, E, 1981 F, W, E, I, NZ 1,2, A, 1982 E, I, F, W, A 1,2, 1983 E, NZ, 1984 W, E, I, F, R, 1985 I, F, W, E, 1986 F, W, E, I, R, 1987 I, F, W, E, [F]
Sampson, R W F (London Scottish) 1939 W, 1947 W
Sanderson, G A (Royal HSFP) 1907 W, I, E, 1908 I
Sanderson, J L P (Edinburgh Acads) 1873 E
Schulze, D G (London Scottish) 1905 E, 1907 I, E, 1908 W, I, E, 1909 W, I, E, 1910 W, I, E, 1911 W
Scobie, R M (Royal Military Coll) 1914 W, I, E
Scotland, K J F (Heriot's FP, Cambridge U, Leicester) 1957 F, W, I, E, 1958 E, 1959 F, W, I, E, 1960 F, W, I, E, 1961 F, SA, W, I, E, 1962 F, W, I, E, 1963 F, W, I, E, 1965 F
Scott, D M (Langholm, Watsonians) 1950 I, E, 1951 W, I, E, SA, 1952 F, W, I, 1953 F
Scott, J M B (Edinburgh Acads) 1907 E, 1908 W, I, E, 1909 W, I, E, 1910 F, W, I, E, 1911 F, W, I, 1912 W, I, E, SA, 1913 W, I, E
Scott, J S (St Andrew's U) 1950 E
Scott, J W (Stewart's Coll FP) 1925 F, W, I, E, 1926 F, W, I, E, 1927 F, W, I, E, A, 1928 F, W, E, 1929 E, 1930 F
Scott, M (Dunfermline) 1992 A 2
Scott, R (Hawick) 1898 I, 1900 I, E
Scott, S (Edinburgh, Borders) 2000 NZ 2 (R), US (t+R), 2001 It (R), I (R), Tg (R), NZ (R), 2002 US (R), R(R), Fj(R), 2004 Sm(R), A1(R)
Scott, T (Langholm, Hawick) 1896 W, 1897 I, E, 1898 I, E, 1899 I, W, E, 1900 W, I, E
Scott, T M (Hawick) 1893 E, 1895 W, I, E, 1896 W, E, 1897 I, E, 1898 I, E, 1900 W, I
Scott, W P (W of Scotland) 1900 I, E, 1902 I, E, 1903 W, I, E, 1904 W, I, E, 1905 W, I, E, NZ, 1906 W, I, E, SA, 1907 W, I, E
Scoular, J G (Cambridge U) 1905 NZ, 1906 W, I, E, SA
Selby, J A R (Watsonians) 1920 W, I
Shackleton, J A P (London Scottish) 1959 E, 1963 F, W, 1964 NZ, W, 1965 I, SA
Sharp, A V (Bristol) 1994 E, I, F, Arg 1,2 SA
Sharp, G (Stewart's FP, Army) 1960 F, 1964 F, NZ, W
Shaw, G D (Sale) 1935 NZ, 1936 W, 1937 W, I, E, 1939 I
Shaw, I (Glasgow HSFP) 1937 I
Shaw, J N (Edinburgh Acads) 1921 W, I
Shaw, R W (Glasgow HSFP) 1934 W, I, E, 1935 W, I, E, NZ, 1936 W, I, E, 1937 W, I, E, 1938 W, I, E, 1939 W, I, E
Shedden, D (W of Scotland) 1972 NZ, 1973 F, W, I, E, P, 1976 W, E, I, 1977 I, F, W, 1978 I, F, W
Shepherd, R J S (Melrose) 1995 WS, 1996 I, F, W, E, NZ 1,2, A, It, 1997 W, E, I, F, SA, 1998 It, I, W (R), Fj (t), A 1,2
Shiel, A G (Melrose, Edinburgh) 1991 [I (R), WS], 1993 I, F, W, E, NZ, 1994 Arg 1,2, SA, 1995 R, [Iv, F, NZ], WS, 2000 I, NZ 1(R),2
Shillinglaw, R B (Gala, Army) 1960 I, E, SA, 1961 F, SA
Simmers, B M (Glasgow Acads) 1965 F, W, 1966 A, 1967 F, W, I, 1971 F (R)
Simmers, W M (Glasgow Acads) 1926 W, I, E, 1927 F, W, I, E, A, 1928 F, W, I, E, 1929 F, W, I, E, 1930 F, W, I, E, 1931 F, W, I, E, 1932 SA, W, I, E
Simpson, G L (Kirkcaldy, Glasgow) 1998 A 1,2, 1999 Arg (R), R, [SA, U, Sm, NZ], 2000 It, I, NZ 1(R), 2001 I, Tg (R), Arg (R), NZ
Simpson, J W (Royal HSFP) 1893 I, E, 1894 W, I, E, 1895 W, I, E, 1896 W, I, 1897 E, 1899 W, E
Simpson, R S (Glasgow Acads) 1923 I
Simson, E D (Edinburgh U, London Scottish) 1902 E, 1903 W, I, E, 1904 W, I, E, 1905 W, I, E, NZ, 1906 W, I, E, 1907 W, I, E
Simson, J T (Watsonians) 1905 NZ, 1909 W, I, E, 1910 F, W, 1911 I
Simson, R F (London Scottish) 1911 E
Sloan, A T (Edinburgh Acads) 1914 W, 1920 F, W, I, E, 1921 F, W, I, E
Sloan, D A (Edinburgh Acads, London Scottish) 1950 F, W, E, 1951 W, I, E, 1953 F
Sloan, T (Glasgow Acads, Oxford U) 1905 NZ, 1906 W, SA, 1907 W, E, 1908 W, 1909 I
Smeaton, P W (Edinburgh Acads) 1881 I, 1883 I, E

Smith, A R (Oxford U) 1895 W, I, E, 1896 W, I, 1897 I, E, 1898 I, E, 1900 I, E

Smith, A R (Cambridge U, Gosforth, Ebbw Vale, Edinburgh Wands) 1955 W, I, E, 1956 F, W, I, E, 1957 F, W, I, E, 1958 F, W, A, I, 1959 F, W, I, E, 1960 F, W, I, E, SA, 1961 F, SA, W, I, E, 1962 F, W, I, E

Smith, C J (Edinburgh) 2002 C, US (R), 2004 Sm(t&R), A1(R),2(R),3(R),J(R), 2005 Arg(R),Sm,NZ(R), 2006 F(R), W(R), E(R), I(R),It(R),SA 1(R),2

Smith, D W C (London Scottish) 1949 F, W, I, E, 1950 F, W, I, 1953 I

Smith, E R (Edinburgh Acads) 1879 I

Smith, G K (Kelso) 1957 I, E, 1958 F, W, A, 1959 F, W, I, E, 1960 F, W, I, E, 1961 F, SA, W, I, E

Smith, H O (Watsonians) 1895 W, 1896 W, I, E, 1898 I, E, 1899 W, I, E, 1900 E, 1902 E

Smith, I R (Gloucester, Moseley) 1992 E, I, W, A 1,2, 1994 E (R), I, F, Arg 1,2, 1995 [Iv], WS, 1996 I, F, W, E, NZ 1,2, A, It, 1997 E, I, F, A, SA

Smith, I S (Oxford U, Edinburgh U) 1924 W, I, E, 1925 F, W, I, E, 1926 F, W, I, E, 1927 F, I, E, 1929 F, W, I, E, 1930 F, W, I, 1931 F, W, I, E, 1932 SA, W, I, E, 1933 W, E, I

Smith I S G (London Scottish) 1969 SA, 1970 F, W, I, E, 1971 F, W, I

Smith, M A (London Scottish) 1970 W, I, E, A

Smith, R T (Kelso) 1929 F, W, I, E, 1930 F, W, I

Smith, S H (Glasgow Acads) 1877 I, 1878 E

Smith, T J (Gala) 1983 E, NZ, 1985 I, F

Smith T J (Watsonians, Dundee HSFP, Glasgow, Brive, Northampton) 1997 E, I, F, 1998 SA, 1999 W, E, It, I, Arg, R, [SA, U, Sm, NZ], 2000 It, I, F, W, E, NZ 1,2, US, A, Sm, 2001 F, W, E, It, I, Tg, Arg, NZ, 2002 E, It, I, F, W, R, SA, Fj, 2003 I 1, F, W 1, E, It 1,2, [J, US, F, Fj, A], 2004 W, E, Sm, A1, 2, 2005 F, I, It, W, E

Sole, D M B (Bath, Edinburgh Acads) 1986 F, W, 1987 I, F, W, E, [F, Z, R, NZ], 1988 I, F, W, E, A, 1989 W, E, I, F, Fj, R, 1990 I, F, W, E, NZ 1,2, Arg, 1991 F, W, E, I, R, [J, I, WS, E, NZ], 1992 E, I, F, W, A 1,2

Somerville, D (Edinburgh Inst FP) 1879 I, 1882 I, 1883 W, I, E, 1884 W

Southwell, H F G (Edinburgh) 2004 Sm(t&R), A1, 2, 3(R), J, A4, SA, 2005 F, I, It, W, E, R(R), Arg(R), Sm(R), NZ, 2006 F, W, E, I, It, SA 1,2

Speirs, L M (Watsonians) 1906 SA, 1907 W, I, E, 1908 W, I, E, 1910 F, W, E

Spence, K M (Oxford U) 1953 I

Spencer, E (Clydesdale) 1898 I

Stagg, P K (Sale) 1965 F, W, E, SA, 1966 F, W, I, E, A, 1967 F, W, I, E, NZ, 1968 F, W, I, E, A, 1969 F, W, I (R), SA, 1970 F, W, I, E, A

Stanger, A G (Hawick) 1989 Fj, R, 1990 I, F, W, E, NZ 1,2, Arg, 1991 F, W, E, I, R, [J, Z, I, WS, E, NZ], 1992 E, I, F, W, A 1,2, 1993 I, F, W, E, NZ, 1994 W, E, I, F, SA, 1995 R, [Iv], 1996 NZ 2, A, It, 1997 W, E, I, F, A, SA, 1998 It, I (R), F, W, E

Stark, D A (Boroughmuir, Melrose, Glasgow Hawks) 1993 I, F, W, E, 1996 NZ 2(R), It (R), 1997 W (R), E, SA

Steel, J F (Glasgow) 2000 US, A, 2001 I, Tg, NZ

Steele, W C C (Langholm, Bedford, RAF, London Scottish) 1969 E, 1971 F, W, I, E (2[1C]), 1972 F, W, E, NZ, 1973 F, W, I, E, 1975 I, F, W, E, NZ (R), 1976 W, E, I, 1977 E

Stephen, A E (W of Scotland) 1885 W, 1886 I

Steven, P D (Heriot's FP) 1984 A, 1985 F, W, E

Steven, R (Edinburgh Wands) 1962 I

Stevenson, A K (Glasgow Acads) 1922 F, 1923 F, W, E

Stevenson, A M (Glasgow U) 1911 F

Stevenson, G D (Hawick) 1956 E, 1957 F, 1958 F, W, A, I, E, 1959 W, I, E, 1960 W, I, E, SA, 1961 F, SA, W, I, E, 1963 F, W, I, 1964 E, 1965 F

Stevenson, H J (Edinburgh Acads) 1888 W, I, 1889 W, I, 1890 W, I, E, 1891 W, I, E, 1892 W, I, E, 1893 I, E

Stevenson, L E (Edinburgh U) 1888 W

Stevenson, R C (London Scottish) 1897 I, E, 1898 E, 1899 I, W, E

Stevenson, R C (St Andrew's U) 1910 F, I, E, 1911 F, W, I

Stevenson, W H (Glasgow Acads) 1925 F

Stewart, A K (Edinburgh U) 1874 E, 1876 E

Stewart, A M (Edinburgh Acads) 1914 W

Stewart, B D (Edinburgh Acads, Edinburgh) 1996 NZ 2, A, 2000 NZ 1,2

Stewart, C A R (W of Scotland) 1880 I, E

Stewart, C E B (Kelso) 1960 W, 1961 F

Stewart, J (Glasgow HSFP) 1930 F

Stewart, J L (Edinburgh Acads) 1921 I

Stewart M J (Northampton) 1996 It, 1997 W, E, I, F, A, SA, 1998 It, I, F, W, Fj (R), 2000 It, I, F, W, E, NZ 1(R), 2001 F, W, E, It, I, Tg, Arg, NZ, 2002 E, It, I, F, W, C, US, R(R)

Stewart, M S (Stewart's Coll FP) 1932 SA, W, I, 1933 W, E, I, 1934 W, I, E

Stewart, W A (London Hospital) 1913 F, W, I, 1914 W

Steyn, S S L (Oxford U) 1911 E, 1912 I

Strachan, G M (Jordanhill) 1971 E (C) (R), 1973 W, I, E, P

Stronach, R S (Glasgow Acads) 1901 W, E, 1905 W, I, E

Stuart, C D (W of Scotland) 1909 I, 1910 F, W, I, E, 1911 I, E

Stuart, L M (Glasgow HSFP) 1923 F, W, I, E, 1924 F, 1928 E, 1930 I, E

Suddon, N (Hawick) 1965 W, I, E, SA, 1966 A, 1968 E, A, 1969 F, W, I, 1970 I, E, A

Sutherland, W R (Hawick) 1910 W, E, 1911 F, E, 1912 F, W, E, SA, 1913 F, W, I, E, 1914 W

Swan, J S (Army, London Scottish, Leicester) 1953 E, 1954 F, NZ, I, E, W, 1955 F, W, I, E, 1956 F, W, I, E, 1957 F, W, 1958 F

Swan, M W (Oxford U, London Scottish) 1958 F, W, A, I, E, 1959 F, W, I

Sweet, J B (Glasgow HSFP) 1913 E, 1914 I

Symington, A W (Cambridge U) 1914 W, E

Tait, A V (Kelso, Newcastle, Edinburgh) 1987 [F(R), Z, R, NZ], 1988 I, F, W, E, 1997 I, F, A, 1998 It, I, F, W, E, SA, 1999 W (R), E, It, I, F, Arg, R, [A, U, NZ]

Tait, J G (Edinburgh Acads) 1880 I, 1885 I 2

Tait, P W (Royal HSFP) 1935 E

Taylor, E G (Oxford U) 1927 W, A

Taylor, R C (Kelvinside-West) 1951 W, I, E, SA

Taylor, S M (Edinburgh) 2000 US, A, 2001 E, It, I, NZ (R), 2002 E, It, I, F, W, C, US, R, SA, Fj, 2003 I 1, F, W 1, E, It 1, SA 1,2, It 2, I 2, [J,US,F,Fj,A], 2004 W,E,It,F,I, 2005 It,W,E,Arg,Sm,NZ, 2006 F,W,E,I,It

Telfer, C M (Hawick) 1968 A, 1969 F, W, I, E, 1972 F, W, E, 1973 W, I, E, P, 1974 W, E, I, 1975 A, 1976 F

Telfer, J W (Melrose) 1964 F, NZ, W, I, E, 1965 F, W, I, 1966 F, W, I, E, 1967 W, I, E, 1968 E, A, 1969 F, W, I, E, SA, 1970 F, W, I

Tennent, J M (W of Scotland) 1909 W, I, E, 1910 F, W, E

Thom, D A (London Scottish) 1934 W, 1935 W, I, E, NZ

Thom, G (Kirkcaldy) 1920 F, W, I, E

Thom, J R (Watsonians) 1933 W, E, I

Thomson, A E (United Services) 1921 F, W, E

Thomson, A M (St Andrew's U) 1949 I

Thomson, B E (Oxford U) 1953 F, W, I

Thomson, I H M (Heriot's FP, Army) 1951 W, I, 1952 F, W, I, 1953 I, E

Thomson, J S (Glasgow Acads) 1871 E

Thomson, R H (London Scottish, PUC) 1960 I, E, SA, 1961 F, SA, W, I, E, 1963 F, W, I, E, 1964 F, NZ, W

Thomson, W H (W of Scotland) 1906 SA

Thomson, W J (W of Scotland) 1899 W, E, 1900 W

Timms, A B (Edinburgh U, Edinburgh Wands) 1896 W, 1900 W, I, 1901 W, I, E, 1902 W, E, 1903 W, E, 1904 I, E, 1905 I, E

Tod, H B (Gala) 1911 F

Tod, J (Watsonians) 1884 W, I, E, 1885 W, I 1,2, 1886 W, I, E

Todd, J K (Glasgow Acads) 1874 E, 1875 E

Tolmie, J M (Glasgow HSFP) 1922 E

Tomes, A J (Hawick) 1976 E, I, 1977 E, 1978 I, F, W, E, NZ, 1979 W, E, I, F, NZ, 1980 F, W, E, 1981 F, W, E, I, NZ 1,2, R, A, 1982 E, I, F, W, A 1,2, 1983 I, F, W, 1984 W, E, I, F, R, A, 1985 W, E, 1987 I, F, E (R), [F, Z, R, NZ]

Torrie, T J (Edinburgh Acads) 1877 E

Townsend, G P J (Gala, Northampton, Brive, Castres, Borders) 1993 E (R), 1994 W, E, I, F, Arg 1,2, 1995 C, I, F, W, E, WS, 1996 I, F, W, E, NZ 1,2, A, It, 1997 W, E, I, F, A, SA, 1998 It, I, F, W, E, Fj, A 1,2, SA (R), 1999 W, E, It, I, F, [SA, U, Sp (R), Sm, NZ], 2000 It, I, F, W, E, NZ 1,2, US, A, Sm, 2001 F, It, I,

Arg, NZ, 2002 E, It, I, F, W, R(R), SA(R), Fj, 2003 I 1(R), F, W 1, E, It 1, SA 1,2, W 2, [J(R),US,F,Fj,A]
Tukalo, I (Selkirk) 1985 I, 1987 I, F, W, E, [F, Z, R, NZ], 1988 F, W, E, A, 1989 W, E, I, F, Fj, 1990 I, F, W, E, NZ 1, 1991 I, R, [J, Z, I, WS, E, NZ], 1992 E, I, F, W, A 1,2
Turk, A S (Langholm) 1971 E (R)
Turnbull, D J (Hawick) 1987 [NZ], 1988 F, E, 1990 E (R), 1991 F, W, E, I, R, [Z], 1993 I, F, W, E, 1994 W
Turnbull, F O (Kelso) 1951 F, SA
Turnbull, G O (W of Scotland) 1896 I, E, 1897 I, E, 1904 W
Turnbull, P (Edinburgh Acads) 1901 W, I, E, 1902 W, I, E
Turner, F H (Oxford U, Liverpool) 1911 F, W, I, E, 1912 F, W, I, E, SA, 1913 F, W, I, E, 1914 I, E
Turner, J W C (Gala) 1966 W, A, 1967 F, W, I, E, NZ, 1968 F, W, I, E, A, 1969 F, 1970 E, A, 1971 F, W, I, E (2[1C])

Usher, C M (United Services, Edinburgh Wands) 1912 E, 1913 F, W, I, E, 1914 E, 1920 F, W, I, E, 1921 W, E, 1922 F, W, I, E
Utterson, K N (Borders) 2003 F, W 1, E(R)

Valentine, A R (RNAS, Anthorn) 1953 F, W, I
Valentine, D D (Hawick) 1947 I, E
Veitch, J P (Royal HSFP) 1882 E, 1883 I, 1884 W, I, E, 1885 I 1,2, 1886 E
Villar, C (Edinburgh Wands) 1876 E, 1877 I, E

Waddell, G H (London Scottish, Cambridge U) 1957 E, 1958 F, W, A, I, E, 1959 F, W, I, E, 1960 I, E, SA, 1961 F, 1962 F, W, I, E
Waddell, H (Glasgow Acads) 1924 F, W, I, E, 1925 I, E, 1926 F, W, I, E, 1927 F, W, I, E, 1930 W
Wade, A L (London Scottish) 1908 E
Wainwright, R I (Edinburgh Acads, West Hartlepool, Watsonians, Army, Dundee HSFP) 1992 I (R), F, A 1,2, 1993 NZ, 1994 W, E, 1995 C, I, F, W, E, R, [Iv, Tg, F, NZ], WS, 1996 I, F, W, E, NZ 1,2, 1997 W, E, I, F, SA, 1998 It, I, F, W, E, Fj, A 1,2
Walker, A (W of Scotland) 1881 I, 1882 E, 1883 W, I, E
Walker, A W (Cambridge U, Birkenhead Park) 1931 F, W, I, E, 1932 I
Walker, J G (W of Scotland) 1882 E, 1883 W
Walker, M (Oxford U) 1952 F
Walker, N (Borders) 2002 R, SA, Fj
Wallace, A C (Oxford U) 1923 F, 1924 F, W, E, 1925 F, W, I, E, 1926 F
Wallace, W M (Cambridge U) 1913 E, 1914 W, I, E
Wallace, M I (Glasgow High Kelvinside) 1996 A, It, 1997 W
Walls, W A (Glasgow Acads) 1882 E, 1883 W, I, E, 1884 W, I, E, 1886 W, I, E
Walter, M W (London Scottish) 1906 I, E, SA, 1907 W, I, 1908 W, I, 1910 I
Walton, P (Northampton, Newcastle) 1994 E, I, F, Arg 1,2, 1995 [Iv], 1997 W, E, I, F, SA (R), 1998 I, F, SA, 1999 W, E, It, I, F (R), Arg, R, [SA (R), U (R), Sp]
Warren, J R (Glasgow Acads) 1914 I
Warren, R C (Glasgow Acads) 1922 W, I, 1930 W, I, E
Waters, F H (Cambridge U, London Scottish) 1930 F, W, I, E, 1932 SA, W, I
Waters, J A (Selkirk) 1933 W, E, I, 1934 W, I, E, 1935 W, I, E, NZ, 1936 W, I, E, 1937 W, I, E
Waters, J B (Cambridge U) 1904 I, E
Watherston, J G (Edinburgh Wands) 1934 I, E
Watherston, W R A (London Scottish) 1963 F, W, I
Watson, D H (Glasgow Acads) 1876 E, 1877 I, E
Watson, W S (Boroughmuir) 1974 W, E, I, F, 1975 NZ, 1977 I, F, W, 1979 I, F
Watt, A G J (Glasgow High Kelvinside) 1991 [Z], 1993 I, NZ, 1994 Arg 2(t & R)
Watt, A G M (Edinburgh Acads) 1947 F, W, I, A, 1948 F, W
Weatherstone, T G (Stewart's Coll FP) 1952 E, 1953 I, E, 1954 F, NZ, I, E, W, 1955 F, 1958 W, A, I, E, 1959 W, I, E
Webster, S (Edinburgh) 2003 I 2(R), 2004 W(R),E,It,F,I,Sm,A1,2, 2005 It,NZ(R), 2006 F(R), W(R),I(R),It(R),SA 1(R),2
Weir, G W (Melrose, Newcastle) 1990 Arg, 1991 R, [J, Z, I, WS, E, NZ], 1992 E, I, F, W, A 1,2, 1993 I, F, W, E, NZ, 1994 W (R), E, I, F, SA, 1995 F (R), W, E, R, [Iv, Tg, F, NZ], WS, 1996 I, F, W, E, NZ 1,2, A, It (R), 1997 W, E, I, F, 1998 It, I, F, W, E, SA, 1999 W, Arg (R), R (R), [SA (R), Sp, Sm, NZ], 2000 It (R), I (R), F
Welsh, R (Watsonians) 1895 W, I, E, 1896 W
Welsh, R B (Hawick) 1967 I, E
Welsh, W B (Hawick) 1927 A, 1928 F, W, I, 1929 I, E, 1930 F, W, I, E, 1931 F, W, I, E, 1932 SA, W, I, E, 1933 W, E, I
Welsh, W H (Edinburgh U) 1900 I, E, 1901 W, I, E, 1902 W, I, E
Wemyss, A (Gala, Edinburgh Wands) 1914 W, I, 1920 F, E, 1922 F, W, I
West, L (Edinburgh U, West Hartlepool) 1903 W, I, E, 1905 I, E, NZ, 1906 W, I, E
Weston, V G (Kelvinside Acads) 1936 I, E
White, D B (Gala, London Scottish) 1982 F, W, A 1,2, 1987 W, E, [F, R, NZ], 1988 I, F, W, E, A, 1989 W, E, I, F, Fj, R, 1990 I, F, W, E, NZ 1,2, 1991 F, W, E, I, R, [J, Z, I, WS, E, NZ], 1992 E, I, F, W
White, D M (Kelvinside Acads) 1963 F, W, I, E
White, J P R (Glasgow, Sale) 2000 E, NZ 1,2, US (R), A (R), Sm, 2001 F (R), I, Tg, Arg, NZ, 2002 E, It, I, F, W, C, US, SA(R), Fj, 2003 F(R), W 1, E, It 1, SA 1,2, It 2, [J, US(R), F, Fj(R), A], 2004 W(R), E, It, F, I, Sm, A1, 2, J(R), A4(R), SA, 2005 F, I, E, Arg, Sm, NZ, 2006 F, W, E, I, It, SA 1,2
White, T B (Edinburgh Acads) 1888 W, I, 1889 W
Whittington, T P (Merchistonians) 1873 E
Whitworth, R J E (London Scottish) 1936 I
Whyte, D J (Edinburgh Wands) 1965 W, I, E, SA, 1966 F, W, I, E, A, 1967 F, W, I, E
Will, J G (Cambridge U) 1912 F, W, I, E, 1914 W, I, E
Wilson, A W (Dunfermline) 1931 F, I, E
Wilson, A W (Glasgow) 2005 R(R)
Wilson, G A (Oxford U) 1949 F, W, E
Wilson, G R (Royal HSFP) 1886 E, 1890 W, I, E, 1891 I
Wilson, J H (Watsonians) 1953 I
Wilson, J S (St Andrew's U) 1931 F, W, I, E, 1932 E
Wilson, J S (United Services, London Scottish) 1908 I, 1909 W
Wilson, R (London Scottish) 1976 E, I, 1977 E, I, F, 1978 I, F, 1981 R, 1983 I
Wilson, R L (Gala) 1951 F, W, I, E, SA, 1953 F, W, E
Wilson, R W (W of Scotland) 1873 E, 1874 E
Wilson, S (Oxford U, London Scottish) 1964 F, NZ, W, I, E, 1965 W, I, E, SA, 1966 F, W, I, A, 1967 F, W, I, E, NZ, 1968 F, W, I, E
Wood, A (Royal HSFP) 1873 E, 1874 E, 1875 E
Wood, G (Gala) 1931 W, I, 1932 W, I, E
Woodburn, J C (Kelvinside Acads) 1892 I
Woodrow, A N (Glasgow Acads) 1887 I, W, E
Wotherspoon, W (W of Scotland) 1891 I, 1892 I, 1893 W, E, 1894 W, I, E
Wright, F A (Edinburgh Acads) 1932 E
Wright, H B (Watsonians) 1894 W
Wright, K M (London Scottish) 1929 F, W, I, E
Wright, P H (Boroughmuir) 1992 A 1,2, 1993 F, W, E, 1994 W, 1995 C, I, F, W, E, R, [Iv, Tg, F, NZ], 1996 W, E, NZ 1
Wright, R W J (Edinburgh Wands) 1973 F
Wright, S T H (Stewart's Coll FP) 1949 E
Wright, T (Hawick) 1947 A
Wyllie, D S (Stewart's-Melville FP) 1984 A, 1985 W (R), E, 1987 I, F, [F, Z, R, NZ], 1989 R, 1991 R, [J (R), Z], 1993 NZ (R), 1994 W (R), E, I, F

Young, A H (Edinburgh Acads) 1874 E
Young, E T (Glasgow Acads) 1914 E
Young, R G (Watsonians) 1970 W
Young, T E B (Durham) 1911 F
Young, W B (Cambridge U, London Scottish) 1937 W, I, E, 1938 W, I, E, 1939 W, I, E, 1948 E

SCOTLAND: DOMESTIC RUGBY

HAWKS SOAR TO ANOTHER TROPHY

Glasgow Hawks became only the third side in the history of Scottish rugby to complete a hat-trick of league titles when they claimed the BT Premiership One crown for the third successive year.

The Hawks wrapped up the title in February and finished 10 points clear of nearest challengers Watsonians to emulate the achievements of Hawick in the 1970s and 1980s and Melrose in the early 1990s in winning the league three years in succession.

Under new coach David Wilson, Glasgow lost just three times during another dominant campaign in which they were never in any real danger of being toppled as champions and averaged nearly 30 points a game.

Wilson, who left relegated GHA in the summer, was brought in to replace Peter Wright, the new Scotland Under-19 coach but if Glasgow's Premiership rivals hoped a change in management would unsettle the Hawks on the pitch, they were to be disappointed.

"Of course I was under pressure following in the footsteps of Peter," Wilson said after his side beat Boroughmuir to confirm them as champions once again.

"But I am a firm believer in the fact that I am only as good as the players I have got and the players must take the credit for leading the way in the championship. They are a very special group."

The destiny of the title was in little doubt after the first month of the campaign. The Hawks began with a 47–17 victory at Melrose to spell out their title intentions and were relatively untroubled in their first home game of the season, beating Stewart's Melville FP 20–7 to go top of the table.

Their first real test of the campaign came on the third weekend with a visit to Edinburgh to face Watsonians. It proved to be a season-defining, nine-try thriller which Glasgow almost contrived to lose but clung on to win.

Leading 21–7 at Myreside at half-time, the Hawks seemed to be cruising to victory but Watsonians battled back after the break and when wing James Easton scored in the 72nd minute to give the home side the lead for the first time, it seemed they had thrown away the points. But with just seconds remaining substitute lock Steve Begley crashed over and Glasgow had conjured up an unlikely 28–25 win.

"To lead 21–7 at half-time and then take our foot off the pedal in the second half is just unacceptable," Wilson said after his side's great escape. "I thought the forwards in the first half were immense but we started to struggle in the second half and there's plenty to work on."

The work, however, paid off and the Hawks embarked on a 10–match unbeaten run that stretched into December. It was only ended when Watsonians were the visitors to Anniesland looking for revenge for September's dramatic reverse. And this time it was Watsonians who produced the late inspirational intervention when centre Bryan Rennie scored in injury-time to give the visitors a 17–12 victory. Glasgow had suffered their first defeat of the campaign and their lead at the top of the table was cut to eight points.

"Hawks are still an outstandingly fine team," said Watsonians player-coach Cammy Mather after his side's win. "They may well win the league at a canter, but it's been good to show they are not invincible."

A narrow 8–6 win at Ayr the following week got the Hawks back to winning ways and although a second defeat at Heriots in early January followed, Glasgow still had their own destiny in their hands. A surprise 17–17 draw at Aberdeen GSFP in February meant the celebratory champagne had to be kept on ice for a little longer but the title-winning party finally got into full swing later in the month when Glasgow beat Boroughmuir 24–19 at Meggetland.

Tries from props Peter Dalton and Gavin Mories and centres Stewart Smith and Ricky Munday were enough to steer Glasgow to victory and the Hawks were Premiership champions once again.

"To win three championships in an area of Scotland which is renowned for its football is particularly special," said a delighted Wilson. "I'm thankful to Brian Simmers and John Roxburgh for giving me the opportunity to work with such a special set of players. Hopefully we can build on this for next season, but meanwhile we'll enjoy the night."

Glasgow, however, were denied a famous league and cup double and it was Watsonians who made up for their Premiership disappointment with a 31–15 win over Currie in the final at Murrayfield in April.

Currie put Glasgow out 25–14 in the second round en route to the final but it was Watsonians who emerged victorious to win the club's first BT Cup final and help erase memories of losing final appearances in both 1996 and 2003.

The Edinburgh side were in control throughout the match and led 19–0 at the break with tries from scrum-half Jamie Blackwood, playing his last game for the club, skipper Alan Nash and centre Bryan Rennie.

Currie fought back after the break and capitalised on the sin binning of Watsonians prop Paul Tait to narrow the gap but they were never within striking distance of their opponents. Further scores from man-of-the-match

Blackwood and a second from Rennie re-established the gap between the two sides and it was Watsonians who were celebrating at the final whistle.

"Today has brought a fantastic season to the perfect end," said cpatain Nash after he collected the cup. "With Cammy [Mather] coming on board and changing things there's a never give up feeling with Watsonians at the moment.

"To come out on top today was a fantastic performance. Everyone came out of their shell and it was a privilege and honour to be on the pitch with them."

BT PREMIERSHIP ONE

FINAL LEAGUE TABLE

	P	W	D	L	F	A	BP	Pts
Glasgow Hawks	22	18	1	3	643	349	16	90
Watsonians	22	17	1	4	535	381	10	80
Aberdeen GSFP	22	12	1	9	554	466	15	65
Currie	22	9	1	12	495	418	15	53
Hawick	22	12	0	10	388	429	5	53
Melrose	22	11	0	11	487	535	9	53
Ayr	22	10	1	11	403	400	9	51
Heriots	22	9	0	13	549	570	15	51
Boroughmuir	22	9	1	12	505	541	12	50
Stewart's Melville FP	22	11	0	11	422	545	4	48
Biggar	22	7	0	15	423	584	7	35
Stirling County	22	4	0	18	384	570	9	25

BT PREMIERSHIP TWO WINNERS

Dundee HSFP

BT PREMIERSHIP THREE WINNERS

Hamilton

BT DIVISION ONE

Perthshire

BT DIVISION TWO

Morgan Academy FP

BT DIVISION THREE

Falkirk

BT DIVISION FOUR

Dumfries

BT DIVISION FIVE (EAST)

Hawick Linden

BT DIVISION FIVE (WEST) A

Marr

BT DIVISION FIVE (WEST) B

Uddingston

BT DIVISION FIVE (CALEDONIA) A

Strathmore

BT DIVISION FIVE (CALEDONIA) AA

Mackie Academy FP

BT DIVISION FIVE (CALEDONIA) B

Panmure

BT CUP FINAL

29 April, Murrayfield, Edinburgh

CURRIE 15 (1G, 1PG, 1T)
WATSONIANS 31 (3G, 2T)

CURRIE: D Flockhart; G Caldwell, B Cairns, D Officer, C Browne; D Raw, G Calder; A Reekie, G Scott, A Edwards, P Huntly, C Black, B Miller, R Weston, M Cairns (captain) Substitutions: R Snedden for Calder (36 mins); K McShane for Browne (66 mins); A Muir for B Cairns (79 mins); S Burnett for M Cairns (81 mins); B Morrison for Scott (82 mins)

SCORERS TRIES: Cairns, McShane Conversion: Raw Penalty Goal: Raw

WATSONIANS: A Nash (captain); A Turnbull, B Rennie, B Hennessey, C McWilliam; J Easton, J Blackwood; K Koertz, S Lawrie, P Tait, I Dryburgh, D Payne, G Brown, I Sinclair, G Hills Substitutions: S Stevenson for Hills (48 mins); J Thrush for Payne (63 mins); W Campbell for McWilliam (79 mins)

SCORERS TRIES: McWilliam (2), Easton, Blackwood, Renney Conversions: Hennessy (3)

YELLOW CARD Tait (46 mins)

REFEREE M Changleng (Gala)

SOUTH AFRICA

SOUTH AFRICA'S TEST RECORD

OPPONENTS	DATE	VENUE	RESULT
Scotland	10 June	H	**Won** 36-16
Scotland	17 June	H	**Won** 29-15
France	24 June	H	**Lost** 26-36
Australia	15 July	A	**Lost** 0-49
New Zealand	22 July	A	**Lost** 17-35
Australia	5 August	A	**Lost** 18-20
New Zealand	26 August	H	**Lost** 26-45
New Zealand	2 Sept	H	**Won** 21-20
Australia	9 Sept	H	**Won** 24-16

LIGHT AT THE END OF THE TUNNEL

By Francois Pienaar

I **think like most** Springbok fans, I'd have to describe 2006 as a difficult period for the team. There were one or two real low points, not least the 49–0 Tri-Nations defeat to Australia in Brisbane, and one massive high for Jake White's side when they beat the All Blacks in

Rustenburg but overall I think the team probably fell a bit short of what they would have been hoping to achieve.

If you look briefly beyond the 'warm-up' games against Scotland and France in June and forward to the Tri-Nations, it came down to whether the Springboks could recapture the Tri-Nations title and whatever positives and negatives White can take from the tournament, the fact is South Africa did not win the competition.

Success in the Tri-Nations is always the real measure of any Springboks team and they weren't able to do the business. It would have taken a monumental effort for any side to have denied New Zealand the title but event though the Springboks produced that one great result in Rustenburg thanks to a late penalty from Andre Pretorius, they never looked like potential champions.

It wasn't a disastrous campaign but it also wasn't one in which they seemed capable of mounting a serious challenge.

But before the Tri-Nations, it was Scotland and then France.

The two-Test series against Scotland was one of stark opposites for both teams. The Springboks had been out of action for six months while Scotland were at the end of another long, hard season and all of what was an under-strength squad must had thoughts of a well-deserved holiday when the tour was over.

Jake White was looking to fine tune for the Tri-Nations. Of course, the results and the performance were important but you really couldn't get two sides at more contrasting stages of their seasons.

South Africa won the first Test 36–16 in Durban and the second in Port Elizabeth 29–15 but I'd have to say the coach Frank Hadden and the Scotland fans probably went away from both matches the happier. Scotland wanted to blood new players without getting played off the park and that's exactly what they achieved.

Yes, it was two wins for the Springboks but the team played OK at best and even though they knew there were bigger challenges to come, they must also have known the two performances could have been better. Most Test teams start their seasons with a little ring rustiness and South Africa definitely looked like a side that hadn't played together for a few months.

France arrived with a lot of new faces in their squad but were full of confidence after regaining the Six Nations title and even with some inexperienced players in their ranks, they looked to me like a powerful outfit.

In the end they were too strong for South Africa and the 36–26 scoreline in favour of France at Newlands proved a reminder of the work White and his coaching team had in front of them. France accepted the

Getty Images

Springboks coach Jake White had to lead his side back from a record-breaking 49–0 defeat in Australia.

physical challenge up front and showed a bit more ambition and ability out wide. They will definitely be hard to beat at home in the World Cup next year.

The Tri-Nations began in July in Brisbane with the 49–0 mauling by the Wallabies, which left everyone in South Africa stunned. Australia were exceptional, but it was a massive blow for White and the team and a terrible way to start the tournament. I'm sure they felt they'd let themselves down badly and it meant they began the competition on a huge downward spiral. To their credit, they were to finish the campaign much stronger than the way they began it, but it was impossible to gloss over such a heavy defeat.

If you have aspirations to be a great side you simply cannot afford to lose like that. There were just no excuses.

The next two games for Springboks were also on the road – the All Blacks in Wellington and a rematch with the Wallabies in Sydney. Both games were considerably closer than the Brisbane debacle, but both still ended in Springbok defeats. Three games in and no wins.

A lot of people have argued South Africa have a mental block, a psychological problem with playing away from home, but I don't agree. It's true they have won just once outside South Africa in both the 2005 and 2006 Tri-Nations, but in my mind that is a reflection on how tough it is to beat good teams in their own country rather than a reflection on some supposed Springbok weakness. The All Blacks have shown the rest

Getty Images

John Smit's leadership helped South Africa to bounce back in the Tri-Nations with wins over New Zealand and Australia.

how to win on the road in recent years and it's been that knack more than anything else that has made them the number one team in the world.

The second half of the Tri-Nations was definitely more encouraging. Three successive home games were always going to provide an opportunity to get a couple of good results and build confidence and that was ultimately what happened.

I was at the first match at Loftus Versfeld for the New Zealand game and although it was a 45–26 win for the Blacks, there were signs that the team was turning the corner. There was more conviction and ambition in their play and I was confident they would get a first win under their belt before the end of the tournament.

It came in the next game – the 21–20 win over the Blacks at Rustenburg and the whole country breathed a sigh of relief. It may have been a dead rubber for New Zealand, but I'm sure White and his team didn't care. It was a performance full of courage and guts and just what everyone had been waiting for.

The final game against the Australians at Ellis Park was another dead rubber, but again no-one cared as South Africa ran out 24–16 winners. The Springboks had picked themselves up after a dreadful start to the tournament and proved they could play.

But as I said at the start, I'm sure Jake White will have been disappointed with the way the year went. He's two years into the job – and he should definitely be given the chance to take the team to the World

Cup – but I know he has high aspirations and the performances didn't live up to them.

But that is not to say there were not positives and I think he came away with answers to some of his selection dilemmas.

At full-back, there was debate about whether South Africa should experiment with some other players. White started with Percy Montgomery in the first four Tri-Nations games, but gave both Ruan Pienaar and Jaque Fourie some game time. I'm sure Montgomery has an important role to play in future squads, but it was a good move on White's part to have a look at his other options.

At fly-half White used three different players – Jaco van der Westhuyzen, Butch James and Andre Pretorius – and it was Pretorius who stepped up to he plate and made a big difference in the last two Tri-Nations games after his return from injury. The question is, can he now produce that level of performance over the next three, four or five games?

The injured Schalk Burger was a big loss in the back row, but my main concern would be White still does not know who should be playing eight. It's a pivotal position in terms of distribution and linking the forwards and backs, but the place in my opinion is still up for grabs.

At lock Victor Matfield had a good tournament and again proved himself an athletic lineout jumper, who secured plenty of ball. He had three different partners in the second row during the Tri-Nations – Danie Rossouw, Albert van den Berg and Johann Muller – but Matfield was a big plus for me.

Some questioned John Smit's captaincy, this has always been a South African past time. I believe he should definitely lead the side into the World Cup. He enjoyed some successes and I think he's the type of player and man who will have learnt a great deal from the defeats as well. He's still relatively inexperienced in terms of international captaincy and I think those who have suggested a change of leadership are being short-sighted.

Not all the questions were answered, but White did increase his selection options and appears to have the confidence of his players, which is crucial. He's still building, but there were definite signs of genuine progress after a difficult start to the year.

SOUTH AFRICA INTERNATIONAL STATISTICS

(UP TO 30TH SEPTEMBER 2006)

MATCH RECORDS

MOST CONSECUTIVE TEST WINS

17	1997	A2, It, F 1, 2, E, S,	1998	I 1, 2,W 1, E 1, A 1, NZ 1, 2, A 2 W 2, S, I 3
15	1994	Arg 1, 2, S, W	1995	WS, A, R, C, WS F, NZ, W, It, E, 1996 Fj

MOST CONSECUTIVE TEST WITHOUT DEFEAT

Matches	Wins	Draws	Periods
17	17	0	1997 to 1998
16	15	1	1994 to 1996
15	12	3	1960 to 1963

MOST POINTS IN A MATCH

BY THE TEAM

Pts.	Opponent	Venue	Year
134	Uruguay	E London	2005
101	Italy	Durban	1999
96	Wales	Pretoria	1998
74	Tonga	Cape Town	1997
74	Italy	Port Elizabeth	1999
72	Uruguay	Perth	2003
68	Scotland	Murrayfield	1997
62	Italy	Bologna	1997
61	Australia	Pretoria	1997

BY A PLAYER

Pts.	Player	Opponent	Venue	Year
34	J H de Beer	England	Paris	1999
31	P C Montgomery	Wales	Pretoria	1998
30	T Chavhanga	Uruguay	E London	2005
29	G S du Toit	Italy	Port Elizabeth	1999
28	G K Johnson	W Samoa	Johannesburg	1995
26	J H de Beer	Australia	Pretoria	1997
26	P C Montgomery	Scotland	Murrayfield	1997
25	J T Stransky	Australia	Bloemfontein	1996
25	C S Terblanche	Italy	Durban	1999

MOST TRIES IN A MATCH

BY THE TEAM

Tries	Opponent	Venue	Year
21	Uruguay	E London	2005
15	Wales	Pretoria	1998
15	Italy	Durban	1999
12	Tonga	Cape Town	1997
12	Uruguay	Perth	2003
11	Italy	Port Elizabeth	1999
10	Ireland	Dublin	1912
10	Scotland	Murrayfield	1997

BY A PLAYER

Tries	Player	Opponent	Venue	Year
6	T Chavhanga	Uruguay	E London	2005
5	C S Terblanche	Italy	Durban	1999
4	C M Williams	W Samoa	Johannesburg	1995
4	P W G Rossouw	France	Parc des Princes	1997
4	C S Terblanche	Ireland	Bloemfontein	1998

MOST CONVERSIONS IN A MATCH

BY THE TEAM

Cons	Opponent	Venue	Year
13	Italy	Durban	1999
13	Uruguay	E London	2005
9	Scotland	Murrayfield	1997
9	Wales	Pretoria	1998
8	Italy	Port Elizabeth	1999
7	Scotland	Murrayfield	1951
7	Tonga	Cape Town	1997
7	Italy	Bologna	1997
7	France	Parc des Princes	1997
7	Italy	Genoa	2001
7	Samoa	Pretoria	2002
7	Samoa	Brisbane	2003

BY A PLAYER

Cons	Player	Opponent	Venue	Year
9	P C Montgomery	Wales	Pretoria	1998
8	P C Montgomery	Scotland	Murrayfield	1997
8	G S du Toit	Italy	Port Elizabeth	1999
8	G S du Toit	Italy	Durban	1999
7	A O Geffin	Scotland	Murrayfield	1951
7	J M F Lubbe	Tonga	Cape Town	1997
7	H W Honiball	Italy	Bologna	1997
7	H W Honiball	France	Parc des Princes	1997
7	A S Pretorius	Samoa	Pretoria	2002
7	J N B van der Westhuyzen	Uruguay	E London	2005

MOST PENALTIES IN A MATCH

BY THE TEAM

Pens	Opponent	Venue	Year
8	Scotland	Port Elizabeth	2006
7	France	Pretoria	1975
7	France	Cape Town	2006
6	Australia	Bloemfontein	1996
6	Australia	Twickenham	1999
6	England	Pretoria	2000
6	Australia	Durban	2000
6	France	Johannesburg	2001
6	Scotland	Johannesburg	2003

BY A PLAYER

Pens	Player	Opponent	Venue	Year
7	P C Montgomery	Scotland	Port Elizabeth	2006
7	P C Montgomery	France	Cape Town	2006
6	G R Bosch	France	Pretoria	1975
6	J T Stransky	Australia	Bloemfontein	1996
6	J H de Beer	Australia	Twickenham	1999
6	A J J van Straaten	England	Pretoria	2000
6	A J J van Straaten	Australia	Durban	2000
6	P C Montgomery	France	Johannesburg	2001
6	L J Koen	Scotland	Johannesburg	2003

MOST DROPPED GOALS IN A MATCH

BY THE TEAM

Drops	Opponent	Venue	Year
5	England	Paris	1999
3	S America	Durban	1980
3	Ireland	Durban	1981
3	Scotland	Murrayfield	2004

BY A PLAYER

Drops	Player	Opponent	Venue	Year
5	J H de Beer	England	Paris	1999
3	H E Botha	S America	Durban	1980
3	H E Botha	Ireland	Durban	1981
3	J N B van der Westhuyzen	Scotland	Murrayfield	2004
2	B L Osler	N Zealand	Durban	1928
2	H E Botha	NZ Cavaliers	Cape Town	1986
2	J T Stransky	N Zealand	Johannesburg	1995
2	J H de Beer	N Zealand	Johannesburg	1997
2	P C Montgomery	N Zealand	Cardiff	1999

MOST CAPPED PLAYERS

Caps	Player	Career Span
89	J H van der Westhuizen	1993 to 2003
80	P C Montgomery	1997 to 2006
77	M G Andrews	1994 to 2001
70	J P du Randt	1994 to 2006
66	A G Venter	1996 to 2001
62	B J Paulse	1999 to 2006
60	J W Smit	2000 to 2006
54	A-H le Roux	1994 to 2002
54	V Matfield	2001 to 2006
47	J T Small	1992 to 1997
46	J C van Niekerk	2001 to 2006
43	J Dalton	1994 to 2002
43	P W G Rossouw	1997 to 2003
42	G H Teichmann	1995 to 1999
40	P A van den Berg	1999 to 2006
39	D W Barry	2000 to 2006
39	C P J Krige	1999 to 2003
38	F C H du Preez	1961 to 1971
38	J H Ellis	1965 to 1976
38	K Otto	1995 to 2000
38	A H Snyman	1996 to 2006

MOST CONSECUTIVE TESTS

Tests	Player	Career span
39	G H Teichmann	1996 to 1999
39	J W Smit	2003 to 2006
26	A H Snyman	1996 to 1998
26	A N Vos	1999 to 2001
25	S H Nomis	1967 to 1972
25	A G Venter	1997 to 1999
25	A-H le Roux	1998 to 1999

MOST TESTS AS CAPTAIN

Tests	Player	Career span
36	G H Teichmann	1996 to 1999
35	J W Smit	2003 to 2006
29	J F Pienaar	1993 to 1996
22	D J de Villiers	1965 to 1970
18	C P J Krigé	1999 to 2003
16	A N Vos	1999 to 2001
15	M du Plessis	1975 to 1980
11	J F K Marais	1971 to 1974

MOST POINTS IN TESTS

Pts	Player	Tests	Career
654	P C Montgomery	80	1997 to 2006
312	H E Botha	28	1980 to 1992
240	J T Stransky	22	1993 to 1996
221	A J J van Straaten	21	1999 to 2001
190	J H van der Westhuizen	89	1993 to 2003
181	J H de Beer	13	1997 to 1999
156	H W Honiball	35	1993 to 1999
145	L J Koen	15	2000 to 2003
138	A S Pretorius	21	2002 to 2006
130	P J Visagie	25	1967 to 1971
130	B J Paulse	62	1999 to 2006

MOST TRIES IN TESTS

Tries	Player	Tests	Career
38	J H van der Westhuizen	89	1993 to 2003
26*	B J Paulse	62	1999 to 2006
21	P W G Rossouw	43	1997 to 2003
20	J T Small	47	1992 to 1997
19	D M Gerber	24	1980 to 1992
19	C S Terblanche	37	1998 to 2003
19	P C Montgomery	80	1997 to 2006
16	B G Habana	22	2004 to 2006
14	C M Williams	27	1993 to 2000

* includes a penalty try

MOST CONVERSIONS IN TESTS

Cons	Player	Tests	Career
98	P C Montgomery	80	1997 to 2006
50	H E Botha	28	1980 to 1992
38	H W Honiball	35	1993 to 1999
33	J H de Beer	13	1997 to 1999
30	J T Stransky	22	1993 to 1996
25	G S du Toit	14	1998 to 2006
25	A S Pretorius	21	2002 to 2006
23	A J J van Straaten	21	1999 to 2001
23	L J Koen	15	2000 to 2003
20	P J Visagie	25	1967 to 1971

MOST PENALTY GOALS IN TESTS

Pens	Player	Tests	Career
115	P C Montgomery	80	1997 to 2006
55	A J J van Straaten	21	1999 to 2001
50	H E Botha	28	1980 to 1992
47	J T Stransky	22	1993 to 1996
31	L J Koen	15	2000 to 2003
27	J H de Beer	13	1997 to 1999
25	H W Honiball	35	1993 to 1999
23	G R Bosch	9	1974 to 1976
22	A S Pretorius	21	2002 to 2006
19	P J Visagie	25	1967 to 1971

MOST DROPPED GOALS IN TESTS

DGs	Player	Tests	Career
18	H E Botha	28	1980 to 1992
8	J H de Beer	13	1997 to 1999
6	P C Montgomery	80	1997 to 2006
5	J D Brewis	10	1949 to 1953
5	P J Visagie	25	1967 to 1971
4	B L Osler	17	1924 to 1933
4	A S Pretorius	21	2002 to 2006

TRI NATIONS RECORDS

RECORD	DETAIL		SET
Most points in season	148	in four matches	1997
Most tries in season	18	in four matches	1997
Highest Score	61	61-22 v Australia (h)	1997
Biggest win	39	61-22 v Australia (h)	1997
Highest score conceded	55	35-55 v N Zealand (a)	1997
Biggest defeat	49	0-49 v Australia (a)	2006
Most points in matches	176	P C Montgomery	1997 to 2006
Most points in season	64	J H de Beer	1997
Most points in match	26	J H de Beer	v Australia (h),1997
Most tries in matches	6	M C Joubert	2001 to 2004
Most tries in season	3	P C Montgomery	1997
	3	M C Joubert	2002
	3	M C Joubert	2004
	3	J de Villiers	2004
	3	B G Habana	2005
	3	J Fourie	2006
	3	P F du Preez	2006
Most tries in match	3	M C Joubert	v New Zealand (h) 2004
Most cons in matches	21	P C Montgomery	1997 to 2006
Most cons in season	12	J H de Beer	1997
Most cons in match	6	J H de Beer	v Australia (h),1997
Most pens in matches	35	P C Montgomery	1997 to 2006
Most pens in season	13	A J J van Straaten	2000
	13	A J J van Straaten	2001
Most pens in match	6	J T Stransky	v Australia (h),1996
	6	A J J van Straaten	v Australia (h),2000

MISCELLANEOUS RECORDS

RECORD	HOLDER	DETAIL
Longest Test Career	J M Powell/B H Heatlie/ D M Gerber/H E Botha	1891-1903/1891-1903/ 1980-1992/1980-1992
Youngest Test Cap	A J Hartley	18 yrs 18 days in 1891
Oldest Test Cap	W H Morkel	36 yrs 258 days in 1921

CAREER RECORDS OF SOUTH AFRICA INTERNATIONAL PLAYERS (PLAYERS CAPPED SINCE THE START OF RWC 2003 UP TO 30 SEPTEMBER 2006)

PLAYER BACKS	DEBUT	CAPS	T	C	P	D	PTS
D W Barry	2000 v C	39	3	0	0	0	15
G Bobo	2003 v S	5	0	0	0	0	0
H M Bosman	2005 v W	3	0	2	1	0	7
T Chavhanga	2005 v U	1	6	0	0	0	30
M Claassens	2004 v W	6	0	0	0	0	0
J H Conradie	2002 v W	15	2	0	0	1	13
G M Delport	2000 v C	18	3	0	0	0	15
N A de Kock	2001 v It	10	2	0	0	0	10
J de Villiers	2002 v F	24	11	0	0	0	55
P F du Preez	2004 v I	30	6	0	0	0	30
G S du Toit	1998 v I	14	5	25	11	0	108
J Fourie	2003 v U	26	13	0	0	0	65
W W Greeff	2002 v Arg	11	4	4	0	1	31
B G Habana	2004 v E	22	16	0	0	0	80
D J Hougaard	2003 v U	5	2	10	5	1	48
A D James	2001 v F	13	0	1	10	0	32
C A Jantjes	2001 v It	10	3	1	0	0	17
E R Januarie	2005 v U	12	2	0	0	0	10
M C Joubert	2001 v NZ	30	9	0	0	0	45
W Julies	1999 v Sp	9	2	0	0	0	10
L J Koen	2000 v A	15	0	23	31	2	145
R I P Loubscher	2002 v W	4	0	0	0	0	0
H Mentz	2004 v I	2	0	0	0	0	0
P C Montgomery	1997 v BI	80	19	98	115	6	654
G P Müller	2003 v A	6	1	0	0	0	5
A Z Ndungane	2006 v A	5	0	0	0	0	0
W Olivier	2006 v S	9	0	0	0	0	0
B J Paulse	1999 v It	62	26*	0	0	0	130
R Pienaar	2006 v NZ	3	0	0	0	0	0
J-P R Pietersen	2006 v A	1	0	0	0	0	0
A S Pretorius	2002 v W	21	2	25	22	4	138
R B Russell	2002 v W	23	8	0	0	0	40

A H Snyman	1996 v NZ	38	10	0	0	0	50
C S Terblanche	1998 v I	37	19	0	0	0	95
J H van der Westhuizen	1993 v Arg	89	38	0	0	0	190
J N B van der Westhuyzen	2000 v NZ	32	5	7	1	3	51
A K Willemse	2003 v S	11	2	0	0	0	10
FORWARDS							
E P Andrews	2004 v I	21	0	0	0	0	0
R E Bands	2003 v S	11	2	0	0	0	10
C J Bezuidenhout	2003 v NZ	4	0	0	0	0	0
C S Boome	1999 v It	20	2	0	0	0	10
B J Botha	2006 v NZ	3	0	0	0	0	0
G van G Botha	2005 v A	2	0	0	0	0	0
J P Botha	2002 v F	31	6	0	0	0	30
G J J Britz	2004 v I	11	0	0	0	0	0
S W P Burger	2003 v Gg	27	3	0	0	0	15
D Coetzee	2002 v Sm	15	1	0	0	0	5
G Cronjé	2003 v NZ	3	0	0	0	0	0
J Cronjé	2004 v I	27	4	0	0	0	20
Q Davids	2002 v W	9	0	0	0	0	0
V T Dlulane	2004 v W	1	0	0	0	0	0
J P du Randt	1994 v Arg	70	4	0	0	0	20
C P J Krige	1999 v It	39	2	0	0	0	10
V Matfield	2001 v It	54	5	0	0	0	25
G J Muller	2006 v S	6	0	0	0	0	0
M C Ralepelle	2006 v NZ	1	0	0	0	0	0
S J Rautenbach	2002 v W	14	1	0	0	0	5
D J Rossouw	2003 v U	17	5	0	0	0	25
D Santon	2003 v A	4	0	0	0	0	0
H Scholtz	2002 v A	5	1	0	0	0	5
L D Sephaka	2001 v US	23	0	0	0	0	0
M H Shimange	2004 v W	9	0	0	0	0	0
J W Smit	2000 v C	60	2	0	0	0	10
J H Smith	2003 v S	27	2	0	0	0	10
P J Spies	2006 v A	4	0	0	0	0	0
G G Steenkamp	2004 v S	8	1	0	0	0	5
S Tyibilika	2004 v S	8	3	0	0	0	15
P A van den Berg	1999 v It	40	4	0	0	0	20
C J van der Linde	2002 v S	30	0	0	0	0	0
J C van Niekerk	2001 v NZ	46	8	0	0	0	40
A J Venter	2000 v W	25	0	0	0	0	0
P J Wannenburg	2002 v F	16	2	0	0	0	10

* Paulse's figures include a penalty try awarded against Wales in 2002

SOUTH AFRICAN INTERNATIONAL PLAYERS

(UP TO 30TH SEPTEMBER 2006)

Entries in square brackets denote matches played in RWC Finals.

Ackermann, D S P (WP) 1955 BI 2,3,4, 1956 A 1,2, NZ 1,3, 1958 F 2
Ackermann, J N (NT, BB) 1996 Fj, A 1, NZ 1, A 2, 2001 F 2(R), It 1, NZ 1(R), A 1
Aitken, A D (WP) 1997 F 2(R), E, 1998 I 2(R), W 1(R), NZ 1,2(R), A 2(R)
Albertyn, P K (SWD) 1924 BI 1,2,3,4
Alexander, F A (GW) 1891 BI 1,2
Allan, J (N) 1993 A 1(R), Arg 1,2(R), 1994 E 1,2, NZ 1,2,3, 1996 Fj, A 1, NZ 1, A 2, NZ 2
Allen, P B (EP) 1960 S
Allport, P H (WP) 1910 BI 2,3
Anderson, J W (WP) 1903 BI 3
Anderson, J H (WP) 1896 BI 1,3,4
Andrew, J B (Tvl) 1896 BI 2
Andrews, E P (WP) 2004 I1, 2, W1(t&R), PI, NZ1, A1, NZ2, A2, W2, I3, E, 2005 F1,A2, NZ2(t), Arg(R), F3(R), 2006 S1,2,F,A1(R),NZ1(t)
Andrews, K S (WP) 1992 E, 1993 F 1,2, A 1(R), 2,3, Arg 1(R), 2, 1994 NZ 3
Andrews, M G (N) 1994 E 2, NZ 1,2,3, Arg 1,2, S, W, 1995 WS, [A, WS, F, NZ], W, It, E, 1996 Fj, A 1, NZ 1, A 2, NZ 2,3,4,5, Arg 1,2, F 1,2, W, 1997 Tg (R), BI 1,2, NZ 1, A 1, NZ 2, A 2, It, F 1,2, E, S, 1998 I 1,2, W 1, E 1, A 1, NZ 1,2, A 2, W 2, S, I 3, E 2, 1999 NZ 1,2(R), A 2(R), [S, U, E, A 3, NZ 3], 2000 A 2, NZ 2, A 3, Arg, I, W, E 3, 2001 F 1,2, It 1, NZ 1, A 1,2, NZ 2, F 3, E
Antelme, M J G (Tvl) 1960 NZ 1,2,3,4, 1961 F
Apsey, J T (WP) 1933 A 4,5, 1938 BI 2
Ashley, S (WP) 1903 BI 2
Aston, F T D (Tvl) 1896 BI 1,2,3,4
Atherton, S (N) 1993 Arg 1,2, 1994 E 1,2, NZ 1,2,3, 1996 NZ 2
Aucamp, J (WT) 1924 BI 1,2

Baard, A P (WP) 1960 I
Babrow, L (WP) 1937 A 1,2, NZ 1,2,3
Badenhorst, C (OFS) 1994 Arg 2, 1995 WS (R)
Bands, R E (BB) 2003 S 1,2, Arg (R), A 1, NZ 1, A 2, NZ 2, [U,E,Sm(R),NZ(R)]
Barnard, A S (EP) 1984 S Am 1,2, 1986 Cv 1,2
Barnard, J H (Tvl) 1965 S, A 1,2, NZ 3,4
Barnard, R W (Tvl) 1970 NZ 2(R)
Barnard, W H M (NT) 1949 NZ 4, 1951 W
Barry, D W (WP) 2000 C, E 1,2, A 1(R), NZ 1, A 2, 2001 F 1,2, US (R), 2002 W 2, Arg, Sm, NZ 1, A 1, NZ 2, A 2, 2003 A 1, NZ 1, A 2, [U,E,Sm,NZ], 2004 PI,NZ1, A1,NZ2, A2,W2,I3,E,Arg(t), 2005 F1,2,A1,NZ2,W(R), F3(R), 2006 F
Barry, J (WP) 1903 BI 1,2,3
Bartmann, W J (Tvl, N) 1986 Cv 1,2,3,4, 1992 NZ, A, F, 1,2
Bastard, W E (N) 1937 A 1, NZ 1,2,3, 1938 BI 1,3
Bates, A J (WT) 1969 E, 1970 NZ 1,2, 1972 E
Bayvel, P C R (Tvl) 1974 BI 2,4, F 1,2, 1975 F 1,2, 1976 NZ 1,2,3,4
Beck, J J (WP) 1981 NZ 2(R), 3(R), US
Bedford, T P (N) 1963 A 1,2,3,4, 1964 W, F, 1965 I, A 1,2, 1968 BI 1,2,3,4, F 1,2, 1969 A 1,2,3,4, S, E, 1970 I, W, 1971 F 1,2
Bekker, H J (WP) 1981 NZ 1,3
Bekker, H P J (NT) 1952 E, F, 1953 A 1,2,3,4, 1955 BI 2,3,4, 1956 A 1,2, NZ 1,2,3,4
Bekker, M J (NT) 1960 S
Bekker, R P (NT) 1953 A 3,4
Bekker, S (NT) 1997 A 2(t)
Bennett, R G (Border) 1997 Tg (R), BI 1(R), 3, NZ 1, A 1, NZ 2
Bergh, W F (SWD) 1931 W, I, 1932 E, S, 1933 A 1,2,3,4,5, 1937 A 1,2, NZ 1,2,3, 1938 BI 1,2,3
Bestbier, A (OFS) 1974 F 2(R)
Bester, J J N (WP) 1924 BI 2,4
Bester, J L A (WP) 1938 BI 2,3
Beswick, A M (Bor) 1896 BI 2,3,4
Bezuidenhout, C E (NT) 1962 BI 2,3,4
Bezuidenhout, C J (MP) 2003 NZ 2(R), [E,Sm,NZ]
Bezuidenhout, N S E (NT) 1972 E, 1974 BI 2,3,4, F 1,2, 1975 F 1,2, 1977 Wld
Bierman, J N (Tvl) 1931 I
Bisset, W M (WP) 1891 BI 1,3
Blair, R (WP) 1977 Wld
Bobo, G (GL) 2003 S 2(R), Arg, A 1(R), NZ 2, 2004 S(R)
Boome, C S (WP) 1999 It 1,2, W, NZ 1(R), A 1, NZ 2, A 2, 2000 C, E 1,2, 2003 S 1(R),2(R), Arg (R), A 1(R), NZ 1(R), A 2, NZ 2(R), [U(R),Gg,NZ(R)]
Bosch, G R (Tvl) 1974 BI 2, F 1,2, 1975 F 1,2, 1976 NZ 1,2,3,4
Bosman, H M (FS) 2005 W,F3, 2006 A1(R)
Bosman, N J S (Tvl) 1924 BI 2,3,4
Botha, B J (N) 2006 NZ2(R),3,A3
Botha, D S (NT) 1981 NZ 1
Botha, G van G (BB) 2005 A3(R), F3(R)
Botha, H E (NT) 1980 S Am 1,2, BI 1,2,3,4, S Am 3,4, F, 1981 I 1,2, NZ 1,2,3, US, 1982 S Am 1,2, 1986 Cv 1,2,3,4, 1989 Wld 1,2, 1992 NZ, A, F 1,2, E
Botha, J A (Tvl) 1903 BI 3
Botha, J P (BB) 2002 F, 2003 S 1,2, A 1, NZ 1, A 2(R), [U,E,Gg,Sm,NZ], 2004 I1,PI, NZ1,A1,NZ2,A2,W2,I3,E, S,Arg, 2005 A1,2,3,NZ1,A4,NZ2,Arg,W,F3
Botha, J P F (NT) 1962 BI 2,3,4
Botha, P H (Tvl) 1965 A 1,2
Boyes, H C (GW) 1891 BI 1,2
Brand, G H (WP) 1928 NZ 2,3, 1931 W, I, 1932 E, S, 1933 A 1,2,3,4,5, 1937 A 1,2, NZ 2,3, 1938 BI 1
Bredenkamp, M J (GW) 1896 BI 1,3
Breedt, J C (Tvl) 1986 Cv 1,2,3,4, 1989 Wld 1,2, 1992 NZ, A
Brewis, J D (NT) 1949 NZ 1,2,3,4, 1951 S, I, W, 1952 E, F, 1953 A 1
Briers, T P D (WP) 1955 BI 1,2,3,4, 1956 NZ 2,3,4
Brink D J (WP) 1906 S, W, E
Brink, R (WP) 1995 [R, C]
Britz, G J J (FS, WP) 2004 I1(R),2(R),W1(R),PI,A1,NZ2, A2(R),I3(t),S(t&R),Arg(R), 2005 U

Britz, W K (N) 2002 W 1
Brooks, D (Bor) 1906 S
Brosnihan, W (GL, N) 1997 A 2, 2000 NZ 1(t+R), A 2(t+R), NZ 2(R), A 3(R), E 3(R)
Brown, C B (WP) 1903 BI 1,2,3
Brynard, G S (WP) 1965 A 1, NZ 1,2,3,4, 1968 BI 3,4
Buchler, J U (Tvl) 1951 S, I, W, 1952 E, F, 1953 A 1,2,3,4, 1956 A 2
Burdett, A F (WP) 1906 S, I
Burger, J M (WP) 1989 Wld 1,2
Burger, M B (NT) 1980 BI 2(R), S Am 3, 1981 US (R)
Burger, S W P (WP) 1984 E 1,2, 1986 Cv 1,2,3,4
Burger, S W P (WP) 2003 [Gg(R),Sm(R),NZ(R)], 2004 I1, 2,W1,PI,NZ1,A1,NZ2,A2, W2,I3,E, 2005 F1,2,A1,2(R), 3(R),NZ1,A4,NZ2,Arg(R),W,F3, 2006 S1,2
Burger, W A G (Bor) 1906 S, I, W, 1910 BI 2

Carelse, G (EP) 1964 W, F, 1965 I, S, 1967 F 1,2,3, 1968 F 1,2, 1969 A 1,2,3,4, S
Carlson, R A (WP) 1972 E
Carolin, H W (WP) 1903 BI 3, 1906 S, I
Carstens, P D (N) 2002 S, E
Castens, H H (WP) 1891 BI 1
Chavhanga, T (WP) 2005 U
Chignell, T W (WP) 1891 BI 3
Cilliers, G D (OFS) 1963 A 1,3,4
Cilliers, N V (WP) 1996 NZ 3(t)
Claassen, J T (WT) 1955 BI 1,2,3,4, 1956 A 1,2, NZ 1,2,3,4, 1958 F 1,2, 1960 S, NZ 1,2,3, W, I, 1961 E, S, F, I, A 1,2, 1962 BI 1,2,3,4
Claassen, W (N) 1981 I 1,2, NZ 2,3, US, 1982 S Am 1,2
Claassens, M (FS) 2004 W2(R),S(R),Arg(R), 2005 Arg(R),W,F3
Clark, W H G (Tvl) 1933 A 3
Clarkson, W A (N) 1921 NZ 1,2, 1924 BI 1
Cloete, H A (WP) 1896 BI 4
Cockrell, C H (WP) 1969 S, 1970 I, W
Cockrell, R J (WP) 1974 F 1,2, 1975 F 1,2, 1976 NZ 1,2, 1977 Wld, 1981 NZ 1,2(R), 3, US
Coetzee, D (BB) 2002 Sm, 2003 S 1,2, Arg, A 1, NZ 1, A 2, NZ 2, [U,E,Sm(R),NZ(R)], 2004 S(R),Arg(R), 2006 A1(R)
Coetzee, J H H (WP) 1974 BI 1, 1975 F 2(R), 1976 NZ 1,2,3,4
Conradie, J H (WP) 2002 W 1,2, Arg (R), Sm, NZ 1, A 1, NZ 2(R), A 2(R), S, E, 2004 W1(R),PI,NZ2,A2, 2005 Arg
Cope, D K (Tvl) 1896 BI 2
Cotty, W (GW) 1896 BI 3
Crampton, G (GW) 1903 BI 2
Craven, D H (WP) 1931 W, I, 1932 S, 1933 A 1,2,3,4,5, 1937 A 1,2, NZ 1,2,3, 1938 BI 1,2,3,
Cronjé, G (BB) 2003 NZ 2, 2004 I2(R),W1(R)
Cronjé, J (BB) 2004 I1,2,W1,PI,NZ1,A1,NZ2(R),A2(t&R), S(t&R),Arg, 2005 U,F1,2,A1, 3,NZ1(R),2(t),Arg,W,F3, 2006 S2(R),F(R),A1(t&R),NZ1,A2,NZ2,A3(R)
Cronje, P A (Tvl) 1971 F 1,2, A 1,2,3, 1974 BI 3,4
Crosby, J H (Tvl) 1896 BI 2
Crosby, N J (Tvl) 1910 BI 1,3
Currie, C (GW) 1903 BI 2

D'Alton, G (WP) 1933 A 1
Dalton, J (Tvl, GL, Falcons) 1994 Arg 1(R), 1995 [A, C], W, It, E, 1996 NZ 4(R),5, Arg 1,2, F 1,2, W, 1997 Tg (R), BI 3, NZ 2, A 2, It, F 1,2, E, S, 1998 I 1,2, W 1, E 1, A 1, NZ 1,2, A 2, W 2, S, I 3, E 2, 2002 W 1,2, Arg, NZ 1, A 1, NZ 2, A 2, F, E
Daneel, G M (WP) 1928 NZ 1,2,3,4, 1931 W, I, 1932 E, S
Daneel, H J (WP) 1906 S, I, W, E
Davidson, C D (N) 2002 W 2(R), Arg, 2003 Arg, NZ 1(R), A 2
Davids, Q (WP) 2002 W 2, Arg (R), Sm (R), 2003 Arg, 2004 I1(R),2,W1,PI(t&R), NZ1(R)
Davison, P M (EP) 1910 BI 1
De Beer, J H (OFS) 1997 BI 3, NZ 1, A 1, NZ 2, A 2, F 2(R), S, 1999 A 2, [S, Sp, U, E, A 3]
De Bruyn, J (OFS) 1974 BI 3
De Jongh, H P K (WP) 1928 NZ 3
De Klerk, I J (Tvl) 1969 E, 1970 I, W
De Klerk, K B H (Tvl) 1974 BI 1,2,3(R), 1975 F 1,2, 1976 NZ 2(R), 3,4, 1980 S Am 1,2, BI 2, 1981 I 1,2
De Kock, A N (GW) 1891 BI 2
De Kock, D (Falcons) 2001 It 2(R), US
De Kock, J S (WP) 1921 NZ 3, 1924 BI 3
De Kock, N A (WP) 2001 It 1, 2002 Sm (R), NZ 1(R),2, A 2, F, 2003 [U(R),Gg,Sm(R), NZ(R)]
Delport, G M (GL, Worcester) 2000 C (R), E 1(t+R), A 1, NZ 1, A 2, NZ 2, A 3, Arg, I, W, 2001 F 2, It 1, 2003 A 1, NZ 2, [U,E,Sm,NZ]
Delport, W H (EP) 1951 S, I, W, 1952 E, F, 1953 A 1,2,3,4
De Melker, S C (GW) 1903 BI 2, 1906 E
Devenish, C E (GW) 1896 BI 2
Devenish, G St L (Tvl) 1896 BI 2
Devenish, G E (Tvl) 1891 BI 1
De Villiers, D I (Tvl) 1910 BI 1,2,3
De Villiers, D J (WP, Bol) 1962 BI 2,3, 1965 I, NZ 1,3,4, 1967 F 1,2,3,4, 1968 BI 1,2,3,4, F 1,2, 1969 A 1,4, E, 1970 I, W, NZ 1,2,3,4
De Villiers, H A (WP) 1906 S, W, E
De Villiers, H O (WP) 1967 F 1,2,3,4, 1968 F 1,2, 1969 A 1,2,3,4, S, E, 1970 I, W
De Villiers, J (WP) 2002 F, 2004 PI,NZ1,A1,NZ2,A2, W2(R),E, 2005 U,F1,2,A1,2,3, NZ1,A4,NZ2,Arg,W,F3, 2006 S1,NZ2,3,A3
De Villiers, P du P (WP) 1928 NZ 1,3,4, 1932 E, 1933 A 4, 1937 A 1,2, NZ 1
Devine, D (Tvl) 1924 BI 3, 1928 NZ 2
De Vos, D J J (WP) 1965 S, 1969 A 3, S
De Waal, A N (WP) 1967 F 1,2,3,4
De Waal, P J (WP) 1896 BI 4
De Wet, A E (WP) 1969 A 3,4, E
De Wet, P J (WP) 1938 BI 1,2,3
Dinkelmann, E E (NT) 1951 S, I, 1952 E, F, 1953 A 1,2
Dirksen, C W (NT) 1963 A 4, 1964 W, 1965 I, S, 1967 F 1,2,3,4, 1968 BI 1,2
Dlulane, V T (MP) 2004 W2(R)
Dobbin, F J (GW) 1903 BI 1,2, 1906 S, W, E, 1910 BI 1, 1912 S, I, W
Dobie, J A R (Tvl) 1928 NZ 2
Dormehl, P J (WP) 1896 BI 3,4
Douglass, F W (EP) 1896 BI 1
Drotské, A E (OFS) 1993 Arg 2, 1995 [WS (R)], 1996 A 1(R), 1997 Tg, BI 1,2,3(R), NZ 1, A 1, NZ 2(R), 1998 I 2(R), W 1(R), I 3(R), 1999 It 1,2, W, NZ 1, A 1, NZ 2, A 2, [S, Sp (R), U, E, A 3, NZ 3]
Dryburgh, R G (WP) 1955 BI 2,3,4, 1956 A 2, NZ 1,4, 1960 NZ 1,2
Duff, B R (WP) 1891 BI 1,2,3
Duffy, B A (Bor) 1928 NZ 1
Du Plessis, C J (WP) 1982 S Am 1,2, 1984 E 1,2, S Am 1,2, 1986 Cv 1,2,3,4, 1989 Wld 1,2
Du Plessis, D C (NT) 1977 Wld, 1980 S Am 2
Du Plessis, F (Tvl) 1949 NZ 1,2,3
Du Plessis, M (WP) 1971 A 1,2,3, 1974 BI 1,2, F 1,2, 1975 F 1,2, 1976 NZ 1,2,3,4, 1977 Wld, 1980 S Am 1,2, BI 1,2,3,4, S Am 4, F
Du Plessis, M J (WP) 1984 S Am 1,2, 1986 Cv 1,2,3,4, 1989 Wld 1,2
Du Plessis, N J (WT) 1921 NZ 2,3, 1924 BI 1,2,3
Du Plessis, P G (NT) 1972 E
Du Plessis, T D (NT) 1980 S Am 1,2
Du Plessis, W (WP) 1980 S Am 1,2, BI 1,2,3,4, S Am 3,4, F, 1981 NZ 1,2,3, 1982 S Am 1,2

Du Plooy, A J J (EP) 1955 BI 1
Du Preez, F C H (NT) 1961 E, S, A 1,2, 1962 BI 1,2,3,4, 1963 A 1, 1964 W, F, 1965 A 1,2, NZ 1,2,3,4, 1967 F 4, 1968 BI 1,2,3,4, F 1,2, 1969 A 1,2, S, 1970 I, W, NZ 1,2,3,4, 1971 F 1,2, A 1,2,3
Du Preez, G J D (GL) 2002 Sm (R), A 1(R)
Du Preez, J G H (WP) 1956 NZ 1
Du Preez, P F (BB) 2004 I1, 2, W1, PI(R), NZ1, A1, NZ2(R), A2(R), W2, I3, E, S, Arg, 2005 U(R), F1, 2(R), A1(R), 2(R), 3, NZ1(R), A4(R), 2006 S1, 2, F, A1(R), NZ1, A2, NZ2, 3, A3
Du Preez, R J (N) 1992 NZ, A, 1993 F 1,2, A 1,2,3
Du Rand, J A (R, NT) 1949 NZ 2,3, 1951 S, I, W, 1952 E, F, 1953 A 1,2,3,4, 1955 BI 1,2,3,4, 1956 A 1,2, NZ 1,2,3,4
Du Randt, J P (OFS, FS) 1994 Arg 1,2, S, W, 1995 WS, [A, WS, F, NZ], 1996 Fj, A 1, NZ 1, A 2, NZ 2,3,4, 1997 Tg, BI 1,2,3, NZ 1, A 1, NZ 2, A 2, It, F 1,2, E, S, 1999 NZ 1, A 1, NZ 2, A 2, [S, Sp (R), U, E, A 3, NZ 3], 2004 I1,2,W1,PI,NZ1,A1,NZ2,A2,W2,I3,E, S(R),Arg(R), 2005 U(R),F1,A1,NZ1,A4,NZ2,Arg,W(R),F3, 2006 S1,2,F,A1, NZ1,A2, NZ2,3,A3
Du Toit, A F (WP) 1928 NZ 3,4
Du Toit, B A (Tvl) 1938 BI 1,2,3
Du Toit, G S (GW, WP) 1998 I 1, 1999 It 1,2, W (R), NZ 1,2, 2004 I1,W1(R),A1(R), S(R),Arg, 2006 S1(R),2(R),F(R)
Du Toit, P A (NT) 1949 NZ 2,3,4, 1951 S, I, W, 1952 E, F
Du Toit, P G (WP) 1981 NZ 1, 1982 S Am 1,2, 1984 E 1,2
Du Toit, P S (WP) 1958 F 1,2, 1960 NZ 1,2,3,4, W, I, 1961 E, S, F, I, A 1,2
Duvenhage, F P (GW) 1949 NZ 1,3

Edwards, P (NT) 1980 S Am 1,2
Ellis, J H (SWA) 1965 NZ 1,2,3,4, 1967 F 1,2,3,4, 1968 BI 1,2,3,4, F 1,2, 1969 A 1,2,3,4, S, 1970 I, W, NZ 1,2,3,4, 1971 F 1,2, A 1,2,3, 1972 E, 1974 BI 1,2,3,4, F 1,2, 1976 NZ 1
Ellis, M C (Tvl) 1921 NZ 2,3, 1924 BI 1,2,3,4
Els, W W (OFS) 1997 A 2(R)
Engelbrecht, J P (WP) 1960 S, W, I, 1961 E, S, F, A 1,2, 1962 BI 2,3,4, 1963 A 2,3, 1964 W, F, 1965 I, S, A 1,2, NZ 1,2,3,4, 1967 F 1,2,3,4, 1968 BI 1,2, F 1,2, 1969 A 1,2
Erasmus, F S (NT, EP) 1986 Cv 3,4, 1989 Wld 2
Erasmus, J C (OFS, GL) 1997 BI 3, A 2, It, F 1,2, S, 1998 I 1,2, W 1, E 1, A 1, NZ 2, A 2, S, W 2, I 3, E 2, 1999 It 1,2, W, A 1, NZ 2, A 2, [S, U, E, A 3, NZ 3], 2000 C, E 1, A 1, NZ 1,2, A 3, 2001 F 1,2
Esterhuizen, G (GL) 2000 NZ 1(R),2, A 3, Arg, I, W (R), E 3(t)
Etlinger, T E (WP) 1896 BI 4

Ferreira, C (OFS) 1986 Cv 1,2
Ferreira, P S (WP) 1984 S Am 1,2
Ferris, H H (Tvl) 1903 BI 3
Fleck R F (WP) 1999 It 1,2, NZ 1(R), A 1, NZ 2(R), A 2, [S, U, E, A 3, NZ 3], 2000 C, E 1,2, A 1, NZ 1, A 2, NZ 2, A 3, Arg, I, W, E 3, 2001 F 1(R),2, It 1, NZ 1, A 1,2, 2002 S, E
Forbes, H H (Tvl) 1896 BI 2
Fourie, C (EP) 1974 F 1,2, 1975 F 1,2
Fourie, J (GL) 2003 [U,Gg,Sm(R),NZ(R)], 2004 I2,E(R),S,Arg, 2005 U(R),F2(R),A1(R), 2,3,NZ1,A4,NZ2,Arg,W,F3, 2006 S1,A1,NZ1,A2,NZ2,3,A3
Fourie, T T (SET) 1974 BI 3
Fourie, W L (SWA) 1958 F 1,2
Francis, J A J (Tvl) 1912 S, I, W, 1913 E, F
Frederickson, C A (Tvl) 1974 BI 2, 1980 S Am 1,2
Frew, A (Tvl) 1903 BI 1
Froneman, D C (OFS) 1977 Wld
Froneman, I L (Bor) 1933 A 1
Fuls, H T (Tvl, EP) 1992 NZ (R), 1993 F 1,2, A 1,2,3, Arg 1,2
Fry, S P (WP) 1951 S, I, W, 1952 E, F, 1953 A 1,2,3,4, 1955 BI 1,2,3,4
Fynn, E E (N) 2001 F 1, It 1(R)
Fyvie, W (N) 1996 NZ 4(t & R), 5(R), Arg 2(R)

Gage, J H (OFS) 1933 A 1
Gainsford, J L (WP) 1960 S, NZ 1,2,3,4, W, I, 1961 E, S, F, A 1,2, 1962 BI 1,2,3,4, 1963 A 1,2,3,4, 1964 W, F, 1965 I, S, A 1,2, NZ 1,2,3,4, 1967 F 1,2,3
Garvey, A C (N) 1996 Arg 1,2, F 1,2, W, 1997 Tg, BI 1,2,3(R), A 1(t), It, F 1,2, E, S, 1998 I 1,2, W 1, E1, A 1, NZ 1,2 A 2, W 2, S, I 3, E 2, 1999 [Sp]
Geel, P J (OFS) 1949 NZ 3
Geere, V (Tvl) 1933 A 1,2,3,4,5
Geffin, A O (Tvl) 1949 NZ 1,2,3,4, 1951 S, I, W
Geldenhuys, A (EP) 1992 NZ, A, F 1,2
Geldenhuys, S B (NT) 1981 NZ 2,3, US, 1982 S Am 1,2, 1989 Wld 1,2
Gentles, T A (WP) 1955 BI 1,2,4, 1956 NZ 2,3, 1958 F 2
Geraghty, E M (Bor) 1949 NZ 4
Gerber, D M (EP, WP) 1980 S Am 3,4, F, 1981 I 1,2, NZ 1,2,3, US, 1982 S Am 1,2, 1984 E 1,2, S Am 1,2, 1986 Cv 1,2,3,4, 1992 NZ, A, F 1,2, E
Gerber, H J (WP) 2003 S 1,2
Gerber, M C (EP) 1958 F 1,2, 1960 S
Gericke, F W (Tvl) 1960 S
Germishuys, J S (OFS, Tvl) 1974 BI 2, 1976 NZ 1,2,3,4, 1977 Wld, 1980 S Am 1,2, BI 1,2,3,4, S Am 3,4, F, 1981 I 1,2, NZ 2,3, US
Gibbs, B (GW) 1903 BI 2
Goosen, C P (OFS) 1965 NZ 2
Gorton, H C (Tvl) 1896 BI 1
Gould, R L (N) 1968 BI 1,2,3,4
Gray, B G (WP) 1931 W, 1932 E, S, 1933 A 5
Greeff, W W (WP) 2002 Arg (R), Sm, NZ 1, A 1, NZ 2, A 2, F, S, E, 2003 [U,Gg]
Greenwood, C M (WP) 1961 I
Greyling, P J F (OFS) 1967 F 1,2,3,4, 1968 BI 1, F 1,2, 1969 A 1,2,3,4, S, E, 1970 I, W, NZ 1,2,3,4, 1971 F 1,2, A 1,2,3, 1972 E
Grobler, C J (OFS) 1974 BI 4, 1975 F 1,2
Guthrie, F H (WP) 1891 BI 1,3, 1896 BI 1

Habana, B G (GL, BB) 2004 E(R),S,Arg, 2005 U,F1,2,A1,2, 3,NZ1,A4,NZ2,Arg,W,F3, 2006 S2,F,A1,NZ1,A2,NZ2,3
Hahn, C H L (Tvl) 1910 BI 1,2,3
Hall, D B (GL) 2001 F 1,2, NZ 1, A 1,2, NZ 2, It 2, E, US, 2002 Sm, NZ 1,2, A 2
Halstead, T M (N) 2001 F 3, It 2, E, US (R), 2003 S 1,2
Hamilton, F (EP) 1891 BI 1
Harris, T A (Tvl) 1937 NZ 2,3, 1938 BI 1,2,3
Hartley, A J (WP) 1891 BI 3
Hattingh, H (NT) 1992 A (R), F 2(R), E, 1994 Arg 1,2
Hattingh, L B (OFS) 1933 A 2
Heatlie, B H (WP) 1891 BI 2,3, 1896 BI 1,4, 1903 BI 1,3
Hendricks, M (Bol) 1998 I 2(R), W 1(R)
Hendriks, P (Tvl) 1992 NZ, A, 1994 S, W, 1995 [A, R, C], 1996 A 1, NZ 1, A 2, NZ 2,3,4,5
Hepburn, T B (WP) 1896 BI 4
Heunis, J W (NT) 1981 NZ 3(R), US, 1982 S Am 1,2, 1984 E 1,2, S Am 1,2, 1986 Cv 1,2,3,4, 1989 Wld 1,2
Hill, R A (R) 1960 W, I, 1961 I, A 1,2, 1962 BI 4, 1963 A 3
Hills, W G (NT) 1992 F 1,2, E, 1993 F 1,2, A 1
Hirsch, J G (EP) 1906 I, 1910 BI 1
Hobson, T E C (WP) 1903 BI 3
Hoffman, R S (Bol) 1953 A 3
Holton, D N (EP) 1960 S
Honiball, H W (N) 1993 A 3(R), Arg 2, 1995 WS (R),

1996 Fj, A 1, NZ 5, Arg 1,2, F 1,2, W, 1997 Tg, BI 1,2,3(R), NZ 1(R), A 1(R), NZ 2, A 2, It, F 1,2, E, 1998 W 1(R), E 1, A 1, NZ 1,2, A 2, W 2, S, I 3, E 2, 1999 [A 3(R), NZ 3]
Hopwood, D J (WP) 1960 S, NZ 3,4, W, 1961 E, S, F, I, A 1,2, 1962 BI 1,2,3,4, 1963 A 1,2,4, 1964 W, F, 1965 S, NZ 3,4
Hougaard, D J (BB) 2003 [U(R),E(R),Gg,Sm,NZ]
Howe, B F (Bor) 1956 NZ 1,4
Howe-Browne, N R F G (WP) 1910 BI 1,2,3
Hugo, D P (WP) 1989 Wld 1,2
Human, D C F (WP) 2002 W 1,2, Arg (R), Sm (R)
Hurter, M H (NT) 1995 [R, C], W, 1996 Fj, A 1, NZ 1,2,3, 4,5, 1997 NZ 1,2, A 2

Immelman, J H (WP) 1913 F

Jackson, D C (WP) 1906 I, W, E
Jackson, J S (WP) 1903 BI 2
Jacobs, A A (Falcons) 2001 It 2(R), US, 2002 W 1(R), Arg, Sm (R), NZ 1(t+R), A 1(R), F, S, E (R)
James, A D (N) 2001 F 1,2, NZ 1, A 1,2, NZ 2, 2002 F (R), S, E, 2006 NZ1,A2,NZ2,3(R)
Jansen, E (OFS) 1981 NZ 1
Jansen, J S (OFS) 1970 NZ 1,2,3,4, 1971 F 1,2, A 1,2,3, 1972 E
Jantjes, C A (GL) 2001 It 1, A 1,2, NZ 2, F 3, It 2, E, US, 2005 Arg,W
Januarie, E R (GL) 2005 U,F2,A1,2,3(R),NZ1,A4,NZ2, 2006 S1(R),2(R),F(R),A1
Jennings, C B (Bor) 1937 NZ 1
Johnson, G K (Tvl) 1993 Arg 2, 1994 NZ 3, Arg 1, 1995 WS, [R, C, WS]
Johnstone, P G A (WP) 1951 S, I, W, 1952 E, F, 1956 A 1, NZ 1,2,4
Jones, C H (Tvl) 1903 BI 1,2
Jones, P S T (WP) 1896 BI 1,3,4
Jordaan, N (BB) 2002 E (R)
Jordaan, R P (NT) 1949 NZ 1,2,3,4
Joubert, A J (OFS, N) 1989 Wld 1(R), 1993 A 3, Arg 1, 1994 E 1,2, NZ 1,2(R), 3, Arg 2, S, W, 1995 [A, C, WS, F, NZ], W, It, E, 1996 Fj, A 1, NZ 1,3,4,5, Arg 1,2, F 1,2, W, 1997 Tg, BI 1,2, A 2
Joubert, M C (Bol, WP) 2001 NZ 1, 2002 W 1,2, Arg (R), Sm, NZ 1, A1, NZ 2, A 2, F (R), 2003 S 2, Arg, A 1, 2004 I1,2,W1,PI,NZ1,A1,NZ2,A2,W2,I3,E,S,Arg, 2005 U,F1,2, A1
Joubert, S J (WP) 1906 I, W, E
Julies, W (Bol, SWD, GL) 1999 [Sp], 2004 I1,2,W1,S,Arg, 2005 A2(R),3(t), 2006 F(R)

Kahts, W J H (NT) 1980 BI 1,2,3, S Am 3,4, F, 1981 I 1,2, NZ 2, 1982 S Am 1,2
Kaminer, J (Tvl) 1958 F 2
Kayser, D J (EP, N) 1999 It 2(R), A 1(R), NZ 2, A 2, [S, Sp (R), U, E, A 3], 2001 It 1(R), NZ 1(R), A 2(R), NZ 2(R)
Kebble, G R (N) 1993 Arg 1,2, 1994 NZ 1(R), 2
Kelly, E W (GW) 1896 BI 3
Kempson, R B (N, WP, Ulster) 1998 I 2(R), W 1, E 1, A 1, NZ 1,2 A 2, W 2, S, I 3, E 2, 1999 It 1,2, W, 2000 C, E 1,2, A 1, NZ 1, A 2,3, Arg, I, W, E 3, 2001 F 1,2(R), NZ 1, A 1,2, NZ 2, 2003 S 1(R),2(R), Arg, A 1(R), NZ 1(R), A 2
Kenyon, B J (Bor) 1949 NZ 4
Kipling, H G (GW) 1931 W, I, 1932 E, S, 1933 A 1,2,3,4,5
Kirkpatrick, A I (GW) 1953 A 2, 1956 NZ 2, 1958 F 1, 1960 S, NZ 1,2,3,4, W, I, 1961 E, S, F
Knight, A S (Tvl) 1912 S, I, W, 1913 E, F
Knoetze, F (WP) 1989 Wld 1,2
Koch, A C (Bol) 1949 NZ 2,3,4, 1951 S, I, W, 1952 E, F, 1953 A 1,2,4, 1955 BI 1,2,3,4, 1956 A 1, NZ 2,3, 1958 F 1,2, 1960 NZ 1,2
Koch, H V (WP) 1949 NZ 1,2,3,4
Koen, L J (GL, BB) 2000 A 1, 2001 It 2, E, US, 2003 S 1,2, Arg, A 1, NZ 1, A 2, NZ 2, [U,E,Sm(R),NZ(R)]
Kotze, G J M (WP) 1967 F 1,2,3,4
Krantz, E F W (OFS) 1976 NZ 1, 1981 I 1,
Krige, C P J (WP) 1999 It 2, W, NZ 1, 2000 C (R), E 1(R),2, A 1(R), NZ 1, A 2, NZ 2, A 3, Arg, I, W, E 3, 2001 F 1,2, It 1(R), A 1(t+R), It 2(R), E (R), 2002 W 2, Arg, Sm, NZ 1, A 1, NZ 2, A 2, F, S, E, 2003 Arg, A 1, NZ 1, A 2, NZ 2, [E,Sm,NZ]
Krige, J D (WP) 1903 BI 1,3, 1906 S, I, W
Kritzinger, J L (Tvl) 1974 BI 3,4, F 1,2, 1975 F 1,2, 1976 NZ 4
Kroon, C M (EP) 1955 BI 1
Kruger, P E (Tvl) 1986 Cv 3,4
Kruger, R J (NT, BB) 1993 Arg 1,2, 1994 S, W, 1995 WS, [A, R, WS, F, NZ], W, It, E, 1996 Fj, A 1, NZ 1, A 2, NZ 2,3,4,5, Arg 1,2, F 1,2, W, 1997 Tg, BI 1,2, NZ 1, A 1, NZ 2, 1999 NZ 2, A 2(R), [Sp, NZ 3(R)]
Kruger, T L (Tvl) 1921 NZ 1,2, 1924 BI 1,2,3,4, 1928 NZ 1,2
Kuhn, S P (Tvl) 1960 NZ 3,4, W, I, 1961 E, S, F, I, A 1,2, 1962 BI 1,2,3,4, 1963 A 1,2,3, 1965 I, S

Labuschagne, J J (GL) 2000 NZ 1(R), 2002 W 1,2, Arg, NZ 1, A 1, NZ 2, A2, F, S, E
La Grange, J B (WP) 1924 BI 3,4
Larard, A (Tvl) 1896 BI 2,4
Lategan, M T (WP) 1949 NZ 1,2,3,4, 1951 S, I, W, 1952 E, F, 1953 A 1,2
Laubscher, T G (WP) 1994 Arg 1,2, S, W, 1995 It, E
Lawless, M J (WP) 1964 F, 1969 E (R), 1970 I, W
Ledger, S H (GW) 1912 S, I, 1913 E, F
Leonard, A (WP, SWD) 1999 A 1, [Sp]
Le Roux, A H (OFS, N) 1994 E 1, 1998 I 1,2, W 1(R), E 1(R), A 1(R), NZ 1(R),2(R), A 2(R), W 2(R), S (R), I 3(R), E 2(t+R), 1999 It 1(R),2(R), W (R), NZ 1(R), A 1(R), NZ 2(R), A 2(R), [S(R), Sp, U (R), E (R), A 3(R), NZ 3(R)], 2000 E 1(t+R),2(R), A 1(R),2(R), NZ 2, A 3(R), Arg (R), I (t), W (R), E 3(R), 2001 F 1(R),2, It 1, NZ 1(R), A 1(R),2(R), NZ 2(R), F 3, It 2, E, US (R), 2002 W 1(R),2(R), Arg, NZ 1(R), A 1(R), NZ 2(R), A 2(R)
Le Roux, H P (Tvl) 1993 F 1,2, 1994 E 1,2, NZ 1,2,3, Arg 2, S, W, 1995 WS [A, R, C (R), WS, F, NZ], W, It, E, 1996 Fj, NZ 2, Arg 1,2, F 1,2, W
Le Roux, J H S (Tvl) 1994 E 2, NZ 1,2
Le Roux, M (OFS) 1980 BI 1,2,3,4, S Am 3,4, F, 1981 I 1
Le Roux, P A (WP) 1906 I, W, E
Little, E M (GW) 1891 BI 1,3
Lochner, G P (WP) 1955 BI 3, 1956 A 1,2, NZ 1,2,3,4, 1958 F 1,2
Lochner, G P (EP) 1937 NZ 3, 1938 BI 1,2
Lockyear, R J (GW) 1960 NZ 1,2,3,4, 1960 I, 1961 F
Lombard, A C (EP) 1910 BI 2
Lombard, F (FS) 2002 S, E
Lötter, D (Tvl) 1993 F 2, A 1,2
Lotz, J W (Tvl) 1937 A 1,2, NZ 1,2,3, 1938 BI 1,2,3
Loubscher, R I P (EP, N) 2002 W 1, 2003 S 1, [U(R),Gg]
Loubser, J A (WP) 1903 BI 3, 1906 S, I, W, E, 1910 BI 1,3
Lourens, M J (NT) 1968 BI 2,3,4
Louw, F H (WP) 2002 W 2(R), Arg, Sm
Louw, J S (Tvl) 1891 BI 1,2,3
Louw, M J (Tvl) 1971 A 2,3
Louw, M M (WP) 1928 NZ 3,4, 1931 W, I, 1932 E, S, 1933 A 1,2,3,4,5, 1937 A 1,2, NZ 2,3, 1938 BI 1,2,3
Louw, R J (WP) 1980 S Am 1,2, BI 1,2,3,4 S Am 3,4, F, 1981 I 1,2, NZ 1,3, 1982 S Am 1,2, 1984 E 1,2, S Am 1,2
Louw, S C (WP) 1933 A 1,2,3,4,5, 1937 A 1, NZ 1,2,3, 1938 BI 1,2,3
Lubbe, E (GW) 1997 Tg, BI 1

Luyt, F P (WP) 1910 BI 1,2,3, 1912 S, I, W, 1913 E
Luyt, J D (EP) 1912 S, W, 1913 E, F
Luyt, R R (W P) 1910 BI 2,3, 1912 S, I, W, 1913 E, F
Lyons, D J (EP) 1896 BI 1
Lyster, P J (N) 1933 A 2,5, 1937 NZ 1

McCallum, I D (WP) 1970 NZ 1,2,3,4, 1971 F 1,2, A 1,2,3, 1974 BI 1,2
McCallum, R J (WP) 1974 BI 1
McCulloch, J D (GW) 1913 E, F
MacDonald, A W (R) 1965 A 1, NZ 1,2,3,4
Macdonald, D A (WP) 1974 BI 2
Macdonald, I (Tvl) 1992 NZ, A, 1993 F 1, A 3, 1994 E 2, 1995 WS (R)
McDonald, J A J (WP) 1931 W, I, 1932 E, S
McEwan, W M C (Tvl) 1903 BI 1,3
McHardy, E E (OFS) 1912 S, I, W, 1913 E, F
McKendrick, J A (WP) 1891 BI 3
Malan, A S (Tvl) 1960 NZ 1,2,3,4, W, I, 1961 E, S, F, 1962 BI 1, 1963 A 1,2,3, 1964 W, 1965 I, S
Malan, A W (NT) 1989 Wld 1,2, 1992 NZ, A, F 1,2, E
Malan, E (NT) 1980 BI 3(R), 4
Malan, G F (WP) 1958 F 2, 1960 NZ 1,3,4, 1961 E, S, F, 1962 BI 1,2,3, 1963 A 1,2,4, 1964 W, 1965 A 1,2, NZ 1,2
Malan, P (Tvl) 1949 NZ 4
Mallett, N V H (WP) 1984 S Am 1,2
Malotana K (Bor) 1999 [Sp]
Mans, W J (WP) 1965 I, S
Marais, C F (WP) 1999 It 1(R),2(R), 2000 C, E 1,2, A 1, NZ 1, A 2, NZ 2, A 3, Arg (R), W (R)
Marais, F P (Bol) 1949 NZ 1,2, 1951 S, 1953 A 1,2
Marais, J F K (WP) 1963 A 3, 1964 W, F, 1965 I, S, A 2, 1968 BI, 1,2,3,4, F 1,2, 1969 A 1,2,3,4, S, E, 1970 I, W, NZ 1,2,3,4, 1971 F 1,2, A 1,2,3, 1974 BI 1,2,3,4, F 1,2
Maré, D S (Tvl) 1906 S
Marsberg, A F W (GW) 1906 S, W, E
Marsberg, P A (GW) 1910 BI 1
Martheze, W C (GW) 1903 BI 2, 1906 I, W
Martin, H J (Tvl) 1937 A 2
Matfield, V (BB) 2001 It 1(R), NZ 1, A 2, NZ 2, F 3, It 2, E, US, 2002 W 1, Sm, NZ 1, A 1, NZ 2(R), 2003 S 1,2, Arg, A 1, NZ 1, A 2, NZ 2, [U, E, Sm ,NZ], 2004 I1, 2, W1, NZ2, A2, W2, I3, E, S, Arg, 2005 F1, 2, A1, 2, 3, NZ1, A4, NZ2, Arg, W, F3, 2006 S1, 2, F, A1, NZ1, A2, NZ2, 3, A3
Mellet, T B (GW) 1896 BI 2
Mellish, F W (WP) 1921 NZ 1,3, 1924 BI 1,2,3,4
Mentz, H (N) 2004 I1,W1(R)
Merry, J (EP) 1891 BI 1
Metcalf, H D (Bor) 1903 BI 2
Meyer, C du P (WP) 1921 NZ 1,2,3
Meyer, P J (GW) 1896 BI 1
Meyer, W (OFS, GL) 1997 S (R), 1999 It 2, NZ 1(R), A 1(R), 2000 C (R), E 1, NZ 1(R),2(R), Arg, I, W, E 3, 2001 F 1(R),2, It 1, F 3(R), It 2, E, US (t+R), 2002 W 1,2, Arg, NZ 1,2, A 2, F
Michau, J M (Tvl) 1921 NZ 1
Michau, J P (WP) 1921 NZ 1,2,3
Millar, W A (WP) 1906 E, 1910 BI 2,3, 1912 I, W, 1913 F
Mills, W J (WP) 1910 BI 2
Moll, T (Tvl) 1910 BI 2
Montini, P E (WP) 1956 A 1,2
Montgomery, P C (WP, Newport) 1997 BI 2,3, NZ 1, A 1, NZ 2, A 2, F 1,2, E, S, 1998 I 1,2, W 1, E 1, A 1, NZ 1,2, A 2, W 2, S, I 3, E 2, 1999 It 1,2, W, NZ 1, A 1, NZ 2, A 2, [S, U, E, A 3, NZ 3], 2000 C, E 1,2, A 1, NZ 1, A 2(R), Arg, I, W, E 3, 2001 F 1, 2(t), It 1, NZ 1, F 3(R), It 2(R), 2004 I2,W1,PI,NZ1,A1,NZ2,A2,W2, I3,E,S, 2005 U,F1,2,A1,2, 3,NZ1,A4,NZ2,Arg,W,F3, 2006 S1,2,F,A1,NZ1,A2,NZ2
Moolman, L C (NT) 1977 Wld, 1980 S Am 1,2, BI 1,2,3,4, S Am 3,4, F, 1981 I 1,2, NZ 1,2,3, US, 1982 S Am 1,2, 1984 S Am 1,2, 1986 Cv 1,2,3,4
Mordt, R H (Z-R, NT) 1980 S Am 1,2, BI 1,2,3,4, S Am 3,4, F, 1981 I 2, NZ 1,2,3, US, 1982 S Am 1,2, 1984 S Am 1,2
Morkel, D A (Tvl) 1903 BI 1
Morkel, D F T (Tvl) 1906 I, E, 1910 BI 1,3, 1912 S, I, W, 1913 E, F
Morkel, H J (WP) 1921 NZ 1
Morkel, H W (WP) 1921 NZ 1,2
Morkel, J A (WP) 1921 NZ 2,3
Morkel, J W H (WP) 1912 S, I, W, 1913 E, F
Morkel, P G (WP) 1912 S, I, W, 1913 E, F, 1921 NZ 1,2,3
Morkel, P K (WP) 1928 NZ 4
Morkel, W H (WP) 1910 BI 3, 1912 S, I, W, 1913 E, F, 1921 NZ 1,2,3
Morkel, W S (Tvl) 1906 S, I, W, E
Moss, C (N) 1949 NZ 1,2,3,4
Mostert, P J (WP) 1921 NZ 1,2,3, 1924 BI 1,2,4, 1928 NZ 1,2,3,4, 1931 W, I, 1932 E, S
Mulder, J C (Tvl, GL) 1994 NZ 2,3, S, W, 1995 WS, [A, WS, F, NZ], W, It, E, 1996 Fj, A 1, NZ 1, A 2, NZ 2,5, Arg 1,2, F 1,2, W, 1997 Tg, BI 1, 1999 It 1(R),2, W, NZ 1, 2000 C(R), A 1, E 3, 2001 F 1, It 1
Muller, G H (WP) 1969 A 3,4, S, 1970 W, NZ 1,2,3,4, 1971 F 1,2, 1972 E, 1974 BI 1,3,4
Muller, G J (N) 2006 S1(R),NZ1(R),A2,NZ2,3,A3
Muller, G P (GL) 2003 A 2, NZ 2, [E,Gg(R),Sm,NZ]
Muller, H L (OFS) 1986 Cv 4(R), 1989 Wld 1(R)
Muller, H S V (Tvl) 1949 NZ 1,2,3,4, 1951 S, I, W, 1952 E, F, 1953 A 1,2,3,4
Muller, L J J (N) 1992 NZ, A
Muller, P G (N) 1992 NZ, A, F 1,2, E, 1993 F 1,2, A 1,2,3, Arg 1,2, 1994 E 1,2, NZ 1, S, W, 1998 I 1,2, W 1, E 1, A 1, NZ 1,2, A 2, 1999 It 1, W, NZ 1, A 1, [Sp, E, A 3, NZ 3]
Muir, D J (WP) 1997 It, F 1,2, E, S
Myburgh, F R (EP) 1896 BI 1
Myburgh, J L (NT) 1962 BI 1, 1963 A 4, 1964 W, F, 1968 BI 1,2,3, F 1,2, 1969 A 1,2,3,4, E, 1970 I, W, NZ 3,4
Myburgh, W H (WT) 1924 BI 1

Naude, J P (WP) 1963 A 4, 1965 A 1,2, NZ 1,3,4, 1967 F 1,2,3,4, 1968 BI 1,2,3,4
Ndungane, A Z (BB) 2006 A1,2,NZ2,3,A3
Neethling, J B (WP) 1967 F 1,2,3,4, 1968 BI 4, 1969 S, 1970 NZ 1,2
Nel, J A (Tvl) 1960 NZ 1,2, 1963 A 1,2, 1965 A 2, NZ 1,2,3,4, 1970 NZ 3,4
Nel, J J (WP) 1956 A 1,2, NZ 1,2,3,4, 1958 F 1,2
Nel, P A R O (Tvl) 1903 BI 1,2,3
Nel, P J (N) 1928 NZ 1,2,3,4, 1931 W, I, 1932 E, S, 1933 A 1,3,4,5, 1937 A 1,2, NZ 2,3
Nimb, C F (WP) 1961 I
Nomis, S H (Tvl) 1967 F 4, 1968 BI 1,2,3,4, F 1,2, 1969 A 1,2,3,4, S, E, 1970 I, W, NZ 1,2,3,4, 1971 F 1,2, A 1,2,3, 1972 E
Nykamp, J L (Tvl) 1933 A 2

Ochse, J K (WP) 1951 I, W, 1952 E, F, 1953 A 1,2,4
Oelofse, J S A (Tvl) 1953 A 1,2,3,4
Oliver, J F (Tvl) 1928 NZ 3,4
Olivier, E (WP) 1967 F 1,2,3,4, 1968 BI 1,2,3,4, F 1,2, 1969 A 1,2,3,4, S, E
Olivier, J (NT) 1992 F 1,2, E, 1993 F 1,2 A 1,2,3, Arg 1, 1995 W, It (R), E, 1996 Arg 1,2, F 1,2, W
Olivier, W (BB) 2006 S1(R),2,F,A1,NZ1,A2,NZ2(R),3,A3
Olver, E (EP) 1896 BI 1
Oosthuizen, J J (WP) 1974 BI 1, F 1,2, 1975 F 1,2, 1976 NZ 1,2,3,4

Oosthuizen, O W (NT, Tvl) 1981 I 1(R), 2, NZ 2,3, US, 1982 S Am 1,2, 1984 E 1,2
Osler, B L (WP) 1924 BI 1,2,3,4, 1928 NZ 1,2,3,4, 1931 W, I, 1932 E, S, 1933 A 1,2,3,4,5
Osler, S G (WP) 1928 NZ 1
Otto, K (NT, BB) 1995 [R, C (R), WS (R)], 1997 BI 3, NZ 1, A 1, NZ 2, It, F 1,2, E, S, 1998 I 1,2, W 1, E 1, A 1, NZ 1,2, A 2, W 2, S, I 3, E 2, 1999 It 1, W, NZ 1, A 1, [S (R), Sp, U, E, A 3, NZ 3], 2000 C, E 1,2, A 1
Oxlee, K (N) 1960 NZ 1,2,3,4, W, I, 1961 S, A 1,2, 1962 BI 1,2,3,4, 1963 A 1,2,4, 1964 W, 1965 NZ 1,2

Pagel, G L (WP) 1995 [A (R), R, C, NZ (R)], 1996 NZ 5(R)
Parker, W H (EP) 1965 A 1,2
Partridge, J E C (Tvl) 1903 BI 1
Paulse, B J (WP) 1999 It 1,2, NZ 1, A 1,2(R), [S (R), Sp, NZ 3], 2000 C, E 1,2, A 1, NZ 1, A 2, NZ 2, A 3, Arg, W, E 3, 2001 F 1,2, It 1, NZ 1, A 1,2, NZ 2, F 3, It 2, E, 2002 W 1,2, Arg, Sm (R), A 1, NZ 2, A 2, F, S, E, 2003 [Gg], 2004 I1,2,W1,PI,NZ1,A1,NZ2,A2, W2,I3,E, 2005 A2,3,NZ1,A4,F3, 2006 S1,2,A1(R),NZ1,3(R),A3(R)
Payn, C (N) 1924 BI 1,2
Pelser, H J M (Tvl) 1958 F 1, 1960 NZ 1,2,3,4, W, I, 1961 F, I, A 1,2
Pfaff, B D (WP) 1956 A 1
Pickard, J A J (WP) 1953 A 3,4, 1956 NZ 2, 1958 F 2
Pienaar, J F (Tvl) 1993 F 1,2, A 1,2,3, Arg 1,2, 1994 E 1,2, NZ 2,3, Arg 1,2, S, W, 1995 WS, [A, C, WS, F, NZ], W, It, E, 1996 Fj, A 1, NZ 1, A 2, NZ 2
Pienaar, R (N) 2006 NZ2(R),3(R),A3(R)
Pienaar, Z M J (OFS) 1980 S Am 2(R), BI 1,2,3,4, S Am 3,4, F, 1981 I 1,2, NZ 1,2,3
Pietersen, J-P R (N) 2006 A3
Pitzer, G (NT) 1967 F 1,2,3,4, 1968 BI 1,2,3,4, F 1,2, 1969 A 3,4
Pope, C F (WP) 1974 BI 1,2,3,4, 1975 F 1,2, 1976 NZ 2,3,4
Potgieter, H J (OFS) 1928 NZ 1,2
Potgieter, H L (OFS) 1977 Wld
Powell, A W (GW) 1896 BI 3
Powell, J M (GW) 1891 BI 2, 1896 BI 3, 1903 BI 1,2
Prentis, R B (Tvl) 1980 S Am 1,2, BI 1,2,3,4, S Am 3,4, F, 1981 I 1,2
Pretorius, A S (GL) 2002 W 1,2, Arg, Sm, NZ 1, A 1, NZ 2, F, S (R), E, 2003 NZ 1(R), A 1, 2005 A2,3,NZ1,A4,NZ2,Arg, 2006 NZ2(R),3,A3
Pretorius, N F (Tvl) 1928 NZ 1,2,3,4
Prinsloo, J (Tvl) 1958 F 1,2
Prinsloo, J (NT) 1963 A 3
Prinsloo, J P (Tvl) 1928 NZ 1
Putter, D J (WT) 1963 A 1,2,4

Raaff, J W E (GW) 1903 BI 1,2, 1906 S, W, E, 1910 BI 1
Ralepelle, M C (BB) 2006 NZ2(R)
Ras, W J de Wet (OFS) 1976 NZ 1(R), 1980 S Am 2(R)
Rautenbach, S J (WP) 2002 W 1(R),2(t+R), Arg (R), Sm, NZ 1(R), A 1, NZ 2(R), A 2(R), 2003 [U(R),Gg,Sm,NZ], 2004 W1,NZ1(R)
Reece-Edwards, H (N) 1992 F 1,2, 1993 A 2
Reid, A (WP) 1903 BI 3
Reid, B C (Bor) 1933 A 4
Reinach, J (OFS) 1986 Cv 1,2,3,4
Rens, I J (Tvl) 1953 A 3,4
Retief, D F (NT) 1955 BI 1,2,4, 1956 A 1,2, NZ 1,2,3,4
Reyneke, H J (WP) 1910 BI 3
Richards, A R (WP) 1891 BI 1,2,3
Richter, A (NT) 1992 F 1,2, E, 1994 E 2, NZ 1,2,3, 1995 [R, C, WS (R)]
Riley, N M (ET) 1963 A 3
Riordan, C A (Tvl) 1910 BI 1,2
Robertson, I W (R) 1974 F 1,2, 1976 NZ 1,2,4
Rodgers, P H (NT, Tvl) 1989 Wld 1,2, 1992 NZ, F 1,2
Rogers, C D (Tvl) 1984 E 1,2, S Am 1,2
Roos, G D (WP) 1910 BI 2,3
Roos, P J (WP) 1903 BI 3, 1906 I, W, E
Rosenberg, W (Tvl) 1955 BI 2,3,4, 1956 NZ 3, 1958 F 1
Rossouw, C L C (Tvl, N) 1995 WS, [R, WS, F, NZ], 1999 NZ 2(R), A 2(t), [Sp, NZ 3(R)]
Rossouw, D H (WP) 1953 A 3, 4
Rossouw, D J (BB) 2003 [U,Gg,Sm(R),NZ], 2004 E(R),S,Arg, 2005 U,F1,2,A1,W(R), F3(R), 2006 S1,2,F,A1
Rossouw, P W G (WP) 1997 BI 2,3, NZ 1, A 1, NZ 2(R), A 2(R), It, F 1,2, E, S, 1998 I 1,2, W 1, E 1, A 1, NZ 1,2, A 2, W 2, S, I 3, E 2, 1999 It 1, W, NZ 1, A 1(R), NZ 2, A 2, [S, U, E, A 3], 2000 C, E 1,2, A 2, Arg (R), I, W, 2001 F 3, US, 2003 Arg
Rousseau, W P (WP) 1928 NZ 3,4
Roux, F du T (WP) 1960 W, 1961 A 1,2, 1962 BI 1,2,3,4, 1963 A 2, 1965 A 1,2, NZ 1,2,3,4, 1968 BI 3,4, F 1,2 1969 A 1,2,3,4, 1970 I, NZ 1,2,3,4
Roux, J P (Tvl) 1994 E 2, NZ 1,2,3, Arg 1, 1995 [R, C, F (R)], 1996 A 1(R), NZ 1, A 2, NZ 3
Roux, O A (NT) 1969 S, E, 1970 I, W, 1972 E, 1974 BI 3,4
Roux, W G (BB) 2002 F (R), S, E
Russell, R B (MP, N) 2002 W 1(R),2, Arg, A 1(R), NZ 2(R), A 2, F, E (R), 2003 Arg (R), A 1(R), NZ 1, A 2(R), 2004 I2(t&R),W1,NZ1(R),W2(R),Arg(R), 2005 U(R),F2(R), A1(t),Arg(R),W(R), 2006 F

Samuels, T A (GW) 1896 BI 2,3,4
Santon, D (Bol) 2003 A 1(R), NZ 1(R), A 2(t), [Gg(R)]
Sauermann, J T (Tvl) 1971 F 1,2, A 1, 1972 E, 1974 BI 1
Schlebusch, J J J (OFS) 1974 BI 3,4, 1975 F 2
Schmidt, L U (NT) 1958 F 2, 1962 BI 2
Schmidt, U L (NT, Tvl) 1986 Cv 1,2,3,4, 1989 Wld 1,2, 1992 NZ, A, 1993 F 1,2, A 1,2,3, 1994 Arg 1,2, S, W
Schoeman, J (WP) 1963 A 3,4, 1965 I, S, A 1, NZ 1,2
Scholtz, C P (WP, Tvl) 1994 Arg 1, 1995 [R, C, WS]
Scholtz, H (FS) 2002 A 1(R), NZ 2(R), A 2(R), 2003 [U(R),Gg]
Scholtz, H H (WP) 1921 NZ 1,2
Schutte, P J W (Tvl) 1994 S, W
Scott, P A (Tvl) 1896 BI 1,2,3,4
Sendin, W D (GW) 1921 NZ 2
Sephaka, L D (GL) 2001 US, 2002 Sm, NZ 1, A 1, NZ 2, A 2, F, 2003 S 1,2, A 1, NZ 1, A 2(t+R), NZ 2, [U,E(t&R),Gg], 2005 F2,A1,2(R),W, 2006 S1(R),NZ3(t&R),A3(R)
Serfontein, D J (WP) 1980 BI 1,2,3,4, S Am 3,4, F, 1981 I 1,2, NZ 1,2,3, US, 1982 S Am 1,2, 1984 E 1,2, S Am 1,2
Shand, R (GW) 1891 BI 2,3
Sheriff, A R (Tvl) 1938 BI 1,2,3
Shimange, M H (FS, WP) 2004 W1(R),NZ2(R),A2(R),W2(R), 2005 U(R),A1(R),2(R), Arg(R), 2006 S1(R)
Shum, E H (Tvl) 1913 E
Sinclair, D J (Tvl) 1955 BI 1,2,3,4
Sinclair, J H (Tvl) 1903 BI 1
Skene, A L (WP) 1958 F 2
Skinstad, R B (WP, GL) 1997 E (t), 1998 W 1(R), E 1(t), NZ 1(R),2(R), A 2(R), W 2(R), S, I 3, E 2, 1999 [S, Sp (R), U, E, A 3], 2001 F 1(R),2(R), It 1, NZ 1, A 1,2, NZ 2, F 3, It 2, E, 2002 W 1,2, Arg, Sm, NZ 1, A 1, NZ 2, A 2, 2003 Arg (R)
Slater, J T (EP) 1924 BI 3,4, 1928 NZ 1
Smal, G P (WP) 1986 Cv 1,2,3,4, 1989 Wld 1,2
Small, J T (Tvl, N, WP) 1992 NZ, A, F 1,2, E, 1993 F 1,2, A 1,2,3, Arg 1,2, 1994 E 1,2, NZ 1,2,3(t), Arg 1, 1995 WS, [A, R, F, NZ], W, It, E (R), 1996 Fj, A 1, NZ 1, A 2, NZ 2, Arg 1,2, F 1,2, W, 1997 Tg, BI 1, NZ 1(R), A 1(R), NZ 2, A 2, It, F 1,2, E, S
Smit, F C (WP) 1992 E
Smit, J W (N) 2000 C (t), A 1(R), NZ 1(t+R), A 2(R), NZ

2(R), A 3(R), Arg, I, W, E 3, 2001 F 1,2, It 1, NZ 1(R), A 1(R),2(R), NZ 2(R), F 3(R), It 2, E, US (R), [U(R),E(t&R), Gg,Sm,NZ], 2004 I1,2,W1,PI,NZ1,A1,NZ2,A2,W2,I3,E, S,Arg, 2005 U,F1,2,A1,2,3, NZ1,A4,NZ2,Arg,W,F3, 2006 S1,2,F,A1,NZ1,A2,NZ2,3,A3
Smith, C M (OFS) 1963 A 3,4, 1964 W, F, 1965 A 1,2, NZ 2
Smith, C W (GW) 1891 BI 2, 1896 BI 2,3
Smith, D (GW) 1891 BI 2
Smith D J (Z-R) 1980 BI 1,2,3,4
Smith, G A C (EP) 1938 BI 3
Smith, J H (FS) 2003 S 1(R),2(R), A 1, NZ 1, A 2, NZ 2, [U,E,Sm,NZ], 2004 W2, 2005 U(R), F2(R), A2, 3, NZ1, A4, NZ2, Arg, W, F3, 2006 S1, 2, F, A1, NZ1, A2
Smith, P F (GW) 1997 S (R), 1998 I 1(t),2, W 1, NZ 1(R),2(R), A 2(R), W 2, 1999 NZ 2
Smollan, F C (Tvl) 1933 A 3,4,5
Snedden, R C D (GW) 1891 BI 2
Snyman, A H (NT, BB, N) 1996 NZ 3,4, Arg 2(R), W (R), 1997 Tg, BI 1,2,3, NZ 1, A 1, NZ 2, A 2, It, F 1,2, E, S, 1998 I 1,2, W 1, E 1, A 1, NZ 1,2, A 2, W 2, S, I 3, E 2, 1999 NZ 2, 2001 NZ 2, F 3, US, 2002 W 1, 2003 S 1, NZ 1, 2006 S1,2
Snyman, D S L (WP) 1972 E, 1974 BI 1,2(R), F 1,2, 1975 F 1,2, 1976 NZ 2,3, 1977 Wld
Snyman, J C P (OFS) 1974 BI 2,3,4
Sonnekus, G H H (OFS) 1974 BI 3, 1984 E 1,2
Sowerby, R S (N) 2002 Sm (R)
Spies, J J (NT) 1970 NZ 1,2,3,4
Spies, P J (BB) 2006 A1,NZ2,3,A3
Stander, J C J (OFS) 1974 BI 4(R), 1976 NZ 1,2,3,4
Stapelberg, W P (NT) 1974 F 1,2
Starke, J J (WP) 1956 NZ 4
Starke, K T (WP) 1924 BI 1,2,3,4
Steenkamp, G G (FS) 2004 S,Arg, 2005 U,F2(R),A2,3, NZ1(R),A4(R)
Steenekamp, J G A (Tvl) 1958 F 1
Stegmann, A C (WP) 1906 S, I
Stegmann, J A (Tvl) 1912 S, I, W, 1913 E, F
Stewart, C (WP) 1998 S, I 3, E 2
Stewart, D A (WP) 1960 S, 1961 E, S, F, I, 1963 A 1,3,4, 1964 W, F, 1965 I
Stofberg, M T S (OFS, NT, WP) 1976 NZ 2,3, 1977 Wld, 1980 S Am 1,2, BI 1,2,3,4, S Am 3,4, F, 1981 I 1,2, NZ 1,2, US, 1982 S Am 1,2, 1984 E 1,2
Strachan, L C (Tvl) 1932 E, S, 1937 A 1,2, NZ 1,2,3, 1938 BI 1,2,3
Stransky, J (N, WP) 1993 A 1,2,3, Arg 1, 1994 Arg 1,2, 1995 WS, [A, R (t), C, F, NZ], W, It, E, 1996 Fj (R), NZ 1, A 2, NZ 2,3,4,5(R)
Straeuli, R A W (Tvl) 1994 NZ 1, Arg 1,2, S, W, 1995 WS, [A, WS, NZ (R)], E (R)
Strauss, C P (WP) 1992 F 1,2, E, 1993 F 1,2, A 1,2,3, Arg 1,2, 1994 E 1, NZ 1,2, Arg 1,2
Strauss, J A (WP) 1984 S Am 1,2
Strauss, J H P (Tvl) 1976 NZ 3,4, 1980 S Am 1
Strauss, S S F (GW) 1921 NZ 3
Strydom, C F (OFS) 1955 BI 3, 1956 A 1,2, NZ 1,4, 1958 F 1,
Strydom, J J (Tvl, GL) 1993 F 2, A 1,2,3, Arg 1,2, 1994 E 1, 1995 [A, C, F, NZ], 1996 A 2(R), NZ 2(R), 3,4, W (R), 1997 Tg, BI 1,2,3, A 2
Strydom, L J (NT) 1949 NZ 1,2
Styger, J J (OFS) 1992 NZ (R), A, F 1,2, E, 1993 F 2(R), A 3(R)
Suter, M R (N) 1965 I, S
Swanepoel, W (OFS, GL) 1997 BI 3(R), A 2(R), F 1(R), 2, E, S, 1998 I 2(R), W 1(R), E 2(R), 1999 It 1,2(R), W, A 1, [Sp, NZ 3(t)], 2000 A 1, NZ 1, A 2, NZ 2, A 3
Swart, J (WP) 1996 Fj, NZ 1(R), A 2, NZ 2,3,4,5, 1997 BI 3(R), It, S (R)
Swart, J J N (SWA) 1955 BI 1
Swart, I S (Tvl) 1993 A 1,2,3, Arg 1, 1994 E 1,2, NZ 1,3, Arg 2(R), 1995 WS, [A, WS, F, NZ], W, 1996 A 2

Taberer, W S (GW) 1896 BI 2
Taylor, O B (N) 1962 BI 1
Terblanche, C S (Bol, N) 1998 I 1,2, W 1, E 1, A 1, NZ 1,2, A 2, W 2, S, I 3, E 2, 1999 It 1(R),2, W, A 1, NZ 2(R), [Sp, E (R), A 3(R), NZ 3], 2000 E 3, 2002 W 1,2, Arg, Sm, NZ 1, A 1,2(R), 2003 S 1,2, Arg, A 1, NZ 1, A 2, NZ 2, [Gg]
Teichmann, G H (N) 1995 W, 1996 Fj, A 1, NZ 1, A 2, NZ 2,3,4,5, Arg 1,2, F 1,2, W, 1997 Tg, BI 1,2,3, NZ 1, A 1, NZ 2, A 2, It, F 1,2 E, S, 1998 I 1,2, W 1, E 1, A 1, NZ 1,2, A 2, W 2, S, I 3, E 2, 1999 It 1, W, NZ 1
Theron, D F (GW) 1996 A 2(R), NZ 2(R), 5, Arg 1,2, F 1,2, W, 1997 BI 2(R), 3, NZ 1(R), A 1, NZ 2(R)
Theunissen, D J (GW) 1896 BI 3
Thompson, G (WP) 1912 S, I, W
Tindall, J C (WP) 1924 BI 1, 1928 NZ 1,2,3,4
Tobias, E G (SARF, Bol) 1981 I 1,2, 1984 E 1,2, S Am 1,2
Tod, N S (N) 1928 NZ 2
Townsend, W H (N) 1921 NZ 1
Trenery, W E (GW) 1891 BI 2
Tromp, H (NT) 1996 NZ3,4, Arg 2(R), F 1(R)
Truter, D R (WP) 1924 BI 2,4
Truter, J T (N) 1963 A 1, 1964 F, 1965 A 2
Turner, F G (EP) 1933 A 1,2,3, 1937 A 1,2, NZ 1,2,3, 1938 BI 1,2,3
Twigge, R J (NT) 1960 S
Tyibilika, S (N) 2004 S,Arg, 2005 U,A2,Arg, 2006 NZ1,A2,NZ2

Ulyate, C A (Tvl) 1955 BI 1,2,3,4, 1956 NZ 1,2,3
Uys, P de W (NT) 1960 W, 1961 E, S, I, A 1,2, 1962 BI 1,4, 1963 A 1,2, 1969 A 1(R), 2
Uys, P J (Pumas) 2002 S

Van Aswegen, H J (WP) 1981 NZ 1, 1982 S Am 2(R)
Van Biljon, L (N) 2001 It 1(R), NZ 1, A 1,2, NZ 2, F 3, It 2(R), E (R), US, 2002 F (R), S, E (R), 2003 NZ 2(R)
Van Broekhuizen, H D (WP) 1896 BI 4
Van Buuren, M C (Tvl) 1891 BI 1
Van de Vyver, D F (WP) 1937 A 2
Van den Berg, D S (N) 1975 F 1,2, 1976 NZ 1,2
Van den Berg, M A (WP) 1937 A 1, NZ 1,2,3
Van den Berg, P A (WP, GW, N) 1999 It 1(R),2, NZ 2, A 2, [S, U (t+R), E (R), A 3(R), NZ 3(R)], 2000 E 1(R), A 1, NZ 1, A 2, NZ 2(R), A 3(t+R), Arg, I, W, E 3, 2001 F 1(R),2, A 2(R), NZ 2(R), US, 2004 NZ1, 2005 U,F1,2, A1(R),2(R),3(R),4(R),Arg(R), F3(R), 2006 S2(R),A1(R), NZ1,A2(R),NZ2(R),A3(R)
Van den Bergh, E (EP) 1994 Arg 2(t & R)
Van der Linde, A (WP) 1995 It, E, 1996 Arg 1(R), 2(R), F 1(R), W (R), 2001 F 3(R)
Van der Linde, C J (FS) 2002 S (R), E(R), 2004 I1(R),2(R), PI(R),A1(R),NZ2(t&R), A2(R),W2(R),I3(R),E(t&R),S,Arg, 2005 U,F1(R),2,A1(R),3,NZ1,A4,NZ2,Arg,W,F3, 2006 S2(R),F(R),A1,NZ1,A2,NZ2
Van der Merwe, A J (Bol) 1955 BI 2,3,4, 1956 A 1,2, NZ 1,2,3,4, 1958 F 1, 1960 S, NZ 2
Van der Merwe, A V (WP) 1931 W
Van der Merwe, B S (NT) 1949 NZ 1
Van der Merwe, H S (NT) 1960 NZ 4, 1963 A 2,3,4, 1964 F
Van der Merwe, J P (WP) 1970 W
Van der Merwe, P R (SWD, WT, GW) 1981 NZ 2,3, US, 1986 Cv 1,2, 1989 Wld 1
Vanderplank, B E (N) 1924 BI 3,4
Van der Schyff, J H (GW) 1949 NZ 1,2,3,4, 1955 BI 1
Van der Watt, A E (WP) 1969 S (R), E, 1970 I
Van der Westhuizen, J C (WP) 1928 NZ 2,3,4, 1931 I
Van der Westhuizen, J H (WP) 1931 I, 1932 E, S

Van der Westhuizen, J H (NT, BB) 1993 Arg 1,2, 1994 E 1,2(R), Arg 2, S, W, 1995 WS, [A, C (R), WS, F, NZ], W, It, E, 1996 Fj, A 1,2(R), NZ 2,3(R), 4,5, Arg 1,2, F 1,2, W, 1997 Tg, BI 1,2,3, NZ 1, A 1, NZ 2, A 2, It, F 1, 1998 I 1,2, W 1, E 1, A 1, NZ 1,2, A 2, W 2, S, I 3, E 2, 1999 NZ 2, A 2, [S, Sp (R), U, E, A 3, NZ 3], 2000 C, E 1,2, A 1(R), NZ 1(R), A 2(R), Arg, I, W, E 3, 2001 F 1,2, It 1(R), NZ 1, A 1,2, NZ 2, F 3, It 2, E, US (R), 2003 S 1,2, A 1, NZ 1, A 2(R), NZ 2, [U,E,Sm,NZ]

Van der Westhuyzen, J N B (MP, BB) 2000 NZ 2(R), 2001 It 1(R), 2003 S 1(R),2, Arg, A 1, 2003 [E,Sm,NZ], 2004 I1,2,W1,PI,NZ1,A1,NZ2,A2,W2,I3,E,S,Arg, 2005 U,F1,2, A1,4(R),NZ2(R), 2006 S1,2,F,A1

Van Druten, N J V (Tvl) 1924 BI 1,2,3,4, 1928 NZ 1,2,3,4

Van Heerden, A J (Tvl) 1921 NZ 1,3

Van Heerden, F J (WP) 1994 E 1,2(R), NZ 3, 1995 It, E, 1996 NZ 5(R), Arg 1(R),2(R), 1997 Tg, BI 2(t+R),3(R), NZ 1(R),2(R), 1999 [Sp]

Van Heerden, J L (NT, Tvl) 1974 BI 3,4, F 1,2, 1975 F 1,2, 1976 NZ 1,2,3,4, 1977 Wld, 1980 BI 1,3,4, S Am 3,4, F

Van Heerden, J L (BB) 2003 S 1,2, A 1, NZ 1, A 2(t)

Van Jaarsveld, C J (Tvl) 1949 NZ 1

Van Jaarsveldt, D C (R) 1960 S

Van Niekerk, J A (WP) 1928 NZ 4

Van Niekerk, J C (GL, WP) 2001 NZ 1(R), A 1(R), NZ 2(t+R), F 3(R), It2, US, 2002 W 1(R),2(R), Arg (R), Sm, NZ 1, A 1, NZ 2, A 2, F, S, E, 2003 A 2, NZ 2, [U,E,Gg, Sm], 2004 NZ1(R),A1(t),NZ2,A2,W2,I3,E,S,Arg(R), 2005 U(R),F2(R),A1(R),2,3,NZ1,A4, NZ2, 2006 S1,2,F,A1, NZ1(R),A2(R)

Van Reenen, G L (WP) 1937 A 2, NZ 1

Van Renen, C G (WP) 1891 BI 3, 1896 BI 1,4

Van Renen, W (WP) 1903 BI 1,3

Van Rensburg, J T J (Tvl) 1992 NZ, A, E, 1993 F 1,2, A 1, 1994 NZ 2

Van Rooyen, G W (Tvl) 1921 NZ 2,3

Van Ryneveld, R C B (WP) 1910 BI 2,3

Van Schalkwyk, D (NT) 1996 Fj (R), NZ 3,4,5, 1997 BI 2,3, NZ 1, A 1

Van Schoor, R A M (R) 1949 NZ 2,3,4, 1951 S, I, W, 1952 E, F, 1953 A 1,2,3,4

Van Straaten, A J J (WP) 1999 It 2(R), W, NZ 1(R), A 1, 2000 C, E 1,2, NZ 1, A 2, NZ 2, A 3, Arg (R), I (R), W, E 3, 2001 A 1,2, NZ 2, F 3, It 2, E

Van Vollenhoven, K T (NT) 1955 BI 1,2,3,4, 1956 A 1,2, NZ 3

Van Vuuren, T F (EP) 1912 S, I, W, 1913 E, F

Van Wyk, C J (Tvl) 1951 S, I, W, 1952 E, F, 1953 A 1,2,3,4, 1955 BI 1

Van Wyk, J F B (NT) 1970 NZ 1,2,3,4, 1971 F 1,2, A 1,2,3, 1972 E, 1974 BI 1,3,4, 1976 NZ 3,4

Van Wyk, S P (WP) 1928 NZ 1,2

Van Zyl, B P (WP) 1961 I

Van Zyl, C G P (OFS) 1965 NZ 1,2,3,4

Van Zyl, D J (WP) 2000 E 3(R)

Van Zyl, G H (WP) 1958 F 1, 1960 S, NZ 1,2,3,4, W, I, 1961 E, S, F, I, A 1,2, 1962 BI 1,3,4

Van Zyl, H J (Tvl) 1960 NZ 1,2,3,4, I, 1961 E, S, I, A 1,2

Van Zyl, P J (Bol) 1961 I

Veldsman, P E (WP) 1977 Wld

Venter, A G (OFS) 1996 NZ 3,4,5, Arg 1,2, F 1,2, W, 1997 Tg, BI 1,2,3, NZ 1, A 1, NZ 2, It, F 1,2, E, S, 1998 I 1,2, W 1, E 1, A 1, NZ 1,2, A 2, W 2, S (R), I 3(R), E 2(R), 1999 It 1,2(R), W (R), NZ 1, A 1, NZ 2, A 2, [S, U, E, A 3, NZ 3], 2000 C, E 1,2, A 1, NZ 1, A 2, NZ 2, A 3, Arg, I, W, E 3, 2001 F 1, It 1, NZ 1, A 1,2, NZ 2, F 3(R), It 2(R), E (t+R), US (R)

Venter, A J (N) 2000 W (R), E 3(R), 2001 F 3, It 2, E, US, 2002 W 1,2, Arg, NZ 1(R),2, A 2, F, S (R), E, 2003 Arg, 2004 PI,NZ1,A1,NZ2(R),A2,I3,E, 2006 NZ3,A3

Venter, B (OFS) 1994 E 1,2, NZ 1,2,3, Arg 1,2, 1995 [R, C, WS (R), NZ (R)], 1996 A 1, NZ 1, A 2, 1999 A 2, [S, U]

Venter, F D (Tvl) 1931 W, 1932 S, 1933 A 3

Versfeld, C (WP) 1891 BI 3

Versfeld, M (WP) 1891 BI 1,2,3

Vigne, J T (Tvl) 1891 BI 1,2,3

Viljoen, J F (GW) 1971 F 1,2, A 1,2,3, 1972 E

Viljoen, J T (N) 1971 A 1,2,3

Villet, J V (WP) 1984 E 1,2

Visagie, I J (WP) 1999 It 1, W, NZ 1, A 1, NZ 2, A 2, [S, U, E, A 3, NZ 3], 2000 C, E 2, A 1, NZ 1, A 2, NZ 2, A 3, 2001 NZ 1, A 1,2, NZ 2, F 3, It 2(R), E (t+R), US, 2003 S 1(R),2(R), Arg

Visagie, P J (GW) 1967 F 1,2,3,4, 1968 BI 1,2,3,4, F 1,2, 1969 A 1,2,3,4, S, E, 1970 NZ 1,2,3,4, 1971 F 1,2, A 1,2,3

Visagie, R G (OFS, N) 1984 E 1,2, S Am 1,2, 1993 F 1

Visser, J de V (WP) 1981 NZ 2, US

Visser, M (WP) 1995 WS (R)

Visser, P J (Tvl) 1933 A 2

Viviers, S S (OFS) 1956 A 1,2, NZ 2,3,4

Vogel, M L (OFS) 1974 BI 2(R)

Von Hoesslin, D J B (GW) 1999 It 1(R),2, W (R), NZ 1, A 1(R)

Vos, A N (GL) 1999 It 1(t+R),2, NZ 1(R),2(R), A 2, [S (R), Sp, E (R), A 3(R), NZ 3], 2000 C, E 1,2, A 1, NZ 1, A 2, NZ 2, A 3, Arg, I, W, E 3, 2001 F 1,2, It 1, NZ 1, A 1,2, NZ 2, F 3, It 2, E, US

Wagenaar, C (NT) 1977 Wld

Wahl, J J (WP) 1949 NZ 1

Walker, A P (N) 1921 NZ 1,3, 1924 BI 1,2,3,4

Walker, H N (OFS) 1953 A 3, 1956 A 2, NZ 1,4

Walker, H W (Tvl) 1910 BI 1,2,3

Walton, D C (N) 1964 F, 1965 I, S, NZ 3,4, 1969 A 1,2, E

Wannenburg, P J (BB) 2002 F (R), E, 2003 S 1,2, Arg, A 1(t+R), NZ 1(R), 2004 I1,2, W1,PI(R), 2006 S1(R),F,NZ2(R), 3,A3

Waring, F W (WP) 1931 I, 1932 E, 1933 A 1,2,3,4,5

Wegner, N (WP) 1993 F 2, A 1,2,3

Wentzel, M van Z (Pumas) 2002 F (R), S

Wessels, J J (WP) 1896 BI 1,2,3

Whipp, P J M (WP) 1974 BI 1,2, 1975 F 1, 1976 NZ 1,3,4, 1980 S Am 1,2

White, J (Bor) 1931 W, 1933 A 1,2,3,4,5, 1937 A 1,2, NZ 1,2

Wiese, J J (Tvl) 1993 F 1, 1995 WS, [R, C, WS, F, NZ], W, It, E, 1996 NZ 3(R), 4(R), 5, Arg 1,2, F 1,2, W

Willemse, A K (GL) 2003 S 1,2, NZ 1, A 2, NZ 2, [U,E,Sm,NZ], 2004 W2,I3

Williams, A E (GW) 1910 BI 1

Williams, A P (WP) 1984 E 1,2

Williams, C M (WP, GL) 1993 Arg 2, 1994 E 1,2, NZ 1,2,3, Arg 1,2, S, W, 1995 WS, [WS, F, NZ], It, E, 1998 A 1(t), NZ 1(t), 2000 C (R), E 1(t),2(R), A 1(R), NZ 2, A 3, Arg, I, W (R)

Williams, D O (WP) 1937 A 1,2, NZ 1,2,3, 1938 BI 1,2,3

Williams, J G (NT) 1971 F 1,2, A 1,2,3, 1972 E, 1974 BI 1,2,4, F 1,2, 1976 NZ 1,2

Wilson, L G (WP) 1960 NZ 3,4, W, I, 1961 E, F, I, A 1,2, 1962 BI 1,2,3,4, 1963 A 1,2,3,4, 1964 W, F, 1965 I, S, A 1,2, NZ 1,2,3,4

Wolmarans, B J (OFS) 1977 Wld

Wright, G D (EP, Tvl) 1986 Cv 3,4, 1989 Wld 1,2, 1992 F 1,2, E

Wyness, M R K (WP) 1962 BI 1,2,3,4, 1963 A 2

Zeller, W C (N) 1921 NZ 2,3

Zimerman, M (WP) 1931 W, I, 1932 E, S

THE 2005 CURRIE CUP

By Francois Pienaar

Before we reflect on the Currie Cup in 2005, I think it's important to look back at the history of the competition over the last decade. The competition has undergone so much upheaval in the last 10 years and only by remembering what has changed over that time can you get a proper perspective on the tournament now.

In my early playing days for Transvaal, the Currie Cup was the pre-eminent rugby event in South Africa. The years of isolation for the Springboks made the Currie Cup the closest we got to Test match rugby and fans would make pilgrimages of thousands of kilometres to watch their provinces play.

Professionalism and the end of the boycott changed all that and the Currie Cup's star began to wane. Fans could watch the Springboks on the international stage and the introduction of the Super 12 in 1996 created a new, higher layer of competition and the popularity of the Currie Cup suffered.

To make matters worse, the rebranding and regionalisation of the teams along the lines of an American Football franchise initially alienated a lot of the fans. Many of the supporters lost their traditional sense of loyalty to a team because rivals were merged in uneasy alliances and fans didn't understand why. The changes took a lot of time to bed down and for a while the Currie Cup went backwards both in terms of attendances and the quality of rugby on offer.

The point to all this is that I now think the competition is in rude health again and 2005 was a great year for the Currie Cup. The passion for the competition in the streets is there again and the fans have grown used to the changes and the teams have developed a new fans base. The fact that both semi-finals were 50,000 sell-outs within two hours of the tickets going on sale tells its own story.

On the pitch, there were few surprises in the semi-final lines-ups with the Bulls, the three-time defending champions coached by Heyneke Meyer, Eugene Eloff's Lions, Western Province, coached by Kobus van der Merwe and Robbie Erasmus' Cheetahs making it through to the last four.

The Bulls cruised through to the knockout phase, winning all eight games en route to the semis and most people had them down as hot favourites to land their fourth Currie Cup crown in succession. The Bulls' pack was typically physical and robust and they simply steam-rollered everything in their way, amassing plenty of points and big scorelines.

The Lions lost home and away to Western Province, who in turn were beaten twice by the Lions. The Cheetahs by comparison limped into the last four, winning just four out of their eight matches and going down home and away to both the Lions and the Bulls. At this stage, there was little evidence in the league phase to suggest anyone could stop the Bulls.

The first semi-final was a repeat of the 2004 last four clash between Western Province and the Cheetahs at Newlands and it was no surprise it was a tight one. The Cheetahs exploited a sluggish start by WP and although van der Merwe's side opened the scoring with an early penalty, a try, conversion and three penalties were enough to give the Cheetahs a 16–11 win and a place in the final for the second successive year.

Many people considered the second semi-final in Pretoria between the Bulls and the Lions as the final in all but name. Under Meyer, the Bulls were the team to beat and on paper at least the Lions were definitely the next best team in the competition.

In fact, it was Eloff's team who were out of the blocks quickest, narrowly leading 17–16 at the break, but the bigger and more powerful Blues pack began to grind the Lions down in the second half and they emerged reasonably comfortable 31–23 winners. The 2005 final would be a repeat of 2004.

As I said, few people could see beyond the Bulls for the title before the semi-finals and they were even hotter favourites going into the final itself. Loftus Versfeld was their home ground, they were unbeaten and they were the defending champions. Everyone except the Cheetahs' fans expected the Bulls to walk away with it.

The contrast in styles of the two teams was stark as well. The Bulls relied on their forward power and the pack's aggression while the Cheetahs favoured a more expansive, exciting brand of rugby.

In the end it was the more ambitious Cheetahs who threw the form book out of the window, got revenge for their defeat in the 2004 final and emerged 29–25 winners in Pretoria. It was a result as shocking at it was refreshing.

For me, there were three main factors in the Cheetahs' triumph. The first was the tactical acumen of Erasmus. He had watched the Bulls pack bully their opposition all season and his side lost to them twice en route to the knockout stages. Erasmus picked the biggest pack he could and he named three props on the bench so he had enough cover to counter the Bulls' chief strength. It was a brilliant move and the Cheetahs' forwards matched fire with fire in a brutal match-up and to a large extent the tactic worked.

Another big reason for the Cheetahs' win was what I perceived as over confidence on the Bulls' part. They picked Wynand Olivier at centre even though he wasn't 100 per cent fit and they made substitutions to give players a game before the match was won. They forgot the golden lesson of playing for the full 80 minutes and they paid the price. At one point the Bulls were 22–9 up but they became complacent and the Cheetahs did not need a second invitation to snatch the trophy away from them. You have got to play to the final whistle.

The third and final factor in the Cheetahs' win was good old-fashioned luck. Bryan Habana was yellow carded 15 minutes from time to give them a glimmer of hope and then, trailing 25–22, they were on the right end of a piece of good fortune that decided the match. A box kick from the Cheetahs caused panic in the Bulls' defence, a mix up between Johan Roets and Fourie du Preez saw the pair collide and the loose ball fall to substitute Meyer Bosman, who raced over for the try that gave Erasmus' side the trophy. No-one could deny it was a slice of luck but they had probably earned it over the first 70 minutes of the match.

So overall, I thought 2005 was a great year for the Currie Cup. There was some great rugby played, the crowds flocked to the games and without burdening any individual player with a mention, I thought there was some real talent on show.

If I have a gripe, it would the continuing failure to transfer the talent that was so obviously on show in the Currie Cup into the national team. The Springboks have been struggling for too long at Test level but there is no shortage of potential international players in the country. Something is going wrong between Currie Cup and international level. I'm not going to point fingers but I don't for a minute believe all the provinces are geared to creating the best Springbok side possible.

But that is the only negative I can think of. It was good for the competition to see someone beat the Bulls after their recent dominance and even the so-called smaller teams seem to have got stronger. The minnows are growing up every year.

On the coaching side, I believe the future is bright and the Currie Cup confirmed South Africa has a number of young coaches coming through, coaches who should be aspiring to work at Test level in the next five years.

Robbie Erasmus at the Cheetahs for one was superb. He showed a willingness to think outside the box and try the unusual and he got his rewards for his innovative approach. I was also impressed with Franz Ludeke at the Lions and although they didn't make the semi-final stage, I thought Dick Muir's Sharks side played some exciting rugby that reminded me of their vintage period 20 years ago. Gary Gold at the Stormers also did some good work in my opinion, although the team wasn't really at its best.

GROUP STANDINGS

GROUP A

	Pld	Pts
Blue Bulls	8	37
Lions	8	30
Sharks	8	19
Cavaliers	8	12

GROUP B

WP	8	26
Cheetahs	8	20
Griquas	8	10
Leopards	8	7

SEMI-FINALS

15 October, Newlands, Cape Town

WESTERN PROVINCE 11 (2PG, 1T)
CHEETAHS 16 (1G, 3PG)

WESTERN PROVINCE: E Rose; E Seconds, J de Villiers, De Wet Barry, Z Ryland; P Grant, N de Kock; E Andrews, H Shimange, P Barnard, R Skeate, G Britz, S Burger, H Gerber, J van Niekerk

SUBSTITUTES: H Edmonds, JD Moller, R Linde, A Badenhorst, B Conradie, W Greeff, G Theron

SCORERS TRY: Conradie Penalty Goals: Grant, Rose

CHEETAHS: B Fortuin; P Burger, C Kruger, B Goodes, S Zweni; W de Waal, M Claassens; W du Preez, N Drotske, J du Plessis, B du Plooy, B Pieterse, H Scholtz, J Smith, R van der Merwe

SUBSTITUTES: O le Roux, CJ van der Linde, C van Zyl, K Floors, F Oelschig, M Bosman, A Hollenbach

SCORERS TRY: De Waal Conversion: De Waal Penalty Goals: De Waal (3)

YELLOW CARD Scholtz (37 mins)

REFEREE T Henning

15 October, Loftus Versfeld, Pretoria

BLUE BULLS 31 (2G, 4PG, 1T)
LIONS 23 (2G, 3PG)

BLUE BULLS: J Roets; A Ndungane, JP Nel, W Olivier, B Habana; M Steyn, F du Preez; K Lensing, G Botha, A Human, B Botha, V Matfield, J Cronje, P Wannenburg, A Leonard

SUBSTITUTES: W Roux, D Coetzee, D Rossouw, J Wasserman, H Adams, D Hougaard, R van der Bergh

SCORERS TRIES: Wannenburg, Leonard, Ndungane Conversions: Steyn (2) Penalty Goals: Steyn (4)

LIONS: C Jantjes; W Human, J Fourie, W Julies, J Muller; A Pretorius, Nicholas Eyre; P van Niekerk, L van Biljon, M Hurter, T Hall, W Stoltz, G Vosloo, W van Heerden, C Grobbelaar

SUBSTITUTES: S Brits, L Sephaka, KJ Tromp, E Joubert, J Vermaak, N Fourie, G Esterhuizen

SCORERS TRIES: Julies (2) Conversions: Pretorius (2) Penalty Goals: Pretorius (3)

REFEREE M Lawrence

FINAL

22 October, Loftus Versfeld, Pretoria

BLUE BULLS 25 (1G, 5PG, 1DG)
CHEETAHS 29 (2G, 5PG)

BLUE BULLS: J Roets; A Ndungane, JP Nel, W Olivier, B Habana; M Steyn, F du Preez; K Lensing, G Botha, A Human, B Botha, V Matfield, J Cronje, P Wannenburg, A Leonard

SUBSTITUTES: D Coetzee, W Roux, D Rossouw, J Wasserman, H Adams, D Hougaard, R van der Bergh

SCORERS TRY: Ndungane Conversion: Steyn Penalty Goals: Steyn (4), Hougaard Drop Goal: Roets

YELLOW CARDS Matfield (36 mins), Habana (65 mins)

CHEETAHS: B Fortuin; E Fredericks, C Kruger, B Goodes, P Burger; W de Waal, M Claassens; W du Preez, N Drotske, J du Plessis, C van Zyl, B Pieterse, H Scholtz, J Smith, R van der Merwe

SUBSTITUTES: O le Roux, O du Randt, CJ van der Linde, K Floors, F Oelschig, M Bosman

SCORERS TRIES: Fortuin, Bosman Conversions: de Waal (2) Penalty Goals: de Waal (5)

YELLOW CARD du Randt (36 mins)

REFEREE J Kaplan

TONGA

TONGA'S TEST RECORD

OPPONENTS	DATE	VENUE	RESULT
Japan	4 June	A	**Won** 57–16
Fiji	10 June	N	**Won** 24–23
Cook Islands	24 June	H	**Won** 77–10
Samoa	1 July	N	**Lost** 0–36
Cook Islands	8 July	H	**Won** 90–0

TONGA GIVEN NEW LEACH OF LIFE

By Jeremy Duxbury

Many wished Adam Leach good luck when the Australian took over the reins from legendary loose forward Viliami Ofahengaue as Tonga's national coach in May this year – he inherited a 12-Test losing streak that stretched back to the 2003 Rugby World Cup under Jim Love.

"Don't change your coach so close to the 2007 World Cup," was the warning call to the Tonga Rugby Union.

Yet Leach assembled his men in haste for the newly formed IRB Pacific 5 Nations, and promptly won their opening two matches – a 57–16 spanking of Japan in Fukuoka, and a narrow but important 24–23 victory against Fiji in Gosford, Tonga's adopted home for the tournament.

And so the old adage "Beware the Tongan Warrior" proved accurate once more.

When major rugby unions consider the Pacific Islands, the tendency quite usually is to imagine small tropical islands with not much around but sand, sea and rugby. And in Tonga's case, the image may not be so far removed from reality, especially as Tonga is only a quarter the size of Fiji and has just a tenth of the population.

In terms of rugby infrastructure, facilities and size of chequebook, Fiji and Samoa are echelons behind nations like New Zealand and Australia. So, consider if you can, how Tonga fits into this picture – population 90,000, landmass 748 square kilometers.

This huge difference in size – Samoa is also four times as big and has double the population – means that in many sporting battles Tonga tends to take up the role of the underdog, a position the Friendly Islanders appear quite content to assume.

This happy-go-lucky approach to life belies the immense natural strength and ferocious pride of the Tongan Warriors, especially on the rugby field.

In recent years, the Tongan age grade teams have been quite the dominant force in the region whilst their elders have struggled to find many positives to take home. Last November's 48–0 loss to Italy in Prato was probably the Ikale Tahi's nadir.

The new cross-border IRB Pacific Rugby Cup in April was designed to lift the standard of the domestic game in Fiji, Samoa and Tonga.

Tonga picked their two teams – Tautahi Gold and Tau'uta Reds – from the players involved in the local Aoniu Datec Cup, held amongst six teams and won by Kolofoou Magic.

But Tonga's teams in the PRC lacked experience compared with their Fijian and Samoan counterparts, some of whom had played at full international level. And as this happened before Leach had arrived in the country, it wasn't much good to him in selection terms.

The Tau'uta Reds finished fourth, thanks to one outstanding 17–14 victory over a vastly more experienced Fiji Barbarians in Nadi, and the Tautahi Gold propped up the bottom of the table in sixth.

Leach's Test squad was thus drawn mostly from European-based players, such as Sale No 8 Epeli Taione, Saracens wing Tevita Vaikona, and Perpignan flanker Viliami Vaki.

But there was also some Super 14 influence in skipper and openside flanker Nili Latu, hooker Aleki Lutui (both with the Chiefs), and retiring tighthead prop Tevita Taumoepeau, now with English side Worcester.

Tonga's Pacific 5 Nations began with the long journey to Fukuoka in Western Japan. An even first half saw the Ikale Tahi hold a slender 15–13 lead at the break. But the Tongans came together in the second period, which Japan coach Jean-Pierre Elissalde later described as a "nightmare".

Tonga ran away 57–16 winners, outscoring their hosts eight tries to one to record the Kingdom's first Test victory in three years. Relief.

Leach admitted that his time spent coaching in Japan had helped considerably as they knew Japan's "strengths and weaknesses."

One week later in dreadful conditions on Australia's Central Coast, his team dug deep to shock Fiji 24–23 with a late try from Lutui and awkward conversion from Pierre Hola sealing the points.

The match was far from pretty, but that didn't concern Leach who savored his second victory in the competition as Tonga led the table alongside the Junior All Blacks. Who would have thought?

Now the Ikale Tahi were gaining in confidence. Going to New Plymouth to play a team hovering below the All Blacks, Leach admitted that they were building game by game and a win was not out of the question.

Twenty-one points from pivot Jimmy Gopperth ended Tonga's brief dream as the New Zealanders triumphed 38–10, by no means a walloping these days. Another try to Lutui and two successful kicks from Hola was all Tonga had to show for their efforts.

Before completing their Pacific 5 Nations schedule, Tonga had to fly off to Rarotonga for the first of two 2007 Rugby World Cup qualifying matches against the Cook Islands.

Buoyed by their newly found form, Leach's men devoured their minnow opponents 77–10 in a 13-try rout; not quite what the Cooks had in mind as they attempt to break into Tier 2 rugby.

Leach admitted that his selection was "starting to reflect our best team with the current players available," but warned of player fatigue with the continuous flying around.

And eight days later, he was proved correct as Tonga slumped 36–0 to Michael Jones's Manu Samoa in Gosford. The game was scoreless for half an hour as the Ikale Tahi held firm, but the Samoans wore down their opponents in the closing stages to grab second spot in the table behind the Junior All Blacks.

Though Tonga ended up fourth, the competitiveness of the warriors had returned.

And to celebrate, they enjoyed a 90–0 massacre of the Cooks in Nuku'alofa as Leach's charges picked up 14 tries in the final repechage match in Oceania before taking on the number two team in Asia for a spot at next year's World Cup.

Most fittingly, and to underline the wonderful nature of these Friendly Islanders, powerhouse prop Tevita Taumoepeau kicked the final conversion of the match as he retired from international rugby after nine years in the Tongan team.

"Tevita has served both king and country admirably over the years," Leach said. "And his legacy of dedication to Tongan rugby, scrummaging and personal commitment will live on."

TONGA INTERNATIONAL STATISTICS

(TO 30TH SEPTEMBER 2006)

Compiled by John Lea (leajr@xtra.co.nz)

This data is unverified, as some match records remain incomplete. Player appearances may be understated in some cases, and some scorers of points in earlier matches have not been identified.

MATCH RECORDS

MOST CONSECUTIVE TEST WINS

4 2002 Papua New Guinea 1,2, 2003 South Korea 1,2

MOST CONSECUTIVE TESTS WITHOUT DEFEAT

Matches	Wins	Draws	Periods
4	4	0	2002 to 2003

MOST POINTS IN A MATCH

BY THE TEAM

Pts.	Opponent	Venue	Year
119	South Korea	Nuku'alofa	2003
90	Cook Islands	Nuku'alofa	2006
84	Papua New Guinea	Port Moresby	2002
82	South Korea	Seoul	1999
77	Cook Islands	Rarotonga	2006
75	South Korea	Seoul	2003
68	Cook Islands	Nuku'alofa	1997

BY A PLAYER

Pts.	Player	Opponent	Venue	Year
44	P Hola	South Korea	Nuku'alofa	2003
27	S Tu'ipolutu	South Korea	Seoul	1999
24	P Hola	Papua New Guinea	Port Moresby	2002
23	K Tonga	Cook Islands	Nuku'alofa	1997
20	B Kivalu	South Korea	Nuku'alofa	2003

MOST TRIES IN A MATCH

BY THE TEAM

Tries	Opponent	Venue	Year
17	South Korea	Nuku'alofa	2003
14	Cook Islands	Nuku'alofa	2006
13	Cook Islands	Rarotonga	2006
12	Papua New Guinea	Port Moresby	2002
12	South Korea	Seoul	2003
11	South Korea	Seoul	1999
10	Cook Islands	Nuku'alofa	1997

BY A PLAYER

Tries	Player	Opponent	Venue	Year
4	B Kivalu	South Korea	Nuku'alofa	2003
3	S Hala'unga	Western Samoa	Apia	1957
3	S Taumalolo	Cook Islands	Nuku'alofa	1997
3	S Koloi	South Korea	Seoul	1999
3	S Taumalolo	Georgia	Tbilisi	1999
3	T Vaikona	Cook Islands	Nuku'alofa	2006
3	V Hakalo	Cook Islands	Rarotonga	2006

MOST CONVERSIONS IN A MATCH

BY THE TEAM

Cons	Opponent	Venue	Year
17	South Korea	Nuku'alofa	2003
10	Cook Islands	Nuku'alofa	2006
9	Cook Islands	Nuku'alofa	1997
9	Papua New Guinea	Port Moresby	2002
8	South Korea	Seoul	1999

BY A PLAYER

Cons	Player	Opponent	Venue	Year
17	P Hola	South Korea	Nuku'alofa	2003
9	K Tonga	Cook Islands	Nuku'alofa	1997
9	P Hola	Papua New Guinea	Port Moresby	2002
9	F Apikatoa	Cook Islands	Nuku'alofa	2006
8	S Tu'ipolutu	South Korea	Seoul	1999

MOST PENALTIES IN A MATCH

BY THE TEAM

Pens	Opponent	Venue	Year
5	Scotland	Murrayfield	2001
4	Japan	Tokyo	1995
4	Fiji	Nuku'alofa	2001
4	Samoa	Nuku'alofa	2005

BY A PLAYER

Pens	Player	Opponent	Venue	Year
4	S Tu'ipolutu	Japan	Tokyo	1995
4	S Tu'ipolutu	Scotland	Murrayfield	2001
4	K Tonga	Fiji	Nuku'alofa	2001
4	F Apikatoa	Samoa	Nuku'alofa	2005

MOST DROP GOALS IN A MATCH

BY THE TEAM AND BY A PLAYER

Drops	Player	Opponent	Venue	Year
1	V Afeaki	Fiji	Suva	1997
1	S Tu'ipolutu	Italy	Leicester	1999
1	P Hola	Fiji	Nadi	2002
1	P Hola	Papua New Guinea	Port Moresby	2002
1	SM Tu'ipolutu	France	Toulouse	2005
1	P Hola	Fiji	Gosford	2006

MOST CAPPED PLAYERS

Caps	Player	Career span
42	E Vunipola	1990 to 2005
41	B Kivalu	1998 to 2005
36	M Vunipola	1987 to 1999
36	F Vunipola	1991 to 2001
28	F Valu	1973 to 1987
27	S Martens	1998 to 2003
27	P Hola	1998 to 2006
26	I Fatani	1992 to 2000
26	V Vaki	2001 to 2006
25	V Ma'asi	1997 to 2005
25	T Taumoepeau	1999 to 2006

MOST POINTS IN TESTS

Pts	Player	Tests	Career
222	P Hola	27	1998 to 2006
190	S Tu'ipolutu	20	1993 to 2003
115	S Taumaolo	24	1996 to 2006
107	K Tonga	13	1996 to 2001
60	F Tatafu	23	1996 to 2002
57	F Apikatoa	10	2004 to 2006
54	V Ma'ake	20	1973 to 1980
50	E Vunipola	42	1990 to 2005

MOST TRIES IN TESTS

Tries	Player	Tests	Career
13	S Taumalolo	24	1996 to 2006
12	F Tatafu	23	1996 to 2002
11	P Hola	27	1998 to 2006
9	B Kivalu	41	1998 to 2005
8	E Vunipola	42	1990 to 2005
8	T Tulia	9	2002 to 2005

MOST CONVERSIONS IN TESTS

Cons	Player	Tests	Career
55	P Hola	27	1998 to 2006
36	S Tu'ipolutu	20	1993 to 2003
30	K Tonga	13	1996 to 2001
18	F Apikatoa	10	2004 to 2006
12	V Ma'ake	20	1973 to 1980

MOST PENALTY GOALS IN TESTS

Pens	Player	Tests	Career
30	S Tu'ipolutu	20	1993 to 2003
16	P Hola	27	1998 to 2006
14	K Tonga	13	1996 to 2001
13	T Lovo	10	1986 to 1990
12	S Taumalolo	24	1996 to 2006
10	V Ma'ake	20	1973 to 1980

MOST DROP GOALS IN TESTS

Drops	Player	Tests	Career
3	P Hola	27	1998 to 2006
1	V Afeaki	6	1997 to 2002
1	S Tu'ipolutu	20	1993 to 2003
1	SM Tu'ipolutu	23	1997 to 2006

URUGUAY

URUGUAY'S TEST RECORD

OPPONENTS	DATE	VENUE	RESULT
Argentina	8 July	A	**Lost** 0–26
Chile	22 July	H	**Won** 43–15

NEW DAY DAWNS FOR LOS TEROS

By Frankie Deges

For some teams, playing in a World Cup final is a part of their accustomed existence. For others, such as the Uruguayan Teros, it spells that difference between surviving or disappearing: it gives them a sense of purpose and belonging. Looking at cold numbers brings confirmation of the impact participation in Rugby World Cup 1999 and 2003 has had in the small South American nation.

When Los Teros played in their first tournament in 1999, the playing base was of only 1,100 players (age group and adult players). They were the smallest of playing nations and rugby was centred in Montevideo

Adam Pretty/Getty Images

Uruguay claimed a famous victory at the 2003 World Cup, beating Georgia.

with one club in their First Division from outside the nation's capital. The three home qualifying matches (against Chile, Portugal and eventually Morocco) were played at the Carrasco Polo Club ground in front of a small crowd, no bigger than 1,500 spectators.

Four years later, after an emotional run to Australia 2003 – which required three consecutive, home wins against Canada, USA and Chile to book the tickets for the World Cup – the playing numbers had more than doubled, with approximately 2,500 players at all levels. Rugby was now being played outside of Montevideo thanks to a large development programme, and there were some 7,000 spectators cramming the derelict River Plate Stadium in Montevideo to support Los Teros in their quest for a place in Australia '03.

Their second World Cup confirmed that Los Teros were no flash in the pan; beating the Georgian Lelos in Sydney brought some of the most remembered clips of that tournament. In front of the biggest "home" support – some 15,000 Uruguayan ex-pats attended that game – the celebrations made history, with players jumping into the stands to join in the celebrations with their supporters.

Back home, the growth continued and even if the last couple of seasons the game somewhat stalled for a variety of reasons, the playing numbers today stand at a healthy 5,000 players – in eight seasons since 1999, it represents an exponential growth and a testament to what Rugby World Cup has meant, the hard work of countless of

Uruguayan rugby-loving amateurs and the vision of the International Rugby Board.

When Los Teros beat Chile 43–15 to confirm they are the second best team in South America – behind Argentina – the team was playing in a new home at Parque Central – a refurbished ground, home of Nacional FC which could become Los Teros home for years to come – and in front of 11,500 spectators. The expectation will now be to have more than 15,000 spectators for the next RWC qualifying match – stretching the home record of the game against Chile.

Uruguay has not had the luxury of a big fixture list in 2006; in fact, the only two internationals played prior to this book being published were in the Rugby World Cup qualifying rounds against Argentina and Chile.

The team went through a six-month preparation process, which proved difficult. A 12-day training camp was organised in February for almost 50 players including all Uruguayans playing overseas. Later in the season, three of the most experienced players were no longer part of the team for internal reasons. Losing the experience of Pablo Lemoine, Nicolás Brignoni and Juan Carlos Bado – veterans of both World Cup campaigns – was at the time seen as suicidal. Also gone was Australian Paul Healy, who had been in Uruguay assisting with the preparation of the team.

The solid work of coaches Fernando Silva and Nicolás Inciarte (who had been assistant coach in RWC '99) was put to the test. Theirs was a team that only had two players currently playing overseas – captain Rodrigo Capo Ortega, a lock in Castres Olympique and number eight for his nation, and flanker Hernán Ponte at Rouen (both in France), whilst veteran prop Diego Lamelas is a First Division player in Buenos Aires. After playing a couple of warm-up matches against Argentine teams – their source of close competition as distances are cruel to Uruguay – the Teros crossed the River Plate to Buenos Aires for the one-off test against Los Pumas.

This was always going to be a game in which Argentina was to qualify for France 2007. Under atrocious weather and in the presence of the Webb Ellis Cup, Los Teros nonetheless gave a strong-hearted performance in losing 26–0. This game gave Rodrigo Capo Ortega's team sufficient encouragement to work hard over the following two weeks before the game against Chile.

In the region, this has been always a big game for both teams – even if Uruguay has had the upper hand in the last thirty years. With a smaller playing base, Los Teros have always found ways to beat Los Cóndores, and the game in Montevideo once again confirmed history.

With an experienced squad – eight players had two World Cups in their

CV and another six had also been in Australia three years ago – the game against Chile confirmed how important a World Cup is for Uruguay. The team played with passion and intelligence – it seemed that with the smell of a probable World Cup trip in their nostrils, the players grow in stature.

Two tries in the first quarter set the tone for the remainder of the game. The strength of flanker Nicolás Grillé (he was nursing a horrible knee gash from the game against Los Pumas and three days before the Chilean test was unable to walk) epitomized the Tero attitude. He scored two tries, his hard tackle on a Chilean player generated a third and gave the last pass for a fourth – with five tries in all, his contribution can't be underestimated.

This game did not confirm that Uruguay goes to the World Cup. For that, they had to patiently wait for the outcome of the Canada v USA match in Newfoundland, later tackle the loser in a home and away series to determine the team that advances to Pool A.

Although Uruguay would love nothing more than to qualify there and then, the lack of matches they play each season would also see it in their best interest that if they don't, the Repechage system would give them precious match mileage.

"We don't have sufficient Test matches which is a problem for us," explains captain Rodrigo Capo Ortega. "In Europe, Africa, even North America, they have more exposure to top level rugby, whilst we only play a handful of games a season."

The sky seems to be the limit for Uruguayan rugby. A third World Cup looms on the horizon for Los Teros which should enable the growth of the game to continue. Even if the national team seems to have mutated little in the past decade, rugby has left the confines of Montevideo and is now played throughout the country.

The Oriental Republic of Uruguay has a population of 3.5 million and an area of 68,000 square kilometers. Politically divided in 19 departments, rugby is being played in an organized way in at least sixteen of these. Women's rugby is also growing, with four teams (only one comes from Montevideo). Whereas in 1999 only people involved with rugby knew about the game, now Los Teros have become a recognizable team – one of the few national sides that are successful, as the soccer team failed to reach the FIFA World Cup. Schools are also committed to rugby.

The domestic club scene has been dominated for many years by the Carrasco Polo Club, champions uninterruptedly since 1990. Of the three championship scheduled for 2006, they had already won the first two and have reached the final of the third by virtue of their performance this year. Without eleven players in the national squad, they still managed to win the 55th Anniversary Cup final the day after the Test against Chile, confirming their top placing with a 24–8 win against Champagnat.

URUGUAYAN INTERNATIONAL STATISTICS

COMPILED BY HUGH COPPING

MOST POINTS IN A MATCH

BY THE TEAM

Pts.	Opponent	Venue	Year
93	Paraguay	Montevideo	1998
92	Venezuela	Santiago	2004
81	Paraguay	Mendoza	2002
77	Brazil	Montevideo	1981
67	Paraguay	Asuncion	1993
67	Paraguay	Asuncion	1997

BY A PLAYER

Pts.	Player	Opponent	Venue	Year
29	Juan Menchaca	Chile	Montevideo	2002
28	Marcelo Nicola Horta	Paraguay	Asuncion	1993
27	Oscar Bacot	Paraguay	Montevideo	1971
23	Federico Sciarra	Paraguay	Asuncion	1998
22	Federico Sciarra	Argentina	Posadas	1995
22	Juan Menchaca	Paraguay	Montevideo	2001

MOST TRIES IN A MATCH

BY THE TEAM

Tries	Opponent	Venue	Year
15	Paraguay	Montevideo	1998
13	Brazil	Montevideo	1981
12	Paraguay	Mendoza	2002
10	Paraguay	Montevideo	1971
10	Brazil	Santiago	1979
10	Paraguay	Asuncion	1993

BY A PLAYER

Tries	Player	Opponent	Venue	Year
4	Benjamin Bono	Paraguay	Mendoza	2002
4	Carlos Bonaso	Brazil	Montevideo	1981
4	Michael Smith	Brazil	Santiago	1979
4	Diego Ormaechea	Brazil	Montevideo	1991

MOST CONVERSIONS IN A MATCH

BY THE TEAM

Cons	Opponent	Venue	Year
9	Paraguay	Mendoza	2002
9	Paraguay	Montevideo	1998
8	Brazil	Montevideo	1981
7	Paraguay	Montevideo	2001
7	Paraguay	Asuncion	1993
7	Brazil	Santiago	1979

BY A PLAYER

Cons	Player	Opponent	Venue	Year
8	Jose Peirano	Brazil	Montevideo	1981
7	Juan Menchaca	Paraguay	Montevideo	2001
6	Ricardo Sierra	Paraguay	Mendoza	2002
6	Rafael Ubilla	Paraguay	Montevideo	1981
6	Federico Sciarra	Paraguay	Montevideo	1998
6	Oscar Bacot	Paraguay	Montevideo	1971
6	Marcelo Nicola Horta	Chile	Santiago	1991
6	Santiago Silva	Chile	Montevideo	1992
6	Santiago Silva	Brazil	Sao Paulo	1993

MOST PENALTIES IN A MATCH

BY THE TEAM

Pens	Opponent	Venue	Year
7	Chile	Tucumán	1977
6	Chile	Montevideo	1997
6	Morocco	Casablanca	1999
6	Argentina	Posadas	1995
6	Argentina	Santiago	1987
6	Chile	Mendoza	2002
6	Chile	Buenos Aires	1983

BY A PLAYER

Pens	Player	Opponent	Venue	Year
6	Federico Sciarra	Argentina	Posadas	1995
6	Rafael Silva	Argentina	Santiago	1987
6	Juan Menchaca	Chile	Mendoza	2002
6	Rafael Ubilla	Chile	Buenos Aires	1983
5	Federico Sciarra	Morocco	Casablanca	1999
5	Federico Sciarra	Chile	Montevideo	1998
5	Juan Menchaca	Argentina	Kingston	2001
5	Juan Menchaca	Chile	Montevideo	2002
5	Sebastián Aguirre	Chile	Montevideo	2003

MOST DROP GOALS IN A MATCH

BY THE TEAM

Drops	Opponent	Venue	Year
4	Chile	Montevideo	2002
3	Chile	Santiago	1991
2	Chile	Santiago	1979
2	Chile	Sao Paulo	1964

BY A PLAYER

Drops	Player	Opponent	Venue	Year
4	Juan Menchaca	Chile	Montevideo	2002
2	Rafael Ubilla	Chile	Santiago	1979
2	Cesar Cat	Chile	Santiago	1991

MOST CAPPED PLAYERS

Caps	Player
53	Diego Aguirre
53	Diego Ormaechea
50	Pedro Vecino
48	Mario Lame
46	Juan Carlos Bado

LEADING TRY SCORERS

Tries	Player
30	Diego Ormaechea
13	Alfonso Cardoso
12	Federico Sciarra
10	Pedro Vecino
9	Pablo Costábile
8	Marcelo Nicola Horta

LEADING CONVERSIONS SCORERS

Cons	Player
35	Marcelo Nicola Horta
31	Federico Sciarra
24	Juan Menchaca
14	Jose Peirano
14	Santiago Silva
14	Diego Aguirre

LEADING PENALTY SCORERS

Pens	Player
47	Juan Menchaca
42	Federico Sciarra
26	Jorge Zerbino
19	Diego Aguirre
16	Marcelo Nicola Horta
16	Rafael Ubilla

LEADING DROP GOAL SCORERS

Drops	Player
5	Juan Menchaca
4	Rafael Ubilla
2	Armando Lerma
2	Cesar Cat
2	Pablo Iturria

LEADING POINT SCORERS

Pts	Player
246	Federico Sciarra
234	Juan Menchaca
152	Marcelo Nicola Horta
136	Diego Ormaechea
120	Diego Aguirre

USA

USA'S TEST RECORD

OPPONENTS	DATE	VENUE	RESULT
NZ Maori	7 June	N	**Lost** 74–6
Canada	17 June	A	**Lost** 33–18
Barbados	1 July	H	**Won** 91–0
Canada	12 Aug	A	**Lost** 56–7

TOUGH TIMES IN THE STATES

By Kurt Oeler

The USA's 2006 season illustrated the saying 'it's darkest before dawn', as the Eagles suffered record defeats to the New Zealand Maori and archrival Canada. The latter, a 56–7 Rugby World Cup qualifying match, consigned America to a home-and-away series against Uruguay. But there were hints of sunlight in the IRB North America 4 competition, which made a promising start in bridging the gap between

Getty Images

Dan Lyle was one of a number of people to depart USA Rugby in 2006.

amateur club rugby and the Test level, as well as USA Rugby's installing a new board of directors.

Kicking off in May, the cross-border tournament instantly became the USA's most significant representative competition. Though first-year scheduling conflicts with domestic play-offs saw some senior players miss the first round in Vancouver, Jim Love's Falcons gave a good account of themselves and many were newly drafted into the national team, including wings Brian Barnard and Jeff Hullinger. Less so the Hawks, who were embarrassed in their opener against Canada West.

Interim USA national coach Peter Thorburn might have sympathised with the Hawks' birth pangs. Taking the helm from Tom Billups, who had resigned in protest of continuing national team budget cuts, the former New Zealand selector quickly discovered that the Eagles had been punching above their weight, based on the standard of club play and the lack of anything in between. "The club scene doesn't see them under pressure a lot. Players don't learn and don't train as hard if they know they are going to have comfortable wins," he observed, underscoring the NA4's potential.

Thorburn fielded nine new internationals (including replacements) in the opening match of June's Barclays Churchill Cup. The 28–13 loss to Ireland A flattered to deceive. Michael Bradley's second string enjoyed the majority of possession, scoring three times in the opening quarter before succumbing to Santa Clara, California's 90-degree heat.

Six changes were made for the Maori fixture as Thorburn looked things over. Poor continuity compounded set piece problems, and the defence yielded 12 tries in a 74–6 mismatch. The result compared unfavorably with 2004's 69–31 away loss to the New Zealanders.

Then on to Edmonton, Alberta, for a fifth-place match against Canada, who began the contest one place below the USA in the IRB rankings. Flanker Todd Clever's 47th-minute touchdown brought the visitors to within 18–11, but the Americans then conceded 15 unanswered points and fell 33–18. Sadly, two of Canada's four tries were scored while the Maple Leafs were a man down.

The Churchill record – three tries (two scored in injury time) and 37 points scored against 135 points conceded – was offset by July's RWC qualifier against Barbados. Backs Hullinger and Phil Eloff, returning after two seasons spoiled by injury, each scored a hat trick in a 91–0 romp over the West Indies champions. Player unhappiness over Billups' departure seemed to be dissipating as Thorburn settled in.

Then followed the NA4's second leg, which saw the debuts of such veteran internationals as lock Alec Parker and half-back Kimball Kjar. But Thorburn insisted that European professionals including centres Paul Emerick and Albert Tuipulotu (both Parma) and number eight Kort Schubert (Cardiff Blues) also take part, while Canada rested its front-line internationals. The Falcons reached the final against Canada West, which claimed the inaugural title 31–20 in muggy Columbus, Ohio.

Some momentum and greater expectations therefore preceded August's RWC qualifier against Canada in Newfoundland, especially since it doubled as the annual Can-Am Match, an increasingly sharp rivalry. From 1977 to 1994, Canada dominated the series 14–4, but since the dawn of professionalism USA had rallied to a 6–5 edge. This time, Canada raced to a 27–0 half-time lead, on route to the biggest win in the contest's 30-year-history. Clever's try, his third of a fine season, was the lone bright spot.

"A lot of things we've been trying to do fell by the wayside, like players staying on their feet at the breakdown. I'm not saying we're the architects of own destruction, but we didn't fire," Thorburn said immediately afterward.

Why had the Eagles declined by 50 points since 2005's 20–19 Can-Am triumph in Edmonton? Back in June, Thorburn had estimated that the majority of the Churchill squad would be selected for the Canadian qualifier. Instead he capped 17 debutants and 38 overall in five matches – before going with something very like the 2005 line-up. In addition to being unsettled, the team may have been tired: players were unused to the NA4's extra demands, and Thorburn had scrummaged the week before the match. The coach himself contended Canada's greater number of professional players plying their trade abroad was the difference, though there was nothing new there.

Whatever the case, the IRB's long-term strategic investment for establishing a domestic high-performance infrastructure was indispensable to the 2006 season. (The three-year, £1.5 million grant is in addition to monies for the NA4 competition.) The acknowledged financial shortcomings of chief executive Doug Arnot, who departed mid-year, meant that the Test calendar simply could not have proceeded without the IRB's grant, which also was applied to the university-level All-Americans, the Under-19s, the (newly established) Under-17s, and sundry player and coaching development initiatives. But the upheaval cost America its first generation of European professionals in Billups, Dave Hodges, and Dan Lyle, who took rugby jobs outside the union.

The import of the £500,000 NA4 grant also was hard to underestimate. Players competed in an unprecedented amount of high-level rugby, providing the country an important developmental platform. One lesson learned: domestic amateurs could not afford to attend all of the summer's national team and the NA4 assemblies: some had already used up their vacation time before the start of the qualifiers. But there was considerable unease that every cross-border or international-level coach, from the Eagles to the NA4 sides to the Under-17 team, was foreign-born; were domestic coaches missing valuable leadership experience?

If 2006's Test results cannot be separated from the boardroom, then the connection is a source of hope for the future. In March USA Rugby adopted an ambitious strategic plan that paved the way for culminating a long-rumbling endeavour to reduce the union's unwieldy 26-person board down to nine members. In came men like Kevin Roberts, the former New Zealand RU director who is the New York-based chairman of advertising giant Saatchi & Saatchi, and Tom Wacker, a London investment banker who served as the IRB's chief executive at a time when rugby union was transitioning to the pro era – valuable experience for the contemporary American game.

Additionally, there were signs of American rugby delivering "mainstream" athletes to the international arena. Hullinger, a second-year football convert, rated highly on Thorburn's list of newcomers, while John Tarpoff returned, improved by two years' hiatus playing gridiron, until a knee injury sidelined him for the qualifiers. Along with Clever, the St. Louis Bombers prop was among the Eagles' best in 2006.

Centre Eloff's recovery from injury lent much-needed depth to a midfield already including pros Tuipulotu and Emerick, but it was a forgettable campaign, by his own standards, for captain Schubert, forced into surgery before the Uruguay matches.

By next year, the US expects to be able to call on a clutch of players newly placed in England's National One.

USA INTERNATIONAL STATISTICS

MATCH RECORDS UP TO 20TH SEPTEMBER 2006

OVERALL MATCH RECORD

Played	Won	Lost	Drawn	PF	PA
147	45	100	2	2,892	4,210

MOST CONSECUTIVE TESTS WITHOUT DEFEAT

Matches	Wins	Draws	Periods
4	4	0	2003

MOST POINTS IN A MATCH

BY THE TEAM

Pts.	Opponent	Venue	Year
91	Barbados	Palo Alto	2006
74	Japan	San Francisco	1996
69	Japan	San Francisco	2003
62	Spain	Madrid	2003
61	Portugal	Lisbon	1998
60	Uruguay	Montevideo	1989
60	Bermuda	Devonshire	1994

BY A PLAYER

Pts.	Player	Opponent	Venue	Year
26	C O'Brien	Uruguay	Montevideo	1989
26	M Hercus	Barbados	Palo Alto	2006
25	C O'Brien	Bermuda	Devonshire	1994
25	M Alexander	Hong Kong	San Francisco	1996
24	M Alexander	Japan	San Francisco	1996
22	M Hercus	Spain	Madrid	2003
20	V Anitoni	Japan	San Francisco	1996
20	B Hightower	Japan	San Francisco	1997
20	V Anitoni	Portugal	Lisbon	1998

MOST TRIES IN A MATCH

BY THE TEAM

Tries	Opponent	Venue	Year
13	Barbados	Palo Alto	2006
11	Uruguay	Montevideo	1989
11	Japan	San Francisco	1996
11	Japan	San Francisco	2003
9	Tunisia	Pebble Beach	1987
9	Bermuda	Devonshire	1994
9	Portugal	Lisbon	1998

BY A PLAYER

Tries	Player	Opponent	Venue	Year
4	V Anitoni	Japan	San Francisco	1996
4	B Hightower	Japan	San Francisco	1997
4	V Anitoni	Portugal	Lisbon	1998
3	G Hein	Tunisia	Pebble Beach	1987
3	C O'Brien	Uruguay	Montevideo	1989
3	K Cross	Japan	San Francisco	2003
3	P Eloff	Barbados	Palo Alto	2006
3	J Hullinger	Barbados	Palo Alto	2006

MOST CONVERSIONS IN A MATCH

BY THE TEAM

Cons	Opponent	Venue	Year
13	Barbados	Palo Alto	2006
8	Uruguay	Montevideo	1989
8	Japan	San Francisco	1996
7	Japan	San Francisco	2003
6	Bermuda	Devonshire	1994
6	Spain	Fort Lauderdale	2003

BY A PLAYER

Cons	Player	Opponent	Venue	Year
13	M Hercus	Barbados	Palo Alto	2006)
8	M Alexander	Japan	San Francisco	1996
7	C O'Brien	Uruguay	Montevideo	1989
7	M Hercus	Japan	San Francisco	2003
6	C O'Brien	Bermuda	Devonshire	1994
6	M Hercus	Spain	Fort Lauderdale	2003

MOST PENALTIES IN A MATCH

BY THE TEAM

Pens	Opponent	Venue	Year
6	Canada	Hamilton	1996
5	Canada	Chicago	1984
5	Australia XV	Riverside	1993
5	Uruguay	Toronto	1996
5	Fiji	San Francisco	1999
5	Scotland	Brisbane	2003

BY A PLAYER

Pens	Player	Opponent	Venue	Year
6	M Alexander	Canada	Hamilton	1996
5	R Nelson	Canada	Chicago	1984
5	C O'Brien	Australia XV	Riverside	1993
5	M Alexander	Uruguay	Toronto	1996
5	K Dalzell	Fiji	San Francisco	1999
5	M Hercus	Scotland	Brisbane	2003

MOST DROP GOALS IN A MATCH

BY THE TEAM

DGs	Opponent	Venue	Year
1	13 occasions	—	—

BY A PLAYER

DGs	Player	Opponent	Venue	Year
1	13 players	—	—	—

MOST CAPPED PLAYERS

Caps	Player	Career span
62	L Gross	1996 to 2003
54	D Hodges	1996 to 2004
48	K Schubert	2000 to 2006
46	V Anitoni	1992 to 2000
45	D Lyle	1994 to 2003
44	T Billups	1993 to 1999
44	A Parker	1996 to 2006
42	K Dalzell	1996 to 2003
39	M Scharrenberg	1993 to 1999
39	M MacDonald	2000 to 2006

MOST CONSECUTIVE TESTS

Tests	Player	Span
42	K Schubert	2001 to 2006
36	D Hodges	1998 to 2003
26	V Anitoni	1997 to 1999
23	T Billups	1997 to 1999
22	K Swords	1987 to 1991
22	L Gross	1997 to 1999

MOST TESTS AS CAPTAIN

Caps	Captain	Career span
28	D Hodges	2000 to 2003
24	D Lyle	1996 to 2003
18	K Schubert	2003 to 2006
12	T Billups	1998 to 1999
9	E Burlingham	1983 to 1987

MOST TESTS IN INDIVIDUAL POSITIONS

#	Player	Tests	Span
15	R Nelson	23	1983 to 1991
	K Shuman	23	1997 to 2001
11/14	V Anitoni	41	1992 to 2000
12/13	M Scharrenberg	39	1993 to 1999
10	M Hercus	29	2002 to 2006
9	K Dalzell	42	1996 to 2003
1/3	M MacDonald	39	2000 to 2006
2	T Billups	44	1993 to 1999
4/5	L Gross	61	1996 to 2003
6/7	D Hodges	32	1996 to 2004
	K Schubert	32	2000 to 2006
8	D Lyle	31	1994 to 2003

MOST POINTS IN TESTS

Points	Player	Tests	Career
331	M Hercus	30	2002 to 2006
286	M Alexander	24	1995 to 1998
144	C O'Brien	20	1988 to 1994
143	M Williams	37	1987 to 1999
130	V Anitoni	46	1992 to 2000
109	K Dalzell	42	1996 to 2003
100	G Wells	12	2000 to 2001
65	R Nelson	25	1983 to 1991
63	L Wilfley	20	2000 to 2003
63	F Viljoen	12	2004 to 2006
56	A Bachelet	33	1993 to 1998

MOST TRIES IN TESTS

Tries	Player	Tests	Career Span
26	V Anitoni	46	1992 to 2000
10	P Eloff	30	2000 to 2006
9	M Hercus	30	2002 to 2006
9	R Van Zyl	13	2003 to 2004
8	M Scharrenberg	39	1993 to 1999
8	K Dalzell	42	1996 to 2003
8	B Hightower	17	1997 to 1999
7	C O'Brien	20	1988 to 1994
7	A Bachelet	33	1993 to 1998
6	T Takau	25	1994 to 1999
6	D Lyle	45	1994 to 2003
6	A Saulala	20	1997 to 1999

MOST CONVERSIONS IN TESTS			
Cons	Player	Tests	Career
65	M Hercus	30	2002 to 2006
45	M Alexander	24	1995 to 1998
24	C O'Brien	20	1988 to 1994
14	G Wells	12	2000 to 2001
13	M Williams	37	1987 to 1999

MOST DROP GOALS IN TESTS			
DGs	Player	Tests	Career
3	M Hercus	30	2002 to 2006
2	D Horton	3	1986 to 1987
2	M Alexander	24	1995 to 1998
2	G Wells	12	2000 to 2001
1	4 players	—	—

MOST PENALTY GOALS IN TESTS			
Pens	Player	Tests	Career
55	M Alexander	24	1995 to 1998
49	M Hercus	30	2002 to 2006
35	M Williams	37	1987 to 1999
22	C O'Brien	20	1988 to 1994
22	G Wells	12	2000 to 2001

CAREER RECORDS FOR USA INTERNATIONAL PLAYERS

(UP TO 20TH SEPTEMBER 2006)

BACKS	DEBUT	CAPS	T	C	P	D	PTS
B Barnard	2006 v I*	4	0	0	0	0	0
P Eloff	2000 v J	30	10	0	0	0	50
P Emerick	2002 v Sp	21	5	0	0	0	25
C Erskine	2006 v C	1	0	0	0	0	0
V Esikia	2006 v I*	4	2	0	0	0	10
M Hercus	2002 v S	30	9	65	49	3	331
J Hullinger	2006 v I*	3	2	0	0	0	10
J Kelly	2006 v M	3	0	0	2	0	6
K Kjar	2000 v Arg	16	2	0	0	0	10
T Meek	2006 v I*	4	0	0	0	0	0
J Nash	2006 v M	2	0	0	0	0	0
M Palefau	2005 v C	8	3	0	0	0	15
S Sika	2003 v Fj	12	3	0	0	0	15
M Timoteo	2000 v Tg	31	3	0	0	0	15
A Tuilevuka	2006 v I*	3	1	1	0	0	7
A Tuipulotu	2004 v C	12	4	0	0	0	20
F Viljoen	2004 v Ru	14	1	8	14	0	63

FORWARDS	DEBUT	CAPS	T	C	P	D	PTS
M Aylor	2006 v I*	4	0	0	0	0	0
P Bell	2006 v I*	5	0	0	0	0	0
T Clever	2003 v Arg	11	3	0	0	0	15
M French	2005 v Wales	3	0	0	0	0	0
C Hansen	2005 v C	4	0	0	0	0	0
S Lawrence	2006 v C	3	0	0	0	0	0
O Lentz	2006 v I*	3	0	0	0	0	0
M MacDonald	2000 v Fj	39	3	0	0	0	0
M Mangan	2005 v C	10	0	0	0	0	0
H Mexted	2006 v Ba	1	0	0	0	0	0
C Osentowski	2005 v It	9	0	0	0	0	0
A Parker	1996 v HK	44	1	0	0	0	5
T Petruzzella	2004 v M	10	1	0	0	0	5
A Russell	2006 v C	1	0	0	0	0	0
B Schoener	2006 v Sm	3	0	0	0	0	0
K Schubert	2000 v J	48	4	0	0	0	20
L Stanfill	2005 v C	2	0	0	0	0	0
J Stencel	2006 v C	1	0	0	0	0	0
J Tarpoff	2002 v S	13	0	0	0	0	0
J Vitale	2006 v C	1	0	0	0	0	0
M Wyatt	2003 v Arg	16	3	0	0	0	15

Tabulated as Caps, Tries, Conversions, Penalty Goals, Dropped Goals, Points

* Denotes the opponent fielded an 'A' side not recognized as an international XV

WALES

By Iain Spragg

WALES'S TEST RECORD

OPPONENTS	DATE	VENUE	RESULT
England	4 February	A	**Lost** 13–47
Scotland	12 February	H	**Won** 28–18
Ireland	26 February	A	**Lost** 5–31
Italy	11 March	H	**Drew** 18–18
France	18 March	H	**Lost** 16–21
Argentina	11 June	A	**Lost** 25–27
Argentina	17 June	A	**Lost** 27–45

HARDER SECOND TIME AROUND

To lose one coach during a Six Nations campaign may be unfortunate. To lose a second within months of the first simply looks like carelessness. To have to install a third before the season is out is pure soap opera.

But that, in short, is the story of Wales' woeful season.

Stu Forster/Getty Images

Mike Ruddock was one of three Wales team coaches in 2006.

Of course, it all began with such justified optimism. Mike Ruddock's side welcomed in 2006 with Wales' first Grand Slam since 1978 safely tucked under their collective belts, a successful summer tour to North America behind them and a first victory over Australia for 18 years – a 24–22 triumph in Cardiff in November – to their credit. The New Year promised to be a good one.

And then things began to crumble around them. Wales kicked off their Six Nations campaign against the English at Twickenham but any hopes the champions had of emulating their famous victory in Cardiff 12 months earlier quickly evaporated. Wales, missing half-a-dozen key players through injury or suspension, were about to experience a painful reality check.

England bullied the game from the start and although the visitors only trailed 15–10 at the break, the writing was on the wall soon after the restart when Martyn Williams was sin-binned. England took full advantage, scored four tries to add to the two they worked in the first half and ran out handsome 47–13 winners. The 2006 Six Nations already looked like being a distinctly tougher proposition for Wales than its 2005 counterpart.

"The sin-binning of Martyn Williams was a crucial moment, as that allowed England to turn the power on," Ruddock said after the heavy defeat. "With a 14–man Wales team they really put us to the sword and ran away with it – and that really hurts.

Getty Images

The 28–18 win over Scotland was Wales' only win in the 2006 RBS Six Nations.

"At the same time you have to respect that England played some good rugby but that moment went against us. It was a tough afternoon for us. I guess we just have to take it on the chin. We dished it out last year when we won the Grand Slam and now we have to regroup quickly for next week against Scotland."

The clash with the Scots in Cardiff afforded Ruddock and his troops an early opportunity to bounce back and they seized it with both hands. Scotland huffed and puffed but when Scott Murray was red carded for kicking Ian Gough midway through the first half, the contest was over and two tries from skipper Gareth Thomas set up a 28–18 win. It seemed Wales had decided to join the party after all.

And then came the bombshell that rocked the Principality. Just two days after the Scotland game, the WRU called a press conference in Cardiff to announce Ruddock had resigned as coach with immediate effect. The man who led his country to the Grand Slam less than a year earlier had left.

Almost as soon as the announcement was made, the speculation over the shock news began. The WRU stuck limpet-like to the line that Ruddock had quit to spend more time with his young family while the cynics began whispering about a breakdown in talks between the coach and his employers about a contract extension.

"This has been a tough decision to make but I have decided to put my family first," Ruddock insisted when the news broke. "The intense

Stu Foster/Getty Images

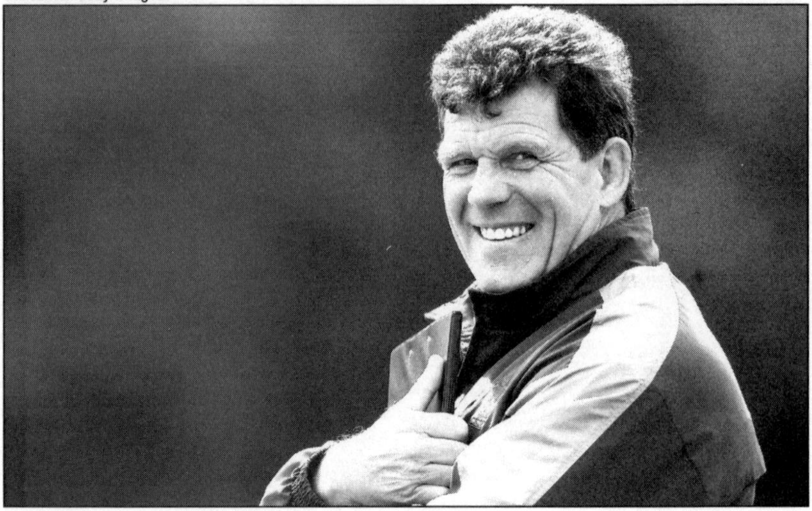

Gareth Jenkins ended the season, smiling, and in charge of Wales.

build-up to the World Cup means more time away from my family. That is something I'd like to avoid.

"I have found during my two years as coach that the position is more than a job. That has meant I have spent long periods away from my family."

What was crystal clear was the timing of the announcement could not have been worse. Shorn of a clutch of leading players, Wales were now bereft of a head coach and although the WRU went for continuity when they appointed Australian skills coach Scott Johnson as caretaker, it was impossible not to see the upheavals undermining the team's Six Nations campaign.

And so it proved. Wales were toothless in their next game against Ireland at Lansdowne Road and although they drew first blood with a try from Mark Jones, it was all one-way traffic after that and they were soundly beaten 31–5.

It got worse still the following month when Italy came to Cardiff. Johnson's Wales started brightly but faded badly in the second half and the two sides were locked at 18–18 at the final whistle to give Italy their first ever Championship point away from home.

"It's not for me to say whether Mike Ruddock leaving was why we've performed like this, I'm out to coach the side," Johson said after the stalemate. "I'm here for a short time and I'll try to do my best to get the best out of the boys."

Wales restored a degree of pride in their final game, pushing eventual champions France close in Cardiff before going down 21–16 but even that improved performance could not paper over the cracks. After the highs of 2005, the Six Nations had been a disaster.

And there was still more upheaval to come. Six days after the France game, Johnson confirmed what everyone else had always suspected when he announced he was leaving the Principality to take up the job as Australia's attack coach. Wales, facing a tough two-Test series in Argentina in the summer, now had no coach whatsoever.

The search for Wales' third coach since the start of the year was a quick one and in late April Gareth Jenkins was unveiled as the new man. The Llanelli Scarlets director of rugby was handed a two-year contract and was quick to acknowledge he would have the briefest of honeymoon periods in his new role.

"I know that the clock is ticking towards my first international in Argentina in 45 days' time," Jenkins said. "I can't wait to get started. It is a new and exciting challenge for me and I am greatly looking forward to it as we build towards the 2007 Rugby World Cup in France.

"I'm a proud Welshman at the moment. This is something which I have aspired to for a long, long time. It is a job I would have been disappointed at not filling at some stage of my career."

Jenkins's obvious enthusiasm was soon tempered by reality, however, when he was forced to take an inexperienced and unfamiliar squad to Argentina. The long list of absentees was to be a pivotal factor in the series.

The first Test against the Pumas in Puerto Madryn was close throughout. Wing Mark Jones opened Wales' account and tries from debutantes Ian Evans and James Hook also followed but Argentina took advantage of the sin-binning of both Gavin Thomas and Alix Popham midway through the first half, scored a total of three tries of their own and emerged 27–25 winners. Jenkins' international career had begun with defeat but the new coach remained defiant at the final whistle.

"It is not the result we wanted, because we believed all week we could have got a win here," he said. "But I am full of admiration for the spirit, intent and commitment of a young team.

"They did everything we asked of them in training, and I couldn't have asked any more of them in the match. It has been a huge effort and we are not out of this Test series. It was more than positive and we will go in there realising we can win the game next week."

Unfortunately for Wales, the second Test in Buenos Aires was an even bigger mountain to climb for Jenkins' young side than the first had been.

From the start Argentina showed a vision with the ball in hand that surprised Wales and once Gonzalo Tiesi collected Hook's charged down kick for the Pumas' first try, there was no going back for the visitors.

Flanker Fernandez Lobbe extended the advantage, Gareth Delve hit back for Jenkins' side and then Tiesi grabbed his second of the match. But the real star of the show was Pumas fly-half Federico Todeschini, who kicked eight penalties and three conversions for a match-winning 30–point haul. Late tries from Shane Williams and Lee Byrne gave the final 45–27 scoreline a flattering gloss but the truth was Wales' young hopefuls had been comprehensively outplayed and Argentina had their first ever series win over the men in red.

"No excuses, they made it very difficult for us," admitted stand-in skipper Duncan Jones. "We also caused a lot of problems for ourselves, but that's not to detract from the Argentineans, they deserved it.

"We had a lot of youngsters on this trip who will have learnt a lot, but today we're all very down."

Jenkins added: "There were a lot of things different to last week and the better side won, for sure. Our lineout didn't work, the set piece was under pressure and we didn't have the same go-forward to compete.

"Argentina were purposeful, aggressive, physical and impressive – and they had all the ball. Playing defensive rugby tires you, we were off the pace."

WALES INTERNATIONAL STATISTICS

MATCH RECORDS UP TO 30TH SEPTEMBER 2006

MOST CONSECUTIVE TEST WINS

11	1907 I, 1908 E,S,F,I,A, 1909 E,S,F,I, 1910 F
10	1999 F1,It,E,Arg 1,2,SA,C,F2,Arg 3,J
8	1970 F, 1971 E,S,I,F, 1972 E,S,F
8	2004 J, 2005 E,It,F,S,I,US,C

MOST CONSECUTIVE TESTS WITHOUT DEFEAT

Matches	Wins	Draws	Periods
11	11	0	1907 to 1910
10	10	0	1999 to 1999
8	8	0	1970 to 1972
8	8	0	2004 to 2005

MOST POINTS IN A MATCH

BY THE TEAM

Pts.	Opponent	Venue	Year
102	Portugal	Lisbon	1994
98	Japan	Cardiff	2004
81	Romania	Cardiff	2001
77	U S A	Hartford	2005
70	Romania	Wrexham	1997
66	Romania	Cardiff	2004
64	Japan	Cardiff	1999
64	Japan	Osaka	2001
60	Italy	Treviso	1999
60	Canada	Toronto	2005
58	Fiji	Cardiff	2002
57	Japan	Bloemfontein	1995
55	Japan	Cardiff	1993

BY A PLAYER

Pts.	Player	Opponent	Venue	Year
30	N R Jenkins	Italy	Treviso	1999
29	N R Jenkins	France	Cardiff	1999
28	N R Jenkins	Canada	Cardiff	1999
28	N R Jenkins	France	Paris	2001
28	G L Henson	Japan	Cardiff	2004
27	N R Jenkins	Italy	Cardiff	2000
27	C Sweeney	U S A	Hartford	2005
26	S M Jones	Romania	Cardiff	2001
24	N R Jenkins	Canada	Cardiff	1993
24	N R Jenkins	Italy	Cardiff	1994
24	G L Henson	Romania	Wrexham	2003
23	A C Thomas	Romania	Wrexham	1997
23	N R Jenkins	Argentina	Llanelli	1998
23	N R Jenkins	Scotland	Murrayfield	2001
22	N R Jenkins	Portugal	Lisbon	1994
22	N R Jenkins	Japan	Bloemfontein	1995
22	N R Jenkins	England	Wembley	1999
22	S M Jones	Canada	Cardiff	2002

MOST TRIES IN A MATCH

BY THE TEAM

Tries	Opponent	Venue	Year
16	Portugal	Lisbon	1994
14	Japan	Cardiff	2004
11	France	Paris	1909
11	Romania	Wrexham	1997
11	Romania	Cardiff	2001
11	U S A	Hartford	2005
10	France	Swansea	1910
10	Japan	Osaka	2001
10	Romania	Cardiff	2004
9	France	Cardiff	1908
9	Japan	Cardiff	1993
9	Japan	Cardiff	1999
9	Japan	Tokyo	2001
9	Canada	Toronto	2005

BY A PLAYER

Tries	Player	Opponent	Venue	Year
4	W Llewellyn	England	Swansea	1899
4	R A Gibbs	France	Cardiff	1908
4	M C R Richards	England	Cardiff	1969
4	I C Evans	Canada	Invercargill	1987
4	N Walker	Portugal	Lisbon	1994
4	G Thomas	Italy	Treviso	1999
4	S M Williams	Japan	Osaka	2001
4	T G L Shanklin	Romania	Cardiff	2004
4	C L Charvis	Japan	Cardiff	2004

MOST CONVERSIONS IN A MATCH

BY THE TEAM

Cons	Opponent	Venue	Year
14	Japan	Cardiff	2004
11	Portugal	Lisbon	1994
11	U S A	Hartford	2005
10	Romania	Cardiff	2001
8	France	Swansea	1910
8	Japan	Cardiff	1999
8	Romania	Cardiff	2004
7	France	Paris	1909
7	Japan	Osaka	2001

BY A PLAYER

Cons	Player	Opponent	Venue	Year
14	G L Henson	Japan	Cardiff	2004
11	N R Jenkins	Portugal	Lisbon	1994
11	C Sweeney	U S A	Hartford	2005
10	S M Jones	Romania	Cardiff	2001
8	J Bancroft	France	Swansea	1910
8	N R Jenkins	Japan	Cardiff	1999
7	S M Jones	Japan	Osaka	2001
7	S M Jones	Romania	Cardiff	2004
6	J Bancroft	France	Paris	1909
6	G L Henson	Romania	Wrexham	2003
6	C Sweeney	Canada	Toronto	2005

MOST PENALTIES IN A MATCH

BY THE TEAM

Pens	Opponent	Venue	Year
9	France	Cardiff	1999
8	Canada	Cardiff	1993
7	Italy	Cardiff	1994
7	Canada	Cardiff	1999
7	Italy	Cardiff	2000
6	France	Cardiff	1982
6	Tonga	Nuku'alofa	1994
6	England	Wembley	1999
6	Canada	Cardiff	2002

BY A PLAYER

Pens	Player	Opponent	Venue	Year
9	N R Jenkins	France	Cardiff	1999
8	N R Jenkins	Canada	Cardiff	1993
7	N R Jenkins	Italy	Cardiff	1994
7	N R Jenkins	Canada	Cardiff	1999
7	N R Jenkins	Italy	Cardiff	2000
6	G Evans	France	Cardiff	1982
6	N R Jenkins	Tonga	Nuku'alofa	1994
6	N R Jenkins	England	Wembley	1999
6	S M Jones	Canada	Cardiff	2002

MOST DROP GOALS IN A MATCH

BY THE TEAM

Drops	Opponent	Venue	Year
3	Scotland	Murrayfield	2001
2	Scotland	Swansea	1912
2	Scotland	Cardiff	1914
2	England	Swansea	1920
2	Scotland	Swansea	1921
2	France	Paris	1930
2	England	Cardiff	1971
2	France	Cardiff	1978
2	England	Twickenham	1984
2	Ireland	Wellington	1987
2	Scotland	Cardiff	1988
2	France	Paris	2001

BY A PLAYER

Drops	Player	Opponent	Venue	Year
3	N R Jenkins	Scotland	Murrayfield	2001
2	J Shea	England	Swansea	1920
2	A Jenkins	Scotland	Swansea	1921
2	B John	England	Cardiff	1971
2	M Dacey	England	Twickenham	1984
2	J Davies	Ireland	Wellington	1987
2	J Davies	Scotland	Cardiff	1988
2	N R Jenkins	France	Paris	2001

MOST CAPPED PLAYERS

Caps	Player	Career Span
92	G O Llewellyn	1989 to 2004
88	Gareth Thomas	1995 to 2006
87	N R Jenkins	1991 to 2002
84	C L Charvis	1996 to 2006
72	I C Evans	1987 to 1998
62	M E Williams	1996 to 2006
59	R Howley	1996 to 2002
58	G R Jenkins	1991 to 2000
56	S M Jones	1998 to 2006
55	J P R Williams	1969 to 1981
54	R N Jones	1986 to 1995
53	G O Edwards	1967 to 1978
53	I S Gibbs	1991 to 2001
52	L S Quinnell	1993 to 2002
51	D Young	1987 to 2001
46	T G R Davies	1966 to 1978
46	P T Davies	1985 to 1995
45	D J Peel	2001 to 2006
45	D R James	1996 to 2006
44	K J Jones	1947 to 1957
44	G R Williams	2000 to 2005

MOST CONSECUTIVE TESTS

Tests	Player	Career span
53	G O Edwards	1967 to 1978
43	K J Jones	1947 to 1956
39	G Price	1975 to 1983
38	T M Davies	1969 to 1976
33	W J Bancroft	1890 to 1901

MOST TESTS AS CAPTAIN

Tests	Player	Career span
28	I C Evans	1991 to 1995
22	R Howley	1998 to 1999
22	C L Charvis	2002 to 2004
19	J M Humphreys	1995 to 2003
18	A J Gould	1889 to 1897
14	D C T Rowlands	1963 to 1965
14	W J Trew	1907 to 1913

MOST POINTS IN TESTS

Points	Player	Tests	Career
1049	N R Jenkins	87	1991 to 2002
506	S M Jones	56	1998 to 2006
304	P H Thorburn	37	1985 to 1991
211	A C Thomas	23	1996 to 2000
180	Gareth Thomas	88	1995 to 2006
166	P Bennett	29	1969 to 1978
157	I C Evans	72	1987 to 1998

MOST TRIES IN TESTS

Tries	Player	Tests	Career
36	Gareth Thomas	88	1995 to 2006
33	I C Evans	72	1987 to 1998
26	S M Williams	39	2000 to 2006
20	G O Edwards	53	1967 to 1978
20	T G R Davies	46	1966 to 1978
20	C L Charvis	84	1996 to 2006
18	G R Williams	44	2000 to 2005
17	R A Gibbs	16	1906 to 1911
17	J L Williams	17	1906 to 1911
17	K J Jones	44	1947 to 1957

MOST CONVERSIONS IN TESTS

Cons	Player	Tests	Career
130	N R Jenkins	87	1991 to 2002
91	S M Jones	56	1998 to 2006
43	P H Thorburn	37	1985 to 1991
38	J Bancroft	18	1909 to 1914
30	A C Thomas	23	1996 to 2000
29	G L Henson	18	2001 to 2006
20	W J Bancroft	33	1890 to 1901
20	I R Harris	25	2001 to 2004

MOST PENALTY GOALS IN TESTS

Penalties	Player	Tests	Career
235	N R Jenkins	87	1991 to 2002
95	S M Jones	56	1998 to 2006
70	P H Thorburn	37	1985 to 1991
36	P Bennett	29	1969 to 1978
35	S P Fenwick	30	1975 to 1981
32	A C Thomas	23	1996 to 2000
22	G Evans	10	1981 to 1983

MOST DROP GOALS IN TESTS

Drops	Player	Tests	Career
13	J Davies	32	1985 to 1997
10	N R Jenkins	87	1991 to 2002
8	B John	25	1966 to 1972
7	W G Davies	21	1978 to 1985

INTERNATIONAL CHAMPIONSHIP RECORDS

RECORD	DETAIL		SET
Most points in season	151	in five matches	2005
Most tries in season	21	in four matches	1910
Highest Score	49	49–14 v France	1910
Biggest win	35	49–14 v France	1910
Highest score conceded	60	26–60 v England	1998
Biggest defeat	51	0–51 v France	1998
Most appearances	45	G O Edwards	1967–1978
Most points in matches	406	N R Jenkins	1991–2001
Most points in season	74	N R Jenkins	2001
Most points in match	28	N R Jenkins	v France, 2001
Most tries in matches	18	G O Edwards	1967–1978
Most tries in season	6	M C R Richards	1969
Most tries in match	4	W Llewellyn	v England, 1899
	4	M C R Richards	v England, 1969
Most cons in matches	46	S M Jones	2000–2006
Most cons in season	12	S M Jones	2005
Most cons in match	8	J Bancroft	v France, 1910
Most pens in matches	93	N R Jenkins	1991–2001
Most pens in season	16	P H Thorburn	1986
	16	N R Jenkins	1999
Most pens in match	7	N R Jenkins	v Italy, 2000
Most drops in matches	8	J Davies	1985–1997
Most drops in season	5	N R Jenkins	2001
Most drops in match	3	N R Jenkins	v Scotland, 2001

MISCELLANEOUS RECORDS

RECORD	HOLDER	DETAIL
Longest Test Career	G O Llewellyn	1989 to 2004
Youngest Test Cap	N Biggs	18 yrs 49 days in 1888
Oldest Test Cap	T H Vile	38 yrs 152 days in 1921

CAREER RECORDS OF WALES INTERNATIONAL PLAYERS (PLAYERS CAPPED SINCE THE START OF RWC 2003 UP TO 30TH SEPTEMBER 2006)

PLAYER	DEBUT	CAPS	T	C	P	D	PTS
BACKS							
L M Byrne	2005 v NZ	10	1	0	0	0	5
G J Cooper	2001 v F	31	6	0	0	0	30
C D Czekaj	2005 v C	2	1	0	0	0	5
B Davies	2006 I	1	0	0	0	0	0
G R Evans	1998 v SA	4	1	0	0	0	5
I R Harris	2001 v Arg	25	1	20	21	0	108
G L Henson	2001 v J	18	3	29	17	1	127
J Hook	2006 v Arg	2	1	2	2	0	15
D R James	1996 v A	45	13	0	0	0	65
M A Jones	2001 v E	22	9	0	0	0	45
Matthew Jones	2005 v C	1	0	0	0	0	0
S M Jones	1998 v SA	56	6	91	95	3	506
H Luscombe	2003 v S	15	2	0	0	0	10
C S Morgan	2002 v I	10	3	0	0	0	15
K A Morgan	1997 v US	36	10	0	0	0	50
S T Parker	2002 v R	18	5	0	0	0	25
D J Peel	2001 v J	45	4	0	0	0	20
M Phillips	2003 v R	14	2	0	0	0	10
J P Robinson	2001 v J	15	5	0	0	0	25
N J Robinson	2003 v I	12	2	3	3	1	28
T J Selley	2005 v US	1	1	0	0	0	5
T G L Shanklin	2001 v J	33	15	0	0	0	75
C Sweeney	2003 v It	27	2	18	4	1	61
M Taylor	1994 v SA	52	12	0	0	0	60
Gareth Thomas	1995 v J	88	36	0	0	0	180
M J Watkins	2003 v It	18	0	0	0	0	0
A Williams	2003 v R	4	0	0	0	0	0
G R Williams	2000 v I	44	18	0	0	0	90
S M Williams	2000 v F	39	26	0	0	0	130
FORWARDS							
H Bennett	2003 v I	10	0	0	0	0	0
B G J Broster	2005 v US	2	1	0	0	0	5
L C Charteris	2004 v SA	6	0	0	0	0	0
C L Charvis	1996 v A	84	20	0	0	0	100
B J Cockbain	2003 v R	22	1	0	0	0	5

Mefin Davies	2002 v SA	37	2	0	0	0	10
G L Delve	2006 v S	4	1	0	0	0	5
B R Evans	1998 v SA	27	0	0	0	0	0
Ian Evans	2006 v Arg	2	1	0	0	0	5
J A Forster	2004 v Arg	1	1	0	0	0	5
I M Gough	1998 v SA	32	1	0	0	0	5
R Hibbard	2006 v Arg	2	0	0	0	0	0
C L Horsman	2005 v NZ	4	0	0	0	0	0
G D Jenkins	2002 v R	37	3	0	0	0	15
A M Jones	2006 v E	2	0	0	0	0	0
A R Jones	2003 v E	33	1	0	0	0	5
A W Jones	2006 v Arg	2	0	0	0	0	0
D A R Jones	2002 v Fj	29	2	0	0	0	10
D J Jones	2001 v A	29	0	0	0	0	0
D L Jones	2000 v Sm	3	0	0	0	0	0
R P Jones	2004 v SA	8	1	0	0	0	5
Steve Jones	2001 v J	5	0	0	0	0	0
G O Llewellyn	1989 v NZ	92	5	0	0	0	24
R C McBryde	1994 v Fj	37	1	0	0	0	5
D R Morris	1998 v Z	18	1	0	0	0	5
M J Owen	2002 v SA	33	2	0	0	0	10
A J Popham	2003 v A	17	2	0	0	0	10
R Pugh	2005 v US	1	1	0	0	0	5
M Rees	2005 v US	2	0	0	0	0	0
R A Sidoli	2002 v SA	35	2	0	0	0	10
R Sowden-Taylor	2005 v It	3	0	0	0	0	0
G M Thomas	2001 v J	18	4	0	0	0	20
I D Thomas	2000 v Sm	30	1*	0	0	0	5
J Thomas	2003 v A	24	4	0	0	0	20
Rhys Thomas	2006 v Arg	1	0	0	0	0	0
T R Thomas	2005 v US	11	0	0	0	0	0
M E Williams	1996 v Bb	62	8	0	0	1	43
C P Wyatt	1998 v Z	38	2	0	0	0	10
J Yapp	2005 v E	8	0	0	0	0	0

* Iestyn Thomas's figures include a penalty try awarded against Fiji in 2002.

WALES INTERNATIONAL PLAYERS

UP TO 30TH SEPTEMBER 2006

Note: Years given for International Championship matches are for second half of season; eg 1972 means season 1971–72. Years for all other matches refer to the actual year of the match. Entries in square brackets denote matches played in RWC Finals.

Ackerman, R A (Newport, London Welsh) 1980 NZ, 1981 E, S, A, 1982 I, F, E, S, 1983 S, I, F, R, 1984 S, I, F, E, A, 1985 S, I, F, E, Fj

Alexander, E P (Llandovery Coll, Cambridge U) 1885 S, 1886 E, S, 1887 E, I

Alexander, W H (Llwynypia) 1898 I, E, 1899 E, S, I, 1901 S, I

Allen, A G (Newbridge) 1990 F, E, I

Allen, C P (Oxford U, Beaumaris) 1884 E, S

Andrews, F (Pontypool) 1912 SA, 1913 E, S, I

Andrews, F G (Swansea) 1884 E, S

Andrews, G E (Newport) 1926 E, S, 1927 E, F, I

Anthony, C T (Swansea, Newport, Gwent Dragons) 1997 US 1(R),2(R), C (R), Tg (R), 1998 SA 2, Arg, 1999 S, I (R), 2001 J 1,2, I (R), 2002 I, F, It, E, S, 2003 R (R)

Anthony, L (Neath) 1948 E, S, F

Appleyard, R C (Swansea) 1997 C, R, Tg, NZ, 1998 It, E (R), S, I, F

Arnold, P (Swansea) 1990 Nm 1, 2, Bb, 1991 E, S, I, F 1, A, [Arg, A], 1993 F (R), Z 2, 1994 Sp, Fj, 1995 SA, 1996 Bb (R)

Arnold, W R (Swansea) 1903 S

Arthur, C S (Cardiff) 1888 I, M, 1891 E

Arthur, T (Neath) 1927 S, F, I, 1929 E, S, F, I, 1930 E, S, I, F, 1931 E, S, F, I, SA, 1933 E, S

Ashton, C (Aberavon) 1959 E, S, I, 1960 E, S, I, 1962 I

Attewell, S L (Newport) 1921 E, S, F

Back, M J (Bridgend) 1995 F (R), E (R), S, I

Badger, O (Llanelli) 1895 E, S, I, 1896 E

Baker, A (Neath) 1921 I, 1923 E, S, F, I

Baker, A M (Newport) 1909 S, F, 1910 S

Bancroft, J (Swansea) 1909 E, S, F, I, 1910 F, E, S, I, 1911 E, F, I, 1912 E, S, I, 1913 I, 1914 E, S, F

Bancroft, W J (Swansea) 1890 S, E, I, 1891 E, S, I, 1892 E, S, I, 1893 E, S, I, 1894 E, S, I, 1895 E, S, I, 1896 E, S, I, 1897 E, 1898 I, E, 1899 E, S, I, 1900 E, S, I, 1901 E, S, I

Barlow, T M (Cardiff) 1884 I

Barrell, R J (Cardiff) 1929 S, F, I, 1933 I

Bartlett, J D (Llanelli) 1927 S, 1928 E, S

Bassett, A (Cardiff) 1934 I, 1935 E, S, I, 1938 E, S

Bassett, J A (Penarth) 1929 E, S, F, I, 1930 E, S, I, 1931 E, S, F, I, SA, 1932 E, S, I

Bateman, A G (Neath, Richmond, Northampton) 1990 S, I, Nm 1,2, 1996 SA, 1997 US, S, F, E, R, NZ, 1998 It, E, S, I, 1999 S, Arg 1,2, SA, C, [J, A (R)], 2000 It, E, S, I, Sm, US, SA, 2001 E (R), It (t), R, I, Art (R), Tg

Bater, J (Ospreys) 2003 R (R)

Bayliss, G (Pontypool) 1933 S

Bebb, D I E (Carmarthen TC, Swansea) 1959 E, S, I, F, 1960 E, S, I, F, SA, 1961 E, S, I, F, 1962 E, S, F, I, 1963 E, F, NZ, 1964 E, S, F, SA, 1965 E, S, I, F, 1966 F, A, 1967 S, I, F, E

Beckingham, G (Cardiff) 1953 E, S, 1958 F

Bennett, A M (Cardiff) 1995 [NZ] SA, Fj

Bennett, H (Ospreys) 2003 I 2(R), S 2(R), [C(R),Tg(R)], 2004 S(R),F(R),Arg 1(R),2,SA1(R), 2006 Arg 2

Bennett, I (Aberavon) 1937 I

Bennett, P (Cardiff Harlequins) 1891 E, S, 1892 S, I

Bennett, P (Llanelli) 1969 F (R), 1970 SA, S, F, 1972 S (R), NZ, 1973 E, S, I, F, A, 1974 S, I, F, E, 1975 S (R), I, 1976 E, S, I, F, 1977 I, F, E, S, 1978 E, S, I, F

Bergiers, R T E (Cardiff Coll of Ed, Llanelli) 1972 E, S, F, NZ, 1973 E, S, I, F, A, 1974 E, 1975 I

Bevan, G W (Llanelli) 1947 E

Bevan, J A (Cambridge U) 1881 E

Bevan, J C (Cardiff, Cardiff Coll of Ed) 1971 E, S, I, F, 1972 E, S, F, NZ, 1973 E, S

Bevan, J D (Aberavon) 1975 F, E, S, A

Bevan, S (Swansea) 1904 I

Beynon, B (Swansea) 1920 E, S

Beynon, G E (Swansea) 1925 F, I

Bidgood, R A (Newport) 1992 S, 1993 Z 1,2, Nm, J (R)

Biggs, N W (Cardiff) 1888 M, 1889 I, 1892 I, 1893 E, S, I, 1894 E, I

Biggs, S H (Cardiff) 1895 E, S, 1896 S, 1897 E, 1898 I, E, 1899 S, I, 1900 I

Birch, J (Neath) 1911 S, F

Birt, F W (Newport) 1911 E, S, 1912 E, S, I, SA, 1913 E

Bishop, D J (Pontypool) 1984 A

Bishop, E H (Swansea) 1889 S

Blackmore, J H (Abertillery) 1909 E

Blackmore, S W (Cardiff) 1987 I, [Tg (R), C, A]

Blake, J (Cardiff) 1899 E, S, I, 1900 E, S, I, 1901 E, S, I

Blakemore, R E (Newport) 1947 E

Bland, A F (Cardiff) 1887 E, S, I, 1888 S, I, M, 1890 S, E, I

Blyth, L (Swansea) 1951 SA, 1952 E, S

Blyth, W R (Swansea) 1974 E, 1975 S (R), 1980 F, E, S, I

Boobyer, N (Llanelli) 1993 Z 1(R),2, Nm, 1994 Fj, Tg, 1998 F, 1999 It (R)

Boon, R W (Cardiff) 1930 S, F, 1931 E, S, F, I, SA, 1932 E, S, I, 1933 E, I

Booth, J (Pontymister) 1898 I

Boots, J G (Newport) 1898 I, E, 1899 I, 1900 E, S, I, 1901 E, S, I, 1902 E, S, I, 1903 E, S, I, 1904 E

Boucher, A W (Newport) 1892 E, S, I, 1893 E, S, I, 1894 E, 1895 E, S, I, 1896 E, I, 1897 E

Bowcott, H M (Cardiff, Cambridge U) 1929 S, F, I, 1930 E, 1931 E, S, 1933 E, I

Bowdler, F A (Cross Keys) 1927 A, 1928 E, S, I, F, 1929 E, S, F, I, 1930 E, 1931 SA, 1932 E, S, I, 1933 I

Bowen, B (S Wales Police, Swansea) 1983 R, 1984 S, I, F, E, 1985 Fj, 1986 E, S, I, F, Fj, Tg, WS, 1987 [C, E, NZ], US, 1988 E, S, I, F, WS, 1989 S, I

Bowen, C A (Llanelli) 1896 E, S, I, 1897 E

Bowen, D H (Llanelli) 1883 E, 1886 E, S, 1887 E

Bowen, G E (Swansea) 1887 S, I, 1888 S, I

Bowen, W (Swansea) 1921 S, F, 1922 E, S, I, F

Bowen, Wm A (Swansea) 1886 E, S, 1887 E, S, I, 1888 M, 1889 S, I, 1890 S, E, I, 1891 E, S

Brace, D O (Llanelli, Oxford U) 1956 E, S, I, F, 1957 E, 1960 S, I, F, 1961 I

Braddock, K J (Newbridge) 1966 A, 1967 S, I

Bradshaw, K (Bridgend) 1964 E, S, I, F, SA, 1966 E, S, I, F

Brew, N R (Gwent Dragons) 2003 R

Brewer, T J (Newport) 1950 E, 1955 E, S

Brice, A B (Aberavon) 1899 E, S, I, 1900 E, S, I, 1901 E, S, I, 1902 E, S, I, 1903 E, S, I, 1904 E, S, I

Bridges, C J (Neath) 1990 Nm 1,2, Bb, 1991 E (R), I, F 1, A

Bridie, R H (Newport) 1882 I
Britton, G R (Newport) 1961 S
Broster, B G J (Saracens) 2005 US(R),C
Broughton, A S (Treorchy) 1927 A, 1929 S
Brown, A (Newport) 1921 I
Brown, J (Cardiff) 1925 I
Brown, J A (Cardiff) 1907 E, S, I, 1908 E, S, F, 1909 E
Brown, M (Pontypool) 1983 R, 1986 E, S, Fj (R), Tg, WS
Bryant, D J (Bridgend) 1988 NZ 1,2, WS, R, 1989 S, I, F, E
Bryant, J (Celtic Warriors) 2003 R (R)
Buchanan, A (Llanelli) 1987 [Tg, E, NZ, A], 1988 I
Buckett, I M (Swansea) 1994 Tg, 1997 US 2, C
Budgett, N J (Ebbw Vale, Bridgend) 2000 S, I, Sm (R), US, SA, 2001 J 1(R),2, 2002 I, F, It, E, S
Burcher, D H (Newport) 1977 I, F, E, S
Burgess, R C (Ebbw Vale) 1977 I, F, E, S, 1981 I, F, 1982 F, E, S
Burnett, R (Newport) 1953 E
Burns, J (Cardiff) 1927 F, I
Bush, P F (Cardiff) 1905 NZ, 1906 E, SA, 1907 I, 1908 E, S, 1910 S, I
Butler, E T (Pontypool) 1980 F, E, S, I, NZ (R), 1982 S, 1983 E, S, I, F, R, 1984 S, I, F, E, A
Byrne, L M (Llanelli Scarlets) 2005 NZ(R),Fj,SA, 2006 E(t&R),S(t&R),I,It,F,Arg 1,2

Cale, W R (Newbridge, Pontypool) 1949 E, S, I, 1950 E, S, I, F
Cardey, M D (Llanelli) 2000 S
Carter, A J (Newport) 1991 E, S
Cattell, A (Llanelli) 1883 E, S
Challinor, C (Neath) 1939 E
Charteris, L C (Newport Gwent Dragons) 2004 SA2(R),R, 2005 US,C,NZ(R),Fj
Charvis, C L (Swansea, Tarbes, Newcastle) 1996 A 3(R), SA, 1997 US, S, I, F, 1998 It (R), E, S, I, F, Z (R), SA 1,2, Arg, 1999 S, I, F 1, It, E, Arg 1, SA, F 2, [Arg 3, A], 2000 F, It (R), E, S, I, Sm, US, SA, 2001 E, S, F, It, R, I, Arg, Tg, A, 2002 E (R), S, SA 1,2, R, Fj, C, NZ, 2003 It, E 1(R), S 1(R), I 1, F,A, NZ, E 2, S 2, [C,Tg,It,NZ,E], 2004 S,F,E,It,Arg 1,2,SA1,2,R,NZ,J, 2005 US,C,NZ,SA,A, 2006 E,S,I,It
Clapp, T J S (Newport) 1882 I, 1883 E, S, 1884 E, S, I, 1885 E, S, 1886 S, 1887 E, S, I, 1888 S, I
Clare, J (Cardiff) 1883 E
Clark, S S (Neath) 1882 I, 1887 I
Cleaver, W B (Cardiff) 1947 E, S, F, I, A, 1948 E, S, F, I, 1949 I, 1950 E, S, I, F
Clegg, B G (Swansea) 1979 F
Clement, A (Swansea) 1987 US (R), 1988 E, NZ 1, WS (R), R, 1989 NZ, 1990 S (R), I (R), Nm 1,2, 1991 S (R), A (R), F 2, [WS, A], 1992 I, F, E, S, 1993 I (R), F, J, C, 1994 S, I, F, Sp, C (R), Tg, WS, It, SA, 1995 F, E, [J, NZ, I]
Clement, W H (Llanelli) 1937 E, S, I, 1938 E, S, I
Cobner, T J (Pontypool) 1974 S, I, F, E, 1975 F, E, S, I, A, 1976 E, S, 1977 F, E, S, 1978 E, S, I, F, A 1
Cockbain, B J (Celtic Warriors, Ospreys) 2003 R, [C,It,NZ,E], 2004 S,I,F,E,Arg 1,2,SA2,NZ, 2005 E,It,F,S,I,US,C(R),NZ,Fj
Coldrick, A P (Newport) 1911 E, S, I, 1912 E, S, F
Coleman, E (Newport) 1949 E, S, I
Coles, F C (Pontypool) 1960 S, I, F
Collins, J (Aberavon) 1958 A, E, S, F, 1959 E, S, I, F, 1960 E, 1961 F
Collins, R G (S Wales Police, Cardiff, Pontypridd) 1987 E (R), I, [I, E, NZ], US, 1988 E, S, I, F, R, 1990 E, S, I, 1991 A, F 2, [WS], 1994 C, Fj, Tg, WS, R, It, SA, 1995 F, E, S, I
Collins, T (Mountain Ash) 1923 I
Conway-Rees, J (Llanelli) 1892 S, 1893 E, 1894 E
Cook, T (Cardiff) 1949 S, I
Cooper, G J (Bath, Celtic Warriors, Newport Gwent Dragons) 2001 F, J 1,2, 2003 E 1, S 1, I 1, F(R), A, NZ, E 2, [C,Tg,It(t&R),NZ,E], 2004 S, I, F, E, It, R(R), NZ(R), J, 2005 E(R),It(R),F(R),NZ(R),Fj,SA,A, 2006 E(R)
Cooper, V L (Llanelli) 2002 C, 2003 I 2(R), S 2
Cope, W (Cardiff, Blackheath) 1896 S
Copsey, A H (Llanelli) 1992 I, F, E, S, A, 1993 E, S, I, J, C, 1994 E (R), Pt, Sp (R), Fj, Tg, WS (R)
Cornish, F H (Cardiff) 1897 E, 1898 I, E, 1899 I
Cornish, R A (Cardiff) 1923 E, S, 1924 E, 1925 E, S, F, 1926 E, S, I, F
Coslett, K (Aberavon) 1962 E, S, F
Cowey, B T V (Welch Regt, Newport) 1934 E, S, I, 1935 E
Cresswell, B (Newport) 1960 E, S, I, F
Cummins, W (Treorchy) 1922 E, S, I, F
Cunningham, L J (Aberavon) 1960 E, S, I, F, 1962 E, S, F, I, 1963 NZ, 1964 E, S, I, F, SA
Czekaj, C D (Cardiff Blues) 2005 C, 2006 Arg 1(R)

Dacey, M (Swansea) 1983 E, S, I, F, R, 1984 S, I, F, E, A, 1986 Fj, Tg, WS, 1987 F (R), [Tg]
Daniel, D J (Llanelli) 1891 S, 1894 E, S, I, 1898 I, E, 1899 E, I
Daniel, L T D (Newport) 1970 S
Daniels, P C T (Cardiff) 1981 A, 1982 I
Darbishire, G (Bangor) 1881 E
Dauncey, F H (Newport) 1896 E, S, I
Davey, C (Swansea) 1930 F, 1931 E, S, F, I, SA, 1932 E, S, I, 1933 E, S, 1934 E, S, I, 1935 E, S, I, NZ, 1936 S, 1937 E, I, 1938 E, I
David, R J (Cardiff) 1907 I
David, T P (Llanelli, Pontypridd) 1973 F, A, 1976 I, F
Davidge, G D (Newport) 1959 F, 1960 S, I, F, SA, 1961 E, S, I, 1962 F
Davies, A (Cambridge U, Neath, Cardiff) 1990 Bb (R), 1991 A, 1993 Z 1,2, J, C, 1994 Fj, 1995 [J, I]
Davies, A C (London Welsh) 1889 I
Davies, A E (Llanelli) 1984 A
Davies, B (Llanelli) 1895 E, 1896 E
Davies, B (Llanelli Scarlets) 2006 I(R)
Davies, C (Cardiff) 1947 S, F, I, A, 1948 E, S, F, I, 1949 F, 1950 E, S, I, F, 1951 E, S, I
Davies, C (Llanelli) 1988 WS, 1989 S, I (R), F
Davies, C H A (Llanelli, Cardiff) 1957 I, 1958 A, E, S, I, 1960 SA, 1961 E
Davies, C L (Cardiff) 1956 E, S, I
Davies, C R (Bedford, RAF) 1934 E
Davies, D (Bridgend) 1921 I, 1925 I
Davies, D B (Llanelli) 1907 E
Davies, D B (Llanelli) 1962 I, 1963 E, S
Davies, D G (Cardiff) 1923 E, S
Davies, D H (Neath) 1904 S
Davies, D H (Aberavon) 1924 E
Davies, D I (Swansea) 1939 E
Davies, D J (Neath) 1962 I
Davies, D M (Somerset Police) 1950 E, S, I, F, 1951 E, S, I, F, SA, 1952 E, S, I, F, 1953 I, F, NZ, 1954 E
Davies, E (Aberavon) 1947 A, 1948 I
Davies, E (Maesteg) 1919 NZA
Davies, E G (Cardiff) 1912 E, F
Davies, E G (Cardiff) 1928 F, 1929 E, 1930 S
Davies, G (Swansea) 1900 E, S, I, 1901 E, S, I, 1905 E, S, I
Davies, G (Cambridge U, Pontypridd) 1947 S, A, 1948 E, S, F, I, 1949 E, S, F, 1951 E, S
Davies, G (Llanelli) 1921 F, I, 1925 F
Davies, H (Swansea) 1898 I, E, 1901 S, I
Davies, H (Swansea, Llanelli) 1939 S, I, 1947 E, S, F, I
Davies, H (Neath) 1912 E, S
Davies, H (Bridgend) 1984 S, I, F, E
Davies, H J (Cambridge U, Aberavon) 1959 E, S
Davies, H J (Newport) 1924 S
Davies, I T (Llanelli) 1914 S, F, I
Davies, J (Neath, Llanelli, Cardiff) 1985 E, Fj, 1986 E, S, I, F, Fj, Tg, WS, 1987 F, E, S, I, [I, Tg (R), C, E, NZ, A], 1988 E, S, I, F, NZ 1,2, WS, R, 1996 A 3, 1997 US (t), S (R), F (R), E
Davies, Rev J A (Swansea) 1913 S, F, I, 1914 E, S, F, I
Davies, J D (Neath, Richmond) 1991 I, F 1, 1993 F (R), Z 2, J, C, 1994 S, I, F, E, Pt, Sp, C, WS, R, It, SA, 1995 F, E, [J, NZ, I] SA, 1996 It, E, S, I, F 1, A 1, Bb, F 2, It, 1998 Z, SA 1
Davies, J H (Aberavon) 1923 I
Davies, L (Swansea) 1939 S, I
Davies, L (Bridgend) 1966 E, S, I

Davies, L B (Neath, Cardiff, Llanelli) 1996 It, E, S, I, F 1, A 1, Bb, F 2, It (R), 1997 US 1,2, C, R, Tg, NZ (R), 1998 E (R), I, F, 1999 C, 2001 I, 2003 It
Davies, L M (Llanelli) 1954 F, S, 1955 I
Davies, M (Swansea) 1981 A, 1982 I, 1985 Fj
Davies, Mefin (Pontypridd, Celtic Warriors, Gloucester) 2002 SA 2(R), R, Fj, 2003 It, S 1(R), I 1(R), F, A(R), NZ(R), I 2, R, [Tg,NZ(R),E(R)], 2004 S,F,It(R),Arg 1,2(R),SA1,2(R),R,NZ, J, 2005E,It,F,S,I,C(R),NZ,SA(R),A(t), 2006 S(R),I(R),It(R),F(R)
Davies, M J (Blackheath) 1939 S, I
Davies, N G (London Welsh) 1955 E
Davies, N G (Llanelli) 1988 NZ 2, WS, 1989 S, I, 1993 F, 1994 S, I, E, Pt, Sp, C, Fj, Tg (R), WS, R, It, 1995 E, S, I, Fj, 1996 E, S, I, F 1, A 1,2, Bb, F 2, 1997 E
Davies, P T (Llanelli) 1985 E, Fj, 1986 E, S, I, F, Fj, Tg, WS, 1987 F, E, I, [Tg, C, NZ], 1988 WS, R, 1989 S, I, F, E, NZ, 1990 F, E, S, 1991 I, F 1, A, F 2, [WS, Arg, A], 1993 F, Z 1, Nm, 1994 S, I, F, E, C, Fj (R), WS, R, It, 1995 F, I
Davies, R H (Oxford U, London Welsh) 1957 S, I, F, 1958 A, 1962 E, S
Davies, S (Treherbert) 1923 I
Davies, S (Swansea) 1992 I, F, E, S, A, 1993 E, S, I, Z 1(R),2, Nm, J, 1995 F, [J, I], 1998 I (R), F
Davies, T G R (Cardiff, London Welsh) 1966 A, 1967 S, I, F, E, 1968 E, S, 1969 S, I, F, NZ 1,2, A, 1971 E, S, I, F, 1972 E, S, F, NZ, 1973 E, S, I, F, A, 1974 S, F, E, 1975 F, E, S, I, 1976 E, S, I, F, 1977 I, F, E, S, 1978 E, S, I, A 1,2
Davies, T J (Devonport Services, Swansea, Llanelli) 1953 E, S, I, F, 1957 E, S, I, F, 1958 A, E, S, F, 1959 E, S, I, F, 1960 E, SA, 1961 E, S, F
Davies, T M (London Welsh, Swansea) 1969 S, I, F, E, NZ 1,2, A, 1970 SA, S, E, I, F, 1971 E, S, I, F, 1972 E, S, F, NZ, 1973 E, S, I, F, A, 1974 S, I, F, E, 1975 F, E, S, I, A, 1976 E, S, I, F
Davies, W (Cardiff) 1896 S
Davies, W (Swansea) 1931 SA, 1932 E, S, I
Davies, W A (Aberavon) 1912 S, I
Davies, W G (Cardiff) 1978 A 1,2, NZ, 1979 S, I, F, E, 1980 F, E, S, NZ, 1981 E, S, A, 1982 I, F, E, S, 1985 S, I, F
Davies, W T H (Swansea) 1936 I, 1937 E, I, 1939 E, S, I
Davis, C E (Newbridge) 1978 A 2, 1981 E, S
Davis, M (Newport) 1991 A
Davis, W E N (Cardiff) 1939 E, S, I
Dawes, S J (London Welsh) 1964 I, F, SA, 1965 E, S, I, F, 1966 A, 1968 I, F, 1969 E, NZ 2, A, 1970 SA, S, E, I, F, 1971 E, S, I, F
Day, H C (Newport) 1930 S, I, F, 1931 E, S
Day, H T (Newport) 1892 I, 1893 E, S, 1894 S, I
Day, T B (Swansea) 1931 E, S, F, I, SA, 1932 E, S, I, 1934 S, I, 1935 E, S, I
Deacon, J T (Swansea) 1891 I, 1892 E, S, I
Delahay, W J (Bridgend) 1922 E, S, I, F, 1923 E, S, F, I, 1924 NZ, 1925 E, S, F, I, 1926 E, S, I, F, 1927 S
Delaney, L (Llanelli) 1989 I, F, E, 1990 E, 1991 F 2, [WS, Arg, A], 1992 I, F, E
Delve, G L (Bath) 2006 S(R),I(R),Arg 1(R),2(R)
Devereux, D (Neath) 1958 A, E, S
Devereux, J A (S Glamorgan Inst, Bridgend) 1986 E, S, I, F, Fj, Tg, WS, 1987 F, E, S, I, [I, C, E, NZ, A], 1988 NZ 1,2, R, 1989 S, I
Diplock, R (Bridgend) 1988 R
Dobson, G (Cardiff) 1900 S
Dobson, T (Cardiff) 1898 I, E, 1899 E, S
Donovan, A J (Swansea) 1978 A 2, 1981 I (R), A, 1982 E, S
Donovan, R (S Wales Police) 1983 F (R)
Douglas, M H J (Llanelli) 1984 S, I, F
Douglas, W M (Cardiff) 1886 E, S, 1887 E, S
Dowell, W H (Newport) 1907 E, S, I, 1908 E, S, F, I
Durston, A (Bridgend) 2001 J 1,2
Dyke, J C M (Penarth) 1906 SA
Dyke, L M (Penarth, Cardiff) 1910 I, 1911 S, F, I

Edmunds, D A (Neath) 1990 I (R), Bb
Edwards, A B (London Welsh, Army) 1955 E, S
Edwards, B O (Newport) 1951 I
Edwards, D (Glynneath) 1921 E
Edwards, G O (Cardiff, Cardiff Coll of Ed) 1967 F, E, NZ, 1968 E, S, I, F, 1969 S, I, F, E, NZ 1,2, A, 1970 SA, S, E, I, F, 1971 E, S, I, F, 1972 E, S, F, NZ, 1973 E, S, I, F, A, 1974 S, I, F, E, 1975 F, E, S, I, A, 1976 E, S, I, F, 1977 I, F, E, S, 1978 E, S, I, F
Eidman, I H (Cardiff) 1983 S, R, 1984 I, F, E, A, 1985 S, I, Fj, 1986 E, S, I, F
Elliott, J E (Cardiff) 1894 I, 1898 I, E
Elsey, W J (Cardiff) 1895 E
Emyr, Arthur (Swansea) 1989 E, NZ, 1990 F, E, S, I, Nm 1,2, 1991 F 1,2, [WS, Arg, A]
Evans, A (Pontypool) 1924 E, I, F
Evans, B (Swansea) 1933 S
Evans, B (Llanelli) 1933 E, S, 1936 E, S, I, 1937 E
Evans, B R (Swansea, Cardiff Blues) 1998 SA 2(R), 1999 F 1, It, E, Arg 1,2, C, [J (R), Sm (R), A (R)], 2000 Sm, US, 2001 J 1(R), 2002 SA 1,2, R(R), Fj, C, NZ, 2003 It, E 1, S 1, I 2, R, 2004 F(R),E(t),It(R)
Evans, B S (Llanelli) 1920 E, 1922 E, S, I, F
Evans, C (Pontypool) 1960 E
Evans, D (Penygraig) 1896 S, I, 1897 E, 1898 E
Evans, D B (Swansea) 1926 E
Evans, D D (Cheshire, Cardiff U) 1934 E
Evans, D P (Llanelli) 1960 SA
Evans, D W (Cardiff) 1889 S, I, 1890 E, I, 1891 E
Evans, D W (Oxford U, Cardiff, Treorchy) 1989 F, E, NZ, 1990 F, E, S, I, Bb, 1991 A (R), F 2(R), [A (R)], 1995 [J (R)]
Evans, E (Llanelli) 1937 E, 1939 S, I
Evans, F (Llanelli) 1921 S
Evans, G (Cardiff) 1947 E, S, F, I, A, 1948 E, S, F, I, 1949 E, S, I
Evans, G (Maesteg) 1981 S (R), I, F, A, 1982 I, F, E, S, 1983 F, R
Evans, G L (Newport) 1977 F (R), 1978 F, A 2(R)
Evans, G R (Llanelli) 1998 SA 1, 2003 I 2, S 2, [NZ]
Evans, Ian (Ospreys) 2006 Arg 1,2
Evans, I (London Welsh) 1934 S, I
Evans, I (Swansea) 1922 E, S, I, F
Evans, I C (Llanelli, Bath) 1987 F, E, S, I, [I, C, E, NZ, A], 1988 E, S, I, F, NZ 1,2, 1989 I, F, E, 1991 E, S, I, F 1, A, F 2, [WS, Arg, A], 1992 I, F, E, S, A, 1993 E, S, I, F, J, C, 1994 S, I, E, Pt, Sp, C, Fj, Tg, WS, R, 1995 E, S, I, [J, NZ, I], SA, Fj, 1996 It, E, S, I, F 1, A 1,2, Bb, F 2, A 3, SA, 1997 US, S, I, F, 1998 It
Evans, I L (Llanelli) 1991 F 2(R)
Evans, J (Llanelli) 1896 S, I, 1897 E
Evans, J (Blaina) 1904 E
Evans, J (Pontypool) 1907 E, S, I
Evans, J D (Cardiff) 1958 I, F
Evans, J E (Llanelli) 1924 S
Evans, J R (Newport) 1934 E
Evans, O J (Cardiff) 1887 E, S, 1888 S, I
Evans, P D (Llanelli) 1951 E, F
Evans, R (Cardiff) 1889 S
Evans, R (Bridgend) 1963 S, I, F
Evans, R L (Llanelli) 1993 E, S, I, F, 1994 S, I, F, E, Pt, Sp, C, Fj, WS, R, It, SA, 1995 F, [NZ, I (R)]
Evans, R T (Newport) 1947 F, I, 1950 E, S, I, F, 1951 E, S, I, F
Evans, S (Swansea, Neath) 1985 F, E, 1986 Fj, Tg, WS, 1987 F, E, [I, Tg]
Evans, T (Swansea) 1924 I
Evans, T G (London Welsh) 1970 SA, S, E, I, 1972 E, S, F
Evans, T H (Llanelli) 1906 I, 1907 E, S, I, 1908 I, A, 1909 E, S, F, I, 1910 F, E, S, I, 1911 E, S, F, I
Evans, T P (Swansea) 1975 F, E, S, I, A, 1976 E, S, I, F, 1977 I
Evans, V (Neath) 1954 I, F, S
Evans, W (Llanelli) 1958 A
Evans, W F (Rhymney) 1882 I, 1883 S
Evans, W G (Brynmawr) 1911 I
Evans, W H (Llwynypia) 1914 E, S, F, I
Evans, W J (Pontypool) 1947 S
Evans, W R (Bridgend) 1958 A, E, S, I, F, 1960 SA, 1961 E, S, I, F, 1962 E, S, I
Everson, W A (Newport) 1926 S

Faulkner, A G (Pontypool) 1975 F, E, S, I, A, 1976 E, S, I, F, 1978 E, S, I, F, A 1,2, NZ, 1979 S, I, F

Faull, J (Swansea) 1957 I, F, 1958 A, E, S, I, F, 1959 E, S, I, 1960 E, F
Fauvel, T J (Aberavon) 1988 NZ 1(R)
Fear, A G (Newport) 1934 S, I, 1935 S, I
Fender, N H (Cardiff) 1930 I, F, 1931 E, S, F, I
Fenwick, S P (Bridgend) 1975 F, E, S, A, 1976 E, S, I, F, 1977 I, F, E, S, 1978 E, S, I, F, A 1,2, NZ, 1979 S, I, F, E, 1980 F, E, S, I, NZ, 1981 E, S
Finch, E (Llanelli) 1924 F, NZ, 1925 F, I, 1926 F, 1927 A, 1928 I
Finlayson, A A J (Cardiff) 1974 I, F, E
Fitzgerald, D (Cardiff) 1894 S, I
Ford, F J V (Welch Regt, Newport) 1939 E
Ford, I (Newport) 1959 E, S
Ford, S P (Cardiff) 1990 I, Nm 1,2, Bb, 1991 E, S, I, A
Forster, J A (Newport Gwent Dragons) 2004 Arg 1
Forward, A (Pontypool, Mon Police) 1951 S, SA, 1952 E, S, I, F
Fowler, I J (Llanelli) 1919 NZA
Francis, D G (Llanelli) 1919 NZA, 1924 S
Francis, P (Maesteg) 1987 S
Funnell, J S (Ebbw Vale) 1998 Z (R), SA 1

Gabe, R T (Cardiff, Llanelli) 1901 I, 1902 E, S, I, 1903 E, S, I, 1904 E, S, I, 1905 E, S, I, NZ, 1906 E, I, SA, 1907 E, S, I, 1908 E, S, F, I
Gale, N R (Swansea, Llanelli) 1960 I, 1963 E, S, I, NZ, 1964 E, S, I, F, SA, 1965 E, S, I, F, 1966 E, S, I, F, A, 1967 E, NZ, 1968 E, 1969 NZ 1(R),2, A
Gallacher, I S (Llanelli) 1970 F
Garrett, R M (Penarth) 1888 M, 1889 S, 1890 S, E, I, 1891 S, I, 1892 E
Geen, W P (Oxford U, Newport) 1912 SA, 1913 E, I
George, E E (Pontypridd, Cardiff) 1895 S, I, 1896 E
George, G M (Newport) 1991 E, S
Gething, G I (Neath) 1913 F
Gibbs, A (Newbridge) 1995 I, SA, 1996 A 2, 1997 US 1,2, C
Gibbs, I S (Neath, Swansea) 1991 E, S, I, F 1, A, F 2, [WS, Arg, A], 1992 I, F, E, S, A, 1993 E, S, I, F, J, C, 1996 It, A 3, SA, 1997 US, S, I, F, Tg, NZ, 1998 It, E, S, SA 2, Arg, 1999 S, I, F 1, It, E, C, F 2, [Arg 3, J, Sm, A], 2000 I, Sm, US, SA, 2001 E, S, F, It
Gibbs, R A (Cardiff) 1906 S, I, 1907 E, S, 1908 E, S, F, I, 1910 F, E, S, I, 1911 E, S, F, I
Giles, R (Aberavon) 1983 R, 1985 Fj (R), 1987 [C]
Girling, B E (Cardiff) 1881 E
Goldsworthy, S J (Swansea) 1884 I, 1885 E, S
Gore, J H (Blaina) 1924 I, F, NZ, 1925 E
Gore, W (Newbridge) 1947 S, F, I
Gough, I M (Newport, Pontypridd, Newport Gwent Dragons) 1998 SA 1, 1999 S, 2000 F, It (R), E (R), S, I, Sm, US, SA, 2001 E, S, F, It, Tg, A, 2002 I (R), F (R), It, S, 2003 R, 2005 It(R),US(R),SA,A, 2006 E,S,I,It,F,Arg 1,2
Gould, A J (Newport) 1885 E, S, 1886 E, S, 1887 E, S, I, 1888 S, 1889 I, 1890 S, E, I, 1892 E, S, I, 1893 E, S, I, 1894 E, S, 1895 E, S, I, 1896 E, S, I, 1897 E
Gould, G H (Newport) 1892 I, 1893 S, I
Gould, R (Newport) 1882 I, 1883 E, S, 1884 E, S, I, 1885 E, S, 1886 E, 1887 E, S
Graham, T C (Newport) 1890 I, 1891 S, I, 1892 E, S, 1893 E, S, I, 1894 E, S, 1895 E, S
Gravell, R W R (Llanelli) 1975 F, E, S, I, A, 1976 E, S, I, F, 1978 E, S, I, F, A 1,2, NZ, 1979 S, I, 1981 I, F, 1982 F, E, S
Gray, A J (London Welsh) 1968 E, S
Greenslade, D (Newport) 1962 S
Greville, H G (Llanelli) 1947 A
Griffin, Dr J (Edinburgh U) 1883 S
Griffiths, C (Llanelli) 1979 E (R)
Griffiths, D (Llanelli) 1888 M, 1889 I
Griffiths, G (Llanelli) 1889 I
Griffiths, G M (Cardiff) 1953 E, S, I, F, NZ, 1954 I, F, S, 1955 I, F, 1957 E, S
Griffiths, J (Swansea) 2000 Sm (R)
Griffiths, J L (Llanelli) 1988 NZ 2, 1989 S
Griffiths, M (Bridgend, Cardiff, Pontypridd) 1988 WS, R, 1989 S, I, F, E, NZ, 1990 F, E, Nm 1,2, Bb, 1991 I, F 1,2, [WS, Arg, A], 1992 I, F, E, S, A, 1993 Z 1,2, Nm, J, C, 1995 F (R), E, S, I, [J, I], 1998 SA 1
Griffiths, V M (Newport) 1924 S, I, F
Gronow, B (Bridgend) 1910 F, E, S, I
Gwilliam, J A (Cambridge U, Newport) 1947 A, 1948 I, 1949 E, S, I, F, 1950 E, S, I, F, 1951 E, S, I, SA, 1952 E, S, I, F, 1953 E, I, F, NZ, 1954 E
Gwynn, D (Swansea) 1883 E, 1887 S, 1890 E, I, 1891 E, S
Gwynn, W H (Swansea) 1884 E, S, I, 1885 E, S

Hadley, A M (Cardiff) 1983 R, 1984 S, I, F, E, 1985 F, E, Fj, 1986 E, S, I, F, Fj, Tg, 1987 S (R), I, [I, Tg, C, E, NZ, A], US, 1988 E, S, I, F
Hall, I (Aberavon) 1967 NZ, 1970 SA, S, E, 1971 S, 1974 S, I, F
Hall, M R (Cambridge U, Bridgend, Cardiff) 1988 NZ 1(R),2, WS, R, 1989 S, I, F, E, NZ, 1990 F, E, S, 1991 A, F 2, [WS, Arg, A], 1992 I, F, E, S, A, 1993 E, S, I, 1994 S, I, F, E, Pt, Sp, C, Tg, R, It, SA, 1995 F, S, I, [J, NZ, I]
Hall, W H (Bridgend) 1988 WS
Hancock, F E (Cardiff) 1884 I, 1885 E, S, 1886 S
Hannan, J (Newport) 1888 M, 1889 S, I, 1890 S, E, I, 1891 E, 1892 E, S, I, 1893 E, S, I, 1894 E, S, I, 1895 E, S, I
Harding, A F (London Welsh) 1902 E, S, I, 1903 E, S, I, 1904 E, S, I, 1905 E, S, I, NZ, 1906 E, S, I, SA, 1907 I, 1908 E, S
Harding, G F (Newport) 1881 E, 1882 I, 1883 E, S
Harding, R (Swansea, Cambridge U) 1923 E, S, F, I, 1924 I, F, NZ, 1925 F, I, 1926 E, I, F, 1927 E, S, F, I, 1928 E
Harding, T (Newport) 1888 M, 1889 S, I
Harris, C A (Aberavon) 1927 A
Harris, D J E (Pontypridd, Cardiff) 1959 I, F, 1960 S, I, F, SA, 1961 E, S
Harris, I R (Cardiff) 2001 Arg, Tg, A, 2002 I, It (R), E, S (R), Fj(R), C(R), NZ(R), 2003 It, E 1(R), S 1(R), I 1(R), F, I 2, S 2, [C,Tg,It,E], 2004 S,I,F,It
Hathway, G F (Newport) 1924 I, F
Havard, Rev W T (Llanelli) 1919 NZA
Hawkins, F (Pontypridd) 1912 I, F
Hayward, B I (Ebbw Vale) 1998 Z (R), SA 1
Hayward, D (Newbridge) 1949 E, F, 1950 E, S, I, F, 1951 E, S, I, F, SA, 1952 E, S, I, F
Hayward, D J (Cardiff) 1963 E, NZ, 1964 S, I, F, SA
Hayward, G (Swansea) 1908 S, F, I, A, 1909 E
Hellings, R (Llwynypia) 1897 E, 1898 I, E, 1899 S, I, 1900 E, I, 1901 E, S
Henson, G L (Swansea, Ospreys) 2001 J 1(R), R, 2003 NZ(R), R, 2004 Arg 1,2,SA1,2,R,NZ, J, 2005 E,It,F,S,I, 2006 I(R),F(R)
Herrerá, R C (Cross Keys) 1925 S, F, I, 1926 E, S, I, F, 1927 E
Hiams, H (Swansea) 1912 I, F
Hibbard, R (Ospreys) 2006 Arg 1(R),2(R)
Hickman, A (Neath) 1930 E, 1933 S
Hiddlestone, D D (Neath) 1922 E, S, I, F, 1924 NZ
Hill, A F (Cardiff) 1885 S, 1886 E, S, 1888 S, I, M, 1889 S, 1890 S, I, 1893 E, S, I, 1894 E, S, I
Hill, S D (Cardiff) 1993 Z 1,2, Nm, 1994 I (R), F, SA, 1995 F, SA, 1996 A 2, F 2(R), It, 1997 E
Hinam, S (Cardiff) 1925 I, 1926 E, S, I, F
Hinton, J T (Cardiff) 1884 I
Hirst, G L (Newport) 1912 S, 1913 S, 1914 E, S, F, I
Hodder, W (Pontypool) 1921 E, S, F
Hodges, J J (Newport) 1899 E, S, I, 1900 E, S, I, 1901 E, S, 1902 E, S, I, 1903 E, S, I, 1904 E, S, 1905 E, S, I, NZ, 1906 E, S, I
Hodgson, G T R (Neath) 1962 I, 1963 E, S, I, F, NZ, 1964 E, S, I, F, SA, 1966 S, I, F, 1967 I
Hollingdale, H (Swansea) 1912 SA, 1913 E
Hollingdale, T H (Neath) 1927 A, 1928 E, S, I, F, 1930 E
Holmes, T D (Cardiff) 1978 A 2, NZ, 1979 S, I, F, E, 1980 F, E, S, I, NZ, 1981 A, 1982 I, F, E, 1983 E, S, I, F, 1984 E, 1985 S, I, F, E, Fj
Hook, J (Ospreys) 2006 Arg 1(R),2
Hopkin, W H (Newport) 1937 S
Hopkins, K (Cardiff, Swansea) 1985 E, 1987 F, E, S, [Tg, C (R)], US
Hopkins, P L (Swansea) 1908 A, 1909 E, I, 1910 E
Hopkins, R (Maesteg) 1970 E (R)

Hopkins, T (Swansea) 1926 E, S, I, F
Hopkins, W J (Aberavon) 1925 E, S
Horsman, C L (Worcester) 2005 NZ(R),Fj,SA,A
Howarth, S P (Sale, Newport) 1998 SA 2, Arg, 1999 S, I, F 1, It, E, Arg 1,2, SA, C, F 2, [Arg 3, J, Sm, A], 2000 F, It, E
Howells, B (Llanelli) 1934 E
Howells, W G (Llanelli) 1957 E, S, I, F
Howells, W H (Swansea) 1888 S, I
Howley, R (Bridgend, Cardiff) 1996 E, S, I, F 1, A 1,2, Bb, F 2, It, A 3, SA, 1997 US, S, I, F, E, Tg (R), NZ, 1998 It, E, S, I, F, Z, SA 2, Arg, 1999 S, I, F 1, It, E, Arg 1,2, SA, C, F 2, [Arg 3, J, Sm, A], 2000 F, It, E, Sm, US, SA, 2001 E, S, F, R, I, Arg, Tg, A, 2002 I, F, It, E, S
Hughes, D (Newbridge) 1967 NZ, 1969 NZ 2, 1970 SA, S, E, I
Hughes, G (Penarth) 1934 E, S, I
Hughes, H (Cardiff) 1887 S, 1889 S
Hughes, K (Cambridge U, London Welsh) 1970 I, 1973 A, 1974 S
Hullin, W (Cardiff) 1967 S
Humphreys, J M (Cardiff, Bath) 1995 [NZ, I], SA, Fj, 1996 It, E, S, I, F 1, A 1,2, Bb, It, A 3, SA, 1997 S, I, F, E, Tg (R), NZ (R), 1998 It (R), E (R), S (R), I (R), F (R), SA 2, Arg, 1999 S, Arg 2(R), SA (R), C, [J (R)], 2003 E 1, I 1
Hurrell, J (Newport) 1959 F
Hutchinson, F (Neath) 1894 I, 1896 S, I
Huxtable, R (Swansea) 1920 F, I
Huzzey, H V P (Cardiff) 1898 I, E, 1899 E, S, I
Hybart, A J (Cardiff) 1887 E

Ingledew, H M (Cardiff) 1890 I, 1891 E, S
Isaacs, I (Cardiff) 1933 E, S

Jackson, T H (Swansea) 1895 E
James, B (Bridgend) 1968 E
James, C R (Llanelli) 1958 A, F
James, D (Swansea) 1891 I, 1892 S, I, 1899 E
James, D R (Treorchy) 1931 F, I
James, D R (Bridgend, Pontypridd, Llanelli Scarlets) 1996 A 2(R), It, A 3, SA, 1997 I, Tg (R), 1998 F (R), Z, SA 1,2, Arg, 1999 S, I, F 1, It, E, Arg 1,2, SA, F 2, [Arg 3, Sm, A], 2000 F, It (R), I (R), Sm (R), US, SA, 2001 E, S, F, It, R, I, 2002 I, F, It, E, S (R), NZ(R), 2005 SA,A, 2006 I,F
James, E (Swansea) 1890 S, 1891 I, 1892 S, I, 1899 E
James, M (Cardiff) 1947 A, 1948 E, S, F, I
James, P (Ospreys) 2003 R
James, T O (Aberavon) 1935 I, 1937 S
James, W J (Aberavon) 1983 E, S, I, F, R, 1984 S, 1985 S, I, F, E, Fj, 1986 E, S, I, F, Fj, Tg, WS, 1987 E, S, I
James, W P (Aberavon) 1925 E, S
Jarman, H (Newport) 1910 E, S, I, 1911 E
Jarrett, K S (Newport) 1967 E, 1968 E, S, 1969 S, I, F, E, NZ 1,2, A
Jarvis, L (Cardiff) 1997 R (R)
Jeffery, J J (Cardiff Coll of Ed, Newport) 1967 NZ
Jenkin, A M (Swansea) 1895 I, 1896 E
Jenkins, A (Llanelli) 1920 E, S, F, I, 1921 S, F, 1922 F, 1923 E, S, F, I, 1924 NZ, 1928 S, I
Jenkins, D M (Treorchy) 1926 E, S, I, F
Jenkins, D R (Swansea) 1927 A, 1929 E
Jenkins, E (Newport) 1910 S, I
Jenkins, E M (Aberavon) 1927 S, F, I, A, 1928 E, S, I, F, 1929 F, 1930 E, S, I, F, 1931 E, S, F, I, SA, 1932 E, S, I
Jenkins, G D (Pontypridd, Celtic Warriors, Cardiff Blues) 2002 R, NZ(R), 2003 E 1(R), S 1(R), I 1, F, A, NZ, I 2(R), E 2, [C, Tg, It(R), NZ(R), E(R)], 2004 S(R), I(R), F, E, It, Arg 1(R), 2(R), SA1, 2(R), R, NZ, J, 2005 E, It, F, S, I, 2006 E(R), S(R), I(R), It(R), F(R)
Jenkins, G R (Pontypool, Swansea) 1991 F 2, [WS (R), Arg, A], 1992 I, F, E, S, A, 1993 C, 1994 S, I, F, E, Pt, Sp, C, Tg, WS, R, It, SA, 1995 F, E, S, I, [J], SA (R), Fj (t), 1996 E (R), 1997 US, US 1, C, 1998 S, I, F, Z, SA 1(R), 1999 I (R), F 1, It, E, Arg 1,2, SA, F 2, [Arg 3, J, Sm, A], 2000 F, It, E, S, I, Sm, US, SA
Jenkins, J C (London Welsh) 1906 SA
Jenkins, J L (Aberavon) 1923 S, F
Jenkins, L H (Mon TC, Newport) 1954 I, 1956 E, S, I, F
Jenkins, N R (Pontypridd, Cardiff) 1991 E, S, I, F 1, 1992 I, F, E, S, 1993 E, S, I, F, Z 1,2, Nm, J, C, 1994 S, I, F, E, Pt, Sp, C, Tg, WS, R, It, SA, 1995 F, E, S, I, [J, NZ, I], SA, Fj, 1996 F 1, A 1,2, Bb, F 2, It, A 3(R), SA, 1997 S, I, F, E, Tg, NZ, 1998 It, E, S, I, F, SA 2, Arg, 1999 S, I, F 1, It, E, Arg 1,2, SA, C, F 2, [Arg 3, J, Sm, A], 2000 F, It, E, I (R), Sm (R), US (R), SA, 2001 E, S, F, It, 2002 SA 1(R),2(R), R
Jenkins, V G J (Oxford U, Bridgend, London Welsh) 1933 E, I, 1934 S, I, 1935 E, S, NZ, 1936 E, S, I, 1937 E, 1938 E, S, 1939 E
Jenkins, W (Cardiff) 1912 I, F, 1913 S, I
John, B (Llanelli, Cardiff) 1966 A, 1967 S, NZ, 1968 E, S, I, F, 1969 S, I, F, E, NZ 1,2, A, 1970 SA, S, E, I, 1971 E, S, I, F, 1972 E, S, F
John, D A (Llanelli) 1925 I, 1928 E, S, I
John, D E (Llanelli) 1923 F, I, 1928 E, S, I
John, E R (Neath) 1950 E, S, I, F, 1951 E, S, I, F, SA, 1952 E, S, I, F, 1953 E, S, I, F, NZ, 1954 E
John G (St Luke's Coll, Exeter) 1954 E, F
John, J H (Swansea) 1926 E, S, I, F, 1927 E, S, F, I
John, P (Pontypridd) 1994 Tg, 1996 Bb (t), 1997 US (R), US 1,2, C, R, Tg, 1998 Z (R), SA 1
John, S C (Llanelli, Cardiff) 1995 S, I, 1997 E (R), Tg, NZ (R), 2000 F (R), It (R), E (R), Sm (R), SA (R), 2001 E (R), S (R), Tg (R), A, 2002 I, F, It (R), S (R)
Johnson, T A (Cardiff) 1921 E, F, I, 1923 E, S, F, 1924 E, S, NZ, 1925 E, S, F
Johnson, W D (Swansea) 1953 E
Jones, A H (Cardiff) 1933 E, S
Jones, A M (Llanelli Scarlets) 2006 E(t&R),S(R)
Jones, A R (Ospreys) 2003 E 2(R), S 2, [C(R), Tg(R), It, NZ, E], 2004 S,I,Arg 1, 2, SA1, 2,R,NZ,J(t&R), 2005 E,It,F,S,I,US,NZ,Fj(R),SA(t&R),A(R), 2006 E,S,I,It,F,Arg 1,2
Jones, A W (Ospreys) 2006 Arg 1,2
Jones, B (Abertillery) 1914 E, S, F, I
Jones, Bert (Llanelli) 1934 S, I
Jones, Bob (Llwynypia) 1901 I
Jones, B J (Newport) 1960 I, F
Jones, B Lewis (Devonport Services, Llanelli) 1950 E, S, I, F, 1951 E, S, SA, 1952 E, I, F
Jones, C W (Cambridge U, Cardiff) 1934 E, S, I, 1935 E, S, I, NZ, 1936 E, S, I, 1938 E, S, I
Jones, C W (Bridgend) 1920 E, S, F
Jones, D (Neath) 1927 A
Jones, D (Aberavon) 1897 E
Jones, D (Swansea) 1947 E, F, I, 1949 E, S, I, F
Jones, D (Treherbert) 1902 E, S, I, 1903 E, S, I, 1905 E, S, I, NZ, 1906 E, S, SA
Jones, D (Newport) 1926 E, S, I, F, 1927 E
Jones, D (Llanelli) 1948 E
Jones, D (Cardiff) 1994 SA, 1995 F, E, S, [J, NZ, I], SA, Fj, 1996 It, E, S, I, F 1, A 1,2, Bb, It, A 3
Jones, D A R (Llanelli Scarlets) 2002 Fj, C, NZ, 2003 It(R), E 1, S 1, I 1, F, NZ, E 2, [C, Tg,It,NZ(R),E], 2004 S,I,F,E,It,Arg 2,SA1,2,R,NZ,J, 2005 E,Fj, 2006 F(R)
Jones, D J (Neath/Ospreys) 2001 A (R), 2002 I (R), F (R), 2003 I 2, S 2, [C, It], 2004 S, E, It, Arg1, 2, SA1(R), 2,R(R), NZ(t&R), J, 2005 US, C, NZ, SA, A, 2006 E, S, I, It, F, Arg 1, 2
Jones, D K (Llanelli, Cardiff) 1962 E, S, F, I, 1963 E, F, NZ, 1964 E, S, SA, 1966 E, S, I, F
Jones, D L (Ebbw Vale, Celtic Warriors, Cardiff Blues) 2000 Sm, 2003 R (R), 2004 SA1
Jones, D P (Pontypool) 1907 I
Jones, E H (Neath) 1929 E, S
Jones, E L (Llanelli) 1930 F, 1933 E, S, I, 1935 E
Jones, Elvet L (Llanelli) 1939 S
Jones, G (Ebbw Vale) 1963 S, I, F
Jones, G (Llanelli) 1988 NZ 2, 1989 F, E, NZ, 1990 F
Jones, G G (Cardiff) 1930 S, 1933 I
Jones, G H (Bridgend) 1995 SA
Jones, H (Penygraig) 1902 S, I
Jones, H (Neath) 1904 I
Jones, H (Swansea) 1930 I, F
Jones, Iorwerth (Llanelli) 1927 A, 1928 E, S, I, F
Jones, I C (London Welsh) 1968 I
Jones, Ivor E (Llanelli) 1924 E, S, 1927 S, F, I, A, 1928 E, S, I, F, 1929 E, S, F, I, 1930 E, S

Jones, J (Aberavon) 1901 E
Jones, J (Swansea) 1924 F
Jones, Jim (Aberavon) 1919 NZA, 1920 E, S, 1921 S, F, I
Jones, J A (Cardiff) 1883 S
Jones, J P (Tuan) (Pontypool) 1913 S
Jones, J P (Pontypool) 1908 A, 1909 E, S, F, I, 1910 F, E, 1912 E, F, 1913 F, I, 1920 F, I, 1921 E
Jones, K D (Cardiff) 1960 SA, 1961 E, S, I, 1962 E, F, 1963 E, S, I, NZ
Jones, K J (Newport) 1947 E, S, F, I, A, 1948 E, S, F, I, 1949 E, S, I, F, 1950 E, S, I, F, 1951 E, S, I, F, SA, 1952 E, S, I, F, 1953 E, S, I, F, NZ, 1954 E, I, F, S, 1955 E, S, I, F, 1956 E, S, I, F, 1957 S
Jones, K P (Ebbw Vale) 1996 Bb, F 2, It, A 3, 1997 I (R), E, 1998 S, I, F (R), SA 1
Jones, K W J (Oxford U, London Welsh) 1934 E
Jones, Matthew (Ospreys) 2005 C(R)
Jones, M A (Neath, Ebbw Vale) 1987 S, 1988 NZ 2(R), 1989 S, I, F, E, NZ, 1990 F, E, S, I, Nm 1,2, Bb, 1998 Z
Jones, M A (Llanelli Scarlets) 2001 E (R), S, J 1, 2002 R, Fj, C, NZ, 2003 It, I 1, A, NZ, E 2, [C,Tg,It,E], 2006 E,S,I,It,Arg 1,2
Jones, P (Newport) 1912 SA, 1913 E, S, F, 1914 E, S, F, I
Jones, P B (Newport) 1921 S
Jones, R (Swansea) 1901 I, 1902 E, 1904 E, S, I, 1905 E, 1908 F, I, A, 1909 E, S, F, I, 1910 F, E
Jones, R (London Welsh) 1929 E
Jones, R (Northampton) 1926 E, S, F
Jones, R (Swansea) 1927 A, 1928 F
Jones, R B (Cambridge U) 1933 E, S
Jones, R E (Coventry) 1967 F, E, 1968 S, I, F
Jones, R G (Llanelli, Cardiff) 1996 It, E, S, I, F 1, A 1, 1997 US (R), S (R), US 1,2, R, Tg, NZ
Jones, R L (Llanelli) 1993 Z 1,2, Nm, J, C
Jones, R N (Swansea) 1986 E, S, I, F, Fj, Tg, WS, 1987 F, E, S, I, [I, Tg, E, NZ, A], US, 1988 E, S, I, F, NZ 1, WS, R, 1989 I, F, E, NZ, 1990 F, E, S, I, 1991 E, S, F 2, [WS, Arg, A], 1992 I, F, E, S, A, 1993 E, S, I, 1994 I (R), Pt, 1995 F, E, S, I, [NZ, I]
Jones, R P (Ospreys) 2004 SA2,NZ(R),J, 2005 E(R), F, S, I, US
Jones, S (Neath, Newport Gwent Dragons) 2001 J 1(R), 2004 SA2,R(R),NZ(R),J(R)
Jones, S M (Llanelli Scarlets, Clermont Auvergne) 1998 SA 1(R), 1999 C (R), [J (R)], 2000 It (R), S, I, 2001 E, F (R), J 1,2, R, I, Arg, Tg, A, 2002 I, F, It, S, SA 1,2, R(R), Fj, C, NZ, 2003 S 1, I 1, F, A, NZ, E 2, [Tg, It(R), NZ, E], 2004 S, I, F, E, It, SA2, R, NZ, 2005 E, It, F, S, I, NZ, SA, A, 2006 E, S, I, It, F
Jones, S T (Pontypool) 1983 S, I, F, R, 1984 S, 1988 E, S, F, NZ 1,2
Jones, Tom (Newport) 1922 E, S, I, F, 1924 E, S
Jones, T B (Newport) 1882 I, 1883 E, S, 1884 S, 1885 E, S
Jones, W (Cardiff) 1898 I, E
Jones, W (Mountain Ash) 1905 I
Jones, W I (Llanelli, Cambridge U) 1925 E, S, F, I
Jones, W J (Llanelli) 1924 I
Jones, W K (Cardiff) 1967 NZ, 1968 E, S, I, F
Jones-Davies, T E (London Welsh) 1930 E, I, 1931 E, S
Jones-Hughes, J (Newport) 1999 [Arg 3(R), J], 2000 F
Jordan, H M (Newport) 1885 E, S, 1889 S
Joseph, W (Swansea) 1902 E, S, I, 1903 E, S, I, 1904 E, S, 1905 E, S, I, NZ, 1906 E, S, I, SA
Jowett, W F (Swansea) 1903 E
Judd, S (Cardiff) 1953 E, S, I, F, NZ, 1954 E, F, S, 1955 E, S
Judson, J H (Llanelli) 1883 E, S

Kedzlie, Q D (Cardiff) 1888 S, I
Keen, L (Aberavon) 1980 F, E, S, I
Knight, P (Pontypridd) 1990 Nm 1,2, Bb (R), 1991 E, S
Knill, F M D (Cardiff) 1976 F (R)

Lamerton, A E H (Llanelli) 1993 F, Z 1,2, Nm, J
Lane, S M (Cardiff) 1978 A 1(R),2, 1979 I (R), 1980 S, I
Lang, J (Llanelli) 1931 F, I, 1934 S, I, 1935 E, S, I, NZ, 1936 E, S, I, 1937 E
Lawrence, S (Bridgend) 1925 S, I, 1926 S, I, F, 1927 E
Law, V J (Newport) 1939 I
Legge, W S G (Newport) 1937 I, 1938 I
Leleu, J (London Welsh, Swansea) 1959 E, S, 1960 F, SA
Lemon, A (Neath) 1929 I, 1930 S, I, F, 1931 E, S, F, I, SA, 1932 E, S, I, 1933 I
Lewis, A J L (Ebbw Vale) 1970 F, 1971 E, I, F, 1972 E, S, F, 1973 E, S, I, F
Lewis, A L P (Cardiff) 1996 It, E, S, I, A 2(t), 1998 It, E, S, I, F, SA 2, Arg, 1999 F 1(R), E (R), Arg 1(R),2(R), SA (R), C (R), [J (R), Sm (R), A (R)], 2000 Sm (R), US (R), SA (R), 2001 F (R), J 1,2, 2002 R(R)
Lewis, A R (Abertillery) 1966 E, S, I, F, A, 1967 I
Lewis, B R (Swansea, Cambridge U) 1912 I, 1913 I
Lewis, C P (Llandovery Coll) 1882 I, 1883 E, S, 1884 E, S
Lewis, D H (Cardiff) 1886 E, S
Lewis, E J (Llandovery) 1881 E
Lewis, E W (Llanelli, Cardiff) 1991 I, F 1, A, F 2, [WS, Arg, A], 1992 I, F, S, A, 1993 E, S, I, F, Z 1,2, Nm, J, C, 1994 S, I, F, E, Pt, Sp, Fj, WS, R, It, SA, 1995 E, S, I, [J, I], 1996 It, E, S, I, F 1
Lewis, G (Pontypridd, Swansea) 1998 SA 1(R), 1999 It (R), Arg 2, C, [J], 2000 F (R), It, S, I, Sm, US (t+R), 2001 F (R), J 1,2, R, I
Lewis, G W (Richmond) 1960 E, S
Lewis, H (Swansea) 1913 S, F, I, 1914 E
Lewis, J G (Llanelli) 1887 I
Lewis, J M C (Cardiff, Cambridge U) 1912 E, 1913 S, F, I, 1914 E, S, F, I, 1921 I, 1923 E, S
Lewis, J R (S Glam Inst, Cardiff) 1981 E, S, I, F, 1982 F, E, S
Lewis, M (Treorchy) 1913 F
Lewis, P I (Llanelli) 1984 A, 1985 S, I, F, E, 1986 E, S, I
Lewis, T W (Cardiff) 1926 E, 1927 E, S
Lewis, W (Llanelli) 1925 F
Lewis, W H (London Welsh, Cambridge U) 1926 I, 1927 E, F, I, A, 1928 F
Llewellyn, D S (Ebbw Vale, Newport) 1998 SA 1(R), 1999 F 1(R), It (R), [J (R)]
Llewellyn, G D (Neath) 1990 Nm 1,2, Bb, 1991 E, S, I, F 1, A, F 2
Llewellyn, G O (Neath, Harlequins, Ospreys, Narbonne) 1989 NZ, 1990 E, S, I, 1991 E, S, A (R), 1992 I, F, E, S, A, 1993 E, S, I, F, Z 1,2, Nm, J, C, 1994 S, I, F, E, Pt, Sp, C, Tg, WS, R, It, SA, 1995 F, E, S, I, [J, NZ, I], 1996 It, E, S, I, F 1, A 1,2, Bb, F 2, It, A 3, SA, 1997 US, S, I, F, E, US 1,2, NZ, 1998 It, E, 1999 C (R), [Sm], 2002 E (R), SA 1,2, R(R), Fj, C, NZ, 2003 E 1(R), S 1(R), I 1, F, A, NZ, I 2, S 2(R), [C,Tg,It,E(R)], 2004 S, F(R), E(R), It, Arg 1, 2, SA1, R, NZ
Llewellyn, P D (Swansea) 1973 I, F, A, 1974 S, E
Llewellyn, W (Llwynypia) 1899 E, S, I, 1900 E, S, I, 1901 E, S, I, 1902 E, S, I, 1903 I, 1904 E, S, I, 1905 E, S, I, NZ
Llewelyn, D B (Newport, Llanelli) 1970 SA, S, E, I, F, 1971 E, S, I, F, 1972 E, S, F, NZ
Lloyd, A (Bath) 2001 J 1
Lloyd, D J (Bridgend) 1966 E, S, I, F, A, 1967 S, I, F, E, 1968 S, I, F, 1969 S, I, F, E, NZ 1, A, 1970 F, 1972 E, S, F, 1973 E, S
Lloyd, E (Llanelli) 1895 S
Lloyd, G L (Newport) 1896 I, 1899 S, I, 1900 E, S, 1901 E, S, 1902 S, I, 1903 E, S, I
Lloyd, P (Llanelli) 1890 S, E, 1891 E, I
Lloyd, R A (Pontypool) 1913 S, F, I, 1914 E, S, F, I
Lloyd, T (Maesteg) 1953 I, F
Lloyd, T C (Neath) 1909 F, 1913 F, I, 1914 E, S, F, I
Loader, C D (Swansea) 1995 SA, Fj, 1996 F 1, A 1,2, Bb, F 2, It, A 3, SA, 1997 US, S, I, F, E, US 1, R, Tg, NZ
Lockwood, T W (Newport) 1887 E, S, I
Long, E C (Swansea) 1936 E, S, I, 1937 E, S, 1939 S, I
Luscombe, H (Newport Gwent Dragons) 2003 S 2(R), 2004 Arg 1, 2, SA1, 2, R, J, 2005 E, It, S(t&R), 2006 E, S, I, It, F
Lyne, H S (Newport) 1883 S, 1884 E, S, I, 1885 E

McBryde, R C (Swansea, Llanelli, Neath, Llanelli Scarlets) 1994 Fj, SA (t), 1997 US 2, 2000 I (R), 2001 E, S, F, It, R, I, Arg, Tg, A, 2002 I, F, It, E, S (R), SA 1,2, C, NZ, 2003 A, NZ, E 2, S 2, [C,It,NZ,E], 2004 I, E, It, 2005 It(R), F(R), S(R), I(R)
McCall, B E W (Welch Regt, Newport) 1936 E, S, I
McCarley, A (Neath) 1938 E, S, I
McCutcheon, W M (Swansea) 1891 S, 1892 E, S, 1893 E, S, I, 1894 E

McIntosh, D L M (Pontypridd) 1996 SA, 1997 E (R)
Madden, M (Llanelli) 2002 SA 1(R), R, Fj(R), 2003 I 1(R), F(R)
Maddock, H T (London Welsh) 1906 E, S, I, 1907 E, S, 1910 F
Maddocks, K (Neath) 1957 E
Main, D R (London Welsh) 1959 E, S, I, F
Mainwaring, H J (Swansea) 1961 F
Mainwaring, W T (Aberavon) 1967 S, I, F, E, NZ, 1968 E
Major, W C (Maesteg) 1949 F, 1950 S
Male, B O (Cardiff) 1921 F, 1923 S, 1924 S, I, 1927 E, S, F, I, 1928 S, I, F
Manfield, L (Mountain Ash, Cardiff) 1939 S, I, 1947 A, 1948 E, S, F, I
Mann, B B (Cardiff) 1881 E
Mantle, J T (Loughborough Colls, Newport) 1964 E, SA
Margrave, F L (Llanelli) 1884 E, S
Marinos, A W N (Newport, Gwent Dragons)) 2002 I (R), F, It, E, S, SA 1,2, 2003 R
Marsden-Jones, D (Cardiff) 1921 E, 1924 NZ
Martin, A J (Aberavon) 1973 A, 1974 S, I, 1975 F, E, S, I, A, 1976 E, S, I, F, 1977 I, F, E, S, 1978 E, S, I, F, A 1,2, NZ, 1979 S, I, F, E, 1980 F, E, S, I, NZ, 1981 I, F
Martin, W J (Newport) 1912 I, F, 1919 NZA
Mason, J (Pontypridd) 1988 NZ 2(R)
Mathews, Rev A A (Lampeter) 1886 S
Mathias, R (Llanelli) 1970 F
Matthews, C (Bridgend) 1939 I
Matthews, J (Cardiff), 1947 E, A, 1948 E, S, F, 1949 E, S, I, F, 1950 E, S, I, F, 1951 E, S, I, F
May, P S (Llanelli) 1988 E, S, I, F, NZ 1,2, 1991 [WS]
Meek, N N (Pontypool) 1993 E, S, I
Meredith, A (Devonport Services) 1949 E, S, I
Meredith, B V (St Luke's Coll, London Welsh, Newport) 1954 I, F, S, 1955 E, S, I, F, 1956 E, S, I, F, 1957 E, S, I, F, 1958 A, E, S, I, 1959 E, S, I, F, 1960 E, S, F, SA, 1961 E, S, I, 1962 E, S, F, I
Meredith, C C (Neath) 1953 S, NZ, 1954 E, I, F, S, 1955 E, S, I, F, 1956 E, I, 1957 E, S
Meredith, J (Swansea) 1888 S, I, 1890 S, E
Merry, A E (Pill Harriers) 1912 I, F
Michael, G (Swansea) 1923 E, S, F
Michaelson, R C B (Aberavon, Cambridge U) 1963 E
Miller, F (Mountain Ash) 1896 I, 1900 E, S, I, 1901 E, S, I
Mills, F M (Swansea, Cardiff) 1892 E, S, I, 1893 E, S, I, 1894 E, S, I, 1895 E, S, I, 1896 E
Moon, R H StJ B (Llanelli) 1993 F, Z 1,2, Nm, J, C, 1994 S, I, F, E, Sp, C, Fj, WS, R, It, SA, 1995 E (R), 2000 S, I, Sm (R), US (R), 2001 E (R), S (R)
Moore, A P (Cardiff) 1995 [J], SA, Fj, 1996 It
Moore, A P (Swansea) 1995 SA (R), Fj, 1998 S, I, F, Z, SA 1, 1999 C, 2000 S, I, US (R), 2001 E (R), S, F, It, J 1,2, R, I, Arg, Tg, A, 2002 F, It, E, S
Moore, S J (Swansea, Moseley) 1997 C, R, Tg
Moore, W J (Bridgend) 1933 I
Morgan, C H (Llanelli) 1957 I, F
Morgan, C I (Cardiff) 1951 I, F, SA, 1952 E, S, I, 1953 S, I, F, NZ, 1954 E, I, S, 1955 E, S, I, F, 1956 E, S, I, F, 1957 E, S, I, F, 1958 E, S, I, F
Morgan, C S (Cardiff Blues) 2002 I, F, It, E, S, SA 1,2, R(R), 2003 F, 2005 v US
Morgan, D (Swansea) 1885 S, 1886 E, S, 1887 E, S, I, 1889 I
Morgan, D (Llanelli) 1895 I, 1896 E
Morgan, D R R (Llanelli) 1962 E, S, F, I, 1963 E, S, I, F, NZ
Morgan, E (Llanelli) 1920 I, 1921 E, S, F
Morgan, Edgar (Swansea) 1914 E, S, F, I
Morgan, E T (London Welsh) 1902 E, S, I, 1903 I, 1904 E, S, I, 1905 E, S, I, NZ, 1906 E, S, I, SA, 1908 F
Morgan, F L (Llanelli) 1938 E, S, I, 1939 E
Morgan, H J (Abertillery) 1958 E, S, I, F, 1959 I, F, 1960 E, 1961 E, S, I, F, 1962 E, S, F, I, 1963 S, I, F, 1965 E, S, I, F, 1966 E, S, I, F, A
Morgan, H P (Newport) 1956 E, S, I, F
Morgan, I (Swansea) 1908 A, 1909 E, S, F, I, 1910 F, E, S, I, 1911 E, F, I, 1912 S
Morgan, J L (Llanelli) 1912 SA, 1913 E
Morgan, K A (Pontypridd, Swansea, Newport Gwent Dragons) 1997 US 1,2, C, R, NZ, 1998 S, I, F, 2001 J 1, 2, R, I, Arg, Tg, A, 2002 I, F, It, E, S, SA 1, 2, 2003 E 1, S 1, [C, It], 2004 J(R), 2005 E(R), It(R), F, S, I, US, C, NZ, Fj
Morgan, M E (Swansea) 1938 E, S, I, 1939 E
Morgan, N (Newport) 1960 S, I, F
Morgan, P E J (Aberavon) 1961 E, S, F
Morgan, P J (Llanelli) 1980 S (R), I, NZ (R), 1981 I
Morgan, R (Newport) 1984 S
Morgan, T (Llanelli) 1889 I
Morgan, W G (Cambridge U) 1927 F, I, 1929 E, S, F, I, 1930 I, F
Morgan, W L (Cardiff) 1910 S
Moriarty, R D (Swansea) 1981 A, 1982 I, F, E, S, 1983 E, 1984 S, I, F, E, 1985 S, I, F, 1986 Fj, Tg, WS, 1987 [I, Tg, C (R), E, NZ, A]
Moriarty, W P (Swansea) 1986 I, F, Fj, Tg, WS, 1987 F, E, S, I, [I, Tg, C, E, NZ, A], US, 1988 E, S, I, F, NZ 1
Morley, J C (Newport) 1929 E, S, F, I, 1930 E, I, 1931 E, S, F, I, SA, 1932 E, S, I
Morris, D R (Neath, Swansea, Leicester) 1998 Z, SA 1(R),2(R), 1999 S, I, It (R), 2000 US, SA, 2001 E, S, F, It, Arg, Tg, A, 2004 Arg 1(R),2(R),SA1(R)
Morris, G L (Swansea) 1882 I, 1883 E, S, 1884 E, S
Morris, H T (Cardiff) 1951 F, 1955 I, F
Morris, J I T (Swansea) 1924 E, S
Morris, M S (S Wales Police, Neath) 1985 S, I, F, 1990 I, Nm 1, 2, Bb, 1991 I, F 1, [WS (R)], 1992 E
Morris, R R (Swansea, Bristol) 1933 S, 1937 S
Morris, S (Cross Keys) 1920 E, S, F, I, 1922 E, S, I, F, 1923 E, S, F, I, 1924 E, S, F, NZ, 1925 E, S, F
Morris, W (Abertillery) 1919 NZA, 1920 F, 1921 I
Morris, W (Llanelli) 1896 S, I, 1897 E
Morris, W D (Neath) 1967 F, E, 1968 E, S, I, F, 1969 S, I, F, E, NZ 1,2, A, 1970 SA, S, E, I, F, 1971 E, S, I, F, 1972 E, S, F, NZ, 1973 E, S, I, A, 1974 S, I, F, E
Morris, W J (Newport) 1965 S, 1966 F
Morris, W J (Pontypool) 1963 S, I
Moseley, K (Pontypool, Newport) 1988 NZ 2, R, 1989 S, I, 1990 F, 1991 F 2, [WS, Arg, A]
Murphy, C D (Cross Keys) 1935 E, S, I
Mustoe, L (Cardiff) 1995 Fj, 1996 A 1(R),2, 1997 US 1,2, C, R (R), 1998 E (R), I (R), F (R)

Nash, D (Ebbw Vale) 1960 SA, 1961 E, S, I, F, 1962 F
Newman, C H (Newport) 1881 E, 1882 I, 1883 E, S, 1884 E, S, 1885 E, S, 1886 E, 1887 E
Nicholas, D L (Llanelli) 1981 E, S, I, F
Nicholas, T J (Cardiff) 1919 NZA
Nicholl, C B (Cambridge U, Llanelli) 1891 I, 1892 E, S, I, 1893 E, S, I, 1894 E, S, 1895 E, S, I, 1896 E, S, I
Nicholl, D W (Llanelli) 1894 I
Nicholls, E G (Cardiff) 1896 S, I, 1897 E, 1898 I, E, 1899 E, S, I, 1900 S, I, 1901 E, S, I, 1902 E, S, I, 1903 I, 1904 E, 1905 I, NZ, 1906 E, S, I, SA
Nicholls, F E (Cardiff Harlequins) 1892 I
Nicholls, H (Cardiff) 1958 I
Nicholls, S H (Cardiff) 1888 M, 1889 S, I, 1891 S
Norris, C H (Cardiff) 1963 F, 1966 F
Norster, R L (Cardiff) 1982 S, 1983 E, S, I, F, 1984 S, I, F, E, A, 1985 S, I, F, E, Fj, 1986 Fj, Tg, WS, 1987 F, E, S, I, [I, C, E], US, 1988 E, S, I, F, NZ 1, WS, 1989 F, E
Norton, W B (Cardiff) 1882 I, 1883 E, S, 1884 E, S, I

Oakley, R L (Gwent Dragons) 2003 I 2, S 2(R)
O'Connor, A (Aberavon) 1960 SA, 1961 E, S, 1962 F, I
O'Connor, R (Aberavon) 1957 E
O'Neill, W (Cardiff) 1904 S, I, 1905 E, S, I, 1907 E, I, 1908 E, S, F, I
O'Shea, J P (Cardiff) 1967 S, I, 1968 S, I, F
Oliver, G (Pontypool) 1920 E, S, F, I
Osborne, W T (Mountain Ash) 1902 E, S, I, 1903 E, S, I
Ould, W J (Cardiff) 1924 E, S
Owen, A (Swansea) 1924 E
Owen, G D (Newport) 1955 I, F, 1956 E, S, I, F
Owen, M J (Pontypridd, Newport Gwent Dragons) 2002 SA 1,2, R, C(R), NZ(R), 2003 It, I 2, S 2, 2004 S(R), I(R), F, E, It,

Arg 1, 2, SA2, R, NZ, J, 2005 E, It, F, S, I,NZ, Fj, SA, A, 2006 E, S, I, It, F
Owen, R M (Swansea) 1901 I, 1902 E, S, I, 1903 E, S, I, 1904 E, S, I, 1905 E, S, I, NZ, 1906 E, S, I, SA, 1907 E, S, 1908 F, I, A, 1909 E, S, F, I, 1910 F, E, 1911 E, S, F, I, 1912 E, S

Packer, H (Newport) 1891 E, 1895 S, I, 1896 E, S, I, 1897 E
Palmer, F (Swansea) 1922 E, S, I
Parfitt, F C (Newport) 1893 E, S, I, 1894 E, S, I, 1895 S, 1896 S, I
Parfitt, S A (Swansea) 1990 Nm 1(R), Bb
Parker, D S (Swansea) 1924 I, F, NZ, 1925 E, S, F, I, 1929 F, I, 1930 E
Parker, S T (Pontypridd, Celtic Warriors, Newport Gwent Dragons, Ospreys) 2002 R, Fj, C, NZ, 2003 E 2, [C, It, NZ], 2004 S, I, Arg 1, 2, SA1, 2, NZ, 2005 Fj, SA,A
Parker, T (Swansea) 1919 NZA, 1920 E, S, I, 1921 E, S, F, I, 1922 E, S, I, F, 1923 E, S, F
Parker, W (Swansea) 1899 E, S
Parks, R D (Pontypridd, Celtic Warriors) 2002 SA 1(R), Fj(R), 2003 I 2, S 2
Parsons, G W (Newport) 1947 E
Pascoe, D (Bridgend) 1923 F, I
Pask, A E I (Abertillery) 1961 F, 1962 E, S, F, I, 1963 E, S, I, F, NZ, 1964 E, S, I, F, SA, 1965 E, S, I, F, 1966 E, S, I, F, A, 1967 S, I
Payne, G W (Army, Pontypridd) 1960 E, S, I
Payne, H (Swansea) 1935 NZ
Peacock, H (Newport) 1929 S, F, I, 1930 S, I, F
Peake, E (Chepstow) 1881 E
Pearce, G P (Bridgend) 1981 I, F, 1982 I (R)
Pearson, T W (Cardiff, Newport) 1891 E, I, 1892 E, S, 1894 S, I, 1895 E, S, I, 1897 E, 1898 I, E, 1903 E
Peel, D J (Llanelli Scarlets) 2001 J 2(R), R (R), Tg (R), 2002 I (R), It (R), E (R), S (R), SA 1,2, R, Fj, C, NZ, 2003 It, S 1(R), I 1(R), F, NZ(R), I 2, S 2, [C(R), Tg(R), It, NZ(R), E(R)], 2004 S(R), I(R), F(R), E(R), It(R), Arg 1, 2, SA1, 2, R, NZ, 2005 E, It, F, S, I, 2006 E, S, I, It
Pegge, E V (Neath) 1891 E
Perego, M A (Llanelli) 1990 S, 1993 F, Z 1, Nm (R), 1994 S, I, F, E, Sp
Perkins, S J (Pontypool) 1983 S, I, F, R, 1984 S, I, F, E, A, 1985 S, I, F, E, Fj, 1986 E, S, I, F
Perrett, F L (Neath) 1912 SA, 1913 E, S, F, I
Perrins, V C (Newport) 1970 SA, S
Perry, W (Neath) 1911 E
Phillips, A J (Cardiff) 1979 E, 1980 F, E, S, I, NZ, 1981 E, S, I, F, A, 1982 I, F, E, S, 1987 [C, E, A]
Phillips, B (Aberavon) 1925 E, S, F, I, 1926 E
Phillips, D H (Swansea) 1952 F
Phillips, H P (Newport) 1892 E, 1893 E, S, I, 1894 E, S
Phillips, H T (Newport) 1927 E, S, F, I, A, 1928 E, S, I, F
Phillips, K H (Neath) 1987 F, [I, Tg, NZ], US, 1988 E, NZ 1, 1989 NZ, 1990 F, E, S, I, Nm 1,2, Bb, 1991 E, S, I, F 1, A
Phillips, L A (Newport) 1900 E, S, I, 1901 S
Phillips, M (Llanelli Scarlets, Cardiff Blues) 2003 R, 2004 Arg 1(R), 2(R), J(R), 2005 US, C, NZ, Fj(R), SA(R), 2006 S(R), It(R), F, Arg 1, 2
Phillips, R (Neath) 1987 US, 1988 E, S, I, F, NZ 1,2, WS, 1989 S, I
Phillips, W D (Cardiff) 1881 E, 1882 I, 1884 E, S, I
Pickering, D F (Llanelli) 1983 E, S, I, F, R, 1984 S, I, F, E, A, 1985 S, I, F, E, Fj, 1986 E, S, I, F, Fj, 1987 F, E, S
Plummer, R C S (Newport) 1912 S, I, F, SA, 1913 E
Pook, T (Newport) 1895 S
Popham, A J (Leeds, Llanelli Scarlets) 2003 A (R), I 2, R, S 2, [Tg, NZ], 2004 I(R), It(R), SA1, J(R), 2005 C, Fj(R), 2006 E(R), It(R), F, Arg 1, 2
Powell, G (Ebbw Vale) 1957 I, F
Powell, J (Cardiff) 1906 I
Powell, J (Cardiff) 1923 I
Powell, R D (Cardiff) 2002 SA 1(R),2(R), C(R)
Powell, R W (Newport) 1888 S, I
Powell, W C (London Welsh) 1926 S, I, F, 1927 E, F, I, 1928 S, I, F, 1929 E, S, F, I, 1930 S, I, F, 1931 E, S, F, I, SA, 1932 E, S, I, 1935 E, S, I
Powell, W J (Cardiff) 1920 E, S, F, I
Price, B (Newport) 1961 I, F, 1962 E, S, 1963 E, S, F, NZ, 1964 E, S, I, F, SA, 1965 E, S, I, F, 1966 E, S, I, F, A, 1967 S, I, F, E, 1969 S, I, F, NZ 1,2, A
Price, G (Pontypool) 1975 F, E, S, I, A, 1976 E, S, I, F, 1977 I, F, E, S, 1978 E, S, I, F, A 1,2, NZ, 1979 S, I, F, E, 1980 F, E, S, I, NZ, 1981 E, S, I, F, A, 1982 I, F, E, S, 1983 E, I, F
Price, M J (Pontypool, RAF) 1959 E, S, I, F, 1960 E, S, I, F, 1962 E
Price, R E (Weston-s-Mare) 1939 S, I
Price, T G (Llanelli) 1965 E, S, I, F, 1966 E, A, 1967 S, F
Priday, A J (Cardiff) 1958 I, 1961 I
Pritchard, C (Pontypool) 1928 E, S, I, F, 1929 E, S, F, I
Pritchard, C C (Newport, Pontypool) 1904 S, I, 1905 NZ, 1906 E, S
Pritchard, C M (Newport) 1904 I, 1905 E, S, NZ, 1906 E, S, I, SA, 1907 E, S, I, 1908 E, 1910 F, E
Proctor, W T (Llanelli) 1992 A, 1993 E, S, Z 1,2, Nm, C, 1994 I, C, Fj, WS, R, It, SA, 1995 S, I, [NZ], Fj, 1996 It, E, S, I, A 1,2, Bb, F 2, It, A 3, 1997 E(R), US 1,2, C, R, 1998 E (R), S, I, F, Z, 2001 A
Prosser, D R (Neath) 1934 S, I
Prosser, G (Neath) 1934 E, S, I, 1935 NZ
Prosser, G (Pontypridd) 1995 [NZ]
Prosser, J (Cardiff) 1921 I
Prosser, T R (Pontypool) 1956 S, F, 1957 E, S, I, F, 1958 A, E, S, I, F, 1959 E, S, I, F, 1960 E, S, I, F, SA, 1961 I, F
Prothero, G J (Bridgend) 1964 S, I, F, 1965 E, S, I, F, 1966 E, S, I, F
Pryce-Jenkins, T J (London Welsh) 1888 S, I
Pugh, C (Maesteg) 1924 E, S, I, F, NZ, 1925 E, S
Pugh, J D (Neath) 1987 US, 1988 S (R), 1990 S
Pugh, P (Neath) 1989 NZ
Pugh, R (Ospreys) 2005 US(R)
Pugsley, J (Cardiff) 1910 E, S, I, 1911 E, S, F, I
Pullman, J J (Neath) 1910 F
Purdon, F T (Newport) 1881 E, 1882 I, 1883 E, S

Quinnell, D L (Llanelli) 1972 F (R), NZ, 1973 E, S, A, 1974 S, F, 1975 E (R), 1977 I (R), F, E, S, 1978 E, S, I, F, A 1, NZ, 1979 S, I, F, E, 1980 NZ
Quinnell, J C (Llanelli, Richmond, Cardiff) 1995 Fj, 1996 A 3(R), 1997 US (R), S (R), I (R), E (R), 1998 SA 2, Arg, 1999 I, F 1, It, E, Arg 1,2, SA, C, F 2, [Arg 3, J, A], 2000 It, E, 2001 S (R), F (R), It (R), J 1,2, R (R), I (R), Arg, 2002 I, F
Quinnell, L S (Llanelli, Richmond) 1993 C, 1994 S, I, F, E, Pt, Sp, C, WS, 1997 US, S, I, F, E, 1998 It, E, S (R), Z, SA 2, Arg, 1999 S, I, F 1, It, E, Arg 1,2, SA, C, F 2, [Arg 3, Sm, A], 2000 F, It, E, Sm, US, SA, 2001 E, S, F, It, Arg, Tg, A, 2002 I, F, It, E, R, C(R)

Radford, W J (Newport) 1923 I
Ralph, A R (Newport) 1931 F, I, SA, 1932 E, S, I
Ramsey, S H (Treorchy) 1896 E, 1904 E
Randell, R (Aberavon) 1924 I, F
Raybould, W H (London Welsh, Cambridge U, Newport) 1967 S, I, F, E, NZ, 1968 I, F, 1970 SA, E, I, F (R)
Rayer, M A (Cardiff) 1991 [WS (R), Arg, A (R)], 1992 E (R), A, 1993 E, S, I, Z 1, Nm, J (R), 1994 S (R), I (R), F, E, Pt, C, Fj, WS, R, It
Rees, Aaron (Maesteg) 1919 NZA
Rees, Alan (Maesteg) 1962 E, S, F
Rees, A M (London Welsh) 1934 E, 1935 E, S, I, NZ, 1936 E, S, I, 1937 E, S, I, 1938 E, S
Rees, B I (London Welsh) 1967 S, I, F
Rees, C F W (London Welsh) 1974 I, 1975 A, 1978 NZ, 1981 F, A, 1982 I, F, E, S, 1983 E, S, I, F
Rees, D (Swansea) 1968 S, I, F
Rees, Dan (Swansea) 1900 E, 1903 E, S, 1905 E, S
Rees, E B (Swansea) 1919 NZA
Rees, H (Cardiff) 1937 S, I, 1938 E, S, I
Rees, H E (Neath) 1979 S, I, F, E, 1980 F, E, S, I, NZ, 1983 E, S, I, F
Rees, J (Swansea) 1920 E, S, F, I, 1921 E, S, I, 1922 E, 1923 E, F, I, 1924 E
Rees, J I (Swansea) 1934 E, S, I, 1935 S, NZ, 1936 E, S, I, 1937 E, S, I, 1938 E, S, I
Rees, L M (Cardiff) 1933 I

Rees, M (Llanelli Scarlets) 2005 US, 2006 Arg 1
Rees, P (Llanelli) 1947 F, I
Rees, P M (Newport) 1961 E, S, I, 1964 I
Rees, R (Swansea) 1998 Z
Rees, T (Newport) 1935 S, I, NZ, 1936 E, S, I, 1937 E, S
Rees, T A (Llandovery) 1881 E
Rees, T E (London Welsh) 1926 I, F, 1927 A, 1928 E
Rees-Jones, G R (Oxford U, London Welsh) 1934 E, S, 1935 I, NZ, 1936 E
Reeves, F (Cross Keys) 1920 F, I, 1921 E
Reynolds, A (Swansea) 1990 Nm 1,2(R), 1992 A (R)
Rhapps, J (Penygraig) 1897 E
Rice-Evans, W (Swansea) 1890 S, 1891 E, S
Richards, B (Swansea)1960 F
Richards, C (Pontypool) 1922 E, S, I, F, 1924 I
Richards, D S (Swansea) 1979 F, E, 1980 F, E, S, I, NZ, 1981 E, S, I, F, 1982 I, F, 1983 E, S, I, R (R)
Richards, E G (Cardiff) 1927 S
Richards, E S (Swansea) 1885 E, 1887 S
Richards, H D (Neath) 1986 Tg (R), 1987 [Tg, E (R), NZ]
Richards, I (Cardiff) 1925 E, S, F
Richards, K H L (Bridgend) 1960 SA, 1961 E, S, I, F
Richards, M C R (Cardiff) 1968 I, F, 1969 S, I, F, E, NZ 1,2, A
Richards, R (Aberavon) 1913 S, F, I
Richards, R (Cross Keys) 1956 F
Richards, T L (Maesteg) 1923 I
Richardson, S J (Aberavon) 1978 A 2(R), 1979 E
Rickards, A R (Cardiff) 1924 F
Ring, J (Aberavon) 1921 E
Ring, M G (Cardiff, Pontypool) 1983 E, 1984 A, 1985 S, I, F, 1987 I, [I, Tg, A], US, 1988 E, S, I, F, NZ 1,2, 1989 NZ, 1990 F, E, S, I, Nm 1,2, Bb, 1991 E, S, I, F 1,2, [WS, Arg, A]
Ringer, J (Bridgend) 2001 J 1(R),2(R)
Ringer, P (Ebbw Vale, Llanelli) 1978 NZ, 1979 S, I, F, E, 1980 F, E, NZ
Roberts, C (Neath) 1958 I, F
Roberts, D E A (London Welsh) 1930 E
Roberts, E (Llanelli) 1886 E, 1887 I
Roberts, E J (Llanelli) 1888 S, I, 1889 I
Roberts, G J (Cardiff) 1985 F (R), E, 1987 [I, Tg, C, E, A]
Roberts, H M (Cardiff) 1960 SA, 1961 E, S, I, F, 1962 S, F, 1963 I
Roberts, J (Cardiff) 1927 E, S, F, I, A, 1928 E, S, I, F, 1929 E, S, F, I
Roberts, M G (London Welsh) 1971 E, S, I, F, 1973 I, F, 1975 S, 1979 E
Roberts, T (Newport, Risca) 1921 S, F, I, 1922 E, S, I, F, 1923 E, S
Roberts, W (Cardiff) 1929 E
Robins, J D (Birkenhead Park) 1950 E, S, I, F, 1951 E, S, I, F, 1953 E, I, F
Robins, R J (Pontypridd) 1953 S, 1954 F, S, 1955 E, S, I, F, 1956 E, F, 1957 E, S, I, F
Robinson, I R (Cardiff) 1974 F, E
Robinson, J P (Cardiff Blues) 2001 J 1(R),2(R), Arg (R), Tg (R), A, 2002 I, Fj(R), C, NZ, 2003 A, NZ, I 2, S 2, 2006 Arg 1,2
Robinson, M F D (Swansea) 1999 S, I, F 1, Arg 1
Robinson, N J (Cardiff Blues) 2003 I 2, R, 2004 Arg 1(R),2,SA1, 2005 US,C,NZ(R),Fj, 2006 S(R),Arg 1,2
Rocyn-Jones, D N (Cambridge U) 1925 I
Roderick, W B (Llanelli) 1884 I
Rogers, P J D (London Irish, Newport, Cardiff) 1999 F 1, It, E, Arg 1,2, SA, C, F 2, [Arg 3, J, Sm, A], 2000 F, It, E, S, I, SA
Rosser, M A (Penarth) 1924 S, F
Rowland, E M (Lampeter) 1885 E
Rowlands, C F (Aberavon) 1926 I
Rowlands, D C T (Pontypool) 1963 E, S, I, F, NZ, 1964 E, S, I, F, SA, 1965 E, S, I, F
Rowlands, G (RAF, Cardiff) 1953 NZ, 1954 E, F, 1956 F
Rowlands, K A (Cardiff) 1962 F, I, 1963 I, 1965 I, F
Rowles, G R (Penarth) 1892 E
Rowley, M (Pontypridd) 1996 SA, 1997 US, S, I, F, R
Roy, W S (Cardiff) 1995 [J (R)]
Russell, S (London Welsh) 1987 US

Samuel, D (Swansea) 1891 I, 1893 I
Samuel, F (Mountain Ash) 1922 S, I, F
Samuel, J (Swansea) 1891 I
Scourfield, T (Torquay) 1930 F
Scrine, G F (Swansea) 1899 E, S, 1901 I
Selley, T J (Llanelli Scarlets) 2005 US(R)
Shanklin, J L (London Welsh) 1970 F, 1972 NZ, 1973 I, F
Shanklin, T G L (Saracens, Cardiff Blues) 2001 J 2, 2002 F, It, SA 1(R),2(R),R, Fj, 2003 It, E 1, S 1, I 1, F(t+R), A, NZ, S 2, [Tg,NZ], 2004 I(R),F(R),E,It(R),Arg 1(R),2, SA1, 2(R), R, NZ, J, 2005 E, It, F, S, I
Shaw, G (Neath) 1972 NZ, 1973 E, S, I, F, A, 1974 S, I, F, E, 1977 I, F
Shaw, T W (Newbridge) 1983 R
Shea, J (Newport) 1919 NZA, 1920 E, S, 1921 E
Shell, R C (Aberavon) 1973 A (R)
Sidoli, R A (Pontypridd, Celtic Warriors, Cardiff Blues) 2002 SA 1(R), 2(R), R, Fj, NZ, 2003 It, E 1, S 1, I 1, F, A, NZ, E 2, [C(R), Tg, It(R), NZ, E], 2004 I, It(R), 2005 E, It, F, S, I, C, NZ, Fj(R), SA, A, 2006 E, S, I, It, F
Simpson, H J (Cardiff) 1884 E, S, I
Sinkinson, B D (Neath) 1999 F 1, It, E, Arg 1,2, SA, F 2, [Arg 3, J, Sm, A], 2000 F, It, E, 2001 R (R), I, Arg (R), Tg, A, 2002 It (R)
Skrimshire, R T (Newport) 1899 E, S, I
Skym, A (Llanelli) 1928 E, S, I, F, 1930 E, S, I, F, 1931 E, S, F, I, SA, 1932 E, S, I, 1933 E, S, I, 1935 E
Smith, J S (Cardiff) 1884 E, I, 1885 E
Smith, R (Ebbw Vale) 2000 F (R)
Sowden-Taylor, R (Cardiff Blues) 2005 It(R),C(R),NZ(R)
Sparks, B (Neath) 1954 I, 1955 E, F, 1956 E, S, I, 1957 S
Spiller, W J (Cardiff) 1910 S, I, 1911 E, S, F, I, 1912 E, F, SA, 1913 E
Squire, J (Newport, Pontypool) 1977 I, F, 1978 E, S, I, F, A 1, NZ, 1979 S, I, F, E, 1980 F, E, S, I, NZ, 1981 E, S, I, F, A, 1982 I, F, E, 1983 E, S, I, F
Stadden, W J W (Cardiff) 1884 I, 1886 E, S, 1887 I, 1888 S, M, 1890 S, E
Stephens, C (Bridgend) 1998 E (R), 2001 J 2(R)
Stephens, C J (Llanelli) 1992 I, F, E, A
Stephens, G (Neath) 1912 E, S, I, F, SA, 1913 E, S, F, I, 1919 NZA
Stephens, I (Bridgend) 1981 E, S, I, F, A, 1982 I, F, E, S, 1984 I, F, E, A
Stephens, Rev J G (Llanelli) 1922 E, S, I, F
Stephens, J R G (Neath) 1947 E, S, F, I, 1948 I, 1949 S, I, F, 1951 F, SA, 1952 E, S, I, F, 1953 E, S, I, F, NZ, 1954 E, I, 1955 E, S, I, F, 1956 S, I, F, 1957 E, S, I, F
Stock, A (Newport) 1924 F, NZ, 1926 E, S
Stone, P (Llanelli) 1949 F
Strand-Jones, J (Llanelli) 1902 E, S, I, 1903 E, S
Sullivan, A C (Cardiff) 2001 Arg, Tg
Summers, R H B (Haverfordwest) 1881 E
Sutton, S (Pontypool, S Wales Police) 1982 F, E, 1987 F, E, S, I, [C, NZ (R), A]
Sweeney, C (Pontypridd, Celtic Warriors, Newport Gwent Dragons) 2003 It(R), E 1, NZ(R), I 2, S 2, [C, It, NZ(t&R), E(t)], 2004 I(R), F(R), E(R), It(R), Arg 1, SA1(R), 2(R), R(R), J, 2005 It(R), F(t), S(R), US, C, NZ, Fj(R), SA(t&R), A(R)
Sweet-Escott, R B (Cardiff) 1891 S, 1894 I, 1895 I

Tamplin, W E (Cardiff) 1947 S, F, I, A, 1948 E, S, F
Tanner, H (Swansea, Cardiff) 1935 NZ, 1936 E, S, I, 1937 E, S, I, 1938 E, S, I, 1939 E, S, I, 1947 E, S, F, I, 1948 E, S, F, I, 1949 E, S, I, F
Tarr, D J (Swansea, Royal Navy) 1935 NZ
Taylor, A R (Cross Keys) 1937 I, 1938 I, 1939 E
Taylor, C G (Ruabon) 1884 E, S, I, 1885 E, S, 1886 E, S, 1887 E, I
Taylor, H T (Cardiff) 1994 Pt, C, Fj, Tg, WS (R), R, It, SA, 1995 E, S, [J, NZ, I], SA, Fj, 1996 It, E, S, I, F 1, A 1,2, It, A 3
Taylor, J (London Welsh) 1967 S, I, F, E, NZ, 1968 I, F, 1969 S, I, F, E, NZ 1, A, 1970 F, 1971 E, S, I, F, 1972 E, S, F, NZ, 1973 E, S, I, F
Taylor, M (Pontypool, Swansea, Llanelli Scarlets, Sale) 1994 SA, 1995 F, E, SA (R), 1998 Z, SA 1,2, Arg, 1999 I, F 1, It, E, Arg 1,2, SA, F 2, [Arg 3, J, Sm, A], 2000 F, It, E, S, Sm, US, 2001 E, S, F, It, 2002 S, SA 1,2, 2003 E 1, S 1, I 1, F,

A, NZ, E 2, [C(R),Tg, NZ, E], 2004 F, E, It, R(R), 2005 I, US, C, NZ

Thomas, A (Newport) 1963 NZ, 1964 E

Thomas, A C (Bristol, Swansea) 1996 It, E, S, I, F 2(R), SA, 1997 US, S, I, F, US 1,2, C, R, NZ (t), 1998 It, E, S (R), Z, SA 1, 2000 Sm, US, SA (R)

Thomas, A G (Swansea, Cardiff) 1952 E, S, I, F, 1953 S, I, F, 1954 E, I, F, 1955 S, I, F

Thomas, Bob (Swansea) 1900 E, S, I, 1901 E

Thomas, Brian (Neath, Cambridge U) 1963 E, S, I, F, NZ, 1964 E, S, I, F, SA, 1965 E, 1966 E, S, I, 1967 NZ, 1969 S, I, F, E, NZ 1,2

Thomas, C (Bridgend) 1925 E, S

Thomas, C J (Newport) 1888 I, M, 1889 S, I, 1890 S, E, I, 1891 E, I

Thomas, D (Aberavon) 1961 I

Thomas, Dick (Mountain Ash) 1906 SA, 1908 F, I, 1909 S

Thomas, D J (Swansea) 1904 E, 1908 A, 1910 E, S, I, 1911 E, S, F, I, 1912 E

Thomas, D J (Swansea) 1930 S, I, 1932 E, S, I, 1933 E, S, 1934 E, 1935 E, S, I

Thomas, D L (Neath) 1937 E

Thomas, E (Newport) 1904 S, I, 1909 S, F, I, 1910 F

Thomas, G (Llanelli) 1923 E, S, F, I

Thomas, G (Newport) 1888 M, 1890 I, 1891 S

Thomas, G (Bridgend, Cardiff, Celtic Warriors, Toulouse) 1995 [J, NZ, I], SA, Fj, 1996 F 1, A 1,2, Bb, F 2, It, A 3, 1997 US, S, I, F, E, US 1, 2, C, R, Tg, NZ, 1998 It, E, S, I, F, SA 2, Arg, 1999 F 1(R), It, E, Arg 2, SA, F 2, [Arg 3, J (R), Sm, A], 2000 F, It, E, S, I, US (R), SA, 2001 E, F, It, J 1,2, R, Arg, Tg, A, 2002 E, R, Fj, C, NZ, 2003 It, E 1, S 1, I 1, F, I 2, E 2, [C,It,NZ(R),E], 2004 S,I,F,E,It,SA2,R,NZ, 2005 E, It, F, NZ, SA, A, 2006 E, S

Thomas, G M (Bath, Ospreys, Llanelli Scarlets) 2001 J 1,2, R, I (R), Arg, Tg (R), A (R), 2002 S (R), SA 2(R),R(R), 2003 It(R), E 1, S 1, F, E 2(R), R, 2006 Arg 1,2

Thomas, H (Llanelli) 1912 F

Thomas, H (Neath) 1936 E, S, I, 1937 E, S, I

Thomas, H W (Swansea) 1912 SA, 1913 E

Thomas, I (Bryncethin) 1924 E

Thomas, I D (Ebbw Vale, Llanelli Scarlets) 2000 Sm, US (R), SA (R), 2001 J 1,2, R, I, Arg (R), Tg, 2002 It, E, S, SA 1,2, Fj, C, NZ, 2003 It, E 1, S 1, I 1, F, A, NZ, E 2, [Tg, NZ, E], 2004 I, F

Thomas, J (Swansea, Ospreys) 2003 A, NZ(R), E 2(R), R, [It(R), NZ, E], 2004 S(t&R), I, F, E, Arg 2(R), SA1(R), R(t&R), J, 2005 E(R), It, F(R), S(R), US, C, NZ, 2006 It(R), F(R)

Thomas, J D (Llanelli) 1954 I

Thomas, L C (Cardiff) 1885 E, S

Thomas, M C (Newport, Devonport Services) 1949 F, 1950 E, S, I, F, 1951 E, S, I, F, SA, 1952 E, S, I, F, 1953 E, 1956 E, S, I, F, 1957 E, S, 1958 E, S, I, F, 1959 I, F

Thomas, M G (St Bart's Hospital) 1919 NZA, 1921 S, F, I, 1923 F, 1924 E

Thomas, N (Bath) 1996 SA (R), 1997 US 1(R),2, C (R), R, Tg, NZ, 1998 Z, SA 1

Thomas, R (Pontypool) 1909 F, I, 1911 S, F, 1912 E, S, SA, 1913 E

Thomas, Rhys (Newport Gwent Dragons) 2006 Arg 2(R)

Thomas, R C C (Swansea) 1949 F, 1952 I, F, 1953 S, I, F, NZ, 1954 E, I, F, S, 1955 S, I, 1956 E, S, I, 1957 E, 1958 A, E, S, I, F, 1959 E, S, I, F

Thomas, R L (London Welsh) 1889 S, I, 1890 I, 1891 E, S, I, 1892 E

Thomas, S (Llanelli) 1890 S, E, 1891 I

Thomas, T R (Cardiff Blues) 2005 US(R),C,NZ(R),Fj,SA,A, 2006 E,S,I,It,F

Thomas, W D (Llanelli) 1966 A, 1968 S, I, F, 1969 E, NZ 2, A, 1970 SA, S, E, I, F, 1971 E, S, I, F, 1972 E, S, F, NZ, 1973 E, S, I, F, 1974 E

Thomas, W G (Llanelli, Waterloo, Swansea) 1927 E, S, F, I, 1929 E, 1931 E, S, SA, 1932 E, S, I, 1933 E, S, I

Thomas, W H (Llandovery Coll, Cambridge U) 1885 S, 1886 E, S, 1887 E, S, 1888 S, I, 1890 E, I, 1891 S, I

Thomas, W J (Cardiff) 1961 F, 1963 F

Thomas, W J L (Llanelli, Cardiff) 1995 SA, Fj, 1996 It, E, S, I, F 1, 1996 Bb (R), 1997 US

Thomas, W L (Newport) 1894 S, 1895 E, I

Thomas, W T (Abertillery) 1930 E

Thompson, J F (Cross Keys) 1923 E

Thorburn, P H (Neath) 1985 F, E, Fj, 1986 E, S, I, F, 1987 F, [I, Tg, C, E, NZ, A], US, 1988 S, I, F, WS, R (R), 1989 S, I, F, E, NZ, 1990 F, E, S, I, Nm 1,2, Bb, 1991 E, S, I, F 1, A

Titley, M H (Bridgend, Swansea) 1983 R, 1984 S, I, F, E, A, 1985 S, I, Fj, 1986 F, Fj, Tg, WS, 1990 F, E

Towers, W H (Swansea) 1887 I, 1888 M

Travers, G (Pill Harriers, Newport) 1903 E, S, I, 1905 E, S, I, NZ, 1906 E, S, I, SA, 1907 E, S, I, 1908 E, S, F, I, A, 1909 E, S, I, 1911 S, F, I

Travers, W H (Newport) 1937 S, I, 1938 E, S, I, 1939 E, S, I, 1949 E, S, I, F

Treharne, E (Pontypridd) 1881 E, 1883 E

Trew, W J (Swansea) 1900 E, S, I, 1901 E, S, 1903 S, 1905 S, 1906 S, 1907 E, S, 1908 E, S, F, I, A, 1909 E, S, F, I, 1910 F, E, S, 1911 E, S, F, I, 1912 S, 1913 S, F

Trott, R F (Cardiff) 1948 E, S, F, I, 1949 E, S, I, F

Truman, W H (Llanelli) 1934 E, 1935 E

Trump, L C (Newport) 1912 E, S, I, F

Turnbull, B R (Cardiff) 1925 I, 1927 E, S, 1928 E, F, 1930 S

Turnbull, M J L (Cardiff) 1933 E, I

Turner, P (Newbridge) 1989 I (R), F, E

Uzzell, H (Newport) 1912 E, S, I, F, 1913 S, F, I, 1914 E, S, F, I, 1920 E, S, F, I

Uzzell, J R (Newport) 1963 NZ, 1965 E, S, I, F

Vickery, W E (Aberavon) 1938 E, S, I, 1939 E

Vile, T H (Newport) 1908 E, S, 1910 I, 1912 I, F, SA, 1913 E, 1921 S

Vincent, H C (Bangor) 1882 I

Voyle, M J (Newport, Llanelli, Cardiff) 1996 A 1(t), F 2, 1997 E, US 1,2, C, Tg, NZ, 1998 It, E, S, I, F, Arg (R), 1999 S (R), I (t), It (R), SA (R), F 2(R), [J, A (R)], 2000 F (R)

Wakeford, J D M (S Wales Police) 1988 WS, R

Waldron, R (Neath) 1965 E, S, I, F

Walker, N (Cardiff) 1993 I, F, J, 1994 S, F, E, Pt, Sp, 1995 F, E, 1997 US 1,2, C, R (R), Tg, NZ, 1998 E

Waller, P D (Newport) 1908 A, 1909 E, S, F, I, 1910 F

Walne, N J (Richmond, Cardiff) 1999 It (R), E (R), C

Walters, N (Llanelli) 1902 E

Wanbon, R (Aberavon) 1968 E

Ward, W S (Cross Keys) 1934 S, I

Warlow, J (Llanelli) 1962 I

Waters, D R (Newport) 1986 E, S, I, F

Waters, K (Newbridge) 1991 [WS]

Watkins, D (Newport) 1963 E, S, I, F, NZ, 1964 E, S, I, F, SA, 1965 E, S, I, F, 1966 E, S, I, F, 1967 I, F, E

Watkins, E (Neath) 1924 E, S, I, F

Watkins, E (Blaina) 1926 S, I, F

Watkins, E (Cardiff) 1935 NZ, 1937 S, I, 1938 E, S, I, 1939 E, S

Watkins, H (Llanelli) 1904 S, I, 1905 E, S, I, 1906 E

Watkins, I J (Ebbw Vale) 1988 E (R), S, I, F, NZ 2, R, 1989 S, I, F, E

Watkins, L (Oxford U, Llandaff) 1881 E

Watkins, M J (Newport) 1984 I, F, E, A

Watkins, M J (Llanelli Scarlets) 2003 It(R), E 1(R), S 1(R), I 1(R), R, S 2, 2005 US(R), C(R), Fj, SA(R), A, 2006 E, S, I, It, F, Arg 1, 2(R)

Watkins, S J (Newport, Cardiff) 1964 S, I, F, 1965 E, S, I, F, 1966 E, S, I, F, A, 1967 S, I, F, E, NZ, 1968 E, S, 1969 S, I, F, E, NZ 1, 1970 E, I

Watkins, W R (Newport) 1959 F

Watts, D (Maesteg) 1914 E, S, F, I

Watts, J (Llanelli) 1907 E, S, I, 1908 E, S, F, I, A, 1909 S, F, I

Watts, W (Llanelli) 1914 E

Watts, W H (Newport) 1892 E, S, I, 1893 E, S, I, 1894 E, S, I, 1895 E, I, 1896 E

Weatherley, D J (Swansea) 1998 Z

Weaver, D (Swansea) 1964 E

Webb, J (Abertillery) 1907 S, 1908 E, S, F, I, A, 1909 E, S, F, I, 1910 F, E, S, I, 1911 E, S, F, I, 1912 E, S

Webb, J E (Newport) 1888 M, 1889 S

Webbe, G M C (Bridgend) 1986 Tg (R), WS, 1987 F, E, S, [Tg], US, 1988 F (R), NZ 1, R
Webster, R E (Swansea) 1987 [A], 1990 Bb, 1991 [Arg, A], 1992 I, F, E, S, A, 1993 E, S, I, F
Wells, G T (Cardiff) 1955 E, S, 1957 I, F, 1958 A, E, S
Westacott, D (Cardiff) 1906 I
Wetter, H (Newport) 1912 SA, 1913 E
Wetter, J J (Newport) 1914 S, F, I, 1920 E, S, F, I, 1921 E, 1924 I, NZ
Wheel, G A D (Swansea) 1974 I, E (R), 1975 F, E, I, A, 1976 E, S, I, F, 1977 I, E, S, 1978 E, S, I, F, A 1,2, NZ, 1979 S, I, 1980 F, E, S, I, 1981 E, S, I, F, A, 1982 I
Wheeler, P J (Aberavon) 1967 NZ, 1968 E
Whitefoot, J (Cardiff) 1984 A (R), 1985 S, I, F, E, Fj, 1986 E, S, I, F, Fj, Tg, WS, 1987 F, E, S, I, [I, C]
Whitfield, J (Newport) 1919 NZA, 1920 E, S, F, I, 1921 E, 1922 E, S, I, F, 1924 S, I
Whitson, G K (Newport) 1956 F, 1960 S, I
Wilkins, G (Bridgend) 1994 Tg
Williams, A (Bridgend, Swansea) 1990 Nm 2(R), 1995 Fj (R)
Williams, A (Ospreys, Bath) 2003 R (R), 2005 v US(R), C(R), 2006 Arg 2(R)
Williams, B (Llanelli) 1920 S, F, I
Williams, B H (Neath, Richmond, Bristol) 1996 F 2, 1997 R, Tg, NZ, 1998 It, E, Z (R), SA 1, Arg (R), 1999 S (R), I, It (R), 2000 F (R), It (R), E (t+R), 2001 R (R), I (R), Tg (R), A (R), 2002 I (R), F (R), It (R), E (R), S
Williams, B L (Cardiff) 1947 E, S, F, I, A, 1948 E, S, F, I, 1949 E, S, I, 1951 I, SA, 1952 S, 1953 E, S, I, F, NZ, 1954 S, 1955 E
Williams, B R (Neath) 1990 S, I, Bb, 1991 E, S
Williams, C (Llanelli) 1924 NZ, 1925 E
Williams, C (Aberavon, Swansea) 1977 E, S, 1980 F, E, S, I, NZ, 1983 E
Williams, C D (Cardiff, Neath) 1955 F, 1956 F
Williams, D (Llanelli) 1998 SA 1(R)
Williams, D (Ebbw Vale) 1963 E, S, I, F, 1964 E, S, I, F, SA, 1965 E, S, I, F, 1966 E, S, I, A, 1967 F, E, NZ, 1968 E, 1969 S, I, F, E, NZ 1,2, A, 1970 SA, S, E, I, 1971 E, S, I, F
Williams, D B (Newport, Swansea) 1978 A 1, 1981 E, S
Williams, E (Neath) 1924 NZ, 1925 F
Williams, E (Aberavon) 1925 E, S
Williams, F L (Cardiff) 1929 S, F, I, 1930 E, S, I, F, 1931 F, I, SA, 1932 E, S, I, 1933 I
Williams, G (Aberavon) 1936 E, S, I
Williams, G (London Welsh) 1950 I, F, 1951 E, S, I, F, SA, 1952 E, S, I, F, 1953 NZ, 1954 E
Williams, G (Bridgend) 1981 I, F, 1982 E (R), S
Williams, G J (Bridgend, Cardiff) 2003 It(R), E 1(R), S 1, F(R), E 2(R)
Williams, G P (Bridgend) 1980 NZ, 1981 E, S, A, 1982 I
Williams, G R (Cardiff Blues) 2000 I, Sm, US, SA, 2001 S, F, It, R (R), I (R), Arg, Tg (R), A (R), 2002 F (R), It (R), E (R), S, SA 1,2, R, Fj, C, NZ, 2003 It, E 1, S 1, I 1, F, A, NZ, E 2, [Tg,It(R)], 2004 S,I,F,E,It,Arg1,R,J, 2005 F(R),S,US,C
Williams, J (Blaina) 1920 E, S, F, I, 1921 S, F, I
Williams, J F (London Welsh) 1905 I, NZ, 1906 S, SA
Williams, J J (Llanelli) 1973 F (R), A, 1974 S, I, F, E, 1975 F, E, S, I, A, 1976 E, S, I, F, 1977 I, F, E, S, 1978 E, S, I, F, A 1,2, NZ, 1979 S, I, F, E
Williams, J L (Cardiff) 1906 SA, 1907 E, S, I, 1908 E, S, I, A, 1909 E, S, F, I, 1910 I, 1911 E, S, F, I
Williams, J P R (London Welsh, Bridgend) 1969 S, I, F, E, NZ 1,2, A, 1970 SA, S, E, I, F, 1971 E, S, I, F, 1972 E, S, F, NZ, 1973 E, S, I, F, A, 1974 S, I, F, 1975 F, E, S, I, A, 1976 E, S, I, F, 1977 I, F, E, S, 1978 E, S, I, F, A 1,2, NZ, 1979 S, I, F, E, 1980 NZ, 1981 E, S
Williams, L (Llanelli, Cardiff) 1947 E, S, F, I, A, 1948 I, 1949 E
Williams, L H (Cardiff) 1957 S, I, F, 1958 E, S, I, F, 1959 E, S, I, 1961 F, 1962 E, S
Williams, M (Newport) 1923 F
Williams, M E (Pontypridd, Cardiff Blues) 1996 Bb, F 2, It (t), 1998 It, E, Z, SA 2, Arg, 1999 S, I, C, J, [Sm], 2000 E (R), 2001 E, S, F, It, 2002 I, F, It, E, S, SA 1,2, Fj, C, NZ, 2003 It, E 1, S 1, I 1, F, A, NZ, E 2, [C, Tg(R), It, E(R)], 2004 S, I, F(t&R), E(R), It, SA2(t&R), R(R), NZ(R), J(R), 2005 E, It, F, S, I, Fj, SA, A, 2006 E, S, I, It, F
Williams, O (Bridgend) 1990 Nm 2
Williams, O (Llanelli) 1947 E, S, A, 1948 E, S, F, I
Williams, R (Llanelli) 1954 S, 1957 F, 1958 A
Williams, R D G (Newport) 1881 E
Williams, R F (Cardiff) 1912 SA, 1913 E, S, 1914 I
Williams, R H (Llanelli) 1954 I, F, S, 1955 S, I, F, 1956 E, S, I, 1957 E, S, I, F, 1958 A, E, S, I, F, 1959 E, S, I, F, 1960 E
Williams, S (Llanelli) 1947 E, S, F, I, 1948 S, F
Williams, S A (Aberavon) 1939 E, S, I
Williams, S M (Neath, Cardiff, Northampton) 1994 Tg, 1996 E (t), A 1,2, Bb, F 2, It, A 3, SA, 1997 US, S, I, F, E, US 1,2(R), C, R (R), Tg (R), NZ (t+R), 2002 SA 1,2, R, Fj(R), 2003 It, E 1, S 1, F(R)
Williams, S M (Neath, Ospreys) 2000 F (R), It, E, S, I, Sm, SA (R), 2001 J 1,2, I, 2003 R, [NZ,E], 2004 S, I, F, E, It, Arg 1, 2, SA1, 2, NZ, J, 2005 E, It, F, S, I, NZ, Fj, SA, A, 2006 E, S, It, F, Arg 1, 2
Williams, T (Pontypridd) 1882 I
Williams, T (Swansea) 1888 S, I
Williams, T (Swansea) 1912 I, 1913 F, 1914 E, S, F, I
Williams, Tudor (Swansea) 1921 F
Williams, T G (Cross Keys) 1935 S, I, NZ, 1936 E, S, I, 1937 S, I
Williams, W A (Crumlin) 1927 E, S, F, I
Williams, W A (Newport) 1952 I, F, 1953 E
Williams, W E O (Cardiff) 1887 S, I, 1889 S, 1890 S, E
Williams, W H (Pontymister) 1900 E, S, I, 1901 E
Williams, W O G (Swansea, Devonport Services) 1951 F, SA, 1952 E, S, I, F, 1953 E, S, I, F, NZ, 1954 E, I, F, S, 1955 E, S, I, F, 1956 E, S, I
Williams, W P J (Neath) 1974 I, F
Williams-Jones, H (S Wales Police, Llanelli) 1989 S (R), 1990 F (R), I, 1991 A, 1992 S, A, 1993 E, S, I, F, Z 1, Nm, 1994 Fj, Tg, WS (R), It (t), 1995 E (R)
Willis, W R (Cardiff) 1950 E, S, I, F, 1951 E, S, I, F, SA, 1952 E, S, 1953 S, NZ, 1954 E, I, F, S, 1955 E, S, I, F
Wiltshire, M L (Aberavon) 1967 NZ, 1968 E, S, F
Windsor, R W (Pontypool) 1973 A, 1974 S, I, F, E, 1975 F, E, S, I, A, 1976 E, S, I, F, 1977 I, F, E, S, 1978 E, S, I, F, A 1,2, NZ, 1979 S, I, F
Winfield, H B (Cardiff) 1903 I, 1904 E, S, I, 1905 NZ, 1906 E, S, I, 1907 S, I, 1908 E, S, F, I, A
Winmill, S (Cross Keys) 1921 E, S, F, I
Wintle, M E (Llanelli) 1996 It
Wintle, R V (London Welsh) 1988 WS (R)
Wooller, W (Sale, Cambridge U, Cardiff) 1933 E, S, I, 1935 E, S, I, NZ, 1936 E, S, I, 1937 E, S, I, 1938 S, I, 1939 E, S, I
Wyatt, C P (Llanelli) 1998 Z (R), SA 1(R),2, Arg, 1999 S, I, F 1, It, E, Arg 1,2, SA, C (R), F 2, [Arg 3, J (R), Sm, A], 2000 F, It, E, US, SA, 2001 E, R, I, Arg (R), Tg (R), A (R), 2002 I, It (R), E, S (R), 2003 A(R), NZ(t+R), E 2, [Tg(R),NZ(R)]
Wyatt, G (Pontypridd, Celtic Warriors) 1997 Tg, 2003 R (R)
Wyatt, M A (Swansea) 1983 E, S, I, F, 1984 A, 1985 S, I, 1987 E, S, I

Yapp, J (Cardiff Blues) 2005 E(R), It(R), F(R),S(R), I(R), C(R), Fj, 2006 Arg 1(R)
Young, D (Swansea, Cardiff) 1987 [E, NZ], US, 1988 E, S, I, F, NZ 1,2, WS, R, 1989 S, NZ, 1990 F, 1996 A 3, SA, 1997 US, S, I, F, E, R, NZ, 1998 It, E, S, I, F, 1999 I, E (R), Arg 1(R),2(R), SA, C (R), F 2, [Arg 3, J, Sm, A], 2000 F, It, E, S, I, 2001 E, S, F, It, R, I, Arg
Young, G A (Cardiff) 1886 E, S
Young, J (Harrogate, RAF, London Welsh) 1968 S, I, F, 1969 S, I, F, E, NZ 1, 1970 E, I, F, 1971 E, S, I, F, 1972 E, S, F, NZ, 1973 E, S, I, F
Young, P (Gwent Dragons) 2003 R (R)

WALES: DOMESTIC RUGBY

ALL BLACKS STAY ON A HIGH

It was business as usual in Wales as Neath successfully defended their Principality Building Society Premiership title with a completely dominant league campaign that left the division's 15 other clubs trailing in their slipstream.

The Welsh All Blacks' second Premiership title in two years was achieved at a canter and second-placed Bridgend found themselves a decidedly distant 15 points adrift of their rivals at the end of what was essentially a one-horse race for honours.

The campaign began for Neath at The Gnoll in early September with the visit of Llanelli, who had ended their 15-game winning streak the previous season. Expectations of the All Blacks were sky high but coach Rowland Phillips refused to get carried away.

"We have created some momentum and the aim will be to keep that going this season," the former Wales back row forward said. "We like the taste of success, but we are not setting ourselves any targets of winning the league or cups – we will simply focus on the next step in front of us. The chief aim is to continue to improve with the performances paramount."

His caution proved to be misplaced. Even though the Scarlets drew first blood with a well-taken try from full-back Lee Byrne, it was the Blacks who dominated the rest of the encounter, which the club dedicated to the memory of former captain Martyn Davies, who died in the summer after playing over 500 games for Neath in the 1970s.

Scores from prop Paul Jones and wing Aled Bevan gave the home side the platform and when prolific fly-half James Hook charged down a clearing kick from his elder brother and opposite number Michael for a try, the result was never in doubt. Prop Cai Griffiths added a fourth try in the 30–10 victory and the defending champions were off.

The second match of the season was a trip to Sardis Road to face Pontypridd, who were brimming with confidence after their opening day 30–17 win away at Pontypool.

The game was a titanic clash between the rival packs but it was the home side that got their noses in front with scores from hooker Ben Phillips and two from wing Chris Clayton. The Blacks replied with tries from Steve Thomas and Gareth Morris but deep into the second-half Pontypridd still led 22–21. The next score would prove crucial and it was the home side that got it, Dai Flanagan landing a late penalty to complete a 25–21 win. The champions had been beaten.

"Not many teams will take on and beat Neath in the way we did," said Pontypridd manager Wayne Cullen. "If anything the scoreline flattered our opponents as we had the chances to put more points on the board."

Neath's title defence was briefly looking shaky. "The defeat at Pontypridd has concentrated our minds and there is a great determination within the squad to get back on track," Phillips admitted. "I don't think we'll be the only side to lose at Sardis Road but we are used to winning at Neath and defeat never comes easy."

The result was to be the defining moment in the club's season. The following week they held on for a tight 15–10 win over Glamorgan Wanderers to get the Pontypridd result out of their system and never looked back. Twenty-six Premiership games followed and all 26 ended with wins for Neath – including a 22–10 defeat of Pontypridd at The Gnoll in January.

The title was wrapped up at the end of April when Bridgend were the visitors to The Gnoll. The Blacks emerged 40–19 winners and the champions had defended their crown. An astonishing 33–29 defeat at home to Bedwas in the final match slightly tarnished Neath's final record but they were in truth far superior to any other side in the league.

"We seem to have the right balance of experience and youth," said captain Steve Martin. "At times this season we have fielded 10 or 11 players under the age of 23, with a few older ones like myself to back them up.

"Retaining a title is always a tough ask but everyone has rolled up their sleeves and just two defeats in 30 league matches speaks for itself."

There was, however, to be no Premiership and Konica Minolta Cup double for the Welsh All Blacks even though Phillips' side fought through to the final at Millennium Stadium in May to face Pontypridd once again.

It was the Premiership runners-up who scored the first of the six tries on the day as wing Matthew Nuthall produced a fine solo effort to open Pontypridd's account. Flanker Andrew Llewellyn hit back for Neath before centre Dafydd Lockyer and wing Scott Roberts scored Pontypridd's second and third soon after the break.

Veteran replacement prop Paul Jones got the Blacks back into it before what appeared to the match's defining moment. Pontypridd fly-half Dai Flanagan threw out a speculative pass which was intercepted by his opposite number James Hook who ran in for a converted try to give Neath a 25–23 lead.

But Flanagan was not finished and after Pontypridd had marched into Neath territory deep into injury-time, he unleashed a redeeming, not to mention match winning drop goal. After losing last season's final by a single point to Llanelli, Pontypridd were finally the cup winners.

"I really went from zero to hero in the space of a few minutes," said a relieved Flanagan after the final whistle. "But you can't fault the whole team's efforts as it was them who got us from our own line to Neath's territory right at the end to get me within sight. It was just a case of catch and kick. Thankfully I didn't have time to think of anything else."

Ponty coach Simon King added: "Neath struggled to live with our width and pace and I think we more than matched them up front. I think we put them under more pressure than they've been used to and I never thought we were out of it – even right at the end."

FINAL LEAGUE TABLE

	P	W	D	L	F	A	Pts
Neath	30	28	0	2	1070	421	84
Bridgend	30	23	0	7	709	587	69
Pontypridd	30	21	0	9	788	560	63
Aberavon	30	19	0	11	748	596	57
Newport	30	19	0	11	623	610	57
Llanelli	30	18	0	12	589	599	54
Swansea	30	16	0	14	849	713	48
Bedwas	30	12	2	16	562	702	38
Cross Keys	30	12	0	18	513	608	36
Cardiff	30	11	0	19	646	726	33
Glamorgan W	30	10	2	18	607	738	32
Ebbw Vale	30	10	1	19	583	686	31
Llandovery	30	10	0	20	597	692	30
Maesteg	30	9	1	20	573	785	28
Carmarthen	30	9	1	20	546	821	28
Pontypool	30	8	3	19	473	632	27

ASDA DIVISION ONE

Bonymaen

ASDA DIVISION TWO EAST

Bargoed

ASDA DIVISION TWO WEST

Dunvant

ASDA DIVISION THREE EAST

Abergavenny

ASDA DIVISION THREE SOUTH EAST

Ynysybwl

ASDA DIVISION THREE SOUTH WEST

Tonna

ASDA DIVISION THREE WEST

Penclawdd

ASDA DIVISION FOUR EAST

Newport HSOB

ASDA DIVISION FOUR SOUTH EAST

Penallta

ASDA DIVISION FOUR NORTH

Mold

ASDA DIVISION FOUR SOUTH WEST

Heol Y Cyw

ASDA DIVISION FOUR WEST

Pontarddulais

ASDA DIVISION FIVE SOUTH EAST

Porth Harlequins

ASDA DIVISION FIVE EAST

Machen

ASDA DIVISION FIVE NORTH

Llandudno

ASDA DIVISION FIVE SOUTH WEST

BP Llandarcy

ASDA DIVISION FIVE WEST

Burry Port

KONICA MINOLTA CUP

18 February, 2006	
Aberavon 7 **Newport** 15	**Bonymaen** 16 **Cardiff** 23
Builth Wells 28 **Nant Conwy** 15	**Dunvant** 24 **Maesteg** 39
Glamorgan Wanderers 19 **Swansea** 24	**Llandovery** 43 **UWIC** 11
Neath 51 **Llangennech** 7	**Cross Keys** 5 **Pontypridd** 44

QUARTER-FINALS

1 April, 2006	
Cardiff 10 **Llandovery** 0	**Maesteg** 27 **Newport** 8
Pontypridd 28 **Builth Wells** 20	**Swansea** 13 **Neath** 33

SEMI-FINALS

21 April, 2006
Cardiff 13 **Pontypridd** 23
23 April, 2006
Neath 50 **Maesteg** 9

FINAL

6 May, Millennium Stadium, Cardiff

PONTYPRIDD 26 (1G 2PG 1DG 2T)†
NEATH 25 (2G 2PG 1T)

Pontypridd: M.Stoddart; C Clayton, T Riley, D Lockyer, M Nuthall; D Flanagan, G Jones; S Williams, B Phillips, S Roberts, C Dicomidis, G Harrington, L Evans, N Strong (captain), R Shellard

Substitutions: J Pocock for Stoddart; P Matthews for Lockyer(temp); R Harford for Williams; L Davies for Phillips; A Powell for Evans; W O'Connor for Harrington

Scorers Tries: Nuthall, Lockyer, Clayton Conversion: Flanagan Penalty Goals: Flanagan (2) Dropped Goal: Flanagan

Neath: G Morris; S Thomas, A Bevan, W Mitchell, R Johnston; J Hook, P Horgan; C Griffiths, E Shervington, C Mitchell, S Martin (captain), M Morgan, A Llewellyn, D McShane, J McPhail

Substitutions N Clapham for Morris; J Spratt for Bevan; M Roberts for Horgan; G Price for Shervington; P Jones for Mitchell; B Davies for Llewellyn; H Jenkins for McShane

Scorers Tries: Llewellyn, Jones, Hook Conversions: Hook (2) Penalty Goals: Hook (2)

Referee N Owens (Pontyberem)

THE COMBINED TEAMS

A RICH HISTORY TO PROTECT

By Stuart Farmer

The history of rugby union, perhaps more than any other sport, has been enriched by the participation of multi-national combined teams. Right from Alfred Shaw and Arthur Shrewsbury's pioneering British tour to Australia and New Zealand in 1888, a venture which would eventually evolve into the now famous British and Irish Lions brand which is rolled out every four years (and dealt with elsewhere in this publication), the sport has been enriched with the exploits of such teams.

Vying with the Lions for the most recognisable combined team image is the Barbarians, who were formed in 1890 in Bradford, and who undertook seven matches last season.

BRITISH BARBARIANS IN 2005/06

Combined Services	15 Nov	Newbury	**Won** 45–6
East Midlands	15 Mar	Bedford	**Won** 63–17
Leicester	17 Mar	Leicester	**Won** 52–42
Royal Navy	4 Apr	Plymouth	**Won** 31–10
England XV	28 May	Twickenham	**Lost** 19–46
Scotland XV	31 May	Murrayfield	**Lost** 19–66
Georgia	4 Jun	Tbilisi	**Won** 28–19

The Barbarians calendar has changed much with the advent of professionalism; gone are the four match Easter tours to South Wales to play Penarth, Cardiff, Swansea and Newport, and the annual Christmas fixture with Leicester Tigers – all that remains unchanged from the amateur days is the annual Mobbs Memorial match against East Midlands. The Baabaas have reorganised their calendar with an annual encounter against the Combined Services to celebrate Remembrance Day, a rescheduling of the Leicester match to later in the season and an annual end of season tour in which they currently take on England and Scotland. The Barbarians have kept up their tradition of pioneering visits to all corners of the globe to promote the game of rugby union and this was further extended to break new ground by the trip to Georgia in June.

Last season the Baabaas despatched their first four opponents with relative ease; Cardiff Blues lock Craig Quinnell helping himself to five tries in the game against the East Midlands and thus becoming the first Barbarian to score five tries in the 85 year history of the Mobbs Memorial match. In addition he became the first Baabaa for 30 years to score five tries in a game as well as being the first forward in the history of the club to accomplish the feat.

At the end of season tour Bob Dwyer was once more appointed head coach for the England match, which the Barbarians lost for the first time since 2002. England's James Simpson-Daniel ran in two tries and fly-half Olly Barkley contributed 21 points, whereas the Barbarians 19 points were tallied by tries from Olivier Magne, Bruce Reihana and Matt Burke, who also added two conversions. Leicester coach Pat Howard replaced Dwyer at the helm and took a much changed team to Scotland and Georgia. The Baabaas incurred a big loss at Murrayfield with Scotland wing Chris Paterson accumulating a massive 31 points on his own, from two tries and a ten out of ten kicking performance, but won 28–19 in Tbilisi with replacement Steve Hanley crossing for

Jamie McDonald/Getty Images

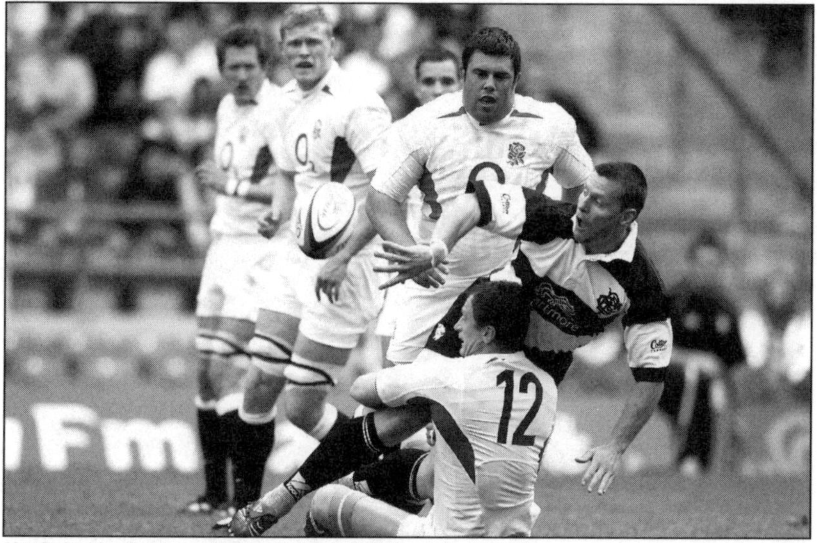

Matt Burke (above) was one of the world stars in Barbarians colours in 2006.

two five pointers. The game against Georgia was the fifth game in the Barbarians history when their opponents have accorded full test status and awarded caps; the others were two games against Wales in Cardiff in 1990 and 1996, a visit to Rhodesia in 1969 and a game against Zimbabwe in Harare in 1994.

Meanwhile, Dwyer took virtually the same team that played against England to South Africa under the "World XV" banner to first play the Springboks at Johannesburg in an uncapped trial game and then facing a Western Province XV as a testimonial match for ex-Spingbok captain Corne Krige, in a contest similar to the match against Saracens XV on 21 May as part of Richard Hill's testimonial season. The World team won the two testimonial matches, 64–14 against Saracens and 49–31 against Western Province, and narrowly lost the "international" at Ellis Park 30–27, thanks to nine penalty goals from South African full-back Percy Montgomery and another from wing Gaffie du Toit, the World XV running in tries from Isa Nacewa and skipper Justin Marshall added to 17 points from full-back Matt Burke.

Whilst the South Africa match was not accorded test status, World XVs have contested six previous matches where their opponents awarded full test caps: in 1977 the Springboks won a one-off test 45–24 in Pretoria to celebrate the opening of the newly reconstructed Loftus Versfeld, and also narrowly took an exciting two game series played in Cape Town and Johannesburg 12 years later to commemorate the centenary of the

John Gichigi/Getty Images

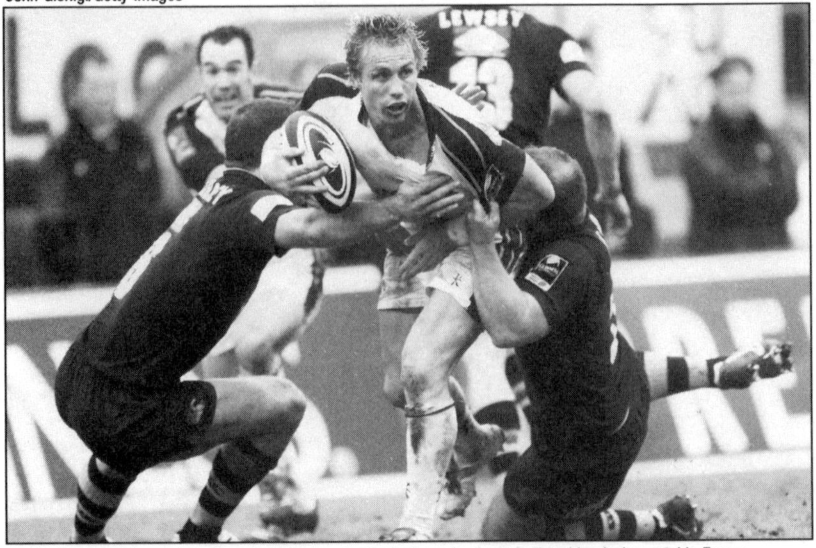

Justin Marshall skippered the French Barbarians in 2005, the only player in the side playing outside France.

South African Rugby Board. In 1992 New Zealand won a three game series against a World XV, to mark the centenary of the New Zealand Rugby Board, after losing the first test 28–14 in Christchurch.

Sixty-four new Barbarians made their debut for the club this season, whilst international players from Tonga, Samoa, Portugal, Fiji, USA, Canada, Zimbabwe, France, Australia, South Africa and New Zealand all turned out for the invitation side.

The Barbarians club has fostered offshoots in New Zealand, Australia, South Africa, South America and Fiji, whilst the French Barbarians made one appearance last season in a game against Australia A on 1 November in Bordeaux and were skippered by the only player plying his trade outside France – Justin Marshall – but also included Canadian lock Mike James and Fijian speedster Sireli Bobo. Biarritz Hooker Benoit August grabbed two tries but his side lost 12–42, with New South Wales full-back Cameron Shepherd adding 17 points with the boot for Australia.

Whilst strictly speaking they are not a multi-national team the New Zealand Maori are a side who are definitely combined and have certainly enriched the world of rugby union from the moment of their first official match in 1910.

Last season they won all four matches they contested and carried off the Churchill Cup for the second time in three years. They have in fact won their last eleven matches, with England being the last team to defeat them: 23–9 in New Plymouth on 9 June 2003.

NEW ZEALAND MAORI IN 2006

New South Wales	2 Jun	Sydney	**Won** 20–16
United States	7 Jun	Santa Clara	**Won** 74–6
Ireland A	10 Jun	Santa Clara	**Won** 27–6
Scotland A	17 Jun	Edmonton	**Won** 52–17

At the height of South Africa's exile from test rugby, during which time they played no home tests for almost three years between 1977–80, the Springboks arranged a visit by a combined South American side, nicknamed "the Jaguars" in preparation for the British Lions tour beginning in May 1980. The 26 man South American touring team skippered by the great Hugo Porta and comprising 22 Argentineans plus one player each from Uruguay, Paraguay, Brazil and Chile, tested their hosts to the full but lost the two test series 9–24 and 9–18. There followed three other similar two-test series between South America and South Africa over the next two years, with the Jaguars winning one test 21–12 at Bloemfontein in April 1982 – Porta scoring all of South America's points. It is interesting to note that across those eight tests only two non-Argentineans turned out for the side, both in the final test at Newlands in 1984 – the Uruguayan prop John Bird and Spanish lock Tomas Pardo Vidal. Pardo was one of two Spaniards included as guests in the South American squad!

The rugby football unions of England in 1971, Scotland in 1973 and Ireland in 1974 all celebrated their centenaries with full capped one-off matches against various President's XVs. England lost 11–28 at Twickenham to a strong side captained by Brian Lochore for which speedy All Black wing Bryan Williams scored a hat trick of tries. Scotland won their celebration match 27–16, the SRU President's XV being skippered by New Zealand back rower Alex "Grizz" Wyllie. A year later at Lansdowne Road Ireland drew 18-all against a star studded IRFU President's XV for whom all the points were scored by Welshmen – tries from J.J. Williams and Gareth Edwards and ten points from the boot of Phil Bennett.

This forthcoming season we look forward to a first ever visit to the northern hemisphere of the Pacific Islanders, an amalgam of the best players from Samoa, Tonga and Fiji. The combined team's only previous forays into test rugby resulted in losses against each of the Tri-Nations in July 2004, 14–29 to Australia in Adelaide, 26–41 to New Zealand in Albany, and 24–38 to South Africa in Gosford, New South Wales. Future All Black back rower, Tonga born Sione Lauaki, scored a try in

Ross Land/Getty Images

The New Zealand Maori (here, with Coach Matt Te Pou, after beating the Lions in 2005) have one of the best records in international rugby and if they were ever given a place in the World Cup, are good enough to make the quarter-finals.

each match whilst another player capped for New Zealand the following year, Fiji born wing Sitiveni Sivivatu, crossed for a brace of tries in each of the games against New Zealand and South Africa. In addition the prolific Sivivatu also scored five tries in the Islanders' wins in their two warm-up matches against a Queensland XV (48–29) and New South Wales (68–21). The Islanders are scheduled to meet Wales, Scotland and Ireland in successive weekends in November 2006.

HEINEKEN CUP

AT LAST, IT'S MUNSTER!

By Iain Spragg

Richard Heathcote/Getty Images

There ain't no stopping us now! Munster are finally European champions.

Munster had waited over a decade to taste European glory but when they finally fulfilled their quest to lift the Heineken Cup in May after beating Biarritz, the 11 years of disappointment, near misses and setbacks were quickly forgotten. Munster were finally the kings of Europe.

They had certainly paid their dues. Beaten finalists in both 2000 and 2002, there had also been three losing semi-finals along the way before their long anticipated triumph in Cardiff and the celebrations that followed the final whistle in the Millennium Stadium reflected the collective relief of the Munster players and fans alike. The Irish side were no longer the nearly men of Europe.

"This bunch of guys have had tough experiences over the years but have tried to learn every time they have lost," said coach Declan Kidney after his side's historic win in the Welsh capital.

"That experience of losing helped them today. They're fully aware that in sport you lose more than you win but they've learnt from every defeat."

Munster and Biarritz's separate paths to the final, however, were far from assured when the group phase of the competition got under way in October.

Kidney's team travelled to England to tackle Sale but fell foul of the boot of Charlie Hodgson, who kicked 17 points in the Sharks 27–13 victory. Munster's European challenge was already looking distinctly shaky.

"I don't think they really deserved a winning margin like that," said skipper Anthony Foley. "But fair play to Sale for the win – they took every opportunity and we just let ourselves down with a couple of silly mistakes.

"It's frustrating because we'd worked so hard and then gave away two soft second-half tries."

The early signs were no more encouraging for Biarritz who were surprise 22–10 losers to Saracens at Vicarage Road. The odds of a Biarritz and Munster final were getting longer by the minute.

But with home advantage for both sides in the second round of games it was a different story. Munster had little difficulty disposing of Castres Olympique 42–16 at fortress Thomond Park while Biarritz were equally untroubled in their 33–19 win over Ulster.

"After last week's result at Saracens, the difference today was we played great rugby in the first 20 minutes," said Biarritz coach Patrice Lagisquet. "We put in such an effort then there was a lot of indiscipline on our part. But we came back to take the initiative."

The rest of the group phase proved to be a stroll as four more wins proved enough for both sides to top their respective groups and earn all-important home advantage in the quarter-finals. Munster, in fact, had to rely on their superior points difference to condemn second-place Sale to an away trip in the last eight – a visit to the Estadio Anoeta to face Biarritz.

The game was agonisingly tight from the start and after 80 minutes Sereli Bobo's first-half try was the only thing that seperated the Premiership leaders and the Frenchmen as Biarritz held on for an 11–6 win. Lagisquet's team were through to their third consecutive Heineken Cup semi-final although his Sale counterpart and compatriot Philippe Saint-Andre was less than impressed by Biarritz's performance.

"Home advantage won them the game," he said. "I think we would have won at Edgeley Park. They were extremely well organised in defence and didn't give us any room to play."

Munster were drawn against Perpignan in their quarter-final and confidence was high of another win at Thomond Park, where the team had never lost in European competition. Their eventual 19–10 victory, however, was far from the dominant display Munster and their supporters had grown accustomed to at home.

Dave Rogers/Getty Images

Bath – and Duncan Bell [above] – went further than any other English club, losing 18–9 to Biarritz in the semi-finals.

"It was far from vintage but we are just happy to get the win," said man-of-the-match Paul O'Connell. "It was a long way off our performance against Sale but that is the way it is when you have not played together for so long. I think it must be 10 weeks since that team played together."

The win set up a mouth watering all Ireland semi-final clash with Leinster at Lansdowne Road. Ireland would definitely be represented in the final. The only question was which of the two provincial rivals would make it through.

Most people predicted a tight game. The two sides' earlier Celtic League meetings had gone to the home side and there appeared to be little to choose between them on paper.

The match itself proved to be far more one-sided than anyone had imagined. Munster were out of the blocks fastest with a Ronan O'Gara penalty and Denis Leamy try in the first 10 minutes and Leinster never really recovered. Munster added second-half tries from O'Gara and Trevor Halstead while all Leinster could muster in reply was two Felipe Contepomi penalties either side of the break. Kidney's side ran out comfortable 30–6 winners and Munster were through to their third Heineken Cup final.

"There was quite a stiff breeze out there and I thought a 13-point lead at half-time might be a point or two, too small," said Kidney, who had been the Leinster coach the previous season.

"And you are never sure that your defence is going to hold up against a team that has such a good attack as the Leinster backline."

The second semi-final was an Anglo-French affair as Biarritz faced Bath, the 1998 champions. The French side had yet to reach the Heineken Cup final and they were acutely aware that Bath, struggling in the Premiership and a shadow of the side that had lifted the trophy eight years ago, were there for the taking.

The game in San Sebastian quickly became a war of attrition and a battle between the two respective kickers – Biarritz scrum-half Dimitri Yachvili and Bath fly-half Chris Malone – and it was the former who emerged with the honours.

Biarritz struck first in the fourth minute with the first of five Yachvili penalties and although Malone kept Bath in touch with three penalties of his own, the West Country side were never able to get their noses in front and a Damien Traille drop goal for the French wrapped up an 18–9 win and a final showdown with Munster.

There were, however, mutterings from Bath of French foul play and predetermined skull duggery at the final whistle, accusations Biarritz were quick to refute.

"We will not feel guilty with the way we played today," Lagisquet said defiantly. "Bath were organised to be negative, maybe because they have struggled in the English Premiership this season."

A month later Biarritz had forgotten all the verbal barbs as they prepared to tackle Munster at the Millennium Stadium in the final. Whatever the result, there would be a new name on the Heineken Cup.

The game was certainly worthy of a final and exploded into life as early as the second minute when Biarritz wing Sireli Bobo danced over for the game's first try, which Yachvili converted.

Munster were forced to regroup and got a foothold in the game with an O'Gara penalty on 10 minutes. Seven minutes later centre Trevor Halstead wriggled over for the first of Munster's two tries on the day and the Irishmen were in the lead. Peter Stringer added the second before the break and at half-time, Kidney's team held a precarious 17–10 advantage.

The second-half failed to yield any further tries for either side but the entertainment did not suffer and the 74,000-strong crowd were on the edge of their seats as the match ebbed and flowed.

O'Gara and Yachvili traded further penalties and with 10 minutes left on the clock, Munster led 20–19. But there was just enough time for one more successful O'Gara kick and Munster were home and dry 23–19. The men in red had become only the second Irish side since Ulster in 1999 to be crowned European champions and had completed the second leg of what was to become an unique Irish hat-trick with Ireland landing the Triple Crown, Munster the Heineken Cup and (a

Dave Rogers/Getty Images

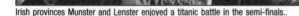

Irish provinces Munster and Lenster enjoyed a titanic battle in the semi-finals..

week later) Ulster winning the Celtic League. Munster finally had the prize they had always coveted.

"When Biarritz came back at us the fans never got on our back," said winning captain Anthony Foley. "Our crowd wouldn't be silenced today and at times out there it was awesome to see the amount of red in the stadium.

"Over the years the fans been putting their hands in their pocket to follow us around Europe and it's great that we can give them some silverware. We all just feel like one, that's the big thing about this team."

"I've been in a ground twice when the opposition's captain has lifted the trophy. To be the one to go up there and pick up the silverware is a great feeling.

"I felt we deserved it over the year. As a player there is nothing that will ever surpass your first international cap. That is the ultimate. But what we achieved today is magnificent. It's a journey which is not over yet – it's just another station on the way.

"We can kick on from here and if we do we can compete for this trophy for a number of years to come."

RESULTS

GROUP PHASE

ROUND ONE

21 October, 2005

Sale Sharks 27 **Munster** 13

Ulster 27 **Benetton Treviso** 0

Bourgoin 16 **Glasgow Warriors** 3

22 October, 2005

Cardiff Blues 40 **Leeds Tykes** 13

Calvisano 6 **Perpignan** 25

Leicester Tigers 57 **ASM Clermont Auvergne** 23

Toulouse 50 **Llanelli Scarlets** 28

Leinster 19 **Bath Rugby** 22

Castres Olympique 29 **Dragons** 24

23 October, 2005

Edinburgh Gunners 32 **London Wasps** 31

Ospreys 13 **Stade Francais** 8

Saracens 22 **Biarritz Olympique** 10

ROUND TWO

28 October, 2005

Dragons 11 **Sale Sharks** 38

Leeds Tykes 33 **Calvisano** 16

Perpignan 37 **Cardiff Blues** 14

29 October, 2005

Benetton Treviso 17 **Saracens** 30

Stade Francais 12 **Leicester Tigers** 6

Bath Rugby 39 **Bourgoin** 12

Llanelli Scarlets 15 **Edinburgh Gunners** 13

Biarritz Olympique 33 **Ulster** 19

Munster 42 **Castres Olympique** 16

30 October, 2005

Glasgow Warriors 20 **Leinster** 33

London Wasps 15 **Toulouse** 15

Clermont Auvergne 34 **Ospreys** 14

ROUND THREE

9 December, 2005	
Ulster 19 **Saracens** 10	**Castres Olympique** 16 **Sale Sharks** 20
10 December, 2005	
Dragons 8 **Munster** 24	**Calvisano** 10 **Cardiff Blues** 25
Bath Rugby 31 **Glasgow Warriors** 26	**ASM Clermont Auvergne** 12 **Stade Francais** 16
Edinburgh Gunners 13 **Toulouse** 20	**Leinster** 53 **Bourgoin** 7
11 December 2005	
Llanelli Scarlets 21 **London Wasps** 13	**Leeds Tykes** 21 **Perpignan** 20
Leicester Tigers 30 **Ospreys** 12	**Biarritz Olympique** 34 **Benetton Treviso** 7

ROUND FOUR

16 December, 2005	
Glasgow Warriors 10 **Bath Rugby** 29	**Sale Sharks** 35 **Castres Olympique** 3
Toulouse 35 **Edinburgh Gunners** 13	
17 December, 2005	
Saracens 18 **Ulster** 10	**Benetton Treviso** 24 **Biarritz Olympique** 38
Cardiff Blues 43 **Calvisano** 16	**Bourgoin** 30 **Leinster** 28
Munster 30 **Dragons** 18	**Stade Francais** 47 **ASM Clermont Auvergne** 28
Perpignan 12 **Leeds Tykes** 8	
18 December, 2005	
Ospreys 15 **Leicester Tigers** 17	**London Wasps** 48 **Llanelli Scarlets** 18

ROUND FIVE

13 January, 2006	
Ulster 8 **Biarritz Olympique** 24	**Bourgoin** 9 **Bath Rugby** 22
Castres Olympique 9 **Munster** 46	
14 January, 2006	
Cardiff Blues 3 **Perpignan** 21	**Toulouse** 19 **London Wasps** 13
Edinburgh Gunners 33 **Llanelli Scarlets** 32	**Ospreys** 26 **ASM Clermont Auvergne** 12
Leinster 46 Glasgow Warriors 22	
15 January, 2006	
Calvisano 0 **Leeds Tykes** 20	**Sale Sharks** 30 **Dragons** 10
Leicester Tigers 29 **Stade Francais** 22	**Saracens** 35 **Benetton Treviso** 30

ROUND SIX

20 January, 2006	
ASM Clermont Auvergne 27 **Leicester Tigers** 40	**Stade Francais** 43 **Ospreys** 10
21 January, 2006	
Llanelli Scarlets 42 **Toulouse** 49	**London Wasps** 53 **Edinburgh Gunners** 17
Benetton Treviso 26 **Ulster** 43	**Biarritz Olympique** 43 **Saracens** 13
Dragons 28 **Castres Olympique** 17	**Munster** 31 **Sale Sharks** 9
22 January, 2006	
Leeds Tykes 48 **Cardiff Blues** 3	**Perpignan** 45 **Calvisano** 0
Bath Rugby 23 **Leinster** 35	**Glasgow Warriors** 50 **Bourgoin** 35

FINAL GROUP STANDINGS

POOL ONE

	P	W	D	L	F	A	Pts
Munster	6	5	0	1	186	87	23
Sale Sharks	6	5	0	1	159	84	23
Dragons	6	1	0	5	99	168	6
Castre Olympique	6	1	0	5	90	195	6

POOL FOUR

	P	W	D	L	F	A	Pts
Biarritz Olympique	6	5	0	1	182	93	24
Saracens	6	4	0	2	128	129	17
Ulster	6	3	0	3	126	111	14
Benetton Treviso	6	0	0	6	104	207	3

POOL TWO

	P	W	D	L	F	A	Pts
Perpignan	6	5	0	1	160	52	23
Leeds Tykes	6	4	0	2	143	91	20
Cardiff Blues	6	3	0	3	128	145	15
Calvisano	6	0	0	6	48	191	0

POOL FIVE

	P	W	D	L	F	A	Pts
Bath Rugby	6	5	0	1	166	111	23
Leinster	6	4	0	2	214	124	22
Bourgoin	6	2	0	4	109	195	9
Glasgow Warriors	6	1	0	5	131	190	6

POOL THREE

	P	W	D	L	F	A	Pts
Leicester Tigers	6	5	0	1	179	111	24
Stade Francais	6	4	0	2	148	98	20
Ospreys	6	2	0	4	90	144	9
Clermont Auvergne	6	1	0	5	136	200	6

POOL SIX

	P	W	D	L	F	A	Pts
Toulouse	6	5	1	0	188	124	25
London Wasps	6	2	1	3	173	118	14
Llanelli Scarlets	6	2	0	4	152	206	12
Edinburgh Gunners	6	2	0	4	121	186	11

KNOCKOUT PHASE

QUARTER-FINALS

1 April, 2006	
Leicester Tigers 12 **Bath Rugby** 15	**Toulouse** 35 **Leinster** 41
Munster 19 **Perpignan** 10	
2 April, 2006	
Biarritz Olympique 11 **Sale Sharks** 6	

SEMI-FINALS

22 April, Estadio Anoeta, San Sebastian

BIARRITZ OLYMPIQUE 18 (5PG, 1DG)
BATH RUGBY 9 (3PG)

Biarritz Olympique: N Brusque; J–B Gobelet, P Bidabe, D Traille, S Bobo; J Peyrelongue, D Yachvili; P V Balan, B August (captain), C Johnson, J Thion, D Couzinet, S Betsen, T Dusautoir, I Harinordoquy Subsitutions: B Lecouls for Johnson (53 mins); O Olibeau for Couzinet (58 mins); C Johnson for Betsen (temp 66 to 76 mins).

SCORERS *Penalty Goals*: Yachvili (5) *Drop Goal*: Traille

YELLOW CARD BALAN (62 mins)

BATH RUGBY: M Stephenson; A Higgins, A Crockett, O Barkley, D Bory; C Malone, N Walshe; T Filise, L Mears, D Bell, S Borthwick (captain), D Grewcock, A Beattie, M Lipman, I Feaunati Substitutions: E Fuimaono for Stephenson (43 mins); S Finau for Higgins (61 mins); G Delve for Feaunati (64 mins); A Williams for Walshe (67 mins); D Barnes for Filise (69 mins); P Short for Beattie (71 mins)

SCORERS *Penalty Goals:* Malone (3)

YELLOW CARD GREWCOCK (62 mins)

REFEREE: A Rolland (Ireland)

23 April, Lansdowne Road, Dublin

LEINSTER 6 (2PG) MUNSTER 30 (3G, 3PG)

LEINSTER: G DEMPSEY; S Horgan, B O'Driscoll (captain), G D'Arcy, D Hickie; F Contepomi, G Easterby; R Corrigan, B Blaney, W Green, B Williams, M O'Kelly, C Jowitt, K Gleeson, J Heaslip Substitutions: E Miller for Jowitt (57 mins); R McCormack for Corrigan (72 mins)

SCORERS *Penalty Goals*: Contepomi (2)

MUNSTER: S Payne; A Horgan, J Kelly, T Halstead, I Dowling; R O'Gara, P Stringer; F Pucciariello, J Flannery, J Hayes, D O'Callaghan, P O'Connell, D Leamy, D Wallace, A Foley (captain) Substitutions: R Henderson for Kelly (14 mins); T O'Leary for Henderson (68 mins); F Roche for Foley (76 mins)

SCORERS *Tries*: Leamy, O'Gara, Halstead *Conversions*: O'Gara (3) *Penalty Goals*: O'Gara (3)

YELLOW CARD PUCCIARIELLO (76 mins)

REFEREE J Jutge (France)

FINAL

20 May, Millennium Stadium, Cardiff

BIARRITZ OLYMPIQUE 19 (1G, 4PG) MUNSTER 23 (2G, 3PG)

BIARRITZ OLYMPIQUE: N Brusque; J–B Gobelet, P Bidabe, D Traille, S Bobo; J Peyrelongue, D Yachvili; P V Balan, B August, C Johnson, J Thion, D Couzinet, S Betsen, I Harinordoquy, T Lievremont (captain) Substitutions: O Olibeau for Couzinet (45 mins); T Dusautoir for Lievremont (52 mins); F Martin Arramburu for Traille (53 mins); B Lecouls for Johnson (63 mins); B Noirot for August (67 mins); C Johnson for Balan (74 mins)

SCORERS *Try*: Bobo *Conversion*: Yachvili *Penalty Goals*: Yachvili (4)

MUNSTER: S Payne; A Horgan, J Kelly, T Halstead, I Dowling; R O'Gara, P Stringer; M Horan, J Flannery, J Hayes, D O'Callaghan, P O'Connell, D Leamy, D Wallace, A Foley (captain) Subsitutions: F Pucciariello for Horan (63 mins); M O'Driscoll for Foley (71 mins); A Quinlan for O'Connell (76 mins)

SCORERS *Tries:* Halstead, Stringer *Conversions*: O'Gara (2) *Penalty Goals*: O'Gara (3)

REFEREE C White (England)

EUROPEAN CHALLENGE CUP

DOWN TO THE WIRE

Dave Rogers/Getty Images

Glory, glory Gloucester as they get their hands on European silverware.

Gloucester maintained the English stranglehold on Europe's second tier cup competition with a dramatic extra-time victory over London Irish in the Challenge Cup final.

The Cherry and Whites edged out the Exiles at the Stoop courtesy of James Forrester's try in the first minute of the second half of extra time to give Gloucester their first ever piece of European silverware and extend the Premiership's complete dominance of the competition.

Victory for the West Country club made it six English wins in succession, dating back to Harlequins' victory over Narbonne in 2001, and brought to a climax a competition that produced a deluge of points in the early stages, some enthralling rugby and yet another new format for Europe's secondary knockout tournament.

The 2005–06 Challenge Cup saw the introduction of a six-match pool stage for the 20 competing clubs from six countries before the quarter-finals. Any fears that the new group phase, in contrast to the previous all-or-nothing knockout phase, would create a negative or defensive mindset were soon dispelled.

The 10th season of the competition kicked off in October and it quickly became obvious few of the teams were prepared to play the percentages. Agen scored a half century of points at Overmach Parma, Newcastle beat Brive 51–19 at Kingston Park while Connacht were the round's biggest winners, centre Keith Matthews helping himself to a hat-trick in his side's one-sided 62–17 victory over Spanish side Catania.

Connacht's performance paled into insignificance, however, compared to Gloucester's display in the second round against the hapless Romanians Bucuresti. Played at Kingsholm, the match was an unfortunate mismatch and once Luke Narraway had crossed in the fourth minute for the first of Gloucester's 15 tries, there was no way back for the visitors. England wing James Simpson-Daniel scored four and Dean Ryan's side had laid down their Challenge Cup marker with a resounding 106–3 victory.

But it was not just Gloucester who were finding the competition to their liking and both Brive and London Irish recorded big wins to emphasise the free-scoring start to the competition.

The third round of pool fixtures took place in December and once again the matches were dominated by attacking, positive rugby that kept the crowds entertained and those unfortunate to be operating the scoreboards extremely busy.

Montpellier sparked the latest points glut with a 74–12 demolition of Catania in France, Gloucester again found a rich vein of form in their 74–3 victory at Toulon while Newcastle travelled to L'Aquila and returned home 86–0 winners.

The Falcons made it three wins out of three in the competition in their 11-try rout as openside Cory Harris crossed twice in Italy.

"The match gave us the chance to do some quality work on our forward play," said Newcastle director of rugby Rob Andrew. "In fact we deliberately overplayed that area so that we could give the pack a work-out instead of giving the ball to the backs all the time. It's difficult to judge a game like that in the grand scheme of things, but I think we did very well."

The points continued to flow in the next three rounds of games and it was invariably the increasingly dominant English sides scoring them. Gloucester, Newcastle, Bristol and London Irish all helped themselves to further half centuries and it was little surprise that the end of the group stage saw all five pools comfortably headed by Premiership representatives.

The top five and the three best runners-up went through to the quarter-finals but there was to be no stopping the English juggernaut in the knockout phase.

Newcastle comfortably saw off the challenge of Connacht 23–3 at Kingston Park in their last eight clash, before Worcester edged out Northampton 34–25 at Franklin Gardens.

The stage was then set for Gloucester and London Irish to once again turn on the style.

The Cherry and Whites faced Brive at Kingsholm and were quickly back in their European stride, outscoring their French visitors seven tries to one in a resounding 46–13 win.

"The win was pleasing as it gives us the home tie against Worcester," said Gloucester coach Dean Ryan. "It was very obvious that we had one eye on the future and developing and at the same time trying to get us through knockout football, which is never easy.

"I think it is crucial that we support these young fellows because I'm convinced the long-term dividend is huge. There is a risk in the knockout game that some of the mistakes they are going to make happen in that game – but that is the risk we have to be prepared to take."

The pressure was now on London Irish to complete an all-Premiership semi-final line-up but if the Exiles felt any nerves whatsoever, they certainly were not on show as they demolished Bayonne 48–5 at the Madejski Stadium to progress to the last four.

"Once they crumbled, I thought we were ruthless with our execution in the second half and it was an outstanding performance," said Exiles head coach Brian Smith.

"By the last 20 minutes, they ran out of gas which was part of our plan. They hit us on a day when we were prepared to play good, positive rugby."

The semi-finals in April paired Gloucester with Worcester and Newcastle with the Irish and produced two close encounters that could not have been further removed from some of the competition's earlier, one-sided clashes.

The first semi-final at Kingsholm was a nip-and-tuck affair from the first whistle. The Cherry and Whites surged into an early lead with tries from James Simpson-Daniel and Anthony Allen but Worcester hit back with scores from Shane Drahm and Pat Sanderson to lead 17–15 at the break.

The second-half developed into a battle of the kickers between Gloucester's Ryan Lamb and Drahm and with only seven minutes on the clock, the Warriors had edged themselves into a 23–21 lead before a converted Mark Foster try and third Lamb penalty sealed it for the home side.

"We got ourselves into a winning position but we were not positive enough," said Worcester coach John Brain at the final whistle. "They crept back into it and the players are obviously gutted because they gave their everything and just didn't do enough to win."

A day later Irish travelled to Newcastle for what was to be an equally tight game.

Leading 15–3 at the break after tries from Robbie Russell and Topsy Ojo, the Exiles seemed to be coasting towards the final when they added further scores from Sailosi Tagicakibau and Gonzalo Tiesi in the second-half to leave Newcastle trailing 27–3.

But the Falcons staged a strong second-half fightback on their home ground, scoring three tries but the Irish clung on for a 27–22 win and a trip to the Twickenham Stoop.

The final in May began tentatively before Barry Everitt notched up the first of 19 points on the day with two unanswered penalties for the Irish. Gloucester hit back with tries from Mark Foster and Andy Hazell to establish the Cherry and Whites in the match. Delon Armitage then crossed for the Exiles and when the two sides headed for their respective dressing rooms after 40 minutes of rain-soaked action, Gloucester found themselves in a 18–13 lead.

The West Country side became firm favourites after the break when Argentine Juan Manuel Leguizamon was yellow-carded for flooring Peter Richards with an outstretched arm on 48 minutes and a long-range James Simpson-Daniel try seemed to have wrapped it up.

But the Exiles refused to lie down and took the match into extra-time after Olivier Magne and then Robbie Russell crashed over from close range. Everitt, in fact, could have won it for Irish but missed his attempted conversion of Russell's score.

Everitt did rediscover his form in the first-half of extra-time with a successful penalty to edge the Exiles in front but number eight James Forrester, overlooked for England's summer tour to Australia the week before, delivered the coup de grace for Gloucester early in the second half when he collected his own hack through to touch down for a decisive five points. Everitt had two further chances with a penalty and drop goal to snatch victory but they both missed and Gloucester were able to celebrate their first European triumph.

"It was all a bit of a blur," said Forrester after his match-winning contribution. "I remember it being a good try but having watched it on the video it looks a bit clumsy.

"I thought I had over-kicked it, the dead ball area looked longer than it was but I just got in there. The line crept up on me and I was panicking but I just got in."

CHALLENGE CUP RESULTS

22 October, 2005	
Worcester 36 **Montpellier** 18	**Section Paloise** 13 **London Irish** 20
Overmach Parma 23 **Agen** 50	**Northampton** 47 **Viadana** 25
Newcastle 51 **Brive** 19	**Narbonne** 20 **Bristol** 13
L'Aquila 25 **Borders** 32	**Connacht** 62 **Catania** 17
Bucuresti 16 **Toulon** 20	**Bayonne** 10 **Gloucester** 26
28 October, 2005	
Montpellier 16 **Connacht** 19	
29 October, 2005	
Toulon 19 **Bayonne** 28	**Gloucester** 106 **Bucuresti** 3
Catania 14 **Worcester** 19	**Brive** 64 **L'Aquila** 22
Agen 23 **Section Paloise** 6	
30 October, 2005	
London Irish 64 **Overmach Parma** 0	**Bristol** 36 **Northampton** 28
Borders 11 **Newcastle** 26	
9 December, 2005	
Viadana 23 **Bristol** 39	**Montpellier** 74 **Catania** 12
10 December, 2005	
Worcester 30 **Connacht** 20	**Toulon** 3 **Gloucester** 74
Section Paloise 29 **Overmach Parma** 3	**Northampton** 32 **Narbonne** 20
L'Aquila 0 **Newcastle** 86	**Bucuresti** 10 **Bayonne** 38
11 December, 205	
London Irish 29 **Agen** 21	**Borders** 25 **Brive** 22
16 December, 2005	
Narbonne 7 **Northampton** 22	**Bayonne** 45 **Bucuresti** 6
17 December, 2005	
Overmach Parma 20 **Section Paloise** 11	**Gloucester** 66 **Toulon** 5
Connacht 22 **Worcester** 21	**Brive** 34 **Borders** 28
Agen 24 **London Irish** 32	
18 December, 2005	
Newcastle 90 **L'Aquila** 14	**Catania** 37 **Montpellier** 34
Bristol 89 **Viadana** 5	
13 January, 2006	
Bayonne 62 **Toulon** 0	

14 January, 2006

Worcester 44 **Catania** 8

Overmach Parma 11 **London Irish** 19

Narbonne 29 **Viadana** 14

Bucuresti 13 **Gloucester** 27

Section Paloise 36 **Agen** 12

Northampton 45 **Bristol** 8

L'Aquila 19 **Brive** 47

15 January, 2006

Newcastle 47 **Borders** 20

20 January, 2006

Catania 28 **Connacht** 24

21 January, 2006

Toulon 17 **Bucuresti** 23

Gloucester 32 **Bayonne** 19

Borders 39 **L'Aquila** 23

London Irish 75 **Section Paloise** 12

Brive 17 **Newcastle** 24

Agen 33 **Overmach Parma** 17

22 January, 2006

Bristol 18 Narbonne 29

FINAL GROUP TABLES

POOL ONE

	P	W	D	L	F	A	BP	Pts
Northampton	6	4	0	1	174	96	5	25
Narbonne	6	4	0	2	125	113	2	18
Bristol	6	3	0	3	203	150	4	16
Viadana	6	0	0	5	81	224	1	1

POOL TWO

	P	W	D	L	F	A	BP	Pts
London Irish	6	6	0	0	239	81	3	27
Agen	6	3	0	3	163	143	2	14
Section Paloise	6	2	0	4	107	153	3	11
O'mach Parma	6	1	0	5	74	206	0	4

POOL THREE

	P	W	D	L	F	A	BP	Pts
Gloucester	6	6	0	0	331	53	5	29
Bayonne	6	4	0	2	202	93	4	20
Bucuresti	6	1	0	5	71	253	1	5
Toulon	6	1	0	5	64	269	1	5

POOL FOUR

	P	W	D	L	F	A	BP	Pts
Newcastle	6	6	0	0	324	81	4	28
Brive	6	3	0	3	203	169	6	18
Borders	6	3	0	3	155	177	3	15
L'Aquila	6	0	0	6	103	358	1	1

POOL FIVE

	P	W	D	L	F	A	BP	Pts
Worcester	6	5	0	1	181	103	4	24
Connacht	6	4	0	2	190	122	4	20
Catania	6	2	0	4	116	257	2	10
Montpellier	6	1	0	5	173	178	4	8

QUARTER-FINALS

31 March, 2006	
Newcastle 23 **Connacht** 3	
1 April, 2006	
Northampton 25 **Worcester** 34	**Gloucester** 46 **Brive** 13
2 April, 2006	
London Irish 48 **Bayonne** 5	

SEMI-FINALS

22 April, Kingsholm, Gloucester

GLOUCESTER 31 (2G, 4PG, 1T)
WORCESTER WARRIORS 21 (1G, 2PG, 1T 1DG)

GLOUCESTER: O Morgan; J Simpson-Daniel, M Tindall, A Allen, M Foster; R Lamb, P Richards; P Collazo, M Davies, G Powell, A Eustace, A Brown, P Buxton (captain), A Hazell, J Forrester

SUBSTITUTIONS: J Bailey for Foster (temp 18 to 20 mins); L Mercier for Morgan (41 mins); Bailey for Simpson-Daniel (41 mins); L Narraway for Buxton (41 mins); J Pendlebury for Hazell (temp 65 to 69 mins); J Forster for Powell (66 mins); Pendlebury for Eustace (69 mins)

SCORERS TRIES: Simpson-Daniel, Allen, Foster Conversions: Lamb (2) Penalty Goals: Lamb (3), Mercier

WORCESTER WARRIORS: N Le Roux; U Oduoza, D Rasmussen, T Lombard, G Trueman; S Drahm, M Powell; T Windo, C Fortey, T Taumoepeau, P Murphy, C Gillies, P Sanderson (captain), T Harding, K Horstmann Substitutions: L Fortey for Taumoepeau (temp 39 to 41 mins); S Vaili for Harding (66 mins); E O'Donoghue for Murphy (74 mins); L Fortey for Taumoepeau (80 mins)

SCORERS TRIES: Drahm, Sanderson Conversion: Drahm Penalty Goals: Drahm (2) Drop Goal: Drahm

REFEREE C Berdos (France)

23 April, Kingston Park, Newcastle

NEWCASTLE FALCONS 22 (2G, 1PG, 1T)
LONDON IRISH 27 (2G, 1PG, 2T)

NEWCASTLE FALCONS: M Burke; T May, M Tait, J Noon, A Elliott; D Walder, J Grindal; M Ward, A Long, R Morris, A Perry, G Parling, M McCarthy, B Woods, C Charvis (captain) Substitutions: M Thompson for Long (33 mins); J Wilkinson for Walder (33 mins); J Williams for Ward (41 mins); H Charlton for Grindal (57 mins); M Ward for Morris (66 mins); O Finegan for Perry (70 mins); C Harris for Woods (81 mins)

SCORERS TRIES: Woods, May, Tait Conversions: Wilkinson (2) Penalty Goal: Burke

LONDON IRISH: D Armitage; T Ojo, G Tiesi, M Catt (captain), S Tagicakibau; R Flutey, P Hodgson; N Hatley, R Russell, F Rautenbach, B Casey, K Roche, D Danaher, O Magne, P Murphy Substitutions: R Skuse for Rautenbach (41 mins); D Paice for Russell (41 mins); K Dawson for Magne (49 mins); M Collins for Hatley (53 mins); D Edwards for Hodgson (66 mins); N Kennedy for Casey (66 mins); S Geraghty for Flutey (70 mins)

SCORERS TRIES: Russell, Ojo, Tagicakibau, Tiesi Conversions: Flutey (2) Penalty Goal: Flutey

YELLOW CARD DANAHER (74mins)

REFEREE N Owens (Wales)

FINAL

21 May, Twickenham Stoop, London

GLOUCESTER 36 (2G, 4PG, 2T)
LONDON IRISH 34 (2G, 4PG, 1T, 1DG)

GLOUCESTER: R Thirlby; J Simpson-Daniel, M Tindall, A Allen, M Foster; R Lamb, P Richards; P Collazo, M Davies, J Forster, J Pendlebury, A Brown, P Buxton (captain), A Hazell, J Forrester Substitutions: L Mercier for Lamb (46 mins); G Powell for Forster (47 mins); A Eustace for Pendlebury (80 mins); L Narraway for Hazell (80 mins); O Azam for Collazo (80 mins); J Bailey for Thirlby (82 mins)

SCORERS TRIES: Hazell, Foster, Simpson-Daniel, Forrester Conversions: Lamb, Mercier Penalty Goals: Lamb (2), Mercier (2)

LONDON IRISH: D Armitage; T Ojo, M Catt (captain), R Flutey, S Tagicakibau; B Everitt, P Hodgson; N Hatley, R Russell, R Skuse, B Casey, N Kennedy, K Roche, O Magne, J Leguizamon Substitutions: D Paice for Hatley (41 mins); M Collins for Skuse (61 mins); D Danaher for Magne (74 mins); P Murphy for Collins (80 mins); G Tiesi for Flutey (80 mins); B Willis for Hodgson (90 mins)

SCORERS TRIES: Armitage, Magne, Russell Conversions: Everitt (2) Penalty Goals: Everitt (4) Drop Goal: Everitt

YELLOW CARD J Leguizamon (47 mins)

REFEREE N Whitehouse (Wales)

POWERGEN CUP
WASPS CLAIM FIRST TITLE

Dave Rogers/Getty Images

Wasps start the party after lifting the first Anglo-Welsh Powergen Cup trophy.

The initial omens for the revamped Powergen Cup were not good. A new-look knockout competition featuring the 12 English Premiership sides and the four Welsh regional outfits, the tournament was a bold move by both the English and Welsh unions to revive interest in domestic cup rugby.

It wasn't, however, supposed to be so divisive.

The problems began in May when details of the inaugural Anglo-Welsh Cup were announced. It soon became clear the Welsh sides had signed up for fixtures that clashed with their existing Celtic League commitments and a huge political row erupted.

The Ireland and Scotland unions were incensed by the news as relations hit rock bottom and the Welsh sides were acrimoniously expelled from the Celtic League. To add insult to injury, Wales' Celtic cousins then threatened to set up their own two-nation tournament.

Peace was finally restored when the Welsh agreed to find a financial sweetener to placate the Irish and Scottish – as well as to play their disputed Celtic League matches in midweek to ease the potential fixture congestion. The Powergen Cup could now make its debut without any further complications.

The opening fixture of the competition was played at the end of September and saw the Newport-Gwent Dragons entertain Leicester at Rodney Parade. It was to prove to be a mouth-watering opener for the tournament.

The Dragons drew first blood with a try from fly-half Craig Warlow and went further ahead when wing Ben Breeze crossed. The Tigers fought back with scores either side of the break from Shane Jennings and Leon Lloyd but Warlow's boot – he finished the match with a full house of try, conversion, penalty (three in total) and a drop goal – kept the home side in the driving seat and they held on for a 24–15 victory.

"Leicester brought down quite a strong side and we matched them in every department," said Warlow. "We scrapped really well for every ball and the win was based on forward supremacy. When a big team like Leicester comes down it really makes you focus and we were top in everything we did – the mistakes were very low."

Tigers' coach Pat Howard added: "If the Welsh teams turn up for it like the Dragons did tonight, the competition has a great future. They were hungry."

There was further Welsh joy in the opening pool games for Cardiff, who beat Saracens 37–20 at The Arms Park and Llanelli, who overcame Leeds 28–7 thanks to tries from Tal Selley, Iestyn Thomas and Matthew Watkins. The Opsreys, in contrast, were beaten 23–7 by Gloucester at Kingsholm.

The second round of games a week later were a different story. Llanelli maintained their 100 per cent record with a narrow 22–20 win over Newcastle at Stradey Park but had to rely on a 75th minute penalty from Gareth Bowen for the points. The three other Welsh sides, however, were all beaten as the English clubs took their revenge.

The competition then went into hibernation for two months before December's final – and decisive – fixtures to decide the group winners and semi-final line-up.

In Group A, it was Bath who emerged victorious after a West Country derby against Gloucester at the Recreation Ground. Both sides went into the game with two wins from two but it was the home side who progressed to the knockout stages thanks to 13 points from Olly Barkley in a 21–12 win.

Wasps, meanwhile, wrapped up Group B after convincingly beating Saracens 42–8 to take maximum points and book their semi-final spot.

Group C saw Llanelli also finish unbeaten at the top after dispatching an under strength Sale side 24–23.

In Group D, however, there was an altogether more dramatic climax as Leicester and Northampton slugged it out at Welford Road. Needing to beat the Saints by at least seven points, scoring four tries in the process for the crucial bonus point, the Tigers held their nerve and pounded their way to a four-try, 29–16 win.

"It was really physical and Northampton made it tough," said a relieved Pat Howard after the game. "They came out with a great deal of passion. It wasn't perfect by any means but our goal was four tries and we did what we set out to do."

The draw for the semi-finals paired Premiership heavyweights Wasps and Leicester together, while Llanelli would face Bath, with both games played at the Millennium Stadium in March.

The all-English showdown was a thriller despite an uninspiring first half which saw Wasps establish a nine-point advantage courtesy of three penalties from the boot of fly-half Jeremy Staunton.

Leicester replied through flying wing Tom Varndell and crossed again soon after half-time when Leon Lloyd scored but Staunton's boot kept the scoreboard ticking over for the Londoners and when late replacement Ayoola Erinle sprinted in from 70 metres, Wasps were home and dry. The Tigers added a third try late on but the 17 points from Staunton proved the difference and Wasps were 22–17 winners.

"It is important that when you are playing well and not scoring tries you need penalties to keep the scoreboard moving," said Wasps boss Ian McGeechan. "Those penalties gave us the points our rugby in the first half deserved. Without them it could well have been a different story. In the second half we had to dig in because Leicester were doing well and it takes a lot out of you."

But if Wasps' semi-final triumph was dramatic, it was nothing compared to the fare served up by Llanelli and Bath later the same day in the Welsh capital.

The match was a pulsating clash with the lead changing hands with nerve-inducing regularity. Bath led 16–7 at half-time after Alex Crockett's try and three Chris Malone penalties but the Scarlets came storming back after the break through Mark Jones and Regan King scores and edged into a 24–23 lead.

Malone put Bath back briefly in the driving seat with another penalty but Llanelli hit back with just eight minutes to go when Mike Hercus kicked three points. Malone then scuffed a match-winning drop goal in the dying minutes and the Scarlets were through to the final.

"We've come unstuck a few times in semi-finals in Europe, but we put a lot of effort into today," said Llanelli captain Simon Easterby. "We gave 100 per cent, dug deep and the reward is the win and we're delighted. We've showed we can mix it with the best, but we've got to remember we haven't won the tournament yet."

The final took place a month later at Twickenham but although the game was watched by a 57,000-strong crowd, it could not quite reproduce the drama and tension of the two semi-finals.

The form book suggested a close game. The two teams had already met twice in the group phase of the Heineken Cup with each winning their home fixture and there was little to choose between them before kick-off.

Llanelli were on the board first with a try from full-back Barry Davies, which Mike Hercus converted. Hercus and Mark van Gisbergen then traded penalties before Wasps' opening try from Tom Voyce sent the teams in level at 10–10 at the break.

The second-half, however, was all Wasps despite the persistent drizzle that made expansive handling a gamble and when Voyce crossed for his second try, they were almost out of sight. Two van Gisbergen penalties and an Alex King drop goal late on went unanswered by Llanelli and Wasps coasted to a 26–10 victory.

"The previous finals helped us," said victorious captain Lawrence Dallaglio. "We were far from our best but we showed what champions are about today.

"When you start the season there are only three trophies available so to win one is very pleasing. We now have a trophy in the cabinet."

Defeat was a bitter pill to swallow for Scarlets director of rugby Gareth Jenkins who was forced to watch Wasps strangle the life out of the game in the second-half.

"It was a lost opportunity," he said. "There were 17 points in that first half for us, and we ended up going in 10–10 at half-time. Wasps scored a good try at the beginning of the second half, and the weather then became a major factor.

"It was nearly impossible to play `catch-up' rugby. They turned the screw and in the end they deserved to win. But if we had scored 17 points in that first half I wonder whether Wasps could have played `catch-up' rugby more effectively than us."

His opposite number Ian McGeechan, however, was delighted to have landed his first piece of silverware since joining the club.

"There was a huge legacy here and I am delighted to become a part of it,'" he said. "It is a great feeling. This is the first club trophy I have ever won and it is a bit special. I knew that when I woke up this morning because I was pretty nervous."

POWERGEN CUP RESULTS

30 September, 2005	
Dragons 24 **Leicester** 15	
1 October, 2005	
Worcester 7 **Northampton** 22	**Gloucester** 23 **Ospreys** 7
Cardiff 37 **Saracens** 20	**Bath** 25 **Bristol** 10
2 October, 2005	
Newcastle 34 **Sale** 9	**London Irish** 26 **Wasps** 30
Leeds 7 **Llanelli** 28	
7 October, 2005	
Wasps 40 **Cardiff** 19	**Sale** 45 **Leeds** 10
8 October, 2005	
Northampton 32 **Dragons** 7	**Leicester** 42 **Worcester** 16
9 October, 2005	
Saracens 32 **London Irish** 13	**Ospreys** 20 **Bath** 27
Llanelli 22 **Newcastle** 20	**Bristol** 6 **Gloucester** 34
2 December, 2005	
Leeds 18 **Newcastle** 18	**Llanelli** 24 **Sale** 23
3 December, 2005	
Dragons 33 **Worcester** 10	**Leicester** 29 **Northampton** 16
Bath 21 **Gloucester** 12	
4 December, 2005	
Wasps 42 **Saracens** 8	**London Irish** 27 **Cardiff** 23
Bristol 28 **Ospreys** 43	

GROUP A

	P	W	D	L	F	A	BP	Pts
Bath	3	3	0	0	73	42	0	12
Gloucester	3	2	0	1	69	34	1	9
Ospreys	3	1	0	2	70	78	2	6
Bristol	3	0	0	3	44	102	1	1

GROUP C

	P	W	D	L	F	A	BP	Pts
Llanelli	3	3	0	0	74	50	0	12
Newcastle	3	1	1	1	72	49	2	8
Sale	3	1	0	2	77	68	2	6
Leeds	3	0	1	2	35	91	0	2

GROUP B

	P	W	D	L	F	A	BP	Pts
Wasps	3	3	0	0	112	53	2	14
Cardiff	3	1	0	2	79	87	2	6
Saracens	3	1	0	2	60	92	1	5
Lon Irish	3	1	0	2	66	85	1	5

GROUP D

	P	W	D	L	F	A	BP	Pts
Leicester	3	2	0	1	86	56	2	10
Northmpt'n	3	2	0	1	70	43	1	9
Dragons	3	2	0	1	64	57	0	8
Worcester	3	0	0	3	33	97	0	0

SEMI-FINALS

4 March, Millennium Stadium, Cardiff

WASPS 22 (1G, 5PG) LEICESTER 17 (1G, 2T)

WASPS: T Voyce; J Lewsey, F Waters, S Abbott, A Erinle: J Staunton, E Reddan; A McKenzie, R Ibanez, T Payne, S Shaw, R Birkett, J Worsley, J O'Connor, L Dallaglio (captain) Substitutions: J Dawson for McKenzie (52 mins); J Brooks for Abbott (70 mins); M Dawson for Reddan (70 mins); A McKenzie for Payne (88 mins)

SCORERS *Try*: Erinle *Conversion*: Staunton *Penalty Goals*: Staunton (5)

LEICESTER: S Vesty; G Murphy, L Lloyd, D Hipkiss, T Varndell; A Goode, A Healey; G Rowntree, G Chuter, J White, L Deacon, B Kay M Corry (captain), L Moody, H Tuilagi Substitutions: S Jennings for Tuilagi (36 mins); H Ellis for Healey (68 mins); L Cullen for Kay (79 mins); M Holford for Rowntree (84 mins)

SCORERS *Tries*: Varndell, Lloyd, Hipkiss *Conversion*: Goode

REFEREE: N Owens (Wales)

4 March, Millennium Stadium, Cardiff

BATH 26 (2G, 4PG) LLANELLI 27 (3G, 2PG)

BATH: M Perry; A Higgins, A Crockett, J Maddock, S Finau; C Malone, N Walshe; D Flatman, L Mears, D Bell, S Borthwick (captain), D Grewcock, A Beattie, M Lipman, Z Feaunati Substitutions: N Abendanon for Finau (47 mins); P Short for Feaunati (74 mins); G Delve for Grewcock (76 mins); C Loader for Bell (78 mins)

SCORERS *Tries*:Crockett, Maddock *Conversions*: Malone (2) *Penalty Goals*: Malone (4)

LLANELLI: B Davies; M Jones, M Watkins, R King, D James; M Hercus, C Stuart-Smith; C Dunlea, M Rees, J Davies, I Afeaki, A Jones, S Easterby (captain), G Thomas, A Popham Substitutions: M Madden for Dunlea (66 mins); A Gravelle for Rees (71 mins); G Quinnell for Afeaki (71 mins); D Jones for Popham (73 mins); L Byrne for M Jones (76 mins)

SCORERS *Tries*: Dunlea, King, M Jones *Conversions*: Hercus (3) *Penalty Goals*: Hercus (2)

YELLOW CARD HIGGINS (55 mins)

REFEREE M Changleng (Scotland).

FINAL

9 April, Twickenham, London

LLANELLI 10 (1G, 1PG)
WASPS 26 (2G, 3PG, 1DG)

LLANELLI: B Davies; M Jones, M J Watkins, R King, D James; M Hercus, C Stuart-Smith; P John, M Rees, J Davies, I Afeaki, A Jones, S Easterby (captain), G Thomas, A Popham Substitutions: M Madden for J Davies (64 mins)

SCORERS *Try*: B Davies *Conversion*: Hercus *Penalty Goal*: Hercus

WASPS: M van Gisbergen; P Sackey, J Lewsey, S Abbott, T Voyce; J Staunton, E Reddan; A McKenzie, R Ibanez, T Payne, S Shaw, R Birkett, J Worsley, J O'Connor, L Dallaglio (captain) Substitutions: D Leo for J O'Connor (1 min); A King for Staunton (54 mins); M Dawson for Reddan (54 mins); J Ward for Ibanez (54 mins); P Bracken for McKenzie (57 mins); J Haskell for Worsley (78 mins); D Jones for S Easterby (40 mins); A Gravelle for M Rees (76 mins), V Cooper for I Afeaki (70 mins)

SCORERS *Tries*: Voyce (2) *Conversions*: van Gisbergen (2) *Penalty Goals*: van Gisbergen (3) Drop Goal: King

REFEREE A Lewis (Ireland)

Ross Land/Getty Images

Crusaders captain Richie McCaw holds the inaugural Super 14 trophy aloft.

SUPER 14

NEW TROPHY, SAME WINNER

By John Eales

Simon Fergusson/Getty Images

The first Super 14 trophy headed to New Zealand, won by the Canterbury Crusaders.

The inaugural Super 14 season may have finished in familiar fashion with the Crusaders taking the trophy back to Canterbury once again but I thought the new-look format was a genuine success and bringing in two new teams definitely gave the competition a new lease of life.

I like the idea of an expanded tournament. In the old days of the Super 12, there were only 11 games per side per season. Bringing in the two additional teams mean there are now 13 games, which I feel gives the competition a bit more depth and credibility. I always felt 11 games were too few to genuinely test all the side's credentials before a knockout phase and the two extra matches are definitely a step in the right direction.

But I still feel the competition has missed a trick by not inviting one of the Pacific Islands to play and rebranding as the Super 15. It's a missed opportunity for southern hemisphere rugby and whether it was a combined islands side or the winner of a round robin knockout, I think the tournament would benefit. It's long overdue Argentina were allowed to play in the Tri-Nations and it's equally short-sighted that we are still waiting to see a side from Samoa, Fiji or Tonga competing in a Super whatever. It would generate a lot of excitement and it would also encourage rugby development on the islands.

But back to the first Super 14 season. At the risk of generalising, I thought the standard was good for the most part of the tournament, although there was criticism from some quarters that defences were too dominant and the matches weren't producing enough free-flowing, try-scoring rugby.

Rugby is always a balance between attack and defence but personally I thought the games on offer this season were very watchable. It's true there weren't as many matches with 40, 50 or 60 points being scored but that doesn't mean that standards have dropped. I'd always prefer to watch a tight, anxious 20–16 game with just a couple of tries rather than a half century hammering. Criticism of a certain style of play is very subjective and merely pointing out that less tries or fewer points have been scored doesn't necessarily prove anything.

Previous Super 12 campaigns have produced a glut of points and I think it becomes easy to expect that year after year. Lots of points doesn't always mean good rugby is being played and the inaugural Super 14 season proved that. There were plenty of tight, nip-and-tuck games, which for me is an important sign of healthy competition.

It's hard if not impossible to argue the Crusaders weren't worthy champions again. To reach a fifth consecutive final and defend your crown is no mean achievement and the fact they lost just once all tournament – a 28–17 loss to the Stormers in Cape Town – tells its own story.

They blew the Bulls away in the semi-final in Christchurch and although the Hurricanes gave them a bit more to think about in the final, I don't think they were ever in any real danger of getting beaten. The fog made the final in Christchurch a bit of a lottery but for me the Crusaders were always in control of the game. I suppose that kind of coolness comes from having been in that situation before and knowing what you have to do to close out an important match.

An all-Kiwi final suggests that the New Zealand sides completely dominated the competition but it wasn't quite as clear cut as that. There's no doubt that the Kiwi sides are still ahead of the Australians and South Africans in terms of their tight play, particularly in the scrum, but I think the gap is beginning to close. The other teams can't catch up overnight but the momentum is building. The overall intensity of scrummaging by all the teams in the tournament was definitely improved on previous years.

From an Australian point of view, I thought the competition was a mixed bag. I'm sure the Brumbies will have been disappointed not to make the semi-finals. They contrived to lose their last two games and miss out on the knockout stages, which let the Bulls in, and they didn't live up to their potential. They were so close but choked when it mattered.

The Reds were never going to make a big impact after losing so many players in the close season but I was impressed with the Force. The new franchise may have only won one game and finished bottom of the table, which doesn't look very positive on the face of it, but it's important not to forget they got a draw with the Crusaders in Perth and lost a lot of their other games only by a handful of points. I'm sure the Force management will have been quietly pleased with their debut season. A few astute signings and I'm sure they'll come back next season stronger and more competitive.

The big Australian disappointment though was the Waratahs. I thought they were a better side than the one beaten by the Crusaders in last year's final but they blew the semi-final against the Hurricanes. They had the potential to beat the Crusaders in the final but didn't give themselves the opportunity to prove it. It was a campaign full of 'what ifs?' which ultimately failed to deliver the big prize I'm sure the players and management had set their sights on.

It was a respectable season for the South Africans overall. The Bulls came in fourth and the Sharks fifth, which was encouraging, and I felt all the South African teams looked to be finally coming to terms with playing away from home. The South Africans have never been great travellers in the competition but they all seemed much less fearful on the road this season.

The new Cheetahs franchise did well to get five wins in their first season and I thought the Sharks were a good side to watch going forward, which is no doubt down to David Campese's influence on the coaching set-up.

The thing that really struck me with the South Africans was the variety of styles their sides adopt. The Kiwi or Aussie sides tend to play in roughly the same way as their country rivals but the Springbok teams all seem to do their own thing. There's plenty of quality players in South Africa, particularly in the back row at the moment, but national coach Jake White must have one of the hardest jobs in world rugby moulding all the disparate styles and tactical approaches when he gets the players together to play for the Springboks.

In terms of individual performances over the season, I didn't think there were many new faces who really stood out. In fact, it was the old hands for me like Tana Umaga and Manu Nonu who turned in the best performances when it mattered.

I thought it was Umaga's best season for a couple of years and Nonu proved he isn't just a crash and bash merchant all the time. He showed plenty of skill for the Hurricanes and was one of the standout performers of the competition for me.

Having said that about the more experienced players, the young Queensland fly-half Berrick Barnes did show a lot of potential. He's got a lot of tricks and if he can continue his development next season and beyond, he could become some player.

So that was the inaugural Super 14 season. The Cruaders victory in the final made it nine titles out of a possible 11 for New Zealand sides, which means South Africa are still waiting for a winning side while Australia can still only point to the Brumbies' two triumphs in 2001 and 2004.

I said earlier I thought the gap between the likes of the Hurricanes and the Crusaders and the rest was narrowing but I'm not sure if the chasing pack will be ready to overhaul them next season. I think it would give the competition a shot in the arm for the trophy to leave New Zealand but until a side is ready to stand up and take it away from the Kiwis, I can't see it going very far.

SUPER 14 RESULTS

February 10: **Blues** 19 **Hurricanes** 37 (Auckland). February 11: **Western Force** 10 **Brumbies** 25 (Perth), **Cheetahs** 18 **Bulls** 30 (Bloemfontein), **Crusaders** 38 **Highlanders** 15 (Christchurch), **Reds** 12 **Waratahs** 16 (Brisbane). February 12: **Cats** 12 **Stormers** 23 (Johannesburg), **Sharks** 30 **Chiefs** 21 (Durban). February 17: **Highlanders** 25 **Blues** 13 (Dunedin). February 18: **Cats** 21 **Chiefs** 16 (Johannesburg), **Bulls** 21 **Brumbies** 27 (Pretoria), **Hurricanes** 29 **Western Force** 5 (New Plymouth), **Reds** 21 **Crusaders** 47 (Brisbane). February 19: **Sharks** 26 **Cheetahs** 27 (Durban), **Stormers** 26 **Waratahs** 32 (Cape Town). February 24: **Hurricanes** 29 **Cats** 16 (Wellington). February 25: **Stormers** 15 **Brumbies** 15 (Cape Town), **Western Force** 9 **Chiefs** 26 (Perth), **Crusaders** 22 **Sharks** 20 (Timaru), **Reds** 20 **Blues** 21 (Brisbane). February 26: **Bulls** 26 **Waratahs** 17 (Pretoria), **Cheetahs** 12 **Highlanders** 17 (Blomfontein). March 3: **Chiefs** 35 **Reds** 17 (Hamilton), **Brumbies** 28 **Cats** 7 (Canberra). March 4: **Waratahs** 31 **Sharks** 16 (Sydney), **Crusaders** 39 **Blues** 10 (Christchurch). March 5: **Stormers** 15 **Highlanders** 30 (Cape Town), **Cheetahs** 27 **Hurricanes** 25 (Blomfontein). March 10: **Chiefs** 19 **Crusaders** 25 (Hamilton), **Waratahs** 50 **Cats** 3 (Sydney). March 11: **Brumbies** 35 **Sharks** 30 (Canberra), **Reds** 29 **Western Force** 18 (Brisbane). March 12: **Bulls** 23 **Highlanders** 16 (Pretoria), **Stormers** 19 **Hurricanes** 23 (Cape Town). March 17: **Crusaders** 43 **Cats** 15 (Christchurch). March 18: **Western Force** 7 **Waratahs** 32 (Perth), **Bulls** 23 **Hurricanes** 26 (Pretoria), **Blues** 26 **Brumbies** 15 (Auckland), **Highlanders** 11 **Sharks** 26 (Dunedin). March 19: **Stormers** 25 **Cheetahs** 31 (Cape Town). March 24: **Hurricanes** 23 **Sharks** 17 (Wellington), **Waratahs** 43 **Blues** 9 (Sydney). March 25: **Cheetahs** 10 **Reds** 6 (Blomfontein), **Brumbies** 28 **Chiefs** 26 (Canberra), **Highlanders** 16 **Cats** 14 (Invercargill). March 26: **Western Force** 21 **Bulls** 30 (Perth). March 31: **Blues** 30 **Bulls** 17 (Auckland), **Waratahs** 26 **Cheetahs** 3 (Sydney), **Western Force** 25 **Stormers** 26 (Perth). April 1: **Hurricanes** 11 **Crusaders** 20 (Wellington), **Chiefs** 16 **Highlanders** 13 (Hamilton). April 2: **Sharks** 36 **Reds** 28 (Durban). April 7: **Crusaders** 17 **Waratahs** 11 (Christchurch). April 8: **Highlanders** 25 **Western Force** 22 (Dunedin), **Chiefs** 26 **Bulls** 26 (Hamilton), **Blues** 32 **Stormers** 15 (Auckland), **Brumbies** 53 **Cheetahs** 20 (Canberra). April 9: **Cats** 16 **Reds** 23 (Johannesburg). April 14: **Blues** 39 **Western Force** 8 (Auckland). April 15: **Crusaders** 53 **Cheetahs** 17 (Christchurch), **Chiefs** 30 **Stormers** 20 (Mt Maung). April 16: **Cats** 8 **Sharks** 36 (Johannesburg), **Highlanders** 13 **Hurricanes** 29 (Dunedin), **Waratahs** 37 **Brumbies** 14 (Sydney). April 21: **Chiefs** 33 **Cheetahs** 32 (Hamilton), **Reds** 20 **Stormers** 24 (Brisbane), **Western Force** 23 **Crusaders** 23 (Perth). April 22: **Brumbies** 21 **Hurricanes** 16 (Canberra). April 23: **Sharks** 32 **Blues** 15 (Durban), **Bulls** 46 **Cats** 17 (Pretoria). April 28: **Highlanders** 3 **Waratahs** 20 (Dunedin). April 29: **Cats** 34 **Western Force** 34 (Johannesburg), **Hurricanes** 35 **Chiefs** 10 (Wellington), **Brumbies** 36 **Reds** 0 (Canberra). April 30: **Cheetahs** 33 **Blues** 34 (Bloemfontein), **Bulls** 34 **Sharks** 27 (Pretoria), **Stormers** 28 **Crusaders** 17 (Cape Town). May 5: **Hurricanes** 26 **Reds** 22 (Wellington), **Bulls** 17 **Crusaders** 35 (Pretoria), **Chiefs** 37 **Waratahs** 33 (Hamilton), **Brumbies** 26 **Highlanders** 28 (Canberra). May 7: **Cheetahs** 14 **Western Force** 16 (Bloemfontein), **Sharks** 24 **Stormers** 17 (Durban), **Cats** 34 **Blues** 33 (Johannesburg). May 12: **Crusaders** 33 **Brumbies** 3 (Christchurch), **Reds** 22 **Highlanders** 16 (Townsville). May 13: **Sharks** 41 **Western Force** 25 (Durban), **Blues** 9 **Chiefs** 30 (Auckland), **Waratahs** 14 **Hurricanes** 19 (Sydney). May 14: **Cheetahs** 28 **Cats** 23 (Bloemfontein) and **Stormers** 10 **Bulls** 43 (Cape Town)

FINAL TABLE

	P	W	D	L	F	A	BP1	BP2	Pts
Crusaders	13	11	1	1	412	210	5	0	51
Hurricanes	13	10	0	3	328	226	5	2	47
Waratahs	13	9	0	4	362	192	6	3	45
Bulls	13	7	1	5	355	290	5	3	38
Sharks	13	7	0	6	361	297	5	5	38
Brumbies	13	8	1	4	326	269	3	1	38
Chiefs	13	7	1	5	325	298	3	3	36
Blues	13	6	0	7	290	348	4	1	29
Highlanders	13	6	0	7	228	276	0	3	27
Cheetahs	13	5	0	8	272	367	3	4	27
Stormers	13	4	1	8	263	334	1	4	23
Reds	13	4	0	9	240	320	1	5	22
Cats	13	2	1	10	220	405	2	3	15
W.Force	13	1	2	10	223	373	2	2	12

SEMI-FINALS

19 May Westpac Stadium, Wellington

HURRICANES 16 (1G, 3PG)
WARATAHS 14 (3PG, 1T)

HURRICANES: I Toeava; L Fa'atau, M Nonu, T Umaga, S Paku; D Holwell, P Weepu; J Schwalger, A Hore, N Tialata, P Tito, J Eaton, J Collins, C Masoe, R So'oialo (captain) Substitutes: L Mahoney, J McDonnell, L Andrews, T Waldrom, B Haami, J Gopperth, T Ellison

SCORERS TRY: Fa'atau Conversion: Holwell Penalty Goals: Weepu, Holwell, Gopperth

WARATAHS: M Rogers; P Hewat, M Turinui, S Norton-Knight, L Tuqiri; D Halangahu, C Whitaker (captain); B Robinson, A Freier, A Baxter, A Kanaar, D Vickerman, R Elsom, P Waugh, S Hoiles

SUBSTITUTES: T Polota-Nau, M Dunning, W Caldwell, D Lyons, W Palu, B Sheehan, B Jacobs

SCORERS TRY: Hewat Penalty Goals: Hewat (3)

REFEREE J Kaplan (South Africa)

20 May, Jade Stadium, Christchurch

CRUSADERS 35 (2G, 1PG, 3T, 1DG)
BULLS 15 (1G, 1PG, 1T)

CRUSADERS: L MacDonald; R Gear, C Laulala, A Mauger, S Hamilton; D Carter, A Ellis; W Crockett, C Flynn, G Somerville, C Jack, R Thorne, J Leo'o, R McCaw (captain), M Tuiali'I

SUBSTITUTES: T Kopelani, C Johnstone, R Filipo, T Latimer, K Senio, C McIntyre, C Ralph

SCORERS TRIES: Gear (2), Jack, Flynn, Mauger Conversions: Carter (2), Penalty Goal: Carter Drop Goal: Carter

BULLS: J van der Westhuyzen; B Habana, JP Nel, W Olivier, F Welsh; M Steyn, F du Preez; W Roux, G Botha, D Thiart, B Botha, V Matfield (captain), J Cronje, T Dlulane, P Wannenburg

SUBSTITUTES: A Strauss, J Engels, D Rossouw, P Spies, F van Schouwenburg, H Adams, A Ndungane

SCORERS TRIES: Habana, Spies Conversion: Steyn Penalty Goal: Steyn

REFEREE S Dickinson (Australia)

FINAL

27 May, Jade Stadium, Christchurch

CRUSADERS 19 (1G, 4PG)
HURRICANES 12 (4PG)

Crusaders: L MacDonald; R Gear, C Laulala, A Mauger, S Hamilton; D Carter, K Senio; W Crockett, C Flynn, G Somerville, C Jack, R Filipo, R Thorne, R McCaw (captain), M Tuiali'I

SUBSTITUTES: T Kopelani, C Johnstone, J Leo'o, T Latimer, S Brett, C McIntyre, C Ralph

SCORERS TRY: Laulala Conversion: Carter Penalty Goals: Carter (4)

HURRICANES: I Toeava; L Fa'atau, M Nonu, T Umaga, S Paku; D Holwell, P Weepu; J Schwalger, A Hore, N Tialata, P Tito, J Eaton, J Collins, C Masoe, R So'oialo (captain)

SUBSTITUTES: L Mahoney, J McDonnell, L Andrews, T Waldrom, B Haami, J Gopperth, T Ellison

SCORERS PENALTY GOALS: Gopperth (2), Weepu, Holwell

REFEREE J Kaplan (South Africa)

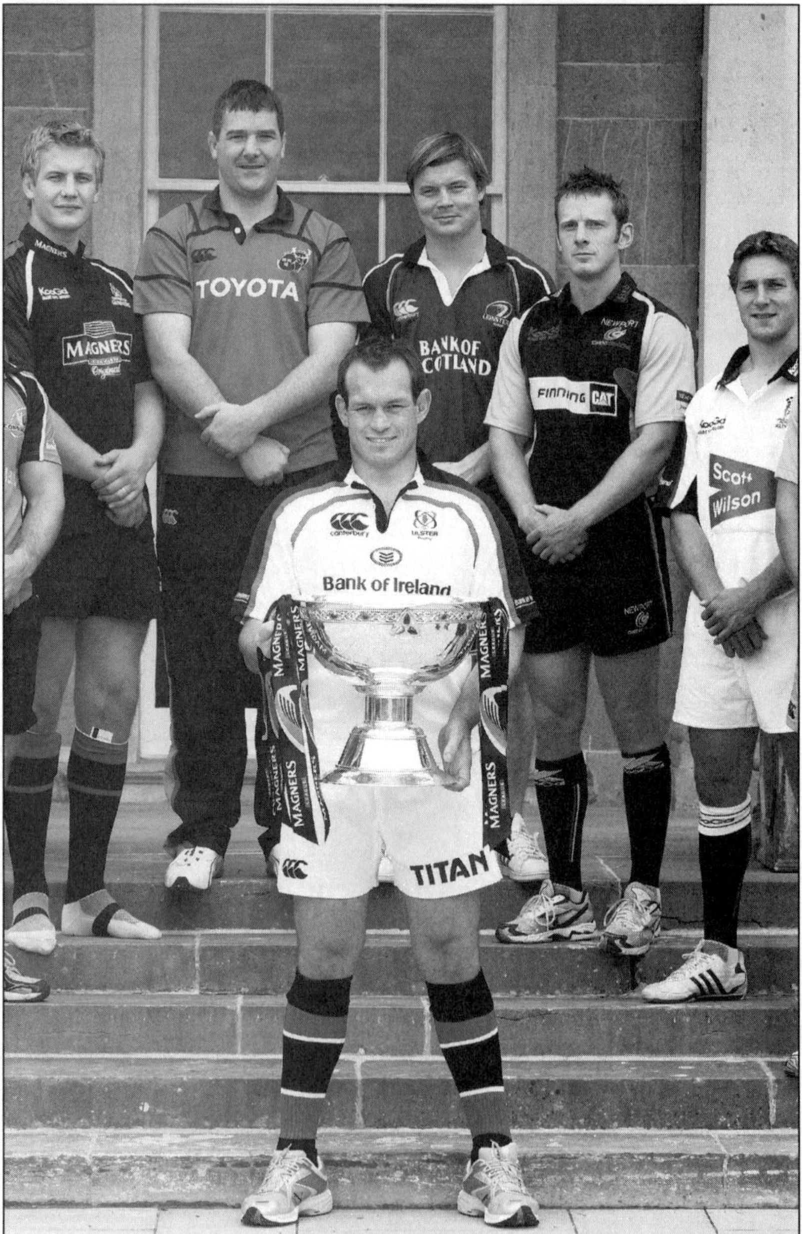

Ulster got their hands on the Celtic League trophy in 2006, the competition renamed, for 2006–07, The Magners League.

CELTIC LEAGUE

ULSTER EYES ARE SMILING

The fifth season of the Celtic League began in controversy and recrimination and ended with incredible drama and heartache. Ulster were crowned champions for the first time and Leinster were denied a second triumph on the last day of an enthralling campaign.

That the race for the title was only decided in the final two minutes of the final round of matches was tribute to a gripping tournament which was dominated by Irish sides but it nearly never took place after a pre-season political row which threatened to split the three Celtic nations.

The dispute over the four Welsh regional sides' participation in the inaugural Anglo-Welsh Cup was only resolved after their Celtic League expulsion and eventual readmittance by the Irish and Scottish unions. A competition that briefly seemed destined to be consigned to the dustbin of history was saved.

Which was fortunate for Ulster but ultimately heartbreaking for Leinster, who were on course to win the tournament until the 78th minute of Ulster's final game against the Ospreys. With the Irishmen trailing 17–16, Ulster looked dead and buried but despondency turned to delight when David Humphreys landed a long-range drop goal to win the match 19–17 and lift Ulster above their provincial rivals in the table and take the title.

After 22 games played over nine months, Ulster had snatched it from Leinster at the death.

The season began in September, however, with little indication of the high drama to follow. Ulster started their campaign with a hard-fought 25–22 victory over Cardiff at the Arms Park while Leinster were narrowly beaten 22–20 by the Ospreys.

Wins over Edinburgh Gunners and the Dragons followed to maintain Ulster's unbeaten start but their title credentials were to be severely tested in early October when they travelled to Donnybrook to face Leinster.

Both sides scored two tries apiece in a passionate clash but it was the boot of fly-half Felipe Contepomi that proved crucial and his six penalties to Humphreys' three gave the home side a 30–23 win. Ulster's unbeaten record was gone and they dropped to third in the table behind early pacesetters Edinburgh and Munster.

"Just because we have lost one match, it doesn't mean that all the good work of the last few weeks is undone," said Ulster coach Mark McCall after his side's reverse.

"Although we didn't play as well against Leinster, there are a number of winnable games coming up if we play well enough. We have to concentrate on the Connacht game now and will prepare well for that.

"It is a big game for us, I expect a big crowd at Ravenhill and it is important that we bounce back to winning ways as soon as possible."

Connacht were duly dispatched 36–10 the following week at Ravenhill and Ulster were back on track. Leinster, in contrast, reverted to losing ways when they went down 33–9 to Munster at Musgrave Park and the Red Army were back on top of the table.

The next pivotal clash of the campaign came in December when Ulster made the trip to Munster knowing defeat would put a serious dent in their title ambitions.

Ulster stormed into a 20–3 half-time lead and despite Munster's spirited second-half fightback, they clung on for a 20–17 victory that ended the home side's 18-game unbeaten run in the competition at Musgrave Park that dated back to 2004.

" Munster played very well in the second half, they came at us hard and it's not easy to come here and get an away win," McCall acknowledged after the match. "To single out any player tonight would be wrong, the team effort was huge and everyone gave everything."

Boxing Day was the date for the return between Ulster and Leinster at Ravenhill but any hopes McCall's side had of avenging their defeat at Donnybrook in October were dashed by second-half tries from Gordon D'Arcy and Girvan Dempsey in a 24–9 win and the return from injury of Brian O'Driscoll. Leinster had done the double over their provincial rivals and Ulster's title challenge was faltering.

"I felt pretty good out there," said O'Driscoll. "It wasn't the quickest game in the world which probably suited me. It's a game that I've been looking forward to and it's great to get it under my belt.

"It's only 30 minutes play so you can't get too far ahead of yourself. It's going to take five or six games to get the match-fitness but hopefully I'll get a bit more pitch-time against Munster at the weekend."

The Ireland captain started the all-important Munster game – played on New Year's Eve – but it was fly-half Felipe Contepomi who proved to be Leinster's match-winner in front of a crowd of 14,155, a new record attendance for a Celtic League match.

The Argentinean number 10 scored 25 points, including two of Leinster's four tries, to beat the league leaders 35–23 which, coupled with Ulster's 22–12 reverse at Connacht, blew the title race wide open.

"We battled back and kept in touch but made mistakes trying things," said Munster skipper Anthony Foley after his side's second defeat in three. "Leinster scored at crucial times and we can't take all the blame for they played a lot of good rugby and defended well when we attacked. It's hard to take because with three minutes to go we're going for the win and suddenly we're conceding a bonus point."

The New Year, however, saw contrasting fortunes for the three Irish challengers.

Leinster suffered defeats at Llanelli and the Dragons in January while Munster were surprisingly beaten at home by Edinburgh in February as both sides began to display nerves. Ulster, in sharp contrast, began to show real title form and embarked an eight-match winning streak – including a 27–3 win over fading Munster in March – that stretched through to May which put them in the driving seat and, more significantly, on top of the Celtic League table. The run was only interrupted by the penultimate game of the campaign at Llanelli – a 12–12 stalemate when a win with a bonus point would have wrapped up the title.

The battle would go down to the final round of matches.

"The title is very much in our hands," said McCall. "We need a victory next week to secure the title and for us to come here and not be beaten was a great effort."

That victory, however, so nearly slipped through Ulster's grasp.

With Leinster playing at Edinburgh and Ulster visiting the Ospreys, both title hopefuls faced potentially perilous away trips on the same day.

But there were to be no scares in the Scottish capital for Leinster thanks to two tries from O'Driscoll and a 16-point haul from Contepomi. The Gunners were dispatched 31–8, the points were in the bag and the destination of the title was now in Ulster's hands.

The first-half against the Ospreys all went according to plan with the vistors' 13–10 up thanks to Matt McCullough's try and David Humphreys two penalties and conversion. The silverware was within touching distance.

It was after the break that things began to go wrong for the Irish. Humphreys added his third penalty but when Jason Spice scored a converted try for the Ospreys with a mere four minutes left, Ulster found themselves trailing 17–16 with the clock running down.

Cue Humphreys, who waited until the 78th minute to try his luck with a long range drop goal that cannoned off both posts before going over. Ulster had won the match 19–17 and the Celtic League title ahead of Leinster by just one point.

"When I struck it, I was turning away – there was a drift in the wind and it started swinging," said Humphreys after his match-winning intervention. "I just stood there saying 'please!' but I knew it was over.

"When Spice scored we knew there was 10 minutes left and they didn't have to work for either of their tries. We just said 'no panic'. We just have to create one more chance.

"And thankfully we did that and then it was just a matter of field position. And thankfully the kick went over. People have asked me how this compares with winning the European Cup in 1999 and it is hard to look back. In sport you have to look forward and enjoy every success for what it is."

Coach McCall added: "It tells you all you need to know about David Humphreys that he bounced back from a couple of kicks he would usually knock over to drop a goal like that to win the game.

"I take my hat off to the players for the effort they have put in all season and for the defence they showed in this game. It is a privilege to be involved with them and they deserve to win this title."

CELTIC LEAGUE RESULTS

September 2: **Llanelli Scarlets** 15 **Edinburgh Gunners** 21, **Munster** 9 **Border Reivers** 7, **Glasgow Warriors** 15 **Dragons** 21. September 3: **Connacht** 13 **Cardiff Blues** 9, **Ospreys** 22 **Leinster** 20. September 9: **Cardiff Blues** 22 **Ulster** 25. September 10: **Edinburgh Gunners** 34 **Connacht** 3, **Leinster** 26 **Glasgow Warriors** 21, **Munster** 37 **Ospreys** 10. September 11: **Border Reivers** 15 **Llanelli Scarlets** 24. September 13: **Ospreys** 15 **Dragons** 9. September 14: **Cardiff Blues** 20 **Llanelli Scarlets** 16. September 16: **Leinster** 33 **Dragons** 14, **Ulster** 30 **Edinburgh Gunners** 23. September 17: **Llanelli Scarlets** 25 **Connacht** 17, **Glasgow Warriors** 32 **Munster** 10. September 18: **Border Reivers** 16 **Ospreys** 6. September 23: **Munster** 14 **Llanelli Scarlets** 13. September 24: **Connacht** 15 **Border Reivers** 17, **Dragons** 19 **Ulster** 22, **Glasgow Warriors** 23 **Cardiff Blues** 28. September 25: **Edinburgh Gunners** 24 **Ospreys** 18.. September 30: **Edinburgh Gunners** 28 **Glasgow Warriors** 12. October 1: **Connacht** 19 **Munster** 44, **Leinster** 30 **Ulster** 23. October 7: **Ulster** 36 **Connacht** 10, **Border Reivers** 23 **Edinburgh Gunners** 11. October 9: **Munster** 33 **Leinster** 9. October 14: **Ospreys** 18 **Connacht** 17, **Edinburgh Gunners** 17 **Dragons** 15. October 15: **Leinster** 34 Cardff Blues 15, **Border Reivers** 0 **Ulster** 27. October 16: **Llanelli Scarlets** 24 **Glasgow Warriors** 20. November 4: **Ulster** 12 **Ospreys** 20, **Cardiff Blues** 16 **Munster** 18, **Glasgow Warriors** 30 **Connacht** 15. November 6: **Leinster** 13 **Edinburgh Gunners** 27, **Dragons** 20 **Border Reivers** 16. December 3: **Connacht** 9 **Leinster** 21, **Munster** 17 **Ulster** 20. December 4: **Glasgow Warriors** 46 **Edinburgh Gunners** 6. December, 22: **Ospreys** 9 **Cardiff Blues** 28. December 23: **Dragons** 16 **Llanelli Scarlets** 28. December 26: **Edinburgh Gunners** 30 **Border Reivers** 25, **Ulster** 19 **Leinster** 24. December 27: **Cardiff Blues** 41 **Dragons** 23, **Munster** 36 **Connacht** 17. December 31: **Leinster** 35 **Munster** 23. **Border Reivers** 24 **Glasgow Warriors** 13, **Connacht** 22 **Ulster** 12. January 1: **Dragons** 24 **Ospreys** 14. January 2: **Llanelli Scarlets** 32 **Cardiff Blues** 13. January 6: **Dragons** 27 **Connacht** 19. January 7: **Ulster** 25 **Glasgow Warriors** 23, **Llanelli Scarlets** 20 **Leinster** 18, **Edinburgh Gunners** 17 **Munster** 18. January 8: **Border Reivers** 26 **Cardiff Blues** 23. January 27: **Cardiff Blues** 9 **Edinburgh Gunners** 13, **Glasgow Warriors** 8 **Ospreys** 22, **Leinster** 62 **Border Reivers** 14, **Ulster** 30 **Llanelli Scarlets** 13. January 28: **Munster** 10 **Dragons** 8. February 17: **Ospreys** 22 **Border Reivers** 18, **Edinburgh Gunners** 23 **Ulster** 31. February 18: **Connacht** 33 **Llanelli Scarlets** 19, **Munster** 20 **Glasgow Warriors** 26, **Dragons** 31 **Leinster** 18. March 3: **Cardiff Blues** 40 **Ospreys** 14, **Glasgow Warriors** 8 **Border Reivers** 20, **Ulster** 27 **Munster** 3. March 5: **Leinster** 16 **Connacht** 13. March 24: **Cardiff Blues** 31 **Glasgow Warriors** 3, **Border Reivers** 9 **Connacht** 11. March 25l: **Ulster** 24 **Dragons** 17. March 26: **Ospreys** 24 **Edinburgh Gunners** 17. March 27: **Llanelli Scarlets** 30 **Ospreys** 17. April 7: **Dragons** 23 **Munster** 17, **Edinburgh Gunners** 10 **Cardiff Blues** 21, **Border Reivers** 34 **Leinster** 35. April 8: **Ospreys** 16 **Glasgow Warriors** 13. April 14: **Leinster** 30 **Llanelli Scarlets** 22. April 15: **Connacht** 15 **Dragons** 10, **Cardiff Blues** 46 **Border Reivers** 11, **Glasgow Warriors** 18 **Ulster** 27, **Munster** 36 **Edinburgh Gunners** 15. April 18: **Ospreys** 25 **Llanelli Scarlets** 13. April 19: **Dragons** 13 **Cardiff Blues** 18. April 22: **Llanelli Scarlets** 36 **Dragons** 17. April 28: **Dragons** 32 **Glasgow Warriors** 18, **Border Reivers** 25 **Munster** 41, **Edinburgh Gunners** 35 **Llanelli Scarlets** 18. April 29: **Cardiff Blues** 30 **Connacht** 12, **Leinster**

38 **Ospreys** 21. May 5: **Connacht** 16 **Edinburgh Gunners** 22, **Ospreys** 27 **Munster** 10, **Ulster** 26 **Cardiff Blues** 17. May 6: **Llanelli Scarlets** 30 **Border Reivers** 26. May 7: **Glasgow Warriors** 18 **Leinster** 21. May 9: **Llanelli Scarlets** 18 **Munster** 6. May 12: **Connacht** 16 **Ospreys** 44, **Glasgow Warriors** 17 **Llanelli Scarlets** 10, **Ulster** 63 **Border Reivers** 17. May 13: **Dragons** 11 **Edinburgh Gunners** 37. May 14: **Cardiff Blues** 40 **Leinster** 31. May 19: **Llanelli Scarlets** 12 **Ulster** 12. May 26: **Connacht** 33 **Glasgow Warriors** 7, **Edinburgh Gunners** 8 **Leinster** 31, **Ospreys** 17 **Ulster** 19, **Border Reivers** 43 **Dragons** 5. May 27: **Munster** 37 **Cardiff Blues** 8.

FINAL TABLE

	P	W	D	L	F	A	BP	Pts
Ulster	22	15	1	4	510	347	5	75
Leinster	22	14	0	6	545	427	10	74
Munster	22	12	0	8	439	372	10	66
Cardiff	22	11	0	9	475	389	11	63
Edinburgh	22	11	0	9	418	415	8	60
Llanelli	22	10	1	9	418	402	7	57
Ospreys	22	11	0	9	381	409	3	55
Dragons	22	7	0	13	355	456	9	45
Borders	22	7	0	13	386	501	8	44
Connacht	22	6	0	14	325	466	5	37
Glasgow	22	5	0	15	371	439	9	37

PACIFIC FIVE NATIONS

ALL BLACKS IN DRIVING SEAT

By Dominic Rumbles

Getty Images

The triumphant Junior All Blacks with their Japanese rivals, following their 38–8 victory in Dunedin.

An international tournament featuring Fiji, Japan, Samoa and Tonga, the Pacific 5 Nations was guaranteed to attract considerable interest in its first season. There were interesting match ups across the four rounds, the inclusion of star names and promising young guns, and the prospect of a double-header to whet the appetite. Yet it was the inclusion of New Zealand's 'B' team, the Junior All Blacks, that was to raise a few eyebrows. With the full Test team taking on summer tourists, the Maori side competing in the Churchill Cup and the Under 21's participating in the IRB Under 21 World Championship, the question remained would the Juniors be able to compete with Test opposition?

The answer was an unequivocal 'yes'. If doubts of their competitiveness hung over the Junior All Blacks before the tournament kicked off then they had certainly vanished midway through the first half of an entertaining encounter in the atmosphere-charged cauldron of the National Stadium in Suva. Twenty Six thousand fans had turned up to

Getty Images

Samoa provided the shock of the tournament, beating Tonga 36–0 in Gosford.

see what was one of the strongest Fiji teams in recent times go head to head with the Junior All Blacks. The juniors, inspired by captain Cory Flynn, secured maximum points to take the match 35–17 seemingly without getting out of second gear.

If the opening match had raised the odd eyebrow, then the second match was to prove no different. Tonga, one of the pre-tournament favourites to be scrapping to avoid bottom place, were about to embark on an outstanding tournament. Under new head coach Adam Leach, the Tongans began their first major march up the IRB Rankings since 2003 (they were to go from 20th to a lofty 16th during the Pacific 5 Nations), with a resounding 57–16 victory away to Japan to top the Round One table. The margin of victory, although impressive considering a lack of recent Test outings, was perhaps only tarred by how disappointing the Japanese were.

Manu Samoa head coach Michael Jones had high hopes that his side might shock the Junior All Blacks at North Harbour Stadium as the Samoans made their tournament bow in Round Two. Instead the former All Black witnessed a drubbing when Samoa fell 56–12 as the Junior All Blacks continued their winning run. Number eight Nick Williams scored a brace and Jimmy Gopperth hinted at what was to come, scoring 26 points on debut, including a fine try. Samoa, buoyed by the return of a number of Test stars and success of Savai'i Samoa at the recent IRB Pacific Rugby Cup, were simply outgunned. The match of the round though was an epic between Tonga and Fiji, which the Tongans narrowly won. Trailing 17–23 with just five minutes left on the clock, the home side rallied to send replacement Aleki Lutui over for a score out wide. Pierre Hola's conversion sealed the victory.

The Round Two results effectively set up the Junior All Blacks v Tonga in the first double-header match in New Plymouth as the Pacific 5 Nations decider despite there being three rounds to come. It was evident that Tonga, on a high after back to back victories, would be the only team capable of challenging the dominant Kiwis, but Adam Leach's side were disappointing on the day as the New Zealanders cruised to the title. Rising star Gopperth was again on song, scoring 21 points, including two tries as the Kiwis ran out comfortable 38–10 winners. In the weekend's other match, Samoa, still reeling from the opening round loss, rallied to defeat Japan 53–9, scoring eight tries in the process. It was a crushing defeat for a young home grown Japan side, who without the record-breaking Daisuke Ohata lacked a cutting edge behind a workman pack.

The mood in the Japan camp improved considerably when they travelled to Dunedin for the Round Four match against the all-conquering Junior All Blacks. The result, a 38–8 victory for Cory Flynn's side, combined with Samoa's defeat to Fiji, confirmed the Junior All Blacks as inaugural IRB Pacific 5 Nations, but it was Japan's vast improvement that caught the eye as pride and passion returned to their performance. Wataru Ikeda's try was just reward for a battling effort which renewed hope that they would be able to sign off the competition with a victory.

Samoa, the only side able to threaten the Junior All Blacks' seemingly inevitable champion status, encountered a determined Fiji side in a remarkable match at a packed National Stadium. Comfortably leading 17–5, and on course for a their first victory in the tournament, Wayne Pivac's Fiji had talisman flanker Mosese Luveitasau sent off after just 27 minutes following a brawl with Seilala Mapusa. The game was turned on its head. Samoa launched wave upon wave of attacks and Eliota Fuimaono-Sapolu's try shortly after the interval reduced the deficit to just two points. However, despite exerting phenomenal pressure, Samoa could not break the back of spirited 14-man Fiji and the home side held on for a deserved 23–20 victory to finally get their campaign up and running.

The final round was played out without the Junior All Blacks who, having played all their fixtures, had already claimed the title and so it was down to Fiji, Samoa and Tonga to play for best of the Pacific nations, while Japan wanted some pride. Samoa and Fiji signed off in style with Samoa providing the shock of the tournament, defeating Tonga 36–0 in Gosford, to claim the coveted 'best of the rest' prize. The manner of the defeat though must have rankled Leach and his Tonga side, who had made considerable progress during the tournament. The final match of the competition was played in Osaka where Fiji were pushed all the way by a much improved Japan side. The 29–15 victory brought down the curtain on the inaugural competition and elevated Fiji above Tonga and into third in the final standings. It was indeed a satisfactory conclusion to the tournament for Pivac's side who have shown steady improvements as they build towards RWC 2007.

The tournament made a successful introduction onto the world rugby calendar. It achieved all that the IRB had intended it to do, providing increased test level competition for the Pacific Nations, while also producing thrilling matches along the way. However, it was the inclusion of a number of locally-produced players who broke through on to the Test arena in the competition, which pleased the IRB. Rugby in the Pacific is very much alive and kicking.

IRB PACIFIC 5 NATIONS FINAL STANDINGS

	P	W	PD	BP	Pts
Junior All Blacks	4	4	120	4	20
Samoa	4	2	38	3	11
Fiji	4	2	–2	2	10
Tonga	4	2	–22	1	9
Japan	4	0	–129	0	0

LEADING SCORERS		
James Gopperth	JAB	47
Seremaia Baikeinuku	FJI	40
Cameron McIntyre	JAB	32
Pierre Hola	Tonga	31
Anthony Tuitavake	JAB	20
Loki Crichton	Samoa	16
John Senio	Samoa	15
Anitele'a Tuilagi	Samoa	15
Nick Williams	JAB	15

Getty Images

The trophy is in the safe hands of Junior All Blacks captain Cory Flynn.

PACIFIC NATIONS CUP

SAMOA BREAK NEW GROUND

By Dominic Rumbles

The first of the IRB's new Tournaments to be played in 2006, the Pacific Rugby Cup made an entertaining debut on the international Rugby calendar as the competition went right down to the wire with Savai'i Samoa crowned inaugural winners after defeating Fiji Warriors in a tense, but exciting Grand Final in Apia.

The competition, which kick-started an unprecedented amount of international rugby from May through to July, was just one element of the IRB's US$50 million global strategic investment programme that was launched in August 2005 and is the first of its kind in the Pacific.

Six new teams were created; Fiji Barbarians, Fiji Warriors, Upolu Samoa, Savai'i Samoa and Tau'uta Reds and Tautahi Gold from Tonga. Each team comprising 30 locally-based players and each designed to provide the national team coaching staff with the opportunity to see their players in action at a level that bridged the gap between domestic rugby and the IRB Pacific 5 Nations.

"The Pacific Rugby Cup provides an opportunity for more local players to experience competitive Rugby on the Islands," explained Manu Samoa's head coach Michael Jones before the tournament. "As coaches we now have a clear development pathway in place for locally based players to progress into the test team – it is an exciting development."

If the legendary former All Black was excited before the Pacific Rugby Cup kicked off, he had plenty to smile about after its completion. Not only did his Savai'i side claim the title after defeating Fiji Warriors in the final, but the competition also proved successful as a selection tool with a strong number of players going on to play test Rugby during the Pacific 5 Nations.

Across the board The Pacific Rugby Cup was typical Pacific Rugby, tough and uncompromising with a liberal dose of attacking flair, producing competitive encounters throughout the competition's five rounds. Round One set the tone with three close encounters played in front of strong crowds across the islands.

The competition made its debut with wins for Tautahi Gold, Fiji Warriors and Savai'i Samoa, ensuring that the honours were spread evenly over the three nations. In the all-Fijian affair in Nasori, Fiji Warriors defeated Fiji Barbarians 22–14 to head the Round One standings. Savai'i Samoa defeated Tau'uta Reds 18–13 away from home to open strongly, while Upolu Samoa edged out Tautahi Gold 20–18 to ensure that Tonga had a winning representative on the opening day.

By Round Two it was apparent that Savai'i Samoa would be the team to beat. Despite playing in front of nearly 4000 vociferous fans at an atmosphere-charged Teufaiva Stadium, Savai'i withstood a strong second half comeback to prevail 26–13 to move to the top of the standings as the competition's only undefeated side. While Savaii scraped through, Fiji Warriors did not fair so well. In heavy conditions the Warriors laboured to an 8–8 draw with Upolu Samoa. Replacement full-back Emosi Vucagn scored a dramatic last minute try to secure a share of the points for the Warriors. The third match of the weekend was no less competitive. Tonga's Tau'uta Reds edged out Fiji Barbarians 17–14 to secure its first win of the competition.

If the Warriors laboured against Upolu Samoa, they bounced back in style in Round Three to defeat Tautahi Gold 32–16 in Nasori. Mosese Luveitasau was the stand out performer for the Warriors, scoring two tries in a bonus-point victory ensuring that the Warriors maintained their 100% record in the competition. The result lifted the Warriors to the top of the table owing to Savai'i's shock defeat against bottom side Fiji Barbarians. The Barbarians, who defended superbly, held on for a 14–13 victory to claim their first points of the competition. The third match of the round was no less tense. Upolu Samoa came from behind against Tau'uta Reds to secure a 20–19 victory that lifted the Samoan side to third in the standings. Trailing 12–3 late in the first half, the home side rallied to score three second half tries to take the points.

Round Four saw normal service resumed for Savai'i as the Samoan side defeated Fiji Warriors 27–21 in an entertaining match to place themselves in pole position to secure a place in the final with one round remaining. The Samoans, who out-muscled their opponents in the scrums, had to withstand a late fightback from the Fijians, who managed to secure a valuable losing bonus point with the last play of the game when the visitors were awarded a penalty try. Fiji Barbarians, buoyed by their victory in the previous round, continued to show impressive signs of improvement, defeating Upolu Samoa 30–15 to move up to third in the table with a bonus-point victory. In the all-Tongan affair Tau'uta Reds' emerged from a tense encounter to defeat Tautahi Gold 13–8 to keep their chances of qualifying for the final alive.

The final round of action, played in front of good crowds finished with both Savai'i and the Warriors qualifying for the Grand Final. Savai'i, who did not play until the following day, were assured a place in the final after Fiji Barbarians could only muster a 5–5 draw against Tautahi Gold ending the Fijian side's slim hopes of making the final. The result meant that Savai'i could not be overhauled, but the question was whether it would be the Samoan side or the Fijian side that would finish as top seeds and secure vital home advantage for the Grand Final the following week. Fiji Warriors, who still needed a victory to make the final, made easy work of despatching Tau'uta Reds 29–8, securing a bonus point to put pressure on Savai'i. However, the Samoan side who had been consistent throughout gained a bonus point against Upolu Samoa to claim the top spot.

The scene was set for a thrilling final at the Marist Ground. Savai'i, who averaged 24 points per match over the five rounds, possessed the best pack in the competition, but Fiji Warriors possessed the dangerous strike runners. A low scoring final was won by Savai'i 10–5, but the score did not do the match justice. In monsoon conditions the standard of rugby was exceptional. Both sides defended outstandingly, but it was Savai'i's superior forward dominance that saw the home side to victory to lift the inaugural trophy.

The full effect of the Pacific Rugby Cup was felt long after the final whistle had sounded at the Marist Ground. Several players progressed from the competition to compete in the IRB Pacific 5 Nations, proving the value of the competition in preparing locally based players on the islands for Test rugby, while burgeoning attendances, competitive matches and increased standards ensured that the Pacific Rugby Cup will play an important part in the rugby calendar for Fiji, Samoa and Tonga for years to come.

20 May, 2006

PACIFIC RUGBY CUP FINAL, AT MARIST GROUNDS, APIA

SAVAI'I SAMOA: Alesana Laumea; Tauvaga Faafou, Henry Bryce, Pati Fetuai, Esera Lauina; Rambo Tavana (Key Anufe 63), Ioane Evalu; Jake Grey, Villiamu Villiamu (Lafoga Aoelua 61), Rudy Levasa, Luti Pese, Lale Latu, Ulia Ulia (Manaia Salavea 80), Iosefa Taina (Filisoa Faaiu 45), Egelani Fale.

NOT USED: Robert Johnstone, Gafa Siona, Mika Viane.

TRY – Henry Bryce. **CON** – Rambo Tavana. **PEN** – Rambo Tavana.

FIJI WARRIORS: Norman Ligairi; Napolioni Vonawale, Kameli Ratuvou, Julian Vulakoro (Tevita Latianara 80), Mosese Luveitasau; Josevata Tora, Emosi Vucago (Aporosa Vata 80); Apisai Nagi, Sunia Koto (capt) (Maciu Vakaruru 80), Apisai Turukawa (Sikeli Gavidi 68), Isoa Domolailal, Jone Qovu (Wame Lewaravu 69), Kini Salabogi, Akapusi Qera, Sisa Koyamaibole (Etonia Naba 80).

NOT USED: Jiuta Lutumailagi.

TRY – Kiniviliame Salabogi.

REFEREE: Eva Mafi (Tonga).

TOUCHJUDGES: Siaola Tangifua (Tonga) and Peter Ah Kuoi (Samoa).

IRB NATIONS CUP

PUMAS HERALD NEW DAWN

By Dominic Rumbles

IRB

Argentina A are the first side to celebrate winning the IRB Nations Cup.

While the Pacific 5 Nations, North America 4 and Pacific Rugby Cup were aimed at providing greater clarity in terms of the amount of Test rugby for Tier 2 sides and also completing a clear pathway for player development from club or provincial to Test level, the IRB Nations Cup made its bow in order to provide certainty for Tier 1 A sides as well as a higher level of competitive Test level Rugby for Tier 3 Unions.

Over the past couple of years Tier 1 A side fixtures had been on the decline as Unions looked to cost saving. However, the introduction of

Portugal made Argentina A work hard for their final win, before doing down 19–24.

the IRB Nations Cup alongside an expanded Barclays Churchill Cup and the Junior All Blacks inclusion in the new Pacific 5 Nations, reversed that trend in emphatic fashion in 2006.

Round One at the impressive University of Lisbon Stadium was played in front of an encouraging crowd of over 1500 despite it being a public holiday in Portugal. While the majority of the home support, whether out of curiosity or genuine rugby interest, were awaiting game two between the home side and Russia, the opening game of the tournament was to be the most significant in terms of where the eventual silverware would be going.

On paper Argentina A, containing a sprinkling of international calibre players like Pablo Cardinali, Hernan Senillosa and Bernardo Stortoni, were comfortable 26–11 winners, scoring four tries and enjoying the better of the physical exchanges against Italy A. However, in truth Patricio Noreiga's outfit were made to work extremely hard for their victory by an Italian side that despite gaining plentiful possession, lacked the finishing edge of their opponents.

Argentina A relied on strength in the set piece to dominate and established a 12–6 lead at the interval following tries by Saracens bound Tomas De Vedia and Hernan Senillosa, but Italy A fought back after the break scoring through impressive scrum half Pietro Travagli to pull his side within a point. However, Italy A's inability to punish their opponents let Argentina A off the hook as they rallied to score two late tries to take the spoils.

The second match was no less entertaining. Eagerly awaited, a vociferous Lisbon support were expecting their side to get off to a winning start. After all Portugal had finished above Russia in the FIRA-AER Nations Cup. However, nobody had told the Russians to stick to the script. Russia, a Union identified by the IRB for additional funding, are a team on the move, and it showed against Portugal as the visitors scored five tries on the way to an emphatic 37–17 victory.

Round Two pitted the two undefeated sides together, while Portugal and Italy A were looking to restore some pride after Round One disappointment. In the event Argentina A's superior firepower and experience up front was to be the difference as the 64–6 victory over Russia all but assured a top place finish in the IRB Nations Cup with one round to be played.

Argentina A did not have it all their own way. Indeed Noreiga's side only led 22–6 at the interval as a spirited Russia side caused their opponents a number of problems at the breakdown. However, Russian legs tired after the interval and Argentina A scored five tries as Juan Gauthier completed a hat-trick of scores to complete the victory.

Portugal responded to the Round One shock defeat in style, completing an impressive 26–26 draw against Italy A. Indeed, it really should have been maximum points for the hosts who established a 26–9 advantage deep in the second half and were good value for their lead. Live on Portuguese television, it looked as though Portugal would record a remarkable victory, but Italy A rallied and made the most of their superior fitness as Luciano Orquera scored two tries deep in injury time to spare his side's blushes.

The final round saw Argentina A predictably crowned inaugural IRB Nations Cup champions, but rather unpredictably were subjected to enormous pressure by a much improved Portugal side. In the competition's most competitive round of matches Argentina A nosed past Portugal 24–19, while Italy A made hard work of overcoming Russia 32–29.

Leading 22–10 at the interval, Italy A appeared to be in complete control of the match, but Russia nearly pulled off a remarkable victory, scoring three second half tries to leave the Italians hanging on at the end.

Despite finishing bottom of the pile, Portugal produced the performance of the Tournament to hold Argentina A to a 24–19 victory. Roared on by the Lisbon support, Portugal established a deserved 16–6 half time lead as the impressive Goncarlo Malheiro scored a wonderful try. However, Argentina once again displayed great composure to score 13 points without reply to seal the victory.

Indeed the competitiveness of the final round of matches proved the worth of the IRB Nations Cup on the global Rugby calendar. It had comprehensively set out its objective of providing a high level of competition for both the A sides and the Tier 3 Test sides, while also helping to foster the increasing popularity of the Game in Portugal. Indeed as a result of the success of the inaugural Tournament, the IRB is already considering the possibility of including more A sides in the 2007 Tournament.

IRB NATIONS CUP FINAL STANDINGS

	P	W	D	L	PF	PA	PD	BP	PTS
1 ARGENTINA A	3	3	0	0	114	36	78	2	14
2 ITALY A	3	1	1	1	69	81	-12	1	7
3 RUSSIA	3	1	0	2	72	113	-45	3	7
4 PORTUGAL	3	0	1	2	62	87	-25	1	4

IRB Nations Cup Results	
Argentina A 26	**Italy A** 11
Portugal 17	**Russia** 37
Portugal 26	**Italy A** 26
Argentina A 64	**Russia** 6
Italy A 32	**Russia** 29
Portugal 19	**Argentina A** 25

WEST MAKE HISTORY

By Dominic Rumbles

IRB

Eric Wilson's Canada West were the first champions of the IRB North America 4 competition.

The inaugural International Rugby Board North America 4 competition made a successful debut with Canada West taking the spoils defeating US Falcons 31–22 in an entertaining Grand Final in Ohio.

The competition, a key element of the IRB's US$ 50 million global strategic investment programme, was introduced to provide locally based players in Canada and USA with the opportunity to showcase their talents in a high-intensity, cross-border competition. It was also geared towards providing the two Unions with a clear development pathway for players from club rugby through to the full test arena.

On both counts the competition did not disappoint. Right from the outset, it was clear that the North America 4 was going to be a valuable and important addition to the rugby calendar. While it unearthed a whole host of home-grown talent over the course of the five competition rounds, it also provided the national coaches with selection headaches when preparing for the Barclays Churchill Cup and important Rugby World Cup 2007 qualifying matches.

The narrow gap between the two nations in the IRB Rankings (Canada and USA were separated by just one place heading in to the competition), suggested that the action would be tight. However, it was clear from round one that out of the newly formed teams, Canada East, Canada West, US Falcons and US Hawks, the balance of experienced players had been tilted towards just two teams – Canada West and US Falcons.

The opening round of the competition threw up few surprises. The US Falcons were comfortable 29–14 winners over Canada East, while West, comprising mainly players from Canada's hot-bed of rugby in the Vancouver region, started ominously, handing out a 98–0 humiliation to US Hawks in round one in a match that yielded four tries for flanker Adam Kleeberger.

While there may have been some early concerns about the rather one-sided rugby in the competition's infancy stages, there were no such concerns about the appeal of the tournament as the Canadian Rugby public turned out in strong numbers to watch the opening three rounds with 1500 witnessing the round two clash between Canada East and Canada West. In an exciting match, which East led from kick-off, West eventually salvaged a draw at the death as Geoff Warden's try, converted by the impressive Ed Fairhurst, saved the Canadian side's blushes. The Falcons though could not capitalise on West's dropped points and were rather unpredictably well beaten 33–22 by round one whipping boys the US Hawks. The competition was now up and running.

The final match of the Canada leg saw the home sides prevail with Canada East defeating US Hawks 34–11 and Canada West returning to winning ways to top the standings with a close-fought 25–24 victory over US Falcons. West, leading 22–14 at the interval, looked to be in control of the match, but the Falcons hit back scoring a try deep in injury time through hooker Patrick Bell and had Enrico Ferri kicked the resulting conversion the Falcons would have recorded notable victories over both the Canadian sides.

Following a month break for the Barclays Churchill Cup and Rugby World Cup qualifiers against Barbados, the IRB North America 4 resumed in July with Canada West looking to become the first side to book a place in the final. Their opponents US Hawks may have been the most-improved outfit of the opening leg, but they provided little resistance against a strong West side that ran in eight tries to book a place in the final with a resounding 46–7 victory. In the round's other match, US Falcons maintained their quest for a final spot, but left it late with a narrow 25–24 victory over Canada East in a match that was decided by the sin-binning of Carl Pocock late in the game.

West, having already qualified for the Grand Final and resting key players, made 15 changes to the starting lineup for the round five match against Canada East and it was therefore no surprise that they were comfortably defeated 34–18 in a rather one-sided encounter. The second match was much more competitive. Requiring at least a point to progress to the final, US Falcons had to come from behind to seal the all important victory. Trailing 17–14 at half time against a determined US Hawks outfit, the Falcons rallied to score 31 points without reply in the second half to win 45–17.

The lineup for the final could not have been better for the competition's organisers, pitting Canada West against USA Falcons in a match that took on additional significance ahead of the decisive Rugby World Cup qualifier between Canada and USA in St. Johns a month later.

Finals Day proved to be a spectacle for both players and supporters alike. The impressive Ohio State University provided the backdrop for the back to back matches which commenced with the consolation final between Canada East and USA Hawks. The match, which East comfortably won 34–18, was to be a sign of what was to come in the Grand Final with Canada taking the spoils. East's fly half Derek Daypuck was crucial in his side's victory scoring a try on his way to finishing as the competition's top points scorer with 78 points. However, the match also highlighted how far the Hawks had progressed since their 98–0 drubbing at the hands of Canada West in the opening round, highlighting the undoubted value of the competition as a development tool

In the main event West, the favourites, looked to be running away with the final after establishing a 21–3 lead early in the second half, but a dogged Falcons side came right back into the game with tries in rapid succession from Jason Pye and Mark Aylor to cut the deficit to 24–13 to set up a rousing finale. However, an experienced West side rallied to set up Akio Tyler for his hat-trick try to seal a memorable victory.

While West celebrated a deserved victory, the IRB were understandably happy with what was a highly competitive event that had also served to capture the imagination of the North American Rugby public. The tournament had fulfilled its objective of providing locally-based players with the platform to advance their own Test credentials, and the national team coaches were quick to underline the importance of the tournament in relation to the development of national sides.

"This was an incredibly successful North America 4 competition, said USA Interim Men's National Head Coach Peter Thorburn. "It clearly defined the steps that USA Rugby needs to take next and identified some very good, young, prospects for future national team sides."

"It goes without saying that the North America 4 and Churchill Cup are both a huge benefit. They are invaluable. Without both it would have been nearly impossible to put a competitive squad together and create an atmosphere of inclusiveness in American rugby, which is key."

"We receive queries almost daily from players both in the U.S. and those based overseas wanting to know the process for breaking into the national squad. Now, with the addition of the North America 4 we can say that there is a clear pathway from club rugby through to the national side."

IRB NORTH AMERICA 4 RESULTS

ROUND ONE	
20th May, Rotary Stadium, Abbotsford	**US Falcons** 29, **Canada East** 14
Canada West 98, **USA Hawks** 0	
ROUND TWO	
24th May, Thunderbird Stadium, Vancouver,	**US Hawks** 33, **US Falcons** 22
Canada West 28 vs. **Canada East** 28	
ROUND THREE	
27th May, Centennial Stadium, Victoria,	**Canada East** 34 vs. **USA Hawks** 11
Canada West 25 vs. **USA Falcons** 24	
ROUND FOUR	
26th July, Fred Beekman Park, Columbus, Ohio, United States	**Canada East** 34, **Canada West** 18
USA Falcons 45, **USA Hawks** 17	
ROUND FIVE	
29 July, Fred Beekman Park, Columbus, Ohio,	Third Place Play off
Canada East 34, **USA Hawks** 18	

NORTH AMERICA 4 FINAL

29 July, Fred Beekman Park, Columbus, Ohio,

CANADA WEST 31 (3G, 2T)
USA FALCONS 22 (2G, 1P, 1T)

CANADA WEST: P Dessaulles, M Lawson, G Cooke (Franklin@47), S Hunter, T Hotson, N Meechan, A Kleeberger, M Jones, E Fairhurst (capt), D Spicer, B Henderson, C Baumberg, A Tyler, T LaCarte, DTH Van der Merwe. *Substitutions*: G Warden for D Spicer (40 mins) S Franklin for G Cooke (47 mins), I Smortchevsky (51 mins), D Biddle for M Jones (56 mins), D Hall for T Hotson (64 mins), H Buydens for C Baumberg (78 mins)

SCORERS *Tries*: Van der Merwe (2), La Carte, Cooke, Tyler. *Conversions:* Fairhurst (2), Baumberg

USA FALCONS: J Vitale, P Bell (capt.), J Tarpoff, H Mexted, A Parker, R Rosser (Rader@68), J Albury, M Aylor, 9. K Kjar, A Locke, S Jones, V Esikia, A Osbourne, B Barnard, J Pye.: *Substitutions:* S Erkine for K Kjar(40 mins), (A Tuilevuka for S Jones 47 mins), B Schoener for H Mexted (50 mins), M Radar for R Rosser (68 mins):

SCORERS *Tries:* Pye, Aylor, Erskine. *Conversions:* Bell, Tuilevuka. *Penalty Goal*: Bell;

REFEREE Phil Smith, Canada

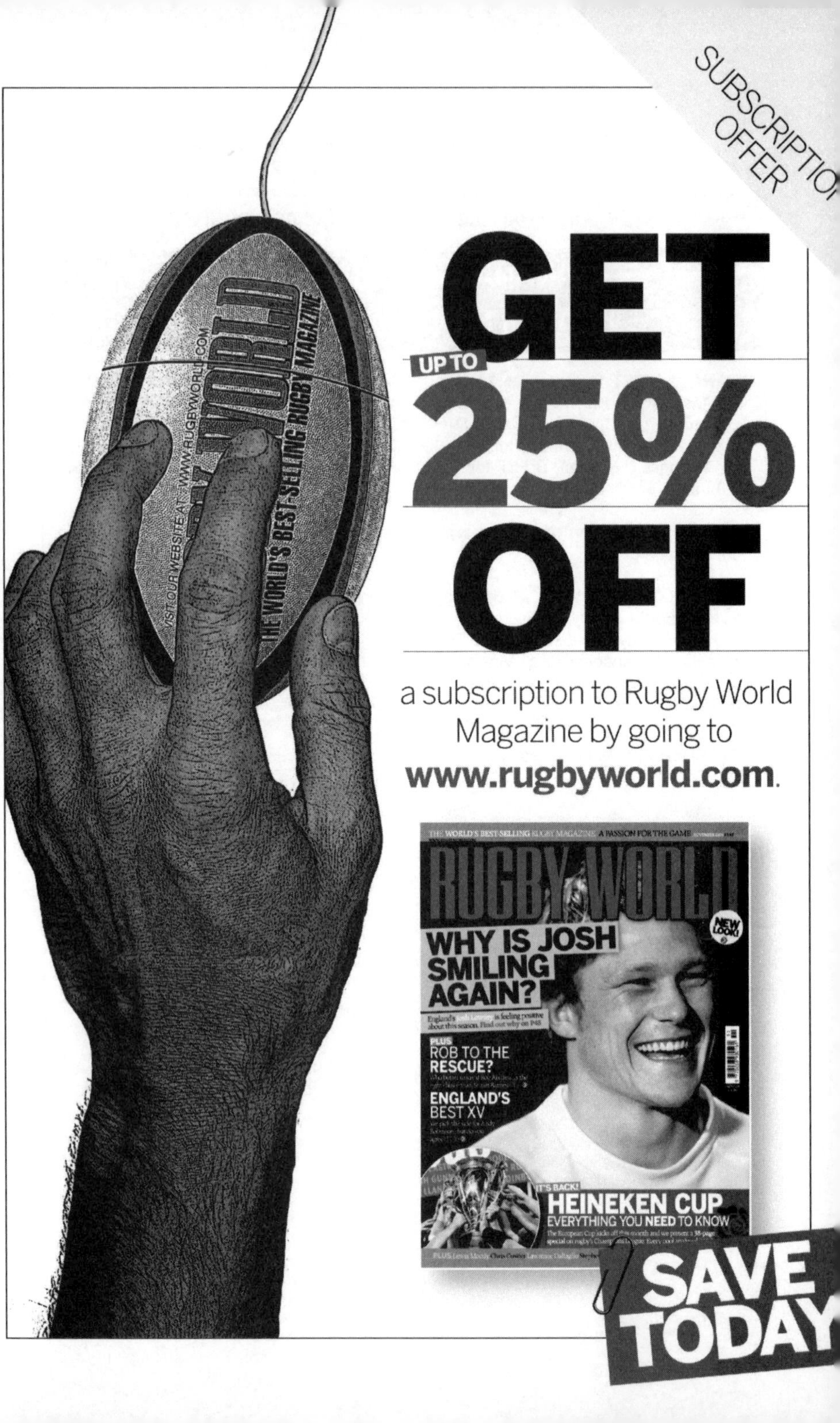
SUBSCRIPTION OFFER
GET
UP TO
25%
OFF
a subscription to Rugby World Magazine by going to
www.rugbyworld.com.
VISIT OUR WEBSITE AT WWW.RUGBYWORLD.COM
RUGBY WORLD
THE WORLD'S BEST-SELLING RUGBY MAGAZINE
RUGBY WORLD
NEW LOOK!
WHY IS JOSH SMILING AGAIN?
PLUS
ROB TO THE RESCUE?
ENGLAND'S BEST XV
IT'S BACK!
HEINEKEN CUP
EVERYTHING YOU NEED TO KNOW
SAVE TODAY

REFEREES

NEW AGE FOR WHISTLE-BLOWERS

By Greg Thomas

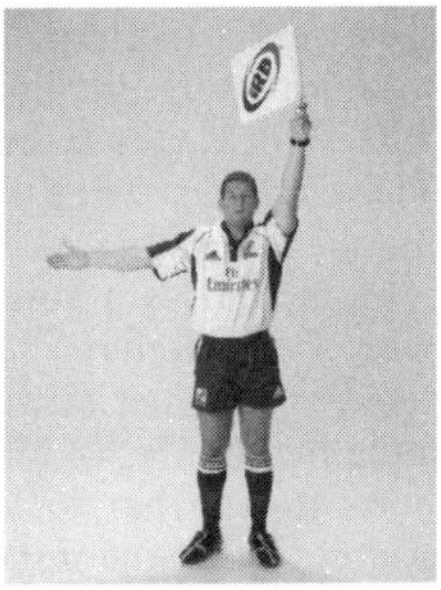

The IRB is currently in the process of examining every law of the game and even trying some experimental law variations.

IRB Referee Manager Paddy O'Brien is part of the Law Project Group who are trialling a number of the variations at Stellenbosch University. The aims of the group are: to determine if the laws can be simplified to assist coach, player, referees and spectators; to reduce the subjectivity of refereeing; and to provide an environment where players and coaches determine the outcome of matches.

"The role of Referee Manager primarily encompasses the management and implementation of the referee programme for international rugby," said O'Brien, who refereed 36 Test matches over a 10-year career that started in 1995, with the Scotland v England game.

"A major part of this work is the management of the elite referee panel that until April 2006 comprised of A, B and C panels. Presently this has been streamlined to an elite panel of 20 referees from around the world. There is also a second panel of 15 referees from which touch judge appointments and television match officials are made. All match appointments for Tier 1 and 2 Test matches are made from these panels."

Until 1996 a rota system was employed for match appointments but today this has changed to a merit-based system that ensures the best referees are refereeing the top matches.

The merit-based selection process is managed by O'Brien via The IRB Referee Selection Committee that comprises four selectors – Steve Hilditch (Ireland), Michelle Lamoulie (France), Dick Byers (Australia), Bob Francis (New Zealand), a Chairman – Council Member David Pickering and Kevin Bowring (RFU), a former Wales coach, who represents the coaching viewpoint at selection.

"All referees are assessed when they take the field for a Test match," explained O'Brien. "Until recently this was done by numerous referee assessors appointed from unions around the world. From November this year the four selectors - all former international referees - will attend (on rotation) all Tier 1 and 2 Tests and Under-19 and Under-21 World Championships matches to watch and report on referee performance.

"At the annual April meeting appointments are made for the June test window and the Tri-Nations, while in November appointments are made for the November Test window and the Six Nations. At these meetings the selectors have at their disposal via the referee database full reports on each referee, including match performance assessments, coach feedback fitness reports and non-compliance issues – areas of a referees' potential weakness areas, e.g., tackle area, lineout or scrum."

Collation of all referee reports from international matches – from coaches (who provide feedback via referee performance forms after each Test) and performance reviewers – is a crucial to the selection process.

Another recent innovation is the decision to appoint just 12 referees for the 2007 World Cup to ensure greater consistency and uniformity of decision-making. These referees will take control of more games and will take the field for a similar number of games as the players over the seven-week tournament.

"As well as a constant dialogue with the referees I also have regular contact with Tier 1 Referee Managers," said O'Brien. "Every year in London all the elite referees together with the managers attend a conference to review the refereeing 'aide memoir' – an interpretation document for referees of the Laws, e.g. the Law book states what constitutes a scrum and how it should form, etc, but the memoir sets out what the mind set of the referee should be at scrum time and what needs to be monitored. This document is reviewed each year at the conference."

An important consideration for the IRB Referee Manager is the area of succession planning to ensure there is a process by which referees are given the necessary training and experience so that they can progress to the elite referee panel. The IRB Sevens World Series and Under-19 and Under-21 World Championships are the perfect training ground and emerging referees are selected for such tournaments and assessed. This process has already assisted in identifying up and coming talent. One of the present aims is to identify suitable referees at this stage of their career that will allow their development and training for the 2011 and 2015 RWC."

Talent identification is not restricted to the senior unions either. For the 2006-07 IRB Sevens World Series a Portuguese, a Japanese and a Tongan referee have all been selected as core referees for the eight tournament series. Such tournaments are now played in front of crowds exceeding 30,000 and provide developing referees with invaluable experience in environments that are commonplace at the elite level.

The continued development of technology as already seen television match officials become the norm at senior level and technology also plays a part in the development of coaching and playing methods. Coaches spend hours pouring over videos and devising new tactics. Referees have to be aware of such changes and be ready. A good example is the lineout which for many years was largely uncontested. Now they are hotly contested and referees have to be trained to deal with this major-contest area. Keeping an eye on such changes is therefore vital and the IRB game analysis team work with O'Brien in this area.

The judiciary process is another facet of a referee's responsibilities. "I have a duty of care to ensure all international referees fully understand the citing and judiciary procedures that may be implemented following matches," said O'Brien. "Referees are often called to appear at post-match hearings and after every match they have to complete a match report which becomes an important document for any subsequent usage. There is also an important monitoring process as part of this that ensures all stakeholders conform to the relevant laws and appropriate sanctions are applied in terms of dangerous and foul play."

INTERNATIONAL REFEREES

DISMISSALS IN MAJOR INTERNATIONAL MATCHES

Up to 30 September 2006 in major international matches. These cover all matches for which the eight senior members of the International Board have awarded caps, and also all matches played in Rugby World Cup final stages.

A E Freethy	sent off	C J Brownlie (NZ)	E v NZ	1925
K D Kelleher	sent off	C E Meads (NZ)	S v NZ	1967
R T Burnett	sent off	M A Burton (E)	A v E	1975
W M Cooney	sent off	J Sovau (Fj)	A v Fj	1976
N R Sanson	sent off	G A D Wheel (W)	W v I	1977
N R Sanson	sent off	W P Duggan (I)	W v I	1977
D I H Burnett	sent off	P Ringer (W)	E v W	1980
C Norling	sent off	J-P Garuet (F)	F v I	1984
K V J Fitzgerald	sent off	H D Richards (W)	NZ v W	*1987
F A Howard	sent off	D Codey (A)	A v W	*1987
K V J Fitzgerald	sent off	M Taga (Fj)	Fj v E	1988
O E Doyle	sent off	A Lorieux (F)	Arg v F	1988
B W Stirling	sent off	T Vonolagi (Fj)	E v Fj	1989
B W Stirling	sent off	N Nadruku (Fj)	E v Fj	1989
F A Howard	sent off	K Moseley (W)	W v F	1990
F A Howard	sent off	A Carminati (F)	S v F	1990
F A Howard	sent off	A Stoop (Nm)	Nm v W	1990
A J Spreadbury	sent off	A Benazzi (F)	A v F	1990
C Norling	sent off	P Gallart (F)	A v F	1990
C J Hawke	sent off	F E Mendez (Arg)	E v Arg	1990
E F Morrison	sent off	C Cojocariu (R)	R v F	1991
J M Fleming	sent off	P L Sporleder (Arg)	WS v Arg	*1991
J M Fleming	sent off	M G Keenan (WS)	WS v Arg	*1991
S R Hilditch	sent off	G Lascubé (F)	F v E	1992
S R Hilditch	sent off	V Moscato (F)	F v E	1992
D J Bishop	sent off	O Roumat (Wld)	NZ v Wld	1992
E F Morrison	sent off	J T Small (SA)	A v SA	1993
I Rogers	sent off	M E Cardinal (C)	C v F	1994
I Rogers	sent off	P Sella (F)	C v F	1994
D Mené	sent off	J D Davies (W)	W v E	1995
S Lander	sent off	F Mahoni (Tg)	F v Tg	*1995
D T M McHugh	sent off	J Dalton (SA)	SA v C	*1995
D T M McHugh	sent off	R G A Snow (C)	SA v C	*1995
D T M McHugh	sent off	G L Rees (C)	SA v C	*1995
J Dumé	sent off	G R Jenkins (W)	SA v W	1995
W J Erickson	sent off	V B Cavubati (Fj)	NZ v Fj	1997
W D Bevan	sent off	A G Venter (SA)	NZ v SA	1997
C Giacomel	sent off	R Travaglini (Arg)	F v Arg	1997

REFEREES

W J Erickson	sent off	D J Grewcock (E)	NZ v E	1998
S R Walsh	sent off	J Sitoa (Tg)	A v Tg	1998
R G Davies	sent off	M Giovanelli (It)	S v It	1999
C Thomas	sent off	T Leota (Sm)	Sm v F	1999
C Thomas	sent off	G Leaupepe (Sm)	Sm v F	1999
S Dickinson	sent off	J-J Crenca (F)	NZ v F	1999
E F Morrison	sent off	M Vunibaka (Fj)	Fj v C	*1999
A Cole	sent off	D R Baugh (C)	C v Nm	*1999
W J Erickson	sent off	N Ta'ufo'ou (Tg)	E v Tg	*1999
P Marshall	sent off	B D Venter (SA)	SA v U	*1999
P C Deluca	sent off	W Cristofoletto (It)	F v It	2000
J I Kaplan	sent off	A Troncon (It)	It v I	2001
R Dickson	sent off	G Leger (Tg)	W v Tg	2001
P C Deluca	sent off	N J Hines (S)	US v S	2002
P D O'Brien	sent off	M C Joubert (SA)	SA v A	2002
P D O'Brien	sent off	J J Labuschagne (SA)	E v SA	2002
S R Walsh	sent off	V Ma'asi (Tg)	Tg v I	2003
N Williams	sent off	S D Shaw (E)	NZ v E	2004
S J Dickinson	sent off	P C Montgomery (SA)	W v SA	2005
S M Lawrence	sent off	L W Moody (E)	E v Sm	2005
S M Lawrence	sent off	A Tuilagi (Sm)	E v Sm	2005
S R Walsh	sent off	S Murray (S)	W v S	2006

* Matches in World Cup final stages

THE DIRECTORY

UNIONS IN MEMBERSHIP OF THE IRB

ANDORRA - FEDERACIÓ ANDORRANA DE RUGBY
Region: FIRA-AER
Founded: 1986
IRB Member: 1991
www.**vpcrugby**.org
Phone: +37 682 2232
FAX: +376864564
Add: Baixada del Moli
No.31 Casal de L'Esport del MICG, Andorra La Vella
AD 500, ANDORRA

ARABIAN GULF - ARABIAN GULF R.F.U.
Region: ARFU
Founded: 1984
IRB Member: 1990
www.**agrfu**.com
Phone: +971 434 52677
FAX: +971 434 52688
PO Box 65785
Office 2066, Dune centre
Al Diyafa Street, Satwa, Dubai
United Arab Emirates
ARABIAN GULF

ARGENTINA - UNION ARGENTINA DE RUGBY
Region: CONSUR
Founded: 1899
IRB Member: 1987
www.**uar**.com.ar
Phone: +541 1 4383 2211
FAX: +541 1 4383 2211102
Avda Rivadavia 1227 EP
Buenos Aires, Capital Federal, 1033
ARGENTINA

AUSTRALIA - AUSTRALIAN R.U.
Region: FORU
Founded: 1949
IRB Member: 1949
www.**rugby**.com.au
Phone: +61 2 99563444
FAX: +61299553299
Level 30, 2 Park Street
Sydney, NSW2060, AUSTRALIA

AUSTRIA - OSTERREICHISCHER RUGBY VERBAND
Region: FIRA-AER
Founded: 1990
IRB Member: 1992
www.**rugby-austria**.at
Phone: 43 1 92 58 21 27
FAX: 43 1 492 58 21 43
Schneiders Vienna
Koppstrassee 27/29
Vienna
A-1160
AUSTRIA

BAHAMAS - BAHAMAS R.U
Region: NAWIRA
Founded: 1973
IRB Member: 1996
www.**rugbybahamas**.com
Phone: +1242 323 2165
FAX: +12423937451
Bahamas Rugby Football Union
PO Box N-7213
Nassau, BAHAMAS

BARBADOS - BARBADOS R.F.U
Region: NAWIRA
Founded: 1965
IRB Member: 1995
www.**rugbybarbados**.com
Phone: +1 246 437 3836
FAX: +12464373838
The Plantation Complex
St Laurence Main Road
Christ Church
Barbados (W.I.), BARBADOS

BELGUIM - FÉDÉRATION BELGE DE RUGBY
Region: **FIRA-AER**
Founded: 1931
IRB Member: 1988
www.**rugby**.be
Phone: 00 32 2 479 9332
FAX: 00 32 2 476 2282
Avenue de Marathon 135C
Boite 5, Brussels
B-1020, BELGIUM

BERMUDA - BERMUDA R.F.U
Region: NAWIRA
Founded: 1964
IRB Member: 1992
www.bermudarfu.com
Phone: +1 441 2950071
FAX: +14412924649
P.O Box HM 1909
Hamilton, HM BX, BERMUDA

BOSNIA AND HERZEGOVINA - R.F.U. OF BOSNIA & HERZEGOVINA
Region: FIRA-AER
Founded: 1992
IRB Member: 1996
Phone: +387 32 41 6323
FAX: +387 32 41 6323
Ragbi Savez Bosne I Hercegovine
Bulevar Kralja Tvrtka 1 7200 Zenica, Bosnia & Herzegovina
BOSNIA & HERZEGOVINA

BOTSWANA - BOTSWANA R.U.
Region: CAR
Founded: 1992
IRB Member: 1994
Phone: 00267 360 4272
FAX: 00267 390 7410
P.O BOX 1920
GABORONE, BOTSWANA

BRAZIL - ASSOCIAÇÃO BRASILEIRA DE RUGBY
Region: CONSUR
Founded: 1972
IRB Member: 1995
www.brasilrugby.com.br
Phone: +55 11 3864 1336
FAX: +551138681703
R. Da Germaine Burchard
451 - s.53 - Agua Branca
Sao Paulo
CEP: 05002-62, BRAZIL

BULGARIA - BULGARIAN RUGBY FEDERATION
Region: FIRA-AER
Founded: 1962
IRB Member: 1992
Phone: 00 359 2 958 5847/62
FAX: 00 359 2 958 0137
Bulgarian Rugby Federation
75 Vassil Levski Blvd
Sofia, BULGARIA

CAMEROON - FÉDÉRATION CAMEROUNAISE DE RUGBY - (FECARUGBY)
Region: CAR
Founded: 1997
IRB Member: 1999
Phone: +2379913267
FAX: +2372205594
BP 15464
Yaoundé, CAMEROON

CANADA - RUGBY CANADA
Region: NAWIRA
Founded: 1965
IRB Member: 1987
www.rugbycanada.ca
Phone: +1 905 780 8998
FAX: +14163521243
Toronto Office
40 Vogell Road Ontario
Richmond Hill
L4B 3N6, CANADA

CAYMAN ISLANDS - CAYMAN R.U.
Region: NAWIRA
Founded: 1971
IRB Member: 1977
www.caymanrugby.com
Phone: +1 345 949 7960
FAX: +1 345 946 5786
PO Box 1161 GT
Grand Cayman British West Indies
Cayman Islands ,CAYMAN

CHILE - FEDERACIÓN DE RUGBY DE CHILE
Region: CONSUR
Founded: 1935
IRB Member: 1991
www.feruchi.cl
Phone: +562 275 9314
FAX: +5622751248
Av. Larrain 11. 095,La Reina
Santiago, CHILE

CHINA - CHINA R.U. **Region:** ARFU
Founded: 1996
IRB Member: 1997
Phone: +86 10 671 450 78
FAX: +86 10 671 62 993
N°9 Tiyuguan Road
Chongwen District, Beijing
100763, CHINA

CHINESE TAPEI - CHINESE TAIPEI R.F.U.
Region: ARFU
Founded: 1946
IRB Member: 1986
Phone: +886 2877 22 159/167
FAX: +886 2877 22 171
Chinese Taipei Rugby Football Union
Room 808 8F N020, Chu Lun Street
Taipei, 104, CHINESE TAIPEI

COLUMBIA - PRO FEDERACIÓN COLOMBIANA DE RUGBY
Region: CONSUR
IRB Member: 1999
scorpions.simplement.com/
columbia.htm
Phone: +571 520 5236
FAX: +571 525 235
Transversal 15 # 126a - 81 Apto 102, Bogota,
COLOMBIA

COOK ISLANDS - COOK ISLANDS RU
Region: FORU
Founded: 1989
IRB Member: 1995
www.rugby.co.ck
Phone: +682 25854
FAX: 68225853
P.O. Box 898
Rarotonga, COOK ISLANDS

CROATIA - HRVATSKI RAGBIJASKI SAVEZ
Region: FIRA-AER
Founded: 1962
IRB Member: 1992
www.rugby.hr
Phone: +385 1 365 0250
FAX: +38513092921
Trg Kresimira Cosica 11, Zagreb
10000, CROATIA

CZECH REPUBLIC - CESKA RUGBYOVA UNIE
Region: FIRA-AER
Founded: 1926
IRB Member: 1988
www.rugbyunion.cz
Phone: +42 02 33351 341
FAX: +420233351341
Mezi Stadiony PS 40
Praha 6, 160 17
CZECH REPUBLIC

DENMARK - DANSK R.U.
Region: FIRA-AER
Founded: 1950
IRB Member: 1988
www.rugby.dk
Phone: +4543262800
FAX: +4543262801
Idraettens Hus
Brondby Stadion 20
Brondby, DK-2605 - Brondby
DENMARK

ENGLAND - THE RUGBY FOOTBALL UNION
Region: FIRA-AER
Founded: 1871
IRB Member: 1890
www.rfu.com
Phone: +44 208 8922000
FAX: +442088913814
Rugby House, Rugby Road
Twickenham, TWI IDS
ENGLAND

FIJI - FIJI R.U.
Region: FORU
Founded: 1913
IRB Member: 1987
www.fijirugbyunion.com
Phone: +679 3302 787
FAX: +679 3300 936
35 Gordon Street PO Box 1234
Suva, FIJI

FINLAND - SUOMEN RUGBY - LITTO
Region: FIRA-AER
Founded: 1968
IRB Member: 2001
www.rugbyfinland.com
Phone: 00 358 40 732 5436
Spjutvagen 7
Borga/Porvoo
06150, FINLAND

FRANCE - FÉDÉRATION FRANÇAISE DE RUGBY
Region: FIRA-AER
Founded: 1919
IRB Member: 1978
www.ffr.fr
Phone: 331 5321 1515
FAX: 0033144919109
Fédération française de rugby
9 Rue de Liège
Paris, 75009, FRANCE

GEORGIA - GEORGIA RUGBY UNION
Region: FIRA-AER
Founded: 1961
IRB Member: 1992
www.**rugby**.ge
Phone: 00 995 32 294 754
FAX: 00 995 32 294 763
49A Chavchavadze Ave
Sports Department, Tbilisi
0162, GEORGIA

GERMANY - DEUTSCHER RUGBY VERBAND
Region: FIRA-AER
Founded: 1900
IRB Member: 1988
www.**rugby**.de
Phone: +49 511 14763
FAX: +495111610206
P.O. Box 1566
Lower Saxony, Hannover
30015, GERMANY

GUAM - GUAM RUGBY FOOTBALL UNION
Region: ARFU
Founded: 1997
IRB Member: 1998
www.**rugbyonguam**.com
Phone: +1 671 477 7250
FAX: +16714721264
Guam Rugby Football Union
Po Box 7246 Tamuning, Guam
96931, GUAM

GUYANA - GUYANA R.F.U.
Region: NAWIRA
Founded: 1920
IRB Member: 1995
Phone: +592 623-8186
FAX: +592 226 0240
Guyana Rugby Football Union
P.O. Box 101730
Georgetown, GUYANA

HONG KONG - HONG-KONG R.F.U.
Region: ARFU
Founded: 1953
IRB Member: 1988
www.**hkrugby**.com
Phone: 00 852 2504 8311
FAX: 00 852 2576 7237
Rooms 2001, Olympic House, 1 Stadium Path
So Kon Po Causeway Bay
Causeway Bay, HONG KONG

HUNGARY - MAGYAR ROGBI SZOVETSEG
Region: FIRA-AER
Founded: 1990
IRB Member: 1991
www.**rugby**.hu
Phone: +36 1 460 6887
FAX: 0036 1 460 6888
Magyar Rogbi Szovetseg
Istvanmezei ut 1-3, Budapest
H -1146, HUNGARY

INDIA - INDIAN R.F.U.
Region: ARFU
Founded: 1968
IRB Member: 2001
www.**irfu**.org
Phone: +9122 2209 6357
FAX: +912222091822
2nd Flr Nawab House
M. Karve 63 M K Road - Marine Lines, Mumbai
400002, INDIA

IRELAND - IRISH RUGBY FOOTBALL UNION
Region: FIRA-AER
Founded: 1874
IRB Member: 1886
www.**irishrugby**.ie
Phone: +353 1 647 3800
FAX: 016473801
Irish Rugby Football Union
62 Lansdowne Road Ballsbridge
Dublin 4, IRELAND

ISRAEL - ISRAEL RU
Region: FIRA-AER
Founded: 1971
IRB Member: 1988
www.**israel-rugby**.org.il
Phone: +972 9 7422 062
FAX: +97297422062
Israel Rugby Football Union
PO Box 560, Raanana
43104, ISRAEL

ITALY-FEDERAZIONE ITALIANA RUGBY
Region: FIRA-AER
Founded: 1928
IRB Member: 1987
www.**federugby**.it
Phone: +3906452131 02 /37
FAX: +39 06 452131.76
Federazione Italiana Rugby
Stadio Olimpico Curva Nord
Roma, 00194, ITALY

IVORY COAST - D'IVORIE COTE
Region: CAR
Founded: 1961
IRB Member: 1988
Phone: +225 20 21 2083
FAX: +225 20347 107
Federation Ivoirienne de Rugby
01 BP 2357 Abidjan
01 Cote d'Ivorie, IVORY COAST

JAMAICA
Region: NAWIRA
Founded: 1946
IRB Member: 1996
Phone: +1 876 925 6703
FAX: +18769311743
Jamaica Rugby Union,
PO Box 144
Kingston 5, JAMAICA

JAPAN - JAPAN RUGBY FOOTBALL UNION
Region: ARFU
Founded: 1926
IRB Member: 1987
www.**rugby-japan**.jp
Phone: +813 3401 3323
FAX: +81354105523
Japan Rugby Football Union
2-8-35 Kitaaoyama Minato-Ku
Tokyo, 107-0061, JAPAN

KAZAKHSTAN - KAZAKHSTAN R.U.
Region: ARFU
Founded: 1993
IRB Member: 1997
Phone: 00 7 333 236 7079
FAX: +73272507357
Kazakhstan Rugby Football Union
Apt. 4 7 Kashgarskaya Street
Almaty, 480083, KAZAKHSTAN

KENYA - KENYA R.F.U.
Region: CAR
Founded: 1923
IRB Member: 1990
www.**kenyarfu**.com
Phone: +254203876438
FAX: + 2542574425
RFUEA Grounds
Ngong Road P.O. Box 48322
Nairobi, KENYA

KOREA - KORÉA R.U.
Region: ARFU
Founded: 1945
IRB Member: 1988
rugby.**sports**.or.kr
Phone: +822 420 4244
FAX: +8224204246
Korea Rugby Union
Olympic Building 88 Oryun-Dong, Songpa-Gu,
KOREA

LATVIA - LATVIAN RUGBY FEDERATION
Region: FIRA-AER
Founded: 1960
IRB Member: 1991
Phone: +371 722 0320
FAX: +3717320180
Pulkv.Brieza Str.19/1, RIGA
LV-1010, LATVIA

LITHUANIA - LITHUANIAN RUGBY UNION
Region: FIRA-AER
Founded: 1961
IRB Member: 1992
www.**litrugby**.lt
Phone: 003752335474
FAX: +3752335474
6 rue Zemaites, Vilnius Lithuania
2600, LITHUANIA

LUXEMBOURG - FÉDÉRATION LUXEMBOURGEOISE DE RUGBY
Region: FIRA-AER
Founded: 1974
IRB Member: 1991
www.**rugby**.lu
Phone: +352 29 7598
FAX: +352 29 7598
Boite Postale 1965
L-1019 LUXEMBOURG-GARE
LUXEMBOURG

MADAGASCAR - FÉDÉRATION MALAGASY DE RUGBY
Region: CAR
Founded: 1963
IRB Member: 1998
Phone: 00 261 202268869
FAX: 00 261 202268869
Fédération Malagasy de Rugby
Lot VE 50 Ambatonakanga
Antananarivo, 101
MADAGASCAR

MALAYSIA-MALAYSIAN R.U.
Region: ARFU
Founded: 1927
IRB Member: 1988
www.mru.org.my
Phone: +603 2031 8336
FAX: +60320788336
Malaysian Rugby Union
Suite 1.12 Wisma OCM
Kuala Lumpar, 50150, MALAYSIA

MALTA - MALTA RFU
Region: FIRA-AER
Founded: 1991
IRB Member: 2000
www.maltarugby.com
Phone: +356 99495966
FAX: +35621317743
Malta Rugby Football Union
241 Tower Road Sliema SLM 05
Gzira, Malta, MALTA

MOLDOVA - FEDERATION OF RUGBY MOLDOVA
Region: FIRA-AER
Founded: 1992
IRB Member: 1994
Phone: +3 73 22222 674
FAX: +37322222674
Str Columna 106, Chisinau
MD 2012, MOLDOVA

MONACO - FÉDÉRATION MONÉGASQUE DE RUGBY
Region: FIRA-AER
Founded: 1996
IRB Member: 1998
www.monaco-rugby.com
Phone: +377 97 77 1568
FAX: 08658143426
"le Formentor", 27 avenue Princesse Grace,
Monaco
98000, MONACO

MOROCCO - FÉDÉRATION ROYALE MAROCAINE DE RUGBY
Region: CAR
Founded: 1956
IRB Member: 1988
Phone: +212 22 94 82 47
FAX: +21222369060
Federation Royale Marocaine de Rugby
Complexe Sportif Mohamed V Porte 9, Casablanca,
MOROCCO

NAMIBIA - NAMIBIA RU
Region: CAR
Founded: 1990
IRB Member: 1990
www.geocities.com/VNamRugby
Phone: +264 61251 775
FAX: +26461251028
Namibia Rugby Union PO Box 138
Lichtenstein Street Olympia
Windhoek, NAMIBIA

NETHERLANDS - NETHERLANDS RUGBY BOARD
Region: FIRA-AER
Founded: 1932
IRB Member: 1988
www.rugby.nl
Phone: 0031 (0) 20 48 08 100
FAX: 0031 (0) 20 48 08 101
Nederlandse Rugby Bond
Bok de Korverweg 6, Amsterdam
1067 HR, NETHERLANDS

NEW ZEALAND - NEW ZEALAND R.F.U.
Region: FORU
Founded: 1892
IRB Member: 1949
www.allblacks.com
Phone: +644 499 4995
FAX: 006444994224
New Zealand Rugby Football Union
1 Hinemoa Street Centre Port
Wellington, NEW ZEALAND

NIGERIA - NIGERIA RUGBY FOOTBALL FEDERATION
Region: CAR
Founded: 1998
IRB Member: 2001
Phone: +234 01 585 0529
FAX: 00234015850530
Federal Ministry Of Sports & Social Development
National Stadium PO Box 1381 Marina, Lagos,
NIGERIA

NIUE ISLANDS - NIUE RU
Region: FORU
Founded: 1952
IRB Member: 1999
nru.virtualave.net
Phone: +683 4153
FAX: +683 4322
Niue Rugby Football Union
PO Box 11 Alofi
Niue Island, NIUE ISLANDS

NORWAY - NORWEGIAN R U
Region: FIRA-AER
Founded: 1982
IRB Member: 1993
www.rugby.no
Phone: +47 21 02 98 45
FAX: +47 21 02 98 46
Serviceboks 1 Ullevaal Stadion
Oslo, N-0840, NORWAY

PAPUA NEW GUINEA
Region: FORU
Founded: 1963
IRB Member: 1993
Phone: +675 323 4212
FAX: +6753234211
Papua New Guinea Rugby Football Union
Shop Front 2, Gateway Hotel Morea-Tobo
RoadP.O. Box 864
Port Moresby
PAPUA NEW GUINEA

PARAGUAY - UNION DE RUGBY DEL PARAGUAY
Region: CONSUR
Founded: 1970
IRB Member: 1989
Phone: +595 21 496 390
FAX: +59521496390
Union de Rugby del Paraguay
Independencia Nacional 250 casi Palma 1er Piso
Asuncion, PARAGUAY

PERU - FEDERACION RUGBY DE PERU
Region: CONSUR
Founded: 1997
IRB Member: 1999
Phone: +51 1 241 2349
Union Peruana de Rugby
Av. Miguel Dasso 126 ofic. 305
Lima, 27, PERU

POLAND - POLISH R.U.
Region: FIRA-AER
Founded: 1957
IRB Member: 1988
www.pzrugby.pl
Phone: 48 22 835 3587
FAX: 0048228651046
Polski Zwiazek Rugby
Marymoncka 34, Warszawa
01-813, POLAND

PORTUGAL - FEDERAÇÃO PORTUGUESA DE RUGBY
Region: FIRA-AER
Founded: 1926
IRB Member: 1988
www.fpr.pt
Phone: 00 351 21 799 1690
FAX: 00 351 21 793 6135
Federacao Portuguesa de Rugby
Rua Julieta Ferrao NR12-3rd Floor
Lisboa, 1600-131, PORTUGAL

ROMANIA - ROMANIAN RUGBY FEDERATION
Region: FIRA-AER
Founded: 1931
IRB Member: 1997
www.rugby.ro
Phone: +40 2 1 224 54 82
FAX: 0040213192449
Federatia Romana de Rugby
Bd. Marasti No. 18-20
Bucharest, ROMANIA

RUSSIA - R.U. OF RUSSIA
Region: FIRA-AER
Founded: 1936
IRB Member: 1990
www.rugby.ru
Phone: 007 495 6370003
FAX: 00 7095 725 4680
Rugby Union of Russia
8 Luzhneckaya Naberezhnaya
Moscow, 119992, RUSSIA

SAMOA - SAMOA RUGBY FOOTBALL UNION
Region: FORU
Founded: 1924
IRB Member: 1988
www.manusamoa.com.ws
Phone: 00685 26 792
FAX: 0068525009
Samoa Rugby Football Union
Cross Island Road
Malifa, SAMOA

SCOTLAND - SCOTTISH R.U.
Region: FIRA-AER
Founded: 1873
IRB Member: 1886
www.sru.org.uk
Phone: 44 131 346 5000
FAX: +441313465001
Scottish Rugby Union
Murrayfield, Edinburgh
EH12 5PJ, SCOTLAND

SENEGAL - FÉDÉRATION SÉNÉGALAISE DE RUGBY
Region: CAR
Founded: 1960
IRB Member: 1999
Phone: 221 821 5858
FAX: 002218218651
Fédération Sénégalaise De Rugby
73 rue Amadou Ndoye
Dakar, SENEGAL

SERBIA AND MONTENEGRO - RUGBY UNION OF SERBIA AND MONTENEGRO
Region: FIRA-AER
Founded: 1954
IRB Member: 1988
Phone: +381 11 324 5743
FAX: +381113245743
Rugby Union of Serbia and Montenegro Terazije
Terazije 35/111 PO Box 1013
Belgrade
SERBIA AND MONTENEGRO

SINGAPORE - SINGAPORE R.U.
Region: ARFU
Founded: 1948
IRB Member: 1989
www.sru.org.sg
Phone: 00 656 4694038
FAX: 00 656 467 0283
Singapore Rugby Union
301 Toa Payoh Lor.6 Toa Payoh Swimming Complex
319 392, SINGAPORE

SLOVENIA - RUGBY ZVEZA SLOVENIJE
Region: FIRA-AER
Founded: 1989
IRB Member: 1996
Phone: +386 1 230 2322
FAX: +386 1 232 1154
Rugby Zveza Slovenije
c/o Studio Mi
Linhartova 8 - 1000 Ljubljana
SLOVENIA

SOLOMON ISLANDS - SOLOMON ISLANDS R.U. FEDERATION
Region: FORU
Founded: 1963
IRB Member: 1999
Phone: 00 677 215 95
FAX: 00 677 215 96
Solomon Islands Rugby Union Federation, PO Box 642
Honaria, SOLOMON ISLANDS

SOUTH AFRICA - SOUTH AFRICA R.F.U.
Region: CAR
Founded: 1889
IRB Member: 1949
www.sarugby.co.za
Phone: 00 27 21 659 6700
FAX: 00 27 21 686 3907
5th Floor, Sports Science Institute
Boundary Road PO Box 99 Newlands 7725
Newlands, 7700, SOUTH AFRICA

SPAIN - FEDERACION ESPANOLA DE RUGBY
Region: FIRA-AER
Founded: 1923
IRB Member: 1988
www.ferugby.com
Phone: 00 34 91 541 49 78/88
FAX: 00 34 91 559 09 86
Federacion Espanola de Rugby
Ferraz 16-4, Madrid
28008, SPAIN

SRI LANKA - SRI LANKA R.F.U.
Region: ARFU
Founded: 1908
IRB Member: 1988
www.srilankarugby.com
Phone: +9411 266 73 21
FAX: +9411 2667320
7 A Reid Avenue
Colombo, 07, SRI LANKA

ST. LUCIA - ST. LUCIA R.F.U.
Region: NAWIRA
Founded: 1996
IRB Member: 1996
Phone: 00 1 758 45 03896
FAX: 00 1 758 452 4794
St. Lucia Rugby Football Union
Hill Top PO Box 614
Castries, ST. LUCIA

ST. VINCENT AND GRANADA - ST. VINCENT AND THE GRENADINES R.U.
Region: NAWIRA
Founded: 1998
IRB Member: 2003
Phone: 1 784 457 5135
FAX: 1 784 457 4396
PO BOX 1034
Kingstown
St. Vincent & the Grenadines
ST. VINCENT & THE GRENADINES

SWAZILAND - SWAZILAND R.U.
Region: CAR
Founded: 1995
IRB Member: 1998
www.**swazilandrugb**.com
Phone: +268 505 2886
FAX: +2685052886
Swaziland Rugby Union
c/o Homecentre 8 Mhlakuvane Street Manzini,
Mbabane, SWAZILAND

SWEDEN - SVENSKA RUGBY FORBUNDET
Region: FIRA-AER
Founded: 1932
IRB Member: 1988
www.**rugby**.se
Phone: 004686996524
FAX: 004686996527
Idrottens Hus
S-114 73 Stockholm, Stockholm, 114 73, SWEDEN

SWITZERLAND - FÉDÉRATION SUISSE DE RUGBY
Region: FIRA-AER
Founded: 1972
IRB Member: 1988
www.**rugby**.ch
Phone: 00 41 31 301 23 88
FAX: 0041 31 301 23 88
Swiss Rugby Union
Pavillonweg 3, 3012 Bern
PO Box 7705 - 3001 Berb, SWITZERLAND

TAHITI - FÉDÉRATION TAHITIENNE DE RUGBY DE POLYNESIE FRANCAISE
Region: FORU
Founded: 1989
IRB Member: 1994
Phone: 689 48 12 28/689 42 04 10
FAX: N/A
Federation Tahitienne de Rugby de Polynesie
Francaise
(Tahiti Rugby Union) B.P. 650 Papeete
PapeeteTahiti 98714
French Polynesia, TAHITI

THAILAND - THAI R.U.
Region: ARFU
Founded: 1938
IRB Member: 1989
www.**thai-tru**.com
Phone: 662 215 3839
FAX: 006622141712
Thai Rugby Union
Thephasdin Stadium Rama 1 Rd.
Bangkok, 10330, THAILAND

TONGA - TONGA RFU
Region: FORU
Founded: 1923
IRB Member: 1987
Phone: 676 26 045
FAX: 676 26 044
Tonga Rugby Football Union
P.O. Box 369 Nuku'alofa, TONGA

TRINIDAD AND TOBAGO - TRINIDAD AND TOBAGO R.F.U.
Region: NAWIRA
Founded: 1928
IRB Member: 1992
www.**ttrfu**.com
Phone: 1 868 628 9048
FAX: 1 868 628 9049
Trinidad and Tobago Rugby Football Union
PO Box 5090 Tragarete Road Post Office
Woodbrook, Trinidad and Tobago,
TRINIDAD & TOBAGO

FÉDÉRATION TUNISIENNE DE RUGBY
Region: CAR
Founded: 1972
IRB Member: 1988
Phone: 00 216 71 755 066/517
FAX: 00 216 71 751 737
Federation Tunisienne de Rugby
Boite Postale 318 - 1004 El Menzah, Tunis,
TUNISIA

UGANDA - UGANDA R.F.U.
Region: CAR
Founded: 1955
IRB Member: 1977
www.**urfu**.org
Phone: +256 41 259 280
FAX: +25641259280
Uganda Rugby Union
PO Box 22108
Kampala, UGANDA

UKRAINE - NATIONAL RUGBY FEDERATION OF UKRAINE
Region: FIRA-AER
Founded: 1991
IRB Member: 1992
www.**rugby**.org.ua
Phone: 00 380 44 2896748
FAX: 00 380 44 2891494
National Rugby Federation of Ukraine105 st
Frunze2nd Floor of the Spartak Stadium
42 Rue Esplanadna str.
Kiev, 01023, UKRAINE

URUGUAY - UNION DE RUGBY DEL URUGUAY
Region: CONSUR
Founded: 1951
IRB Member: 1989
www.uru.org.uy
Phone: +5982 712 3826/3648
FAX: +59827106082
Union de Rugby del Uruguay
Bulevard Artigas 420
Montevideo, 11300, URUGUAY

USA - UNITED STATES OF AMERICA RUGBY
Region: NAWIRA
Founded: 1975
IRB Member: 1987
www.usarugby.org
Phone: +1 303 539 0300
FAX: +13035390311
USA Rugby Football Union
1033 Walnut Street, Ste.200
Boulder, CO 80302, USA

VANUATU - VANUATU R.F.U.
Region: FORU
Founded: 1980
IRB Member: 1999
Phone: +678 424 93
FAX: +67823529
Vanuatu Rugby Football Union
PO Box 284 / 1584
Port Vila, VANUATU

VENEZUELA-FEDERACIÓN VENEZOLANA DE RUGBY
Region: CONSUR
Founded: 1991
IRB Member: 1998
Phone: 00584168087366
FAX: +582129767575
Carretera hacia Fila de Mariches
Centro de Servicios La Florencia, allado del Restauante
Riskos via Urbanizacion , Miranda, 1070, VENEZUELA

WALES - WELSH R.U.
Region: FIRA-AER
Founded: 1881
IRB Member: 1886
www.wru.co.uk
Phone: +44 8700138600
FAX: +442920822474
Welsh Rugby Union
1st Floor Golate House 101 St. Mary's Street, Cardiff
CF10 1GE, WALES

ZAMBIA - ZAMBIA R.F.U.
Region: CAR
Founded: 1975
IRB Member: 1995
Phone: 00 260 223 1604
FAX: 00 260 223 1604
Zambia Rugby Football Union
Room 116 1st Floor Sanlam Building, Kitwe, ZAMBIA

ZIMBABWE - ZIMBABWE R.U.
Region: CAR
Founded: 1895
IRB Member: 1987
www.zimsevensrugby.com
Phone: 00263 4740 562
FAX: 00263 4778 242
The National Sports Stadium
Bay 26, Office Y105 Harare, Harare
Y105, ZIMBABWE

AMERICAN SAMOA – AMERICAN SAMOA R.F.U
Region: FORU
IRB Associate Member: 2005

ARMENIA - ARMENIA R.F.U
Region: FIRA-AER
IRB Associate Member: 2004
Phone: 0037 42 553671
FAX: 003742151090
9 Abovian str,
Yerevan, 375001, ARMENIA

AZERBAIJAN - AZERBAIJAN R.U
Region: FIRA-AER
IRB Associate Member: 2004
Phone: 00994502122704
FAX: 00994124973745
c/o Amerada Hess ACG Ltd
10-33 Izmir Str, Hyatt Tower II, 5th Floor, AZ
1004 BAKU, Azerbijan, AZERBAIJAN

BRITISH VIRGIN ISLANDS
Region: NAWIRA
IRB Associate Member: 2001
Phone: 00 1 284 494 4388
FAX: 00 1 284 494 3088
C/o Smith-Hughes Raworth and McKenzin, BOX
173 Road Town, Tortola

BURUNDI - BURUNDI RFU
Region: CAR
IRB Associate Member: 2004
Place de Independance
BP 1103, Bujumbuna, BURUNDI

CAMBODIA - CAMBODIA FEDERATION OF RUGBY
Region: ARFU
IRB Associate Member: 2004
Cambodian Federation of Rugby
74 Boulevard Preah Sihanouk
CAMBODIA

GHANA - GHANA RUGBY UNION
Region: CAR
IRB Associate Member: 2004
Phone: 0023321661058
FAX: 0023321689789
PO Box GP 1272
ACCRA Ghana, GHANA

KRYGYZSTAN - KRYGYZSTAN RUGBY UNION
Region: ARFU
IRB Associate Member: 2004
Phone: 0073272334992
FAX: 0073272507357
7 Kashgarskaya Street
Àpt 4 Almaty Kazakhstan 480083, Kazakhstan
480083, KYRGYZSTAN

LAO - LAO RUGBY UNION
Region: ARFU
IRB Associate Member: 2004
Lao Rugby Union
c/o- Sodetour 086 Phonexay Street, Ban Fay
Vientiane, Lao P.D.R, LAO

MALI - MALI RFU
Region: CAR
IRB Associate Member: 2004
PO Box 91, Stade Omnisports
Modibo Keita, MALI

MAURITANIA - FÉDÉRATION MAURITANIENNE DE RUGBY
Region: CAR
IRB Associate Member: 2003
Phone: 0022 26 433617
FAX: 0022 26 430028
BP 3201 Nouakchott
Mauritania, MAURITANIA

MAURITIUS - RUGBY UNION MAURITIUS
Region: CAR
IRB Associate Member: 2004
www.**mauritiusrugby**.mu
Phone: 002304835471
FAX: 002304835471
Lot. DG01, Ruisseau Créole
Rivière Noire, MAURITIUS

MEXICO - FEDERACIÓN MEXICANA DE RUGBY A.C
Region: NAWIRA
Founded: 1972
IRB Member: 2003
www.**mexrugby**.com
Phone: 00525552764439
FAX: 00525552764439
Villahermosa 21 – B
Colonia Condesa, Mexico
06100, MEXICO

MONGOLIA - MONGOLIA RUGBY UNION
Region: ARFU
IRB Associate Member: 2004
Phone: 0097611343625
FAX: 0097611343817
Khan Uul District
Chinggis Avenue Erel Complex
MONGOLIA

PAKISTAN - PAKISTAN RUGBY UNION
Region: ARFU
IRB Associate Member: 2004
www.pakistanrugby.com
Phone: 0092425751999
FAX: 0092425712109
Servis House
2 Main Gulberg
Lahore
54662
PAKISTAN

PHILIPPINES - PHILIPPINES RUGBY FOOTBALL UNION
Region: ARFU
Founded: 1998
IRB Member: 2004
www.prfu.com
Phone: +632 8528171
c/o The PRFU Secretariat
12 Sunset Drive Los Tamaraos Village NAIA Rd
Paranaque
Metro Manila
PHILLIPINES

RWANDA - RWANDA RUGBY FEDERATION
Region: CAR
IRB Associate Member: 2004
Phone: 00250503481
FAX: 00250503478
Rwanda P.BOX 3264
Kigali RWANDA

TANZANIA - TANZANIA RUGBY UNION
Region: CAR
IRB Associate Member: 2004
IRB Member: 2004
Phone: 00255272508917
FAX: 00255272508434
PO Box 1182
Arusha
TANZANIA

TOGO - FÉDÉRATION TOGOLAISE DE RUGBY
Region: CAR
Founded: 2001
IRB Member: 2004
Phone: +228 2227513
FAX: +228 2227369
BP 7512, Lomé, TOGO

UZBEKISTAN - UZBEKISTAN RUGBY FOOTBALL UNION
Region: ARFU
IRB Associate Member: 2004
Phone: (+998 712) 97-97-49
FAX: (+998 712) 97-97-49
1,Lisunova Str, h.119 apartment 27, Tashkent,
700204, UZBEKISTAN

REGIONAL ASSOCIATIONS

ARFU (ASIA)
Asian Rugby Football Union
Flat 40C, Tower 6 Sorrento, Union Square
No. 1 Austin Road, Kowloon
Hong Kong, ARFU

CAR (AFRICA)
C/O Aziz Bougja
116 rue Damremont 75018 Paris
Paris, CAR

CONSUR (SOUTH AMERICA)
c/o Union Argentina de Rugby
Rivadavia 1227, entre piso 1033 Capital Federal
Buenos Aires, Argentina

FIRA-AER (EUROPE)
9 Rue de Liege
75009 Paris, Paris, France

FORU (OCEANIA)
c/o Andy Conway
Level 7 Rugby House
Rugby House
181 Miller Street, North Sydney NSW 2060

NAWIRA (NORTH AMERICA AND THE WEST INDIES)
C/O Legacy Financial
Suite 104, Savannah Court 10B Queens Park West
Port of Spain, Trinidad, NAWIRA

KEY FIXTURES FOR 2007

KICK OFFS ARE UK & IRELAND

RIGHT AT TIME OF GOING TO PRESS. UPDATES ON IRB.COM

RBS SIX NATIONS

Saturday 3 February
Italy v **France**: 1.30pm
(Stadio Flaminio, Rome)
England v **Scotland**: 4pm
(Twickenham)

Sunday 4 February
Wales v **Ireland**: 3pm
(Millennium Stadium, Cardiff)

Saturday 10 February
England v **Italy**:1.30
(Twickenham)
Scotland v **Wales**:3.30
(Murrayfield, Edinburgh)

Sunday 11 February
Ireland v **France**: 3pm
(Croke Park, Dublin)

Saturday 24 February
Scotland v **Italy**: 3pm
(Murrayfield, Edinburgh)
Ireland v **England**: 5.30pm
(Croke Park, Dublin)
France v **Wales**, 8pm
(Stade de France, Paris)

Saturday 10 March
Scotland v **Ireland**: 1.30pm
(Murrayfield, Edinburgh)
Italy v **Wales**: 3.30pm
(Stadio Flaminio, Rome)

Sunday 11 March
England v **France** : 3pm
(Twickenham)

Saturday 17 March
Italy v **Ireland**: 1.30pm
(StadioFlaminio, Rome)
France v **Scotland**: 3.30pm
(Stade de France, Paris
Wales v **England**: 5.30pm
(Millennium Stadium, Cardiff)

RUGBY WORLD CUP

* Updates and ticket details from www.rugbyworldcup.com

Friday 7 September
France v **Argentina (Pool D)**
Stade de France

Saturday 8 September
New Zealand v **Europe** 1 **(C)**
Marseille
Australia v **Asia** 1 **(B)**
Lyon
England v **Americas** 3 **(A)**
Lens

Sunday 9 September
Wales v **Canada (B)**
Nantes
South Africa v **Samoa (A)**
Parc des Princes
Scotland v **Repechage** 1 **(C)**
St Etienne
Ireland v **Africa** 1 **(D)**
Bordeaux

Tuesday 11 September
Argentina v **Europe** 3 **(D)**
Lyon

Wednesday 12 September
Americas 3 v **Repechage 2 (A)**
Montpellier
Asia 1 v **Fiji (B)**
Toulouse
Europe 1 v **Europe 2 (C)**
Marseille

Friday 14 September
England v **South Africa (A)**
Stade de France

Saturday 15 September
New Zealand v **Repechage 1 (C)**
Lyon
Wales v **Australia (B)**
Cardiff
Ireland v **Europe 3 (D)**
Bordeaux

Sunday 16 September
Fiji v **Canada (B)**
Cardiff
Samoa v **Repechage 2 (A)**
Montpellier
France v **Africa 1 (D)**
Toulouse

Tuesday 18 September
Scotland v **Europe 2 (C)**
Edinburgh

Wednesday 19 September
Europe 1 v **Repechage 1 (C)**
Parc des Princes

Thursday 20 September
Wales v **Asia 1 (B)**
Cardiff

Friday 21 September
France v **Ireland (D)**
Stade de France

Saturday 22 September
South Africa v **Repechage 2 (A)**
Lens
England v **Samoa (A)**
Nantes
Argentina v **Africa 1 (D)**
Marseille

Sunday 23 September
Australia v **Fiji (B)**
Montpellier
Scotland v **New Zealand (C)**
Edinburgh

Tuesday 25 September
Canada v **Asia 1 (B)**
Bordeaux
Europe 2 v **Repechage 1 (C)**
Toulouse

Wednesday 26 September
Europe 3 v **Africa 1 (D)**
Lens
Samoa v **Americas 3 (A)**
St Etienne

Friday 28 September
England v **Repechage 2 (A)**
Parc des Princes

Saturday 29 September
New Zealand v **Europe 2 (C)**
Toulouse
Australia v **Canada (B)**
Bordeaux
Wales v **Fiji (B)**
Nantes
Scotland v **Europe 1 (C)**
St Etienne

Sunday 30 September
France v **Europe** 3 (D)
Marseille
Ireland v **Argentina** (D)
Parc des Princes
South Africa v **Americas** 3 (A)
Montpellier

QUARTER-FINALS
Saturday 6 October
Winner Pool B v **R-Up Pool A**
Marseille (42)
Winner Pool C v **R-Up Pool D**
Cardiff (43)

Sunday 7 October
Winner Pool A v **R-Up Pool B**
Marseille (44)
Winner Pool D v **R-Up Pool C**
Stade de France (45)

SEMI-FINALS
Saturday 13 October
Winner Match 42 v **Winner** 43
Stade de France
Sunday 14 October
Winner Match 44 v **Winner** 45
Stade de France

THIRD-FOURTH PLAY-OFF
Friday 19 October
Parc des Princes

WORLD CUP FINAL
Saturday 20 October
Stade de France

Ian Waldie/Getty Images

Who'll be holding this trophy on 20 October? Rugby's greatest prize.